D1064881

WEST'S ENCYCLOPEDIA *of* AMERICAN LAW

2ND EDITION

WEST'S ENCYCLOPEDIA *of* AMERICAN LAW

2ND EDITION

VOLUME 12

PRIMARY DOCUMENTS

THOMSON

GALE

Detroit • San Die... • San Francisco • New Haven, Conn. • Waterville, Maine • London • Munich

...TEXAS COMMUNITY COLLEGE
...ING RESOURCE CENTER
...PLEASANT TEXAS 75...

WITHDRAWN

West's Encyclopedia of American Law, 2nd Edition

Project Editors
Jeffrey Lehman
Shirelle Phelps

Editorial
Andrew C. Claps, Pamela A. Dear, Jason M. Everett, Lynn U. Koch, John F. McCoy, Jeffrey Wilson, Jennifer M. York, Ralph Zerbonia

Research
Barbara McNeil

Editorial Support Services
Ryan Cartmill, Mark Hefner, Sue Petrus

Data Capture
Katrina Coach, Nikita Greene, Beverly Jendrowski, Elizabeth Pilette, Beth Richardson

Indexing Services
Lynne Maday

Permissions
Margaret A. Chamberlain

Imaging and Multimedia
Dean Dauphinais, Leitha Etheridge-Sims, Mary Grimes, Lezlie Light, Dan Newell, David G. Oblender, Chris O'Bryan

Product Design
Cynthia Baldwin, Kate Scheible

Composition and Electronic Capture
Evi Seoud, Mary Beth Trimper

Manufacturing
Rhonda Williams

© 2005 Thomson Gale, a part of The Thomson Corporation.

Thomson and Star Logo are trademarks and Gale is a registered trademark used herein under license.

For more information, contact
The Gale Group, Inc.
27500 Drake Rd.
Farmington Hills, MI 48331-3535
Or you can visit our Internet site at
http://www.gale.com

ALL RIGHTS RESERVED
No part of this work covered by the copyright hereon may be reproduced or used in any form or by any means—graphic, electronic, or mechanical, including photocopying, recording, taping, Web distribution, or information storage retrieval systems—without the written permission of the publisher.

This publication is a creative work fully protected by all applicable copyright laws, as well as by misappropriation, trade secret, unfair condition, and other applicable laws. The authors and editors of this work have added value to the underlying factual material herein through one or more of the following: coordination, expression, arrangement, and classification of the information.

For permission to use material from this product, submit your request via Web at http://www.gale-edit.com/permission or you may download our Permissions Request form and submit your request by fax of mail to:

Permissions Department
The Gale Group, Inc.
27500 Drake Rd.
Farmington Hills, MI 48331-3535
Permissions Hotline:
248-699-8006 or 800-877-4253, ext. 8006
Fax: 248-699-8074 or 800-762-4058

Inside cover photographs reproduced by permission of the Library of Congress (Thurgood Marshall).

Since this page cannot legibly accommodate all copyright notices, the acknowledgments constitute an extension of the copyright notice.

While every effort has been made to ensure the reliability of the information presented in this publication, The Gale Group, Inc. does not guarantee the accuracy of the data contained herein. The Gale Group, Inc. accepts no payment for listing; and inclusion in the publication of any organization, agency, institution, publication service, or individual does not imply endorsement of the editors or publisher. Errors brought to the attention of the publisher and verified to the satisfaction of the publisher will be corrected in future editions.

Library of Congress Cataloging-in-Publication Data
West's encyclopedia of American law / Jeffrey Lehman, editor, Shirelle Phelps, editor.— 2nd ed.
p. cm.
Includes bibliographical references and index.
ISBN 0-7876-6367-0 (hardcover set : alk. paper)
1. Law—United States—Encyclopedias. 2. Law—United States—Popular works. I. Lehman, Jeffrey. II. Phelps, Shirelle.
KF154.W47 2004
349.73'03—dc22

2004004918

ISBN 0-7876-6367-0 (set), ISBN 0-7876-6368-9 (vol. 1), ISBN 0-7876-6369-7 (vol. 2), ISBN 0-7876-6370-0 (vol. 3), ISBN 0-7876-6371-9 (vol. 4), ISBN 0-7876-6372-7 (vol. 5), ISBN 0-7876-6373-5 (vol. 6), ISBN 0-7876-6374-3 (vol. 7), ISBN 0-7876-6375-1 (vol. 8), ISBN 0-7876-6376-X (vol. 9), ISBN 0-7876-6377-8 (vol. 10), ISBN 0-7876-6378-6 (vo1. 11), ISBN 0-7876-6379-4 (vol. 12), ISBN 0-7876-9420-7 (vol. 13)

This title is also available as an e-book. ISBN 0-7876-9373-1 (set)
Contact your Gale sales representative for ordering information.

Printed in the United States of America
10 9 8 7 6 5 4 3 2 1

DEDICATION

West's Encyclopedia of American Law (WEAL) is dedicated to librarians and library patrons throughout the United States and beyond. Your interest in the American legal system helps to expand and fuel the framework of our Republic.

CONTENTS

The U.S. legal system is admired around the world for the freedoms it allows the individual and the fairness with which it attempts to treat all persons. On the surface, it may seem simple, yet those who have delved into it know that this sytem of federal and state constitutions, statutes, regulations, and common-law decisions is elaborate and complex. It derives from the English common law, but includes principles older than England, along with some principles from other lands. The U.S. legal system, like many others, has a language all its own, but too often it is an unfamiliar language: many concepts are still phrased in Latin. The second edition of *West's Encyclopedia of American Law (WEAL)* explains legal terms and concepts in everyday language, however. It covers a wide variety of persons, entities, and events that have shaped the U.S. legal system and influenced public perceptions of it.

MAIN FEATURES OF THIS SET

Entries

This encyclopedia contains nearly 5,000 entries devoted to terms, concepts, events, movements, cases, and persons significant to U.S. law. Entries on legal terms contain a definition of the term, followed by explanatory text if necessary. Entries are arranged alphabetically in standard encyclopedia format for ease of use. A wide variety of additional features, listed later in this preface, provide interesting background and supplemental information.

Definitions Every entry on a legal term is followed by a definition, which appears at the beginning of the entry and is italicized. The Dictionary and Indexes volume includes a glossary containing all the definitions from *WEAL*.

Further Readings To facilitate further research, a list of Further Readings is included at the end of a majority of the main entries.

Cross-References *WEAL* provides two types of cross-references, within and following entries. Within the entries, terms are set in small capital letters—for example, LIEN—to indicate that they have their own entry in the encyclopedia. At the end of the entries, related entries the reader may wish to explore are listed alphabetically by title.

Blind cross-reference entries are also included to direct the user to other entries throughout the set.

In Focus Essays

In Focus essays accompany related entries and provide additional facts, details, and arguments on particularly interesting, important, or controversial issues raised by those entries. The subjects covered include hotly contested issues, such as abortion, capital punishment, and gay rights; detailed processes, such as the Food and Drug Administration's approval process for new drugs; and important historical or social issues, such as debates over the formation of the U.S. Constitution.

Sidebars

Sidebars provide brief highlights of some interesting facet of accompanying entries. They complement regular entries and In Focus essays by adding informative details. Sidebar topics include the Million Man March and the branches of the U.S. armed services. Sidebars appear at the top of a text page and are set in a box.

Biographies

WEAL profiles a wide variety of interesting and influential people—including lawyers, judges, government and civic leaders, and historical and modern figures—who have played a part in creating or shaping U.S. law. Each biography includes a timeline, which shows important moments in the subject's life as well as important historical events of the period. Biographies appear alphabetically by the subject's last name.

ADDITIONAL FEATURES OF THIS SET

Enhancements Throughout *WEAL*, readers will find a broad array of photographs, charts, graphs, manuscripts, legal forms, and other visual aids enhancing the ideas presented in the text.

Indexes *WEAL* features a cases index and a cumulative general index in a separate volume.

Appendixes

Three appendix volumes are included with *WEAL*, containing hundreds of pages of docu-ments, laws, manuscripts, and forms fundamental to and characteristic of U.S. law.

Milestone Cases in the Law

A special Appendix volume entitled Milestones in the Law, allows readers to take a close look at landmark cases in U.S. law. Readers can explore the reasoning of the judges and the arguments of the attorneys that produced major decisions on important legal and social issues. Included in each Milestone are the opinions of the lower courts; the briefs presented by the parties to the U.S. Supreme Court; and the decision of the Supreme Court, including the majority opinion and all concurring and dissenting opinions for each case.

Primary Documents

There is also an Appendix volume containing more than 60 primary documents, such as the English Bill of Rights, Martin Luther King Jr.'s Letter from Brimingham Jail, and several presidential speeches.

Citations

Wherever possible, *WEAL* entries include citations for cases and statutes mentioned in the text. These allow readers wishing to do additional research to find the opinions and statutes cited. Two sample citations, with explanations of common citation terms, can be seen below and opposite.

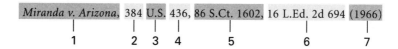

1. *Case title.*   The title of the case is set in italics and indicates the names of the parties. The suit in this sample citation was between Ernesto A. Miranda and the state of Arizona.
2. *Reporter volume number.*   The number preceding the reporter name indicates the reporter volume containing the case. (The volume number appears on the spine of the reporter, along with the reporter name.)
3. *Reporter name.*   The reporter name is abbreviated. The suit in the sample citation is from the reporter, or series of books, called *U.S. Reports,* which contains cases from the U.S. Supreme Court. (Numerous reporters publish cases from the federal and state courts.)

4. *Reporter page.*   The number following the reporter name indicates the reporter page on which the case begins.
5. *Additional reporter citation.*   Many cases may be found in more than one reporter. The suit in the sample citation also appears in volume 86 of the *Supreme Court Reporter,* beginning on page 1602.
6. *Additional reporter citation.*   The suit in the sample citation is also reported in volume 16 of the *Lawyer's Edition,* second series, beginning on page 694.
7. *Year of decision.*   The year the court issued its decision in the case appears in parentheses at the end of the cite.

Brady Handgun Violence Prevention Act, Pub. L. No. 103–159, 107 Stat. 1536 (18 U.S.C.A. §§ 921–925A)

1   2   3 4 5 6 7   8

1. *Statute title.*
2. *Public law number.* In the sample citation, the number 103 indicates that this law was passed by the 103d Congress, and the number 159 indicates that it was the 159th law passed by that Congress.
3. *Reporter volume number.* The number preceding the reporter name indicates the reporter volume containing the statute.
4. *Reporter name.* The reporter name is abbreviated. The statute in the sample citation is from *Statutes at Large.*
5. *Reporter page.* The number following the reporter name indicates the reporter page on which the statute begins.

6. *Title number.* Federal laws are divided into major sections with specific titles. The number preceding a reference to the *U.S. Code Annotated* is the title number. title 18 of the U.S. Code is Crimes and Criminal Procedure.
7. *Additional reporter.* The statute in the sample citation may also be found in the *U.S. Code Annotated.*
8. *Section number.* The section numbers following a reference to the *U.S. Code Annotated* indicate where the statute appears in that reporter.

Editorial Reviewers

Matthew C. Cordon
Frederick K. Grittner
Stephanie Schmitt
Linda Tashbook
M. Uri Toch

Contributing Authors

James Cahoy
Matthew C. Cordon
Richard J. Cretan
Mark Engsberg
Frederick K. Grittner
Lauri R. Harding
David R. Johnstone
Theresa J. Lippert
Frances T. Lynch
George A. Milite
Melodie Monahan
Kelle Sisung
Scott D. Slick

**Contributors to
Previous Edition**

Richard Abowitz
Paul Bard
Joanne Bergum
Michael Bernard
Gregory A. Borchard
Susan Buie

Terry Carter
Sally Chatelaine
Joanne Smestad Claussen
Richard Cretan
Lynne Crist
Paul D. Daggett
Susan L. Dalhed
Lisa M. DelFiacco
Suzanne Paul Dell'Oro
Dan DeVoe
Joanne Engelking
Sharon Fischlowitz
Jonathan Flanders
Lisa Florey
Robert A. Frame
John E. Gisselquist
Russell L. Gray III
Frederick K. Grittner
Victoria L. Handler
Heidi L. Headlee
James Heidberg
Clifford P. Hooker
Marianne Ashley Jerpbak
Andrew Kass
Margaret Anderson Kelliher
Christopher J. Kennedy
Anne E. Kevlin
Ann T. Laughlin
Laura Ledsworth-Wang
Linda Lincoln

Gregory Luce
David Luiken
Jennifer Marsh
Sandra M. Olson
Anne Larsen Olstad
William Ostrem
Lauren Pacelli
Randolph C. Park
Gary Peter
Michele A. Potts
Reinhard Priester
Christy Rain
Brian Roberts
Debra J. Rosenthal
Mary Lahr Schier
Mary Scarbrough
Theresa L. Schulz
John Scobey
James Slavicek
Scott D. Slick
David Strom
Wendy Tien
Douglas Tueting
Richard F. Tyson
Christine Ver Ploeg
George E. Warner
Anne Welsbacher
Eric P. Wind
Lindy T. Yokanovich

CONTENTS

APPENDIX: PRIMARY DOCUMENTS

FOUNDATIONS
OF U.S. LAW

ENGLISH LAW

THE COLONIAL PERIOD

CONFLICT AND RESOLUTION

ORIGINS OF U.S. GOVERNMENT

ENGLISH LAW

- MAGNA CHARTA
- ENGLISH BILL OF RIGHTS
- SECOND TREATISE ON GOVERNMENT

The development of U.S. law is rooted in English political and legal history. The colonial settlers of North America were primarily from England, and until the 1760s they viewed themselves as English rather than "American." They brought with them the English COMMON LAW and the English constitutional tradition.

Unlike the United States, England has never had a written constitution. Instead, the English constitutional tradition is based on the substance and procedures of the common law, along with key documents, such as Magna Charta and the English Bill of Rights. In the seventeenth and eighteenth centuries, political philosophers, especially JOHN LOCKE, challenged the absolute authority of the monarchy and introduced the democratic idea that the people have a right to a government that meets their needs. These documents and ideas assumed great importance as the American colonists moved toward independence in the 1770s. In this sense English ideas paved the way for the American Revolution and the writing of the U.S. Constitution.

ENGLISH LAW

MAGNA CHARTA

The document that has come to be known as Magna Charta (spelled variously as "charta" or "carta"), or Great Charter, is recognized as a fundamental part of the English constitutional tradition. Although it is not a constitution, it contains provisions on criminal law that were incorporated into the Bill of Rights of the U.S. Constitution.

In 1215 King John of England (1199–1216) fought more than forty English barons and their followers in a civil war. The king had angered the barons by extracting revenues based on their feudal obligations in order to fight a war in France. After John lost the war, the barons rebelled against the king.

The rebels first demanded that the king confirm the Charter of Henry I, a coronation charter from 1100 in which King Henry I had promised to abolish all evil customs that oppressed the realm. Additional grievances were added to the charter, which King John was forced to accept at Runnymede in June 1215, after the rebels occupied London.

Magna Charta contains sixty-three chapters. Many of the chapters defined the king's feudal rights over his vassals, preventing the king from arbitrarily collecting revenue from the barons. Chapter 39 established the right to due process of law, and in chapter 40 the king promised that he would not sell, deny, or delay justice to anyone.

Magna Charta did not resolve the dispute between the barons and King John. Within months they were fighting again. In August 1215 the charter was annulled by Pope Innocent III, John's feudal overlord, on the grounds that it had been executed under duress. In 1216, however, after John's death the charter was reissued with some modifications. At the conclusion of the civil war in 1217, it was reissued again with minor revisions. This version of Magna Charta became part of the English constitutional tradition; confirmed by later kings and interpreted by Parliament, it is still revered as a symbol of English liberties.

———ɱ———

Magna Charta

John, by the grace of God, king of England, lord of Ireland, duke of Normandy and Aquitaine, count of Anjou, to all his archbishops, bishops, abbots, earls, barons, justiciars, foresters, sheriffs, stewards, servants, and all bailiffs and faithful men, health. Know that we by looking to God, and for the health of our soul, and of all our ancestors and heirs, to the honor of God, and the exaltation of his holy Church, and the rectifying of our realm by the counsel of our venerable fathers, Stephen, archbishop of Canterbury, primate of all England and cardinal of the holy Roman Church; Henry, archbishop of Dublin; William of London, Peter of Winchester, Joscelin of Bath and Glastonbury, Hugh of Lincoln, Walter of Worcester, William of Coventry and Benedict of Rochester, bishops; Master Pandulf, subdeacon of our lord pope and servant; brother Eymeric, master of the knights of the Temple in England; and of nobles, William Marshall, Earl of Pembroke; William, Earl of Salisbury; William, Earl Warrenne;

William, Earl of Arundel; Alan of Galway, constable of Scotland; Warin, son of Gerold; Peter, son of Herbert; Hubert de Burg, seneschal of Poitou; Hugh de Neville; Matthew, son of Herbert; Thomas Basset; Alan Basset; Philip de Albini; Robert de Ropley; John Marshall; John, son of Hugh; and others our lieges.

CHAPTER 1

First, we grant to God, and by this our present charter we confirm, for us and our heirs forever, that the English church be free, and have its rights whole and its liberties unimpaired; *and so we will to be observed, which appears from the fact that we have of pure and free will, before difference arose between us and our barons, granted, and by our charter confirmed, freedom of elections, which is conceived greatest and most necessary for the English church, and have got it confirmed from our lord Pope Innocent III, which we will observe ourselves and will to be observed in good faith by our heirs forever.*[1] We have granted to all free men of our realm, for ourself and our heirs forever, all these underwritten liberties to have and to hold, for themselves and their heirs, from us and our heirs.

CHAPTER 2

If any of our earls or barons, or other tenant of us in chief by military service, die, and when he dies, his heir be of full age, and owe a relief, he shall have his inheritance by the old relief, to wit, the heir, or heirs of an earl, for the whole barony of an earl by P100; the heir or heirs of a baron, the whole barony by P100; the heir or heirs of a knight for a whole military fee by 100*s*. at most, and he who owes less should pay less according to the ancient custom of fees.

CHAPTER 3

If the heir of any of these be below age, and be in wardship, when he comes to full age he shall have his inheritance without relief or fine.

CHAPTER 4

The guardians of the land of any heir, who is below age, shall not take from the land of the heir more than reasonable exits [revenues], and reasonable customs, and reasonable services, and this without destruction and waste of men or property; and if we commit the wardship of any such land to the sheriff or any one else, who is to answer to us for the exits, and he made destruction or waste of his wardship, we will

take recompense of him, and the land shall be committed to two lawful and discreet men of that fee, who will answer to us of the exits, or to him to whom we have assigned them; and if we have given or sold to any one the wardship of any such land, and he does destruction or waste, he shall lose his wardship, and give it to two lawful and discreet men of that fee, who shall in like manner answer to us as is aforesaid.

CHAPTER 5

The guardian, as long as he have wardship of the land, shall keep up houses, parks, stews, pools, mills, and other things belonging to that land, from the exits of the same land, and restore to the heir, when he comes to full age, all that land stocked with teams, according to what the season of teams demands, and the exits of the land can reasonably sustain.[2]

CHAPTER 6

Heirs shall be married without disparagement, *so that before they contract matrimony it be communicated to the kinsmen in blood of the heir.*

CHAPTER 7

A widow after the death of her husband shall at once and without hindrance have her marriage and inheritance, nor give anything for her dower, or for her marriage, or for her inheritance, which inheritance she and her husband had on the day of her husband's death, and she shall remain in her husband's home for forty days after his death, within which her dower shall be assigned to her.[3]

CHAPTER 8

No widow shall be forced to marry as long as she wills to live without a husband, so that she

---

Source: Selections from *The Second Treatise on Government*, 5 J. Locke, WORKS (1823). The footnotes have been renumbered.

[1] The full text of the Charter of 1215 has been included here. Sections that were omitted in later versions of the charter are printed in italic type on this and subsequent pages. Unless otherwise indicated, the omissions were made in 1216. Important alterations and additions have been indicated in the notes.

[2] A clause added in 1216 stipulated that the chapter also applied to ecclesiastical properties except that those wardships should not be sold.

[3] In 1217 a clause was added that guaranteed a widow one-third of her husband's lands unless a smaller dower had been assigned at the time of the marriage. In 1225 chapters 7 and 8 were combined into one.

give security that she will not marry without our assent, if she hold from us, or without the assent of the lord from whom she holds, if she holds from another.

CHAPTER 9

Neither we nor our bailiffs will seize any land or rent for any debt, as long as the chattels of the debtor suffice for paying the debt, nor shall the sureties of the debtor be distrained, as long as that debtor in chief suffices for the payment of the debt, and if the debtor in chief fail in paying the debt, not having whence to pay, the sureties shall answer for the debt, and if they will, shall have the land and rents of the debtor till they are satisfied of the debt which they paid for him, unless the debtor in chief show that he is quit thence against these sureties.

CHAPTER 10

If anyone borrows anything from the Jews, more or less, and dies before the debt is paid, the debt shall not bear usury as long as the heir is under age, from whoever he holds it, and if that debt fall into our hands we will take only the chattel contained in the deed.

CHAPTER 11

And if anyone die and owes a debt to the Jews, his wife shall have her dower and pay nothing of that debt, and if the children of the dead man are under age, necessaries shall be provided for them according to the holding of the dead man, and the debt shall be paid from the residue, the service of the lords saved, and in the same way shall it be done with debts which are owed to other than Jews.

CHAPTER 12

No scutage or aid shall be laid on our realm except by the common counsel of our realm, unless for ransoming our person, and making our eldest son a knight, and marrying our eldest daughter once, and this must only be a reasonable aid, and so shall it be with the aids of the city of London.

CHAPTER 13

And the city of London shall have all its ancient liberties and its free customs, *both by land and by water.* Besides we will and grant that all other cities, and burghs [boroughs], and vills [towns], and ports shall have all their liberties and free customs.

CHAPTER 14

And to have a common counsel of our realm on assessing an aid other than in the three aforenamed cases, or assessing a scutage, we will cause to be summoned archbishops, bishops, abbots, earls, and greater barons, singly by our letters, and we will also cause to be summoned in general, by our sheriffs and bailiffs, all those who hold of us in chief, at a certain day, to wit, at least forty days after, and a certain place; and in all letters of summons we will express the cause of summons, and when summons is made the business assigned for the day shall proceed according to the council of those who are present, though not all who are summoned come.

CHAPTER 15

We will grant to no one in future that he take aid from his free men, except to ransom his person, to make his eldest son a knight, and to marry his eldest daughter once, and for this there shall only be a reasonable aid.

CHAPTER 16

No one shall be distrained to do a greater service for a knight's fee, or any other frank [free] tenement than is due from it.

CHAPTER 17

Common pleas shall not follow our court, but shall be held in some certain place.

CHAPTER 18

Recognizances of novel disseisin, mort d'ancestor, and darrein presentment shall not be taken except in their own counties and in this manner; we, or, if we be out of the realm, our chief justiciar, will send two justices to each county four times in the year, who, with four knights of each county, elected by the county, shall take in the county and day and place the aforenamed assises of the county.[4]

CHAPTER 19

And if the aforesaid assises of the county cannot be taken on that day, so many knights and free tenants shall remain of those who were at the county on that day, by whom judgments

---

[4] In 1217 the text was changed to say that justices (number unspecified) would be sent through each county once a year to hold assises with knights of the county (number unspecified). A separate chapter was created that stipulated that assises involving darrein presentment should always be held before the justices of the bench.

can be sufficiently effected, according as the business is great or small.

CHAPTER 20

A free man shall not be amerced for a small offense unless according to the measure of the offense, and for a great offense he shall be amerced according to the greatness of the offense, saving his tenement, and the merchant in the same manner, saving his merchandise, and the villein shall be amerced in the same manner, saving his tools of husbandry, if they fall into our mercy, and none of the aforenamed mercies shall be imposed except by the oath of reputable men of the vicinage.

CHAPTER 21

Earls and barons shall not be amerced but by their equals, and only according to the measure of the offense.

CHAPTER 22

No cleric shall be amerced *of his lay tenement,* except according to the measure of the other aforesaid, and not according to the size of his ecclesiastical benefice.[5]

CHAPTER 23

No vill or man shall be distrained to make bridges at rivers, unless he who of old, or by right, is bound to do so.

CHAPTER 24

No sheriff, constable, coroners, or others of our bailiffs shall hold pleas of our crown.

CHAPTER 25

All counties, hundreds, wapentakes, and ridings shall be at the old farms [rents] without any increase, saving the manors of our demesne.

CHAPTER 26

If anyone holding a lay fee [fief] of us dies, and the sheriff or our bailiff shows our letters patent of the summonses of a debt which the dead man owed us, it shall be lawful for our sheriff or bailiff to attach and enroll the chattels of the dead man found in this fee to the value of the debt by the view of lawful men, so that nothing be moved thence till our debt which is clear be paid us, and the residue shall be left to the executors to fulfill the testament of the deceased, and if nothing be owed us by the deceased, all his chattels shall go to the deceased, save the reasonable shares to his wife and children.

CHAPTER 27

If any free man die intestate, his chattels shall be distributed by his nearest relations and friends, by the view of the church, save the debts due to each which the deceased owed.

CHAPTER 28

No constable, or other bailiff of ours, shall take the corn or chattels of anyone, unless he forthwith pays money for them, or can have any respite by the good will of the seller.[6]

CHAPTER 29

No constable shall distrain any knight to give money for the wardship of a castle [military service in the garrison of a castle], if he be willing to perform that wardship in his own person, or by some other reputable man, if he cannot do it himself for some reasonable cause, and if we have led or sent him to an army, he shall be quit of the wardship, according to the length of time that he is with us in the army.

CHAPTER 30

No sheriff or bailiff of ours, or any other, shall take horses and carts of any free man for carrying, except by the will of the free man.[7]

CHAPTER 31

Neither we nor our bailiffs will take any wood for our castles, or other our works, except by consent of the man whose wood it is.

CHAPTER 32

We will not hold the lands of those who are convict of felony, except for one year and one day, and then the lands shall be returned to the lords of the fees.

---

[5] In 1225 chapters 20, 21, and 22 were combined in a single chapter.

[6] In 1216 the chapter was modified to say that constables and their bailiffs should not take the goods of anyone who is not from the village where the castle is located unless they pay cash or make arrangements to pay later; persons from the village should be paid in three weeks. In 1217 the three weeks was changed to forty days.

[7] In 1216 the chapter was modified to say that the horses and carts should not be taken unless the owner received a specified amount of money. In 1217 a chapter was inserted that prohibited bailiffs from taking carts from the demesne of a cleric, a knight, or a lady. In 1225 chapters 30 and 31 from the Charter of 1215 and the new chapter were combined into a single chapter.

CHAPTER 33

All kidells [fish-weirs] shall for the future be wholly taken away from the Thames and the Medway, and through all England, except at the coast of the sea.

CHAPTER 34

The writ which is called *praecipe* for the future shall not issue to anyone about any tenement from which a free man may lose his court.

CHAPTER 35

There shall be one measure of wine throughout our whole realm, and one measure of beer, and one measure of corn, to wit, the London quarter, and one breadth of dyed cloth, and russet and haberget cloth, to wit, two ells within the lists, and of weights it shall be as of measures.

CHAPTER 36

Nothing shall be given or taken hereafter for the writ of inquisition on life or limb, but it shall be granted freely, and not denied.

CHAPTER 37

If anyone holds of us by fee-farm, either by socage or by burgage, or of any other land by military service, we shall not have the wardship of the heir or his land which belongs to another's fee, because of that fee-farm, or socage or burgage, nor shall we have wardship of that fee-farm, or socage or burgage, unless the fee-farm itself owes military service. We shall not either have wardship of heir or any land, which he holds of another by military service, by reason of some petty serjeanty which he holds of us, by the service of paying us knives, or arrows, or the like.

CHAPTER 38

No bailiff in future shall put anyone to law by his mere word, without trustworthy witnesses brought forward for it.

CHAPTER 39

No free man shall be seized, or imprisoned, or disseised, or outlawed, or exiled, or injured in any way, nor will we enter on him or send against him except by the lawful judgment of his peers, or by the law of the land.[8]

CHAPTER 40

We will sell to no one, or deny to no one, or put off right or justice.

CHAPTER 41

All merchants shall have safe conduct and security to go out of England or come into England, and to stay in, and go through England, both by land and water, for buying or selling, without any evil tolls, by old and right customs, except in time of war; and if they be of the land at war against us, and if such shall be found in our land, at the beginning of war, they shall be attached without loss of person or property, until it be known by us or our chief justiciar how the merchants of our land are treated who are found then in the land at war with us; and if ours be safe there, others shall be safe here.[9]

CHAPTER 42

It shall be lawful for anyone hereafter to go out of our realm, and return, safe and sound, by land or by water, saving fealty to us, except in time of war for some short time, for the common weal of the realm, except imprisoned men, and outlaws according to the law of the realm, and as natives of a land at war against us, and to the merchants of whom is done as is aforesaid.

CHAPTER 43

If any person holds of any escheat, as of the honor of Wallingford, Nottingham, Boulogne, Lancaster, or of other escheats which are in our hands, and they are baronies, and he dies, his heir shall not pay any other relief, or do us any other service but that which he would do for the baron, if the barony were in the hand of a baron, and we similarly will hold him in the same way that the baron held him.[10]

CHAPTER 44

Men who dwell without the forest shall not come hereafter before our justices of the forest, by common summonses, unless they are in plea, or sureties of one or more, who are attached for the forest.[11]

---

[8] In 1217 the words "of his freehold liberties or free customs" were inserted after "disseised." In 1225 the words "in the future" were inserted after "No free man shall," and the chapter and the one following it were joined together.

[9] In 1216 the words "unless formerly they have been publicly prohibited" were inserted after "All merchants."

[10] In 1217 a sentence added at the end of the chapter stipulated that the king would not have an escheat or wardship by reason of such an escheat or barony unless the person who held the property was a tenant-in-chief for other property.

[11] Chapter 44 of the Charter of 1215 was retained in the Charter of 1216, but in 1217 it was transferred to the separate Charter of the Forest. In 1217 a new chapter was inserted at

CHAPTER 45

We will not make justices, constables, sheriffs, or bailiffs except from those who know the law of the realm, and are willing to keep it.

CHAPTER 46

All barons who have founded abbeys, whence they have charters of the kings of England, or ancient tenure, shall have their custody while vacant, as they ought to have it.

CHAPTER 47

All forests which have been afforested in our time shall be forthwith deforested, and so with the rivers which have been forbidden by us in our time.[12]

CHAPTER 48

All ill customs of forests and warrens, and foresters and warreners, sheriffs and their servants, rivers and their keepers, shall be forthwith inquired into in each county by twelve sworn knights of the same county, who should be chosen by the reputable men of the same county; and, within forty days after the inquest is over, they shall be wholly done away by them, never to be recalled, so we know this first, or our justiciar, if we are not in England.

CHAPTER 49

We will forthwith return all hostages and charters which were delivered to us by the English as security of peace or faithful service.

CHAPTER 50

We will wholly remove from their bailiwicks the relations of Gerard de Athée so that hereafter they shall have no bailiwick in England, Engelard de Cigogné, Andrew, Peter, and Guy de Chanceux, Geoffrey de Martigny and his brothers, Philip Mark and his brothers, and Geoffrey his nephew, and all their following.

CHAPTER 51

And immediately after the restoration of peace, we will remove from the realm all foreign knights, bowmen, officers, and mercenaries who came with horses and arms to the harm of the realm.

---

this point that stipulated that no free man should give or sell so much of his land that he would be prevented from doing the full service due from the fief.

[12] In 1217 the first clause was transferred to the Charter of the Forest; the second clause became a separate chapter.

CHAPTER 52

If anyone has been disseised or deprived by us without lawful judgment of his peers, from lands, castles, liberties, or his right, we will forthwith restore him; and if a dispute arise about this, judgment shall then be made by twenty-five barons, of whom mention is made below, for the security of peace, and of all those matters of which a man has been disseised or deprived without the lawful judgment of his peers, by King Henry our father, or by King Richard our brother, which lands we have in our hands, or which others have, which we ought to warrant, we will have respite up to the common term of the crusaders, those being excepted of which the plea was raised or inquisition was made by our order, before the taking of our cross, and when we return from our journey, or if we chance to remain from our journey, we will forthwith show full justice thence.

CHAPTER 53

We will have the same respite, and in the same way, about exhibiting justice of deforesting or maintaining the forests, which Henry our father, or Richard our brother afforested, and of the wardship of the lands which are of another's fee, of which thing we have hitherto had the wardship, by reason of the fee, because someone held of us by military service, and of the abbeys which were founded on the fee of another than our own, in which the lord of the fee says he has the right; and when we return, or if we stay from our journey, we will afford full justice to those who complain of these things.

CHAPTER 54

No one shall be seized or imprisoned for the appeal of a woman about the death of any other man but her husband.

CHAPTER 55

All fines which have been made unjustly and against the law of the land with us, and all amercements made unjustly and against the law of the land, shall be wholly excused, or it shall be done with them by the judgment of twenty-five barons, of whom mention will be made below on the security of the peace, or by the judgment of the greater part of them, along with the aforenamed Stephen, archbishop of Canterbury, if he can be present, and others whom he wills to summon to him, and if he be unable to be present, nevertheless the business shall go on without him, so that if one or more of the aforenamed twenty-five barons are in a like suit, they may be removed as far as this judgment is concerned, and others be appointed, elected, and sworn for this matter only, by the residue of the same twenty-five.

CHAPTER 56

If we have disseised or deprived the Welsh of their lands or liberties or other goods, without lawful judgment of their peers, in England or in Wales, let these things be forthwith restored, and if a dispute arise upon this, let it be thereafter settled in the march by the judgment of their peers; on tenements in England according to the law of England; on tenements in Wales according to the law of Wales; on tenements in the march according to the law of the march. The Welshmen shall do the same to us and ours.[13]

CHAPTER 57

In all these matters in which anyone of the Welsh was disseised or deprived without lawful judgment of his peers, by King Henry our father, or King Richard our brother, which we have in our hands, or which others hold, and which we ought to warrant, we will have respite to the common term of the crusaders, those excepted in which our plea has been raised, or inquisition has been made by our order, before we took the cross; but, when we return, or if by chance we wait from our journey, we will show full justice to them thence, according to the laws of Wales, and the aforesaid parties.

CHAPTER 58

We will restore the son of Llewellyn forthwith, and all the hostages of Wales, and the charters which have been delivered to us for the security of peace.

CHAPTER 59

We will do to Alexander, king of Scots, about his sisters, and restoring his hostages, and his liberties, and his right, according to the form in which we have dealt with our other barons of England, unless they are bound to other matters by the charters which we have of William his father, once king of the Scots, and this shall be by judgment of their peers in our court.

CHAPTER 60

All these aforesaid customs and liberties which we have granted to be held in our realm, as far as belongs to us, towards our own, all in our realm, both clergy and lay, shall observe, as far as belongs to them, towards their own.

CHAPTER 61

But since, for the sake of God and for the bettering of our realm, and for better quieting the discord which has arisen between us and our barons, we have ganted all the aforesaid, wishing to enjoy them in pure and firm security forever, we make and grant them the underwritten security: viz. that the barons choose twenty-five barons from the realm, whom they will, who should with all their power keep, hold, and cause to be kept, the peace and liberties which we grant them, and by this our present charter confirm, so that, if we, or our justiciar, or our bailiffs, or any of our servants, do wrong in any case to anyone, or we transgress any of the articles of peace and security, and the offense is shown to four out of the aforenamed twenty-five barons, those four barons shall come to us, or our justiciar, if we are out of the realm, to show the wrong; they shall seek that we cause that wrong to be rectified without delay. And if we do not rectify the wrong, or if we are without the realm, our justiciar does not rectify it within forty days from the time in which it was shown to us or our justiciar, if we are without the realm, the aforesaid four barons shall bring the case before the rest of the twenty-five barons, and those twenty-five barons, with the commonalty of the whole realm, shall distrain and distress us, in every way they can, to wit, by the capture of castles, lands, possessions, and other ways in which they can, till right is done according to their will, saving our person and that of our queen and our children; and, when right is done, they shall obey us as before. And whoever of the land wishes, may swear that he will obey the orders of the aforesaid twenty-five barons, in carrying out all the aforesaid, and that he will distress us as far as he can, with them, and we give publicly and freely license to all to swear who wills, and we will forbid no one to swear. But all those in the land who will not, by themselves and of their own accord, swear to the twenty-five barons about distraining and distressing us with them, we will cause them to swear by our orders, as is aforesaid. And if any one of the twenty-five barons dies, or quits the country, or in any way is hindered from being able to carry out the aforesaid, the remainder of the aforesaid twenty-five barons may choose another into his place, at their discretion, who shall be sworn in like manner with the rest. In all those matters which are committed to the barons

---

[13] Chapter 56 was retained in the Charter of 1216 but was omitted thereafter.

to carry out, if these twenty-five happen to be present and differ on any one point, or others summoned by them will not or cannot be present, that must be had settled and fixed which the majority of those who are present provides or decides, just as if all the twenty-five agreed on it, and the aforesaid twenty-five shall swear that they will faithfully keep all the aforesaid, and cause them to be kept with all their power. And we will ask nothing from anyone, by ourselves or any other, by which any one of these grants and liberties shall be revoked or lessened; and if we do obtain any such thing, it shall be vain and void, and we will never use it by ourselves or by another.

CHAPTER 62

And all ill will, wrath, and rancor, which has arisen between us and our men, clerics and laymen, from the time of the discord, we fully have remitted and condoned to all. Besides, all the offenses done by reason of the same discord, from Easter in the sixteenth year of our reign to the renewal of peace, we wholly remit to all, clerics and laymen, and as far as we are concerned fully have condoned. And, moreover, we have caused letters patent to be made to them, in witness of this, of lord Stephen, archbishop of Canterbury, of lord Henry, archbishop of Dublin, and of the aforesaid bishops, and of Master Pandulf, as the aforenamed security and grants.

CHAPTER 63

Wherefore we will and firmly order that the English church should be free, and that the men of our realm should have and hold all the aforenamed liberties, rights, and grants, well and in peace, freely and quietly, fully and completely, for them and their heirs, from us and our heirs, in all things and places, forever, as is aforesaid. It is sworn both by us, and on the part of the barons, that all these aforesaid shall be kept in good faith and without ill meaning. Witnesses, the above-named and many others. Given by our hand, in the meadow which is called Runnymede, between Windsor and Staines, on the fifteenth day of June, in the seventeenth year of our reign.[14]

---

[14] Several chapters were added in 1217 that regulated the sheriff's tourn (tour through the hundreds, or subdivisions, of a county to hold court) and view of frankpledge; made it illegal for anyone to give land to a religious house and receive it back to hold as a tenant; established that scutage should be taken as it had been during the reign of King Henry II (1154–1189); and decreed that all adulterine castles (castles built without the king's permission) that had been erected since the beginning of the war between John and the barons should be destroyed. All but the last chapter were retained in 1225.

ENGLISH LAW

ENGLISH BILL OF RIGHTS

An Act Declaring the Rights and Liberties of the Subject
and Settling the Succession of the Crown

The English Bill of Rights grew out of the Glorious Revolution of 1688. During the revolution King James II abdicated and fled from England. He was succeeded by his daughter, Mary, and her husband, William of Orange, a Dutch prince. Parliament proposed a Declaration of Rights and presented it to William and Mary on February 13, 1689. Only after they accepted the declaration did Parliament proclaim them king and queen of England. Parliament then added several clauses to the declaration and formally enacted the amended bill as the Bill of Rights on December 16, 1689.

The Bill of Rights combined past grievances against the deposed king with a more general statement of basic liberties. The statute prohibited the monarch from suspending laws or levying taxes or customs duties without Parliament's consent and prohibited the raising and maintaining of a standing army during peacetime. More importantly, it proclaimed fundamental liberties, including freedom of elections, freedom of debate in Parliament, and freedom from excessive bail and from cruel and unusual punishments. To prevent a recurrence of the religious divisions that beset the Catholic James in ruling a largely Protestant England, the Bill of Rights also barred Roman Catholics from the throne.

The Bill of Rights became one of the cornerstones of the unwritten English constitution. The Bill of Rights has also had a significant impact on U.S. law, with many of its provisions becoming part of the U.S. Constitution and Bill of Rights.

—〰—

English Bill of Rights

Whereas the Lords Spiritual and Temporal and Commons assembled at Westminster, lawfully, fully, and freely representing all the states of people of this realm, did upon the thirteenth day of February in the year of our Lord one thousand six hundred eighty-eight present unto their Majesties, then called and known by the names and style of William and Mary, prince and princess of Orange, being present in their proper persons, a certain declaration in writing made by the said Lords and Commons in the words following, viz:[1]

Whereas the late King James the Second, by the assistance of divers evil councilors, judges, and ministers employed by him, did endeavor to subvert and extirpate the Protestant religion and the laws and liberties of the kingdom;

By assuming and exercising a power of dispensing with and suspending of laws and the execution of laws without consent of Parliament;

By committing and prosecuting divers worthy prelates for humbly petitioning to be excused from concurring to the said assumed power;

By issuing and causing to be executed a commission under the great seal for erecting a

---

Source: Selections from *The Second Treatise on Government*, 5 J. Locke, WORKS (1823). The footnotes have been renumbered.

[1] English monarchs styled themselves king or queen of France between 1340 and 1801. The custom began when the English became embroiled in the Hundred Years War with France and King Edward III of England, whose mother was a French princess, claimed the French throne.

court called the Court of Commissioners for Ecclesiastical Causes;

By levying money for and to the use of the Crown by pretense of prerogative for other time and in other manner than the same was granted by Parliament;

By raising and keeping a standing army within this kingdom in time of peace without consent of Parliament and quartering soldiers contrary to law;

By causing several good subjects being Protestants to be disarmed at the same time when papists were both armed and employed contrary to law;

By violating the freedom of election of members to serve in Parliament;

By prosecutions in the Court of King's Bench for matters and causes cognizable only in Parliament and by divers other arbitrary and illegal courses;

And whereas of late years, partial, corrupt, and unqualified persons have been returned and served on juries in trials, and particularly divers jurors in trials for high treason which were not freeholders;

And excessive bail hath been required of persons committed in criminal cases to elude the benefit of the laws made for the liberty of the subjects;

And excessive fines have been imposed;

And illegal and cruel punishments inflicted;

And several grants and promises made of fines and forfeitures before any conviction or judgment against the persons upon whom the same were to be levied;

All which are utterly and directly contrary to the known laws and statutes and freedom of this realm.

And whereas the said late King James the Second having abdicated the government, and the throne being thereby vacant, his Highness the prince of Orange (whom it hath pleased Almighty God to make the glorious instrument of delivering this kingdom from popery and arbitrary power) did, by the advice of the Lords Spiritual and Temporal and divers principal persons of the Commons, cause letters to be written to the Lords Spiritual and Temporal being Protestants and other letters to the several counties, cities, universities, boroughs, and cinque ports for the choosing of such persons to repre-

sent them as were of right to be sent to Parliament, to meet and sit at Westminster upon the two-and-twentieth day of January in this year one thousand six hundred eighty and eight, in order to such an establishment as that their religion, laws, and liberties might not again be in danger of being subverted; upon which letters, elections have been accordingly made.

And thereupon the said Lords Spiritual and Temporal and Commons, pursuant to their respective letters and elections being now assembled in a full and free representative of this nation, taking into their most serious consideration the best means for attaining the ends aforesaid, do in the first place (as their ancestors in like case have usually done) for the vindicating and asserting their ancient rights and liberties, declare

That the pretended power of suspending of laws or the execution of laws by regal authority without consent of Parliament is illegal;

That the pretended power of dispensing with laws or the execution of laws by regal authority, as it hath been assumed and exercised of late, is illegal;

That the commission for erecting the late Court of Commissioners for Ecclesiastical Causes, and all other commissions and courts of like nature, are illegal and pernicious;

That levying money for or to the use of the Crown by pretense of prerogative without grant of Parliament, for longer time or in other manner than the same is or shall be granted, is illegal;

That it is the right of the subjects to petition the king, and all commitments and prosecutions for such petitioning are illegal;

That the raising or keeping a standing army within the kingdom in time of peace, unless it be with consent of Parliament, is against law;

That the subjects which are Protestants may have arms for their defense suitable to their conditions and as allowed by law;

That election of members of Parliament ought to be free;

That the freedom of speech and debates or proceedings in Parliament ought not to be impeached or questioned in any court or place out of Parliament;

That excessive bail ought not to be required, nor excessive fines imposed, or cruel and unusual punishments inflicted;

That jurors ought to be duly impaneled and returned, and jurors which pass upon men in trials for high treason ought to be freeholders;

That all grants and promises of fines and forfeitures of particular persons before conviction are illegal and void;

And that, for redress of all grievances and for the amending, strengthening, and preserving of the laws, Parliaments ought to be held frequently.

And they do claim, demand, and insist upon all and singular the premises as their undoubted rights and liberties, and no declarations, judgments, doings, or proceedings to the prejudice of the people in any of the said premises ought in any wise to be drawn hereafter into consequence or example. To which demand of their rights, they are particularly encouraged by the declaration of his Highness the prince of Orange, as being the only means for obtaining a full redress and remedy therein. Having therefore an entire confidence that his said Highness the prince of Orange will perfect the deliverance so far advanced by him and will still preserve them from the violation of their rights which they have here asserted and from all other attempts upon their religion, rights, and liberties, the said Lords Spiritual and Temporal and Commons assembled at Westminster do resolve that William and Mary, prince and princess of Orange, be and be declared king and queen of England, France, and Ireland and the dominions thereunto belonging,[2] to hold the Crown and royal dignity of the said kingdom and dominions to them, the said prince and princess, during their lives and the life of the survivor of them; and that the sole and full exercise of the regal power be only in and executed by the said prince of Orange in the names of the said prince and princess during their joint lives, and after their deceases the said Crown and royal dignity of the said kingdoms and dominions to be to the heirs of the body of the said princess, and for default of such issue to the Princess Anne of Denmark and the heirs of her body, and for default of such issue to the heirs of the body of the said prince of Orange. And the Lords Spiritual and Temporal and Commons do pray the said prince and princess to accept the same accordingly; and that the oaths hereafter mentioned be taken by all persons of whom the oaths of allegiance and supremacy might be required by law, instead of them; and that the said oaths of allegiance and supremacy be abrogated:

I, A. B., do sincerely promise and swear that I will be faithful and bear true allegiance to their Majesties King William and Queen Mary. So help me God.

I, A. B., do swear that I do from my heart abhor, detest, and abjure as impious and heretical this damnable doctrine and position, that princes excommunicated or deprived by the pope or any authority of the see of Rome may be deposed or murdered by their subjects or any other whatsoever. And I do declare that no foreign prince, person, prelate, state, or potentate hath or ought to have any jurisdiction, power, superiority, preeminence, or authority, ecclesiastical or spiritual, within this realm. So help me God.

Upon which their said Majesties did accept the Crown and royal dignity of the kingdoms of England, France, and Ireland and the dominions thereunto belonging, according to the resolution and desire of the said Lords and Commons contained in the said declaration. And thereupon their Majesties were pleased that the said Lords Spiritual and Temporal and Commons, being the two Houses of Parliament, should continue to sit and, with their Majesties' royal concurrence, make effectual provision for the settlement of the religion, laws, and liberties of this kingdom, so that the same for the future might not be in danger again of being subverted. To which the said Lords Spiritual and Temporal and Commons did agree and proceed to act accordingly.

Now in pursuance of the premises, the said Lords Spiritual and Temporal and Commons in Parliament assembled, for the ratifying, confirming, and establishing the said declaration and the articles, clauses, matters, and things therein contained by the force of a law made in due form by authority of Parliament, do pray that it may be declared and enacted that all and singular the rights and liberties asserted and claimed in the said declaration are the true ancient and indubitable rights and liberties of the people of this kingdom and so shall be esteemed, allowed, adjudged, deemed, and taken to be; and that all and every the particulars aforesaid shall be firmly and strictly holden and observed as they are expressed in the said declaration; and all officers and ministers whatsoever shall serve their Majesties and their successors according to the same in all times to come. And the said Lords Spiritual and Temporal and Commons, seriously considering how it hath pleased Almighty God in his marvelous providence and merciful goodness to this nation to

ENGLISH LAW

ENGLISH BILL OF
RIGHTS

provide and preserve their said Majesties' royal persons most happily to reign over us upon the throne of their ancestors, for which they render unto him from the bottom of their hearts their humblest thanks and praises, do truly, firmly, assuredly, and in the sincerity of their hearts think, and do hereby recognize, acknowledge, and declare that King James the Second having abdicated the government and their Majesties having accepted the Crown and royal dignity as aforesaid, their said Majesties did become, were, are, and of right ought to be by the laws of this realm our sovereign liege lord and lady, king and queen of England, France, and Ireland and the dominions thereunto belonging; in and to whose princely persons, the royal state, Crown, and dignity of the said realms with all honors, styles, titles, regalities, prerogatives, powers, jurisdictions, and authorities to the same belonging and appertaining are most fully, rightfully, and entirely invested and incorporated, united and annexed.

And for preventing all questions and divisions in this realm by reason of any pretended titles to the Crown, and for preserving a certainty in the succession thereof, in and upon which the unity, peace, tranquility, and safety of this nation doth under God wholly consist and depend, the said Lords Spiritual and Temporal and Commons do beseech their Majesties that it may be enacted, established, and declared that the Crown and regal government of the said kingdoms and dominions, with all and singular the premises thereunto belonging and appertaining, shall be and continue to their said Majesties and the survivor of them during their lives and the life of the survivor of them; and that the entire, perfect, and full exercise of the regal power and government be only in and executed by his Majesty in the names of both their Majesties during their joint lives; and after the deceases, the said Crown and premises shall be and remain to the heirs of the body of her Majesty and, for default of such issue, to her Royal Highness the Princess Anne of Denmark and the heirs of her body and, for default of such issue, to the heirs of the body of his said Majesty. And thereunto the said Lords Spiritual and Temporal and Commons do in the name of all the people aforesaid most humbly and faithfully submit themselves, their heirs, and posterities forever and do faithfully promise that they will stand to maintain and defend their said Majesties and also the limitation and succession

of the Crown, herein specified and contained, to the utmost of their powers with their lives and estates against all persons whatsoever that shall attempt any thing to the contrary.

And whereas it hath been found by experience that it is inconsistent with the safety and welfare of this Protestant kingdom to be governed by a popish prince, or by any king or queen marrying a papist, the said Lords Spiritual and Temporal and Commons do further pray that it may be enacted that all and every person and persons that is, are, or shall be reconciled to, or shall hold communion with, the see or church of Rome, or shall profess the popish religion or shall marry a papist, shall be excluded and be forever incapable to inherit, possess, or enjoy the Crown and government of this realm and Ireland and the dominions thereunto belonging or any part of the same, or to have, use, or exercise any regal power, authority, or jurisdiction within the same. And in all and every such case or cases, the people of these realms shall be and are hereby absolved of their allegiance. And the said Crown and government shall from time to time descend to and be enjoyed by such person or persons being Protestants, as should have inherited and enjoyed the same in case the said person or persons so reconciled, holding communion, or professing or marrying as aforesaid were naturally dead. And that every king and queen of this realm, who at any time hereafter shall come to and succeed in the imperial Crown of this kingdom, shall on the first day of the meeting of the first Parliament next after his or her coming to the Crown, sitting in his or her throne in the House of Peers, in the presence of the Lords and Commons therein assembled, or at his or her coronation before such person or persons who shall administer the coronation oath to him or her at the time of his or her taking the said oath (which shall first happen), make, subscribe, and audibly repeat the declaration mentioned in the statute made in the thirtieth year of the reign of King Charles the Second entitled *An act for the more effectual preserving the king's person and government by disabling papists from sitting in either House of Parliament*. But if it shall happen that such a king or queen upon his or her succession to the Crown of this realm shall be under the age of twelve years, then every such king or queen shall make, subscribe, and audibly repeat the said declaration at his or her coronation, or the first day of the meeting of the first

Parliament as aforesaid which shall first happen after such king or queen shall have attained the said age of twelve years. All which their Majesties are contented and pleased shall be declared, enacted, and established by authority of this present Parliament and shall stand, remain, and be the law of this realm forever. And the same are by their said Majesties, by and with the advice and consent of the Lords Spiritual and Temporal and Commons in Parliament assembled and by the authority of the same, declared, enacted, and established accordingly.

And be it further declared and enacted by the authority aforesaid that, from and after this present session of Parliament, no dispensation by *non obstante* of or to any statute, or any part thereof, shall be allowed but that the same shall be held void and of no effect, except a dispensation be allowed of in such statutes, and except in such cases as shall be specially provided for by one or more bill or bills to be passed during this present session of Parliament.

Provided that no charter or grant or pardon granted before the three-and-twentieth day of October in the year of our Lord one thousand six hundred eighty-nine shall be anyway impeached or invalidated by this act, but that the same shall be and remain of the same force and effect in law and no other than as if this act had never been made.

ENGLISH LAW

ENGLISH BILL OF
RIGHTS

ENGLISH LAW

SECOND TREATISE ON GOVERNMENT

John Locke, 1690

The Englishman JOHN LOCKE is regarded as one of the world's most important political philosophers, and his "Second Treatise on Government" has proved to be one of the seminal documents on the liberal political state. The U.S. system of government was built on Locke's ideas, including such core premises as the ultimate sovereignty of the people, the necessity of restraints on the exercise of arbitrary power by the executive or the legislature, and the revocability of the social contract by the people when power has been arbitrarily used against them. The Declaration of Independence and the U.S. Constitution are testaments to many of Locke's core ideas.

The "Second Treatise" (the second part of *Two Treatises on Government*) was written during the period preceding the abdication of King James II. Locke's work, which was published in 1690, became a justification for the Glorious Revolution of 1688, when government was reformed along the lines outlined by Locke in his *Two Treatises*. As a result of these reforms, England became a constitutional monarchy under Parliament's control. Greater measures of religious toleration and freedom of expression and thought were permitted, as set out in the English Bill of Rights.

In part, the *Two Treatises* were an attack upon political absolutism. The first treatise refuted the theory of the divine right of kings, which posited that monarchs derived their authority from God. The second treatise, however, has had the more lasting impact on the United States, for it sets out a theory of politics that found its way into U.S. law.

Locke maintained that people are naturally tolerant and reasonable, but that without a governing force, a certain amount of chaos and other inconveniences will occur. In his view all people are inherently equal and free to pursue "life, liberty, health, and property." To do this, they engage in a social contract in which they consent to give up a certain amount of power to a government dedicated to maintaining the well-being of the whole. At the same time, however, individuals' right to freedom of thought, speech, and worship must be preserved. In addition, the government must preserve citizens' private property.

Locke believed that the government is the trustee of the people's power and that it exercises power specifically for the purpose of serving the people. If the government abuses that trust, however, the people have a right to revoke the trust and assume the reins of government themselves or place them in new hands. This idea provided justification for the American Revolution in 1776.

Thomas Jefferson drew upon Locke's ideas of the law of nature, popular sovereignty, and the sanctity of the right of private property in writing the Declaration of Independence. The U.S. Constitution, with its separation of church and state and its guarantee of personal freedoms, reflects Locke's influence as well.

—ɯ—

Second Treatise on Government

CHAPTER VII.

Of Political or Civil Society.

§ 77. God having made man such a creature, that in his own judgment it was not good for him to be alone, put him under strong obligations of necessity, convenience, and inclination, to drive him into society, as well as fitted him with understanding and language to continue and enjoy it. The first society was between man and wife, which gave beginning to that between parents and children; to which, in time, that between master and servant came to be added: and though all these might, and commonly did meet together, and make up but one family, wherein the master or mistress of it had some sort of rule proper to a family; each of these, or all together, came short of political society, as we shall see, if we consider the different ends, ties, and bounds of each of these.

* * *

§ 85. Master and servant are names as old as history, but given to those of far different condition; for a free-man makes himself a servant to another, by selling him, for a certain time, the service he undertakes to do, in exchange for wages he is to receive: and though this commonly puts him into the family of his master, and under the ordinary discipline thereof: yet it gives the master but a temporary power over him, and no greater than what is contained in the contract between them. But there is another sort of servants, which by a peculiar name we call slaves, who being captives taken in a just war, are by the right of nature subjected to the absolute dominion and arbitrary power of their masters. These men having, as I say, forfeited their lives, and with it their liberties, and lost their estates; and being in the state of slavery, not capable of any property; cannot in that state be considered as any part of civil society; the chief end whereof is the preservation of property.

§ 86. Let us therefore consider a master of a family with all these subordinate relations of wife, children, servants, and slaves, united under the domestic rule of a family; which, what resemblance soever it may have in its order, offices, and number too, with a little commonwealth, yet is very far from it, both in its constitution, power, and end: or if it must be thought a monarchy, and the pater-familias the absolute monarch in it, absolute monarchy will have but a very shattered and short power, when it is plain, by what has been said before, that the master of the family has a very distinct and differently limited power, both as to time and extent, over those several persons that are in it: for excepting the slave (and the family is as much a family, and his power as pater-familias as great, whether there be any slaves in his family or no), he has no legislative power of life and death over any of them, and none too but what a mistress of a family may have as well as he. And he certainly can have no absolute power over the whole family, who has but a very limited one over every individual in it. But how a family, or any other society of men, differ from that which is properly political society, we shall best see by considering wherein political society itself consists.

§ 87. Man being born, as has been proved, with a title to perfect freedom, and uncontrolled enjoyment of all the rights and privileges of the law of nature, equally with any other man, or number of men in the world, hath by nature a power, not only to preserve his property, that is, his life, liberty, and estate, against the injuries and attempts of other men; but to judge of and punish the breaches of that law in others, as he is persuaded the offence deserves, even with death itself, in crimes where the heinousness of the fact, in his opinion, requires it. But because no political society can be, nor subsist, without having in itself the power to preserve the property, and, in order thereunto, punish the offences of all those of that society; there, and there only is political society, where every one of the members hath quitted this natural power, resigned it up into the hands of the community in all cases that exclude him not from appealing for protection to the law established by it. And thus all private judgment of every particular member being excluded, the community comes to be umpire, by settled standing rules, indifferent, and the same to all parties; and by men having authority from the community, for the execution of those rules, decides all the differences that may happen between any members of that society concerning any matter of right; and punishes those offences which any member hath committed against the society, with such penalties as the law has established: whereby it is easy to discern who are, and who are not, in political society together. Those who are united into one body, and have a common established law and judicature to appeal to, with authority to decide controversies between them, and punish offenders, are in civil society one with another: but those who have no such common appeal, I mean on earth, are still in the state of nature, each being, where there is no other, judge for himself, and executioner: which is, as I have before showed it, the perfect state of nature.

§ 88. And thus the commonwealth comes by a power to set down what punishment shall belong to the several transgressions which they think worthy of it, committed amongst the members of that society, (which is the power of making laws) as well as it has the power to punish any injury done unto any of its members, by any one that is not of it, (which is the power of war and peace:) and all this for the preservation of the property of all the members of that society, as far as is possible. But though every man who has entered into civil society, and is become a member of any commonwealth, has thereby quitted his power to punish offences against the law of nature, in prosecution of his own private judgment; yet with the judgment of offences, which he has given up to the legislative in all cases, where he can appeal to the magistrate, he has given a right to the commonwealth to employ his force, for the execution of the judgments of the commonwealth, whenever he shall be called to it; which indeed are his own judgments, they being made by himself, or his representative. And herein we have the original of the legislative and executive power of civil society, which is to judge by standing laws, how far offences are to be punished, when committed within the commonwealth; and also to determine, by occasional judgments founded on the present circumstances of the fact, how far injuries from without are to be vindicated; and in both these to employ all the force of all the members, when there shall be need.

§ 89. Whenever therefore any number of men are so united into one society, as to quit every one his executive power of the law of nature, and to resign it to the public, there and there only is a political or civil society. And this is done, wherever any number of men, in the state of nature, enter into society to make one people, one body politic, under one supreme government; or else when any one joins himself to, and incorporates with any government already made: for hereby he authorizes the society, or, which is all one, the legislative thereof, to

make laws for him, as the public good of the society shall require; to the execution whereof, his own assistance (as to his own degrees) is due. And this puts men out of a state of nature into that of a commonwealth, by setting up a judge on earth, with authority to determine all the controversies, and redress the injuries that may happen to any member of the commonwealth; which judge is the legislative, or magistrate appointed by it. And wherever there are any number of men, however associated, that have no such decisive power to appeal to, there they are still in the state of nature.

§ 90. Hence it is evident, that absolute monarchy, which by some men is counted the only government in the world, is indeed inconsistent with civil society, and so can be no form of civil government at all: for the end of civil society being to avoid and remedy those inconveniences of the state of nature which necessarily follow from every man being judge in his own case, by setting up a known authority, to which every one of that society may appeal upon any injury received, or controversy that may arise, and which every one of the society ought to obey;[66] wherever any persons are, who have not such an authority to appeal to, for the decision of any difference between them, there those persons are still in the state of nature; and so is every absolute prince, in respect of those who are under his dominion.

§ 91. For he being supposed to have all, both legislative and executive power in himself alone, there is no judge to be found, no appeal lies open to any one, who may fairly, and indifferently, and with authority decide, and from whose decision relief and redress may be expected of any injury or inconveniency, that may be suffered from the prince, or by his order: so that such a man, however entitled, czar, or grand seignior, or how you please, is as much in the state of nature, with all under his dominion, as he is with the rest of

---

Source: Selections from *The Second Treatise on Government*, 5 J. Locke, WORKS (1823). The footnotes have been renumbered.

[66] "The public power of all society is above every soul contained in the same society; and the principal use of that power is to give laws unto all that are under it which laws in such cases we must obey, unless there be reason showed which may, necessarily enforce that the law of reason, or of God, doth enjoin the contrary" (Hooker's *Eccl. Pol.* lib. i. sect. 16). [Ed. note] In the Keble edition of Hooker's Works, the appropriate citation for this passage would be Book I, chapter xvi, § 5.

mankind: for wherever any two men are, who have no standing rule, and common judge to appeal to on earth, for the determination of controversies of right betwixt them, there they are still in the state of nature[67], and under all the inconveniences of it, with only this woeful difference to the subject, or rather slave of an absolute prince: that whereas in the ordinary state of nature he has a liberty to judge of his right, and, according to the best of his power, to maintain it; now, whenever his property is invaded by the will and order of his monarch, he has not only no appeal, as those in society ought to have, but, as if he were degraded from the common state of rational creatures, is denied a liberty to judge of, or to defend his right: and so is exposed to all the misery and inconveniences, that a man can fear from one, who being in the unrestrained state of nature, is yet corrupted with flattery, and armed with power.

§ 92. For he that thinks absolute power purifies men's blood, and corrects the baseness of human nature, need read but the history of this, or any other age, to be convinced of the contrary. He that would have been insolent and injurious in the woods of America, would not probably be much better in a throne; where perhaps learning and religion shall be found out to justify all that he shall do to his subjects, and the sword presently silence all those that dare question it: for what the protection of absolute monarchy is, what kind of fathers of their countries it makes princes to be, and to what a degree of happiness and security it carries civil society, where this sort of government is grown to perfection; he that will look into the late relation of Ceylon may easily see.

§ 93. In absolute monarchies indeed, as well as other governments of the world, the subjects have an appeal to the law, and judges to decide any controversies, and restrain any violence that may happen betwixt the subjects themselves, one amongst another. This every one thinks necessary, and believes he deserves to be thought a declared enemy to society and mankind who should go about to take it away. But whether this be from a true love of mankind and society, and such a charity as we all owe one to another, there is reason to doubt: for this is no more than what

every man, who loves his own power, profit, or greatness, may and naturally must do, keep those animals from hurting or destroying one another, who labour and drudge only for his pleasure and advantage; and so are taken care of, not out of any love the master has for them, but love of himself, and the profit they bring him: for if it be asked, what security, what fence is there, in such a state, against the violence and oppression of this absolute ruler? the very question can scarce be borne. They are ready to tell you, that it deserves death only to ask after safety. Betwixt subject and subject, they will grant, there must be measures, laws, and judges, for their mutual peace and security: but as for the ruler, he ought to be absolute, and is above all such circumstances; because he has power to do more hurt and wrong, it is right when he does it. To ask how you may be guarded from harm, or injury, on that side where the strongest hand is to do it, is presently the voice of faction and rebellion: as if when men quitting the state of nature entered into society, they agreed that all of them but one should be under the restraint of laws, but that he should still retain all the liberty of the state of nature, increased with power, and made licentious by impunity. This is to think, that men are so foolish, that they take care to avoid what mischiefs may be done them by polecats, or foxes; but are content, nay think it safety, to be devoured by lions.

§ 94. But whatever flatterers may talk to amuse people's understandings, it hinders not men from feeling; and when they perceive that any man, in what station soever, is out of the bounds of the civil society which they are of, and that they have no appeal on earth against any harm they may receive from him, they are apt to think themselves in the state of nature in respect of him whom they find to be so; and to take care, as soon as they can, to have that safety and security in civil society for which it was instituted, and for which only they entered into it. And therefore, though perhaps at first (as shall be showed more at large hereafter in the following part of this discourse), some one good and excellent man having got a pre-eminency amongst the rest, had this deference paid to his goodness and virtue, as to a kind of natural authority, that the chief rule, with arbitration of their differences, by a tacit consent devolved into his hands, without any other caution but the assurance they had of his uprightness and wisdom; yet when time, giving authority, and (as

---

[67] [Ed. note] In a footnote, Locke here quotes a long passage from Hooker, LAWS OF ECCLESIASTICAL POLITY, Bk. I, c. x, § 4.

WITHDRAWN

some men would persuade us) sacredness to customs, which the negligent and unforeseeing innocence of the first ages began, had brought in successors of another stamp; the people finding their properties not secure under the government as then it was[68] (whereas government has no other end but the preservation of property), could never be safe nor at rest, nor think themselves in civil society, till the legislature was placed in collective bodies of men, call them senate, parliament, or what you please. By which means every single person became subject, equally with other the meanest men, to those laws which he himself, as part of the legislative, had established; nor could any one, by his own authority, avoid the force of the law when once made; nor by any pretence of superiority plead exemption, thereby to license his own, or the miscarriages of any of his dependents. "No man in civil society can be exempted from the laws of it:"[69] for if any man may do what he thinks fit, and there be no appeal on earth, for redress or security against any harm he shall do; I ask, whether he be not perfectly still in the state of nature, and so can be no part or member of that civil society; unless any one will say the state of nature and civil society are one and the same thing, which I have never yet found any one so great a patron of anarchy as to affirm.

CHAPTER VIII.

Of the Beginning of Political Societies.

§ 95. Men being, as has been said, by nature all free, equal, and independent, no one can be put out of this estate, and subjected to the political power of another, without his own consent. The only way whereby any one divests himself of his natural liberty, and puts on the bonds of civil society, is by agreeing with other men to join and unite into a community, for their comfortable, safe, and peaceable living one amongst another, in a secure enjoyment of their properties, and a greater security against any that are not of it. This any number of men may do, because it injures not the freedom of the rest; they are left as they were in the liberty of the state of nature. When any number of men have so consented to make one community or government, they are thereby

presently incorporated, and make one body politic, wherein the majority have a right to act and conclude the rest.

§ 96. For when any number of men have, by the consent of every individual, made a community, they have thereby made that community one body, with a power to act as one body, which is only by the will and determination of the majority; for that which acts any community being only the consent of the individuals of it, and it being necessary to that which is one body to move one way; it is necessary the body should move that way whither the greater force carries it, which is the consent of the majority: or else it is impossible it should act or continue one body, one community, which the consent of every individual that united into it agreed that it should; and so every one is bound by that consent to be concluded by the majority. And therefore we see that in assemblies, empowered to act by positive laws, where no number is set by that positive law which empowers them, the act of the majority passes for the act of the whole, and of course determines; as having, by the law of nature and reason, the power of the whole.

§ 97. And thus every man, by consenting with others to make one body politic under one government, puts himself under an obligation to every one of that society to submit to the determination of the majority, and to be concluded by it; or else this original compact, whereby he with others incorporate into one society, would signify nothing, and be no compact, if he be left free, and under no other ties than he was in before in the state of nature. For what appearance would there be of any compact? what new engagement, if he were no farther tied by any decrees of the society than he himself thought fit, and did actually consent to? This would be still as great a liberty as he himself had before his compact, or any one else in the state of nature hath, who may submit himself and consent to any acts of it if he thinks fit.

§ 98. For if the consent of the majority shall not, in reason, be received as the act of the whole, and conclude every individual, nothing but the consent of every individual can make any thing to be the act of the whole: but such a consent is next to impossible ever to be had, if we consider the infirmities of health, and avocations of business, which in a number, though much less than that of a commonwealth, will necessarily keep many away from the public

---

[68] [Ed. note] In a footnote, Locke here quotes from Hooker, LAWS OF ECCLESIASTICAL POLITY, Bk. I, c. x, § 5.

[69] "Civil law, being the act of the whole body politic, doth therefore over-rule each several part of the same body" (Hooker, *Ibid.*). [Ed. note] Bk. I, c. x, § 13.

assembly. To which if we add the variety of opinions, and contrariety of interests which unavoidably happen in all collections of men, the coming into society upon such terms would be only like Cato's coming into the theatre, only to go out again.[70] Such a constitution as this would make the mighty leviathan of a shorter duration than the feeblest creatures, and not let it outlast the day it was born in: which cannot be supposed, till we can think that rational creatures should desire and constitute societies only to be dissolved: for where the majority cannot conclude the rest, there they cannot act as one body, and consequently will be immediately dissolved again.

§ 99. Whosoever therefore out of a state of nature unite into a community, must be understood to give up all the power necessary to the ends for which they unite into society, to the majority of the community, unless they expressly agreed in any number greater than the majority. And this is done by barely agreeing to unite into one political society, which is all the compact that is, or needs be, between the individuals that enter into, or make up a commonwealth. And thus that which begins and actually constitutes any political society, is nothing but the consent of any number of freemen capable of a majority, to unite and incorporate into such a society. And this is that, and that only, which did or could give beginning to any lawful government in the world.

§ 100. To this I find two objections made.

First, "That there are no instances to be found in story, of a company of men independent and equal one amongst another, that met together, and in this way began and set up a government."

Secondly, "It is impossible of right, that men should do so, because all men being born under

government, they are to submit to that, and are not at liberty to begin a new one."

§ 101. To the first there is this to answer, that it is not at all to be wondered, that history gives us but a very little account of men that lived together in the state of nature. The inconveniences of that condition, and the love and want of society, no sooner brought any number of them together, but they presently united and incorporated, if they designed to continue together. And if we may not suppose men ever to have been in the state of nature, because we hear not much of them in such a state, we may as well suppose the armies of Salmanasser[71] or Xerxes were never children, because we hear little of them till they were men, and embodied in armies. Government is every where antecedent to records, and letters seldom come in amongst a people till a long continuation of civil society has, by other more necessary arts, provided for their safety, ease, and plenty: and then they begin to look after the history of their founders, and search into their original, when they have outlived the memory of it: for it is with commonwealths as with particular persons, they are commonly ignorant of their own births and infancies: and if they know any thing of their original, they are beholden for it to the accidental records that others have kept of it. And those that we have of the beginning of any politics in the world, excepting that of the Jews, where God himself immediately interposed, and which favours not at all paternal dominion, are all either plain instances of such a beginning as I have mentioned, or at least have manifest footsteps of it.

§ 102. He must show a strange inclination to deny evident matter of fact, when it agrees not with his hypothesis, who will not allow, that the beginnings of Rome and Venice were by the uniting together of several men free and independent one of another, amongst whom there

---

[70] [Ed. note] The reference of course is to Cato the Elder (Marcus, 234–149 B.C.) who was called Cato the Censor because of his opposition to the introduction into Rome of Greek refinement and luxury. This is the same Cato who continually urged the destruction of Carthage, an event which finally occurred three years after his death.

[71] [Ed. note] Undoubtedly a reference to Shalmaneser V (or IV), King of Assyria (727–22 B.C.) who defeated the Israelites (the inhabitants of the Northern Kingdom of Israel consisting of ten of the twelve tribes of Israel). He besieged the capital, Samaria, which fell to his successor Sargon II, who carried the inhabitants off to captivity in Assyria. These

incidents are referred to in II Kings (in the Catholic Bible, IV Kings) 17. As "Salmanazar," he has achieved a certain measure of immortality by providing the name of an oversized bottle of wine holding 9.6 liters or the equivalent of 12 regular-size bottles of champagne (about ten U.S. quarts). Xerxes (d. 465 B.C.), who is mentioned next in the text is of course the "Great King" (of Persia) who led the second Persian invasion of Greece. He forced the pass at Thermopylae and burned Athens, but was defeated in the famous sea battle of Salamis (480 B.C.); after he returned to Asia Minor, his Army was routed at the battle of Plataea in 479 B.C.

was no natural superiority or subjection. And if Josephus Acosta's[72] word may be taken, he tells us, that in many parts of America there was no government at all. "There are great and apparent conjectures," says he, "that these men, speaking of those of Peru, for a long time had neither kings nor commonwealths, but lived in troops, as they do this day in Florida, the Cheriquanas, those of Brasil, and many other nations, which have no certain kings, but as occasion is offered, in peace or war, they choose their captains as they please," l. i. c. *25.* If it be said that every man there was born subject to his father, or the head of his family; that the subjection due from a child to a father took not away his freedom of uniting into what political society he thought fit, has been already proved. But be that as it will, these men, it is evident, were actually free; and whatever superiority some politicians now would place in any of them, they themselves claimed it not, but by consent were all equal, till by the same consent they set rulers over themselves. So that their politic societies all began from a voluntary union, and the mutual agreement of men freely acting in the choice of their governors and forms of government.

§ 103. And I hope those who went away from Sparta with Palantus, mentioned by Justin,[73] l. iii. c. 4, will be allowed to have been freemen, independent one of another, and to have set up a government over themselves, by their own consent. Thus I have given several examples out of history, of people free and in the state of nature, that being met together incorporated and began a commonwealth. And if the want of such instances be an argument to prove that governments were not, nor could not be so begun, I suppose the contenders for paternal empire were better let it alone than urge it against natural liberty: for if they can give so

many instances out of history, of governments begun upon paternal right, I think (though at best an argument from what has been, to what should of right be, has no great force) one might, without any great danger, yield them the cause. But if I might advise them in the case, they would do well not to search too much into the original of governments, as they have begun *de facto;* lest they should find, at the foundation of most of them, something very little favourable to the design they promote, and such a power as they contend for.

§ 104. But to conclude, reason being plain on our side, that men are naturally free, and the examples of history showing, that the governments of the world, that were begun in peace, had their beginning laid on that foundation, and were made by the consent of the people; there can be little room for doubt, either where the right is, or what has been the opinion or practice of mankind about the first erecting of governments.

§ 105. I will not deny that if we look back as far as history will direct us, towards the original of commonwealths, we shall generally find them under the government and administration of one man. And I am also apt to believe, that where a family was numerous enough to subsist by itself, and continued entire together, without mixing with others, as it often happens, where there is much land and few people, the government commonly began in the father: for the father having, by the law of nature, the same power with every man else to punish, as he thought fit, any offences against that law, might thereby punish his transgressing children, even when they were men, and out of their pupilage; and they were very likely to submit to his punishment, and all join with him against the offender in their turns, giving him thereby power to execute his sentence against any transgression, and so in effect make him the lawmaker and governor over all that remained in conjunction with his family. He was fittest to be trusted; paternal affection secured their property and interest under his care; and the custom of obeying him in their childhood, made it easier to submit to him rather than to any other. If, therefore, they must have one to rule them, as government is hardly to be avoided amongst men that live together, who so likely to be the man as he that was their common father, unless negligence, cruelty, or any other defect of mind or body made him unfit for it? But when either

---

[72] [Ed. note] José de Acosta, c.1539–1600, a Spanish Jesuit missionary who spent about fifteen years in the Spanish possessions in the new world, principally Peru, and who wrote *Historia Natural y Moral de las Indias (A Natural and Moral History of the Indians)*, translated into English in 1604 and reprinted in 1880.

[73] [Ed. note] The reference is to Marcus Junianus Justinus, a Roman historian of the third century A.D. (or possibly later) whose major work was a summary of an earlier history, now lost, of Gnaeus Pompeius Trogus, who flourished around the first century B.C. to the first century A.D. The event described in the text was the founding of Tarentum (modern Taranto) in Southern Italy by dissatisfied Spartans under Phalanthus at around 708 B.C. This was the only colony ever founded by Sparta.

the father died, and left his next heir, for want of age, wisdom, courage, or any other qualities, less fit for rule, or where several families met and consented to continue together, there, it is not to be doubted, but they used their natural freedom to set up him whom they judged the ablest, and most likely to rule well over them. Conformable hereunto, we find the people of America, who (living out of the reach of the conquering swords and spreading domination of the two great empires of Peru and Mexico) enjoyed their own natural freedom, though, *cœteris paribus,* they commonly prefer the heir of their deceased king; yet if they find him any way weak or incapable, they pass him by, and set up the stoutest and bravest man for their ruler.

§ 106. Thus, though looking back as far as records give us any account of peopling the world, and the history of nations, we commonly find the government to be in one hand; yet it destroys not that which I affirm, viz. that the beginning of politic society depends upon the consent of the individuals, to join into, and make one society; who, when they are thus incorporated, might set up what form of government they thought fit. But this having given occasion to men to mistake, and think that by nature government was monarchical, and belonged to the father; it may not be amiss here to consider, why people in the beginning generally pitched upon this form: which though perhaps the father's preeminency might, in the first institution of some commonwealth, give a rise to, and place in the beginning the power in one hand; yet it is plain that the reason that continued the form of government in a single person, was not any regard or respect to paternal authority; since all petty monarchies, that is, almost all monarchies, near their original, have been commonly, at least upon occasion, elective.

§ 107. First then, in the beginning of things, the father's government of the childhood of those sprung from him, having accustomed them to the rule of one man, and taught them that where it was exercised with care and skill, with affection and love to those under it, it was sufficient to procure and preserve to men all the political happiness they sought for in society; it was no wonder that they should pitch upon, and naturally run into that form of government, which from their infancy they had been all accustomed to; and which, by experience, they had found both easy and safe. To which, if we

add, that monarchy being simple, and most obvious to men, whom neither experience had instructed in forms of government, nor the ambition or insolence of empire had taught to beware of the encroachments of prerogative, or the inconveniencies of absolute power, which monarchy in succession was apt to lay claim to, and bring upon them; it was not at all strange that they should not much trouble themselves to think of methods of restraining any exorbitancies of those to whom they had given the authority over them, and of balancing the power of government, by placing several parts of it in different hands. They had neither felt the oppression of tyrannical dominion, nor did the fashion of the age, nor their possessions, or way of living (which afforded little matter for covetousness or ambition), give them any reason to apprehend or provide against it; and therefore it is no wonder they put themselves into such a frame of government, as was not only, as I said, most obvious and simple, but also best suited to their present state and condition, which stood more in need of defence against foreign invasions and injuries, than of multiplicity of laws. The equality of a simple poor way of living, confining their desires within the narrow bounds of each man's small property, made few controversies, and so no need of many laws to decide them, or variety of officers to superintend the process, or look after the execution of justice, where there were but few trespasses, and few offenders. Since then those who liked one another so well as to join into society, cannot but be supposed to have some acquaintance and friendship together, and some trust one in another; they could not but have greater apprehensions of others than of one another: and therefore their first care and thought cannot but be supposed to be, how to secure themselves against foreign force. It was natural for them to put themselves under a frame of government which might best serve to that end, and choose the wisest and bravest man to conduct them in their wars, and lead them out against their enemies, and in this chiefly be their ruler.

§ 108. Thus we see that the kings of the Indians in America, which is still a pattern of the first ages in Asia and Europe, whilst the inhabitants were too few for the country, and want of people and money gave men no temptation to enlarge their possessions of land, or contest for wider extent of ground, are little more than generals of their armies; and though they command absolutely in war, yet at home and in time of peace they exercise very little dominion, and have but a very moderate sovereignty; the resolutions of peace and war being ordinarily either in the people, or in a council. Though the war itself, which admits not of plurality of governors, naturally devolves the command into the king's sole authority.

* * *

[Section 109 contains a discussion of illustrations taken from the history of Israel as contained in the Old Testament.]

§ 110. Thus, whether a family by degrees grew up into a commonwealth, and the fatherly authority being continued on to the elder son, every one in his turn growing up under it, tacitly submitted to it; and the easiness and equality of it not offending any one, every one acquiesced, till time seemed to have confirmed it, and settle a right of succession by prescription: or whether several families, or the descendants of several families, whom chance, neighbourhood, or business brought together, uniting into society: the need of a general, whose conduct might defend them against their enemies in war, and the great confidence the innocence and sincerity of that poor but virtuous age (such as are almost all those which begin governments, that ever come to last in the world) gave men of one another, made the first beginners of commonwealths generally put the rule into one man's hand, without any other express limitation or restraint, but what the nature of the thing and the end of government required: whichever of those it was that at first put the rule into the hands of a single person, certain it is that nobody was intrusted with it but for the public good and safety, and to those ends, in the infancies of commonwealths, those who had it, commonly used it. And unless they had done so, young societies could not have subsisted; without such nursing fathers, tender and careful of the public weal, all governments would have sunk under the weakness and infirmities of their infancy, and the prince and the people had soon perished together.

§ 111. But though the golden age (before vain ambition, and *amor sceleratus habendi,* evil concupiscence, had corrupted men's minds into a mistake of true power and honour) had more virtue, and consequently better governors, as well as less vicious subjects; and there was then no stretching prerogative on the one side, to

oppress the people; nor consequently on the other, any dispute about privilege, to lessen or restrain the power of the magistrate; and so no contest betwixt rulers and people about governors or government: yet, when ambition and luxury in future ages[74] would retain and increase the power, without doing the business for which it was given; and, aided by flattery, taught princes to have distinct and separate interests from their people; men found it necessary to examine more carefully the original and rights of government, and to find out ways to restrain the exorbitancies, and prevent the abuses of that power, which they having intrusted in another's hands only for their own good, they found was made use of to hurt them.

§ 112. Thus we may see how probable it is, that people that were naturally free, and by their own consent either submitted to the government of their father, or united together out of different families to make a government, should generally put the rule into one man's hands, and choose to be under the conduct of a single person, without so much as by express conditions limiting or regulating his power, which they thought safe enough in his honesty and prudence: though they never dreamed of monarchy being *jure divino,* which we never heard of among mankind, till it was revealed to us by the divinity of this last age; nor ever allowed paternal power to have a right to dominion, or to be the foundation of all government. And thus much may suffice to show, that, as far as we have any light from history, we have reason to conclude, that all peaceful beginnings of government have been laid in the consent of the people. I say peaceful, because I shall have occasion in another place to speak of conquest, which some esteem a way of beginning of governments.

The other objection I find urged against the beginning of politics, in the way I have mentioned, is this, viz.

§ 113. "That all men being born under government, some or other, it is impossible any of them should ever be free, and at liberty to unite together, and begin a new one, or ever be able to erect a lawful government."

If this argument be good, I ask, how came so many lawful monarchies into the world? for if

---

[74] [Ed. note] In a footnote, Locke here quotes again (*see* note 67, *supra*) but at greater length from Hooker, LAWS OF ECCLESIASTICAL POLITY, Bk. I, c. x, § 5.

any body, upon this supposition, can show me any one man in any age of the world free to begin a lawful monarchy, I will be bound to show him ten other free men at liberty at the same time to unite and begin a new government under a regal, or any other form; it being demonstration, that if any one, born under the dominion of another, may be so free as to have a right to command others in a new and distinct empire, every one that is born under the dominion of another may be so free too, and may become a ruler, or subject of a distinct separate government. And so by this their own principle, either all men, however born, are free, or else there is but one lawful prince, one lawful government in the world. And then they have nothing to do, but barely to show us which that is; which when they have done, I doubt not but all mankind will easily agree to pay obedience to him.

§ 114. Though it be a sufficient answer to their objection, to show that it involves them in the same difficulties that it doth those they use it against; yet I shall endeavour to discover the weakness of this argument a little farther.

"All men, 'say they,' are born under government, and therefore they cannot be at liberty to begin a new one. Every one is born a subject to his father, or his prince, and is therefore under the perpetual tie of subjection and allegiance." It is plain mankind never owned nor considered any such natural subjection that they were born in, to one or to the other, that tied them, without their own consents, to a subjection to them and their heirs.

§ 115. For there are no examples so frequent in history, both sacred and profane, as those of men withdrawing themselves, and their obedience, from the jurisdiction they were born under, and the family or community they were bred up in, and setting up new governments in other places; from whence sprang all that number of petty commonwealths in the beginning of ages, and which always multiplied as long as there was room enough, till the stronger, or more fortunate, swallowed the weaker; and those great ones again breaking to pieces, dissolved into lesser dominions. All which are so many testimonies against paternal sovereignty, and plainly prove that it was not the natural right of the father descending to his heirs, that made governments in the beginning, since it was impossible, upon that ground, there should have been so many little kingdoms; all must have

been but only one universal monarchy, if men had not been at liberty to separate themselves from their families and the government, be it what it will, that was set up in it, and go and make distinct commonwealths and other governments, as they thought fit.

§ 116. This has been the practice of the world from its first beginning to this day; nor is it now any more hinderance to the freedom of mankind, that they are born under constituted and ancient polities, that have established laws and set forms of government, than if they were born in the woods, amongst the unconfined inhabitants that run loose in them: for those who would persuade us, that "by being born under any government, we are naturally subjects to it," and have no more any title or pretence to the freedom of the state of nature; have no other reason (bating that of paternal power, which we have already answered) to produce for it, but only because our fathers or progenitors passed away their natural liberty, and thereby bound up themselves and their posterity to a perpetual subjection to the government which they themselves submitted to. It is true, that whatever engagement or promises any one has made for himself, he is under the obligation of them, but cannot, by any compact whatsoever, bind his children or posterity: for his son, when a man, being altogether as free as the father, any "act of the father can no more give away the liberty of the son," than it can of any body else: he may indeed annex such conditions to the land he enjoyed as a subject of any commonwealth, as may oblige his son to be of that community, if he will enjoy those possessions which were his father's; because that estate being his father's property; he may dispose or settle it as he pleases.

§ 117. And this has generally given the occasion to mistake in this matter; because commonwealths not permitting any part of their dominions to be dismembered, nor to be enjoyed by any but those of their community, the son cannot ordinarily enjoy the possessions of his father, but under the same terms his father did, by becoming a member of the society; whereby he puts himself presently under the government he finds there established, as much as any other subject of that commonwealth. And thus "the consent of freemen, born under government, which only makes them members of it," being given separately in their turns, as each comes to be of age, and not in a multitude together; people take no notice of it, and thinking it not done at all, or not necessary, conclude they are naturally subjects as they are men.

§ 118. But it is plain governments themselves understand it otherwise; they claim "no power over the son, because of that they had over the father;" nor look on children as being their subjects, by their fathers being so. If a subject of England have a child by an English woman in France, whose subject is he? Not the king of England's; for he must have leave to be admitted to the privileges of it: nor the king of France's; for how then has his father a liberty to bring him away, and breed him as he pleases? and who ever was judged as a traitor or deserter, if he left or warred against a country, for being barely born in it of parents that were aliens there? It is plain then, by the practice of governments themselves, as well as by the law of right reason, that "a child is born a subject of no country or government."[75] He is under his father's tuition and authority till he comes to age of discretion; and then he is a freeman, at liberty what government he will put himself under, what body politic he will unite himself to: for if an Englishman's son, born in France, be at liberty, and may do so, it is evident there is no tie upon him by his father's being a subject of this kingdom; nor is he bound up by any compact of his ancestors. And why then hath not his son, by the same reason, the same liberty, though he be born any where else? Since the power that a father hath naturally over his children is the same, wherever they be born, and the ties of natural obligations are not bounded by the positive limits of kingdoms and commonwealths.

§ 119. Every man being, as has been showed, naturally free, and nothing being able to put him into subjection to any earthly power, but only his own consent; it is to be considered, what

shall be understood to be a sufficient declaration of a man's consent, to make him subject to the laws of any government. There is a common distinction of an express and a tacit consent, which will concern our present case. Nobody doubts but an express consent of any man entering into any society, makes him a perfect member of that society, a subject of that government. The difficulty is, what ought to be looked upon as a tacit consent, and how far it binds, i.e. how far any one shall be looked on to have consented, and thereby submitted to any government, where he has made no expressions of it at all. And to this I say, that every man, that hath any possessions, or enjoyment of any part of the dominions of any government, doth thereby give his tacit consent, and is as far forth obliged to obedience to the laws of that government, during such enjoyment, as any one under it; whether this his possession be of land, to him and his heirs for ever, or a lodging only for a week; or whether it be barely travelling freely on the highway; and, in effect, it reaches as far as the very being of any one within the territories of that government.

§ 120. To understand this the better, it is fit to consider, that every man, when he at first incorporates himself into any commonwealth, he, by his uniting himself thereunto, annexes also, and submits to the community those possessions which he has, or shall acquire, that do not already belong to any other government: for it would be a direct contradiction for any one to enter into society with others for the securing and regulating of property, and yet to suppose his land, whose property is to be regulated by the laws of the society, should be exempt from the jurisdiction of that government, to which he himself, the proprietor of the land, is a subject. By the same act therefore, whereby any one unites his person, which was before free, to any

---

[75] [Ed. note] In this connection it should be noted that Locke derives the power of sovereign nations to punish aliens who commit crimes within their borders from the right of every man in the state of nature to punish those who violate the laws of nature.

... I desire them to resolve me by what right any prince or state can put to death or punish an alien for any crime he commits in their country. It is certain their laws, by virtue of any sanction they receive from the promulgated will of the legislative, reach not a stranger: they speak not to him, nor, if they did, is he bound to harken to them. The legislative authority, by which they are in force over the subjects of that commonwealth, hath no power over him. Those who have the supreme power of

making laws in England, France, or Holland, are to an Indian but like the rest of the world, men without authority: and therefore, if by the law of nature every man hath not a power to punish offences against it, as he soberly judges the case to require, I see not how the magistrates of any community can punish an alien of another country; since, in reference to him, they can have no more power than what every man naturally may have over another.

J. Locke, The Second Treatise on Government Para. 9 [5 J. Locke, WORKS 342 (1823 ed.) from which these readings were taken]. Locke seems driven to this a priori rejection of the ius sanguinis and ius soli as legitimate bases of jurisdiction by his insistence that governmental power can only originate from consent.

commonwealth, by the same he unites his possessions, which were before free, to it also: and they become, both of them, person and possession, subject to the government and dominion of that commonwealth, as long as it hath a being. Whoever, therefore, from thenceforth, by inheritance, purchase, permission, or otherways, enjoys any part of the land so annexed to, and under the government of that commonwealth, must take it with the condition it is under; that is, of submitting to the government of the commonwealth, under whose jurisdiction it is, as far forth as any subject of it.

§ 121. But since the government has a direct jurisdiction only over the land, and reaches the possessor of it (before he has actually incorporated himself in the society) only as he dwells upon, and enjoys that; the obligation any one is under, by virtue of such enjoyment, to "submit to the government, begins and ends with the enjoyment:" so that whenever the owner, who has given nothing but such a tacit consent to the government, will, by donation, sale, or otherwise, quit the said possession, he is at liberty to go and incorporate himself into any other commonwealth; or to agree with others to begin a new one, in *vacuis locis*, in any part of the world they can find free and unpossessed: whereas he that has once, by actual agreement, and any express declaration, given his consent to be of any commonwealth, is perpetually and indispensably obliged to be, and remain unalterably a subject to it, and can never be again in the liberty of the state of nature; unless, by any calamity, the government he was under comes to be dissolved, or else by some public act cuts him off from being any longer a member of it.

§ 122. But submitting to the laws of any country, living quietly, and enjoying privileges and protection under them, makes not a man a member of that society: this is only a local protection and homage due to and from all those, who, not being in a state of war, come within the territories belonging to any government, to all parts whereof the force of its laws extends. But this no more makes a man a member of that society, a perpetual subject of that commonwealth, than it would make a man a subject to another, in whose family he found it convenient to abide for some time; though, whilst he continued in it, he were obliged to comply with the laws, and submit to the government he found there. And thus we see, that foreigners, by living all their lives under another government, and enjoying the privileges and protection of it, though they are bound, even in conscience, to submit to its administration, as far forth as any denison; yet do not thereby come to be subjects or members of that commonwealth. Nothing can make any man so, but his actually entering into it by positive engagement, and express promise and compact. This is that which I think concerning the beginning of political societies, and that consent which makes any one a member of any commonwealth.

CHAPTER IX.

Of the Ends of Political Society and Government.

§ 123. If man in the state of nature be so free as has been said; if he be absolute lord of his own person and possessions, equal to the greatest, and subject to nobody, why will he part with his freedom, why will he give up this empire, and subject himself to the dominion and control of any other power? To which it is obvious to answer, that though in the state of nature he hath such a right yet the enjoyment of it is very uncertain, and constantly exposed to the invasion of others; for all being kings as much as he, every man his equal, and the greater part no strict observers of equity and justice, the enjoyment of the property he has in this state is very unsafe, very unsecure. This makes him willing to quit a condition, which, however free, is full of fears and continual dangers: and it is not without reason that he seeks out, and is willing to join in society with others, who are already united, or have a mind to unite, for the mutual preservation of their lives, liberties and estates, which I call by the general name property.

§ 124. The great and chief end, therefore, of men's uniting into commonwealths, and putting themselves under government, is the preservation of their property. To which in the state of nature there are many things wanting.

First, There wants an established, settled, known law, received and allowed by common consent to be the standard of right and wrong, and the common measure to decide all controversies between them: for though the law of nature be plain and intelligible to all rational creatures: yet men being biassed by their interest, as well as ignorant for want of studying it, are not apt to allow of it as a law binding to them in the application of it to their particular cases.

§ 125. Secondly, In the state of nature there wants a known and indifferent judge, with authority to determine all differences according to the established law: for every one in that state being both judge and executioner of the law of nature, men being partial to themselves, passion and revenges very apt to carry them too far, and with too much heat, in their own cases; as well as negligence and unconcernedness, to make them too remiss in other men's.

§ 126. Thirdly, In the state of nature there often wants power to back and support the sentence when right, and to give it due execution. They who by any injustice offend, will seldom fail, where they are able, by force to make good their injustice; such resistance many times makes the punishment dangerous, and frequently destructive to those who attempt it.

§ 127. Thus mankind, notwithstanding all the privileges of the state of nature, being but in an ill condition, while they remain in it, are quickly driven into society. Hence it comes to pass, that we seldom find any number of men live any time together in this state. The inconveniencies that they are therein exposed to, by the irregular and uncertain exercise of the power every man has of punishing the transgressions of others, make them take sanctuary under the established laws of government, and therein seek the preservation of their property. It is this makes them so willingly give up every one his single power of punishing, to be exercised by such alone as shall be appointed to it amongst them; and by such rules as the community, or those authorized by them to that purpose, shall agree on. And in this we have the original right of both the legislative and executive power, as well as of the governments and societies themselves.

§ 128. For in the state of nature, to omit the liberty he has of innocent delights, a man has two powers.

The first is to do whatsoever he thinks fit for the preservation of himself and others within the permission of the law of nature: by which law, common to them all, he and all the rest of mankind are one community, make up one society, distinct from all other creatures. And, were it not for the corruption and viciousness of degenerate men, there would be no need of any other; no necessity that men should separate from this great and natural community, and by positive agreements combine into smaller and divided associations.

The other power a man has in the state of nature, is the power to punish the crimes committed against that law. Both these he gives up when he joins in a private, if I may so call it, or particular politic society, and incorporates into any commonwealth, separate from the rest of mankind.

§ 129. The first power, viz. "of doing whatsoever he thought fit for the preservation of himself" and the rest of mankind, he gives up to be regulated by laws made by the society, so far forth as the preservation of himself and the rest of that society shall require; which laws of the society in many things confine the liberty he had by the law of nature.

§ 130. Secondly, The power of punishing he wholly gives up, and engages his natural force (which he might before employ in the execution of the law of nature, by his own single authority, as he thought fit), to assist the executive power of the society, as the law thereof shall require: for being now in a new state, wherein he is to enjoy many conveniences, from the labour, assistance, and society of others in the same community, as well as protection from its whole strength; he is to part also with as much of his natural liberty, in providing for himself, as the good, prosperity, and safety of the society shall require; which is not only necessary, but just, since the other members of the society do the like.

§ 131. But though men, when they enter into society, give up the equality, liberty, and executive power they had in the state of nature, into the hands of the society, to be so far disposed of by the legislative as the good of the society shall require; yet it being only with an intention in every one the better to preserve himself, his liberty and property (for no rational creature can be supposed to change his condition with an intention to be worse); the power of the society, or legislative constituted by them, can never be supposed to extend farther than the common good; but is obliged to secure every one's property, by providing against those three defects above-mentioned, that made the state of nature so unsafe and uneasy. And so whoever has the legislative or supreme power of any commonwealth, is bound to govern by established standing laws, promulgated and known to the people, and not by extemporary decrees; by indifferent and upright judges, who are to decide controversies by those laws; and to employ the force of the community at home, only in the execution of such laws; or abroad to prevent or redress foreign injuries, and secure the community from inroads and invasion. And all this to be directed to no other end but the peace, safety, and public good of the people.

CHAPTER X.

Of the Forms of a Commonwealth.

§ 132. The majority having, as has been showed, upon men's first uniting into society, the whole power of the community naturally in them, may employ all that power in making laws for the community from time to time, and executing those laws by officers of their own appointing; and then the form of the government is a perfect democracy: or else may put the power of making laws into the hands of a few select men, and their heirs or successors; and then it is an oligarchy: or else into the hands of one man, and then it is a monarchy: if to him and his heirs, it is an hereditary monarchy: if to him only for life, but upon his death the power only of nominating a successor to return to them, an elective monarchy. And so accordingly of these the community may make compounded and mixed forms of government, as they think good. And if the legislative power be at first given by the majority to one or more persons only for their lives, or any limited time, and then the supreme power to revert to them again; when it is so reverted, the community may dispose of it again anew into what hands they please, and so constitute a new form of government: for the form of government depending upon the placing the supreme power, which is the legislative (it being impossible to conceive that an inferior power should prescribe to a superior, or any but the supreme make laws), according as the power of making laws is placed, such is the form of the commonwealth.

§ 133. By commonwealth, I must be understood all along to mean, not a democracy, or any form of government, but any independent community, which the Latines signified by the word *civitas;* to which the word which best answers in our language is commonwealth, and most properly expresses such a society of men, which community or city in English does not: for there may be subordinate communities in government; and city amongst us has a quite different notion from commonwealth: and therefore, to avoid ambiguity, I crave leave to use the word commonwealth in that sense, in which I find it used

by king James the First; and I take it to be its genuine signification; which if any body dislike, I consent with him to change it for a better.

CHAPTER XI.

Of the Extent of the legislative Power.

§ 134. The great end of men's entering into society being the enjoyment of their properties in peace and safety, and the great instrument and means of that being the laws established in that society; the first and fundamental positive law of all commonwealths is the establishing of the legislative power; as the first and fundamental natural law, which is to govern even the legislative itself, is the preservation of the society, and (as far as will consist with the public good) of every person in it. This legislative is not only the supreme power of the commonwealth, but sacred and unalterable in the hands where the community have once placed it; nor can any edict of any body else, in what form soever conceived, or by what power soever backed, have the force and obligation of a law, which has not its sanction from that legislative which the public has chosen and appointed: for without this the law could not have that which is absolutely necessary to its being a law, the consent of the society; over whom nobody can have a power to make laws, but by their own consent, and by authority received from them.[76] And therefore all the obedience, which by the most solemn ties any one can be obliged to pay, ultimately terminates in this supreme power, and is directed by those laws which it enacts: nor can any oaths to any foreign power whatsoever, or any domestic subordinate power, discharge any member of the society from his obedience to the legislative, acting pursuant to their trust; nor oblige him to any obedience contrary to the laws so enacted, or farther than they do allow; it being ridiculous to imagine one can be tied ultimately to obey any power in the society which is not supreme.

§ 135. Though the legislative, whether placed in one or more, whether it be always in being, or only by intervals, though it be the supreme power in every commonwealth; yet,

---

[76] [Ed. note] Locke, in a footnote here quotes several passages from Hooker, *Laws of Ecclesiastical Polity*, Bk. I, c. x, § 8. The quoted passages include the famous sentence "Laws they are not therefore which public approbation hath not made so."

First, It is not, nor can possibly be absolutely arbitrary over the lives and fortunes of the people: for it being but the joint power of every member of the society given up to that person or assembly which is legislator; it can be no more than those persons had in a state of nature before they entered into society, and gave up to the community: for nobody can transfer to another more power than he has in himself; and nobody has an absolute arbitrary power over himself, or over any other, to destroy his own life, or take away the life or property of another. A man, as has been proved, cannot subject himself to the arbitrary power of another; and having in the state of nature no arbitrary power over the life, liberty, or possession of another, but only so much as the law of nature gave him for the preservation of himself and the rest of mankind; this is all he doth, or can give up to the commonwealth, and by it to the legislative power, so that the legislative can have no more than this. Their power, in the utmost bounds of it, is limited to the public good of the society. It is a power that hath no other end but preservation, and therefore can never have a right to destroy, enslave, or designedly to impoverish the subjects.[77] The obligations of the law of nature cease not in society, but only in many cases are drawn closer, and have by human laws known penalties annexed to them, to enforce their observation. Thus the law of nature stands as an eternal rule to all men, legislators as well as others. The rules that they make for other men's actions must, as well as their own and other men's actions be conformable to the law of nature, *i.e.* to the will of God, of which that is a declaration; and the "fundamental law of nature being the preservation of mankind, no human sanction can be good or valid against it."

§ 136. Secondly, The legislative or supreme authority cannot assume to itself a power to rule by extemporary, arbitrary decrees; but is bound to dispense justice, and to decide the rights of the subject, by promulgated, standing laws, and known authorized judges.[78] For the law of nature being unwritten, and so nowhere to be found, but in the minds of men, they who, through passion, or interest, shall miscite, or misapply it, cannot so easily be convinced of their mistake, where there is no established judge: and so it serves not, as it ought, to determine the rights, and fence the properties of those that live under it; especially where every one is judge, interpreter, and executioner of it

too, and that in his own case: and he that has right on his side, having ordinarily but his own single strength, hath not force enough to defend himself from injuries, or to punish delinquents. To avoid these inconveniences, which disorder men's properties in the state of nature, men unite into societies, that they may have the united strength of the whole society to secure and defend their properties, and may have standing rules to bound it, by which every one may know what is his. To this end it is that men give up all their natural power to the society which they enter into, and the community put the legislative power into such hands as they think fit; with this trust, that they shall be governed by declared laws, or else their peace, quiet, and property will still be at the same uncertainty as it was in the state of nature.

§ 137. Absolute arbitrary power, or governing without settled standing laws, can neither of them consist with the ends of society and government, which men would not quit the freedom of the state of nature for, and tie themselves up under, were it not to preserve their lives, liberties, and fortunes, and by stated rules of right and property to secure their peace and quiet. It cannot be supposed that they should intend, had they a power so to do, to give to any one, or more, an absolute arbitrary power over their persons and estates, and put a force into the magistrate's hand to execute his unlimited will arbitrarily upon them. This were to put themselves into a worse condition than the state of nature, wherein they had a liberty to defend their right against the injuries of others, and were upon equal terms of force to maintain it, whether invaded by a single man, or many in combination. Whereas by supposing they have given up themselves to the absolute arbitrary power and will of a legislator, they have dis-

---

[77] [Ed. note] Locke here, in a footnote, inserts a rather lengthy quote from Hooker, *Laws of Ecclesiastical Polity*, Bk. I, c. x, § 1.

[78] "Human laws are measures in respect of men whose actions they must direct, howbeit such measures they are as have also their higher rules to be measured by, which rules are two, the law of God, and the law of nature; so that laws human must be made according to the general laws of nature, and without contradiction to any positive law of Scripture, otherwise they are ill-made" (Hooker's *Eccl. Pol.* lib. iii. sect. 9). [Bk. III, c. ix, § 2. In this passage, Hooker cites St. Thomas, *Summa Theologica*, Pt. II (1st Pt.), Q. 95, Art. 3, reprinted at p. 118, *supra*.] "To constrain men to anything inconvenient doth seem unreasonable" (*Ibid.* lib. i. sect. 10). [Bk. I, c. x, § 7].

armed themselves, and armed him, to make a prey of them when he pleases; he being in a much worse condition, who is exposed to the arbitrary power of one man, who has the command of 100,000, than he that is exposed to the arbitrary power of 100,000 single men; nobody being secure that his will, who has such a command, is better than that of other men, though his force be 100,000 times stronger. And therefore, whatever form the commonwealth is under, the ruling power ought to govern by declared and received laws, and not by extemporary dictates and undetermined resolutions; for then mankind will be in a far worse condition than in the state of nature, if they shall have armed one or a few men with the joint power of a multitude, to force them to obey at pleasure the exorbitant and unlimited degrees of their sudden thoughts, or unrestrained, and till that moment unknown wills, without having any measures set down which may guide and justify their actions: for all the power the government has being only for the good of the society, as it ought not to be arbitrary and at pleasure, so it ought to be exercised by established and promulgated laws; that both the people may know their duty, and be safe and secure within the limits of the law; and the rulers too kept within their bounds, and not be tempted, by the power they have in their hands, to employ it to such purposes, and by such measures, as they would not have known, and own not willingly.

§ 138. Thirdly, The supreme power cannot take from any man part of his property without his own consent: for the preservation of property being the end of government, and that for which men enter into society, it necessarily supposes and requires, that the people should have property, without which they must be supposed to lose that, by entering into society, which was the end for which they entered into it; too gross an absurdity for any man to own. Men therefore in society having property, they have such right to the goods, which by the law of the community are theirs, that nobody hath a right to take their substance or any part of it from them, without their own consent: without this they have no property at all; for I have truly no property in that, which another can by right take from me, when he pleases, against my consent. Hence it is a mistake to think, that the supreme or legislative power of any commonwealth can do what it will, and dispose of the estates of the subject arbitrarily, or take any part of them at

pleasure. This is not much to be feared in governments where the legislative consists, wholly or in part, in assemblies which are variable, whose members, upon the dissolution of the assembly, are subjects under the common laws of their country, equally with the rest. But in governments where the legislative is in one lasting assembly always in being, or in one man, as in absolute monarchies, there is danger still that they will think themselves to have a distinct interest from the rest of the community; and so will be apt to increase their own riches and power, by taking what they think fit from the people: for a man's property is not at all secure, though there be good and equitable laws to set the bounds of it between him and his fellow-subjects, if he who commands those subjects have power to take from any private man what part he pleases of his property, and use and dispose of it as he thinks good.

§ 139. But government, into whatsoever hands it is put, being, as I have before showed, entrusted with this condition, and for this end, that men might have and secure their properties; the prince, or senate, however it may have power to make laws for the regulating of property between the subjects one amongst another, yet can never have a power to take to themselves the whole or any part of the subject's property without their own consent: for this would be in effect to leave them no property at all. And to let us see, that even absolute power, where it is necessary, is not arbitrary by being absolute, but is still limited by that reason, and confined to those ends, which required it in some cases to be absolute, we need look no farther than the common practice of martial discipline: for the preservation of the army, and in it of the whole commonwealth, requires an absolute obedience to the command of every superior officer, and it is justly death to disobey or dispute the most dangerous or unreasonable of them; but yet we see, that neither the serjeant, that could command a soldier to march up to the mouth of a cannon, or stand in a breach, where he is almost sure to perish, can command that soldier to give him one penny of his money; nor the general, that can condemn him to death for deserting his post, or for not obeying the most desperate orders, can yet, with all his absolute power of life and death, dispose of one farthing of that soldier's estate, or seize one jot of his goods; whom yet he can command any thing, and hang for the least disobedience; because such a blind obedience is necessary to that end for which the commander has his power, viz. the preservation of the rest; but the disposing of his goods has nothing to do with it.

§ 140. It is true, governments cannot be supported without great charge, and it is fit every one who enjoys his share of the protection, should pay out of his estate his proportion for the maintenance of it. But still it must be with his own consent, *i.e.* the consent of the majority, giving it either by themselves, or their representatives chosen by them: for if any one shall claim a power to lay and levy taxes on the people by his own authority, and without such consent of the people, he thereby invades the fundamental law of property, and subverts the end of government: for what property have I in that which another may by right take, when he pleases, to himself?

§ 141. Fourthly, The legislative cannot transfer the power of making laws to any other hands: for it being but a delegated power from the people, they who have it cannot pass it over to others. The people alone can appoint the form of the commonwealth, which is by constituting the legislative, and appointing in whose hands that shall be. And when the people have said, we will submit to rules, and be governed by laws made by such men, and in such forms, nobody else can say other men shall make laws for them; nor can the people be bound by any laws but such as are enacted by those whom they have chosen, and authorized to make laws for them. The power of the legislative being derived from the people by a positive voluntary grant and institution, can be no other than what that positive grant conveyed, which being only to make laws, and not to make legislators, the legislative can have no power to transfer their authority of making laws and place it in other hands.

§ 142. These are the bounds which the trust that is put in them by the society, and the law of God and nature, have set to the legislative power of every commonwealth, in all forms of government.

First, They are to govern by promulgated established laws, not to be varied in particular cases, but to have one rule for rich and poor, for the favourite at court, and the countryman at plough.

Secondly, These laws also ought to be designed for no other end ultimately, but the good of the people.

Thirdly, They must not raise taxes on the property of the people, without the consent of the people, given by themselves or their deputies. And this properly concerns only such governments where the legislative is always in being, or at least where the people have not reserved any part of the legislative to deputies, to be from time to time chosen by themselves.

Fourthly, The legislative neither must nor can transfer the power of making laws to any body else, or place it any where, but where the people have.

CHAPTER XII.

Of the legislative, executive, and federative Power of the Commonwealth.

§ 143. The legislative power is that, which has a right to direct how the force of the commonwealth shall be employed for preserving the community and the members of it. But because those laws which are constantly to be executed, and whose force is always to continue, may be made in a little time, therefore there is no need that the legislative should be always in being, not having always business to do. And because it may be too great a temptation to human frailty, apt to grasp at power, for the same persons who have the power of making laws, to have also in their hands the power to execute them; whereby they may exempt themselves from obedience to the laws they make, and suit the law, both in its making and execution, to their own private advantage, and thereby come to have a distinct interest from the rest of the community, contrary to the end of society and government: therefore in well ordered commonwealths, where the good of the whole is so considered, as it ought, the legislative power is put into the hands of divers persons, who, duly assembled, have by themselves or jointly with others, a power to make laws; which when they have done, being separated again, they are themselves subject to the laws they have made; which is a new and near tie upon them, to take care that they make them for the public good.

§ 144. But because the laws, that are at once, and in a short time made, have a constant and lasting force, and need a perpetual execution, or an attendance thereunto; therefore it is necessary there should be a power always in being, which should see to the execution of the laws that are made, and remain in force. And thus the legislative and executive power come often to be separated.

§ 145. There is another power in every commonwealth, which one may call natural, because it is that which answers to the power every man naturally had before he entered into society: for though in a commonwealth, the members of it are distinct persons still in reference to one another, and as such are governed by the laws of the society; yet in reference to the rest of mankind, they make one body, which is, as every member of it before was, still in the state of nature with the rest of mankind. Hence it is, that the controversies that happen between any man of the society with those that are out of it, are managed by the public; and an injury done to a member of their body engages the whole in the reparation of it. So that, under this consideration, the whole community is one body in the state of nature, in respect of all other states or persons out of its community.

§ 146. This therefore contains the power of war and peace, leagues and alliances, and all the transactions with all persons and communities without the commonwealth; and may be called federative, if any one pleases. So the thing be understood, I am indifferent as to the name.

§ 147. These two powers, executive and federative, though they be really distinct in themselves, yet one comprehending the execution of the municipal laws of the society within itself, upon all that are parts of it; the other the management of the security and interest of the public without, with all those that it may receive benefit or damage from; yet they are always almost united. And though this federative power in the well or ill management of it be of great moment to the commonwealth, yet it is much less capable to be directed by antecedent, standing, positive laws, than the executive; and so must necessarily be left to the prudence and wisdom of those whose hands it is in, to be managed for the public good: for the laws that concern subjects one amongst another, being to direct their actions, may well enough precede them. But what is to be done in reference to foreigners, depending much upon their actions, and the variation of designs, and interests, must be left in great part to the prudence of those who have this power committed to them, to be managed by the best of their skill, for the advantage of the commonwealth.

§ 148. Though, as I said, the executive and federative power of every community be really distinct in themselves, yet they are hardly to be separated, and placed at the same time in the hands of distinct persons: for both of them requiring the force of the society for their exercise, it is almost impracticable to place the force of the commonwealth in distinct, and not subordinate hands; or that the executive and federative power should be placed in persons that might act separately, whereby the force of the public would be under different commands; which would be apt some time or other to cause disorder and ruin.

CHAPTER XIII.

Of the Subordination of the Powers of the Commonwealth.

§ 149. Though in a constituted commonwealth, standing upon its own basis, and acting according to its own nature, that is, acting for the preservation of the community, there can be but one supreme power, which is the legislative, to which all the rest are and must be subordinate; yet the legislative being only a fiduciary power to act for certain ends, there remains still "in the people a supreme power to remove or alter the legislative," when they find the legislative act contrary to the trust reposed in them: for all power given with trust for the attaining an end, being limited by that end: whenever that end is manifestly neglected or opposed, the trust must necessarily be forfeited, and the power devolve into the hands of those that gave it, who may place it anew where they shall think best for their safety and security. And thus the community perpetually retains a supreme power of saving themselves from the attempts and designs of any body, even of their legislators, whenever they shall be so foolish, or so wicked, as to lay and carry on designs against the liberties and properties of the subject: for no man, or society of men, having a power to deliver up their preservation, or consequently the means of it, to the absolute will and arbitrary dominion of another; whenever any one shall go about to bring them into such a slavish condition, they will always have a right to preserve what they have not a power to part with; and to rid themselves of those who invade this fundamental, sacred, and unalterable law of self-preservation, for which they entered into society. And thus the community may be said in this respect to be always the supreme power, but not as considered under any form of government, because this power of the people can never take place till the government be dissolved.

§ 150. In all cases, whilst the government subsists, the legislative is the supreme power: for what can give laws to another, must needs be superior to him; and since the legislative is no otherwise legislative of the society, but by the right it has to make laws for all the parts, and for every member of the society, prescribing rules to their actions, and giving power of execution, where they are transgressed; the legislative must needs be the supreme, and all other powers, in any members or parts of the society, derived from and subordinate to it.

§ 151. In some commonwealths, where the legislative is not always in being, and the executive is vested in a single person, who has also a share in the legislative; there that single person in a very tolerable sense may also be called supreme; not that he has in himself all the supreme power, which is that of law-making; but because he has in him the supreme execution, from whom all inferior magistrates derive all their several subordinate powers, or at least the greatest part of them: having also no legislative superior to him, there being no law to be made without his consent, which cannot be expected should ever subject him to the other part of the legislative, he is properly enough in this sense supreme. But yet it is to be observed, that though oaths of allegiance and fealty are taken to him, it is not to him as supreme legislator, but as supreme executor of the law, made by a joint power of him with others: allegiance being nothing but an obedience according to law, which when he violates, he has no right to obedience, nor can claim it otherwise than as the public person invested with the power of the law; and so is to be considered as the image, phantom, or representative of the commonwealth, acted by the will of the society, declared in its laws; and thus he has no will, no power, but that of the law. But when he quits this representation, this public will, and acts by his own private will, he degrades himself, and is but a single private person without power, and without will, that has no right to obedience; the members owing no obedience but to the public will of the society.

§ 152. The executive power, placed any where but in a person that has also a share in the legislative, is visibly subordinate and account-

able to it, and may be at pleasure changed and displaced; so that it is not the supreme executive power that is exempt from subordination: but the supreme executive power vested in one, who having a share in the legislative, has no distinct superior legislative to be subordinate and accountable to, farther than he himself shall join and consent; so that he is no more subordinate than he himself shall think fit, which one may certainly conclude will be but very little. Of other ministerial and subordinate powers in a commonwealth we need not speak, they being so multiplied with infinite variety, in the different customs and constitutions of distinct commonwealths, that it is impossible to give a particular account of them all. Only thus much, which is necessary to our present purpose, we may take notice of concerning them, that they have no manner of authority, any of them, beyond what is by positive grant and commission delegated to them, and are all of them accountable to some other power in the commonwealth.

§ 153. It is not necessary, no, nor so much as convenient, that the legislative should be always in being; but absolutely necessary that the executive power should; because there is not always need of new laws to be made, but always need of execution of the laws that are made. When the legislative hath put the execution of the laws they make into other hands, they have a power still to resume it out of those hands, when they find cause, and to punish for any male administration against the laws. The same holds also in regard of the federative power, that and the executive being both ministerial and subordinate to the legislative, which, as has been showed, in a constituted commonwealth is the supreme. The legislative also in this case being supposed to consist of several persons, (for if it be a single person, it cannot but be always in being, and so will, as supreme, naturally have the supreme executive power, together with the legislative) may assemble, and exercise their legislature, at the times that either their original constitution, or their own adjournment, appoints, or when they please; if neither of these hath appointed any time, or there be no other way prescribed to convoke them: for the supreme power being placed in them by the people, it is always in them, and they may exercise it when they please, unless by their original constitution they are limited to certain seasons, or by an act of their supreme power they have adjourned to a certain time; and when that time comes, they have a right to assemble and act again.

§ 154. If the legislative, or any part of it, be made up of representatives chosen for that time by the people, which afterwards return into the ordinary state of subjects, and have no share in the legislature but upon a new choice, this power of choosing must also be exercised by the people, either at certain appointed seasons, or else when they are summoned to it; and in this latter case the power of convoking the legislative is ordinarily placed in the executive, and has one of these two limitations in respect of time: that either the original constitution requires their assembling and acting at certain intervals, and then the executive power does nothing but ministerially issue directions for their electing and assembling according to due forms; or else it is left to his prudence to call them by new elections, when the occasions or exigencies of the public require the amendment of old, or making of new laws, or the redress or prevention of any inconveniences, that lie on, or threaten the people.

§ 155. It may be demanded here, What if the executive power, being possessed of the force of the commonwealth, shall make use of that force to hinder the meeting and acting of the legislative, when the original constitution or the public exigencies require it? I say, using force upon the people without authority, and contrary to the trust put in him that does so, is a state of war with the people, who have a right to reinstate their legislative in the exercise of their power: for having erected a legislative, with an intent they should exercise the power of making laws, either at certain set times, or when there is need of it; when they are hindered by any force from what is so necessary to the society, and wherein the safety and preservation of the people consists, the people have a right to remove it by force. In all states and conditions, the true remedy of force without authority is to oppose force to it. The use of force without authority always puts him that uses it into a state of war, as the aggressor, and renders him liable to be treated accordingly.

§ 156. The power of assembling and dismissing the legislative, placed in the executive, gives not the executive a superiority over it, but is a fiduciary trust placed in him for the safety of the people, in a case where the uncertainty and variableness of human affairs could not bear a steady fixed rule: for it not being possible that the first framers of the government should, by

any foresight, be so much masters of future events as to be able to prefix so just periods of return and duration to the assemblies of the legislative, in all times to come, that might exactly answer all the exigencies of the commonwealth; the best remedy could be found for this defect was to trust this to the prudence of one who was always to be present, and whose business it was to watch over the public good. Constant frequent meetings of the legislative, and long continuations of their assemblies, without necessary occasion, could not but be burdensome to the people, and must necessarily in time produce more dangerous inconveniencies, and yet the quick turn of affairs might be sometimes such as to need their present help; any delay of their convening might endanger the public; and sometimes too their business might be so great, that the limited time of their sitting might be too short for their work, and rob the public of that benefit which could be had only from their mature deliberation. What then could be done in this case to prevent the community from being exposed some time or other to eminent hazard, on one side or the other, by fixed intervals and periods, set to the meeting and acting of the legislative; but to intrust it to the prudence of some, who being present, and acquainted with the state of public affairs, might make use of this prerogative for the public good? and where else could this be so well placed as in his hands, who was intrusted with the execution of the laws for the same end? Thus supposing the regulation of times for the assembling and sitting of the legislative not settled by the original constitution, it naturally fell into the hands of the executive, not as an arbitrary power depending on his good pleasure, but with this trust always to have it exercised only for the public weal, as the occurrences of times and change of affairs might require. Whether settled periods of their convening, or a liberty left to the prince for convoking the legislative, or perhaps a mixture of both, hath the least inconvenience attending it, it is not my business here to inquire; but only to show, that though the executive power may have the prerogative of convoking and dissolving such conventions of the legislative, yet it is not thereby superior to it.

§ 157. Things of this world are in so constant a flux, that nothing remains long in the same state. Thus people, riches, trade, power, change their stations, flourishing mighty cities come to ruin, and prove in time neglected desolate corners, whilst other unfrequented places grow into populous countries, filled with wealth and inhabitants. But things not always changing equally, and private interest often keeping up customs and privileges, when the reasons of them are ceased; it often comes to pass, that in governments, where part of the legislative consists of representatives chosen by the people, that in tract of time this representation becomes very unequal and disproportionate to the reasons it was at first established upon. To what gross absurdities the following of custom, when reason has left it, may lead, we may be satisfied, when we see the bare name of a town, of which there remains not so much as the ruins, where scarce so much housing as a sheepcote, or more inhabitants than a shepherd is to be found, sends as many representatives to the grand assembly of law-makers as a whole county, numerous in people, and powerful in riches. This strangers stand amazed at, and every one must confess needs a remedy; though most think it hard to find one; because the constitution of the legislative being the original and supreme act of the society, antecedent to all positive laws in it, and depending wholly on the people, no inferior power can alter it. And therefore the people, when the legislative is once constituted, having, in such a government as we have been speaking of, no power to act as long as the government stands; this inconvenience is thought incapable of a remedy.

§ 158. *Salus populi suprema lex,* is certainly so just and fundamental a rule, that he, who sincerely follows it, cannot dangerously err. If therefore the executive, who has the power of convoking the legislative, observing rather the true proportion than fashion of representation, regulates not by old custom, but true reason, the number of members in all places that have a right to be distinctly represented, which no part of the people, however incorporated, can pretend to, but in proportion to the assistance which it affords to the public; it cannot be judged to have set up a new legislative, but to have restored the old and true one, and to have rectified the disorders which succession of time had insensibly, as well as inevitably introduced; for it being the interest as well as intention of the people, to have a fair and equal representative; whoever brings it nearest to that, is an undoubted friend to, and establisher of the government, and cannot miss the consent and approbation of the community: prerogative being nothing but a

power in the hands of the prince, to provide for the public good, in such cases, which depending upon unforeseen and uncertain occurrences, certain and unalterable laws could not safely direct; whatsoever shall be done manifestly for the good of the people, and the establishing the government upon its true foundations, is, and always will be, just prerogative. The power of erecting new corporations, and therewith new representatives, carries with it a supposition that in time the measures of representation might vary, and those places have a just right to be represented which before had none; and by the same reason, those cease to have a right, and be too inconsiderable for such a privilege, which before had it. It is not a change from the present state, which perhaps corruption or decay has introduced, that makes an inroad upon the government; but the tendency of it to injure or oppress the people, and to set up one part or party, with a distinction from and an unequal subjection of the rest. Whatsoever cannot but be acknowledged to be of advantage to the society, and people in general, upon just and lasting measures, will always, when done, justify itself; and whenever the people shall choose their representatives upon just and undeniably equal measures, suitable to the original frame of the government, it cannot be doubted to be the will and act of the society, whoever permitted or caused them so to do.

CHAPTER XIV.

Of Prerogative.

§ 159. Where the legislative and executive power are in distinct hands, (as they are in all moderated monarchies and well-framed governments) there the good of the society requires, that several things should be left to the discretion of him that has the executive power: for the legislators not being able to foresee, and provide by laws, for all that may be useful to the community, the executor of the laws having the power in his hands, has by the common law of nature a right to make use of it for the good of the society, in many cases, where the municipal law has given no direction, till the legislative can conveniently be assembled to provide for it. Many things there are, which the law can by no means provide for; and those must necessarily be left to the discretion of him that has the executive power in his hands, to be ordered by him as the public good and advantage shall require:

nay, it is fit that the laws themselves should in some cases give way to the executive power, or rather to this fundamental law of nature and government, viz. That, as much as may be, all the members of the society are to be preserved: for since many accidents may happen, wherein a strict and rigid observation of the laws may do harm; (as not to pull down an innocent man's house to stop the fire, when the next to it is burning) and a man may come sometimes within the reach of the law, which makes no distinction of persons, by an action that may deserve reward and pardon; it is fit the ruler should have a power, in many cases, to mitigate the severity of the law, and pardon some offenders: for the end of government being the preservation of all, as much as may be, even the guilty are to be spared, where it can prove no prejudice to the innocent.

§ 160. This power to act according to discretion for the public good, without the prescription of the law, and sometimes even against it, is that which is called prerogative: for since in some governments the law-making power is not always in being, and is usually too numerous, and so too slow for the despatch requisite to execution; and because also it is impossible to foresee, and so by laws to provide for all accidents and necessities that may concern the public, or to make such laws as will do no harm, if they are executed with an inflexible rigour on all occasions, and upon all persons that may come in their way; therefore there is a latitude left to the executive power, to do many things of choice which the laws do not prescribe.

§ 161. This power, whilst employed for the benefit of the community, and suitably to the trust and ends of the government, is undoubted prerogative and never is questioned; for the people are very seldom or never scrupulous or nice in the point; they are far from examining prerogative, whilst it is in any tolerable degree employed for the use it was meant; that is, for the good of the people, and not manifestly against it: but if there comes to be a question between the executive power and the people, about a thing claimed as a prerogative, the tendency of the exercise of such prerogative to the good or hurt of the people will easily decide that question.

§ 162. It is easy to conceive, that in the infancy of governments, when commonwealths differed little from families in number of people,

they differed from them too but little in number of laws: and the governors being as the fathers of them, watching over them for their good, the government was almost all prerogative. A few established laws served the turn, and the discretion and care of the ruler supplied the rest. But when mistake or flattery prevailed with weak princes to make use of this power for private ends of their own, and not for the public good, the people were fain by express laws to get prerogative determined in those points wherein they found disadvantage from it: and thus declared limitations of prerogative were by the people found necessary in cases which they and their ancestors had left, in the utmost latitude, to the wisdom of those princes who made no other but a right use of it; that is, for the good of their people.

§ 163. And therefore they have a very wrong notion of government, who say, that the people have encroached upon the prerogative, when they have got any part of it to be defined by positive laws: for in so doing they have not pulled from the prince any thing that of right belonged to him, but only declare, that that power which they indefinitely left in his or his ancestors' hands, to be exercised for their good, was not a thing which they intended him when he used it otherwise: for the end of government being the good of the community, whatsoever alterations are made in it, tending to that end, cannot be an encroachment upon any body, since nobody in government can have a right tending to any other end: and those only are encroachments which prejudice or hinder the public good. Those who say otherwise, speak as if the prince had a distinct and separate interest from the good of the community, and was not made for it; the root and source from which spring almost all those evils and disorders which happen in kingly governments. And indeed, if that be so, the people under his government are not a society of rational creatures, entered into a community for their mutual good; they are not such as have set rulers over themselves, to guard and promote that good; but are to be looked on as an herd of inferior creatures under the dominion of a master, who keeps them and works them for his own pleasure or profit. If men were so void of reason, and brutish, as to enter into society upon such terms, prerogative might indeed be, what some men would have it, an arbitrary power to do things hurtful to the people.

ENGLISH LAW

SECOND
TREATISE ON
GOVERNMENT

§ 164. But since a rational creature cannot be supposed, when free, to put himself into subjection to another, for his own harm; (though, where he finds a good and wise ruler, he may not perhaps think it either necessary or useful to set precise bounds to his power in all things) prerogative can be nothing but the people's permitting their rulers to do several things, of their own free choice, where the law was silent, and sometimes too against the direct letter of the law, for the public good; and their acquiescing in it when so done: for as a good prince, who is mindful of the trust put into his hands, and careful of the good of his people, cannot have too much prerogative, that is, power to do good; so a weak and ill prince, who would claim that power which his predecessors exercised without the direction of the law, as a prerogative belonging to him by right of his office, which he may exercise at his pleasure, to make or promote an interest distinct from that of the public; gives the people an occasion to claim their right, and limit that power, which, whilst it was exercised for their good, they were content should be tacitly allowed.

§ 165. And therefore he that will look into the history of England, will find, that prerogative was always largest in the hands of our wisest and best princes; because the people, observing the whole tendency of their actions to be the public good, contested not what was done without law to that end: or, if any human frailty or mistake (for princes are but men, made as others) appeared in some small declinations from that end; yet it was visible, the main of their conduct tended to nothing but the care of the public. The people, therefore, finding reason to be satisfied with these princes, whenever they acted without, or contrary to the letter of the law, acquiesced in what they did, and, without the least complaint, let them enlarge their prerogative as they pleased; judging rightly, that they did nothing herein to the prejudice of their laws, since they acted conformably to the foundation and end of all laws, the public good.

§ 166. Such God-like princes, indeed, had some title to arbitrary power by that argument, that would prove absolute monarchy the best government, as that which God himself governs the universe by; because such kings partook of his wisdom and goodness. Upon this is founded that saying, That the reigns of good princes have been always most dangerous to the liberties of their people: for when their successors, managing the government with different thoughts, would draw the actions of those good rulers into precedent, and make them the standard of their prerogative, as if what had been done only for the good of the people was a right in them to do for the harm of the people, if they so pleased; it has often occasioned contest, and sometimes public disorders, before the people could recover their original right, and get that to be declared not to be prerogative, which truly was never so: since it is impossible that any body in the society should ever have a right to do the people harm; though it be very possible and reasonable that the people should not go about to set any bounds to the prerogative of those kings or rulers, who themselves transgressed not the bounds of the public good; for "prerogative is nothing but the power of doing public good without a rule."

§ 167. The power of calling parliaments in England, as to precise time, place, and duration, is certainly a prerogative of the king, but still with this trust, that it shall be made use of for the good of the nation, as the exigencies of the times, and variety of occasions shall require: for it being impossible to foresee which should always be the fittest place for them to assemble in, and what the best season, the choice of these was left with the executive power, as might be most subservient to the public good, and best suit the ends of parliaments.

§ 168. The old question will be asked in this matter of prerogative, "But who shall be judge when this power is made a right use of?" I answer: between an executive power in being, with such a prerogative, and a legislative that depends upon his will for their convening, there can be no judge on earth; as there can be none between the legislative and the people, should either the executive or the legislative, when they have got the power in their hands, design or go about to enslave or destroy them. The people have no other remedy in this, as in all other cases where they have no judge on earth, but to appeal to heaven: for the rulers, in such attempts, exercising a power the people never put into their hands (who can never be supposed to consent that any body should rule over them for their harm), do that which they have not a right to do. And where the body of the people, or any single man, is deprived of their right, or under the exercise of a power without right, and have no appeal on earth, then they have a liberty to appeal to heaven, whenever they judge the cause of sufficient moment. And therefore, though the people cannot be judge, so as to have, by the constitution of that society, any superior power to determine and give effective sentence in the case; yet they have, by a law antecedent and paramount to all positive laws of men, reserved that ultimate determination to themselves which belongs to all mankind, where there lies no appeal on earth, viz. to judge whether they have just cause to make their appeal to heaven.—And this judgment they cannot part with, it being out of a man's power so to submit himself to another, as to give him a liberty to destroy him; God and nature never allowing a man so to abandon himself, as to neglect his own preservation: and since he cannot take away his own life, neither can he give another power to take it. Nor let any one think this lays a perpetual foundation for disorder; for this operates not till the inconveniency is so great that the majority feel it, and are weary of it, and find a necessity to have it amended. But this the executive power, or wise princes, never need come in the danger of: and it is the thing, of all others, they have most need to avoid, as of all others the most perilous.

* * *

CHAPTER XIX.

Of the Dissolution of Government.

§ 211. He that will with any clearness speak of the dissolution of government, ought in the first place to distinguish between the dissolution of the society and the dissolution of the government. That which makes the community, and brings men out of the loose state of nature into one politic society, is the agreement which every one has with the rest to incorporate, and act as one body, and so be one distinct commonwealth. The usual, and almost only way whereby this union is dissolved, is the inroad of foreign force making a conquest upon them: for in that case (not being able to maintain and support themselves as one entire and independent body), the union belonging to that body which consisted therein, must necessarily cease, and so every one return to the state he was in before, with a liberty to shift for himself, and provide for his own safety, as he thinks fit, in some other society. Whenever the society is dissolved, it is certain the government of that society cannot remain. Thus conquerors' swords often cut up governments by the roots, and mangle societies to pieces, separating the subdued or scattered multitude from the protection of, and dependence on, that society which ought to have preserved them from violence. The world is too well instructed in, and too forward to allow of, this way of dissolving of governments, to need any more to be said of it; and there wants not much argument to prove, that where the society is dissolved, the government cannot remain; that being as impossible, as for the frame of a house to subsist when the materials of it are scattered and dissipated by a whirlwind, or jumbled into a confused heap by an earthquake.

§ 212. Besides this overturning from without, governments are dissolved from within.

First, When the legislative is altered. Civil society being a state of peace, amongst those who are of it from whom the state of war is excluded by the umpirage, which they have provided in their legislative, for the ending all differences that may arise amongst any of them; it is in their legislative, that the members of a commonwealth are united, and combined together into one coherent living body. This is the soul that gives form, life, and unity to the commonwealth: from hence the several members have their mutual influence, sympathy, and connexion: and therefore, when the legislative is broken or dissolved, dissolution and death follows: for, the essence and union of the society consisting in having one will, the legislative, when once established by the majority, has the declaring, and as it were keeping of that will. The constitution of the legislative is the first and fundamental act of society, whereby provision is made for the continuation of their union, under the direction of persons, and bonds of laws, made by persons authorized thereunto, by the consent and appointment of the people; without which no one man, or number of men, amongst them, can have authority of making laws that shall be binding to the rest. When any one, or more, shall take upon them to make laws, whom the people have not appointed so to do, they make laws without authority, which the people are not therefore bound to obey; by which means they come again to be out of subjection, and may constitute to themselves a new legislative, as they think best, being in full liberty to resist the force of those, who without authority would impose any thing upon them. Every one is at the disposure of his own will, when those who had, by the delegation of the society, the declaring of the public will, are excluded from it, and others usurp the place, who have no such authority or delegation.

§ 213. This being usually brought about by such in the commonwealth who misuse the power they have, it is hard to consider it aright, and know at whose door to lay it, without knowing the form of government in which it happens. Let us suppose then the legislative placed in the concurrence of three distinct persons.

1. A single hereditary person, having the constant, supreme, executive power, and with it the power of convoking and dissolving the other two, within certain periods of time.

2. An assembly of hereditary nobility.

3. An assembly of representatives chosen, *pro tempore,* by the people. Such a form of government supposed, it is evident.

§ 214. First, That when such a single person, or prince, sets up his own arbitrary will in place of the laws, which are the will of the society, declared by the legislative, then the legislative is changed: for that being in effect the legislative, whose rules and laws are put in execution, and required to be obeyed; when other laws are set up, and other rules pretended, and enforced, than what the legislative, constituted by the society, have enacted, it is plain that the legislative is changed. Whoever introduces new laws, not being thereunto authorized by the fundamental appointment of the society, or subverts the old; disowns and overturns the power by which they were made, and so sets up a new legislative.

§ 215. Secondly, When the prince hinders the legislative from assembling in its due time, or from acting freely, pursuant to those ends for which it was constituted, the legislative is altered: for it is not a certain number of men, no, nor their meeting, unless they have also freedom of debating, and leisure of perfecting, what is for the good of the society, wherein the legislative consists: when these are taken away or altered, so as to deprive the society of the due exercise of their power, the legislative is truly altered: for it is not names that constitute governments, but the use and exercise of those powers that were intended to accompany them; so that he, who takes away the freedom, or hinders the acting of the legislative in its due seasons, in effect takes away the legislative, and puts an end to the government.

§ 216. Thirdly, When, by the arbitrary power of the prince, the electors, or ways of election,

are altered, without the consent, and contrary to the common interest of the people, there also the legislative is altered: for if others than those whom the society hath authorized thereunto, do choose, or in another way than what the society hath prescribed, those chosen are not the legislative appointed by the people.

§ 217. Fourthly, The delivery also of the people into the subjection of a foreign power, either by the prince or by the legislative, is certainly a change of the legislative, and so a dissolution of the government: for the end why people entered into society being to be preserved one entire, free, independent society, to be governed by its own laws; this is lost, whenever they are given up into the power of another.

§ 218. Why, in such a constitution as this, the dissolution of the government in these cases is to be imputed to the prince, is evident; because he, having the force, treasure, and offices of the state to employ, and often persuading himself, or being flattered by others, that as supreme magistrate he is uncapable of control; he alone is in a condition to make great advances toward such changes, under pretence of lawful authority, and has it in his hands to terrify or suppress opposers, as factious, seditious, and enemies to the government: whereas no other part of the legislative, or people, is capable by themselves to attempt any alteration of the legislative, without open and visible rebellion, apt enough to be taken notice of; which, when it prevails, produces effects very little different from foreign conquest. Besides, the prince in such a form of government having the power of dissolving the other parts of the legislative, and thereby rendering them private persons, they can never in opposition to him, or without his concurrence, alter the legislative by a law, his consent being necessary to give any of their decrees that sanction. But yet, so far as the other parts of the legislative any way contribute to any attempt upon the government, and do either promote, or not (what lies in them) hinder such designs; they are guilty, and partake in this, which is certainly the greatest crime men can be guilty of one towards another.

§ 219. There is one way more whereby such a government may be dissolved, and that is, when he who has the supreme executive power, neglects and abandons that charge, so that the laws already made can no longer be put in execution. This is demonstratively to reduce all to anarchy, and so effectually to dissolve the government: for laws not being made for themselves, but to be, by their execution, the bonds of the society, to keep every part of the body politic in its due place and function; when that totally ceases, the government visibly ceases, and the people become a confused multitude, without order or connexion. Where there is no longer the administration of justice, for the securing of men's rights, nor any remaining power within the community to direct the force, or provide for the necessities of the public; there certainly is no government left. Where the laws cannot be executed, it is all one as if there were no laws; and a government without laws is, I suppose, a mystery in politics, inconceivable to human capacity, and inconsistent with human society.

§ 220. In these and the like cases, when the government is dissolved, the people are at liberty to provide for themselves, by erecting a new legislative, differing from the other, by the change of persons, or form, or both, as they shall find it most for their safety and good: for the society can never, by the fault of another, lose the native and original right it has to preserve itself; which can only be done by a settled legislative, and a fair and impartial execution of the laws made by it. But the state of mankind is not so miserable that they are not capable of using this remedy, till it be too late to look for any. To tell people they may provide for themselves, by erecting a new legislative, when by oppression, artifice, or being delivered over to a foreign power, their old one is gone, is only to tell them, they may expect relief when it is too late, and the evil is past cure. This is in effect no more than to bid them first be slaves, and then to take care of their liberty; and when their chains are on, tell them they may act like freemen. This, if barely so, is rather mockery than relief; and men can never be secure from tyranny, if there be no means to escape it till they are perfectly under it; and therefore it is, that they have not only a right to get out of it, but to prevent it.

§ 221. There is therefore, secondly, another way whereby governments are dissolved, and that is, when the legislative, or the prince, either of them act contrary to their trust.

First, the legislative acts against the trust reposed in them, when they endeavour to invade the property of the subject, and to make themselves, or any part of the community, masters, or arbitrary disposers of the lives, liberties, or fortunes of the people.

§ 222. The reason why men enter into society is the preservation of their property; and the end why they choose and authorize a legislative is, that there may be laws made, and rules set, as guards and fences to the properties of all the members of the society: to limit the power, and moderate the dominion, of every part and member of the society: for since it can never be supposed to be the will of the society that the legislative should have a power to destroy that which every one designs to secure by entering into society, and for which the people submitted themselves to legislators of their own making; whenever the legislators endeavour to take away and destroy the property of the people, or to reduce them to slavery under arbitrary power, they put themselves into a state of war with the people, who are thereupon absolved from any farther obedience, and are left to the common refuge, which God hath provided for all men, against force and violence. Whensoever therefore the legislative shall transgress this fundamental rule of society; and either by ambition, fear, folly, or corruption, endeavour to grasp themselves, or put into the hands of any other, an absolute power over the lives, liberties, and estates of the people; by this breach of trust they forfeit the power the people had put into their hands for quite contrary ends, and it devolves to the people, who have a right to resume their original liberty, and, by the establishment of a new legislative, (such as they shall think fit) provide for their own safety and security, which is the end for which they are in society. What I have said here, concerning the legislative in general, holds true also concerning the supreme executor, who having a double trust put in him, both to have a part in the legislative, and the supreme execution of the law, acts against both, when he goes about to set up his own arbitrary will as the law of the society. He acts also contrary to his trust, when he either employs the force, treasure, and offices of the society to corrupt the representatives, and gain them to his purposes; or openly pre-engages the electors, and prescribes to their choice, such, whom he has, by solicitations, threats, promises, or otherwise, won to his designs; and employs them to bring in such, who have promised beforehand what to vote, and what to enact. Thus to regulate candidates and electors, and new-model the ways of election, what is it but to cut up the government by the roots, and poison the very fountain of public security? for the people having reserved to themselves the choice of their representatives, as the fence to their properties, could do it for no other end, but that they might always be freely chosen, and so chosen, freely act, and advise, as the necessity of the commonwealth and the public good should, upon examination and mature debate, be judged to require. This, those who give their votes before they hear the debate, and have weighed the reasons on all sides, are not capable of doing. To prepare such an assembly as this, and endeavour to set up the declared abettors of his own will, for the true representatives of the people, and the law-makers of the society, is certainly as great a breach of trust, and as perfect a declaration of a design to subvert the government, as is possible to be met with. To which if one shall add rewards and punishments visibly employed to the same end, and all the arts of perverted law made use of, to take off and destroy all that stand in the way of such a design, and will not comply and consent to betray the liberties of their country, it will be past doubt what is doing. What power they ought to have in the society, who thus employ it contrary to the trust that went along with it in its first institution, is easy to determine; and one cannot but see, that he, who has once attempted any such thing as this, cannot any longer be trusted.

§ 223. To this perhaps it will be said, that the people being ignorant, and always discontented, to lay the foundation of government in the unsteady opinion and uncertain humour of the people, is to expose it to certain ruin; and no government will be able long to subsist, if the people may set up a new legislative, whenever they take offence at the old one. To this I answer, quite the contrary. People are not so easily got out of their old forms, as some are apt to suggest. They are hardly to be prevailed with to amend the acknowledged faults in the frame they have been accustomed to. And if there be any original defects, or adventitious ones introduced by time, or corruption; it is not an easy thing to get them changed, even when all the world sees there is an opportunity for it. This slowness and aversion in the people to quit their old constitutions, has in the many revolutions, which have been seen in this kingdom, in this and former ages, still kept us to, or, after some interval of fruitless attempts, still brought us back again to, our old legislative of king, lords, and commons: and whatever provocations have made the crown be taken from some of our princes' heads, they never carried the people so far as to place it in another line.

§ 224. But it will be said, this hypothesis lays a ferment for frequent rebellion. To which I answer,

First, No more than any other hypothesis: for when the people are made miserable, and find themselves exposed to the ill usage of arbitrary power, cry up their governors as much as you will, for sons of Jupiter; let them be sacred and divine, descended, or authorized from heaven; give them out for whom or what you please, the same will happen. The people generally ill-treated, and contrary to right, will be ready upon any occasion to ease themselves of a burden that sits heavy upon them. They will wish, and seek for the opportunity, which in the change, weakness, and accidents of human affairs, seldom delays long to offer itself. He must have lived but a little while in the world, who has not seen examples of this in his time; and he must have read very little, who cannot produce examples of it in all sorts of governments in the world.

§ 225. Secondly, I answer, such revolutions happen not upon every little mismanagement in public affairs. Great mistakes in the ruling part, many wrong and inconvenient laws, and all the slips of human frailty, will be borne by the people without mutiny or murmur. But if a long train of abuses, prevarications, and artifices, all tending the same way, make the design visible to the people, and they cannot but feel what they lie under, and see whither they are going; it is not to be wondered, that they should then rouse themselves, and endeavour to put the rule into such hands which may secure to them the ends for which government was at first erected; and without which, ancient names, and specious forms, are so far from being better, that they are much worse, than the state of nature, or pure anarchy; the inconveniencies, being all as great and as near, but the remedy farther off and more difficult.

§ 226. Thirdly, I answer, that this doctrine of a power in the people of providing for their safety anew, by a new legislative, when their legislators have acted contrary to their trust, by invading their property, is the best fence against rebellion, and the probablest means to hinder it: for rebellion being an opposition, not to persons, but authority, which is founded only in the constitutions and laws of the government; those, whoever they be, who by force break through, and by force justify their violation of them, are truly and properly rebels: for when men, by entering into society and civil government, have excluded force, and introduced laws for the preservation of property, peace, and unity amongst themselves; those who set up force again in opposition to the laws, do *rebellare,* that is, bring back again the state of war, and are properly rebels: which they who are in power, (by the pretence they have to authority, the temptation of force they have in their hands, and the flattery of those about them) being likeliest to do; the properest way to prevent the evil is to show them the danger and injustice of it, who are under the greatest temptation to run into it.

§ 227. In both the fore-mentioned cases, when either the legislative is changed, or the legislators act contrary to the end for which they were constituted, those who are guilty are guilty of rebellion: for if any one by force takes away the established legislative of any society, and the laws by them made pursuant to their trust, he thereby takes away the umpirage, which every one had consented to, for a peaceable decision of all their controversies, and a bar to the state of war amongst them. They, who remove, or change the legislative, take away this decisive power, which nobody can have but by the appointment and consent of the people; and so destroying the authority which the people did, and nobody else can set up, and introducing a power which the people hath not authorized, they actually introduce a state of war, which is that of force without authority; and thus, by removing the legislative established by the society (in whose decisions the people acquiesced and united, as to that of their own will) they untie the knot, and expose the people anew to the state of war. And if those, who by force take away the legislative, are rebels, the legislators themselves, as has been shown, can be no less esteemed so; when they, who were set up for the protection and preservation of the people, their liberties and properties, shall by force invade and endeavour to take them away; and so they putting themselves into a state of war with those who made them the protectors and guardians of their peace, are properly, and with the greatest aggravation, *rebellantes,* rebels.

§ 228. But if they, who say, "it lays a foundation for rebellion," mean that it may occasion civil wars, or intestine broils, to tell the people they are absolved from obedience when illegal attempts are made upon their liberties or properties, and may oppose the unlawful violence of those who were their magistrates, when they invade their properties contrary to the trust put in them; and that therefore this doctrine is not to be allowed, being so destructive to the peace of the world: they may as well say, upon the same ground, that honest men may not oppose robbers or pirates, because this may occasion disorder or bloodshed. If any mischief come in such cases, it is not to be charged upon him who defends his own right, but on him that invades his neighbour's. If the innocent honest man must quietly quit all he has, for peace sake, to him who will lay violent hands upon it, I desire it may be considered, what a kind of peace there will be in the world, which consists only in violence and rapine; and which is to be maintained only for the benefit of robbers and oppressors. Who would not think it an admirable peace betwixt the mighty and the mean, when the lamb, without resistance, yielded his throat to be torn by the imperious wolf? Polyphemus's den gives us a perfect pattern of such a peace, and such a government, wherein Ulysses and his companions had nothing to do, but quietly to suffer themselves to be devoured. And no doubt Ulysses, who was a prudent man, preached up passive obedience, and exhorted them to a quiet submission, by representing to them of what concernment peace was to mankind; and by showing the inconveniencies might happen, if they should offer to resist Polyphemus, who had now the power over them.

§ 229. The end of government is the good of mankind: and which is best for mankind that the people should be always exposed to the boundless will of tyranny; or that the rulers should be sometimes liable to be opposed, when they grow exorbitant in the use of their power, and employ it for the destruction, and not the preservation of the properties of their people?

§ 230. Nor let any one say, that mischief can arise from hence, as often as it shall please a busy head, or turbulent spirit, to desire the alteration of the government. It is true, such men may stir, whenever they please; but it will be only to their own just ruin and perdition: for till the mischief be grown general, and the ill designs of the rulers become visible, or their attempts sensible to the greater part, the people, who are more disposed to suffer than right themselves by resistance, are not apt to stir. The examples of particular injustice or oppression, of here and there an unfortunate man, moves them not. But if they universally have a persuasion, grounded upon manifest evidence, that designs are carrying on against their liberties, and the general course and tendency of things cannot but give them strong suspicions of the evil intention of their governors, who is to be blamed for it? Who can help it, if they, who might avoid it, bring themselves into this suspicion? Are the people to be blamed, if they have the sense of rational creatures, and can think of things no otherwise than as they find and feel them? And is it not rather their fault, who put things into such a posture, that they would not have them thought to be as they are? I grant, that the pride, ambition, and turbulency of private men have sometimes caused great disorders in commonwealths, and factions have been fatal to states and kingdoms. But whether the mischief hath oftener begun in the people's wantonness, and a desire to cast off the lawful authority of their rulers, or in the rulers' insolence, and endeavours to get and exercise an arbitrary power over their people; whether oppression, or disobedience, gave the first rise to the disorder; I leave it to impartial history to determine. This I am sure, whoever, either ruler or subject, by force goes about to invade the rights of either prince or people, and lays the foundation for overturning the constitution and frame of any just government, is highly guilty of the greatest crime, I think, a man is capable of; being to answer for all those mischiefs of blood, rapine, and desolation, which the breaking to pieces of governments bring on a country. And he who does it, is justly to be esteemed the common enemy and pest of mankind, and is to be treated accordingly.

§ 231. That subjects or foreigners, attempting by force on the properties of any people, may be resisted with force, is agreed on all hands. But that magistrates, doing the same thing, may be resisted, hath of late been denied: as if those who had the greatest privileges and advantages by the law, had thereby a power to break those laws, by which alone they were set in a better place than their brethren: whereas their offence is thereby the greater, both as being ungrateful for the greater share they have by the law, and breaking also that trust, which is put into their hands by their brethren.

§ 232. Whosoever uses force without right, as every one does in society, who does it without law, puts himself into a state of war with those against whom he so uses it; and in that state all former ties are cancelled, all other rights cease, and every one has a right to defend himself, and to resist the aggressor. This is so evident, that Barclay[79] himself, that great assertor of the power and sacredness of kings, is forced to confess, that it is lawful for the people, in some cases, to resist their king; and that too in a chapter, wherein he pretends to show, that the divine law shuts up the people from all manner of rebellion. Whereby it is evident, even by his own doctrine, that, since they may in some cases resist, all resisting of princes is not rebellion. . . .

---

[79] [Ed. note] William Barclay, c. 1546–1608; Scottish jurist and political theorist who wrote in Latin. Even more than Filmer, it may be appropriate to say that Locke rescued him from (complete?) oblivion.

THE COLONIAL PERIOD

The development of the law in the thirteen American colonies between 1620 and 1776 was marked by the willingness of the colonists to apply elements of English common law and to devise new, and often simpler, ways of handling legal matters. Because many of the colonial settlements were geographically isolated, the law varied from place to place, and local traditions, customs, religious beliefs, and economic conditions often played major roles in shaping the law.

The Pilgrims who left England in 1620 to settle in Massachusetts were escaping from religious intolerance and persecution. Their religious beliefs, rooted in a strict version of Protestantism, led them to create a government that was dominated by the church leadership. By the beginning of the eighteenth century, however, Massachusetts had become a more heterogeneous and secular society with a growing commercial class that created a demand for trained lawyers and judges.

Other colonies were shaped by different traditions. In Pennsylvania the Quakers played a decisive role in the development of law and social arrangements. In the southern colonies, law became an instrument to support the institution of slavery. Laws in slaveholding colonies presumed that slaves were chattel (personal property) rather than human beings.

THE COLONIAL PERIOD

MAYFLOWER COMPACT

In 1620 the ship *Mayflower* departed from England for the New World. Many of those on board were religious dissenters, known then as Separatists and later as Pilgrims or Puritans, who preferred to separate altogether from the Church of England rather than try to change the church as other dissenters attempted to do. The passengers also included emigrants who were not members of the Separatist congregation. The combined group of Separatists and "strangers," as they were called by the Separatists, had obtained a charter from the Virginia Company of London, giving them permission to settle within the boundaries of the colony of Virginia.

The *Mayflower*, however, did not reach Virginia. Instead, it arrived off the coast of what is now Cape Cod, Massachusetts, which was not within the boundaries of any established colonial government. The strangers asserted that they would not be bound by any laws, but WILLIAM BRADFORD, the Separatists' leader, insisted that all male passengers sign an agreement to abide by the laws that the colonial leaders would establish at the colony they called Plymouth.

On November 21, 1620, forty-one adult male passengers signed the Mayflower Compact. The compact served as a device to preserve order and establish rules for self-government. The signers agreed to combine themselves into a "civil Body Politick" that would enact and obey "just and equal laws" that were made for the "general good of the colony." This commitment to justice and equality would be reiterated in many later documents, including the U.S. Constitution.

Mayflower Compact

In the name of God, amen. We, whose names are underwritten, the loyal subjects of our dread sovereign lord King James, by the grace of God, of Great Britain, France, and Ireland, king, defender of the faith, &c. Having undertaken for the glory of God, and advancement of the Christian faith, and the honor of our king and country, a voyage to plant the first colony in the northern parts of Virginia, do by these presents, solemnly and mutually, in the presence of God and one another, covenant and combine ourselves together into a civil body politic, for our better ordering and preservation and furtherance of the ends aforesaid; and by virtue hereof do enact, constitute, and frame such just and equal laws, ordinances, acts, constitutions, and officers, from time to time, as shall be thought most meet and convenient for the general good of the colony; unto which we promise all due submission and obedience. In witness whereof we have hereunto subscribed our names at Cape Cod the eleventh of November, in the reign of our sovereign lord King James, of England, France, and Ireland, the eighteenth, and of Scotland, the fifty-fourth, anno Domini, 1620.[1]

Source: Ben Perley Poore, ed., *The Federal and State Constitutions, Colonial Charters, and Other Organic Laws of the United States*, vol. 1 (1878), p. 931.

[1] English monarchs styled themselves king or queen of France between 1340 and 1801. The custom began when the English became embroiled in the Hundred Years War with France and King Edward III of England, whose mother was a French princess, claimed the French throne.

Mr. John Carver

Mr. William Bradford

Mr. Edward Winslow

Mr. William Brewster

Isaac Allerton

Miles Standish

John Alden

John Turner

Francis Eaton

James Chilton

John Craxton

John Billington

Joses Fletcher

John Goodman

Mr. Samuel Fuller

Mr. Christopher Martin

Mr. William Mullins

Mr. William White

Mr. Richard Warren

John Howland

Mr. Steven Hopkins

Digery Priest

Thomas Williams

Gilbert Winslow

Edmund Margesson

Peter Brown

Richard Bitteridge

George Soule

Edward Tilly

John Tilly

Francis Cooke

Thomas Rogers

Thomas Tinker

John Ridgdale

Edward Fuller

Richard Clark

Richard Gardiner

Mr. John Allerton

Thomas English

Edward Doten

Edward Liester

**THE COLONIAL
PERIOD**

MAYFLOWER
COMPACT

THE COLONIAL PERIOD

THE LAWS AND LIBERTIES OF MASSACHUSETTS

The Laws and Liberties of Massachusetts, enacted in 1648, served as the basis for civil and criminal law in the colony until the eighteenth century. This code was a revision of a 1641 code known as *The Body of Liberties*, which was written by NATHANIEL WARD, a Puritan minister and teacher. The Laws and Liberties reflect the Puritans' concern that members of the community should live a Christian life true to the principles of the sect. Laws were meant to guide the righteous and punish the wicked, but they were also to be administered fairly. Religious heresy was severely punished as were fornication, adultery, and other behavior that violated the moral teachings of the colonists. Nevertheless, the code mandated that individuals could not be punished or penalized without DUE PROCESS OF LAW.

—⁓—

The Laws and Liberties of Massachusetts

To Our Beloved Brethren and Neighbours
the Inhabitants of the Massachusetts, the Governour,
Assistants and Deputies assembled in the General Court
of that Jurisdiction with grace and peace in our
Lord Jesus Christ

So soon as God had set up Political Government among his people Israel he gave them a body of laws for judgment both in civil and criminal causes. These were brief and fundamental principles, yet withall so full and comprehensive as out of them clear deductions were to be drawn to all particular cases in future times. For a Commonwealth without lawes is like a Ship without rigging and steerage. Nor is it sufficient to have principles or fundamentalls, but these are to be drawn out into so many of their deductions as the time and conditions of that people may have use of. And it is very unsafe & injurious to the body of the people to put them to learn their duty and libertie from generall rules, nor is it enough to have lawes except they be also just. Therefore among other priviledges which the Lord bestowed upon his peculiar people, these he calls them specially to consider of, that God was neerer to them and their lawes were more righteous then other nations. God was sayd to be amongst them or neer to them because of his Ordinances established by himself, and their lawes righteous because himselfe was their Lawgiver: yet in the comparison are implyed two things, first that other nations had something of Gods presence amongst them. Secondly that there was also somewhat of equitie in their lawes, for it pleased the Father (upon the Covenant of Redemption with his Son) to restore so much of his Image to lost man as whereby all nations are disposed to worship God, and to advance righteousness: … They did by nature the things contained in the law of God. But the nations corrupting his Ordinances (both of Religion, and Justice) God withdrew his presence from them proportionably whereby they vvere given up to abominable lusts. … Wheras if they had vvalked according to that light & lavv of nature they might have been preserved from such moral evils and might have injoyed common blessing in all their natural and civil Ordinances: now, if it might have been so with the nations who were so much strangers to the Covenant of Grace, what advantage have they who have interests in this Covenant, and may injoye the special presence of God in the puritie and native simplicitie of all his Ordinances by which he is so neer to his owne people. This hath been no small priviledge, and advantage to us New-England that our Churches, and civil State have been planted and growne up (like two vines) together like that of Israel in the vvilderness by which we were put in minde (and had opportunity put into our hands) not only to gather our Churches, and set up the Ordinances of Christ Jesus in them according to the Apostolick patterne by such lights as the Lord graciously afforded us: but also withall to frame our civil Politie, and lawes according to the rules of his most holy word whereby each do help and strengthen other (the Churches the civil Authoritie, and the Civil Authoritie the Churches) and so both prosper the better without such emulation, and contention for priviledges or priority as have proved the misery (if not ruine) of both in other places.

* * *

These Lawes which were made successively in divers former years, we have reduced under several heads in an alphabeticall method, that so they might the more readilye be found … wherin (upon every occasion) you might readily see the rule which you ought to walke by.

* * *

You have called us from among the rest of our Bretheren and given us power to make the lawes: we must now call upon you to see them executed: remembring that old & true proverb, The execution of the law is the life of the law. If one sort of you viz: non-Freemen should object that you had no hand in calling us to this worke, and therfore think yourselvs not bound to obedience &c. Wee answer that a subsequent, or implicit consent is of like force in this case, as an express precedent power: for in puting your persons and estates into the protection and way of subsistance held forth and exercised within this Jursidiction, you doe tacitly submit to this Government and to all the wholesome lawes thereof[.]

* * *

If any of you meet with some law that seemes not to tend to your particular benefit,

you must consider that lawes are made with respect to the whole people, and not to each particular person: and obedience to them must be yielded with respect to the common welfare, not to thy private advantage, and as thou yeildest obedience to the law for common good, but to thy disadvantage: so another must observe some other law for thy good, though to his own damage; thus must we be content to bear one anothers burden and so fullfill the Law of Christ.

That distinction which is put between the Lawes of God and the lawes of men, becomes a snare to many as it is mis-applyed in the ordering of their obedience to civil Authoritie; for when the Authoritie is of God and that in way of an Ordinance … and when the administration of it is according to deductions, and rules gathered from the word of God, and the clear light of nature in civil nations, surely there is no humane law that tendeth to common good (according to those principles) but the same is mediately a law of God, and that in way of an Ordinance which all are to submit unto and that for conscience sake. . . .

THE
BOOK OF THE GENERAL LAVVES AND
LIBERTYES CONCERNING &C:

Forasmuch as the free fruition of such Liberties, Immunities, priviledges as humanitie, civilitie & christianity call for as due to everie man in his place, & proportion, without impeachment & infringement hath ever been, & ever will be the tranquility & stability of Churches & Comonwealths; & the deniall or deprivall thereof the disturbance, if not ruine of both:

It is therefore ordered by this Court, & Authority thereof, That no mans life shall be taken away; no mans honour or good name shall be stayned; no mans person shall be arrested, restrained, bannished, dismembered nor any wayes punished; no man shall be deprived of his wife or children; no mans goods or estate shal be taken away from him; nor any wayes indamaged under colour of Law or countenance of Authoritie unless it be by the vertue or equity of some expresse law of the Country warranting the same established by a General Court & sufficiently published; or in case of the defect of a law in any particular case by the word of God. And in capital cases, or cases concerning dismembring or banishment according to that word to be judged by the General Court.

THE COLONIAL PERIOD

FRAME OF GOVERNMENT

William Penn, 1682

In 1681 King Charles II of England granted William Penn a large tract of land on the west bank of the Delaware River, which Penn named Pennsylvania in honor of his father. Penn, a member and intellectual leader of the Quakers (Society of Friends), saw Pennsylvania as a refuge for Quakers and other persecuted peoples.

Penn believed in religious toleration on both pragmatic and moral grounds. He thought that a harmonious society, unhampered by intolerance, would be a prosperous society as well. In 1682, before he left England to become the first governor of Pennsylvania, Penn wrote the Frame of Government, which served as the colony's first constitution.

The Frame of Government was an expression of Penn's religious and political ideas. He sought to create a framework that would frustrate political mischief and prevent a ruler from assuming absolute power to the detriment of the community. To prevent absolutism, Penn employed the concept of balancing forces, a concept that the Framers of the U.S. Constitution later would use liberally. Freedom of worship was to be absolute, and all the traditional English rights were to be protected.

In practice, the government outlined in the Frame of Government proved in some respects to be unworkable. Penn, however, had included an amending clause, the first in any written constitution, so that the Frame of Government could be changed as circumstances required.

—◊—

Frame of Government

PREFACE

I know what is said by the several admirers of monarchy, aristocracy and democracy, which are the rule of one, a few, and many, and are the three common ideas of government, when men discourse on the subject. But I chuse to solve the controversy with this small distinction, and it belongs to all three: Any government is free to the people under it (whatever be the frame) where the laws rule, and the people are a party to those laws, and more than this is tyranny, oligarchy, or confusion. . . .

* * *

Governments, like clocks, go from the motion men give them; and as governments are made and moved by men, so by them they are ruined too. Wherefore governments rather depend upon men, than men upon governments. Let men be good, and the government cannot be bad; if it be ill, they will cure it. But, if men be bad, let the government be never so good, they will endeavor to warp and spoil it to their turn.

I know some say, let us have good laws, and no matter for the men that execute them: but let them consider, that though good laws do well, good men do better: for good laws may want good men, and be abolished or evaded by ill men: but good men will never want good laws, nor suffer ill ones. It is true, good laws have some awe upon ill ministers, but that is where they have not power to escape or abolish them, and the people are generally wise and good: but a loose and depraved people (which is the question) love laws and an administration like themselves. That, therefore, which makes a good constitution, must keep it, viz: men of wisdom and virtue, qualities, that because they descend not with worldly inheritances, must be carefully propagated by a virtuous education of youth; for which after ages will owe more to the care and prudence of founders, and the successive magistracy, than to their parents, for their private patrimonies. . . .

* * *

But, next to the power of necessity (which is a solicitor, that will take no denial) this induced me to a compliance, that we have (with reverence to God, and good conscience to men) to the best of our skill contrived and composed to the frame and laws of this government, to the great end of all government, viz: To support power in reverence with the people and to secure the people from the abuse of power; that they may be free by their just obedience, and the magistrates honourable, for their administration: for liberty without obedience is confusion, and obedience without liberty is slavery. To carry this evenness is partly owing to the constitution, and partly to the magistracy: where either of these fail, government will be subject to convulsions; but where both are wanting, it must be totally subverted; then where both meet, the government is like to endure. Which I humbly pray and hope God will please to make the lot of this Pensilvania. Amen.

THE COLONIAL PERIOD

SOUTH CAROLINA SLAVE CODE

The southern colonies relied on slave labor to cultivate the cash crops raised on large plantations. The first slave ships reached the colonies in the 1620s, and by the end of the century, the slave trade between West Africa and the southern colonies was thriving.

The social and legal relations between the English colonists and the African slaves were governed by racial beliefs and economics. Since the first meetings of West Africans and Europeans, Europeans had judged Africans to be their cultural inferiors. This belief shaped the slave codes that the colonies began to enact in the late seventeenth century. Africans were human chattel with no civil rights.

The South Carolina Slave Code of 1740 reflected concerns about controlling slaves. Section X authorized a white person to detain and examine any slave found outside a house or plantation who was not accompanied by a white person. Section XXXVI prohibited slaves from leaving their plantation, especially on Saturday nights, Sundays, and holidays. Slaves who violated the law could be subjected to a "moderate whipping." Section XLV prohibited white persons from teaching slaves to read and write.

Criminal behavior by slaves, especially actions directed against white persons, was severely punished under the code. Section IX provided that in the case of a capital crime, a slave must be brought to trial in a summary proceeding within three days of apprehension. Under section XVII, the killing of a white person by a slave was a capital crime, but section XXXVII treated a white person who killed a slave quite differently.

Willfull murder of a slave was punished by a fine of 700 pounds. Killing a slave "on a sudden heat of passion" resulted in a fine of 350 pounds.

The code did recognize that slaves were entitled to a sufficient level of food, clothing, and shelter. Section XXXVIII permitted a complaint to be filed against a slave owner who was derelict in providing the necessities. A court could order the owner to provide relief to the slaves. Likewise, section XLIV authorized the fining of slave owners who worked their slaves more than fifteen hours a day during the hottest time of the year.

South Carolina Slave Code

AN ACT FOR THE BETTER ORDERING AND GOVERNING [OF]

NEGROES AND OTHER SLAVES IN THIS PROVINCE

Whereas in his majesty's plantations in America, slavery has been introduced and allowed; and the people commonly called negroes, Indians, mulatos and mestizos have [been] deemed absolute slaves, and the subjects of property in the hands of particular persons the extent of whose power over slaves ought to be settled and limited by positive laws so that the slaves may be kept in due subjection and obedience, and the owners and other persons having the care and government of slaves, may be restrained from exercising too great rigour and cruelty over them; and that the public peace and order of this Province may be preserved:

Be it enacted, that all negroes, Indians (free Indians in amity with this government, and negroes, mulatos and mestizos who are now free excepted) mulatos or mestizos who now are or shall hereafter be in this Province, and all their issue and offspring born or to be born, shall be and they are hereby declared to be and remain for ever herafter absolute slaves, and shall follow the condition of the mother; and shall be deemed, ... taken, reputed and adjudged in law to be chattels personal in the hands of their owners and possessors and their executors, administrators and assigns to all intents, constructions and purposes whatsoever, Provided that if any negro Indian mulato, or mestizo shall claim his or her freedom, it shall and may be lawful for such negro, Indian, mulato, or mestizo, or any person or persons whatsoever, on his or her behalf to apply to the justices of his Majesty's court of common pleas by petition or motion, either during the sitting of the said court, or before any of the justices of the same court at any time in the vacation. And the said court or any of the justices thereof, shall and they are hereby fully impowered to admit any person so applying, to be guardian for any negro, Indian, mulato or mestizo, claiming his, her or their freedom, and such guardians shall be enabled, intitled and capable in law to bring an action of trespass, in the nature of ravishment of ward against any person who shall claim property in, or who shall be in possession of any such negro, Indian, mulato or mestizo.

* * *

Provided that in any action or suit to be brought in pursuance of the direction of this act the burthen of the proof shall lay upon the plaintiff, and it shall be always presumed, that every negro, Indian, mulato, and mestizo, is a slave unless the contrary can be made appear (the Indians in amity with this government excepted) in which case the burden of the proof shall lie on the defendant.

* * *

III. And for the better keeping slaves in due order and subjection: be it further enacted that no person whatsoever, shall permit or suffer any slave under his or their care or management, and who lives, or is employed in Charlestown, or any other town in this Province to go out of the limits of the said town, or any such slave, who lives in the country to go out of the plantation to which such slave belongs, or in which plantation

such slave is usually employed, without a letter subscribed and directed, or a ticket in the words following. . . .

* * *

V. If any slave who shall be out of the house or plantation where such slave shall live or shall be usually employed, or without some white person in company with such slave, shall refuse to submit or to undergo the examination of any white person, it shall be lawful for any such white Person to pursue, apprehend and moderately correct such slave; and if such slave shall assault and strike such white person, such slave may be lawfully killed.

* * *

IX. And whereas natural justice forbids, that any person of what condition soever should be condemned unheard, and the order of civil government requires that for the due and equal administration of justice, some convenient method and form of trial should be established, Be it therefore enacted, that all crimes and offences which shall be committed by slaves in this Province and for which capital punishment shall or lawfully may be inflicted, shall be heard, examined, tried, adjudged, and finally determined by any 2 justices assigned to keep the peace, and any number of freeholders not less than 3 or more than 5 in the county where the offence shall be committed and can be most conveniently assembled; either of which justices, on complaint made or information received of any such offence committed by a slave, shall commit the offender to the safe custody of the constable of the parish where such offence shall be committed, and shall without delay by warrant under his hand and seal, call to his assistance, and request any one of the nearest justices of the peace to associate with him; and shall by the same warrant summon such a number of the neighbouring freeholders as aforesaid, to assemble and meet together with the said justices, at a certain day and place not exceeding 3 days after the apprehending of such slave or slaves: and the justices and freeholders being so assembled, shall cause the slave accused or charged, to be brought before them, and shall hear the accusations which shall be brought against such slave, and his or her defence, and shall proceed to the examination of witnesses, and other evidence, and finally hear and determine the matter brought before them, in the most summary and expeditious manner; and in case the offender shall be convicted of any crime for which by law the offender ought to suffer death, the said justices shall give judgment, and award and cause execution of their sentence to be done, by inflicting such manner of death, and at such time as the said justices, by and with the consent of the freeholders shall direct, and which they shall judge will be most effectual to deter others from offending in the like manner.

* * *

[XVI.] Be it therefore enacted, that the several crimes and offences hereinafter particularly enumerated, are hereby declared to be felony without the benefit of the clergy, That is to say, If any slave, free negro, mulatto, Indian, or mestizo, shall willfully and maliciously burn or destroy any stack of rice, corn or other grain, of the product, growth or manufacture of this Province; or shall willfully and maliciously set fire to, burn or destroy any tar kiln, barrels of pitch, tar, turpentine or rosin, or any other of the goods or commodities of the growth, produce or manufacture of this Province; or shall feloniously steal, take or carry away any slave, being the property of another, with intent to carry such slave out of this Province; or shall willfully and maliciously poison, or administer any poison to any person, free man, woman, servant or slave; every such slave, free negro, mulatto, Indian (except as before excepted) and mestizo, shall suffer death as a felon.

XVII. Any slave who shall be guilty of homicide of any sort, upon any white person, except by misadventure or in defence of his master or other person under whose care and government such slave shall be, shall upon conviction thereof as aforesaid, suffer death. And every slave who shall raise or attempt to raise an insurrection in this Province, or shall endeavor to delude or entice any slave to run away and leave this Province; every such slave and slaves, and his and their accomplices, aiders and abettors, shall upon conviction as aforesaid suffer death. Provided always, That it shall and may be lawful to and for the justices who shall pronounce sentence against such slaves, and by and with the advice and consent of the freeholders as aforesaid, if several slaves shall receive sentence at one time, to mitigate and alter the sentence of any slave other than such as shall be convicted of the homicide of a white person, who they shall think may deserve mercy, and may inflict such corporal punishment (other than death) on any such

slave, as they in their discretion shall think fit, any thing herein contained to the contrary thereof in any wise notwithstanding. Provided, That one or more of the said slaves who shall be convicted of the crimes or offences aforesaid, where several are concerned, shall be executed for example, to deter others from offending in the like kind.

* * *

XXXIII. And whereas several owners of slaves do suffer their slaves to go and work where they please, upon condition of paying to their owners certain sums of money agreed upon between the owner and slave; which practice occasioned such slaves to pilfer and steal to raise money for their owners, as well as to maintain themselves in drunkenness and evil courses; for prevention of which practices for the future, Be it enacted, that no owner, master or mistress of any slave, after the passing of this act, shall permit or suffer any of his, her or their slaves to go and work out of their respective houses or families, without a ticket in writing under pain of forfeiting the sum of current money, for every such offence.

* * *

XXXVI. And for that as it is absolutely necessary to the safety of this Province, that all due care be taken to restrain the wanderings and meetings of negroes and other slaves, at all times, and more especially on Saturday nights, Sundays and other holidays, and the using and carrying wooden swords, and other mischievous and dangerous weapons, or using and keeping of drums, horns, or other loud instruments, which may call together or give sign or notice to one another of their wicked designs and purposes; and that all masters, overseers and others may be enjoined diligently and carefully to prevent the same, Be it enacted, that it shall be lawfull for all masters, overseers and other persons whomsoever, to apprehend and take up any negro or other slave that shall be found out of the plantation of his or their master or owner, at any time, especially on Saturday nights, Sundays or other holidays, not being on lawful business, and with a letter from their master or a ticket, or not having a white person with them, and the said negro or other slave or slaves correct by a moderate whipping.

XXXVII. And whereas cruelty is not only highly unbecoming those who profess themselves Christians, but is odious in the eyes of all men who have any sense of virtue or humanity; therefore to restrain and prevent barbarity being exercised toward slaves, Be it enacted, That if any person or persons whosoever, shall willfully murder his own slave, or the slave of another person, every such person shall upon conviction thereof, forfeit and pay the sum of £700 current money, and shall be rendered, and is hereby declared altogether and forever incapable of holding, exercising, enjoying or receiving the profits of any office, place or employment civil or military within this Province: ... And if any person shall on a sudden heat of passion, or by undue correction, kill his own slave or the slave of any person, he shall forfeit the sum of £350 current money, And in case any person or persons shall wilfully cut out the tongue, put out the eye, castrate or cruelly scald, burn, or deprive any slave of any limb or member, or shall inflict any other cruel punishment, other than by whipping or beating with a horsewhip, cowskin, switch or small stick, or by putting irons on, or confining or imprisoning such slave; every such person shall for every such offence, forfeit the sum of £100 current money.

XXXVIII. That in case any person in this Province, who shall be owner, or who shall have the care government or charge of any slave, or slaves, shall deny, neglect or refuse to allow such slave or slaves under his or her charge, sufficient cloathing, covering or food, it shall and may be lawfull for any person or persons, on behalf of such slave or slaves, to make complaint to the next neighbouring justice in the parish where such slave or slaves live, or are usually employed; and if there shall be no justice in the parish, then to the next justice in nearest parish: and the said justice shall summon the party against whom such complaint shall be made, and shall enquire of, hear and determine the same: and if the said justice shall find the said complaint to be true, or

that such person will not exculpate or clear himself from the charge, by his or her own oath, which such person shall be at liberty to do in all cases where positive proof is not given of the offence, such justice shall and may make such orders upon the same for the relief of such slave or slaves, as he in his discretion shall think fit, and shall and may let and impose a fine or penalty on any person who shall offend in the premises, in any sum not exceeding £20 current money, for each offence.

* * *

XLIV. And whereas many owners of slaves, and others who have the care, management and overseeing of slaves, do confine them so closely to hard labour; that they have not sufficient time for natural rest—Be it therefore enacted, That if any owner of slaves, or other person who shall have the care, management, or overseeing of any slaves, shall work or put any such slave or slaves to labour, more than 15 hours in 24 hours, from the 25th day of March to the 25th day of September, or more than 14 hours in 24 hours, from the 25th day of September to the 25th day of March; every such person shall forfeit any sum not exceeding or under £20, nor under £5 current money, for every time he, she or they shall offend herein, at the discretion of the justice before whom the complaint shall be made.

XLV. And whereas the having of slaves taught to write, or suffering them to be employed in writing, may be attended with great inconveniences; Be it enacted, that all and every person and persons whatsoever, who shall hereafter teach, or cause any slave or slaves to be taught to write, or shall use or employ any slave as a scribe in any manner of writing whatsoever, hereafter taught to write; every such person and persons shall, for every such offence, forfeit the sum of £100 current money.

CONFLICT AND REVOLUTION

By the 1750s the American colonies had grown in both population and economic strength. Increasingly, the colonists expressed dissatisfaction with Great Britain's control of their political and economic affairs. The colonies chafed under the rules of British mercantilism, the idea that colonies were to be exploited as a source of raw materials and a market for the mother country. The king and Parliament, however, viewed the colonies as part of the empire and sought to maintain the status quo.

The road to the American Revolution began with the French and Indian War (1756–1763), also known as the Seven Years' War. The war was fought to determine whether France or Great Britain would rule North America. Though Britain won the war, relations between Parliament and the colonies were strained. During the war the colonies had asserted their economic independence by trading with the enemy, flagrantly defying customs laws, and evading trade regulations. After the war the British government resolved to bring the colonies into proper subordination and to use them as a source of revenue for repaying the war debt.

Accordingly, Parliament passed a series of acts that required the colonies to pay taxes and import duties on a variety of goods and raw materials. The colonists, however, detested the STAMP ACT and the TOWNSHEND ACTS and refused to comply with them. Ultimately, these acts pushed the colonists to demand more autonomy in governing their affairs.

In 1774 armed conflict began in Massachusetts, and the colonies moved closer to declaring their independence. Nevertheless, many colonists still hoped to reach an accommodation with Britain. Public opinion shifted toward independence, however, when King George III issued orders to put down the colonial rebellion. The CONTINENTAL CONGRESS reacted by enacting the Declaration of the Causes and Necessity of Taking up Arms. In January 1776 THOMAS PAINE, the firebrand pamphleteer, published *Common Sense,* which was a direct attack on the king and a call for independence.

In July 1776 the DECLARATION OF INDEPENDENCE cut the cord with the mother country by asserting the independence of the thirteen colonies. In writing the declaration, THOMAS JEFFERSON borrowed phrases and ideas from the VIRGINIA DECLARATION OF RIGHTS of 1776, which had been adopted a few weeks earlier. The WAR OF INDEPENDENCE lasted from 1775 until 1783, when Britain renounced control of the colonies in the TREATY OF PARIS.

CONFLICT AND REVOLUTION

In 1765 the British Parliament passed the STAMP ACT, which imposed the first direct tax on the American colonies. The revenue measure was intended to help pay off the debt the British had incurred during the French and Indian War and to pay for the continuing defense of the colonies. To Parliament's great surprise, the Stamp Act ignited colonial opposition and outrage, leading to the first concerted effort by the colonists to resist Parliament and British authority.

The Stamp Act was designed to raise almost one-third of the revenue needed to support the military establishment permanently stationed in the colonies at the end of the French and Indian War. The act placed a tax on newspapers, almanacs, pamphlets and broadsides, legal documents of all kinds, insurance policies, ship's papers, licenses, and even playing cards and dice. All these documents and objects had to carry a tax stamp.

In October 1765 nine of the thirteen colonies sent delegates to New York to attend the Stamp Act Congress. The Congress issued a "Declaration of Rights and Grievances" declaring that British subjects in the colonies had the same "rights and liberties" as the king's subjects in Britain. The Congress, noting that the colonies were not represented in Parliament, concluded that no taxes could be constitutionally imposed on them except by their own legislatures. Colonial merchants also organized an effective economic boycott that led to the bankruptcy of some London merchants.

The Stamp Act was repealed in 1766. Nevertheless, Parliament then passed the Declaratory Act, which asserted that Parliament had full authority to make laws that were legally binding on the colonies.

—⁓—

Stamp Act

An Act for Granting and Applying Certain Stamp Duties, and Other Duties, in the British Colonies and Plantations in America, towards Further Defraying the Expenses of Defending, Protecting, and Securing the Same; and for Amending Such Parts of the Several Acts of Parliament Relating to the Trade and Revenues of the Said Colonies and Plantations, as Direct the Manner of Determining and Recovering the Penalties and Forfeitures Therein Mentioned

CHAPTER 1

Whereas by an act made in the last session of Parliament, several duties were granted, continued, and appropriated towards defraying the expenses of defending, protecting, and securing the British colonies and plantations in America; and whereas it is just and necessary that provision be made for raising a further revenue within your Majesty's dominions in America, towards defraying the said expenses, we, your Majesty's most dutiful and loyal subjects, the

Source: Danby Pickering, ed., *The Statutes at Large from Magna Carta to the End of the Eleventh Parliament of Great Britain, Anno 1761: Continued*, vol. 26 (1765), pp. 179–205.

Commons of Great Britain in Parliament assembled, have therefore resolved to give and grant unto your Majesty the several rates and duties hereinafter mentioned; and do most humbly beseech your Majesty that it may be enacted, and be it enacted by the king's most excellent Majesty, by and with the advice and consent of the Lords Spiritual and Temporal and Commons in this present Parliament assembled, and by the authority of the same, that from and after the first day of November, one thousand seven hundred and sixty-five, there shall be raised, levied, collected, and paid unto his Majesty, his heirs, and successors throughout the colonies and plantations in America which now are, or hereafter may be, under the dominion of his Majesty, his heirs, and successors,

For every skin or piece of vellum or parchment or sheet or piece of paper on which shall be engrossed, written, or printed any declaration, plea, replication, rejoinder, demurrer, or other pleading, or any copy thereof, in any court of law within the British colonies and plantations in America, a stamp duty of three pence.

For every skin or piece of vellum or parchment or sheet or piece of paper on which shall be engrossed, written, or printed any special bail and appearance upon such bail in any such court, a stamp duty of two shillings.

For every skin or piece of vellum or parchment or sheet or piece of paper on which shall be engrossed, written, or printed any petition, bill, answer, claim, plea, replication, rejoinder, demurrer, or other pleading in any court of chancery or equity within the said colonies and plantations, a stamp duty of one shilling and six pence.

For every skin or piece of vellum or parchment or sheet or piece of paper on which shall be engrossed, written, or printed any copy of any petition, bill, answer, claim, plea, replication, rejoinder, demurrer, or other pleading in any such court, a stamp duty of three pence.

For every skin or piece of vellum or parchment or sheet or piece of paper on which shall be engrossed, written, or printed any monition, libel, answer, allegation, inventory, or renunciation in ecclesiastical matters in any court of probate, court of the ordinary, or other court exercising ecclesiastical jurisdiction within the said colonies and plantations, a stamp duty of one shilling.

For every skin or piece of vellum or parchment or sheet or piece of paper on which shall be engrossed, written, or printed any copy of any will (other than the probate thereof), monition, libel, answer, allegation, inventory, or renunciation in ecclesiastical matters in any such court, a stamp duty of six pence.

For every skin or piece of vellum or parchment or sheet or piece of paper on which shall be engrossed, written, or printed any donation, presentation, collation, or institution of or to any benefice, or any writ or instrument for the like purpose, or any register, entry, testimonial, or certificate of any degree taken in any university, academy, college, or seminary of learning within the said colonies and plantations, a stamp duty of two pounds.

For every skin or piece of vellum or parchment or sheet or piece of paper, on which shall be engrossed, written, or printed any monition, libel, claim, answer, allegation, information, letter of request, execution, renunciation, inventory, or other pleading, in any admiralty court within the said colonies and plantations, a stamp duty of one shilling.

For every skin or piece of vellum or parchment or sheet or piece of paper on which any copy of any such monition, libel, claim, answer, allegation, information, letter of request, execution, renunciation, inventory, or other pleading shall be engrossed, written, or printed, a stamp duty of six pence.

For every skin or piece of vellum or parchment or sheet or piece of paper on which shall be engrossed, written, or printed, any appeal, writ of error, writ of dower, *ad quod damnum*, certiorari, statute merchant, statute staple, attestation, or certificate by any officer or exemplification of any record or proceeding in any court whatsoever within the said colonies and plantations (except appeals, writs of error, certiorari, attestations, certificates, and exemplifications, for or relating to the removal of any proceedings from before a single justice of the peace), a stamp duty of ten shillings.

For every skin or piece of vellum or parchment or sheet or piece of paper on which shall be engrossed, written, or printed any writ of covenant for levying of fines, writ of entry for suffering a common recovery, or attachment issuing out of, or returnable into, any court within the said colonies and plantations, a stamp duty of five shillings.

For every skin or piece of vellum or parchment or sheet or piece of paper on which shall be engrossed, written, or printed any judgment, decree, sentence, or dismission, or any record of *nisi prius* or *postea,* in any court within the said colonies and plantations, a stamp duty of four shillings.

For every skin or piece of vellum or parchment or sheet or piece of paper on which shall be engrossed, written, or printed any affidavit, common bail or appearance, interrogatory deposition, rule, order, or warrant of any court, or any *dedimus potestatem, capias, subpoena,* summons, compulsory citation, commission, recognizance, or any other writ, process, or mandate, issuing out of, or returnable into, any court or any office belonging thereto or any other proceeding therein whatsoever or any copy thereof or of any record not herein before charged within the said colonies and plantations (except warrants relating to criminal matters and proceedings thereon or relating thereto), a stamp duty of one shilling.

For every skin or piece of vellum or parchment or sheet or piece of paper on which shall be engrossed, written, or printed any license, appointment, or admission of any counselor, solicitor, attorney, advocate, or proctor to practice in any court, or of any notary within the said colonies and plantations, a stamp duty of ten pounds.

For every skin or piece of vellum or parchment or sheet or piece of paper on which shall be engrossed, written, or printed any note or bill of lading, which shall be signed for any kind of goods, wares, or merchandise to be exported from, or any cocket [a document sealed by the Custom House] or clearance granted within, the said colonies and plantations, a stamp duty of four pence.

For every skin or piece of vellum or parchment or sheet or piece of paper on which shall be engrossed, written, or printed letters of marque, or commission for private ships of war, within the said colonies and plantations, a stamp duty of twenty shillings.

For every skin or piece of vellum or parchment or sheet or piece of paper on which shall be engrossed, written, or printed any grant, appointment, or admission of or to any public beneficial office or employment for the space of one year, or any lesser time, of or above the value of twenty pounds per annum sterling money in salary, fees, and perquisites within the said colonies and plantations (except commissions and appointments of officers of the army, navy, ordnance, or militia, of judges, and of justices of the peace), a stamp duty of ten shillings.

For every skin or piece of vellum or parchment or sheet or piece of paper on which any grant of any liberty, privilege, or franchise under the seal of any of the said colonies or plantations, or under the seal or sign manual of any governor, proprietor, or public officer alone or in conjunction with any other person or persons, or with any council, or any council and assembly, or any exemplification of the same, shall be engrossed, written, or printed within the said colonies and plantations, a stamp duty of six pounds.

For every skin or piece of vellum or parchment or sheet or piece of paper on which shall be engrossed, written, or printed any license for retailing of spirituous liquors, to be granted to any person who shall take out the same within the said colonies and plantations, a stamp duty of twenty shillings.

For every skin or piece of vellum or parchment or sheet or piece of paper on which shall be engrossed, written, or printed any license for retailing of wine, to be granted to any person who shall not take out a license for retailing of spirituous liquors within the said colonies and plantations, a stamp duty of four pounds.

For every skin or piece of vellum or parchment or sheet or piece of paper on which shall be engrossed, written, or printed any license for retailing of wine, to be granted to any person who shall take out a license for retailing of spirituous liquors within the said colonies and plantations, a stamp duty of three pounds.

For every skin or piece of vellum or parchment or sheet or piece of paper on which shall be engrossed, written, or printed any probate of a will, letters of administration, or of guardianship for any estate above the value of twenty pounds sterling money; within the British colonies and plantations upon the continent of America, the islands belonging thereto, and the Bermuda and Bahama islands, a stamp duty of five shillings.

For every skin or piece of vellum or parchment or sheet or piece of paper on which shall be engrossed, written, or printed any such probate, letters of administration or of guardianship within all other parts of the British dominions in America, a stamp duty of ten shillings.

For every skin or piece of vellum or parchment or sheet or piece of paper on which shall be engrossed, written, or printed any bond for securing the payment of any sum of money, not exceeding the sum of ten pounds sterling money, within the British colonies and plantations upon the continent of America, the islands belonging thereto, and the Bermuda and Bahama islands, a stamp duty of six pence.

For every skin or piece of vellum or parchment or sheet or piece of paper on which shall be engrossed, written, or printed any bond for securing the payment of any sum of money above ten pounds, and not exceeding the sum of twenty pounds sterling money, within such colonies, plantations, and islands, a stamp duty of one shilling.

For every skin or piece of vellum or parchment or sheet or piece of paper on which shall be engrossed, written, or printed any bond for securing the payment of any sum of money above twenty pounds, and not exceeding forty pounds sterling money, within such colonies, plantations, and islands, a stamp duty of one shilling and six pence.

For every skin or piece of vellum or parchment or sheet or piece of paper on which shall be engrossed, written, or printed any order or warrant for surveying or setting out any quantity of land, not exceeding one hundred acres, issued by any governor, proprietor, or any public officer alone, or in conjunction with any other person or persons, or with any council or any council and assembly, within the British colonies and plantations in America, a stamp duty of six pence.

For every skin or piece of vellum or parchment or sheet or piece of paper on which shall be engrossed, written, or printed any such order or warrant for surveying or setting out any quantity of land above one hundred, and not exceeding two hundred acres, within the said colonies and plantations, a stamp duty of one shilling.

For every skin or piece of vellum or parchment or sheet or piece of paper on which shall be engrossed, written, or printed any such order or warrant for surveying or setting out any quantity of land above two hundred, and not exceeding three hundred and twenty acres, and

in proportion for every such order or warrant for surveying or setting out every other three hundred and twenty acres within the said colonies and plantations, a stamp duty of one shilling and six pence.

For every skin or piece of vellum or parchment or sheet or piece of paper on which shall be engrossed, written, or printed any original grant or any deed, mesne conveyance, or other instrument whatsoever by which any quantity of land not exceeding one hundred acres shall be granted, conveyed, or assigned within the British colonies and plantations upon the continent of America, the islands belonging thereto, and the Bermuda and Bahama islands (except leases for any term not exceeding the term of twenty-one years), a stamp duty of one shilling and six pence.

For every skin or piece of vellum or parchment or sheet or piece of paper on which shall be engrossed, written, or printed any such original grant or any such deed, mesne conveyance, or other instrument whatsoever by which any quantity of land above one hundred, and not exceeding two hundred acres, shall be granted, conveyed, or assigned within such colonies, plantations, and islands, a stamp duty of two shillings.

For every skin or piece of vellum or parchment or sheet or piece of paper on which shall be engrossed, written, or printed any such original grant or any such deed, mesne conveyance, or other instrument whatsoever by which any quantity of land above two hundred, and not exceeding three hundred and twenty acres, shall be granted, conveyed, or assigned, and in proportion for every such grant, deed, mesne conveyance, or other instrument, granting, conveying, or assigning, every other three hundred and twenty acres within such colonies, plantations, and islands, a stamp duty of two shillings and six pence.

For every skin or piece of vellum or parchment or sheet or piece of paper on which shall be engrossed, written, or printed any such original grant or any such deed, mesne conveyance, or other instrument whatsoever by which any quantity of land not exceeding one hundred acres shall be granted, conveyed, or assigned within all other parts of the British dominions in America, a stamp duty of three shillings.

For every skin or piece of vellum or parchment or sheet or piece of paper on which shall be engrossed, written, or printed any such original grant or any such deed, mesne conveyance, or other instrument whatsoever by which any quantity of land above one hundred, and not exceeding two hundred acres, shall be granted, conveyed, or assigned within the same parts of the said dominions, a stamp duty of four shillings.

For every skin or piece of vellum or parchment or sheet or piece of paper on which shall be engrossed, written, or printed any such original grant or any such deed, mesne conveyance, or other instrument whatsoever whereby any quantity of land above two hundred, and not exceeding three hundred and twenty acres, shall be granted, conveyed, or assigned, and in proportion for every such grant, deed, mesne conveyance, or other instrument, granting, conveying, or assigning every other three hundred and twenty acres within the same parts of the said dominions, a stamp duty of five shillings.

For every skin or piece of vellum or parchment or sheet or piece of paper on which shall be engrossed, written, or printed any grant, appointment, or admission of or to any public beneficial office or employment, not herein before charged, above the value of twenty pounds per annum sterling money in salary, fees, and perquisites, or any exemplification of the same, within the British colonies and plantations upon the continent of America, the islands belonging thereto, and the Bermuda and Bahama islands (except commissions of officers of the army, navy, ordnance, or militia, and of justices of the peace), a stamp duty of four pounds.

For every skin or piece of vellum or parchment or sheet or piece of paper on which shall be engrossed, written, or printed any such grant, appointment, or admission, of or to any such public beneficial office or employment, or any exemplification of the same, within all other parts of the British dominions in America, a stamp duty of six pounds.

For every skin or piece of vellum or parchment or sheet or piece of paper on which shall be engrossed, written, or printed any indenture, lease, conveyance, contract, stipulation, bill of sale, charter party, protest, articles of apprenticeship, or covenant (except for the hire of servants not apprentices, and also except such other matters as are herein before charged) within the British colonies and plantations in America, a stamp duty of two shillings and six pence.

For every skin or piece of vellum or parchment or sheet or piece of paper on which any warrant or order for auditing any public accounts, beneficial warrant, order, grant, or certificate under any public seal, or under the seal or sign manual of any governor, proprietor, or public officer alone, or in conjunction with any other person or persons, or with any council or any council and assembly not herein before charged, or any passport or let-pass, surrender of office, or policy of assurance shall be engrossed, written, or printed within the said colonies and plantations (except warrants or orders for the service of the navy, army, ordnance, or militia, and grants of offices under twenty pounds per annum in salary, fees, and perquisites), a stamp duty of five shillings.

For every skin or piece of vellum or parchment or sheet or piece of paper on which shall be engrossed, written, or printed any notarial act, bond, deed, letter of attorney, procuration, mortgage, release, or other obligatory instrument not herein before charged within the said colonies and plantations, a stamp duty of two shillings and three pence.

For every skin or piece of vellum or parchment or sheet or piece of paper on which shall be engrossed, written, or printed any register, entry, or enrollment of any grant, deed, or other instrument whatsoever herein before charged within the said colonies and plantations, a stamp duty of three pence.

For every skin or piece of vellum or parchment or sheet or piece of paper on which shall be engrossed, written, or printed any register, entry, or enrollment of any grant, deed, or other instrument whatsoever not herein before charged within the said colonies and plantations, a stamp duty of two shillings.

And for and upon every pack of playing cards and all dice which shall be sold or used within the said colonies and plantations, the several stamp duties following (that is to say):

For every pack of such cards, the sum of one shilling.

And for every pair of such dice, the sum of ten shillings.

And for and upon every paper, commonly called a pamphlet, and upon every newspaper containing public news, intelligence, or occurrences, which shall be printed, dispersed, and made public, within any of the said colonies and plantations, and for and upon such advertisements as are hereinafter mentioned, the respective duties following (that is to say):

For every such pamphlet and paper contained in half a sheet, or any lesser piece of paper, which shall be so printed, a stamp duty of one halfpenny for every printed copy thereof.

For every such pamphlet and paper (being larger than half a sheet and not exceeding one whole sheet), which shall be so printed, a stamp duty of one penny for every printed copy thereof.

For every such pamphlet and paper being larger than one whole sheet and not exceeding six sheets in octavo, or in a lesser page, or not exceeding twelve sheets in quarto, or twenty sheets in folio, which shall be so printed, a duty after the rate of one shilling for every sheet of any kind of paper which shall be contained in one printed copy thereof.

For every advertisement to be contained in any gazette, newspaper, or other paper, or any pamphlet which shall be so printed, a duty of two shillings.

For every almanac or calendar for any one particular year, or for any time less than a year, which shall be written or printed on one side only of any one sheet, skin, or piece of paper, parchment, or vellum within the said colonies and plantations, a stamp duty of two pence.

For every other almanac or calendar for any one particular year, which shall be written or printed within the said colonies and plantations, a stamp duty of four pence.

And for every almanac or calendar written or printed within the said colonies and plantations to serve for several years, duties to the same amount respectively shall be paid for every such year.

For every skin or piece of vellum or parchment or sheet or piece of paper on which any instrument, proceeding, or other matter or thing aforesaid shall be engrossed, written, or printed within the said colonies and plantations in any other than the English language, a stamp duty of double the amount of the respective duties before charged thereon.

And there shall be also paid in the said colonies and plantations a duty of six pence for every twenty shillings, in any sum not exceeding fifty pounds sterling money, which shall be given, paid, contracted, or agreed for, with or in relation to any clerk or apprentice, which shall be put or placed to or with any master or mistress to learn any profession, trade, or employment.

* * *

CHAPTER 12

And be it further enacted by the authority aforesaid that the said several duties shall be under the management of the commissioners, for the time being, of the duties charged on stamped vellum, parchment, and paper in Great Britain: and the said commissioners are hereby empowered and required to employ such officers under them for that purpose as they shall think proper; and to use such stamps and marks to denote the stamp duties hereby charged as they shall think fit; and to repair, renew, or alter the same, from time to time, as there shall be occasion; and to do all other acts, matters, and things necessary to be done for putting this act in execution with relation to the duties hereby charged.

CHAPTER 13

And be it further enacted by the authority aforesaid that the commissioners for managing the said duties, for the time being, shall and may appoint a fit person or persons to attend in every court or public office within the said colonies and plantations to take notice of the vellum, parchment, or paper upon which any of the matters or things hereby charged with a duty shall be engrossed, written, or printed, and of the stamps or marks thereupon, and of all other matters and things tending to secure the said duties; and that the judges in the several courts and all other persons to whom it may appertain shall, at the request of any such officer, make such orders and do such other matters and things for the better securing of the said duties, as shall be lawfully or reasonably desired in that behalf: and every commissioner and other officer, before he proceeds to the execution of any part of this act, shall take an oath in the words, or to the effect following (that is to say):

I A.B. do swear that I will faithfully execute the trust reposed in me, pursuant to an act of Parliament made in the fifth year of the reign of his majesty King George the Third for granting certain stamp duties and other duties in the British colonies and plantations in America without fraud or concealment; and will from time to time true account make of my doing therein and deliver the same to such person or persons as his Majesty, his heirs, or successors shall appoint to receive such account; and will take no fee, reward, or profit for the execution or performance of the said trust or the business relating thereto from any person or persons other than such as shall be allowed by his Majesty, his heirs, and successors, or by some other person or persons under him or them to that purpose authorized.

Or if any such officer shall be of the people commonly called Quakers, he shall take a solemn affirmation to the effect of the said oath; which oath or affirmation shall and may be administered to any such commissioner or commissioners by any two or more of the same commissioners, whether they have or have not previously taken the same: and any of the said commissioners or any justice of the peace within the kingdom of Great Britain, or any governor, lieutenant governor, judge, or other magistrate within the said colonies or plantations, shall and may administer such oath or affirmation to any subordinate officer.

CHAPTER 14

And be it further enacted by the authority aforesaid that the said commissioners and all officers to be employed or entrusted by or under them as aforesaid shall, from time to time, in and for the better execution of their several places and trusts observe such rules, methods, and orders as they respectively shall, from time to time, receive from the high treasurer of Great Britain or the commissioners of the treasury or any three or more of such commissioners for the time being; and that the said commissioners for managing the stamp duties shall take especial care that the several parts of the said colonies and plantations shall, from time to time, be sufficiently furnished with vellum, parchment, and paper, stamped or marked with the said respective duties.

CHAPTER 15

And be it further enacted by the authority aforesaid that if any person or persons shall sign, engross, write, print, or sell, or expose to sale or cause to be signed, engrossed, written, printed, or sold or exposed to sale in any of the said colonies or plantations or in any other part of his Majesty's dominions any matter or thing for which the vellum, parchment, or paper is hereby charged to pay any duty before the same shall be marked or stamped with the marks or stamps to be provided as aforesaid, or upon which there shall not be some stamp or mark resembling the same; or shall sign, engross, write, print, or sell, or expose to sale or cause to be signed, engrossed, written, printed, or sold or exposed to sale any matter or thing upon any vellum, parchment, or paper that shall be marked or stamped for any lower duty than the duty by this act made payable in respect thereof; every such person so offending shall, for every such offense, forfeit the sum of ten pounds.

CHAPTER 16

And be it further enacted by the authority aforesaid that no matter or thing whatsoever by this act charged with the payment of a duty shall be pleaded or given in evidence or admitted in any court within the said colonies and plantations, to be good, useful, or available in law or equity, unless the same shall be marked or stamped in pursuance of this act with the respective duty hereby charged thereon, or with an higher duty.

CHAPTER 17

Provided nevertheless, and be it further enacted by the authority aforesaid that if any vellum, parchment, or paper containing any deed, instrument, or other matter or thing shall not be duly stamped in pursuance of this act at the time of the signing, sealing, or other execution or the entry or enrollment thereof, any person interested therein, or any person on his or her behalf, upon producing the same to any one of the chief distributors of stamped vellum, parchment, and paper, and paying to him the sum of ten pounds for every such deed, instrument, matter, or thing, and also double the amount of the duties payable in respect thereof, shall be entitled to receive from such distributor vellum, parchment, or paper stamped pursuant to this act to the amount of the money so paid; a certificate being first written upon every such piece of vellum, parchment, or paper, expressing the name and place of abode of the person by or on whose behalf such payment is made, the general purport of such deed, instrument, matter, or thing, the names of the parties therein and of the witnesses (if any) thereto, and the date thereof, which certificate shall be signed by the said distributor; and the vellum, parchment, or paper shall be then annexed to such deed, instrument, matter, or thing, by or in the presence of such distributor, who shall impress a seal upon wax to be affixed on the part where such annexation shall be made in the presence of a magistrate, who shall attest such signature and sealing; and the deed, instrument, or other matter or thing from thenceforth shall and may, with the vellum, parchment, or paper so annexed, be admitted and allowed in evidence in any court whatsoever and shall be as valid and effectual as if the proper stamps had been impressed thereon at the time of the signing, sealing, or other execution or entry or enrollment thereof: and the said distributor shall once in every six months, or oftener if required by the commissioners for managing the stamp duties, send to such commissioners true copies of all such certificates and an account of the number of pieces of vellum, parchment, and paper so annexed and of the respective duties impressed upon every such piece.

CHAPTER 18

And be it further enacted by the authority aforesaid that if any person shall forge, counterfeit, erase, or alter any such certificate, every such person so offending shall be guilty of felony and shall suffer death as in cases of felony without the benefit of clergy.

CHAPTER 19

And be it further enacted by the authority aforesaid that if any person or persons shall, in the said colonies or plantations or in any other part of his Majesty's dominions, counterfeit or forge any seal, stamp, mark, type, device, or label to resemble any seal, stamp, mark, type, device, or label which shall be provided or made in pursuance of this act; or shall counterfeit or resemble the impression of the same upon any vellum, parchment, paper, cards, dice, or other matter or thing thereby to evade the payment of any duty hereby granted; or shall make, sign, print, utter, vend, or sell any vellum, parchment, or paper or other matter or thing with such counterfeit mark or impression thereon, knowing such mark or impression to be counterfeited; then every person so offending shall be adjudged a felon and shall suffer death as in cases of felony without the benefit of clergy.

CHAPTER 20

And it is hereby declared that upon any prosecution or prosecutions for such felony, the dye, tool, or other instrument made use of in counterfeiting or forging any such seal, stamp, mark, type, device, or label, together with the vellum, parchment, paper, cards, dice, or other matter or thing having such counterfeit impression, shall, immediately after the trial or convic-

tion of the party or parties accused, be broke, defaced, or destroyed in open court.

CHAPTER 21

And be it further enacted by the authority aforesaid that if any register, public officer, clerk, or other person in any court, registry, or office within any of the said colonies or plantations shall, at any time after the said first day of November, one thousand seven hundred and sixty-five, enter, register, or enroll any matter or thing hereby charged with a stamp duty, unless the same shall appear to be duly stamped; in every such case such register, public officer, clerk, or other person shall, for every such offense, forfeit the sum of twenty pounds.

* * *

CHAPTER 49

And be it further enacted by the authority aforesaid that the high treasurer of Great Britain, or the commissioners of his Majesty's treasury, or any three or more of such commissioners, for the time being shall once in every year at least set the prices at which all sorts of stamped vellum, parchment, and paper shall be sold by the said commissioners for managing the stamp duties and their officers; and that the said commissioners for the said duties shall cause such prices to be marked upon every such skin and piece of vellum and parchment and sheet and piece of paper: and if any officer or distributor to be appointed by virtue of this act shall sell, or cause to be sold, any vellum, parchment, or paper for a greater or higher price or sum than the price or sum so set or affixed thereon; every such officer or distributor shall, for every such offense, forfeit the sum of twenty pounds.

CHAPTER 50

And be it also enacted by the authority aforesaid that several officers who shall be respectively employed in the raising, receiving, collecting, or paying the several duties hereby charged within the said colonies and plantations shall every twelve months or oftener, if thereunto required by the said commissioners for managing the said duties, exhibit his and their respective account and accounts of the said several duties upon oath, or if a Quaker upon affirmation, in the presence of the governor, or commander in chief, or principal judge of the colony or plantation where such officers shall be respectively resident, in such manner as the high treasurer, or the commissioners of the treasury, or any three or more of such commissioners for the time being shall, from time to time, direct and appoint, in order that the same may be immediately afterwards transmitted by the said officer or officers to the commissioners for managing the said duties, to be comptrolled and audited according to the usual course and form of comptrolling and auditing the accounts of the stamp duties arising within this kingdom: and if any of the said officers shall neglect or refuse to exhibit any such account, or to verify the same upon oath or affirmation, or to transmit any such account so verified to the commissioners for managing the said duties in such manner, and within such time, as shall be so appointed or directed; or shall neglect or refuse to pay, or cause to be paid into the hands of the receiver general of the stamp duties in Great Britain, or to such other person or persons as the high treasurer, or commissioners of the treasury, or any three or more of such commissioners for the time being shall, from time to time, nominate or appoint, the monies respectively raised, levied, and received by such officers under the authority of this act, at such times, and in such manner as they shall be respectively required by the said high treasurer, or commissioners of the treasury; or if any such officers shall divert, detain, or misapply all or any part of the said monies so by them respectively raised, levied, and received, or shall knowingly return any person or persons *insuper* for any monies or other things duly answered, paid, or accounted for by such person or persons, whereby he or they shall sustain any damage or prejudice; in every such case, every such officer shall be liable to pay treble the value of all and every sum and sums of money so diverted or misapplied; and shall also be liable to pay treble damages to the party grieved, by returning him *insuper*.

CHAPTER 51

And be it further enacted by the authority aforesaid that the commissioners, receiver or receivers general, or other person or persons who shall be respectively employed in Great Britain in the directing, receiving, or paying the monies arising by the duties hereby granted shall, and are hereby required, between the tenth day of October and the fifth day of January following, and so from year to year, yearly, at those times, to exhibit their respective accounts there-

of to his Majesty's auditors of the imprest in England for the time being, or one of them, to be declared before the high treasurer or commissioners of the treasury and chancellor of the exchequer for the time being, according to the course of the exchequer.

CHAPTER 52

And be it further enacted by the authority aforesaid that if the said commissioners for managing the said duties, or the said receiver or receivers general, shall neglect or refuse to pay into the exchequer all or any of the said monies in such manner as they are required by this act to pay the same, or shall divert or misapply any part thereof, then they, and every of them so offending, shall be liable to pay double the value of all and every sum and sums of money so diverted or misapplied.

CHAPTER 53

And be it further enacted by the authority aforesaid that the comptroller or comptrollers for the time being of the duties hereby imposed shall keep perfect and distinct accounts in books fairly written of all the monies arising by the said duties; and if any such comptroller or comptrollers shall neglect his or their duty therein, then he or they, for every such offense, shall forfeit the sum of one hundred pounds.

CHAPTER 54

And be it further enacted by the authority aforesaid that all the monies which shall arise by the several rates and duties hereby granted (except the necessary charges of raising, collecting, recovering, answering, paying, and accounting for the same, and the necessary charges from time to time incurred in relation to this act, and the execution thereof) shall be paid into the receipt of his Majesty's exchequer, and shall be entered separate and apart from all other monies, and shall be there reserved to be from time to time disposed of by Parliament towards further defraying the necessary expenses of defending, protecting, and securing the said colonies and plantations.

CHAPTER 55

And whereas it is proper that some provision should be made for payment of the necessary expenses which have been and shall be incurred in relation to this act and the execution thereof; and of the orders and rules to be established under the authority of the same before the said duties shall take effect, or the monies arising thereby shall be sufficient to discharge such expenses; be it therefore enacted by the authority aforesaid that his Majesty may, and he is hereby empowered by any warrant or warrants under his royal sign manual, at any time or times before the twentieth day of April, one thousand seven hundred and sixty-six, to cause to be issued and paid out of any of the surpluses, excesses, overplus monies, and other revenues composing the fund commonly called *The sinking fund* (except such monies of the said sinking fund as are appropriated to any particular use or uses, by any former act or acts of Parliament in that behalf) such sum and sums of money as shall be necessary to defray the said expenses; and the monies so issued shall be reimbursed by payment into the exchequer of the like sum or sums out of the first monies which shall arise by virtue of this act; which monies, upon the payment thereof into the exchequer, shall be carried to the account, and made part of the said fund.

CHAPTER 56

And it is hereby further enacted and declared that all the powers and authorities by this act granted to the commissioners for managing the duties upon stamped vellum, parchment, and paper shall and may be fully and effectually carried into execution by any three or more of the said commissioners, anything herein before contained to the contrary notwithstanding.

CHAPTER 57

And be it further enacted by the authority aforesaid that all forfeitures and penalties incurred after the twenty-ninth day of September, one thousand seven hundred and sixty-five, for offenses committed against an act passed in the fourth year of the reign of his present Majesty, entitled, *An act for granting certain duties in the British colonies and plantations in America;* for continuing, amending, and making perpetual an act passed in the sixth year of the reign of his late Majesty King George the Second, entitled, *An act for the better securing and encouraging the trade of his Majesty's sugar colonies in America;* for applying for produce of such duties, and of the duties to arise by virtue of the said act towards defraying the expenses of defending, protecting, and securing the said colonies and plantations; for explaining an act

made in the twenty-fifth year of the reign of King Charles the Second, entitled, *An act for the encouragement of the Greenland and Eastland trades, and for the better securing the plantation trade;* and for altering and disallowing several drawbacks on exports from this kingdom, and more effectually preventing the clandestine conveyance of goods to and from the said colonies and plantations, and improving and securing the trade between the same and Great Britain, and for offenses committed against any other act or acts of Parliament relating to the trade or revenues of the said colonies of plantations; shall and may be prosecuted, sued for, and recovered in any court of record, or in any court of admiralty in the respective colony or plantation where the offense shall be committed, or in any court of vice admiralty appointed or to be appointed, and which shall have jurisdiction within such colony, plantation, or place (which courts of admiralty or vice admiralty are hereby respectively authorized and required to proceed, hear, and determine the same) at the election of the informer or prosecutor.

CHAPTER 58

And it is hereby further enacted and declared by the authority aforesaid that all sums of money granted and imposed by this act as rates or duties, and also all sums of money imposed as forfeitures or penalties, and all sums of money required to be paid, and all other monies herein mentioned shall be deemed and taken to be sterling money of Great Britain, and shall be collected, recovered, and paid to the amount of the value which such nominal sums bear in Great Britain; and that such monies shall and may be received and taken according to the proportion and value of five shillings and six pence the ounce in silver; and that all the forfeitures and penalties hereby inflicted, and which shall be incurred in the said colonies and plantations, shall and may be prosecuted, sued for, and recovered in any court of record, or in any court of admiralty in the respective colony or plantation where the offense shall be committed, or in any court of vice admiralty appointed or to be appointed, and which shall have jurisdiction within such colony, plantation, or place (which courts of admiralty or vice admiralty are hereby respectively authorized and required to proceed, hear, and determine the same) at the election of the informer or prosecutor; and that from and after the twenty-ninth day of September, one thousand seven hundred and sixty-five, in all cases where any suit or prosecution shall be commenced and determined for any penalty or forfeiture inflicted by this act, or by the said act made in the fourth year of his present Majesty's reign, or by any other act of Parliament relating to the trade or revenues of the said colonies or plantations in any court of admiralty in the respective colony or plantation where the offense shall be committed, either party, who shall think himself aggrieved by such determination, may appeal from such determination to any court of vice admiralty appointed or to be appointed, and which shall have jurisdiction within such colony, plantation, or place (which court of vice admiralty is hereby authorized and required to proceed, hear, and determine such appeal) any law, custom, or usage to the contrary notwithstanding; and the forfeitures and penalties hereby inflicted, which shall be incurred in any other part of his Majesty's dominions, shall and may be prosecuted, sued for, and recovered with full costs of suit in any court of record within the kingdom, territory, or place where the offense shall be committed, in such and the same manner as any debt or damage, to the amount of such forfeiture or penalty, can or may be sued for and recovered.

CHAPTER 59

And it is hereby further enacted that all the forfeitures and penalties hereby inflicted shall be divided, paid, and applied as follows; (that is to say) one-third part of all such forfeitures and penalties recovered in the said colonies and plantations shall be paid into the hands of one of the chief distributors of stamped vellum, parchment, and paper residing in the colony or plantation wherein the offender shall be convicted, for the use of his Majesty, his heirs, and successors; one-third part of the penalties and forfeitures so recovered, to the governor or commander in chief of such colony or plantation; and the other third part thereof to the person who shall inform or sue for the same; and that one moiety of all such penalties and forfeitures recovered in any other part of his Majesty's dominions shall be to the use of his Majesty, his heirs, and successors, and the other moiety thereof to the person who shall inform or sue for the same.

CHAPTER 60

And be it further enacted by the authority aforesaid that all the offenses which are by this act made felony and shall be committed within any part of his Majesty's dominions, shall and may be heard, tried, and determined before any court of law within the respective kingdom, territory, colony, or plantation where the offense shall be committed, in such and the same manner as all other felonies can or may be heard, tried, and determined in such court.

CHAPTER 61

And be it further enacted by the authority aforesaid that all the present governors or commanders in chief of any British colony or plantation shall, before the said first day of November, one thousand seven hundred and sixty-five, and all who hereafter shall be made governors or commanders in chief of the said colonies or plantations, or any of them, before their entrance into their government shall take a solemn oath to do their utmost that all and every the clauses contained in this present act be punctually and bona fide observed, according to the true intent and meaning thereof, so far as appertains unto the said governors or commanders in chief, respectively, under the like penalties, forfeitures, and disabilities, either for neglecting to take the said oath, or for wittingly neglecting to do their duty accordingly, as are mentioned and expressed in an act made in the seventh and eighth year of the reign of King William the Third, entitled, *An act for preventing frauds and regulating abuses in the plantation trade;* and the said oath hereby required to be taken shall be administered by such person or persons as hath or have been, or shall be appointed to administer the oath required to be taken by the said act made in the seventh and eighth year of the reign of King William the Third.

CHAPTER 62

And be it further enacted by the authority aforesaid that all records, writs, pleadings, and other proceedings in all courts whatsoever, and all deeds, instruments, and writings whatsoever, hereby charged, shall be engrossed and written in such manner as they have been usually accustomed to be engrossed and written, or are now engrossed and written within the said colonies and plantations.

CHAPTER 63

And it is hereby further enacted that if any person or persons shall be sued or prosecuted, either in Great Britain or America, for anything done in pursurance of this act, such person and persons shall and may plead the general issue, and give this act and the special matter in evidence; and if it shall appear so to have been done, the jury shall find for the defendant or defendants: and if the plaintiff or plaintiffs shall become nonsuited, or discontinue his or their action after the defendant or defendants shall have appeared, or if judgment shall be given upon any verdict or demurrer against the plaintiff or plaintiffs, the defendant or defendants shall recover treble costs and have the like remedy for the same, as defendants have in other cases by law.

CONFLICT AND REVOLUTION

TOWNSHEND ACTS

Parliament wasted little time in attempting to reassert its authority over the colonies. Between June 15 and July 2, 1767, it enacted four measures to raise revenue to pay the salaries of British governors and other officials in the colonies so that these officials would be independent of the colonial legislatures, which had been paying their salaries. The statutes came to be known as the Townshend Acts after Charles Townshend, the chancellor of the exchequer, who sponsored them.

The Townshend Acts accomplished four things. One act suspended the New York legislature until it complied with the Quartering Act of 1765, which required legislatures to house and provide supplies to British troops stationed in the colonies. Another act imposed import duties on tea, lead, paper, paint, and glass, while a third act allowed tea to be imported to the colonies free of the taxes that were levied in Great Britain. The fourth act restructured the customs service in the colonies, placing its headquarters in Boston.

As with the STAMP ACT, the colonies met the new legislation with widespread opposition. The colonists saw the acts as a threat to their rights to govern themselves and levy taxes through colonial legislatures. Angry colonists threatened customs collectors and evaded the duties, while colonial merchants refused to import British goods. The situation in Boston escalated, culminating in the BOSTON MASSACRE on March 5, 1770, in which five men were killed.

On the same day as the massacre, Parliament repealed all the import duties except that on tea, lifted the requirements of the Quartering Act,

and ordered the removal of troops from Boston. Nevertheless, the Townshend Acts had had devastating effects on relations between the British government and the colonies. Colonists continued to argue that taxation without representation was not legitimate and began to discuss the necessity of political independence.

—⚬—

Townshend Acts

An Act for Restraining and Prohibiting the Governor, Council, and House of Representatives of the Province of New York, until Provision Shall Have Been Made for Furnishing the King's Troops with All the Necessaries Required by Law, from Passing or Assenting to Any Act of Assembly, Vote, or Resolution for Any Other Purpose

[CHAPTER 1]

Whereas an act of Parliament was made in the fifth year of his present Majesty's reign, entitled, *An act to amend and render more effectual, in his Majesty's dominions in America, an act passed in this present session of Parliament, entitled, An act for punishing mutiny and desertion and for the better payment of the army and their quarters;* wherein several directions were given, and rules and regulations established and appointed for the supplying his Majesty's troops

---

Source: Danby Pickering, ed., *The Statutes at Large from Magna Carta to the End of the Eleventh Parliament of Great Britain, Anno 1761: Continued*, vol. 27 (1768), pp. 505–512.

in the British dominions in America with such necessaries as are in the said act mentioned during the continuance thereof, from the twenty-fourth day of March, one thousand seven hundred and sixty-five, until the twenty-fourth day of March, one thousand seven hundred and sixty-seven; and whereas the House of Representatives of his Majesty's province of New York in America have, in direct disobedience of the authority of the British legislature, refused to make provision for supplying the necessaries and in the manner required by the said act; and an act of assembly hath been passed within the said province for furnishing the barracks in the cities of New York and Albany with firewood and candles, and the other necessaries therein mentioned, for his Majesty's forces inconsistent with the provisions and in opposition to the directions of the said act of Parliament; and whereas by an act made in the last session, entitled, *An act to amend and render more effectual, in his Majesty's dominions in America, an act passed in this present session of Parliament entitled, An act for punishing mutiny and desertion, and for the better payment of the army and their quarters, the like directions, rules, and regulations were given and established for supplying with necessaries his Majesty's troops within the said dominions during the continuance of such act, from the twenty-fourth day of* March, *one thousand seven hundred and sixty-six, until the twenty-fourth day of* March, *one thousand seven hundred and sixty-eight;* which act was, by an act made in this present session of Parliament, entitled, *An act for further continuing an act of the last session of Parliament entitled, An act to amend and render more effectual, in his Majesty's dominions in America, an act passed in this present session of Parliament entitled, An act for punishing mutiny and desertion, and for the better payment of the army and their quarters, further continued until the twenty-fourth day of* March, *one thousand seven hundred and sixty-nine.* In order therefore to enforce within the said province of New York the supplying of his Majesty's troops with the necessaries and in the manner required by the said acts of Parliament, may it please your Majesty that it may be enacted; and be it enacted by the King's most excellent Majesty, by and with the advice and consent of the Lords Spiritual and Temporal and Commons, in this present Parliament assembled, and by the authority of the same that from and after the first day of October, one thousand

seven hundred and sixty-seven, until provision shall have been made by the said assembly of New York for furnishing his Majesty's troops within the said province with all such necessaries as are required by the said acts of Parliament, or any of them, to be furnished for such troops, it shall not be lawful for the governor, lieutenant governor, or person presiding or acting as governor or commander in chief, or for the council for the time being, within the colony, plantation, or province of New York in America, to pass, or give his or their assent to, or concurrence in, the making or passing of any act of assembly; or his or their assent to any order, resolution, or vote in concurrence with the House of Representatives for the time being within the said colony, plantation, or province; or for the said House of Representatives to pass or make any bill, order, resolution, or vote (orders, resolutions, or votes for adjourning such house only, excepted) of any kind, for any other purpose whatsoever; and that all acts of assembly, orders, resolutions, and votes whatsoever, which shall or may be passed, assented to, or made contrary to the tenor and meaning of this act after the said first day of October, one thousand seven hundred and sixty-seven, within the said colony, plantation, or province before and until provision shall have been made for supplying his Majesty's troops with necessaries as aforesaid, shall be and are hereby declared to be null and void, and of no force or effect whatsoever.

CHAPTER 2

Provided nevertheless, and it is hereby declared to be the true intent and meaning of this act that nothing herein before contained shall extend, or be construed to extend, to hinder, prevent, or invalidate the choice, election, or approbation of a speaker of the House of Representatives for the time being within the said colony, plantation, or province.

An Act for Granting Certain Duties in the British Colonies and Plantations in America; for Allowing a Drawback of the Duties of Customs upon the Exportation from This Kingdom of Coffee and Cocoa Nuts of the Produce of the Said Colonies or Plantations; for Discontinuing the Drawbacks Payable on China Earthenware Exported to America; and for More Effectually Preventing the Clandestine Running of Goods in the Said Colonies and Plantations

[CHAPTER 1]

Whereas it is expedient that a revenue should be raised in your Majesty's dominions in America for making a more certain and adequate provision for defraying the charge of the administration of justice and the support of civil government in such provinces where it shall be found necessary; and towards further defraying the expenses of defending, protecting, and securing the said dominions; we, your Majesty's most dutiful and loyal subjects, the Commons of Great Britain in Parliament assembled have therefore resolved to give and grant unto your Majesty the several rates and duties hereinafter mentioned; and do most humbly beseech your Majesty that it may be enacted, and be it enacted by the king's most excellent Majesty, by and with the advice and consent of the Lords Spiritual and Temporal and Commons in this present Parliament assembled, and by the authority of the same that from and after the twentieth day of November, one thousand seven hundred and sixty-seven, there shall be raised, levied, collected, and paid unto his Majesty, his heirs, and successors for and upon the respective goods herein after mentioned which shall be imported from Great Britain into any colony or plantation in America which now is, or hereafter may be, under the dominion of his Majesty, his heirs, or successors, the several rates and duties following; that is to say,

For every hundredweight avoirdupois of crown, plate, flint, and white glass, four shillings and eight pence.

For every hundredweight avoirdupois of green glass, one shilling and two pence.

For every hundredweight avoirdupois of red lead, two shillings.

For every hundredweight avoirdupois of white lead, two shillings.

For every hundredweight avoirdupois of painters colors, two shillings.

For every poundweight avoirdupois of tea, three pence.

For every ream of paper usually called or known by the name of Atlas Fine, twelve shillings.

For every ream of paper called Atlas Ordinary, six shillings.

For every ream of paper called Bastard, or Double Copy, one shilling and six pence.

For every single ream of blue paper for sugar bakers, ten pence half-penny.

For every ream of paper called Blue Royal, one shilling and six pence.

For every bundle of brown paper containing forty quires, not made in Great Britain, six pence.

CHAPTER 2

And it is hereby further enacted by the authority aforesaid that all other paper (not being particularly rated and charged in this act) shall pay the several and respective duties that are charged by this act upon such paper as is nearest above in size and goodness to such unrated paper.

CHAPTER 3

And be it declared and enacted by the authority aforesaid that a ream of paper chargeable by this act shall be understood to consist of twenty quires, and each quire of twenty such sheets.

CHAPTER 4

And it is hereby further enacted by the authority aforesaid that the said rates and duties charged by this act upon goods imported into any British American colony or plantation shall be deemed and are hereby declared to be sterling money of Great Britain; and shall be collected, recovered, and paid to the amount of the value which such nominal sums bear in Great Britain; and that such monies may be received and taken according to the proportion and value of five shillings and six pence the ounce in silver; and shall be raised, levied, collected, paid, and recovered in the same manner and form and by such rules, ways, and means and under such penalties and forfeitures as any other duties now payable to his Majesty upon goods imported into the said colonies or plantations, may be raised, levied, collected, paid, and recovered by any act or acts of Parliament now in force, as fully and effectually to all intents and purposes, as if the several clauses, powers, directions, penalties, and forfeitures relating thereto were particularly repeated and again enacted in the body of this present act: and that all the monies that shall arise by the said duties (except the necessary charges of raising, collecting, levying, recovering, answering, paying, and accounting for the same) shall be applied in the first place, in such manner as is hereinafter mentioned, in making a

CONFLICT AND
REVOLUTION

TOWNSHEND
ACTS

more certain and adequate provision for the charge of the administration of justice and the support of civil government in such of the said colonies and plantations where it shall be found necessary; and that the residue of such duties shall be paid into the receipt of his Majesty's exchequer, and shall be entered separate and apart from all other monies paid or payable to his Majesty, his heirs, or successors; and shall be there reserved, to be from time to time disposed of by Parliament towards defraying the necessary expenses of defending, protecting, and securing the British colonies and plantations in America.

CHAPTER 5

And be it further enacted by the authority aforesaid that his Majesty and his successors shall be, and are hereby empowered from time to time, by any warrant or warrants under his or their royal sign manual or sign manuals, countersigned by the high treasurer, or any three or more of the commissioners of the treasury for the time being, to cause such monies to be applied out of the produce of the duties granted by this act as his Majesty or his successors shall think proper or necessary for defraying the charges of the administration of justice and the support of the civil government within all or any of the said colonies or plantations.

CHAPTER 6

And whereas the allowing a drawback of all the duties of customs upon the exportation from this kingdom of coffee and cocoa nuts, the growth of the British dominions in America may be a means of encouraging the growth of coffee and cocoa in the said dominions, be it therefore enacted by the authority aforesaid that from and after the said twentieth day of November, one thousand seven hundred and sixty-seven, upon the exportation of any coffee or cocoa nuts, of the growth or produce of any British colony or plantation in America, from this kingdom as merchandise, the whole duties of customs payable upon the importation of such coffee or cocoa nuts shall be drawn back and repaid in such manner, and under such rules, regulations, penalties, and forfeitures as any drawback or allowance, payable out of the duties of customs upon the exportation of such coffee or cocoa nuts, was, could, or might be paid before the passing of this act; any law, custom, or usage to the contrary notwithstanding.

CHAPTER 7

And it is hereby further enacted by the authority aforesaid that no drawback shall be allowed for any china earthenware sold after the passing of this act as the sale of the united company of merchants of England trading to the East Indies, which shall be entered for exportation from Great Britain to any part of America; any law, custom, or usage to the contrary notwithstanding.

CHAPTER 8

And it is hereby further enacted by the authority aforesaid that if any china earthenware sold after the passing of this act at the sale of the said united company shall be entered for exportation to any part of America as china earthen ware that had been sold at the sale of the said company before that time, or, if any china earthenware shall be entered for exportation to any parts beyond the seas other than to some part of America in order to obtain any drawback thereon, and the said china earthenware shall nevertheless be carried to any part of America and landed there, contrary to the true intent and meaning of this act; that then, in each and every such case the drawback shall be forfeited; and the merchant or other person making such entry and the master or person taking the charge of the ship or vessel on board which the said goods shall be loaden for exportation shall forfeit double the amount of the drawback paid, or to be paid for the same, and also treble the value of the said goods; one moiety to and for the use of his Majesty, his heirs, and successors; and the other moiety to such officer of the customs as shall sue for the same; to be prosecuted, sued for, and recovered in such manner and form, and by the same rules and regulations, as other penalties inflicted for offenses against the laws relating to the customs may be prosecuted, sued for, and recovered by any act or acts of Parliament now in force.

CHAPTER 9

And for the more effectual preventing the clandestine running of goods in the British dominions in America, be it further enacted by the authority aforesaid that from and after the said twentieth day of November, one thousand seven hundred and sixty-seven, the master or other person having or taking the charge or command of every ship or vessel arriving in any British colony or plantation in America shall, before he proceeds with his vessel to the place of unlading, come directly to the customhouse for the port of district where he arrives and make a just and true entry, upon oath, before the collector and comptroller, or other principal officer of the customs there, of the burthen [burden], contents, and lading of such ship or vessel with the particular marks, numbers, qualities, and contents of every parcel of goods therein laden, to the best of his knowledge; also where and in what port she took in her lading; of what country built; how manned; who was master during the voyage, and who are owners thereof; and whether any and what goods during the course of such voyage had or had not been discharged out of such ship or vessel, and where: and the master or other person having or taking the charge or command of every ship or vessel going out from any British colony or plantation in America, before he shall take in or suffer to be taken into or laden on board any such ship or vessel any goods, wares, or merchandises to be exported shall in like manner enter and report outwards such ship or vessel, with her names and burden, of what country built, and how manned, with the names of the master and owners thereof, and to what port or place he intends to pass or sail. And before he shall depart with such ship or vessel out of any such colony or plantation, he shall also bring and deliver unto the collector and comptroller, or other principal officer of the customs at the port or place where he shall lade, a content in writing under his hand of the name of every merchant, or other person, who shall have laden or put on board any such ship or vessel any goods or merchandise, together with the marks and numbers of such goods or merchandise; and such master or person having or taking the charge or command of every such ship or vessel, either coming into or going out of any British colony or plantation as aforesaid, whether such ship or vessel shall be laden or in ballast, or otherwise, shall likewise publicly in the open customhouse, to the best of his knowledge, answer upon oath to such questions as shall be demanded of him by the collector and comptroller, or other principal officer of the customs for such port or place, concerning such ship or vessel and the destination of her voyage, or concerning any goods or merchandise that shall or may be laden on board her, upon forfeiture of one hundred pounds sterling money of Great Britain for each and every default or neglect; to be sued for, prosecuted, recovered, and

divided in the same manner and form by the same rules and regulation in all respects as other pecuniary penalties for offenses against the laws relating to the customs or trade of his Majesty's colonies in America, may, by any act or acts of Parliament now in force, be prosecuted, sued for, recovered, and divided.

CHAPTER 10

And whereas by an act of Parliament made in the fourteenth year of the reign of King Charles the Second, entitled *An act for preventing frauds and regulating abuses in his Majesty's customs* and several other acts now in force, it is lawful for any officer of his Majesty's customs, authorized by writ of assistance under the seal of his Majesty's Court of Exchequer, to take a constable, headborough, or other public officer inhabiting near unto the place and in the daytime to enter and go into any house, shop, cellar, warehouse, or room or other place and, in case of resistance, to break open doors, chests, trunks, and other package there to seize, and from thence to bring, any kind of goods or merchandise whatsoever prohibited or uncustomed and to put and secure the same in his Majesty's storehouse next to the place where such seizure shall be made. And whereas by an act made in the seventh and eighth years of the reign of King William the Third, entitled, *An act for preventing frauds, and regulating abuses in the plantation trade,* it is, amongst other things, enacted that the officers for collecting and managing his Majesty's revenue and inspecting the plantation trade in America shall have the same powers and authorities to enter houses or warehouses to search and seize goods prohibited to be imported or exported into or out of any of the said plantations, or for which any duties are payable, or ought to have been paid; and that the like assistance shall be given to the said officers in the execution of their office, as, by the said recited act of the fourteenth year of King Charles the Second, is provided for the officers in England. But no authority being expressly given by the said act made in the seventh and eighth years of the reign of King William the Third to any particular court to grant such writs of assistance for the officers of the customs in the said plantations, it is doubted whether such officers can legally enter houses and other places on land to search for and seize goods in the manner directed by the said recited acts. To obviate such doubts for the future, and in order to carry the intention of the said recited acts into effectual execution, be it enacted, and it is hereby enacted by the authority aforesaid, that from and after the said twentieth day of November, one thousand seven hundred and sixty-seven, such writs of assistance to authorize and empower the officers of his Majesty's customs to enter and go into any house, warehouse, shop, cellar, or other place in the British colonies or plantations in America to search for and seize prohibited or uncustomed goods in the manner directed by the said recited acts shall and may be granted by the said superior or supreme court of justice having jurisdiction within such colony or plantation, respectively.

CHAPTER 11

And be it further enacted by the authority aforesaid that if any action or suit shall be commenced, either in Great Britain or America, against any person or persons for anything done in pursuance of this act, the defendant or defendants in such action or suit may plead the general issue and give this act and the special matter in evidence at any trial to be had thereupon; and that the same was done in pursuance and by the authority of this act. And if it shall appear so to have been done, the jury shall find for the defendant or defendants. And if the plaintiff shall be nonsuited, or discontinue his action after the defendant or defendants shall have appeared, or if judgment shall be given upon any verdict or demurrer against the plaintiff, the defendant or defendants shall recover treble costs and have the like remedy for the same as defendants have in other cases by law.

An Act to Enable His Majesty to Put the Customs, and Other Duties, in the British Dominions in America, and the Execution of the Laws Relating to Trade There, under the Management of Commissioners to be Appointed for that Purpose, and to be Resident in the Said Dominions

[CHAPTER 1]

Whereas in pursuance of an act of Parliament made in the twenty-fifth year of the reign of King Charles the Second, entitled, *An act for the encouragement of the Greenland and Eastland trades, and for the better securing the plantation trade,* the rates and duties imposed by that, and several subsequent acts of Parliament upon various goods imported into, or exported from the British colonies and plantations in America, have been put under the management of the commissioners of the customs in England for the time being, by and under the authority and directions of the high treasurer, or commissioners of the treasury for the time being; and whereas the officers appointed for the collection of the said rates and duties in America are obliged to apply to the said commissioners of the customs in England for their special instructions and directions, upon every particular doubt and difficulty which arises in relation to the payment of the said rates and duties, whereby all persons concerned in the commerce and trade of the said colonies and plantations are greatly obstructed and delayed in the carrying on and transacting of their business; and whereas the appointing of commissioners to be resident in some convenient part of his Majesty's dominions in America, and to be invested with such powers as are now exercised by the commissioners of the customs in England by virtue of the laws in being, would relieve the said merchants and traders from the said inconveniences, tend to the encouragement of commerce and to the better securing of the said rates and duties, by the more speedy and effectual collection thereof; be it therefore enacted by the King's most excellent Majesty, by and with the advice and consent of the Lords Spiritual and Temporal and Commons in this present Parliament assembled and by the authority of the same, that the customs and other duties imposed by any act or acts of Parliament upon any goods or merchandises brought or imported into, or exported or carried from any British colony or plantation in America, may from time to time be put under the management and direction of such commissioners to reside in the said plantations, as his Majesty, his heirs, and successors, by his or their commission or commissions under the great seal of Great Britain, shall judge to be most for the advantage of trade and security of the revenue of the said British colonies; any law, custom, or usage to the contrary notwithstanding.

CHAPTER 2

And it is hereby further enacted by the authority aforesaid that the said commissioners to be appointed, or any three or more of them, shall have the same powers and authorities for carrying into execution the several laws relating to the revenues and trade of the said British colonies in America, as were, before the passing of this act, exercised by the commissioners of the customs in England, by virtue of any act or acts of Parliament now in force, and it shall and may be lawful to and for his Majesty, his heirs, and successors, in such commission or commissions, to make provision for putting in execution the several laws relating to the customs and trade of the said British colonies; any law, custom, or usage to the contrary notwithstanding.

CHAPTER 3

Provided always, and it is hereby further enacted by the authority aforesaid, that all deputations and other authorities granted by the commissioners of the customs in England before the passing of this act, or which may be granted by them before any commission or commissions shall issue in pursuance of this act, to any officer or officers acting in the said colonies or plantations shall continue in force as fully, to all intents and purposes, as if this act had not been made, until the deputation, or other authorities so granted to such officer or officers, respectively, shall be revoked, annulled, or made void by the high treasurer of Great Britain, or commissioners of the treasury for the time being.

An Act for Taking Off the Inland Duty of One Shilling per Pound Weight upon All Black and Singlo Teas Consumed in Great Britain; and for Granting a Drawback upon the Exportation of Teas to Ireland and the British Dominions in America, for a Limited Time, upon Such Indemnification to Be Made in Respect Thereof by the East India Company, as Is Therein Mentioned; for Permitting the Exportation of Teas in Smaller Quantities Than One Lot to Ireland, or the Said Dominions in America; and for Preventing Teas Seized and Condemned from Being Consumed in Great Britain

[CHAPTER 1]

Whereas by an act of Parliament made in the eighteenth year of the reign of his late Majesty King George the Second, entitled, *An act for repealing the present inland duty of four shillings per poundweight upon all tea sold in Great Britain, and for granting to his Majesty certain other inland duties in lieu thereof; and for better securing the duty upon tea and other duties of excise; and for pursuing offenders out of one county into another;* an inland duty of one shilling per poundweight avoirdupois, and in that proportion for a greater or lesser quantity, was imposed and charged upon all tea to be sold in

Great Britain; and also a further duty of twenty-five pounds for every one hundred pounds of the gross price at which such teas should be sold at the public sales of the united company of merchants of England trading to the East Indies, and proportionably for a greater or lesser sum; which duties were to commence from the twenty-fourth day of June, one thousand seven hundred and forty-five, over and above all customs, subsidies, and duties, payable to his Majesty for the same, upon importation thereof, to be paid in manner as in the said act is directed; and whereas by an act of Parliament made in the twenty-first year of his said late Majesty's reign, tea was allowed to be exported from this kingdom to Ireland and his Majesty's plantations in America without payment of the said inland duties; and whereas the taking off the said inland duty of one shilling per poundweight upon black and singlo teas, granted by the said act, and the allowing, upon the exportation of all teas which shall be exported to Ireland and his Majesty's plantations in America, the whole of the duty paid upon the importation thereof into this kingdom, appear to be the most probable and expedient means of extending the consumption of teas legally imported within this kingdom, and of increasing the exportation of teas to Ireland and to his Majesty's plantations in America, which are now chiefly furnished by foreigners in a course of illicit trade; and whereas the united company of merchants of England trading to the East Indies are willing and desirous to indemnify the public, in such manner as is hereinafter provided, with respect to any diminution of the revenue which shall or may happen from this experiment. We, your Majesty's most dutiful and loyal subjects, the Commons of Great Britain in Parliament assembled, do therefore most humbly beseech your Majesty, that it may be enacted; and be it enacted by the King's most excellent Majesty, by and with the advice and consent of the Lords Spiritual and Temporal and Commons in this present Parliament assembled and by the authority of the same, that for and during the space of five years, to be computed from the fifth day of July, one thousand seven hundred and sixty-seven, the said inland duty of one shilling per poundweight upon teas shall not be paid for or in respect of any bohea, congo, souchong, or pekoe teas, commonly called black teas, or any teas known by the denomination of singlo teas, which shall be cleared for consumption within

Great Britain, out of the warehouses of the united company of merchants of England trading to the East Indies, or their successors; but that all such teas so to be cleared, whether the same have been already, or shall be hereafter, sold by the said company, or their successors, shall be and are hereby freed and discharged during the said term from the said inland duty.

CHAPTER 2

And it is hereby further enacted by the authority aforesaid, that for and during the like space of five years, to be computed from the fifth day of July, one thousand seven hundred and sixty-seven, there shall be drawn back and allowed for all teas exported from this kingdom as merchandise to Ireland, or any of the British colonies or plantations in America, the whole duties of customs payable upon the importation of such teas; which drawback or allowance, with respect to such teas as shall be exported to Ireland, shall be made to the exporter in such manner, and under such rules, regulations, securities, penalties, and forfeitures, as any drawback or allowance is now payable out of the duty of customs upon the exportation of foreign goods to Ireland; and with respect to such teas as shall be exported to the British colonies and plantations in America, the said drawback or allowance shall be made in such manner, and under such rules, regulations, penalties, and forfeitures, as any drawback or allowance payable out of the duty of customs upon foreign goods exported to foreign parts was, could, or might be made before the passing of this act (except in such cases as are otherwise provided for by this act).

CHAPTER 3

Provided always, and it is hereby enacted by the authority aforesaid, that the drawback allowed by this act shall not be paid or allowed for any teas which shall not be exported directly from the warehouse or warehouses wherein the same shall be lodged, pursuant to the directions of an act made in the tenth year of the reign of his late Majesty King George the First.

CHAPTER 4

And, for making good any diminution which may happen in the revenues of customs and excise by the discontinuance of the said duty and the allowance of the said drawback during the term aforesaid, be it enacted by the authority aforesaid, that on or before the first day of

September, one thousand seven hundred and sixty-eight, and on or before the first day of September in each of the four succeeding years, a true and exact account shall be taken, slated, and made up by the proper officers of the customs and excise, respectively, of the net produce of all the duties of customs for and in respect of teas sold by the said company, or their successors, and also of the net produce of the duties of excise upon teas cleared out of the warehouses belonging to the said company, or their successors, within the year, ending the fifth day of July immediately preceding the taking, stating, and making up, such account; and that a sum, which shall be equal to the annual net produce of the duties of customs paid upon the importation of teas which were exported to Ireland and the British colonies and plantations in America, upon an average for five years preceding the fifth day of July, one thousand seven hundred and sixty-seven, shall be deducted from the total of the net produce, so stated, of the said duties of customs and excise in the said account, for the year ending the said fifth day of July, one thousand seven hundred and sixty-eight, and for each of the said four succeeding years, respectively; and if, after such deduction shall have been made, the remaining sum shall not amount to such a sum as shall be equal to the annual net produce of all the duties of customs for and in respect of teas sold by the said company; and also to the annual net produce of the duties of excise upon teas cleared out of the warehouses of the said company on an average for five years preceding the said fifth day of July, one thousand seven hundred and sixty-seven; then, and in every such case, from time to time, as often as such case shall so happen, the said company, or their successors, within forty days after a copy of such yearly account respectively shall have been delivered to their chairman, deputy chairman, secretary, cashier, or accomptant [accountant] general shall advance and pay, for every such year, respectively, into the receipt of his Majesty's exchequer, for his Majesty's use, such sum of money as shall, with the monies remaining in such respective annual account after the deduction aforesaid shall have been made, amount to such a sum as shall be equal to the annual net produce of all the said duties of customs and excise upon teas, on the said average of five years preceding the said fifth day of July, one thousand seven hundred and sixty-seven; so as the money to be paid by the said company, or their successors, in pursuance of this act, shall not, in any one of the said five years, exceed such a sum as shall be equal to the annual net amount of the said inland duty of one shilling per pound weight upon teas cleared from the warehouses of the said company for consumption within Great Britain; and also to the annual net amount of the duties of customs paid on the importation of teas which were exported to Ireland and the British colonies and plantations in America upon an average for five years preceding the said fifth day of July, one thousand seven hundred and sixty-seven.

CHAPTER 5

And be it further enacted by the authority aforesaid, that in case the said united company of merchants of England trading to the East Indies, or their successors, shall make failure in any of the payments hereby directed, required, or appointed to be made into the receipt of his Majesty's exchequer, in the manner, or on or before the respective times herein before limited or appointed for that purpose; that then, from time to time, as often as such case shall so happen, the money, whereof such failure in payment shall be made, shall and may be recovered to his Majesty's use, by action of debt, or upon the case, bill, suit, or information, in any of his Majesty's courts of record at Westminster; wherein no essoin, protection, privilege, or wager of law shall be allowed, or any more than one imparlance; in which action, bill, suit, or information, it shall be lawful to declare that the said united company of merchants of England trading to the East Indies, or their successors, are indebted to his Majesty the monies of which they shall have made default in payment, according to the form of this statute, and have not paid the same, which shall be sufficient; and in or upon such action, bill, suit, or information, there shall be further recovered to his Majesty's use, against the said united company of merchants of England trading to the East Indies, or their successors, damages, after the rate of twelve pounds per centum per annum, for the respective monies so unpaid, contrary to this act, together with full costs of suit; and the said united company, and their successors, and all their stock, funds, and all other their estate and property whatsoever and wheresoever shall be and are hereby made subject and liable to the payment of such monies, damages, and costs.

CHAPTER 6

And be it further enacted by the authority aforesaid, that all the monies which shall be paid into the receipt of his Majesty's exchequer in pursuance of this act shall be applied to such uses and purposes, and in such proportions, as the present duties on teas are now made applicable.

CHAPTER 7

And whereas by an act made in the twenty-first year of the reign of his late Majesty, entitled, *An act for permitting tea to be exported to Ireland, and his Majesty's plantations in America, without paying the inland duties charged thereupon by an act of the eighteenth year of his present Majesty's reign; and for enlarging the time for some of the payments to be made on the subscription of six millions three hundred thousand pounds, by virtue of an act of this session of Parliament,* it is enacted, that from and after the first day of June, one thousand seven hundred and forty-eight, no tea should be exported to the kingdom of Ireland, or to any of his Majesty's plantations in America, in any chest, cask, tub, or package whatsoever, other than that in which it was originally imported into Great Britain, nor in any less quantities than in the entire lot or lots in which the same was sold at the sale of the said united company, under the penalty of the forfeiture of such tea and the package containing the same; and whereas the prohibiting the exportation of tea in any less quantity than one entire lot has been very inconvenient to merchants and traders and tends to discourage the exportation of tea to Ireland, and the said colonies; be it therefore enacted by the authority aforesaid, that from and after the fifth day of July, one thousand seven hundred and sixty-seven, the said recited clause shall be, and is hereby, repealed.

CHAPTER 8

And be it further enacted by the authority aforesaid, that from and after the said fifth day of July, one thousand seven hundred and sixty-seven, no tea shall be exported to the kingdom of Ireland, or to any of his Majesty's plantations in America, in any chest, cask, tub, or package whatsoever other than that in which it was originally imported into Great Britain; nor in any less quantity than the whole and entire quantity contained in any chest, cask, tub, or package in which the same was sold at the public sale of the united company of merchants of England trading to the East Indies; under the penalty of the forfeiture of such tea, and the package containing the same, which shall and may be seized by any officer of the customs; and such forfeiture shall be recovered and applied in such and the same manner, as any of the penalties or forfeitures mentioned in the said act, made in the twenty-first year of the reign of his late Majesty, are thereby directed to be recovered and applied; and all tea exported under the authority of this act is hereby freed and discharged from the payment of the inland duties of excise, in such and the same manner, and shall be subject to the same rules and regulations, as are mentioned, appointed, and prescribed by the said act, in relation to tea exported by virtue thereof.

CHAPTER 9

And be it enacted by the authority aforesaid, that from and after the twenty-fourth day of July, one thousand seven hundred and sixty-seven, all teas which shall be seized and condemned for being illegally imported, or for any other cause, shall not be sold for consumption within this kingdom, but shall be exported to Ireland, or to the British colonies in America; and that no such teas, after the sale thereof, shall be delivered out of any warehouse belonging to his Majesty, otherwise than for exportation as aforesaid, or be exported in any package containing a less quantity than fifty pounds weight; which exportation shall be made in like manner, and under the same rules, regulations, penalties, and forfeitures, except in respect to the allowance of any drawback, as are by this act prescribed, appointed, and inflicted in relation to the exportation of teas sold by the said company; and upon the like bond and security as is required by the said act made in the twenty-first year of the reign of his late Majesty King George the Second, to be approved of by the commissioners of the customs or excise in England for the time being, or any three of them, respectively, or by such person or persons as they shall respectively appoint for that purpose.

CHAPTER 10

And be it further enacted by the authority aforesaid, that if any action or suit shall be commenced against any person or persons for anything by him or them done or executed in pursuance of this act, the defendant or defendants in such action or suit shall and may plead the general issue, and give this act, and the special matter, in evidence, at any trial to be had thereupon; and that the same was done in pursuance and by the authority of this act; and if afterwards a verdict shall pass for the defendant or defendants, or the plaintiff or plaintiffs shall become nonsuited, or discontinue his, her, or their action or prosecution, or judgment shall be given against him, her or them, upon demurrer, or otherwise, then such defendant or defendants shall have treble costs awarded to him or them against such plaintiff or plaintiffs.

CONFLICT AND REVOLUTION

DECLARATION OF THE CAUSES AND NECESSITY OF TAKING UP ARMS

A declaration by the representatives of the united colonies of North America, now met in Congress at Philadelphia, setting forth the causes and necessity of their taking up arms

Following the outbreak of hostilities in Concord and Lexington, Massachusetts, in April 1775, the Second Continental Congress met in Philadelphia. The Congress created the Continental Army, appointed GEORGE WASHINGTON commander, and, on July 8, adopted the Declaration of the Causes and Necessity of Taking up Arms.

JOHN DICKINSON, a delegate from Pennsylvania, was the principal author of the declaration. Although the declaration describes the actions by the British government that had angered the colonists and justifies the need to resist the British with arms, it does not proclaim a desire to break with the mother country. Instead the declaration expresses the need to conserve old liberties and the old order "in defence of the freedom that is our birth right and which we ever enjoyed until the late violation of it."

—⚍—

Declaration of the Causes and Necessity of Taking up Arms

If it was possible for men, who exercise their reason to believe, that the divine Author of our existence intended a part of the human race to hold an absolute property in, and an unbounded power over others, marked out by his infinite goodness and wisdom, as the objects of a legal domination never rightfully resistible, however severe and oppressive, the inhabitants of these colonies might at least require from the parliament of Great-Britain some evidence, that this dreadful authority over them, has been granted to that body. But a reverence for our Creator, principles of humanity, and the dictates of common sense, must convince all those who reflect upon the subject, that government was instituted to promote the welfare of mankind, and ought to be administered for the attainment of that end. The legislature of Great-Britain, however, stimulated by an inordinate passion for a power not only unjustifiable, but which they know to be peculiarly reprobated by the very constitution of that kingdom, and desparate of success in any mode of contest, where regard should be had to truth, law, or right, have at length, deserting those, attempted to effect their cruel and impolitic purpose of enslaving these colonies by violence, and have thereby rendered it necessary for us to close with their last appeal from reason to arms. Yet, however blinded that assembly may be, by their intemperate rage for unlimited domination, so to sight justice and the opinion of mankind, we esteem ourselves bound by obligations of respect to the rest of the world, to make known the justice of our cause. Our forefathers, inhabitants of the island of Great-Britain, left their native land, to seek on these shores a residence for civil and religious freedom. At the expense of their blood, at the hazard of their fortunes, without the least charge to the country from which they removed, by unceasing labour, and an unconquerable spirit, they effected settlements in the distant and unhospitable wilds of America, then filled with numerous and warlike barbarians.—Societies or

CONFLICT AND
REVOLUTION

DECLARATION
OF THE CAUSES
AND NECESSITY
OF TAKING UP
ARMS

governments, vested with perfect legislatures, were formed under charters from the crown, and an harmonious intercourse was established between the colonies and the kingdom from which they derived their origin. The mutual benefits of this union became in a short time so extraordinary, as to excite astonishment. It is universally confessed, that the amazing increase of the wealth, strength, and navigation of the realm, arose from this source; and the minister, who so wisely and successfully directed the measures of Great-Britain in the late war, publicly declared, that these colonies enabled her to triumph over her enemies.—Towards the conclusion of that war, it pleased our sovereign to make a change in his counsels.—From that fatal movement, the affairs of the British empire began to fall into confusion, and gradually sliding from the summit of glorious prosperity, to which they had been advanced by the virtues and abilities of one man, are at length distracted by the convulsions, that now shake it to its deepest foundations.—The new ministry finding the brave foes of Britain, though frequently defeated, yet still contending, took up the unfortunate idea of granting them a hasty peace, and then subduing her faithful friends.

These colonies were judged to be in such a state, as to present victories without bloodshed, and all the easy emoluments of statuteable plunder.—The uninterrupted tenor of their peaceable and respectful behaviour from the beginning of colonization, their dutiful, zealous, and useful services during the war, though so recently and amply acknowledged in the most honourable manner by his majesty, by the late king, and by parliament, could not save them from the meditated innovations.—Parliament was influenced to adopt the pernicious project, and assuming a new power over them, have in the course of eleven years, given such decisive specimens of the spirit and consequences attending this power, as to leave no doubt concerning the effects of acquiescence under it. They have undertaken to give and grant our money without our consent, though we have ever exercised an exclusive right to dispose of our own property; statutes have been passed for extending the jurisdiction of courts of admiralty and vice-admiralty beyond their ancient limits; for depriving us of the accustomed and inestimable privilege of trial by jury, in cases affecting both life and property; for suspending the legislature of one of the colonies; for interdicting all commerce to the capital of another; and for altering fundamentally the form of government established by charter, and secured by acts of its own legislature solemnly confirmed by the crown; for exempting the "*murderers*" of colonists from legal trial, and in effect, from punishment; for erecting in a neighbouring province, acquired by the joint arms of Great-Britain and America, a despotism dangerous to our very existence; and for quartering soldiers upon the colonists in time of profound peace. It has also been resolved in parliament, that colonists charged with committing certain offences, shall be transported to England to be tried. But why should we enumerate our injuries in detail? By one statute it is declared, that parliament can "*of right make laws to bind us in all cases whatsoever.*" What is to defend us against so enormous, so unlimited a power? Not a single man of those who assume it, is chosen by us; or is subject to our control or influence; but, on the contrary, they are all of them exempt from the operation of such laws, and an American revenue, if not diverted from the ostensible purposes for which it is raised, would actually lighten their own burdens in proportion, as they increase ours. We saw the misery to which such despotism would reduce us. We for ten years incessantly and ineffectually besieged the throne as supplicants; we reasoned, we remonstrated with parliament, in the most mild and decent language.

Administration sensible that we should regard these oppressive measures as freemen ought to do, sent over fleets and armies to enforce them. The indignation of the Americans was roused, it is true; but it was the indignation of a virtuous, loyal, and affectionate people. A Congress of delegates from the United Colonies was assembled at Philadelphia, on the fifth day of last September. We resolved again to offer an humble and dutiful petition to the King, and also addressed our fellow-subjects of Great-Britain. We have pursued every temperate, every respectful measure; we have even proceeded to break off our commercial intercourse with our fellow-subjects, as the last peaceable admonition, that our attachment to no nation upon earth should supplant our attachment to liberty.—This, we flattered ourselves, was the ultimate step of the controversy: but subsequent events have shewn, how vain was this hope of finding moderation in our enemies.

Several threatening expressions against the colonies were inserted in his majesty's speech; our petition, tho' we were told it was a decent one, and that his majesty had been pleased to receive it graciously, and to promise laying it before his parliament, was huddled into both houses among a bundle of American papers, and there neglected. The lords and commons in their address, in the month of February, said, that *"a rebellion at that time actually existed within the province of Massachusetts-Bay; and that those concerned with it, had been countenanced and encouraged by unlawful combinations and engagements, entered into by his majesty's subjects in several of the other colonies; and therefore they besought his majesty, that he would take the most effectual measures to inforce due obediance to the laws and authority of the supreme legislature."*— Soon after, the commercial intercourse of whole colonies, with foreign countries, and with each other, was cut off by an act of parliament; by another several of them were intirely prohibited from the fisheries in the seas near their coasts, on which they always depended for their sustenance; and large reinforcements of ships and troops were immediately sent over to general Gage.

Fruitless were all the entreaties, arguments, and eloquence of an illustrious band of the most distinguished peers, and commoners, who nobly and strenuously asserted the justice of our cause, to stay, or even to mitigate the heedless fury with which these accumulated and unexampled outrages were hurried on.—equally fruitless was the interference of the city of London, of Bristol, and many other respectable towns in our favor. Parliament adopted an insidious manoeuvre calculated to divide us, to establish a perpetual auction of taxations where colony should bid against colony, all of them uninformed what ransom would redeem their lives; and thus to extort from us, at the point of the bayonet, the unknown sums that should be sufficient to gratify, if possible to gratify, ministerial rapacity, with the miserable indulgence left to us of raising, in our own mode, the prescribed tribute. What terms more rigid and humiliating could have been dictated by remorseless victors to conquered enemies? in our circumstances to accept them, would be to deserve them.

Soon after the intelligence of these proceedings arrived on this continent, general Gage, who in the course of the last year had taken possession of the town of Boston, in the province of

Massachusetts-Bay, and still occupied in it a garrison, on the 19th day of April, sent out from that place a large detachment of his army, who made an unprovoked assault on the inhabitants of the said province, at the town of Lexington, as appears by the affidavits of a great number of persons, some of whom were officers and soldiers of that detachment, murdered eight of the inhabitants, and wounded many others. From thence the troops proceeded in warlike array to the town of Concord, where they set upon another party of the inhabitants of the same province, killing several and wounding more, until compelled to retreat by the country people suddenly assembled to repel this cruel aggression. Hostilities, thus commenced by the British troops, have been since prosecuted by them without regard to faith or reputation.—The inhabitants of Boston being confined within that town by the general their governor, and having, in order to procure their dismission, entered into a treaty with him, it was stipulated that the said inhabitants having deposited their arms with their own magistrate, should have liberty to depart, taking with them their other effects. They accordingly delivered up their arms, but in open violation of honour, in defiance of the obligation of treaties, which even savage nations esteemed sacred, the governor ordered the arms deposited as aforesaid, that they might be preserved for their owners, to be seized by a body of soldiers; detained the greatest part of the inhabitants in the town, and compelled the few who were permitted to retire, to leave their most valuable effects behind.

By this perfidy wives are separated from their husbands, children from their parents, the aged and the sick from their relations and friends, who wish to attend and comfort them; and those who have been used to live in plenty and even elegance, are reduced to deplorable distress.

The general, further emulating his ministerial masters, by a proclamation bearing date on the 12th day of June, after venting the grossest falsehoods and calumnies against the good people of these colonies, proceeds to *"declare them all, either by name or description, to be rebels and traitors, to supercede the course of the common law, and instead thereof to publish and order the use and exercise of the law martial."*—His troops have butchered our countrymen, have wantonly burnt Charlestown, besides a considerable num-

CONFLICT AND
REVOLUTION

DECLARATION
OF THE CAUSES
AND NECESSITY
OF TAKING UP
ARMS

CONFLICT AND
REVOLUTION

DECLARATION
OF THE CAUSES
AND NECESSITY
OF TAKING UP
ARMS

ber of houses in other places; our ships and vessels are seized; the necessary supplies of provisions are intercepted, and he is exerting his utmost power to spread destruction and devastation around him.

We have received certain intelligence, that general Carleton, the governor of Canada, is instigating the people of that province and the Indians to fall upon us; and we have but too much reason to apprehend, that schemes have been formed to excite domestic enemies against us. In brief, a part of these colonies now feel, and all of them are sure of feeling, as far as the vengeance of administration can inflict them, the complicated calamities of fire, sword and famine. We are reduced to the alternative of chusing an unconditional submission to the tyranny of irritated ministers, or resistance by force.—The latter is our choice.—We have counted the cost of this contest, and find nothing so dreadful as voluntary slavery.—Honour, justice, and humanity, forbid us tamely to surrender that freedom which we received from our gallant ancestors, and which our innocent posterity have a right to receive from us. We cannot endure the infamy and guilt of resigning succeeding generations to that wretchedness which inevitably awaits them, if we basely entail hereditary bondage upon them.

Our cause is just. Our union is perfect. Our internal resources are great, and, if necessary, foreign assistance is undoubtedly attainable.—We gratefully acknowledge, as signal instances of the Divine favour towards us, that his Providence would not permit us to be called into this severe controversy, until we were grown up to our present strength, had been previously exercised in warlike operation, and possessed of the means of defending ourselves. With hearts fortified with these animating reflections, we most solemnly, before God and the world, declare, that, exerting the utmost energy of those powers, which our

beneficent Creator hath graciously bestowed upon us, the arms we have been compelled by our enemies to assume, we will, in defiance of every hazard, with unabating firmness and perseverance, employ for the preservation of our liberties; being with one mind resolved to die freemen rather than to live slaves.

Lest this declaration should disquiet the minds of our friends and fellow-subjects in any part of the empire, we assure them that we mean not to dissolve that union which has so long and so happily subsisted between us, and which we sincerely wish to see restored.—Necessity has not yet driven us into that desperate measure, or induced us to excite any other nation to war against them.—We have not raised armies with ambitious designs of separating from Great-Britain, and establishing independent states. We fight not for glory or for conquest. We exhibit to mankind the remarkable spectacle of a people attacked by unprovoked enemies, without any imputation or even suspicion of offence. They boast of their privileges and civilization, and yet proffer no milder conditions than servitude or death.

In our own native land, in defence of the freedom that is our birthright, and which we ever enjoyed till the late violation of it—for the protection of our property, acquired solely by the honest industry of our fore-fathers and ourselves, against violence actually offered, we have taken up arms. We shall lay them down when hostilities shall cease on the part of the aggressors, and all danger of their being renewed shall be removed, and not before.

With an humble confidence in the mercies of the supreme and impartial Judge and Ruler of the Universe, we most devoutly implore his divine goodness to protect us happily through this great conflict, to dispose our adversaries to reconciliation on reasonable terms, and thereby to relieve the empire from the calamities of civil war.

CONFLICT AND REVOLUTION

COMMON SENSE

Thomas Paine, 1776

In January 1776 THOMAS PAINE published his fifty-page pamphlet *Common Sense.* It called for political independence and the establishment of a republican government. The pamphlet created a sensation, as much for its passionate rhetoric as for its political views. It sold more than 500,000 copies within a few months and is credited with creating the political momentum that led to the issuance of the DECLARATION OF INDEPENDENCE on July 4, 1776.

In *Common Sense,* Paine turned his vitriol on King George III and the institution of the monarchy, calling the king a "royal brute" and a "crowned ruffian." Insisting that people did not have to live under such a regime, he declared "that in America the law is king."

—⁓—

Common Sense

This is supposing the present race of kings in the world to have had an honorable origin; whereas it is more than probable, that, could we take off the dark covering of antiquity and trace them to their first rise, we should find the first of them nothing better than the principal ruffian of some restless gang; whose savage manners or preeminence in subtility obtained him the title of chief among plunderers: and who by increasing in power and extending his depredations, overawed the quiet and defenceless to purchase their safety by frequent contributions. . . .

* * *

England since the conquest hath known some few good monarchs, but groaned beneath a much larger number of bad ones; yet no man in his senses can say that their claim under William the Conqueror is a very honorable one. A French bastard landing with an armed banditti and establishing himself king of England against the consent of the natives is in plain terms a very paltry rascally original. It certainly hath no divinity in it. However it is needless to spend much time in exposing the folly of herditary rights: if there were any so weak as to believe it, let them promiscuously worship the ass and the lion, and welcome. I shall neither copy their humility, nor disturb their devotion. . . . The plain truth is, that the antiquity of English monarchy will not bear looking into.

* * *

In England a king hath little more to do than to make war and give away places; which, in plain terms, is to empoverish the nation and set it together by the ears. A pretty business indeed for a man to be allowed eight hundred thousand sterling a year for, and worshipped into the bargain! Of more worth is one honest man to society, and in the sight of God, than all the crowned ruffians that ever lived.

* * *

But where, say some, is the king of America? I'll tell you, he reigns above, and doth not make havoc of mankind like the royal brute of Great Britain. Yet that we may not appear to be defec-

Selections from *Common Sense* by Thomas Paine.

tive even in earthly honors, let a day be solemnly set apart for proclaiming the charter; let it be brought forth placed on the divine law, the Word of God; let a crown be placed thereon, by which the world may know, that so far as we approve of monarchy, that in America the law is king. For as in absolute governments the king is law, so in free countries the law ought to be king; and there ought to be no other. But lest any ill use should afterwards arise, let the crown at the conclusion of the ceremony be demolished, and scattered among the people whose right it is.

CONFLICT AND REVOLUTION

VIRGINIA DECLARATION OF RIGHTS

The VIRGINIA DECLARATION OF RIGHTS was adopted by the Virginia colonial constitutional convention on June 12, 1776. Its sixteen sections enumerated specific civil liberties that could not be legitimately taken away by government.

Most of the Declaration of Rights was written by GEORGE MASON, a plantation owner, real estate speculator, and neighbor of GEORGE WASHINGTON. A strong believer in human liberty and limited government, Mason crafted a document that guaranteed the citizens of Virginia, upon achieving independence from Great Britain, all the civil liberties they had lost under British rule.

The Declaration of Rights enumerates specific civil liberties, including freedom of the press, the free exercise of religion, and the injunction that "no man be deprived of his liberty, except by the law of the land or the judgement of his peers." Other provisions prohibited excessive bail or cruel and unusual punishments, required authorities to have evidence and good cause before obtaining a search warrant to enter a place, guaranteed the right to trial by jury, and said that a "well regulated militia" should be "under strict subordination" to the civilian government. Many of these provisions were later incorporated into the Bill of Rights.

―――〰―――

Virginia Declaration of Rights

I

That all men are by nature equally free and independent, and have certain inherent rights, of which, when they enter into a state of society, they cannot, by any compact, deprive or divest their posterity; namely, the enjoyment of life and liberty, with the means of acquiring and possessing property, and pursuing and obtaining happiness and safety.

II

That all power is vested in, and consequently derived from, the people; that magistrates are their trustees and servants, and at all times amenable to them.

III

That government is, or ought to be, instituted for the common benefit, protection, and security of the people, nation, or community; of all the various modes and forms of government that is best, which is capable of producing the greatest degree of happiness and safety and is most effectually secured against the danger of maladministration; and that, whenever any government shall be found inadequate or contrary to these purposes, a majority of the community hath an indubitable, unalienable, and indefeasible right to reform, alter, or abolish it, in such manner as shall be judged most conducive to the public weal.

IV

That no man, or set of men, are entitled to exclusive or separate emoluments or privileges

---

Source: Ben Perley Poore, ed., *The Federal and State Constitutions, Colonial Charters, and Other Organic Laws of the United States,* vol. 2 (1878), pp. 1908–1909.

from the community, but in consideration of public services; which, not being descendible, neither ought the offices of magistrate, legislator, or judge to be hereditary.

V

That the legislative and executive powers of the state should be separate and distinct from the judicative; and, that the members of the two first may be restrained from oppression by feeling and participating the burthens of the people, they should, at fixed periods, be reduced to a private station, return into that body from which they were originally taken, and the vacancies be supplied by frequent, certain, and regular elections in which all, or any part of the former members, to be again eligible, or ineligible, as the laws shall direct.

VI

That elections of members to serve as representatives of the people in assembly ought to be free; and that all men, having sufficient evidence of permanent common interest with, and attachment to, the community have the right of suffrage and cannot be taxed or deprived of their property for public uses without their own consent or that of their representatives so elected, nor bound by any law to which they have not, in like manner, assented, for the public good.

VII

That all power of suspending laws, or the execution of laws, by any authority without consent of the representatives of the people is injurious to their rights and ought not to be exercised.

VIII

That in all capital or criminal prosecutions a man hath a right to demand the cause and nature of his accusation to be confronted with the accusers and witnesses, to call for evidence in his favor, and to a speedy trial by an impartial jury of his vicinage, without whose unanimous consent he cannot be found guilty, nor can he be compelled to give evidence against himself; that no man be deprived of his liberty except by the law of the land or the judgment of his peers.

IX

That excessive bail ought not to be required, nor excessive fines imposed; nor cruel and unusual punishments inflicted.

X

That general warrants, whereby any officer or messenger may be commanded to search suspected places without evidence of a fact committed, or to seize any person or persons not named, or whose offense is not particularly described and supported by evidence, are grievous and oppressive and ought not be granted.

XI

That in controversies respecting property and in suits between man and man, the ancient trial by jury is preferable to any other and ought to be held sacred.

XII

That the freedom of the press is one of the greatest bulwarks of liberty and can never be restrained but by despotic governments.

XIII

That a well regulated militia, composed of the body of the people, trained to arms, is the proper, natural, and safe defense of a free state; that standing armies, in time of peace, should be avoided as dangerous to liberty; and that, in all cases, the military should be under strict subordination to, and governed by, the civil power.

XIV

That the people have a right to uniform government; and therefore, that no government separate from, or independent of, the government of Virginia, ought to be erected or established within the limits thereof.

XV

That no free government, or the blessings of liberty, can be preserved to any people but by a firm adherence to justice, moderation, temperance, frugality, and virtue and by frequent recurrence to fundamental principles.

XVI

That religion, or the duty which we owe to our Creator and the manner of discharging it, can be directed only by reason and conviction, not by force or violence; and therefore, all men are equally entitled to the free exercise of religion, according to the dictates of conscience; and that it is the mutual duty of all to practice Christian forbearance, love, and charity towards each other.

CONFLICT AND REVOLUTION

DECLARATION OF INDEPENDENCE

In Congress, July 4, 1776
The Unanimous Declaration of the thirteen united States of America

The DECLARATION OF INDEPENDENCE, perhaps the most famous document in U.S. history, was adopted by the Second Continental Congress on July 4, 1776. The preparation of the declaration began on June 11, when Congress appointed a committee composed of THOMAS JEFFERSON, JOHN ADAMS, BENJAMIN FRANKLIN, ROBERT R. LIVINGSTON, and ROGER SHERMAN. Jefferson actually wrote the declaration, appropriating some of the language in the VIRGINIA DECLARATION OF RIGHTS. Jefferson's famous phrase concerning "life, liberty, and the pursuit of happiness" is a slight reworking of the wording of the Virginia declaration.

After debate on Jefferson's draft, the Congress made several changes, yet the document remained an expression of the liberal political ideas articulated by JOHN LOCKE and others. The second section, with its reference to "He," is an indictment of the actions of King George III. Like *Common Sense,* this section destroyed the aura surrounding the monarchy and helped move the colonists toward psychological as well as political independence from Great Britain.

For the members of the CONTINENTAL CONGRESS, the declaration served as a vehicle for publicizing their grievances and winning support for the revolutionary cause. It affirmed the natural rights of all people and the right of the colonists to "dissolve the political bands" with the British government. Later generations have laid more stress on the political ideals expressed in the declaration and, in particular,

have found inspiration in the phrase "all men are created equal."

Declaration of Independence

When in the Course of human events, it becomes necessary for one people to dissolve the political bands which have connected them with another, and to assume among the powers of the earth, the separate and equal station to which the Laws of Nature and of Nature's God entitle them, a decent respect to the opinions of mankind requires that they should declare the causes which impel them to the separation.—We hold these truths to be self-evident, that all men are created equal, that they are endowed by their Creator with certain unalienable Rights, that among these are Life, Liberty and the pursuit of Happiness.—That to secure these rights, Governments are instituted among Men, deriving their just powers from the consent of the governed.—That whenever any Form of Government becomes destructive of these ends, it is the Right of the People to alter or to abolish it, and to institute new Government, laying its foundation on such principles and organizing its powers in such form, as to them shall seem most likely to effect their Safety and Happiness. Prudence, indeed, will dictate that Governments long established should not be changed for light and transient causes; and accordingly all experience hath shown, that mankind are more disposed to suffer, while evils

Source: *The United States Government Manual.*

CONFLICT AND
REVOLUTION

DECLARATION
OF
INDEPENDENCE

are sufferable, than to right themselves by abolishing the forms to which they are accustomed. But when a long train of abuses and usurpations, pursuing invariably the same Object evinces a design to reduce them under absolute Despotism, it is their right, it is their duty, to throw off such Government, and to provide new Guards for their future security.—Such has been the patient sufferance of these Colonies; and such is now the necessity which constrains them to alter their former Systems of Government. The history of the present King of Great Britain is a history of repeated injuries and usurpations, all having in direct object the establishment of an absolute Tyranny over these States. To prove this, let Facts be submitted to a candid world.—He has refused his Assent to Laws, the most wholesome and necessary for the public good.—He has forbidden his Governors to pass Laws of immediate and pressing importance, unless suspended in their operation till his Assent should be obtained; and when so suspended, he has utterly neglected to attend to them.—He has refused to pass other Laws for the accommodation of large districts of people, unless those people would relinquish the right of Representation in the Legislature, a right inestimable to them and formidable to tyrants only.—He has called together legislative bodies at places unusual, uncomfortable, and distant from the depository or their public Records, for the sole purpose of fatiguing them into compliance with his measures.—He has dissolved Representative Houses repeatedly, for opposing with manly firmness his invasions on the rights of the people.—He has refused for a long time, after such dissolutions, to cause others to be elected; whereby the Legislative powers, incapable of Annihilation, have returned to the People at large for their exercise; the State remaining in the mean time exposed to all the dangers of invasion from without, and convulsions within.—He has endeavored to prevent the population of these States; for that purpose obstructing the Laws for Naturalization of Foreigners; refusing to pass others to encourage their migration hither, and raising the conditions of new Appropriations of Lands.—He has obstructed the Administration of Justice, by refusing his Assent to Laws for establishing Judiciary powers.—He has made Judges dependent on his Will alone, for the tenure of their offices, and the amount and payment of their salaries.—He has erected a multitude of New Offices, and sent hither swarms of Officers to harrass our people, and eat out their substance.—He has kept among us, in times of peace, Standing Armies, without the Consent of our legislatures.—He has affected to render the Military independent of and superior to the Civil power.—He has combined with others to subject us to a jurisdiction foreign to our constitution, and unacknowledged by our laws; giving his Assent to their Acts of pretended Legislation:—For quartering large bodies of armed troops among us:—For protecting them, by a mock Trial, from punishment for any Murders which they should commit on the Inhabitants of these States:—For cutting off our Trade with all parts of the world:—For imposing Taxes on us without our Consent:—For depriving us in many cases, of the benefits of Trial by Jury:—For transporting us beyond Seas to be tried for pretended offences:—For abolishing the free System of English Laws in a neighbouring Province, establishing therein an Arbitrary government, and enlarging its Boundaries so as to render it at once an example and fit instrument for introducing the same absolute rule into these Colonies:—For taking away our Charters, abolishing our most valuable Laws, and altering fundamentally the Forms of our Governments:—For suspending our own Legislatures, and declaring themselves invested with power to legislate for us in all cases whatsoever.—He has abdicated Government here, by declaring us out of his Protection and waging War against us.—He has plundered our seas, ravaged our Coasts, burnt our towns, and destroyed the lives of our people.—He is at this time transporting large Armies of foreign Mercenaries to compleat the works of death, desolation and tyranny, already begun with circumstances of Cruelty & perfidy scarcely paralleled in the most barbarous ages, and totally unworthy the Head of a civilized nation.—He has constrained our fellow Citizens taken Captive on the high Seas to bear Arms against their Country, to become the executioners of their friends and Brethren, or to fall themselves by their Hands.—He has excited domestic insurrections amongst us, and has endeavored to bring on the inhabitants of our frontiers, the merciless Indian Savages, whose known rule of warfare, is an undistinguished destruction of all ages, sexes and conditions. In every state of these Oppressions We have Petitioned for Redress in the most humble terms. Our repeated Petitions have been answered only by repeated injury. A Prince, whose character is thus marked by every act which may define a

Tyrant, is unfit to be the ruler of a free people. Nor have We been wanting in attentions to our British brethren. We have warned them from time to time of attempts by their legislature to extend an unwarrantable jurisdiction over us. We have reminded them of the circumstances of our emigration and settlement here. We have appealed to their native justice and magnanimity, and we have conjured them by the ties of our common kindred to disavow these usurpations, which would inevitably interrupt our connections and correspondence. They too have been deaf to the voice of justice and consanguinity. We must, therefore, acquiesce in the necessity, which denounces our Separation, and hold them, as we hold the rest of mankind, Enemies in War, in Peace Friends.—

WE, THEREFORE, the REPRESENTATIVES of the UNITED STATES OF AMERICA, in General Congress, Assembled, appealing to the Supreme Judge of the world for the rectitude of our intentions, do, in the Name, and by Authority of the good People of these Colonies, solemnly publish and declare, That these United Colonies are, and of Right ought to be FREE AND INDEPENDENT STATES; that they are Absolved from all Allegiance to the British Crown, and that all political connection between them and the State of Great Britain, is and ought to be totally disolved; and that as Free and Independent States, they have full Power to levy War, conclude Peace, contract Alliances, establish Commerce, and to do all other Acts and Things which Independent States may of right do.—And for the support of this Declaration, with a firm reliance on the protection of Divine Providence, we mutually pledge to each other our Lives, our Fortunes and our sacred Honor.

John Hancock	Benj. Harrison	Lewis Morris
Button Gwinnett	Thos. Nelson, Jr.	Richd. Stockton
Lyman Hall	Francis Lightfoot Lee	Jno. Witherspoon
Geo. Walton	Carter Braxton	Fras. Hopkinson
Wm. Hooper	Robt. Morris	John Hart
Joseph Hewes	Benjamin Rush	Abra. Clark
John Penn	Benj. Franklin	Josiah Bartlett
Edward Rutledge	John Morton	Wm. Whipple
Thos. Heyward, Jr.	Geo. Clymer	Saml. Adams
Thomas Lynch, Jr.	Jas. Smith	John Adams
Arthur Middleton	Geo. Taylor	Robt. Treat Paine
Samuel Chase	James Wilson	Elbridge Gerry
Wm. Paca	Geo. Ross	Step. Hopkins
Thos. Stone	Caesar Rodney	William Ellery
Charles Carroll of	Geo. Read	Roger Sherman
Carrollton	Tho. M. Kean	Sam. Huntington
George Wythe	Wm. Floyd	Wm. Williams
Richard Henry Lee	Phil. Livington	Oliver Wolcott
Th. Jefferson	Frans. Lewis	Matthew Thornton

CONFLICT AND REVOLUTION

TREATY OF PARIS

The TREATY OF PARIS of 1783 ended the WAR OF INDEPENDENCE and granted the thirteen colonies political freedom. A preliminary treaty between Great Britain and the United States had been signed in 1782, but the final agreement was not signed until September 3, 1783.

Peace negotiations began in Paris, France, in April 1782. The U.S. delegation included BENJAMIN FRANKLIN, JOHN ADAMS, JOHN JAY, and Henry Laurens, while the British were represented by Richard Oswald and Henry Strachey. The negotiators concluded the preliminary treaty on November 30, 1782, but the agreement was not effective until Great Britain concluded treaties with France and Spain concerning foreign colonies.

In the final agreement, the British recognized the independence of the United States. The treaty established generous boundaries for the United States; U.S. territory now extended from the Atlantic Ocean to the Mississippi River in the west, and from the Great Lakes and Canada in the north to the 31st parallel in the south. The U.S. fishing fleet was guaranteed access to the fisheries off the coast of Newfoundland with their plentiful supply of cod.

Navigation of the Mississippi River was to be open to both the United States and Great Britain. Creditors of both countries were not to be impeded from collecting their debts, and Congress was to recommend to the states that loyalists to the British cause during the war should be treated fairly and their rights and confiscated property restored.

Treaty of Paris

In the name of the most holy and undivided Trinity.

It having pleased the Divine Providence to dispose the hearts of the most serene and most potent Prince George the Third, by the grace of God, king of Great Britain, France, and Ireland, defender of the faith, duke of Brunswick and Lunebourg, arch-treasurer and prince elector of the Holy Roman Empire etc., and of the United States of America, to forget all past misunderstandings and differences that have unhappily interrupted the good correspondence and friendship which they mutually wish to restore, and to establish such a beneficial and satisfactory intercourse, between the two countries upon the ground of reciprocal advantages and mutual convenience as may promote and secure to both perpetual peace and harmony; and having for this desirable end already laid the foundation of peace and reconciliation by the Provisional Articles signed at Paris on the 30th of November 1782, by the commissioners empowered on each part, which articles were agreed to be inserted in and to constitute the Treaty of Peace proposed to be concluded between the Crown of Great Britain and the said United States, but which treaty was not to be concluded until terms of peace should be agreed upon between Great Britain and France and his Britannic Majesty

Source: United States. Department of State, *Treaties and Other International Agreements of the United States of America, 1776–1949* (compiled under the direction of Charles I. Bevans), vol. 12 (1974), pp. 8–12.

should be ready to conclude such treaty accordingly; and the treaty between Great Britain and France having since been concluded, his Britannic Majesty and the United States of America, in order to carry into full effect the Provisional Articles above mentioned, according to the tenor thereof, have constituted and appointed, that is to say his Britannic Majesty on his part, David Hartley, Esqr., member of the Parliament of Great Britain, and the said United States on their part, John Adams, Esqr., late a commissioner of the United States of America at the court of Versailles, late delegate in Congress from the state of Massachusetts, and chief justice of the said state, and minister plenipotentiary of the said United States to their high mightinesses the States General of the United Netherlands; Benjamin Franklin, Esqr., late delegate in Congress from the state of Pennsylvania, president of the convention of the said state, and minister plenipotentiary from the United States of America at the court of Versailles; John Jay, Esqr., late president of Congress and chief justice of the state of New York, and minister plenipotentiary from the said United States at the court of Madrid; to be the plenipotentiaries for the concluding and signing the present definitive treaty; who after having reciprocally communicated their respective full powers have agreed upon and confirmed the following articles.

ARTICLE 1

His Britannic Majesty acknowledges the said United States, viz., New Hampshire, Massachusetts Bay, Rhode Island and Providence Plantations, Connecticut, New York, New Jersey, Pennsylvania, Delaware, Maryland, Virginia, North Carolina, South Carolina and Georgia, to be free sovereign and independent states, that he treats with them as such, and for himself, his heirs, and successors, relinquishes all claims to the government, propriety, and territorial rights of the same and every part thereof.

ARTICLE 2

And that all disputes which might arise in future on the subject of the boundaries of the said United States may be prevented, it is hereby agreed and declared, that the following are and shall be their boundaries, viz.: from the northwest angle of Nova Scotia, viz., that angle which is formed by a line drawn due north from the source of St. Croix River to the highlands; along the said highlands which divide those rivers that

empty themselves into the river St. Lawrence, from those which fall into the Atlantic Ocean, to the northwesternmost head of Connecticut River; thence down along the middle of that river to the forty-fifth degree of north latitude; from thence by a line due west on said latitude until it strikes the river Iroquois or Cataraquy; thence along the middle of said river into Lake Ontario; through the middle of said lake until it strikes the communication by water between that lake and Lake Erie; thence along the middle of said communication into Lake Erie, through the middle of said lake until it arrives at the water communication between that lake and Lake Huron; thence along the middle of said water communication into the Lake Huron, thence through the middle of said lake to the water communication between that lake and Lake Superior; thence through Lake Superior northward of the Isles Royal and Phelipeaux to the Long Lake; thence through the middle of said Long Lake and the water communication between it and the Lake of the Woods, to the said Lake of the Woods; thence through the said lake to the most northwestern point thereof, and from thence on a due west course to the river Mississippi; thence by a line to be drawn along the middle of the said river Mississippi until it shall intersect the northernmost part of the thirty-first degree of north latitude. South, by a line to be drawn due east from the determination of the line last mentioned in the latitude of thirty-one degrees north of the equator, to the middle of the river Apalachicola or Catahouche; thence along the middle thereof to its junction with the Flint River, thence straight to the head of Saint Mary's River; and thence down along the middle of Saint Mary's River to the Atlantic Ocean; east, by a line to be drawn along the middle of the river Saint Croix, from its mouth in the Bay of Fundy to its source, and from its source directly north to the aforesaid highlands which divide the rivers that fall into the Atlantic Ocean from those which fall into the river Saint Lawrence; comprehending all islands within twenty leagues of any part of the shores of the United States, and lying between lines to be drawn due east from the points where the aforesaid boundaries between Nova Scotia on the one part and East Florida on the other shall, respectively, touch the Bay of Fundy and the Atlantic Ocean, excepting such islands as now are or heretofore have been within the limits of the said province of Nova Scotia.

CONFLICT AND
REVOLUTION

TREATY OF
PARIS

ARTICLE 3

It is agreed that the people of the United States shall continue to enjoy unmolested the right to take fish of every kind on the Grand Bank and on all the other banks of Newfoundland, also in the Gulf of Saint Lawrence and at all other places in the sea, where the inhabitants of both countries used at any time heretofore to fish. And also that the inhabitants of the United States shall have liberty to take fish of every kind on such part of the coast of Newfoundland as British fishermen shall use, (but not to dry or cure the same on that island) and also on the coasts, bays, and creeks of all other of his Britannic Majesty's dominions in America; and that the American fishermen shall have liberty to dry and cure fish in any of the unsettled bays, harbors, and creeks of Nova Scotia, Magdalen Islands, and Labrador, so long as the same shall remain unsettled, but so soon as the same or either of them shall be settled, it shall not be lawful for the said fishermen to dry or cure fish at such settlement without a previous agreement for that purpose with the inhabitants, proprietors, or possessors of the ground.

ARTICLE 4

It is agreed that creditors on either side shall meet with no lawful impediment to the recovery of the full value in sterling money of all bona fide debts heretofore contracted.

ARTICLE 5

It is agreed that Congress shall earnestly recommend it to the legislatures of the respective states to provide for the restitution of all estates, rights, and properties, which have been confiscated belonging to real British subjects; and also of the estates, rights, and properties of persons resident in districts in the possession of his Majesty's arms and who have not borne arms against the said United States. And that persons of any other description shall have free liberty to go to any part or parts of any of the thirteen United States and therein to remain twelve months unmolested in their endeavors to obtain the restitution of such of their estates, rights, and properties as may have been confiscated; and that Congress shall also earnestly recommend to the several states a reconsideration and revision of all acts or laws regarding the premises, so as to render the said laws or acts perfectly consistent not only with justice and equity but with that spirit of conciliation which on the return of the blessings of peace should universally prevail. And that Congress shall also earnestly recommend to the several states that the estates, rights, and properties, of such last mentioned persons shall be restored to them, they refunding to any persons who may be now in possession the bona fide price (where any has been given) which such persons may have paid on purchasing any of the said lands, rights, or properties since the confiscation.

And it is agreed that all persons who have any interest in confiscated lands, either by debts, marriage settlements, or otherwise, shall meet with no lawful impediment in the prosecution of their just rights.

ARTICLE 6

That there shall be no future confiscations made nor any prosecutions commenced against any person or persons for, or by reason of, the part which he or they may have taken in the present war, and that no person shall on that account suffer any future loss or damage, either in his person, liberty, or property; and that those who may be in confinement on such charges at the time of the ratification of the treaty in America shall be immediately set at liberty, and the prosecutions so commenced be discontinued.

ARTICLE 7

There shall be a firm and perpetual peace between his Britannic Majesty and the said states, and between the subjects of the one and the citizens of the other, wherefore all hostilities both by sea and land shall from henceforth cease. All prisoners on both sides shall be set at liberty, and his Britannic Majesty shall with all convenient speed, and without causing any destruction, or carrying away any Negroes or other property of the American inhabitants, withdraw all his armies, garrisons, and fleets from the said United States, and from every post, place, and harbor within the same; leaving in all fortifications, the American artillery that may be therein; and shall also order and cause all archives, records, deeds, and papers belonging to any of the said states, or their citizens, which in the course of the war may have fallen into the hands of his officers, to be forthwith restored and delivered to the proper states and persons to whom they belong.

ARTICLE 8

The navigation of the river Mississippi, from its source to the ocean, shall forever remain free and open to the subjects of Great Britain and the citizens of the United States.

ARTICLE 9

In case it should so happen that any place or territory belonging to Great Britain or to the United States should have been conquered by the arms of either from the other before the arrival of the said Provisional Articles in America, it is agreed that the same shall be restored without difficulty and without requiring any compensation.

ARTICLE 10

The solemn ratifications of the present treaty expedited in good and due form shall be exchanged between the contracting parties in the space of six months or sooner, if possible, to be computed from the day of the signature of the present treaty. In witness whereof we the undersigned, their ministers plenipotentiary, have in their name and in virtue of our full powers, signed with our hands the present definitive treaty and caused the seals of our arms to be affixed thereto.

Done at Paris, this third day of September in the year of our Lord, one thousand seven hundred and eighty-three.

D. Hartley [Seal]

John Adams [Seal]

B. Franklin [Seal]

John Jay [Seal]

ORIGINS OF U.S. GOVERNMENT

- ARTICLES OF CONFEDERATION
- NORTHWEST ORDINANCE
- THE VIRGINIA, OR RANDOLPH, PLAN
- THE NEW JERSEY, OR PATERSON, PLAN
- CONSTITUTION OF THE UNITED STATES
- BILL OF RIGHTS
- FEDERALIST, NUMBER 10
- FEDERALIST, NUMBER 78
- THE VIRGINIA AND KENTUCKY RESOLVES
- MONROE DOCTRINE

After declaring their independence in 1776, the thirteen states had to determine both what type of central government they should form and how the individual states would be related to that central government. Their initial efforts to answer those questions resulted in the ARTICLES OF CONFEDERATION. The Articles were drafted in 1776 but were modified during the ratification process, which ended when the Articles went into effect on March 1, 1781.

The Articles of Confederation created a weak national government, which lacked both an executive and a judicial branch. The national government consisted only of a Congress, which prosecuted the end of the WAR OF INDEPENDENCE and negotiated the TREATY OF PARIS. By the end of the war, however, the Congress of the Confederation of the States found itself receiving less cooperation from the individual states. The Congress did enact the NORTHWEST ORDINANCE in 1787, which provided for the government of the Northwest Territory and established a procedure by which states could be carved out of the territory.

Dissatisfaction with the Articles of Confederation grew during the 1780s until Congress finally summoned a convention to amend and revise the Articles. All of the states except Rhode Island sent delegates to the convention, which convened in Philadelphia, Pennsylvania, in May 1787. A fundamental problem for the delegates was resolving a split between the states that favored a strong national government and those that preferred the strong state governments established by the Articles of Confederation.

As the convention debated the issues, it soon became apparent that a stronger national government was needed and that the Articles of Confederation would have to be replaced. A major conflict developed, however, between the large states, which favored a legislature apportioned by population, and the small states, which preferred a system under which each state would have an equal vote. The large states proposed the Virginia Plan, also known as the Randolph Plan, and the small states offered the New Jersey, or Paterson, Plan. At first, neither side would yield on the issue of representation. Finally, ROGER SHERMAN, along with OLIVER ELLSWORTH, proposed the Connecticut, or Great, Compromise, which called for a bicameral legislature with proportional representation in the lower house and equal representation in the upper house.

The U.S. Constitution was completed on September 17, 1787. It established three branches of government (legislative, executive, judicial) with an intricate set of checks and balances aimed at preventing one branch of government from gaining absolute control. The separation of powers is one of the hallmarks of the Constitution. The Framers did not, however, resolve the question of slavery. Southern states won the Three-fifths Compromise, which allowed them to count each slave as three-fifths of a white person in apportioning the House of Representatives and the electoral college.

Though opponents of the Constitution argued that it gave too much power to the national government, it was ratified by the requisite number of states by June 1788. GEORGE MASON, drafter of the VIRGINIA DECLARATION OF RIGHTS, and other STATES' RIGHTS advocates opposed ratification because the Constitution included no guarantees of basic personal liberties. In response, the first Congress convened under the Constitution in 1789 enacted the first ten amendments to the Constitution, known as the BILL OF RIGHTS.

During the ratification battle of 1787 and 1788, ALEXANDER HAMILTON, JAMES MADISON, and JOHN JAY wrote eighty-five short essays in support of the Constitution. The essays, known as the FEDERALIST PAPERS, sought to convince the voters of New York to persuade their legislators to vote in favor of the proposed federal constitution. The writers so clearly articulated the reasoning and scope of many of the constitutional provisions that the *Federalist Papers* have taken on lasting historical and legal significance.

The early years of the Republic saw a clash between the Federalists, led by Hamilton, and the Republicans, led by Thomas Jefferson. Jefferson and other proponents of strong state governments accused Hamilton and other advocates of a strong national government of going beyond the constitutional restrictions on the power of the national government. This debate escalated after the federal ALIEN AND SEDITION ACTS (1 Stat. 570, 596) were enacted in 1798. Jefferson and Madison prepared resolves, or resolutions, for the Virginia and Kentucky legislatures that proposed a "compact" theory of the U.S. Constitution. Under this theory state legislatures possessed all powers not specifically granted to the federal government, and states had the right to pass upon the constitutionality of federal legislation.

In the first years of the new nation, it was unclear whether the Supreme Court had the right to review an executive or legislative act and invalidate it if the act was contrary to constitutional principles. Article III of the Constitution was silent on the subject, but the Supreme Court settled the issue in 1803, when it ruled in MARBURY V. MADISON, 5 U.S. (1 Cranch) 137, 2 L. Ed. 60, that a particular act of Congress was unconstitutional.

The United States entered the field of international relations in 1823, when President JAMES MONROE enunciated a statement on foreign policy that has come to be known as the MONROE DOCTRINE. The Monroe Doctrine asserted U.S. dominance over the Western Hemisphere and warned European nations not to interfere with the free nations of the region.

ORIGINS OF U.S. GOVERNMENT

ARTICLES OF CONFEDERATION

The Articles of Confederation were the first constitution of the United States. During 1776–1777, a congressional committee led by JOHN DICKINSON of Pennsylvania (who had drafted the Declaration of the Causes and Necessity of Taking up Arms in 1775) wrote the Articles and submitted them to the states for ratification in 1777. Ratification was delayed by disputes between the states with extensive western lands and the "landless" states such as Maryland. On March 1, 1781, after the landed states agreed to cede their lands to Congress, the new government came into existence.

The Articles of Confederation reflected the new nation's fear of centralized power and authority. Under the Articles the states were more powerful than the central government, which consisted only of a Congress. Each state had one vote in Congress, with that vote determined by a delegation of from two to seven representatives. Though the Congress had the authority to regulate foreign affairs, wage war, and maintain the postal system, it had no power to levy and collect taxes or regulate interstate commerce.

Critics of the Articles multiplied until finally, in 1787, Congress summoned a convention to draft a revised constitution. On March 4, 1789, the new U.S. Constitution took effect, superseding the Articles of Confederation.

Articles of Confederation

To all to whom these Presents shall come, we the undersigned Delegates of the States affixed to our Names send greeting

Whereas the Delegates of the United States of America in Congress assembled did on the fifteenth day of November in the Year of our Lord One Thousand Seven Hundred and Seventy-seven, and in the Second Year of the Independence of America agree to certain articles of Confederation and perpetual Union between the States of Newhampshire, Massachusetts-bay, Rhode-island, and Providence Plantations, Connecticut, New York, New Jersey, Pennsylvania, Delaware, Maryland, Virginia, North-Carolina, South-Carolina and Georgia in the Words following, viz.

Articles of Confederation and perpetual Union between the States of New Hampshire, Massachusetts-bay, Rhode-island and Providence Plantations, Connecticut, New-York, New-Jersey, Pennsylvania, Delaware, Maryland, Virginia, North-Carolina, South-Carolina and Georgia

ARTICLE I

The stile of this confederacy shall be "The United States of America."

Source: Ben Perley Poore, ed., *The Federal and State Constitutions, Colonial Charters, and Other Organic Laws of the United States,* vol. 1 (1878), pp. 7–12.

ARTICLE II

Each State retains its sovereignty, freedom and independence, and every power, jurisdiction and right, which is not by this confederation expressly delegated to the United States, in Congress assembled.

ARTICLE III

The said States hereby severally enter into a firm league of friendship with each other, for their common defense, the security of their liberties, and their mutual and general welfare, binding themselves to assist each other, against all force offered to, or attacks made upon them, or any of them, on account of religion, sovereignty trade or any other pretence whatever.

ARTICLE IV

The better to secure and perpetuate mutual friendship and intercourse among the people of the different States in this Union, the free inhabitants of each of these States, paupers, vagabonds and fugitives from justice excepted, shall be entitled to all privileges and immunities of free citizens in the several States; and the people of each State shall have free ingress and regress to and from any other State, and shall enjoy therein all the privileges of trade and commerce, subject to the same duties, impositions and restrictions as the inhabitants thereof respectively, provided that such restrictions shall not exceed so far as to prevent the removal of property imported into any State, to any other State of which the owner is an inhabitant; provided also that no imposition, duties or restriction shall be laid by any State, on the property of the United States, or either of them.

If any person guilty of, or charged with treason, felony, or other high misdemeanor in any State, shall flee from justice, and be found in any of the United States, he shall upon demand of the Governor or Executive power, of the State from which he fled, be delivered up and removed to the State having jurisdiction of his offense.

Full faith and credit shall be given in each of these States to the records, acts and judicial proceedings to the courts and magistrates of every other State.

ARTICLE V

For the more convenient management of the general interests of the United States, delegates shall be annually appointed in such manner as the legislature of each State shall direct, to meet in Congress on the first Monday in November, in every year, with a power reserved to each State, to recall its delegates, or any of them, at any time within the year, and to send others in their stead, for the remainder of the year.

No State shall be represented in Congress by less than two, nor by more than seven members; and no person shall be capable of being a delegate for more than three years in any term of six years; nor shall any person, being a delegate, be capable of holding any office under the United States, for which he, or another for his benefit receives any salary, fees or emolument of any kind.

Each State shall maintain its own delegates in a meeting of the States, and while they act as members of the committee of the States.

In determining questions in the United States, in Congress assembled, each State shall have one vote.

Freedom of speech and debate in Congress shall not be impeached or questioned in any court, or place out of Congress, and the members of Congress shall be protected in their persons from arrests and imprisonments, during the time of their going to and from, and attendance on Congress, except for treason, felony, or breach of the peace.

ARTICLE VI

No State without the consent of the United States in Congress assembled, shall send any embassy to, or receive any embassy from, or enter into any conference, agreement, alliance or treaty with any king, prince or state; nor shall any person holding any office or profit or trust under the United States, or any of them, accept of any present, emolument, office or title of any kind whatever from any king, prince or foreign state; nor shall the United States in Congress assembled or any of them, grant any title of nobility.

No two or more States shall enter into any treaty, confederation or alliance whatever between them, without the consent of the United States in Congress assembled, specifying accurately the purposes for which the same is to be entered into, and how long it shall continue.

No State shall lay any imposts or duties, which may interfere with any stipulations in treaties, entered into by the United States in Congress assembled, with any king, prince or state, in pursuance of any treaties already proposed by Congress, to the courts of France and Spain.

No vessels of war shall be kept up in time of peace by any State, except such number only, as shall be deemed necessary by the United States in Congress assembled, for the defence of such State, or its trade; nor shall any body of forces be kept up by any State, in time of peace, except such number only, as in the judgment of the United States, in Congress assembled, shall be deemed requisite to garrison the forts necessary for the defence of such State; but every State shall always keep up a well regulated and disciplined militia, sufficiently armed and accoutered, and shall provide and constantly have ready for use, in public stores, a due number of field pieces and tents, and a proper quantity of arms, ammunition and camp equipage.

No State shall engage in any way without the consent of the United States in Congress assembled, unless such State be actually invaded by enemies, or shall have received certain advice of a resolution being formed by some nation of Indians to invade such State, and the danger is so imminent as not to admit of a delay, till the United States in Congress assembled can be consulted: nor shall any State grant commissions to any ships or vessels of war, nor letters of marque or reprisal, except it be after a declaration of war by the United States in Congress assembled, and then only against the kingdom or state and the subject thereof, against which war has been so declared and under such regulations as shall be established by the United States in Congress assembled, unless such State be infested by pirates, in which case vessels of war may be fitted out for that occasion, and kept so long as the danger shall continue, or until the United States in Congress assembled shall determine otherwise.

ARTICLE VII

When land-forces are raised by any State for the common defence, all officers of or under the rank of colonel, shall be appointed by the Legislature of each State respectively by whom such forces shall be raised, or in such manner as such State shall direct, and all vacancies shall be filled up by the State which first made the appointment.

ARTICLE VIII

All charges of war, and all other expenses that shall be incurred for the common defence or general welfare, and allowed by the United States in Congress assembled, shall be defrayed out of a common treasury, which shall be sup-

plied by the several States, in proportion to the value of all land within each State, granted to or surveyed for any person, as such land and the buildings and improvements thereon shall be estimated according to such mode as the United States in Congress assembled, shall from time to time direct and appoint.

The taxes for paying that proportion shall be laid and levied by the authority and direction of the Legislatures of the several States within the time agreed upon by the United States in Congress Assembled.

ARTICLE IX

The United States in Congress assembled, shall have the sole and exclusive right and power of determining on peace and war, except in the cases mentioned in the sixth article—of sending and receiving ambassadors—entering into treaties and alliances, provided that no treaty of commerce shall be made whereby the legislative power of the respective States shall be restrained from imposing such imposts and duties on foreigners, as their own people are subjected to, or from prohibiting the exportation or importation of any species of goods or commodities whatsoever—of establishing rules for deciding in all cases, what captures on land or water shall be legal, and in what manner prizes taken by land or naval forces in the service of the United States shall be divided or appropriated—of granting letters of marque and reprisal in times of peace—appointing courts for trial of piracies and felonies committed on the high seas and establishing courts for receiving and determining finally appeals in all cases of captures, provided that no member of Congress shall be appointed a judge of any of the said courts.

The United States in Congress assembled shall also be the last resort on appeal in all disputes and differences now subsisting or that hereafter may arise between two or more States concerning boundary, jurisdiction or any other cause whatever; which authority shall always be exercised in the manner following. Whenever the legislative or executive authority or lawful agent of any State in controversy with another shall present a petition to Congress, stating the matter in question and praying for a hearing, notice thereof shall be given by order of Congress to the legislative or executive authority of the other State in controversy, and a day assigned for the appearance of the parties by their lawful agents, who shall then be directed to appoint by joint consent, commissioners or judges to constitute a court for hearing and determining the matter in question: but if they cannot agree, Congress shall name three persons out of each of the United States, and from the list of such persons each party shall alternately strike out one, the petitioners beginning, until the number shall be reduced to thirteen; and from that number not less than seven, nor more than nine names as Congress shall direct, shall, in the presence of Congress be drawn out by lot, and the persons whose names shall be so drawn or any five of them, shall be commissioners or judges, to hear and finally determine the controversy, so always as a major part of the judges who shall hear the cause shall agree in the determination: and if either party shall neglect to attend at the day appointed, without showing reasons, which Congress shall judge sufficient, or being present shall refuse to strike, the Congress shall proceed to nominate three persons out of each State, and the Secretary of Congress shall strike in behalf of such party absent or refusing; and the judgment and sentence of the court to be appointed, in the manner before prescribed, shall be final and conclusive; and if any of the parties shall refuse to submit to the authority of such court, or to appear or defend their claim or cause, the court shall nevertheless proceed to pronounce sentence, or judgment, which shall in like manner be final and decisive, the judgment or sentence and other proceedings being in either case transmitted to Congress, and lodged among the acts of Congress for the security of the parties concerned: provided that every commissioner, before he sits in judgment, shall take an oath to be administered by one of the judges of the supreme court of the State where the cause shall be tried, "well and truly to hear and determine the matter in question, according to the best of his judgment, without favour, affection or hope of reward:" provided also that no State shall be deprived of territory for the benefit of the United States.

All controversies concerning the private right of soil claimed under different grants of two or more States, whose jurisdiction as they may respect such lands, and the States which passed such grants are adjusted, the said grants or either of them being at the same time claimed to have originated antecedent to such settlement of jurisdiction, shall on the petition of either party to the Congress of the United States, be finally determined as near as may be in the same manner as is before prescribed for deciding disputes respecting territorial jurisdiction between different States.

The United States in Congress assembled shall also have the sole and exclusive right and power of regulating the alloy and value of coin struck by their own authority, or by that of the respective States.—fixing the standard of weights and measures throughout the United States.—regulating the trade and managing all affairs with the Indians, not members of any of the States, provided that the legislative right of any State within its own limits be not infringed or violated—establishing and regulating post-offices from one State to another, throughout all the United States, and exacting such postage on the papers passing thro' the same as may be requisite to defray the expenses of the said office— appointing all officers of the land forces, in the service of the United States, excepting regimental officers—appointing all the officers of the naval forces, and commissioning all officers whatever in the service of the United States— making rules for the government and regulation of the said land and naval forces, and directing their operations.

The United States in Congress assembled shall have authority to appoint a committee, to sit in the recess of Congress, to be denominated "a Committee of the States," and to consist of one delegate from each State; and to appoint such other committees and civil officers as may be necessary for managing the general affairs of the United States under their direction—to appoint one of their number to preside, provided that no person be allowed to serve in the office of president more than one year in any term of three years; to ascertain the necessary sums of money to be raised for the service of the United States, and to appropriate and apply the same for defraying the public expenses—to borrow money or emit bills on the credit of the United States transmitting every half year to the respective States an account of the sums of money so borrowed or emitted,—to build and equip a navy—to agree upon the number of land forces, and to make requisitions from each State for its quota, in proportion to the number of white inhabitants in such State; which requisition shall be binding, and thereupon the Legislature of each State shall appoint the regimental officers, raise the men and cloath, arm

ORIGINS OF U.S. GOVERNMENT

ARTICLES OF CONFEDERATION

and equip them in a soldier like manner, at the expense of the United States; and the officers and men so cloathed, armed and equipped shall march to the place appointed, and within the time agreed on by the United States in Congress assembled: but if the United States in Congress assembled shall, on consideration of circumstances judge proper that any State should not raise men, or should raise a smaller number than its quota, and that any other State should raise a greater number of men than the quota thereof, such extra number shall be raised, officered, cloathed, armed and equipped in the same manner as the quota of such State, unless the legislature of such State shall judge that such extra number cannot be safely spared out of the same, in which case they shall raise officer, cloath, arm and equip as many of such extra number as they judge can be safely spared. And the officers and men so cloathed, armed, and equipped, shall march to the place appointed, and within the time agreed on by the United States in Congress assembled.

The United States in Congress assembled shall never engage in a war, nor grant letters of marque and reprisal in time of peace, nor enter into any treaties or alliances, nor coin money, nor regulate the value thereof, nor ascertain the sums and expenses necessary for the defence and welfare of the United States, or any of them, nor emit bills, nor borrow money on the credit of the United States, nor appropriate money, nor agree upon the number of vessels of war, to be built or purchased, or the number of land or sea forces to be raised, nor appoint a commander in chief of the army or navy, unless nine States assent to the same: nor shall a question on any other point, except for adjourning from day to day be determined, unless by the votes of a majority of the United States in Congress assembled.

The Congress of the United States shall have power to adjourn to any time within the year, and to any place within the United States, so that no period of adjournment be for a longer duration than the space of six months, and shall publish the journal of their proceedings monthly, except such parts thereof relating to treaties, alliances or military operations, as in their judgment require secrecy; and the yeas and nays of the delegates of each State on any question shall be entered on the journal, when it is desired by any delegate; and the delegates of a State, or any of them, at his or her request shall be furnished

with a transcript of the said journal, except such parts as are above excepted, to lay before the Legislatures of the several States.

ARTICLE X

The committee of the States, or any nine of them, shall be authorized to execute in the recess of Congress, such of the powers of Congress as the United States in Congress assembled, by the consent of nine States, shall from time to time think expedient to vest them with; provided that no power be delegated to the said committee, for the exercise of which, by the articles of confederation, the voice of nine States in the Congress of the United States assembled is requisite.

ARTICLE XI

Canada acceding to this confederation, and joining in the measures of the United States, shall be admitted into, and entitled to all the advantages of this Union: but no other colony shall be admitted into the same, unless such admission be agreed to by nine States.

ARTICLE XII

All bills of credit emitted, monies borrowed and debts contracted by, or under the authority of Congress, before the assembling of the United States, in pursuance of the present confederation, shall be deemed and considered as a charge against the United States, for payment and satisfaction whereof the said United States, and the public faith are hereby solemnly pledged.

ARTICLE XIII

Every State shall abide by the determinations of the United States in Congress assembled, on all questions which by this confederation are submitted to them. And the articles of this confederation shall be inviolably observed by every State, and the Union shall be perpetual; nor shall any alteration at any time hereafter be made in any of them; unless such alteration be agreed to in a Congress of the United States, and be afterwards confirmed by the Legislatures of every State.

And whereas it has pleased the Great Governor of the world to incline the hearts of the Legislatures we respectively represent in Congress, to approve of, and to authorize us to ratify the said articles of confederation and perpetual union. Know ye that we the undersigned delegates, by virtue of the power and authority to us given for that purpose, do by these presents, in the name and in behalf of our respective constituents, fully and entirely ratify and confirm each and every of the said articles of confederation and perpetual union, and all and singular the matters and things therein contained: and we do further solemnly plight and engage the faith of our respective constituents, that they shall abide by the determinations of the United States in Congress assembled, on all questions, which by the said confederation are submitted to them. And that the articles thereof shall be inviolably observed by the States we re[s]pectively represent, and that the Union shall be perpetual.

In witness whereof we have hereunto set our hands in Congress.

Done at Philadelphia in the State of Pennsylvania the ninth day of July in the year of our Lord one thousand seven hundred and seventy-eight, and in the third year of the independence of America.

On the part and behalf of the State of New Hampshire

JOSIAH BARTLETT, August 8th, 1778.

JOHN WENTWORTH, Junr.,

On the part and behalf of the State of Massachusetts Bay

JOHN HANCOCK,   FRANCIS DANA,

SAMUEL ADAMS,   JAMES LOVELL,

ELBRIDGE GERRY,   SAMUEL HOLTEN.

On the part and behalf of the State of Rhode Island and Providence Plantations

WILLIAM ELLERY,   JOHN COLLINS.

HENRY MARCHANT,

On the part and behalf of the State of Connecticut

ROGER SHERMAN,   TITUS HOSMER,

SAMUEL HUNTINGTON,

OLIVER WOLCOTT,   ANDREW ADAMS.

On the part and behalf of the State of New York

JAS. DUANE,   WM. DUER,

FRA. LEWIS,   GOUV. MORRIS.

On the part and in behalf of the State of New Jersey, Novr. 26, 1778

JNO. WITHERSPOON,   NATHL. SCUDDER.

On the part and behalf of the State of Pennsylvania

ROBT. MORRIS,   WILLIAM CLINGAN,

DANIEL ROBERDEAU,   JOSEPH REED,

JONA. BAYARD SMITH, 22d July, 1778.

On the part & behalf of the State of Delaware

THO. M'KEAN, Feby. 12, 1779.

NICHOLAS VAN DYKE.

JOHN DICKINSON, May 5th, 1779

On the part and behalf of the State of Maryland

JOHN HANSON, Mar. 1, 1781.

DANIEL CARROLL, March 1, 1781.

On the part and behalf of the State of Virginia

RICHARD HENRY LEE,   JNO. HARVIE,

JOHN BANISTER,   THOMAS ADAMS,

FRANCIS LIGHTFOOT LEE.

On the part and behalf of the State of No. Carolina

JOHN PENN, July 21st, 1778.

CORNS. HARNETT,   JNO. WILLIAMS.

On the part & behalf of the State of South Carolina

HENRY LAURENS,   RICHD. HUTSON,

WILLIAM HENRY DRAYTON,

JNO. MATHEWS,   THOS. HEYWARD, Junr.

On the part & behalf of the State of Georgia

JNO. WALTON, 24th July, 1778.

EDWD. TELFAIR

EDWD. LANGWORTHY.

ORIGINS OF U.S. GOVERNMENT

ARTICLES OF CONFEDERATION

ORIGINS OF U.S. GOVERNMENT

NORTHWEST ORDINANCE

An Ordinance for the Government of the Territory of the United States Northwest of the River Ohio

The Northwest Ordinance (officially the Ordinance of 1787) was enacted by the Congress of the Confederation of the States on July 13, 1787. This statute provided for the government of the Northwest Territory, an area bounded by the Ohio and Mississippi Rivers and the Great Lakes, and created a procedure by which states could be established within this territory and admitted to the Union. Congress was spurred to enact the ordinance when the Ohio Company of Associates, a group of land speculators, made plans to purchase more than one million acres in the territory.

The Northwest Ordinance set several important precedents. It established that unlike many nations, which left their new territories in a position inferior to the old, the United States would admit new states to the Union on an equal basis with the original states. The ordinance also set aside land in each township for schools, thus setting a precedent for federal support to education. In addition, the ordinance prohibited slavery in the territory and included the first full statement of U.S. Indian policy, which stressed that "utmost good faith shall always be observed toward the Indians."

Northwest Ordinance

Be it ordained by the United States in Congress assembled that the said territory, for the purposes of temporary government, be one district, subject, however, to be divided into two dis-

tricts, as future circumstances may, in the opinion of Congress, make it expedient.

Be it ordained by the authority aforesaid that the estates both of resident and nonresident proprietors in the said territory, dying intestate, shall descend to and be distributed among their children and the descendants of a deceased child in equal parts, the descendants of a deceased child or grandchild to take the share of their deceased parent in equal parts among them; and where there shall be no children or descendants, then in equal parts to the next of kin, in equal degree; and among collaterals, the children of a deceased brother or sister of the intestate shall have, in equal parts among them, their deceased parent's share; and there shall, in no case, be a distinction between kindred of the whole and half blood; saving in all cases to the widow of the intestate, her third part of the real estate for life, and one-third part of the personal estate; and this law relative to descents and dower shall remain in full force until altered by the legislature of the district. And until the governor and judges shall adopt laws as hereinafter mentioned, estates in the said territory may be devised or bequeathed by wills in writing, signed and sealed by him or her in whom the estate may be (being of full age) and attested by three witnesses;—and real estates may be conveyed by lease and release, or bargain and sale, signed,

Source: Francis Newton Thorpe, ed., *The Federal and State Constitutions, Colonial Charters, and Other Organic Laws of the States, Territories, and Colonies Now or Heretofore Forming the United States of America*, vol. 2 (1909), pp. 957–962.

sealed, and delivered by the person, being of full age, in whom the estate may be, and attested by two witnesses, provided such wills be duly proved, and such conveyances be acknowledged, or the execution thereof duly proved, and be recorded within one year after proper magistrates, courts, and registers shall be appointed for that purpose; and personal property may be transferred by delivery, saving, however, to the French and Canadian inhabitants, and other settlers of the Kaskaskies, Saint Vincents, and the neighboring villages, who have heretofore professed themselves citizens of Virginia, their laws and customs now in force among them, relative to the descent and conveyance of property.

Be it ordained by the authority aforesaid that there shall be appointed from time to time, by Congress, a governor whose commission shall continue in force for the term of three years, unless sooner revoked by Congress; he shall reside in the district and have a freehold estate therein, in one thousand acres of land, while in the exercise of his office.

There shall be appointed from time to time, by Congress, a secretary whose commission shall continue in force for four years, unless sooner revoked; he shall reside in the district and have a freehold estate therein, in five hundred acres of land, while in the exercise of his office. It shall be his duty to keep and preserve the acts and laws passed by the legislature, and the public records of the district, and the proceedings of the governor in his executive department, and transmit authentic copies of such acts and proceedings every six months to the secretary of Congress. There shall also be appointed a court, to consist of three judges, any two of whom to form a court, who shall have a common-law jurisdiction, and reside in the district and have each therein a freehold estate, in five hundred acres of land, while in the exercise of their offices; and their commissions shall continue in force during good behavior.

The governor and judges, or a majority of them, shall adopt and publish in the district such laws of the original states, criminal and civil, as may be necessary and best suited to the circumstances of the district, and report them to Congress from time to time, which laws shall be in force in the district until the organization of the general assembly therein, unless disapproved of by Congress; but afterwards the legislature

shall have authority to alter them as they shall think fit.

The governor, for the time being, shall be commander in chief of the militia, appoint and commission all officers in the same below the rank of general officers; all general officers shall be appointed and commissioned by Congress.

Previous to the organization of the general assembly the governor shall appoint such magistrates and other civil officers in each county or township as he shall find necessary for the preservation of the peace and good order in the same. After the general assembly shall be organized, the powers and duties of magistrates and other civil officers shall be regulated and defined by the said assembly; but all magistrates and other civil officers, not herein otherwise directed shall, during the continuance of this temporary government, be appointed by the governor.

For the prevention of crimes and injuries, the laws to be adopted or made shall have force in all parts of the district, and for the execution of process, criminal and civil, the governor shall make proper divisions thereof; and he shall proceed from time to time, as circumstances may require, to lay out the parts of the district in which the Indian titles shall have been extinguished, into counties and townships, subject, however, to such alterations as may thereafter be made by the legislature.

So soon as there shall be five thousand free male inhabitants of full age in the district, upon giving proof thereof to the governor they shall receive authority, with time and place, to elect representatives from their counties or townships to represent them in the general assembly: provided that for every five hundred free male inhabitants there shall be one representative, and so on, progressively, with the number of free male inhabitants, shall the right of representation increase until the number of representatives shall amount to twenty-five; after which the number and proportion of representatives shall be regulated by the legislature: provided that no person be eligible or qualified to act as a representative unless he shall have been a citizen of one of the United States three years and be a resident in the district, or unless he shall have resided in the district three years; and in either case, shall likewise hold in his own right, in fee simple, two hundred acres of land within the same: provided also that a freehold in fifty acres of land in the district, having been a citizen of one of the states, and being resident in the district, or the like freehold and two years' residence in the district, shall be necessary to qualify a man as an elector of a representative.

The representatives thus elected shall serve for the term of two years; and in case of the death of a representative, or removal from office, the governor shall issue a writ to the county or township for which he was a member to elect another in his stead, to serve for the residue of the term.

The general assembly or legislature shall consist of the governor, legislative council, and a house of representatives. The legislative council shall consist of five members, to continue in office five years, unless sooner removed by Congress; any three of whom to be a quorum: and the members of the council shall be nominated and appointed in the following manner, to wit: As soon as representatives shall be elected the governor shall appoint a time and place for them to meet together, and when met they shall nominate ten persons, residents in the district, and each possessed of a freehold in five hundred acres of land, and return their names to Congress, five of whom Congress shall appoint and commission to serve as aforesaid; and whenever a vacancy shall happen in the council, by death or removal from office, the house of representatives shall nominate two persons, qualified as aforesaid, for each vacancy and return their names to Congress, one of whom Congress shall appoint and commission for the residue of the term; and every five years, four months at least before the expiration of the time of service of the members of the council, the said house shall nominate ten persons, qualified as aforesaid, and return their names to Congress, five of whom Congress shall appoint and commission to serve as members of the council five years, unless sooner removed. And the governor, legislative council, and house of representatives shall have authority to make laws in all cases for the good government of the district, not repugnant to the principles and articles in this ordinance established and declared. And all bills, having passed by a majority in the house and by a majority in the council, shall be referred to the governor for his assent; but no bill or legislative act whatever shall be of any force without his assent. The governor shall have power to convene, prorogue, and dissolve the

general assembly when, in his opinion, it shall be expedient.

The governor, judges, legislative council, secretary, and such other officers as Congress shall appoint in the district shall take an oath or affirmation of fidelity and of office; the governor before the president of Congress, and all other officers before the governor. As soon as a legislature shall be formed in the district, the council and house, assembled in one room, shall have authority by joint ballot to elect a delegate to Congress who shall have a seat in Congress, with a right of debating, but not of voting, during this temporary government.

And for extending the fundamental principles of civil and religious liberty, which form the basis whereon these republics, their laws and constitutions, are erected; to fix and establish those principles as the basis of all laws, constitutions, and governments which forever hereafter shall be formed in the said territory; to provide also for the establishment of states, and permanent government therein, and for their admission to a share in the Federal councils on an equal footing with the original states, at as early periods as may be consistent with the general interest:

It is hereby ordained and declared by the authority aforesaid that the following articles shall be considered as articles of compact, between the original states and the people and states in the said territory, and forever remain unalterable, unless by common consent, to wit:

ARTICLE I

No person, demeaning himself in a peaceable and orderly manner, shall ever be molested on account of his mode of worship or religious sentiments in the said territory.

ARTICLE II

The inhabitants of the said territory shall always be entitled to the benefits of the writs of habeas corpus and of the trial by jury; of a proportionate representation of the people in the legislature and of judicial proceedings according to the course of the common law. All persons shall be bailable, unless for capital offenses, where the proof shall be evident or the presumption great. All fines shall be moderate; and no cruel or unusual punishments shall be inflicted. No man shall be deprived of his liberty or property, but by the judgment of his peers, or the law of the land, and should the public exigencies make it necessary for the common preservation to take any person's property, or to demand his particular services, full compensation shall be made for the same. And in the just preservation of rights and property, it is understood and declared that no law ought ever to be made or have force in the said territory that shall in any manner whatever interfere with or affect private contracts, or engagements, bona fide, and without fraud previously formed.

ARTICLE III

Religion, morality, and knowledge being necessary to good government and the happiness of mankind, schools and the means of education shall forever be encouraged. The utmost good faith shall always be observed towards the Indians; their lands and property shall never be taken from them without their consent; and in their property, rights, and liberty they never shall be invaded or disturbed, unless in just and lawful wars authorized by Congress; but laws founded in justice and humanity shall from time to time be made for preventing wrongs being done to them, and for preserving peace and friendship with them.

ARTICLE IV

The said territory, and the states which may be formed therein, shall forever remain a part of this confederacy of the United States of America, subject to the Articles of Confederation, and to such alterations therein as shall be constitutionally made; and to all the acts and ordinances of the United States in Congress assembled, conformable thereto. The inhabitants and settlers in the said territory shall be subject to pay a part of the Federal debts contracted or to be contracted, and a proportional part of the expenses of government to be apportioned on them by Congress, according to the same common rule and measure by which apportionments thereof shall be made on the other states; and the taxes for paying their proportion shall be laid and levied by the authority and direction of the legislatures of the district, or districts, or new states, as in the original states, within the time agreed upon by the United States in Congress assembled. The legislatures of those districts, or new states, shall never interfere with the primary disposal of the soil by the United States in Congress assembled, nor with any regulations Congress may find necessary for securing the title in such soil to the bona fide purchasers.

No tax shall be imposed on land the property of the United States; and in no case shall nonresident proprietors be taxed higher than residents. The navigable waters leading into the Mississippi and Saint Lawrence and the carrying places between the same shall be common highways and forever free, as well to the inhabitants of the said territory as to the citizens of the United States, and those of any other states that may be admitted into the confederacy, without any tax, impost, or duty therefore.

ARTICLE V

There shall be formed in the said territory not less than three nor more than five states; and the boundaries of the states, as soon as Virginia shall alter her act of cession and consent to the same, shall become fixed and established as follows, to wit: The western state in the said territory shall be bounded by the Mississippi, the Ohio, and the Wabash rivers; a direct line drawn from the Wabash and Post Vincents, due north to the territorial line between the United States and Canada; and by the said territorial line to the Lake of the Woods and Mississippi. The middle state shall be bounded by the said direct line, the Wabash from Post Vincents to the Ohio, by the Ohio, by a direct line drawn due north from the mouth of the Great Miami to the said territorial line, and by the said territorial line. The eastern state shall be bounded by the last-mentioned direct line, the Ohio, Pennsylvania, and the said territorial line: provided, however, and it is further understood and declared, that the boundaries of these three states shall be subject so far to be altered that, if Congress shall hereafter find it expedient, they shall have authority to form one or two states in that part of the said territory which lies north of an east and west line drawn through the southerly bend or extreme of Lake Michigan. And whenever any of the said states shall have sixty thousand free inhabitants therein, such state shall be admitted by its delegates into the Congress of the United States, on an equal footing with the original states in all respects whatever; and shall be at liberty to form a permanent constitution and state government: provided the constitution and government so to be formed shall be republican, and in conformity to the principles contained in these articles, and, so far as it can be consistent with the general interest of the confederacy, such admission shall be allowed at an earlier period, and when there may be a less number of free inhabitants in the state than sixty thousand.

ARTICLE VI

There shall be neither slavery nor involuntary servitude in the said territory, otherwise than in punishment of crimes, whereof the party shall have been duly convicted: provided always that any person escaping into the same, from whom labor or service is lawfully claimed in any one of the original states, such fugitive may be lawfully reclaimed and conveyed to the person claiming his or her labor or service as aforesaid.

Be it ordained by the authority aforesaid that the resolutions of the 23d of April, 1784, relative to the subject of this ordinance, be, and the same are hereby, repealed and declared null and void.

Done by the United States, in Congress assembled, the 13th day of July, in the year of our Lord one thousand seven hundred and eighty-seven, and of their sovereignty and independence the twelfth.

ORIGINS OF U.S. GOVERNMENT

THE VIRGINIA, OR RANDOLPH, PLAN

At the Constitutional Convention in 1787, a deep division emerged between the large, more populated states and the smaller states over the apportionment of the national legislature. The Virginia Plan, also known as the Randolph Plan, after its sponsor, EDMUND JENNINGS RANDOLPH, called for a two-house legislature with representation of each state based on its population or wealth.

ROGER SHERMAN, along with OLIVER ELLSWORTH, proposed the Connecticut, or Great, Compromise. This plan created a bicameral legislature with proportional representation in the lower house and equal representation in the upper house. All revenue measures would originate in the lower house. The compromise was accepted, and the Constitution was soon approved by the convention.

—⟋⟍—

The Virginia, or Randolph, Plan

[Virginia Governor Edmund Randolph] then commented on the difficulty of the crisis, and the necessity of preventing the fulfillment of the prophecies of the American downfall.

He observed that in revising the federal system we ought to inquire 1. into the properties, which such a government ought to possess, 2. the defects of the confederation, 3. the danger of our situation & 4. the remedy.

1. The Character of such a government ought to secure 1. against foreign invasion: 2. against dissensions between members of the Union, or seditions in particular states: 3. to procure to the several States various blessings, of which an isolated situation was incapable: 4. to be able to defend itself against incroachment: & 5. to be paramount to the state constitutions.

* * *

He then proceeded to enumerate the defects: 1. that the confederation produced no security against foreign invasion; congress not being permitted to prevent a war nor to support it by their own authority—Of this he cited many examples; most of which tended to shew, that they could not cause infractions of treaties or of the law of nations, to be punished: that particular states might by their conduct provoke war without controul; and that neither militia nor draughts being fit for defence on such occasions, inlistments only could be successful, and these could not be executed without money. 2. that the federal government could not check the quarrels between states, nor a rebellion in any, not having constitutional power nor means to interpose according to the exigency:

3. that there were many advantages, which the U.S. might acquire, which were not attainable under the confederation—such as a productive impost—counteraction of the commercial regulations of other nations—pushing of commerce ad libitum—etc.etc.

4. that the federal government could not defend itself against the incroachments from the states.

5. that it was not even paramount to the state constitutions, ratified, as it was in ma[n]y of the states.

3. He next reviewed the danger of our situation, appealed to the sense of the best friends of the U.S.—the prospect of anarchy from the laxity of government every where; and to other considerations.

4. He then proceeded to the remedy; the basis of which he said must be the republican principle.

He proposed as conformable to his ideas the following resolutions, which he explained one by one... .

1. Resolved that the Articles of Confederation ought to be so corrected & enlarged as to accomplish the objects proposed by their institution; namely, "common defence, security of liberty, and general welfare."

2. Resolved therefore that the rights of suffrage in the National Legislature ought to be proportioned to the Quotas of contribution, or to the number of free inhabitants, as the one or the other rule may seem best in different cases.

3. Resolved that the National Legislature ought to consist of two branches.

4. Resolved that the members of the first branch of the National Legislature ought to be elected by the people of the several States every for the term of [.]

* * *

5. Resolved that the members of the second branch of the National Legislature ought to be elected by those of the first, out of a proper number of persons nominated by the individual Legislatures[.]

* * *

6. Resolved that each branch ought to possess the right of originating Acts; that the National Legislature ought to be empowered to enjoy the Legislative Rights vested in Congress by the Confederation & moreover to legislate in all cases to which the separate States are incompetent, or in which the harmony of the United States may be interrupted by the exercise of individual Legislation; to negative all laws passed by the several States, contravening in the opinion of the National Legislature the articles of Union; and to call forth the force of the Union against any member of the Union failing to fulfill its duty under the articles thereof.

7. Resolved that a National Executive be instituted; to be chosen by the National Legislature for the term of years, to receive punctually at stated times, a fixed compensation for the services rendered, in which no increase or diminution shall be made so as to affect the Magistracy, existing at the time of increase or diminution, and to be ineligible a second time; and that besides a general authority to execute the National laws, it ought to enjoy the Executive rights vested in Congress by the Confederation.

8. Resolved that the Executive and a convenient number of the National Judiciary, ought to compose a Council of revision with authority to examine every act of the National Legislature before it shall operate, & every act of a particular Legislature before a Negative thereon shall be final; and that the dissent of the said Council shall amount to a rejection, unless the Act of the National Legislature be again passed, or that of a particular Legislature be again negatived by of the members of each branch.

9. Resolved that a National Judiciary be established to consist of one or more supreme tribunals, and of inferior tribunals to be chosen by the National Legislature, to hold their offices during good behaviour; and to receive punctually at stated times fixed compensation for their services, in which no increase or diminution shall be made so as to affect the persons actually in office at the time of such increase or diminution; that the jurisdiction of the inferior tribunals shall be to hear & determine in the first instance, and of the supreme tribunal to hear and determine in the dernier resort, all piracies & felonies on the high seas, captures from an enemy, cases in which foreigners or citizens of other States applying to such jurisdictions may be interested, or which respect the collection of the National revenue; impeachments of any National officers, and questions which may involve the national peace and harmony.

* * *

Mr. Wilson. He wished for vigor in the Government, but he wished that vigorous authority to flow immediately from the legitimate source of all authority. The Government ought to possess not only first the force, but secondly the mind or sense of the people at large. The Legislature ought to be the most exact transcript of the whole Society. Representation is made necessary only because it is impossible for the people to act collectively. The opposition was to be expected he said from the Governments, not from the Citizens of the States. The latter had parted as was observed (by

Mr. King) with all the necessary powers; and it was immaterial to them, by whom they were exercised, if well exercised. The State officers were to be the losers of power. The people he supposed would be rather more attached to the national Government than to the State Governments as being more important in itself, and more flattering to their pride. There is no danger of improper elections if made by large districts. Bad elections proceed from the smallness of the districts which give an opportunity to bad men to intrigue themselves into office.

* * *

Colonel Mason. Under the existing Confederacy, Congress represent the States not the people of the States; their acts operate on the States, not on the individuals. The case will be changed in the new plan of Government. The people will be represented; they ought therefore to choose the Representatives. The requisites in actual representation are that the Representatives should sympathize with their constituents; should think as they think, & feel as they feel; and that for these purposes should even be residents among them. Much he said had been alleged against democratic elections. He admitted that much might be said; but it was to be considered that no Government was free from imperfections & evils; and that improper elections in many instances, were inseparable from Republican Governments. But compare these with the advantage of this Form in favor of the rights of the people, in favor of human nature. He was persuaded there was a better chance for proper elections by the people, if divided into large districts, than by the State Legislatures.

ORIGINS OF U.S. GOVERNMENT

THE VIRGINIA, OR RANDOLPH, PLAN

ORIGINS OF U.S. GOVERNMENT

THE NEW JERSEY, OR PATERSON, PLAN

At the Constitutional Convention in 1787, a deep division emerged between the large, more populated states and the smaller states over the apportionment of the national legislature. WILLIAM PATERSON, a delegate from New Jersey, proposed an apportionment plan on behalf of the small states that would allow each state to have one vote in a unicameral Congress.

ROGER SHERMAN, along with OLIVER ELLSWORTH, proposed the Connecticut, or Great, Compromise. This plan created a bicameral legislature with proportional representation in the lower house and equal representation in the upper house. All revenue measures would originate in the lower house. The compromise was accepted, and the Constitution was soon approved by the convention.

—⁜—

The New Jersey, or Paterson, Plan

Mr. Paterson, said as he had on a former occasion given his sentiments on the plan proposed by Mr. Randolph he would now avoiding repetition as much as possible give his reasons in favor of that proposed by himself. He preferred it because it accorded 1. with the powers of the Convention, 2. with the sentiments of the people. If the confederacy was radically wrong, let us return to our States, and obtain larger powers, not assume them of ourselves.

* * *

… If the sovereignty of the States is to be maintained, the Representatives must be drawn immediately from the States, not from the people: and we have no power to vary the idea of equal sovereignty. The only expedient that will cure the difficulty, is that of throwing the States into Hotchpot.

* * *

Mr. Wilson entered into a contrast of the principal points of the two plans so far he said as there had been time to examine the one last proposed. These points were 1. in the Virginia plan there are two & in some degree three branches in the Legislature: in the plan from N.J. there is to be a single legislature only—2. Representation of the people at large is the basis of the one:—the State Legislatures, the pillars of the other—3. proportional representation prevails in one:—equality of suffrage in the other—4. A single Executive Magistrate is at the head of the one:—a plurality is held out in the other.—5. in the one the majority of the people of the U.S. must prevail:—in the other a minority may prevail. 6. the National Legislature is to make laws in all cases to which the separate States are incompetent &—:—in place of this Congress are to have additional power in a few cases only—7. A negative on the laws of the States:—in place of this coertion to be substituted—8. The Executive to be removable on impeachment & conviction;—in one plan: in the other to be removeable at the instance of majority of the Executives of the States—9. Revision of the laws provided for in one:—no such check in the other—10. inferior national tribunals in one:—none such in the other. 11. In the one jurisdiction of National tribunals to extend etc.—; an appellate jurisdiction only allowed in the other. 12. Here the jurisdiction is to extend to all cases affecting the National peace & harmony: there, a few cases only are marked out. 13. finally the ratification is in this way to be by the people themselves:— in that by the legislative authorities according to the thirteenth article of Confederation.

ORIGINS OF U.S.
GOVERNMENT

THE NEW
JERSEY, OR
PATERSON.
PLAN

ORIGINS OF U.S. GOVERNMENT

CONSTITUTION OF THE UNITED STATES

The U.S. Constitution was drafted in 1787 in Philadelphia by delegates to the CONSTITUTIONAL CONVENTION. The delegates decided soon after their arrival that the ARTICLES OF CONFEDERATION could not be saved through amendment and that an entirely new constitution should be written to replace it. The document that emerged from the convention was the product of a series of compromises.

Once the Constitution had been offered to the states for ratification, critics opposed it on several grounds. Most importantly, they argued that the Constitution created an overly powerful central government that could abuse the rights of citizens and criticized the Framers for failing to include a bill of rights. To win over the opposition, the supporters of the Constitution agreed that the enactment of a bill of rights should be among the business of the first Congress. By June 21, 1788, the requisite nine states had ratified the Constitution. Virginia and New York ratified it a few days later, while North Carolina did so in 1789 and Rhode Island agreed to the Constitution in 1790.

Since the Constitution went into effect in 1789, only twenty-seven amendments have been added to correct deficiencies in the original document or to adapt it to changing needs and principles.

—⁂—

Constitution of the United States

We the People of the United States, in Order to form a more perfect Union, establish Justice, insure domestic Tranquility, provide for the common defence, promote the general Welfare, and secure the Blessings of Liberty to ourselves and our Posterity, do ordain and establish this Constitution for the United States of America.

ARTICLE I

Section 1. All legislative Powers herein granted shall be vested in a Congress of the United States, which shall consist of a Senate and House of Representatives.

Section 2. The House of Representatives shall be composed of Members chosen every second Year by the People of the several States, and the Electors in each State shall have the Qualifications requisite for Electors of the most numerous Branch of the State Legislature.

No Person shall be a Representative who shall not have attained to the Age of twenty five Years, and been seven Years a Citizen of the United States, and who shall not, when elected, be an Inhabitant of that State in which he shall be chosen.

Representatives *and direct Taxes* shall be apportioned among the several States which may be included within this Union, according to their respective Numbers, *which shall be determined by adding to the whole Number of free Persons, including those bound to Service for a Term of Years, and excluding Indians not taxed, three fifths of all other Persons.*[1] The actual Enumeration shall be made within three Years after the first Meeting of the Congress of the United States, and within every subsequent Term of ten Years, in such Manner as they shall by Law direct. The Number of Representatives shall not exceed one for every thirty Thousand, but each State shall have at Least one Representative; *and until such enumerations shall be made, the State of New Hampshire shall be entitled to chuse three, Massachusetts eight, Rhode-Island and Providence Plantations one, Connecticut five, New-York six, New Jersey four, Pennsylvania eight, Delaware one, Maryland six, Virginia ten, North Carolina five, South Carolina five, and Georgia three.*

When vacancies happen in the Representation from any State, the Executive Authority thereof shall issue Writs of Election to fill such Vacancies.

The House of Representatives shall chuse their speaker and other Officers; and shall have the sole Power of Impeachment.

Section 3. The Senate of the United States shall be composed of two Senators from each State, *chosen by the Legislature thereof,*[2] for six Years; and each Senator shall have one Vote.

Immediately after they shall be assembled in Consequence of the first Election, they shall be divided as equally as may be into three Classes. The Seats of the Senators of the first Class shall be vacated at the Expiration of the second Year, of the second Class at the Expiration of the fourth Year, and of the third Class at the Expiration of the sixth Year, so that one third may be chosen every second Year; *and if Vacancies happen by Resignation, or otherwise, during the Recess of the Legislature of any State, the Executive thereof may make temporary Appointments until the next Meeting of the Legislature, which shall then fill such Vacancies.*[3]

No Person shall be a Senator who shall not have attained to the Age of thirty Years, and been nine Years a Citizen of the United States, and who shall not, when elected, be an Inhabitant of that State for which he shall be chosen.

The Vice President of the United States shall be President of the Senate, but shall have no Vote, unless they be equally divided.

The Senate shall chuse their other Officers, and also a President pro tempore, in the Absence of the Vice President, or when he shall exercise the Office of President of the United States.

The Senate shall have the sole Power to try all Impeachments. When sitting for that Purpose, they shall be on Oath or Affirmation. When the President of the United States is tried, the Chief Justice shall preside: And no Person shall be convicted without the concurrence of two thirds of the Members present. Judgment in Cases of Impeachment shall not extend further than to removal from Office, and disqualification to hold and enjoy any Office of honor, Trust or Profit under the United States: but the Party convicted shall nevertheless be liable and subject to Indictment, Trial, Judgment and Punishment, according to law.

Section 4. The Times, Places and Manner of holding Elections for Senators and Representatives, shall be prescribed in each State by the Legislature thereof; but the Congress may at any time by Law make or alter such Regulations, except as to the Places of chusing Senators.

The Congress shall assemble at least once in every Year, *and such Meeting shall be on the first Monday in December,*[4] unless they shall by Law appoint a different Day.

Section 5. Each House shall be the Judge of the Elections, Returns and Qualifications of its own Members, and a Majority of each shall constitute a Quorum to do business; but a smaller Number may adjourn from day to day, and may be authorized to compel the Attendance of absent Members, in such Manner, and under such Penalties as each House may provide.

Each House may determine the Rules of its Proceedings, punish its Members for disorderly Behaviour, and, with the Concurrence of two thirds, expel a Member.

Each House shall keep a journal of its Proceedings, and from time to time publish the same, excepting such Parts as may in their Judgment require Secrecy; and the yeas and Nays of the Members of either House on any question shall, at the Desire of one fifth of those Present, be entered on the Journal.

Neither House, during the Session of Congress, shall, without the Consent of the

---

Source: *The United States Government Manual.*

[1] Provisions that have been changed by amendments or other legislation or have become obsolete have been printed in italic type. The Sixteenth Amendment overturned the provision on direct taxes. The provision on apportionment was overturned by the Thirteenth Amendment, which abolished slavery, and by the Fourteenth Amendment, which stipulated that all persons excluding Indians should be counted. Since 1940 Indians have also been counted.

[2] Changed by the Seventeenth Amendment.

[3] Modified by the Seventeenth Amendment.

[4] Changed by the Twentieth Amendment, Section 2, to January 3.

other, adjourn for more than three days, nor to any other place than that in which the two Houses shall be sitting.

Section 6. The Senators and Representatives shall receive a Compensation for their Services, to be ascertained by Law, and paid out of the Treasury of the United States. They shall in all Cases, except Treason, Felony and Breach of the Peace, be privileged from Arrest during their Attendance at the Session of their respective Houses, and in going to and returning from the same; and for any Speech or Debate in either House, they shall not be questioned in any other Place.

No Senator or Representative shall, during the Time for which he was elected, be appointed to any civil Office under the Authority of the United States, which shall have been created, or the Emoluments whereof shall have been encreased during such time; and no Person holding any Office under the United States, shall be a Member of either House during his Continuance in Office.

Section 7. All Bills for raising Revenue shall originate in the House of Representatives; but the Senate may propose or concur with Amendments as on other Bills.

Every Bill which shall have passed the House of Representatives and the Senate, shall, before it become a Law, be presented to the President of the United States; If he approve he shall sign it, but if not he shall return it, with his Objections to that House in which it shall have originated, who shall enter the Objections at large on their Journal, and proceed to reconsider it. If after such Reconsideration two thirds of that House shall agree to pass the Bill, it shall be sent, together with the Objections, to the other House, by which it shall likewise be reconsidered, and if approved by two thirds of that House, it shall become a Law. But in all such Cases the Votes of both Houses shall be determined by yeas and Nays, and the Names of the Persons voting for and against the Bill shall be entered on the Journal of each House respectively. If any Bill shall not be returned by the President within ten Days (Sundays excepted) after it shall have been presented to him, the Same shall be a Law, in like Manner as if he had signed it, unless the Congress by their Adjournment prevent its Return, in which Case it shall not be a Law.

Every Order, Resolution, or Vote to which the Concurrence of the Senate and House of Representatives may be necessary (except on a question of Adjournment) shall be presented to the President of the United States; and before the Same shall take Effect, shall be approved by him, or being disapproved by him, shall be repassed by two thirds of the Senate and House of Representatives, according to the Rules and Limitations prescribed in the Case of a Bill.

Section 8. The Congress shall have Power To lay and collect Taxes, Duties, Imposts and Excises, to pay the Debts and provide for the common Defence and general Welfare of the United States; but all duties, Imposts and Excises shall be uniform throughout the United States;

To borrow Money on the Credit of the United States;

To regulate Commerce with foreign Nations, and among the several States, *and with the Indian Tribes;*[5]

To establish an uniform Rule of Naturalization, and uniform Laws on the subject of Bankruptcies throughout the United States;

To coin Money, regulate the Value thereof, and of foreign Coin, and fix the Standard of Weights and Measures;

To provide for the Punishment of counterfeiting the Securities and current Coin of the United States;

To establish Post Offices and post Roads;

To promote the Progress of Science and useful Arts, by securing for limited Times to Authors and Inventors exclusive Right to their respective Writings and Discoveries;

To constitute Tribunals inferior to the supreme Court;

To define and punish Piracies and Felonies committed on the high Seas, and Offences against the Law of Nations;

To declare War, *grant Letters of Marque and Reprisal,*[6] and make rules concerning Captures on Land and Water;

To raise and support Armies, but no Appropriation of Money to that Use shall be for a longer Term than two Years;

To provide and maintain a Navy;

---

[5] Formal treaty arrangements with the Indians were abandoned after 1871.

[6] The Declaration of Paris in 1856 and other treaties have outlawed letters of marque and reprisal.

To make rules for the Government and Regulation of the land and naval Forces;

To provide for calling forth the Militia to execute the Laws of the Union, suppress Insurrections and repel Invasions;

To provide for organizing, arming, and disciplining, the Militia, and for governing such Part of them as may be employed in the Service of the United States, reserving to the States respectively, the Appointment of the Officers, and the Authority of training the Militia according to the discipline prescribed by Congress;

To exercise exclusive Legislation in all Cases whatsoever, over such District (not exceeding ten Miles square), as may, by Cession of particular States, and the Acceptance of Congress, become the Seat of the Government of the United States,[7] and to exercise like Authority over all Places purchased by the Consent of the Legislature of the State in which the Same shall be for the Erection of Forts, Magazines, Arsenals, dock-Yards, and other needful Buildings;—And

To make all Laws which shall be necessary and proper for carrying into Execution the foregoing Powers, and all other Powers vested by this Constitution in the Government of the United States, or in any Department or Officer thereof.

Section 9. The Migration or Importation of such Persons as any of the States now existing shall think proper to admit, shall not be prohibited by the Congress prior to the Year one thousand eight hundred and eight, but a Tax or duty may be imposed on such Importation, not exceeding ten dollars for each Person.

The Privilege of the Writ of Habeas Corpus shall not be suspended, unless when in Cases of Rebellion or Invasion the public Safety may require it.

No Bill of Attainder or ex post facto Law shall be passed.

No Capitation, or other direct, Tax shall be laid, unless in Proportion to the Census or Enumeration herein before directed to be taken.[8]

No Tax or Duty shall be laid on Articles exported from any State.

No Preference shall be given by any Regulation of Commerce or Revenue to the Ports of one State over those of another: nor shall Vessels bound to, or from, one State, be obliged to enter, clear, or pay Duties in another.

No money shall be drawn from the Treasury, but in Consequence of Appropriations made by Law; and a regular Statement and Account of the Receipts and Expenditures of all public Money shall be published from time to time.

No Title of Nobility shall be granted by the United States: And no Person holding any Office of Profit or Trust under them, shall, without the Consent of the Congress, accept of any present, Emolument, Office, or Title, of any kind whatever, from any King, Prince, or foreign State.

Section 10. No State shall enter into any Treaty, Alliance, or Confederation; grant Letters of Marque and Reprisal; coin Money; emit Bills of Credit; make any Thing but gold and silver Coin a Tender in Payment of Debts; pass any Bill of Attainder, ex post facto Law, or Law impairing the Obligation of Contracts, or grant any Title of Nobility.

No State shall, without the Consent of the Congress, lay any Imposts or Duties on Imports or Exports, except what may be absolutely necessary for executing its inspection Laws: and the net Produce of all Duties and Imposts, laid by any State on Imports or Exports, shall be for the Use of the Treasury of the United States; and all such Laws shall be subject to the Revision and Control of the Congress.

No State shall, without the Consent of Congress, lay any Duty of Tonnage, keep Troops, or Ships of War in time of Peace, enter into any Agreement or Compact with another State, or with a foreign Power, or engage in War, unless actually invaded, or in such imminent Danger as will not admit of delay.

ARTICLE II

Section 1. The executive Power shall be vested in a President of the United States of America. He shall hold his Office during the Term of four Years, and, together with the Vice President, chosen for the same term, be elected, as follows

Each State shall appoint, in such Manner as the Legislature thereof may direct, a Number of Electors, equal to the whole Number of Senators and Representatives to which the State may be entitled in the Congress: but no Senator or Representative, or Person holding an Office of

---

[7] Modified by the District of Columbia Home Rule Act of 1973.

[8] Changed by the Sixteenth Amendment which permits a Federal income tax, and the Twenty-fourth Amendment, which prohibits Federal pollution.

Trust or Profit under the United States, shall be appointed an Elector.

The Electors shall meet in their respective States, and vote by Ballot for two Persons, of whom one at least shall not be an Inhabitant of the same State with themselves. And they shall make a List of all the Persons voted for, and of the Number of Votes for each; which List they shall sign and certify, and transmit sealed to the Seat of the Government of the United States, directed to the President of the Senate. The President of the Senate shall, in the Presence of the Senate and House of Representatives, open all the Certificates, and the Votes shall then be counted. The Person having the greatest Number of Votes shall be the President, if such Number be a Majority of the whole Number of Electors appointed; and if there be more than one who have such Majority, and have an equal Number of Votes, then the House of Representatives shall immediately chuse by Ballot one of them for President; and if no Person have a Majority, then from the five highest on the List the said House shall in like Manner chuse the President. But in chusing the President, the Votes shall be taken by States, the Representation from each State having one Vote; A quorum for this Purpose shall consist of a Member or Members from two thirds of the States, and a Majority of all the States shall be necessary to a Choice. In every Case, after the Choice of the President, the Person having the greatest Number of Votes of the Electors shall be the Vice President. But if there should remain two or more who have equal Votes, the Senate shall chuse from them by Ballot the Vice President.[9]

The Congress may determine the Time of chusing the Electors, and the Day on which they shall give their Votes; which Day shall be the same throughout the United States.

No Person except a natural born Citizen, *or a Citizen of the United States, at the time of the Adoption of this Constitution,* shall be eligible to the Office of President; neither shall any Person be eligible to that Office who shall not have attained to the Age of thirty five Years, and been fourteen Years a Resident within the United States.

In Case of the Removal of the President from Office, or of his Death, Resignation, or Inability to discharge the Powers and Duties of the said Office, the Same shall devolve on the Vice President, *and the Congress may by Law provide for the Case of Removal, Death, Resignation*

or Inability, both of the President and Vice President, declaring what Officer shall then act as President, and such Officer shall act accordingly, until the Disability be removed, or a President shall be elected.[10]

The President shall, at stated Times, receive for his Services, a Compensation, which shall neither be encreased nor diminished during the Period for which he shall have been elected, and he shall not receive within that Period any other Emolument from the United States, or any of them.

Before he enter on the Execution of his Office, he shall take the following Oath or Affirmation:—"I do solemnly swear (or affirm) that I will faithfully execute the Office of President of the United States, and will to the best of my Ability, preserve, protect and defend the Constitution of the United States."

Section 2. The President shall be Commander in Chief of the Army and Navy of the United States, and of the Militia of the several States, when called into the actual Service of the United States; he may require the Opinion, in writing, of the principal Officer in each of the executive Departments, upon any Subject relating to the Duties of their respective Offices, and he shall have Power to grant Reprieves and Pardons for Offences against the United States, except in Cases of Impeachment.

He shall have Power, by and with the Advice and Consent of the Senate, to make Treaties, provided two thirds of the Senators present concur; and he shall nominate, and by and with the Advice and Consent of the Senate, shall appoint Ambassadors, other public Ministers and Consuls, Judges of the Supreme Court, and all other Officers of the United States, whose Appointments are not herein otherwise provided for, and which shall be established by Law: but the Congress may by Law vest the Appointment of such inferior Officers, as they think proper, in the President alone, in the Courts of Law, or in the Heads of Departments.

The President shall have Power to fill up all Vacancies that may happen during the Recess of the Senate, by granting Commissions which shall expire at the End of their next Session.

---

[9] Modified by the Twelfth and Twenty-third Amendments.
[10] Clarified by the Presidential Succession Act of 1947 and by the Twenty-fifth Amendment.

Section 3. He shall from time to time give to the Congress Information of the State of the Union, and recommend to their Consideration such Measures as he shall judge necessary and expedient; he may, on extraordinary Occasions, convene both Houses, or either of them, and in Case of Disagreement between them, with Respect to the Time of Adjournment, he may adjourn them to such Time as he shall think proper; he shall receive Ambassadors and other public Ministers; he shall take Care that the Laws be faithfully executed, and shall Commission all the Officers of the United States.

Section 4. The President, Vice President and all civil Officers of the United States, shall be removed from Office on Impeachment for, and Conviction of, Treason, Bribery, or other High Crimes and Misdemeanors.

ARTICLE III

Section 1. The judicial Power of the United States, shall be vested in one supreme Court, and in such inferior Courts as the Congress may from time to time ordain and establish. The Judges, both of the supreme and inferior Courts, shall hold their Offices during good Behaviour, and shall, at stated Times, receive for their Services, a Compensation, which shall not be diminished during their Continuance in Office.

Section 2. The judicial Power shall extend to all Cases, in Law and Equity, arising under this Constitution, the Laws of the United States, and Treaties made, or which shall be made, under their Authority;—to all Cases affecting Ambassadors, other public Ministers and Consuls;—to all Cases of admiralty and maritime Jurisdiction;—to Controversies to which the United States shall be a Party;—to Controversies between two or more States; *between a State and Citizens of another State;*[11]— between Citizens of different States;—between Citizens of the same State claiming Lands under Grants of different States, and between a State, or the Citizens thereof, and foreign States, Citizens or Subjects.

In all Cases affecting Ambassadors, other public Ministers and Consuls, and those in which a State shall be Party, the supreme Court shall have original Jurisdiction. In all the other Cases before mentioned, the supreme Court shall have appellate Jurisdiction, both as to Law and Fact, with such Exceptions, and under such Regulations as the Congress shall make.

The Trial of all Crimes, except in Cases of Impeachment, shall be by Jury; and such Trial shall be held in the State where the said Crimes shall have been committed; but when not committed within any State, the Trial shall be at such Place or Places as the Congress may by Law have directed.

Section 3. Treason against the United States, shall consist only in levying War against them, or in adhering to their Enemies, giving them Aid and Comfort. No Person shall be convicted of Treason unless on the Testimony of two Witnesses to the same overt Act, or on Confession in open Court.

The Congress shall have Power to declare the Punishment of Treason, but no Attainder of Treason shall work Corruption of Blood, or Forfeiture except during the Life of the Person attainted.

ARTICLE IV

Section 1. Full Faith and Credit shall be given in each State to the public Acts, Records, and judicial Proceedings of every other State. And the Congress may by general Laws prescribe the Manner in which such Acts, Records, and Proceedings shall be proved, and the Effect thereof.

Section 2. The Citizens of each State shall be entitled to all Privileges and Immunities of Citizens in the several States.

A Person charged in any State with Treason, Felony, or other Crime, who shall flee from Justice, and be found in another State, shall on Demand of the executive Authority of the State from which he fled, be delivered up, to be removed to the State having Jurisdiction of the Crime.

No person held to Service or Labour in one State, under the Laws thereof, escaping into another, shall, in Consequence of any Law or Regulation therein, be discharged from such Service of Labour, but shall be delivered up on Claim of the Party to whom such Service or Labour may be due.[12]

Section 3. New States may be admitted by the Congress into this Union; but no new State shall be formed or erected within the Jurisdiction of any other State; nor any State be formed by the Junction of two or more States, or Parts of States, without the Consent of the Legislatures of the States concerned as well as of the Congress.

---

[11] Changed by the Eleventh Amendment.

[12] Made obsolete by the Thirteenth Amendment.

The Congress shall have Power to dispose of and make all needful Rules and Regulations respecting the Territory or other Property belonging to the United States; and nothing in this Constitution shall be so construed as to Prejudice any Claims of the United States, or of any particular State.

Section 4. The United States shall guarantee to every State in this Union a Republican Form of Government, and shall protect each of them against Invasion; and on Application of the Legislature, or of the Executive (when Legislature cannot be convened) against domestic Violence.

ARTICLE V

The Congress, whenever two thirds of both Houses shall deem it necessary, shall propose Amendments to this Constitution, or, on the Application of the Legislatures of two thirds of the several States, shall call a Convention for proposing Amendments, which, in either Case, shall be valid to all Intents and Purposes, as Part of this Constitution, when ratified by the Legislatures of three fourths of the several States, or by Conventions in three fourths thereof, as the one or the other Mode of Ratification may be proposed by the Congress; Provided *that no Amendment which may be made prior to the Year One thousand eight hundred and eight shall in any Manner affect the first and fourth Clauses in the Ninth Section of the first Article; and* that no State, without its Consent, shall be deprived of its equal Suffrage in the Senate.

ARTICLE VI

All Debts contracted and Engagements entered into, before the Adoption of this Constitution, shall be as valid against the United States under this Constitution, as under the Confederation.

This Constitution, and the Laws of the United States which shall be made in Pursuance thereof; and all Treaties made, or which shall be made, under the Authority of the United States, shall be the supreme Law of the Land; and the Judges in every State shall be bound thereby, any Thing in the Constitution or Laws of any State to the Contrary notwithstanding.

The Senators and Representatives before mentioned, and the Members of the several State Legislatures, and all executive and judicial Officers, both of the United States and of the several States, shall be bound by Oath or Affirmation, to support this Constitution; but no religious Test shall ever be required as a Qualification to any Office or public Trust under the United States.

ARTICLE VII

The Ratification of the Conventions of nine States, shall be sufficient for the Establishment of this Constitution between the States so ratifying the Same.

Done in Convention by the Unanimous Consent of the States present the Seventeenth Day of September in the Year of our Lord one thousand seven hundred and Eighty seven and of the Independence of the United States of America the Twelfth In witness whereof We have hereunto subscribed our Names,

Gº Washington—Presidᵗ and deputy from Virginia

New Hampshire	John Langdon
	Nicholas Gilman
Massachusetts	Nathaniel Gorham
	Rufus King
Connecticut	Wᵐ Samˡ Johnson
	Roger Sherman
New York	Alexander Hamilton
New Jersey	Wil: Livingston
	David Brearley.
	Wᵐ Paterson.
	Jona: Dayton
Pennsylvania	B Franklin
	Thomas Mifflin
	Robᵗ Morris
	Geo. Clymer
	Thoˢ. FitzSimons
	Jared Ingersoll
	James Wilson
	Gouv Morris
Delaware	Geo: Read
	Gunning Bedford jun
	John Dickinson
	Richard Bassett
	Jaco: Broom
Maryland	James McHenry
	Dan of Sᵗ Thoˢ. Jenifer
	Danˡ Carroll

Virginia	John Blair—
	James Madison Jr.
North Carolina	Wm Blount
	Richd Dobbs Spaight.
	Hu Williamson
South Carolina	J. Rutledge
	Charles Cotesworth Pinckney
	Charles Pinckney
	Pierce Butler.
Georgia	William Few
	Abr Baldwin

AMENDMENTS

(The first ten amendments were ratified December 15, 1791, and form what is known as the "Bill of Rights.")

AMENDMENT 1

Congress shall make no law respecting an establishment of religion, or prohibiting the free exercise thereof; or abridging the freedom of speech, or of the press; or the right of the people peaceably to assemble, and to petition the Government for a redress of grievances.

AMENDMENT 2

A well regulated Militia, being necessary to the security of a free State, the right of the people to keep and bear Arms, shall not be infringed.

AMENDMENT 3

No Soldier shall, in time of peace be quartered in any house, without the consent of the Owner, nor in time of war, but in a manner to be prescribed by law.

AMENDMENT 4

The right of the people to be secure in their persons, houses, papers, and effects, against unreasonable searches and seizures, shall not be violated, and no Warrants shall issue, but upon probable cause, supported by Oath or affirmation, and particularly describing the place to be searched, and the persons or things to be seized.

AMENDMENT 5

No person shall be held to answer for a capital, or otherwise infamous crime, unless on a presentment or indictment of a Grand Jury, except in cases arising in the land or naval forces, or in the Militia, when in actual service in time of War or public danger; nor shall any person be subject for the same offence to be twice put in jeopardy of life or limb; nor shall be compelled in any criminal case to be a witness against himself, nor be deprived of life, liberty, or property, without due process of law; nor shall private property be taken for public use, without just compensation.

AMENDMENT 6

In all criminal prosecutions, the accused shall enjoy the right to a speedy and public trial, by an impartial jury of the State and district wherein the crime shall have been committed, which district shall have been previously ascertained by law, and to be informed of the nature and cause of the accusation; to be confronted with the witnesses against him; to have compulsory process for obtaining witnesses in his favor, and to have the Assistance of Counsel for his defence.

AMENDMENT 7

In Suits at common law, where the value in controversy shall exceed twenty dollars, the right of trial by jury shall be preserved, and no fact tried by a jury, shall be otherwise re-examined in any Court of the United States, than according to the rules of the common law.

AMENDMENT 8

Excessive bail shall not be required, nor excessive fines imposed, nor cruel and unusual punishments inflicted.

AMENDMENT 9

The enumeration in the Constitution, of certain rights, shall not be construed to deny or disparage others retained by the people.

AMENDMENT 10

The powers not delegated to the United States by the Constitution, nor prohibited by it to the States, are reserved to the States respectively, or to the people.

AMENDMENT 11

(Ratified February 7, 1795)

The Judicial power of the United States shall not be construed to extend to any suit in law or equity, commenced or prosecuted against one of the United States by Citizens of another State, or by Citizens or Subjects of any Foreign State.

ORIGINS OF U.S. GOVERNMENT

CONSTITUTION OF THE UNITED STATES

AMENDMENT 12

(Ratified July 27, 1804)

The Electors shall meet in their respective states and vote by ballot for President and Vice-President, one of whom, at least, shall not be an inhabitant of the same state with themselves; they shall name in their ballots the person voted for as President, and in distinct ballots the person voted for as Vice-President, and they shall make distinct lists of all persons voted for as President, and of all persons voted for as Vice-President, and of the number of votes for each, which lists they shall sign and certify, and transmit sealed to the seat of the government of the United States, directed to the President of the Senate;—The President of the Senate shall, in the presence of the Senate and House of Representatives, open all the certificates and the votes shall then be counted;—The person having the greatest number of votes for President, shall be the President, if such number be a majority of the whole number of Electors appointed; and if no person have such majority, then from the persons having the highest numbers not exceeding three on the list of those voted for as President, the House of Representatives shall choose immediately, by ballot, the President. But in choosing the President, the votes shall be taken by states, the representation from each state having one vote; a quorum for this purpose shall consist of a member or members from two-thirds of the states, and a majority of all the states shall be necessary to a choice. And if the House of Representatives shall not choose a President whenever the right of choice shall devolve upon them, before the fourth day of March next following, then the Vice-President shall act as President, as in the case of the death or other constitutional disability of the President.—The person having the greatest number of votes as Vice-President, shall be the Vice-President, if such number be a majority of the whole number of Electors appointed, and if no person have a majority, then from the two highest numbers on the list, the Senate shall choose the Vice-President; a quorum for the purpose shall consist of two-thirds of the whole number of Senators, and a majority of the whole number shall be necessary to a choice. But no person constitutionally ineligible to the office of President shall be eligible to that of Vice-President of the United States.

AMENDMENT 13

(Ratified December 6, 1865)

Section 1. Neither slavery nor involuntary servitude, except as a punishment for crime whereof the party shall have been duly convicted, shall exist within the United States, or any place subject to their jurisdiction.

Section 2. Congress shall have power to enforce this article by appropriate legislation.

AMENDMENT 14

(Ratified July 9, 1868)

Section 1. All persons born or naturalized in the United States, and subject to the jurisdiction thereof, are citizens of the United States and of the State wherein they reside. No State shall make or enforce any law which shall abridge the privileges or immunities of citizens of the United States; nor shall any State deprive any person of life, liberty, or property, without due process of law; nor deny to any person within its jurisdiction the equal protection of the laws.

Section 2. Representatives shall be apportioned among the several States according to their respective numbers, counting the whole number of persons in each State, excluding Indians not taxed. But when the right to vote at any election for the choice of electors for President and Vice President of the United States, Representatives in Congress, the Executive and Judicial officers of a State, or the members of the Legislature thereof, is denied to any of the male inhabitants of such State, being twenty-one years of age, and citizens of the United States, or in any way abridged, except for participation in rebellion, or other crime, the basis of representation therein shall be reduced in the proportion which the number of such male citizens shall bear to the whole number of male citizens twenty-one years of age in such State.

Section 3. No person shall be a Senator or Representative in Congress, or elector of President and Vice President, or hold any office, civil or military, under the United States, or under any State, who, having previously taken an oath, as a member of Congress, or as an officer of the United States, or as a member of any State legislature, or as an executive or judicial officer of any State, to support the Constitution of the United States, shall have engaged in insurrection or rebellion against the same, or given aid or comfort to the enemies thereof. But

Congress may by a vote of two-thirds of each House, remove such disability.

Section 4. The validity of the public debt of the United States, authorized by law, including debts incurred for payment of pensions and bounties for services in suppressing insurrection or rebellion, shall not be questioned. But neither the United States nor any State shall assume or pay any debt or obligation incurred in aid of insurrection or rebellion against the United States, or any claim for the loss or emancipation of any slave; but all such debts, obligations and claims shall be held illegal and void.

Section 5. The Congress shall have power to enforce, by appropriate legislation, the provisions of this article.

AMENDMENT 15

(Ratified February 3, 1870)

Section 1. The right of citizens of the United States to vote shall not be denied or abridged by the United States or by any State on account of race, color, or previous condition of servitude.

Section 2. The Congress shall have power to enforce this article by appropriate legislation.

AMENDMENT 16

(Ratified February 3, 1913)

The Congress shall have power to lay and collect taxes on incomes, from whatever source derived, without apportionment among the several States, and without regard to any census or enumeration.

AMENDMENT 17

(Ratified April 8, 1913)

The Senate of the United States shall be composed of two Senators from each State, elected by the people thereof for six years; and each Senator shall have one vote. The electors in each State shall have the qualifications requisite for electors of the most numerous branch of the State legislatures.

When vacancies happen in the representation of any State in the Senate, the executive authority of such State shall issue writs of election to fill such vacancies: Provided, That the legislature of any State may empower the executive thereof to make temporary appointments until the people fill the vacancies by election as the legislature may direct.

This amendment shall not be so construed as to affect the election or term of any Senator chosen before it becomes valid as part of the Constitution.

AMENDMENT 18

(Ratified January 16, 1919. Repealed December 5, 1933, by Amendment 21.)

Section 1. After one year from the ratification of this article the manufacture, sale, or transportation of intoxicating liquors within, the importation thereof into, or the exportation thereof from the United States and all territory subject to the jurisdiction thereof for beverage purposes is hereby prohibited.

Section 2. The Congress and the several States shall have concurrent power to enforce this article by appropriate legislation.

Section 3. This article shall be inoperative unless it shall have been ratified as an amendment to the Constitution by the legislatures of the several States as provided in the Constitution, within seven years from the date of the submission hereof to the States by the Congress.

AMENDMENT 19

(Ratified August 18, 1920)

The right of citizens of the United States to vote shall not be denied or abridged by the United States or by any State on account of sex.

Congress shall have power to enforce this article by appropriate legislation.

AMENDMENT 20

(Ratified January 23, 1933)

Section 1. The terms of the President and Vice President shall end at noon on the 20th day of January, and the terms of Senators and Representatives at noon on the 3d day of January, of the years in which such terms would have ended if this article had not been ratified; and the terms of their successors shall then begin.

Section 2. The Congress shall assemble at least once in every year, and such meeting shall begin at noon on the 3d day of January, unless they shall by law appoint a different day.

Section 3. If, at the time fixed for the beginning of the term of the President, the President elect shall have died, the Vice President elect shall become President. If a President shall not have been chosen before the time fixed for the beginning of his term, or if the President elect shall have failed to qualify, then the Vice President elect shall act as President until a President shall have qualified; and the Congress may by law provide for the case wherein neither a President elect nor a Vice President elect shall have qualified, declaring who shall then act as President, or the manner in which one who is to act shall be selected, and such person shall act accordingly until a President or Vice President shall have qualified.

Section 4. The Congress may by law provide for the case of the death of any of the persons from whom the House of Representatives may choose a President whenever the right of choice shall have devolved upon them, and for the case of the death of any of the persons from whom the Senate may choose a Vice President whenever the right of choice shall have devolved upon them.

Section 5. Sections 1 and 2 shall take effect on the 15th day of October following the ratification of this article.

Section 6. This article shall be inoperative unless it shall have been ratified as an amendment to the Constitution by the legislatures of three-fourths of the several States within seven years from the date of its submission.

AMENDMENT 21

(Ratified December 5, 1933)

Section 1. The eighteenth article of amendment to the Constitution of the United States is hereby repealed.

Section 2. The transportation or importation into any State, Territory, or possession of the United States for delivery or use therein of intoxicating liquors, in violation of the laws thereof, is hereby prohibited.

Section 3. This article shall be inoperative unless it shall have been ratified as an amendment to the Constitution by conventions in the several States, as provided in the Constitution, within seven years from the date of the submission hereof to the States by the Congress.

AMENDMENT 22

(Ratified February 27, 1951)

Section 1. No person shall be elected to the office of the President more than twice, and no person who has held the office of President, or acted as President, for more than two years of a term to which some other person was elected President shall be elected to the office of the President more than once. But this Article shall not apply

to any person holding the office of President when this Article was proposed by the Congress, and shall not prevent any person who may be holding the office of President, or acting as President, during the term within which this Article becomes operative from holding the office of President or acting as President during the remainder of such term.

Section 2. This article shall be inoperative unless it shall have been ratified as an amendment to the Constitution by the legislatures of three-fourths of the several States within seven years from the date of its submission to the States by the Congress.

AMENDMENT 23

(Ratified March 29, 1961)

Section 1. The District constituting the seat of Government of the United States shall appoint in such manner as the Congress may direct:

A number of electors of President and Vice President equal to the whole number of Senators and Representatives in Congress to which the District would be entitled if it were a State, but in no event more than the least populous State; they shall be in addition to those appointed by the States, but they shall be considered, for the purposes of the election of President and Vice President, to be electors appointed by a State; and they shall meet in the District and perform such duties as provided by the twelfth article of amendment.

Section 2. The Congress shall have power to enforce this article by appropriate legislation.

AMENDMENT 24

(Ratified January 23, 1964)

Section 1. The right of citizens of the United States to vote in any primary or other election for President or Vice President, for electors for President or Vice President, or for Senator or Representative in Congress, shall not be denied or abridged by the United States or any State by reason of failure to pay any poll tax or other tax.

Section 2. The Congress shall have power to enforce this article by appropriate legislation.

AMENDMENT 25

(Ratified February 10, 1967)

Section 1. In case of the removal of the President from office or of his death or resignation, the Vice President shall become President.

Section 2. Whenever there is a vacancy in the office of the Vice President, the President shall nominate a Vice President who shall take office upon confirmation by a majority vote of both Houses of Congress.

Section 3. Whenever the President transmits to the President pro tempore of the Senate and the Speaker of the House of Representatives his written declaration that he is unable to discharge the powers and duties of his office, and until he transmits to them a written declaration to the contrary, such powers and duties shall be discharged by the Vice President as Acting President.

Section 4. Whenever the Vice President and a majority of either the principal officers of the executive departments or of such other body as Congress may by law provide, transmit to the President pro tempore of the Senate and the Speaker of the House of Representatives their written declaration that the President is unable to discharge the powers and duties of his office, the Vice President shall immediately assume the powers and duties of the office as Acting President.

Thereafter, when the President transmits to the President pro tempore of the Senate and the Speaker of the House of Representatives his written declaration that no inability exists, he shall resume the powers and duties of his office unless the Vice President and a majority of either the principal officers of the executive department or of such other body as Congress may by law pro- vide, transmit within four days to the President pro tempore of the Senate and the Speaker of the House of Representatives their written declaration that the President is unable to discharge the powers and duties of his office. Thereupon Congress shall decide the issue, assembling within forty-eight hours for that purpose if not in session. If the Congress, within twenty-one days after receipt of the latter written declaration, or, if Congress is not in session, within twenty-one days after Congress is required to assemble, determines by two-thirds vote of both Houses that the President is unable to discharge the powers and duties of his office, the Vice President shall continue to discharge the same as Acting President; otherwise, the President shall resume the powers and duties of his office.

AMENDMENT 26

(Ratified July 1, 1971)

Section 1. The right of citizens of the United States, who are eighteen years of age or older, to vote shall not be denied or abridged by the United States or by any State on account of age.

Section 2. The Congress shall have the power to enforce this article by appropriate legislation.

AMENDMENT 27

(Ratified May 7, 1992)

No law, varying the compensation for the services of the Senators and Representatives, shall take effect, until an election of Represen- tatives shall have intervened.

ORIGINS OF U.S. GOVERNMENT

CONSTITUTION OF THE UNITED STATES

ORIGINS OF U.S. GOVERNMENT

BILL OF RIGHTS

The Bill of Rights, which consists of the first ten amendments to the U.S. Constitution, was drafted by the first Congress of the new government in 1789 and went into effect on December 15, 1791, when Virginia became the eleventh state to ratify the amendments.

The Bill of Rights followed a tradition in Anglo-American law of drawing up a list of basic rights to which all the people in the state were entitled. The English Bill of Rights, enacted in 1689, included the right to petition the government with grievances, the right to trial by jury, and the right not to be subjected to cruel and unusual punishments. In 1774 the First Continental Congress drew up a Declaration of Rights, which included such liberties as freedom of the press and a prohibition against standing armies in peacetime.

The VIRGINIA DECLARATION OF RIGHTS, enacted in 1776, quickly became the model for other states. By 1781 eight states had enacted bills of rights, and four others had included statements guaranteeing individual rights either in the prefaces to their constitutions or in supplementary statutes. The ARTICLES OF CONFEDERATION did not include a bill of rights, however. The drafters of the Articles believed that the protection of individual rights was a state responsibility.

At the 1787 CONSTITUTIONAL CONVENTION, EDMUND RANDOLPH and GEORGE MASON of Virginia and Elbridge Gerry of Massachusetts sought unsuccessfully to include a bill of rights in the new constitution. Most delegates took the view that the state bills of rights would continue to protect individual rights at the state level and that

Congress would resist any attempts to infringe upon individual liberties at the federal level.

When the lack of a bill of rights became an issue in the ratification process, James Madison promised that the first Congress would enact a bill of rights as part of its business. As a member of the first House of Representatives, Madison reminded the members of this pledge. He drafted much of the final document, using Mason's VIRGINIA DECLARATION OF RIGHTS as a model.

The Bill of Rights plays a central role in the protection of civil liberties and civil rights. When enacted, the ten amendments applied only to the actions of the federal government. In a long series of decisions, however, the U.S. Supreme Court has ruled that almost all the provisions in the Bill of Rights also apply to the states. Therefore, the Bill of Rights safeguards the basic rights of individuals from encroachment by all levels of government.

—⟋⟍—

Bill of Rights

AMENDMENT 1

Congress shall make no law respecting an establishment of religion, or prohibiting the free exercise thereof; or abridging the freedom of speech, or of the press; or the right of the people peaceably to assemble, and to petition the Government for a redress of grievances.

Source: *The United States Government Manual.*

AMENDMENT 2

A well regulated Militia, being necessary to the security of a free State, the right of the people to keep and bear Arms, shall not be infringed.

AMENDMENT 3

No Soldier shall, in time of peace be quartered in any house, without the consent of the Owner, nor in time of war, but in a manner to be prescribed by law.

AMENDMENT 4

The right of the people to be secure in their persons, houses, papers, and effects, against unreasonable searches and seizures, shall not be violated, and no Warrants shall issue, but upon probable cause, supported by Oath or affirmation, and particularly describing the place to be searched, and the persons or things to be seized.

AMENDMENT 5

No person shall be held to answer for a capital, or otherwise infamous crime, unless on a presentment or indictment of a Grand jury, except, in cases arising in the land or naval forces, or in the Militia, when in actual service in time of War or public danger; nor shall any person be subject for the same offence to be twice put in jeopardy of life or limb; nor shall be compelled in any criminal case to be a witness against himself, nor be deprived of life, liberty, or property, without due process of law; nor shall private property be taken for public use, without just compensation.

AMENDMENT 6

In all criminal prosecutions, the accused shall enjoy the right to a speedy and public trial, by an impartial jury of the State and district wherein the crime shall have been committed, which district shall have been previously ascertained by law, and to be informed of the nature and cause of the accusation; to be confronted with the witnesses against him; to have compulsory process for obtaining Witnesses in his favor, and to have the Assistance of Counsel for his defence.

AMENDMENT 7

In Suits at common law, where the value in controversy shall exceed twenty dollars, the right of trial by jury shall be preserved, and no fact tried by a jury, shall be otherwise reexamined in any Court of the United States, than according to the rules of the common law.

AMENDMENT 8

Excessive bail shall not be required, nor excessive fines imposed, nor cruel and unusual punishments inflicted.

AMENDMENT 9

The enumeration in the Constitution, of certain rights, shall not be construed to deny or disparage others retained by the people.

AMENDMENT 10

The powers not delegated to the United States by the Constitution, nor prohibited by it to the States, are reserved to the States respectively, or to the people.

ORIGINS OF U.S. GOVERNMENT

BILL OF RIGHTS

ORIGINS OF U.S. GOVERNMENT

FEDERALIST, NUMBER 10

James Madison, 1787

The *Federalist Papers* were published by ALEXANDER HAMILTON, JAMES MADISON, and JOHN JAY to help convince the citizens of New York that ratification of the U.S. Constitution was justified. The essays not only discuss many of the Constitution's provisions but also elaborate on the authors' own vision of the proper role of a national government.

Madison's first essay, *Federalist,* no. 10, is the most frequently quoted of the group. In it, Madison discussed the idea of political factions. At the time it was commonly agreed that democratic society needed to prevent factions because they would ultimately undermine the government and lead to violence. Madison agreed that factions can divide government but came to the opposite conclusion: the more factions, the better. In Madison's view more factions would make it less likely that any one party or coalition of parties would be able to gain control of government and invade the rights of other citizens. The system of checks and balances contained in the Constitution was part of Madison's plan for frustrating factions.

—m—

Federalist, Number 10

Among the numerous advantages promised by a well constructed Union, none deserve to be more accurately developed than its tendency to break and control the violence of faction. The friend of popular governments, never finds himself so much alarmed for their character and fate, as when he contemplates their propensity to this dangerous vice. He will not fail therefore to set a due value on any plan which, without violating the principles to which he is attached, provides a proper cure to it. The instability, injustice and confusion introduced into the public councils, have in truth been the mortal diseases under which popular governments have every where perished; as they continue to be the favorite and fruitful topics from which the adversaries to liberty derive their most specious declamations. The valuable improvements made by the American Constitutions on the popular models, both ancient and modern, cannot certainly be too much admired; but it would be an unwarrantable partiality, to contend that they have as effectually obviated the danger on this side as was wished and expected. Complaints are every where heard from our most considerate and virtuous citizens, equally the friends of public and private faith, and of public and personal liberty; that our governments are too unstable; that the public good is disregarded in the conflicts of rival parties; and that measures are too often decided, not according to the rules of justice, and the rights of the minor party; but by the superior force of an interested and overbearing majority. However anxiously we may wish that these complaints had no foundation, the evidence of known facts will not permit us to deny that they are in some degree true. It will be found indeed, on a candid review of our situation, that some of the distresses under which we labor, have been erroneously charged on the operation of our governments; but it will be found, at the same time, that other causes will not alone account for many of our heaviest misfortunes; and particularly, for the prevailing and increasing distrust of public engagements, and alarm for private rights, which are echoed from one end of the continent to the other. These must be chiefly, if not wholly, effects of the unsteadiness and injustice, with which a factious spirit has tainted our public administrations.

By a faction I understand a number of citizens, whether amounting to a majority or minority of the whole, who are united and actuated by some common impulse of passion, or of interest, adverse to the rights of other citizens, or to the permanent and aggregate interest of the community.

* * *

As long as the reason of man continues fallible, and he is at liberty to exercise it, different opinions will be formed. As long as the connection subsists between his reason and his self-love, his opinions and passions will have a reciprocal influence on each other; and the former will be objects to which the latter will attach themselves. The diversity in the faculties of men from which the rights of property originate, is not less an insuperable obstacle to a uniformity of interests. The protection of these faculties is the first object of Government. From the protection of different and unequal faculties of acquiring property, the possession of different degrees and kinds of property immediately results; and from the influence of these on the sentiments and views of the respective proprietors, ensues a division of the society into different interests and parties.

The latent causes of faction are thus sown in the nature of man; and we see them every where brought into different degrees of activity, according to the different circumstances of civil society. A zeal for different opinions concerning religion, concerning Government and many other points, as well of speculation as of practice; and attachment to different leaders ambitiously contending for pre-eminence and power; or to persons of other descriptions whose fortunes have been interesting to the human passions, have in turn divided mankind into parties, inflamed them with mutual animosity, and rendered them much more disposed to vex and oppress each other, than to co-operate for their common good. So strong is this propensity of mankind to fall into mutual animosities, that where no substantial occasion presents itself, the most frivolous and fanciful distinctions have

been sufficient to kindle their unfriendly passions, and excite their most violent conflicts. But the most common and durable source of factions, has been the various and unequal distribution of property. Those who hold, and those who are without property, have ever formed distinct interests in society. Those who are creditors, and those who are debtors, fall under a like discrimination. A landed interest, a manufacturing interest, a mercantile interest, a monied interest, with many lesser interests, grow up of necessity in civilized nations, and divide them into different classes, actuated by different sentiments and views. The regulation of these various and interfering interests forms the principal task of modern Legislation, and involves the spirit of party and faction in the necessary and ordinary operations of Government.

* * *

The inference to which we are brought, is, that the causes of faction cannot be removed; and that relief is only to be sought in the means of controlling its effects.

If a faction consists of less than a majority, relief is supplied by the republican principle, which enables the majority to defeat its sinister views by regular vote: It may clog the administration, it may convulse the society; but it will be unable to execute and mask its violence under the forms of the Constitution. When a majority is included in a faction, the form of popular government on the other hand enables it to sacrifice to its ruling passion or interest, both the public good and the rights of other citizens. To secure the public good, and private rights, against the danger of such a faction, and at the same time to preserve the spirit and the form of popular government, is then the great object to which our enquiries are directed: Let me add that it is the great desideratum, by which alone this form of government can be rescued from the opprobrium under which it has so long labored, and be recommended to the esteem and adoption of mankind.

By what means is this object attainable? Evidently by one of two only. Either the existence of the same passion or interest in a majority at the same time, must be prevented; or the majority, having such co-existent passion or interest, must be rendered, by their number and local situation, unable to concert and carry into effect schemes of oppression. If the impulse and the opportunity be suffered to coincide, we well know that neither moral nor religious motives can be relied on as an

ORIGINS OF U.S. GOVERNMENT

FEDERALIST, NUMBER 10

adequate control. They are not found to be such on the injustice and violence of individuals, and lose their efficacy in proportion to the number combined together; that is, in proportion as their efficacy becomes needful.

From this view of the subject, it may be concluded, that a pure Democracy, by which I mean, a Society, consisting of a small number of citizens, who assemble and administer the Government in person, can admit of no cure for the mischiefs of faction. A common passion or interest will, in almost every case, be felt by a majority of the whole; a communication and concert results from the form of Government itself; and there is nothing to check the inducements to sacrifice the weaker party, or an obnoxious individual. Hence it is, that such Democracies have ever been spectacles of turbulence and contention; have ever been found incompatible with personal security, or the rights of property; and have in general been as short in their lives, as they have been violent in their deaths. Theoretic politicians, who have patronized this species of Government, have erroneously supposed, that by reducing mankind to a perfect equality in their political rights, they would, at the same time, be perfectly equalized and assimilated in their possessions, their opinions, and their passions.

A Republic, by which I mean a Government in which the scheme of representation takes place, opens a different prospect, and promises the cure for which we are seeking. Let us examine the points in which it varies from pure Democracy, and we shall comprehend both the nature of the cure, and the efficacy which it must derive from the Union.

The two great points of difference between a Democracy and a Republic are, first, the delegation of the Government, in the latter, to a small number of citizens elected by the rest: secondly, the greater number of citizens, and greater sphere of country, over which the latter may be extended.

The effect of the first difference is, on the one hand to refine and enlarge the public views, by passing them through the medium of a chosen body of citizens, whose wisdom may best discern the true interest of their country, and whose patriotism and love of justice, will be least likely to sacrifice it to temporary or partial considerations. Under such a regulation, it may well happen that the public voice pronounced by the representatives of the people, will be more con-

sonant to the public good, than if pronounced by the people themselves convened for the purpose. On the other hand, the effect may be inverted. Men of factious tempers, of local prejudices, or of sinister designs, may by intrigue, by corruption or by other means, first obtain the suffrages, and then betray the interests of the people. The question resulting is, whether small or extensive Republics are most favorable to the election of proper guardians of the public weal: and it is clearly decided in favor of the latter by two obvious considerations.

In the first place it is to be remarked that however small the Republic may be, the Representatives must be raised to a certain number, in order to guard against the cabals of a few; and that however large it may be, they must be limited to a certain number, in order to guard against the confusion of a multitude. Hence the number of Representatives in the two cases, not being in proportion to that of the Constituents, and being proportionally greatest in the small Republic, it follows, that if the proportion of fit characters, be not less, in the large than in the small Republic, the former will present a greater option, and consequently a greater possibility of a fit choice.

In the next place, as each Representative will be chosen by a greater number of citizens in the large than in the small Republic, it will be more difficult for unworthy candidates to practise with success the vicious arts, by which elections are too often carried; and the suffrages of the people being more free, will be more likely to centre on men who possess the most attractive merit, and the most diffusive and established characters.

* * *

The other point of difference is, the greater number of citizens and extent of territory which may be brought within the compass of Republican, than of Democratic Government; and it is this circumstance principally which renders factious combinations less to be dreaded in the former, than in the latter. The smaller the society, the fewer probably will be the distinct parties and interests composing it; the fewer the distinct parties and interests, the more frequently will a majority be found of the same party; and the smaller the number of individuals composing a majority, and the smaller the compass within which they are placed, the more easily will they concert and execute their plans of oppression. Extend the sphere, and you take in a greater variety of parties and interests; you make it less probable that a majority of the whole will have a common motive to invade the rights of other citizens; or if such a common motive exists, it will be more difficult for all who feel it to discover their own strength, and to act in unison with each other.

ORIGINS OF U.S. GOVERNMENT

FEDERALIST, NUMBER 10

ORIGINS OF U.S. GOVERNMENT

FEDERALIST, NUMBER 78

Alexander Hamilton, 1788

The *Federalist Papers* were published by ALEXANDER HAMILTON, JAMES MADISON, and JOHN JAY to help convince the citizens of New York that ratification of the U.S. Constitution was justified. The essays not only discuss many of the Constitution's provisions but also elaborate on the authors' own vision of the proper role of a national government.

In *Federalist,* no. 78, Hamilton discussed the role of the judiciary. He defended the concept of judicial review, which was generally regarded as neither legitimate nor desirable by most political leaders. Hamilton also defended the independence of the judiciary and the need for judicial discretion.

—ɯ—

Federalist, Number 78

According to the plan of the convention, all the judges who may be appointed by the United States are to hold their offices during good behaviour, which is conformable to the most approved of the state constitutions; and among the rest, to that of this state. Its propriety having been drawn into question by the adversaries of that plan, is no light symptom of the rage for objection which disorders their imaginations and judgments. The standard of good behaviour for the continuance in office of the judicial magistracy is certainly one of the most valuable of the modern improvements in the practice of government. In a monarchy it is an excellent barrier to the depotism of the prince: In a republic it is a no less excellent barrier to the encroachments and oppressions of the representative body. And it is the best expedient which can be devised in any government, to secure a steady, upright and impartial administration of the laws.

Whoever attentively considers the different departments of power must perceive, that in a government in which they are separated from each other, the judiciary, from the nature of its functions, will always be the least dangerous to the political rights of the constitution; because it will be least in a capacity to annoy or injure them. The executive not only dispenses the honors, but holds the sword of the community. The legislature not only commands the purse, but prescribes the rules by which the duties and rights of every citizen are to be regulated. The judiciary on the contrary has no influence over either the sword or the purse, no direction either of the strength or of the wealth of the society, and can take no active resolution whatever. It may truly be said to have neither Force nor Will, but merely judgment; and must ultimately depend upon the aid of the executive arm even for the efficacy of its judgments.

This simple view of the matter suggests several important consequences. It proves incontestibly that the judiciary is beyond comparison the weakest of the three departments of power; that it can never attack with success either of the other two; and that all possible care is requisite to enable it to defend itself against their attacks. It equally proves, that though individual oppression may now and then proceed from the courts of justice, the general liberty of the people can never be endangered from that quarter: I mean, so long as the judiciary remains truly distinct from both the legislative and executive. For I agree that "there is no liberty, if the power of judging be not separated from the legislative and executive powers." And it proves, in the last place, that as liberty can have nothing to fear from the judiciary alone, but would have everything to fear from its union with either of the other departments; that as all the effects of such an union must ensue from a dependence of the former on the latter, notwithstanding a nominal and apparent separation; that as from the natural feebleness of the judiciary, it is in continual jeopardy of being overpowered, awed or influenced by its coordinate branches; and that as nothing can contribute so much to its firmness and independence, as permanency in office, this quality may therefore be justly regarded as an indispensable ingredient in its constitution; and in a great measure as the citadel of the public justice and the public security.

The complete independence of the courts of justice is peculiarly essential in a limited constitution. By a limited constitution I understand one which contains certain specified exceptions to the legislative authority; such for instance as that it shall pass no bills of attainder, no ex post facto laws, and the like. Limitations of this kind can be preserved in practice no other way than through the medium of the courts of justice; whose duty it must be to declare all acts contrary to the manifest tenor of the constitution void. Without this, all the reservations of particular rights or privileges would amount to nothing.

Some perplexity respecting the right of the courts to pronounce legislative acts void, because contrary to the constitution, has arisen from an imagination that the doctrine would imply a superiority of the judiciary to the legislative power. It is urged that the authority which can declare the acts of another void, must necessarily be superior to the one whose acts may be declared void. As this doctrine is of great importance in all the American constitutions, a brief discussion of the grounds on which it rests cannot be unacceptable.

There is no position which depends on clearer principles, than that every act of a delegated authority, contrary to the tenor of the commission under which it is exercised, is void. No legislative act therefore contrary to the constitution can be valid. To deny this would be to

affirm that the deputy is greater than his principal; that the servant is above his master; that the representatives of the people are superior to the people themselves; that men acting by virtue of powers may do not only what their powers do not authorise, but what they forbid.

If it be said that the legislative body are themselves the constitutional judges of their own powers, and that the construction they put upon them is conclusive upon the other departments, it may be answered, that this cannot be the natural presumption, where it is not to be collected from any particular provisions in the constitution. It is not otherwise to be supposed that the constitution could intend to enable the representatives of the people to substitute their will to that of their constituents. It is far more rational to suppose that the courts were designed to be an intermediate body between the people and the legislature, in order, among other things, to keep the latter within the limits assigned to their authority. The interpretation of the laws is the proper and peculiar province of the courts. A constitution is in fact, and must be, regarded by the judges as a fundamental law. It therefore belongs to them to ascertain its meaning as well as the meaning of any particular act proceeding from the legislative body. If there should happen to be an irreconcileable variance between the two, that which has the superior obligation and validity ought of course to be preferred; or in other words, the constitution ought to be preferred to the statute, the intention of the people to the intention of their agents.

Nor does this conclusion by any means suppose a superiority of the judicial to the legislative power. It only supposes that the power of the people is superior to both; and that where the will of the legislature declared in its statutes, stands in opposition to that of the people declared in the constitution, the judges ought to be governed by the latter, rather than the former. They ought to regulate their decisions by the fundamental laws, rather than by those which are not fundamental.

This exercise of judicial discretion in determining between two contradictory laws, is exemplified in a familiar instance. It not uncommonly happens, that there are two statutes existing at one time, clashing in whole or in part with each other, and neither of them containing any repealing clause or expression. In such a case, it is the province of the courts to liquidate and fix their meaning and operation; so far as they can by any fair construction be reconciled to each other; reason and law conspire to dictate that this should be done. Where this is impracticable, it becomes a matter of necessity to give effect to one, in exclusion of the other. The rule which has obtained in the courts for determining their relative validity is that the last in order of time shall be preferred to the first. But this is mere rule of construction, not derived from any positive law, but from the nature and reason of the thing. It is a rule not enjoined upon the courts by legislative provision, but adopted by themselves, as consonant to truth and propriety, for the direction of their conduct as interpreters of the law. They thought it reasonable, that between the interfering acts of an equal authority, that which was the last indication of its will, should have the preference.

But in regard to the interfering acts of a superior and subordinate authority, of an original and derivative power, the nature and reason of the thing indicate the converse of that rule as proper to be followed. They teach us that the prior act of a superior ought to be preferred to the subsequent act of an inferior and subordinate authority; and that, accordingly, whenever a particular statute contravenes the constitution, it will be the duty of the judicial tribunals to adhere to the latter, and disregard the former.

It can be of no weight to say, that the courts on the pretense of a repugnancy, may substitute their own pleasure to the constitutional intentions of the legislature. This might as well happen in the case of two contradictory statutes; or it might as well happen in every adjudication upon any single statute. The courts must declare the sense of the law; and if they should be disposed to exercise will instead of judgment, the consequence would equally be the substitution of their pleasure to that of the legislative body. The observation, if it proved anything, would prove that there ought to be no judges distinct from that body.

If then the courts of justice are to be considered as the bulwarks of a limited constitution against legislative encroachments, this consideration will afford a strong argument for the permanent tenure of judicial offices, since nothing will contribute so much as this to that independent spirit in the judges, which must be essential to the faithful performance of so arduous a duty.

This independence of the judges is equally requisite to guard the constitution and the rights of individuals from the effects of those ill humours which the arts of designing men, or the influence of particular conjunctures, sometimes disseminate among the people themselves, and which, though they speedily give place to better information and more deliberate reflection, have a tendency in the mean time to occasion dangerous innovations in the government, and serious oppressions of the minor party in the community. Though I trust the friends of the proposed constitution will never concur with its enemies in questioning that fundamental principle of republican government, which admits the right of people to alter or abolish the established constitution whenever they find it inconsistent with their happiness; yet it is not to be inferred from this principle, that the representatives of the people, whenever a momentary inclination happens to lay hold of a majority of their constituents incompatible with the provisions in the existing constitution, would on that account be justifiable in a violation of those provisions; or that the courts would be under a greater obligation to connive at infractions in this shape, than when they had proceeded wholly from the cabals of the representative body. Until the people have by some solemn and authoritative act annulled or changed the established form, it is binding upon themselves collectively, as well as individually; and no presumption, or even knowledge of their sentiments, can warrant their representatives in a departure from it, prior to such an act.

ORIGINS OF U.S. GOVERNMENT

THE VIRGINIA AND KENTUCKY RESOLVES

In 1798 JAMES MADISON wrote the VIRGINIA RESOLVES, and THOMAS JEFFERSON wrote the KENTUCKY RESOLVES. These legislative resolutions challenged the legitimacy of the federal ALIEN AND SEDITION ACTS of 1798. Enacted as internal security laws, these acts restricted aliens and limited freedom of the press on the assumption that the United States might soon be at war with France.

Madison and Jefferson argued that Congress did not have the express constitutional authority to deport aliens nor to prosecute persons for seditious libel. They asserted in the resolves that state legislatures had the right to determine whether the federal government was complying with the mandate of the Constitution. In the second of the Kentucky Resolves, Jefferson contended that the "sovereign and independent states" had the right to "interpose" themselves between their citizens and improper national legislative actions and to "nullify" acts of Congress they deemed unconstitutional.

The resolves became an important component of Southern political resistance in the nineteenth century. These ideas ultimately became the legal justification for the secession of the Southern states from the Union in 1861.

—⁂—

The Virginia and Kentucky Resolves

KENTUCKY RESOLVE

November 10, 1798

1. Resolved, That the several states composing the United States of America are not united on the principle of unlimited submission to their general government; but that, by compact, under the style and title of a Constitution for the United States, and of amendments thereto, they constituted a general government for special purposes, delegated to that government certain definite powers, reserving, each state to itself, the residuary mass of right to their own self-government; and that whensoever the general government assumes undelegated powers, its acts are unauthoritative, void, and no force; that to this compact each state acceded as a state, and is an integral party; that this government, created by this compact, was not made the exclusive or final judge of the extent of the powers delegated to itself, since that would have made its discretion, and not the Constitution, the measure of its powers; but that, as in all other cases of compact among parties having no common judge, each party has an equal right to judge for itself, as well of infractions as the mode and measure of redress.

2. Resolved, That the Constitution of the United States having delegated to Congress a power to punish treason, counterfeiting the securities and current coin of the United States, piracies and felonies committed on the high seas, and offences against the laws of nations, and no other crimes whatever; and it being true, as a general principle, and one of the amendments to the Constitution having also declared "that the powers not delegated to the United States by the Constitution, nor prohibited by it to the states, are reserved to the states respec-

tively, or to the people,"—therefore, also, the [Sedition Act] (and all other their acts which assume to create, define, or punish crimes other than those enumerated in the Constitution,) are altogether void, and of no force; and that the power to create, define, and punish, such other crimes is reserved, and of right appertains, solely and exclusively, to the respective states, each within its own territory.

3. Resolved, That it is true, as a general principle, and is also expressly declared by one of the amendments to the Constitution, that "the powers not delegated to the United States by the Constitution, nor prohibited by it to the states, are reserved to the states respectively, or to the people;" and that, no power over the freedom of religion, freedom of speech, or freedom of the press, being delegated to the United States by the Constitution, nor prohibited by it to the states, all lawful powers respecting the same did of right remain, and were reserved to the states, or to the people; . . . . That therefore the act of the Congress of the United States, passed on the 14th of July, 1798, entitled "An Act in Addition to the Act entitled 'An Act for the Punishment of certain Crimes against the United States,'" which does abridge the freedom of the press, is not law, but is altogether void, and of no force.

* * *

7. Resolved, That the construction applied by the general government [of the necessary-and-proper clause] goes to the destruction of all the limits prescribed to their power by the Constitution; that words meant by that instrument to be subsidiary only to the execution of the limited powers, ought not to be so construed as themselves to give unlimited powers, nor a part so to be taken as to destroy the whole residue of the instrument[.]

* * *

In questions of power, then, let no more be said of confidence in man, but bind him down from mischief by the chains of the Constitution. That this commonwealth does therefore call on its co-states for an expression of their sentiments on the acts concerning aliens, and for the punishment of certain crimes herein before specified, plainly declaring whether these acts are or are not authorized by the federal compact. And it doubts not that their sense will be so announced as to prove their attachment to limited government, whether general or particular,

and that the rights and liberties of their co-states will be exposed to no dangers by remaining embarked on a common bottom with their own; but they will concur with this commonwealth in considering the said acts as so palpably against the Constitution as to amount to an undisguised declaration, that the compact is not meant to be the measure of the powers of the general government, but that it will proceed in the exercise over these states of all powers whatsoever. That they will view this as seizing the rights of the states, and consolidating them in the hands of the general government, with a power assumed to bind the states, not merely in cases made federal, but in all cases whatsoever, by laws made not with their consent, but by others against their consent; that this would be to surrender the form of government we have chosen, and live under one deriving its powers from its own will, and not from our authority; and that the co-states, recurring to their natural rights not made federal, will concur in declaring these void and of no force, and will each unite with this commonwealth in requesting their repeal at the next session of Congress.

Thomas Jefferson

VIRGINIA RESOLVE
December 21, 1798

That this Assembly doth explicitly and peremptorily declare, that it views the powers of the federal government as resulting from the compact to which the states are parties, as limited by the plain sense and intention of the instrument constituting that compact, as no further valid than they are authorized by the grants enumerated in that compact; and that, in case of a deliberate, palpable, and dangerous exercise of other powers, not granted by the said compact, the states, who are parties thereto, have the right, and are in duty bound, to interpose, for arresting the progress of the evil, and for maintaining, within their respective limits, the authorities, rights and liberties, appertaining to them.

That the General Assembly doth also express its deep regret, that a spirit has, in sundry instances, been manifested by the federal government to enlarge it powers by forced constructions of the constitutional charter which defines them; and that indications have appeared of a design to expound certain general phrases (which, having been copied from the very limited grant of powers in the former

Articles of Confederation, were the less liable to be misconstrued) so as to destroy the meaning and effect of the particular enumeration which necessarily explains and limits the general phrases, and so as to consolidate the states, by degrees, into one sovereignty, the obvious tendency and inevitable result of which would be, to transform the present republican system of the United States into an absolute, or, at best, a mixed monarchy.

James Madison

KENTUCKY RESOLVE

November 14, 1799

Resolved, That this commonwealth considers the federal Union, upon the terms and for the purposes specified in the late compact, conducive to the liberty and happiness of the several states: That it does now unequivocally declare its attachment to the Union, and to that compact, agreeably to its obvious and real intention, and will be among the last to seek its dissolution: That, if those who administer the general government be permitted to transgress the limits fixed by that compact, by a total disregard to the special delegations of power therein contained, an annihilation of the state governments, and the creation, upon their ruins, of a general consolidated government, will be the inevitable consequence: That the principle and construction, contended for by sundry of the state legislatures, that the general government is the exclusive judge of the extent of the powers delegated to it, stop not short of despotism—since the discretion of those who administer the government, and not the Constitution, would be the measure of their powers: That the several states who formed that instrument, being sovereign and independent, have the unquestionable right to judge of the infraction; and, That a nullification, by those sovereignties, of all unauthorized acts done under color of that instrument, is the rightful remedy: That this commonwealth does, under the most deliberate reconsideration declare, that the said Alien and Sedition Laws, are in their opinion, palpable violations of the said Constitution; and however cheerfully it may be disposed to surrender its opinion to a majority of its sister states, in matters of ordinary or doubtful policy, yet, in momentous regulations like the present, which so vitally wound the best rights of the citizen, it would consider a silent acquiescence as highly criminal: That, although this commonwealth, as a party to the federal compact, will bow to the laws of the Union, yet it does, at the same time, declare, that it will not now, or ever hereafter, cease to oppose, in a constitutional manner, every attempt, at what quarter soever offered, to violate that compact: And finally, in order that no pretext or arguments may be drawn from a supposed acquiescence, on the part of this commonwealth, in the constitutionality of those laws, and be thereby used as precedents for similar future violations of the federal compact, this commonwealth now enter against them in solemn Protest.

Thomas Jefferson

ORIGINS OF U.S.
GOVERNMENT

THE VIRGINIA
AND KENTUCKY
RESOLVES

ORIGINS OF U.S. GOVERNMENT

MONROE DOCTRINE

On December 23, 1823, in his annual message to Congress, President JAMES MONROE made a statement on foreign policy that came to be known as the Monroe Doctrine. At that time the United States feared that Russia intended to establish colonies in Alaska and, more importantly, that the continental European states would intervene in Central and South America to help Spain recover its former colonies, which had won their independence in a series of wars in the early nineteenth century.

President Monroe announced that North and South America were closed to colonization, that the United States would not become involved in European wars or colonial wars in the Americas, and, most importantly, that any intervention by a European power in the independent states of the Western Hemisphere would be viewed by the United States as an unfriendly act against the United States.

Later presidents reiterated the Monroe Doctrine. In the early twentieth century, it was extended to justify U.S. intervention in the states of Latin America.

―∭―

Monroe Doctrine

Fellow citizens of the Senate and House of Representatives:

Many important subjects will claim your attention during the present session, of which I shall endeavor to give, in aid of your deliberations, a just idea in this communication. I undertake this duty with diffidence, from the vast extent of the interests on which I have to treat and of their great importance to every portion of our Union. I enter on it with zeal from a thorough conviction that there never was a period since the establishment of our revolution when, regarding the condition of the civilized world and its bearing on us, there was greater necessity for devotion in the public servants to their respective duties, or for virtue, patriotism, and union in our constituents.

Meeting in you a new Congress, I deem it proper to present this view of public affairs in greater detail than might otherwise be necessary. I do it, however, with peculiar satisfaction, from a knowledge that in this respect I shall comply more fully with the sound principles of our government. The people being with us exclusively the sovereign, it is indispensable that full information be laid before them on all important subjects, to enable them to exercise that high power with complete effect. If kept in the dark, they must be incompetent to it. We are all liable to error, and those who are engaged in the management of public affairs are more subject to excitement and to be led astray by their particular interests and passions than the great body of our constituents, who, living at home in the pursuit of their ordinary avocations, are calm but deeply interested spectators of events and of the conduct of those who are parties to them. To the

Source: James D. Richardson, ed., *A Compilation of the Messages and Papers of the Presidents,* vol. 2 (1897), pp. 207–219.

people every department of the government and every individual in each are responsible, and the more full their information the better they can judge of the wisdom of the policy pursued and of the conduct of each in regard to it. From their dispassionate judgment much aid may always be obtained, while their approbation will form the greatest incentive and most gratifying reward for virtuous actions and the dread of their censure the best security against the abuse of their confidence. Their interests in all vital questions are the same, and the bond, by sentiment as well as by interest, will be proportionably strengthened as they are better informed of the real state of public affairs, especially in difficult conjunctures. It is by such knowledge that local prejudices and jealousies are surmounted, and that a national policy, extending its fostering care and protection to all the great interests of our Union, is formed and steadily adhered to. . . .

At the proposal of the Russian imperial government, made through the minister of the emperor residing here, a full power and instructions have been transmitted to the minister of the United States at St. Petersburg to arrange by amicable negotiation the respective rights and interests of the two nations on the northwest coast of this continent. A similar proposal had been made by his imperial Majesty to the government of Great Britain, which has likewise been acceded to. The government of the United States has been desirous by this friendly proceeding of manifesting the great value which they have invariably attached to the friendship of the emperor and their solicitude to cultivate the best understanding with his government. In the discussions to which this interest has given rise and in the arrangements by which they may terminate the occasion has been judged proper for asserting, as a principle in which the rights and interests of the United States are involved, that the American continents, by the free and independent condition which they have assumed and maintain, are henceforth not to be considered as subjects for future colonization by any European powers. . . .

It was stated at the commencement of the last session that a great effort was then making in Spain and Portugal to improve the condition of the people of those countries, and that it appeared to be conducted with extraordinary moderation. It need scarcely be remarked that the result has been so far very different from what was then anticipated. Of events in that quarter of the globe, with which we have so much intercourse and from which we derive our origin, we have always been anxious and interested spectators. The citizens of the United States cherish sentiments the most friendly in favor of the liberty and happiness of their fellow men on that side of the Atlantic. In the wars of the European powers in matters relating to themselves, we have never taken any part, nor does it comport with our policy so to do. It is only when our rights are invaded or seriously menaced that we resent injuries or make preparation for our defense. With the movements in this hemisphere we are of necessity more immediately connected, and by causes which must be obvious to all enlightened and impartial observers. The political system of the allied powers is essentially different in this respect from that of America. This difference proceeds from that which exists in their respective governments; and to the defense of our own, which has been achieved by the loss of so much blood and treasure, and matured by the wisdom of their most enlightened citizens, and under which we have enjoyed unexampled felicity, this whole nation is devoted. We owe it, therefore, to candor and to the amicable relations existing between the United States and those powers to declare that we should consider any attempt on their part to extend their system to any portion of this hemisphere as dangerous to our peace and safety. With the existing colonies or dependencies of any European power, we have not interfered and shall not interfere. But with the governments who have declared their independence and maintained it, and whose independence we have, on great consideration and on just principles, acknowledged, we could not view any interposition for the purpose of oppressing them, or controlling in any other manner their destiny, by any European power in any other light than as the manifestation of an unfriendly disposition toward the United States. In the war between those new governments and Spain, we declared our neutrality at the time of their recognition, and to this we have adhered, and shall continue to adhere, provided no change shall occur which, in the judgment of the competent authorities of this government, shall make a corresponding change on the part of the United States indispensable to their security.

The late events in Spain and Portugal show that Europe is still unsettled. Of this important fact no stronger proof can be adduced than that the allied powers should have thought it proper, on any principle satisfactory to themselves, to have interposed by force in the internal concerns of Spain. To what extent such interposition may be carried, on the same principle, is a question in which all independent powers whose governments differ from theirs are interested, even those most remote, and surely none more so than the United States. Our policy in regard to Europe, which was adopted at an early stage of the wars which have so long agitated that quarter of the globe, nevertheless remains the same, which is, not to interfere in the internal concerns of any of its powers; to consider the government *de facto* as the legitimate government for us; to cultivate friendly relations with it, and to preserve those relations by a frank, firm, and manly policy, meeting in all instances the just claims of every power, submitting to injuries from none. But in regard to those continents, circumstances are eminently and conspicuously different. It is impossible that the allied powers should extend their political system to any portion of either continent without endangering our peace and happiness; nor can anyone believe that our southern brethren, if left to themselves, would adopt it of their own accord. It is equally impossible, therefore, that we should behold such interposition in any form with indifference. If we look to the comparative strength and resources of Spain and those new governments, and their distance from each other, it must be obvious that she can never subdue them. It is still the true policy of the United States to leave the parties to themselves in the hope that other powers will pursue the same course.

CIVIL RIGHTS

SLAVERY

FROM SEGREGATION
TO CIVIL RIGHTS

WOMEN'S RIGHTS

NATIVE AMERICAN RIGHTS

SLAVERY

Slavery was introduced to the American colonies in the 1620s. By 1700 the slave population, located primarily in the southern colonies, had grown dramatically. After independence, the United States debated whether slavery should be allowed to continue. Though the NORTHWEST ORDINANCE of 1787 banned slavery in the western territories, the Framers of the U.S. Constitution did not outlaw it. For the most part the Constitution ignored the issue, but the Three-fifths Compromise permitted southern states to count each slave as three-fifths of a white person for legislative APPORTIONMENT.

The invention of the cotton gin by Eli Whitney, which revolutionized cotton processing and vastly increased the profitability of cotton growing, and the LOUISIANA PURCHASE of 1803 forced the United States to consider whether slavery should be confined to the Southern states or extended to the new states carved out of the territory west of the Mississippi River. Legislative compromises succeeded in holding the Union together until mid-century. The *Dred Scott* case (DRED SCOTT V. SANDFORD, 60 U.S. [19 How.] 393, 15 L. Ed. 691 [1857]), however, destroyed the legal basis for compromise by holding that Congress could not prohibit slavery in the territories.

Abolitionist opposition to slavery increased after *Dred Scott*. ABRAHAM LINCOLN's hostility to slavery, expressed in his "House Divided" speech, frightened the Southern states. His election as president in 1860 led to the secession of the Southern states and the U.S. CIVIL WAR. Though Lincoln saw the preservation of the Union as his main goal, he recognized that slavery had to be ended. The EMANCIPATION PROCLAMATION of January 1, 1863, decreed the freedom of slaves in Southern territories, but it took the THIRTEENTH AMENDMENT, ratified in December 1865, to abolish slavery in the United States.

SLAVERY

Missouri Compromise

The Missouri Compromise of 1820 was a congressional agreement that regulated the extension of SLAVERY in the United States for thirty years. Under the agreement, the territory of Missouri was admitted as a slave state, the territory of Maine was admitted as a free state, and the boundaries of slavery were limited to the same latitude as the southern boundary of Missouri, 36°30' north latitude.

By 1818 the rapid growth in population in the North had left the Southern states, for the first time, with less than 45 percent of the seats in the U.S. House of Representatives. The U.S. Senate was evenly balanced between eleven slave and eleven free states. Therefore, Missouri's 1818 application for statehood, if approved, would give the slave states a majority in the Senate and reduce the Northern majority in the House.

In 1819 the free territory of Maine applied for statehood. Speaker of the House HENRY CLAY of Kentucky saw this event as an opportunity to maintain the balance of free and slave states. He made it clear to Northern representatives that Maine would not be admitted without an agreement to admit Missouri. Clay persuaded opponents of slavery to drop efforts to ban it in the territories. In return, the Southern states agreed to limit slavery to the territory below 36°30' north latitude. Under this provision the unsettled portions of the LOUISIANA PURCHASE north and west of Missouri would be free from slavery. The only area remaining for further expansion of slavery would be the territory that would become Arkansas and Oklahoma. To preserve the sectional equality in the Senate, Missouri and Maine were to be admitted to the Union simultaneously. Clay managed to pass the compromise in the House by a three-vote margin.

In 1821 Missouri complicated matters, however, by inserting a provision into its state constitution that prohibited free blacks and mulattoes from entering the state. Northern representatives objected to this language and refused to give final approval for statehood until it was removed. Clay then negotiated a second compromise that removed the offensive language from the Missouri constitution and substituted a provision that prohibited Missouri from discriminating against citizens from other states. Left unsettled was the question of who was a citizen. With this change Missouri and Maine were admitted to the Union.

—m—

Missouri Compromise

An Act to Authorize the People of the Missouri Territory to Form a Constitution and State Government, and for the Admission of Such State into the Union on an Equal Footing with the Original States, and to Prohibit Slavery in Certain Territories

Source: *Statutes at Large,* vol. 6 (1822), pp. 545–548, 645; Ben Perley Poore, ed., *The Federal and State Constitutions, Colonial Charters, and Other Organic Laws of the United States,* vol. 2 (1878), pp. 1107–1108.

[SECTION 1]

Be it enacted by the Senate and House of Representatives of the United States of America, in Congress assembled, that the inhabitants of that portion of the Missouri territory included within the boundaries hereinafter designated, be, and they are hereby, authorized to form for themselves a constitution and state government and to assume such name as they shall deem proper; and the said state, when formed, shall be admitted into the Union, upon an equal footing with the original states, in all respects whatsoever.

SECTION 2

And be it further enacted, that the said state shall consist of all the territory included within the following boundaries, to wit: beginning in the middle of the Mississippi River, on the parallel of thirty-six degrees of north latitude; thence west, along that parallel of latitude, to the St. Francis River; thence up, and following the course of that river, in the middle of the main channel thereof, to the parallel of latitude of thirty-six degrees and thirty minutes; thence west, along the same, to a point where the said parallel is intersected by a meridian line passing through the middle of the mouth of the Kansas River, where the same empties into the Missouri River, thence, from the point aforesaid north, along the said meridian line, to the intersection of the parallel of latitude which passes through the rapids of the river Des Moines, making the said line to correspond with the Indian boundary line; thence east, from the point of intersection last aforesaid, along the said parallel of latitude, to the middle of the channel of the main fork of the said river Des Moines; thence down and along the middle of the main channel of the said river Des Moines, to the mouth of the same, where it empties into the Mississippi River; thence, due east, to the middle of the main channel of the Mississippi River; thence down, and following the course of the Mississippi River, in the middle of the main channel thereof, to the place of beginning: provided, the said state shall ratify the boundaries aforesaid. And provided also, that the said state shall have concurrent jurisdiction on the river Mississippi and every other river bordering on the said state, so far as the said rivers shall form a common boundary to the said state; and any other state or states, now or hereafter to be formed and bounded by the same, such rivers to be common to both; and that the river Mississippi and the navigable rivers and waters leading into the same shall be common highways, and forever free, as well to the inhabitants of the said state as to other citizens of the United States, without any tax, duty, impost, or toll, therefore, imposed by the said state.

SECTION 3

And be it further enacted, that all free white male citizens of the United States, who shall have arrived at the age of twenty-one years, and have resided in said territory three months previous to the day of election, and all other persons qualified to vote for representatives to the general assembly of the said territory, shall be qualified to be elected, and they are hereby qualified and authorized to vote, and choose representatives to form a convention, who shall be apportioned amongst the several counties as follows:

From the county of Howard, five representatives. From the county of Cooper, three representatives. From the county of Montgomery, two representatives. From the county of Pike, one representative. From the county of Lincoln, one representative. From the county of St. Charles, three representatives. From the county of Franklin, one representative. From the county of St. Louis, eight representatives. From the county of Jefferson, one representative. From the county of Washington, three representatives. From the county of St. Genevieve, four representatives. From the county of Madison, one representative. From the county of Cape Girardeau, five representatives. From the county of New Madrid, two representatives. From the county of Wayne, and that portion of the county of Lawrence which falls within the boundaries herein designated, one representative.

And the election for the representatives aforesaid shall be holden on the first Monday and two succeeding days of May next, throughout the several counties aforesaid in the said territory, and shall be, in every respect, held and conducted in the same manner and under the same regulations as is prescribed by the laws of the said territory regulating elections therein for members of the general assembly, except that the returns of the election in that portion of Lawrence County included in the boundaries aforesaid shall be made to the county of Wayne, as is provided in other cases under the laws of said territory.

SECTION 4

And be it further enacted, that the members of the convention thus duly elected, shall be, and they are hereby authorized to meet at the seat of government of said territory on the second Monday of the month of June next; and the said convention, when so assembled, shall have power and authority to adjourn to any other place in the said territory, which to them shall seem best for the convenient transaction of their business; and which convention, when so met, shall first determine by a majority of the whole number elected, whether it be, or be not, expedient at that time to form a constitution and state government for the people within the said territory, as included within the boundaries above designated; and if it be deemed expedient, the convention shall be, and hereby is, authorized to form a constitution and state government; or, if it be deemed more expedient, the said convention shall provide by ordinance for electing representatives to form a constitution or frame of government; which said representatives shall be chosen in such manner, and in such proportion as they shall designate; and shall meet at such time and place as shall be prescribed by the said ordinance; and shall then form for the people of said territory, within the boundaries aforesaid, a constitution and state government: provided, that the same, whenever formed, shall be republican and not repugnant to the Constitution of the United States; and that the legislature of said state shall never interfere with the primary disposal of the soil by the United States, nor with any regulations Congress may find necessary for securing the title in such soil to the bona fide purchasers; and that no tax shall be imposed on lands the property of the United States; and in no case shall nonresident proprietors be taxed higher than residents.

SECTION 5

And be it further enacted, that until the next general census shall be taken, the said state shall be entitled to one representative in the House of Representatives of the United States.

SECTION 6

And be it further enacted, that the following propositions be, and the same are hereby, offered to the convention of the said territory of Missouri, when formed, for their free acceptance or rejection, which, if accepted by the convention, shall be obligatory upon the United States:

1. That section numbered sixteen in every township, and when such section has been sold

or otherwise disposed of, other lands equivalent thereto and as contiguous as may be shall be granted to the state for the use of the inhabitants of such township for the use of schools.

2. That all salt springs, not exceeding twelve in number, with six sections of land adjoining to each, shall be granted to the said state for the use of said state, the same to be selected by the legislature of the said state, on or before the first day of January, in the year one thousand eight hundred and twenty-five; and the same, when so selected, to be used under such terms, conditions, and regulations as the legislature of said state shall direct. Provided, that no salt spring, the right whereof now is, or hereafter shall be, confirmed or adjudged to any individual or individuals, shall, by this section, be granted to the said state: and provided also, that the legislature shall never sell or lease the same, at any one time, for a longer period than ten years, without the consent of Congress.

3. That 5 percent of the net proceeds of the sale of lands lying within the said territory or state, and which shall be sold by Congress from and after the first day of January next, after deducting all expenses incident to the same, shall be reserved for making public roads and canals, of which three-fifths shall be applied to those objects within the state, under the direction of the legislature thereof; and the other two-fifths in defraying, under the direction of Congress, the expenses to be incurred in making of a road or roads, canal or canals, leading to the said state.

4. That four entire sections of land be, and the same are hereby, granted to the said state, for the purpose of fixing their seat of government thereon; which said sections shall, under the direction of the legislature of said state, be located, as near as may be, in one body, at any time, in such townships and ranges as the legislature aforesaid may select, on any of the public lands of the United States. Provided, that such locations shall be made prior to the public sale of the lands of the United States surrounding such location.

5. That thirty-six sections, or one entire township, which shall be designated by the president of the United States, together with the other lands heretofore reserved for that purpose, shall be reserved for the use of a seminary of learning, and vested in the legislature of said state, to be appropriated solely to the use of such

seminary by the said legislature. Provided, that the five foregoing propositions herein offered, are on the condition that the convention of the said state shall provide by an ordinance, irrevocable without the consent of the United States, that every and each tract of land sold by the United States, from and after the first day of January next, shall remain exempt from any tax laid by order or under the authority of the state, whether for state, county, or township, or any other purpose whatever, for the term of five years from and after the day of sale; and further, that the bounty lands granted, or hereafter to be granted, for military services during the late war shall, while they continue to be held by the patentees or their heirs, remain exempt as aforesaid from taxation for the term of three years from and after the date of the patents, respectively.

SECTION 7

And be it further enacted, that in case a constitution and state government shall be formed for the people of the said territory of Missouri, the said convention or representatives, as soon thereafter as may be, shall cause a true and attested copy of such constitution, or frame of state government, as shall be formed or provided, to be transmitted to Congress.

SECTION 8

And be it further enacted, that in all that territory ceded by France to the United States under the name of Louisiana, which lies north of thirty-six degrees and thirty minutes north latitude, not included within the limits of the state contemplated by this act, slavery and involuntary servitude, otherwise than in the punishment of crimes whereof the parties shall have been duly convicted, shall be, and is hereby, forever prohibited. Provided always, that any person escaping into the same, from whom labor or service is lawfully claimed in any state or territory of the United States, such fugitive may be lawfully reclaimed and conveyed to the person claiming his or her labor or service as aforesaid.

Approved, March 6, 1820.

SECTIONS OF THE MISSOURI CONSTITUTION OF 1820 DEALING WITH SLAVERY

SECTION 26

The general assembly shall not have power to pass laws—

1. For the emancipation of slaves without the consent of their owners; or without paying them, before such emancipation, a full equivalent for such slaves so emancipated; and,

2. To prevent bona fide immigrants to this state, or actual settlers therein, from bringing from any of the United States, or from any of their territories, such persons as may there be deemed to be slaves, so long as any persons of the same description are allowed to be held as slaves by the laws of this state.

They shall have power to pass laws—

1. To prohibit the introduction into this state of any slaves who may have committed any high crime in any other state or territory;

2. To prohibit the introduction of any slave for the purpose of speculation, or as an article of trade or merchandise;

3. To prohibit the introduction of any slave, or the offspring of any slave, who heretofore may have been, or who hereafter may be, imported from any foreign country into the United States, or any territory thereof, in contravention of any existing statute of the United States; and,

4. To permit the owners of slaves to emancipate them, saving the right of creditors, where the person so emancipating will give security that the slave so emancipated shall not become a public charge.

It shall be their duty, as soon as may be, to pass such laws as may be necessary—

1. To prevent free Negroes and mulattoes from coming to and settling in this state, under any pretext whatsoever; and,

2. To oblige the owners of slaves to treat them with humanity and to abstain from all injuries to them extending to life or limb.

SECTION 27

In prosecutions for crimes, slaves shall not be deprived of an impartial trial by jury, and a slave convicted of a capital offense shall suffer the same degree of punishment, and no other, that would be inflicted on a white person for a like offense; and courts of justice, before whom slaves shall be tried, shall assign them counsel for their defense.

SECTION 28

Any person who shall maliciously deprive of life or dismember a slave shall suffer such punishment as would be inflicted for the like offense if it were committed on a free white person.

RESOLUTION PROVIDING FOR THE ADMISSION OF THE STATE OF MISSOURI INTO THE UNION, ON A CERTAIN CONDITION

Resolved by the Senate and House of Representatives of the United States of America, in Congress assembled, that Missouri shall be admitted into this Union on an equal footing with the original states in all respects whatever upon the fundamental condition that the fourth clause of the twenty-sixth section of the third article of the constitution submitted on the part of said state to Congress shall never be construed to authorize the passage of any law, and that no law shall be passed in conformity there-

to, by which any citizen, of either of the states in this Union, shall be excluded from the enjoyment of any of the privileges and immunities to which such citizen is entitled under the Constitution of the United States. Provided, that the legislature of the said state, by a solemn public act, shall declare the assent of the said state to the said fundamental condition and shall transmit to the president of the United States, on or before the fourth Monday in November next, an authentic copy of the said act; upon the receipt whereof, the president, by proclamation, shall announce the fact; whereupon, and without any further proceeding on the part of Congress, the admission of the said state into this Union shall be considered as complete.

Approved, March 2, 1821.

SLAVERY

MISSOURI
COMPROMISE

SLAVERY

WILMOT PROVISO

The Wilmot Proviso was an unsuccessful congressional amendment, offered for the first time in 1846, that sought to ban slavery in the territories acquired from Mexico after the Mexican War. Named after its sponsor, Democratic Representative DAVID WILMOT of Pennsylvania, the proviso never passed both houses of Congress, but it did ignite an intense national debate over slavery that led to the creation of the antislavery Republican party in 1854.

In August 1846 President JAMES K. POLK asked Congress for $2 million to help him negotiate peace and settle the boundary with Mexico. Polk sought the acquisition of Texas and other Mexican territories. Wilmot quickly offered his amendment, which he attached to Polk's funding measure. The House approved the bill and sent it to the Senate for action. The Senate, however, adjourned before discussing the issue.

When the next Congress convened, a new appropriations bill for $3 million was presented, but the Wilmot Proviso was again attached to the measure. The House passed the bill, and the Senate was forced to consider the proposal. Under the leadership of Senator JOHN C. CALHOUN of South Carolina and other proslavery senators, the Senate refused to accept the Wilmot amendment and approved the funds for the negotiations without the proviso.

Though the amendment was never enacted, it became a rallying point for opponents of slavery. The creation of the REPUBLICAN PARTY in 1854 was based on an antislavery platform that endorsed the Wilmot Proviso.

***

Wilmot Proviso

Provided, that, as an express and fundamental condition to the acquisition of any territory from the Republic of Mexico by the United States, by virtue of any treaty which may be negotiated between them, and to the use by the executive of the moneys herein appropriated, neither slavery nor involuntary servitude shall ever exist in any part of said territory, except for crime, whereof the party shall first be duly convicted.

Source: *Congressional Globe*, 29th Congress, 1st session (August 12, 1846), p. 1217.

SLAVERY

COMPROMISE OF 1850

The Compromise of 1850 is the name given to a series of congressional statutes enacted in September 1850 in an attempt to resolve long-standing disputes over slavery. Southern slave owners had long demanded a more stringent fugitive slave law while Northern abolitionists insisted that slavery should be abolished in the District of Columbia. The unsuccessful WILMOT PROVISO of 1846–1847 also revealed deep opposition to the expansion of slavery into the newly acquired Mexican territories. The debate over slavery intensified in 1849 when California applied for admission to the Union as a free state. Concern grew over the possibility that some Southern states might secede, leading to the dissolution of the Union.

Senator HENRY CLAY of Kentucky, aided by Senators DANIEL WEBSTER of Massachusetts and STEPHEN A. DOUGLAS of Illinois, proposed a compromise that passed the Congress after much difficulty. The compromise consisted of five statutes. One statute created the New Mexico Territory, and a second created the Utah Territory. Both statutes left it up to the inhabitants to decide whether to enter the Union as a free state or a slave state. This approach, whose leading advocate was Douglas, became known as "popular sovereignty." A third statute admitted California to the Union as a free state, and a fourth statute prohibited bringing slaves into the District of Columbia for sale or transportation. The fifth statute was the most controversial, for it established a more rigorous fugitive slave law. The strengthening of federal enforcement of the FUGITIVE SLAVE ACT (9 Stat. 462)

angered many Northerners and led to growing sectional conflict.

—⟋⟋⟍—

Compromise of 1850

An Act Proposing to the State of Texas the Establishment of Her Northern and Western Boundaries, the Relinquishment by the Said State of All Territory Claimed by Her Exterior to Said Boundaries, and of All Her Claims upon the United States, and to Establish a Territorial Government for New Mexico

[Section 1]

Be it enacted by the Senate and House of Representatives of the United States of America in Congress assembled, that the following propositions shall be, and the same hereby are, offered to the state of Texas, which, when agreed to by the said state, in an act passed by the general assembly, shall be binding and obligatory upon the United States, and upon the said state of Texas: provided, the said agreement by the said general assembly shall be given on or before the first day of December, eighteen hundred and fifty:

1. The state of Texas will agree that her boundary on the north shall commence at the point at which the meridian of one hundred degrees west from Greenwich is intersected by the parallel of thirty-six degrees thirty minutes

Source: *Statutes at Large,* vol. 9 (1851), pp. 446–458, 462–465, 467–468.

north latitude, and shall run from said point due west to the meridian of one hundred and three degrees west from Greenwich; thence her boundary shall run due south to the thirty-second degree of north latitude; thence on the said parallel of thirty-two degrees of north latitude to the Rio Bravo del Norte, and thence with the channel of said river to the Gulf of Mexico.

2. The state of Texas cedes to the United States all her claim to territory exterior to the limits and boundaries which she agrees to establish by the first article of this agreement.

3. The state of Texas relinquishes all claim upon the United States for liability of the debts of Texas, and for compensation or indemnity for the surrender to the United States of her ships, forts, arsenals, custom houses, custom house revenue, arms and munitions of war, and public buildings with their sites, which became the property of the United States at the time of the annexation.

4. The United States, in consideration of said establishment of boundaries, cession of claim to territory, and relinquishment of claims, will pay to the state of Texas the sum of ten millions of dollars in a stock bearing 5 percent interest, and redeemable at the end of fourteen years, the interest payable half-yearly at the treasury of the United States.

5. Immediately after the president of the United States shall have been furnished with an authentic copy of the act of the general assembly of Texas accepting these propositions, he shall cause the stock to be issued in favor of the state of Texas, as provided for in the fourth article of this agreement: provided, also, that no more than five millions of said stock shall be issued until the creditors of the state holding bonds and other certificates of stock of Texas for which duties on imports were specially pledged, shall first file at the treasury of the United States releases of all claim against the United States for or on account of said bonds or certificates in such form as shall be prescribed by the secretary of the treasury and approved by the president of the United States: provided, that nothing herein contained shall be construed to impair or qualify anything contained in the third article of the second section of the "joint resolution for annexing Texas to the United States," approved March first, eighteen hundred and forty-five, either as regards the number of states that may hereafter be formed out of the state of Texas, or otherwise.

Section 2

And be it further enacted, that all that portion of the territory of the United States bounded as follows: beginning at a point in the Colorado River where the boundary line with the republic of Mexico crosses the same; thence eastwardly with the said boundary line to the Rio Grande; thence following the main channel of said river to the parallel of the thirty-second degree of north latitude; thence east with said degree to its intersection with the one hundred and third degree of longitude west of Greenwich; thence north with said degree of longitude to the parallel of thirty-eighth degree of north latitude; thence west with said parallel to the summit of the Sierra Madre; thence south with the crest of said mountains to the thirty-seventh parallel of north latitude; thence west with said parallel to its intersection with the boundary line of the state of California; thence with said boundary line to the place of beginning—be, and the same is hereby, erected into a temporary government, by the name of the territory of New Mexico. Provided, that nothing in this act contained shall be construed to inhibit the government of the United States from dividing said territory into two or more territories, in such manner and at such times as Congress shall deem convenient and proper, or from attaching any portion thereof to any other territory or state. And provided, further, that, when admitted as a state, the said territory, or any portion of the same, shall be received into the Union, with or without slavery, as their constitution may prescribe at the time of their admission.

Section 3

And be it further enacted, that the executive power and authority in and over said territory of New Mexico shall be vested in a governor, who shall hold his office for four years, and until his successor shall be appointed and qualified, unless sooner removed by the president of the United States. The governor shall reside within said territory, shall be commander in chief of the militia thereof, shall perform the duties and receive the emoluments of superintendent of Indian affairs, and shall approve all laws passed by the legislative assembly before they shall take effect; he may grant pardons for offenses against the laws of said territory, and reprieves for offenses against the laws of the United States, until the decision of the president can be made known thereon; he shall commission all officers who shall be appointed to office under the laws of the said territory and shall take care that the laws be faithfully executed.

Section 4

And be it further enacted, that there shall be a secretary of said territory, who shall reside therein, and hold his office for four years, unless sooner removed by the president of the United States; he shall record and preserve all the laws and proceedings of the legislative assembly hereinafter constituted and all the acts and proceedings of the governor in his executive department; he shall transmit one copy of the laws and one copy of the executive proceedings, on or before the first day of December in each year, to the president of the United States, and, at the same time, two copies of the laws to the speaker of the House of Representatives and the president of the Senate, for the use of Congress. And, in case of the death, removal, resignation, or other necessary absence of the governor from the territory, the secretary shall have, and he is hereby authorized and required to execute and perform all the powers and duties of the governor during such vacancy or necessary absence, or until another governor shall be duly appointed to fill such vacancy.

Section 5

And be it further enacted, that the legislative power and authority of said territory shall be vested in the governor and a legislative assembly. The legislative assembly shall consist of a council and house of representatives. The council shall consist of thirteen members, having the qualifications of voters as hereinafter prescribed, whose term of service shall continue two years. The house of representatives shall consist of twenty-six members, possessing the same qualifications as prescribed for members of the council, and whose term of service shall continue one year. An apportionment shall be made, as nearly equal as practicable, among the several counties or districts, for the election of the council and house of representatives, giving to each section of the territory representation in the ratio of its population (Indians excepted), as nearly as may be. And the members of the council and of the house of representatives shall reside in, and be inhabitants of, the district for which they may be elected respectively. Previous to the first election, the governor shall cause a census or enumeration of the inhabitants of the several counties and dis-

tricts of the territory to be taken, and the first election shall be held at such time and places and be conducted in such manner, as the governor shall appoint and direct; and he shall, at the same time, declare the number of the members of the council and house of representatives to which each of the counties or districts shall be entitled under this act. The number of persons authorized to be elected having the highest number of votes in each of said council districts, for members of the council, shall be declared by the governor to be duly elected to the council; and the person or persons authorized to be elected having the greatest number of votes for the house of representatives, equal to the number to which each county or district shall be entitled, shall be declared by the governor to be duly elected members of the house of representatives. Provided, that in case of a tie between two or more persons voted for, the governor shall order a new election to supply the vacancy made by such tie. And the persons thus elected to the legislative assembly shall meet at such place and on such day as the governor shall appoint; but thereafter, the time, place, and manner of holding and conducting all elections by the people, and the apportioning the representation in the several counties or districts to the council and house of representatives according to the population, shall be prescribed by law, as well as the day of the commencement of the regular sessions of the legislative assembly: provided, that no one session shall exceed the term of forty days.

Section 6

And be it further enacted, that every free white male inhabitant, above the age of twenty-one years, who shall have been a resident of said territory at the time of the passage of this act, shall be entitled to vote at the first election and shall be eligible to any office within the said territory; but the qualifications of voters and of holding office, at all subsequent elections, shall be such as shall be prescribed by the legislative assembly. Provided, that the right of suffrage, and of holding office, shall be exercised only by citizens of the United States, including those recognized as citizens by the treaty with the republic of Mexico, concluded February second, eighteen hundred and forty-eight.

Section 7

And be it further enacted, that the legislative power of the territory shall extend to all rightful

SLAVERY

COMPROMISE OF
1850

subjects of legislation, consistent with the Constitution of the United States and the provisions of this act; but no law shall be passed interfering with the primary disposal of the soil; no tax shall be imposed upon the property of the United States; nor shall the lands or other property of nonresidents be taxed higher than the lands or other property of residents. All the laws passed by the legislative assembly and governor shall be submitted to the Congress of the United States, and, if disapproved, shall be null and of no effect.

Section 8

And be it further enacted, that all township, district, and county officers, not herein otherwise provided for, shall be appointed or elected, as the case may be, in such manner as shall be provided by the governor and legislative assembly of the territory of New Mexico. The governor shall nominate and, by and with the advice and consent of the legislative council, appoint all officers not herein otherwise provided for; and in the first instance the governor alone may appoint all said officers, who shall hold their offices until the end of the first session of the legislative assembly, and shall lay off the necessary districts for members of the council and house of representatives, and all other officers.

Section 9

And be it further enacted, that no member of the legislative assembly shall hold, or be appointed to, any office which shall have been created, or the salary or emoluments of which shall have been increased while he was a member, during the term for which he was elected, and for one year after the expiration of such term; and no person holding a commission or appointment under the United States, except postmasters, shall be a member of the legislative assembly, or shall hold any office under the government of said territory.

Section 10

And be it further enacted, that the judicial power of said territory shall be vested in a supreme court, district courts, probate courts, and in justices of the peace. The supreme court shall consist of a chief justice and two associate justices, any two of whom shall constitute a quorum, and who shall hold a term at the seat of government of said territory annually, and they shall hold their offices during the period of four years. The said territory shall be divided into three judicial districts, and a district court shall be held in each of said districts by one of the justices of the supreme court, at such time and place as may be prescribed by law; and the said judges shall, after their appointments, respectively, reside in the districts which shall be assigned them. The jurisdiction of the several courts herein provided for, both appellate and original, and that of the probate courts and of justices of the peace, shall be as limited by law. Provided, that justices of the peace shall not have jurisdiction of any matter in controversy when the title or boundaries of land may be in dispute, or where the debt or sum claimed shall exceed one hundred dollars; and the said supreme and district courts, respectively, shall possess chancery as well as common-law jurisdiction. Each district court, or the judge thereof, shall appoint its clerk, who shall also be the register in chancery and shall keep his office at the place where the court may be held. Writs of error, bills of exception, and appeals shall be allowed in all cases from the final decisions of said district courts to the supreme court, under such regulations as may be prescribed by law, but in no case removed to the supreme court shall trial by jury be allowed in said court. The supreme court, or the justices thereof, shall appoint its own clerk, and every clerk shall hold his office at the pleasure of the court for which he shall have been appointed. Writs of error and appeals from the final decisions of said supreme court shall be allowed, and may be taken to the Supreme Court of the United States, in the same manner and under the same regulations as from the circuit courts of the United States, where the value of the property or the amount in controversy, to be ascertained by the oath or affirmation of either party, or other competent witness, shall exceed one thousand dollars; except only that in all cases involving title to slaves, the said writs of error or appeals shall be allowed and decided by the said Supreme Court without regard to the value of the matter, property, or title in controversy; and except also that a writ of error or appeal shall also be allowed to the Supreme Court of the United States from the decision of the said supreme court created by this act, or of any judge thereof, or of the district courts created by this act, or of any judge thereof, upon any writ of habeas corpus involving the question of personal freedom; and each of the said district courts shall have and exercise the same jurisdiction in all cases arising under the Constitution and laws of the United States as is vested in the circuit and district courts of the United States; and the said supreme and district courts of the said territory, and the respective judges thereof, shall and may grant writs of habeas corpus in all cases in which the same are grantable by the judges of the United States in the District of Columbia; and the first six days of every term of said courts, or so much thereof as shall be necessary, shall be appropriated to the trial of causes arising under the said Constitution and laws; and writs of error and appeals in all such cases shall be made to the supreme court of said territory, the same as in other cases. The said clerk shall receive in all such cases the same fees which the clerks of the district courts of Oregon Territory now receive for similar services.

Section 11

And be it further enacted, that there shall be appointed an attorney for said territory, who shall continue in office for four years, unless sooner removed by the president, and who shall receive the same fees and salary as the attorney of the United States for the present territory of Oregon. There shall also be a marshal for the territory appointed, who shall hold his office for four years, unless sooner removed by the president, and who shall execute all processes issuing from the said courts when exercising their jurisdiction as circuit and district courts of the United States; he shall perform the duties, be subject to the same regulation and penalties, and be entitled to the same fees as the marshal of the district court of the United States for the present territory of Oregon, and shall, in addition, be paid two hundred (dollars) annually as a compensation for extra services.

Section 12

And be it further enacted, that the governor, secretary, chief justice and associate justices, attorney, and marshal shall be nominated and, by and with the advice and consent of the Senate, appointed by the president of the United States. The governor and secretary, to be appointed as aforesaid, shall, before they act as such, respectively take an oath or affirmation, before the district judge, or some justice of the peace in the limits of said territory, duly authorized to administer oaths and affirmations by the laws now in force therein, or before the chief jus-

tice or some associate justice of the Supreme Court of the United States, to support the Constitution of the United States, and faithfully to discharge the duties of their respective offices; which said oaths, when so taken, shall be certified by the person by whom the same shall have been taken, and such certificates shall be received and recorded by the said secretary among the executive proceedings; and the chief justice and associate justices, and all other civil officers in said territory, before they act as such, shall take a like oath or affirmation, before the said governor or secretary, or some judge or justice of the peace of the territory, who may be duly commissioned and qualified; which said oath or affirmation shall be certified and transmitted, by the person taking the same to the secretary, to be by him recorded as aforesaid; and afterwards, the like oath or affirmation shall be taken, certified, and recorded in such manner and form as may be prescribed by law. The governor shall receive an annual salary of fifteen hundred dollars as governor, and one thousand dollars as superintendent of Indian affairs. The chief justice and associate justices shall each receive an annual salary of eighteen hundred dollars. The secretary shall receive an annual salary of eighteen hundred dollars. The said salaries shall be paid quarter-yearly, at the treasury of the United States. The members of the legislative assembly shall be entitled to receive three dollars each per day during their attendance at the sessions thereof, and three dollars each for every twenty miles' travel in going to and returning from the said sessions, estimated according to the nearest usually traveled route. There shall be appropriated annually the sum of one thousand dollars, to be expended by the governor, to defray the contingent expenses of the territory; there shall also be appropriated annually a sufficient sum to be expended by the secretary of the territory, and upon an estimate to be made by the secretary of the treasury of the United States, to defray the expenses of the legislative assembly, the printing of the laws, and other incidental expenses; and the secretary of the territory shall annually account to the secretary of the treasury of the United States for the manner in which the aforesaid sum shall have been expended.

Section 13

And be it further enacted, that the legislative assembly of the territory of New Mexico shall

SLAVERY

COMPROMISE OF
1850

hold its first session at such time and place in said territory as the governor thereof shall appoint and direct; and at said first session, or as soon thereafter as they shall deem expedient, the governor and legislative assembly shall proceed to locate and establish the seat of government for said territory at such place as they may deem eligible; which place, however, shall thereafter be subject to be changed by the said governor and legislative assembly.

Section 14

And be it further enacted, that a delegate to the House of Representatives of the United States, to serve during each Congress of the United States, may be elected by the voters qualified to elect members of the legislative assembly, who shall be entitled to the same rights and privileges as are exercised and enjoyed by the delegates from the several other territories of the United States to the said House of Representatives. The first election shall be held at such time and places, and be conducted in such manner, as the governor shall appoint and direct; and at all subsequent elections, the times, places, and manner of holding the elections shall be prescribed by law. The person having the greatest number of votes shall be declared by the governor to be duly elected, and a certificate thereof shall be given accordingly; provided, that such delegate shall receive no higher sum for mileage than is allowed by law to the delegate from Oregon.

Section 15

And be it further enacted, that when the lands in said territory shall be surveyed under the direction of the government of the United States, preparatory to bringing the same into market, sections numbered sixteen and thirty-six in each township in said territory shall be, and the same are hereby, reserved for the purpose of being applied to schools in said territory, and in the states and territories hereafter to be erected out of the same.

Section 16

And be it further enacted, that temporarily and until otherwise provided by law, the governor of said territory may define the judicial districts of said territory, and assign the judges who may be appointed for said territory to the several districts, and also appoint the times and places for holding courts in the several counties or sub-

divisions in each of said judicial districts, by proclamation to be issued by him; but the legislative assembly, at their first or any subsequent session, may organize, alter, or modify such judicial districts, and assign the judges, and alter the times and places of holding the courts, as to them shall seem proper and convenient.

Section 17

And be it further enacted, that the Constitution, and all laws of the United States which are not locally inapplicable, shall have the same force and effect within the said territory of New Mexico as elsewhere within the United States.

Section 18

And be it further enacted, that the provisions of this act be, and they are hereby, suspended until the boundary between the United States and the state of Texas shall be adjusted; and when such adjustment shall have been effected, the president of the United States shall issue his proclamation, declaring this act to be in full force and operation, and shall proceed to appoint the officers herein provided to be appointed in and for said territory.

Section 19

And be it further enacted, that no citizen of the United States shall be deprived of his life, liberty, or property, in said territory, except by the judgment of his peers and the laws of the land.

Approved, September 9, 1850.

AN ACT FOR THE ADMISSION OF THE STATE OF CALIFORNIA INTO THE UNION

Whereas the people of California have presented a constitution and asked admission into the Union, which constitution was submitted to Congress by the president of the United States, by message dated February thirteenth, eighteen hundred and fifty, and which, on due examination, is found to be republican in its form of government:

[Section 1]

Be it enacted by the Senate and House of Representatives of the United States of America in Congress assembled, that the state of California shall be one, and is hereby declared to be one, of the United States of America, and admitted into the Union on an equal footing with the original states in all respects whatever.

Section 2

And be it further enacted, that, until the representatives in Congress shall be apportioned according to an actual enumeration of the inhabitants of the United States, the state of California shall be entitled to two representatives in Congress.

Section 3

And be it further enacted, that the said state of California is admitted into the Union upon the express condition that the people of said state, through their legislature or otherwise, shall never interfere with the primary disposal of the public lands within its limits, and shall pass no law and do no act whereby the title of the United States to, and right to dispose of, the same shall be impaired or questioned; and that they shall never lay any tax or assessment of any description whatsoever upon the public domain of the United States, and in no case shall nonresident proprietors, who are citizens of the United States, be taxed higher than residents; and that all the navigable waters within the said state shall be common highways, and forever free, as well to the inhabitants of said state as to the citizens of the United States, without any tax, impost, or duty therefore: provided, that nothing herein contained shall be construed as recognizing or rejecting the propositions tendered by the people of California as articles of compact in the ordinance adopted by the convention which formed the constitution of that state.

Approved, September 9, 1850.

AN ACT TO ESTABLISH A TERRITORIAL GOVERNMENT FOR UTAH

Be it enacted by the Senate and House of Representatives of the United States of America in Congress assembled, that all that part of the territory of the United States included within the following limits, to wit: bounded on the west by the state of California, on the north by the territory of Oregon, and on the east by the summit of the Rocky Mountains, and on the south by the thirty-seventh parallel of north latitude, be, and the same is hereby, created into a temporary government, by the name of the territory of Utah; and, when admitted as a state, the said territory, or any portion of the same, shall be received into the Union, with or without slavery, as their constitution may prescribe at the time of their admission: provided, that nothing in this act contained shall be construed to inhib-

it the government of the United States from dividing said territory into two or more territories, in such manner and at such times as Congress shall deem convenient and proper, or from attaching any portion of said territory to any other state or territory of the United States.

* * *

Section 14

And be it further enacted, that the sum of five thousand dollars be, and the same is hereby, appropriated out of any moneys in the treasury not otherwise appropriated, to be expended by and under the direction of the said governor of the territory of Utah, in the purchase of a library, to be kept at the seat of government for the use of the governor, legislative assembly, judges of the supreme court, secretary, marshal, and attorney of said territory, and such other persons, and under such regulations, as shall be prescribed by law.

AN ACT TO AMEND, AND SUPPLEMENTARY TO, THE ACT ENTITLED "AN ACT RESPECTING FUGITIVES FROM JUSTICE, AND PERSONS ESCAPING FROM THE SERVICE OF THEIR MASTERS," APPROVED FEBRUARY TWELFTH, ONE THOUSAND SEVEN HUNDRED AND NINETY-THREE

[Section 1]

Be it enacted by the Senate and House of Representatives of the United States of America in Congress assembled, that the persons who have been, or may hereafter be, appointed commissioners, in virtue of any act of Congress, by the circuit courts of the United States, and who, in consequence of such appointment, are authorized to exercise the powers that any justice of the peace, or other magistrate of any of the United States, may exercise in respect to offenders for any crime or offense against the United States, by arresting, imprisoning, or bailing the same under and by virtue of the thirty-third section of the act of the twenty-fourth of September, seventeen hundred and eighty-nine, entitled "An act to establish the judicial courts of the United States," shall be, and are hereby, authorized and required to exercise and discharge all the powers and duties conferred by this act.

SLAVERY

COMPROMISE OF 1850

Section 2

And be it further enacted, that the superior court of each organized territory of the United States shall have the same power to appoint commissioners to take acknowledgments of bail and affidavits, and to take depositions of witnesses in civil causes, which is now possessed by the circuit court of the United States; and all commissioners, who shall hereafter be appointed for such purposes by the superior court of any organized territory of the United States, shall possess all the powers, and exercise all the duties, conferred by law upon the commissioners appointed by the circuit courts of the United States for similar purposes and shall moreover exercise and discharge all the powers and duties conferred by this act.

Section 3

And be it further enacted, that the circuit courts of the United States and the superior courts of each organized territory of the United States shall from time to time enlarge the number of commissioners, with a view to afford reasonable facilities to reclaim fugitives from labor and to the prompt discharge of the duties imposed by this act.

Section 4

And be it further enacted, that the commissioners above named shall have concurrent jurisdiction with the judges of the circuit and district courts of the United States, in their respective circuits and districts within the several states, and the judges of the superior courts of the territories, severally and collectively, in termtime and vacation; and shall grant certificates to such claimants, upon satisfactory proof being made, with authority to take and remove such fugitives from service or labor, under the restrictions herein contained, to the state or territory from which such persons may have escaped or fled.

Section 5

And be it further enacted, that it shall be the duty of all marshals and deputy marshals to obey and execute all warrants and precepts issued under the provisions of this act, when to them directed; and should any marshal or deputy marshal refuse to receive such warrant, or other process, when tendered, or to use all proper means diligently to execute the same, he shall, on conviction thereof, be fined in the sum of one thousand dollars, to the use of such claimant, on the motion of such claimant, by the circuit or district court for the district of such marshal; and after arrest of such fugitive by such marshal or his deputy, or whilst at any time in his custody under the provisions of this act, should such fugitive escape, whether with or without the assent of such marshal or his deputy, such marshal shall be liable, on his official bond, to be prosecuted for the benefit of such claimant, for the full value of the service or labor of said fugitive in the state, territory, or district whence he escaped. And the better to enable the said commissioners, when thus appointed, to execute their duties faithfully and efficiently in conformity with the requirements of the Constitution of the United States and of this act, they are hereby authorized and empowered, within their counties respectively, to appoint, in writing under their hands, any one or more suitable persons, from time to time, to execute all such warrants and other process as may be issued by them in the lawful performance of their respective duties; with authority to such commissioners, or the persons to be appointed by them, to execute process as aforesaid, to summon and call to their aid the bystanders, or *posse comitatus* of the proper county, when necessary to ensure a faithful observance of the clause of the Constitution referred to, in conformity with the provisions of this act; and all good citizens are hereby commanded to aid and assist in the prompt and efficient execution of this law, whenever their services may be required, as aforesaid, for that purpose; and said warrants shall run, and be executed by said officers, anywhere in the state within which they are issued.

Section 6

And be it further enacted, that when a person held to service or labor in any state or territory of the United States has heretofore or shall hereafter escape into another state or territory of the United States, the person or persons to whom such service or labor may be due or his, her, or their agent or attorney, duly authorized by power of attorney in writing, acknowledged and certified under the seal of some legal officer or court of the state or territory in which the same may be executed, may pursue and reclaim such fugitive person, either by procuring a warrant from some one of the courts, judges, or commissioners aforesaid, of the proper circuit, district, or county, for the apprehension of such fugitive from service or labor or by seizing and arresting such fugitive, where the same can be done without process, and by taking, or causing such person to be taken, forthwith before such court, judge, or commissioner, whose duty it shall be to hear and determine the case of such claimant in a summary manner; and upon satisfactory proof being made, by deposition or affidavit in writing, to be taken and certified by such court, judge, or commissioner, or by other satisfactory testimony, duly taken and certified by some court, magistrate, justice of the peace, or other legal officer authorized to administer an oath and take depositions under the laws of the state or territory from which such person owing service or labor may have escaped, with a certificate of such magistracy or other authority, as aforesaid, with the seal of the proper court or officer thereto attached, which seal shall be sufficient to establish the competency of the proof, and with proof, also by affidavit, of the identity of the person whose service or labor is claimed to be due as aforesaid, that the person so arrested does in fact owe service or labor to the person or persons claiming him or her, in the state or territory from which such fugitive may have escaped as aforesaid, and that said person escaped, to make out and deliver to such claimant, his or her agent or attorney, a certificate setting forth the substantial facts as to the service or labor due from such fugitive to the claimant, and of his or her escape from the state or territory in which such service or labor was due, to the state or territory in which he or she was arrested, with authority to such claimant, or his or her agent or attorney, to use such reasonable force and restraint as may be necessary, under the circumstances of the case, to take and remove such fugitive person back to the state or territory whence he or she may have escaped as aforesaid. In no trial or hearing under this act shall the testimony of such alleged fugitive be admitted in evidence; and the certificates in this and the first (fourth) section mentioned, shall be conclusive of the right of the person or persons in whose favor granted, to remove such fugitive to the state or territory from which he escaped, and shall prevent all molestation of such person or persons by any process issued by any court, judge, magistrate, or other person whomsoever.

Section 7

And be it further enacted, that any person who shall knowingly and willingly obstruct, hinder, or prevent such claimant, his agent or attorney, or any person or persons lawfully assisting him, her, or them, from arresting such a fugitive from service or labor, either with or without process as aforesaid, or shall rescue, or attempt to rescue, such fugitive from service or labor, from the custody of such claimant, his or her agent or attorney, or other person or persons lawfully assisting as aforesaid, when so arrested, pursuant to the authority herein given and declared; or shall aid, abet, or assist such person so owing service or labor as aforesaid, directly or indirectly, to escape from such claimant, his agent or attorney, or other person or persons legally authorized as aforesaid; or shall harbor or conceal such fugitive, so as to prevent the discovery and arrest of such person, after notice or knowledge of the fact that such person was a fugitive from service or labor as aforesaid, shall, for either of said offenses, be subject to a fine not exceeding one thousand dollars and imprisonment not exceeding six months, by indictment and conviction before the district court of the United States for the district in which such offense may have been committed, or before the proper court of criminal jurisdiction, if committed within any one of the organized territories of the United States; and shall moreover forfeit and pay, by way of civil damages to the party injured by such illegal conduct, the sum of one thousand dollars, for each fugitive so lost as aforesaid, to be recovered by action of debt, in any of the district or territorial courts aforesaid, within whose jurisdiction the said offense may have been committed.

Section 8

And be it further enacted, that the marshals, their deputies, and the clerks of the said district and territorial courts, shall be paid, for their services, the like fees as may be allowed to them for similar services in other cases; and where such services are rendered exclusively in the arrest, custody, and delivery of the fugitive to the claimant, his or her agent or attorney, or where such supposed fugitive may be discharged out of custody for the want of sufficient proof as aforesaid, then such fees are to be paid in the whole by such claimant, his agent or attorney; and in all cases where the proceedings are before a commissioner, he shall be entitled to a fee of ten dollars in full for his services in each case, upon the delivery of the said certificate to the claimant, his or her agent or attorney; or a fee of five dollars in cases where the proof shall not, in the opinion of such commissioner, warrant such certificate and delivery, inclusive of all services incident to such arrest and examination, to be paid, in either case, by the claimant, his or her agent or attorney. The person or persons authorized to execute the process to be issued by such commissioners for the arrest and detention of fugitives from service or labor as aforesaid shall also be entitled to a fee of five dollars each for each person he or they may arrest and take before any such commissioner as aforesaid, at the instance and request of such claimant, with such other fees as may be deemed reasonable by such commissioner for such other additional services as may be necessarily performed by him or them: such as attending at the examination, keeping the fugitive in custody, and providing him with food and lodging during his detention, and until the final determination of such commissioner; and, in general, for performing such other duties as may be required by such claimant, his or her attorney or agent, or commissioner in the premises, such fees to be made up in conformity with the fees usually charged by the officers of the courts of justice within the proper district or county, as near as may be practicable, and paid by such claimants, their agents or attorneys, whether such supposed fugitives from service or labor be ordered to be delivered to such claimants by the final determination of such commissioners or not.

Section 9

And be it further enacted, that, upon affidavit made by the claimant of such fugitive, his agent or attorney, after such certificate has been issued, that he has reason to apprehend that such fugitive will be rescued by force from his or their possession before he can be taken beyond the limits of the state in which the arrest is made, it shall be the duty of the officer making the arrest to retain such fugitive in his custody and to remove him to the state whence he fled, and there to deliver him to said claimant, his agent, or attorney. And to this end, the officer aforesaid is hereby authorized and required to employ so many persons as he may deem necessary to overcome such force and to retain them in his service so long as circumstances may require. The said officer and his assistants, while

so employed, to receive the same compensation, and to be allowed the same expenses, as are now allowed by law for transportation of criminals, to be certified by the judge of the district within which the arrest is made, and paid out of the treasury of the United States.

Section 10

And be it further enacted, that when any person held to service or labor in any state or territory, or in the District of Columbia, shall escape therefrom, the party to whom such service or labor shall be due, his, her, or their agent or attorney, may apply to any court of record therein, or judge thereof in vacation, and make satisfactory proof to such court, or judge in vacation, of the escape aforesaid, and that the person escaping owed service or labor to such party. Whereupon the court shall cause a record to be made of the matters so proved, and also a general description of the person so escaping, with such convenient certainty as may be; and a transcript of such record, authenticated by the attestation of the clerk and of the seal of the said court, being produced in any other state, territory, or district in which the person so escaping may be found, and being exhibited to any judge, commissioner, or other officer authorized by the law of the United States to cause persons escaping from service or labor to be delivered up, shall be held and taken to be full and conclusive evidence of the fact of escape, and that the service or labor of the person escaping is due to the party in such record mentioned. And upon the production by the said party of other and further evidence if necessary, either oral or by affidavit, in addition to what is contained in the said record of the identity of the person escaping, he or she shall be delivered up to the claimant. And the said court, commissioner, judge, or other person authorized by this act to grant certificates to claimants of fugitives, shall, upon the production of the record and other evidences aforesaid, grant to such claimant a certificate of his right to take any such person identified and proved to be owing service or labor as aforesaid, which certificate shall authorize such claimant to seize or arrest and transport such person to the state or territory from which he escaped: provided, that nothing herein contained shall be construed as requiring the production of a transcript of such record as evidence as aforesaid. But in its absence the claim shall be heard and determined upon other satisfactory proofs, competent in law.

Approved, September 18, 1850.

AN ACT TO SUPPRESS THE SLAVE TRADE IN THE DISTRICT OF COLUMBIA

[Section 1]

Be it enacted by the Senate and House of Representatives of the United States of America in Congress assembled, that from and after the first day of January, eighteen hundred and fifty-one, it shall not be lawful to bring into the District of Columbia any slave whatever, for the purpose of being sold, or for the purpose of being placed in depot, to be subsequently transferred to any other state or place to be sold as merchandise. And if any slave shall be brought into the said district by its owner, or by the authority or consent of its owner, contrary to the provisions of this act, such slave shall thereupon become liberated and free.

Section 2

And be it further enacted, that it shall and may be lawful for each of the corporations of the cities of Washington and Georgetown, from time to time, and as often as may be necessary, to abate, break up, and abolish any depot or place of confinement of slaves brought into the said district as merchandise, contrary to the provisions of this act, by such appropriate means as may appear to either of the said corporations expedient and proper. And the same power is hereby vested in the Levy Court of Washington County, if any attempt shall be made, within its jurisdictional limits, to establish a depot or place of confinement for slaves brought into the said district as merchandise for sale contrary to this act.

Approved, September 20, 1850.

SLAVERY

KANSAS-NEBRASKA ACT

An Act to Organize the Territories of Nebraska and Kansas

The Kansas-Nebraska Act of 1854 was the third and last of the series of compromises enacted before the U.S. CIVIL WAR in an attempt to resolve the question of whether SLAVERY should be permitted in the western territories. Senator STEPHEN A. DOUGLAS of Illinois, drafted the legislation that revoked the MISSOURI COMPROMISE of 1820, which had banned slavery north of 36°30' latitude. Douglas applied the doctrine of popular sovereignty to the Kansas and Nebraska Territories, as he had successfully urged Congress to do in the COMPROMISE OF 1850. The 1850 law left to New Mexico and Utah the decision of whether to enter the Union as free or slave states.

The Kansas-Nebraska Act failed to end the national conflict over slavery. Antislavery forces viewed the statute as a capitulation to the South, and many abandoned the Whig and Democratic parties to form the REPUBLICAN PARTY. Kansas soon became a battleground over slavery. On May 25, 1856, the militant abolitionist JOHN BROWN led a raid against proslavery supporters at Pottawatomie Creek, Kansas, killing five persons. The violence between the abolitionists and those who were proslavery soon gave the territory the name "Bleeding Kansas."

—✳—

Kansas-Nebraska Act

[SECTION 1]

Be it enacted by the Senate and House of Representatives of the United States of America in Congress assembled, that all that part of the territory of the United States included within the following limits, except such portions thereof as are hereinafter expressly exempted from the operations of this act, to wit: beginning at a point in the Missouri River where the fortieth parallel of north latitude crosses the same; thence west on said parallel to the east boundary of the territory of Utah, on the summit of the Rocky Mountains; thence on said summit northward to the forty-ninth parallel of north latitude; thence east on said summit northward to the forty-ninth parallel of north latitude; thence east on said parallel to the western boundary of the territory of Minnesota; thence southward on said boundary to the Missouri River; thence down the main channel of said river to the place of beginning, be, and the same is hereby, created into a temporary government by the name of the territory of Nebraska; and when admitted as a state or states, the said territory, or any portion of the same, shall be received into the Union with or without slavery, as their constitution may prescribe at the time of their admission. Provided, that nothing in this act contained shall be construed to inhibit the government of the United States from dividing said territory into two or more territories, in such manner and at such times as Congress shall deem convenient and proper, or from attaching any portion of said territory to any other state or territory of the United States. Provided further, that nothing in this act contained shall be construed to impair the rights of person or property now pertaining to the

Source: *Statutes at Large*, vol. 10 (1855), pp. 277–290.

Indians in said territory, so long as such rights shall remain unextinguished by treaty between the United States and such Indians, or to include any territory which, by treaty with any Indian tribe, is not, without the consent of said tribe, to be included within the territorial limits or jurisdiction of any state or territory; but all such territory shall be excepted out of the boundaries, and constitute no part of the territory of Nebraska, until said tribe shall signify their assent to the president of the United States to be included within the said territory of Nebraska, or to affect the authority of the government of the United States to make any regulations respecting such Indians, their lands, property, or other rights by treaty, law, or otherwise, which it would have been competent to the government to make if this act had never passed.

SECTION 2

And be it further enacted, that the executive power and authority in and over said territory of Nebraska shall be vested in a governor, who shall hold his office for four years, and until his successor shall be appointed and qualified, unless sooner removed by the president of the United States. The governor shall reside within said territory and shall be commander in chief of the militia thereof. He may grant pardons and respites for offenses against the laws of said territory and reprieves for offenses against the laws of the United States, until the decision of the president can be made known thereon; he shall commission all officers who shall be appointed to office under the laws of the said territory and shall take care that the laws be faithfully executed.

SECTION 3

And be it further enacted, that there shall be a secretary of said territory, who shall reside therein and hold his office for five years, unless sooner removed by the president of the United States; he shall record and preserve all the laws and proceedings of the legislative assembly hereinafter constituted and all the acts and proceedings of the governor in his executive department; he shall transmit one copy of the laws and journals of the legislative assembly within thirty days after the end of each session and one copy of the executive proceedings and official correspondence semiannually, on the first days of January and July in each year, to the president of the United States and two copies of the laws to the president of the Senate and to the speaker of the House of Representatives, to be deposited in the libraries of Congress; and in case of the death, removal, resignation, or absence of the governor from the territory, the secretary shall be, and he is hereby, authorized and required to execute and perform all the powers and duties of the governor during such vacancy or absence, or until another governor shall be duly appointed and qualified to fill such vacancy.

SECTION 4

And be it further enacted, that the legislative power and authority of said territory shall be vested in the governor and a legislative assembly. The legislative assembly shall consist of a council and house of representatives. The council shall consist of thirteen members having the qualifications of voters, as hereinafter prescribed, whose term of service shall continue two years. The house of representatives shall, at its first session, consist of twenty-six members, possessing the same qualifications as prescribed for members of the council, and whose term of service shall continue one year. The number of representatives may be increased by the legislative assembly, from time to time, in proportion to the increase of qualified voters; provided, that the whole number shall never exceed thirty-nine. An apportionment shall be made, as nearly equal as practicable, among the several counties or districts, for the election of the council and representatives, giving to each section of the territory representation in the ratio of its qualified voters as nearly as may be. And the members of the council and of the house of representatives shall reside in, and be inhabitants of, the district or county or counties for which they may be elected, respectively. Previous to the first election, the governor shall cause a census, or enumeration of the inhabitants and qualified voters of the several counties and districts of the territory, to be taken by such persons and in such mode as the governor shall designate and appoint; and the persons so appointed shall receive a reasonable compensation therefore. And the first election shall be held at such time and places and be conducted in such manner, both as to the persons who shall superintend such election and the returns thereof, as the governor shall appoint and direct; and he shall at the same time declare the number of members of the council and house of representatives to which each of the counties or districts shall be entitled under this act. The persons having the highest number of legal votes in each of said council districts for members of the council shall be declared by the governor to be duly elected to the council; and the persons having the highest number of legal votes for the house of representatives shall be declared by the governor to be duly elected members of said house. Provided, that in case two or more persons voted for shall have an equal number of votes, and in case a vacancy shall otherwise occur in either branch of the legislative assembly, the governor shall order a new election; and the persons thus elected to the legislative assembly shall meet at such place and on such day as the governor shall appoint; but thereafter, the time, place, and manner of holding and conducting all elections by the people and the apportioning the representation in the several counties or districts to the council and house of representatives, according to the number of qualified voters, shall be prescribed by law, as well as the day of the commencement of the regular sessions of the legislative assembly; provided, that no session in any one year shall exceed the term of forty days, except the first session, which may continue sixty days.

SECTION 5

And be it further enacted, that every free white male inhabitant above the age of twenty-one years who shall be an actual resident of said territory and shall possess the qualifications hereinafter prescribed shall be entitled to vote at the first election and shall be eligible to any office within the said territory; but the qualifications of voters, and of holding office, at all subsequent elections, shall be such as shall be prescribed by the legislative assembly. Provided, that the right of suffrage and of holding office shall be exercised only by citizens of the United States and those who shall have declared on oath their intention to become such and shall have taken an oath to support the Constitution of the United States and the provisions of this act; and provided further, that no officer, soldier, seaman, or marine, or other person in the army or navy of the United States, or attached to troops in the service of the United States, shall be allowed to vote or hold office in said territory by reason of being on service therein.

SECTION 6

And be it further enacted, that the legislative power of the territory shall extend to all rightful subjects of legislation consistent with the Constitution of the United States and the provisions of this act; but no law shall be passed interfering with the primary disposal of the soil; no tax shall be imposed upon the property of the United States; nor shall the lands or other property of nonresidents be taxed higher than the lands or other property of residents. Every bill which shall have passed the council and house of representatives of the said territory shall, before it become a law, be presented to the governor of the territory; if he approve, he shall sign it; but if not, he shall return it with his objections to the house in which it originated, who shall enter the objections at large on their journal and proceed to reconsider it. If, after such reconsideration, two-thirds of that house shall agree to pass the bill, it shall be sent, together with the objections, to the other house, by which it shall likewise be reconsidered, and if approved by two-thirds of that house, it shall become a law. But in all such cases the votes of both houses shall be determined by yeas and nays, to be entered on the journal of each house respectively. If any bill shall not be returned by the governor within three days (Sundays excepted) after it shall have been presented to him, the same shall be a law in like manner as if he had signed it, unless the assembly, by adjournment, prevents its return, in which case it shall not be a law.

SECTION 7

And be it further enacted, that all township, district, and county officers, not herein otherwise provided for, shall be appointed or elected, as the case may be, in such manner as shall be provided by the governor and legislative assembly of the territory of Nebraska. The governor shall nominate and, by and with the advice and consent of the legislative council, appoint all officers not herein otherwise provided for; and in the first instance the governor alone may appoint all said officers, who shall hold their offices until the end of the first session of the legislative assembly, and shall lay off the necessary districts for members of the council and house of representatives and all other officers.

SECTION 8

And be it further enacted, that no member of the legislative assembly shall hold, or be appointed to, any office which shall have been created, or the salary or emoluments of which shall have been increased, while he was a member, during the term for which he was elected, and for one year after the expiration of such term; but this restriction shall not be applicable to members of the first legislative assembly; and no person holding a commission or appointment under the United States, except postmasters, shall be a member of the legislative assembly, or hold any office under the government of said territory.

SECTION 9

And be it further enacted, that the judicial power of said territory shall be vested in a supreme court, district courts, probate courts, and in justices of the peace. The supreme court shall consist of a chief justice and two associate justices, any two of whom shall constitute a quorum, and who shall hold a term at the seat of government of said territory annually, and they shall hold their offices during the period of four years, and until their successor shall be appointed and qualified. The said territory shall be divided into three judicial districts, and a district court shall be held in each of said districts by one of the justices of the supreme court at such times and places as may be prescribed by law; and the said judges shall, after their appointments, respectively, reside in the districts which shall be assigned them. The jurisdiction of the several courts herein provided for, both appellate and original, and that of the probate courts and of justices of the peace, shall be as limited by law: provided, that justices of the peace shall not have jurisdiction of any matter in controversy when the title or boundaries of land may be in dispute, or where the debt or sum claimed shall exceed one hundred dollars; and the said supreme and districts courts, respectively, shall possess chancery as well as commonlaw jurisdiction. Each district court, or the judge thereof, shall appoint its clerk, who shall also be the register in chancery, and shall keep his office at the place where the court may be held. Writs of error, bills of exception, and appeals shall be allowed in all cases from the final decisions of said district courts to the supreme court, under such regulations as may be prescribed by law; but in no case removed to the supreme court shall trial by jury be allowed in said court. The supreme court, or the justices thereof, shall appoint its own clerk, and every clerk shall hold his office at the pleasure of the court for which he shall have been appointed. Writs of error and appeals from the final decisions of said supreme court shall be allowed, and may be taken to the Supreme Court of the United States, in the same manner and under the same regulations as from the circuit courts of the United States, where the value of the property, or the amount in controversy, to be ascertained by the oath or affirmation of either party or other competent witness, shall exceed one thousand dollars; except only that in all cases involving title to slaves, the said writs of error or appeals shall be allowed and decided by the said supreme court, without regard to the value of the matter, property, or title in controversy; and except also that a writ of error or appeal shall also be allowed to the Supreme Court of the United States, from the decision of the said supreme court created by this act, or of any judge thereof, or of the district courts created by this act, or of any judge thereof, upon any writ of habeas corpus, involving the question of personal freedom. Provided, that nothing herein contained shall be construed to apply to or affect the provisions to the "Act respecting fugitives from justice, and persons escaping from the service of their masters," approved February twelfth, seventeen hundred and ninety-three, and the "Act to amend and supplementary to the aforesaid act," approved September eighteen, eighteen hundred and fifty; and each of the said district courts shall have and exercise the same jurisdiction in all cases arising under the Constitution and laws of the United States as is vested in the circuit and district courts of the United States; and the said supreme and district courts of the said territory, and the respective judges thereof, shall and may grant writs of habeas corpus in all cases in which the same are granted by the judges of the United States in the District of Columbia; and the first six days of every term of said courts, or so much thereof as shall be necessary, shall be appropriated to the trial of causes arising under the said constitution and laws and writs of error and appeal in all such cases shall be made to the supreme court of said territory, the same as in other cases. The said clerk shall receive in all such cases the same fees which the clerks of the district courts of Utah Territory now receive for similar services.

SECTION 10

And be it further enacted, that the provisions of an act entitled "An act respecting fugitives from justice, and persons escaping from the service of their masters," approved February twelve, seventeen hundred and ninety-three, and

SLAVERY

KANSAS-
NEBRASKA ACT

the provisions of the act entitled "An act to amend, and supplementary to, the aforesaid act," approved September eighteen, eighteen hundred and fifty, be, and the same are hereby, declared to extend to and be in full force within the limits of said territory of Nebraska.

SECTION 11

And be it further enacted, that there shall be appointed an attorney for said territory, who shall continue in office for four years, and until his successor shall be appointed and qualified, unless sooner removed by the president, and who shall receive the same fees and salary as the attorney of the United States for the present territory of Utah. There shall also be a marshal for the territory appointed, who shall hold his office for four years, and until his successor shall be appointed and qualified, unless sooner removed by the president, and who shall execute all processes issuing from the said courts when exercising their jurisdiction as circuit and district courts of the United States; he shall perform the duties, be subject to the same regulation and penalties, and be entitled to the same fees, as the marshal of the district court of the United States for the present territory of Utah, and shall, in addition, be paid two hundred dollars annually as a compensation for extra services.

SECTION 12

And be it further enacted, that the governor, secretary, chief justice and associate justices, attorney, and marshal shall be nominated and, by and with the advice and consent of the Senate, appointed by the president of the United States. The governor and secretary to be appointed as aforesaid shall, before they act as such, respectively take an oath or affirmation before the district judge or some justice of the peace in the limits of said territory, duly authorized to administer oaths and affirmations by the laws now in force therein, or before the chief justice, or some associate justice of the Supreme Court of the United States, to support the Constitution of the United States and faithfully to discharge the duties of their respective offices, which said oaths, when so taken, shall be certified by the person by whom the same shall have been taken; and such certificates shall be received and recorded by the said secretary among the executive proceedings; and the chief justice and associate justices, and all other civil officers in said territory, before they act as such, shall take a

like oath or affirmation before the said governor or secretary, or some judge or justice of the peace of the territory, who may be duly commissioned and qualified, which said oath or affirmation shall be certified and transmitted by the person taking the same to the secretary, to be by him recorded as aforesaid; and afterwards, the like oath or affirmation shall be taken, certified, and recorded, in such manner and form as may be prescribed by law. The governor shall receive an annual salary of two thousand five hundred dollars. The chief justice and associate justices shall each receive an annual salary of two thousand dollars. The secretary shall receive an annual salary of two thousand dollars. The said salaries shall be paid quarter-yearly, from the dates of the respective appointments, at the treasury of the United States; but no such payment shall be made until said officers shall have entered upon the duties of their respective appointments. The members of the legislative assembly shall be entitled to receive three dollars each per day during their attendance at the sessions thereof and three dollars each for every twenty miles' travel in going to and returning from the said sessions, estimated according to the nearest usually travelled route; and an additional allowance of three dollars shall be paid to the presiding officer of each house for each day he shall so preside. And a chief clerk, one assistant clerk, a sergeant-at-arms, and doorkeeper may be chosen for each house; and the chief clerk shall receive four dollars per day, and the said other officers three dollars per day during the session of the legislative assembly; but no other officers shall be paid by the United States; provided, that there shall be but one session of the legislature annually, unless, on an extraordinary occasion, the governor shall think proper to call the legislature together. There shall be appropriated annually the usual sum, to be expended by the governor, to defray the contingent expenses of the territory, including the salary of a clerk of the executive department; and there shall also be appropriated annually a sufficient sum, to be expended by the secretary of the territory, and upon an estimate to be made by the secretary of the treasury of the United States, to defray the expenses of the legislative assembly, the printing of the laws, and other incidental expenses; and the governor and secretary of the territory shall, in the disbursement of all moneys entrusted to them, be governed solely by the instructions of the secretary of the treasury of the United States and shall, semiannually, account to the said secretary for the manner in which the aforesaid moneys shall have been expended; and no expenditure shall be made by said legislative assembly for objects not specially authorized by the acts of Congress, making the appropriations, nor beyond the sums thus appropriated for such objects.

SECTION 13

And be it further enacted, that the legislative assembly of the territory of Nebraska shall hold its first session at such time and place in said territory as the governor thereof shall appoint and direct; and at said first session, or as soon thereafter as they shall deem expedient, the governor and legislative assembly shall proceed to locate and establish the seat of government for said territory at such place as they may deem eligible; which place, however, shall thereafter be subject to be changed by the said governor and legislative assembly.

SECTION 14

And be it further enacted, that a delegate to the House of Representatives of the United States, to serve for the term of two years, who shall be a citizen of the United States, may be elected by the voters qualified to elect members of the legislative assembly, who shall be entitled to the same rights and privileges as are exercised and enjoyed by the delegates from the several other territories of the United States to the said House of Representatives, but the delegate first elected shall hold his seat only during the term of the Congress to which he shall be elected. The first election shall be held at such time and places and be conducted in such manner as the governor shall appoint and direct; and at all subsequent elections the times, places, and manner of holding the elections shall be prescribed by law. The person having the greatest number of votes shall be declared by the governor to be duly elected; and a certificate thereof shall be given accordingly. That the Constitution, and all laws of the United States which are not locally inapplicable, shall have the same force and effect within the said territory of Nebraska as elsewhere within the United States, except the eighth section of the act preparatory to the admission of Missouri into the Union, approved March sixth, eighteen hundred and twenty, which, being inconsistent with the principle of nonintervention by Congress with slavery in the states and territories, as recognized by the legislation of eighteen

hundred and fifty, commonly called the Compromise Measures, is hereby declared inoperative and void; it being the true intent and meaning of this act not to legislate slavery into any territory or state, nor to exclude it therefrom, but to leave the people thereof perfectly free to form and regulate their domestic institutions in their own way, subject only to the Constitution of the United States: provided, that nothing herein contained shall be construed to revive or put in force any law or regulation which may have existed prior to the act of March sixth, eighteen hundred and twenty, either protecting, establishing, prohibiting, or abolishing slavery.

SECTION 15

And be it further enacted, that there shall hereafter be appropriated, as has been customary for the territorial governments, a sufficient amount, to be expended under the direction of the said governor of the territory of Nebraska, not exceeding the sums heretofore appropriated for similar objects, for the erection of suitable public buildings at the seat of government, and for the purchase of a library, to be kept at the seat of government for the use of the governor, legislative assembly, judges of the supreme court, secretary, marshal, and attorney of said territory, and such other persons, and under such regulations, as shall be prescribed by law.

SECTION 16

And be it further enacted, that when the lands in the said territory shall be surveyed under the direction of the government of the United States, preparatory to bringing the same into market, sections numbered sixteen and thirty-six in each township in said territory shall be, and the same are hereby, reserved for the purpose of being applied to schools in said territory and in the states and territories hereafter to be erected out of the same.

SECTION 17

And be it further enacted, that, until otherwise provided by law, the governor of said territory may define the judicial districts of said territory and assign the judges who may be appointed for said territory to the several districts; and also appoint the times and places for holding courts in the several counties or subdivisions in each of said judicial districts by proclamation, to be issued by him; but the legislative assembly, at their first or any subsequent session, may organize, alter, or modify such judicial districts and assign the judges and alter the times and places of holding the courts, as to them shall seem proper and convenient.

SECTION 18

And be it further enacted, that all officers to be appointed by the president, by and with the advice and consent of the Senate, for the territory of Nebraska, who, by virtue of the provisions of any law now existing, or which may be enacted during the present Congress, are required to give security for moneys that may be entrusted with them for disbursement, shall give such security at such time and place and in such manner as the secretary of the treasury may prescribe.

SECTION 19

And be it further enacted, that all that part of the territory of the United States included within the following limits, except such portions thereof as are hereinafter expressly exempted from the operations of this act, to wit, beginning at a point on the western boundary of the state of Missouri, where the thirty-seventh parallel of north latitude crosses the same; thence west on said parallel to the eastern boundary of New Mexico; thence north on said boundary to latitude thirty-eight; thence following said boundary westward to the east boundary of the territory of Utah, on the summit of the Rocky Mountains; thence northward on said summit to the fortieth parallel of latitude; thence east on said parallel to the western boundary of the state of Missouri; thence south with the western boundary of said state to the place of beginning, be, and the same is hereby, created into a temporary government by the name of the territory of Kansas; and when admitted as a state or states, the said territory, or any portion of the same, shall be received into the Union with or without slavery, as their constitution may prescribe at the time of their admission: provided, that nothing in this act contained shall be construed to inhibit the government of the United States from dividing said territory into two or more territories, in such manner and at such times as Congress shall deem convenient and proper, or from attaching any portion of said territory to any other state or territory of the

United States. Provided further, that nothing in this act contained shall be construed to impair the rights of person or property now pertaining to the Indians in said territory, so long as such rights shall remain unextinguished by treaty between the United States and such Indians, or to include any territory which, by treaty with any Indian tribe, is not, without the consent of said tribe, to be included within the territorial limits or jurisdiction of any state or territory; but all such territory shall be excepted out of the boundaries and constitute no part of the territory of Kansas, until said tribe shall signify their assent to the president of the United States to be included within the said territory of Kansas, or to affect the authority of the government of the United States to make any regulation respecting such Indians, their lands, property, or other rights by treaty, law, or otherwise, which it would have been competent to the government to make if this act had never passed.

[Sections 20–30 and 32–36 are identical to the sections establishing a territorial government for Nebraska and have therefore been omitted.]

SECTION 31

And be it further enacted, that the seat of government of said territory is hereby located temporarily at Fort Leavenworth; and that such portions of the public buildings as may not be actually used and needed for military purposes may be occupied and used, under the direction of the governor and legislative assembly, for such public purposes as may be required under the provisions of this act.

SECTION 37

And be it further enacted, that all treaties, laws, and other engagements made by the government of the United States with the Indian tribes inhabiting the territories embraced within this act, shall be faithfully and rigidly observed, notwithstanding anything contained in this act; and that the existing agencies and superintendencies of said Indians be continued with the same powers and duties which are now prescribed by law, except that the president of the United States may, at his discretion, change the location of the office of superintendent.

Approved, May 30, 1854.

SLAVERY

DRED SCOTT V. SANDFORD

The U.S. Supreme Court attempted to resolve the legal status of African Americans in *Dred Scott v. Sandford*. Chief Justice ROGER TANEY's belief that the Court could settle the issue proved mistaken, however. The decision heightened tensions and convinced abolitionists that the legal system was immoral.

Dred Scott was a slave owned by an army surgeon, John Emerson, who resided in Missouri. In 1836 Emerson took Scott to Fort Snelling, in what is now Minnesota, but then was a territory in which slavery had been expressly forbidden by the Missouri Compromise of 1820. In 1846 Scott sued for his freedom in Missouri state court, arguing that his residence in a free territory had released him from slavery. The Missouri Supreme Court rejected his argument, and Scott appealed to the U.S. Supreme Court.

The Court heard arguments on *Dred Scott* in 1855 and 1856. The Court could have disposed of the case on narrower grounds by holding that Scott had not become free through his temporary stay with Emerson in free territory. Instead, Taney decided that the Court needed to address the broader issue of the status of slavery in the territories. He wrote a tortuous opinion, arguing that because of the attitudes toward slavery and African Americans that prevailed in 1787–1789, when the Constitution was drafted and ratified, a slave was not and never could become a federal citizen. In addition, Taney ruled that the free descendants of slaves were not federal citizens and that property in slaves was entitled to such protection that Congress could not constitutionally forbid slavery in the territories.

The immediate effect of the *Dred Scott* decision was to convince abolitionists that the South and the Supreme Court planned to impose slavery throughout the Union. With the start of the U.S. CIVIL WAR in 1861, it became clear that Taney's decision had failed in its essential purpose.

―⁓―

Dred Scott, Plff. in Er., v. John F.A. Sandford.

(See S. C. 19 How. 393–633.)

Plea in abatement, when may be reviewed—the word "citizen" in the Constitution does not embrace one of the negro race—negro cannot become a citizen—slave not made free by residence in a free state or territory—Declaration of Independence does not include slaves as part of the people—the rights and privileges conferred by the constitution upon citizens do not apply to the negro race—Constitution should have the meaning intended when it was adopted—court may examine other errors besides plea in abatement—Constitution expressly affirms right of property in slaves—Missouri compromise unconstitutional and void.

Where a plea in abatement, by defendant, to the jurisdiction of the court below is overruled on demurrer, and the defendant thereupon pleads in bar, upon which issues were joined and the trial and verdict were in his favor, and the plaintiff thereupon brought the case into this court by writ of error, and the plea and demur-

SLAVERY

rer and judgment of the court below upon it are part of the record; held, that this court has power to review the decision of the court below upon the plea in abatement.

It is therefore the duty of the court to decide whether the facts stated in the plea, are or are not sufficient to show that the plaintiff is not entitled to sue as a citizen in the court of the United States.

The provisions of the Constitution of the United States in relation to the personal rights and privileges to which the citizen of a state should be entitled, do not embrace the negro African race, at that time in this country, or who might afterwards be imported, who had then been or should afterwards be made free in any state.

Such provisions of the Constitution do not put it in the power of a single state to make out one of the negro African race a citizen of the United States, and to endue him with the full rights of citizenship in every other state without their consent.

The Constitution of the United States does not act upon one of the negro race whenever he shall be made free under the laws of a state, and raise him to the rank of a citizen, and immediately clothe him with all the privileges of a citizen of any other state, and in its own courts.

The plaintiff in error was a negro slave, and brought into a free State (Illinois), and in the free territory of the United States for about four years, during which time he was married to another negro slave who also was in said free territory. One of their children (Eliza) was born on the River Mississippi, north of the north line of Missouri, and another of their children was born in the State of Missouri, to which state he had returned.

Held, that the plaintiff in error could not be and was not a citizen of the State of Missouri, within the meaning of the constitution of the United States, and consequently was not entitled to sue in its courts.

The legislation and histories of the times, and the language used in the Declaration of Independence, show that neither the class of persons who had been imported as slaves, nor their descendants, whether they had become free or not, were then acknowledged as part of the people, nor intended to be included in the general words used in that instrument.

The descendants of Africans who were imported into this country and sold as slaves, when they shall become emancipated, or who are born of parents who had become free before their birth, are not citizens of a state in the sense in which the word "citizens" is used in the Constitution of the United States.

The enslaved African race was not intended to be included in, and formed no part of, the people who framed and adopted the Declaration of Independence.

When the framers of the Constitution were conferring special rights and privileges upon the citizens of a state in every other part of the Union, it is impossible to believe that these rights and privileges were intended to be extended to the negro race.

The words of the Constitution should be given the meaning they were intended to bear, when that instrument was framed and adopted.

Where this court has decided against the jurisdiction of the Circuit Court on a plea of abatement, it has still the right to examine any question presented by exception or by the record, and may reverse the judgement for errors committed, and remand the case to the Circuit Court for it to dismiss the case for want of jurisdiction.

The right of property in a slave is distinctly and expressly affirmed in the Constitution.

The Act of Congress which prohibited a citizen from holding and owning property of this kind in the territory of the United States north of the line therein mentioned (thirty-six degrees thirty minutes north latitude), is not warranted by the Constitution, and is therefore void.

Neither Dred Scott himself, nor any of his family were made free by being carried into such territory; even if they had been carried there by their owner with the intention of becoming permanent residents.

Scott was not made free by being taken to Rock Island in the State of Illinois.

As Scott was a slave when taken into the State of Illinois by his owner, and was there held as such, and brought back into Missouri in that character, his status, as free or slave, depended on the laws of Missouri, and not of Illinois. He and his family were not free, by the laws of Missouri, the property of defendant.

Argued Feb. 11, 12, 13 and 14, 1856. May 12, 1856, ordered to be re-argued at the next term.

Re-argued Dec. 15, 16, 17 and 18, 1856. Decided March 6, 1857.

In Error to the Circuit Court of the United States for the District of Missouri.

On November 2, 1853, Dred Scott, by his attorney, filed in the clerk's office of the Circuit Court of the United States for the District of Missouri, the following declaration against the defendant, John F.A. Sandford:

Dred Scott, of St. Louis, in the State of Missouri, and a citizen of the State of Missouri, complains of John F.A. Sandford, of the City of New York, and a citizen of the State of New York, in the plea of trespass for that the defendant heretofore, to wit: on the 1st day of January, A.D. 1853, at St. Louis, in the County of St. Louis and State of Missouri, with force and arms assaulted the plaintiff, and without law or right held him as a slave, and imprisoned him for the space of six hours and more, and then and there did threaten to beat the plaintiff and to hold him in prison, and restrained of liberty, so that by means of such threats the plaintiff was put in fear and could not attend to his business, to wit: $2,500, and other wrongs to the plaintiff then and there did, against the peace and to the damage of the plaintiff $3,000.

And also for that the defendant heretofore, on the 1st day of January, A.D. 1853, with force and arms at St. Louis aforesaid, an assault did make on Harriet Scott, then and still the wife of the plaintiff, and then and there did imprison said Harriet, and hold her as a slave, without law or right, for the space of six hours, and then and there did threaten to beat said Harriet and hold her as a slave, so that by means of the premises said Harriet was put in great fear and pain, and could not and did not attend to the plaintiff's business, and the plaintiff lost and was deprived of the society, comfort and assistance of his wife, and thereby lost great gains and profits, of the value, to wit: of $2,500, and other wrongs to the plaintiff, the defendant then and there did, against the peace and to the plaintiff's damage, $3,000.

And also for that the defendant heretofore, to wit: on the 1st day of January, A.D. 1853, with force and arms at St. Louis aforesaid, made an assault on Eliza Scott and Lizzie Scott, then and still infant daughters and servants of the plaintiff, and then and here imprisoned and held as slaves said Eliza and Lizzie, for a long space of time, to wit: six hours, and then and there did

threaten to beat said Eliza and Lizzie and hold them as slaves and restrained of their liberty, so that by means of the premises, said Eliza and Lizzie were put in great fear, and could not and did not attend to plaintiff's business as otherwise they might and would have done, and the plaintiff thereby lost the comfort, society, service and assistance of his said children and servants, of great value, to wit: $2,500, and other wrongs to the plaintiff, the defendant then and there did against the peace, and to the damage of plaintiff $3,000, and the plaintiff on account of the aforesaid several grievances, brings suit, etc. by his attorney, R.M. Field.

The defendant, by his attorney, filed the following plea:

Plea to the jurisdiction of the court. April Term, 1854.

And the said John F.A. Sandford, in his own proper person, comes and says that this court ought not to have or take further cognizance of the action aforesaid, because he says that said cause of action, and each and every of them, if any such have accrued to the said Dred Scott, accrued to the said Dred Scott out of the jurisdiction of this court and exclusively within the jurisdiction of the courts of the State of Missouri; for that, to wit: the said plaintiff Dred Scott is not a citizen of the State of Missouri, as alleged in his declaration, because he is a negro of African descent, his ancestors were of pure African blood, and were brought into this country and sold as negro slaves, and this the said Sandford is ready to verify; wherefore he prays judgment whether this court can or will take further cognizance of the action aforesaid.

The plea was verified.

The plaintiff filed the following demurrer to this plea:

And now comes the plaintiff and demurs in law to the plea of the defendant to the jurisdiction of the court, and says that the said plea and the matters therein contained are not sufficient in law to preclude the court of its jurisdiction of this case, and that the plaintiff is not bound by law to reply to said plea. Wherefore the plaintiff prays judgment of said plea, and that the defendant answer further to the plaintiff's said action, etc.

On April 24, 1854, the matters of law arising upon the demurrer were argued and submitted to the court. On April 25, the court rendered a decision that the law was for plaintiff on said demurrer, and that the said demurrer be, and the same is hereby sustained.

On May 4, 1854, in accordance with an agreement by the attorneys, the defendant filed pleas, Nos. 1, 2 and 3, to all of which pleas the plaintiff filed replications. Said attorneys also filed an agreement upon the statement of the facts in this case. The pleas are as follows:

1. And the said John F.A. Sandford, by H.A. Garland, his attorney, comes and defends the wrong and injury, when, etc., and says that he is not guilty of the said supposed trespass above laid to his charge, or any part thereof in manner and form as the said Dred Scott hath above thereof complained against him, and of this he, the said Sandford, putteth himself upon the country.

2. And for a further plea in this behalf, as to the making of said assault on said Dred Scott in the first count in said declaration mentioned, imprisoning him and keeping and detaining him in prison, etc., the said Sandford, by leave of the court first obtained, says that the said Dred Scott ought not have or maintain his aforesaid action thereof against him, because he says that before, and at the time when, etc., in the said first count mentioned, the said Dred Scott was a negro slave, the lawful property of the defendant, and as such slave he gently laid his hands upon him, and only restrained him of such liberty as he had a right to do, and this the said Sandford is ready to verify, wherefore he prays judgment whether the said Scott ought to have or maintain his aforesaid action thereof against him.

3. And for a further plea in this behalf, as to making the said assault upon Harriet, the wife, and Eliza and Lizzie, the daughters of the said Dred Scott, in the second and third counts of the said declaration mentioned, and imprisoning them and keeping and detaining them in prison, etc., the said John F.A. Sandford, by leave of the court obtained, says that said Dred Scott out not to have or maintain his aforesaid action thereof against him, because he says that before and at the said time, etc., when etc., in the said second and third counts mentioned, the said Harriet, wife of said Scott, and Eliza and Lizzie, his daughters, were the lawful slaves of the said Sandford, and as such slaves he gently laid his hands upon them and restrained them of their liberty as he had a right to do. And this he is ready to verify. Wherefore he prays judgment, etc.

Garland, for defendant.

The replications are as follows:

The plaintiff, as to the plea of the defendant firstly above pleaded, and whereof he has put himself on the country, doth do like. Field.

And the plaintiff, as to the plea of the defendant secondly above pleaded as to said several trespasses in the introductory part of that plea mentioned and therein attempted to be justified, says that the plaintiff, by reason of anything in that plea alleged, ought not to be barred from having and maintaining his aforesaid action against the defendant, because he says that said defendant at said time, when, etc., of his own wrong, and without the cause by him in his said second plea alleged, committed the said several trespasses in the introductory part of that plea mentioned, in manner and form as the plaintiff has above in his declaration complained, and this the plaintiff prays may be inquired of by the country.

The replication to the third plea was similar to the second.

The agreed statement of facts was as follows:

In the year 1834 the plaintiff was a negro slave belonging to Doctor Emerson, who was a surgeon in the Army of the United States. In that year, 1834, said Doctor Emerson took the plaintiff from the State of Missouri to the military post at Rock Island in the State of Illinois, and held him there as a slave until the month of April or May, 1836. At the time last mentioned, said Doctor Emerson removed the plaintiff from said military post at Rock Island to the military post at Fort Snelling, situate on the west bank of the Mississippi River in the Territory known as Upper Louisiana, acquired by the United States of France, and situate north of the latitude of 36 degrees 30 minutes north, and north of the State of Missouri. Said doctor Emerson held the plaintiff in slavery at said Fort Snelling, from said last-mentioned date until the year 1838.

In the year 1835, Harriet, who is named in the second count of the plaintiff's declaration, was the negro slave of Major Taliaferro, who belonged to the Army of the United States. In that year, 1835, said Major Taliaferro took said Harriet to said Fort Snelling, a military post situated as hereinbefore stated, and kept her there as a slave until the year 1836, and then sold and delivered her as a slave at said Fort Snelling unto the said Doctor Emerson hereinbefore named.

Said Doctor Emerson held said Harriet in slavery at said Fort Snelling until the year 1838.

In the year 1836 the plaintiff and said Harriet, at said Fort Snelling, with the consent of said Doctor Emerson, who then claimed to be heir master and owner, intermarried and took each other for husband and wife, Eliza and Lizzie named in the third count of the plaintiff's declaration, are the fruit of that marriage. Eliza is about fourteen years old, and was born on board of the steamboat Gipsey, north of the north line of the State of Missouri, and upon the River Mississippi. Lizzie is about seven years old, and was born in the State of Missouri, at the military post called Jefferson Barracks.

In the year 1838, said Doctor Emerson remove the plaintiff and said Harriet and their said daughter Eliza from said Fort Snelling to the State of Missouri, where they have ever since resided.

Before the commencement of this suit, said Doctor Emerson sold and conveyed the plaintiff, said Harriet, Eliza and Lizzie, to the defendant as slaves, and the defendant has ever since claimed to hold them, and each of them as slaves.

At the times mentioned in the plaintiff's declaration, the defendant, claiming to be owner as aforesaid, laid his hands upon said plaintiff, Harriet, Eliza and Lizzie, and imprisoned them, doing in this respect, however no more than what he might lawfully do, if they were of right his slaves at such time.

Further proof may be given on the trial for either party.

Mr. R.M. Field, for plaintiff.

Mr. H.A. Garland for defendant.

The case was tried, at the Circuit Court held for the District of Missouri at St. Louis on May 15, 1854, before the court and a jury.

The jury found the following verdict, *viz.*:

"As to the first issue joined in this case, we of the jury find the defendant not guilty; and as to the issue secondly above joined, we of the jury find, that before and at the time when, etc., in the first count mentioned, the said Dred Scott was a negro slave, the lawful property of the defendant. And as to the issue thirdly above joined, we the jury find, that before and at the time when, etc., in the second and third counts mentioned, the said Harriet wife of said Dred Scott, and Eliza and Lizzie the daughters of the

said Dred Scott were negro slaves, the lawful property of the defendant." Whereupon it is now considered by the court, that the plaintiff take nothing by his writ in this case, and that the defendant John F.A. Sandford go hence without day and recover against said plaintiff, Dred Scott, the costs by him expended in the defense of this suit.

A motion for a new trial was made by the attorneys for the plaintiff, which the court overruled. Thereupon the said plaintiff filed a bill of exception, which is as follows:

Dred Scott v. John F.A. Sandford.

April Term, 1854.

On the trial of this cause by the jury, the plaintiff, to maintain the issues on his part, read to the jury, the following agreed statement of facts.

"It is agreed that Dred Scott brought suit for his freedom, in the Circuit Court of St. Louis County; that there was a verdict and judgment in his favor; that on a writ of error to the Supreme Court, the judgment below was reversed, and the same remanded to the Circuit Court, where it has been continued to await the decision of this case.

Mr. Field, for plaintiff.

Mr. Garland, for defendant."

No further testimony was given to the jury by either party. Thereupon the plaintiff moved the court to give the jury, the following instructions:

Plaintiff's Instruction.

The jury are instructed, that upon the facts agreed to by the parties, they ought to find for the plaintiff.

The court refused to give such instruction to the jury, and the plaintiff to such refusal then and there duly excepted. The court then gave the following instruction to the jury, on motion of the defendant:

Defendant's Instruction.

The jury are instructed, that upon the facts in this case the law is with the defendant.

To the giving of such instruction the plaintiff then and there duly excepted.

The jury found the verdict as above. The plaintiff thereupon immediately filed in court the following motion for a new trial:

And now, after verdict, and before judgment, the plaintiff comes and moves the court to set aside the verdict and grant a new trial, because the court misdirected the jury in matter of law on said trial. Field.

The court overruled the said motion and gave judgment on verdict for the defendant; and to such action of the court the plaintiff then and there duly excepted.

The plaintiff writes this bill of exceptions and prays that it may be allowed, and signed and sealed. Field.

Allowed and signed and sealed, May 15, 1854.

R. W. Wells. [seal.]

A writ of error was issued, and in the Supreme Court of the United States, December Term, 1854, the following was filed:

And now comes said plaintiff in error and says that in the record of the proceedings, and in the giving of judgment below, there is manifest error, because the court below gave judgment for the defendant below, when the judgment should have been for plaintiff below, wherefore for said errors and others the plaintiff prays judgment of reversal here, and that he may be restored to all he has lost.

By his attorney, Nathaniel Holmes. Filed, Dec. 30, 1854.

Messrs. M. Blair and Curtis, for the plaintiff in error:

1. The first question is, whether this court will consider the question raised in the Circuit Court by the plea to the jurisdiction, no final judgment having been rendered on the demurrer to that plea, and the defendant having pleaded over after the demurrer was sustained, and the final judgment assigned for error having been rendered on the issue on the merits.

2. Whether, if the ruling of the Circuit Court on the demurrer to the plea in abatement is subject to be reviewed here, the judgment of the court, in holding the plaintiff to be "a citizen" in such sense as to enable him to maintain an action in that character in the courts of the United States, was erroneous.

3. Whether the facts stated in the agreed case entitle the plaintiff and his family to freedom, supposing the 8th section of the Act of 1820, known as the Missouri Compromise, to be constitutional.

4. Whether the said Act is constitutional.

Upon the first point the counsel cited, *Shephard v. Graves*, 14 How. 519; *U. S. v. Boyd*, 5 How. 51; *Smith v. Kernochen*, 7 How. 216; *Sims v. Hundley*, 6 How. 1; *Bailey v. Dozier*, 6 How . 23; *Conard v. Atlantic Ins. Co.* 1 Pet. 386; *De Wolf v. Rabaud*, 1 Pet. 476; *Evans v. Gee*, 11 Pet. 89; 1 Wash. C. C. 70, 80; 2 Sumn. 251; 2 Dall. 341; 4 Dall. 330, and then said: In this case, as in those cited, the declaration gives jurisdiction, and the facts alleged in support of it can only be contested by making an issue as in other cases. If that issue be not made, or be waived in the conduct of the cause according to a well-settled practice of the court, there is no reason in this case more than in any other why the objection should be available at a later stage of the case. If the fact had been that plaintiff was not a resident of Missouri, and that was the reason why he was not a citizen, no advantage could be taken of the fact at any subsequent stage of the case. What difference does it make that another fact is relied on to show that he is not a citizen? It is the right to sue as "a citizen" of Missouri, which is questioned: and it is immaterial whether the right be questioned on account of residence, or on account of any other circumstances which deprives him of the character of a citizen of Missouri.

2. But if the court should be of opinion that the question raised by the plea in abatement, and the demurrer thereto, is not waived, and that the judgment of the Circuit Court therein must be maintained before it will consider the questions affecting his right to freedom, I submit the following considerations in support of the judgment on the demurrer:

The opinion of the court in *Amy v. Smith*, 1 Litt. 326, 4 Ga. 68, that free negroes are not citizens within the meaning of the 2d section of the 4th article of the Constitution, delivered in the spring of 1822, displays no research, logic or learning. On the other hand, the dissenting opinion of Judge Mills, p. 337, is sustained by the views of Judge Washington in *Corfield v. Coryell*, 4 Wash. C. C. 71.

21 Ala. 434; *State v. Manuel*, 4 Dev. & Bat. 24.

The other decisions relied on, Meigs, 339; 1 English, 509, are to the same effect as the decision in *Amy v. Smith*, and simply follow that.

The argument most relied on by those who deny the citizenship of free colored men is, that the Acts of Congress on the subject of naturalization provide for naturalizing white persons only. But even naturalization was not limited to the whites by the Constitution, and it has been extended repeatedly by treaty and Act of Congress to Indians and negroes.

Treaty with Choctaws, art. 14, 20th September , 1830; Treaty with the Cherokees, 12th art. Vol. V. U. S. Laws, 647; Treaties of 1803 for Louisiana, 1819 for Florida, 1847 for California; 21 Ala. 454; and as Judge Gaston says, 4 Dev. & Bat. 24, there is no connection between the subject of citizenship as acquired by birth and that acquired under the laws of Congress, and it would be a dangerous mistake to confound them. That citizenship is acquired by birth, is a well settled common law principle.

Vattel, ch. 19, secs. 212, 313, 314; Justinian, Lib. 1, Tit. 5, sec. 3; Constitution, sec. 5, art. 2.

The Constitution of the United States recognizes but two kinds of free persons, citizens and aliens. Nobody supposes that free negroes are aliens. They must therefore be citizens.

Opinions Atty.-Gen. Vol. IV. p. 417; 3d sec. Act march 6, 1820; 6th sec. Act of 1812, to form a territorial government in Missouri; Militia Act, May 17, 1792; Constitutions of Kentucky, Louisiana, Mississippi, Connecticut and Missouri.

All of the above define the qualifications of electors in terms, "free white male citizens;" and thus show that it is as a class of citizens that the negroes are excluded. These considerations would authorize the conclusion that the framers of the Constitutions and the patriots of that era regarded this class of persons as citizens, and included them in that character in the provisions of the Constitutions; and this is fully confirmed by reference to the laws and records of that day.

Act of Mass. 6th March, 1788; Proposal of South Carolina, Jan. 25, 1778. to amend the 4th article; Journals, Vol. II. p. 606; Journals, Vol. IV. p. 183; Organization of the Western Territory, Resolutions, April 23, 1784; Ordinance 1787, art. 4; 2 Kent's Com. p. 258, note b.

Missouri Rev. Laws of 1845, p. 755, and Code of 1835, allude to free negroes who were "citizens."

No reason can be imagined for permitting a suit between free white persons of different states, for wrongs which the local tribunals were deemed inadequate to redress, which will not apply with equal force to controversies to which a free negro may be a party. They have equal capacity with other citizens to hold property

and carry on business, and therefore to create the mischief against which the national judiciary was provided. The words of a law are to be construed with reference to the object of the law.

16 Pet. 640; 12 Wheat. 441; 16 Pet. 104.

In 1 Paine, C. C. 394, the courts say that a person need not have acquired political rights; it is only necessary that he should have acquired a domicil, to enable him to sue as a citizen; and in 3 Wash. C. C. 546, that "citizenship means nothing but residence."

3. The next question to be considered is, whether Dred and his family, or either of them, was emancipated by being taken to Illinois, and to that part of Louisiana Territory lying north of 36 degrees 30 minutes, and being detained there in the manner described in the agreed case. The eldest child, Eliza, having been born north of the Missouri line, on the boat whilst descending the Mississippi, was free under the Constitution of Illinois, and well settled legal principles.

Constitutions of Illinois, art. 6, secs. 1 and 2; 3 U. S. Stat. at L. p. 544; *Spotts v. Gillaspie*, 6 Rand. (Va.), 572; *Commonwealth v. Holloway*, 2 S. & R. 305.

The Circuit Court decided against the plaintiff on the strength of *Scott v. Emerson*, 15 Mo. 586.

But the question depends on general principles, and the courts of the United States, whilst they will respectfully consider the decisions of the State Court, decide such questions according to their own judgment of the law.

Swift v. Tyson, 16 Pet. 1; *Carpenter v. Ins. Co.* 16 Pet. 511; *Lane v. Vick*, 3 How. 476; *Foxcroft v. Mallett*, 4 How 379.

During the time that Dr. Emerson kept Dred at his station at Rock Island, and Harriet at Fort Snelling, there is no evidence that he had or claimed a residence elsewhere, and this court, in *Ennis v. Smith*, 14 how. 423, "where a party lives, is taken prima facie to be his domicil."

See, also *Sylvia v. Kirby*, 17 Mo. 434.

In the case of *Scott v. Emerson*, 15 Mo. 576, the court base their decision on two grounds:

1st. That by returning to Missouri to reside the master's right, which was suspended during the residence in Illinois, and in the Territory, is revived.

2d. The Constitution of Illinois, and the 8th sec. of the Act of 1820, are penal statutes which

SLAVERY

DRED SCOTT V. SANDFORD

the courts of other States were not bound to enforce.

In support of the first position, *Ex parte Grace*, 2 Hagg. 90; *Commonwealth v. Aves*, 18 Pick. 193, and *Mahoney v. Ashton*, 4 H. & McH. 295, were cited.

These decisions are inapplicable to the case at bar, for the present case the Constitution and Statute of Illinois expressly provide that emancipation shall be the effect of the violation of the provision. The laws under which the above decisions were made were different.

David v. Porter, 4 H. & McH. 418; *Betty v. Horton*, 1 Lee, 615.

The second ground relied upon by the court was equally untenable. See opinion of Judge Gambles, of the same case of *Emerson v. Scott*, "in this State it has been recognized from the beginning of the government as a correct position in law, that the master who takes his slave to reside in a state or territory where slavery is prohibited, emancipates his slave."

Also *McMicken v. Amos*, 4 Rand. 134; *Bank v. Earle*, 13 Pet. 590; *Spencer v. Dennis*, 8 Gill 321.

4. The freedom of Harriet and her daughter Lizzie depends on the validity of the 8th section of the Act of March 6, 1820, entitled "An Act to authorize the people of Missouri Territory to form a constitution and state government," etc.

The section is as follows:

That in all that territory ceded by France to the United States, which lies north of 36 degrees 30 minutes north latitude, not included within the limits of the State contemplated by this Act, slavery and involuntary servitude, otherwise than in the punishment of crimes whereof the party shall have been duly convicted, shall be, and the same is hereby forever prohibited.

Provided, always, that any person escaping into the same, from whom labor or service is lawfully claimed in any State or Territory of the United States, such fugitive may be lawfully reclaimed and conveyed to the person claiming his or her labor or service as aforesaid.

The Validity of this section is denied, on the ground that Congress possessed no power to prohibit slavery in the Territories.

It is not the power to govern the Territories, but the extent of the power which is questioned. Even those who deny any constitutional power on the ground of necessity; but they say where

the necessity stops, there the power ceases. But this concedes the whole question; for it be lawful to legislate at all, the quantum which may be necessary is purely a legislative question; and indeed, whether the Constitution confers directly the legislative power in question or not is immaterial, seeing that it owns the lands, and has power to pass what laws it may deem expedient to dispose of and make them available.

Undoubtedly, for temporary purposes, it is indispensable that provision be made to govern the people in order that the lands shall posses any value, or that what remains after part is sold, may not be seized and confiscated. What would be proper provisions to this end, is not within the scope of judicial inquiry. If it were, it is demonstrable that the provision in question is most judicious, as a mere regulation to facilitate the disposition of public lands.

But it is alleged that the particular provision prohibiting slavery is violative of some part of the Constitution, which establishes the quality of the States and the rights of slave holders to take that species of property into the Territories of the United States. I admit that whether the power of Congress to legislate be given expressly or implication, it is given with the limitation that it shall be exercised in subordination to the Constitution, and that if it be exercised in violation of any provisions of the Constitution, the Act would be void. Subject to this limitation, Congress is at liberty to adopt any means to accomplish its object.

McCulloch v. Maryland, 4 Wheat. 316.

But where is it written in the Constitution that no law shall be passed prohibiting slavery in the territories? Not only was this measure adopted as one deemed advisable and proper to the well government of the territories under both the Confederation and the Constitution, but when the Mississippi Territory was ceded in 1798, it was deemed necessary to stipulate that slavery should not be prohibited, in order to limit the discretion of Congress. The limitation sought to be imposed is one dependent altogether upon state laws, and subjects Congress to the State Legislatures. The Act is now claimed as unconstitutional, because a species of property recognized in the laws of the States cannot be held in the Territories; but it would become constitutional if the States should cease to recognize such property; and again unconstitutional if the States should recognize it again. How the law in question affects the States as States, in any respect, is not perceived; it is not pretended that any State has legislative rights in the Territories.

Pollard v. Hagan, 3 How. 322.

On other subjects, there are difficulties in adjusting the rights of the general and state governments; but there can be no conflict on this. Over the Territories, the general government alone has any power; and in the exercise of that, as of all other powers, is a government of the people. "In form and substance (this court says, it emanates from them, its powers are granted by them, and are to be exercised on them and for their benefit."

On this branch of the subject, the counsel cited the following authorities: Story's Com. Const. Vol. III., pp. 193, 195; 1 Kent's Com. 360; Sergeant, Const. Law, 389; *McCulloch v. Maryland,* 4 Wheat. 422; *Am. Ins. Co. v. Canter,* 1 Pet. 543; *Cherokee Nation v. Georgia,* 5 Pet. 44; *Menard v. Aspasia,* 5 Pet. 505; *Strader v. Graham,* 10 How. 93; *Cross v. Harrison,* 16 How. 193; *Hogg v. Zanesville Canal Co.* 5 Ohio, 410; *Phoebe v. Jay,* Breese, 210; *Spooner v. McConnell,* 1 McL. 341; *Harry v. Decker,* Walker (Miss.) 36; *Rachael v. Walker,* 4 Mo. 350; 3 How 223. And the following Acts of Congress; 1 Stat. at L., pp. 50, 551; 2 Stat. at L., pp. 58, 283, 309, 514; 3 Stat. at L., p. 546; 4 Stat. at L., p. 740; 5 Stat. at L., pp. 10, 235, 797; 9 Stat. at L., pp. 223, 447.

Messrs. H. S. Geyer and R. Johnson, for the defendant in error:

This cause was argued before this court at the December Term, 1855, when it was ordered to be re-argued by counsel for their respective parties, at a next term of court, and especially upon the following points:

1. Whether or not the facts being admitted by the demurrer to the plea to the jurisdiction, the judgment on the demurrer being that the defendant answer over, and the submission of the defendant to that judgment, by pleading over the merits, the appellate court can take notice of these facts thus admitted upon the record, in determining the question of the jurisdiction to the court below, to hear and fully dispose of the case.

2. Whether or not, assuming that the appellate court is bound to take notice of the facts thus appearing upon the record, the plaintiff is a citizen of the State of Missouri within the meaning of the 11th section of the Judiciary Act of 1789.

1. The averment that the plaintiff is a citizen of the State of Missouri, is a necessary averment. If it had been omitted or defectively stated, it would have been error in the Circuit Court to entertain jurisdiction, even though the defendant had not traversed the averment, but pleaded to the merits.

3 Dall. 382; 2 Cranch, 1, 126; *Sullivan v. Fulton Steamboat Co.* 6 Wheat. 450; *Turner v. Enrille,* 4 Dall. 7; *Capron v. Van Noorden,* 2 Cranch, 126.

If the plea demurred to, is to be regarded as a traverse or averment of citizenship of the plaintiff, then the fact on which the plaintiff claims a right to sue in the Circuit Court does not appear by the record; on the contrary, it appears affirmatively that he had no right to sue in that court. The whole question, whether the court could entertain jurisdiction and allow the defendant to plead over, depends on the decision on the demurrer. If that was erroneous, it was error to proceed further, and the defendants pleading over could not give jurisdiction.

2. It appears by the record that the defendant is a negro, born a slave; and therefore, whether he is entitled to freedom or not, by his temporary residence at Rock Island or Fort Snelling, or both, he is not and cannot be a citizen of the State of Missouri, within the meaning of the Constitution, or sec. 11 of the Judiciary Act.

Citizens, within the meaning of art. 3, sec. 2, are citizens of the United States, who are citizens of the state in which they respectively reside.

Read v. Bertrand, 4 Wash. C. C. 516; *Knox v. Greenleaf,* 4 Dall. 360; 3 Story on Const. 565, secs. 1687, 1688; 6 Pet. 761.

Citizens are natives or naturalized. All persons born in the United States are not citizens.

Exceptions are:

First. Children of foreign ambassadors.

Second. Indians.

Third. In general, persons of color.

1 Bouv. Inst. pp. 16, 64; *Amy v. Smith,* 1 Lit. Ky. 334; 2 Kent's Com. p. 258, note b.

Free blacks are not citizens within the provision of the Constitution, art. 4, sec. 2; so held by Dagget, Ch. J., in Connecticut. See note Kent's Com. supra.

See also, *State v. Claiborne,* 1 Meigs, 331; Opinions Atty.Gen. Vol. I. 382, ed. 41; Vol. I. p. 506, ed. 52. "An inquiry into the political grade of the free colored population, under the Constitution of the United States," by John P. Denny.

Persons who are not citizens of the United States by birth, can become such only by virtue of treaty, or in pursuance of some law of the United States.

The power of naturalization is exclusively vested in Congress.

U.S. v. Villato, 2 Dall. 370; *Chirac v. Chirac,* 2 Wheat. 269; *Houston v. Moore,* 5 Wheat. 48.

A slave cannot become a citizen merely by a discharge from bondage.

3. Assuming that the Circuit Court had jurisdiction, the facts, as agreed by the parties, do not establish the right of the plaintiff, his wife and children, or either of them, to freedom.

Sec. 1 of art. 5 of the Constitution of Illinois, and sec. 8 of the Act of 6 March, 1820, do not declare the consequence of bringing a slave within the Territory, embraced. There is no exception or saving in respect to the rights of travelers. The effect of the provision is, in terms, the same, whether a slave is introduced to reside there or for some temporary purpose. Neither clause changes the condition of the slave brought into the Territory embraced by it. The slave is held to be free while he remains within such State or country, only because his owner has not the authority of law to restrain him of his liberty.

The owner's authority is restored if the slave is found within a State or country where slavery exists by law.

The Slave Grace, 2 Hagg. Adm. 94; *Willard v. The People,* 4 Scam. 461; *Graham v. Strader,* 5 B. Mon. 181; 7 B. Mon. 633; *Collins v. America,* 9 B. Mon 565; *Mercer v. Gilman,* 11 B. Mon. 210; *Maria v. Kirby,* 12 B. Mon. 542; *Lewis v. Fullerton,* 1 Rand. 15.

It has been held that where an owner of a slave brings him into a State or country in which slavery does not exist, or is prohibited by law, with the intention to make it his domicil, it operates as an emancipation, and the master cannot resume domain, though the slave return to, or is found in a country where slavery exists by law.

Rankin v. Lydia, 2 A. K. Marsh. 467; *Griffith v. Fanny,* Gilm. (Va.) 143; *Lunsford v. Coquillon,* 2 Mart. N. S. 405; *Josephine v. Poultney,* 1 La. Ann.

329; *Winney v. Whitesides,* 1 Mo. 472; *Milly v. Smith,* 2 Mo. 172; *Nat v. Ruddle,* 8 Mo. 282; *Rachel v. Walker,* 4 Mo. 350; overruled in *Scott v. Emerson,* 15 Mo. 570; *Sylvia v. Kirby,* 17 Mo. 434.

These are cases of emancipation by the voluntary act of the master, binding upon him everywhere, as would be emancipation upon any other proof recognized by law. Slaves, however, attending their owners temporarily sojourning in, or traveling through a State wherein slavery does not exist by law, are not thereby emancipated.

2 A. K. Marsh. 467; *Graham v. Strader,* 5 B. Mon. 181; *Mercer v. Gilman,* 11 B. Mon. 210; *Maria v. Kirby,* 12 B. Mon. 542; *Lewis v. Fullerton,* 1 Rand. 15; *Henry v. Ball,* 1 Wheat. 1; *Spragg v. Mary,* 3 Harr. & J.; *Pocock v. Hendricks,* 8 Gill & J. 421; *The Slave Grace,* 2 Hagg. 94; *Commonwealth v. Aves,* 18 Pick. 193; *Mahoney v. Ashton,* 4 H. & McH. 295.

The present plaintiff in error was held not entitled to his freedom, on the same state of facts as is now in evidence, in *Scott v. Emerson,* 15 Mo. 576.

This decision was affirmed in *Sylvia v. Kirby,* 17 Mo. 434.

By the laws of Missouri, therefore, the claimants are slaves, and these laws must determine their condition in the courts of the United States.

Strader v. Graham, 10 How. 93.

4. No residence of a slave at Fort Snelling could change his condition or devest the title of his owner.

Slavery existed by law in all the territory ceded by France to the United States, and Congress has not the constitutional power to repeal that law, or abolish or prohibit slavery within any part of that Territory.

Sec. 8 of the Act of March 6, 1820, is the first, and almost the only instance of an assumption by Congress of the power to abolish slavery in the Territory. It has never been recognized by this court. It is understood to be claimed that authority of Congress to erect territorial governments is confirmed by art. 4, sec. 3, of the Constitution, which gives the "power to dispose of and make all needful rules and regulations respecting the territory or other property belonging to the United States," or to result from the power to acquire territory; and in either case, it comprehends a power of legislation exclusive, universal, absolute and unlimited.

3 Story, const. secs. 1314, 1315, 1318, 1319, 1320, 1322; 1 Kent's Com. 423.

The clause of the Constitution, however, has been judicially interpreted to be a power to dispose of and make all needful rules and regulations respecting the lands and other property of the United States.

U. S. v. Gratiot, 14 Pet. 526, 537; *Am. Ins. Co. v. Canter,* 1 Pet. 342; see, also, *Federalist,* No. 43.

The subject of the power conferred by art. 4, sec. 3, is property, and the property only of the United States. This power is over unappropriated lands.

To organize a municipal government or corporation for the district or country, to prohibit slavery, is not to make needful rules and regulations respecting the territory or other property belonging within such district; therefore, the power to institute such a government, and more specially an unlimited power to legislate in all cases over the inhabitants in a territory and their property, cannot be deduced from the clause under consideration.

The power of Congress to institute temporary government over any territory, results necessarily from the fact that it is not within the jurisdiction of any particular State, and is within the power and jurisdiction of the United States. It is a power resulting from the necessity of the State, and is limited to the necessity from which it arises; to change the law of property, to emancipate slavery, to abolish slavery where, by the law it exists, to confiscate property, or devest vested rights, cannot be necessary or proper to institution of a temporary government. The power of Congress over the territory belonging to the United States cannot authorize legislation which practically excludes from such territory the people of any portion of the Union, or prevents them from taking with them and holding in such territory any property recognized by the Constitution, and the local laws of the territory.

Mr. Chief Justice Taney delivered the opinion of the court:

This case has been twice argued. After the argument at the last term, differences of opinion were found to exist among the members of the court; and as the questions in controversy are the highest importance, and the court wax at that time much pressed by the ordinary business

of the term, it was deemed advisable to continue the case, and direct a re-argument on some of the points, in order that we might have an opportunity of giving to the whole subject a more deliberate consideration. It has accordingly been again argued by counsel, and considered by the court; and I now proceed to deliver its opinion.

There are two leading questions presented by the record:

1. Had the Circuit court of the United States jurisdiction to hear and determine the case between these parties? And,

2. If it had jurisdiction, is the judgment it has given erroneous or not?

The plaintiff in error, who was also the plaintiff in the court below, was, with his wife and children, held as slaves by the defendant, in the State of Missouri, and he brought this action in the Circuit Court of the United States for that district, to assert the title of himself and his family to freedom.

The declaration is in the form usually adopted in that State to try questions of this description, and contains the averment necessary to give the court jurisdiction; that he and the defendant are citizens of different States; that is, he is a citizen of Missouri, and the defendant a citizen of New York.

The defendant pleaded in abatement to the jurisdiction of the court, that the plaintiff was not a citizen of the State of Missouri, as alleged in his declaration, being a negro of African descent, whose ancestors were of pure African blood, and who were brought into this country and sold as slaves.

To this plea the plaintiff demurred, and the defendant joined in demurrer. The court overruled the plea, and gave judgment that the defendant should answer over. And he thereupon put in sundry pleas in bar, upon which issues were joined, and at the trial the verdict and judgment were in his favor. Whereupon the plaintiff brought this writ of error.

Before we speak of the pleas in bar, it will be proper to dispose of the questions which have arisen on the plea in abatement.

That plea denies the right of the plaintiff to sue in a court of the United States, for the reasons therein stated.

If the question raised by it is legally before us, and the court should be of opinion that the facts stated in it disqualify the plaintiff from becoming a citizen, in the sense in which that word is used in the Constitution of the United States, then the judgment of the Circuit Court is erroneous, and must be reversed.

It is suggested, however, that this plea is not before us; and that as the judgment in the court below on this plea was in favor of the plaintiff, he does not seek to reverse it, or bring it before the court for revision by his writ of error; and also that the defendant waived this defense by pleading over, and thereby admitted the jurisdiction of the court. But in making this objection, we think the peculiar and limited jurisdiction of courts of the United States has not been adverted to. This peculiar and limited jurisdiction had made it necessary, in these courts, to adopt different rules and principles of pleading, so far as jurisdiction is concerned, from those which regulate courts of common law in England and in the different States of the Union which have adopted the common law rules.

In these last mentioned courts, where their character and rank are analogous to that of a circuit court of the United States; in other words, where they are what the law terms courts of general jurisdiction, they are presumed to have jurisdiction unless the contrary appears. No averment in the pleadings of the plaintiff is necessary, in order to give jurisdiction. If the defendant objects to it, he must plead it specially, and unless the fact on which he relies is found to be true by a jury, or admitted to be true by the plaintiff, the jurisdiction cannot be disputed in an appellate court.

Now, it is not necessary to inquire whether in courts of that description a party who pleads over in bar, when a plea to the jurisdiction has been ruled against him, does or does not waive his plea; nor whether upon a judgment in his favor on the pleas in bar, and writ of error brought by the plaintiff, the question upon the plea in abatement would be open for revision in the appellate court. Cases that may have been decided in such courts, or rules that may have been laid down by common law pleaders, can have no influence in the decision in this court. Because, under the constitution and laws of the United States, the rules which govern the pleadings in its courts, in questions of jurisdiction,

stand on different principles and are regulated by different laws.

This difference arises, as we have said, from the peculiar character of the government of the United States. For although it is sovereign and supreme in its appropriate sphere of action, yet it does not possess all the powers which usually belong to the sovereignty of a nation. Certain specified powers, enumerated in the Constitution, have been conferred upon it; and neither the Legislative, Executive nor Judicial Departments of the Government can lawfully exercise any authority beyond the limits marked out by the Constitution. And in regulating the Judicial Department, the cases in which the courts of the United States shall have jurisdiction are particularly and specifically enumerated and defined; and they are not authorized to take cognizance of any case which does not come within the description therein specified. Hence, when a plaintiff sues in a court of the United States, it is necessary that he should show, in his pleading, that the suit he brings is within the jurisdiction of the court, and that he is entitled to sue there. And if he omits to do this, and should, by an oversight of the Circuit Court, obtain a judgment in his favor, the judgment would be reversed in the appellate court for want of jurisdiction in the court below. The jurisdiction would not be presumed, as in the case of a common law, English, or state court, unless the contrary appeared. But the record, when it comes before the appellate court, must show, affirmatively, that the inferior court had authority, under the Constitution, to hear and determine the case. And if the plaintiff claims a right to sue in a circuit court of the United States, under that provision of the Constitution which gives jurisdiction in controversies between citizens of different states, he must distinctly aver in his pleading that they are citizens of different states; and he cannot maintain his suit without showing that fact in the pleading.

This point was decided in the case of *Bingham v. Cabot*, 3 Dall. 382, and ever since adhered to by the court. And in *Jackson v. Ashton*, 8 Pet. 148, it was held that the objection to which it was open could not be waived by the opposite party, because consent of parties could not give jurisdiction.

It is needless to accumulate cases on this subject. Those already referred to, and the cases of *Chapron v. Van Noorden*, in 2 Cranch, 126,

and *Montalet v. Murray,* 4 Cranch, 46, are sufficient to show the rule of which we have spoken.
The case of *Capron v. Van Noorden* strikingly
illustrates the difference between a common law
court and a court of the United States.

If, however, the fact of citizenship is averred
in the declaration, and the defendant does not
deny it, and put it in issue by plea in abatement,
he cannot offer evidence at the trial to disprove
it, and consequently cannot avail himself of the
objection in the appellate court, unless the
defect should be apparent in some other part of
the record. For if there is no plea in abatement,
and the want of jurisdiction does not appear in
any other part of the transcript brought up by
the writ of error, the undisputed averment of
citizenship in the declaration must be taken in
this court to be true. In this case, the citizenship
is averred, but it is denied by the defendant in
the manner required by the rules of pleading,
and the fact upon which the denial is based is
admitted by the demurrer. And if the plea and
demurrer, and judgment of the court below
upon it, are before us upon this record, the question to be decided is, whether the facts stated in
the plea are sufficient to show that the plaintiff is
not entitled to sue as a citizen in a court of the
United States.

We think they are before us. The plea in
abatement and the judgment of the court upon
it, are a part of the judicial proceedings in the
Circuit Court, and are there recorded as such;
and a writ of error always bring us up to the
superior court the whole record of the proceedings in the court below. And in the case of *The
Bank of the U.S. v. Smith,* 11 Wheat. 172, this
court said, that the case being brought up by
writ of error, the whole record was under the
consideration of this court. And this being the
case in the present instance, the plea in abatement is necessarily under consideration; and it
becomes, therefore, our duty to decide whether
the facts stated in the plea are or are not sufficient to show that the plaintiff is not entitled to
sue as a citizen in a court of the United States.

This is certainly a very serious question, and
one that now for the first time has been brought
for decision before this court. But it is brought
here by those who have a right to bring it, and it
is our duty to meet it and decide it.

The question is simply this: can a negro,
whose ancestors were imported into this country and sold as slaves, become a member of the
political community formed and brought into
existence by the Constitution of the United
States, and as such become entitled to all the
rights, and privileges, and immunities, guarantied by that instrument to the citizen. One of
these rights is the privilege of suing in a court of
the United States in the cases specified in the
Constitution.

It will be observed, that the plea applies to
that class of persons only whose ancestors were
negroes of the African race, and imported into
this country, and sold and held as slaves. The
only matter in issue before the court, therefore,
is, whether the descendants of such slaves, when
they shall be emancipated, or who are born of
parents who had become free before their birth,
are citizens of a state, in the sense in which the
word "citizen" is used in the Constitution of the
United States. And this being the only matter in
dispute on the pleadings, the court must be
understood as speaking in this opinion of that
class only that is, of those persons who are the
descendants of Africans who were imported into
this country and sold as slaves.

The situation of this population was altogether unlike that of the Indian race. The latter,
it is true, formed no part of the colonial communities, and never amalgamated with them in
social connections or in government. But
although they were uncivilized, they were yet a
free and independent people, associated together in nations or tribes, and governed by their
own laws. Many of these political communities
were situated in territories to which the white
race claimed the ultimate right of dominion. But
that claim was acknowledged to be subject to the
right of the Indians to occupy it as long as they
thought proper, and neither the English nor
Colonial Governments claimed or exercised any
dominion over the tribe or nation by whom it
was occupied, nor claimed the right to the possession of the territory, until the tribe or nation
consented to cede it. These Indian governments
were regarded and treated as foreign governments, as much so as if an ocean had separated
the red man from the white; and their freedom
has constantly been acknowledged, from the
time of the first emigration to the English
Colonies to the present day, by the different governments which succeeded each other. Treaties
have been negotiated with them, and their
alliance sought for in war; and the people who
compose these Indian political communities

SLAVERY

DRED SCOTT V.
SANDFORD

have always been treated as foreigners not living under our government. It is true that the course of events has brought the Indian tribes within the limits of the United States under subjection to the white race; and it has been found necessary, for their sake as well as our own, to regard them as in a state of pupilage, and to legislate to a certain extent over them and the territory they occupy. But they may, without doubt, like the subjects of any other foreign government, be naturalized by the authority of Congress, and become citizens of a State and of the United States; and if an individual should leave his nation or tribe, and take up his abode among the white population, he would be entitled to all the rights and privileges which would belong to an emigrant from any other foreign people.

We proceed to examine the case as presented by the pleadings.

The words "people of the United States" and "citizens" are synonymous terms, and mean the same thing. They both describe the political body, who, according to our republican institutions, form the sovereignty, and who hold the power and conduct the government through their representatives. They are what we familiarly call the "sovereign people," and every citizen is one of this people, and a constituent member of this sovereignty. The question before us is, whether the class of persons described in the plea in abatement compose a portion of this people, and are constituent members of this sovereignty. We think they are not, and that they are not included, and were not intended to be included, under the word "citizens" in the Constitution, and can, therefore, claim none of the rights and privileges which that instrument provides for and secures to citizens of the United States. On the contrary, they were at that time considered as a subordinate and inferior class of beings, who had been subjugated by the dominant race, and whether emancipated or not, yet remained subject to their authority, and had no rights or privileges but such as those who held the power and the government might choose to grant them.

It is not the province of the court to decide upon the justice or injustice, the policy or impolicy of these laws. The decision of that question belonged to the political or law-making power; to those who formed the sovereignty and framed the Constitution. The duty of the court is to interpret the instrument they have framed, with the best lights we can obtain on the subject, and to administer it as we find it, according to its true intent and meaning when it was adopted.

In discussing this question, we must not confound the rights of citizenship which a state may confer within its own limits, and the rights of citizenship as a member of the Union. It does not by any means follow, because he has all the rights and privileges of the citizen of a state, and yet not be entitled to the rights and privileges of a citizen in any other State. For previous to the adoption of the Constitution of the United States, every State had the undoubted right to confer on whomsoever it pleased the character of a citizen, and to endow him with all its rights. But this character, of course, was confined to the boundaries of the State, and gave him no rights or privileges in other States beyond those secured to him by the laws of nations and the comity of States. Nor have the several States surrendered the power of conferring these rights and privileges by adopting the Constitution of the United States. Each State may still confer them upon an alien, or any one it thinks proper, or upon any class or description of persons; yet he would not be a citizen in the sense in which that word is used in the Constitution of the United States, nor entitled to sue as such in one of its courts, nor to the privileges and immunities of a citizen in the other States. The rights which he would acquire would be restricted to the State which gave them. The Constitution has conferred on Congress the right to establish an uniform rule of naturalization, and this right is evidently exclusive, and has always been held by this court to be so. Consequently, no State, since the adoption of the Constitution, can, by naturalizing an alien, invest him with the rights and privileges secured to a citizen of a State under the federal government, although, so far as the State alone was concerned, he would undoubtedly be entitled to the rights of a citizen, and clothed with all the rights and immunities which the Constitution and laws of the State attached to that character.

It is very clear, therefore, that no State can, by any Act or law of its own, passed, since the adoption of the Constitution, introduce a new member into the political community created by the Constitution of the United States. It cannot make him a member of this community by making him a member of its own. And for the same reason it cannot introduce any person, or description of persons, who were not intended to be embraced in this new political family, which the Constitution brought into existence, but were intended to be excluded from it.

The question then arises, whether the provisions of the Constitution, in relation to the personal rights and privileges to which the citizen of a state should be entitled, embraced the negro African race, at that time in this country, or who might afterwards be imported, who had then or should afterwards be made free in any State; and to put it in the power of a single State to make him a citizen of the United States, and endue him with the full rights of citizenship in every other State without their consent. Does the Constitution of the United States act upon him whenever he shall be made free under the laws of a State, and raised here to the rank of citizen, and immediately clothe him with all the privileges of a citizen in every other State, and in its own courts?

It is true, every person, and every class and description of persons, who were at the time of the adoption of the Constitution recognized as citizens in the several States, became also citizens of this new political body; but none other; it was formed by them, and for them and their posterity, but for no one else. And the personal rights and privileges guarantied to citizens of this new sovereignty were intended to embrace those only who were then members of the several state communities, or who should afterwards, by birthright or otherwise, become members, according to the provisions of the Constitution and the principles on which it was founded. It was the union of those who were at the time members of distinct and separate political communities into one political family, whose power, for certain specified purposes, was to extend over the whole territory of the United States. And it gave to each citizen rights and privileges outside of his State which he did not before possess, and placed him in every other State upon perfect equality with its own citizen as to rights of person and rights of property; it made him a citizen of the United States.

It becomes necessary, therefore, to determine who were citizens of the several States when the Constitution was adopted. And in order to do this, we must recur to the governments and institutions of the thirteen Colonies, when they separated from Great Britain and formed new sovereignties, and took their places in the family of independent nations. We must inquire who, at that time, were recognized as the people or citizens of a State, whose rights and liberties had been outraged by the English Government; and who declared their independence, and assumed the powers of government to defend their rights by force of arms.

In the opinion of the court, the legislation and histories of the times, and the language used in the Declaration of Independence, show, that neither the class of persons who had been imported as slaves, nor their descendants, whether they had become free or not, were then acknowledged as a part of the people, nor intended to be included in the general words used in the memorable instrument.

It is difficult at this day to realize the state of public opinion in relation to that unfortunate race, which prevailed in the civilized and enlightened portions of the world at the time of the Declaration of Independence, and when the Constitution of the United States was framed and adopted. But the public history of every European nation displays it, in a manner too plain to be mistaken.

They had for more than a century before been regarded as beings of an inferior order; and altogether unfit to associate with the white race, either in social or political relations; and so far inferior, that they had no rights which the white man was bound to respect; and that the negro might justly and lawfully be reduced to slavery for his benefit. He was bought and sold, and treated as an ordinary article of merchandise and traffic, whenever a profit could be made by it. This opinion was at the time fixed and universal in the civilized portion of the white race. It was regarded as an axiom in morals as well as in politics, which no one thought of disputing, or supposed to be open to dispute; and men in every grade and position in society daily and habitually acted upon it in their private pursuits, as well as in matters of public concern, without doubting for a moment the correctness of this opinion.

And in no nation was this opinion more firmly fixed or more uniformly acted upon than by the English government and English people. They not only seized them on the coast of Africa, and sold them or held them in slavery for their own use; but they took them as ordinary articles of merchandise to every country where they could make a profit on them, and were far

SLAVERY

DRED SCOTT V. SANDFORD

SLAVERY

DRED SCOTT V.
SANDFORD

more extensively engaged in this commerce than any other nation in the world.

The opinion thus entertained and acted upon in England was naturally impressed upon the colonies they founded on this side of the Atlantic. And, accordingly, a negro of the African race was regarded by them as an article of property, and held, and bought and sold as such, in every one of the thirteen Colonies which united in the Declaration of Independence, and afterwards formed the Constitution of the United States. The slaved were more or less numerous in the different Colonies, as slave labor was found more or less profitable. But no one seems to have doubted the correctness of the prevailing opinion of the time.

The legislation of the different Colonies furnishes positive and indisputable proof of this fact.

It would be tedious, in this opinion to enumerate the various laws they passed upon this subject. It will be sufficient, as a sample of the legislation which then generally prevailed throughout the British Colonies, to give the laws of two of them; one being still a large slaveholding State, and the other the first State in which slavery ceased to exist.

The Province of Maryland, in 1717 (ch. 13, sec. 5), passed a law declaring "that if any free negro or mulatto intermarry with any white woman, or if any white man shall intermarry with any negro or mulatto woman, such negro or mulatto shall be a slave during life, excepting mulattoes born of white women, who, for such intermarriage, shall only become servants for seven years, to be disposed of as the Justices of the County Court, where such marriage so happens, shall think fit; to be applied by them towards the support of a public school within the said county. And any white man or white woman shall become servants during the term of seven years, and shall be disposed of by the justices as aforesaid, and be applied to the uses aforesaid."

The other colonial law to which we refer was passed by Massachusetts in 1705 (chap. 6). It is entitled "An Act for the better preventing of a spurious and mixed issue," etc.; and it provides, that "if any negro or mulatto shall presume to smite or strike any person of the English or other Christian nation, such negro or mulatto shall be severely whipped, at the discretion of the justices before whom the offender shall be convicted."

And "that none of Her Majesty's English or Scottish subjects, nor of any other Christian nation, within this province, shall contract matrimony with any negro or mulatto; nor shall any person duly authorized to solemnize marriage, presume to join any such in marriage, on pain of forfeiting the sum of fifty pounds; one moiety thereof to Her Majesty, for and towards the support of the government within this province, and the other moiety to him or them that shall inform and sue for the same in any of Her Majesty's courts of record within the Province, by will, plaint, or information."

We give both of these laws in the words used by the respective legislative bodies, because the language in which they are framed, as well as the provisions contained in them, show, too plainly to be misunderstood, the degraded condition of this unhappy race. They were still in force when the Revolution began, and are a faithful index to the state of feeling towards the class of persons of whom they speak, and of the position they occupied throughout the thirteen colonies, in the eyes and thoughts of the men who framed the Declaration of Independence and established the State constitutions and governments. They show that a perpetual and impassable barrier was intended to be erected between the white race and the one which they had reduced to slavery, and governed as subjects with absolute and despotic power, and which they then looked upon as so far below them in the scale of created beings, that intermarriages between white persons and negroes or mulattoes were regarded as unnaturally and immoral, and punished as crimes, not only in the parties, but in the person who joined them in marriage. And no distinction in this respect was made between the free negro or mulatto and the slave, but this stigma, of the deepest degradation, was fixed upon the whole race.

We refer to these historical facts for the purpose of showing the fixed opinions concerning that race, upon which the statesmen of that day spoke and acted. It is necessary to do this, in order to determine whether the general terms used in the Constitution of the United States, as to the rights of man and the rights of the people, was intended to include them, or to give to them or their posterity the benefit of any of its provisions.

The language of the Declaration of Independence is equally conclusive.

It begins by declaring that, "when in the course of human events it becomes necessary for one people to dissolve the political bands which have connected them with another, and to assume among the powers of the earth the separate and equal station to which the laws of nature and nature's God entitle them, a decent respect for the opinions of mankind requires that they should declare the causes which impel them to the separation."

It then proceeds to say: "We hold these truths to be self-evident: that all men are created equal; that they are endowed by their Creator with certain inalienable rights; that among them is life, liberty, and pursuit of happiness; that to secure these rights, governments are instituted, deriving their just powers from the consent of the governed."

The general words above quoted would seem to embrace the whole human family, and if they were used in a similar instrument at this day, would be so understood. But it is too clear for dispute, that the enslaved African race were not intended to be included, and formed no part of the people who framed and adopted this Declaration; for if the language, as understood in that day, would embrace them, the conduct of the distinguished men who framed the Declaration of Independence would have been utterly and flagrantly inconsistent with the principles they asserted; and instead of the sympathy of mankind, to which they so confidently appealed, they would have deserved and received universal rebuke and reprobation.

Yet the men who framed this Declaration were great men—high in literary acquirements—high in their sense of honor, and incapable of asserting principles inconsistent with those on which they were acting. They perfectly understood the meaning of the language they used, and how it would be understood by others; and they knew that it would not, in any part of the civilized world, be supposed to embraced the negro race, which, by common consent, had been excluded from civilized governments and the family of nations, and doomed to slavery. The spoke and acted according to the then established doctrines and principles, and in the ordinary language of the day, and no one misunderstood them. The unhappy black race were separated from the white by indelible marks, and laws long before established, and were never thought of or spoken of except as property, and when the claims of the owner or the profit of the trader were supposed to need protection.

This state of public opinion had undergone no change when the Constitution was adopted, as is equally evident from its provisions and language.

The brief preamble sets forth by whom it was formed, for what purposes, and for whose benefit and protection. It declares that it is formed by the people of the United States; that is to say, by those who were members of the different political communities in the several States; and its great object is declared to be to secure the blessings of liberty to themselves and their posterity. It speaks in general terms of the people of the United States, when it is providing for the exercise of the powers granted or the privileges secured to the citizen. It does not define what description of persons are intended to be included under these terms, or who shall be regarded as a citizen and one of the people. It uses them as terms so well understood that no further description or definition was necessary.

But there are two clauses in the Constitution which point directly and specifically to the negro race as a separate class of persons, and show clearly that they were not regarded as a portion of the people of citizens of the government then formed.

One of these clauses reserves to each of the thirteen States the right to import slaves until the year 1808, if it thinks proper. And the importation which it thus sanctions was unquestionably of persons of the race of which we are speaking, as the traffic in slaves in the United States had always been confined to them. And by the other provision the States pledge themselves to each other to maintain the right of property of the master, by delivering up to him any slave who may have escaped from his service, and be found within their respective territories. By the first above-mentioned clause, therefore, the right to purchase and hold this property is directly sanctioned and authorized for twenty years by the people who framed the Constitution. And by the second, they pledge themselves to maintain and uphold the right of the master in the manner specified, as long as the government they then formed should endure. And these two provisions show, conclusively, that neither the description of persons therein referred to, nor their descendants, were embraced in any of the other provisions of the Constitution; for certainly these two

SLAVERY

DRED SCOTT V.
SANDFORD

clauses were not intended to confer on them or their posterity the blessings or liberty, or any of the personal rights so carefully provided for the citizen.

No one of that race had ever migrated to the United States voluntarily; all of them had been brought here as articles of merchandise. The number that had been emancipated at that time were but few in comparison with those held in slavery; and they were identified in the public mind with the race to which they belonged, and regarded as a part of the slave population rather than the free. It is obvious that they were not even in the minds of the framers of the Constitution when they were conferring special rights and privileges upon the citizens of a State in every other part of the Union.

Indeed, when we look to the condition of this race in the several States at the time, it is impossible to believe that these rights and privileges were intended to be extended to them.

It is very true, that in that portion of the Union where the labor of the negro race was found to be unsuited to the climate, and unprofitable to the master, but few slaves were held at the time of the Declaration of Independence; and when the Constitution was adopted, it had entirely worn out in one of them, and measures had been taken for its gradual abolition in several others. But this change had not been produced by any change of opinion in relation to this race; but because it was discovered, from experience, that slave labor was unsuited to the climate and productions of these States: for some of the States, where it had ceased or nearly ceased to exist, were actively engaged in the slave trade, procuring cargoes on the coast of Africa, and transporting them for sale to those parts of the Union where their labor was found to be profitable, and suited to the climate and productions. And this traffic was openly carried on, and fortunes accumulated by it, without reproach from the people of the States where they resided. And it can hardly be supposed that, in the States where it was then countenanced in it worst form—that is, in the seizure and transportation—the people could have regarded those who were emancipated as entitled to equal rights with themselves.

And we may here again refer, in support of this proposition, to the plain and unequivocal language of the laws of the several States, some passed after the Declaration of Independence

and before the Constitution was adopted, and some since the government went into operation.

We need not refer, on this point, particularly to the laws of the present slaveholding States. Their statute books are full of provisions in relation to this class, in the same spirit with the Maryland law which we have before quoted. They have continued to treat them as an inferior class, and to subject them to strict police regulation, drawing a broad line of distinction between the citizen and the slave races, and legislating in relation to them upon the same principle which prevailed at the time of the Declaration of Independence. As relates to these States, it is too plain for argument, that they have never been regarded as a part of the people or citizens of the State, nor supposed to possess any political rights which the dominant race might not withhold or grant at their pleasure. And as long as 1822, the Court of Appeals of Kentucky decided that free negroes and mulattoes were not citizens within the meaning of the Constitution of the United States; and the correctness of this decision is recognized, and the same doctrine affirmed, in 1 Meigs' Tenn. 321.

And if we turn to the legislation of the States where slavery had worn out, or measures taken for its speedy abolition, we shall find the same opinions and principles equally fixed and equally acted upon.

Thus, Massachusetts, in 1786, passed a law similar to the colonial one of which we have spoken. The law of 1786, like the Law of 1705, forbids the marriage of any white person with any negro, Indian or mulatto, and inflicts a penalty of £50 upon anyone who shall join them in marriage; and declares all such marriages absolutely null and void, and degrades thus the unhappy issue of the marriage by fixing upon it the stain of bastardy. And this mark of degradation was renewed, and again impressed upon the race, in the careful and deliberate preparation of their Revised Code published in 1836. This Code forbids any person from joining in marriage any white person with any Indian, negro or mulatto, and subjects the party who shall offend in this respect, to imprisonment, not exceeding six months, in the common jail, or hard labor, and to a fine of not less than fifty nor more than two hundred dollars; and, like the Law of 1786, it declares the marriage to be absolutely null and void. It will be seen that the punishment is increased by the Code upon the person who shall marry them, by adding imprisonment to a pecuniary penalty.

So, too, in Connecticut. We refer more particularly to the legislation of this State, because it was not only among the first to put an end to slavery within its own territory, but was the first to fix a mark of reprobation upon the African slave trade. The law last mentioned was passed in October, 1788, about nine months after the State had ratified and adopted the Present Constitution of the United States; and by that law it prohibited its own citizens, under severe penalties, from engaging in the trade, and declared all policies of insurance on the vessel or cargo made in the State to be null and void. But, up to the time of the adoption of the Constitution, there is nothing in the legislation of the State indicating any change of opinion as to the relative rights and position of the white and black races in this country, or indicating that it meant to place the latter, when free, upon a level with its citizens. And certainly nothing which would have led the slaveholding States to suppose that Connecticut designed to claim for them, under the new Constitution, the equal rights and privileges and rank of citizens in every other state.

The first step taken by Connecticut upon this subject was as early as 1774, when it passed an Act forbidding the further importation of slaves into the State. But the section containing the prohibition is introduced by the following preamble:

"And whereas the increase of slaves in this State is injurious to the poor, and inconvenient."

This recital would appear to have been carefully introduced, in order to prevent any misunderstanding of the motive which induced the Legislature to pass the law, and places it distinctly upon the interest and convenience of the white population—excluding the inference that it might have been intended in any degree for the benefit of the other.

And in the Act of 1784, by which the issue of slaves, born after the time therein mentioned, were to be free at a certain age, the section is again introduced by a preamble assigning a similar motive for the Act. It is in these words:

"Whereas sound policy requires that the abolition of slavery should be effected as soon as may be consistent with the rights of individuals, and the public safety and welfare"—showing

that the right of property on the master was to be protected, and that the measure was one of policy, and to prevent the injury and inconvenience, to the whites, of a slave population in the State.

And still further pursuing its legislation, we find that in the same Statute passed in 1774, which prohibited the further importation of slaves into the State, there is also a provision by which any negro, Indian or mulatto servant, who was found wandering out of the town or place to which he belonged, without a written pass such as is therein described, was made liable to be seized by anyone, and taken before the next authority to be examined and delivered up to his master—who was required to pay the charge which had accrued thereby. And a subsequent section of the same law provides, that if any free negro shall travel without such pass, and shall be stopped, seized or taken up, he shall pay all charges arising thereby. And this law was in full operation when the Constitution of the United States was adopted, and was not repealed till 1797. So that up to that time free negroes and mulattoes were associated with servants and slaves in the police regulations established by the laws of the State.

And again, in 1833, Connecticut passed another law, which made it penal to set up or establish any school in that State for the instruction of persons of the African race not inhabitants of the State, or to instruct or teach in any such school or institution, or board or harbor for that purpose, any such person, without previous consent in writing of the civil authority of the town in which such school or institution might be.

And it appears by the case of *Crandall v. The State*, reported in 10 Conn. 340, that upon an information filed against Prudence Crandall for a violation of this law, one of the points raised in the defense was, that the law was a violation of the Constitution of the United States; and that the persons instructed, although of the African race, were citizens of other States, and therefore entitled to the rights and privileges of citizens in the State of Connecticut. But Chief Justice Daggett, before whom the case was tried, held, that persons of that description were not citizens of a State, within the meaning of the word "citizen" in the Constitution of the United States, and were not, therefore, entitled to the privileges and immunities of citizens in other States.

SLAVERY

DRED SCOTT V.
SANDFORD

The case was carried up to the Supreme Court of Errors of the State, and the question fully argued there. But the case went off upon another point, and no opinion was expressed on this question.

We have made this particular examination into the legislative and judicial action of Connecticut, because, from the early hostility it displayed to the slave trade on the coast of Africa, we may expect to find the laws of that State as lenient and favorable to the subject race as those of any other State in the Union; and if we find that at the time the Constitution was adopted, they were not even there raised to the rank of citizens, but were still held and treated as property, and the laws relating to them passed with reference altogether to the interest and convenience of the white race, we shall hardly find them elevated to a higher rank anywhere else.

A brief notice of the laws of two other States, and we shall pass on to other considerations.

By the laws of New Hampshire, collected and finally passed in 1815, no one was permitted to be enrolled in the militia of the State but free white citizens; and the same provision is found in a subsequent collection of the laws made in 1855. Nothing could more strongly mark the entire repudiation of the African race. The alien is excluded, because, being born in a foreign country, he cannot be a member of the community until he is naturalized. Buy why are the African race, born in the State, not permitted to share in one of the highest duties of the citizen? The answer is obvious; he is not by the institutions and laws of the State numbered among its people. He forms no part of the sovereignty of the State, and is not, therefore, called on to uphold and defend it.

Again in 1822, Rhode Island in its Revised Code, passed a law forbidding persons who were authorized to join persons in marriage from joining in marriage any white person with any negro, Indian or mulatto, under the penalty of $200, and declaring all such marriages absolutely null and void; and the same law was again re-enacted in its Revised Code of 1844. So that, down to the last mentioned period, the strongest mark of inferiority and degradation was fastened upon the African race in that State.

It would be impossible to enumerate and compress, in the space usually allotted to an opinion of a court, the various laws, marking the condition of this race, which were passed from time to time after the Revolution, and before and since the adoption of the Constitution of the United States. In addition to those already referred to, it is sufficient to say that Chancellor Kent, whose accuracy and research no one will question, states in the sixth edition of his Commentaries, published in 1848, 2d vol. 258, note b, that in no part of the country, except Maine, did the African race, in point of fact, participate equally with the whites in the exercise of civil and political rights.

The legislation of the States therefore shows, in a manner not to be mistaken, the inferior and subject condition of that race at the time the Constitution was adopted, and long afterwards, throughout the thirteen States by which that instrument was framed; and it is hardly consistent with the respect due to these States, to suppose that they regarded at that time, as fellow citizens and members of the sovereignty, a class of beings whom they had thus stigmatized; whom, as we are bound, out of respect to the State sovereignties, to assume they had deemed it just and necessary thus to stigmatize, and upon whom they had impressed such deep and enduring marks of inferiority and degradation; or that when they met in convention to form the Constitution, they looked upon them as a portion of their constituents, or designed to include them in the provisions so carefully inserted for the security and protection of the liberties and rights of their citizens. It cannot be supposed that they intended to secure to them rights and privileges, and rank, in the new political body throughout the Union, which every one of them denied within the limits of its own dominion. More especially, it cannot be believed that the large slaveholding States regarded them as included in the word "citizens," or would have consented to a constitution which might compel them to receive them in that character from another State. For if they were so received, and entitled to the privileges and immunities of citizens, it would exempt them from the operation of the special laws and from the police regulations which they considered to be necessary for their own safety. It would give to persons of the negro race, who were recognized as citizens in any one State of the Union, the right to enter every other State whenever they pleased, singly or in companies, without pass or passport, and without obstruction, to sojourn there as long as they pleased, to go where they pleased at every hour of the day or night without molestations, unless they committed some violation of law for which a white man would be punished; and it would give them the full liberty of speech in public and in private upon all subjects upon which its own citizens might speak; to hold public meetings upon political affairs, and to keep and carry arms wherever they went. And all of this would be done in the face of the subject race of the same color, both free and slaves, inevitably producing discontent and insubordination among them, and endangering the peace and safety of the State.

It is impossible, it would seem, to believe that the great men of the slaveholding States, who took so large a share in framing in Constitution of the United States, and exercised so much influence in procuring its adoption, could have been so forgetful or regardless of their own safety and the safety of those who trusted and confided in them.

Besides, this want of foresight and care would have been utterly inconsistent with the caution displayed in providing for the admission of new members into this political family. For, when they gave to the citizens of each State the privileges and immunities of citizens in the several States, they at the same time took from the several States the power of naturalization, and confined that power exclusively to the Federal Government. No state was willing to permit another State to determine who should or should not be admitted as one of its citizens, and entitled to demand equal rights and privileges with their own people, within their own territories. The right of naturalization was therefore, with one accord, surrendered by the States, and confined to the Federal Government. And this power granted to Congress to establish an uniform rule of naturalization is, by the well-understood meaning of the word, confined to persons born in a foreign country, under a foreign government. It is not a power to raise to the rank of a citizen anyone born in the United States, who, from birth or parentage, by the laws of the country, belongs to an inferior and subordinate class. And when we find the States guarding themselves from the indiscreet or improper admission by other states of emigrants from other countries, by giving the power exclusively to Congress, we cannot fail to see that they could never have left with the States a much more important power—that is, the power of transforming into citizens a numerous class of per-

sons, who in that character would be much more dangerous to the peace and safety of a large portion of the Union than the few foreigners one of the States might improperly naturalize. The Constitution, upon its adoption, obviously took from the States all power by any subsequent legislation to introduce as a citizen into the political family of the United States anyone, no matter where he was born, or what might be his character or condition; and it gave to Congress the power to confer this character upon those only who were born outside of the dominions of the United States. And no law of a State, therefore, passed since the Constitution was adopted, can give any right of citizenship outside of its own territory.

A clause, similar to the one in the Constitution, in relation to the rights and immunities of citizens of one State in the other States, was contained in the Articles of Confederation. But there is a difference of language, which is worthy of note. The provision in the Articles of Confederation was, "that the free inhabitants of each of the States, paupers, vagabonds, and fugitives from justice excepted, should be entitled to all the privileges and immunities of free citizens, in the several States."

It will be observed, that under this Confederation each State had the right to decide for itself, and in its own tribunals, whom it would acknowledge as a free inhabitant of another state. The term "free inhabitant," in the generality of its terms, would certainly include one of the African race who had been manumitted. But no example, we think, can be found of his admission to all the privileges of citizenship in any State of the Union after these Articles were formed, and while they continued in force. And notwithstanding the generality of the words "free inhabitants," it is very clear that, according to their accepted meaning in that day, they did not include the African race, whether free or not; for the 5th section of the 9th article provides that Congress should have the power "to agree upon the number of land forces to be raised, and to make requisitions from each State for its quota in proportion to the number of white inhabitants in such State, which requisition should be binding."

Words could hardly have been used which more strongly mark the line of distinction between the citizen and the subject—the free and the subjugated races. The latter were not

SLAVERY

DRED SCOTT V.
SANDFORD

even counted when the inhabitants of a State were to be embodied in proportion to its numbers for the general defense. And it cannot for a moment be supposed, that a class of persons thus separated and rejected from those who formed the sovereignty of the States, were yet intended to be included under the words "free inhabitants," in the preceding article, to whom privileges and immunities were so carefully secured in every State.

But although this clause of the Articles of Confederation is the same in principle with that inserted in the Constitution, yet the comprehensive word "inhabitant," which might be construed to include an emancipated slave, is omitted, and the privilege is confined to "citizens" of the State. And this alteration in words would hardly have been made unless a different meaning was intended to be conveyed, or a possible doubt removed. The just and fair inference is, that as this privilege was about to be placed under the protection of the general government, and the words expounded by its tribunals, and all power in relation to it taken from the State and its courts, it was deemed prudent to describe with precision and caution the persons to whom this high privilege was given—and the word "citizen" was on that account substituted for the words "free inhabitant." The word "citizen" excluded, and no doubt intended to exclude, foreigners who had not become citizens of some one of the States when the Constitution was adopted; and also every description of persons who were not fully recognized as citizens in the several States. This, upon any fair construction of the instruments to which we have referred, was evidently the object and purpose of this change of words.

To all this mass of proof we have still to add, that Congress has repeatedly legislated upon the same construction of the Constitution that we have given. Three laws, two of which were passed almost immediately after the government went into operation, will be abundantly sufficient to show this. The first two are particularly worthy of notice, because many of the men who assisted in framing the Constitution, and took an active part in procuring its adoption, were then in the halls of legislation, and certainly understood what they meant when they used the words "people of the United States" and "citizen" in that well considered instrument.

The first of these Acts is the Naturalization Law, which was passed at the second session of the first Congress, March 26, 1790, and confines the right of becoming citizens "to aliens being free white persons."

Now, the Constitution does not limit the power of Congress in this respect to white persons. And they may, if they think proper, authorize the naturalization of anyone, of any color, who was born under allegiance to another government. But the language of the law above quoted shows that citizenship at that time was perfectly understood to be confined to the white race; and that they alone constituted the sovereignty in the government.

Congress might, as we before said, have authorized the naturalization of Indians, because they were aliens and foreigners. But, in their then untutored and savage state, no one would have thought of admitting them as citizens in a civilized community. And, moreover, the atrocities they had but recently committed, when they were the allies of Great Britain in the Revolutionary War, were yet fresh in the recollection of the people of the United States, and they were even then guarding themselves against the threatened renewal of Indian hostilities. No one supposed then that any Indian would ask for, or was capable of enjoying, the privileges of an American citizen, and the word "white" was not used with any particular reference to them.

Neither was it used with any reference to the African race imported into or born in this country; because Congress had no power to naturalize them, and therefore there was not necessity for using particular words to exclude them.

It would seem to have been used merely because it followed out the line of division which the Constitution has drawn between the citizen race, who formed and held government, and the African race, which they held in subjection and slavery, and governed at their own pleasure.

Another of the early laws of which we have spoken, is the first Militia Law, which was passed in 1792, at the first session of the second Congress. The language of this law is equally plain and significant with the one just mentioned. It directs that every "free able-bodied white male citizen" shall be enrolled in the militia. The word "white" is evidently used to exclude the African race, and the word "citizen" to exclude unnaturalized foreigners, the latter forming no part of the sovereignty; owing it no allegiance, and therefore under no obligation to defend it. The African race, however, born in the country, did owe allegiance to the government, whether they were slave or free; but it is repudiated, and rejected from the duties and obligations of citizenship in marked language.

The third Act to which we have alluded is even still more decisive; it was passed as late as 1813 (2 Stat. 809), and it provides: "That from and after the termination of the war in which the United States are now engaged with Great Britain, it shall not be lawful to employ, on board of any public or private vessels of the United States, any person or persons except citizens of the United States, or person of color, natives of the United States.

Here the line of distinction is drawn in express words. Persons of color, in the judgment of Congress, were not included in the word "citizen," and they are described as another and different class of persons, and authorized to be employed, if born in the United States.

And even as late as 1820 (chap. 104, sec. 8), in the charter to the City of Washington, the Corporation is authorized "to restrain and prohibit the nightly and other disorderly meetings of slaves, free negroes, and mulattoes," thus associating them together in its legislation; and after prescribing the punishment that may be inflicted on the slaves, proceeds in the following words: "And to punish such free negroes and mulattoes by penalties not exceeding twenty dollars for any one offense; and in case of the inability of any such free negro or mulatto to pay any such penalty and cost thereon, to cause him or her to be confined to labor for any time not exceeding six calendar months." And in a subsequent part of the same section, the Act authorizes the Corporation "to prescribe the terms and conditions upon which free negroes and mulattoes may reside in the city."

This law, like the laws of the States, shows that this class of persons were governed by special legislation directed expressly to them, and always connected with provisions for the government of slaves, and not with those for the government of free white citizens. And after such an uniform course of legislation as we have stated, by the Colonies, by the States, and by Congress, running through a period of more than a century, it would seem that to call persons thus marked and stigmatized, "citizens" of the United States, "fellow-citizens," a constituent part of the sovereignty, would be an abuse of terms, and not calculated to exalt the character of an American citizen in the eyes of other nations.

The conduct of the Executive Department of the government has been in perfect harmony upon this subject with this course of legislation. The question was brought officially before the late William Wirt, when he was the Attorney General of the United States, in 1821, and he decided that the words "citizens of the United States" were used in the Acts of Congress in the same sense as in the Constitution; and that free persons of color were not citizens, within the meaning of the Constitution and laws; and his opinion has been confirmed by that of the late Attorney-General, Caleb Cushing, in a recent case, and acted upon by the Secretary of State, who refused to grant passports to them as "citizens of the United States."

But it is said that a person may be a citizens, and entitled to that character, although he does not possess all the rights which may belong to other citizens; as, for example, the right to vote, or to hold particular offices; and that yet, when he goes into another State, he is entitled to be recognized there as a citizen, although the State may measure his rights by the rights which it allows to persons of a like character or class, resident in the State, and refuse to him the full rights of citizenship.

This argument overlooks the language of the provision in the Constitution of which we are speaking.

Undoubtedly, a person may be a citizen, that is, a member of the community who from the sovereignty, although he exercises no share of the political power, and is incapacitated from holding particular offices. Women and minors, who from a part of the political family, cannot vote; and when a property qualification is required to vote or hold a particular office, those who have not the necessary qualification cannot vote or hold the office, yet they are citizens.

So, too, a person may be entitled to vote by the law of the State, who is not a citizen even of the State itself. And in some of the States of the Union foreigners not naturalized are allowed to vote. And the State may give the right to free negroes and mulattoes, but that does not make them citizens of the State, and still less of the United States. And the provision in the

Constitution giving privileges and immunities in other States, does not apply to them.

Neither does it apply to a person who, being the citizen of a State, migrates to another State. For then he becomes subject to the laws of the State in which he lives, and he is no longer a citizen of the State from which he removed. And the State in which he resides may then, unquestionably, determine his status or condition, and place him among the class of persons who are not recognized as citizens, but belong to an inferior and subject race; and may deny him the privileges and immunities enjoyed by its citizens.

But so far as mere rights of person are concerned, the provision in question is confined to citizens of a State who are temporarily in another State without taking up their residence there. It gives them no political rights in the state as to voting or holding office, or in any other respect. For a citizen of one State has no right to participate in the government of another. But if he ranks as a citizen of the State to which he belongs, within the meaning of the Constitution of the United States, then, whenever he goes into another State, the constitution clothes him, as to the rights of person, with all the privileges and immunities which belong to citizens of the State. And if persons of the African race are citizens of a state, and of the United States, they wold be entitled to all of these privileges and immunities in every State, and the State could not restrict them; for they would hold these privileges and immunities, under the paramount authority of the Federal Government, and its courts would be bound to maintain and enforce them, the Constitution and laws of the State to the contrary notwithstanding. And if the State could limit or restrict them, or place the party in an inferior grade, this clause of the constitution would be unmeaning, and could have no operation; and would give no rights to the citizen when in another State. He would have none but what the State itself chose to allow him. This is evidently not the construction or meaning of the clause in question. It guarantees rights to the citizen, and the State cannot withhold them. And these rights are of a character and would lead to consequences which make it absolutely certain that the African race were not included under the name of citizens of a State, and were not in the contemplation of the framers of the Constitution when these privileges and immu-

nities were provided for the protection of the citizen in other States.

The case of *Legrand v. Darnall,* 2 Pet. 664, has been referred to for the purpose of showing that this court has decided that the descendant of a slave may sue as a citizen in a court of the United States; but the case itself shows that the question did not arise and could not have arisen in the case.

It appears from the report that Darnall was born in Maryland, and was the son of a white man by one of his slaves, and his father executed certain instruments to manumit him, and devised to him some landed property in the State. This property Darnall afterwards sold to Legrand, the appellant, who gave his notes for the purchase money. But becoming afterwards apprehensive that the appellee had not been emancipated according to the laws of Maryland, he refused to pay the notes until he could be better satisfied as to Darnall's right to convey. Darnall, in the meantime, had taken up his residence in Pennsylvania, and brought suit on the notes and recovered judgment in the Circuit Court for the District of Maryland.

The whole proceeding, as appears by the report, was an amicable one; Legrand being perfectly willing to pay the money, if he could obtain a title, and Darnall not wishing him to pay unless he could make him a good one. In point of fact, the whole proceeding was under the direction of the counsel who argued the case for the appellee, who was the mutual friend of the parties, and confided in by both of them, and whose only object was to have the rights of both parties established by judicial decision in the most speedy and least expensive manner.

Legrand, therefore, raised no objection to the jurisdiction of the courts in the suit at law, because he was himself anxious to obtain the judgment of the court upon his title. Consequently, there was nothing in the record before the court to show that Darnall was of African descent, and the usual judgment and award of execution was entered. And Legrand thereupon filled his bill on the equity side of the Circuit Court, stating that Darnall was born a slave, and had not been legally emancipated, and could not, therefore, take the land devised to him, nor make Legrand a good title; and praying an injunction to restrain Darnall from proceeding to execution on the judgment, which was granted. Darnall answered, averring in his answer that he was a free man, and capable of conveying a good title. Testimony was taken on this point, and at the hearing the Circuit Court was of opinion that Darnall was a free man and his title good, and dissolved the injunction and dismissed the bill; and that decree was affirmed here, upon the appeal of Legrand.

Now, it is difficult to imagine how any question about the citizenship of Darnall, or his right to sue in that character, can be supposed to have arisen and been decided in that case. The fact that he was of African descent was first brought before the court upon the bill in equity. The suit at law had then passed into judgment and award of execution, and the Circuit Court, as a court of law, had no longer any authority over it. It was a valid and legal judgment, which the court that rendered it had not the power to reverse or set aside. And unless it had jurisdiction as a court of equity to restrain him from using its process as a court of law, Darnall, if he thought proper, would have been at liberty to proceed on his judgment, and compel the payment of the money, although the allegations in the bill were true, and he was incapable of making a title. No other court could have enjoined him, for certainly no State equity court could interfere in what way with the judgment of a circuit court of the United States.

But the Circuit Court as a court of equity certainly had equity jurisdiction over its own judgment as a court of law, without regard to the character of the parties; and had not only the right, but it was its duty—no matter who were the parties in the judgment—to prevent them from proceeding to enforce it by execution, if the court was satisfied that the money was not justly and equitably due. The ability of Darnall to convey did not depend upon his citizenship, but upon his title to freedom. And if he was free, he could hold and convey property, by the laws of Maryland, although he was not a citizen. But if he was by law still a slave, he could not. It was, therefore, the duty of the court, sitting as a court of equity in the latter case, to prevent him from using its process, as a court of common law, to compel the payment of the purchase money, when it was evident that the purchaser must lose the land. But if he was free, and could make a title, it was equally the duty of the court not to suffer Legrand to keep the land, and refuse the payment of the money, upon the ground that Darnall was incapable of suing or being sued as

a citizen in a court of the United States. The character or citizenship of the parties had no connection with the question of jurisdiction, and the matter in dispute had no relation to the citizenship of Darnall. Nor is such a question alluded to in the opinion of the court.

Besides, we are by no means prepared to say that there are not many cases, civil as well as criminal, in which a circuit court of the United States may exercise jurisdiction, although one of the African race is a party; that broad question is not before the court. The question with which we are now dealing is, whether a person of the African race can be a citizen of the United States, and become thereby entitled to a special privilege, by virtue to his title to that character, and which, under the Constitution, no one but a citizen can claim. It is manifest that the case of *Legrand v. Darnall* has no bearing on that question, and can have no application to the case now before the court.

This case, however, strikingly illustrates the consequences that would follow the construction of the Constitution which would give the power contended for, to a State. It would, in effect, give it also to an individual. For if the father of young Darnall had manumitted him in his lifetime, and sent him to reside in a State which recognized him as a citizen, he might have visited and sojourned in Maryland as he pleased, and as long as he pleased, as a citizen and tribunals would be compelled by the paramount authority of the Constitution, to receive him and treat him as one of its citizens, exempt from the laws and police of the state in relation to a person of that description, and allow him to enjoy all the rights and privileges of citizenship, without respect to the laws of Maryland, although such laws were deemed by it absolutely essential to its own safety.

The only two provisions which point to them and include them, treat them as property, and make it the duty of the government to protect it; no other power, in relation to this race, is to be found in the Constitution; and as it is a government of special, delegated powers, no authority beyond these two provisions can be constitutionally exercised. The Government of the United States had no right to interfere for any other purpose but that of protecting the rights of the owner, leaving it altogether with the several States to deal with this race, whether emancipated or not, as each State may think justice, humanity, and the interests and safety of society, require. The States evidently intended to reserve this power exclusively to themselves.

No one, we presume, supposes that any change in public opinion or feeling in relation to this unfortunate race, in the civilized nations of Europe or in this country, should induce the court to give to the words of the Constitution a more liberal construction in their favor than they were intended to bear when the instrument was framed and adopted. Such an argument would be altogether inadmissible in any tribunal called on to interpret it. If any of its provisions are deemed unjust, there is a mode prescribed in the instrument itself by which it may be amended; but while it remains unaltered, it must be construed now as it was understood at the time of its adoption. It is not only the same in words, but the same in meaning, and delegates the same powers to the government, and reserves and secures the same rights and privileges to the citizen; and as long as it continues to exist in its present form, it speaks not only in the same words, but with the same meaning and intent with which it spoke when it came from the hands of its framers, and was voted on and adopted by the people of the United States. Any other rule of construction would abrogate the judicial character of this court, and make it the mere reflex of the popular opinion or passion of the day. This court was not created by the Constitution for such purposes. Higher and graver trusts have been confided to it, and it must not falter in the path of duty.

What the construction was at that time, we think can hardly admit of doubt. We have the language of the Declaration of Independence and of the Articles of Confederation, in addition to the plain words of the Constitution itself; we have the legislation of the different States, before, about the time, and since the Constitution was adopted; we have the legislation of Congress, from the time of its adoption to a recent period; and we have the constant and uniform action of the Executive Department, all concurring together, and leading to the same result. And if anything in relation to the construction of the Constitution can be regarded as settled, it is that which we now give to the word "citizen" and the word "people."

And upon a full and careful consideration of the subject, the court is of opinion that, upon the facts stated in the plea in abatement, Dred Scott was not a citizen of Missouri within the meaning of the Constitution of the United States, and not entitled as such to sue in its courts; and, consequently, that the Circuit Court had no jurisdiction of the case, and that the judgment on the plea in abatement is erroneous.

We are aware that doubts are entertained by some of the members of the court, whether the plea in abatement is legally before the court upon this writ of error; but if that plea is regarded as waived, or out of the case upon any other ground, yet the question as to the jurisdiction of the Circuit Court is presented on the face of the bill of exception itself, taken by the plaintiff at the trial; for he admits that he and his wife were born slaves, but endeavors to make out this title to freedom and citizenship by showing that they were taken by their owner to certain places, hereinafter mentioned, where slavery could not by law exist, and that they thereby became free, and upon their return to Missouri became citizens of that State.

Now, if the removal of which he speaks did not give them their freedom, then by his own admission he is still a slave; and whatever opinions may be entertained in favor of the citizenship of a free person of the African race, no one supposes that a slave is a citizen of the State or of the United States. If, therefore, the acts done by his owner did not make them free persons, he is still a slave, and certainly incapable of suing in the character of a citizen.

The principle of law it too well settled to be disputed, that a court can give no judgment for either party, where it has no jurisdiction; and if, upon the showing of Scott himself, it appeared that he was still a slave, the case ought to have been dismissed, and the judgment against him and in favor of the defendant for costs, is, like that on the plea in abatement, erroneous, and the suit ought to have been dismissed by the Circuit Court for want of jurisdiction in that court.

But, before we proceed to examine this part of the case, it may be proper to notice an objection taken to the judicial authority of this court to decide it; and it has been said, that as this court has decided against the jurisdiction of the Circuit Court on the plea in abatement, it has no right to examine any question presented by the exception; and that anything it may say upon that part of the case will be extrajudicial, and mere obiter dicta.

This is a manifest mistake; there can be no doubt as to the jurisdiction of this court to revise the judgement of a circuit court, and to reverse it for any error of giving judgment in a case over which it had no jurisdiction, or any other material error; and this, too, whether there is a plea in abatement or not.

The objection appears to have arisen from confounding writs of error to a state court, with writs of error to a circuit court of the United States. Undoubtedly, upon a writ of error to state court, unless the record shows a case that gives jurisdiction, the case must be dismissed for want of jurisdiction in this court. And if it is dismissed on that ground, we have no right to examine and decide upon any questions presented by the bill of exceptions, or any other part of the record. But writs of error to a state court, and to a circuit court of the United States, are regulated by different laws, and stand upon entirely different principles. And in a writ of error to a circuit court of the United States, the whole record is before this court for examination and decision; and if the sum in controversy is large enough to give jurisdiction, it is not only the right, but it is the judicial duty of the court, to examine the whole case as presented by the record; and if it appears upon its face that any material error or errors have been committed by the court below, it is the duty of this court to reverse the judgment, and remand the case. And certainly an error in passing a judgment upon the merits in favor of either party, in a case which it was not authorized to try, and over which it had no jurisdiction, is as grave an error as a court can commit.

The plea in abatement is not a plea to the jurisdiction of this court, but to the jurisdiction of the Circuit Court. And it appears by the record before us, that the Circuit Court committed an error, in deciding that it had jurisdiction, upon the facts in the case, admitted by the pleadings. It is the duty of the appellate tribunal to correct this error; but that could not be done by dismissing the case for want of jurisdiction here—for that would leave the erroneous judgment in full force, and the injured party without remedy. And the appellate court, therefore, exercises the power for which alone appellate courts are constituted, by reversing the judgment of the court below for this error. It exercises its proper and appropriate jurisdiction over the judgment and proceedings of the Circuit Court as they appear upon the record brought up by the writ of error.

The correction of one error in the court below does not deprive the appellate court of the power of examining further into the record, and correcting any other material errors which may have been committed by the inferior court. There is certainly no rule of law—nor any practice—nor any decision of a court—which even questions this power in the appellate tribunal. On the contrary, it is the daily practice of this court, and of all appellate courts where they reverse the judgment of an inferior court for error, to correct by its opinions whatever errors may appear on the record material to the case; and they have always held it to be their duty to do so where the silence of the court might lead to misconstruction or future controversy, and the point has been relied on by either side, and argued before the court.

In the case before us, we have already decided that the Circuit Court erred in deciding that it had jurisdiction upon the facts admitted by the pleadings. And it appears that, in the further progress of the case, it acted upon the erroneous principle it had decided on the pleadings, and gave judgment for the defendant, where, upon the facts admitted in the exception, it had no jurisdiction.

We are at a loss to understand upon what principle of law, applicable to appellate jurisdiction, it can be supposed that this court has not judicial authority to correct the last mentioned error because they had before corrected the former; or by what process of reasoning it can be made out, that the error of an inferior court in actually pronouncing judgment for one of the parties, in a case in which it had no jurisdiction, cannot be looked into or corrected by this court, because we have decided a similar question presented in the pleadings. The last point is distinctly presented by the facts contained in the plaintiff's own bill of exceptions, which he himself brings here by this writ of error. It was the point which chiefly occupied the attention of the counsel on both sides in the argument—and the judgment which this court must render upon both errors is precisely the same. It must, in each of them, exercise jurisdiction over the judgment, and reverse it for the errors committed by the court below; and issue a mandate to the Circuit Court to conform its judgment to the opinion pronounced by this court, by dismissing the case for want of jurisdiction in the Circuit Court. This is the constant an invariable practice of this court where it reverses a judgment for want of jurisdiction in the Circuit Court.

It can scarcely be necessary to pursue such a question further. The want of jurisdiction in the court below may appear on the record without any plea in abatement. This is familiarly the case where a court of chancery has exercised jurisdiction in a case where the plaintiff had a plain and adequate remedy at law, and it so appears by the transcript when brought here by appeal. So, also where it appears that a court of admiralty has exercised jurisdiction in a case belonging exclusively to a court of common law. In these cases there is no plea in abatement. And for the same reason, and upon the same principles, where the defect of jurisdiction is patent on the record, this court is bound to reverse the judgment, although the defendant has not pleaded in abatement to the jurisdiction of the inferior court.

The cases of *Jackson v. Ashton*, 8 Pet. 148, and of *Capron v. Van Noorden*, 2 Cranch, 126, to which we have referred in a previous part of this opinion, are directly in point. In the last mentioned case, Capron brought an action against Van Noorden in a circuit court of the United States, without showing, by the usual averments of citizenship, that the court had jurisdiction. There was no plea in abatement put in, and the parties went to trial upon the merits. The court gave judgment in favor of the defendant with costs. The plaintiff thereupon brought his writ of error, and this court reversed the judgment given in favor of the defendant, and remanded the case with directions to dismiss it, because it did not appear by the transcript that the Circuit Court had jurisdiction.

The case before us still more strongly, imposes upon this court the duty of examining whether the court below has not committed an error, in taking jurisdiction and giving a judgment for costs in favor of the defendant; for in *Capron v. Van Noorden* the judgment was reversed, because it did not appear that the parties were citizens of different States. They might or might not be. But in this case it does not appear that the plaintiff was born a slave; and if the facts upon which he relies have not made him free, then it appears affirmatively on the record that he is not a citizen, and consequently his suit against Sandford was not a suit between citizens of different States, and the court had no

authority to pass any judgment between the parties. The suit ought, in this view of it, to have been dismissed by the Circuit Court, and its judgement in favor of Sandford is erroneous, and must be reversed.

It is true that the result either way, by dismissal or by a judgment for the defendant, makes very little, if any difference in a pecuniary or personal point of view to either party. But the fact that the result would be very nearly the same to the parties in either form of judgment, would not justify this court in sanctioning an error in the judgment which is patent on the record, and which, if sanctioned, might be drawn into precedent, and lead to serious mischief and injustice in some future suit.

We proceed, therefore, to inquire whether the facts relied on by the plaintiff entitled him to his freedom.

The case, as he himself states it, on the record, brought here by his writ of error, is this: The plaintiff was a negro slave, belonging to Dr. Emerson, who was a surgeon in the Army of the United States. In the year 1834, he took the plaintiff from the State of Missouri to the military post at Rock Island, in the State of Illinois, and held him there as a slave until the month of April or May, 1836. At the time last mentioned, said Dr. Emerson removed the plaintiff from said military post at Rock Island to the military post at Fort Snelling, situate on the west bank of the Mississippi River, in the Territory known as Upper Louisiana, acquired by the United States of France, and situate north of the latitude of thirty-six degrees thirty minutes north, and north of the State of Missouri. Said Dr. Emerson held the plaintiff in slavery at said Fort Snelling, from said last mentioned date until the year 1838. In the year 1835, Harriet, who is named in the second count of the count of the plaintiff's declaration, was a negro slave of Major Taliaferro, who belonged to the Army of the United States. In that year, 1835, said Major Taliaferro took said Harriet to said Fort Snelling, a military post, situated as hereinbefore stated, and kept her there as a slave until the year 1836, and then sold and delivered her as a slave, at said Fort Snelling, unto the said Dr. Emerson hereinbefore named. Said Dr. Emerson held said Harriet in slavery at said Fort Snelling, until the year 1838. In the year 1836, the plaintiff and Harriet intermarried, at Fort Selling, with the consent of Dr. Emerson, who then claimed to be their master and owner. Eliza and Lizzie, named in the third count of the plaintiffs declaration, are the fruit of that marriage. Eliza is about fourteen years old, and was born on board the steamboat Gipsey, north of the north line of the State of Missouri, and upon the River Mississippi. Lizzie is about seven years old, and was born in the State of Missouri, at the military post called Jefferson Barracks In the year 1838, said Dr. Emerson removed the plaintiff and said Harriet, and their said daughter Eliza, from said Fort Snelling, to the State of Missouri, where they have ever since resided. Before the commencement of this suit, said Dr. Emerson sold and conveyed the plaintiff, and Harriet, Eliza, and Lizzie, to the defendant, as slaves, and the defendant has ever since claimed to hold them, and each of them, as slaves.

In considering this part of the controversy, two questions arise: 1st. Was he, together with his family, free in Missouri by reason of the stay in the territory of the United States hereinbefore mentioned? And 2d. If they were not, is Scott himself free by reason of his removal to Rock Island, in the State of Illinois, as stated in the above admissions?

We proceed to examine the first question.

The Act of Congress, upon which the plaintiff relies, declares that slavery and involuntary servitude, except as a punishment for crime, shall be forever prohibited in all that part of that territory ceded by France, under the name of Louisiana, which lies north of thirty-six degrees thirty minutes north latitude, and not included within the limits of Missouri. And the difficulty which meets us at the threshold of this part of the inquiry is, whether Congress was authorized to pass this law under any of the powers granted to it by the Constitution; for if the authority is not given by that instrument, it is the duty of this court to declare it void and inoperative, and incapable of conferring freedom upon one who is held as a slave under the laws of any one of the States.

The counsel for the plaintiff has laid much stress upon that article in the Constitution which confers on Congress the power "to dispose of and make all needful rules and regulations respecting the territory or other property belonging to the United States;" but, in the judgement of the court, that provision has no bearing on the present controversy, and the power there given, whatever it may be, is confined, and was intended to be confined, to the territory which at that time belonged to, or was claimed by, the United States, and was within their boundaries as settled by the Treaty with Great Britain, and can have no influence upon a territory afterwards acquired from a foreign government. It was a special provision for a known and particular Territory, and to meet a present emergency, and nothing more.

A brief summary of the history of the times, as well as the careful and measured terms in which the article is framed, will show the correctness of this proposition.

It will be remembered that, from the commencement of the Revolutionary War, serious difficulties existed between the States, in relation to the disposition of large and unsettled territories which were included in the chartered limits of some of the States. And some of the other States, and more especially Maryland, which had no unsettled lands, insisted that as the unoccupied lands, if wrested from Great Britain, would owe their preservation to the common purse and the common sword, the money arising from them ought to be applied in just proportion among the several States to pay the expense of the war, and ought not to be appropriated to the use of State in whose chartered limits they might happen to lie, to the exclusion of the other States by whose combined efforts and common expense the territory was defended and preserved against the claim of the British Government.

These difficulties caused much uneasiness during the War, while the issue was in some degree doubtful, and the future boundaries of the United States yet to be defined by treaty, if we achieved our independence.

The majority of the Congress of the Confederation obviously concurred in opinion with the State of Maryland, and desired to obtain from the States which claimed it a cession of this territory, in order that Congress might raise money on this security to carry on the War. This appears by the resolution passed on the 6th of September, 1780 strongly urging the States to cede these lands to the United States, both for the sake of peace and union among themselves, and to maintain the public credit; and this was followed by the resolution of October 10th, 1780, by which Congress pledged itself, that if the lands were ceded, as recommended by the resolution above mentioned, they should be disposed of for the common benefit of the United

SLAVERY

DRED SCOTT V. SANDFORD

States, and be settled and formed into distinct republican States, which should become members of the Federal Union, and have the same rights of sovereignty, and freedom, and independence as other States.

But these difficulties became much more serious after peace took place, and the boundaries of the United States were established. Every State, at that time, felt severely the pressure of its war debt; but in Virginia, and some other States there were large territories of unsettled lands, the sale of which would enable them to discharge their obligations without much inconvenience; while other States which had not such resource, saw before them many years of heavy and burdensome taxation, and the latter insisted, for the reasons before stated, that these unsettled lands should be treated as the common property of the States, and the proceeds applied to their common benefit.

The letters from the statesman of that day will show how mush this controversy occupied their thoughts, and the dangers that were apprehended from it. It was the disturbing element of the time, and fears were entertained that it might dissolve the Confederation by which the States were then united.

These fears and dangers were, however, at once removed, when the State of Virginia, in 1784, voluntarily ceded to the United States the immense tract of country lying northwest of the River Ohio, and which was within the acknowledged limits of the State. The only object of the State, in making this cession, was to put an end to the threatening and exciting controversy, and to enable the Congress of that time to dispose of the lands, and appropriate the proceeds as a common fund for the common benefit of the States. It was not ceded because it was inconvenient to the State to hold and govern it, nor from any expectation that it could be better or more conveniently governed by the United States.

The example of Virginia was soon afterwards followed by other States, and, at the time of the adoption of the Constitution, all of the States, similarly situated, had ceded their unappropriated lands, except North Carolina and Georgia. The main object for which these cessions were desired and made, was on account of their money value, and to put an end to a dangerous controversy, as to who was justly entitled to the proceeds when the lands should be sold. It is necessary to bring this part of the history of

these cessions thus distinctly into view, because it will enable us the better to comprehend the phraseology of the Article of the Constitution so often referred to in the argument.

Undoubtedly the powers of sovereignty and the eminent domain were ceded with the land. This was essential, in order to make it effectual, and to accomplish its objects. But it must be remembered that, at that time, there was no Government of the United States in existence with enumerated and limited powers; what was then called the United States, were thirteen separate, sovereign, independent States, which had entered into a league or confederation for their mutual protection and advantage, and the Congress of the United States was composed of the representatives of these separate sovereignties, meeting together, as equals, to discuss and decide on certain measures which the States, by the Articles of Confederation, had agreed to submit to their decision. But this Confederation had none of the attributes of sovereignty in legislative, executive, or judicial power. It was little more than a congress of ambassadors, authorized to represent separate nations, in matters in which they had a common concern.

It was this Congress that accepted the cession from Virginia. They had no power to accept it under the Articles of Confederation. But they had an undoubted right, as independent sovereignties, to accept any cession of territory for their common benefit, which all of them assented to; and it is equally clear, that as their common property, and having no superior to control them, they had the right to exercise absolute dominion over it, subject only to the restrictions which Virginia had imposed in her Act of Cession. There was, as we have said, no Government of the United States then in existence with special enumerated and limited powers. The territory belonged to sovereignties, who, subject to the limitations above mentioned, had a right to establish any form of government they pleased, by compact or treaty among themselves, and to regulate rights of person and property in the territory as they might deem proper. It was by a Congress, representing the authority of these several and separate sovereignties, and acting under their authority and command (but not from any authority derived from the Articles of Confederation), that the instrument, usually called the Ordinance of 1787, was adopted; regulating in much detail the principles and the laws by which this Territory should be governed; and among other provisions, slavery is prohibited in it. We do not question the power of the States, by agreement among themselves, to pass this Ordinance, nor its obligatory force in the Territory, while the confederation or league of the States in their separate sovereign character continued to exist.

This was the state of things when the Constitution of the United States was formed. The territory ceded by Virginia belonged to the several confederated States as common property, and they had united in establishing in it a system of government and jurisprudence, in order to prepare it for admission as States, according to the terms of the cession. They were about to dissolve this federative Union, and to surrender a portion of their independent sovereignty to a new government, which, for certain purposes, would make the people of the several States one people, and which was to be supreme and controlling within its sphere of action throughout the United States; but this government was to be carefully limited in its powers, and to exercise no authority beyond those expressly granted by the Constitution, or necessarily to be implied from the language of the instrument, and the objects it was intended to accomplish; and as this league of States would, upon the adoption of the new government, cease to have any power over the territory, and the Ordinance they had agreed upon be incapable of execution, and a mere nullity, it was obvious that some provision was necessary to give the new government sufficient power to enable it to carry into effect the objects for which it was ceded, and the compacts and agreements which the States had made each other in the exercise of their powers of sovereignty. It was necessary that the lands should be sold to pay the war debt; that a government and system of jurisprudence should be maintained in it, to protect the citizens of the United States, who should migrate to the Territory, in their rights of person and of property. It was also necessary that the new government, about to be adopted, should be authorized to maintain the claim of the United States to the unappropriated lands in North Carolina and Georgia, which had not then been ceded, but the cession of which was confidently anticipated upon some terms that would be arranged between the general government and these two States. And, moreover, there were many articles of value besides this property in land, such as arms, military stores, munitions, and ships of war, which were the common property of the States, when acting in their independent characters as confederates, which neither the new government nor anyone else would have a right to take possession of or control, without authority from them; and it was to place these things under the guardianship and protection of the new government, and to clothe it with the necessary powers, that the clause was inserted in the Constitution which gives Congress the power "to dispose of and make all needful rules and regulations respecting the territory or other property belonging to the United States." It was intended for a specific purpose, to provide for the things we have mentioned. It was to transfer to the new government the property then held in common by the States, and to give to that government power to apply it to the objects for which it had been destined by mutual agreement among the States before their league was dissolved. It applied only to the property which the States held in common at that time, and has no reference whatever to any territory or other property which the new sovereignty might afterwards itself acquire.

The language used in the clause, the arrangement and combination of the powers, and the somewhat unusual phraseology it uses, when it speaks of the political power to be exercised in the government of the territory, all indicate the design and meaning of the clause to be such as we have mentioned. It does not speak of any Territory, nor of Territories, but uses language which, according to its legitimate meaning, points to a particular thing. The power is given in relation only to the territory of the United States—that is, to a Territory then in existence, and then known or claimed as the territory of the United States. It begins its enumeration of powers by that of disposing, in other words, making sale of the lands, or raising money from them, which, as we have already said, was the main object of the cession, and which is accordingly the first thing provided for in the Article. It then gives the power which was necessarily associated with the disposition and sale of the lands—that is, the power of making needful rules and regulations respecting the Territory. And whatever construction may now be given to these words, everyone, we think, must admit that they are not the word usually employed by statesman in giving supreme power of legislation. They are certainly very unlike the words used in the power granted to legislate over territory which the new government might afterwards itself obtain by cession form a state, either for its seat of government, or for forts, magazines, arsenals, dockyards, and other needful buildings.

And the same power of making needful rules respecting the Territory is, in precisely the same language, applied to the other property belonging to the United States—associating the power over the Territory in this respect with the power over movable or personal property—that is, the ships, arms, and munitions of war, which then belonged in common to the State sovereignties. And it will hardly be said, that this power, in relation to the last mentioned objects, was deemed necessary to be thus specially given to the new government, in order to authorize it to make needful rules and regulations respecting the ships it might itself build, or arms and munitions of war it might itself manufacture or provide for the public service.

No one, it is believed, would think a moment of deriving the power of Congress to make needful rules and regulations in relation to property of this kind from this clause of the Constitution. Nor can it, upon any fair construction, be applied to any property but that which the new government was about to receive from the confederate States. And if this be true as to this property, it must be equally true and limited as to the territory, which is so carefully and precisely coupled with it—and like it referred to as property in the power granted. The concluding words of the clause appear to render this construction irresistible; for, after the provisions we have mentioned, it proceeds to say, "that nothing in the Constitution shall be so construed as to prejudice any claims of the United States, or of any particular State."

Now, as we have before said, all of the States, except North Carolina and Georgia, had made the cession before the Constitution was adopted, according to the resolution of Congress of October 10, 1780. The claims of other States, that the unappropriated lands in these two States should be applied to the common benefit, in like manner, was still insisted on, but refused by the States. And this member of the clause in question evidently applies to them, and can apply to nothing else. It was to exclude the conclusion that either party, by adopting the Constitution, would surrender what they deemed their rights. And when the latter provi-

sion relates so obviously to the unappropriated lands not yet ceded by the States, and the first clause makes provision for those then actually ceded, it is impossible, by any just rule of construction, to make the first provision general, and extend to all territories, which the Federal Government might in any way afterwards acquire, when the latter is plainly and unequivocally confined to a particular territory; which was a part of the same controversy, and involved in the same dispute, and depended upon the same principles. The union of the two provisions in the same clause shows that they were kindred subjects, and that the whole clause is local, and relates only to lands, within the limits of the United States, which had been or then were claimed by a State; and that no other Territory was in the mind of the framers of the Constitution, or intended to be embraced in it. Upon any other construction it would be impossible to account for the insertion of the last provision in the place where it is found, or to comprehend why, or for what object, it was associated with the previous provision.

This view of the subject is confirmed by the manner in which the present Government of the United States dealt with the subject as soon as it came into existence. It must be borne in mind that the same States that formed the Confederation also formed and adopted the new government, to which so large a portion of their former sovereign powers were surrendered. It must also be borne in mind that all of these same States which had then ratified the new Constitution were represented in the Congress which passed the first law for the government of this territory; and many of the members of that legislative body had been deputies from the States under the Confederation—had united in adopting the Ordinance of 1787, and assisted in forming the new government under which they were then acting, and whose powers they were then exercising. And it is obvious from the law they passed to carry into effect the principles and provisions of the Ordinance, that they regarded it as the Act of the States done in the exercise of their legitimate powers at the time. The new government took the territory as it found it, in the condition in which it was transferred, and did not attempt to undo anything that had been done. And among the earliest laws passed under the new government, is one reviving the Ordinance of 1787, which had become inoperative and a nullity upon the adoption of the Constitution. This law introduces no new form or principles for its government, but recites, in the preamble, that it is passed in order that this Ordinance may continue to have full effect, and proceeds to make only those rules and regulations which were needful to adapt it to the new government, into whose hands the power had fallen. It appears, therefore, that this Congress regarded the purposes to which the land in this territory was to be applied, and the form of government and principles of jurisprudence which were to prevail there, while it remained in the territorial state, as already determined on by the States when they had full power and right to make the decision; and that the new government, having received it in this condition, ought to carry substantially into effect the plans and principles which had been previous; adopted by the States, and which no doubt the States anticipated when they surrendered their power to the new government. And if we regard this clause of the Constitution as pointing to this Territory, with a territorial government already established in it, which had been ceded to the States for the purposes hereinbefore mentioned—every word in it is perfectly appropriate and easily understood, and the provisions it contains are in perfect harmony with the objects for which it was ceded, and with the condition of its government as a Territory at the time. We can, then, easily account for the manner in which the first Congress legislated on the subject—and can also understand why this power over the Territory was associated in the same clause with the other property of the United States, and subjected to the like power of making needful rules and regulations. But if the clause is construed in the expanded sense contended for, so as to embrace any territory acquired from a foreign nation by the present government, and to give it in such territory a despotic and unlimited power over persons and property, such as the confederated States might exercise in their common property, it would be difficult to account for the phraseology used, when compared with other grants of power—and also for its association with the other provisions in the same clause.

The Constitution has always been remarkable for the felicity of its arrangement of different subjects, and the perspicuity and appropriateness of the language it uses. But if this clause is construed to extend to territory acquired by the present government from a foreign nation, outside of the limits of any charter from the British Government to a Colony, it would be difficult to say, why it was deemed necessary to give the government the power to sell any vacant lands belonging to the sovereignty which might be found within it; and if this was necessary, why the grant of this power should precede the power to legislate over it and establish a government there; and still more difficult to say, why it was deemed necessary so specially and particularly to grant the power to make needful rules and regulations in relation to any personal or movable property it might acquire there. For the words, "other property," necessarily, by every known rule of interpretation, must mean property of a different description from territory or land. And the difficulty would perhaps be insurmountable in endeavoring to account for the last member of the sentence, which provides that "nothing in this Constitution shall be so construed as to prejudice any claims of the United States or any particular State," or to say how any particular State could have claims in or to a Territory ceded by a foreign government, or to account for associating this provision with the preceding provisions of the clause, with which it would appear to have no connection.

The words "needful rules and regulations" would seem, also, to have been cautiously used for some definite object. They are not the words usually employed by statesman, when they mean to give the powers of sovereignty, or to establish a government, or to authorize its establishment. Thus, in the law to renew and keep alive the Ordinance of 1787, and to reestablish the government, the title of the law is: "An Act to provide for the government of the territory northwest of the River Ohio." And in the Constitution, when granting the power to legislate over the territory that may be selected for the seat of government independently of a state, it does not say Congress shall have power "to make all needful rules and regulations respecting the territory;" but it declares that "Congress shall have power to exercise exclusive legislation in all cases whatsoever over such District (not exceeding ten miles square) as may, by cession of particular States and the acceptance of Congress, become the seat of the Government of the United States.

The words "rules and regulations" are usually employed in the Constitution in speaking of some particular specified power which it means to confer on the government, and not, as we have seen, when granting general powers of legislation. As, for example, in the particular power of Congress "to make rules for the government and regulations of the land and naval forces, or the particular and specific power to regulate commerce;" "to establish an uniform rule of naturalization;" "to coin money and regulate the value thereof." And to construe the words of which we are speaking as a general and unlimited grant of sovereignty over territories which the government might afterwards acquire, is to use them in a sense and for a purpose for which they were not used in any other part of the instrument. But if confined to a particular territory, in which a government and laws had already been established, but which would require some alterations to adapt it to the new government, the words are peculiarly applicable and appropriate for that purpose.

The necessity of this special provision in relation to property and the rights or property held in common by the confederated State, is illustrated by the 1st clause of the 6th article. This clause provides that "all debts, contracts and engagements entered into before the adoption of this Constitution, shall be as valid against the United States under this government as under the Confederation." This provision, like the one under consideration, was indispensable if the new Constitution was adopted. The new government was not a mere change in a dynasty, or in a form of government, leaving the nation or sovereignty the same, and clothed with all the rights, and bound by all the obligations of the preceding one. But, when the present United States came into existence under the new government, it was a new political body, a new nation, then for the first time taking its place in the family of nations. It took nothing by succession from the Confederation. It had no right, as its successor, to any property or rights of property which it had acquired, and was not liable for any of its obligations. It was evidently viewed in this light by the framers of the Constitution. And as the several States would cease to exist in their former confederated character upon the adoption of the Constitution, and could not, in that character, again assemble together, special provisions were indispensable to transfer to the new government the property and rights which at that time they held in common; and at the same time to authorize it to pay taxes and appropriate money to pay the common debt which they had contracted; and this power

could only be given to it by special provisions in the Constitution.

The clause in relation to the territory and other property of the United States provided for the first, and the clause last quoted provided for the other. They have no connection with the general powers and rights of sovereignty delegated to the new government, and can neither enlarge nor diminish them. They were inserted to meet a present emergency, and not to regulate its powers as a government.

Indeed, a similar provision was deemed necessary, in relation to treaties made by the Confederation; and when in the clause next succeeding the one of which we have last spoken, it is declared that treaties shall be the supreme law of the land, care is taken to include, by express words, the Treaties made by the confederate States. The language is: "an all treaties made, or which shall be made, under the authority of the United States, shall be the supreme law of the land."

Whether, therefore, we take the particular clause in question by itself, or in connection with the other provisions of the Constitution, we think it clear, that it applies only to the particular territory of which we have spoken, and cannot, by any just rule of interpretation, be extended to a territory which the new government might afterwards obtain from a foreign nation. Consequently, the power which Congress may have lawfully exercised in this territory, while it remained under a territorial government, and which may have been sanctioned by judicial decision, can furnish no justification and no argument to support a similar exercise of power over territory afterwards acquired by the Federal Government. We put aside, therefore, any argument, drawn from precedents, showing the extent of the power which the general government exercised over slavery in this territory, as altogether inapplicable to the case before us.

But the case of *The American and Ocean Insurance Companies v. Canter,* 1 Pet. 511, has been quoted as establishing a different construction of this clause of the Constitution. There is, however, not the slightest conflict between the opinion now given and the one referred to; and it is only by taking a single sentence out of the latter and separating it form the context, that even an appearance of conflict can be shown. We need not comment on such a mode of expounding an opinion of the court. Indeed it most commonly misrepresents instead of expounding it. And this is fully exemplified in the case referred to, where if one sentence is taken by itself, the opinion would appear to be in direct conflict with that now given; but the words which immediately follow that sentence show that the court did not mean to decide the point, but merely affirmed the power of Congress to establish a government in the Territory, leaving it an open question, whether that power was derived from this clause in the Constitution, or was to be necessarily inferred from a power to acquire territory by cession from a foreign government. The opinion on this part of the case is short, and we give the whole of it to show how well the selection of a single sentence is calculated to mislead.

The passage referred to is in page 542, in which the court, in speaking of the power of Congress to establish a territorial government in Florida until it should become a State, uses the following language:

"In the meantime Florida continues to be a Territory of the United States, governed by that clause of the Constitution which empowers Congress to make all needful rules and regulations respecting the territory or other property of the United States. Perhaps the power of governing a territory belonging to the United States, which has not, by becoming a State, acquired the means of self-government, may result necessarily from the facts that it is not within the jurisdiction of any particular State, and is within the power and jurisdiction of the United States. The right to govern may be the inevitable consequence of the right to acquire territory. Whichever may be the source from which the power is derived, the possession of it is unquestionable."

It is thus clear, from the whole opinion on this point, that the court did not mean to decide whether the power was derived from the clause in the Constitution, or was the necessary consequence of the right to acquire. They do decide that the power in Congress is unquestionable, and in this we entirely concur, and nothing will be found in this opinion to the contrary. The power stands firmly on the latter alternative put by the court, that is, as "the inevitable consequence of the right to acquire territory."

And what still more clearly demonstrates that the court did not mean to decide the question, but leave it open for future consideration, is the fact that the case was decided in the

Circuit Court by Mr. Justice Johnson, and his decision was affirmed by the Supreme Court. His opinion at the Circuit is given in full in a note to the case, and in that opinion he states, in explicit terms, that the clause of the Constitution applies only to the territory then within the limits of the United States, and not to Florida, which had been acquired by cession from Spain. This part of his opinion will be found in the note in page 517 of the report. But he does not dissent from the opinion of the Supreme Court; thereby showing that, in his judgment, as well as that of the court, the case before them did not call for a decision on that particular point, and the court abstained from deciding it. And in a part of its opinion subsequent to the passage we have quoted, where the court speak of the legislative power of Congress in Florida, they still speak with the same reserve. And in page 546, speaking of the power of Congress to authorize the Territorial Legislature to establish courts there, the court say: "They are legislative courts, created in virtue of the general right of sovereignty which exists in the government, or in virtue of that clause which enables Congress to make all needful rules and regulations respecting the territory belonging to the United States."

It has been said that the construction given to this clause is new, and now for the first time brought forward. The case which we are speaking, and which has been so much discussed, shows that the fact is otherwise. It shows that precisely the same question came before Mr. Justice Johnson, at his circuit, thirty years ago—was fully considered by him, and the same construction given by this court. And that upon an appeal from his decision the same question was brought before this court, but was not decided because a decision upon it was not required by the case before the court.

There is another sentence in the opinion which has been commented on, which even in a still more striking manner shows how one may mislead or be misled by taking out a single sentence from the opinion of a court, and leaving out of view what precedes and follows. It is in page 546, near the close of the opinion, in which the court say: "In legislating for them" (the Territories of the United States), "Congress exercises the combined powers of the general and of a state government." And it is said, that as a State may unquestionably prohibit slavery within its territory of the United States, exercising there the powers of a State, as well as the power of the general government.

The examination of this passage in the case referred to, would be more appropriate when we come to consider in another part of this opinion what power Congress can constitutionally exercise in a Territory, over the rights of person or rights of property of a citizen. But, as it is in the same case with passage we have before commented on, we dispose of it now, as it will save the court from the necessity of referring again to the case. And it will be seen upon reading the page in which this sentence is found, that it has not reference, whatever to the power of Congress over rights of person or rights of property—but relates altogether to the power of establishing judicial tribunals to administer the laws constitutionally passed, and defining the jurisdiction they may exercise.

The law of Congress establishing a territorial government in Florida, provided that the Legislature of the Territory should have legislative powers over "all rightful objects of legislation; but no law should be valid which was inconsistent with the laws and Constitution of the United States."

Under the power thus conferred, the Legislature of Florida passed an Act, erecting a tribunal at Key West to decide cases of salvage. And in the case of which we are speaking, the question arose whether the Territorial Legislature could be authorized by Congress to establish such a tribunal, with such powers; and one of the parties, among other objections, insisted that Congress could not under the Constitution authorize the Legislature of the Territory to establish such a tribunal with such powers, but that it must be established by Congress itself; and that a sale of cargo made under its order, to pay salvors, was void, as made without legal authority, and passed no property to the purchaser.

It is disposing of this objection that the sentence relied on occurs, and the court begin that part of the opinion by stating with great precision the point which they are about to decide.

They say: "It has been contended that by the Constitution of the United States, the judicial power of the United States extends to all cases of admiralty and maritime jurisdiction; and that the whole of the judicial power must be vested in one Supreme Court, and in such inferior courts as Congress shall from time to time ordain and establish. Hence it has been argued that Congress cannot vest admiralty jurisdiction in courts created by the Territorial Legislature."

And after thus clearly stating the point before them, and which they were about to decide, they proceed to show that these territorial tribunals were not constitutional courts, but merely legislative, and that Congress might, therefore, delegate the power to the territorial government to establish the court in question; and they conclude that part of the opinion in the following words: "Although admiralty jurisdiction can be exercised in the states in those courts only which are established in pursuance of the 3d article of the Constitution, the same limitation does not extend to the Territories. In legislating for them, Congress exercises the combined powers of the general and state governments."

Thus it will be seen by these quotations from the opinion, that the court, after stating the question it was about to decide, in a manner too plain to be misunderstood, proceeded to decide it, and announced, as the opinion of the tribunal, that in organizing the Judicial Department of the government in a Territory of the United States, Congress does not act under, and is not restricted by, the 3d article in the Constitution, and is not bound, in a Territory, to ordain and establish courts in which the judges hold their offices during good behavior; but may exercise the discretionary power which a state exercises in establishing it's judicial department, and regulating the jurisdiction of its courts, and may authorize the territorial government to establish, or may itself establish, courts in which the judges hold their offices for a term of years only, and may vest in them judicial power upon subjects confided to the judiciary of the United States. And in doing this, Congress undoubtedly exercises the combined power of the general and a state government. It exercises the discretionary power of a state government in authorizing the establishment of a court in which the judges hold their appointments for a term of years only, and not during good behavior; and it exercises the power of the general government in investing that court with admiralty jurisdiction over which the general government had exclusive jurisdiction in the Territory.

No one, we presume, will question the correctness of that opinion; nor is there anything in conflict with it in the opinion now given. The point decided in the case cited has no relation to the question now before the court. That depended on the construction of the 3d article of the Constitution, in relation to the judiciary of the United States, and the power which Congress might exercise in a territory in organizing the Judicial Department of the government. The case before us depends upon other and different provisions of the Constitution, altogether separate and apart from the one above mentioned. The question as to what courts Congress may ordain or establish in a territory to administer laws which the Constitution authorizes it to pass, and what laws it is or is not authorized by the Constitution to pass, are widely different—are regulated by different and separate articles of the Constitution, and stand upon different principles. And we are satisfied that no one who reads attentively the page in Peters' Reports to which we have referred, can suppose that the attention of the court was drawn for a moment to the question now before this court, or that it meant in that case to say that Congress had a right to prohibit a citizen of the United States from taking any property which he lawfully held, into a Territory of the United States.

This brings us to examine by what provisions of the Constitution the present Federal Government under its delegated and restricted powers, is authorized to acquire territory outside of the original limits of the United States, and what powers it may exercise therein over the person or property of a citizen of the United States, while it remains a territory, and until it shall be admitted as one of the States of the Union.

There is certainly no power given by the Constitution to the Federal Government to establish or maintain Colonies bordering on the United States or at a distance, to be ruled and governed at its own pleasure; nor to enlarge its territorial limits in any way, except by the admission of new States. That power is plainly given; and if a new State is admitted it needs no further legislation by Congress, because the Constitution itself defines the relative rights and powers and duties of the State, and the citizens of the State, and the Federal Government. But no power is given to acquire a Territory to be held and governed permanently in that character.

And indeed the power exercised by Congress to acquire territory and establish a government

there, according to its own unlimited discretion, was viewed with great jealousy by the leading statesmen of the day. And in the *Federalist*, No. 38, written by Mr. Madison, he speaks of the acquisition of the Northwestern Territory by the confederated States, by the cession from Virginia and the establishment of a government there, as an exercise of power not warranted by the Articles of Confederation, and dangerous to the liberties of the people. And he urges the adoption of the Constitution as a security and safeguard against such an exercise of power.

We do not mean, however, to question the power of Congress in this respect. The power to expand the territory of the United States by the admission of new States is plainly given; and in the construction of this power by all the departments of the government, it has been held to authorize the acquisition of territory, not fit for admission at the time, but to be admitted as soon as its population and situation would entitle it to admission. It is acquired to become a State, and not to be held as a colony and governed by Congress with absolute authority; and as the propriety of admitting a new State is committed to the sound discretion of Congress, the power to acquire territory for that purpose, to be held by the United States until it is in a suitable condition to become a state upon an equal footing with the other States, must rest upon the same discretion. It is a question for the Political Department of the government, and not the judicial; and whatever the Political Department of the government shall recognize as within the limits of the United States, the Judicial Department is also bound to recognize, and to administer in it the laws of the United States, so far as they apply, and to maintain in the territory the authority and rights of the government; and also the personal rights of property of individual citizens, as secured by the Constitution. All we mean to say on this point is, that as there is no express regulation in the Constitution defining the power which the general government may exercise over the person or property of a citizen in a territory thus acquired, the court must necessarily look to the provisions and principles of the Constitution, and its distribution of powers, for the rules and principles by which its decision must be governed.

Taking this rule to guide us, it may be safely assumed that citizens of the United States who migrate to a territory belonging to the people of the United States, cannot be ruled as mere colonists, dependent upon the will of the general government, and to be governed by any laws it may think proper to impose. The principle upon which our governments rest, and upon which alone they continue to exist, is the union of States, sovereign and independent within their own limits in their internal and domestic concerns, and bound together as one people by a general government, possessing certain enumerated and restricted powers, delegated to it by the people of the several States, and exercising supreme authority within the scope of the powers granted to it, throughout the dominion of the United States. A power, therefore, in the general government to obtain and hold Colonies and dependent Territories, over which they might legislate without restriction, would be inconsistent with its own existence in its present form. Whatever it acquires, it acquires for the benefit of the people of the several States who created it. It is their trustee acting for them, and charged with the duty of promoting the interests of the whole people of the Union in the exercise of the powers specifically granted.

At the time when the Territory in question was obtained by cession from France, it contained no population fit to be associated together and admitted as a State; and it therefore was absolutely necessary to hold possession of it as a Territory belonging to the United States until it was settled and inhabited by a civilized community capable of self-government, and in a condition to be admitted on equal terms with the other States as a member of the Union. But, as we have before said, it was acquired by the general government as the representative and trustee of the people of the United States, and it must, therefore, be held in that character for their common and equal benefit; for it was the people of the several States, acting through the agent and representative, the Federal Government, who in fact acquired the territory in question, and the government holds it for their common use until it shall be associated with the other States as a member of the Union.

But until that time arrives, it is undoubtedly necessary that some government should be established, in order to organize society, and to protect the inhabitants in their persons and property; and as the people of the United States could act in this matter only through the government which represented them, and through

which they spoke and acted when the territory was obtained, it was not only within the scope of its powers, but it was its duty to pass such laws and establish such a government as would enable those by whose authority they acted to reap the advantages anticipated from its acquisition, and to gather there a population which would enable it to assume the position to which it was destined among the States of the Union. The power to acquire, necessarily carries with it the power to preserve and apply to the purposes for which it was acquired. The form of government to be established necessarily rested in the discretion of Congress. It was their duty to establish the one that would be best suited for the protection and security of the citizens of the United States and other inhabitants who might be authorized to take up their abode there, and that must always depend upon the existing condition of the Territory, as to the number and character of its inhabitants, and the situation in the Territory. In some cases a government, consisting of persons appointed by the Federal Government, would best subserve the interests of the Territory, when the inhabitants were few and scattered, and new to one another. In other instances, it would be more advisable to commit the powers of self-government to the people who had settled in the territory, as being the most competent to determine what was best for their own interests. But some form of civil authority would be absolutely necessary to organize and preserve civilized society, and prepare it to become a state; and what is the best form must always depend on the condition of the territory at the time, and the choice of the mode must depend upon the exercise of a discretionary power by Congress acting within the scope of its constitutional authority, and not infringing upon the rights of person or rights of property of the citizen who might go there to reside or for any other lawful purpose. It was acquired by the exercise of this discretion and it must be held and governed in like manner, until it is fitted to be a state.

But the power of Congress over the person or property of a citizen can never be a mere discretionary power under our Constitution and form of government. The powers of the government and the rights and privileges of the citizen are regulated and plainly defined by the Constitution itself. And when the territory becomes a part of the United States, the Federal Government enters into possession in the character impressed upon it by those who created it. It enters upon it with its powers over the citizen strictly defined, and limited by the Constitution, from which it derives its own existence, and by virtue of which alone it continues to exist and acts as a government and sovereignty. It has no power of any kind beyond it; and it cannot, when it enters a territory of the United States, put off its character, and assume discretionary or despotic powers which the Constitution has denied to it. It cannot create for itself a new character separated from the citizens of the United States, and the duties it owes them under the provisions of the Constitution. The territory being a part of the United States, the government and the citizen both enter it under the authority of the Constitution, with their respective rights defined and marked out; and the Federal Government can exercise no power over his person or property, beyond what that instrument confers, nor lawfully deny any right which it has reserved.

A reference to a few of the provisions of the Constitution will illustrate this proposition.

For example, no one, we presume, will contend that Congress can make any law in a territory respecting the establishment of religion or the free exercise thereof, or abridging the freedom of speech or of the press, or the right of the people of the territory peaceably to assemble and to petition the government for the redress of grievances.

Nor can Congress deny to the people the right to keep and bear arms, nor the right to trial by jury, nor compel anyone to be a witness against himself in a criminal proceeding.

These powers, and others in relation to rights of person, which it is not necessary here to enumerate, are, in express and positive terms, denied to the general government; and the rights of private property have been guarded with equal care. Thus the rights of property are united with the rights of person, and placed on the same ground by the fifth amendment to the Constitution, which provides that no person shall be deprived of life, liberty and property, without due process of law. And an Act of Congress which deprives a citizen of the United States of his liberty or property, merely because he came himself or brought his property into a particular Territory of the United States, and who had committed no offense against the laws,

could hardly be dignified with the name of due process of law.

So, too, it will hardly be contended that Congress could by law quarter a soldier in a house in a territory without the consent of the owner, in time of peace; nor in time of war, but in a manner prescribed by law. Nor could they by law forfeit the property of a citizen in a territory who was convicted of treason, for a longer period than the life of the person convicted; nor take private property of public use without just compensation.

The powers over person and property of which we speak are not only not granted to Congress, but are in express terms denied, and they are forbidden to exercise them. And this prohibition is not confined to the States, but the words are general, and extend to the whole territory over which the Constitution gives it power to legislate, including those portions of it remaining under territorial government, as well as that covered by States. It is a total absence of power everywhere within the dominion of the United States, and places the citizens of a territory, so far as these rights are concerned, on the same footing with citizens of the States, and guards them as firmly and plainly against any inroads which the general government might attempt, under the plea of implied or incidental powers. And if Congress itself cannot do this— if it is beyond the powers conferred on the Federal Government—it will be admitted, we presume, that it could not authorize a territorial government to exercise them. It could confer no power on any local government, established by its authority, to violate the provisions of the Constitution.

It seems, however, to be supposed, that there is a difference between property in a slave and other property, and that different rules may be applied to it in expounding the Constitution of the United States. And the laws and usages of nations, and the writings of eminent jurists upon the rights and duties, and the powers which governments may exercise over it, have been dwelt upon in the argument.

But in considering the question before us, it must be borne in mind that there is no law of nations standing between the people of the United States and their governments and interfering with their relation to each other. The powers of the government, and the rights of the citizen under it, are positive and practical regulations plainly written down. The people of the United States have delegated to it certain enumerated powers, and forbidden it to exercise others. It has no power over the person or property of a citizen but what the citizens of the United States have granted. And no laws or usages of other nations, or reasoning of statesmen or jurists upon the relations of master and slave, can enlarge the powers of the government, or take from the citizens the rights they have reserved. And if the Constitution recognizes the right of property of the master in a slave, and makes no distinction between that description of property and other property owned by a citizen, no tribunal, acting under the authority of the United States, whether it be legislative, executive, or judicial, has a right to draw such a distinction, or deny to it the benefit of the provisions and guarantees which have been provided for the protection of private property against the encroachments of the governments.

Now, as we have already said in an earlier part of this opinion, upon a different point, the right of property in a slave is distinctly and expressly affirmed in the Constitution. The right to traffic in it, like an ordinary article of merchandise and property, was guaranteed to the citizens of the United States, in every State that might desire it, for twenty years. And the government in express terms is pledged to protect it in all future time, if the slave escapes from his owner. This is done in plain words—too plain to be misunderstood. And no word can be found in the Constitution which gives Congress a greater power over slave property, or which entitles property of that kind to less protection than property of any other description. The only power conferred is the power coupled with the duty of guarding and protecting the owner in his rights.

Upon these considerations, it is the opinion of the court that the Act of Congress which prohibited a citizen from holding and owning property of this kind in the territory of the United States north of the line therein mentioned, is not warranted by the Constitution, and is therefore void; and that neither Dred Scott himself, nor any of his family, were made free by being carried into this territory; even if they had been carried there by the owner, with the intention of becoming a permanent resident.

We have so far examined the case, as it stands under the Constitution of the United States, and the powers thereby delegated to the Federal Government.

But there is another point in the case which depends on state power and state law. And it is contended, on the part of the plaintiff, that he is made free by being taken to Rock Island, in the State of Illinois, independently of his residence in the territory of the United States; and being so made free he was not again reduced to a state of slavery by being brought back to Missouri.

Our notice of this part of the case will be very brief; for the principle on which it depends was decided in this court, upon much consideration, in the case of *Strader et al. v. Graham*, reported in 10th Howard, 82. In that case, the slaves had been taken from Kentucky to Ohio, with the consent of the owner, and afterwards brought back to Kentucky. And this court held that their status or condition, as free or slave, depended upon the laws of Kentucky, when they were brought back into that State, and not of Ohio; and that this court had no jurisdiction to revise the judgement of a state court upon its own laws. This was the point directly before the court, and the decision that this court had not jurisdiction, turned upon it, as will be seen by the report of the case.

So in this case: as Scott was a slave when taken into the State of Illinois by his owner, and was there held as such, and brought back in that character, his status, as free or slave, depended on the laws of Missouri, and not of Illinois.

It has, however, been urged in the argument, that by the laws of Missouri he was free on this return, and that this case, therefore, cannot be governed by the case of *Strader et al. v. Graham*, where it appeared, by the laws of Kentucky, that the plaintiffs continued to be slaves on their return from Ohio. But whatever doubts or opinions may, at one time, have been entertained upon this subject, we are satisfied, upon a careful examination of all the cases decided in the State courts of Missouri referred to, that it is now firmly settled by the decisions of the highest court in the State, that Scott and his family upon their return were not free, but were, by the laws of Missouri, the property of the defendant; and that the Circuit Court of the United States had no jurisdiction, when, by the laws of the State, the plaintiff was a slave and not a citizen.

Moreover, the plaintiff, it appears, brought a similar action against the defendant in the State court of Missouri, claiming the freedom of himself and his family upon the same grounds and the same evidence upon which he relies in the case before the court. The case was carried before the Supreme Court of the State; was fully argued there; and that court decided that neither the plaintiff nor his family were entitled to freedom, and were still the slaves of the defendant; and reversed the judgment of the inferior State court, which had given a different decision. If the plaintiff supposed that this judgment of the Supreme Court of the State was erroneous, and that this court had jurisdiction to revise and reverse it, the only mode by which he could legally bring it before this court was by writ of error directed to the Supreme Court of the State, requiring it to transmit the record to this court. It this had been done, it is too plain for argument that the writ must have been dismissed for want of jurisdiction in this court. The case of *Strader et al. v. Graham* is directly in point; and, indeed, independent of any decision, the language of the 25th section of the Act of 1789 is too clear and precise to admit of controversy.

But the plaintiff did not pursue the mode prescribed by law for bringing the judgment of a state court before this court for revision, but suffered the case to be remanded to the inferior State court, where it is still continued, and is, by agreement of parties, to await the judgment of this court on the point. All of this appears on the record before us and by the printed report of the case.

And while the case is yet open and pending in the inferior State court, the plaintiff goes into the Circuit Court of the United States, upon the same case and the same evidence, and against the same party, and proceeds to judgment, and then brings here the same case from the Circuit Court, which the law would not have permitted him to bring directly from the State court. And if this court takes jurisdiction in this form, the result, so far as the rights of the respective parties are concerned, is in every respect substantially the same as if it had, in open violation of law, entertained jurisdiction over the judgment of the State court upon a writ of error, and revised and reversed its judgment upon the ground that its opinion upon the question of law was erroneous. It would ill become this court to sanction such an attempt to evade the law, or to exercise an appellate power in this circuitous way, which it is forbidden to exercise in

the direct and regular and invariable forms of judicial proceedings.

Upon the whole, therefore, it is the judgment of this court, that it appears by the record before us that the plaintiff in error is not a citizen of Missouri, in the same sense in which that word is used in the Constitution; and the Circuit Court of the United States, for that reason, had no jurisdiction in the case, and could give no judgment in it.

Its judgment for the defendant must, consequently, be reversed, and a mandate issued directing the suit to be dismissed for want of jurisdiction.

Mr. Justice Wayne:

Concurring as I do entirely in the opinion of the court, as it has been written and read by the Chief Justice—without any qualification of its reasoning or its conclusions—I shall neither read nor file an opinion of my own in this case which I prepared when I supposed it might be necessary and proper for me to do so.

The opinion of the court meets fully and decides every point which was made in the argument of the case by the counsel on either side of it. Nothing belonging to the case has been left undecided, nor has any point been discussed and decided which was not called for by the record, or which was not necessary for the judicial disposition of it, in the way that it has been done, by more than a majority of the court.

In doing this the court neither sought nor made the case. It was brought to us in the course of the administration of the laws which Congress has enacted, for the review of cases from the circuit courts by the Supreme Court.

In our action upon it, we have only discharged our duty as a distinct and efficient department of the government, as the framers of the Constitution meant the judiciary to be, and as the States of the Union and the people of those States intended it should be, when they ratified the Constitution of the United States.

The case involves private rights of value, and constitutional principles of the highest importance, about which there had become such a difference of opinion, that the peace and harmony of the country required the settlement of them by judicial decision.

It would certainly be a subject to regret, that the conclusions of the court have not been assented to by all of its members, if I did not know from its history and my own experience how rarely it has happened that the judges have been unanimous upon constitutional questions of moment, and if our decision in this case had not been made by as large a majority of them as has been usually had on constitutional questions of importance.

Two of the judges, Mr. Justices McLean and Curtis, dissent from the opinion of the court. A third, Mr. Justice Nelson, gives a separate opinion upon a single point in the case, with which I concur, assuming that the Circuit Court had jurisdiction; but he abstains altogether from expressing any opinion upon the 8th section of the Act of 1820 known commonly as the Missouri Compromise Law, and six of us declare that it was unconstitutional.

But it has been assumed, that this court has acted extrajudicially in giving an opinion upon the 8th section Act of 1820, because, as it has decided that the Circuit Court had no jurisdiction of the case, this court has no jurisdiction to examine the case upon its merits.

But the error of such an assertion had arisen in part from a misapprehension of what has been heretofore decided by the Supreme Court, in cases of a like kind with that before us; in part, from a misapplication to the circuit courts of the United States, of the rules of pleading concerning pleas to the jurisdiction which prevail in common law courts; and from its having been forgotten that this case was not brought to this court by appeal or writ of error from a state court, but by a writ of error to the Circuit Court of the United States.

The cases cited by the Chief Justice to show that this court has now only done what it has repeatedly done before in other cases, without any question of its correctness, speak for themselves. The differences between the rules concerning pleas to the jurisdiction in the courts of the United States and common law courts have been stated and sustained by reasoning and adjudged cases; and it has been shown that writs of error to a state court and to the circuit courts of the United States are to be determined by different laws and principles. In the first, it is our duty to ascertain if this court has jurisdiction, under the 25th section of the judiciary Act, to review the case from the State court; and if it shall be found that it has not, the case is at end, so far as this court is concerned; for our power to review the case upon its merits has been

made, by the 25th section, to depend upon its having jurisdiction; when it has not, this court cannot criticize, controvert, or give any opinion upon the merits of a case from a state court.

But in a case brought to this court, by appeal or by writ of error from a circuit court of the United States, we begin a review of it, not by inquiring if this court has jurisdiction, but if that court has it. If the case has been decided by that court upon its merits, but the record shows it to be deficient in those averments which by the law of the United States must be made by the plaintiff in the action, to give the court jurisdiction of his case, we send it back to the court from which it was brought, with directions to be dismissed, though it has been decided there upon its merits.

So, in a case containing the averments by the plaintiff which are necessary to give the Circuit Court jurisdiction, if the defendant shall file his plea in abatement denying the truth of them, and the plaintiff shall demur to it, and the court should erroneously sustain the plaintiff's demurrer, or declare the plea to be insufficient, and doing so require the defendant to answer over by a plea to the merits, and shall decide the case upon such pleading, this court has the same authority to inquire into jurisdiction of that court to do so, and to correct its error in that regard, that it had in the other case to correct its error, in trying a case in which the plaintiff had not made those averments which were necessary to give the court jurisdiction. In both cases the record is resorted to, to determine the point of jurisdiction, but, as the power of review of cases from a federal court, is not limited by the law to a part of the case, this court may correct an error upon the merits; and there is the same reason for correcting an erroneous judgment of the Circuit Court, where the want of jurisdiction appears from any part of the record, that there is for declaring a want of jurisdiction for a want of necessary averments. Any attempt to control the court from doing so by the technical common law rules of pleading in cases of jurisdiction, when a defendant has been denied his plea to it, would tend to enlarge the jurisdiction of the Circuit Court, by limiting this court's review of its judgments in that particular. But I will not argue a point already so fully discussed. I have every confidence in the opinion of the court upon the point of jurisdiction, and do not allow myself to doubt that the error of a contrary conclusion will be fully understood by all who shall read the argument of the Chief Justice.

I have already said that the opinion of the court has my unqualified assent.

Mr. Justice Nelson:

I shall proceed to state the grounds upon which I have arrived at the conclusion that the judgment of the court below should be affirmed. The suit was brought in the court below by the plaintiff, for the purpose of asserting his freedom, and that of Harriet, his wife, and two children.

The defendant pleaded, in abatement to the suit, that the cause of action, if any, accrued to the plaintiff out of the jurisdiction of the court, and exclusively within the jurisdiction of the courts of the State of Missouri; for that the said plaintiff is not a citizen of the State of Missouri, as alleged in the declaration, because he is a negro of African descent; his ancestors were of pure African blood, and were brought into this country and sold as negro slaves.

To this plea the plaintiff demurred, and the defendant joined in demurrer. The court below sustained the demurrer, holding that the plea was insufficient in law to abate the suit.

The defendant then pleaded over in bar of the action.

1. The general issue. 2. That the plaintiff was a negro slave, the lawful property of the defendant. And 3. That Harriet, the wife of said plaintiff, and the two children, were the lawful slaves of the said defendant. Issue was taken upon these pleas, and the cause went down to trial before the court and jury, and an agreed state of facts was presented, upon which the trial proceeded, and resulted in a verdict for the defendant, under the instructions of the court.

The facts agreed upon were substantially as follows:

That in the year 1834, the plaintiff, Scott, was a negro slave of Dr. Emerson, who was a surgeon in the Army of the United States; and in that year he took the plaintiff from the State of Missouri to the military post at Rock Island, in the State of Illinois, and held him there as a slave until the month of April or May 1836. At this date, Dr. Emerson removed, with the plaintiff, from the Rock Island post to the military post at For Snelling, situate on the west bank of the Mississippi River, in the Territory of Upper Louisiana, and north of the latitude thirty-six

degrees thirty minutes, and north of the State of Missouri. That he held the plaintiff in slavery at Fort Snelling, from the last mentioned date until the year 1838.

That in the year 1835, Harriet, mentioned in the declaration, was a negro slave of Major Taliaferro, who belonged to the Army of the United States; and in that year he took her to Fort Snelling, already mentioned, and kept her there as a slave until the year 1836, and then sold and delivered her to Dr. Emerson, who held her in slavery, at Fort Snelling until the year 1838. That in the year 1836 the plaintiff and Harriet were married, at Fort Snelling, with the consent of their master. The two children, Eliza and Lizzie, are the fruit of this marriage. The first is about fourteen years of age, and was born on board the steamboat Gipsey, north of the State of Missouri, and upon the Mississippi River; the other, about seven years of age, was born in the State of Missouri, at the military post called Jefferson Barracks.

In 1838 Dr. Emerson removed the plaintiff Harriet, and their daughter Eliza, from Fort Snelling to the State of Missouri, where they have ever since resided. And that before the commencement of this suit, they were sold by the Doctor to Sandford, the defendant, who has claimed and held them as slaves ever since.

The agreed case also states that the plaintiff brought a suit for his freedom, in the Circuit Court of the State of Missouri, on which a judgment was rendered in his favor; but that, on a writ of error from the Supreme Court of the State, the judgment of the court below was reversed, and the cause remanded to the circuit for a new trial.

On closing the testimony on the court below, the counsel for the plaintiff prayed the court to instruct the jury, upon the agreed state of facts, that they ought to find for the plaintiff; when the court refused, and instructed them that, upon the facts, the law was with the defendant.

With respect to the plea in abatement, which went to the citizenship of the plaintiff, and his competency to bring a suit in the federal courts, the common law rule of pleading is, that upon a judgment against the plea on demurrer, and that the defendant answer over, and the defendant submits to the judgment, and pleads over to the merits, the plea in abatement is deemed to be waived, and is not afterwards to be regarded as a part of the record in deciding upon the rights of the parties. There is some question, however, whether this rule of pleading applies to the peculiar system and jurisdiction of the federal courts. As, in these courts, if the facts appearing on the record show that the Circuit Court had no jurisdiction, its judgment will be reversed in the appellate court for that cause, and the case remanded with directions to be dismissed.

In the view we have taken of the case, it will not be necessary to pass upon this question, and we shall therefore proceed at once to an examination of the case upon its merits. The questions upon the merits, in general terms, is whether or not the removal of the plaintiff, who was a slave, with this master, from the State of Missouri to the State of Illinois, with a view to a temporary residence, and after such residence and return to the slave State, such residence in the free State works an emancipation.

As appears from an agreed statement of facts, this question has been before the highest court of the State of Missouri, and a judgment rendered that this residence in the free State has no such effect; but, on the contrary, that his original condition continued unchanged.

The court below, the Circuit Court of the United States for Missouri, in which this suit was afterwards brought, followed the decision of the State court, and rendered a like judgment against the plaintiff.

The argument against these decisions is, that the laws of Illinois, forbidding slavery within her territory, had the effect to set the slave free while residing in that State, and to impress upon him the condition and status of a freeman; and that, by force of these laws, this status and condition accompanied him on his return to the slave State, and of consequence he could not be there held as a slave.

This question has been examined in the courts of several of the slaveholding States, and different opinions expressed and conclusions arrived at. We shall hereafter refer to some of them, and to the principles upon which they are founded. Our opinion is, that the question is one which belongs to each State to decide for itself, either by its Legislature or courts of justice; and hence, in respect to the case before us, to the State of Missouri law, and which, when determined by that State, it is the duty of the federal courts to follow it. In other words, except in cases where the power is restrained by the Constitution of the United States, the law of the State is supreme over the subject of slavery within its jurisdiction.

As a practical illustration of the principle, we may refer to the legislation of the free States in abolishing slavery, and prohibiting its introduction into their territories. Confessedly, except as restrained by the Federal Constitution, they exercised, and rightfully, complete and absolute power over the subject. Upon what principle, then, can it be denied to the State of Missouri? The power flows from the sovereign character of the States of this Union; sovereign, not merely as respects the federal government—except as they have consented to its limitation—but sovereign as respects each other. Whether, therefore, the State of Missouri will recognize or give effect to the laws of Illinois within her territories, on the subject of slavery, is a question for her to determine. Nor is there any constitutional power in this government that can rightfully control her.

Every State or nation possesses an exclusive sovereignty and jurisdiction within her own territory; and her laws effect and bind all property and persons residing within it. It may regulate the manner and circumstances under which property is held, and the condition, capacity and state, of all persons therein; and, also, the remedy and modes of administering justice. And it is equally true, that no State or nation can effect or bind property out of its territory, or persons residing within it. No State, therefore, can enact laws to operate beyond its own dominions, and, if it attempts to do so, it may be lawfully refused obedience. Such laws can have no inherent authority extraterritorially. This is the necessary result of the independence of distinct and separate sovereignties.

Now, it follows from these principles, that whatever force or effect the laws of one State or nation may have in the territories of another, must depend solely upon the laws and municipal regulations of the latter, upon its own jurisprudence and polity, and upon its own express or tacit consent.

Judge Story observes, in his *Conflict of Laws*, p. 24, "that a State may prohibit the operation of all foreign laws, and the rights growing out of them, within its territories." "And that when its code speaks positively on the subject, it must be obeyed by all persons who are within reach of its sovereignty; when its customary unwritten or common law speaks directly on the subject, it is equally to be obeyed."

Nations, from convenience and comity, and from mutual interest, and a sort of moral necessity to do justice, recognize and administer the laws of other countries. But, of the nature, extent and utility, of them, respecting property, or the state and conditions of persons within her territories, each nation judges for itself; and is never bound, even upon the ground of comity, to recognize them, if prejudicial to her own interests. The recognition if purely from comity, and not from any absolute or paramount obligation.

Judge Story again observes (398), "that the true foundation and extent of the obligation of the laws of one nation within another is the voluntary consent of the latter, and is inadmissible whey they are contrary to its known interests." And he adds, "in the silence of any positive rule affirming or denying or restraining the operation of the foreign laws, courts of justice presume the tacit adoption of them by their own government, unless they are repugnant to its policy or prejudicial to its interests." See, also, 2 Kent's Com. p. 457; 13 Pet. 519, 589.

These principles fully establish that it belongs to the sovereign State of Missouri to determine by her laws the question of slavery within her jurisdiction, subject only to such limitations as may be found in the Federal Constitution; and, further, that the laws of other States of the Confederacy, whether enacted by their Legislatures or expounded by their courts, can have no operation within her territory, or effect rights growing out of her own laws on the subject. This is the necessary result of the independent and sovereign character of the State. The principle is not peculiar to the State of Missouri, but is equally applicable to each State belonging to the Confederacy. The laws of each have no extraterritorial operation within the jurisdiction of another, except such as may be voluntarily conceded by her laws or courts of justice. To the extent of such concession upon the rule of comity of nations, the foreign law may operate, as it then becomes a part of the municipal law of the State. When determined that the foreign law shall have effect, the municipal law of the State retires, and gives place to the foreign law.

In view of these principles, let us examine a little more closely the doctrine of those who maintain that the law of Missouri is not to govern the status and condition of the plaintiff. They insist that the removal and temporary res-

idence with his master in Illinois, where slavery is inhibited, had the effect to set him free, and that the same effect is to be given to the law of Illinois, within the State of Missouri, after his return. Why was he set free in Illinois? Because the law of Missouri, under which he was held as a slave, had no operation by its own force extraterritorially; and the State of Illinois refused to recognize its effect within her limits, upon principles of comity, as a state of slavery was inconsistent withe her laws, and contrary to her policy. But, how is the case different on the return of the plaintiff to the State of Missouri? Is she bound to recognize and enforce the law of Illinois? For, unless she is, the status and condition of the slave upon his return remains the same as originally existed. Has the law of Illinois any greater force within the jurisdiction of Missouri, than the laws of the latter within that of the former? Certainly not. They stand upon an equal footing. Neither has any force extraterritorially, except what may be voluntarily conceded to them.

It has been supposed, by the counsel for the plaintiff, that a rule laid down by Huberus had some bearing upon that question. Huberus observes that "personal qualities, impressed by the laws of any place, surround and accompany the person wherever he goes, with this effect: that in every place he enjoys and is subject to the same law which other persons of his class elsewhere enjoy or are subject to." De Confl. Leg. lib. 1, tit. 3, sec. 12; 4 Dall. 375, n; 1 Story, Com. Laws, pp. 59, 60.

The application sought to be given to the rule was this; that as Dred Scott was free while residing in the State of Illinois, by the laws of that State, on his return to the State of Missouri he carried with him the personal qualities of freedom, and that the same effect must be given to his status there as in the former State. But the difficulty in the case is in the total misapplication of the rule.

These personal qualities, to which Huberus refers, are those impressed upon the individual by the law of the domicil; it is this that the author claims should be permitted to accompany the person into whatever country he might go, and should supersede the law of the place where he had taken up a temporary residence.

Now, as the domicil of Scott was in the State of Missouri, where he was a slave, and from whence he was taken by his master into Illinois for a temporary residence, according to the doctrine of Huberus, the law of his domicil would have accompanied him, and during his residence there he would remain in the same condition as in the State of Missouri. In order to have given effect to the rule, as claimed in the argument, it should have been first shown that a domicil had been acquired in the free State, which cannot be pretended upon the agreed facts in the case. But the true answer to the doctrine of Huberus is, that the rule, in any aspect in which it may be reviewed, has no bearing upon either side of the question before us, even if conceded to the extent laid down by the author; for he admits that foreign governments give effect to these laws of the domicil no further than they are consistent with their own laws, and not prejudicial to their own subjects; in other words, their force and effect depend upon the law of comity of the foreign government. We should add, also, that this general rule of Huberus, referred to, has not been admitted in the practice of nations, nor is it sanctioned by the most approved jurists of international law. Story, Com. secs. 91, 96, 103, 104; 2 Kent's Com. pp. 457, 458; 1 Burge, Con. Laws, pp. 12, 127.

We come now to the decision of this court in the case of *Strader et al. v. Graham*, 10 How. p. 82. The case came up form the Court of Appeals, in the State of Kentucky. The question in the case was, whether certain slaves of Graham, a resident of Kentucky, who had been employed temporarily at several places in the State of Ohio, with their master's consent, and had returned to Kentucky into his service, had thereby become entitled to their freedom. The Court of Appeals held that they had not. The law was brought to this court under the 25th section of the Judiciary Act. This court held that it had no jurisdiction, for the reason, the question was one that belonged exclusively to the State of Kentucky. The Chief Justice, in delivering the opinion of the court, observed that "every State has an undoubted right to determine the status or domestic and social condition of the persons domiciled within its territory, except in so far as the powers of the States in this respect are restrained, or duties and obligations imposed upon them by the Constitution of the United States. There is nothing in the Constitution of the United States, he observes, that can in any degree control the law of Kentucky upon this subject. And the condition of the negroes, therefore, as to freedom or slavery, after their return,

depended altogether upon the laws of that State, and could not be influenced by the laws of Ohio. It was exclusively in the power of Kentucky to determine, for herself, whether their employment in another State should or should not make them free on their return."

It has been supposed, in the argument on the part of the plaintiff, that the 8th section of the Act of Congress passed March 6, 1820 (3 stat. al L. p. 544), which prohibited slavery north of thirty-six degrees thirty minutes, within which the plaintiff and his wife temporarily resided at Fort Snelling, possessed some superior virtue and effect, extraterritorially and within the State of Missouri, beyond that of the laws of Illinois, or those of Ohio in the case of *Strader et al. v. Graham*. A similar ground was taken and urged upon the court in the case just mentioned, under the Ordinance of 1787, which was enacted during the time of the Confederation, and re-enacted by Congress after the adoption of the Constitution, with some amendments adapting it to the new government. 1 Stat. at L. p. 50.

In answer to this ground, the Chief Justice, in delivering the opinion of the court, observed: The argument assumes that the six articles which that Ordinance declares to be perpetual, are still in force in the States since formed within the territory, and admitted into the Union. If this proposition could be maintained, it would not alter the question; for the Regulations of Congress, under the old Confederation or the present Constitution, for the government of a particular territory, could have no force beyond its limits. It certainly could not restrict the power of the States, within their respective territories, nor in any manner interfere with their laws and institutions, nor give this court control over them.

"The Ordinance in question," he observes, "if still in force, could have no more operation than the laws of Ohio, in the State of Kentucky, and could not influence the decision upon the rights of the master of the slaves in that State."

This view, thus authoritatively declared, furnishes a conclusive answer to the distinction attempted to be set up between the extraterritorial effect of a state law and the Act of Congress in question.

It must be admitted that Congress possesses no power to regulate or abolish slavery within the States; and that if this Act had attempted any such legislation, it would have been a nullity.

And yet the argument, here, if there be any force in it, leads to the result, that effect may be given to such legislation; for it is only by giving the Act of Congress operation within the State of Missouri, that it can have any effect upon the question between the parties. Having no such effect directly, it will be difficult to maintain, upon any consistent reasoning, that it can be made to operate indirectly upon the subject.

The argument, we think, in any aspect in which it may be reviewed, is utterly destitute of support upon any principles of constitutional law, as, according to that, Congress has no power whatever over the subject of slavery within the State; and is also subversive of the established doctrine of international jurisprudence, as, according to that, it is an axiom that the laws of one government have no force within the limits of another, or extraterritorially, except from the consent of the latter.

It is perhaps not unfit to notice, in this connection, that many of the most eminent statesmen and jurists of the country entertain the opinion that this provision of the Act of Congress, even within the territory to which it relates, was not authorized by any power under the Constitution. The doctrine here contended for, not only upholds its validity in the territory, but claims for it effect beyond and within the limits of a sovereign state—an effect, as insisted, that displaces the laws of the State, and substitutes its own provisions in their place.

The consequences of any such construction are apparent. If Congress possesses the power, under the Constitution, to abolish slavery in a territory, it must necessarily possess the like power to establish it. It cannot be a one sided power, as may suit the convenience or particular views of the advocates. It is a power, if it exists at all, over the whole subject; and then, upon the process of reasoning which seeks to extend its influence beyond the territory, and within the limits of a state, if Congress should establish, instead of abolish, slavery, we do not see but that, if a slave should be removed from the territory into a free State his status would accompany him, and continue, notwithstanding its laws against slavery. The laws of the free State, according to the argument, would be displaced, and the Act of Congress, in its effect, be substituted in their place. We do not see how this conclusion could be avoided, if the construction against which we are contending should prevail.

We are satisfied, however it is unsound, and that the true answer to it is, that even conceding, for the purposes of the argument, that this provision of the Act of Congress is valid within the territory for which it was enacted, it can have no operation or effect beyond its limits, or within the jurisdiction of a state. It can neither displace its laws nor change the status or condition of its inhabitants.

Our conclusion, therefore, is, upon this branch of the case, that the question involved is one depending solely upon the law of Missouri, and that the federal court sitting in the State, and trying the case before us, was bound to follow it.

The remaining question for consideration is: what is the law of the State of Missouri on this subject. And it would be a sufficient answer to refer to the judgment of the highest court of the State in the very case, were it not due to that tribunal to state somewhat at large the course of decision and the principles involved, on account of some diversity of opinion in the cases. As we have already stated, this case was originally brought in the Circuit Court of the State, which resulted in a judgment for the plaintiff. The case was carried up to the Supreme Court for revision. That court reversed the judgement below, and remanded the cause to the Circuit, for a new trial. In that state of the proceeding, a new suit was brought by the plaintiff in the Circuit Court of the United States, and tried upon the issues and agreed case before us, and a verdict and judgment for the defendant, that court following the decision of the Supreme Court of the State.

The judgment of the Supreme Court is reported in the 15 Mo. p. 576. The court placed the decision upon the temporary residence of the master with the slaves in the State and territory to which they removed, and their return to the slave State; and upon the principles of international law, that foreign laws have no extraterritorial force, except such as the State within which they are sought to be enforced may see fit to extend to them, upon the doctrine of comity of nations.

This is the substance of the grounds of the decision.

The same question has been twice before that court since, and the same judgment given. 15 Mo. 595; 17 Ib. 434. It must be admitted, therefore, as the settled law of the State, and, according to the decision in the case of *Strader et al. v. Graham,* 10 How. 82, is conclusive of the case in this court.

It is said, however, that the previous cases and course of decision in the State of Missouri on this subject were different, and that the courts had held the slave to be free on his return from a temporary residence in the free State. We do not see, were this to be admitted, that the circumstance would show that the settled course of decision at the time this case was tried in the court below, was not to be considered the law of the State. Certainly, it must be, unless the first decision of a principle of law by a state court is to be permanent and irrevocable. The idea seems to be, that the courts of a state are not to change their opinions, or, if they do, the first decision is to be regarded by this court as the law of the State. It is certain, if this be so, in the case before us, it is an exception to the rule governing this court in all other cases. But what court has not changed its opinions? What judge has not changed his?

Waiving, however, this view, and turning to the decisions of the courts of Missouri, it will be found that there is no discrepancy between the earlier and the present cases upon this subject. There are some eight of them reported previous to the decision in the case before us, which was decided in 1852. The last of the earlier cases was decided in 1836. In each on of these, with two exceptions, the master or mistress removed into the free State with the slave, with a view to a permanent residence—in other words, to make that his or her domicil. And in several of the cases, this removal and permanent residence were relied on as the ground of the decision in favor of the plaintiff. All these states, therefore, are not necessarily in conflict with it. In one of the tow excepted cases, the master had hired the slave in the State of Illinois from 1817 to 1825. In the other, the master was an officer in the army, and removed with his slave to the military post of Fort Snelling, and at Prairie du Chien, in Michigan, temporarily, while acting under the orders of his government. It is conceded the decision in this case was departed from in the case before us, and in those that have followed it. But it is to be observed that these subsequent cases are in conformity with those in all the slave States bordering on the free—in Kentucky, 2 Marsh. 476; 5 B. Monroe, 176; 9 Ib. 565,—in Virginia, 1 Rand. 15; 1 Leigh, 172; 10 Grat. 495,—in Maryland, 4 Harr. & McH. 295, 322,

325. In conformity, also, with the law of England on this subject, *Ex parte Grace,* 2 Hagg Adm. 94, and with the opinions of the most eminent jurists of the country. Story's Confl. 396 a; 5 Kent's Com. 258 n; 18 Pick. 193, Chief Justice Shaw. Sec Corresp. between Lord Stowell and Judge Story, 1 vol. Life of Story, p. 552, 558.

Lord Stowell, in communicating his opinions in the case of *The Slave Grace* to the Judge Story, states, in his letter, what the question was before him, namely: "Whether the emancipation of a slave brought to England insured a complete emancipation to him on his return to his own country, or whether it only operated as a suspension of slavery in England, and is original character devolved on him again upon his return." He observed, "the question had never been examined since an end was put to slavery fifty years ago," having reference to the decision of Lord Mansfield in the case of Somersett, but the practise, he observed, "has regularly been, that on his return to this own country, the slave resume his original character as a slave." And so Lord Stowell held in the case.

Judge Story, in his letter in reply, observes: "I have read with great attention your judgement in the slave case, etc. Upon the fullest consideration which I have been able to give the subject, I entirely concur in your views. If I had been called upon to pronounce a judgement in a like case, I should have certainly arrived at the same result." Again he observes: "In my native State (Massachusetts), the state of slavery is not recognized as legal; and yet, if a slave should come hither, and afterwards return to his own home, we should certainly think that the local law attached upon him and this servile character would be reintegrated."

We may remark in this connection, that the case before the Maryland court, already referred to, and which was decided in 1799, presented the same question as that before Lord Stowell and received a similar decision. Tis was nearly thirty years before the decision in that case, which was in 1828. The Court of Appeals observed, in deciding the Maryland case, that "however the laws of Great Britain in such instances, operating upon such persons there, might interfere so as to prevent the exercise of certain acts by the masters, not permitted, as in the case of Somersett, yet, upon the bringing Ann Joice into this State (then the Province of Maryland), the relation of master and slave continued in its extent, as authorized by the laws of this State." And Luther Martin, one of the counsel in that case, stated, on the argument, that the question had been previously decided the same way in the case of slaves returning from a residence in Pennsylvania, where they had become free under her laws.

The State of Louisiana, whose courts had gone further in holding the slave free on his return from a residence in a free State than the courts of her sister States, has settled the law, by an Act of her Legislature, in conformity with the law of the court of Missouri in the case before us. Sess. Law, 1846.

The case before Lord Stowell presented much stronger features for giving effect to the law of England in the case of *The Slave Grace* than exists in the cases that have arisen in this country, for in that case the slave returned to a colony of England over which the imperial government exercised supreme authority. Yet, on the return of the slave to the colony, from a temporary residence in England, he held that the original condition of the slave attached. The question presented in cases arising here, is as to the effect and operation to be given to the laws of a foreign State, on the return of the slave within an independent sovereignty.

Upon the whole, it must be admitted that the current of authority, both in England and in this country, is in accordance with the law as declared by the courts of Missouri in the case before us, and we think the court below was not only right, but bound to follow it.

Some question has been made as to the character of the residence in this case in the free State. But we regard the facts a set forth in the agreed case as decisive. The removal of Dr. Emerson from Missouri to the military posts was in the discharge of his duties as surgeon in the army, and under the orders of his government. He was liable at any moment to be recalled, as he was in 1838, and ordered to another post. The same is also true as it respects Major Taliaferro. In such a case, the officer goes to his post for a temporary purpose, to remain there for an uncertain time, and not for the purpose of fixing his permanent abode. The question we think too plain to require argument. The case of *The Attorney General v. Napier*, 6 Welsb. H. & G. Exch. 216, illustrates and applies the principle in the case of an officer of the English army.

A question has been alluded to, on the argument, namely: the right of the master with his slave of transit into or through a free State, on business or commercial pursuits, or in the exercise of a federal right, or the discharge of a federal duty, being a citizen of the United States, which is not before us. This question depends upon different considerations and principles from the one in hand, and turns upon the rights and privileges secured to a common citizen of the republic, under the Constitution of the United States. When that question arises, we shall be prepared to decide it.

Our conclusion is, that the judgment of the court below should be affirmed.

Mr. Justice Grier:

I concur in the opinion delivered by Mr. Justice Nelson on the questions discussed by him.

I also concur with the opinion of the court as delivered by the Chief Justice, that the Act of Congress of 6th March, 1820, is unconstitutional and void; and that, assuming the facts as stated in the opinion, the plaintiff cannot sue as a citizen of Missouri in the courts of the United States. But, that the record shows a prima facie case of jurisdiction, requiring the court to decide all the questions properly arising in it; and as the decision of the pleas in bar shows that the plaintiff is a slave, and therefore not entitled to sue in a court of the United States, the form of the judgment is of little importance; for whether the judgment be affirmed or dismissed for want of jurisdiction, it is justified by the decision of the court, and is the same in effect between the parties to the suit.

Mr. Justice Daniel:

It may with truth be affirmed, that since the establishment of the several communities now constituting the States of this Confederacy, there never has been submitted to any tribunal within its limits questions surpassing in importance those now claiming the consideration of this court. Indeed it is difficult to imagine, in connection with the systems of polity peculiar to the United States, a conjuncture of graver import than that must be, within which it is aimed to comprise, and to control, not only the faculties and practical operation appropriate to the American Confederacy as such, but also the rights and powers of its separate and independent members, with reference alike to their internal and domestic authority and interests, and the relations they sustain to their confederates.

To my mind it is evident that nothing less than the ambitious and far-reaching pretension to compass these objects of vital concern, is either directly essayed, or necessarily implied in the positions attempted in the argument for the plaintiff in error.

How far these position have any foundation in the nature of the rights and relations of separate, equal and independent governments, or in the provisions of our own federal compact, or the laws enacted under and in pursuance of the authority of that compact, will be presently investigated.

In order correctly to comprehend the tendency and force of these positions, it is proper her succinctly to advert to the facts upon which the questions of law propounded in the argument have arisen.

This was an action of trespass *vi et armis,* instituted in the Circuit Court of the United States for the District of Missouri, in the name of the plaintiff in error, a negro held as a slave, for the recovery of freedom for himself, his wife, and two children, also negroes.

To the declaration in this case that defendant below, who is also the defendant in error, pleaded in abatement that the court could not take cognizance of the cause because the plaintiff was not a citizen of the State of Missouri, as averred in the declaration, but was a negro of African descent, and that his ancestors were of pure African blood, and were brought into this country and sold as negro slaves; and hence it followed, from the 2d section of the 3d article of the Constitution, which creates the judicial power of the United States, with respect to controversies between citizens of different States, that the Circuit Court could not take cognizance of the action.

To this plea in abatement, a demurrer having been interposed on behalf of the plaintiff, it was sustained by the court. After the decision sustaining the demurrer, the defendant, in pursuance of a previous agreement between counsel, and with the leave of the court, pleaded in bar of the action; 1st, not guilty; 2d, that the plaintiff was a negro slave, the lawful property of the defendant, and as such the defendant gently laid his hands upon him, and thereby had only restrained him, as the defendant had a right to

do; 3d, that with respect to the wife and daughters of the plaintiff, in the second and third counts of the declaration mentioned, the defendant had, as to them, only acted in the same manner, and in virtue of the same legal right.

Issues having been joined upon the above pleas in bar, the following statement, comprising all the evidence in the case, was agreed upon and signed by the counsel of the respective parties, viz:

"In the year 1834, the plaintiff was a negro slave belonging to Dr. Emerson, who was a surgeon in the Army of the United States. In that year, 1834, said Dr. Emerson took the plaintiff from the State of Missouri to the military post at Rock Island, in the State of Illinois, and held him there as a slave until the month of April or May, 1836, At the time last mentioned, said Dr. Emerson removed the plaintiff from said military post at Rock Island to the military post at Fort Snelling, situate on the west bank of the Mississippi River, in the Territory known as Upper Louisiana, acquired by the United States of France, and situate north of the latitude of thirty-six degrees thirty minutes north, and north of the State of Missouri. Said Dr. Emerson held the plaintiff in slavery at said Fort Snelling, from said last mentioned date until the year 1838.

In the year 1835, Harriet, who is named in the second count of the plaintiff's declaration, was the negro slave of Major Taliaferro, who belonged to the Army of the United States. In that year, 1835, said Major Taliaferro took said Harriet to said Fort Snelling, a military post situated as hereinbefore stated, and kept her there as a slave until the year 1836, and then sold and delivered her as a slave at said Fort Snelling unto the said Dr. Emerson, hereinbefore named. Said Dr. Emerson held said Harriet in slavery at said Ford Snelling until the year 1838.

In the year 1836, the plaintiff and said Harriet, at said Fort Snelling, with the consent of said Dr. Emerson, who then claimed to be their master and owner, intermarried and took each other for husband and wife. Eliza and Lizzie, named in the third count of the plaintiff's declaration, are the fruit of that marriage. Eliza is about fourteen years old, and was born on board the steamboat Gipsey, north of the north line of the State of Missouri, and upon the River Mississippi. Lizzie is about seven years old, and was born in the State of Missouri at a military post called Jefferson Barracks.

In the year 1838, said Dr. Emerson removed the plaintiff and said Harriet, and their said daughter Eliza, from said Fort Snelling to the State of Missouri, where they have ever since resided.

Before the commencement of this suit, said Dr. Emerson sold and conveyed the plaintiff, said Harriet, Eliza and Lizzie, to the defendant, as slaves, and the defendant has ever since claimed to hold them and each of them as slaves.

At the time mentioned in the plaintiff's declaration, the defendant, claiming to be owner as aforesaid, laid his hands upon said plaintiff, Harriet, Eliza and Lizzie, and imprisoned them, doing in this respect, however, no more than what he might lawfully do if they were of right his slaves at such times.

Further proof may be given on the trial for either party.

R. M. Field, for plaintiff,

H. A. Garland, for defendant."

"It is agreed that Dred Scott brought suit for his freedom in the Circuit Court of St. Louis County; that there was a verdict and judgment in his favor; that on a writ of error to the Supreme Court, the judgment below was reversed, and the cause remanded to the Circuit Court, where it has been continued to await the decision of this case.

Field, for plaintiff,

Garland, for defendant."

Upon the aforegoing agreed facts, the plaintiff prayed the court to instruct the jury that they ought to find for the plaintiff, and upon the refusal of the instruction thus prayed for, the plaintiff excepted to the court's opinion. The court then, upon the prayer of the defendant, instructed the jury, that upon the facts of this case agreed as above, the law was with the defendant. To this opinion, also, the plaintiff's counsel excepted, as he did to the opinion of the court denying to the plaintiff a new trial after the verdict of the jury in favor of the defendant.

The question first in order presented by the record in his case, is that which arises upon the plea in abatement, and the demurrer to that plea; and upon this question it is my opinion that the demurrer should have been overruled, and the plea sustained.

On behalf of the plaintiff it has been urged, that by the pleas interposed in bar of a recovery in the court below (which pleas both in fact and in law are essentially the same with the objections averred in abatement), the defense in abatement has been displaced or waived; that it could, therefore, no longer be relied on in the Circuit Court, and cannot claim the consideration of this court in reviewing this cause. This position is regarded as wholly untenable. On the contrary, it would seem to follow conclusively from the peculiar character of the courts of the United States, as organized under the Constitution and the statutes, and as defined by numerous and unvarying adjudications from this bench; and there is not one of those courts whose jurisdiction and powers can be deduced from mere custom or tradition; not one, whose jurisdiction and powers must not be traced palpably to, and invested exclusively by, the constitution and statutes of the United States; not one, that is not bound, therefore, at all times, and at all stages of its proceedings, to look and to regard the special and declared extent and bounds of its commission and authority. There is no such tribunal of the United States as a court of general jurisdiction, in the sense in which that phrase is applied to the superior courts under the common law; and even with respect to the courts existing under that system, it is a well settled principle, that consent can never give jurisdiction.

The principles above stated, and the consequences regularly deducible from them, have, as already remarked, been repeatedly and unvaryingly propounded from this bench. Beginning with the earliest decisions of this court, we have the cases of *Bingham v. Cabot et al.* 3 Dall. 382; *Turner v. Enrille,* 4 Dall. 7; *Abercrombie v. Dupuis et al.* 1 Cranch, 343; *Wood v. Wagnon,* 2 Cranch, 9; *The United States v. The Brig Union et al.* 4 Cranch, 216; *Sulivan v. The Fulton Steamboat Company,* 5 Wheat. 450; *Mollan et al. v. Torrence,* 9 Wheat. 537; *Brown v. Keene,* 8 Pet. 112, and *Jackson v. Ashton,.* 8 Pet. 148; ruling, uniform and unbroken current, the doctrine that it is essential to the jurisdiction of the courts of the United States, that the facts upon which it is founded should appear upon the record. Nay, to such an extent and so inflexibly has this requisite to the jurisdiction been enforced, that in the case of *Capron v. Van Noorden,* 2 Cranch, 126, it is declared, that the plaintiff in this court may assign for error his own omission in the pleadings in the court below, where they go to the jurisdiction. This doctrine has been, if possible, more strikingly illustrated in a latter decision, the case of *The State of R.I. v. The State of Mass.* 12 Pet. 657, 755

In this case, on p. 718 of the volume, this court, with reference to a motion to dismiss the cause for want of jurisdiction, have said: "However late this objection has been made or may be made, in any cause in an inferior or appellate court of the United States, it must be considered and decided before any court can move and farther step in the cause, as any movement is necessarily to exercise the jurisdiction. Jurisdiction is the power to hear and determine the subject matter in controversy between the parties to a suit; to adjudicate or exercise any judicial power over them. The question is, whether on the case before the court their action is judicial or extrajudicial; with or without the authority of law to render a judgment or decree upon the rights of the litigant parties. A motion to dismiss a cause pending in the courts of the United States, is not analogous to a pleas to the jurisdiction of a court of common law or equity in England; there, the superior courts have a general jurisdiction over all persons within the realm, and all causes of action between them. It depends on the subject matter, whether the jurisdiction shall be exercised by a court of law or equity; but that court to which it appropriately belongs can act judicially upon the party and the subject of the suit, unless it shall be made apparent to the court that the judicial determination of the case has been withdrawn from the court of general jurisdiction to an inferior and limited one. It is a necessary presumption that the court of general jurisdiction can act upon the given case; when nothing to the contrary appears; hence has arisen the rule that the party claiming an exemption from its process must set out the reason by a special plea in abatement, and show that some inferior court of law or equity has the exclusive cognizance of the case; otherwise the superior court must proceed in virtue of its general jurisdiction. A motion to dismiss, therefore, cannot be entertained, as it does not disclose a case of exception; and if a plea in abatement is put in, it must not only make out the exception, but point to the particular court to which the case belongs. There are other classes of cases where the objection to the jurisdiction is of a different nature, as on a bill in chancery, that the subject matter is cognizable only by the King in Council, or that the parties defendant cannot be brought before any municipal court on account

of their sovereign character or the nature of the controversy; or to the very common cases which present the question, whether the case belong to a court of law or equity. To such cases, a plea in abatement would not be applicable, because the plaintiff could not sue in an inferior court. The objection goes to a denial of any jurisdiction of a municipal court in the one class of cases, and to the jurisdiction of any court of equity or of law in the other, on which last the court decides according to its discretion.

"An objection to jurisdiction on the ground of exemption from the process of the court in which the suit is brought, or the manner in which a defendant is brought into it, is waived by appearance and pleading to issue; but when the objection goes to the power of the court over the parties or the subject matter, the defendant need not, for he cannot give the plaintiff a better writ. Where an inferior court can have no jurisdiction of a case of law or equity, the ground of objection is not taken by plea in abatement, as an exception of the given case from the otherwise general jurisdiction of the court; appearance does not cure the defect of judicial power, and it may be relied on by plea, answer, demurrer, or at the trial or hearing. As denial of jurisdiction over the subject matter of a suit between parties within the realm, over which and whom the court has power to act, cannot be successful in an English court of general jurisdiction, a motion like the present could not be sustained consistently with the principles of its constitution. But as this court is one of limited and special original jurisdiction, its action must be confined to the particular cases, controversies, and parties over which the Constitution and laws have authorized it to act; any proceedings without the limits prescribed is coram non judice, and its action a nullity. And whether the want or excess of power is objected to by a party, or is apparent to the court, it must surcease its action or proceed extrajudicially."

In the constructing of pleadings either in abatement or in bar, every fact or position constituting a portion of the public law, or of known or general history, is necessarily implied. Such fact or position need not be specially averred and set forth; it is what the world at large and every individual are presumed to know— nay, are bound to know and to be governed by.

If, on the other hand, there exists facts or circumstance by which a particular case would be withdrawn or exempted from the influence of public law or necessary historical knowledge, such facts and circumstances form an exception to the general principle, and these must be specially set forth and established by those who would avail themselves of such exception.

Now, the following are truths which a knowledge of the history of the world, and particularly of that of our own country, compels us to know—that the African negro race never have been acknowledged as belonging to the family of nations; that as amongst them there never has been known or recognized by the inhabitants of other countries anything partaking of the character of nationality, or civil or political polity; that this race has been by all the nations of Europe regarded as subjects of capture or purchase; as subjects of commerce or traffic; and that the introduction of that race into section of this country was not as members of civil or political society, but as slaves, as property in the strictest sense of the term.

In the plea in abatement, the character or capacity of citizen on the part of the plaintiff is denied; and the causes which show the absence of that character or capacity are set forth by averment. The verity of those causes, according to the settled rules of pleading, being admitted by the demurrer, it only remained for the Circuit Court to decide upon their legal sufficiency to abate the plaintiff's action. And it now becomes the province of this court to determine whether the plaintiff below (and in error here), admitted to be a negro of African descent, whose ancestors were of pure African blood, and were brought into this country and sold as negro slaves—such being his status, and such the circumstances surrounding his position—whether he can by correct legal induction from that status and those circumstances, be clothed with the character and capacities of a citizen of the State of Missouri.

It may be assumed as a postulate, that to a slave, as such, there appertains and can appertain no relation, civil or political, with the State or the government. He is himself strictly property, to be used in subserviency to the interests, the convenience or the will, of his owner; and to suppose, with respect of the former, the existence of any privilege or discretion, or of any obligation to others incompatible with the magisterial rights just defined, would be by implication, if not directly, to deny the relation of master and slave,

since none can possess and enjoy as his own, that which another has a paramount right and power to withhold. Hence it follows necessarily, that a slave, the peculium or property of a master, and possessing within himself no civil nor political rights or capacities, cannot be a citizen. For who, it may be asked, is a citizen? What do the character and status of citizen import? Without fear of contradiction, it does not import the condition of being private property, the subject of individual power and ownership. Upon a principle of etymology alone, the term "citizen," as derived from civitas, conveys the ideas of connection or identification with the State or government, and a participation of its functions. But beyond this, there is not, it is believed, to be found, in the theories of writers on government, or in any actual experiment heretofore tried, an exposition of the term "citizen," which has not been understood as conferring the actual possession and enjoyment, or the perfect right of acquisition and enjoyment, or an entire equality of privileges, civil and political.

Thus Vattel, in the preliminary chapter to his treatise on the Law of the Nations, says: "Nations or State are bodies politic; societies of men united together for the purpose of promoting their mutual safety and advantage, by the joint efforts of their mutual strength. Such a society has her affairs and her interests; she deliberates and takes resolutions in common; thus becoming a moral person, who possesses an understanding and a will peculiar to herself." Again, in the first chapter of the first book of the treatise just quoted, the same writer, after repeating his definition of a State, proceeds to remark, that, "from the very design that induces a number of men to form a society, which has its common interests and which is to act in concert, it is necessary that there should be established a public authority, to order and direct what is to be done by each, in relation to the end of the association. This political authority is the sovereignty." Again this writer remarks: "The authority of all over each member essentially belongs to the body politic or the state."

By this same writer it is also said: "The citizens are the member of the civil society; bound to this society by certain duties, and subject to its authority; they equally participate in its advantages. The natives, or natural born citizens, are those born in the country, of parents who are citizens. As society cannot perpetuate itself otherwise than by the children of the citizens, those children naturally follow the condition of their parents, and succeed to all their rights." Again: "I say, to be of the country, it is necessary to be born of a person who is a citizen; for if he be born there of a foreigner, it will be only the place of birth, and not his country. The inhabitants, as distinguished from citizens, are foreigners who are permitted to settle and stay in the country." Vattel, Book 1, cap. 19, p. 101.

From the views here expressed, and they seem to be unexceptionable, it must follow, that with the slave, with one devoid of rights or capacities, civil or political, there could be no pact; that one thus situated could be no party to, or actor in the association of those possessing free will, power, discretion. He could form no part of the design, no constituent ingredient or portion of a society based upon common, that is, upon equal interests and powers. He could not at the same time be the sovereign and the slave.

But it has been insisted, in argument, that the emancipation of a slave, effected either by the direct act and assent of the master, or by causes operating in contravention of his will, produces a change in the status or capacities of the slave, such as will transform him from a mere subject of property, into a being possessing a social, civil, and political equality with a citizen; in other words, will make him a citizen of the State within which he was, previously to his emancipation, a slave.

It is difficult to perceive by what magic the mere surcease or renunciation of an interest in a subject of property, by an individual possessing that interest, can alter the essential character of that property with respect to persons or communities unconnected with such renunciation. Can it be pretended that an individual in any State, by his single act, though voluntarily or designedly performed, yet without the operation or warrant of the government, perhaps in opposition to its policy or its guaranties, can create a citizen of that State? Much more emphatically may it be asked, how such a result could be accomplished by means wholly extraneous, and entirely foreign to the government of the State. The argument thus urged must lead to these extraordinary conclusions. It is regarded at once as wholly untenable, and as unsustained by the direct authority or by the analogies of history.

The institution of slavery, as it exists and has existed from the period of its introduction into the United States, though more humane and mitigated in character than was the same institution, either under the republic or the empire of Rome, bears both in is tenure and in the simplicity incident to the mode of its exercise, a closer resemblance to Roman slavery than it does to the condition of villanage, as it formerly existed in England. Connected with the latter, there were peculiarities, from custom or positive regulation, which varied it materially from the slavery of the Romans, or from slavery at any period within the United States.

But with regard to slavery amongst the Romans, it is by no means true that emancipation, either during the republic or the empire, conferred, by the act itself, or implied, the status or the rights of citizenship.

The proud title of Roman citizen, with the immunities and rights incident thereto, and as contradistinguished alike from the condition of conquered subjects or of the lower grades of native domestic residents, was maintained throughout the duration of the Republic, and until a late period of the eastern empire and at last was in effect destroyed less by an elevation of the inferior classes than by the degradation of the free, and the previous possessors of rights and immunities civil and political, to the indiscriminate abatement incident to absolute and simple despotism.

By the learned and elegant historian of the decline and fall of the Roman Empire we are told that "In the decline of the Roman Empire, the proud distinctions of the republic were gradually abolished; and the reason or instinct of Justinian completed the simple form of an absolute monarchy. The Emperor could not eradicate the popular reverence which always waits on the possession of hereditary wealth or the memory of famous ancestors. He delighted to honor with titles and emoluments his generals, magistrates and senators, and his precarious indulgence communicated some rays of their glory to their wives and children. But in the eye of the law all Roman citizens were equal, and all subjects of the empire were citizens of Rome. That inestimable character was degraded to an obsolete and empty name. The voice of a Roman could no longer enact his laws, or create the annual ministers of his powers; his constitutional rights might have checked the arbitrary will of a master; and the bold adventurer from Germany or Arabia was admitted with equal favor to the civil and military command which the citizen alone had been once entitled to assume over the conquests of his fathers. The first Caesars had scrupulously guarded the distinction of ingenuous and servile birth, which was decided by the condition of the mother. The slaves who were liberated by a generous master, immediately entered into the middle class of libertini or freedmen; but they could never be enfranchised from the duties of obedience and gratitude; whatever were the fruits of their industry, their patron and his family inherited the third part, or even the whole of their fortune, if they died without children and without a testament. Justinian respected the rights of patrons, but his indulgence removed the badge of disgrace from the two inferior orders of freedman; whoever ceased to be a slave, obtained, without reserve or delay, the station of a citizen; and at length the dignity of an ingenuous birth was created or supposed by the omnipotence of the Emperor.[1]

The above account of slavery and its modifications will be found in strictest conformity with the institutes of Justinian. Thus, (book 1st, title 3d), it is said: "The first general division of persons in respect of their rights is into freeman and slaves." The same title, sec. 4th: "Slaves are born such, or become so. They are born such of bondwomen; they become so either by the law of nations, as by capture, or by the civil law." Section 5th: "In the condition of slaves there is no diversity; but among free persons there are many. Thus some are ingenui or freemen, others libertini or freedmen."

Tit. 4th De. Ingenuis.— "A freeman is who is born free by being born in matrimony, of parents who both are free, or both freed; or of parents one free and the other freed. But one born of a free mother, although the father be a slave or unknown, is free."

Tit. 5th. De Libertinis.—"Freedmen are those who have been manumitted from just servitude."

Section 3d of the same title states that "freedmen were formerly distinguished by a threefold division." But the Emperor proceeds to say: "Our piety leading us to reduce all things into a better state, we have amended our laws, and re-established the ancient usage; for anciently liberty was simple and undivided—

that is, was conferred upon the slave as his manumittor possessed it, admitting this single difference, that the person manumitted became only a freed man, although his manumittor was a free man." And he further declares: "We have made all freed men in general become citizens of Rome, regarding neither the age of the manumitted, nor the manumittor, nor the ancient forms of manumission. We have also introduced many new methods by which slaves may become Roman citizens."

By the references above given it is shown, from the nature and objects of civil and political associations, and upon the direct authority of history, that citizenship was not conferred by the simple fact of emancipation, but that such a result was deduced therefrom in violation of the fundamental principles of free political association; by the exertion of despotic will to establish under a false and misapplied denomination, one equal and universal slavery; and to effect this result required the exertions of absolute power—of a power both in theory and practice, being, in its most plenary acceptation, the sovereignty, the State itself—it could not be produced by a less or inferior authority, much less by the will or the act of one who, with reference to civil and political rights, was himself a slave. The master might abdicate or abandon his interest or ownership in his property, but his act would be a mere abandonment. It seems to involve an absurdity to impute to it the investiture of rights which the sovereignty alone had power to impart. There is not, perhaps, a community in which slavery is recognized, in which the power of emancipation, and the modes of its exercise are not regulated by law—that is, by the sovereign authority; and none can fail to comprehend the necessity for such regulation, for the preservation of order, and even of political and social existence.

By the argument for the plaintiff in error, a power equally despotic is vested in every member of the association, and the most obscure or unworthy individual it comprises may arbitrarily invade and derange its most deliberate and solemn ordinances. At assumptions anomalous as these, so fraught with mischief and ruin, the mind at once is revolted, and goes directly to the conclusions, that to change or to abolish a fundamental principle of the society itself—of the sovereignty; and that none other can admit to a participation of that high attribute. It may fur-

---

[1] Vide Gibbon's *Decline and Fall of the Roman Empire.* London edition of 1825, Vol. III., chap. 44, p. 183.

ther expose the character of the argument urged for the plaintiff, to point out some of the revolting consequences, which it would authorize. If that argument possesses any integrity, it asserts the power in any citizen, or quasi citizen, or a resident foreigner of any one of the States, from a motive either of corruption or caprice, not only to infract the inherent and necessary authority of such state, but also materially to interfere with the organization of the Federal Government, and with the authority of the separate and independent States. He may emancipate his negro slave, by which process he first transforms that slave into a citizen of his own State; he may next, under color of article 4th, section 2d, of the Constitution of the United States, obtrude him, and on terms of civil and political equality, upon any and every State in this Union, in defiance of all regulations of necessity or policy, ordained by those States for their internal happiness or safety. Nay, more: this manumitted slave may, by a proceeding springing from the will or act of his master alone, be mixed up with the institutions of the Federal Government, to which he is not a party, and in opposition to the laws of that government which, in authorizing the extension by naturalization of the rights and immunities of citizens of the United States to those not originally parties to the federal compact, have restricted that boon to free white aliens alone. If the rights and immunities connected with or practiced under the institutions of the United States can by any indirection be claimed or deduced from sources or modes other than the Constitution and laws of the United States, it follows that the power of naturalization vested in Congress is not exclusive—that it has in effect no existence, but is repealed or abrogated.

But it has been strangely contended that the jurisdiction of the Circuit Court might be maintained upon the ground that the plaintiff was a resident of Missouri, and that, for the purpose of vesting the court with jurisdiction over the parties, residence within the State was sufficient.

The first, and to my mind a conclusive reply to this singular argument, is presented in the fact that the language of the Constitution restricts the jurisdiction of the courts to cases in which the parties shall be citizens, and is entirely silent with respect to residence. A second answer to this strange and latitudinous notion is, that it so far stultifies the sages by whom the Constitution

was framed, as to impute to them ignorance of the material distinction existing between citizenship and mere residence or domicil, and of the well known facts, that a person confessedly an alien may be permitted to reside in a country in which he can possess no civil or political rights, or of which he is neither a citizen nor subject; and that for certain purposes a man may have a domicil in different countries, in no one of which he is an actual personal resident.

The correct conclusions upon the question here considered would seem to be these:

That in the establishment of the several communities now the States of this Union, and in the formation of the Federal Government, the African was not deemed politically a person. He was regarded and owned in every State in the Union as property merely, and as such was not and could not be a party or an actor, much less a peer in any compact or form of government established by the States or the United States. That if, since the adoption of the state governments, he has been or could have been elevated to the possession of political rights or powers, this result could have been effected by no authority less potent than that of the sovereignty—the State—exerted to that end, either in the form of legislation, or in some other mode of operation. It could certainly never have been accomplished by the will of an individual operating independently of the sovereign power, and even contravening and controlling that power. That so far as rights and immunities appertaining to citizens have been defined and secured by the Constitution and laws of the United States, the African race is not and never was recognized either by the language or purposes of the former; and it has been expressly excluded by every Act of Congress providing for the creation of citizens by naturalization, these laws, as has already been remarked, being restricted to free white aliens exclusively.

But it is evident that, after the formation of the Federal Government by the adoption of the Constitution, the highest exertion of State power would be incompetent to bestow a character or status created by the Constitution, or conferred in virtue of its authority only. Upon those, therefore, who were not originally parties to the federal compact, or who are not admitted and adopted as parties thereto, in the mode prescribed by its paramount authority, no State could have power to bestow the character or the rights and privileges exclusively reserved by the States for the action of the Federal Government by that compact.

The States, in the exercise of their political power, might, with reference to their peculiar government and jurisdiction, guaranty the rights of person and property, and the enjoyment of civil and political privileges, to those whom they should be disposed to make the objects of their bounty: but they could not reclaim or exert the powers which they had invested exclusively in the government of the United States. They could not add to or change in any respect the class of persons to whom alone the character of citizen of the United States appertained, at the time of the adoption of the Federal Constitution. They could not create citizens of the United States by any direct or indirect proceeding.

According to the view taken of the law, as applicable to the demurrer to the plea in abatement in this cause, the questions subsequently raised upon the several pleas in bar might be passed by, as requiring neither a particular examination, nor an adjudication directly upon them. But as these questions are intrinsically of primary interest and magnitude, and have been elaborately discussed in argument, and as with respect to them the opinions of a majority of the court, including my own, are perfectly coincident, to me it seems proper that they should here be fully considered, and, so far as it is practicable for this court to accomplish such an end, finally put to rest.

The questions, then, to be considered upon the several pleas in bar, and upon the agreed statement of facts between the counsel, are: 1st. Whether the admitted master and owner of the plaintiff, holding him as his slave in the State of Missouri, and in conformity with his rights guarantied to him by the laws of Missouri then and still in force, by carrying with him for his own benefit and accommodation, and as his own slave, the person of the plaintiff during the commorancy of the master within the State of Illinois, had, upon his return with his slave into the State of Missouri, forfeited his rights as master, by reason of any supposed operation of the prohibitory provision in the Constitution of Illinois, beyond the proper territorial jurisdiction of the latter State. 2d. Whether a similar removal of the plaintiff by his master from the State of Missouri, and his retention in service at

a point included within no State, but situated north of thirty-six degrees thirty minutes of north latitude, worked a forfeiture of the right of property of the master, and the manumission of the plaintiff.

In considering the first of these questions, the acts of declarations of the master, as expressive of his purpose to emancipate, may be thrown out of view, since none will deny the right of the owner to relinquish his interest in any subject of property at any time or in any place. The inquiry here bears no relation to acts or declarations of the owner as expressive of his intent or purpose to make such a relinquishment; it is simply a question whether, irrespective of such purpose and in opposition thereto, that relinquishment can be enforced against the owner of property within his own country, in defiance of every guaranty promised by its laws; and this through the instrumentality of a claim to power entirely foreign and extraneous with reference to himself, to the origin and foundation of his title, and to the independent authority of his country. A conclusive negative answer to such an inquiry is at once supplied, by announcing a few familiar and settled principles and doctrines of public law.

Vattel, in his chapter on the general principle of the laws of nations, section 15th, tells us, that "nations being free and independent of each other in the same manner that men are naturally free and independent, the second general law of their society is, that each nation should be left in the peaceable enjoyment of that liberty which she inherits from nature."

"The natural society of nations," says this writer, "cannot subsist unless the natural rights of each be respected." In section 16th he says, "as a consequence of that liberty and independence, it exclusively belongs to each nation to form her own judgment of what her conscience prescribes for her—of what it is proper or improper for her to do; and of course it rests whether she can perform any office for another nation without neglecting a duty she owes to herself. In all cases, therefore, in which a nation has the right of judging what her duty requires, no other nation can compel her to act in such or such a particular manner, for any attempt at such compulsion would be an infringement on the liberty of nations." Again, in section 18th of the same chapter, "nations composed of men, and considered as so many free persons living together in a state of nature, are naturally equal, and inherit from nature the same obligations and rights. Power or weakness does not produce any difference. A small republic is no less a sovereign state than the most powerful kingdom."

So, in section 20: "A nation, then, is mistress of her own actions, so long as they do not affect the proper and perfect rights of any other nation—so long as she is only internally bound, and does not lie under any external and perfect obligation. If she makes an ill use of her liberty, she is guilty of a breach of duty; but other nations are bound to acquiesce in her conduct, since they have no right to dictate to her. Since nations are free, independent, and equal, and since each possesses the right of judging, according to the dictates of her conscience, what conduct she is to pursue, in order to fulfill her duties, the effect of the whole is to produce, at least externally, in the eyes of mankind, perfect equality of rights between nations, in the administration of their affairs, and in the pursuit of their pretensions, without regard to the intrinsic justice of their conduct, of which others have no right to form a definitive judgement."

Chancellor Kent, in the 1st volume of his Commentaries, lecture 2d, after collating the opinions of Grotius, Heineccius, Vattel, and Rutherford, enunciates the following positions as sanctioned by these and other learned publicists, *viz.*: "nations are equal in respect to each other, and entitled to claim equal consideration for their rights, whatever may be their relative dimensions and strength, or however greatly they may differ in government, religion, or manners. This perfect equality and entire independence of all distinct States is a fundamental principle of public law. It is a necessary consequence of this equality, that each nation has a right to govern itself as it may think proper, and no one nation is entitled to dictate a form of government or religion, or a course of internal policy to another." This writer gives some instances of the violation of this great national immunity, and amongst them the constant interference by the ancient Romans, under the pretext of settling disputes between their neighbors, but with the real purpose of reducing those neighbors to bondage; the interference of Russia, Prussia, and Austria, for the dismemberment of Poland; the more recent invasion of Naples by Austria in 1821, and of Spain by the French Government in 1823, under the excuse of suppressing a danger-

ous spirit of international revolution and reform.

With reference to this right of self-government in independent sovereign States, an opinion has been expressed, which, whilst it concedes this right as inseparable from, and as a necessary attribute of sovereignty and independence, asserts, nevertheless, some implied and paramount authority of a supposed international law, to which this right of self-government must be regarded and exerted as subordinate; and from which independent and sovereign States can be exempted only by a protest, or by some public and formal rejection of that authority. With all respect for those by whom this opinion has been professed, I am constrained to regard it as utterly untenable, as palpably inconsistent, and as presenting in argument a complete *felo de se*.

Sovereignty, independence, and a perfect right of self-government, can signify nothing less than a superiority to and an exemption from all claims by any extraneous power, however expressly they may be asserted, and render all attempts to enforce such claims merely attempts at usurpation. Again; could such claims from extraneous sources be regarded as legitimate, the effort to resist or evade them, by protest or denial, would be as irregular and unmeaning as it would be futile. It could in nowise affect the question of superior right. For the position here combated, no respectable authority has been, and none, it is thought, can be adduced. It is certainly irreconcilable with the doctrines already cited from the writers upon public law.

Neither the case of James Somersett, 20 Howell's St. Tr. so often vaunted as the proud evidence of devotion to freedom under a government which has done as much perhaps to extend the reign of slavery as all the world besides; nor does any decision founded upon the authority of Somersett's case, when correctly expounded, assail or impair the principle of national equality, enunciated by each and all of the publicists already referred to. In the case of Somersett, although the applicant for the habeas corpus and the individual claiming property in that applicant were both subjects and residents within the British Empire, yet the decision cannot be correctly understood as ruling absolutely and under all circumstances against the right of property in the claimant. That decision goes no farther than to determine, that within the realm of England there was no authority to justify the detention of an individual in private bondage. If the decision in Somersett's case had gone beyond that point, it would have presented the anomaly of a repeal by laws enacted for and limited in their operation to the realm alone, of other laws and institutions established for places and subjects without limits of the realm of England; laws and institutions at that very time, and long subsequently, sanctioned and maintained under the authority of the British Government, and which the full and combined action of the King and Parliament was required to abrogate.

But could the decision in Somersett's case be correctly interpreted as ruling the doctrine which it has been attempted to deduce from it, still that doctrine must be considered as having been overruled by the lucid and able opinion of Lord Stowell in the more recent case of The Slave Grace, reported in the second volume of Haggard, p. 94; in which opinion, whilst it is conceded by the learned judge that there existed no power to coerce the slave whilst in England, that yet, upon her return to the Island of Antigua, her status as a slave was revived, or, rather, that the title of the owner to the slave as property had never been extinguished, but had always existed in that Island. If the principle of this decision be applicable as between different portions of one and the same empire, with how much more force does it apply as between nations or governments entirely separate, and absolutely independent of each other? For in this precise attitude the States of this Union stand with reference to this subject, and with reference to the tenure of every description of property vested under their laws and held within their territorial jurisdiction.

A strong illustration of the principle ruled by Lord Stowell, and of the effect of that principle, even in a case of express contract, is seen in the case of *Lewis v. Fullerton*, decided by the Supreme Court of Virginia, and reported in the first volume of Randolph, p. 15. The case was this: a female slave, the property of a citizen in the State of Ohio, was taken from his possession under a writ of habeas corpus, and set at liberty. Soon, or immediately after, by agreement between this slave and her master, a deed was executed in Ohio by the latter, containing a stipulation that this slave should return to Virginia, and after a service of two years in that State should there be free. The law of Virginia regulat-

ing emancipation required that deeds of emancipation should, within a given time from their date, be recorded in the courts of the county in which the grantor resided, and declared that deeds with regard to which this requisite was not complied with should be void. Lewis, an infant son of this female, under the rules prescribed in such cases, brought an action, in *forma pauperis*, in one of the courts of Virginia, for the recovery of his freedom, claimed in virtue of the transactions above mentioned. Upon an appeal to the Supreme Court from a judgement against the plaintiff, Roane, Justice, in delivering the opinion of the court, after disposing of other questions discussed in that case, remarks:

"As to the deed of emancipation contained in the record, that deed, taken in connection with the evidence offered in support of it, shows that it had a reference to the State of Virginia; and the testimony shows that it formed a part of this contract, whereby the slave Milly was to be brought back (as she was brought back) into the State of Virginia. Her object was, therefore, to secure her freedom by the deed within the State of Virginia, after the time should have expired for which she had intended herself, and when she should be found abiding within the State of Virginia.

If, then, this contract had an eye to the State of Virginia for its operation and effect, the *lex loci* ceased to operate. In that case it must, to have its effect, conform to the laws of Virginia. It is insufficient under those laws to effectuate an emancipation, for want of a due recording in the county court, as was decided in the case of *Givens v. Mann*, 6 Munf. 190, in this court. It is also ineffectual within the Commonwealth of Virginia for another reason. The *lex loci* is also to be taken subject to the exception, that it is not to be enforced in another country, when it violates some moral duty or the policy of that country, or is not consistent with a positive right secured to a third person or party by the laws of that country in which it is sought to be enforced. In such a case we are told, 'magis jus nostrum quam jus alienum servemus.'" Huberus, tom. 2. lib. 1, tit. 3; 2 Fonblanque, p. 444. "That third party, in this instance, is the Commonwealth of Virginia, and her policy and interests are also to be attended to. These turn the scale against the *lex loci* in the present instance."

The second or last mentioned position assumed for the plaintiff under the pleas in bar, as it rests mainly if not solely upon the provision of the Act of Congress of March 6, 1820, prohibiting slavery in Upper Louisiana north of thirty-six degrees thirty minutes north latitude, popularly called the Missouri Compromise, that assumption renews the question, formerly so zealously debated, as to the validity of the provision in the Act of Congress, and upon the constitutional competency of Congress to establish it.

Before proceeding, however, to examine the validity of the prohibitory provision of the law, it may, so far as the rights involved in this cause are concerned, be remarked, that conceding to that provision the validity of a legitimate exercise of power, still this concession could by no rational interpretation imply the slightest authority for its operation beyond the territorial limits comprised within its terms; much less could there be inferred from it a power to destroy or in any degree to control rights, either of person or property, entirely within the bounds of a distinct and independent sovereignty—rights invested and fortified by the guaranty of that sovereignty. These surely would remain in all their integrity, whatever effect might be ascribed to the prohibition within the limits defined by its language.

But beyond and in defiance of this conclusion, inevitable and undeniable as it appears, upon every principle of justice or sound induction, it has been attempted to convert this prohibitory provision of the Act of 1820 not only into a weapon with which to assail the inherent—the necessary inherent—powers of independent sovereign governments, but into a means of forfeiting that equality of rights and immunities which are the birthright or the donative from the Constitution of every citizen of the United States within the length and breadth of the nation. In this attempt, there is asserted power in Congress, whether from incentives or interest, ignorance, faction, partiality or prejudice, to bestow upon a portion of the citizens of this nation that which is the common property and privilege of all—the power, in fine, of confiscation, in retribution for no offense, or, if for an offense, for that of accidental locality only.

It may be that, with respect to future cases, like the one now before the court, there is felt an assurance of the impotence of such a pretension; still, the fullest conviction of the result can impart to it no claim to forbearance, nor dispense with the duty of antipathy and disgust at

its sinister aspect, whenever it may be seen to scowl upon the justice, the order, the tranquillity, and fraternal feeling, which are the surest, nay, the only means, of promoting or preserving the happiness and prosperity of the nation, and which were the great and efficient incentives to the formation of this government.

The power of Congress to impose the prohibition in the 8th section of the Act of 1820 has been advocated upon an attempted construction of the 2d clause of the 3d section of the 4th article of the Constitution, which declares that "Congress shall have the power to dispose of and to make all needful rules and regulations respecting the territory and other property belonging to the United States."

In the discussions in both houses of Congress, at the time of adopting this 8th section of the Act of 1820, great weight was given to the peculiar language of this clause, *viz.*: territory and other property belonging to the United States, as going to show that the power of disposing of and regulating, thereby vested in Congress, was restricted to a proprietary interest in the territory or land comprised therein, and did not extend to the personal or political rights of citizens or settlers, inasmuch as this phrase in the Constitution, "territory or other property," identified territory with property, and inasmuch as citizens or persons could not be property, and especially were not property belonging to the United States. And upon every principle or reason or necessity, this power to dispose of and to regulate the territory of the nation could be designed to extend no farther than to its preservation and appropriation to the uses of those to whom it belonged, *viz.*: the nation. Scarcely anything more illogical or extravagant can be imagined than the attempt to deduce from this provision in the Constitution a power to destroy or in any wise to impair the civil and political rights of the citizens of the United States, and much more so the power to establish inequalities amongst those citizens by creating privileges in one class of those citizens, and by the disfranchisement of other portions or classes, by degrading them from the position they previously occupied.

There can exist no rational or natural connection or affinity between a pretension like this and the power vested by the Constitution in Congress with regard to the territories; on the contrary, there is an absolute incongruity between them.

But whatever the power vested in Congress, and whatever the precise subject to which that power extended, it is clear that the power related to a subject appertaining to the United States, and one to be disposed of and regulated for the benefit and under the authority of the United States. Congress was made simply the agent or trustee for the United States, and could not, without a breach of trust and a fraud, appropriate the subject of the trust to any other beneficiary or *cestui que trust* than the United States, or to the people of the United States, upon equal grounds, legal or equitable. Congress could not appropriate that subject to any one class or portion of the people, to the exclusion of others, politically and constitutionally equals; but every citizen would if anyone could claim it, have the like rights of purchase, settlement, occupation, or any other right, in the national territory.

Nothing can be more conclusive to show the equality of this with every other right in all the citizens of the United States, and the iniquity and absurdity of the pretension to exclude or to disfranchise a portion of them because they are the owners of slaves, than the fact that the same instrument, which imparts to Congress its very existence and its every function, guaranties to the slaveholder the title to his property, and gives him the right to its reclamation throughout the entire extent of the nation; and farther, that the only private property which the Constitution has specifically recognized, and has imposed it as a direct obligation both on the States and the Federal Government to protect and enforce, is the property of the master in his slave; no other right of property is placed by the Constitution upon the same high ground, nor shielded by a similar guaranty.

Can there be imputed to the sages and patriots by whom the Constitution was framed, or can there be detected in the text of that Constitution, or in any rational construction or implication deducible therefrom, a contradiction so palpable as would exist between a pledge to the slaveholder of an equality with his fellow-citizens, and of the formal and solemn assurance for the security and enjoyment of his property, and a warrant given, as it were, *uno flatu*, to another, to rob him of that property, or to subject him to proscription and disfranchisement for processing or for endeavoring to retain it?

The injustice and extravagance necessarily implied in a supposition like this, cannot be rationally imputed to the patriotic or the honest, or to those who were merely sane.

A conclusion in favor of the prohibitory power in Congress, as asserted in the 8th section of the Act of 1820, has been attempted, as deducible from the precedent of the Ordinance of the Convention of 1787, concerning the cession by Virginia of the territory northwest of the Ohio; the provision in which Ordinance, relative to slavery, it has been attempted to impose upon other and subsequently acquired territory.

The first circumstance which, in the consideration of this provision, impresses itself upon my mind, is its utter futility and want of authority. This court has, in repeated instances, ruled, that whatever may have been the force according to this Ordinance of 1787 at the period of its enactment, its authority and effect ceases, and yielded to the paramount authority of the Constitution, from the period of the adoption of the latter. Such is the principle ruled in the cases of *Pollard's Lessee v. Hagan*, 3 How 212; *Permoli v. New Orleans*, 3 How. 589; *Strader v. Graham*, 10 How. 82. But apart from the superior control of the Constitution, and anterior to the adoption of that instrument, it is obvious that the inhibition in question never had and never could have any legitimate and binding force. We may seek in vain for any power in the convention, either to require or to accept a condition or restriction upon the cession like that insisted on; a condition inconsistent with, and destructive of the object of the grant. The cession was, as recommended by the old Congress in 1780, made originally and completed in terms to the United States, i.e., for the people, all the people, of the United States. The condition subsequently sought to be annexed in 1787 (declared, too, to be perpetual and immutable), being contradictory to the terms and destructive of the purposes of the cession, and after the cession was consummated, and the powers of the ceding party terminated, and the rights of the grantees, the people of the United States, vested, must necessarily, so far, have been *ab initio* void. With respect to the power of the convention to impose this inhibition, it seems to be pertinent in this place to recur to the opinion of one contemporary with the establishment of the government, and whose distinguished services in the formation and adoption of our national charter, point him out as the *artifex maximus* of our federal system. James Madison, in the year 1819, speaking with reference to the prohibitory power claimed by Congress, then threatening the very existence of the Union, remarks of the language of the 2d clause of the 3d section of article 4th of the Constitution, "that it cannot be well extended beyond a power over the territory as property, and the power to make provisions really needful or necessary for the government of settlers, until ripe for admission into the Union."

Again he says, "with respect to what has taken place in the Northwest Territory, it may be observed that the Ordinance giving it its distinctive character on the subject of slaveholding proceeded from the old Congress, acting with the best intentions, but under a charter which contains no shadow of the authority exercised; and it remains to be decided how far the states formed within the Territory, and admitted into the Union, are on a different footing from its other member as to their legislative sovereignty. As to the power of admitting new States into the federal compact, the questions offering themselves are, whether Congress can attach conditions, or the new States concur in conditions, which after admission would abridge or enlarge the constitutional rights of legislation common to other States; whether Congress can, by a compact with a new State, take power either to or from itself, or place the new member above or below the equal rank and rights possessed by the others; whether all such stipulations expressed or implied would not be nullities, and be so pronounced when brought to a practical test. It falls within the scope of your inquiry to state the fact, that there was a proposition in the convention to discriminate between the old and the new States by an article in the Constitution. The proposition, happily, was rejected. The effect of such a discrimination is sufficiently evident."[2]

In support of the Ordinance of 1787, there may be adduced the semblance at least of obligation deducible from compact, the form of assent or agreement between the grantor and grantee; but this form of similitude, as is justly remarked by Mr. Madison, is rendered null by the absence of power or authority in the contracting parties, and by the more intrinsic and essential defect of incompatibility with the

rights and avowed purposes of those parties, and with their relative duties and obligations to others. If, then, with the attendant formalities of assent or compact, the restrictive power claimed was void as to the immediate subject of the Ordinance, how much more unfounded must be the pretension to such a power as derived from that source (*viz.*: the Ordinance of 1787), with respect to territory acquired by purchase or conquest under the supreme authority of the Constitution—territory not the subject of mere donation, but obtained in the name of all, by the combined efforts and resources of all, and with no condition annexed or pretended.

In conclusion, my opinion is, that the decision of the Circuit Court, upon the law arising upon the several pleas in bar, is correct, but that it is erroneous in having sustained the demurrer to the plea in abatement of the jurisdiction; that for this error the decision of the Circuit Court should be reversed, and the cause remanded to that court, with instructions to abate the action, for the reason set forth and pleaded in the plea in abatement.

In the foregoing examination of this cause, the circumstance that the questions involved therein had been previously adjudged between these parties by the court of the State of Missouri, has not been adverted to; for although it has been ruled by this court, that in instances of concurrent jurisdiction, the court first obtaining possession or cognizance of the controversy should retain and decide it, yet, as in this case there had been no plea, either of a former judgment or of autre action pendent, it was thought that the fact of a prior decision, however conclusive it might have been if regularly pleaded, could not be incidentally taken into view.

Mr. Justice Campbell:

I concur in the judgment pronounced by the Chief Justice, but the importance of the cause, the expectation and interest it has awakened, and the responsibility involved in its determination, induce me to file a separate opinion.

The case shows that the plaintiff, in the year 1834, was a negro slave in Missouri, the property of Dr. Emerson, a surgeon in the Army of the United States. In 1834, his master took him to the military station at Rock Island, on the border of Illinois, and in 1836 to Fort Snelling, in the present Minnesota, then Wisconsin Territory. While at Fort Snelling, the plaintiff married a slave who was there with her master, and two

---

[2] Letter from James Madison to Robert Walsh, November 27th, 1819, on the subject of the Missouri Compromise.

children have been born of this connection; one during the journey of the family in returning to Missouri, and the other after their return to that State.

Since 1838, the plaintiff and the members of his family have been in Missouri in the condition of slaves. The object of this suit is to establish their freedom. The defendant, who claims the plaintiff and his family, under the title of Dr. Emerson, denied the jurisdiction of the Circuit Court, by the plea that the plaintiff was a negro of African blood, the descendant of Africans who had been imported and sold in this country as slaves, and thus he had no capacity as a citizen of Missouri to maintain a suit in the Circuit Court. The court sustained a demurrer to this plea; a trial was then had upon the general issue, and special pleas to the effect that the plaintiff and his family were slaves belonging to the defendant.

My opinion in this case is not affected by the plea to the jurisdiction, and I shall not discuss the questions it suggests. The claim of the plaintiff to freedom depends upon the effect to be given to his absence from Missouri, in company with his master, in Illinois and Minnesota, and this effect is to be ascertained by a reference to the laws of Missouri. For the trespass complained of was committed upon one claiming to be a freeman and a citizen, in that State, and who had been living for years under the dominion of its laws. And the rule is, that whatever is a justification where the thing is done, must be a justification in the forum where the case is tried.

20 How. St. Tri. 234; Cowp. S. C. 161.

The Constitution of Missouri recognizes slavery as a legal condition, extends guaranties to the masters of slaves, and invites immigrants to introduce them, as property, by a promise of protection. The laws of the State charge the master with the custody of the slave, and provide for the maintenance and security of their relation.

The Federal Constitution and the Acts of Congress provide for the return of escaping slaves within the limits of the Union. No removal of the slave beyond the limits of the State, against the consent of the master, nor residence there in another condition, would be regarded as an effective manumission by the courts of Missouri, upon his return to the State. "Sicut liberis captis status restituitur sic servus domino." Nor can the master emancipate the slave within the State except through the agency of a public authority. The inquiry arises,

whether the manumission of the slave is effected by his removal, with the consent of the master, to community where the law of slavery does not exist, in a case where neither the master nor slave discloses a purpose to remain permanently, and where both parties have continued to maintain their existing relations. What is the law of Missouri in such a case? Similar inquiries have arisen in a great number of suits, and the discussions in the State courts have relieved the subject of much of its difficulty.

12 B. M. Ky. 545; *Foster v. Foster*, 10 Gratt. Va. 485; 4 Hrr. & McH. Md. 295; *Scott v. Emerson* 15 Mo. 576; 4 Rich. S. C. 186; 17 Mo. 434; 15 Mo. 596; 5 B. M. 173; 8 B. M. 540, 633; 9 B. M. 565; 5 Leigh, 614; 1 Rand. 15; 18 Pick. 193.

The result of these discussions is, that, in general, the status, or civil and political capacity of a person, is determined, in the first instance, by the law of the domicil where he is born; that the legal effect on persons, arising from the operation of the law of that domicil, is not indelible, but that a new capacity or status may be acquired by a change of domicil. That questions of status are closely connected with considerations arising out of the social and political organization of the State where they originate, and each sovereign power must determine them within its own territories.

A large class of cases has been decided upon the second of the propositions above stated, in the Southern and Western courts—cases in which the law of the actual domicil was adjudged to have altered the native condition and status of the slave, although he had never actually possessed the status of freedom in that domicil.

Rankin v. Lydia, 2 A. K. Marsh. 467; *Harny v. Decker*, Walk. Miss. 36; 4 Mart. 385; 1 Mo. 472; *Hunter v. Fulcher*, 1 Leigh, 172.

I do not impugn the authority of these cases. No evidence is found in the record to establish the existence of a domicil acquired by the master and slave, either in Illinois or Minnesota. The master is described as an officer of the army, who was transferred from one station to another, along the Western frontier, in the line of his duty, and who, after performing the usual tours of service, returned to Missouri; these slaves returned to Missouri with him, and had been there for near fifteen years, in that condition, when this suit was instituted. But absence, in the performance of military duty, without more, is a fact of no importance in determining a question of a change of domicil. Questions of that kind depend upon acts and intentions, and are ascertained from motives, pursuits, the condition of the family, and fortune of the party, and no change will be inferred, unless evidence shows that one domicil was abandoned, and there was an intention to acquire another.

11 L. & Eq. 6; 6 exch. 217; 6 M. & W. 511; 2 Curt. Ecc. 368.

The cases first cited deny the authority of a foreign law to dissolve relations which have been legally contracted in the State where the parties are, and have their actual domicil—relations which were never questioned during their absence from that State—relations which are consistent with the native capacity and condition of the respective parties, and with the policy of the State where they reside; but which relations were inconsistent with the policy or laws of the State or Territory within which they had been for a time, and from which they had returned, with these relations undisturbed. It is upon the assumption, that the law of Illinois or Minnesota was indelibly impressed upon the slave, and its consequences carried into Missouri, that the claim of the plaintiff depends. The importance of the case entitles the doctrine on which it rests to a careful examination.

It will be conceded, that in countries where no law or regulation prevails, opposed to the existence and consequences of slavery, persons who are born in that condition in a foreign State, would not be liberated by the accident of their introgression. The relation of domestic slavery is recognized in the law of nations, and the interference of the authorities of one State with the rights of a master belonging to another, without a valid cause is a violation of that law.

Wheat. Law of Na. 724; 5 Stats. at L. 601; calh. Sp. 378; Reports of the Com. U. S. and G. B. 187, 238, 241.

The public law of Europe formerly permitted a master to reclaim his bondsman, within a limited period, wherever he could find him, and one of the capitularies of Charlemagne abolishes the rule of prescription. He directs, "that wheresoever, within the bounds of Italy, either the runaway slave of the King, or of the church, or of any other man, shall be found by his master, he shall be restored without any bar or prescription of years; yet upon the provision that the master be a Frank or German, or of any other nation (foreign); but if he be a Lombard or a Roman, he

shall acquire or receive his slaves by that law which has been established from ancient times among them." Without referring for precedents abroad, or to the colonial history, for similar instances, the history of the Confederation and Union affords evidence to attest the existence of this ancient law. In 1783, Congress directed General Washington to continue his remonstrances to the commander of the British forces respecting the permitting negroes belonging to the citizens of these States to leave New York, and to insist upon the discontinuance of that measure. In 1788, the resident minister of the United States at Madrid was instructed to obtain from the Spanish Crown orders to its governors in Louisiana and Florida, "to permit and facilitate the apprehension of fugitive slaves from the States, promising that the States would observe the like conduct respecting fugitives from Spanish subjects." The committee that made the report of this resolution consisted of Hamilton, Madison an Sedgwick (2 Hamilton's Works, 473); and the clause in the Federal Constitution providing for the restoration of fugitive slaves is a recognition of this ancient right, and of the principle that a change of place does not effect a change of condition. The diminution of the power of a master to reclaim his escaping bondsman in Europe commenced in the enactment of laws of prescription in favor of privileged communes. Bremen, Spire, Worms, Vienna, and Ratisbon, in Germany; Carcassonne, Beziers, Toulouse, and Paris, in France, acquired privileges on this subject at an early period. The Ordinance of William the Conqueror, that a residence of any of the servile population of England, for a year and a day, without being claimed, in any city, burgh, walled town, or castle of the King, should entitle them to perpetual liberty, is a specimen of these laws.

The earliest publicist who has discussed this subject is Bodin, a jurist of the sixteenth century, whose work was quoted in the early discussions of the courts in France and England on this subject. He says: "In France, although there be some remembrance of old servitude, yet it is not lawful here to make a slave or to buy any one of others, in so much as the slaves of strangers, as soon as they set their foot within France, become frank and free, as was determined by an old decree of the court of Paris against an ambassador of Spain, who had brought a slave with him into France." He states another case, which arose in the City of Toulouse, of a

Genoese merchant, who had carried a slave into that city on his voyage from Spain; and when the matter was brought before the magistrates, the "procureur of the city, out of the records, showed certain ancient privileges given unto them of Toulouse, wherein it was granted that slaves, so soon as they should come into Toulouse, should be free." These cases were cited with much approbation in the discussion of the claims of the West India slaves of Verdelin for freedom, in 1738, before the judges in admiralty (15 Causes Celébrés, p. 1; 2 Masse Droit Com. sec. 58) and were reproduced before Lord Mansfield, in the cause of Somersett, in 1772. Of the cases cited by Bodin, it is to be observed that Charles V. of France exempted all the inhabitants of Paris from serfdom, or other feudal incapacities, in 1371, and this was confirmed by several of his successors (3 Dulaire Hist. de Par. 546; Broud. Cout. de Par. 21), and the Ordinance of Toulouse is preserved as follows: "Civitas Tholosana fuit et erit sine fine libera, adeo ut servi et ancillæ sclavi et sclavæ, dominos habentes, cum rebus vel sine rebus suis, and Tholosam vel infrà terminos extra urbem terminatos accedentes acquirant libertatem."

Hist. de Langue, tome 3, p. 69; Ibid. 6, p. 8; Loysel Inst. b. 1. sec. 6.

The decisions were made upon special ordinances, or charters, which contained positive prohibitions of slavery, and where liberty had been granted as a privilege; and the history of Paris furnishes but little support for the boast that she was a "*sacro sancta civitas*," where liberty always had an asylum, or for the "self-complacent rhapsodies" of the French advocates in the case of Verdelin, which amused the grave lawyers who argued the case of Somersett. The case of Verdelin was decided upon a special ordinance, which prescribed the conditions on which West India slaves might be introduced into France, and which had been disregarded by the master.

The case of Somersett was that of a Virginia slave carried to England by his master in 1770, and who remained there two years. For some cause, he was confined on a vessel destined to Jamaica, where he was to be sold. Lord Mansfield, upon a return to a habeas corpus, states the question involved. "Here, the person of the slave himself," he says, "is the immediate subject of inquiry. Can any dominion, authority or coercion be exercised in this country, accord-

ing to the American laws?" He answers: "The difficulty of adopting the relation, without adopting it in all its consequences, is indeed extreme, and yet many of those consequences are absolutely contrary to the municipal law of England." Again he says: "The return states that the slave departed, and refused to serve; whereupon, he was kept to be sold abroad." "So high an act of dominion must be recognized by the law of the country where it is used. The power of the master over his slave has been extremely different in different countries." "The state of slavery is of such a nature, that it is incapable of being introduced on any reasons, moral or political, but only by positive law, which preserves its force long after the reasons, occasion, and time itself, from whence it was created, are erased from the memory. It is so odious, that nothing can be suffered to support it but positive law." That there is a difference in the systems of States, which recognize and which do not recognize the institution of slavery, cannot be disguised. Constitutional law, punitive law, police, domestic economy, industrial pursuits, and amusements, the modes of thinking and of belief of the population of the respective communities, all show the profound influence exerted upon society by this single arrangement. This influence was discovered in the Federal Convention, in the deliberations on the plan of the Constitution. Mr. Madison observed, "that the States were divided into different interests, not by their difference of size, but by other circumstances; the most material of which resulted partly from climate, but principally from the effects of their having or not having slaves. These two causes concur in forming the great division of interests in the United States."

The question to be raised with the opinion of Lord Mansfield, therefore, is not in respect to the incongruity of the two systems, but whether slavery was absolutely contrary to the law of England; for if it was so, clearly, the American laws could not operate there. Historical research ascertains that at the date of the Conquest the rural population of England were generally in a servile condition, and under various names, denoting slight variances in condition, they were sold with the land like cattle, and were a part of its living money. Traces of the existence of African slaves are to be found in the early chronicles. Parliament, in the time of Richard II., and also of Henry VIII., refused to adopt a general law of emancipation. Acts of emancipation by

SLAVERY

DRED SCOTT V.
SANDFORD

the last-named monarch and by Elizabeth are preserved.

The African slave trade had been carried on, under the unbounded protection of the Crown, for near two centuries, when the case of Somersett was heard, and no motion for its suppression had ever been submitted to Parliament, while it was forced upon and maintained in unwilling colonies by the Parliament and Crown of England at that moment. Fifteen thousand negro slaves were then living in that island, where they had been publicly sold for near a century in the markets of London. In the northern part of the kingdom of Great Britain there existed a class of from 30,000 to 40,000 persons of whom the Parliament said, in 1775 (15 George III, chap. 28) "many colliers, coal heavers, and salters, are in a state of slavery or bondage, bound to the collieries and salt works, where they work for life, transferable with the collieries and salt works when their original masters have no use for them; and whereas the emancipating or setting free the colliers, coal heavers, and salters, in Scotland, who are now in a state of servitude, gradually and upon reasonable conditions, would be the means of increasing the number of colliers, coal heavers, and salters, to the great benefit of the public, without doing any injury to the present masters, and would remove the reproach of allowing such a state of servitude to exist in a free country." etc.: and again, in 1799, "they declare that many colliers and coal heavers still continue in a state of bondage." No statute, from the Conquest till the 15 George III., had been passed upon the subject of personal slavery. These facts have led the most eminent civilian of England to question the accuracy of this judgment, and to insinuate that in this judgment the offense of *ampliare jurisdictionem* by private authority was committed by the eminent magistrate who pronounced it.

This sentence is distinguishable from those cited from the French courts in this: that there positive prohibitions existed against slavery, and the right to freedom was conferred on the immigrant slave by positive law; whereas here the consequences of slavery merely—that is, the public policy— were found to be contrary to the law of slavery. The case of *The Slave Grace*, 2 Hagg. 94, with four others, came before Lord Stowell in 1827, by appeals from the West India vice admiralty courts. They were cases of slaves who had returned to those islands, after a residence in Great Britain, and where the claim to freedom was first presented in the colonial forum. The learned judge in that case said: "This suit fails in its foundation. She (Grace) was not a free person; no injury is done her by her continuance in slavery, and she has no pretensions to any other station than that which was enjoyed by every slave of a family. If she depends upon such freedom conveyed by a mere residence in England, she complains of a violation of right which she possessed no longer than whilst she resided in England, but which totally expired when that residence ceased, and she was imported into Antigua."

The decision of Lord Mansfield was, "that so high an act of dominion" as the master exercises over his slave, in sending him abroad for sale, could not be exercised in England under the American laws, and contrary to the spirit of their own.

The decision of Lord Stowell is, that the authority of the English laws terminated when the slave departed from England. That the laws of England were not imported into Antigua, with the slave, upon her return, and that the colonial forum had no warrant for applying a foreign code to dissolve relations which had existed between persons belonging to that island, and which were legal according to its own system. There is no distinguishable difference between the case before us and that determined in the admiralty of Great Britain.

The complaint here, in my opinion, amounts to this: that the judicial tribunals of Missouri have not denounced as odious the Constitution and laws under which they are organized, and have not superseded them on their own private authority, for the purpose of applying the laws of Illinois, or those passed by Congress for Minnesota, in their stead. The 8th section of the Act of Congress of the 6th March, 1820 (3 Stat. at L. 545), entitled, "An Act to authorize the people of Missouri to form a State government," etc., etc., is referred to as affording the authority to this court to pronounce the sentence which the Supreme Court of Missouri felt themselves constrained to refuse. That section of the Act prohibits slavery in the district of country west of the Mississippi, north of thirty-six degrees thirty minutes north latitude, which belonged to the ancient Province of Louisiana, not included in Missouri.

It is a settled doctrine of this court, that the Federal Government can exercise no power over the subject of slavery within the States, nor control the intermigration of slaves, other than fugitives, among the States. Nor can that government affect the duration of slavery within the States, other than by a legislation over the foreign slave trade. The power of Congress to adopt the section of the Act above cited must, therefore, depend upon some condition of the Territories which distinguishes them from States, and subjects them to a control more extended. The 3d section of the 4th article of the Constitution is referred to as the only and all-sufficient grant to support this claim. It is, that "new States may be admitted by the Congress to this Union; but no new State shall be formed or erected within the jurisdiction of any other State, not any State be formed by the junction of two or more States, or parts of States, without the consent of the Legislatures of the States concerned, as well as of the Congress. The Congress shall have power to dispose of and make all needful rules and regulations respecting the territory, or other property belonging to the United States; and nothing in this Constitution shall be so construed as to prejudice any claims of the United States, or of any particular State."

It is conceded, in the decisions of this court, that Congress may secure the rights of the United States in the public domain, provide for the sale or lease of any part of it, and establish the validity of the titles of the purchasers, and may organize territorial governments, with powers of legislation.

3 How. 212; 12 How. 1; Pet. 511; 13 Pet. 436; 16 How. 164.

But the recognition of a plenary power in Congress to dispose of the public domain, or to organize a government over it, does not imply a corresponding authority to determine the internal polity, or to adjust the domestic relations, or the persons who may lawfully inhabit the territory in which it is situated. A supreme power to make needful rules respecting the public domain, and a similar power of framing laws to operate upon persons and things within the territorial limits where it lies, are distinguished by broad lines of demarcation in American history. This court has assisted us to define them. In *Johnson v. McIntosh*, 8 Wheat. 543–605, they say: "According to the theory of the British Constitution, all vacant lands are vested in the Crown; and the exclusive power to grant them is admitted to reside in the Crown, as a branch of the royal prerogative.

All the lands we hold were originally granted by the Crown, and the establishment of a royal government has never been considered as impairing its right to grant lands within the chartered limits of such colony."

And the British Parliament did claim a supremacy of legislation co-extensive with the absoluteness of the dominion of the sovereign over the crown lands. The American doctrine, to the contrary, is embodied in two brief resolutions of the people of Pennsylvania, in 1774: 1st. "That the inhabitants of these Colonies are entitled to the same rights and liberties, within the Colonies, that the subjects born in England are entitled within the realm." 2d. "That the power assumed by Parliament to bind people of these Colonies by statutes, in all cases whatever, is unconstitutional, and therefore the source of these unhappy difficulties." The Congress of 1774, in their statement of rights and grievances, affirm "a free and exclusive power of legislation" in their several provincial Legislatures, "in all cases of taxation and internal polity, subject only to the negative of their sovereign, in such manner as has been heretofore used and accustomed." 1 Jour. Cong. 32

The unanimous consent of the people of the Colonies, then, to the power of their sovereign, "to dispose of and make all needful rules and regulations respecting the territory" of the Crown, in 1774, was deemed by them as entirely consistent with opposition, remonstrance, the renunciation of allegiance, and proclamation of civil war, in preference to submission to his claim of supreme power in the Territories.

I pass now to the evidence afforded during the Revolution and Confederation. The American Revolution was not a social revolution. It did not alter the domestic condition or capacity of persons within the Colonies, not was it designed to disturb the domestic relations existing among them. It was a political revolution, by which thirteen dependent Colonies became thirteen independent States. "The Declaration of Independence was not," says Justice Chase, "a declaration that the united Colonies jointly, in a collective capacity, were independent States, etc., etc., etc., but that each of them was a sovereign and independent State: that is, that each of them had a right to govern itself by its own authority and its own laws, without any control from any other power on earth."

3 Dall. 199; 4 Cranch, 212,

These sovereign and independent States, being united as a Confederation, by various public acts of cession, became jointly interested in territory, and concerned to dispose of and make all needful rules and regulations respecting it. It is a conclusion not open to discussion in this court, "that there was no territory within the (original) United States, that was claimed by them in any other right than that of some of the confederate States." *Harcourt v. Gaillard*, 12 Wheat. 523. "The question whether the vacant lands within the United States," says Chief Justice Marshall, "became joint property, or belonged to the separate States, was a momentous question, which threatened to shake the American Confederacy to its foundations. This important and dangerous question has been compromised, and the compromise is not now to be contested." 6 Cranch, 87.

The cessions of the States to the Confederation were made on the condition that the territory ceded should be laid out and formed into distinct republican States which would be admitted as members to the Federal Union, having the same rights of sovereignty, freedom and independence, as the other States. The first effort to fulfill this trust was made in 1785, by the offer of a charter or compact to the inhabitants who might come to occupy the land.

Those inhabitants were to form for themselves temporary state governments, founded on the constitutions of any of the States, but to be alterable—at the will of their Legislature; and permanent governments were to succeed these, whenever the population became sufficiently numerous to authorize the State to enter the Confederacy; and Congress assumed to obtain powers from the States to facilitate this object. Neither in the deeds of cession of the States, nor in this compact, was a sovereign power for Congress to govern the Territories asserted. Congress retained power, by this Act, "to dispose of and to make rules and regulations respecting the public domain," but submitted to the people to organize a government harmonious with those of the confederate States.

The next stage in the progress of colonial government was the adoption of the Ordinance of 1787, by eight States, in which the plan of a territorial government, established by Act of Congress, is first seen. This was adopted while the Federal Convention to form the Constitution was sitting. The plan placed the government in the hands of a governor, secretary, and judges, appointed by Congress, and conferred power on them to select suitable laws from the codes of the States, until the population should equal 5,000. A legislative council, elected by the people, was then to be admitted to a share of the legislative authority, under the supervision of Congress; and States were to be formed whenever the number of the population should authorize the measure.

This Ordinance was addressed to the inhabitants as a fundamental compact, and six of its articles define the conditions to be observed in their Constitution and laws. These conditions were designed to fulfill the trust in the agreements of cession, that the States to be formed of the ceded Territories should be "distinct republican States." This Ordinance was submitted to Virginia in 1788, and the 5th article, embodying as it does a summary of the entire Act, was specifically ratified and confirmed by that State. This was an incorporation of the Ordinance into her Act of Cession. It was conceded, in the argument, that the authority of Congress was not adequate to the enactment of the ordinance, and that it cannot be supported upon the Articles of Confederation. To a part of the engagements, the assent of nine states was required, and for another portion no provision had been made in those Articles. Mr. Madison said, in a writing nearly contemporary but before the Confirmatory Act of Virginia, "Congress have proceeded to form new states, to erect temporary governments, to appoint officers for them, and to prescribe the conditions on which such States shall be admitted into the Confederacy; all this has been done, and done without the least color of constitutional authority." Federalist, No. 38. Richard Henry Lee, one of the committee who reported the Ordinance to Congress, transmitted it to General Washington (15th July, 1787), saying: "It seemed necessary, for the security of property among uninformed and perhaps licentious people, as the greater part of those who go there are, that a strong-toned government should exist, and the rights of property be clearly defined." The consent of all the States represented in Congress, the consent of inhabitants of the territory, all concur to support the authority of this enactment. It is apparent, in the frame of the Constitution, that the Convention recognized its validity, and adjusted parts of their work with reference to it.

The authority to admit new States into the Union, the omission to provide distinctly for territorial governments, and the clause limiting the foreign slave trade to States then existing, which might not prohibit it, show that they regarded this territory as provided with a government and organized permanently with a restriction on the subject of slavery. Justice Chase, in the opinion already cited, says of the government before, and it is in some measure true during the Confederation, "that the powers of Congress originated from necessity, and arose out of and were only limited by events, or, in other words, they were revolutionary in their very nature. Their extent depended upon the exigencies and necessities of public affairs;" and there is only one rule of construction, in regard to the acts done, which will fully support them, *viz.*: that the powers actually exercised were rightfully exercised, wherever they were supported by the implied sanction of the State Legislatures, and by the ratifications of the people.

The clauses in the 3d section of the 4th article of the Constitution, relative to the admission of new States, and the disposal and regulation of the territory of the United States, were adopted without debate in the Convention.

There was a warm discussion on the clauses that relate to the subdivision of the States, and the reservation of the claims of the United States and each of the States from any prejudice. The Maryland members revived the controversy in regard to the Crown lands of the Southwest. There was nothing to indicate any reference to a government of territories not included within the limits of the Union; and the whole discussion demonstrates that the Convention was consciously dealing with a Territory whose condition, as to government, had been arranged by a fundamental and unalterable compact.

An examination of this clause of the Constitution, by the light of the circumstances in which the Convention was placed, will aid us to determine its significance. The first clause is, "that new States may be admitted by the Congress into this Union." The condition of Kentucky, Vermont, Rhode Island and the new States to be formed in the Northwest, suggested this, as a necessary addition to the powers of Congress. The next clause, providing for the subdivision of States, and the parties to consent to such an alteration, was required, by the plans on foot, for changes in Massachusetts, New York, Pennsylvania, North Carolina and Georgia. The clause which enables Congress to dispose of and make regulations respecting the public domain, was demanded by the exigencies of an exhausted treasury and a disordered finance, for relief by sales, and the preparation for sales, of the public lands; and the last clause, that nothing in the Constitution should prejudice the claims of the United States or a particular State, was to quiet the jealousy and irritation of those who had claimed for the United States all the unappropriated lands. I look in vain, among the discussions of the time for the assertion of a supreme sovereignty for Congress over the territory then belonging to the United States, or that they might thereafter acquire. I seek in vain for an enunciation that a consolidated power had been inaugurated, whose subject comprehended an empire, and which had no restriction but the discretion of Congress. This disturbing element of the Union entirely escaped the apprehensive provisions of Samuel Adams, George Clinton, Luther Martin, and Patrick Henry; and, in respect to dangers from power vested in a central government over distant settlements, colonies, or provinces, their instincts were always alive. Not a word escaped them, to warn their countrymen that here was a power to threaten the landmarks of this federative Union, and with them the safeguards of popular and constitutional liberty; or that under this Article there might be introduced, on our soil, a single government over a vast extent of country—a government foreign to the persons over whom it might be exercised and capable of binding those not represented by statutes, in all cases whatever. I find nothing to authorize these enormous pretensions, nothing in the expositions of the friends of the Constitution, nothing in the expressions of alarm by its opponents—expressions which have since been developed as prophecies. Every portion of the United States was then provided with a municipal government, which this Constitution was not designed to supersede, but merely to modify as to its condition.

The compacts of cession by North Carolina and Georgia, are subsequent to the Constitution. They adopt the Ordinance of 1787, except the clause respecting slavery. But the precautionary repudiation of that article forms an argument quite as satisfactory to the advocates for federal power, as its introduction would have done. The refusal of a power to Congress to legislate in one place, seems to justify the seizure of the same power when another place for its exercise is found.

This proceeds from a radical error, which lies at the foundation of much of this discussion. It is, that the Federal Government may lawfully do whatever is not directly prohibited by the Constitution. This would have been a fundamental error, if no amendments to the Constitution had been made. But the final expression of the will of the people of the States, in the 10th Amendment, is, that the powers of the Federal Government are limited to the grants of the Constitution.

Before the cession of Georgia was made, Congress asserted rights, in respect to a part of her territory, which require a passing notice. In 1798 and 1800, Acts for the settlement of limits with Georgia, and to establish a government in the Mississippi Territory were adopted. A territorial government was organized, between the Chattahoochee and Mississippi Rivers. This was within the limits of Georgia. These Acts dismembered Georgia. They established a separate government on her soil, while they rather derisively professed, "that the establishment of that government shall in no respect impair the rights of the State of Georgia, either to the jurisdiction or soil of the territory." The Constitution provided that the importation of such persons as any of the existing States shall think proper to admit, shall not be prohibited by Congress before 1808. By these enactments, a prohibition was placed upon the importation of slaves into Georgia, although her Legislature had made none.

This court have repeatedly affirmed the paramount claim of Georgia to this territory. They have denied the existence of any title in the United States. 6 Cranch. 87; 12 Wheat. 523; 3 How. 212; 13 How. 381. Yet these Acts were cited in the argument as precedents to show the power of Congress in the Territories. These Statutes were the occasion of earnest expostulation and bitter remonstrance on the part of the authorities of the State, and the memory of their injustice and wrong remained long after the legal settlement of the controversy by the compact of 1802. A reference to these Acts terminates what I have to say upon the constitutions of the territory within the original limits of the United States. These constitutions were framed by the concurrence of the States making the cessions, and Congress, and were tendered to immigrants who might be attracted to the vacant territory. The legislative

powers of the officers of this government were limited to the selection of laws from the States; and provision was made for the introduction of popular institutions, and their emancipation from federal control, whenever a suitable opportunity occurred. The limited reservation of legislative power to the officers of the Federal Government was excused on the plea of necessity; and the probability is, that the clauses respecting slavery embody some compromise among the statesmen of that time; beyond these, the distinguishing features of the system which the patriots of the Revolution had claimed as their birthright, from Great Britain, predominated in them.

The acquisition of Louisiana, in 1803, introduced another system into the United States. This vast Province was ceded by Napoleon, and its population had always been accustomed to a viceroyal government, appointed by the Crowns of France or Spain. To establish a government constituted on similar principles, and with like conditions, was not an unnatural proceeding.

But there was a great difficulty in finding constitutional authority for the measure. The 3d section of the 4th article of the Constitution, was introduced into the Constitution on the motion of Mr. Gouverneur Morris. In 1803, he was appealed to for information in regard to its meaning. "I am very certain I had it not in contemplation to insert a decree de coercendo imperio in the Constitution of America.* * * I knew then, as well as I do now, that all North America must at length be annexed to us. Happy, indeed, if the lust of dominion stop here. It would, therefore, have been perfectly Utopian to oppose a paper restriction to the violence of popular sentiment, in a popular government." 3 Mor. Writ. 185. A few days later, he makes another reply to his correspondents, "I perceive," he says, "I mistook the drift of your inquiry, which substantially is whether Congress can admit, as a new State, territory which did not belong to the United States when the Constitution was made. In my opinion, they cannot. I always thought, when we should acquire Canada and Louisiana, it would be proper to govern them as provinces, and allow them no voice in our councils. In wording the 3d section of the 4th article, I went as far as circumstances would permit, to establish the exclusion. Candor obliges me to add my belief, that had it been more pointedly expressed, a strong opposition would have been made." 3 Mor. Writ.

192. The first territorial government of Louisiana was an Imperial one, founded upon a French or Spanish model. For a time, the Governor, judges, legislative council, marshal, secretary, and officers of the militia, were appointed by the President[3]

Besides these anomalous arrangements, the acquisition gave rise to jealous inquiries, as to the influence it would exert in determining the men and States that were to be "the arbiters and the rulers" of the destinies of the Union; and unconstitutional opinions, having for their aim to promote sectional divisions, were announced and developed. "Something," said an eminent statesman, "something has suggested to the members of Congress the policy of acquiring geographical majorities. This is a very direct step towards disunion, for it must foster the geographical enmities by which alone it can be effected. This something must be a contemplation of particular advantages to be derived from such majorities; and is it not notorious that they consist of nothing else but usurpations over persons and property, by which they can regulate the internal wealth and prosperity of States and individuals?"

The most dangerous of the efforts to employ geographical political power, to perpetuate a geographical preponderance in the Union, is to be found in the deliberations upon the Act of the 6th of March, 1820, before cited. The attempt consisted of a proposal to exclude Missouri from a place in the Union, unless her people would adopt a constitution containing a prohibition upon the subject of slavery, according to a prescription of Congress. The sentiment is now general, if not universal, that Congress had no constitutional power to impose the restriction. This was frankly admitted at the bar in the course of this argument. The principles which this court have pronounced condemn the pretension then made on behalf of the Legislative Department. In *Groves v. Slaughter*, 15 Pet., the Chief Justice said: "The power over this subject is exclusively with the several States, and each of them has a right to decide for itself whether it will or will not allow persons of this description to be brought within its limits." Justice McLean said: "The Constitution of the United States operates alike in all the States, and one State has the same power over the subject of slavery as every other State." In *Pollard's Lessee v. Hagan*, 3 How. 212, the court say: "The United States have no constitutional capacity to exercise municipal jurisdiction, sov-

ereignty, or eminent domain, within the limits of a State or elsewhere, except in cases where it is delegated, and the court denies the faculty of the Federal Government to add to its powers by treaty or compact."

This is a necessary consequence, resulting from the nature of the Federal Constitution, which is a federal compact among the States, establishing a limited government, with powers delegated by the people of distinct and independent communities, who reserved to their state governments, and to themselves, the powers they did not grant. This claim to impose a restriction upon the people of Missouri involved a denial of the constitutional relations between the people of the States and Congress, and affirmed a concurrent right for the latter, with their people to constitute the social and political system of the new States. A successful maintenance of this claim would have altered the basis of the Constitution. The new States would have become members of a Union defined in part by the Constitution and in part by Congress. They would not have been admitted to "this Union." Their sovereignty would have been restricted by Congress as well as the Constitution. The demand was unconstitutional and subversive, but was prosecuted with an energy, and aroused such animosities among the people, that patriots, whose confidence had not failed during the Revolution, began to despair for the Constitution.[4] Amid the utmost violence of this extraordinary contest, the expedient contained in the 8th section of this Act was proposed, to moderate it, and to avert the catastrophe it menaced. It was not seriously

---

[3] Mr. Varnum said: "The bill provided such a government as had never been known in the United States." Mr.Eustis: "The government laid down in this bill is certainly a new thing in the United States." Mr. Lucas: "It has been remarked, that this bill establishes elementary principles never previously introduced in the government of any territory of the United States. Granting the truth of this observation," etc. etc. Mr. Macon: "My first objection to the principle contained in this section is, that it establishes species of government unknown to the United States." Mr. Boyle: "Were the President an angel instead of a man, I would not clothe him with this power." Mr. G. W. Campbell: "On examining the section, it will appear that it really establishes a complete despotism." Mr. Sloan: "Can anything be more repugnant to the principles of just government? Can anything be more despotic?—Annals of Congress, 1803–'4.

[4] Mr. Jefferson wrote: "The Missouri question is the most portentous one that ever threatened our Union. In the gloomiest moments of the Revolutionary War, I never had any apprehension equal to that I feel from this source."

debated, nor were its constitutional aspects severely scrutinized by Congress. For the first time, in the history of the country, has its operation been embodied in a case at law, and been presented to this court for their judgment. The inquiry is, whether there are conditions in the constitutions of the Territories which subject the capacity and status of persons within their limits to the direct action of Congress. Can Congress determine the condition and status of persons who inhabit the Territories?

The Constitution permits Congress to dispose of and to make all needful rules and regulations respecting the territory of other property belonging to the United States. This power applies as well to territory belonging to the United States within the States, as beyond them. It comprehends all the public domain, wherever it may be. The argument is, that the power to make "all needful rules and regulations" "is a power of legislation," "a full legislative power;" "that it includes all subjects of legislation in the territory," and is without any limitations, except the positive prohibitions which affect all the powers of Congress. Congress may then regulate or prohibit slavery upon the public domain within the new States, and such a prohibition would permanently affect the capacity of a slave, whose master might carry him to it. And why not? Because no power has been conferred on Congress. This is a conclusion universally admitted. But the power to "make rules and regulations respecting the territory" is not restrained by State lines, nor are there any constitutional prohibitions upon its exercise in the domain of the United States within the States; and whatever rules and regulations respecting territory Congress may constitutionally make, are supreme and are not dependent on the situs of "the territory."

The author of the *Farmer's Letters*, so famous in the ante-revolutionary history, thus states the argument made by the American loyalists to legislate in all cases whatever over the Colonies: "It has been urged with great vehemence against us," he says, "and it seems to be thought their fort, by our adversaries, that a power of regulation is a power of legislation; and a power of legislation, if constitutional, must be universal and supreme, in the utmost sense of the word. It is, therefore, concluded that the Colonies, by acknowledging the power of regulation, acknowledged every other power."

This sophism imposed upon a portion of the patriots of that day. Chief Justice Marshall, in his *Life of Washington*, says "that many of the best informed men in Massachusetts had, perhaps adopted the opinion of the parliamentary right of internal government over the Colonies;" "that the English statute book furnishes many instances of its exercise;" "that in no case recollected, was their authority openly controverted;" and "that the General Court of Massachusetts, on a late occasion, openly recognized the principle."

Marsh. Wash. Vol. II. pp. 75, 76.

But the more eminent men of Massachusetts rejected it; and another patriot of the time employs the instance to warn us of "the stealth with which oppression approaches," and "the enormities towards which precedents travel." And the people of the United States, as we have seen, appealed to the last argument, rather than acquiesce in their authority. Could it have been the purpose of Washington and his illustrious associates, by the use of ambiguous, equivocal, and expansive words, such as "rules," "regulations," "territory," to re-establish in the Constitution of their country that fort which had been prostrated amid the toils and with the sufferings and sacrifices of seven years of war? Are there words to be understood as the Norths, the Grenvilles, Hillsboroughs, Hutchinsons, and Dunmores—in a word, as George III. would have understood them—or are we to look for their interpretation to Patrick Henry or Samuel Adams, to Jefferson, and Jay, and Dickinson; to the sage Franklin, or to Hamilton, who from his early manhood was engaged in combating British constructions of such words? We know that the resolution of Congress of 1780 contemplated that the new States to be formed under their recommendation were to have the same rights of sovereignty, freedom and independence, as the old. That every resolution, cession, compact and ordinance, of the States, observed the same liberal principle. That the Union of the Constitution is a Union formed of equal States; and that new States, when admitted, were to enter "this Union." Had another Union been proposed in "any pointed manner," it would have encountered not only "strong" but successful opposition. The disunion between Great Britain and her colonies originated in the antipathy of the latter to "rules and regulations" made by a remote power respecting their internal policy. In forming the Constitution, this fact was ever present in the minds of its authors. The people were assured by their most trusted statesman "that the jurisdiction of the Federal Government is limited to certain enumerated objects, which concern all members of the republic," and "that the local or municipal authorities form distinct portions or supremacy, no more subject within their respective spheres to the general authority, than the general authority is subject to them within its own sphere." Still, this did not content them. Under the lead of Hancock and Samuel Adams, of Patrick Henry and George Mason, they demanded an explicit declaration that no more power was to be exercised than they had delegated. And the 9th and 10th Amendments to the Constitution were designed to include the reserved rights of the States, and the people, within all the sanctions of that instrument, and to bind the authorities, state and federal, by the judicial oath it prescribes, to their recognition and observance. Is it probable, therefore, that the supreme and irresponsible power, which is now claimed for Congress over boundless territories, the use of which cannot fail to react upon the political system of the States, to its subversion, was ever within the contemplation of the statesmen who conducted the counsels of the people in the formation of this Constitution? When the questions that came to the surface upon the acquisition of Louisiana were presented to the mind of Jefferson, he wrote: "I had rather ask an enlargement of power from the nation, where it is found necessary, than to assume it by a construction which would make our powers boundless. Our peculiar security is in the possession of a written Constitution. Let us not make it blank paper by construction. I say the same as to the opinion of those who consider the grant of the treaty-making power as boundless. If it is, then we have no Constitution. If it has bounds, they can be no others than the definitions of the powers which that instrument gives. It specifies and delineates the operations permitted to the Federal Government, and gives the powers necessary to carry them into execution." The publication of the journals of the Federal Convention in 1819, of the debates reported by Mr. Madison in 1840, and the mass of private correspondence of the early statesmen before and since, enable us to approach the discussion of the aims of those who made the Constitution, with some insight and confidence.

I have endeavored, with the assistance of these, to find a solution for the grave and difficult question involved in this inquiry. My opinion is, that the claim for Congress of supreme power in the Territories, under the grant to "dispose of and make all needful rules and regulations respecting territory," is not supported by the historical evidence drawn from the Revolution, the Confederation, or the deliberations which preceded the ratifications of the Federal Constitution. The Ordinance of 1787 depended upon the action of the Congress of the Confederation, the assent of the State of Virginia, and the acquiescence of the people who recognized the validity of that plea of necessity, which supported so many of the Acts of the governments of that time; and the Federal Government accepted the Ordinance as a recognized and valid engagement of the Confederation.

In referring to the precedents of 1798 and 1800, I find the Constitution was plainly violated by the invasion of the rights of a sovereign State, both of soil and jurisdiction; and in reference to that of 1804, the wisest statesmen protested against it, and the President more than doubted its policy and the power of the government.

Mr. John Qunicy Adams, at a later period, says of the last Act, "that the President found Congress mounted to the pitch of passing those acts, without inquiring where they acquired the authority, and he conquered his own scruples as they had done theirs." But this court cannot undertake for themselves the same conquest. They acknowledge that our peculiar security is in the possession of a written Constitution, and they cannot make it blank paper by construction.

They look to its delineation of the operations of the Federal Government, and they must not exceed the limits it marks out, in their administration. The court have said "that Congress cannot exercise municipal jurisdiction, sovereignty, or eminent domain, within the limits of a state or elsewhere, beyond what has been delegated." We are then to find the authority for supreme power in the Territories in the Constitution. What are the limits upon the operations of a government invested with the legislative, executive and judiciary powers, and charged with the power to dispose of and to make all needful rules and regulations respecting a vast public domain? The feudal system would have recognized the claim made on behalf of the Federal Government for supreme power over persons and things in the Territories, as an incident to this title—that is, the title to dispose of and make rules and regulations respecting it.

The Norman lawyers or William the Conqueror would have yielded an implicit assent to the doctrine, that a supreme sovereignty is an inseparable incident to a grant, to dispose of and to make all needful rules and regulations respecting the public domain. But an American patriot, in contrasting the European and American systems, may affirm, "that European sovereigns give lands to their colonists, but reserve to themselves a power to control their property, liberty and privileges; but the American Government sells the lands belonging to the people of the several States (i. e., United States) to their citizens, who are already in the possession of personal and political rights, which the government did not give, and cannot take away." And the advocates for government sovereignty in the Territories have been compelled to abate a portion of the presentations originally made in its behalf, and to admit that the constitutional prohibitions upon Congress operate in the Territories. But a constitutional prohibition is not requisite to ascertain a limitation upon the authority of the several departments of the Federal Government. Nor are the States or people restrained by any enumertaion of definition of their rights or liberties.

To impair or diminish either, the Department must produce an authority from the people themselves, in their Constitution; and as we have seen, a power to make rules and regulations respecting the public domain does not confer a municipal sovereignty over persons and thing upon it. But as this is "thought their fort" by our adversaries, I propose a more definite examination of it. We have seen, Congress does not dispose of or make rules and regulations respecting domain belonging to themselves, but belonging to the United States.

These conferred on their mandatory, Congress, authority to dispose of the territory which belonged to them in common; and to accomplish that object beneficially and effectually, they gave an authority to make suitable rules and regulations respecting it. When the power of disposition is fulfilled, the authority to make rules and regulations terminates, for it attaches only upon territory "belonging to the United States."

Consequently, the power to make rules and regulations, from the nature of the subject, is restricted to such administrative and conservatory Acts as are needful for the preservation of the public domain, and its preparation for sale or disposition. The system of land surveys; the reservations for schools, internal improvements, military sites, and public buildings; the preemption claims of settlers; the establishment of land offices and boards of inquiry, to determine the validity of land titles; the modes of entry and sale, and of conferring titles; the protection of the lands from trespass and waste; the partition of the public domain into municipal subdivisions, having reference to the erection of territorial governments and States; and perhaps the selection, under their authority, of suitable laws for the protection of the settlers, until there may be a sufficient number of them to form a self-sustaining municipal government—these important rules and regulations will sufficiently illustrate the scope and operation of the 3d section of the 4th article of the Constitution. But this clause in the Constitution does not exhaust the powers of Congress within the territorial subdivisions, or over the persons who inhabit them. Congress may exercise there all the powers of government which belong to them as the Legislature of the United States, of which these Territories make a part. *Loughborough v. Blake,* 5 Wheat. 317. Thus the laws of taxation, for the regulation of foreign, federal and Indian commerce, and so for the abolition of the slave trade, for the protection of copyrights and inventions, for the establishment of postal communication and courts of justice, and for the punishment of crimes, are as operative there as within the States. I admit that to mark the bounds for the jurisdiction of the Government of the United States within the Territory, and of its power in respect to persons and things within the municipal subdivisions it has created, is a work of delicacy and difficulty, and, in a great measure is beyond the cognizance of the Judiciary Department of that government. How much municipal power may be exercised by the people of the Territory, before their admission to the Union, the courts of justice cannot decide. This must depend, for the most part, on political considerations, which cannot enter into the determination of a case of law or equity. I do not feel called upon to define the jurisdiction of Congress. It is sufficient for the decision of this case to ascertain whether the residuary sovereignty of the States or people has been invaded by the 8th section of the Act of 6th March, 1820, I have cited, in so far as it concerns the capacity and status of persons in the condition and circumstances of the plaintiff and his family.

These States, at the adoption of the Federal Constitution, were organized communities, having distinct systems of municipal law, which, though derived from a common source, and recognizing in the main similar principles, yet in some respects had become unlike, and on a particular subject promised to be antagonistic.

Their systems provided protection for life, liberty and property, among their citizens, and for the determination of the condition and capacity of the persons domiciled within their limits. These institutions, for the most part, were placed beyond the control of the Federal Government. The Constitution allows Congress to coin money, and regulate its value; to regulate foreign and federal commerce; to secure, for a limited period, to authors and inventors a property in their writings and discoveries; and to make rules concerning captures in war; and within the limits of these powers, it has exercised, rightly, to a greater or less extent, the power to determine what shall and what shall not be property.

But the great powers of war and negotiation, finance, postal communication and commerce, in general, when employed in respect to the property of a citizen, refer to, and depend upon, the municipal laws of the States, to ascertain and determine what is property, and the rights of the owner, and the tenure by which it is held.

Whatever these Constitutions and laws validly determine to be property, it is the duty of the Federal Government, through the domain of jurisdiction merely federal, to recognize to be property.

And this principle follows from the structure of the respective governments, state and federal, and their reciprocal relations. They are different agents and trustees of the people of the several States, appointed with different powers and with distinct purposes, but whose Acts, within the scope of their respective jurisdictions, are mutually obligatory. They are respectively the depositories of such powers of legislation as the people were willing to surrender, and their duty is to cooperate within their several jurisdictions to maintain the rights of the same citizens under both governments, unimpaired. A proscription,

therefore, of the constitution and laws of one or more States, determining property, on the part of the Federal Government, by which the stability of its social system may be endangered, is plainly repugnant to the conditions on which the Federal Constitution was adopted, or which that government was designed to accomplish. Each of the States surrendered its powers of war and negotiation, to raise armies and to support a navy, and all these powers are sometime required to preserve a State from disaster and ruin. The Federal Government was constituted to exercise these powers for the preservation of the States, respectively, and to secure to all their citizens the enjoyment of the rights which were not surrendered to the Federal Government. The provident care of the statesmen who projected the Constitution was signalized by such a distribution of the powers of government as to exclude many of the motives and opportunities for promoting provocations and spreading discord among the States, and for guarding against those partial combinations, so destructive of the community of interest, sentiment and feeling, which are so essential to the support of the Union. The distinguishing features of their system consist in the exclusion of the Federal Government from the local and internal concerns of, and in the establishment of an independent internal government within, the States. And it is a significant fact in the history of the United States, that those controversies which have been productive of the greatest animosity, and have occasioned most peril to the peace of the Union, have had their origin in the well-sustained opinion of a minority among the people, that the Federal Government had overstepped its constitutional limits to grant some exclusive privilege, or disturb the legitimate distribution of property or power among the States or individuals. Nor can a more signal instance of this be found than is furnished by the Act before us. No candid or rational man can hesitate to believe, that if the subject of the 8th section of the Act of March, 1820, had never been introduced into Congress and made the basis of legislation, no interest common to the Union would have been seriously affected. And certainly the creation, within this Union, or large confederacies of unfriendly and frowning States, which has been the tendency, and, to an alarming extent, the result, produced by the agitation arising from it, does not commend it to the patriot or statesman. This court have determined that intermigration of slaves

SLAVERY

DRED SCOTT V. SANDFORD

was not committed to the jurisdiction or control of Congress. Wherever a master is entitled to go within the United States, his slave may accompany him, without any impediment from, or fear of, Congressional legislation or interference. The question then arises, whether Congress, which can exercise no jurisdiction over the relations of master and slave within the limits of the Union, and is bound to recognize and respect the rights and relations that validity exist under the constitutions and laws of the States, can deny the exercise of those rights, and prohibit the continuance of those relations within the Territories.

And the citation of state statutes prohibiting the immigration of slaves, and of the decisions of state courts enforcing the forfeiture of the master's title in accordance with their rule, only darkens the discussion. For the question is, have Congress the municipal sovereignty in the territories which the State Legislatures have derived from the authority of the people, and exercise in the States.

And this depends upon the construction of the article in the Constitution before referred to.

And, in my opinion, that clause confers no power upon Congress to dissolve the relations of the master and slave on the domain of the United States either within or without any of the States.

The 8th section of the Act of Congress of the 6th of March, 1820, did not, in my opinion, operate to determine the domestic condition and status of the plaintiff and his family during their sojourn in Minnesota Territory, or after their return to Missouri.

The question occurs as to the judgment to be given in this case. It appeared upon the trial that the plaintiff, in 1834, was in a state of slavery in Missouri, and he had been in Missouri for near fifteen years in that condition, when this suit was brought. Nor does it appear that he at any time possessed another state or condition, de facto. His claim to freedom depends upon his temporary elocation, from the domicil of his origin, in company with his master, to communities where the law of slavery did not prevail. My examination is confined to the case, as it was submitted upon uncontested evidence, upon appropriate issues to the jury, and upon the instructions given and refused by the court upon that evidence. My opinion is, that the opinion of the Circuit Court was correct upon all the claims involved in those issues, and that the verdict of

the jury was justified by the evidence and instructions.

The jury have returned that the plaintiff and his family are slaves.

Upon this record, it is apparent that this is not a controversy between citizens of different States; and that the plaintiff, at no period of the life which has been submitted to the view of the court, has had capacity to maintain a suit in the courts of the United States. And in so far as the argument of the Chief Justice upon the plea in abatement has a reference to the plaintiff or his family, in any of the conditions or circumstances of their lives as presented in the evidence, I concur in that portion of his opinion. I concur in the judgment which expresses the conclusion that the Circuit Court should not have rendered a general judgment.

The capacity of the plaintiff to sue is involved in the pleas in bar, and the verdict of the jury discloses an incapacity under the Constitution. Under the Constitution of the United States, his is an incapacity to sue in their courts, while, by the laws of Missouri, the operation of the verdict would be more extensive. I think it a safe conclusion to enforce the lesser disability imposed by the Constitution of the United States, and leave to the plaintiff all his rights in Missouri. I think the judgment should be affirmed on the ground that the Circuit Court had not jurisdiction, or that the case should be reversed and remanded that the suit may be dismissed.

Mr. Justice Catron:

The defendant pleaded to the jurisdiction of the Circuit Court, that the plaintiff was a negro of African blood; the descendant of Africans, who had been imported and sold in this country as slaves, and thus had no capacity as a citizen of Missouri to maintain a suit in the Circuit Court. The court sustained a demurrer to this plea, and a trial was had upon the pleas, of general issue, and also that the plaintiff and his family were slaves, belonging to the defendant. In this trial a verdict was given for the defendant.

The judgment of the Circuit Court upon the plea in abatement is not open, in my opinion, to examination in this court upon the plaintiff's writ.

The judgment was given for him conformably to the prayer or his demurrer. He cannot assign an error in such a judgment.

Tidd's Pr. 1163; 2 Williams' Saund. 46a; 2 Iredell, N. C. 87; 2 W. & S. 391.

Nor does the fact that the judgment was given on a plea to the jurisdiction, avoid the application of this rule.

Capron v. Van Noorden, 2 Cranch, 126; 6 Wend. 465; 7 Met. 598; 5 Pike, 1005.

The declaration discloses a case within the jurisdiction of the court—a controversy between citizens of different States. The plea in abatement, impugning these jurisdictional averments, was waived when the defendant answered to the declaration by pleas to the merits. The proceedings on that plea remain a part of the technical record, to show the history of the case, but are not open to the review of this court by a writ of error. The authorities are very conclusive on this point.

Shepherd v. Graves, 14 How. 505; *Bailey v. Dozier,* 6 How. 23; 1 Stewart (Ala.), 46; 10 Ben. Monroe (Ky.) 555; 2 Stew. (Ala.) 370, 443; 2 Scam. (Ill.) 78.

Nor can the court assume, as admitted facts, the averments of the plea from the confession of the demurrer. That confession was for a single object, and cannot be used for any other purpose than to test the validity of the plea. *Tompkins v. Ashby,* 1 Moo. & Mal. 32; 33 Me. 96, 100.

There being nothing in controversy here but the merits, I will proceed to discuss them.

The plaintiff claims to have acquired property in himself, and became free, by being kept in Illinois during two years.

The Constitution, laws, and policy, of Illinois, are somewhat peculiar respecting slavery. Unless the master becomes an inhabitant of that State, the slaves he takes there do not acquire their freedom; and if they return with their master to the slave State of his domicil, they cannot assert their freedom after their return. For the reasons and authorities on this point, I refer to the opinion of my brother Nelson with which I not only concur, but think his opinion is the most conclusive argument on the subject within my knowledge.

It is next insisted for the plaintiff, that his freedom (and that of his wife and eldest child) was obtained by force of the Act of Congress of 1820, usually known as the Missouri Compromise Act, which declares: "That in all that territory ceded by France to the United States, which lies north of thirty-six degrees

thirty minutes north latitude, slavery and involuntary servitude shall be, and are hereby forever prohibited."

From this prohibition, the Territory now constituting the State of Missouri was excepted; which exception to the stipulation gave it the designation of a compromise.

The first question presented on this Act is, whether Congress has power to make such compromise. For, if power was wanting, then no freedom could be acquired by the defendant under the Act.

That Congress has no authority to pass laws and bind men's rights beyond the powers conferred by the Constitution, is not open to controversy. But it is insisted that, by the Constitution, Congress has power to legislate for and govern the Territories of the United States, and that, by force of the power to govern, laws could be enacted, prohibiting slavery in any portion of the Louisiana Territory; and, of course, to abolish slavery in all parts of it, whilst it was, or is, governed as a Territory.

My opinion is, that Congress is vested with power to govern the Territories of the United States by force of the 3d section of the 4th article of the Constitution. And I will state my reasons for this opinion.

Almost every provision in that instrument has a history that must be understood, before the brief and sententious language employed can be comprehended in the relations its authors intended. We must bring before us the state of things presented to the Convention, and in regard to which it acted, when the compound provision was made, declaring: 1st. That "new States may be admitted by the Congress into this Union." 2d. "The Congress shall have power to dispose of and make all needful rules and regulations respecting the territory or other property belonging to the United States. And nothing in this Constitution shall be so construed as to prejudice any claims of the United States, or any particular State."

Having ascertained the historical facts giving rise to these provisions, the difficulty of arriving at the true meaning of the language employed will be greatly lessened.

The history of these facts is substantially as follows:

The King of Great Britain, by his proclamation of 1763, virtually claimed that the country west of the mountains had been conquered from France, and ceded to the Crown of Great Britain by the Treaty of Paris of that year, and he says: "We reserve it under our sovereignty, protection, and dominion, for the use of the Indians."

This country was conquered from the Crown of Great Britain, and surrendered to the United States by the Treaty of Peace of 1783. The colonial charters of Virginia, North Carolina and Georgia, included it. Other States set up pretensions of claim to some portions of the territory north of the Ohio, but they were of no value, as I suppose. 5 Wheat. 375.

As this vacant country had been won by the blood and treasure of all the States, those whose charters did not reach it, insisted that the country belonged to the States united, and that the land should be disposed of for the benefit of the whole; and to which end, the Western Territory should be ceded to the States united. The contest was stringent and angry, long before the Convention convened, and deeply agitated that body. As a matter of justice, and to quiet the controversy, Virginia consented to cede the country north of the Ohio as early as 1783; and in 1784 the deed of cession was executed, by her delegates in the Congress of the Confederation, conveying to the United States, in Congress assembled, for the benefit of said States, "all right, title and claim, as well of soil as of jurisdiction, which this Commonwealth hath to the territory or tract of country within the limits of the Virginia charter, situate, lying, and being to the northwest of the River Ohio." In 1787 (July 13), the Ordinance was passed by the old Congress to govern the Territory.

Massachusetts had ceded her pretension of claim to western territory in 1785, Connecticut hers in 1786, and New York had ceded hers. In August, 1787, South Carolina ceded to the Confederation her pretension of claim to territory west of that State. And North Carolina was expected to cede hers, which she did do, in April, 1790. And so Georgia was confidently expected to cede her large domain, now constituting the territory of the States of Alabama and Mississippi.

At the time the Constitution was under consideration, there had been ceded to the United States, or was shortly expected to be ceded, all the western country, from the British Canada line to Florida, and from the head of the Mississippi almost to its mouth, except that portion which now constitutes the State of Kentucky.

Although Virginia had conferred on the Congress of the Confederation power to govern the territory north of the Ohio, still, it cannot be denied, as I think, that power was wanting to admit a new State under the Articles of Confederation.

With these facts prominently before the Convention, they proposed to accomplish these ends:

1st. To give power to admit new States.

2d. To dispose of the public lands in the Territories, and such as might remain undisposed of in the new States after they were admitted.

And third, to give power to goven to different Territories as incipient States, not of the Union, and fit them for admission. No one in the Convention seems to have doubted that these power were necessary. As early as the third day of its session (May 29th), Edmund Randolph brought forward a set of resolutions containing nearly all the germs of the Constitution, the 10th of which is as follows:

"Resolved, That provision ought to be made for the admission of the States lawfully arising within the limits of the United States, whether from a voluntary junction of government and territory or otherwise, with the consent of a number of voices in the National Legislature less than the whole."

August 18th, Mr. Madison submitted, in order to be referred to the committee of detail, the following powers as proper to be added to those of the General Legislature:

"To dispose of the unappropriated lands of the United States." "To institute temporary governments for new States arising therein." 3 Madison Papers, 1353.

These, with the resolution, that a district for the location of the seat of government should be provided, and some others, were referred, without a dissent, to the committee of detail, to arrange and put them into satisfactory language.

Gouverneur Morris constructed the clauses, and combined the views of a majority on the two provisions, to admit new States; and second, to dispose of the public lands, and to govern the Territories, in the mean time, between the cessions of the States and the admission into the Union of new States arising in the ceded territory.

3 Madison Papers, 1456 to 1466.

It was hardly possible to separate the power "to make all needful rules and regulations" respecting the government of the territory and the disposition of the public lands.

North of the Ohio, Virginia conveyed the lands, and vested the jurisdiction in the thirteen original States, before the Constitution was formed. She had the sole title and sole sovereignty, and the same power to cede, on any terms she saw proper, that the King of England had to grant the Virginia Colonial Charter of 1609, or to grant the Charter of Pennsylvania to William Penn. The thirteen States, through their representatives and deputed ministers in the old Congress, had the same right to govern that Virginia had before the cession. Baldwin's constitutional Views, 90. And the 6th article of the Constitution adopted all engagements entered into by the Congress of the Confederation, as valid against the United States; and that the laws, made in pursuance of the new Constitution, to carry out this engagement, should be the supreme law of the land, and the judges bound thereby. To give the compact, and the Ordinance, which was part of it, full effect under the new government, the Act of August 7th, 1789, was passed, which declares, "Whereas in order that the Ordinance of the United States in Congress assembled, for the government of the territory northwest of the River Ohio, may have full effect, it is requisite that certain provisions should be made, so as to adapt the same to the present Constitution of the United States." It is then provided that the Governor and other offices should be appointed by the President, with the consent of the Senate; and be subject to removal, etc., in like manner that they were by the old Congress, whose functions had ceased.

By the powers to govern, given by the Constitution, those amendments to the Ordinance could be made, but Congress guardedly abstained from touching the compact of Virginia, further than to adapt it to the new Constitution.

It is due to myself to say, that it is asking much of a judge, who has for nearly twenty years been exercising jurisdiction, from the western Missouri line to the Rocky Mountains, and, on this understanding of the Constitution, inflicting the extreme penalty of death for crimes committed where the direct legislation of Congress was the only rule, to agree that he had been all the while acting in mistake, as an usurper.

More than sixty years have passed away since Congress has exercised power to govern the Territories, by its legislation directly, or by territorial charters, subject to repeal at all times, and it is now too late to call that power into question, if this court could disregard its own decisions; which it cannot do, as I think. It was held in the case of *Cross v. Harrison*, 16 How. 193, 194, that the sovereignty of California was in the United States, in virtue of the Constitution, by which power had been given to Congress to dispose of and make all needful rules and regulations respecting the territory or other property belonging to the United States, with the power to admit new States into the Union. That decision followed preceding ones, there cited. The question was then presented, how it was possible for the judicial mind to conceive that the United States Government, created solely by the Constitution, could, by a lawful treaty, acquire territory over which the acquiring power had no jurisdiction to hold and govern it, by force of the instrument under whose authority the country was acquired; and the foregoing was the conclusion of this court on the proposition. What was there announced, was most deliberately done, and with a purpose. The only question here is, as I think, how far the power of Congress is limited.

As to the Northwest Territory, Virginia had the right to abolish slavery there; and she did so agree in 1787, with the other States in the Congress of the Confederation, by assenting to and adopting the Ordinance of 1787, for the government of the Northwest Territory. She did this also by an act of her Legislature, passed afterwards, which was a treaty in fact.

Before the new Constitution was adopted, she had as much right to treat and agree as any European government had. And, having excluded slavery, the new government was bound by that engagement by Article six of the new Constitution. This only meant that slavery should not exist whilst the United States exercised the power of government, in the territorial form; for, when a State came in, it might do so, with or without slavery.

My opinion is, that Congress had no power, in face of the compact between Virginia and the twelve other States to force slavery into the

Northwest Territory, because there, it was bound to that "engagement," and could not break it.

In 1790, North Carolina ceded her western territory, now the State of Tennessee, and stipulated that the inhabitants thereof should enjoy all the privileges and advantages of the Ordinance for governing the territory north of the Ohio River, and that Congress should assume the government, and accept the cession, under the express conditions contained in the Ordinance: Provided, "That no regulation made, or to be made, by Congress, shall tend to emancipate slaves."

In 1802, Georgia ceded her western territory to the United States, with the provision that the Ordinance of 1787 should in all its parts extend to the territory ceded, "that article only excepted which forbids slavery." Congress had no more power to legislate slavery out from the North Carolina and Georgia cessions, than it had power to legislate slavery in, north of the Ohio. No power existed in Congress to legislate at all, affecting slavery, in either case. The inhabitants, as respected this description of property, stood protected, whilst they were governed by Congress, in like manner that they were protected before the cession was made and when they were respectively, parts of North Carolina and Georgia.

And how does the power of Congress stand west of the Mississippi River? The country there was acquired from France, by Treaty, in 1803. It declares, that the First Consul, in the name of the French Republic, doth hereby cede to the United States, in full sovereignty, the Colony or Province of Louisiana, with all the rights and appurtenances of the said Territory. And, by article 3d, that "the inhabitants of the ceded territory shall be incorporated in the Union of the United States, and admitted as soon as possible, according to the principles of the Federal Constitution, to the enjoyment of all the rights, advantages and immunities, of citizens of the United States; and, in the mean time, they shall be maintained and protected in the free enjoyment of their liberty, property, and the religion which they profess."

Louisiana was a Province where slavery was not only lawful, but where property in slaves was the most valuable of all personal property. The Province was ceded as a unit, with an equal right pertaining to its inhabitants, in every part thereof, to own slaves. It was, to a great extent, a vacant country, having in it few civilized inhabitants. No one portion of the Colony, of a proper size for a State of the Union, had a sufficient number of inhabitants to claim admission into the Union. To enable the United States to fulfill the Treaty, additional population was indispensable, and obviously desired with anxiety by both sides, so that the whole country should, as soon as possible, become States of the Union. And for this contemplated future population, the Treaty as expressly provided as it did for the inhabitants residing in the province when the Treaty was made. All these were to be protected "in the mean time;" that is to say, at all times, between the date of the Treaty and the time when the portion of the Territory where the inhabitants resided was admitted into the Union as a State.

At the date of the Treaty, each inhabitant had the right to the free enjoyment of his property, alike with his liberty and his religion, in every part of Louisiana; the Province then being one Country, he might go everywhere in it, and carry his liberty, property, and religion, with him, and in which he was to be maintained and protected, until he became a citizen of a State of the Union of the United States. This cannot be denied by the original inhabitants and their descendants. And, if it be true that immigrants were equally protected, it must follow that they can also stand on the Treaty.

The settled doctrine in the State courts of Louisiana is, that a French subject coming to the Orleans Territory, after the Treaty of 1803 was made, and before Louisiana was admitted into the Union, and being an inhabitant at the time of the admission, became a citizen of the United States by that Act; that he was one of the inhabitants contemplated by the 3d article of the Treaty, which referred to all the inhabitants embraced within the new State on it admission.

That this is the true construction, I have no doubt.

If power existed to draw a line at thirty-six degrees thirty minutes north, so Congress had equal power to draw the line on the thirtieth degree—that is, due west from the City of New Orleans—and to declare that north of that line slavery should never exist. Suppose this had been done before 1812, when Louisiana came into the Union, and the question of infraction of the Treaty had then been presented on the present assumption of power to prohibit slavery, who doubts what the decision of this court would have been on such an Act of Congress; yet, the difference between the supposed line, and that on thirty-six degrees thirty minutes north, is only in the degree of grossness presented by the lower line.

The Missouri compromise line of 1820 was very aggressive; it declared that slavery was abolished forever throughout a country reaching from the Mississippi River to the Pacific Ocean, stretching over thirty-two degrees of longitude, and twelve and a half degrees of latitude on its eastern side, sweeping over four fifths, to say no more, of the original Province of Louisiana.

That the United States Government stipulated in favor of the inhabitants to the extent here contended for has not been seriously denied, as far as I know; but the argument is, that Congress had authority to repeal the 3d article of the Treaty of 1803, in so far as it secured the right to hold slave property, in a portion of the ceded territory, leaving the right to exist in other parts. In other words, that Congress repeal the 3d article entirely, at its pleasure. This I deny.

The compacts with North Carolina and Georgia were Treaties also, and stood on the same footing of the Louisiana Treaty; on the assumption of power to repeal the one, it must have extended to all, and Congress could have excluded the slaveholder of North Carolina from the enjoyment of his lands in the Territory, now the State, of Tennessee, where the citizens of the mother State were the principal proprietors.

And so in the case of Georgia. Her citizens could have been refused the right to emigrate to the Mississippi or Alabama Territory, unless they left their most valuable and cherished property behind them.

The Constitution was framed in reference to facts then existing or likely to arise: the instrument looked to no theories of government. In the vigorous debates in the Convention, as reported by Mr. Madison and others, surrounding facts, and the condition and necessities of the country, gave rise to almost every provision; and among those facts, it was prominently true, that Congress dare not be intrusted with power to provide that, if North Carolina or Georgia ceded her western territory, the citizens of the State (in either case) could be prohibited, at the pleasure of Congress, from removing to their lands, then granted to a large extent, in the country likely

to be ceded, unless they left their slaves behind. That such an attempt, in the face of a population fresh from the war of the Revolution, and then engaged in war with the great confederacy of Indians, extending from the mouth of the Ohio to the Gulf of Mexico, would end in open revolt, all intelligent men knew.

In view of these facts, let us inquire how the question stands by the terms of the Constitution, aside from the Treaty. How it stood in public opinion when the Georgia cession was made, in 1802, is apparent from the fact that no guaranty was required by Georgia of the United States for the protection of slave property. The Federal Constitution was relied on, to secure the rights of Georgia and her citizens during the territorial condition of the country. She relied on the indisputable truths, that the States were by the Constitution made equals in political rights, and equals in the right to participate in the common property of all the States united, and held in trust for them. The Constitution having provided that "The citizens of each State shall be entitled to all privileges and immunities of citizens of the several States," the right to enjoy the territory as equals was reserved to the States, and to the citizens of the States, respectively. The cited clause is not that citizens of the United States shall have equal privileges in the Territories, but the citizens of each State shall come there in right of his State, and enjoy the common property. He secures his equality through the equality of his State, by virtue of that great fundamental condition of the Union—the equality of the States.

Congress cannot do indirectly what the Constitution prohibits directly. If the slaveholder is prohibited from going to the Territory with his slaves, who are parts of his family in name and in fact, it will follow that men owning lawful property in their own States, carrying with them the equality of their State to enjoy the common property, may be told, you cannot come here with your slaves, and he will be held out at the border. By this subterfuge, owners of slave property, to the amount of thousands of millions, might be almost as effectually excluded from removing into the Territory of Louisiana north of thirty-six degrees thirty minutes, as if the law declared that owners of slaves, as a class, should be excluded, even if their slaves were left behind.

Just as well might Congress have said to those of the North, you shall not introduce into the territory south of said line your cattle or horses, as the country is already overstocked; nor can you introduce your tools of trade, or machines as the policy of Congress is to encourage the culture of sugar and cotton, south of the line, and so to provide that the Northern people shall manufacture for those of the South, and barter for the staple articles slave labor produces. And thus the Northern farmer and mechanic would be held out, as the slaveholder was for thirty years, by the Missouri restriction.

If Congress could prohibit one species of property, lawful throughout Louisiana when it was acquired, and lawful in the State from whence it was brought, so Congress might exclude any or all property.

The case before us will illustrate the construction contended for. Dr. Emerson was a citizen of Missouri; he had an equal right to go to the Territory with every citizen of other States. This is undeniable, as I suppose. Scott was Dr. Emerson's lawful property in Missouri; he carried his Missouri title with him; and the precise question here is, whether Congress had the power to annul that title. It is idle to say, that if Congress could not defeat the title directly, that it might be done indirectly, by drawing a narrow circle around the slave population of Upper Louisiana, and declaring that if the slave went beyond it he should be free. Such assumption is mere evasion, and entitled to no consideration. And it is equally idle, to contend that because Congress has express power to regulate commerce among the Indian tribes, and to prohibit intercourse with the Indians, that therefore Dr. Emerson's title might be defeated within the country ceded by the Indians to the United States as early as 1805, and which embraces Fort Snelling. Am. State Papers, Vol. I. p. 734. We must meet the question whether Congress had the power to declare that a citizen of a State, carrying with him his equal rights, secured to him through his State, could be stripped of his goods and slaves, and be deprived of any participation in the common property. If this be the true meaning of the Constitution, equality of rights to enjoy a common country (equal to a thousand miles square) may be cut off by a geographical line, and a great portion of our citizens excluded from it.

Ingenious, indirect evasions of the Constitution have been attempted and defeated heretofore. In the *Passenger Cases*, 7 How. 283, the attempt was made to impose a tax on the masters, crews and passengers of vessels, the Constitution having prohibited a tax on the vessel itself; but this court held the attempt to be a mere evasion, and pronounced the tax illegal.

I admit that Virginia could, and lawfully did, prohibit slavery northwest of the Ohio, by her charter of cession, and that the Territory was taken by the United States with this condition imposed. I also admit that France could, by the Treaty of 1803, have prohibited slavery in any part of the ceded Territory, and imposed it on the United States as a fundamental condition of the cession, in the mean time, till new States were admitted into the Union.

I concur with Judge Baldwin, that federal power is exercised over all the territory within the United States, pursuant to the Constitution; and the conditions of the cession, whether it was a part of the original territory of a State of the Union, or of a foreign state, ceded by deed or treaty; the right of the United States in or over it depends on the contract of cession, which operates to incorporate as well the territory as its inhabitants into the Union.

Baldwin's Constitutional Views, 84.

My opinion is, that the 3d article of the Treaty of 1803, ceding Louisiana to the United States, stands protected by the Constitution, and cannot be repealed by Congress.

And, secondly, that the Act of 1820, known as the Missouri Compromise, violates the most leading feature of the Constitution—a feature on which the Union depends, and which secures to the respective States and their citizens an entire equality of rights, privileges and immunities.

On these grounds, I hold the Compromise Act to have been void; and consequently, that the plaintiff, Scott, can claim no benefit under it.

For the reasons above stated, I concur with my brother judges that the plaintiff, Scott, is a slave, and was so when this suit was brought.

Mr. Justice McLean, dissenting:

This case is before us on a writ of error from the Circuit Court for the District of Missouri.

An action of trespass was brought, which charges the defendant with an assault and imprisonment of the plaintiff, and also of Harriet Scott, his wife, Eliza and Lizzie, his two children, on the ground that they were his slaves, which was without right on his part, and against law.

The defendant filed a plea in abatement, "that said causes of action, and each and every of them, if any such accrued to the said Dred Scott accrued out of the jurisdiction of this court, and exclusively within the jurisdiction of the courts of the State of Missouri, for that, to wit: said plaintiff, Dred Scott, is not a citizen of the State of Missouri, as alleged in his declaration, because he is a negro of African descent, his ancestors were of pure African blood; and were brought into this country and sold as negro slaves; and this the said Sandford is ready to verify; wherefore he prays judgment whether the court can or will take further cognizance of the action aforesaid."

To this a demurrer was filed, which, on argument, was sustained by the court, the plea in abatement being held insufficient; the defendant was ruled to plead over. Under this rule he pleaded: 1. Not guilty; 2. That Dred Scott was a negro slave, the property of the defendant; and 3. That Harriet, the wife, and Eliza and Lizzie, the daughters of the plaintiff, were the lawful slaves of the defendant.

Issue was joined on the first plea, and replications of *de injuria* were filed to the other pleas.

The parties agreed to the following facts: in the year 1834, the plaintiff was a negro slave belonging to Dr. Emerson, who was a surgeon in the Army of the United States. In that year, Dr. Emerson took the plaintiff from the State of Missouri to the post of Rock Island, in the State of Illinois, and held him there as a slave until the month of April or May, 1836. At the time last mentioned, Dr. Emerson removed the plaintiff from Rock Island to the military post at Fort Snelling, situate on the west bank of the Mississippi River, in the Territory known as Upper Louisiana., acquired by the United States of France, and situate north of latitude thirty-six degrees thirty minutes north, and north of the State of Missouri. Dr. Emerson held the plaintiff in slavery, at Fort Snelling, from the last-mentioned date until the year 1838.

In the year 1835, Harriet, who is named in the second count of the plaintiff's declaration, was the negro slave of Major Taliaferro, who belonged to the Army of the United States. In that year, Major Taliaferro took Harriet to Fort Snelling, a military post situated as hereinbefore

stated, and kept her there as a slave until the year 1836, and then sold and delivered her as a slave, at Fort Snelling, unto Dr. Emerson, who held her in slavery, at that place, until the year 1838.

In the year 1836, the plaintiff and Harriet were married at Fort Snelling, with the consent of Dr. Emerson, who claimed to be their master and owner. Eliza and Lizzie, named in the third count of the plaintiff's declaration, are the fruit of that marriage. Eliza is about fourteen years old, and was born on board the steamboat Gipsey, north of the north line of the State of Missouri, and upon the River Mississippi. Lizzie is about seven years old, and was born in the State of Missouri, at the military post called Jefferson Barracks.

In the year 1838, Dr. Emerson removed the plaintiff and said Harriet and their daughter Eliza from Fort Snelling to the State of Missouri, where they have ever since resided.

Before the commencement of the suit, Dr. Emerson sold and conveyed the plaintiff, Harriet, Eliza and Lizzie, to the defendant, as slaves, and he has ever since claimed to hold them as slaves.

At the times mentioned in the plaintiff's declaration, the defendant, claiming to be the owner, laid his hands upon said plaintiff, Harriet, Eliza and Lizzie, and imprisoned them; doing in this respect, however, no more than he might lawfully do, if they were of right his slaves at such times.

In the first place, the plea to the jurisdiction is not before us, on this writ of error. A demurrer to the plea was sustained, which ruled the plea bad, and the defendant, on leave, pleaded over.

The decision on the demurrer was in favor of the plaintiff; and as the plaintiff prosecutes this writ of error, he does not complain of the decision on the demurrer. The defendant might have complained of this decision, as against him, and have prosecuted a writ of error, to reverse it. But as the case, under the instruction of the court to the jury, was decided in his favor, of course he had no ground of complaint.

But it is said, if the court, on looking at the record, shall clearly perceive that the Circuit Court had no jurisdiction, it is a ground for the dismissal of the case. This may be characterized as rather a sharp practice, and one which seldom, if ever, occurs. No case was cited in the argument as authority, and not a single case precisely in point is recollected in our reports. The pleadings do not show a want of jurisdiction. This want of jurisdiction can only be ascertained by a judgment on the demurrer to the special plea. No such case, it is believed, can be cited. But if this rule of practice is to be applied in this case, and the plaintiff in error is required to answer and maintain as well the points ruled in his favor, as to show the error of those ruled against him, he has more than an ordinary duty to perform. Under such circumstances, the want of jurisdiction in the Circuit Court must be so clear as not to admit of doubt. Now, the plea which raises the question of jurisdiction, in my judgment, is radically defective. The gravamen of the plea is this: "That the plaintiff is a negro of African descent, his ancestors being of pure African blood, and were brought into this country, and sold as negro slaves."

There is no averment in this plea which shows or conduces to show an inability in the plaintiff to sue in the Circuit Court. It does not allege that the plaintiff had his domicil in any other State, nor that he is not a free man in Missouri. He is averred to have had a negro ancestry, but this does not show that he is not a citizen of Missouri, within the meaning of the Act of Congress authorizing him to sue in the Circuit Court. It has never been held necessary, to constitute a citizen within the Act, that he should have the qualifications of an elector. Females and minors may sue in the Federal courts, and so may any individual who has a permanent domicil in the State under whose laws his rights are protected, and to which he owes allegiance.

Being born under our Constitution and laws, no naturalization is required, as one of foreign birth, to make him a citizen. The most general and appropriate definition of the term "citizen" is "a freeman." Being a freeman, and having his domicil in a State different from that of the defendant, he is a citizen within the Act of Congress, and the courts of the Union are open to him.

It has often been held, that the jurisdiction, as regards parties, can only be exercised between citizens of different States, and that a mere residence is not sufficient; but this has been said to distinguish a temporary from a permanent residence.

To constitute a good plea to the jurisdiction, it must negative those qualities and rights which enable an individual to sue in the Federal courts.

This has not been done; and on this ground the plea was defective, and the demurrer was properly sustained. No implication can aid a plea in abatement or in bar; it must be complete in itself; the facts stated, if true, must abate or bar the right of the plaintiff to sue. This is not the character of the above plea. The facts stated, if admitted, are not inconsistent with other facts, which may be presumed, and which bring the plaintiff within the Act of Congress.

The pleader has not the boldness to allege that the plaintiff is a slave, as that would assume against him the matter in controversy, and embrace the entire merits of the case in a plea to the jurisdiction. But beyond the facts set out in the plea, the court, to sustain it, must assume the plaintiff to be a slave, which is decisive on the merits. This is a short and an effectual mode of deciding the cause; but I am yet to learn that it is sanctioned by any known rule of pleading.

The defendant's counsel complain, that if the court take jurisdiction on the ground that the plaintiff is free, the assumption is against the right of the master. This argument is easily answered. In the first place, the plea does not show him to be a slave; it does not follow that a man is not free whose ancestors were slaves. The reports of the Supreme Court of Missouri show that this assumption has many exceptions; and there is no averment in the plea that the plaintiff is not within them.

By all the rules of pleading, this is a fatal defect in the plea. If there be doubt, what rule of construction has been established in the slave States? In *Jacob v. Sharp*, Meigs' Tenn. 114, the court held, when there was doubt as to the construction of a will which emancipated a slave, "it must be construed to be subordinate to the higher and more important right of freedom."

No injustice can result to the master, from an exercise of jurisdiction in this cause. Such a decision does not in any degree affect the merits of the case; it only enables the plaintiff to assert his claims to freedom before this tribunal. If the jurisdiction be ruled against him, on the ground that he is a slave, it is decisive of his fate.

It has been argued that, if a colored person be made a citizen of a State, he cannot sue in the Federal court. The Constitution declares that federal jurisdiction "may be exercised between citizens of different States," and the same is provided in the Act of 1789. The above argument is properly met, by saying that the Constitution was intended to be a practical instrument; and where its language is too plain to be misunderstood, the argument ends.

In *Chirac v. Chirac*, 2 Wheat. 261, 15 U.S., this court says: "That the power of naturalization is exclusively in Congress does not seem to be, and certainly ought not to be, controverted." No person can legally be made a citizen of a State, and consequently a citizen of the United States, of foreign birth, unless he be naturalized under the Acts of Congress. Congress has power "to establish a uniform rule of naturalization."

It is a power which belongs exclusively to Congress, as intimately connected with our federal relations. A State may authorize foreigners to hold real estate within its jurisdiction, but it has no power to naturalize foreigners, and give them the rights of citizens. Such a right is opposed to the Acts of Congress on the subject of naturalization, and subversive of the federal powers. I regret that any countenance should be given from this bench to a practice like this in some of the States, which has no warrant in the Constitution.

In the argument, it was said that a colored citizen would not be an agreeable member of society. This is more a matter of taste than of law. Several of the States have admitted persons of color to the right of suffrage, and in this view have recognized them as citizens; and this has been done in the slave as well as the free States. On the question of citizenship, it must be admitted that we have not been very fastidious. Under the late Treaty with Mexico, we have made citizens of all grades, combinations, and colors. The same was done in the admission of Louisiana and Florida. No one ever doubted, and no court ever held, that the people of these Territories did not become citizens under the Treaty. They have exercised all the rights of citizens, without being naturalized under the Acts of Congress.

There are several important principles involved in this case, which have been argued, and which may be considered under the following heads:

1. The locality of slavery, as settled by this court and the courts of the States.

2. The relation which the Federal Government bears to slavery in the States.

3. The power of Congress to establish territorial governments, and to prohibit the introduction of slavery therein.

4. The effect of taking slaves into a new State or Territory, and so holding them, where slavery is prohibited.

5. Whether the return of a slave under the control of his master, after being entitled to his freedom, reduces him to his former condition.

6. Are the decisions of the Supreme Court of Missouri, on the questions before us, binding on this court, within the rule adopted?

In the course of my judicial duties, I have had occasion to consider and decide several of the above points.

1. As to the locality of slavery. The civil law throughout the Continent of Europe, it is believed, without an exception, is, that slavery can exist only within the territory where it is established; and that, if a slave escapes, or is carried beyond such territory, his master cannot reclaim him, unless by virtue of some express stipulations.

Grotius, lib. 2, chap. 15, 5, 1; lib. 10. chap. 10 2, 1; Wicqueposts Ambassador, lib. 1, p. 418; 4 Martin, 385; case of *The Creole in the House of Lords*, 1842; 1 Phillimore on International Law, 316, 335.

There is no nation in Europe which considers itself bound to return to his master a fugitive slave, under the civil law or the law of nations. On the contrary, the slave is held to be free where there is no treaty obligation, or compact in some other form, to return him to his master. The Roman law did not allow freedom to be sold. An ambassador or any other public functionary could not take a slave to France, Spain, or any other country of Europe, without emancipating him. A number of slaves escaped from a Florida plantation, and were received on board of ship by Admiral Cochrane. By the King's Bench, they were held to be free. 2 B. & C. 440.

In the great and leading case of *Prigg v. The State of Pennsylvania*, 16 Pet. 594, 41 U.S., this court say that, by the general law of nations, no nation is bound to recognize the state of slavery, as found within its territorial dominions, where it is in opposition to its own policy and institutions, in favor of the subjects of other nations where slavery is organized. If it does it, it is as a matter of comity, and not as a matter of international right. The state of slavery is deemed to be a mere municipal regulation, founded upon and limited to the range of the territorial laws. This was fully recognized in Somersett's case, Lafft's

Rep. 1, 20 Howell's State Trials, 79, which was decided before the American Revolution.

There was some contrariety of opinion among the judges on certain points ruled in Prigg's case, but there was none in regard to the great principle, that slavery is limited to the range of the laws under which it is sanctioned.

No case in England appears to have been more thoroughly examined than that of Somersett. The judgment pronounced by Lord Mansfield was the judgment of the Court of King's Bench. The cause was argued at great length, and with great ability, by Hargrave and others, who stood among the most eminent counsel in England. It was held under advisement from term to term, and a due sense of its importance was felt and expressed by the Bench.

In giving the opinion of the court, Lord Mansfield said:

"The state of slavery is of such a nature that it is incapable of being introduced on any reasons, moral or political, but only by positive law, which preserves its force long after the reasons, occasion, and time itself, from whence it was created, is erased from the memory; it is of a nature that nothing can be suffered to support it but positive law."

He referred to the contrary opinion of Lord Hardwicke, in October, 1749, as Chancellor: "That he and Lord Talbot, when Attorney and Solicitor-General, were of opinion that no such claim, as here presented, for freedom, was valid."

The weight of this decision is sought to be impaired, from the terms in which it was described by the exuberant imagination of Curran. The words of Lord Mansfield, in giving the opinion of the court, were such as were fit to be used by a great judge, in a most important case. It is a sufficient answer to all objections to that judgement, that it was pronounced before the Revolution, and that it was considered by this court as the highest authority. For near a century, the decision in Somersett's case has remained the law of England. The case of *The Slave Grace*, decided by Lord Stowell in 1827, does not, as has been supposed, overrule the judgment of Lord Mansfield. Lord Stowell held that, during the residence of the slave in England, "No dominion, authority, or coercion, can be exercised over him." Under another head, I shall have occasion to examine the opinion in the case of Grace.

To the position, that slavery can only exist except under the authority of law, it is objected, that in few if in any instances has it been established by statutory enactment. This is no answer to the doctrine laid down by the court. Almost all the principles of the common law had their foundation in usage. Slavery was introduced into the Colonies of this country by Great Britain at an early period of their history, and it was protected and cherished, until it became incorporated into the colonial policy. It is immaterial whether a system of slavery was introduced by express law, or otherwise, if it have the authority of law. There is no slave state where the institution is not recognized and protected by statutory enactments and judicial decisions. Slaves are made property by the laws of the slave States, and as such are liable to the claims of creditors; they descend to heirs, are taxed, and in the South they are a subject of commerce.

In the case of *Rankin v. Lydia*, 2. A. K. Marsh, 467, Judge Mills, speaking for the Court of Appeals of Kentucky, says: "In deciding the question (of slavery), we disclaim the influence of the general principles of liberty, which we all admire, and conceive it ought to be decided by the law as it is, and not as it ought to be. Slavery is sanctioned by the laws of this State, and the right to hold slaves under our municipay regulations is unquestionable. But we view this as a right existing by positive law of a municipal character, without foundation in the law of nature, or the unwritten and common law."

I will now consider the relation which the Federal Government bears to slavery in the States:

Slavery is emphatically a state institution. In the 9th section of the 1st article of the Constitution, it is provided "that the migration or importation of such persons as any of the States now existing shall think proper to admit, shall not be prohibited by the Congress prior to the year 1808, but a tax or duty may be imposed on such importation, not exceeding ten dollars for each."

In the Convention, it was proposed by a committee of eleven to limit the importation of slaves to the year 1800, when Mr. Pinckney moved to extend the time to the year 1808. This motion was carried—New Hampshire, Massachusetts, Connecticut, Maryland, North Carolina, South Carolina and Georgia voting in the affirmative; and New Jersey, Pennsylvania and Virginia, in the negative. In opposition to the motion, Mr. Madison said: "Twenty years will produce all the mischief that can be apprehended from the liberty to import slaves; so long a term will be more dishonorable to the American character than to say nothing about it in the Constitution." Madison Papers.

The provision in regard to the slave trade shows clearly that Congress considered slavery a state institution, to be continued and regulated by its individual sovereignty; and to conciliate that interest, the slave trade was continued twenty years, not as a general measure, but for the "benefit of such States as shall think proper to encourage it."

In the case of *Groves v. Slaughter*, 15 Pet. 449, 40 U.S. Messrs. Clay and Webster contended that, under the commercial power, Congress had a right to regulate the slave trade among the several States, but the court held that Congress had no power to interfere with slavery as it exists in the States, or to regulate what is called the slave trade among them. If this trade were subject to the commercial power, it would follow that Congress could abolish or establish slavery in every State of the Union.

The only connection which the Federal Government holds with slaves in a State, arises from that provision of the Constitution which declares that "No person held to service in one State, under the laws thereof, escaping into another, shall, in consequence of any law or regulation therein, be discharged from such service or labor, but shall be delivered up, on claim of the party to whom such service or labor may be due."

This being a fundamental law of the Federal Government, it rests mainly for its execution, as has been held, on the judicial power of the Union; and so far as the rendition of fugitives from labor has become a subject of judicial action, the federal obligation has been faithfully discharged.

In the formation of the Federal Constitution, care was taken to confer no power on the Federal Government, to interfere with this institution in the States. In the provision respecting the slave trade, in fixing the ratio of representation, and providing for the reclamation of fugitives from labor, slaves were referred to as persons, and in no other respect are they considered in the Constitution.

We need not refer to the mercenary spirit which introduced the infamous traffic in slaves, to show the degradation of negro slavery in our country. This system was imposed upon our colonial settlements by the mother country, and it is due to truth to say that the commercial Colonies and States were chiefly engaged in the traffic. But we know as a historical fact, that James Madison, that great and good man, a leading member in the Federal Convention, was solicitous to guard the language of that instrument so as not to convey the idea that there could be property in man.

I prefer the lights of Madison, Hamilton, and Jay, as a means of construing the Constitution in all its bearings, rather than to look behind that period, into a traffic which is now declared to be piracy, and punished with death by Christian nations. I do not like to draw the sources of our domestic relations from so dark a ground. Our independence was a great epoch in the history of freedom; and while I admit the government was not made especially for the colored race, yet many of them were citizens of the New England States, and exercised the rights of suffrage when the Constitution was adopted, and it was not doubted by any intelligent person that its tendencies would greatly ameliorate their condition.

Many of the States, on the adoption of the Constitution, or shortly afterward, took measures to abolish slavery within their respective jurisdictions; and it is a well-known fact that a belief was cherished by the leading men, South as well as North, that the institution of slavery would gradually decline, until it would become extinct. The increased value of slave labor, in the culture of cotton and sugar, prevented the realization of this expectation. Like all other communities and states, the South were influenced by what they considered to be their own interests.

But if we are to turn our attention to the dark ages of the world, why confine our view to colored slavery? On the same principles white men were made slaves. All slavery has its origin in power, and is against right.

The power of Congress to establish territorial governments, and to prohibit the introduction of slavery therein, is the next point to be considered.

After the cession of western territory by Virginia and other States, to the United States,

SLAVERY

DRED SCOTT V.
SANDFORD

the public attention was directed to the best mode of disposing of it for the general benefit.

While is attendance on the Federal Convention, Mr. Madison, in a letter to Edmund Randolph, dated the 22d April, 1787, says: "Congress are deliberating on the plan most eligible for disposing of the western territory not yet surveyed. Some alteration will probably be made in the ordinance on that subject." And in the same letter he says: "The inhabitants of the Illinois complain of the land jobbers, etc., who are purchasing titles among them. Those of St. Vincent's complain of the defective criminal and civil justice among them, as well as of military protection." And on the next day he writes to Mr. Jefferson: "The government of the settlements on the Illinois and Wabash is a subject very perplexing in itself, and rendered more so by our ignorance of the many circumstances on which a right judgment depends. The inhabitants at those places claim protection against the savages, and some provision for both civil and criminal justice."

In May, 1787, Mr. Edmund Randolph submitted to the Federal Convention certain propositions, as the basis of a Federal Government, among which was the following:

"Resolved, that provision ought to be made for the admission of States lawfully arising within the limits of the United States, whether from a voluntary junction of government and territory or otherwise, with the consent of a number of voices in the National Legislature less that the whole."

Afterward, Mr. Madison submitted to the Convention, in order to be referred to the committee of detail, the following powers, as proper to be added to those of general legislation: "To dispose of the unappropriated lands of the United States. To institute temporary governments for new States arising therein. To regulate affairs with the Indians, as well within as without the limits of the United States."

Other propositions were made in reference to the same subjects, which it would be tedious to enumerate. Mr. Gouverneur Morris proposed the following:

"The Legislature shall have power to dispose of and make all needful rules and regulations respecting the territory or other property belonging to the United States; and nothing in this Constitution contained shall be so construed as to prejudice any claims either of the United States or of any particular State."

This was adopted as a part of the Constitution, with two verbal alterations—Congress was substituted for Legislature, and the word "either" was stricken out.

In the organization of the new government, but little revenue for a series of years was expected from commerce. The public lands were considered as the principal resource of the country for the payment of the Revolutionary debt. Direct taxation was the means relied on to pay the current expenses of the government. The short period that occurred between the cession of western lands to the Federal Government by Virginia and other States, and the adoption of the Constitution, was sufficient to show the necessity of a proper land system and a temporary government. This was clearly seen by propositions and remarks in the Federal Convention, some of which are above cited, by the passage of the Ordinance of 1787, and the adoption of that instrument by Congress, under the Constitution, which gave to it validity.

It will be recollected that the deed of cession of western territory was made to the United States by Virginia in 1784, and that it required the territory ceded to be laid out into States, that the land should be disposed of for the common benefit of the States, and that all right, title, and claim, as well of soil as of jurisdiction, were ceded; and this was the form of cession from other States.

On the 13th of July, the Ordinance of 1787 was passed, "for the government of the United States territory northwest of the River Ohio," with but one dissenting vote. This instrument provided there should be organized in the territory not less than three, nor more than five, States, designating their boundaries. It was passed while the Federal Convention was in session, about two months before the Constitution was adopted by the Conventions. The members of the Convention must, therefore, have been well acquainted with the provisions of the Ordinance. It provided for a temporary government, as initiatory to the formation of state governments. Slavery was prohibited in the territory.

Can anyone suppose that the eminent men of the Federal Convention could have overlooked or neglected a matter so vitally important to the country, in the organization of temporary governments for the vast territory northwest of the River Ohio? In the 3d section of the 4th article of the Constitution, they did make provision for the admission of new States, the sale of the public lands, and the temporary government of the territory. Without a temporary government, new States could not have been formed nor could the public lands have been sold.

If the 3d section were before us now for consideration for the first time, under the facts stated, I could not hesitate to say there was adequate legislative power given in it. The power to make all needful rules and regulations is a power to legislate. This no one will controvert, as Congress cannot make "rules and regulations," except by legislation. But it is argued that the word "territory" is used as synonymous with the word "land"; and that the rules and regulations of Congress are limited to the disposition of lands and other property belonging to the United States. That this is not the true construction of the section, appears from the fact that in the first line of the section "the power to dispose of the public lands" is given expressly, and, in addition, to make all needful rules and regulations. The power to dispose of it is complete in itself, and requires nothing more. It authorizes Congress to use the proper means within its discretion, and any further provision for this purpose would be a useless verbiage. As a composition, the Constitution is remarkably free from such a charge.

In the discussion of the power of Congress to govern a territory, in the case of *The Atlantic Insurance Company v. Canter*, 1 Pet. 511; 7 Curt. 685, Chief Justice Marshall, speaking for the court, said, in regard to the people of Florida, "they do not, however, participate in political power; they do not share in the government till Florida shall become a state; in the mean time, Florida continues to be a territory of the United States, governed by virtue of that clause in the Constitution which empowers Congress 'to make all needful rules and regulations respecting the territory or other property belonging to the United States.'"

And he adds, "perhaps the power of governing a territory belonging to the United States, which has not, by becoming a state, acquired the means of self-government, may result necessarily from the fact that it is not within the jurisdiction of any particular State, and is within the

power and jurisdiction of the United States. The right to govern may be the inevitable consequence of the right to acquire territory; whichever may be the source whence the power is derived, the possession of it is unquestioned." And in the close of the opinion, the court say, "in legislating for them [the territories], Congress exercises the combined powers of the general and state governments."

Some consider the opinion to be loose and inconclusive; others that it is obiter dicta; and the last sentence is objected to as recognizing absolute power in Congress over Territories. The learned and eloquent Wirt, who, in the argument of a cause before the court, had occasion to cite a few sentences from an opinion of the Chief Justice, observed, "no one can mistake the style, the words so completely match the thought."

I can see no want of precision in the language of the Chief Justice; his meaning cannot be mistaken. He states, first, the 3d section as giving power to Congress to govern the territories, and two other grounds from which the power may also be implied. The objection seems to be, that the Chief Justice did not say which of the grounds stated he considered the source of the power. He did not specifically state this, but he did say, "whichever may be the source whence the power is derived, the possession of it is unquestioned." No opinion of the court could have been expressed with a stronger emphasis; the power in Congress is unquestioned. But those who have undertaken to criticise the opinion, consider it without authority, because the Chief Justice did not designate specially the power. This is a singular objection. If the power be unquestioned, it can be a matter of no importance on which ground it is exercised.

The opinion clearly was not *obiter dicta*. The turning point in the case was, whether Congress had power to authorize the Territorial Legislature of Florida to pass the law under which the Territorial Court was established, whose decree was brought before this court for revision. The power of Congress, therefore, was the point in issue.

The word "territory," according to Worcester means "land, country, a district of country, under a temporary government." The words "territory or other property," as used, do imply, from the use of the pronoun other, that territory was used as descriptive of land; but does it follow that it was not used also as descriptive of a district of country? In both of these senses it belonged to the United States—as land, for the purpose of sale; as territory, for the purpose of government.

But, if it be admitted that the word "territory" as used means land, and nothing but land, the power of Congress to organize a temporary government is clear. It has power to make all needful regulations respecting the public lands, and the extent of those "needful regulations" depends upon the direction of Congress, where the means are appropriate to the end, and do not conflict with any of the prohibitions of the Constitution. If a temporary government be deemed needful, necessary, requisite, or is wanted, Congress has power to establish it. This court says, in *McCulloch v. The State of Maryland*, 4 Wheat. 316 "If a certain means to carry into effect any of the powers expressly given by the Constitution to the government of the Union be an appropriate measure, not prohibited by the Constitution, the degree of its necessity is a question of legislative discretion, not of judicial cognizance.

The power to establish post offices and post roads gives power to Congress to make contracts for the transportation of the mail, and to punish all who commit depredations upon it in its transit, or at its places of distribution. Congress has power to regulate commerce, and, in the exercise of its discretion, to lay an embargo, which suspends commerce; so under the same power, harbors, lighthouses, breakwaters, etc., are constructed.

Did Chief Justice Marshall, in saying that Congress governed a Territory, by exercising the combined powers of the federal and state governments, refer to unlimited discretion? A government which can make white men slaves? Surely, such a remark in the argument must have been inadvertently uttered. On the contrary, there is no power in the Constitution by which Congress can make either white or black men slaves. In organizing the government of a territory, Congress is limited to means appropriate to the attainment of the constitutional object. No powers can be exercised which are prohibited by the Constitution, or which are contrary to its spirit; so that, whether the object may be the protection of the persons and property of purchasers of the public lands, or of communities who have been annexed to the Union by conquest or purchase, they are initiatory to the

establishment of state governments, and no more power can be claimed or exercised, than is necessary to the attainment of the end. This is the limitation of all the federal powers.

But Congress has no power to regulate the internal concerns of a State, as of a Territory; consequently, in providing for the government of a Territory, to some extent, the combined powers of the federal and state governments are necessarily exercised.

If Congress should deem slaves or free colored persons injurious to the population of a free Territory, as conducing to lessen the value of the public lands, or on any other ground connected with the public interest, they have the power to prohibit them from becoming settlers in it. This can be sustained on the ground of a sound national policy, which is so clearly shown in our history by practical results, that it would seem no considerate individual can question it. And, as regards any unfairness of such a policy to our Southern brethren, as urged in the argument, it is only necessary to say that, with one fourth of the federal population of the Union, they have in the slave States a larger extent of fertile territory than is included in the free States; and it is submitted, if masters of slaves be restricted from bringing them into free territory, that the restriction on the free citizens of non-slaveholding States, by bringing slaves into free territory, is four times greater than that complained of by the South. But, not only so; some three or four hundred thousand holders of slaves, by bringing them into free territory, impose a restriction on twenty millions of the free States. The repugnancy to slavery would probably prevent fifty or a hundred freemen from settling in a slave Territory, where one slaveholder would be prevented from settling in a free Territory.

This remark is made in answer to the argument urged, that a prohibition of slavery in the free Territories is inconsistent with the continuance of the Union. Where a territorial government is established in a slave Territory, it has uniformly remained in that condition until the people form a State constitution; the same course where the Territory is free, both parties acting in good faith, would be attended with satisfactory results.

The sovereignty of the Federal Government extends to the entire limits of our territory. Should any foreign power invade our jurisdiction, it would be repelled. There is a law of Congress to punish our citizens for crimes committed in districts of country where there is no organized government. Criminals are brought to certain Territories or States, designated in the law, for punishment. Death has been inflicted in Arkansas and in Missouri, on individuals, for murders committed beyond the limit of any organized Territory or State; and no one doubts that such a jurisdiction was rightfully exercised. If there be a right to acquire territory, there necessarily must be an implied power to govern it. When the military force of the Union shall conquer a country, may not Congress provide for the government of such country? This would be an implied power essential to the acquisition of new territory. This power has been exercised, without doubt of its constitutionality on territory acquired by conquest and purchases.

And when there is a large district of country within the United States and not within any state government, if it be necessary to establish a temporary government to carry out a power expressly vested in Congress—as the disposition of the public lands—may not such government be instituted by Congress? How do we read the Constitution? Is it not a practical instrument?

In such cases, no implication of a power can arise which is inhibited by the Constitution, or which may be against the theory of its construction. As my opinion rests on the 3d section, these remarks are made as an intimation that the power to establish a temporary government may arise, also, on the other two grounds stated in the opinion of the court in the insurance case, without weakening the 3d section

I would here simply remark, that the Constitution was formed for our whole country. An expansion or contraction of our territory required no change in the fundamental law. When we consider the men who laid the foundation of our government and carried it into operation, the men who occupied the Bench, who filled the halls of legislation and the Chief Magistracy, it would seem, if any question could be settled clear of all doubt, it was the power of Congress to establish territorial governments. Slavery was prohibited in the entire Northwestern Territory, with the approbation of leading men, South and North; but this prohibition was not retained when this Ordinance was adopted for the government of southern Territories, where slavery existed. In a late

republication of a letter of Mr. Madison, dated November 27, 1819, speaking of this power of Congress to prohibit slavery in a Territory, he infers there is no such power, from the fact that it has not been exercised. This is not a very satisfactory argument against any power, as there are but few, if any subjects on which the constitutional powers of Congress are exhausted. It is true, as Mr. Madison states, that Congress, in the Act to establish a government in the Mississippi Territory, prohibited the importation of slaves into it from foreign parts; but it is equally true, that in the Act erecting Louisiana into two Territories, Congress declared, "it shall not be lawful for any person to bring into Orleans Territory, from any port or place within the limits of the United States, any slave which shall have been imported, except by a citizen of the United States who settles in the Territory, under the penalty of the freedom of such slave." The inference of Mr. Madison, therefore, against the power of Congress, is of no force, as it was founded on a fact supposed, which did not exist.

It is refreshing to turn to the early incidents of our history, and learn wisdom from the acts of the great men who have gone to their account. I refer to a report in the House of Representatives, by John Randolph, of Roanoke, as chairman of a committee, in March, 1803—fifty-four years ago. From the Convention held at Vincennes, in Indiana, by their president, and from the people of the Territory, a petition was presented to Congress, praying the suspension of the provision which prohibited slavery in that Territory. The report stated "that the rapid population of the State of Ohio sufficiently evinces, in the opinion of your committee, that the labor of slaves is not necessary to promote the growth and settlement of colonies in that region. That this labor, demonstrably the dearest of any, can only be employed to advantage in the cultivation of products more valuable than any known to that quarter of the United States; that the committee deem it highly dangerous and inexpedient to impair a provision wisely calculated to promote the happiness and prosperity of the Northwestern country, and to give strength and security to that extensive frontier. In the salutary operation of this sagacious and benevolent restraint, it is believed that the inhabitants will, at no very distant day, find ample remuneration for a temporary privation of labor and of emigration."

SLAVERY

DRED SCOTT V. SANDFORD

SLAVERY

DRED SCOTT V.
SANDFORD

1 vol. State Papers, Public Lands, 160.

The judicial mind of this country, State and Federal, has agreed on no subject, within its legitimate action, with equal unanimity, as on the power of Congress to establish territorial governments. No court, State or Federal, no judge or statesman, is known to have had any doubts on this question for nearly sixty years after the power was exercised. Such governments have been established from the sources of the Ohio to the Gulf of Mexico, extending to the Lakes on the north and the Pacific Ocean on the west, and from the lines of Georgia to Texas.

Great interests have grown up under the territorial laws over a country more than five times greater in extent than the original thirteen States; and these interests, corporate or otherwise, have been cherished and consolidated by a benign policy, without anyone supposing the law-making power had united with the judiciary, under the universal sanction of the whole country, to usurp a jurisdiction which did not belong to them. Such as discovery at this late date is more extraordinary than anything which has occurred in the judicial history of this or any other country. Texas, under a previous organization, was admitted as a State; but no State can be admitted into the Union which has not been organized under some form of government. Without temporary governments, our public lands could not have been sold, nor our wilderness reduced to cultivation, and the population protected; nor could our flourishing States, west and south, have been formed.

What do the lessons of wisdom and experience teach, under such circumstances, if the new light, which has so suddenly and unexpectedly burst upon us, be true? Acquiescence; acquiescence under a settled construction of the Constitution for sixty years, though it may be erroneous; which has secured to the country an advancement and prosperity beyond the power of computation.

An act of James Madison, when President, forcibly illustrates this policy. He had made up his opinion that Congress had no power under the Constitution to establish a National Bank. In 1815, Congress passed a bill to establish a bank. He vetoed the bill, on objections other than constitutional. In his message, he speaks as a wise statesman and Chief Magistrate, as follows:

"Waiving the question of the constitutional authority of the Legislature to establish an incorporated bank, as being precluded, in my judgement, by the repeated recognitions under varied circumstances of the validity of such an institution, in acts of the Legislature, Executive, and Judicial branches of the Government, accompanied by indications, in different modes, of a concurrence of the general will of the nation."

Has this impressive lesson of practical wisdom become lost to the present generation?

If the great and fundamental principles of our Government are never to be settled, there can be no lasting prosperity. The Constitution will become a floating waif on the billows of popular excitement.

The prohibition of slavery north of thirty-six degrees thirty minutes, and of the State of Missouri, contained in the Act admitting that State into the Union, was passed by a vote of 134, in the House of Representatives, to 42. Before Mr. Monroe signed the Act, it was submitted by him to his Cabinet, and they held the restriction of slavery in a Territory to be within the constitutional powers of Congress. It would be singular, if in 1804 Congress had power to prohibit the introduction of slaves in Orleans Territory from any other part of the Union, under the penalty of freedom to the slave, if the same power embodied in the Missouri Compromise, could not be exercised in 1820.

But this law of Congress, which prohibits slavery north of Missouri and of thirty-six degrees thirty minutes, is declared to have been null and void by my brethren. And this opinion is founded mainly, as I understand, on the distinction drawn between the Ordinance of 1787 and the Missouri compromise line. In what does the distinction consist? The Ordinance, it is said, was a compact entered into by the confederated States before the adoption of the Constitution; and that in the cession of territory, authority was given to establish a territorial government.

It is clear that the Ordinance did not go into operation by virtue of the authority of the Confederation, but by reason of its modification and adoption by Congress under the Constitution. It seems to be supposed, in the opinion of the court, that the articles of cession placed it on a different footing from Territories subsequently acquired. I am unable to perceive the force of this distinction. That the Ordinance was intended for the government of the Northwestern Territory, and was limited to such Territory, is admitted. It was extended to southern

Territories, with modifications, by Acts of Congress, and to some northern Territories. But the Ordinance was made valid by the Act of Congress, and without such Act could have been of no force. It rested for its validity on the Act of Congress, the same, in my opinion, as the Missouri compromise line.

If Congress may establish a territorial government in the exercise of its discretion, it is a clear principle that a court cannot control that discretion. This being the case, I do not see on what ground the Act is held to be void. It did not purport to forfeit property, or take it for public purposes. It only prohibited slavery; in doing which, it followed the Ordinance of 1787.

I will now consider the fourth head, which is: "The effect of taking slaves into a State or Territory, and so holding them, where slavery is prohibited."

If the principle laid down in the case of *Prigg v. The State of Pennsylvania* is to be maintained, and it is certainly to be maintained until overruled, as a law of this court, there can be no difficulty on this point. In that case, the court says: "The state of slavery is deemed to be a mere municipal regulation, founded upon and limited to the range of the territorial laws." If this be so, slavery can exist nowhere except under the authority of law, founded on usage having the force of law, or by statutory recognition. And the court further says: "It is manifest, from this consideration, that if the Constitution had not contained the clause requiring the rendition of fugitives from labor, every non-slaveholding State in the Union would have been at liberty to have declared free all runaway slaves coming within its limits, and to have given them entire immunity and protection against the claims of the masters."

Now, if a slave abscond, he may be reclaimed, but if he accompany his master into a State or Territory where slavery is prohibited, such slave cannot be said to have left the service of his master where his services were legalized. And if slavery be limited to the range of the territorial laws, how can the slave be coerced to serve in a State or Territory, not only without the authority of law, but against its express provisions? What gives the master the right to control the will of his slave? The local law, which exists in some form. But where there is no such law, can the master control the will of the slave by force? Where no slavery exists, the presumption,

without regard to color, is in favor of freedom. Under such a jurisdiction, may the colored man be levied on as the property of his master by a creditor? On the decease of the master, does the slave descend to his heirs as property? Can the master sell him? Any one or all of these acts may be done to the slave, where he is legally held to service. But where the law does not confer this power, it cannot be exercised.

Lord Mansfield held that a slave brought into England was free. Lord Stowell agreed with Lord Mansfield in this respect, and that the slave could not be coerced in England; but on her voluntary return to Antigua, the place of her slave domicil, her former status attached. The law of England did not prohibit slavery, but did not authorize it. The jurisdiction which prohibits slavery is much stronger in behalf of the slave within it, than where it only does not authorize it.

By virtue of what law is it, that a master may take his slave into free territory, and exact from him the duties of a slave? The law of the territory does not sanction it. No authority can be claimed under the Constitution of the United States, or any law of Congress. Will it be said that the slave is taken as property, the same as other property which the master may own? To this I answer, that colored persons are made property by the law of the State, and no such power has been given to Congress. Does the master carry with him the law of the State from which he removes into the Territory? And does that enable him to coerce his slave in the Territory? Let us test this theory. If this may be done by a master from one slave State, it may be done by a master from every other slave State. This right is supposed to be connected with the person of the master, by virtue of the local law. Is it transferable? May it be negotiated, as a promissory noted or bill of exchange? If it be assigned to a man from a free State, may he coerce the slave by virtue of it? What shall this thing be denominated? Is it personal or real property? Or is it an indefinable fragment of sovereignty, which every person carries with him from his late domicil? One thing is certain, that its origin has been very recent, and it is unknown to the laws of any civilized country.

A slave is brought to England from one of its islands, where slavery was introduced and maintained by the mother country. Although there is no law prohibiting slavery in England, yet there is no law authorizing it; and, for near a century, its courts have declared that the slave there is free from the coercion of the master. Lords Mansfield and Stowell agree upon this point, and there is no dissenting authority.

There is no other description of property which was not protected in England, brought from one of its slave islands. Does not this show that property in a human being does not arise from nature or from the common law, but, in the language of this court, "it is a mere municipal regulation, founded upon and limited to the range of the territorial laws?" This decision is not a mere argument, but it is the end of the law, in regard to the extent of slavery. Until it shall be overturned, it is not a point for argument; it is obligatory on myself and by brethren, and on all judicial tribunals over which this court exercises an appellate power.

It is said the Territories are common property of the States, and that every man has a right to go there with his property. This is not controverted. But the court say a slave is not property beyond the operation of the local law which makes him such. Never was a truth more authoritatively and justly uttered by man. Suppose a master of a slave in a British island owned a million of property in England; would that authorize him to take his slaves with him to England? The Constitution, in express terms, recognizes the status of slavery as founded on the municipal law. "No person held to service or labor in one State, under the laws thereof, escaping into another, shall," etc. Now, unless the fugitive escape from a place where, by the municipal law, he is held to labor, this provision affords no remedy to the master. What can be more conclusive than this? Suppose a slave escape from a Territory where slavery is not authorized by law, can he be reclaimed?

In this case, a majority of the court have said that a slave may be taken by his master into a Territory of the United States, the same as a horse, or any other kind of property. It is true, this was said by the court, as also many other things, which are of no authority. Nothing that has been said by them, which has not a direct bearing on the jurisdiction of the court, against which they decided, can be considered as authority. I shall certainly not regard it as such. The question of jurisdiction, being before the court, was decided by them authoritatively, but nothing beyond that question. A slave is not a mere chattel. He bears the impress of his Maker, and is amenable to the laws of God and man; and he is destined to an endless existence.

Under this head I shall chiefly rely on the decisions of the Supreme Courts of the Southern States, and especially of the State of Missouri.

In the 1st and 2d sections of the 6th article of the Constitution of Illinois, it is declared that neither slavery nor involuntary servitude shall hereafter be introduced into this State, otherwise than for the punishment of crimes whereof the party shall have been duly convicted; and in the 2d section it is declared that any violation of this article shall effect the emancipation of such person from his obligation to service. In Illinois, a right of transit through the State is given the master with his slaves. This is a matter which, as a I suppose, belongs exclusively to the State.

The Supreme Court of Illinois, in the case of *Jarrot v. Jarrot*, 2 Gilman, 7, said:

"After the conquest of this Territory by Virginia, she ceded it to the United States, and stipulated that the titles and possessions, right and liberties of the French settlers, should be guarantied to them. This, it has been contended, secured them in the possession of those negroes as slaves which they held before that time, and that neither Congress nor the Convention had power to deprive them of it; or, in other words, that the Ordinance and Constitution should not be so interpreted and understood as applying to such slaves, when it is therein declared that there shall be neither slavery nor involuntary servitude in the Northwest Territory, nor in the State of Illinois, otherwise than in the punishment of crimes. But it was held that those rights could not be thus protected, but must yield to the Ordinance and Constitution."

The first slave case decided by the Supreme Court of Missouri, contained in the reports, was *Winny v. Whitesides*, 1 Mo. 473, at October Term, 1824. It appeared that, more than twenty-five years before, the defendant, with her husband, had removed from Carolina to Illinois, and brought with them the plaintiff; that they continued to reside in Illinois three or four years, retaining the plaintiff as a slave; after which, they removed to Missouri, taking her with them.

The court held, that if a slave be detained in Illinois until he be entitled to freedom, the right of the owner does not revive when he finds the negro in a slave State.

That when a slave is taken to Illinois by his owner, who takes up his residence there, the slave is entitled to freedom.

In the case of *Lagrange v. Chouteau*, 2 Mo. 20 at May Term, 1828, it was decided that the Ordinance of 1787 was intended as a fundmental law for those who may choose to live under it, rather than as a penal statute.

That any sort of residence contrived or permitted by the legal owner of the slave, upon the faith of secret trusts or contracts, in order to defeat or evade the Ordinance, and thereby introduced slavery de facto, would entitle such slave to freedom.

In *Julia v. McKinney*, 3 Mo. 270, it was held, where a slave was settled in the State of Illinois, but with an intention on the part of the owner to be removed at some future day, that hiring said slave to a person to labor for one or two days, and receiving the pay for the hire, the slave is entitled to her freedom, under the 2d section of the 6th article of the Constitution of Illinois.

Rachel v. Walker, 4 Mo. 350, June Term, 1836, is a case involving, in every particular, the principles of the case before us. Rachel sued for her freedom; and it appeared that she had been bought as a slave in Missouri, by Stockton an officer of the army, taken to Fort Snelling, where he was stationed, and she was retained there as a slave a year; and then Stockton removed to Prairie du Chien, taking Rachel with him as a slave, where he continued to hold her three years, and then he took her to the State of Missouri, and sold her as a slave.

"Fort Snelling was admitted to be on the west side of the Mississippi River, and north of the State of Missouri, in the territory of the United States. That Prairie du Chien was in the Michigan Territory, on the east side of the Mississippi River. Walker, the defendant, held Rachel under Stockton."

The court said, in this case:

"The officer lived in Missouri Territory, at the time he bought the slave; he sent to a slave-holding country and procured her; this was his voluntary act, done without any other reason than that of his convenience; and he and those claiming under him must be holden to abide the consequences of introducing slavery both in Missouri Territory and Michigan, contrary to law; and on that ground Rachel was declared to be entitled to freedom."

In answer to the argument that, as an officer of the army, the master had a right to take his slave into free territory, the court said no authority of law or the government compelled him to keep the plaintiff there as a slave.

"Shall it be said, that because an officer of the army owns slaves in Virginia, that when, as officer and soldier, he is required to take the command of a fort in the non-slave-holding States or Territories, he thereby has a right to take with him as many slaves as will suit his interests or convenience? It surely cannot be law. If this be true, the court say, then it is also true that the convenience or supposed convenience of the officer repeals, as to him and others who have the same character, the Ordinance and the Act of 1821, admitting Missouri into the Union, and also the prohibition of the several laws and constitutions of the non-slaveholding States.

In *Wilson v. Melvin*, 4 Mo. 592, it appeared the defendant left Tennessee with an intention of residing in Illinois, taking his negroes with him. After a month's stay in Illinois, he took his negroes to St. Louis, and hired them, then returned to Illinois. On these facts, the inferior court instructed the jury that the defendant was a sojourner in Illinois. This the Supreme Court held was error, and the judgment was reversed.

The case of *Dred Scott v. Emerson*, 15 Mo. 576, March Term, 1852, will now be stated. This case involved the identical question before us, Emerson having, since the hearing, sold the plaintiff to Sandford, the defendant.

Two of the judges ruled the case, the Chief Justice dissenting. It cannot be improper to state the grounds of the opinion of the court, and the dissent.

The court says: "Cases of this kind are not strangers in our court. Persons have been frequently here adjudged to be entitled to their freedom, on the ground that their masters held them in slavery in Territories or States in which that institution is prohibited. From the first case decided in our court, it might be inferred that this result was brought about by a presumed assent of the master, from the fact of having voluntarily taken his slave to a place where the relation of master and slave did not exist. But subsequent cases base the right to 'exact the forfeiture of emancipation,' as they term it, on the ground, it would seem, that it was the duty of the courts of this State to carry into effect the constitution and laws of other States and Territories, regardless of the rights, the policy, or the institutions, of the people of this State."

And the court say that the States of the Union, in their municipal concerns, are regarded as foreign to each other; that the courts of one State do not take notice of the laws of other States, unless proved as facts, and that every State has the right to determine how far its comity to other States shall extend; and it is laid down, that when there is no act of manumission decreed to the free State, the courts of the slave States cannot be called to give effect to the law of the free State. Comity, it alleges, between States, depends upon the discretion of both, which may be varied by circumstances. And it is declared by the court, "that times are not as they were when the former decisions on this subject were made." Since then, not only individuals but States have been possessed with a dark and fell spirit in relation to slavery, whose gratification is sought in the pursuit of measures whose inevitable consequence must be the overthrow and destruction of our government. Under such circumstances, it does not behoove the State of Missouri to show the least countenance to any measure which might gratify this spirit. She is willing to assume her full responsibility for the existence of slavery within her limits, nor does she seek to share or divide it with others.

Chief Justice Gamble dissented from the other two judges. He says:

"In every slaveholding State in the Union, the subject of emancipation is regulated by statute; and the forms are prescribed in which it shall be effected. Whenever the forms required by the laws of the State in which the master and slave are resident are complied with, the emancipation is complete, and the slave is free. If the right of the person thus emancipated is subsequently drawn in question in another State, it will be ascertained and determined by the law of the State in which the slave and his former master resided; and when it appears that such law has been complied with, the right to freedom will be fully sustained in the courts of all the slaveholding States, although the act of emancipation may not be in the form required by law in which the court sits.

"In all such cases, courts continually administer the law of the country where the right was acquired; and when that law becomes known to the court, it is just as much a matter of course to decide the rights of the parties according to its requirements, as it is to settle the title of real estate situated in our State by its own laws."

This appears to me a most satisfactory answer to the argument of the court. Chief Justice continues:

"The perfect equality of the different States lies at the foundation of the Union. As the institution of slavery in the States is one over which the Constitution of the United States gives no power to the general government, it is left to be adopted or rejected by the several States, as they think best; nor can any one State, or number of States, claim the right to interfere with any other State upon the question of admitting or excluding this institution.

"A citizen of Missouri, who removes with his slave to Illinois, has no right to complain that the fundamental law of that State to which he removes, and in which he makes his residence, dissolves the relation between him and his slave. It is as much his own voluntary act, as if he had executed a deed of emancipation. No one can pretend ignorance of this constitutional provision, and," he says, "the decisions which have heretofore been made in this State, and in many other slaveholding States, give effect to this and other similar provisions, on the ground that the master, by making the free State the residence of his slave, has submitted his right to the operation of the law of such State; and this," he says, "is the same in law as a regular deed of emancipation."

He adds:

"I regard the question as conclusively settled by repeated adjudications of this court, and, if I doubted or denied the propriety of those decisions, I would not feel myself anymore at liberty to overturn them, than I would any other series of decisions by which the law of any other question was settled. There is with me," he says, "nothing in the law relating to slavery which distinguishes it from the law on any other subject, or allows any more accommodation to the temporary public excitements which are gathered around it."

"In this State," he says, "it has been recognized from the beginning of the government as a correct position in law, that a master who takes his slave to reside in a State or Territory where slavery is prohibited, thereby emancipates his slave." These decisions, which come down to the year 1837, seemed to have so fully settled the question, that since that time there has been no case bringing it before the court for any reconsideration, until the present. In the case of "*Winny v. Whitesides*, 1 Mo. 473, the question was made in the argument, "whether one nation would execute the penal laws of another," and the court replied in this language (Huberus, quoted in 4 Dallas), which says, "personal rights or disabilities obtained or communicated by the laws of any particular place are of a nature which accompany the person wherever he goes;" and the Chief Justice observed, in the case of *Rachel v. Walker*, 4 Mo. 350, the Act of Congress called the Missouri Compromise was held as operative as the Ordinance of 1787.

When Dred Scott, his wife and children, were removed from Fort Snelling to Missouri, in 1838, they were free as the law was then settled, and continued for fourteen years afterwards, up to 1852, when the above decision was made. Prior to this, for nearly thirty years, as Chief Justice Gamble declares, the residence of a master with his slave in the State of Illinois, or the Territory north of Missouri, where slavery was prohibited by the Act called the Missouri Compromise, would manumit the slave as effectually as if he had executed a deed of emancipation; and that an officer of the army who takes his slave into that State or Territory; and holds him there as a slave, liberates him the same as any other citizen—and down to the above time it was settled by numerous and uniform decisions; and that on the return of the slave to Missouri, his former condition of slavery did not attach. Such was the settled law of Missouri until the decision of *Scott v. Emerson*.

In the case of *Sylvia v. Kirby*, 17 Mo. 434, the court followed the above decision, observing that it was similar in all respects to the case of *Scott v. Emerson*.

This court follows the established construction of the statutes of a State by its Supreme Court. Such a construction is considered as a part of the Statute, and we follow it to avoid two rules of property in the same State. But we do not follow the decisions of the Supreme Court of a State beyond a statutory construction as a rule of decision for this court. State decisions are always viewed with respect and treated as authority; but we follow the settled construction of the statutes,

not because it is of binding authority, but in pursuance of a rule of judicial policy.

But there is no pretense that the case of *Dred Scott v. Emerson* turned upon the construction of a Missouri Statute; nor was there any established rule of property which could have rightfully influenced in the decision. On the contrary, the decision overruled the settled law for nearly thirty years.

This is said by my brethren to be a Missouri question; but there is nothing which gives it this character, except that it involves the right to persons claimed as slaves who reside in Missouri, and the decision was made by the Supreme Court of that State. It involves a right claimed under an Act of Congress and the Constitution of Illinois, and which cannot be decided without the consideration and construction of those laws. But the Supreme Court of Missouri held, in this case, that it will not regard either of those laws, without which there was no case before it; and Dred Scott, having been a slave, remains a slave. In this respect it is admitted this is a Missouri question—a case which has but one side, if the Act of Congress and the Constitution of Illinois are not recognized.

And does such a case constitute a rule of decision for this court—a case to be followed by this court? The course of decision so long and so uniformly maintained established a comity or law between Missouri and the free States and Territories where slavery was prohibited, which must be somewhat regarded in this case. Rights sanctioned for twenty-eight years ought not and cannot be repudiated, with any semblance of justice, by one or two decisions, influenced, as declared, by a determination to counteract the excitement against slavery in the free States.

The courts of Louisiana having held, for a series of years, that where a master took his slave to France, or any free state, he was entitled to freedom, and that on bringing him back the status of slavery did not attach, the Legislature of Louisiana declared by an Act that the slave should not be made free under such circumstances. This regulated the rights of the master from the time the Act took effect. But the decision of the Missouri court, reversing a former decision, affects all previous decisions, technically, made on the same principles, unless such decisions are protected by the lapse of time or the Statute of Limitations. Dred Scott and his family, beyond all controversy, were free under the decisions made for twenty-eight years, before the case of *Scott v. Emerson*. This was the undoubted law of Missouri for fourteen years after Scott and his family were brought back to that State. And the grave question arises, whether this law may be so disregarded as to enslave free persons. I am strongly inclined to think that a rule of decision so well settled as not to be questioned, cannot be annulled by a single decision of the court. Such rights may be inoperatives under the decision in future; but I cannot well perceive how it can have the same effect in prior cases.

It is admitted, that when a former decision is reversed, the technical effect of the judgment is to make all previous adjudications on the same question erroneous. But the case before us was not that the law had been erroneously construed, but that, under the circumstances which then existed, that law would not be recognized; and the reason for this is declared to be the excitement against the institution of slavery in the free States. While I lament this excitement as much as anyone, I cannot assent that it shall be made a basis for judicial action.

In 1816, the common law, by statute, was made a part of the law of Missouri; and that includes the great principles of international law. These principles cannot be abrogated by judicial decisions. It will require that same exercise of power to abolish the common law, as to introduce it. International law is founded in the opinions generally received and acted on by civilized nations, and enforced by moral sanctions. It becomes a more authoritative system when it results from special compacts, founded on modified rules adapted to the exigencies of human society; it is in fact an international morality, adapted to the best interests of nations. And in regard to the States of this Union, on the subject of slavery, it is eminently fitted for a rule of action, subject to the Federal Constitution.

"The laws of nations are but the natural rights of man applied to nations." Vattel.

If the common law have the force of a statutory enactment in Missouri, it is clear, as it seems to me, that a slave who, by a residence in Illinois in the service of his master, becomes entitled to his freedom, cannot again be reduced to slavery by returning to his former domicil in a slave State. It is unnecessary to say what legislative power might do by a general Act in such a case, but it would be singular if a freeman could be made a slave by the exercise of a judicial discretion. And it would be still more extraordinary if this could be done, not only in the absence of special legislation, but in a State where the common law is in force.

It is supposed by some that the 3d article in the Treaty of Cession of Louisiana to this country, by France, in 1803, may have some bearing on this question. The article referred to provides "that the inhabitants of the ceded Territory shall be incorporated into the Union, and enjoy all the advantages of citizens of the United States, and in the mean time they shall be maintained and protected in the free enjoyment of their liberty, property, and the religion they profess."

As slavery existed in Louisiana at the time of the cession, it is supposed this is a guaranty that there should be no change in its condition.

The answer to this is, in the first place, that such a subject does not belong to the treaty-making power; and any such arrangement would have been nugatory. And, in the second place, by no admissible construction can the guaranty be carried further than the protection of property in slaves at that time in the ceded Territory. And this has been complied with. The organization of the slave States of Louisiana, Missouri and Arkansas, embraced every slave in Louisiana at the time of the cession. This removes every ground of objection under the Treaty. There is, therefore, no pretense, growing out of the Treaty, that any part of the Territory of Louisiana, as ceded, beyond the organized States, is slave territory.

Under the fifth head, we were to consider whether the status of slavery attached to the plaintiff and wife on their return to Missouri.

This doctrine is not asserted in the late opinion of the Supreme Court of Missouri, and up to 1852 the contrary doctrine was uniformly maintained by that court.

In its late decision, the court say that it will not give effect in Missouri to the laws of Illinois, or the law of Congress called the Missouri Compromise. This was the effect of the decision, though its terms were, that the court would not take notice, judicially, of those laws.

In 1851, the Court of Appeals of South Carolina recognized the principle, that a slave, being taken to a free State, became free. *Commonwealth v. Pleasant*, 10 Leigh, 697. In *Betty v. Horton*, the Court of Appeals held that the freedom of the slave was acquired by the action of the laws of Massachusetts, by the said slave being taken there. 5 Leigh, 615.

The slave States have generally adopted the rule, that where the master, by a residence with his slave in a State or Territory where slavery is prohibited, the slave was entitled to his freedom everywhere. This was the settled doctrine of the Supreme Court of Missouri. It has been so held in Mississippi, in Virginia, in Louisiana, formerly in Kentucky, Maryland, and in other States.

The law, where a contract is made and is to be executed, governs it. This does not depend upon comity, but upon the law of the contract. And if, in the language of the Supreme Court of Missouri, the master, by taking his slave to Illinois, and employing him there as a slave, emancipates him as effectually as by a deed of emancipation, is it possible that such an act is not matter for adjudication in any slave State where the master may take him? Does not the master assent to the law when he places himself under it in a free State?

The States of Missouri and Illinois are bounded by a common line. The one prohibits slavery, the other admits it. This has been done by the exercise of that sovereign power which appertains to each. We are bound to respect the institutions of each, as emanating from the voluntary action of the people. Have the people of either any right to disturb the relations of the other? Each State rests upon the basis of its own sovereignty, protected by the Constitution. Our Union has been the foundation of our prosperity and national glory. Shall we not cherish and maintain it? This can only be done by respecting the legal rights of each State.

If a citizen of a free State shall entice or enable a slave to escape from the service of his master, the law holds him responsible, not only for the loss of the slave, but he is liable to be indicted and fined for the misdemeanor. And I am bound here to say that I have never found a jury in the four States which constitute my circuit, which have not sustained this law, where the evidence required them to sustain it. And it is proper that I should also say that more cases have arisen in my circuit by reason of its extent and locality, than in all other parts of the Union. This has been done to vindicate the sovereign rights of the Southern States, and protect the legal interests of our brethren of the South.

Let these facts be contrasted with the case now before the court. Illinois has declared in the most solemn and impressive form that there shall be neither slavery not involuntary servitude in that State, and that any slave brought into it, with a view of becoming a resident, shall be emancipated. And effect has been given to this provision of the Constitution by the decision of the Supreme Court of that State. With a full knowledge of these facts, a slave is brought from Missouri to Rock Island, in the State of Illinois, and is retained there as a slave for two years, and then taken to Fort Snelling, where slavery is prohibited by the Missouri Compromise Act, and there he is detained two years longer in a state of slavery. Harriet, his wife, was also kept at the same place four years as a slave, having been purchased in Missouri. They were then removed to the State of Missouri, and sold as slaves, and in the action before us they are not only claimed as slaves, but a majority of my brethren have held that on their being returned to Missouri the status of slavery attached to them.

I am not able to reconcile this result with the respect due to the State of Illinois. Having the same rights of sovereignty as the State of Missouri in adopting a constitution, I can perceive no reason why the institutions of Illinois should not receive the same consideration as those of Missouri. Allowing to my brethren the same right of judgment that I exercise myself, I must be permitted to say that it seems to me the principle laid down will enable the people of a slave State to introduce slavery into a free State, for a longer or shorter time, as may suit their convenience; and by returning the slave to the State whence he was brought, by force or otherwise, the status of slavery attaches, and protects the rights of the master, and defies the sovereignty of the free State. There is no evidence before us that Dred Scott and his family returned to Missouri voluntarily. The contrary is inferable from the agreed case: "In the year 1838, Dr. Emerson removed the plaintiff and said Harriet, and their daughter Eliza, from Fort Snelling to the State of Missouri, where they have ever since resided." This is the agreed case; and can it be inferred from this that Scott and family returned to Missouri voluntarily? He was removed; which shows that he was passive, as a slave, having exercised no volition on the subject. He did not resist the master by absconding or force. But that was not sufficient to bring him within Lord Stowell's

SLAVERY

DRED SCOTT V.
SANDFORD

decision; he must have acted voluntarily. It would be a mockery of law and an outrage on his rights to coerce his return, and then claim that it was voluntary, and on that ground that his former status of slavery attached.

If the decision be placed on this ground, it is a fact for a jury to decide, whether the return was voluntary, or else the fact should be distinctly admitted. A presumption against the plaintiff in this respect, I say with confidence is not authorized from the facts admitted.

In coming to the conclusion that a voluntary return by Grace to her former domicil, slavery attached, Lord Stowell took great pains to show that England forced slavery upon her Colonies, and that it was maintained by numerous Acts of Parliament and public policy, and, in short, that the system of slavery was not only established by Great Britain in her West Indian colonies, but that it was popular and profitable to many of the wealthy and influential people of England, who were engaged in trade, or owned and cultivated plantations in the Colonies. No one can read his elaborate views and not be struck with the great difference between England and her Colonies, and the free and slave States of this Union. While slavery in the Colonies of England is subject to the power of the mother country, our States, especially in regard to slavery, are independent, resting upon their own sovereignties, and subject only to international laws, which apply to independent States.

In the case of Williams, who was a slave in Granada, having run away, came to England, Lord Stowell said: "The four judges all concur in this—that he was a slave in Granada, though a free man in England, and he would have continued a free man in all other parts of the world except Granada."

Strader v. Graham, 10 How. 82, and 18 Curt. 305, has been cited as having a direct bearing in the case before us. In that case the court say: "It was exclusively in the power of Kentucky to determine, for itself, whether the employment of slaves in another State should or should not make them free on their return." No question was before the court in that case, except that of jurisdiction. And any opinion given on any other point is obiter dictum, and of no authority. In the conclusion of his opinion, the Chief Justice said: "In every view of the subject, therefore, this court has no jurisdiction of the case,

and the writ of error must on that ground be dismissed."

In the case of *Spencer v. Negro Dennis*, 8 Gill, 321, the court say "Once free, and always free, is the maxim of Maryland law upon the subject. Freedom having once vested, by no compact between the master and the liberated slave, nor by any condition subsequent, attached by the master to the gift of freedom, can a state of slavery be reproduced."

In *Hunter v Fulcher*, 1 Leigh, 172.

"By a Statute of Maryland of 1796, all slaves brought into that State to reside are declared free; a Virginian-born slave is carried by his master to Maryland; the master settled there, and keeps the slave there in bondage for twelve years, the statute in force all the time; then he brings him as a slave to Virginia, and sells him there. Adjudged, in an action brought by the man against the purchaser, that he is free."

Judge Kerr, in the case, says:

"Agreeing, as I do, with the general view taken in this case by my brother Green, I would not add a word, but to mark the exact extent to which I mean to go. The law of Maryland having enacted that slaves carried into that State for sale or to reside shall be free, and the owner of the slave here having carried him to Maryland, and voluntarily submitting himself and the slave to that law, it governs the case."

In every decision of a slave case prior to that of *Dred Scott v. Emerson*, the Supreme Court of Missouri considered it as turning upon the Constitution of Illinois, the Ordinance of 1787, or the Missouri Compromise Act of 1820. The court treated these Acts as in force, and held itself bound to execute them, by declaring the slave to be free who had acquired a domicil under them with the consent of his master.

The late decision reversed this whole line of adjudication, and held that neither the Constitution and laws of the States, nor Acts of Congress in relation to Territories, could be judicially noticed by the Supreme Court of Missouri. This is believed to be in conflict with the decisions of all the courts in the Southern States, with some exceptions of recent cases.

In *Marie Louise v. Marot et. al.* 9 La. 475, it was held, where a slave having been taken to the kingdom of France or other country by the owner, where slavery is not tolerated, operates on the condition of the slave, and produces immediate emancipation; and that, where a slave thus becomes free, the master cannot reduce him again to slavery.

Josephine v. Poultney, 1 La. Ann. 329 "where the owner removes with a slave into a State in which slavery is prohibited, with the intention of residing there, the slave will be thereby emancipated, and their subsequent return to the State of Louisiana cannot restore the relation of master and slave." To the same import are the cases of *Smith v. Smith*, 13 La. 441; *Thomas v. Generis*, 16 La. 483; *Harry et al. v. Decker and Hopkins*, Walk. (Miss.) 36. It was held that "slaves within the jurisdiction of the Northwestern Territory became freemen by virtue of the Ordinance of 1787, and can assert their claim to freedom in the courts of Mississippi." *Griffith v. Fanny*, 1 Virginia, 143. It was decided that a negro held in servitude in Ohio, under a deed executed in Virginia is entitled to freedom by the Constitution of Ohio.

The case of *Rhodes v. Bell*, 2 How. 397, involved the main principle in the case before us. A person residing in Washington City purchased a slave in Alexandria, and brought him to Washington. Washington continued under the law of Maryland, Alexandria under the law of Virginia. The Act of Maryland of November, 1796, 2 Maxcy's Laws, 351, declared anyone who shall bring any negro, mulatto, or other slave, into Maryland, such slave should be free. The above slave, by reason of his being brought into Washington City, was declared by this court to be free. This, it appears to me, is a much stronger case against the slave than the facts in the case of Scott.

In *Bush v. White*, 3 Monroe, 104, the court say:

"That the Ordinance was paramount to the territorial laws, and restrained the legislative power there as effectually as a Constitution in an organized State. It was a public Act of the Legislature of the Union, and a part of the supreme law of the land; and, as such, this court is as much bound to take notice of it as it can be of any other law."

In the case of *Rankin v. Lydia*, 2 A. K. Marsh. 467, before cited, Judge Mills, speaking for the Court of Appeals of Kentucky, says:

"If, by the positive provision in our code, we can and must hold our slaves in the one case, and statutory provisions equally positive decide against that right in the other, and liberate the slave, he must, by an authority equally imperious, be declared free. Every argument which supports the right of the master on one side, based upon the force of written law, must be equally conclusive in favor of the slave, when he can point out in the statute the clause which secures his freedom."

And he further said:

"Free people of color in all the States are, it is believed, quasi citizens, or, at least, denizens. Although none of the States may allow them the privilege of office and suffrage, yet all other civil and conventional rights are secured to them; at least, such rights were evidently secured to them by the Ordinance in question for the government of Indiana. If these rights are vested in that or any other portion of the United States, can it be compatible with the spirit of our confederated government to deny their existence in any other part? Is there less comity existing between State and State, or State and Territory, than exists between the despotic governments of Europe."

These are the words of a learned and great judge, born and educated in a slave State.

I now come to inquire, under the sixth and last head, "whether the decisions of the Supreme Court of Missouri, on the question before us, are binding on this court."

While we respect the learning and high intelligence of the state courts, and consider their decisions, with others, as authority, we follow them only where they give a construction to the state statutes. On this head, I consider myself fortunate in being able to turn to the decision of this court, given by Mr. Justice Grier, in *Pease v. Peck*, a case from the State of Michigan, 18 How. 595, decided in December Term, 1855. Speaking for the court, Judge Grier said:

"We entertain the highest respect for that learned court (the Supreme Court of Michigan), and in any question affecting the construction of their own laws, where we entertain any doubt, would be glad to be relieved from doubt and responsibility by reposing on their decision. There are, it is true, many dicta to be found in our decisions, averring that the courts of the United States are bound to follow the decisions of the state courts on the construction of their own laws. But although this may be correct, yet a rather strong expression of a general rule, it cannot be received as the annunciation of a maxim of universal application. Accordingly, our reports furnish many cases of exceptions of it. In all cases where there is a settled construction of the laws of a State, by its highest judicature established by admitted precedent, it is the practice of the courts of the United States to receive and adopt it, without criticism or further inquiry. When the decisions of the State court are not consistent, we do not feel bound to follow the last, if it is contrary to our own convictions; and much more is this the case where, after a long course of consistent decisions, some new light suddenly springs up, or an excited public opinion has elicited new doctrines subversive of former safe precedent."

These words, it appears to me, have a stronger application to the case before us than they had to the cause in which they were spoken as the opinion of this court; and I regret that they do not seem to be as fresh in the recollection of some of my brethren as in my own. For twenty-eight years, the decisions of the Supreme Court of Missouri were consistent on all the points made in this case. But this consistent course was suddenly terminated, whether by some new light suddenly springing up, or an excited public opinion, or both, it is not necessary to say. In the case of *Scott v. Emerson*, in 1852, they were overturned and repudiated.

This, then, is the very case in which seven of my brethren declared that they would not follow the last decision. On this authority I may well repose. I can desire no other or better basis.

But there is another ground which I deem conclusive, and which I will restate.

The Supreme Court of Missouri refused to notice the Act of Congress or the Constitution of Illinois, under which Dred Scott, his wife and children, claimed that they are entitled to freedom.

This being rejected by the Missouri court, there was no case before it, or at least it was a case with only one side. And this is the case which, in the opinion of this court, we are bound to follow. The Missouri court disregards the express provisions of an Act of Congress and the constitution of a sovereign State, both of which laws for twenty-eight years if had not only regarded, but carried into effect.

If a State court may do this, on a question involving the liberty of a human being, what protection do the laws afford? So far from this being a Missouri question, it is a question, as it would seem, within the 25th sec. of the Judiciary Act, where a right to freedom being set up under the Act of Congress, and the decision being against such right, it may be brought for revision before this court, from the Supreme Court of Missouri.

I think the judgment of the court below should be reversed.

Mr. Justice Curtis, dissenting:

I dissent from the opinion pronounced by the Chief Justice, and from the judgment which the majority of the court think it proper to render in this case. The plaintiff alleged in his declaration, that he was a citizen of the State of Missouri, and that the defendant was a citizen of the State of New York. It is not doubted that it was necessary to make each of these allegations, to sustain the jurisdiction of the Circuit Court. The defendant denied, by a plea to the jurisdiction, either sufficient or insufficient, that the plaintiff was a citizen of the State of Missouri. The plaintiff demurred to that plea. The Circuit Court adjudged the plea insufficient, and the first question for our consideration is, whether the sufficiency of that plea is before this court for judgment, upon this writ of error. The part of the judicial power of the United States, conferred by Congress on the circuit courts, being limited to certain described cases and controversies, the question whether a particular case is within the cognizance of a circuit court, may be raised by a plea to the jurisdiction of such court. When that question has been raised, the Circuit Court must, in the first instance, pass upon and determine it. Whether its determination be final, or subject to review by this appellate court, must depend upon the will of Congress; upon which body the Constitution has conferred the power, with certain restrictions, to establish inferior courts to determine their jurisdiction, and to regulate the appellate power of this court. The 22d section of the Judiciary Act of 1789, which allows a writ of error from final judgments of circuit courts, provides that there shall be no reversal in this court, on such writ of error, for error in ruling any plea in abatement, other than a plea to the jurisdiction of the court. Accordingly it has been held, from the origin of the court to the present day, that circuit courts have not been made by Congress the final judges of their own jurisdiction in civil cases. And that when a record comes here upon a writ of error or appeal, and, on its inspection, it appears to this court that the Circuit Court had not jurisdiction, its judgment must be reversed, and the cause remanded, to be dismissed for want of jurisdiction.

It is alleged by the defendant in error, in this case, that the plea to the jurisdiction was a sufficient plea; that it shows, on inspection of its allegations, confessed by the demurrer, that the plaintiff was not a citizen of the State of Missouri; that upon this record, it must appear to this court that the case was not within the judicial power of the United States, as defined and granted by the Constitution, because it was not a suit by a citizen of one State against a citizen of another State.

To this it is answered, first, that the defendant, by pleading over, after the plea to the jurisdiction was adjudged insufficient, finally waived all benefit of that plea.

When that plea was adjudged insufficient, the defendant was obliged to answer over. He held no alternative. He could not stop the further progress of the case in the Circuit Court by a writ of error, on which the sufficiency of his plea to the jurisdiction could be tried in this court, because the judgment on that plea was not final, and no writ of error would lie. He was forced to plead to the merits. It cannot be true, then, that he waived the benefit of his plea to the jurisdiction by answering over. Waiver includes consent. Here, there was no consent. And if the benefit of the plea was finally lost, it must be, not by any waiver, but because the laws of the United States have not provided any mode of reviewing the decision of the Circuit Court on such a plea, when that decision is against the defendant. This is not the law. Whether the decision of the Circuit Court on a plea to the jurisdiction be against the plaintiff, or against the defendant, the losing party may have any alleged error in law, in ruling such a plea examined in this court on a writ of error, when the matter in controversy exceeds the sum or value of $2,000. If the decision be against the plaintiff, and his suit dismissed for want of jurisdiction, the judgment is technically final, and he may at once sue out his writ of error.

Mollan v. Torrance, 9 Wheat. 537.

If the decision be against the defendant, though he must answer over, and wait for a final judgment in the cause, he may then have his writ of error, and upon it obtain the judgment of this court on any question of law apparent on the record, touching the jurisdiction. The fact that he pleaded over to the merits, under compulsion, can have no effect on his right to object to the jurisdiction. If this were not so, the condition of the two parties would be grossly unequal. For if a plea to the jurisdiction were ruled against the plaintiff, he could at once take his writ of error and have the ruling reviewed here; while, if the same plea were ruled against the defendant, he must not only wait for a final judgment, but could in no event have the ruling of the Circuit Court upon the plea reviewed by this court. I know of no ground for saying that the laws of the United States have thus discriminated between the parties to a suit in its courts.

It is further objected, that as the judgment of the Circuit Court was in favor of the defendant, and the writ of error in this cause was sued out by the plaintiff, the defendant is not in a condition to assign any error in the record, and therefore this court is precluded from considering the question whether the Circuit Court had jurisdiction.

The practice of this court does not require a technical assignment of errors. See the rule. Upon a writ of error, the whole record is open for inspection; and if any error be found in it, the judgment is reversed.

Bank of U.S. v. Smith, 11 Wheat. 171.

It is true, as a general rule, that the court will not allow a party to rely on anything as cause for reversing a judgment, which was for his advantage. In this, we follow an ancient rule of the common law. But so careful was that law of the preservation of the course of its courts, that it made an exception out of that general rule, and allowed a party to assign for error that which was for his advantage, if it were a departure by the court itself from its settled course of procedure. The cases on this subject are collected in Bac. Abr. Error, H. 4. And this court followed this practice in *Capron v. Van Noorden*, 2 Cranch, 126, where the plaintiff below procured the reversal of a judgment for the defendant, on the ground that the plaintiff's allegations of citizenship had not shown jurisdiction.

But it is not necessary to determine whether the defendant can be allowed to assign want of jurisdiction as an error in a judgment in his own favor. The true question is, not what either of the parties may be allowed to do, but whether this court will affirm or reverse a judgment of the

SLAVERY

DRED SCOTT V.
SANDFORD

Circuit Court on the merits, when it appears on the record, by a plea to the jurisdiction, that it is a case to which the judicial power of the United States does not extend. The course of the court is, where no motion is made by either party, on its own motion, to reverse such a judgment for want of jurisdiction, not only in cases where it is shown, negatively, by a plea to the jurisdiction, that jurisdiction does not exist, but even where it does not appear, affirmatively, that it does exist. *Piquignot v. The Pennsylvania R. R. Co.* 16 How. 104. It acts upon the principle, that the judicial power of the United States must not be exerted in a case to which it does not extend, even if both parties desire to have it exerted. *Cutler v. Rae,* 7 How. 729. I consider, therefore, that when there was a plea to the jurisdiction of the Circuit Court in a case brought here by a writ of error, the first duty of this court is, *sua sponte,* if not moved to it by either party, to examine the sufficiency of that plea; and thus to take care that neither the Circuit Court nor this court shall use the judicial power of the United States in a case to which the Constitution and laws of the United States have not extended that power.

I proceed, therefore, to examine the plea to the jurisdiction.

I do not perceive any sound reason why it is not to be judged by the rules of the common law applicable to such pleas. It is true, where the jurisdiction of the Circuit Court depends on the citizenship of the parties, it is incumbent on the plaintiff to allege on the record the necessary citizenship; but when he has done so, the defendant must interpose a plea in abatement, the allegations whereof show that the court has not jurisdiction; and it is incumbent on him to prove the truth of his plea.

In *Sheppard v. Graves,* 14 How. 505, the rules on this subject are thus stated in the opinion of the court: "That although, in the courts of the United States, it is necessary to set forth the grounds of their cognizance as courts of limited jurisdiction, yet wherever jurisdiction shall be averred in the pleadings, in conformity with the laws creating those courts, it must be taken prima facie, as existing; and it is incumbent on him who would impeach that jurisdiction for causes dehors the pleading, to allege and prove such causes; that the necessity for the allegation, and the burden of sustaining it by proof, both rest upon the party taking the exception." These posi-

tions are sustained by the authorities there cited, as well as by *Wickliffe v. Ownings,* 17 How. 47.

When, therefore, as in this case, the necessary averments as to citizenship are made on the record, and jurisdiction is assumed to exist, and the defendant comes by a plea to the jurisdiction to displace that presumption, he occupies, in my judgment, precisely the position described in Bacon Abr. Abatement: "Abatement, in the general acceptation of the word, signifies a plea, put in by the defendant, in which he shows cause to the court why he should not be impleaded; or, if at all, not in the manner and form he now is."

This being, then, a plea in abatement, to the jurisdiction of the court, I must judge of its sufficiency by those rules of the common law applicable to such pleas.

The plea was as follows: "And the said John F.A. Sandford, in his own proper person, comes and says that this court ought not to have or take further cognizance of the action aforesaid, because he says that said cause of action, and each and every of them (if any such have accrued to the said Dred Scott), accrued to the said Dred Scott out of the jurisdiction of this court, and exclusively within the jurisdiction of the courts of the State of Missouri; for that, to wit: the said plaintiff, Dred Scott, is not a citizen of the State of Missouri, as alleged in his declaration, because he is a negro of African descent; his ancestors were of pure African blood, and were brought into this country and sold as negro slaves; and this the said Sandford is ready to verify. Wherefore, he prays judgment whether this court can or will take further cognizance of the action aforesaid."

The plaintiff demurred, and the judgment of the Circuit Court was, that the plea was insufficient.

I cannot treat this plea as a general traverse of the citizenship alleged by the plaintiff. Indeed, if it were so treated, the plea was clearly bad, for it concludes with a verification, and not to the country, as a general traverse should. And though this defect in a plea in bar must be pointed out by a special demurrer, it is never necessary to demur specially to a plea in abatement; all matters, though of form only, may be taken advantage of upon a general demurrer to such a plea.

Chitty on Pl. 465.

The truth is, that though not drawn with the utmost technical accuracy, it is a special traverse of the plaintiff's allegation of citizenship, and was a suitable and proper mode of traverse under the circumstances. By reference to Mr. Stephen's description of the uses of such a traverse, contained in his excellent analysis of pleadings (Steph. on Pl. 176), it will be seen how precisely this plea meets one of his discriptions. No doubt the defendant might have traversed, by a common or general traverse, the plainiff's allegation that he was a citizen of the State of Missouri; concluding to the country. The issue thus presented being joined, would have involved matter of law, on which the jury must have passed, under the direction of the court. But by traversing the plaintiff's citizenship specially—that is, averring those facts as a decision therefrom—opportunity was given to do what was done; that is, to present directly to the court, by a demurrer, the sufficiency of those facts to negative, in point of law, the plaintiff's allegation of citizenship. This, then, being a special, and not a general or common traverse, the rule is settled, that the facts thus set out in the plea, as the reason or ground of the traverse, must of themselves constitute, in point of law, a negative of the allegation thus traversed. Steph. on Pl. 183; Ch. on Pl. 620. And upon a demurrer to this plea, the question which arises is, whether the facts, that the plaintiff is a negro of African descent, whose ancestors were of pure African blood, and were brought into this country and sold as negro slaves, may all be true, and yet the plaintiff be a citizen of the State of Missouri, within the meaning of the Constitution and laws of the United States, which confer on citizens of one State the right to sue citizens of another State in the circuit courts. Undoubtedly, if these facts, taken together, amount to an allegation that, at the time of action brought, the plaintiff was himself a slave, the plea is sufficient. It has been suggested that the plea, in legal effect, does so aver because, if his ancestors were sold as slaves, the presumption is they continued slaves; and if so, the presumption is, the plaintiff was born a slave; and if so, the presumption is, he continued to be a slave to the time of action brought.

I cannot think such presumptions can be resorted to, to help out defective averments in pleading; especially, in pleading in abatement, where the utmost certainty and precision are required. Chit. Pl. 457. That the plaintiff himself was a slave at the time of action brought, is a substantive fact, having no necessary connection with the fact that his parents were sold as slaves. For they might have been sold after he was born; or the plaintiff himself, if once a slave, might have become a freeman before action was brought.. To aver that his ancestor were sold as slaves, is not equivalent, in point of law to an averment that he was a slave. If it were, he could not even confess and avoid the averment of the slavery of his ancestors, which would be monstrous; and if it be not equivalent in point of law, it cannot be treated as amounting thereto when demurred to; for a demurrer confesses only those substantive facts which are well pleaded, and not other distinct substantive facts which might be inferred therefrom by a jury. To treat an averment that the plaintiff's ancestors were Africans, brought to this country and sold as slaves as amounting to an averment on the record that he was a slave, because it may lay some foundation for presuming so, is to hold that the facts actually aleged may be treated as intended as evidence of another distinct fact not alleged. But, it is a cardinal rule of pleading, laid down in Dowman's case, 9 Rep. b, and in even earlier authorities therein referred to, "that evidence shall never be pleaded, for it only tends to prove matter of fact; and therefore the matter of fact shall be pleaded." Or, as the rule is sometimes stated, pleadings must not be argumentative. Steph. Pl. 384, and authorities cited by him. In Com. Dig. Pleader, E. 3, and Bac. Abr. Pleas I. 5, and Steph. Pl., many decisions under this rule are collected. In trover, for an indenture whereby A granted a manor, it is no plea that A did not grant the manor, for it does not answer the declaration except by argument. Yelv. 223.

So in trespass for taking and carrying away the plaintiff's goods, the defendant pleaded that the plaintiff never had any goods. The court said, "this is an infallible argument that the defendant is not guilty, but it is no plea." Dyer, a 43.

In ejectment, the defendant pleaded a surrender of a copyhold by the hand of Fosset, the steward. The plaintiff replied that Fosset was not steward. The court held this no issue, for it traversed the surrender only argumentatively, Cro. Eliz. 260.

In these cases, and many others reported in the books, the inferences from the facts stated were irresistible. But the court held they did not, when demurred to, amount to such inferable facts. In the case at bar, the inference that the defendant was a slave at the time of action brought, even if it can be made at all, from the fact that his parents were slaves, is certainly not a necessary inference. This case, therefore, is like that of *Digby v. Alexander,* 8 Bing. 416. In that case, the defendant pleaded many facts strongly tending to show that he was once Earl of Stirling; but as there was no positive allegation that he was so at the time of action brought, and as every fact averred might be true, and yet the defendant not have been Earl of Stirling at the time of action brought, the plea was held to be insufficient.

A lawful seisin of land is presumed to continue. But if, in an action of trespass quare clausum, the defendant were to plead that he was lawfully seised of the *locus in quo,* one month before the time of the alleged trespass, I should have no doubt it would be a bad plea. See *Mollan v. Torrance,* 9 Wheat. 537. So if a plea to the jurisdiction, instead of alleging that the plaintiff was a citizen of the same State as the defendant, were to allege that the plaintiff's ancestors were citizens of that State, I think the plea could not be supported. My judgment would be, as it is in this case, that if the defendant meant to aver a particular substantive fact, as existing at the time of action brought, he must do it directly and explicitly, and not by way of inference from certain other averments, which are quite consistent with the countrary hypothesis. I cannot therefore, treat this plea as containing an averment that the plaintiff himself was a slave at the time of action brought; and the inquiry recurs, whether the facts, that he is of African descent, and that his parents were once slaves, are necessarily inconsistent with his own citizenship in the State of Missouri, within the meaning of the Constitution and laws of the United States.

In *Gassies v. Ballon,* 6 Pet. 761, the defendant was described on the record as a naturalized citizen of the United States, residing in Louisiana. The court held this equivalent to an averment that the defendant was a citizen of Louisiana; because a citizen of the United States, residing in any State of the Union, is, for purposes of jurisdiction, a citizen of that State. Now, the plea to the jurisdiction in this case does not controvert the fact that the plaintiff resided in Missouri at the date of the writ. If he did then reside there, and was also a citizen of the United States, no provisions contained in the Constitution or laws

of Missouri can deprive the plaintiff of his right to sue citizens of States other than Missouri, in the courts of the United States.

So that, under the allegations contained in this plea, and admitted by the demurrer, the question is, whether any person of African descent, whose ancestors were sold as slaves in the United States, can be a citizen of the United States. If any such person can be a citizen, this plaintiff has the right to the judgment of the court that he is so; for no cause is shown by the plea, why he is not so, except his descent and the slaverly of his ancestors.

The 1st section of the 2d Article of the Constitution uses the language, "a citizen of the United States at the time of the adoption of the Constitution." One mode of approaching this question is, to inquire who were citizens of the United States at the time of the adoption of the Constitution.

Citizens of the United States at the time of the adoption of the Constitution can have been no other than the citizens of the United States under the Confederation. By the Articles of Confederation, a government was organized, the style whereof was, "The United States of America." This government was in existence when the Constitution was framed and proposed for adoption, and was to be superseded by the new Government of the United States of America, organized under the Constitution. When, therefore, the Constitution speaks of citizenship of the United States, existing at the time of adoption of the Constitution, it must necessarily refer to citizenship under the government which existed prior to and at the time of such adoption.

Without going into any question concerning the powers of the confederation to govern the territory of the United States out of the limits of the States, and consequently to sustain the relation of Government and citizen in respect to the inhabitants of such territory, it may safely be said that the citizens of the several States were citizens of the United States under the Confederation.

That government was simply a confederacy of the several States, possessing a few defined powers over subjects of general concern, each State retaining every power, jurisdiction, and right, not expressly delegated to the United States in Congress assembled. And no power was thus delegated to the government of the

Confederation, to act on any question of citizenship, or to make any rules in respect thereto. The whole matter was left to stand upon the action of the several States, and to the natural consequence of such action, that the citizens of each State should be citizens of that Confederacy into which that State had entered, the style whereof was, "The United States of America."

To determine whether any free persons, descended from Africans held in slavery, were citizens of the United States under the Confederation, and consequently at the time of the adoption of the Constitution of the United States, it is only necessary to know whether any such persons were citizens of either of the States under the Confederation at the time of the adoption of the Constitution.

Of this there can be no doubt. At the time of the ratification of the Articles of Confederation, all free native-born inhabitants of the States of New Hampshire, Massachusetts, New York, New Jersey and North Carolina, though descended from African slaves, were not only citizens of those States, but such of them as had the other necessary qualifications possessed the franchise of electors on equal terms with other citizens.

The Supreme Court of North Carolina, in the case of *The State v. Manuel*, 4 Dev. & Bat. 20, has declared the law of that State on this subject, in terms which I believe to be as sound law in the other States I have enumerated, as it was in North Carolina.

"According to the laws of this State," says Judge Gaston, in delivering the opinion of the court, "all human beings within it, who are not slaves, fall within one of two classes. Whatever distinctions may have existed in the Roman laws between citizens and free inhabitants, they are unknown to our institutions. Before our Revolution, all free persons born within the dominions of the King of Great Britain, whatever their color or complexion, were native-born British subjects—those born out of his allegiance were aliens. Slavery did not exist in England, but it did in the British Colonies. Slaves were not in legal parlance persons, but property. The moment the incapacity, the disqualification of slavery, was removed, they became persons, and were then either British subjects, or not British subjects, according as they were or were not born within the allegiance of the British King. Upon the Revolution, no other change took place in the laws of North Carolina than was consequent on the transition from a Colony dependent on a European King, to a free and sovereign State. Slaves remained slaves. British subjects in North Carolina became North Carolina freemen, and therefore, if born within North Carolina, are citizens of North Carolina, and all free persons born within the State are born citizens of the State. The Constitution extended the elective franchise to every freeman who had arrived at the age of twenty-one, and paid a public tax; and it is a matter of universal notoriety, that, under it, free persons, without regard to color, claimed and exercised the franchise, until it was taken from free men of color a few years since by our amended Constitution."

In *The State v. Newcomb*, 5 Ired. 253, decided in 1844, the same court referred to this case of *The State v. Manuel*, and said: "That case underwent a very laborious investigation, both by the Bar and the Bench. The case was brought here by appeal, and was felt to be one of great importance in principle. It was considered with an anxiety and care worthy of the principle involved, and which give it a controlling influence and authority on all questions of a similar character."

An argument from speculative premises, however well chosen, that the then state of opinion in the Commonwealth of Massachusetts was not consistent with the natural rights of people of color who were born on that soil, and that they were not, by the Constitution of 1780 of that State, admitted to the condition of citizens, would be received with surprise by the people of that State, who know their own political history. It is true, beyond all controversy, that persons of color, descended from African slaves, were by that Constitution made citizens of the State; and such of them as have had the necessary qualifications, have held and exercised the elective franchise, as citizens, from that time to the present. See *Com. v. Aves,* 18 pick. 210.

The Constitution of New Hampshire confered the elective franchise upon "every inhabitant of the State having the necessary qualifications," of which color or descent was not one.

The Constitution of New York gave the right to vote to "every male inhabitant, who shall have resided," etc.; making no discrimination between the colored persons and others. See Con. of N.Y. Art. 2, Rev. Stats. of N. Y. Vol. I. p. 126.

SLAVERY

DRED SCOTT V.
SANDFORD

That of New Jersey, to "all inhabitants of this Colony, of full age, who are worth £50 proclamation money, clear estate."

New York, by its Constitution of 1820, required colored persons to have some qualifications as prerequisites for voting, which white persons need not possess. And New Jersey, by its present Constitution, restricts the right to vote to white male citizens. But these changes can have no other effect upon the present inquiry, except to show, that before they were made, no such restrictions existed; and colored, in common with white persons, were not only citizens of those States, but entitled to the elective franchise on the same qualifications as white persons, as they now are in New Hampshire and Massachusetts. I shall not enter into an examination of the existing opinions of that period respecting the African race, nor into any discussion concerning the meaning of those who asserted, in the Declaration of Independence, that all men are created equal; that they are endowed by their Creator with certain inalienable rights; that among these are life, liberty, and the pursuit of happiness. My own opinion is, that a calm comparison of these assertions of universal abstract truths, and of their own individual opinions and acts, would not leave these men under any reproach of inconsistency; that the great truths they asserted on that solemn occasion, they were ready and anxious to make effectual, wherever a necessary regard to circumstances, which no statesman can disregard without producing more evil than good, would allow; and that it would not be just to them, nor true in itself, to allege that they intended to say that the Creator of all men had endowed the white race, exclusively, with the great natural rights which the Declaration of Independence asserts. But this is not the place to vindicate their memory. As I conceive, we should deal here, not with such disputes, if there can be a dispute concerning this subject, but with those substantial facts evinced by the written constitutions of States, and by the notorious practice under them. And they show, in a manner which no argument can obscure, that in some of the original thirteen States, free colored persons, before and at the time of the formation of the Constitution, were citizens of those States.

The 4th of the fundamental articles of the Confederation was as follows: "The free inhabitants of each of these States, paupers, vaga-bounds and fugitives from justice expected, shall be entitled to all the privileges and immunities of free citizens in the several States."

The fact that free persons of color were citizens of some of the several States, and the consequence, that this 4th Article of the Confederation would have the effect to confer on such persons the privileges and immunities of general citizenship, were not only known to those who framed and adopted those articles, but the evidence is decisive, that the 4th Article was intended to have the effect, and that more restricted language, which would have excluded such persons, was deliberately and purposely rejected.

On the 25th of June, 1778, the Articles of Confederation being under consideration by the Congress, the delegates from South Carolina moved to amend this 4th Article, by inserting after the word "free," and before the word "inhabitants," the word "white," so that the privileges and immunities of general citizenship would be secured only to white persons. Two States voted for the amendment, eight states against it, and the vote of one State was divided. The language of the article stood unchanged, and both its terms of inclusion, "free inhabitants," and the strong implication from its terms of exclusion, "paupers, vagabonds and fugitives from justice," who alone were excepted, it is clear, that under the Confederation, and at the time of the adoption of the Constitution, free colored persons of African descent might be, and, by reason of their citizenship in certain States, were, entitled to the privileges and immunities of general citizenship of the United States.

Did the Constitution of the United States deprive them or their descendants of citizenship?

That Constitution was ordained and established by the people of the United States through the action, in each State, of those persons who were qualified by its laws to act thereon, in behalf of themselves and all other citizens of that State. In some of the States, as we have seen, colored persons were among those qualified by law to act on this subject. These colored persons were not only included in the body of "the people of the United States by whom the Consititution was ordained and established," but in at least five of the States they had the power to act, and doubtless did act, by their suffrages, upon the question of its adoption. It would be strange, if we were to find in that instrument anything which deprived of their citizenship any part of the people of the United States who were among those by whom it was established.

I can find nothing in the Constitution which, *proprio vigore,* deprives of their citizenship any class of persons who were citizens of the United States at the time of its adoption, or who should be native-born citizens of any State after its adoption; nor any power enabling Congress to disfranchise persons born on the soil of any State, and entitled to citizenship of such State by its constitution and laws. And my opinion is, that under the Constitution of the United States, every free person born on the soil of a State, who is a citizen of that State by force of its Constitution or laws, is also a citizen of the United States.

I will proceed to state the grounds of that opinion.

The 1st Section of the 2d Article of the Constitution uses the language, "natural-born citizen." It thus assumes that citizenship may be acquired by birth. Undoubtedly, this language of the Constitution was used in reference to that principle of public law, well-understood in this country at the time of the adoption of the Constitution, which referred citizenship to the place of birth. At the Declaration of Independence, and ever since, the received general doctorine has been, in conformity with the common law, that free persons born within either of the colonies were subjects of the King; that by the Declaration of Independence, and the consequent acquisition of sovereignty by the several States, all such persons ceased to be subjects, and became citizens of the several States, except so far as some of them were disfranchised by the legislative power of the States, or availed themselves, seasonably, of the right to adhere to the British Crown in the civil contest, and thus to continue British subjects. *McIvaine v. Coxe's Lessee,* 4 Cranch, 209; *Inglis v. Sailors' Snug Harbor,* 3 Pet. p. 99; *Shanks v. Dupont,* Ibid, p. 242.

The Constitution having recognized the rule that persons born within the several States, one of four things must be true:

First. That the Constitution itself has described what native-born persons shall or shall not be citizens of the United States; or,

Second. That it has empowered Congress to do so; or,

Third. That all free persons, born within the several States, are citizens of the United States; or,

Fourth. That it is left to each State to determine what free persons, born within its limits, shall be citizens of such State, and thereby be citizens of the United States.

If there be such a thing as citizenship of the United States acquired by birth within the States, which the Constitution expressly recognizes, and no one denies, then these four alternatives embrace the entire subject, and it only remains to select that one which is true.

That the Constitution itself has defined citizenship of the United States by declaring what persons, born within the several States, shall or shall not be pretended. It contains no such declaration. We may dismiss the first alternative, as without doubt unfounded.

Has it empowered Congress to enact what free persons, born within the several States, shall or shall not be citizens of the United States?

Before examining the various provisions of the Constitution which may relate to this question, it is important to consider for a moment the substantial nature of this inquiry. It is, in effect, whether the Constitution has empowered Congress to create privileged classes within the States, who alone can be entitled to the franchises and powers of citizenship of the United States. If it be admitted that the Constitution has enabled Congress to declare what free persons, born within the several States, shall be citizens of the United States, it must, at the same time, be admitted that it is an unlimited power. If this subject is within the control of Congress, it must depend wholly on its discretion. For, certainly, no limits of that discretion can be found in the Constitution, which is wholly silent concerning it; and the necessary consequence is, that the Federal Government may select classes of persons within the several States who alone can be entitled to the political privileges of citizenship of the United States. If this power exists, what persons born within the States may be President or Vice President of the United States, or members of either house of Congress, or hold any office or enjoy any privilege whereof citizenship of the United States is a necessary qualification, must depend solely on the will of Congress. By virtue of it, though Congress can grant no title of nobility, they may create an oligarchy, in whose hands would be concentrated the entire power of the Federal Government.

It is a substantive power, distinct in its nature from all others; capable of affecting not only the relations of the States to the General Government, but of controlling the political condition of the people of the United States. Certainly we ought to find this power granted by the Constitution, at least by some necessary inference, before we can say it does not remain to the States or the people. I proceed, therefore, to examine all the provisions of the Constitution which may have some bearing on this subject.

Among the powers expressly granted to Congress is "the power to establish a uniform rule of naturalization." It is not doubted that this is a power to prescribe a rule for the removal of the disabilities consequent on foreign birth. To hold that it extends further than this, would do violence to the meaning of the term naturalization, fixed in the common law (Co. Litt, & a, 129 a; 2 Ves. Sr. 286; 2 Bl. Com. 293), and in the minds of those who concurred in framing and adopting the Constitution. It was in this sense of conferring on an alien and his issue the rights and powers of a native-born citizen, that it was employed in the Declaration of Independence. It was in this sense it was expounded in the Federalist (No. 42), has been understood by Congress, by the Judiciary (2 Wheat.259, 269; 3 Wash. 313, 322; 12 Wheat. 277), and by commentators on the Constitution. 3 Story's Com. on Const. 1–3; 1 Rawle on Const. 84–88; 1 Tucker's Bl. Com. App. 225–259.

It appears, then, that the only power expressly granted to Congress to legislate concerning citizenship, is confined to the removal of the disabilities of foreign birth.

Whether there be anything in the Constitution from which a broader power may be implied, will best be seen when we come to examine the two other alternatives, which are, whether all free persons, born on the soil of the several States, or only such of them as may be citizens of each State, respectively, are thereby citizens of the United States. The last of these alternatives, in my judgment, contains the truth.

Undoubtedly, as has already been said, it is a principle of public law, recognized by the Constitution itself, that birth on the soil of a country both creates the duties and confers the rights of citizenship. But it must be remembered, that though the Constitution was to form a government, and under it the United States of America were to be one united sovereign nation, to which loyalty and obedience, on the one side, and from which protection and privileges on the other, would be due, yet the several sovereign States, whose people were the citizens, were not only to continue in existence, but with powers unimpaired, except so far as they were granted by the people to the National Government.

Among the powers unquestionably possessed by the several States, was that of determining what persons should and what persons should not be citizens. It was practicable to confer on the government of the Union this entire power. It embraced what may, well enough for the purpose now in view, be divided into three parts: First. The power to remove the disabilities of alienage, either by special acts in reference to each individual case, or by establishing a rule of naturalization to be administered and applied by the courts. Second. Determining what persons should enjoy the privileges of citizenship, in respect to the internal affairs of the several States. Third. What native born persons should be citizens of the United States.

The first named power, that of establishing a uniform rule of naturalization, was granted; and here the grant, according to its terms, stopped. Construing a constitution containing only limited and defined powers of government, the argument derived from this definite and restricted power to establish a rule of naturalization, must be admitted to be exceedingly strong. I do not say it is necessarily decisive. It might be controlled by other parts of the Constitution. But when this particular subject of citizenship was under consideration, and in the clause specially intended to define the extent of power concerning it, we find a particular part of this entire power separated from the residue, and conferred on the General Government, there arises a strong presumption that this is all which is granted, and that the residue is left to the States and to the people. And this presumption is, in my opinion, converted into a certainty by an examination of all such other clauses of the Constitution as touch this subject.

I will examine each which can have any possible bearing on this question.

The 1st clause of the 2d Section of the 3d Article of the Constitution is: "The judicial power shall extend to controversies between a State and citizens of another State between citizens of different States; between citizens of the same State, claiming lands under grants of different States; and between States, or the citizens thereof, and foreign states, citizens or subjects." I do not think this clause has any considerable bearing upon the particular inquiry now under consideration. Its purpose was, to extend the judicial power to those controversies into which local feelings or interests might so enter as to disturb the course of justice, or give rise to suspicions that they had done so, and thus possibly give occasion to jealously or ill will between different States, or a particular State and a foreign nation. At the same time, I would remark, in passing, that it has been held—I do not know that it has ever been supposed—that any citizen of a State could bring himself under this clause and the 11th and 12th sections of the Judiciary Act of 1789, passed in pursuance of it, who was not a citizen of the United States. But I have referred to the clause, only because it is one of the places where citizenship is mentioned by the Constitution. Whether it is entitled to any weight in this inquiry or not, it refers only to citizenship of the several States; it recognizes that; but it does not recognize citizenship of the United States as something distinct therefrom.

As has been said, the purpose of this clause did not necessarily connect it with citizenship of the United States, even if that were something distinct from citizenship of the several States, in the contemplation of the Constitution. This cannot be said of other clauses of the Constitution, which I now proceed to refer to.

"The citizens of each State shall be entitled to all the privileges and immunities of citizens of the several States." Nowhere else in the Constitution is there anything concerning a general citizenship; but here, privileges and immunities to be enjoyed throughout the United States, under and by force of the national compact, are granted and secured. In selecting those who are to enjoy these national rights of citizenship—how are they described? As citizens of each State. It is to them these national rights are secured. The qualification for them is not to be looked for in any provision of the Constitution or laws of the United States. They are to be citizens of the several States, and, as such, the privileges and immunities of general citizenship, derived from and guarantied by the Constitution, are to be enjoyed by them. It would seem that if it had been intended to constitute a class of native born persons within the States, who should derive their citizenship of the

United States from the action of the Federal Government, this was an occasion for referring to them. It cannot be supposed that it was the purpose of this article to confer the privileges and immunities of citizens in all the States upon persons not citizens of the United States.

And if it was intended to secure these rights only to citizens of the United States, how was the Constitution here described such persons? Simply as citizens of each State.

But, further: though, as I shall presently more fully state, I do not think the enjoyment of the elective franchise essential to citizenship, there can be no doubt it is one of the chiefest attributes of citizenship under the American Constitutions; and the just and constitutional possession of this right is decisive evidence of citizenship. The provisions made by a constitution on this subject must therefore be looked to as bearing directly on the question what persons as are allowed by the Constitution to exercise the elective franchise, and thus to participate in the Government of the United States, must be deemed citizens of the United States.

Here, again, the consideration presses itself upon us, that if there was designed to be a particular class of native-born persons within the States, deriving their citizenship from the Constitution and laws of the United States, they should at least have been referred to as those by whom the President and House of Representatives were to be elected, and to whom they should be responsible.

Instead of that, we again find this subject referred to the laws of the several States. The electors of President are to be appointed in such manner as the Legislature of each State may direct, and the qualifications of electors of members of the House of Representatives shall be the same as for electors of the most numerous branch of the State Legislature.

Laying aside, then, the case of aliens, concerning which the Constitution of the United States has provided, and confining our view to free persons born within the several States, we find that the Constitution has recognized the general principle of public law, that allegiance and citizenship depend on the place of birth; that it has not attempted practically to apply this principle by designating the particular classes of persons who should or should not come under it; that when we turn to the Constitution for an answer to the question, what free persons, born within the several States, are citizens of the United States, the only answer we can receive from any of its express provisions is, the citizens of the several States, are to enjoy the privileges and immunities of citizens in every State, and their franchise as electors under the Constitution depends on their citizenship in the several States. Add to this, that the Constitution was ordained by the citizens of the several States; that they were "the people of the United States," for whom and whose posterity the government was declared in the preamble of the Constitution to be made; that each of them was "a citizen of the United States at the time of the adoption of the Constitution," within the meaning of those words in that instrument; that by them the government was to be and was in fact organized; and that no power is conferred on the Government of the Union to discriminate between them, or to disfranchise any of them— the necessary conclusion is, that those persons born within the several States, who, by force of their respective constitutions and laws, are citizens of the State, are thereby citizens of the United States.

It may be proper here to notice some supposed objections to this view of the subject.

It has been often asserted that the Constitution was made exclusively by and for the white race. It has already been shown that in five of the thirteen original States, colored persons then possessed the elective franchise, and were among those by whom the Constitution was ordained and established. If so, it is not true, in point of fact, that the Constitution was made exclusively by the white race. And that it was made exclusively for the white race is, in my opinion, not only an assumption not warranted by anything in the Constitution, but contradicted by its opening declaration, that it was ordained and established by the people of the United States, for themselves and their posterity. And as free colored persons were then citizens of at least five States, and so in every sense part of the people of the United States, they were among those for whom and whose posterity the Constitution was ordained and established.

Again; it has been objected, that if the Constitution has left to the several States the rightful power to determine who of their inhabitants shall be citizens of the United States, the States may make aliens citizens.

The answer is obvious. The Constitution has left to the States the determination what persons, born within their respective limits, shall acquire by birth citizenship of the United States; it has not left to them any power to prescribe any rule for the removal of the disabilities of alienage. This power is exclusively in Congress.

It has been further objected, that if free colored persons, born within a particular State, and made citizens of that State by its constitution and laws, are thereby made citizens of the United States, then, under the 2d section of the 4th article of the Constitution, such persons would be entitled to all the privileges and immunities of citizens in the several States; and if so, then colored persons could vote, and be eligible to not only federal offices, but offices even in those State whose Constitutions and laws disqualify colored persons from voting or being elected to office.

But this position rests upon an assumption which I deem untenable. Its basis is, that no one can be deemed a citizen of the United States who is not entitled to enjoy all the privileges and franchises which are conferred on any citizen. See 1 Lit. Ky. 326. That this is not true, under the Constitution of the United States, seems to me clear.

A naturalized citizen cannot be President of the United States, not a Senator till after the lapse of nine years, nor a Representative till after the lapse of seven years, from his naturalization. Yet, as soon as naturalized, he is certainly a citizen of the United States. Nor is any inhabitant of the District of Columbia, or of either of the Territories, eligible to the office of Senator or Representative in Congress, though they may be citizens of the United States. So, in all the States, numerous persons, though citizens, cannot vote, or cannot hold office, either on account of their age or sex, or the want of the necessary legal qualifications. The truth is, that citizenship, under the Constitution of the United States, is not dependent on the possession of any particular political or even of all civil rights; and any attempt so to define it must lead to error. To what citizens the elective franchise shall be confided, is a question to be determined by each State, in accordance with its own views of the necessities or expediences of its condition. What civil rights shall be enjoyed by its citizens, and whether all shall enjoy the same, or how they may be gained or lost, are to be determined in the same way.

One may confine the right of suffrage to white male citizens; another may extend it to colored persons and females; one may allow all persons above a prescribed age to convey property and transact business; another may exclude married women. But whether native-born women, or persons under age, or under guardianship because insane or spendthrifts, be excluded from voting or holding office, or allowed to do so, I apprehend no one will deny that they are citizens of the United States. Besides this clause of the Constitution does not confer on the citizens of one State, in all other States, specific and enumerated privileges and immunities. They are entitled to such as belong to citizenship, but not such as belong to particular citizens attended by other qualifications. Privileges and immunities which belong to certain citizens of a State, by reason of the operation of causes other than mere citizenship, are not conferred. Thus, if the laws of a State require, in addition to citizenship of the State, some qualification for office, or the exercise of the elective franchise, citizens of all other States, coming thither to reside, and not possessing those qualifications, cannot enjoy those privileges, not because they are not to be deemed entitled to the privileges of citizens of the State in which they reside, but because they, in common with the native-born citizens of that State, must have the qualifications prescribed by law for the enjoyment of such privileges under its constitution and laws. It rests with the States themselves so to frame their constitutions and laws as not to attach a particular privilege or immunity to mere naked citizenship. If one of the States will not deny to any of its own citizens a particular privilege or immunity, if it confer it on all of them by reason of mere naked citizenship, then it may be claimed by every citizen of each State by force of the Constitution; and it must be borne in mind, that the difficulties which attend the allowance of the claims of colored persons to be citizens of the United States are not avoided by saying that, though each State may make them its citizens, they are not thereby made citizens of the United States, because the privileges of general citizenship are secured to the citizens of each State. The language of the Constitution is: "The citizens of each State shall be entitled to all privileges and immunities of citizens in the several States." If each State may

make such persons its citizens, they become, as such, entitled to the benefits of this article, if there be a native-born citizenship of the United States distinct from a native-born citizenship of several states.

There is one view of this article entitled to consideration in this connection. It is manifestly copied from the 4th of the Articles of Confederation, with only slight changes of phraseology, which render its meaning more precise, and dropping the clause which excluded paupers, vagabonds and fugitives from justice, probably because these cases could be dealt with under the police powers of the States, and a special provision therefor was not necessary. It has been suggested, that in adopting it into the Constitution, the words "free inhabitants" were changed for the word "citizens." An examination of the forms of expression commonly used in the state papers of that day, and an attention to the substance of this article of the Confederation, will show that the words "free inhabitants," as then used, were synonymous with citizens. When the Articles of Confederation were adopted, we were in the midst of the War of the Revolution, and there were very few persons then embraced in the words "free inhabitants," who were not born on our soil. It was not a time when many, save the children of the soil, were willing to embark their fortunes in our cause; and though there might be an inaccuracy in the uses of words to call free inhabitants citizens, it was then a technical rather than a substantial difference. If we look into the constitutions and state papers of that period, we find the inhabitants or people of these Colonies or the inhabitants of this State, or Commonwealth, employed to designate those whom we should now denominate "citizens." The substance and purpose of the article prove it was in this sense it used these words: It secures to the free inhabitants of each State the privileges and immunities of free citizens in every State. It is not conceivable that the States should have agreed to extend the privileges of citizenship to persons not entitled to enjoy the privileges of citizens in the States where they dwelt; that under this article there was a class of persons in some of the States, not citizens, to whom were secured all the privileges and immunities of citizens when they went into other States; and the just conclusion is, that though the Constitution cured an inaccuracy of language, it left the substance of this article in

SLAVERY

DRED SCOTT V. SANDFORD

the National Constitution the same as it was in the Articles of Confederation.

The history of this 4th article, respecting the attempt to exclude free persons of color from its operation, has been already stated. It is reasonable to conclude that this history was known to those who framed and adopted the Constitution. That under this 4th article of the Confederation, free persons of color might be entitled to the privileges of general citizenship, if otherwise entitled thereto, is clear. When this article was, in substance, placed in and made part of the Constitution of the United States, with no change in its language calculated to exclude free colored persons from the benefit of its provisions, the presumption is, to say the least, strong, that the practical effect which it was designed to have, and did have, under the former government, it was designed to have, and should have, under the new government.

It may be further objected, that if free colored persons may be citizens of the United States, it depends only on the will of a master whether he will emancipate his slave and thereby make him a citizen. Not so. The master is subject to the will of the State. Whether he shall be allowed to emancipate his slave at all; if so, on what conditions; and what is to be the political status of the freed man, depend , not on the will of the master, but on the will of the State, upon which the political status of all its native-born inhabitants depends. Under the Constitution of the United States, each State has retained this power of determining the political status of its native-born inhabitants, and no exception thereto can be found in the Constitution. And if a master in a slaveholding State should carry his slave into a free State, and there emancipate him, he would not thereby make him a native-born citizen of that State, and consequently no privileges could be claimed by such emancipated slave as a citizen of the United States. For, whatever powers of the States may exercise to confer privileges of citizenship on persons not born on their soil, the Constitution of the United States does not recognize such citizens. As has already been said, it recognizes the great principle of public law, that allegiance and citizenship spring from the place of birth. It leaves to the States the application of that principle to individual cases. It secured to the citizens of each State the privileges and immunities of citizens in every other State. But it does not allow to the States the power to make

aliens citizens, or permit one State to take persons born on the soil of another State, and, contrary to the laws and policy of the States where they were born, make them its citizens, and so citizens of the United States. No such deviation from the great rule of public law was contemplated by the Constitution; and when any such attempt shall be actually made, it is to be met by applying to those rules of law and those principles of good faith which will be sufficient to decide it, and not, in my judgment, by denying that all the free native-born inhabitants of a State, who are its citizens under its constitution and laws, are also citizens of the United States.

It has sometimes been urged that colored persons are shown not to be citizens of the United States, by the fact that the naturalization laws apply only to white persons. But whether a person born in the United States be or be not a citizen, cannot depend on laws which refer only to aliens, and do not affect the status of persons born in the United States. The utmost effect which can be attributed to them is, to show that Congress has not deemed it expedient generally to apply the rule to colored aliens. That they might do so, if thought fit, is clear. The Constitution has not excluded them. And since that has conferred the power on Congress to naturalize colored aliens, it certainly shows that color is not a necessary qualification for citizenship under the Constitution of the United States. It may be added, that the power to make colored persons citizens of the United States, under the Constitution, has been actually exercised in repeated and important instances. See the Treaties with the Choctaws, of Sept. 27, 1830, art. 14; with the Cherokees, of May 23, 1836, art. 12; Treaty of Guadaloupe Hidalgo, Feb. 2, 1848, art. 8.

I do not deem it necessary to review at length the legislation of Congress having more or less bearing on the citizenship of colored persons. It does not seem to me to have any considerable tendency to prove that it has been considered by the Legislative Department of the government, that no such persons are citizens of the United States. Undoubtedly they have been debarred from the exercise of particular rights or privileges extended by white persons, but, I believe, always in terms which, by implication, admit they may be citizens. Thus the Act of may 17, 1792, for the organization of the militia, directs the enrollment of "every free, able-bodied, white male citizen." An assumption that none but white persons are citizens, would be as inconsistent with the just import of this language, as that all citizens are able-bodied, or males.

So the Act of February 28, 1803, 2 Stat. at L. 205, to prevent the importation of certain persons into States, when by the laws thereof their admission is prohibited, in its 1st section forbids all masters of vessels to import or bring "any negro, mulatto, or other person of color, not being a native, a citizen, or registered seaman of the United States," etc.

The Acts of March 3, 1813, sec. 1, 2 Stat. at L. 809, and March 1, 1817, sec. 3, 3 Stat. at L. 351, concerning seamen, certainly imply there may be persons of color, natives of the United States, who are not citizens of the United States. This implication is undoubtedly in accordance with the fact. For not only slaves, but free persons of color, born in some of the States, are not citizens. But there is nothing in these laws inconsistent with the citizenship of persons of color in others of the States, nor with their being citizens of the United States.

Whether much or little weight should be attached to the particular phraseology of these and other laws, which were not passed with any direct reference to this subject, I consider their tendency to be, as already indicated, to show that, in the apprehension of their framers, color was not a necessary qualification of citizenship. It would be strange, if laws were found on our statute book to that effect, when by solemn treaties, large bodies of Mexican and North American Indians, as well as free colored inhabitants of Louisiana, have been admitted to citizenship of the United States.

In the legislative debates which preceded the admission of the State of Missouri into the Union, this question was agitated. Its result is found in the resolution of Congress, of March 5, 1821, for the admission of that State into the Union. The Constitution of Missouri, under which that State applied for admission into the Union, provided, that it should be the duty of the Legislature "to pass laws to prevent free negroes and mulattoes from coming to and settling in the State, under any pretext whatever." One ground of objection to the admission of the State under this Constitution was, that it would require the Legislature to exclude free persons of color, who would be entitled, under the 2d section of the 4th article of the Constitution, not only to come within the State, but to enjoy there the privileges and immunities of citizens. The resolutions of Congress admitting the State was upon the fundamental condition, "that the Constitution of Missouri shall never be construed to authorize the passage of any law, and that no law shall be passed in conformity thereto, by which any citizen of either of the States of this Union shall be excluded from the enjoyment of any of the privileges and immunities to which such citizen is entitled under the Constitution of the United States." It is true, that neither this legislative declaration, nor anything in the Constitution or laws of Missouri, could confer or take away any privilege or immunity granted by the Constitution. But it is also true, that it expresses the then conviction of the legislative power of the United Sates, that free negroes, as citizens of some of the States, might be entitled to the privileges and immunities of citizens in all the States.

The conclusions at which I have arrived on this part of the case are:

First. That the free native-born citizens of each State are citizens of the United States.

Second. That as free colored persons born within some of the States are citizens of those States, such persons are also citizens of the United States.

Third. That every such citizen, residing in any State, has the right to sue and is liable to be sued in the federal courts, as a citizen of that State in which he resides.

Fourth. That as the plea to the jurisdiction in this case shows no facts, except that the plaintiff was of African descent, and his ancestors were sold as slaves, and as these facts are not inconsistent with his citizenship of the United States, and his residence in the State of Missouri, the plea to the jurisdiction was bad and the judgment of the Circuit Court overruling it, was correct.

I dissent, therefore, from that part of the opinion of the majority of the court, in which it is held that a person of African descent cannot be a citizen of the United States; and I regret I must go further, and dissent both from what I deem their assumption of authority to examine the constitutionality of the Act of Congress commonly called the Missouri Compromise Act, and the grounds and conclusions announced in their opinion.

SLAVERY

DRED SCOTT V. SANDFORD

Having first decided that they were bound to consider the sufficiency of the plea to the jurisdiction of the Circuit Court, and having decided that this plea showed that the Circuit Court had not jurisdiction, and consequently that this is a case to which the judicial power of the United States does not extend, they have gone on to examine the merits of the case as they appeared on the trial before the court and jury, on the issues joined on the pleas in bar, and so have reached the question of the power of Congress to pass the Act of 1820. On so grave a subject as this, I feel obliged to say that, in my opinion, such an exertion of judicial power transcends the limits of the authority of the court, as described by its repeated decisions, and, as I understand, acknowledged in this opinion of the majority of the court.

In the course of that opinion, it became necessary to comment on the case of *Legrand v. Darnall,* reported in 2 Pet. 664. In that case, a bill was filed, by one alleged to be a citizen of Maryland, against one alleged to be a citizen of Pennsylvania. The bill stated that the defendant was the son of a white man by one of his slaves; and that the defendant's father devised to him certain lands, the title to which was put in controversy by the bill. These facts were admitted in the answer, and upon these and other facts the court made its decree, founded on the principle that a devise of land by a master to a slave was by implication also a bequest of his freedom. The facts that the defendant was of African descent, and was born a slave, were not only before the court, but entered into the entire substance of its inquiries. The opinion of the majority of my brethren in this case disposes of the case of *Legrand v. Darnall,* by saying, among other things, that as the fact that the defendant was born a slave only came before this court on the bill and answer, it was then too late to raise the question of the personal disability of the party, and therefore that decision is altogether inapplicable in this case.

In this I concur. Since the decision of this court in *Livingston v. Story,* II Pet. 351, the law has been settled, that when the declaration or bill contains the necessary averments of citizenship, this court cannot look at the record, to see whether those averments are true, except so far as they are put in issue by a plea to the jurisdiction. In that case, the defendant denied by his answer that Mr. Livingston was a citizen of New York, as he had alleged in the bill. Both parties went into proofs. The court refused to examine those proofs, with reference to the personal disability of the plaintiff. This is the settled law of the court, affirmed so lately as *Sheppard v. Graves,* 14 How. 505, and *Wickliffe v. Owings* 17 How. 51; see also, *De Wolf v. Rabaud,* I Pet. 476. But I do not understand this to be a rule which the court may depart from at its pleasure. If it be a rule, it is as binding on the court as on the suitors. If it removes from the latter the power to take any objection to the personal disability of a party alleged by the record to be competent, which is not shown by a plea to the jurisdiction, it is because the court are forbidden by law to consider and decide on objections so taken. I do not consider it to be within the scope of the judicial power of the majority of the court to pass upon any question respecting the plaintiff's citizenship in Missouri save that raised by the plea to the jurisdiction; and I do not hold any opinion of this court or any court, binding, when expressed on a question not legitimately before it. *Carroll v. Carroll,* 16 How. 275. The judgment of this court is, that the case is to be dismissed for want of jurisdiction, because the plaintiff was not a citizen of Missouri, as he alleged in his declaration. Into that judgment, according to the settled course of this court, nothing appearing after a plea to the merits can enter. A great question of constitutional law, deeply affecting the peace and welfare of the country, is not, in my opinion, a fit subject to be thus reached.

But as, in my opinion, the Circuit Court had jurisdiction, I am obliged to consider the question whether its judgment on the merits of the case should stand or be reversed.

The residence of the plaintiff in the State of Illinois, and the residence of himself and his wife in the Territory acquired from France lying north of latitude thirty-six degrees thirty minutes, and north of the State of Missouri, are each relied on by the plaintiff in error. As the residence in the Territory affects the plaintiff's wife and children as well as himself, I must inquire what was its effect.

The general question may be stated to be, whether the plaintiff's status, as a slave, was so changed by his residence within that Territory, that he was not a slave in the State of Missouri, at the time this action was brought.

In such cases, two inquiries arise, which may be confounded, but should be kept distinct.

The first is, what was the law of the Territory into which the master and slave went, respecting the relation between them?

The second is, whether the State of Missouri recognizes and allows the effect of that law of the Territory, on the status of the slave, on his return within its jurisdiction.

As to the first of these questions, the will of States and nations, by whose municipal law slavery is not recognized, has been manifested in three different ways.

One is, absolutely to dissolve the relation, and terminate the rights of the master existing under the law of the country whence the parties came. This is said by Lord Stowell, in the case of *The Slave Grace*, 2 Hagg. Ad. 94, and by the Supreme Court of Louisiana in the case of *Maria Louise v. Marot*, 9 La. 473, to be the law of France; and it has been the law of several States of this Union, in respect to slaves introduced under certain conditions.

Wilson v. Isabel, 5 Call, 430; *Hunter v. Fulcher*, 1 Leigh, 172; *Stewart v. Oakes*, 5 Harr. & J. 107.

The second is, where the municipal law of a country not recognizing slavery, it is the will of the State to refuse the master all aid to exercise any control over his slave; and if he attempt to do so, in a manner justifiable only by that relation, to prevent the exercise of that control. But no law exists, designed to operate directly on the relation of master and slave, and put an end to that relation. This is said by Lord Stowell, in the case above mentioned to be the law of England, and by Mr. Chief Justice Shaw, in the case of *The Commonwealth v. Ave*, 18 Pick. 193, to be the law of Massachusetts.

The third is, to make a distinction between the case of a master and his slave only temporarily in the country, amino non manendi, and those who are there to reside for permanent or indefinite purposes. This is said by Mr. Wheaton to be the law of Prussia, and was formerly the statute law of several States of our Union. It is necessary in this case to keep in view this distinction between those countries whose laws are designed to act directly on the status of a slave, and make him a freeman, and those where the master can obtain no aid from the laws to enforce his rights.

It is to the last case only that the authorities, out of Missouri, relied on by defendant, apply, when the residence in the non-slaveholding Territory was permanent. In *The Commonwealth v. Aves*, 18 Pick. 218, Mr. Chief Justice Shaw said: "From the principle above stated on which a slave brought here becomes free, to wit; that he becomes entitled to the protection of our laws, it would seem to follow, as a necessary conclusion, that if the slave waives the protection of those laws, and returns to the State where he is held as a slave, his condition is not changed." It was upon this ground, as is apparent from his whole reasoning, that Sir William Scott rests his opinion in the case of *The Slave Grace*. To use one of his expressions, the effect of the law of England was to put the liberty of the slave into a parenthesis. If there had been an Act of Parliament declaring that a slave coming to England with his master should thereby be deemed no longer to be a slave, it is easy to see that the learned judge could not have arrived at the same conclusion. This distinction is very clearly stated and shown by President Tucker, in his opinion in the case of *Betty v. Horton*, 5 Leigh's Va. 615.

See, also, *Hunter v. Fulcher*, 1 Leigh's Va. 172; *Maria Louise v. Marot*, 9 La. 473; *Smith v. Smith*, 13 la. 441; *Thomas v. Generis*, 16 La. 483; *Rankin v. Lydia*, 2 A. K. Marsh. 467; *Davis v. Tingle*, 8 B. Mon. 539; *Griffeth v. Fanny*, Gilm. Va. 143; *Lunsford v. Coquillon*, 2 Mart. N. S. 405; *Josephine v. Poultney*, 1 La. Ann. 329.

But if the Acts of Congress on this subject are valid, the law of the Territory of Wisconsin, within whose limits the residence of the plaintiff and his wife, and their marriage and the birth of one or both of their children, took place, falls under the first category, and is a law operating directly on the status of the slave. By the 8th section of the Act of March 6, 1820, 3 Stat. at L. 548, it was enacted that within this Territory "slavery and involuntary servitude, otherwise than in the punishment of crimes, whereof the parties shall have been duly convicted, shall be, and is hereby forever prohibited: Provided, always, that any person escaping into the same, from whom labor or service is lawfully claimed in any State or Territory of the United States, such fugitive may be lawfully reclaimed, and conveyed to the person claiming his or her labor or services, as aforesaid."

By the Act of April 20, 1836, 4 Stat. at L. 10, passed in the same month and year of the removal of the plaintiff to Fort Snelling, this part of the Territory ceded by France, where Fort

Snelling is, together with so much of this terri- tory of the United States east of the Mississippi as now constitutes the State of Wisconsin, was brought under the name of the Territory of Wisconsin. By the 18th section of this Act, it was enacted, "That the inhabitants of this Territory shall be entitled to and enjoy all and singular the rights, privileges and advantages, granted and secured to the people of the Territory of the United States northwest of the River Ohio, by the articles of compact contained in the Ordinance for the government of said Territory, passed on the 13th day of July, 1787; and shall be subject to all the restrictions and prohibitions in said articles of compact imposed upon the peo- ple of the said Territory." The 6th article of that compact is, "there shall be neither slavery nor involuntary servitude in the said Territory, oth- erwise than in the punishment of crimes, where- of the party shall have been duly convicted: Provided, always, that any person escaping into the same, from whom labor or service is lawful- ly claimed in any one of the original States, such fugitive may be lawfully reclaimed, and con- veyed to the person claiming his or her labor or service, as aforesaid." By other provisions of this Act establishing the Territory of Wisconsin, the laws of the United States, and the then existing laws of the State of Michigan, are extended over the Territory; the latter being subject to alter- ation and repeal by the legislative power of the Territory created by the Act.

Fort Snelling was within the Territory of Wisconsin, and these laws were extended over it. The Indian title to that site for a military post had been acquired from the Sioux nation as early as September 23, 1805 (Am. State Papers, Indian Affairs, Vol. I. p. 744), and until the erec- tion of the territorial government, the persons at that post were governed by the Rules and Articles of War, and such laws of the United States, including the 8th section of the Act of March 6, 1820, prohibiting slavery, as were applicable to their condition; but after the erec- tion of the Territory, and the extension of the laws of the United States and the laws of Michigan over the whole of the Territory, including this military post, the persons residing there were under the dominion of those laws in all particulars to which the Rules and Articles of War did not apply.

It thus appears that, by these Acts of Congress, not only was a general system of

municipal law borrowed from the State of Michigan, which did not tolerate slavery, but it was positively enacted that slavery and involun- tary servitude, with only one exception, specifi- cally described, should not exist there. It is not simply that slavery is not recognized and cannot be aided by the municipal law. It is recognized for the purpose of being absolutely prohibited, and declared incapable of existing within the Territory, save in the instance of a fugitive slave.

It would not be easy for the Legislature to employ more explicit language to signify its will that the status of slavery should not exist within the Territory, than the words found in the Act of 1820, and in the Ordinance of 1787; and if any doubt could exist concerning their application to cases of masters coming into the Territory with their slaves to reside, that doubt must yield to the inference required by the words of excep- tion. That exception is, of cases of fugitive slaves. An exception from a prohibition marks the extent of the prohibition; for it would be absurd, as well as useless, to except from a prohibition a case not contained within it. 9 Wheat. 200. I must conclude, therefore, that it was the will of Congress that the state of involuntary servitude of a slave, coming into the Territory with his master, should cease to exist. The Supreme Court of Missouri so held in *Rachel v. Walker,* 4 Mo. 350, which was the case of a military officer going into the Territory with two slaves.

But it is a distinct question, whether the law of Missouri recognized and allowed effect to the change wrought in the status of the plaintiff, by force of the laws of the Territory of Wisconsin.

I say the law of Missouri, because a judicial tribunal, in one State or nation, can recognize personal rights acquired by force of the law of any other State or nation, only so far as it is the law of the former State that those rights should be recognized. But, in the absence of positive law to the contrary, the will of every civilized State must be presumed to be to allow such effect to foreign laws as is in accordance with the settled rules of international law. And legal tribunals are bound to act on this presumption. It may be assumed that the motive of the State in allowing such operation to foreign laws is what has been termed comity. But, as has justly been said (per Chief Justice Taney, 13 Pet. 589), it is the comity of the State, not of the court. The judges have nothing to do with the motive of the State. Their duty is simply to ascertain and give effect to its will. And when it is found by them that its will to depart from a rule of international law has not been manifested by the State, they are bound to assume that its will is to give effect to it. Undoubtedly, every sovereign State may refuse to recognize a change, wrought by the law of a foreign State, on the status of a person, while within such foreign State, even in cases where the rules of international law require that recognition. Its will to refuse such recognition may be manifested by what we term statute law, or by the customary law of the State. It is within the province of its judicial tribunals to inquire and adjudge whether it appears, from the statute or customary law of the State, to be the will of the State to refuse to recognize such changes of status by force of foreign law, as the rules of the law of nations require to be recognized. But, in my opinion, it is not within the province of any judicial tribunal to refuse such recognition from any political considerations, or any view it may take of the exterior political relations between the State and one or more foreign States, or any impressions it may have that a change of foreign opinion and action on the subject of slavery may afford a reason why the State should change its own action. To understand and give just effect to such considerations, and to change the action of the State in consequence of them, are functions of diplomatists and legislators, not of judges.

The inquiry to be made on this part of the case is, therefore, whether the State of Missouri has, by its statute, or its customary law, manifested its will to displace any rule of international law, applicable to a change of the status of a slave, by foreign law.

I have not heard it suggested that there was any statute of the State of Missouri bearing on this question. The customary law of Missouri is the common law, introduced by statute in 1816. 1 Ter. Laws, 436. And the common law, as Blackstone says (4 Com. 67) adopts, in its full extent, the law of nations, and holds it to be a part of the law of the land.

I know of no sufficient warrant for declaring that any rule of international law, concerning the recognition, in that State, of a change of status, wrought by an extraterritorial law, has been displaced or varied by the will of the State of Missouri.

I proceed, then, to inquire what the rules of international law prescribe concerning the change of status of the plaintiff wrought by the law of the Territory of Wisconsin.

It is generally agreed by writers upon international law, and the rule has been judicially applied in a great number of cases, that wherever any question may arise concerning the status of a person, it must be determined according to that law which has next previously rightfully operated on and fixed that status. And further, that the laws of a country do not rightfully operate upon and fix the status of persons who are within its limits in itinere, or who are abiding there for definite temporary purposes, as for health, curiosity, or occasional business; that these laws, known to writers on public and private international law as personal statutes, operate only on the inhabitants of the country. Not that it is or can be denied that each independent nation may, if it thinks fit, apply them to all persons within their limits. But when this is done, not in conformity with the principles of international law, other States are not understood to be willing to recognize or allow effect to such applications of personal statutes.

It becomes necessary, therefore, to inquire whether the operation of the laws of the Territory of Wisconsin upon the status of the plaintiff was or was not such an operation as these principles of international law require other States to recognize and allow effect to.

And this renders it needful to attend to the particular facts and circumstances of this case. It appears that this case came on for trial before the Circuit Court and a jury, upon an issue, in substance, whether the plaintiff, together with his wife and children, were the slaves of the defendant.

The court instructed the jury that, "upon the facts in this case, the law is with the defendant." This withdrew from the jury the consideration and decision of every matter of fact. The evidence in the case consisted of written admissions, signed by the counsel of the parties. If the case had been submitted to the judgment of the court, upon an agreed statement of facts, entered of record, in place of a special verdict, it would have been necessary for the court below, and for this court, to pronounce its judgment solely on those facts, thus agreed, without inferring any other facts therefrom. By the rules of the common law applicable to such a case, and by force of the 7th article of the Amendments of the Constitution, this court is precluded from finding any fact not agreed to by the parties on the record. No submission to the court on a statement of facts was made. It was a trial by jury, in which certain admissions, made by the parties were the evidence. The jury were not only competent, but were bound to draw from that evidence every inference which, in their judgment exercised according to the rules of law, it would warrant. The Circuit Court took from the jury the power to draw any inferences form the admissions made by the parties, and decided the case for the defendant. This course can be justified here, if at all, only by its appearing that upon the facts agreed, and all such inferences of fact favorable to the plaintiff's case, as the jury might have been warranted in drawing from those admissions, the law was with the defendant. Otherwise, the plaintiff would be deprived of the benefit of his trial by jury, by whom, for aught we can know, those inferences favorable to his case would have been drawn.

The material facts agreed, bearing on this part of the case, are, that Dr. Emerson, the plaintiff's master, resided about two years at the military post of Fort Snelling, being a surgeon in the Army of the United States, his domicil of origin being unknown; and what, if anything, he had done, to preserve or change his domicil prior to his residence at Rock Island, being also unknown.

Now, it is true, that under some circumstances the residence of a military officer at a particular place, in the discharge of his official duties does not amount to the acquisition of a technical domicil. But it cannot be affirmed, with correctness, that it never does. There being actual residence, and this being presumptive evidence of domicil, all the circumstances of the case must be considered, before a legal conclusion can be reached, that his place of residence is not his domicil. If a military officer, stationed at a particular post, should entertain an exception that his residence there would be indefinitely protracted, and in consequence should remove his family to the place where his duties were to be discharged, form a permanent domestic establishment there, exercise there the civil rights and discharge the civil duties of an inhabitant, while he did no act and manifested no intent to have a domicil elsewhere, I think no one would say that the mere fact that he was himself liable to be called away by the orders of the Government would prevent his acquisition of a technical domicil at the place of the residence of himself and his family. In other words, I do not think a military officer incapable of acquiring a domicil. *Bruce v. Bruce,* 2 Bos. & P. 230; *Monroe v. Douglas,* 5 Madd. Ch. 379. This being so this case stands thus: there was evidence before the jury that Emerson resided about two years at Fort Snelling, in the Territory of Wisconsin. This may or may not have been with such intent as to make it his technical domicil. The presumption is that it was. It is so laid down by this court in *Ennis v. Smith,* 14 How. 400, and the authorities in support of the position are there referred to. His intent was a question of fact for the jury. *Fitchburg v. Winchendon,* 4 Cush 190.

The case was taken from the jury. If they had power to find that the presumption of the necessary intent had not been rebutted, we cannot say on this record, that Emerson had not his technical domicil at Fort Snelling. But, for reason which I shall now proceed to give, I do not deem it necessary in this case to determine the question of the technical domicil of Dr. Emerson.

It must be admitted that the inquiry whether the law of a particular country has rightfully fixed the status of a person, so that in accordance with the principles of international law that status should be recognized in other jurisdictions, ordinarily depends on the question whether the person was domiciled in the country whose laws are asserted to have fixed his status. But, in the United States, questions of this kind may arise, where an attempt to decide solely with reference to technical domicil, tested by the rules which are applicable to changes of places of abode from one country to another, would not be consistent with sound principles. And in my judgment, this is one of those cases.

The residence of the plaintiff, who was taken by his master, Dr. Emerson, as a slave, from Missouri, to the State of Illinois, and thence to the Territory of Wisconsin, must be deemed to have been for the time being, and until he asserted his own separate intention, the same as the residence of his master; and the inquiry, whether the personal statutes of the Territory were rightfully extended over the plaintiff, and ought, in accordance with the rules of international law, to be allowed to fix his status, must depend upon the circumstances under which Dr. Emerson went into that Territory, and remained there;

and upon the further question, whether anything was there rightfully done by the plaintiff to cause those personal statutes to operate on him.

Dr. Emerson was an officer in the Army of the United States. He went into the Territory to discharge his duty to the United States. The place was out of the jurisdiction of any particular State, and within the exclusive jurisdiction of the United States. It does not appear where the domicil of origin of Dr. Emerson was, nor whether or not he had lost it, and gained another domicil, nor of what particular State, if any, he was a citizen.

On what ground can it be denied that all valid laws of the United States, Constitutionally enacted by Congress for the government of the Territory, rightfully extended over an officer of the United States and his servant who went into the Territory to remain there for an indefinite length of time, to take part in its civil or military affairs? They were not foreigners, coming from abroad. Dr. Emerson was a citizen of the country which had exclusive jurisdiction over the Territory; and not only a citizen, but he went there in a public capacity, in the service of the same sovereignty which made the laws. Whatever those laws might be, whether of the kind denominated personal statutes, or not, so far as they were intended by the legislative will, constitutionally expressed, to operate on him and his servant, and on the relations between them, they had a rightful operation, and no other State or country can refuse to allow that those laws might rightfully operate on the plaintiff and his servant, because such a refusal would be a denial that the United States could, by laws constitutionally enacted, govern their own servants, residing on their own territory, over which the United States had the exclusive control, and in respect to which they are an independent sovereign power. Whether the laws now in question were constitutionally enacted, I repeat once more, is a separate question. But, assuming that they were, and that they operated directly on the status of the plaintiff, I consider that no other State or country could question the rightful power of the United States so to legislate, or, consistently with the settled rules of international law could refuse to recognize the effects of such legislation upon the status of their officers and servants, as valid everywhere.

This alone would, in my apprehension, be sufficient to decide this question.

But there are other facts stated on the record which should not be passed over. It is agreed that in the year 1836, the plaintiff, while residing in the Territory, was married, with the consent of Dr. Emerson, to Harriet, named in the declaration as his wife, and that Eliza and Lizzie were the children of that marriage, the first named having been born on the Mississippi River, north of the line of Missouri, and the other having been born after their return to Missouri. And the inquiry is, whether, after the marriage of the plaintiff in the Territory, with the consent of Dr. Emerson, any other State or country can, consistently with the settled rules of international law, refuse to recognize and treat him as a free man, when suing for the liberty of himself, his wife, and the children of that marriage. It is in reference to his status, as viewed in other States and countries, that the contract of marriage and the birth of children becomes strictly material. At the same time, it is proper to observe that the female to whom he was married having been taken to the same military post of Fort Snelling as a slave, and Dr. Emerson claiming also to be her master at the time of her marriage, her status, and that of the children of the marriage, are also affected by the same consideration.

If the laws of Congress governing the Territory of Wisconsin were constitutional and valid laws, there can be no doubt these parties were capable of contracting a lawful marriage, attended with all the usual civil rights and obligations of that condition. In that Territory they were absolutely free persons, having full capacity to enter into the civil contract of marriage.

It is a principle of international law, settled beyond controversy in England and America, that a marriage, valid by the law of the place where it was contracted, and not in fraud of the law of any other place, is valid everywhere: and that no technical domicil at the place of the contract is necessary to make it so. See Bishop on mar. and Div. 125–129, where the cases are collected.

If, in Missouri, the plaintiff were held to be a slave, the validity and operation of his contract of marriage must be denied. He can have no legal rights; of course, not those of a husband and father. And the same is true of his wife and children. The denial of his rights is the denial of theirs. So that, though lawfully married in the Territory, when they came out of it, into the State of Missouri, they were no longer husband and wife; and a child of that lawful marriage,

SLAVERY

DRED SCOTT V.
SANDFORD

SLAVERY

DRED SCOTT V.
SANDFORD

though born under the same dominion where its parents contracted a lawful marriage, is not the fruit of that marriage, nor the child of its father, but subject to the maxim, *partus sequitur ventrem.*

It must be borne in mind that in this case there is no ground for the injury, whether it be the will of the State of Missouri not to recognize the validity of the marriage of a fugitive slave, who escapes into a State or country where slavery is not allowed, and there contracts a marriage; or the validity of such a marriage, where the master, being a citizen of the State of Missouri, voluntarily goes with his slave in itinere, into a State or country which does not permit slavery to exist, and the slave there contracts marriage without the consent of his master; for in this case, it is agreed, Dr. Emerson did consent; and no further question can arise concerning his rights, so far as their assertion is inconsistent with the validity of the marriage. Nor do I know of any ground for the assertion that this marriage was in fraud of any law of Missouri. It has been held by this court, that a bequest of property by a master to his slave, by necessary implication entitles the slave to his freedom; because, only as a freeman could he take and hold the bequest. *Legrand v. Darnall,* 2 Pet. 664. It has also been held, that when a master goes with his slave to reside for an indefinite period in a State where slavery is not tolerated, this operates as an act of manumission; because it is sufficiently expressive of the consent of the master that the slave should be free. 2 Marsh. Ky. 470; 14 Mart. La. 401.

What, then, shall we say of the consent of the master, that the slave may contract a lawful marriage attended with all the civil rights and duties which belong to that relation; that he may enter into a relation which none but a free man can assume—a relation which involves not only the rights and duties of the slave, but those of the other party to the contract, and of their descendants to the remotest generation? In my judgment, there can be no more effectual abandonment of the legal rights of a master over his slave, than by the consent of the master that the slave should enter into a contract of marriage, in a free State, attended by all the civil rights and obligations which belong to that condition.

And any claim by Dr. Emerson, or anyone claiming under him, the effect of which is to deny the validity of this marriage, and the lawful paternity of the children born from it, wherever asserted, is, in my judgment, a claim inconsistent with good faith and sound reason, as well as with the rules of international law. And I go further: in my opinion, a law of the State of Missouri, which should thus annual marriage, lawfully contracted by these parties while resident in Wisconsin, not in fraud of any law of Missouri, or of any right of Dr. Emerson, who consented thereto, would be a law impairing the obligation of a contract, and within the prohibition of the Constitution of the United States. See 4 Wheat. 629, 695, 696.

To avoid misapprehension on this important and difficult subject, I will state, distinctly, the conclusions at which I have arrived. They are:

First. The rules of international law respecting the emancipation of slaves, by the rightful operation of the laws of another State or country upon the status of the slave, while resident in such foreign State or country, are part of the common law of Missouri, and have not been abrogated by any statute law of that State.

Second. The laws of the United States, constitutionally enacted, which operated directly on and changed the status of a slave coming into the Territory of Wisconsin with his master, who went thither to reside for an indefinite length of time, in the performance of his duties as an officer of the United States, had a righful operation on the status of the slave, and it is conformity with the rules of international law that this change of status should be recognized everywhere.

Third. The laws of the United States, in operation in the Territory of Wisconsin at the time of the plaintiff's residence there, did act directly on the status of the plaintiff, and change his status to that of a free man.

Fourth. The plaintiff and his wife were capable of contracting, and, with the consent of Dr. Emerson, did contract a marriage in that Territory, valid under its laws; and the validity of this marriage cannot be questioned in Missouri, save by showing that it was in fraud of the laws of that State, or of some right derived from them; which cannot be shown in this case, because the master consented to it.

Fifth. That the consent of the master that his slave, residing in a country which does not tolerate slavery, may enter into a lawful contract of marriage, attended with the civil rights and duties which belong to that condition, is an effectual act of emancipation. And the law does not enable Dr. Emerson, or anyone claiming under him, to assert a title to the married persons as slaves, and thus destroy the obligation of the contract of marriage, and bastardize their issue, and reduce them to slavery.

But it is insisted that the Supreme Court of Missouri has settled this case by its decision in *Scott v. Emerson,* 15 Mo. 576; and that this decision is in conformity with the weight of authority elsewhere, and with sound principles. If the Supreme Court of Missouri had placed its decision on the ground that it appeared Dr. Emerson never became domiciled in the Territory, and so its laws could not rightfully operate on him and his slave; and the facts that he went there to reside indefinitely, as an officer of the United States, and that the plaintiff was lawfully married there, with Dr. Emerson's consent, were left out of view, the decision would find support in other cases, and I might not be prepared to deny its correctness. But the decision is not rested on this ground. The domicil of Dr. Emerson in that Territory is not questioned in that decision: and it is placed on a broad denial, of the operation, in Missouri, of the law of any foreign State or country, upon the status of a slave, going with his master from Missouri into such foreign State or country, even though they went thither to become, and actually became, permanent inhabitants of such foreign State or country, the laws whereof acted directly on the status of the slave, and changed his status to that of a freeman.

To the correctness of such a decision I cannot assent. In my judgment, the opinion of the majority of the court in that case is in conflict with its previous decisions, with a great weight of judicial authority in other slaveholding States, and with fundamental principles of private international law. Mr. Chief Justice Gamble in his dissenting opinion in that case, said:

"I regard the question as conclusively settled by repeated adjudications of this court; and if I doubted or denied the propriety of those decisions, I would not feel myself any more at liberty to overturn them, than I would any other series of decisions by which the law upon any other question had been settled. There is with me nothing in the law of slavery which distinguishes it from the law on any other subject, or allows any more accommodation to the temporary excitements which have gathered around it

. . . But in the midst of all such excitement, it is proper that the judicial mind, calm and self-balanced, should adhere to principles established when there was no feeling to disturb the view of the legal questions upon which the rights of parties depend."

"In this State, it has been recognized from the beginning of the government as a correct position in law, that the master who takes his slave to reside in a State or Territory where slavery is prohibited, thereby emancipates his slave." *Whinney v. Whitesides,* 1 Mo. 473; *Le Grange v. Chouteau,* 2 Mo. 20; *Milley v. Smith,* 2 Mo.36; *Ralph v. Duncan,* 3 Mo. 194; *Julia v. McKinney,* 3 Mo. 270; *Nat v. Ruddle,* 3 Mo. 400; *Rachel v. Walker,* 4 Mo. 350; *Wilson v. Melvin,* 4 Mo. 592.

Chief Justice Gamble has also examined the decisions of the courts of other States in which slavery is established, and finds them in accordance with these preceding decisions of the Supreme Court of Missouri to which he refers.

It would be a useless parade of learning for me to go over the ground which he has so fully and ably occupied.

But it is further insisted we are bound to follow this decision. I do not think so. In this case, it is to be determined what laws of the United States were in operation in the Territory of Wisconsin, and what was their effect on the status of the plaintiff. Could the plaintiff contract a lawful marriage there? Does any law of the State of Missouri impair the obligation of the contract of marriage, destroy his rights as a husband, bastardize the use of marriage, and reduce them to a state of slavery?

The questions which arise exclusively under the Constitution and laws of the United States, this court, under the Constitution and laws of the United States, has the rightful authority finally to decide. And if we look beyond these questions, we come to the consideration whether the rules of international law, which are part of the laws of Missouri until displaced by some statute not alleged to exist, do or do not require the status of the plaintiff, as fixed by the laws of the Territory of Wisconsin, to be recognized in Missouri. Upon such a question, not depending on any statute or local usage, but on principles of universal jurisprudence, this court has repeatedly asserted it could not hold itself bound by the decisions of State Courts, however great respect might be felt for their learning, ability, and impartiality. See *Swift v. Tyson,* 16

Pet. 1; *Carpenter v. The Providence Ins. Co.* 16 Pet. 495; *Foxcroft v. Mallet,* 4 How. 353; *Rowan v. Runnels,* 5 How. 134.

Some reliance has been placed on the fact that the decision in the Supreme Court of Missouri was between these parties, and the suit there was abandoned to obtain another trial in the courts of the United States.

In *Homer v. Brown,* 16 How. 354, this court made a decision upon the construction of a devise of lands, in direct opposition to the unanimous opinion of the Supreme Court of Massachusetts, between the same parties, respecting the same subject matter—the claimant having become nonsuit in the State Court, in order to bring his action in the Circuit Court of the United States. I did not sit in that case, having been of counsel for one of the parties while at the bar; but, on examining the report of the argument of the counsel for the plaintiff in error, I find they made the point, that this court ought to give effect to the construction put upon by the will by the State Court, to the end that rights respecting lands may be governed by one law, and that the law of the place where the lands are situated; that they referred to the state decision of the case, reported in 3 Cushing, 390, and to many decisions of this court. But this court does not seem to have considered the point of sufficient importance to notice it in their opinions. In *Miller v. Austin,* 13 How. 218, an action was brought by the endorsee of a written promise. The question was, whether it was negotiable under a statute of Ohio. The Supreme Court of that State having decided it was not negotiable, the plaintiff became nonsuit, and brought his action in the Circuit Court of the United States. The decision of the Supreme Court of the State, reported in 4 Ves. L. J. 527, was relied on. This court unanimously held the paper to be negotiable.

When the decisions of the highest court of a State are directly in conflict with each other, it has been repeatedly held, here, that the last decision is not necessarily to be taken as the rule. *State Bank v. Knoop,* 16 How. 369; *Pease v. Peck,* 18 How. 599.

To these considerations I desire to add, that it was not made known to the Supreme Court of Missouri, so far as appears, that the plaintiff was married in Wisconsin with the consent of Dr. Emerson, and it is not made known to us that Dr. Emerson was a citizen of Missouri, a fact to

which that court seem to have attached much importance.

Sitting here to administer the law between these parties, I do not feel at liberty to surrender my own convictions of what the law requires, to the authority of the decision in 15 Missouri Reports.

I have thus far assumed, merely for the purpose of the argument, that the laws of the United States, respecting slavery in this Territory, were Constitutionally enacted by Congress. It remains to inquire whether they are constitutional and binding laws.

In the argument of this part of the case at bar, it was justly considered by all the counsel to be necessary to ascertain the source of the power of Congress over the Territory belonging to the United States. Until this is ascertained, it is not possible to determine the extent of that power. On the one side it was maintained that the Constitution contains no express grant of power to organize and govern what is known to the laws of the United States as a Territory. That whatever power of this kind exists, is derived by implication from the capacity of the United States to hold and acquire territory out of the limits of any State, and the necessity for its having some government.

On the other side it was insisted that the Constitution has not failed to make an express provision for this end, and that it is found in the 3rd Section of the 4th Article of the Constitution.

To determine which of these is the correct view, it is needful to advert to some facts respecting this subject, which existed when the Constitution was framed and adopted. It will be found that these facts not only shed much light on the question, whether the framers of the Constitution omitted to make a provision concerning the power of Congress to organize and govern Territories, but they will also aid in the construction of any provision which may have been made respecting this subject.

Under the Confederation, the unsettled territory within the limits of the United States had been a subject of deep interest. Some of the States insisted that these lands were within their chartered boundaries, and that they had succeeded to the title of the Crown to the soil. On the other hand, it was argued that the vacant lands had been acquired by the United States by the war carried on by them under a common government and for the common interest.

This dispute was further complicated by unsettled questions of boundary among several States. It not only delayed the accession of Maryland to the Confederation, but at one time seriously threatened its existence. 5 Jour. of Cong. 208, 442. Under the pressure of these circumstances, Congress earnestly recommended to the several States a cession of their claims and rights to the United States. 5 Jour. of Cong. 442. And before the Constitution was framed, it had been begun. That by New York had been made on the 1st day of March, 1781; that of Virginia on the 1st day of March, 1784; that of Massachusetts on the 19th day of April, 1785, that of Connecticut on the 14th day of September, 1786; that of South Carolina on the 8th day of August, 1787, while the convention for framing the Constitution was in session.

It is very material to observe, in this connection, that each of these Acts cedes, in terms, to the United States, as well the jurisdiction as the soil.

It is also equally important to note that, when the Constitution was framed and adopted, this plan of vesting in the United States, for the common good, the great tracts of ungranted lands claimed by the several States, in which so deep an interest was felt, was yet incomplete. It remained for North Carolina and Georgia to cede their extensive and valuable claims. These were made, by North Carolina on the 25th day of February, 1790, and by Georgia on the 24th day of April, 1802. The terms of these last mentioned cessions will hereafter be noticed in another connection; but I observe here that each of them distinctly shows, upon its face, that they were not only in execution of the general plan proposed by the Congress of the Confederation, but of a formed purpose of each of these States, existing when the assent of their respective people was given to the Constitution of the United States.

It appears, then, that when the Federal Constitution was framed and presented to the people of the several States for their consideration, the unsettled territory was viewed as justly applicable to the common benefit, so far as it then had or might attain thereafter a pecuniary value; and so far as it might become the seat of new States, to be admitted into the Union upon an equal footing with the original States. And also that relations of the United States to that unsettled territory were of different kinds. The titles of the States of New York, Virginia, Massachusetts, Connecticut and South Carolina, as well of soil as of jurisdiction had been transferred to the United States. North Carolina and Georgia had not actually made transfers, but a confident expectation, founded on their appreciation of the justice of the general claim, and fully justified by the results, was entertained, that these cessions would be made. The Ordinance of 1787 had made provision for the temporary government of so much of the territory, actually ceded, as lay northwest of the River Ohio.

But it must have been apparent, both to the framers of the Constitution and the people of the several States who were to act upon it, that the government thus provided for could not continue, unless the Constitution should confer on the United States the necessary powers to continue it. That temporary government, under the Ordinance, was to consist of certain officers, to be appointed by and responsible to the Congress of the Confederation; their powers had been conferred and defined by the ordinance. So far as it provided for the temporary government of the Territory, it was an ordinary Act of legislation, deriving its force from the legislative power of Congress, and depending for its vitality upon the continuance of that legislative power. But the officers to be appointed for the Northwestern Territory, after the adoption of the Constitution, must necessarily be officers of the United States, and not of the Congress of the Confederation; appointed and commissioned by the President, and exercising powers derived from the United States under the Constitution.

Such was the relation between the United States and the Northwestern Territory, which all reflecting men must have foreseen would exist, when the government created by the Constitution should supersede that of the Confederation. That if the new government should be without power to govern this Territory, it could not appoint and commission officers, and send them into the Territory, to exercise their legislative, judicial and executive power; and that this Territory, which was even then foreseen to be so important, both politically and financially, to all the existing States, must be left not only without the control of the General Government, in respect to its future political relations to the rest of the States, but absolutely without any government, save what its inhabitants, acting in their primary capacity, might from time to time create for themselves.

But this Northwestern Territory was not the only Territory, the soil and jurisdiction whereof were then understood to have been ceded to the United States. The cession by South Carolina, made in August, 1787, was of "all the territory included within the River Mississippi, and a line beginning at that part of the said river which is intersected by the southern boundary of North Carolina, and continuing along the said boundary line until it intersects the ridge or chain of mountains which divides the Eastern from the Western waters; then to be continued along the top of the said ridge of mountains, until it intersects a line to be drawn due west form the head of the southern branch of the Tugaloo River, to the said mountains; and thence to run a due west course to the River Mississippi."

It is true that by subsequent explorations it was ascertained that the source of the Tugaloo River, upon which the title of the South Carolina depended, was so far to the northward, that the transfer conveyed only a narrow slip of land, about twelve miles wide, lying on the top of the ridge of mountains, and extending from the northern boundary of Georgia to the southern boundary of North Carolina. But this was a discovery made long after the cession, and there can be no doubt that the State of South Carolina, in making the cession, and the Congress in accepting it, viewed it as a transfer to the United States of the soil and jurisdiction of an extensive and important part of the unsettled territory ceded by the Crown of Great Britain by the Treaty of Peace, though its quantity or extent then remained to be ascertained.[5]

It must be remembered also, as has been already stated, that not only was there a confident expectation entertained by the other States, that North Carolina and Georgia would complete the plan already so far executed by New York, Virginia, Massachusetts, Connecticut, and South Carolina, but that the opinion was in no small degree prevalent, that the just title to the "back country," as it was termed, had vested in the United States by the Treaty of Peace, and could not rightfully be claimed by an individual State.

There is another consideration applicable to this part of the subject, and entitled, in my judgment, to great weight.

The Congress of the Confederation had assumed the power not only to dispose of the lands ceded, but to institute governments and make laws for their inhabitants. In other words, they had proceeded to act under the cession, which, as we have seen, was as well of the jurisdiction as of the soil. This ordinance was passed on the 13th of July, 1787. The Convention for framing the Constitution was then in session at Philadelphia. The proof is direct and decisive, that it was know to the Convention.[6] It is equally clear that it was admitted and understood not to be within the legitimate powers of the Confederation to pass this Ordinance. *Jefferson's Works*, Vol. IX. pp. 251, 276; *Federalist*, Nos. 38, 43.

The importance of conferring on the new government regular powers commensurate with the objects to be attained, and thus avoiding the alternative of a failure to execute the trust assumed by the acceptance of the cessions made and expected, or its execution by usurpation, could scarcely fail to be perceived. That it was in fact perceived, is clearly shown by the *Federalist* (No. 38), where this very argument is made use of in commendation of the Constitution. Keeping these facts in view, it may confidently be asserted that there is very strong reason to believe, before we examine the Constitution itself, that the necessity for a competent grant of power to hold, dispose of, and govern territory, ceded and expected to be ceded, could not have escaped the attention of those who framed or adopted the Constitution; and that if it did not escape their attention, it would not fail to be adequately provided for.

Any other conclusion would involve the assumption that a subject of the gravest national concern, respecting which the small States felt

---

[5] Note by Mr. Justice Curtis. This statement that some territory did actually pass by this cession, is taken from the opinion of the court, delivered by Mr. Justice Wayne, in the case of *Howard v. Ingersoll*, reported in 13 How. 405. It is an obscure matter, and, on some examination of it, I have been led to doubt whether any territory actually passed this cession. But as the fact is not important to the argument, I have not thought it necessary further to investigate it.

[6] It was published in a newspaper at Philadelphia, in May, and a copy of it was sent by R. H. Lee to Gen. Washington, on the 15th of July. See p. 261, *Cor. of Am. Rev.* Vol. IV., and *Writings of Washington*, Vol. IX. p. 174.

so much jealousy that it had been almost an insurmountable obstacle to the formation of the Confederation, and as to which all the States had deep pecuniary and political interests, and which had been so recently and constantly agitated, was nevertheless overlooked; or that such a subject was not overlooked, but designedly left unprovided for, though it was manifestly a subject of common concern, which belonged to the care of the General Government, and adequate provision for which could not fail to be deemed necessary and proper.

The admission of new States, to be framed out of the ceded territory, early attracted the attention of the Convention. Among the resolutions introduced by Mr. Randolph, on the 29th of May, was one on this subject (Res. No. 10, 5 Elliot, 128), which having been affirmed in Committee of the Whole, on the 5th of June (5 Elliot, 156), and reported to the Convention on the 13th of June (5 Elliot, 190), was referred to the Committee of Detail, to prepare the Constitution, on the 26th of July (5 Elliot, 376). This committee reported an article for the admission of new States "lawfully constituted or established." Nothing was said concerning the power of Congress to prepare or form such States. This omission struck Mr. Madison, who, on the 18th of August (5 Elliott, 439), moved for the insertion of power to dispose of the unappropriated lands of the United States, and to institute temporary governments for new States arising therein.

On the 29th of August (5 Elliot, 492), the report of the committee was taken up, and after debate, which exhibited great diversity of views concerning the proper mode of providing for the subject, arising out of the supposed diversity of interests of the large and small States, and between those which had and those which had not unsettled territory, but no difference of opinion respecting the propriety and necessity of some adequate provision for the subject, Gouverneur Morris moved the clause as it stands in the Constitution. This met with general approbation, and was at once adopted. The whole section is as follows:

"New States may be admitted by the Congress into this Union; but no new States shall be formed or erected within the jurisdiction of any other State, nor any State be formed by the junction of two or more States, or parts of States, without consent of the Legislatures of the States concerned, as well as of Congress."

The Congress shall have power to dispose of, and make all needful rules and regulations respecting the territory or other property belonging to the United States; and nothing in this Constitution shall be so construed as to prejudice any claims of the United States or any particular State."

That Congress has some power to institute temporary governments over the Territory, I believe all agree; and, if it be admitted that the necessity of some power to govern the Territory of the United States could not and did not escape the attention of the Convention and the people, and the necessity is so great that, in the absence of any express grant, it is strong enough to raise an implication of the existence of that power, it would seem to follow that it is also strong enough to afford material aid in construing an express grant of power respecting that Territory; and that they who maintain the existence of the power, without finding any words at all in which it is conveyed, should be willing to receive a reasonable interpretation of language of the Constitution, manifestly intended to relate to the Territory, and to convey to Congress some authority concerning it.

It would seem, also, that when we find the subject matter of the growth and formation and admission of new States, and the disposal of the Territory of these ends, were under consideration, and that some provision therefor was expressly made, it is improbable that it would be, in its terms, a grossly inadequate provision; and that an indispensably necessary power to institute temporary governments, and to legislate for the inhabitants of the Territory, was passed silently by, and left to be deduced from the necessity of the case.

In the argument at the bar, great attention has been paid to the meaning of the word "territory."

Ordinarily, when the territory of a sovereign power is spoken of, it refers to that tract of country which is under the political jurisdiction of that sovereign power. Thus Chief Justice Marshall, in *United States v. Bevans,* 3 Wheat. 386, says: "What, then, is the extent of jurisdiction which a State possess? We answer, without hesitation, the jurisdiction of a State is co-extensive with its territory." Examples might easily be multiplied of this use of the word, but they are unnecessary, because it is familiar. But the word

SLAVERY

DRED SCOTT V. SANDFORD

"territory" is not used in this broad and general sense in this clause of the Constitution.

At the time of the adoption of the Constitution, the United States held a great tract of country northwest of the Ohio; another tract, then of unknown extent, ceded by South Carolina; and a confident expectation was then entertained, and afterwards realized, that they then were or would become the owners of other great tracts, claimed by North Carolina and Georgia. These ceded tracts lay within the limits of the United States, and out of the limits of any particular State; and the cessions embraced the civil and political jurisdiction, and so much of the soil as had not previously been granted to individuals.

These words, "territory belonging to the United States," were not used in the Constitution to describe an abstraction, but to identify and apply to these actual subjects, matter then existing and belonging to the United States, and other similar subjects which might afterwards be acquired; and this being so, all the essential qualities and incidents attending such actual subjects are embraced within the words "territory belonging to the United States," as fully as if each of those essential qualities and incidents had been specifically described.

I say, the essential qualities and incidents. But in determining what were the essential qualities and incidents of the subject with which they were dealing, we must take into consideration not only all the particular facts which were immediately before them, but the great consideration, ever present to the minds of those who framed and adopted the Constitution, that they were making a frame of government for the people of the United States and their posterity, under which they hoped the United States might be, what they have now become, a great and powerful nation, possessing the power to make war and to conclude treaties, and thus to acquire territory. See *Sere v. Pitot,* 6 Cranch, 336; *Am. Ins. Co. v. Canter,* I Pet. 542. With these in view, I turn to examine the clause of the article now in question.

It is said this provision has no application to any territory save that then belonging to the United States. I have already shown that, when the Constitution was framed, a confident expectation was entertained, which was speedily realized, that North Carolina and Georgia would cede their claims to that great Territory which lay west of those States. No doubt has been suggested that the first clause of this same article, which enabled Congress to admit new States, refers to and includes new States to be formed out of this Territory, and expected to be thereafter ceded by North Carolina and Georgia, as well as new States to be formed out of territory northwest of the Ohio, which then had been ceded by Virginia. It must have been seen, therefore, that the same necessity would exist for an authority to dispose of and make all needful regulations respecting this Territory, when ceded, as existed for a like authority respecting territory which had been ceded.

No reason has been suggested why any reluctance should have been felt, by the framers of the Constitution, to apply this provision to all the territory which might belong to the United States, or why any distinction should have been made, founded on the accidental circumstance in no way material as respects the necessity for rules and regulations, or the propriety of conferring on the Congress power to make them. And if we look at the course of the debates in the Convention on this article, we shall find that the then unceded lands, so far from having been left out of view in adopting this article, constituted, in the minds of members, a subject of even paramount importance.

Again; in what an extraordinary position would the limitation of this clause to territory then belonging to the United States, place the Territory which lay within the chartered limits of North Carolina and Georgia. The title to that Territory was then claimed by those States, and by the United States; their respective claims are purposely left unsettled by the express words of this clause; and when cessions were made by those States, they were merely of their claims to this Territory, the United States neither admitting nor denying the validity of those claims; so that it was impossible then, and has ever since remained impossible, to know whether this Territory did or did not then belong to the United States; and, consequently, to know whether it was within or without the authority conferred by this clause, to dispose of and make rules and regulations respecting the territory of the United States. This attributes to the eminent men who acted on this subject a want of ability and forecast, or a want of attention to the known facts upon which they were acting, in which I cannot concur.

There is not, in my judgment, anything in the language, the history, or the subject matter of this article, which restricts its operation to the territory owned by the United States when the Constitution was adopted.

But it is also insisted that provisions of the Constitution respecting territory belonging to the United States do not apply to territory acquired by treaty from a foreign nation. This objection must rest upon the position that the Constitution did not authorize the Federal Government to acquire foreign territory, and consequently has made no provision for its government when acquired; or, that though the acquisition of foreign territory was contemplated by the Constitution, its provisions concerning the admission of new States, and the making of all needful rules and regulations respecting territory belonging to the United States, were not designed to be applicable to territory acquired from foreign nations.

It is undoubtedly true, that at the date of the treaty of 1803, between the United States and France, for the cession of Louisiana, it was made a question, whether the Constitution had conferred on the Executive Department of the Government of the United States power to acquire foreign territory by a treaty.

There is evidence that very grave doubts were then entertained concerning the existence of this power. But that there was then a settled opinion in the executive and legislative branches of the government, that this power did not exist, cannot be admitted, without at the same time imputing to those who negotiated and ratified the Treaty, and passed the laws necessary to carry it into execution, a deliberate and known violation of their oaths to support the Constitution; and whatever doubts may then have existed, the question must now be taken to have been settled. Four distinct acquisitions of foreign territory have been made by as many different treaties, under as many different administrations. Six States, formed on such territory, are now in the Union. Every branch of this government, during a period of more than fifty years, has participated in these transactions. To question their validity now, is vain. As was said by Mr. Chief Justice Marshall, in *The American Insurance Company v. Canter*, 1 Pet. 542, "the Constitution confers absolutely on the government of the Union the powers of making war and of making treaties; consequently, that gov-

ernment possesses the power of acquiring territory, either by conquest or treaty." See *Sere v. Pitot*, 6 Cranch, 336. And I add, it also possesses the power of governing it, when acquired, not by resorting to suppositious powers, nowhere found described in the Constitution, but expressly granted in the authority to make all needful rules and regulations, respecting the Territory of the United States.

There was to be established by the Constitution a frame of government, under which the people of the United States and their posterity were to continue indefinitely. To take one of its provisions, the language of which is broad enough to extend throughout the existence of the government, and embrace all territory belonging to the United States throughout all time, and the purposes and objects of which apply to all Territory of the United States, and narrow it down to territory belonging to the United States when the Constitution was framed, while at the same time it is admitted that the Constitution contemplated and authorized the acquisition, from time to time, of other and foreign territory, seems to me to be an interpretation as inconsistent with the nature and purposes of the instrument, as it is with its language, and I can have no hesitation in rejecting it.

I construe this clause, therefore, as if it had read, Congress shall have power to make all needful rules and regulations respecting the tracts of country, out of the limits of the several States, which the United States have acquired, or may hereafter acquire, by cessions, as well of the jurisdiction as of the soil, so far as the soil may be the property of the party making the cession, at the time of making it.

It has been urged that the words "rules and regulations" are not appropriate terms in which to convey authority to make laws for the government of the Territory.

But it must be remembered that this is a grant of power to the Congress—that it is, therefore, necessarily a grant of power to legislate— and certainly, rules and regulation respecting a particular subject, made by the legislative power of a country, can be nothing but laws. Nor do the particular terms employed, in my judgment, tend in any degree to restrict this legislative power. Power granted to a Legislature to make all needful rules and regulations respecting the

Territory, is a power to pass all needful laws respecting it.

The word regulate, or regulation, is several times used in the Constitution. It is used in the 4th section of the 1st article to describe those laws of the States which prescribe the times, places, and manner, of choosing Senator or Representatives; in the 2d section of the 4th article, to designate the legislative action of a State on the subject of fugitives from service, having a very close relation to the matter of our present inquiry; in the 2d section of the 3d article, to empower Congress to fix the extent of the appellate jurisdiction of this court; and, finally, in the 8th section of the 1st article in the words, "Congress shall have power to regulate commerce."

It is unnecessary to describe the body of legislation which has been enacted under this grant of power; its variety and extent are well known. But it may be mentioned, in passing, that under this power to regulate commerce, Congress has enacted a great system of municipal laws, and extended it over the vessels and crews of the United States on the high seas and in foreign ports, and even over citizens of the United States resident in China; and has established judicatures, with power to inflict even capital punishment within that country.

If, then, this clause does contain a power to legislate respecting the Territory, what are the limits of that power?

To this I answer, that, in common with all the other legislative powers of Congress, it finds limits in the express prohibitions on Congress not to do certain things; that, in the exercise of the legislative power, Congress cannot pass an ex post facto law or bill of attainder; and so in respect to each of the other prohibitions contained in the Constitution.

Besides this, the rules and regulations must be needful. But undoubtedly the question whether a particular rule or regulation be needful, must be finally determined by Congress itself. Whether a law be needful, is a legislative or political, not a judicial, question. Whatever Congress deems needful, is so under the grant of power.

Nor am I aware that it has ever been questioned that laws providing for the temporary government of the settlers on the public lands are needful, not only to prepare them for admission to the Union as States, but even to enable the United States to dispose of the lands.

Without government and social order there can be no property; for without law, its ownership, its use and the power of disposing of it, cease to exist, in the sense in which those words are used and understood in all civilized States.

Since, then, this power was manifestly conferred to enable the United States to dispose of its public lands to settlers, and to admit them into the Union as States, when in the judgment of Congress they should be fitted therefor, since these were the needs provided for, since it is confessed that Government is indispensable to provide for those needs, and the power is, to make all needful rules and regulations respecting the Territory, I cannot doubt that this is a power to govern the inhabitants of the Territory, by such laws as Congress deems needful, until they obtain admission as States.

Whether they should be thus governed solely by laws enacted by Congress, or partly by laws enacted by legislative power conferred by Congress, is one of those questions which depend on the judgment of Congress—a question which of these is needful.

But it is insisted, that whatever other powers Congress may have respecting the Territory of the United States, the subject of negro slavery forms as an exception.

The Constitution declares that Congress shall have power to make "all needful rules and regulation" respecting the Territory belonging to the United States.

The assertion is, though the Constitution says all, it does not mean all—though it says all, without qualification, it means all except such as allow or prohibit slavery. It cannot be doubted that it is incumbent on those who would thus introduce an exception not found in the language of the instrument, to exhibit some solid and satisfactory reason, drawn from the subject matter or the purposes and objects of the clause, the context, or from other provisions of the Constitution, showing that the words employed in this clause are not to be understood, according to their clear, plain, and natural signification.

The subject matter is the Territory of the United States out of the limits of every State, and consequently under the exclusive power of the people of the United States. Their will respecting it, manifested in the Constitution, can be subject to no restriction. The purposes and objects of the clause were the enactment of laws concerning the disposal of the public lands, and the temporary government of the settlers thereon, until new States should be formed. It will not be questioned that, when the Constitution of the United States was framed and adopted, the allowance and the prohibition of negro slavery were recognized subjects of municipal legislation; every State had in some measure acted thereon; and the only legislative Act concerning the Territory—the Ordinance of 1787, which had then so recently been passed—contained a prohibition of slavery. The purpose and object of the clause being to enable Congress to provide a body of municipal law for the government of the settlers, the allowance or the prohibition of slavery comes within the known and recognized scope of that purpose and object.

There is nothing in the context which qualifies the grant of power. The regulations must be "respecting the Territory." An enactment that slavery may or may not exist there, is a regulation respecting the Territory. Regulations must be needful; but is necessarily left to the legislative discretion to determine whether a law be needful. No other clause of the Constitution has been seen by me, which imposes any restriction or makes any exception concerning the power of Congress to allow or prohibit slavery in the territory belonging to the United States.

A practical construction, nearly contemporaneous with the adoption of the Constitution, and continued by repeated instances through a long series of years, may always influence, and in doubtful cases should determine, the judicial mind, on a question of the interpretation of the Constitution. *Stuart v. Laird*, 1 Cranch, 299; *Martin v. Hunter*, 1 Wheat. 304; *Cohens v. Virginia*, 6 Wheat. 264; *Prigg v. Pennsylvania*, 16 Pet. 621; *Cooley v. Port Wardens*, 12 How. 315.

In this view, I proceed briefly to examine the practical construction placed on the clause now in question, so far as it respects the inclusion therein of power to permit or prohibit slavery in the Territories.

It has already been stated, that after the Government of the United States was organized under the Constitution, the temporary government of the Territory northwest of the River Ohio could no longer exist, save under the powers conferred on Congress by the Constitution. Whatever legislative, judicial, or executive authority should be exercised therein could be derived only from the people of the United States under the Constitution. And, accordingly, an Act was passed on the 7th day of August, 1789, 1 Stat. at L. 50, which recites: "Whereas, in order that the Ordinance of the United States in Congress assembled, for the government of the Territory northwest of the River Ohio, may continue to have full effect, it is required that certain provisions should be made, so as to adapt the same to the present Constitution of the United States." It then provides for the appointment by the President of all officers, who, by force of the Ordinance, were to have been appointed by the Congress of the Confederation, and their commission in the manner required by the Constitution; and empowers the Secretary of the Territory to exercise the powers of the Governor in case of the death or necessary absence of the latter.

Here is an explicit declaration of the will the first Congress, of which fourteen members, including Mr. Madison, had been members of the Convention which framed the Constitution, that the Ordinance, one article of which prohibited slavery, "should continue to have good effect." Gen. Washington, who signed this bill, as President, was the President of the Convention.

It does not appear to me to be important, in this connection, that that clause in the Ordinance which prohibited slavery was one of series of articles of what is therein termed a compact. The Congress of the Confederation had no power to make such a compact, nor to act at all on the subject; and after what had been so recently said by Mr. Madison on this subject, in the thirty-eighth number of the *Federalist*, I cannot suppose that he, or any others who voted for this bill, attributed any intrinsic effect to what was denominated in the Ordinance a compact between "the original States and the people and States in the new territory;" there being no new States then in existence in the Territory, with whom a compact could be made, and the few scattered inhabitants, unorganized into a political body, not being capable of becoming a party to a treaty, even if the Congress of the Confederation had had power to make one touching the government of that Territory.

I consider the passage of this law to have been an assertion by the first Congress of the power of the United States to prohibit slavery within this part of the Territory of the United

SLAVERY

DRED SCOTT V. SANDFORD

States; for it clearly shows that slavery was there after to be prohibited there, and it could be prohibited only by an exertion of the power of the United Sates, under the Constitution; no other power being capable of operating within that Territory after the Constitution took effect.

On the 2d of April, 1790, 1 Stat. at L. 106, the first Congress passed an Act accepting a deed of cession by North Carolina of that Territory afterwards erected into the State of Tennessee. The fourth express condition contained in this deed of cession, after providing that the inhabitants of the Territory shall be temporarily governed in the same manner as those beyond the Ohio, is followed by these words: "Provided, always, that no regulations made or to be made by Congress shall tend to emancipate slaves."

This provision shows that it was then understood Congress might make a regulation prohibiting slavery, and that Congress might also allow it to continue to exist in the Territory; and accordingly, when a few days later, Congress passed the Act of May 20th, 1790, 1 Stat. at L. 123, for the government of the Territory south of the River Ohio, it provided, "and the government of the Territory south of the Ohio shall be similar to that now exercised in the Territory northwest of the Ohio, except so far as is otherwise provided in the conditions expressed in an Act of Congress of the present session, entitled 'An Act to accept a cession of the claims of the State of North Carolina to a certain district of western territory.'" Under the government thus established, slavery existed until the Territory became the State of Tennessee.

On the 7th of April, 1798, 1 Stat. at L. 649, an Act was passed to establish a government in the Mississippi Territory in all respects like that exercised in the Territory northwest of the Ohio, "excepting and excluding the last article of the Ordinance made for the government thereof by the late Congress on the 13th day of July, 1787." When the limits of this Territory had been amicably settled with Georgia and the latter ceded all its claim thereto, it was one stipulation in the compact of cession, that the ordinance of July 13th, 1787, "shall in all its parts extend to the Territory contained in the present Act of Cession, that article only excepted which forbids slavery." The government of this Territory was subsequently established and organized under the Act of May 10th, 1800; but so much of the Ordinance as prohibited slavery was not put in operation there.

Without going minutely into the details of each case, I will now give reference to two classes of Acts, in one of which Congress has extended the Ordinance of 1787, including the article prohibiting slavery, over different Territories, and thus exerted its power to prohibit it; in the other, Congress has erected governments over Territories acquired from France and Spain, in which slavery already existed, but refused to apply to them that part of the government under the Ordinance which excluded slavery.

Of the first class are the Act of May 7th, 1800, 2 Stat. at L. 58, for the government of the Indian Territory; the Act of Jan. 11th, 1805, 2 Stat. at L. 309, for the government of Michigan Territory; the Act of May 3d, 1809, 2 Stat. at L. 514, for the government of the Illinois Territory; the Act of April 20th, 1836, 5 Stat. at L. 10, for government of the Territory of Wisconsin; the Act of June 12th, 1838; for the government of the Territory of Iowa; the Act of Aug. 14th, 1848, government of the Territory of Oregon. To These instances should be added the Act of March 6th, 1820, 3 Stat. at L. 548, prohibiting slavery in the Territory acquired from France, being northwest of Missouri, and north of thirty-six degrees thirty minutes north latitude.

Of the second class, in which Congress refused to interfere with slavery already existing under the municipal law of France or Spain, and established governments by which slavery was recognized and allowed, are: the Act of March 26th, 1804, 2 Stat. at L. 283, for the government of Louisiana; the Act of March 2d, 1805, 2 Stat. at L. 322, for the government of the Territory of Orleans; the Act of June 4th, 1812, 3 Stat. at L. 743, for the government of the Missouri Territory; the Act of March 30th, 1822, 3 Stat. at L. 654, for the government of the Territory of Florida. Here are eight distinct instances, beginning with the first Congress, and coming down to the year of 1848, in which Congress has excluded slavery from the Territory of the United States; and six distinct instances in which Congress organized governments of Territories by which slavery was recognized and continued, beginning also with the first Congress, and coming down to the year 1822. These Acts were severally signed by seven Presidents of the United States, beginning with General Washington, and coming regularly down as far as Mr. John

Quincy Adams, thus including all who were in public life when the Constitution was adopted.

If the practical construction of the Constitution contemporaneously with its going into effect, by men intimately acquainted with the history from their personal participation in framing and adopting it, and continued by them through a long series of Acts of the gravest importance, be entitled to weight in the judicial mind on a question of construction, it would seem to be difficult to resist the force of the Acts above adverted to.

It appears, however, from what has taken place at the bar, that notwithstanding the language of the Constitution, and the long line of legislative and executive precedents under it, three different and opposite views are taken of the power of Congress respecting slavery in the Territories.

One is, that though Congress can make a regulation prohibiting slavery in a Territory, they cannot make a regulation allowing it; another is, that it can neither be established nor prohibited by Congress, but that the people of a Territory, when organized by Congress, can establish or prohibit slavery; while the third is, that the Constitution itself secures every citizen who holds slaves, under the laws of any State, the indefeasible right to carry them into any Territory, and there hold them as property.

No particular clause of the Constitution has been referred to at the bar in support of either of these views. The first seems to be rested upon general considerations concerning the social and moral evils of slavery, its relations to republican governments, its inconsistency with the Declaration of Independence and with natural right.

The second is drawn from considerations equally general, concerning the right of self-government, and the nature of the political institutions which have been established by people of the United States.

While the third is said to rest upon the equal right of all citizens to go with their property upon the public domain, and the inequality of a regulation which would admit the property of some and exclude the property of other citizens; and inasmuch as slaves are chiefly held by citizens of those particular States where slavery is established, it is insisted that a regulation excluding slavery from a Territory operates, practically, to make an unjust discrimination between citizens of different States, in respect to their use and enjoyment of the territory of the United States.

With the weight of either of these considerations, when presented to Congress to influence its action, this court has no concern. One or the other may be justly entitled to guide or control the legislative judgment upon what is a needful regulation. The question here is, whether they are sufficient to authorize this court to insert into this clause of the Constitution an exception of the exclusion or allowance of slavery, not found therein, nor in any other part of that instrument. To engraft on any instrument a substantive exception not found in it, must be admitted to be a matter attended with great difficulty. And the difficulty increases with the importance of the instrument, and the magnitude and complexity of the interests involved in its construction. To allow this to be done with the Constitution, upon reasons purely political, renders its judicial interpretation impossible— because judicial tribunals, as such, cannot decide upon political considerations. Political reasons have not the requisite certainty to afford rules of juridical interpretation. They are different in different men. They are different in the same men at different times. And when a strict interpretation of the Constitution, according to the fixed rules which govern the interpretation of laws, is abandoned, and the theoretical opinions of individuals are allowed to control its meaning, we have no longer a Constitution; we are under the government of individual men, who for the time being have power to declare what the Constitution is, according to their own views of what it ought to mean. When such a method of interpretation of the Constitution obtains, in place of a republican government, with limited and defined powers, we have a government which is merely an exponent of the will of Congress; or what, in my opinion, would not be preferable, an exponent of the individual political opinions of the members of this court.

If it can be shown by anything in the Constitution itself that when it confers on Congress the power to make all needful rules and regulations respecting the Territory belonging to the United States, the exclusion or the allowance of slavery was excepted; or if any thing in the history of this provision tends to show that such an exception was intended by those who framed and

SLAVERY

DRED SCOTT V.
SANDFORD

adopted the Constitution to be introduced into it, I hold it to be my duty carefully to consider, and to allow just weight to such considerations in interpreting the positive text of the Constitution. But where the Constitution has said all needful rules and regulations, I must find something more than theoretical reasoning to induce me to say it did not mean all.

There have been eminent instances in this court closely analogous to this one, in which such an attempt to introduce an exception, not found in the Constitution itself, has failed of success.

By the 8th section of the 1st article, Congress has the power of exclusive legislation in all cases whatsoever within this district.

In the case of *Loughborough v. Blake*, 5 Wheat. 324 the question arose, whether Congress has power to impose direct taxes on persons and property. It was insisted, that though the grant of power was in its terms broad enough to include direct taxation, it must be limited by the principle, that taxation and representation are inseparable. It would not be easy to fix on any political truth, better established or more fully admitted in our country, than that taxation and representation must exist together. We went into the War of the Revolution to assert it, and it is incorporated as fundamental into all American Governments. But however true and important this maxim may be, it is not necessarily of universal application. It was for the people of the United States, who ordained the Constitution, to decide whether it should or should not be permitted to operate within this district. Their decision was embodied in the words of the Constitution; and as that maintained no such exception as would permit the maxim to operate in this district, this court interpreting that language, held that the exception did not exist.

Again; the Constitution confers on Congress power to regulate commerce with foreign nations. Under this, Congress passed an Act on the 22d of December, 1807, unlimited in duration, laying an embargo on all ships and vessels in the ports or within the limits and jurisdiction of the United States. No law of the United States ever pressed so severely upon particular States. Though the constitutionality of the law was contested with an earnestness and zeal proportioned to the ruinous effects which were felt from it, and though, as Mr. Chief Justice Marshall has said, 9 Wheat. 192, "a want

of acuteness in discovering objections to a measure to which they felt the most deep-rooted hostility will not be imputed to those who were arrayed in opposition to this" I am not aware that the fact that its prohibited the use of a particular species of property, belonging almost exclusively to citizens of a few States, and this indefinitely, was ever supposed to show that is was unconstitutional. Something much more stringent, as a ground of legal judgment, was relied on—that the power to regulate commerce did not include the power to annihilate commerce.

But the decision was, that under the power to regulate commerce, the power of Congress over the subject was restricted only by those exceptions and limitations contained in the Constitution; and as neither the clause in question, which was a general grant of power to regulate commerce, nor any other clause of the Constitution, imposed any restrictions as to the duration of an embargo, an unlimited prohibition of the use of the shipping of the country was within the power of Congress. On this subject, Mr. Justice Daniel, speaking for the court in the case of *U.S. v. Marigold*, 9 How. 560, says: "Congress are, by the Constitution, vested with power to regulate commerce with foreign nations; and however, at periods of high excitement, an application of the terms 'to regulate commerce,' such as would embrace absolute prohibition, may have been questioned, yet, since the passage of the Embargo and Non-Intercourse Laws, and the repeated judicial sanctions these statutes have received, it can scarcely, at this day, be open to doubt, that every subject falling legitimately within the sphere of commercial regulation may be partially or wholly excluded, when either measure shall be demanded by the safety or the important interests of the entire nation. The power once conceded, it may operate on any and every subject of commerce to which the legislative discretion may apply it."

If power to regulate commerce extends to an indefinite prohibition of the use of all vessels belonging to citizens of the several States, and may operate, without exception, upon every subject of commerce to which the legislative discretion may apply it, upon what grounds can I say that power to make all needful rules and regulations respecting the territory of the United States is subject to an exception of the allowance or prohibition of slavery therein?

While the regulation is one "respecting the Territory," while it is, in the judgment of Congress, "a needful regulation," and is thus completely within the words of the grant, while no other clause of the Constitution can be shown, which requires the insertion of an exception respecting slavery, and while the practical construction for a period of upwards of fifty years forbids such an exception, it would, in my opinion, violate every sound rule of interpretation to force that exception into the Constitution upon the strength of abstract political reasoning, which we are bound to believe the people of the United States thought insufficient to induce them to limit the power of Congress, because what they have said contains no such limitation.

Before I proceed further to notice some other grounds of supposed objection to this power of Congress, I desire to say, that if it were not for my anxiety to insist upon what I deem a correct exposition of the Constitution; if I looked only to the purposes of the argument, the source of the power of Congress asserted in the opinion of the majority of the court would answer those purposes equally well. For they admit that Congress has power to organize and govern the Territories until they arrive at a suitable condition for admission to the Union; they admit, also, that the kind of government which shall thus exist, should be regulated by the condition and wants of each Territory, and that it is necessarily committed to the discretion of Congress to enact such laws for that purpose as that discretion may dictate; and no limit to that discretion has been shown, or even suggested save those positive prohibitions to legislate, which are found in the Constitution.

I confess myself unable to perceive any difference whatever between my own opinion of the general extent of the power of Congress and the opinion of the majority of the court, save that I consider it derivable from the express language of the Constitution, while they hold it to be silently implied from the power to acquire territory. Looking at the power of Congress over the Territories as of the extent just described, what positive prohibition exists in the Constitution, which restrained Congress from enacting a law in 1820 to prohibit slavery north of thirty-six degrees thirty minutes north latitude?

The only one suggested is that clause in the 5th article of the Amendments of the Constitution which declares that no person shall be deprived of his life, liberty, or property, without due process of law. I will now proceed to examine the question, whether this clause is entitled to the effect thus contributed to it. It is necessary, first, to have a clear view of the nature and incidents of that particular species of property which is now in question.

Slavery being contrary to natural right, is created only by municipal law. This is not only plain in itself, and agreed by all writers on the subject, but is inferable from the Constitution, and has been explicitly declared by this court. This Constitution refers to slaves as "persons held to service in one State, under the laws thereof." Nothing can more clearly describe a status created by municipal law. In *Prigg v. Pennsylvania*, 16 Pet. 611, this court said: "The state of slavery is deemed to be a mere municipal regulation, founded on and limited to the range of territorial laws." In *Rankin v. Lydia*, 2 A. K. Marsh, 470, the Supreme Court of Appeals of Kentucky said: "Slavery is sanctioned by the laws of this State, and the right to hold them under the municipal regulations is unquestionable. But we view this as a right existing by positive law of a municipal character, without foundation in the law of nature or the unwritten common law." I am not acquainted with any case or writer questioning the correctness of this doctrine. See, also, 1 Burge, Col., and For. Laws, 738–741, where the authorities are collected.

The status of slavery is not necessarily always attended with the same powers on the part of the master. The master is subject to the supreme power of the State, whose will controls his action towards his slave, and this control must be defined and regulated by the municipal law. In one State, as at one period of the Roman law, it may put the life of the slave into the hand of the master; others, as those of the United States, which tolerate slavery, may treat the slave as a person when the master takes his life; while in others, the law may recognize a right of the slave to be protected from cruel treatment. In other words, the status of slavery embraces every condition, from that in which the slave is known to the law simply as a chattel, with no civil rights, to that in which he is recognized as a person for all purposes, save the compulsory power of directing and receiving the fruits of his labor. Which of these conditions shall attend the status of slavery, must depend on the municipal law which creates and upholds it.

And not only must the status of slavery be created and measured by municipal law, but the rights, powers and obligations which grow out of the status, must be defined, protected and enforced by such laws. The liability of the master for the torts and crimes of his slave, and of third persons for assaulting or injuring or harboring or kidnapping him, the forms and modes of emancipation and sale, their subjection to the debts of the master, succession by the death of the master, suits for freedom, the capacity of the slave to be party to a suit, or to be a witness, with such police regulations as have existed in all civilized States where slavery has been tolerated, are among the subjects upon which municipal legislation becomes necessary when slavery is introduced.

Is it conceivable that the Constitution has conferred the right on every citizen to become a resident on the Territory of the United States with his slaves, and there to hold them as such, but has neither made nor provided for any municipal regulations which are essential to the existence of slavery?

Is it not more rational to conclude that they who framed and adopted the Constitution were aware that persons held to service under the laws of a State are property only to the extent and under the conditions fixed by those laws; that they must cease to be available as property, when their owners voluntarily place them permanently within another jurisdiction, where no municipal laws on the subject of slavery exist; and that, being aware of these principles, and having said nothing to interfere with or displace them, or compel Congress to legislate in any particular manner on the subject, and having empowered Congress to make all needful rules and regulations respecting the Territory of the United States, it was their intention to leave to the discretion of Congress what regulations, if any, should be made concerning slavery therein? Moreover, if the right exists, what are its limits, and what are its conditions? If citizens of the United States have the right to take their slaves to a Territory, and hold them there as slaves, without regard to the laws of the Territory, I suppose this right is not to be restricted to the citizens of slave-holding States. A citizen of a State which does not tolerate slavery can hardly be denied the power of doing the same thing. And what law of slavery does either take with

him to the Territory? If it be said to be those laws respecting slavery which existed in the particular State from which each slave last came, what an anomaly is this? Where else can we find, under the law of any civilized country, the power to introduce and permanently continue diverse systems of foreign municipal law, for holding persons in slavery? I say, not merely to introduce, but permanently to continue these anomalies. For the offspring of the female must be governed by the foreign municipal laws to which the mother was subject: and when any slave is sold or passes by succession on the death of the owner, there must pass with him, by a species of subrogation, and as a kind of unknown *jus in re*, the foreign municipal laws which constituted, regulated, and preserved, the status of the slave before his exportation. Whatever theoretical importance may now be supposed to belong to maintenance of such a right, I feel a perfect conviction that it would, if ever tried, prove to be as impracticable in fact, as it is, in my judgment, monstrous in theory.

I consider the assumption which lies at the basis of this theory to be unsound; not in its just sense, and when properly understood, but in the sense which has been attached to it. That assumption is, that the Territory ceded by France was acquired for the equal benefit of all the citizens of the United States. I agree to the position. But it was acquired for their benefit in their collective, not their individual, capacities. It was acquired for their benefit, as an organized political society, subsisting as "the people of the United States," under the Constitution of the United States; to be administered justly and impartially, and as nearly as possible for the equal benefit of every individual citizen, according to the best judgment and discretion of the Congress; to whose power, as the Legislature of the nation which acquired it, the people of United States have committed its administration. Whatever individual claims may be founded on local circumstances, or sectional differences of condition, cannot, in my opinion, be recognized in this court, without arrogating to the judicial branch of the government powers not committed to it; and which, with all unaffected respect I feel for it, when acting in its proper sphere, I do not think it fitted to wield.

Nor, in my judgment, will the position, that a prohibition to bring slaves into a Territory deprives any one of his property without due process of law, bear examination.

It must be remembered that this restriction on the legislative power is not peculiar to the Constitution of the United States; it was borrowed from Magna Charta; was brought to America by our ancestors, as part of their inherited liberties, and has existed in all the States, usually in the very words of the Great Charter. It existed in every political community in America in 1787, when the Ordinance prohibiting slavery north and west of the Ohio was passed.

And if a prohibition of slavery in a Territory in 1820 violated this principle of Magna Charta, the Ordinance of 1787 also violated it; and what power had, I do not say the Congress of the Confederation alone, but the Legislature of Virginia, or the Legislature of any or all the States of the Confederacy, to consent to such a violation? The people of the States had conferred no such power. I think I may at least say, if the Congress did then violate Magna Charta by the Ordinance, no one discovered that violation. Besides, if the prohibition upon all persons, citizens as well as others, to bring slaves into a Territory, and a declaration that if brought they shall be free, deprives citizens of their property without due process of law, what shall we say of the legislation of many of the slaveholding States which have enacted the same prohibition? As early as October, 1778, a law was passed in Virginia, that thereafter no slave should be imported into that Commonwealth by sea or by land, and that every slave who should be imported should become free. A citizen of Virginia purchased in Maryland a slave who belonged to another citizen of Virginia, and removed with the slave to Virginia. The slave sued for her freedom, and recovered it; as may be seen in *Wilson v. Isbel*, 5 Call. 425. See also, *Hunter v. Hulsher*, 1 Leigh, 172; and a similar law has been recognized as valid in Maryland, in *Stewart v. Oakes*, 5 Harr. & Johns, 107. I am not aware that such laws, though they exist in many States, were ever supposed to be in conflict with the principle of Magna Charta incorporated into the state constitutions. It was certainly understood by the Convention which framed the Constitution, and has been so understood ever since, that, under the power to regulate commerce, Congress could prohibit the importation of slaves; and the exercise of the power was restrained till 1808. A citizen of the United States owns slaves in Cuba, and brings them to the United States, where they are set free by the legislation of Congress. Does this legislation deprive him of his property without due process of law? If so, what becomes of the laws prohibiting the slave trade? If not, how can a similar regulation respecting a Territory violate the 5th Amendment of the Constitution.

Some reliance was placed by the defendant's counsel upon the fact that the prohibition of slavery in this Territory was in the words, "that slavery, &c., shall be, and is hereby forever prohibited." But the insertion of the word "forever" can have no legal effect. Every enactment not expressly limited in its duration continues in force until repealed or abrogated by some competent power, and the use of the word "forever" can give to the law no more durable operation. The argument is, that Congress cannot so legislate as to bind the future States formed out of the Territory, and that in this instance it has attempted to do so. Of the political reasons which may have induced the Congress to use these words, and which caused them to expect that subsequent Legislatures would conform their action to the then general opinion of the country that it ought to be permanent, this court can take no cognizance.

However fit such considerations are to control the action of Congress, and however reluctant a statesman may be disturb what has been settled, every law made by Congress may be repealed, and, saving private rights, and public rights gained by States, its repeal is subject to the absolute will of the same power which enacted it. If Congress had enacted that the crime of murder, committed in this Indian Territory, north of thirty-six degrees thirty minutes, by or on any white man, should forever be punishable with death, it would seem to be an insufficient objection to an indictment, found while it was a Territory, that at some future day States might exist there, and so the law was invalid, because by its terms, it was to continue in force forever. Such as objection rests upon a misapprehension of the province and power of courts respecting the constitutionality of laws enacted by the Legislature.

If the Constitution prescribe one rule, and the law another and different rule, it is the duty of the courts to declare that the Constitution, and not the law, governs the case before them for judgment. If the law include no case save those for which the Constitution has furnished a different rule, or no case which the Legislature has the power to govern, then the law can have no operation. If it includes cases which the Legislature has power to govern, and concerning which the Constitution does not prescribe a different rule, the law governs those cases, though it may, in its terms, attempt to include others, on which it cannot operate. In other words, this court cannot declare void an Act of Congress which constitutionally embraces some cases, though other cases, within its terms, are beyond the control of Congress, or beyond the reach of that particular law. If, therefore, Congress had power to make a law excluding slavery form this Territory while under the exclusive power of the United States, the use of the word "forever" does not invalidate the law, so long as Congress has the exclusive legislative power in the Territory.

But it is further insisted that the Treaty of 1803, between the United States and France, by which this Territory was acquired, has so restrained the constitutional powers of Congress, that it cannot, by law, prohibit the introduction of slavery into that part of this Territory north and west of Missouri, and north of thirty-six degrees thirty minutes north latitude.

By a treaty with a foreign nation, the United States may rightfully stipulate that the Congress will or will not exercise its legislative power in some particular manner, on some particular subject. Such promises, when made, should be voluntarily kept, with the most scrupulous good faith. But that a treaty with a foreign nation can deprive the Congress of any part of the legislative power conferred by the people, so that it no longer can legislate as it was empowered by the Constitution to do, I more than doubt.

The powers of the government do and must remain unimpaired. The responsibility of the government to a foreign nation, for the exercise of those powers, is quite another matter. That responsibility is to be met, and justified to the foreign nation, according to the requirements of the rules of public law; but never upon the assumption that the United States had parted with or restricted any power of acting according to its own free will, governed solely by its own appreciation of its duty.

The 2d section of the 4th article is: "This Constitution, and the laws of the United States which shall be made in pursuance thereof, and all treaties made or which shall be made under the authority of the United States, shall be the supreme law of the land." This has made treaties part of our municipal law; but it has not assigned to them any particular degree of authority, nor declared that laws so enacted shall be irrepealable. No supremacy is assigned to treaties over Acts of Congress. That they are not perpetual, and must be in some way repealable, all will agree.

If the President and the Senate alone possess the power to repeal or modify a law found in a treaty, inasmuch as they can change or abrogate one treaty only by making another inconsistent with the first, the Government of the United States could not act at all, to that effect, without the consent of some foreign government. I do not consider—I am not aware it has ever been considered—that the Constitution has placed our country in this helpless condition. The action of Congress in repealing the Treaties with France by the Act of July 7th, 1798, 1 Stat. at L. 578, was in conformity with these views. In the case of *Taylor et. al. v. Morton,* 2 Curt. Cir. Ct. 454, I had occasion to consider this subject, and I adhere to the views there expressed.

If, therefore, it were admitted that the Treaty between the United States and France did contain an express stipulation that the United States would not exclude slavery from so much of the ceded territory as is now in question, this court could not declare that an Act of Congress excluding it was void by force of the Treaty. Whether or not a case existed sufficient to justify a refusal to execute such a stipulation, would not be a judicial, but a political and legislative question, wholly beyond the authority of this court to try and determine. It would belong to diplomacy and legislation, and not to the administration of existing laws. Such a stipulation in a treaty, to legislate or not to legislate in a particular way, has been repeatedly held in this court to address itself to the political or the legislative power, by whose action thereon this court is bound, *Foster v. Neilson,* 2 Pet. 314; *Garcia v. Lee,* 12 Pet. 519.

But, in my judgment, this Treaty contains no stipulation in any manner affecting the action of the United States respecting the Territory in question. Before examining the language of the Treaty, it is material to bear in mind that the part of the ceded Territory lying north of thirty-six degrees thirty minutes, and west and north of the present State of Missouri, was then a wilderness, uninhabited save by savages, whose possessory title had not then been extinguished.

It is impossible for me to conceive on what ground France could have advanced a claim, or could have desired to advance a claim, to restrain the United States from making any rules and regulations respecting this Territory, which the United States might think fit to make; and still less can I conceive of any reason which would have induced the United States to yield to such a claim. It was to be expected that France would desire to make the change of sovereignty and jurisdiction as little burdensome as possible to the then inhabitants of Louisiana, and might well exhibit even an anxious solicitude to protect their property and persons, and to secure to them and their posterity their religious and political rights; and the United States, as a just government, might readily accede to all proper stipulations respecting those who were about to have their allegiance transferred. But what interest France could have in uninhabited Territory, which, in the language of the Treaty, was to be transferred "forever, and in full sovereignty," to the United States, or how the United States could consent to allow a foreign nation to interfere in its purely internal affairs, in which that foreign nation had no concern whatever, is difficult for me to conjecture. In my judgment, this Treaty contains nothing of the kind.

The 3d article is supposed to have a bearing on the question. It is as follows: "The inhabitants of the ceded Territory shall be incorporated in the Union of the United States, and admitted as soon as possible, according to the principles of the Federal Constitution, to the enjoyment of all the rights, advantages, and immunities, of citizens of the United States; and in the meantime they shall be maintained and protected in the enjoyment of their liberty, property, and the religion they profess."

There are two views of this article, each of which, I think, decisively shows that it was not intended to restrain the Congress from excluding slavery from that part of the ceded Territory then uninhabited. The first is, that, manifestly, its sole object was to protect individual rights of the then inhabitants of the Territory. They are to be "maintained and protected in the free enjoyment of their liberty, property, and the religion they profess." But this Article does not secure to them the right to go upon the public domain ceded by this Treaty, either with or without their

slaves. The right or power of doing this did not exist before or at the time the Treaty was made. The French and Spanish Governments, while they held the country, as well as the United States when they acquired it, always exercised the undoubted right of excluding inhabitants from the Indians country, and of determining when and on what conditions it should be opened to settlers. And a stipulation, that the then inhabitants of Louisiana should be protected in their property, can have no reference to their use of that property, where they had no right, under the Treaty, to go with it, save at the will of the United States. If one who was an inhabitant of Louisiana at the time of the Treaty had afterwards taken property then owned by him, consisting of fire-arms, ammunition, and spirits, and had gone into the Indian country north of thirty-six degrees thirty minutes, to sell them to the Indians, all must agree the 3d article of the Treaty would not have protected him from indictment under the Act of Congress of March 30, 1802, 2 Stat. at L. 139, adopted and extended to this Territory by the Act of March 26, 1804, 2 Stat. at L. 283.

Besides, whatever rights were secured were individual rights. If Congress should pass any law which violated such rights of any individual, and those rights were of such a character as not to be within the lawful control of Congress under the Constitution, that individual could complain, and the Act of Congress, as to such rights of his, would be inoperative; but it would be valid and operative as to all other persons, whose individual rights did not come under the protection of the Treaty. And inasmuch as it does not appear that any inhabitant of Louisiana, whose rights were secured by Treaty, had been injured, it would be wholly inadmissible for this court to assume, first, that one or more such cases may have existed; and second, that if any did exist, the entire law was void—not only as to those cases, if any, in which it could not rightfully operate, but as to all others, wholly unconnected with the Treaty, in which such law could rightfully operate.

But it is quite unnecessary, in my opinion, to pursue this inquiry further, because it clearly appears from the language of the Article, and it has been decided by this court that the stipulation was temporary, and ceased to have any effect when the then inhabitants of the Territory

SLAVERY

DRED SCOTT V.
SANDFORD

of the Louisiana, in whose behalf the stipulation was made, were incorporated into the Union.

In the case of *New Orleans v. De armas et al.* 9 Pet . 224, the question was, whether a title to property, which existed at the date of the Treaty, continued to be protected by the Treaty after the State of Louisiana was admitted to the Union. The 3d article of the Treaty was relied on. Mr. Chief Justice Marshall said: "This article obviously contemplates two objects. One, that Louisiana shall be admitted into the Union as soon as possible, on an equal footing with the other States; and the other, that, till such admission, the inhabitants of the ceded Territory shall be protected in the free enjoyment of their liberty, property and religion. Had any one of these rights been violated while these stipulations continued in force, the individual supposing himself to be injured might have brought his case into this court under the 25th section of the Judicial Act. But this stipulation ceased to operate when Louisiana became a member of the Union, and its inhabitants were "admitted to the enjoyment of all the rights, advantages and immunities of citizens of the United States."

The case of *Chateau v. Marguerita*, 12 Pet. 507, and *Permoli v. New Orleans*, 3 How. 589, are in conformity with this view of the Treaty.

To convert this temporary stipulation of the Treaty, in behalf of French subjects who then inhabited a small portion of Louisiana, into a permanent restriction upon the power of Congress to regulate territory then uninhabited, and to assert that it not only restrains Congress from affecting the rights of property of the then inhabitants, but enable them and all other citizens of the United States to go into any part of the ceded Territory with their slaves and hold them there, is a construction of this Treaty so opposed to its natural meaning, and so far beyond it subject matter and the evident design of the parties, that I cannot assent to it. In my opinion, this Treaty has no bearing on the present question.

For these reasons, I am of opinion that so much of the several Acts of Congress as prohibited slavery and involuntary servitude within that part of the Territory of Wisconsin lying north of thirty-six degrees thirty minutes north latitude, and west of the River Mississippi, were constitutional and valid laws.

I have expressed my opinion, and the reasons therefore, at far greater length than I could have wished, upon the different questions on which I have found it necessary to pass, to arrive at a judgment on the case at bar. These questions are numerous, and the grave importance of some of them required me to exhibit fully the grounds of my opinion. I have touched no question which, in the view I have taken, it was not absolutely necessary for me to pass upon, to ascertain whether the judgement of the Circuit Court should stand or be reversed. I have avoided no question on which the validity of that judgment depends. To have done either more or less, would have been inconsistent with my views of my duty.

In my opinion, the judgment of the Circuit Court should be reversed, and the cause remanded for a new trial.

SLAVERY

"A House Divided" Speech

Abraham Lincoln, June 16, 1858

In 1856 ABRAHAM LINCOLN, an Illinois lawyer and politician, left the WHIG PARTY over the issue of SLAVERY and joined the newly-formed, antislavery REPUBLICAN PARTY. Lincoln was outraged at the KANSAS-NEBRASKA ACT of 1854 and the *Dred Scott* decision. He was particularly displeased with Senator STEPHEN A. DOUGLAS (D-Ill.) for championing the popular sovereignty doctrine, which allowed territories to decide whether to be free or slave states. The *Dred Scott* case suggested that there was no legal way to prevent slavery in the North as well.

The Republicans chose Lincoln as their candidate in the 1858 Illinois senatorial race against Douglas. The campaign was marked by a series of seven brilliant debates between the two contenders. Lincoln advocated loyalty to the Union, regarded slavery as unjust, and was opposed to any further expansion of slavery. He opened his campaign on June 16, 1858, with the declaration "'A house divided against itself cannot stand.' I believe this government cannot endure permanently half *slave* and half *free*." His speech attacked the morality and legitimacy of popular sovereignty and warned that whether slavery could be permitted in the North was still an open question.

Lincoln lost the election due to an unfavorable APPORTIONMENT of legislative seats in Illinois. At that time U.S. senators were elected by a vote of the state legislature. Though Lincoln garnered more popular votes, the legislators chose to reelect Douglas. Despite the loss, Lincoln's firm antislavery position had enhanced his national reputation and helped him win election as president in 1860.

"A House Divided" Speech

"A house divided against itself cannot stand."

I believe this government cannot endure, permanently half *slave* and half *free*.

I do not expect the Union to be *dissolved*—I do not expect the house to *fall*—but I *do* expect it will cease to be divided.

It will become *all* one thing, or *all* the other.

Either the *opponents* of slavery, will arrest the further spread of it, and place it where the public mind shall rest in the belief that it is in course of ultimate extinction; or its *advocates* will push it forward, till it shall become alike lawful in *all* the states, *old* as well as *new*—*North* as well as *South*.

Have we no *tendency* to the latter condition?

Let any one who doubts, carefully contemplate that now almost complete legal combination—piece of *machinery* so to speak—compounded of the Nebraska doctrine, and the Dred Scott decision. . . .

* * *

. . .[The Kansas-Nebraska Act] opened all the national territory to slavery. . . . This . . . had been provided for . . . in the notable argument of "*squatter sovereignty*," otherwise called "*sacred right of self government*," which latter phrase, though expressive of the only rightful basis of any government, was so perverted in this attempted use of it as to amount to just this: That if any *one* man, choose to enslave *another,* no *third* man shall be allowed to object.

* * *

While the Nebraska Bill was passing through Congress, a law case, involving the question of a negro's freedom ... was passing through the U.S. Circuit Court for the District of Missouri; and both Nebraska Bill and law suit were brought to a decision in the same month of May, 1854. The Negro's name was "Dred Scott". . . .

* * *

[The points decided by the *Dred Scott* decision include] that whether the holding a negro in actual slavery in a free state, makes him free, as against the holder, the United States courts will not decide, but will leave to be decided by the courts of any slave state the negro may be forced into by the master.

This point is made, not to be pressed immediately ... [that] the logical conclusion that what Dred Scott's master might lawfully do with Dred Scott, in the free state Illinois, every other master may lawfully do with any other *one,* or one *thousand* slaves, in Illinois, or in any other free state.

* * *

While the opinion of ... Chief Justice Taney, in the Dred Scott case ... expressly declare[s] that the Constitution of the United States neither permits congress nor a territorial legislature to exclude slavery from any United States territory, ... [Taney] *omit*[s] to declare whether or not the same constitution permits a *state,* or the people of a state, to exclude it.

Possibly, this was a mere omission; but who can be quite sure. . . .

The nearest approach to the point of declaring the power of a state over slavery, is made by Judge Nelson. He approaches it more than once, using the precise idea, and *almost* the language too, of the Nebraska Act. On one occasion his exact language is, "except in cases where the power is restrained by the Constitution of the United States, the law of the State is supreme over the subject of slavery within its jurisdiction."

In what *cases* the power of the *states* is so restrained by the U.S. Constitution, is left an *open* question, precisely as the same question, as to the restraint on the power of the *territories* was left open in the Nebraska Act. Put *that* and *that* together, and we have another nice little niche, which we may, ere long, see filled with another Supreme Court decision, declaring that the Constitution of the United States does not permit a *state* to exclude slavery from its limits.

* * *

Such a decision is all that slavery now lacks of being alike lawful in all the states.

Welcome or unwelcome, such decision *is* probably coming, and will soon be upon us, unless the power of the present political dynasty shall be met and overthrown.

We shall *lie down* pleasantly dreaming that the people of Missouri are on the verge of making their state *free;* and we shall *awake* to the *reality,* instead, that the Supreme Court has made *Illinois* a *slave* state.

SLAVERY

EMANCIPATION PROCLAMATION

By the President of the United States of America

President ABRAHAM LINCOLN supported the U.S. CIVIL WAR to preserve the Union, not to end SLAVERY. Though he was personally opposed to slavery, he had been elected on a platform that pledged the continuation of slavery in states where it already existed. Wartime pressures, however, drove Lincoln toward emancipation of the slaves. Military leaders argued that an enslaved labor force in the South allowed the Confederate states to place more soldiers on the front lines. By the summer of 1862, Lincoln had prepared an EMANCIPATION PROCLAMATION, but he did not want to issue it until Union armies had had greater success on the battlefield. He feared that otherwise the proclamation might be seen as a sign of weakness.

The Union army's victory at the Battle of Antietam encouraged the president to issue a preliminary proclamation on September 22, 1862, that announced the abolition of slavery in areas occupied by the Confederacy effective January 1, 1863. The wording of the Emancipation Proclamation on that date made clear that slavery would still be tolerated in the border states and areas occupied by Union troops, so as not to jeopardize the war effort. Lincoln was uncertain that the Supreme Court would uphold the constitutionality of his action, so he lobbied Congress to adopt the THIRTEENTH AMENDMENT, which totally abolished slavery.

Emancipation Proclamation

A PROCLAMATION

Whereas, on the twenty-second day of September, in the year of our Lord one thousand eight hundred and sixty-two, a proclamation was issued by the president of the United States, containing, among other things, the following, to wit:

"That on the first day of January, in the year of our Lord one thousand eight hundred and sixty-three, all persons held as slaves within any state or designated part of a state, the people whereof shall then be in rebellion against the United States, shall be then, thenceforward and forever, free; and the executive government of the United States, including the military and naval authority thereof, will recognize and maintain the freedom of such persons and will do no act or acts to repress such persons, or any of them, in any efforts they may make for their actual freedom.

"That the executive will, on the first day of January aforesaid, by proclamation, designate the states and parts of states, if any, in which the people thereof, respectively, shall then be in rebellion against the United States; and the fact that any state, or the people thereof, shall on that day be in good faith represented in the Congress of the United States, by members chosen thereto at elections wherein a majority of the qualified voters of such states shall have participated,

Source: *Statutes at Large,* vol. 12 (1864), pp. 1268–1269.

shall, in the absence of strong countervailing testimony, be deemed conclusive evidence that such state, and the people thereof, are not then in rebellion against the United States."

Now, therefore, I, Abraham Lincoln, president of the United States, by virtue of the power in me vested as commander in chief of the army and navy of the United States, in time of actual armed rebellion against the authority and government of the United States, and as a fit and necessary war measure for suppressing said rebellion, do, on this first day of January, in the year of our Lord one thousand eight hundred and sixty-three, and in accordance with my purpose so to do, publicly proclaimed for the full period of one hundred days from the day first above mentioned, order and designate as the states and parts of states wherein the people thereof, respectively, are this day in rebellion against the United States, the following, to wit:

Arkansas, Texas, Louisiana (except the parishes of St. Bernard, Plaquemines, Jefferson, St. John, St. Charles, St. James, Ascension, Assumption, Terre Bonne, Lafourche, St. Mary, St. Martin, and Orleans, including the city of New Orleans), Mississippi, Alabama, Florida, Georgia, South Carolina, North Carolina, and Virginia (except the forty-eight counties designated as West Virginia, and also the counties of Berkeley, Accomac, Northampton, Elizabeth City, York, Princess Ann, and Norfolk, including the cities of Norfolk and Portsmouth), and which excepted parts are for the present left precisely as if this proclamation were not issued.

And by virtue of the power and for the purpose aforesaid, I do order and declare that all persons held as slaves within said designated states and parts of states are, and henceforward shall be, free; and that the executive government of the United States, including the military and naval authorities thereof, will recognize and maintain the freedom of said persons.

And I hereby enjoin upon the people so declared to be free to abstain from all violence, unless in necessary self-defense; and I recommend to them that, in all cases when allowed, they labor faithfully for reasonable wages.

And I further declare and make known that such persons, of suitable condition will be received into the armed service of the United States to garrison forts, positions, stations, and other places and to man vessels of all sorts in said service.

And upon this act, sincerely believed to be an act of justice, warranted by the Constitution upon military necessity, I invoke the considerate judgment of mankind and the gracious favor of Almighty God.

In witness whereof, I have hereunto set my hand and caused the seal of the United States to be affixed.

Done at the city of Washington this first day of January, in the year of our Lord one thousand eight hundred and sixty-three, and of the independence of the United States of America the eighty-seventh.

By the President:

Abraham Lincoln

William H. Seward, Secretary of State.

FROM SEGREGATION TO CIVIL RIGHTS

- "THE CIVIL RIGHTS CASES"
- PLESSY V. FERGUSON
- BROWN V. BOARD OF EDUCATION OF TOPEKA, KANSAS
- LETTER FROM BIRMINGHAM CITY JAIL
- "I HAVE A DREAM" SPEECH
- CIVIL RIGHTS ACT OF 1964
- VOTING RIGHTS ACT OF 1965

After the U.S. CIVIL WAR the THIRTEENTH, FOURTEENTH, and FIFTEENTH AMENDMENTS to the U.S. Constitution, along with many pieces of CIVIL RIGHTS legislation, were enacted to protect the rights of the newly freed slaves. Nevertheless, African Americans were soon ensnared in a southern political and legal system that limited their political, economic, and social freedoms.

Initially after the war, during the RECONSTRUCTION era (1865–1876), the former Confederate states were placed under federal military control. During this time African Americans were able to register to vote and to be elected to state and local government posts. This period was also marked by white vigilantism, however, in the form of the KU KLUX KLAN (KKK). The KKK used terror to discourage African Americans from voting or from asserting their other constitutional rights.

The presidential election of 1876 resulted in a deadlocked ELECTORAL COLLEGE and allegations of election fraud. A congressional compromise was reached in which Republican RUTHERFORD B. HAYES became president. In exchange, southern Democrats were rewarded with the withdrawal of federal troops and the end of Reconstruction.

During the 1870s the U.S. Supreme Court was called on to decide the scope of the Fourteenth Amendment. In the CIVIL RIGHTS CASES, 109 U.S. 3, 3 S. Ct. 18, 27 L. Ed. 835 (1883), the Court struck down the CIVIL RIGHTS ACT of 1875, which had been based on the Fourteenth Amendment. The Court held that the amendment prohibited only official, state-sponsored discrimination and did not reach discrimination by private parties. By the 1890s African Americans had lost virtually all their civil rights as southern states, emboldened by the *Civil Rights* cases, passed laws that segregated all public facilities and public transportation on the basis of race. In PLESSY V. FERGUSON, 163 U.S. 537, 16 S. Ct. 1138, 41 L. Ed. 256 (1896), the Supreme Court endorsed "separate-but-equal" laws, holding that they did not violate the Constitution.

Beginning in the 1930s, the National Association for the Advancement of Colored People (NAACP) fought a series of court battles against various aspects of state-sponsored segregation. The NAACP's main focus, however, was the desegregation of public schools. A team of talented attorneys, which included future Supreme Court justice THURGOOD MARSHALL, led the fight. Ultimately, they succeeded in having *Plessy* struck down. In BROWN V. BOARD OF EDUCATION OF TOPEKA, KANSAS, 347 U.S. 483, 74 S. Ct. 686, 98 L. Ed. 873 (1954), the Supreme Court ordered the end of state-sponsored segregated schools.

Despite these legal victories, most African Americans in the South were not able to vote or to exercise their civil rights. In response, MARTIN LUTHER KING JR. started the modern CIVIL RIGHTS MOVEMENT in the 1950s. Instead of lawsuits, he used nonviolent public protests to attract the nation's attention to the conditions under which African Americans were forced to live. King and his followers were jailed for their demonstrations, but by the early 1960s it was clear that legal change must come.

President LYNDON B. JOHNSON pushed for the enactment of the landmark Civil Rights Act of 1964 (42 U.S.C.A. § 2000a et seq.), which prohibited racial and other types of discrimination in employment, education, and public accommodations. The act outlawed both state-sponsored and private segregation in hotels, restaurants, and public transportation. Johnson also introduced the VOTING RIGHTS ACT OF 1965 (42 U.S.C.A. § 1971 et seq.), which ensured protection against discriminatory voting practices. This act changed the South, as African Americans were allowed to register to vote for the first time since Reconstruction.

FROM SEGREGATION TO CIVIL RIGHTS

"THE CIVIL RIGHTS CASES"

The *Civil Rights* cases involved five prosecutions and civil suits from California, Kansas, Missouri, New York, and Tennessee for denying African Americans access to public accommodations (hotels, theaters, and railroad cars) in violation of the Civil Rights Act of 1875. Justice Joseph P. Bradley, writing for the majority of the Supreme Court, held that the Fourteenth Amendment prohibited only official, state-sponsored discrimination and could not reach discrimination practiced by privately owned places of public accommodation.

Justice John M. Harlan, in a dissenting opinion, argued that segregation in public accommodations was a "badge of slavery" for the recently freed African Americans and that the act could be constitutionally justified by looking to the Thirteenth Amendment. This amendment gave Congress the authority to outlaw all "badges and incidents" of slavery. Not until the passage of Title II of the Civil Rights Act of 1964 would the federal government achieve the desegregation of public accommodations.

"The Civil Rights Cases"

UNITED STATES V. STANLEY.

[On a Certificate of Division in Opinion between the Judges of the Circuit Court of the United States for the District of Kansas.]

UNITED STATES V. RYAN.

[In Error to the Circuit Court of the United States for the District of California.]

UNITED STATES V. NICHOLS.

[On a Certificate of Division in Opinion between the Judges of the Circuit Court of the United States for the Western District of Missouri.]

UNITED STATES V. SINGLETON.

[On a Certificate of Division in Opinion between the Judges of the Circuit Court of the United States for the Southern District of New York.]

ROBINSON AND WIFE V. MEMPHIS & CHARLESTON R. CO.

[In Error to the Circuit Court of the United States for the Western District of Tennessee.]

Supreme Court of the United States

3 S.Ct. 18

27 L.Ed. 835

(Cite as: 109 U.S. 3, 3 S.Ct. 18)

October 15, 1883.

Harlan, J., dissents.

Sol. Gen. Phillips, for plaintiff, the United States.

No counsel for defendants, Stanley, Ryan, Nichols, and Singleton.

Wm. M. Randolph, for plaintiffs in error, Robinson and wife.

W. Y. C. Humes, for defendant in error, the Memphis & Charleston R. Co.

Bradley, J.

These cases are all founded on the first and second sections of the act of Congress known as the "Civil Rights Act," passed March 1, 1875, entitled "An act to protect all citizens in their civil and legal rights." 18 St. 335. Two of the

FROM
SEGREGATION
TO CIVIL RIGHTS

"THE CIVIL
RIGHTS CASES"

cases, those against Stanley and Nichols, are indictments for denying to persons of color the accommodations and privileges of an inn or hotel; two of them, those against Ryan and Singleton, are, one an information, the other an indictment, for denying to individuals the privileges and accommodations of a theater, the information against Ryan being for refusing a colored person a seat in the dress circle of Maguire's theater in San Francisco; and the indictment against Singleton being for denying to another person, whose color is not stated, the full enjoyment of the accommodations of the theater known as the Grand Opera House in New York, "said denial not being made for any reasons by law applicable to citizens of every race and color, and regardless of any previous condition of servitude." The case of Robinson and wife against the Memphis & Charleston Railroad Company was an action brought in the Circuit Court of the United States for the Western District of Tennessee, to recover the penalty of $500 given by the second section of the act; and the gravamen was the refusal by the conductor of the railroad company to allow the wife to ride in the ladies' car, for the reason, as stated in one of the counts, that she was a person of African descent. The jury rendered a verdict for the defendants in this case upon the merits under a charge of the court, to which a bill of exceptions was taken by the plaintiffs. The case was tried on the assumption by both parties of the validity of the act of Congress; and the principal point made by the exceptions was that the judge allowed evidence to go to the jury tending to show that the plaintiff, the wife, was an improper person, because she was in company with a young man whom he supposed to be a white man, and on that account inferred that there was some improper connection between them; and the judge charged the jury, in substance, that if this was the conductor's bona fide reason for excluding the woman from the car, they might take it into consideration on the question of the liability of the company. The case is brought here by writ of error at the suit of the plaintiffs. The cases of Stanley, Nichols, and Singleton come up on certificates of division of opinion between the judges below as to the constitutionality of the first and second sections of the act referred to; and the case of Ryan, on a writ of error to the judgment of the Circuit Court for the District of California sustaining a demurrer to the information.

It is obvious that the primary and important question in all the cases is the constitutionality of the law; for if the law is unconstitutional none of the prosecutions can stand.

The sections of the law referred to provide as follows:

"Section 1. That all persons within the jurisdiction of the United States shall be entitled to the full and equal enjoyment of the accommodations, advantages, facilities, and privileges of inns, public conveyances on land or water, theaters, and other places of public amusement; subject only to the conditions and limitations established by law, and applicable alike to citizens of every race and color, regardless of any previous condition of servitude."

"Sec. 2. That any person who shall violate the foregoing section by denying to any citizen, except for reasons by law applicable to citizens of every race and color, and regardless of any previous condition of servitude, the full enjoyment of any of the accommodations, advantages, facilities, or privileges in said section enumerated, or by aiding or inciting such denial, shall, for every such offense, forfeit and pay the sum of $500 to the person aggrieved thereby, to be recovered in an action of debt, with full costs; and shall, also, for every such offense, be deemed guilty of a misdemeanor, and upon conviction thereof shall be fined not less than $500 nor more than $1,000, or shall be imprisoned not less than 30 days nor more than one year: Provided, that all persons may elect to sue for the penalty aforesaid, or to proceed under their rights at common law and by state statutes; and having so elected to proceed in the one mode or the other, their right to proceed in the other jurisdiction shall be barred. But this provision shall not apply to criminal proceedings, either under this act or the criminal law of any state: And provided, further, that a judgment for the penalty in favor of the party aggrieved, or a judgment upon an indictment, shall be a bar to either prosecution respectively."

Are these sections constitutional? The first section, which is the principal one, cannot be fairly understood without attending to the last clause, which qualifies the preceding part. The essence of the law is, not to declare broadly that all persons shall be entitled to the full and equal enjoyment of the accommodations, advantages, facilities, and privileges of inns, public conveyances, and theaters; but that such enjoyment shall not be subject to any conditions applicable only to citizens of a particular race or color, or who had been in a previous condition of servitude. In other words, it is the purpose of the law to declare that, in the enjoyment of the accommodations and privileges of inns, public conveyances, theaters, and other places of public amusement, no distinction shall be made between citizens of different race or color, or between those who have, and those who have not, been slaves. Its effect is to declare that in all inns, public conveyances, and places of amusement, colored citizens, whether formerly slaves or not, and citizens of other races, shall have the same accommodations and privileges in all inns, public conveyances, and places of amusement, as are enjoyed by white citizens; and vice versa. The second section makes it a penal offense in any person to deny to any citizen of any race or color, regardless of previous servitude, any of the accommodations or privileges mentioned in the first section.

Has Congress constitutional power to make such a law? Of course, no one will contend that the power to pass it was contained in the Constitution before the adoption of the last three amendments. The power is sought, first, in the Fourteenth Amendment, and the views and arguments of distinguished senators, advanced while the law was under consideration, claiming authority to pass it by virtue of that amendment, are the principal arguments adduced in favor of the power. We have carefully considered those arguments, as was due to the eminent ability of those who put them forward, and have felt, in all its force, the weight of authority which always invests a law that Congress deems itself competent to pass. But the responsibility of an independent judgment is now thrown upon this court; and we are bound to exercise it according to the best lights we have.

The first section of the Fourteenth Amendment—which is the one relied on—after declaring who shall be citizens of the United States, and of the several states, is prohibitory in its character, and prohibitory upon the states. It declares that "no state shall make or enforce any law which shall abridge the privileges or immunities of citizens of the United States; nor shall any state deprive any person of life, liberty, or property without due process of law; nor deny to any person within its jurisdiction the equal protection of the laws." It is state action of a particular character that is prohibited. Individual invasion of individual right is not the subject-matter of the amendment. It has a deeper and broader scope. It nullifies and makes void all state legislation, and state action of every kind, which impairs the privileges and immunities of citizens of the United States, or which injures them in life, liberty, or property without due process of law, or which denies to any of them the equal protection of the laws. It not only does this, but, in order that the national will, thus declared, may not be a mere *brutum fulmen*, the last section of the amendment invests congress with power to enforce it by appropriate legislation. To enforce what? To enforce the prohibition. To adopt appropriate legislation for correcting the effects of such prohibited state law and state acts, and thus to render them effectually null, void, and innocuous. This is the legislative power conferred upon Congress, and this is the whole of it. It does not invest congress with power to legislate upon subjects which are within the domain of state legislation; but to provide modes of relief against state legislation, or state action, of the kind referred to. It does not authorize Congress to create a code of municipal law for the regulation of private rights; but to provide modes of redress against the operation of state laws, and the action of state officers, executive or judicial, when these are subversive of the fundamental rights specified in the amendment. Positive rights and privileges are undoubtedly secured by the Fourteenth Amendment; but they are secured by way of prohibition against state laws and state proceedings affecting those rights and privileges, and by power given to congress to legislate for the purpose of carrying such prohibition into effect; and such legislation must necessarily be predicated upon such supposed state laws or state proceedings, and be directed to the correction of their operation and effect. A quite full discussion of this aspect of the amendment may be found in *U.S. v. Cruikshank*, 92 U.S. 542; *Virginia v. Rives*, 100 U.S. 313, and *Ex parte Virginia*, Id. 339.

An apt illustration of this distinction may be found in some of the provisions of the original Constitution. Take the subject of contracts, for example. The Constitution prohibited the states from passing any law impairing the obligation of contracts. This did not give to Congress power to provide laws for the general enforcement of contracts; nor power to invest the courts of the United States with jurisdiction over contracts, so as to enable parties to sue upon them in those courts. It did, however, give the power to provide

FROM
SEGREGATION
TO CIVIL RIGHTS

"THE CIVIL
RIGHTS CASES"

FROM
SEGREGATION
TO CIVIL RIGHTS

"THE CIVIL
RIGHTS CASES"

remedies by which the impairment of contracts by state legislation might be counteracted and corrected; and this power was exercised. The remedy which Congress actually provided was that contained in the twenty-fifth section of the Judiciary Act of 1789, giving to the Supreme Court of the United States jurisdiction by writ of error to review the final decisions of state courts whenever they should sustain the validity of a state statute or authority, alleged to be repugnant to the Constitution or laws of the United States. By this means, if a state law was passed impairing the obligation of a contract, and the state tribunals sustained the validity of the law, the mischief could be corrected in this court. The legislation of Congress, and the proceedings provided for under it, were corrective in their character. No attempt was made to draw into the United States courts the litigation of contracts generally, and no such attempt would have been sustained. We do not say that the remedy provided was the only one that might have been provided in that case. Probably Congress had power to pass a law giving to the courts of the United States direct jurisdiction over contracts alleged to be impaired by a state law; and, under the broad provisions of the act of March 3, 1875, giving to the circuit courts jurisdiction of all cases arising under the Constitution and laws of the United States, it is possible that such jurisdiction now exists. But under that or any other law, it must appear, as well by allegation as proof at the trial, that the Constitution had been violated by the action of the state legislature. Some obnoxious state law passed, or that might be passed, is necessary to be assumed in order to lay the foundation of any federal remedy in the case, and for the very sufficient reason that the constitutional prohibition is against state laws impairing the obligation of contracts.

And so in the present case, until some state law has been passed, or some state action through its officers or agents has been taken, adverse to the rights of citizens sought to be protected by the Fourteenth Amendment, no legislation of the United States under said amendment, nor any proceeding under such legislation, can be called into activity, for the prohibitions of the amendment are against state laws and acts done under state authority. Of course, legislation may and should be provided in advance to meet the exigency when it arises, but it should be adapted to the mischief and wrong which the amendment was intended to

provide against; and that is, state laws or state action of some kind adverse to the rights of the citizen secured by the amendment. Such legislation cannot properly cover the whole domain of rights appertaining to life, liberty, and property, defining them and providing for their vindication. That would be to establish a code of municipal law regulative of all private rights between man and man in society. It would be to make Congress take the place of the state legislatures and to supersede them. It is absurd to affirm that, because the rights of life, liberty, and property (which include all civil rights that men have) are by the amendment sought to be protected against invasion on the part of the state without due process of law, Congress may, therefore, provide due process of law for their vindication in every case; and that, because the denial by a state to any persons of the equal protection of the laws is prohibited by the amendment, therefore Congress may establish laws for their equal protection. In fine, the legislation which Congress is authorized to adopt in this behalf is not general legislation upon the rights of the citizens, but corrective legislation; that is, such as may be necessary and proper for counteracting such laws as the states may adopt or enforce, and which by the amendment they are prohibited from making or enforcing, or such acts and proceedings as the states may commit or take, and which by the amendment they are prohibited from committing or taking. It is not necessary for us to state, if we could, what legislation would be proper for Congress to adopt. It is sufficient for us to examine whether the law in question is of that character.

An inspection of the law shows that is makes no reference whatever to any supposed or apprehended violation of the Fourteenth Amendment on the part of the states. It is not predicated on any such view. It proceeds *ex directo* to declare that certain acts committed by individuals shall be deemed offenses, and shall be prosecuted and punished by proceedings in the courts of the United States. It does not profess to be corrective of any constitutional wrong committed by the states; it does not make its operation to depend upon any such wrong committed. It applies equally to cases arising in states which have the justest laws respecting the personal rights of citizens, and whose authorities are ever ready to enforce such laws as to those which arise in states that may have violated the prohibition of the amendment. In other words, it steps into the domain of local jurisprudence, and lays down rules for the conduct of individuals in society towards each other, and imposes sanctions for the enforcement of those rules, without referring in any manner to any supposed action of the state or its authorities.

If this legislation is appropriate for enforcing the prohibitions of the amendment, it is difficult to see where it is to stop. Why may not Congress, with equal show of authority, enact a code of laws for the enforcement and vindication of all rights of life, liberty, and property? If it is supposable that the states may deprive persons of life, liberty, and property without due process of law, (and the amendment itself does suppose this,) why should not Congress proceed at once to prescribe due process of law for the protection of every one of these fundamental rights, in every possible case, as well as to prescribe equal privileges in inns, public conveyances, and theaters. The truth is that the implication of a power to legislate in this manner is based upon the assumption that if the states are forbidden to legislate or act in a particular way on a particular subject, and power is conferred upon Congress to enforce the prohibition, this gives Congress power to legislate generally upon that subject, and not merely power to provide modes of redress against such state legislation or action. The assumption is certainly unsound. It is repugnant to the Tenth Amendment of the Constitution, which declares that powers not delegated to the United States by the Constitution, nor prohibited by it to the states, are reserved to the states respectively or to the people.

We have not overlooked the fact that the fourth section of the act now under consideration has been held by this court to be constitutional. That section declares

> "that no citizen, possessing all other qualifications which are or may be prescribed by law, shall be disqualified for service as grand or petit juror in any court of the United State, or of any state, on account of race, color, or previous condition of servitude; and any officer or other person charged with any duty in the selection or summoning of jurors who shall exclude or fail to summon any citizen for the cause aforesaid, shall, on conviction thereof, be deemed guilty of a misdemeanor, and be fined not more than five thousand dollars. *In Ex parte Virginia*, 100 U.S. 339, it was held that an indictment against a state officer under this section for excluding persons of color from the jury list is sustainable.

But a moment's attention to its terms will show that the section is entirely corrective in its character. Disqualifications for service on juries are only created by the law, and the first part of the section is aimed at certain disqualifying laws, namely, those which make mere race or color a disqualification; and the second clause is directed against those who, assuming to use the authority of the state government, carry into effect such a rule of disqualification. In the Virginia case, the state, through its officer, enforced a rule of disqualification which the law was intended to abrogate and counteract. Whether the statute-book of the state actually laid down any such rule of disqualification or not, the state, through its officer, enforced such a rule; and it is against such state action, through its officers and agents, that the last clause of the section is directed. This aspect of the law was deemed sufficient to divest it of any unconstitutional character, and makes it differ widely from the first and second sections of the same act which we are now considering.

These sections, in the objectionable features before referred to, are different also from the law ordinarily called the "Civil Rights Bill," originally passed April 9, 1866, and re-enacted with some modifications in sections 16, 17, 18, of the enforcement act, passed May 31, 1870. That law, as re-enacted, after declaring that all persons within the jurisdiction of the United States shall have the same right in every state and territory to make and enforce contracts, to sue, be parties, give evidence, and to the full and equal benefit of all laws and proceedings for the security of persons and property as is enjoyed by white citizens, and shall be subject to like punishment, pains, penalties, taxes, licenses, and exactions of every kind, and none other, any law, statute, ordinance, regulation, or custom to the contrary notwithstanding, proceeds to enact that any person who, under color of any law, statute, ordinance, regulation, or custom, shall subject, or cause to be subjected, any inhabitant of any state or territory to the deprivation of any rights secured or protected by the preceding section, (above quoted,) or to different punishment, pains, or penalties, on account of such person being an alien, or by reason of his color or race, than is prescribed for the punishment of citizens, shall be deemed guilty of a misdemeanor, and subject to fine and imprisonment as specified in the act. This law is clearly corrective in its character, intended to counteract and furnish redress against state laws and proceedings, and customs having the force of law, which sanction the wrongful acts specified. In the Revised Statutes, it is true, a very important clause, to-wit, the words "any law, statute, ordinance, regulation, or custom to the contrary not-withstanding," which gave the declaratory section its point and effect, are omitted; but the penal part, by which the declaration is enforced, and which is really the effective part of the law, retains the reference to state laws by making the penalty apply only to those who should subject parties to a deprivation of their rights under color of any statute, ordinance, custom, etc., of any state or territory, thus preserving the corrective character of the legislation. Rev. St. §§ 1977, 1978, 1979, 5510. The civil rights bill here referred to is analogous in its character to what a law would have been under the original constitution, declaring that the validity of contracts should not be impaired, and that if any person bound by a contract should refuse to comply with it under color or pretense that it had been rendered void or invalid by a state law, he should be liable to an action upon it in the courts of the United States, with the addition of a penalty for setting up such an unjust and unconstitutional defense.

In this connection it is proper to state that civil rights, such as are guarantied by the constitution against state aggression, cannot be impaired by the wrongful acts of individuals, unsupported by state authority in the shape of laws, customs, or judicial or executive proceedings. The wrongful act of an individual, unsupported by any such authority, is simply a private wrong, or a crime of that individual; an invasion of the rights of the injured party, it is true, whether they affect his person, his property, or his reputation; but if not sanctioned in some way by the state, or not done under state authority, his rights remain in full force, and may presumably be vindicated by resort to the laws of the state for redress. An individual cannot deprive a man of his right to vote, to hold property, to buy and to sell, to sue in the courts, or to be a witness or a juror; he may, by force or fraud, interfere with the enjoyment of the right in a particular case; he may commit an assault against the person, or commit murder, or use ruffian violence at the polls, or slander the good name of a fellow-citizen; but unless protected in these wrongful acts by some shield of state law or state authority, he cannot destroy or injure the right; he will only render himself amenable to satisfaction or punishment; and amenable therefore to the laws of the state where the wrongful acts are committed. Hence, in all those cases where the constitution seeks to protect the rights of the citizen against discriminative and unjust laws of the state by prohibiting such laws, it is not individual offenses, but abrogation and denial of rights, which it denounces, and for which it clothes the congress with power to provide a remedy. This abrogation and denial of rights, for which the states alone were or could be responsible, was the great seminal and fundamental wrong which was intended to be remedied. And the remedy to be provided must necessarily be predicated upon that wrong. It must assume that in the cases provided for, the evil or wrong actually committed rests upon some state law or state authority for its excuse and perpetration.

Of course, these remarks do not apply to those cases in which Congress is clothed with direct and plenary powers of legislation over the whole subject, accompanied with an express or implied denial of such power to the states, as in the regulation of commerce with foreign nations, among the several states, and with the Indian tribes, the coining of money, the establishment of post-offices and post-roads, the declaring of war, etc. In these cases congress has power to pass laws for regulating the subjects specified, in every detail, and the conduct and transactions of individuals respect thereof. But where a subject is not submitted to the general legislative power of Congress, but is only submitted thereto for the purpose of rendering effective some prohibition against particular state legislation or state action in reference to that subject, the power given is limited by its object, and any legislation by Congress in the matter must necessarily be corrective in its character, adapted to counteract and redress the operation of such prohibited state laws or proceedings of state officers.

If the principles of interpretation which we have laid down are correct, as we deem them to be—and they are in accord with the principles laid down in the cases before referred to, as well as in the recent case of *U.S. v. Harris*, decided at the last term of this court [1 Sup. Ct. Rep. 601]—it is clear that the law in question cannot be sustained by any grant of legislative power made to congress by the Fourteenth Amendment. That amendment prohibits the states from denying to any person the equal protection of the laws, and declares that Congress shall have power to enforce, by appropriate legislation, the provisions of the amendment. The law in question, without any reference to adverse state legislation on the subject, declares that all persons shall be entitled to equal accommodation and privileges of inns, public conveyances, and places of public amusement, and imposes a penalty upon any individual who shall deny to any citizen such equal accommodations and privileges. This is not corrective legislation; it is primary and direct; it takes immediate and absolute possession of the subject of the right of admission to inns, public conveyances, and places of amusement. It supersedes and displaces state legislation on the same subject, or only allows it permissive force. It ignores such legislation, and assumes that the matter is one that belongs to the domain of national regulation. Whether it would not have been a more effective protection of the rights of citizens to have clothed Congress with plenary power over the whole subject, is not now the question. What we have to decide it, whether such plenary power has been conferred upon Congress by the Fourteenth Amendment, and, in our judgment, it has not.

We have discussed the question presented by the law on the assumption that a right to enjoy equal accommodations and privileges in all inns, public conveyances, and places of public amusement, is one of the essential rights of the citizen which no state can abridge or interfere with. Whether it is such a right or not is a different question, which, in the view we have taken of the validity of the law on the ground already stated, it is not necessary to examine.

We have also discussed the validity of the law in reference to cases arising in the states only; and not in reference to cases arising in the territories or the District of Columbia, which are subject to the plenary legislation of Congress in every branch of municipal regulation. Whether the law would be a valid one as applied to the territories and the district is not a question for consideration in the cases before us; they all being cases arising within the limits of states. And whether Congress, in the exercise of its power to regulate commerce among the several states, might or might not pass a law regulating rights in public conveyances passing from one state to another, is also a question which is not now before us, as the sections in question are not conceived in any such view.

But the power of Congress to adopt direct and primary, as distinguished from corrective, legislation on the subject in hand, is sought, in the second place, from the Thirteenth Amendment, which abolishes slavery. This amendment declares

> "that neither slavery, not involuntary servitude, except as a punishment for crime, whereof the party shall have been duly convicted, shall exist within the United States, or any place subject to their jurisdiction;"

and it gives Congress power to enforce the amendment by appropriate legislation.

This amendment, as well as the Fourteenth, is undoubtedly self-executing without any ancillary legislation, so far as its terms are applicable to any existing state of circumstances. By its own unaided force and effect it abolished slavery, and established universal freedom. Still, legislation may be necessary and proper to meet all the various cases and circumstances to be affected by it, and to prescribe proper modes of redress for its violation in letter or spirit. And such legislation may be primary and direct in its character; for the amendment is not a mere prohibition of state laws establishing or upholding slavery, but an absolute declaration that slavery or involuntary servitude shall not exist in any part of the United States.

It is true that slavery cannot exist without law any more than property in lands and goods can exist without law, and therefore the Thirteenth Amendment may be regarded as nullifying all state laws which establish or uphold slavery. But is has a reflex character also, establishing and decreeing universal civil and political freedom throughout the United States; and it is assumed that the power vested in Congress to enforce the article by appropriate legislation, clothes Congress with power to pass all laws necessary and proper for abolishing all badges and incidents of slavery in the United States; and upon this assumption it is claimed that this is sufficient authority for declaring by law that all persons shall have equal accommodations and privileges in all inns, public conveyances, and places of public amusement; the argument being that the denial of such equal accommodations and privileges is in itself a subjection to a species of servitude within the meaning of the amendment. Conceding the major proposition to be true, that Congress has a right to enact all necessary and proper laws for the obliteration and prevention of slavery, with all its badges and

FROM
SEGREGATION
TO CIVIL RIGHTS

"THE CIVIL
RIGHTS CASES"

incidents, is the minor proposition also true, that the denial to any person of admission to the accommodations and privileges of an inn, a public conveyance, or a theater, does subject that person to any form of servitude, or tend to fasten upon him any badge of slavery? If it does not, then power to pass the law is not found in the Thirteenth Amendment.

In a very able and learned presentation of the cognate question as to the extent of the rights, privileges, and immunities of citizens which cannot rightfully be abridged by state laws under the Fourteenth Amendment made in a former case, a long list of burdens and disabilities of a servile character, incident to feudal vassalage in France, and which were abolished by the decrees of the national assembly, was presented for the purpose of showing that all inequalities and observances exacted by one man from another, were servitudes or badges of slavery, which a great nation, in its effort to establish universal liberty, made haste to wipe out and destroy. But these were servitudes imposed by the old law, or by long custom which had the force of law, and or by long custom which had the force of law, and exacted by one man from another without the latter's consent. Should any such servitudes be imposed by a state law, there can be no doubt that the law would be repugnant to the Fourteenth, no less than to the Thirteenth, Amendment; nor any greater doubt that Congress has adequate power to forbid any such servitude from being exacted.

But is there any similarity between such servitudes and a denial by the owner of an inn, a public conveyance, or a theater, of its accommodations and privileges to an individual, even through the denial be founded on the race or color of that individual? Where does any slavery or servitude, or badge or either, arise from such an act of denial? Whether it might not be a denial of a right which, if sanctioned by the state law, would be obnoxious to the prohibitions of the Fourteenth Amendment, is another question. But what has it to do with the question of slavery? It may be that by the Black Code, (as it was called,) in the times when slavery prevailed, the proprietors of inns and public conveyances were forbidden to receive persons of the African race, because it might assist slaves to escape from the control of their masters. This was merely a means of preventing such escapes, and was no part of the servitude itself. A law of that kind could not have any such object now, however justly it might be deemed an invasion of the party's legal right as a citizen, and amenable to the prohibitions of the Fourteenth Amendment.

The long existence of African slavery in this country gave us very distinct notions of what it was, and what were its necessary incidents. Compulsory service of the slave for the benefit of the master, restraint of his movements except by the master's will, disability to hold property, to make contracts, to have a standing in court, to be a witness against a white person, and such like burdens and incapacities were the inseparable incidents of the institution. Severer punishments for crimes were imposed on the slave than on free persons guilty of the same offenses. Congress, as we have seen, by the Civil Rights Bill of 1866, passed in view of the Thirteenth Amendment, before the Fourteenth was adopted, undertook to wipe out these burdens and disabilities, the necessary incidents of slavery, constituting its substance and visible from; and to secure to all citizens of every race and color, and without regard to previous servitude, those fundamental rights which are the essence of civil freedom, namely, the same right to make and enforce contracts, to sue, be parties, give evidence, and to inherit, purchase, lease, sell, and convey property, as is enjoyed by white citizens. Whether this legislation was fully authorized by the Thirteenth Amendment alone, without the support which it afterwards received from the Fourteenth Amendment, after the adoption of which it was re-enacted with some additions, it is not necessary to inquire. It is referred to for purpose of showing that at that time (in 1866) Congress did not assume, under the authority given by the Thirteenth Amendment, to adjust what may be called the social rights of men and races in the community; but only to declare and vindicate those fundamental rights which appertain to the essence of citizenship, and the enjoyment or deprivation of which constitutes the essential distinction between freedom and slavery.

We must not forget that the province and scope of the Thirteenth and Fourteenth Amendments are different: the former simply abolished slavery: the latter prohibited the states from abridging the privileges or immunities of citizens of the United States, from depriving them of life, liberty, or property without due process of law, and from denying to any the equal protection of the laws. The amendments are different, and the powers of Congress under them are different. What Congress has power to do under one, it may not have power to do under one, it may not have power to do under the other. Under the Thirteenth Amendment, it has only to do with slavery and its incidents. Under the Fourteenth Amendment, it has power to counteract and render nugatory all state laws and proceedings which have the effect to abridge any of the privileges or immunities which have the effect to abridge any deprive them of life, liberty, or property without due process of law, or to deny to any of them the equal protection of the laws. Under the Thirteenth Amendment the legislation, so far as necessary or proper to eradicate all forms and incidents of slavery and involuntary servitude, may be direct and primary, operating upon the acts of individuals, whether sanctioned by state legislation or not; under the Fourteenth, as we have already shown, it must necessarily be, and can only be, corrective in its character, addressed to counteract and afford relief against state regulations or proceedings.

The only question under the present head, therefore, is, whether the refusal to any persons of the accommodations of an inn, or a public conveyance, or a place of public amusement, by and individual, and without any sanction or support from any state law or regulation, does inflict upon such persons any manner of servitude, or form of slavery, as those terms are understood in this country? Many wrongs may be obnoxious to the prohibitions of the Fourteenth Amendment which are not, in any just sense, incidents or elements of slavery. Such, for example, would be the taking of private property without due process of law; or allowing persons who have committed certain crimes (horse-stealing, for example) to be seized and hung by the *posse comitatus* without regular trial; or denying to any person, or class of persons, the right to pursue any peaceful avocations allowed to others. What is called class legislation would belong to this category, and would be obnoxious to the prohibitions of the Fourteenth Amendment, but would not to the prohibitions of the Fourteenth when not involving the idea of any subjection of one man of another. The Thirteenth Amendment has respect, not to distinctions of race, or class, or color, but to slavery. The Fourteenth Amendment extends its protection to races and classes, and prohibits any state legislation which has the effect of denying to any race or class, or to any individual, the equal protection of the laws.

Now, conceding, for the sake of the argument, that the admission to an inn, a public conveyance, or a place of public amusement, on equal terms with all other citizens, is the right of every man and all classes of men, is it any more than one of those rights which the states by the Fourteenth Amendment are forbidden to deny to any person? and is the Constitution violated until the denial of the right has some state sanction or authority? Can the act of a mere individual, the owner of the inn, the public conveyance, or place of amusement, refusing the accommodation, be justly regarded as imposing any badge of slavery or servitude upon the applicant, or only as inflicting an ordinary civil injury, properly cognizable by the laws of the state, and presumably subject to redress by those laws until the contrary appears?

After giving to these questions all the consideration which their importance demands, we are forced to the conclusion that such an act of refusal has nothing to do with slavery or involuntary servitude, and that if it is violative of any right of the party, his redress is to be sought under the laws of the state; or, if those laws are adverse to his rights and do not protect him, his remedy will be found in the corrective legislation which Congress has adopted, or may adopt, for counteracting the effect of state laws, or state action, prohibited by the Fourteenth Amendment. It would be running the slavery argument into the ground to make it apply to every act of discrimination which a person may see fit to make as to the guests he will entertain, or as to the people he will take into his coach or cab or car, or admit to his concert or theater, or deal with in other matters of intercourse or business. Innkeepers and public carriers, by the laws of all the states, so far as we are aware, are bound, to the extent of their facilities, to furnish proper accommodation to all unobjectionable persons who in good faith apply for them. If the laws themselves make any unjust discriminations, amenable to the prohibitions of the Fourteenth Amendment, Congress has full power to afford a remedy under that amendment and in accordance with it.

When a man has emerged from slavery, and by the aid of beneficent legislation has shaken off the inseparable concomitants of that state, there must be some stage in the progress of his elevation when he takes the rank of a mere citizen, and ceases to be the special favorite of the laws, and when his rights as a citizen, or a man, are to be protected in the ordinary modes by which other men's rights are protected. There were thousands of free colored people in this country before the abolition of slavery, enjoying all the essential rights of life, liberty, and property the same as white citizens; yet no one, at that time, thought that it was any invasion of their personal status as freemen because they were not admitted to all the privileges enjoyed by white citizens, or because they were subjected to discriminations in the enjoyment of accommodations in inns, public conveyances, and places of amusement. Mere discriminations on account of race or color were not regarded as badges of slavery. If, since that time, the enjoyment of equal rights in all these respects has become established by constitutional enactment, it is not by force of the Thirteenth Amendment, (which merely abolishes slavery,) but by force of the Fourteenth and Fifteenth Amendments.

On the whole, we are of opinion that no countenance of authority for the passage of the law in question can be found in either the Thirteenth or Fourteenth Amendment of the Constitution; and no other ground of authority for its passage being suggested, it must necessarily be declared void, at least so far as its operation in the several states is concerned.

This conclusion disposes of the cases not under consideration. In the cases of *U.S. v. Ryan*, and of *Robinson v. Memphis & C.R. Co.*, the judgments must be affirmed. In the other cases, the answer to be given will be, that the first and second sections of the act of Congress of March 1, 1875, entitled "An act to protect all citizens in their civil and legal rights," are unconstitutional and void, and that judgment should be rendered upon the several indictments in those cases accordingly. And it is so ordered.

Harlan, J., dissenting.

The opinion in these cases proceeds, as it seems to me, upon grounds entirely too narrow and artificial. The substance and spirit of the recent amendments of the Constitution have been sacrificed by a subtle and ingenious verbal criticism. "It is not the words of the law but the internal sense of it that makes the law. The letter of the law is the body; the sense and reason of the law is the soul." Constitutional provisions, adopted in the interest of liberty, and for the purpose of securing, through national legislation, if need be, rights inhering in a state of free-

dom, and belonging to American citizenship, have been so construed as to defeat the ends the people desired to accomplish, which they attempted to accomplish, and which they supposed they had accomplished by changes in their fundamental law. By this I do not mean that the determination of these cases should have been materially controlled by considerations of mere expediency or policy. I mean only, in this form to express an earnest conviction that the court has departed from the familiar rule requiring, in the interpretation of constitutional provisions, that full effect be given to the intent with which they were adopted.

The purpose of the first section of the act of Congress of March 1, 1875, was to prevent race discrimination. It does not assume to define the general conditions and limitations under the general conditions and limitations under which inns, public conveyances, and places of public amusement may be conducted, but only declares that such conditions and limitations, whatever they may be, shall not be applied, by way of discrimination, on account of race, color, or previous condition of servitude. The second section provides a penalty against any one denying, or aiding or inciting the denial, to any citizen that equality of right given by the first section, except for reasons by law applicable to citizens of every race or color, and regardless of any previous condition of servitude.

There seems to be no substantial difference between my brethren and myself as to what was the purpose of Congress; for they say that the essence of the law is, not to declare broadly that all persons shall be entitled to the full and equal enjoyment of the accommodations, advantages, facilities, and privileges of inns, public conveyances, and theaters, but that such enjoyment shall not be subject to any conditions applicable only to citizens of a particular race or color, or who had been in a previous condition of servitude. The effect of the statute, the court says, is that colored citizens, whether formerly slaves or not, and citizens of other races, shall have the same accommodations and privileges in all inns, public conveyances, and places of amusement as are enjoyed by white person, and vice versa.

The court adjudges that Congress is without power, under either the Thirteenth or Fourteenth Amendment, to establish such regulations, and that the first and second sections of the statute are, in all their parts, unconstitutional and void.

Before considering the particular language and scope of these amendments it will be proper to recall the relations which, prior to their adoption, subsisted between the national government and the institution of slavery, as indicated by the provisions of the Constitution, the legislation of Congress, and the decisions of this court. In this mode we may obtain keys with which to open the mind of the people, and discover the thought intended to be expressed.

In section 2 of article 4 of the Constitution it was provided that

> "no person held to service or labor in one state, under the laws thereof, escaping into another, shall, in consequence of any law or regulation therein, be discharged from such service or labor, but shall be delivered up on claim of the party to whom such service or labor may be due."

Under the authority of that clause Congress passed the Fugitive Slave Law of 1793, establishing the mode for the recovery of a fugitive slave, and prescribing a penalty against any person knowingly and willingly obstructing or hindering the master, his agent or attorney, in seizing, arresting, and recovering the fugitive, or who should rescue the fugitive from him, or who should harbor or conceal the slave after notice that he was a fugitive.

In *Prigg v. Com.* 16 Pet 539, this court had occasion to define the powers and duties of congress in reference to fugitives from labor. Speaking by Mr. Justice Story, the court laid down these propositions: That a clause of the Constitution conferring a right should not be so construed as to make it shadowy, or unsubstantial, or leave the citizen without a remedial power adequate for its protection, when another mode, equally accordant with the words and the sense in which they were used, would enforce and protect the right so granted; that Congress is not restricted to legislation for the exertion of tis powers expressly granted; but, for the protection of rights guaranteed by the Constitution, it may employ, through legislation, such means, not prohibited, as are necessary and proper, or such as are appropriate, to attain the ends proposed; that the Constitution recognized the master's right of property in his fugitive slave, and, as incidental thereto, the right of seizing and recovering him, regardless of any state law, or regula-

tion, or local custom whatsoever; and that the right of the master to have his slave, so escaping, delivered up on claim, being guaranteed by the Constitution, the fair implication was that the national government was clothed with appropriate authority and functions to enforce it.

The court said:

> "The fundamental principle, applicable to all cases of this sort, would seem to be that when the end is required the means are given, and when the duty is enjoined the ability to perform it is contemplated to exist on the part of the functionary to whom it is intrusted."

Again:

> "It would be a strange anomaly and forced construction to suppose that the national government meant to rely for the due fulfillment of its own proper duties, and the rights which it intended to secure, upon state legislation, and not upon that of the Union. *A fortiori*, it would be more objectionable to suppose that a power which was to be the same throughout the Union should be confided to state sovereignty, which could not rightfully act beyond its own territorial limits."

The act of 1793 was, upon these grounds, adjudged to be a constitutional exercise of the powers of Congress.

It is to be observed, from the report of Prigg's Case, that Pennsylvania, by her attorney general, pressed the argument that the obligation to surrender fugitive slaves was on the states and for the states, subject to the restriction that they should not pass laws or establish regulations liberating such fugitives; that the Constitution did not take from the states the right to determine the status of all persons within their respective jurisdictions; that it was for the state in which the alleged fugitive was found to determine, through her courts, or in such modes as she prescribed, whether the person arrested was, in fact, a freeman or a fugitive slave; that the sole power of the general government in the premises was, by judicial instrumentality, to restrain and correct, not to forbid and prevent in the absence of hostile state action; and that, for the general government to assume primary authority to legislate on the subject of fugitive slaves, to the exclusion of the state, would be a dangerous encroachment on state sovereignty. But to such suggestions this court turned a deaf ear, and adjudged that primary legislation by Congress to enforce the master's right was authorized by the Constitution.

We next come to the Fugitive Slave Act of 1850, the constitutionality of which rested, as did that of 1793, solely upon the implied power of Congress to enforce the master's rights. The provisions of that act were far in advance of previous legislation. They placed at the disposal of the master seeking to recover his fugitive slave, substantially, the whole power of the nation. It invested commissioners, appointed under the act, with power to summon the *posse comitatus* for the enforcement of its provisions, and commanded "all good citizens" to assist in its prompt and efficient execution whenever their services were required as part of the *posse comitatus*. Without going into the details of that act, it is sufficient to say that Congress omitted from it nothing which the utmost ingenuity could suggest as essential to the successful enforcement of the master's claim to recover his fugitive slave. And this court, in *Ableman v. Booth*, 21 How. 526, adjudged it to be, "in all of its provisions, fully authorized by the Constitution of the United States."

The only other decision prior to the adoption of the recent amendments, to which reference will be made, is *Dred Scott v. Sandford*, 19 How. 393. That suit was instituted in a circuit court of the United States by Dred Scott, claiming to be a citizen of Missouri, the defendant being a citizen of another state. Its object was to assert the title of himself and family to freedom. The defendant pleaded in abatement to the jurisdiction of the court that Scott—being of African descent, whose ancestors, of pure African blood, were brought into this country, and sold as slaves— was not a citizen. The only matter in issue, said the court, was whether the descendants of slaves so imported and sold, when they should be emancipated, or who were born of parents who had become free before their birth, are citizens of a state in the sense in which the word "citizen" is used in the Constitution of the United States.

In determining that question the court instituted an inquiry as to who were citizens of the several states at the adoption of the constitution, and who, at that time, were recognized as the people whose rights and liberties had been violated by the British government. The result was a declaration by this court, speaking through Chief Justice Taney, that the legislation and histories of the times, and the language used in the Declaration of Independence, showed

> "that neither the class of persons who had been imported as slaves, nor their descendants,

whether they had become free or not, were then acknowledged as a part of the people, nor intended to be included in the general words used that instrument:"

that

> "they had for more than a century before been regarded as beings of an inferior race, and altogether unfit to associate with the white race, either in social or political relations, and so far inferior that they had no rights which the white man was bound to respect, and that the negro might justly and lawfully be reduced to slavery for his benefit;"

that he was

> "bought and sold, and treated as an ordinary article of merchandise and traffic, whenever a profit could be made by it;"

and that

> "this opinion was at that time fixed and universal in the civilized portion of the white race. It was regarded as an axiom in morals as well as in politics, which no one thought of disputing, or supposed to be open to dispute; and men in every grade and position in society daily and habitually acted upon it in their private pursuits, as well as in matters of public concern, without for a moment doubting the correctness of this opinion."

The judgment of the court was that the words "people of the United States" and "citizens" meant the same thing, both describing

> "the political body who, according to our republican institutions, form the sovereignty and hold the power and conduct the government through their representatives;"

that

> "they are what we familiarly call the "sovereign people," and every citizen is one of this people and a constituent member of this sovereignty;"

but that the class of persons described in the plea in abatement did not compose a portion of this people, were not

> "included, and were not intended to be included, under the word "citizens" in the Constitution;"

that, therefore, they could

> "claim none of the rights and privileges which that instrument provides for and secures to citizens of the United States;"

that,

> "on the contrary, they were at that time considered as a subordinate and inferior class of beings, who had been subjugated by the

dominant race, and, whether emancipated or not, yet remained subject to their authority, and had no rights or privileges but such as those who held the power and the government might choose to grant them."

Such were relations which, prior to the adoption of the Thirteenth Amendment, existed between the government, whether national or state, and the descendants, whether free or in bondage, of those of African blood who had been imported into this country and sold as slaves.

The first section thereof provides that "neither slavery nor involuntary servitude, except as a punishment for crime, whereof the party shall have been duly convicted, shall exist within the United States, or any place subject to their jurisdiction." Its second section declares that "Congress shall have power to enforce this article by appropriate legislation." This amendment was followed by the Civil Rights Act of April 9, 1866, which, among other things, provided that "all persons born in the United States, and not subject to any foreign power, excluding Indians not taxed, are hereby declared to be citizens of the United States." 14 St. 27. The power of Congress, in this mode, to elevate the race thus liberated to the plane of national citizenship, was maintained, by the supporters of the act of 1866, to be as full and complete as its power, by general statute, to make the children, being of full age, of persons naturalized in this country, citizens of the United States without going through the process of naturalization. The act of 1866, in this respect, was also likened to that of 1843, in which Congress declared

> "that the Stockbridge tribe of Indians, and each and every one of them, shall be deemed to be, and are hereby declared to be, citizens of the United States to all intent and purposes, and shall be entitled to all the rights, privileges, and immunities of such citizens, and shall in all respects be subject to the laws of the United States."

If the act of 1866 was valid, as conferring national citizenship upon all embraced by its terms, then the colored race, liberated by the Thirteenth Amendment, became citizens of the United States prior to the adoption of the Fourteenth Amendment. But, in the view which I take of the present case, it is not necessary to examine this question.

The terms of the Thirteenth Amendment are absolute and universal. They embrace every race which then was, or might thereafter be, within the United States. No race, as such, can be excluded from the benefits or rights thereby conferred. Yet it is historically true that amendment was suggested by the condition, in this country, of that race which had been declared by this court to have had, according to the opinion entertained by the most civilized portion of the white race at the time of the adoption of the constitution, "no rights which the white man was bound to respect," none of the privileges or immunities secured by that instrument to citizens of the United States. It had reference, in a peculiar sense, to a people which (although the larger part of them were in slavery) had been invited by an act of Congress to aid, by their strong right arms, in saving from overthrow a government which, theretofore, by all of its departments, had treated them as an inferior race, with no legal rights or privileges except such as the white race might choose to grant them.

These are the circumstances under which the Thirteenth Amendment was proposed for adoption. They are now recalled only that we may better understand what was in the minds of the people when that amendment was being considered, and what were the mischiefs to be remedied, and the grievances to be redressed.

We have seen that the power of Congress by legislation, to enforce the master's right to have his slave delivered up on claim was implied from the recognition and guaranty of that right in the national constitution. But the power conferred by the Thirteenth Amendment does not rest upon implication or inference. Those who framed it were not ignorant of the discussion, covering many years of the country's history, as to the constitutional power of Congress to enact the fugitive slave laws of 1793 and 1850. When, therefore, it was determined by a change in the fundamental law, to uproot the institution of slavery wherever it existed in this land, and to establish universal freedom, there was a fixed purpose to place the power of Congress in the premises beyond the possibility of doubt. Therefore, *ex industria*, the power to enforce the Thirteenth Amendment, by appropriate legislation, was expressly granted. Legislation for that purpose, it is conceded, may be direct and primary. But to what specific ends may it be directed? This court has uniformly held that the national government has the power, whether expressly given or not, to secure and protect rights conferred or guarantied by the constitution. *U.S. v. Reese*, 92 U.S. 214; *Strauder v. West*

Virginia, 100 U.S. 303. That doctrine ought not now to be abandoned, when the inquiry is not as to an implied power to protect the master's rights, but what may Congress do, under powers expressly granted, for the protection of freedom, and the rights necessarily inhering in a state of freedom.

The Thirteenth Amendment, my brethren concede, did something more than to prohibit slavery as an institution, resting upon distinctions of race, and upheld by positive law. They admit that it established and decreed universal civil freedom throughout the United States. But did the freedom thus established involve nothing more than exemption from actual slavery? Was nothing more intended than to forbid one man from owning another as property? Was it the purpose of the nation simply to destroy the institution, and then remit the race, theretofore held in bondage, to the several states for such protection, in their civil rights, necessarily growing out of freedom, as those states, in their discretion, choose to provide? Were the states, against whose solemn protest the institution was destroyed, to be left perfectly free, so far as national interference was concerned, to make or allow discriminations against that race, as such, in the enjoyment of those fundamental rights that inhere in a state of freedom? Had the Thirteenth Amendment stopped with the sweeping declaration, in its first section, against the existence of slavery and involuntary servitude, except for crime, Congress would have had the power, by implication, according to the doctrines of *Prigg v. Com.*, repeated in *Strauder v. West Virginia*, to protect the freedom thus established, and consequently to secure the enjoyment of such civil rights as were fundamental in freedom. But that it can exert its authority to that extent is now made clear, and was intended to be made clear, by the express grant of power contained in the second section of that amendment.

That there are burdens and disabilities which constitute badges of slavery and servitude, and that the express power delegated to Congress to enforce, by appropriate legislation, the Thirteenth Amendment, may be exerted by legislation of a direct and primary character, for the eradication, not simply of the institution, but of its badges and incidents, are propositions which ought to be deemed indisputable. They lie at the very foundation of the Civil Rights Act of 1866. Whether that act was fully authorized by

the Thirteenth Amendment alone, without the support which it afterwards received from the Fourteenth Amendment, after the adoption of which it was re-enacted with some additions, the court, in its opinion, says it is unnecessary to inquire. But I submit, with all respect to my brethren, that its constitutionality is conclusively shown by other portions of their opinion. It is expressly conceded by them that the Thirteenth Amendment established freedom; that there are burdens and disabilities, the necessary incidents of slavery, which constitute its substance and visible form; that Congress, by the act of 1866, passed in view of the Thirteenth Amendment, before the Fourteenth was adopted, undertook to remove certain burdens and disabilities, the necessary incidents of slavery, and to secure to all citizens of every race and color, and without regard to previous servitude, those fundamental rights which are the essence of civil freedom, namely, the same right to make and enforce contracts, to sue, be parties, give evidence, and to inherit, purchase, lease, sell and convey property as is enjoyed by white citizens; that under the Thirteenth Amendment Congress has to do with slavery and its incidents; and that legislation, so far as necessary or proper to eradicate all forms and incidents of slavery and involuntary servitude, may be direct and primary, operating upon the acts of individuals, whether sanctioned by state legislation or not. These propositions being conceded, it is impossible, as it seems to me, to question the constitutional validity of the Civil Rights Act of 1866. I do not contend that the Thirteenth Amendment invests Congress with authority, by legislation, to regulate the entire body of the civil rights which citizens enjoy, or may enjoy, in the several states. But I do hold that since slavery, as the court has repeatedly declared, was the moving or principal cause of the adoption of that amendment, and since that institution rested wholly upon the inferiority, as a race, of those held in bondage, their freedom necessarily involved immunity from, and protection against, all discrimination against them, because of their race, in respect of such civil rights as belong to freemen of other races. Congress, therefore, under its express power to enforce that amendment, by appropriate legislation, may enact laws to protect that people against the deprivation, on account of their race, of any civil rights enjoyed by other freemen in the same state; and such legislation may be of a direct and primary character, operating upon states, their officers and agents, and also upon, at least, such individuals and corporations as exercise public functions and wield power and authority under the state.

By way of testing the correctness of this position, let us suppose that, prior to the adoption of the Fourteenth Amendment, a state had passed a statute denying to freemen of African descent, resident within its limits, the same rights which were accorded to white persons, of making or enforcing contracts, or of inheriting, purchasing, leasing, selling, and conveying property; or a statute subjecting colored people to severer punishment for particular offenses than was prescribed for white persons, or excluding that race from the benefit of the laws exempting homesteads from execution. Recall the legislation of 1865–66 in some of the states, of which this court, in the *Slaughter-house Cases*, said that it imposed upon the colored race onerous disabilities and burdens; curtailed their rights in the pursuit of life, liberty, and property to such an extent that their freedom was of little value; forbade them to appear in the towns in any other character than menial servants; required them to reside on and cultivate the soil, without the right to purchase or own it; excluded them from many occupations of gain; and denied them the privilege of giving testimony in the courts where a white man was a party. 16 Wall. 57. Can there by any doubt that all such legislation might have been reached by direct legislation upon the part of Congress under its express power to enforce the Thirteenth Amendment? Would any court have hesitated to declare that such legislation imposed badges of servitude in conflict with the civil freedom ordained by that amendment? That it would have been also in conflict with the Fourteenth Amendment, because inconsistent with the fundamental rights of American citizenship, does not prove that it would have been consistent with the Thirteenth Amendment.

What has been said is sufficient to show that the power of Congress under the Thirteenth Amendment is not necessarily restricted to legislation against slavery as an institution upheld by positive law, but may be exerted to the extent at least of protecting the race, so liberated, against discrimination, in respect of legal rights belonging to freemen, where such discrimination is based upon race.

It remains now to inquire what are the legal rights of colored persons in respect of the accommodations, privileges, and facilities of public conveyances, inns, and places of public amusement.

1. As to public conveyances on land and water. In *New Jersey Steam Nav. Co. v. Merchants' Bank*, 6 How. 382, this court, speaking by Mr. Justice Nelson, said that a common carrier is "in the exercise of a sort of public office and has public duties to perform, from which he should not be permitted to exonerate himself without the assent of the parties concerned." To the same effect is *Munn v. Illinois*, 94 U.S. 113. In *Olcott v. Sup'rs*, 16 Wall. 694, it was ruled that railroads are public highways, established, by authority of the state, for the public use; that they are none the less public highways because controlled and owned by private corporations; that it is a part of the function of government to make and maintain highways for the conveyance of the public; that no matter who is the agent, and what is the agency, the function performed is that of the state; that although the owners may be private companies, they may be compelled to permit the public to use these works in the manner in which they can be used; that upon these grounds alone have the courts sustained the investiture of railroad corporations with the state's right of eminent domain, or the right of municipal corporations, under legislative authority, to assess, levy, and collect taxes to aid in the construction of railroads. So in *Town of Queensbury v. Culver*, 19 Wall. 91, it was said that a municipal subscription of railroad stock was in aid of the construction and maintenance of a public highway and for the promotion of a public use. Again, in *Township of Pine Grove v. Talcott*, 19 Wall. 676: "Though the corporation [railroad] was private, its work was public; as much so as if it were to be constructed by the state." To the like effect are numerous adjudications in this and the state courts with which the profession is familiar. The Supreme Judicial Court of Massachusetts, in *Inhabitants of Worcester v. Western R. Corp.* 4 Metc. 566, said, in reference to a certain railroad:

> "The establishment of that great thoroughfare is regarded as a public work, established by public authority, intended for the public use and benefit, the use of which is secured to the whole community, and constitutes, therefore, like a canal, turnpike, or highway, a public easement. * * * It is true that the real and

FROM
SEGREGATION
TO CIVIL RIGHTS

"THE CIVIL
RIGHTS CASES"

personal property necessary to the establishment and management of the railroad is vested in the corporation; but it is in trust for the public."

In *Erie & N. E. R. Co. v. Casey*, 26 Pa. St. 287, the court, referring to an act repealing the charter of a railroad, and under which the state took possession of the road, said, speaking by Black, J.:

> "It is public highway, solemnly devoted to public use. When the lands were taken it was for such use, or they could not have been taken at all. * * * Railroads established upon land taken by the right of eminent domain by authority of the commonwealth, created by her laws as thoroughfares for commerce, are her highways. No corporation has property in them, though it may have franchises annexed to and exercisable within them."

In many courts it has been held that because of the public interest in such a corporation the land of a railroad company cannot be levied on and sold under execution by a creditor. The sum of the adjudged cases is that a railroad corporation is a governmental agency, created primarily for public purposes, and subject to be controlled for the public benefit. It is upon that ground that the state, when unfettered by contract, may regulate, in its discretion, the rates of fares of passengers and freight. And upon this ground, too, the state may regulate the entire management of railroads in all matters affecting the convenience and safety of the public; as, for example, by regulating speed, compelling stops of prescribed length at stations, and prohibiting discriminations and favoritism. If the corporation neglect or refuse to discharge its duties to the public, it may be coerced to do so by appropriate proceedings in the name or in behalf of the state.

Such being the relations these corporations hold to the public, it would seem that the right of a colored person to use an improved public highway, upon the terms accorded to freemen of other races, is as fundamental in the state of freedom, established in this country, as are any of the rights which my brethren concede to be so far fundamental as to be deemed the essence of civil freedom. "Personal liberty consists," says Blackstone, "in the power of locomotion, of changing situation, or removing one's person to whatever place one's own inclination may direct, without restraint, unless by due course of law." But of what value is this right of locomotion, if it may be logged by such burdens as Congress intended by the act of 1875 to remove? They are burdens which lay at the very foundation of the

institution of slavery as it once existed. They are not to be sustained, except upon the assumption that there is still, in this land of universal liberty, a class which may yet be discriminated against, even in respect of rights of a character so essential and so supreme, that, deprived of their enjoyment, in common with others, a freeman is not only branded as one inferior and infected, but, in the competitions of life, is robbed of some of the most necessary means of existence; and all this solely because they belong to a particular race which the nation has liberated. The Thirteenth Amendment alone obliterated the race line, so far as all rights fundamental in a state of freedom are concerned.

As to inns. The same general observations which have been made as to railroads are applicable to inns. The word "inn" has a technical legal signification. It means, in the act of 1875, just what it meant at common law. A mere private boardinghouse is not an inn, nor is its keeper subject to the responsibilities, or entitled to the privileges of a common innkeeper. "To constitute one an innkeeper, within the legal force of that term, he must keep a house of entertainment or lodging for all travelers or wayfarers who might choose to accept the same, being of good character or conduct." Redf. Carr. § 575. Says Judge Story:

> "An innkeeper may be defined to be the keeper of a common inn for the lodging and entertainment of travelers and passengers, their horses and attendants. An innkeeper is bound to take in all travelers and wayfaring person, and to entertain them, if he can accommodate them, for a reasonable compensation; and he must guard their goods with proper diligence. * * * If an innkeeper improperly refuses to receive or provide for a guest, he is liable to be indicted therefor. * * * They [carriers of passengers] are no more at liberty to refuse a passenger, if they have sufficient room and accommodations, than an innkeeper is to refuse suitable room and accommodations to a guest." Story, Bailm §§ 475, 476.

Said Mr. Justice Coleridge, in *Rex v. Ivens*, 7 Car. & P. 213, (32 E. C. L. 495:)

> "An indictment lies against an innkeeper who refuses to receive a guest, he having at the time room in his house; and either the price of the guest's entertainment being tendered to him, or such circumstances occurring as will dispense with that tender. This law is founded in good sense. The innkeeper is not to select his guests. He has no right to say to one, you shall come to my inn, and to anoth-

er you shall not, as every one coming and conducting himself in a proper manner has a right to be received; and for this purpose innkeepers are a sort of public servants, they having in return a kind of privilege of entertaining travelers and supplying them with that they want."

These authorities are sufficient to show a keeper of an inn is in the exercise of a quasi public employment. The law gives him special privileges, and he is charged with certain duties and responsibilities to the public. The public nature of his employment forbids him from discriminating against any person asking admission as a guest on account of the race or color of that person.

3. As to places of public amusement. It may be argued that the managers of such places have no duties to perform with which the public are, in any legal sense, concerned, or with which the public have any right to interfere; and that the exclusion of a black man from a place of public amusement on account of his race, or the denial to him, on that ground, of equal accommodations at such places, violates no legal right for the vindication of which he may invoke the aid of the courts. My answer to that argument is that places of public amusement, within the meaning of the act of 1875, are such as are established and maintained under direct license of the law. The authority to establish and maintain them comes from the public. The colored race is a part of that public. The local government granting the license represents them as well as all other races within its jurisdiction. A license from the public to establish a place of public amusement, imports, in law, equality of right, at such places, among all the members of that public. This must be so, unless it be—which I deny—that the common municipal government of all the people may, in the exertion of its powers, conferred for the benefit of all, discriminate or authorize discrimination against a particular race, solely because of its former condition of servitude.

I also submit whether it can be said—in view of the doctrines of this court as announced in *Munn v. Illinois*, U.S. 123, and reaffirmed in *Peik v. Chicago & N. W. Ry. Co.* 94 U.S. 178—that the management of places of public amusement is a purely private matter, with which government has no rightful concern. In the Munn Case the question was whether the state of Illinois could fix, by law, the maximum of charges for the storage of grain in certain warehouses in that state—the private property of individual citi-

zens. After quoting a remark attributed to Lord Chief Justice Hale, to the effect that when private property is "affected with a public interest it ceases to be *juris privati* only," the court says:

> "Property does become clothed with a public interest when used in a manner to make it of public consequence and affect the community at large. When, therefore, one devotes his property to a use in which the public has an interest, he in effect grants to the public an interest in that use, and must submit to be controlled by the public for the common good to the extent of the interest he has thus created. He may withdraw his grant by discontinuing the use, but, so long as he maintains the use, he must submit to the control."

The doctrines of *Munn v. Illinois* have never been modified by this court, and I am justified, upon the authority of that case, in saying that places of public amusement, conducted under the authority of the law, are clothed with a public interest, because used in a manner to make them of public consequence and to affect the community at large." The law may therefore regulate, to some extent, the mode in which they shall be conducted, and consequently the public have rights in respect of such places which may be vindicated by the law. It is consequently not a matter purely of private concern.

Congress has not, in these matters, entered the domain of state control and supervision. It does not assume to prescribe the general conditions and limitations under which inns, public conveyances, and places of public amusement shall by conducted or managed. It simply declares in effect that since the nation has established universal freedom in this country for all time, there shall be no discrimination, based merely upon race or color, in respect of the legal rights in the accommodations and advantages of public conveyances, inns, and places of public amusement.

I am of opinion that such discrimination is a badge of servitude, the imposition of which Congress may prevent under its power, through appropriate legislation, to enforce the Thirteenth Amendment; and consequently, without reference to its enlarged power under the Fourteenth Amendment, the act of March 1, 1875, is not, in my judgment, repugnant to the Constitution.

It remains now to consider these cases with reference to the power Congress has possessed since the adoption of the Fourteenth Amendment.

FROM
SEGREGATION
TO CIVIL RIGHTS

"THE CIVIL
RIGHTS CASES"

FROM
SEGREGATION
TO CIVIL RIGHTS

"THE CIVIL
RIGHTS CASES"

Before the adoption of the recent amendments it had become, as we have seen, the established doctrine of this court that negroes, whose ancestors had been imported and sold as slaves, could not become citizens of a state, or even of the United States, with the rights and privileges guarantied to citizens by the national constitution; further, that one might have all the rights and privileges of a citizen of a state without being a citizen in the sense in which that word was used in the national constitution, and without being entitled to the privileges and immunities of citizens of the several states. Still further, between the adoption of the Fourteenth Amendment.

Before the adoption of the recent amendments it had become, as we have seen, the established doctrine of this court that negroes, whose ancestors had been imported and sold as slaves, could not become citizens of a state, or even of the United States, with the rights and privileges guarantied to citizens by the national constitution; further, that one might have all the rights and privileges of a citizen of a state without being a citizen in the sense in which that word was used in the national constitution, and without being entitled to the privileges and immunities of citizens of the several states. Still further, between the adoption of the Thirteenth Amendment and the proposal by Congress of the Fourteenth Amendment, on June 16, 1866, the statute-books of several of the states, as we have seen, had become loaded down with enactments which, under the guise of apprentice, vagrant, and contract regulations, sought to keep the colored race in a condition, practically, of servitude. It was openly announced that whatever rights persons of that race might have as freemen, under the guaranties of the national Constitution, they could not become citizens of a state, with the rights belonging to citizens, except by the consent of such state; consequently, that their civil rights, as citizens of the state, depended entirely upon state legislation. To meet this new peril to the black race, that the purposes of the nation might not be doubted or defeated, and by way of further enlargement of the power of Congress, the Fourteenth Amendment was proposed for adoption.

Remembering that this court, in the *Slaughter-house Cases*, declared that the one pervading purpose found in all the recent amendments, lying at the foundation of each, and without which none of them would have been suggested, was

"the freedom of the slave race, the security and firm establishment of that freedom, and the protection of the newly-made freeman and citizen from the oppression of those who had formerly exercised unlimited dominion over him;"

that each amendment was addressed primarily to the grievances of that race—let us proceed to consider the language of the Fourteenth Amendment. Its first and fifth sections are in these words:

"Section 1. All persons born or naturalized in the United States, and subject to the jurisdiction thereof, are citizens of the United States and of the state wherein they reside. No state shall make or enforce any law which shall abridge the privileges or immunities of citizens of the United States; nor shall any state deprive any person of life, liberty, or property without due process of law; nor deny to any person within its jurisdiction the equal protection of the laws."

* * *

"Sec. 5. That Congress shall have power to enforce, by appropriate legislation, the provisions of this article."

It was adjudged in *Strauder v. West Virginia* and *Ex parte Virginia*, 100 U.S. 307, 345, and my brethren concede, that positive rights and privileges were intended to be secured, and are in fact secured, by the Fourteenth Amendment.

But when, under what circumstances, and to what extent may Congress, by means of legislation, exert its power to enforce the provisions of this amendment? The logic of the opinion of the majority of the court—the foundation upon which its whole reasoning seems to rest—is that the general government cannot, in advance of hostile state laws or hostile state proceedings, actively interfere for the protection of any of the rights, privileges, and immunities secured by the Fourteenth Amendment. It is said that such rights, privileges, and immunities are secured by way of prohibition against state laws and state proceedings affecting such rights and privileges, and by power given to Congress to legislate for the purpose of carrying such prohibition into effect; also, that congressional legislation must necessarily be predicated upon such supposed state laws or state proceedings, and be directed to the correction of their operation and effect.

In illustration of its position, the court refers to the clause of the Constitution forbidding the passage by a state of any law impairing the obligation of contracts. The clause does not, I submit, furnish a proper illustration of the scope and effect of the fifth section of the Fourteenth Amendment. No express power is given Congress to enforce, by primary direct legislation, the prohibition upon state laws impairing the obligation of contracts. Authority is, indeed, conferred to enact all necessary and proper laws for carrying into execution the enumerated powers of Congress, and all other powers vested by the Constitution in the government of the United States, or in any department or officer thereof. And, as heretofore shown, there is also, by necessary implication, power in Congress, by legislation, to protect a right derived from the national Constitution. But a prohibition upon a state is not a power in Congress or in the national government. It is simply a denial of power to the state. And the only mode in which the inhibition upon state laws impairing the obligation of contracts can be enforced, is, indirectly, through the courts, in suits where the parties raise some question as to the constitutional validity of such laws. The judicial power of the United States extends to such suits, for the reason that they are suits arising under the Constitution. The Fourteenth Amendment presents the first instance in our history of the investiture of Congress with affirmative power, by legislation, to enforce an express prohibition upon the states. It is not said that the judicial power of the nation may be exerted for the enforcement of that amendment. No enlargement of the judicial power was required, for it is clear that had the fifth section of the Fourteenth Amendment been entirely omitted, the judiciary could have stricken down all state laws and nullified all state proceedings in hostility to rights and privileges secured or recognized by that amendment. The power given it, in terms, by congressional legislation, to enforce the provisions of the amendment.

The assumption that this amendment consists wholly of prohibitions upon state laws and state proceedings in hostility to its provisions, is unauthorized by its language. The first clause of the first section—"all persons born or naturalized in the United States, and subject to the jurisdiction thereof, are citizens of the United States, and of the state wherein they reside"—is of a distinctly affirmative character. In its application to the colored race, previously liberated, it created and granted, as well citizenship of the United States, as citizenship of the state in which they respectively resided. It introduced all of that race, whose ancestors had been imported

and sold as slaves, at once, into the political community known as the "People of the United States." They became, instantly, citizens of the United States, and of their respective states. Further, they were brought, by this supreme act of the nation, within the direct operation of that provision of the Constitution which declares that "the citizens of each state shall be entitled to all privileges and immunities of citizens in the several states." Article 4, §2.

The citizenship thus acquired by that race, in virtue of an affirmative grant by the nation, may be protected, not alone by the judicial branch of the government, but by congressional legislation of a primary direct character; this, because the power of Congress is not restricted to the enforcement of prohibitions upon state laws or state action. It is, in terms distinct and positive, to enforce "the provisions or this article" of amendment; not simply those of a prohibitive character, but the provisions—all of the provisions—affirmative and prohibitive, of the amendment. It is, therefore, a grave misconception to suppose that the fifth section of the amendment has reference exclusively to express prohibitions upon state laws or state action. If any right was created by that amendment, the grant of power, through appropriate legislation, to enforce its provisions authorizes Congress, by means of legislation operating throughout the entire Union, to guard, secure, and protect that right.

It is, therefore, an essential inquiry what, if any, right, privilege, or immunity was given by the nation to colored persons when they were made citizens of the state in which they reside? Did the national grant of state citizenship to that race, of its own force, invest them with any rights, privileges, and immunities whatever? That they became entitled, upon the adoption of the Fourteenth Amendment, "to all privileges and immunities of citizens in the several states," within the meaning of section 2 of article 4 of the Constitution, no one, I suppose, will for a moment question. What are the privileges and immunities to which, by that clause of the Constitution, they became entitled? To this it may be answered, generally, upon the authority of the adjudged cases, that they are those which are fundamental in citizenship in a free government, "common to the citizens in the latter states under their constitutions and laws by virtue of their being citizens." Of that provision it has been said, with the approval of this court,

FROM
SEGREGATION
TO CIVIL RIGHTS

"THE CIVIL
RIGHTS CASES"

FROM
SEGREGATION
TO CIVIL RIGHTS

"THE CIVIL
RIGHTS CASES"

that no other one in the Constitution has tended so strongly to constitute the citizens of the United States one people. *Ward v. Maryland*, 12 Wall. 430; *Corfield v. Coryell*, 4 Wash. C. C. 371; *Paul v. Virginia*, 8 Wall. 180; *Slaughter-house Cases*, 16 Wall. 77.

Although this court has wisely forborne any attempt, by a comprehensive definition, to indicate all the privileges and immunities to which the citizens of each state are entitled of right to enjoy in the several state, I hazard nothing, in view of former adjudications, in saying that no state can sustain her denial to colored citizens of other states, while within her limits, of privileges or immunities, fundamental in republican citizenship, upon the ground that she accords such privileges and immunities only to hear white citizens and withholds them from her colored citizens. The colored citizens of other states, within the jurisdiction of that state, could claim, under the Constitution, every privilege and immunity which that state secures to her white citizens. Otherwise, it would be in the power of any state, by discriminating class legislation against its own citizens of a particular race or color, to withhold from citizens of other states, belonging to that proscribed race, when within her limits, privileges and immunities of the character regarded by all courts as fundamental in citizenship; and that, too, when the constitutional guaranty is that the citizens of each state shall be entitled to "all privileges and immunities of citizens of the several states." No state may, by discrimination against a portion of its own citizens of a particular race, in respect of privileges and immunities fundamental in citizenship, impair the constitutional right of citizens of other states, of whatever race, to enjoy in that state all such privileges and immunities as are there accorded to her most favored citizens. A colored citizen of Ohio or Indiana, being in the jurisdiction of Tennessee, is entitled to enjoy any privilege or immunity, fundamental in citizenship, which is given to citizens of the white race in the latter state. It is not to be supposed that any one will controvert this proposition.

But what was secured to colored citizens of the United States—as between them and their respective states—by the grant to them of state citizenship? With what rights, privileges, or immunities did this grant from the nation invest them? There is one, if there be no others— exemption from race discrimination in respect of

any civil right belonging to citizens of the white race in the same state. That, surely, is their constitutional privilege when within the jurisdiction of other states. And such must be their constitutional right, in their own state, unless the recent amendments be "splendid baubles," thrown out to delude those who deserved fair and generous treatment at the hands of the nation. Citizenship in this country necessarily imports equality of civil rights among citizens of every race in the same state. It is fundamental in American citizenship that, in respect of such rights, there shall be no discrimination by the state, or its officers, or by individuals, or corporations exercising public functions or authority, against any citizen because of his race or previous condition of servitude. In *U.S. v. Cruikshank*, 92 U.S. 555, it was said that "the equality of rights of citizens is a principle of republicanism." And in *Ex parte Virginia*, 100 U.S. 344, the emphatic language of this court is that

> "one great purpose of these amendments was to raise the colored race from that condition of inferiority and servitude in which most of them had previously stood, into perfect equality of civil rights with all other persons within the jurisdiction of the states."

So, in *Strauder v. West Virginia*, Id. 306, the court, alluding to the Fourteenth Amendment, said:

> "This is one of a series of constitutional provisions having a common purpose, namely, securing to a race recently emancipated, a race that through many generations had been held in slavery, all the civil rights that the superior race enjoy."

Again, in *Neal v. Delaware*, 103 U.S. 386, it was ruled that this amendment was designed, primarily, "to secure to the colored race, thereby invested with the rights, privileges, and responsibilities of citizenship, the enjoyment of all the civil rights that, under the law, are enjoyed by white persons."

Much light is thrown upon this part of the discussion by the language of this court in reference to the Fifteenth Amendment. In *U.S. v. Cruikshank* it was said:

> "In *U.S. v. Reese*, 92 U.S. 214, we held that the Fifteenth Amendment has invested the citizens of the United States with a new constitutional right, which is exemption from discrimination in the exercise of the elective franchise on account of race, color, or previous condition of servitude. From this it appears that the right of suffrage is not a necessary attribute of national citizenship, but

that exemption from discrimination in the exercise of that right on account of race, etc., is. The right to vote in the states comes from the states; but the right of exemption from the prohibited discrimination comes from the United States. The first has not been granted or secured by the Constitution of the United States, but the last has been."

Here, in language at once clear and forcible, is stated the principle for which I contend. It can hardly be claimed that exemption from race discrimination, in respect of civil rights, against those to whom state citizenship was granted by the nation, is any less for the colored race a new constitutional right, derived from and secured by the national Constitution, than is exemption from such discrimination in the exercise of the elective franchise. It cannot be that the latter is an attribute of national citizenship, while the other is not essential in national citizenship, or fundamental in state citizenship.

If, then, exemption from discrimination in respect of civil rights is a new constitutional right, secured by the grant of state constitutional right, secured by the grant of state citizenship to colored citizens of the United States, why may not the nation, by means of its own legislation of a primary direct character, guard, protect, and enforce that right? It is a right and privilege which the nation conferred. It did not come from the states in which those colored citizens reside. It has been the established doctrine of this court during all its history, accepted as vital to the national supremacy, that Congress, in the absence of a positive delegation of power to the state legislatures, may by legislation enforce and protect any right derived from or created by the national Constitution. It was so declared in *Prigg v. Com.* It was reiterated in *U.S. v. Reese*, 92 U.S. 214, where the court said that "rights and immunities created by and dependent upon the Constitution of the United States can be protected by Congress. The form and manner of the protection may be such as Congress, in the legitimate exercise of its discretion, shall provide. These may be varied to meet the necessities of the particular right to protected." It was distinctly reaffirmed in *Strauder v. West Virginia*, 100 U.S. 310, where we said that "a right or immunity created by the Constitution or only guarantied by it, even without any express delegation of power, may be protected by Congress." Will any one claim, in view of the declarations of this court in former cases, or even without them,

that exemption of colored citizens within their states from race discrimination, in respect of the civil rights of citizens, is not an immunity created or derived from the national Constitution?

This court has always given a broad and liberal construction to the Constitution, so as to enable Congress, by legislation, to enforce rights secured by that instrument. The legislation Congress may enact, in execution of its power to enforce the provisions of this amendment, is that which is appropriate to protect the right granted. Under given circumstances, that which the court characterizes as corrective legislation might be sufficient. Under other circumstances primary direct legislation may be required. But it is for Congress, not the judiciary, to say which is best adapted to the end to be attained. In *U.S. v. Fisher*, 2 Cranch, 358, this court said that "Congress must possess the choice of means, and must be empowered to use any means which are in fact conducive to the exercise of a power granted by the Constitution." "The sound construction of the Constitution," said Chief Justice Marshall,

> "must allow to the national legislature that discretion, with respect to the means by which the powers it confers are to be carried into execution, which will enable that body to perform the high duties assigned to it in the manner most beneficial to the people. Let the end be legitimate—let it be within the scope of the constitution—and all means which are appropriate, which are plainly adapted to that end, which are not prohibited, but consistent with the letter and spirit of the constitution, are constitutional." *McCulloch v. Maryland*, 4 Wheat. 423.

Must these rules of construction be now abandoned? Are the powers of the national legislature to be restrained in proportion as the rights and privileges, derived from the nation, are more valuable? Are constitutional provisions, enacted to secure the dearest right of freemen and citizens, to be subjected to that rule of construction, applicable to private instruments, which requires that the words to be interpreted must be taken most strongly against those who employ them? Or shall it be remembered that

> "a constitution of government, founded by the people for themselves and their posterity, and for objects of the most momentous nature—for perpetual union, for the establishment of justice, for the general welfare, and for a perpetuation of the blessings of liberty—necessarily requires that every interpretation of its powers should have a

constant reference to these objects? No interpretation of the words in which those powers are granted can be a sound one which narrows down their ordinary import so as to defeat those objects." 1 Story, Const. § 422.

The opinion of the court, as I have said, proceeds upon the ground that the power of Congress to legislate for the protection of the rights and privileges secured by the Fourteenth Amendment cannot be brought into activity except with the view, and as it may become necessary, to correct and annul state laws and state proceedings in hostility to such right and privileges. In the absence of state laws or state action, adverse to such rights and privileges, the nation may not actively interfere for their protection and security. Such I understand to be the position of my brethren. If the grant to colored citizens of the United States of citizenship in their respective states imports exemption from race discrimination, in their states, in respect of the civil rights belonging to citizenship, then, to hold that the amendment remits that right to the states for their protection, primarily, and stays the hands of the nation, until it is assailed by state laws or state proceedings, is to adjudge that the amendment, so far from enlarging the powers of congress—as we have heretofore and it did—not only curtails them, but reverses the policy which the general government has pursued from its very organization. Such an interpretation of the amendment is a denial to Congress of the power, by appropriate legislation, to enforce one of its provisions. In view of the circumstances under which the recent amendments were incorporated into the Constitution, and especially in view of the peculiar character of the new rights they created and secured, it ought not to be presumed that the general government has abdicated its authority, by national legislation, direct and primary in its Character, to guard and protect privileges and immunities secured by that instrument. Such an interpretation of the Constitution ought not to be accepted if it be possible to avoid it. Its acceptance would lead to this anomalous result: that whereas, prior to the amendments, Congress, with the sanction of this court, passed the most stringent laws—operating directly and primarily upon states, and their officers and agents, as well as upon individuals—in vindication of slavery and the right of the master, it may not now, by legislation of a like primary and direct character, guard, protect, and secure the freedom estab-

lished, and the most essential right of the citizenship granted, by the constitutional amendments. I venture, with all respect for the opinion of others, to insist that the national legislature may, without transcending the limits of the Constitution, do for human liberty and the fundamental rights of American citizenship, what it did, with the sanction of this court, for the protection of slavery and the rights of the masters of fugitive slaves. If fugitive slave laws, providing modes and prescribing penalties whereby the master could seize and recover his fugitive slave, were legitimate exertions of an implied power to protect and enforce a right recognized by the constitution, why shall the hands of congress be tied, so that—under an express power, by appropriate legislation, to enforce a constitutional provision, granting citizenship—it may not, by means of direct legislation, bring the whole power of this nation to bear upon states and their officers, and upon such individuals and corporations exercising public functions, as assume to abridge, impair, or deny rights confessedly secured by the supreme law of the land?

It does not seem to me that the fact that, by the second clause of the first section of the Fourteenth Amendment, the states are expressly prohibited from making or enforcing laws abridging the privileges and immunities of citizens of the United States, furnishes any sufficient reason for holding or maintaining that the amendment was intended to deny Congress the power, by general, primary, and direct legislation, of protecting citizens of the United States, being also citizens of their respective states, against discrimination, in respect to their rights as citizens, founded on race, color, or previous condition of servitude. Such an interpretation of the amendment is plainly repugnant to its fifth section, conferring upon Congress power, by appropriate legislation, to enforce, not merely the provisions containing prohibitions upon the states, but all of the provisions, express and implied, of the grant of citizenship in the first clause of the first section of the article. This alone is sufficient for holding that Congress is not restricted to the enactment of laws adapted to counteract and redress the operation of state legislation, or the action of state officers of the character prohibited by the amendment. It was perfectly well known that the great danger to the equal enjoyment by citizens of their rights, as citizens, was to be apprehended, not altogether from unfriendly state legislation, but from the hostile action of corporations and individuals in the states. And it is to be presumed that it was intended, by that section, to clothe Congress with power and authority to meet that danger. If the rights intended to be secured by the act of 1875 are such as belong to the citizen, in common or equally with other citizens in the same state, then it is not to be denied that such legislation is appropriate to the end which Congress is authorized to accomplish, viz., to protect the citizen, in respect of such rights, against discrimination on account of his race. As to the prohibition in the Fourteenth Amendment upon the making or enforcing of state laws abridging the privileges of citizens of the United States, it was impossible for any state to have enforced laws of that character. The judiciary could have annulled all such legislation under the provision that the Constitution shall be the supreme law of the land, anything in the Constitution or laws of any state to the contrary notwithstanding. The states were already under an implied prohibition not to abridge any privilege or immunity belonging to citizens of the United States as such. Consequently, the prohibition upon state laws hostile to the rights belonging to citizens of the United States, was intended only as an express limitation on the powers of the states, and was not intended to diminish, in the slightest degree, the authority which the nation has always exercised, of protecting, by means of its own direct legislation, rights created or secured by the Constitution. The purpose not to diminish the national authority is distinctly negatived by the express grant of power, by legislation, to enforce every provision of the amendment, including that which, by the grant of citizenship in the state, secures exemption from race discrimination in respect of the civil rights of citizens.

It is said that any interpretation of the Fourteenth Amendment different from that adopted by the court, would authorize Congress to enact a municipal code for all the states, covering every matter affecting the life, liberty, and property of the citizens of the several states. Not so. Prior to the adoption of that amendment the constitutions of the several states, without, perhaps, an exception, secured all persons against deprivation of life, liberty, or property, otherwise than by due process of law, and, in some form, recognized the right of all persons to the equal protection of the laws. These rights, therefore, existed before that amendment was proposed or adopted. If, by reason of that fact, it be

assumed that protection in these rights of persons still rests, primarily, with the states, and that Congress may not interfere except to enforce, by means of corrective legislation, the prohibitions upon state laws or state proceedings inconsistent with those rights, it does not at all follow that privileges which have been granted by the nation may not be protected by primary legislation upon the part of Congress. The rights and immunities of persons recognized in the prohibitive clauses of the amendments were always under the protection, primarily, of the states, while rights created by or derived from the United States have always been, and, in the nature of things, should always be, primarily, under the protection of the general government. Exemption from race discrimination in respect of the civil rights which are fundamental in citizenship in a republican government, is, as we have seen, a new constitutional right, created by the nation, with express power in Congress, by legislation, to enforce the constitutional provision from which it is derived. If, in some sense, such race discrimination is a denial of the equal protection of the laws, within the letter of the last clause of the first section, it cannot be possible that a mere prohibition upon state denial of such equal protection to persons within its jurisdiction, or a prohibition upon state laws abridging the privileges and immunities of citizens of the United States, takes from the nation the power which it has uniformly exercised of protecting, by primary direct legislation, those privileges and immunities which existed under the constitution before the adoption of the Fourteenth Amendment, or which have been created by that amendment in behalf of those thereby made citizens of their respective states.

It was said of *Dred Scott v. Sandford* that this court in that case overruled the action of two generations, virtually inserted a new clause in the Constitution, changed its character, and made a new departure in the workings of the federal government. I may be permitted to say that if the recent amendments are so construed that Congress may not, in its own discretion, and independently of the action or non-action of the states, provide, by legislation of a primary and direct character, for the security of rights created by the national Constitution; if it be adjudged that the obligation to protect the fundamental privileges and immunities granted by the Fourteenth Amendment to citizens residing in the several states, rests, primarily, not on the nation, but on the states; if it be further adjudged that individuals and corporations exercising public functions may, without liability to direct primary legislation on the part of Congress, make the race of citizens the ground for denying them that equality of civil rights which the constitution ordains as a principle of republican citizenship—then, not only the foundations upon which the national supremacy has always securely rested will be materially disturbed, but we shall enter upon an era of constitutional law when the rights of freedom and American citizenship cannot receive from the nation that efficient protection which heretofore was accorded to slavery and the rights of the master.

But if it were conceded that the power of Congress could not be brought into activity until the rights specified in the act of 1875 had been abridged or denied by some state law or state action, I maintain that the decision of the court is erroneous. There has been adverse state action within the Fourteenth Amendment as heretofore interpreted by this court. I allude to *Ex parte Virginia*, supra. It appears, in that case, that one Cole, judge of a county court, was charged with the duty, by the laws of Virginia, of selecting grand and petit jurors. The law of the state did not authorize or permit him, in making such selections, to discriminate against colored citizens because of their race. But he was indicated in the federal court, under the act of 1875, for making such discriminations. The attorney general of Virginia contended before us that the state had done its duty, and had not authorized or directed that county judge to do what he was charged with having done, and consequently that the state had not denied to the colored race the equal protection of the laws, and the act of Cole must therefore be deemed his individual act, in contravention of the will of the state. Plausible as this argument was, it failed to convince this court, and after saying that the Fourteenth Amendment had reference to the political body denominated a state, "by whatever instruments or in whatever modes that action may be taken," and that a state acts by its legislative, executive, and judicial authorities, and can act in no other way, we proceeded:

> "The constitutional provision, therefore, must mean that no agency of the state, or of the officers or agents by whom its powers are exerted, shall deny to any person within its jurisdiction the equal protection of the laws. Whoever, by virtue of public position under

a state government, deprives another of property, life, or liberty without due process of law, or denies or takes away the equal protection of the laws, violates the constitutional inhibition; and, as he acts under the name and for the state, and is clothed with the state's power, his act is that of the state. This must be so, or the constitutional prohibition has no meaning. Then the state has clothed one of its agents with power to annual or evade it. But the constitutional amendment was ordained for a purpose. It was to secure equal rights to all persons, and, to insure to all persons the enjoyment of such rights, power was given to Congress to enforce its provisions by appropriate legislation. Such legislation must act upon person, not upon the abstract thing denominated a state, but upon the persons who are the agents of the state, in the denial of the rights which were intended to be secured." 100 U.S. 346, 347

In every material sense applicable to the practical enforcement of the Fourteenth Amendment, railroad corporations, keepers of inns, and managers of places of public amusement are agents of the state, because amenable, in respect of their public duties and functions, to public regulation. It seems to me that, within the principle settled in *Ex parte Virginia*, a denial by these instrumentalities of the state to the citizen, because of his race, of that equality of civil rights secured to him by law, is a denial by the state within the meaning of the Fourteenth Amendment. If it be not, then that race is left, in respect of the civil rights under discussion, practically at the mercy of corporation and individuals wielding power under public authority.

But the court says that Congress did not, in the act of 1866, assume, under the authority given by the Thirteenth Amendment, to adjust what may be called the social rights of men and races in the community. I agree that government has nothing to do with social, as distinguished from technically legal, rights of individuals. No government ever has brought, or ever can bring, its people into social intercourse against their wishes. Whether one person will permit or maintain social relations with another is a matter with which government has not concern. I agree that if one citizen chooses not to hold social intercourse with another, he is not and cannot be made amenable to the law for his conduct in that regard; for no legal right of a citizen is violated by the refusal of others to maintain merely social relations with him, even upon grounds of race. What I affirm is that no state, nor the officers of any state, nor any corporation or individual wielding power under state authority for the public benefit or the public convenience, can, consistently either with the freedom established by the fundamental law, or with that equality of civil rights which now belongs to every citizen, discriminate against freemen or citizens, in their civil rights, because of their race, or because they once labored under disabilities imposed upon them as a race. The rights which Congress, by the act of 1875, endeavored to secure and protect are legal, not social, rights. The right, for instance, of a colored citizen to use the accommodations of a public highway upon the same terms as are permitted to white citizens is no more a social right than his right, under the law, to use the public streets of a city, or a town, or a turnpike road, or a public market, or a post-office, or his right to sit in a public building with others of whatever race, for the purpose of hearing the political questions to the day discussed. Scarcely a day passes without our seeing in this court-room citizens of the white and black races sitting side by side watching the progress of our business. It would never occur to any one that the presence of a colored citizen in a court-house or court-room was an invasion of the social rights of white persons who may frequent such places. And yet such a suggestion would be quite as sound in law—I say it with all respect—as is the suggestion that the claim of a colored citizen to use, upon the same terms as is permitted to white citizens, the accommodations of public highways, or public inns, or places of public amusement, established under the license of the law, is an invasion of the social rights of the white race.

The court, in its opinion, reserves the question whether Congress, in the exercise of its power to regulate commerce among the several states, might or might not pass a law regulating rights in public conveyances passing from one state to another. I beg to suggest that precise question was substantially presented here in the only one of these cases relating to railroads— *Robinson v. Memphis & C. R. Co.* In that case it appears that Mrs. Robinson, a citizen of Mississippi, purchased a railroad ticket entitling her to be carried from Grand Junction, Tennessee, to Lynchburg, Virginia. Might not the act of 1875 be maintained in that case, as applicable at least to commerce between the states, notwithstanding it does not, upon its face, profess to have been passed in pursuance of the power given to Congress to regulate commerce? Has it ever been held that the judiciary should overturn a statute because the legislative department did not accurately recite therein the particular provision of the constitution authorizing its enactment? We have often enforced municipal bonds in aid of railroad subscriptions where they failed to recite the statute authorizing their issue, but recited one which did not sustain their validity. The inquiry in such cases has been, was there in any statute authority for the execution of the bonds? Upon this branch of the case it may be remarked that the state of Louisiana, in 1869, passed a statute giving to passengers, without regard to race or color, equality of right in the accommodations of railroad and street cars, steam-boats, or other water-crafts, stage-coaches, omnibuses, or other vehicles. But in *Hall v. De Cuir*, 95 U.S. 487, that act was pronounced unconstitutional so far as it related to commerce between the state, this court saying that "if the public good requires such legislation it must come from Congress and not from the state." I suggest that it may become a pertinent inquiry whether Congress may, in the exertion of its power to regulate commerce among the states, enforce among passengers on public conveyances quality of right without regard to race, color, or previous condition of servitude, if it be true—which I do not admit—that such legislation would be an interference by government with the social rights of the people.

My brethren say that when a man has emerged from slavery, and by the aid of beneficent legislation has shaken off the inseparable concomitants of that state, there must be some stage in the progress of his elevation when he takes the rank of a mere citizen, and ceases to be the special favorite of the laws, and when his rights as a citizen, or a man, are to be protected in the ordinary modes by which other men's rights are protected. It is, I submit, scarcely just to say that the colored race has been the special favorite of the laws. What the nation, through Congress, has sought to accomplish in reference to that race is, what had already been done in every state in the Union for the white race, to secure and protect rights belonging to them as freemen and citizens; nothing more. The one underlying purpose of congressional legislation has been to enable the black race to take the rank of mere citizens. The difficulty has been to compel a recognition of their legal right to take that rank, and to secure the enjoyment of privileges belonging, under the law, to them as a component part of the people for whose welfare and happiness government is ordained. At every step in this direction the nation has been confronted with class tyranny, which a contemporary English historian says is, of all tyrannies, the most intolerable, "for it is ubiquitous in its operation, and weighs, perhaps, most heavily on those whose obscurity or distance would withdraw them from the notice of a single despot." Today it is the colored race which is denied, by corporations and individuals wielding public authority, rights fundamental in their freedom and citizenship. At some future time it may be some other race that will fall under the ban. If the constitutional amendments be enforced, according to the intent with which, as I conceive, they were adopted, there cannot be, in this republic, any class of human beings in practical subjection to another class, with power in the latter to dole out to the former just such privileges as they may choose to grant. The supreme law of the land has decreed that no authority shall be exercised in this country upon the basis of discrimination, in respect of civil rights, against freemen and citizens because of their race, color, or previous condition of servitude. To that decree—for the due enforcement of which, be appropriate legislation, Congress has been invested with express power—every one must bow, whatever may have been, or whatever now are, his individual views as to the wisdom or policy, either of the recent changes in the fundamental law, or of the legislation which has been enacted to give them effect.

For the reasons stated I feel constrained to withhold my assent to the opinion of the court.

FROM SEGREGATION TO CIVIL RIGHTS

PLESSY V. FERGUSON

At issue in *Plessy v. Ferguson* was an 1890 Louisiana law that required passenger trains operating within the state to provide "equal but separate" accommodations for "white and colored races." The Supreme Court upheld the law by a 7–1 vote, in the process putting a stamp of approval on all laws that mandated racial segregation. In his majority opinion, Justice Henry Billings Brown concluded that the Fourteenth Amendment "could not have intended to abolish distinctions based upon color, or to enforce social, as distinguished from political, equality, or a commingling of the two races upon terms unsatisfactory to either."

Justice John M. Harlan, the lone dissenter, responded that the "arbitrary separation of citizens on the basis of race" was equivalent to imposing a "badge of servitude" on African Americans. He contended that the real intent of the law was not to provide equal accommodations but to compel African Americans "to keep to themselves." This was intolerable because "our Constitution is color-blind, and neither knows nor tolerates classes among citizens." Nevertheless, *Plessy* was the law of the land until 1954.

—⁂—

Plessy v. Ferguson

(May 18, 1896.)

No. 210.

1. An act requiring white and colored persons to be furnished with separate accommodations on railway trains does not violate Const. Amend. 13, abolishing slavery and involuntary servitude. 11 South. 948, affirmed.

2. A state statute requiring railway companies to provide separate accommodations for white and colored persons, and making a passenger insisting on occupying a coach or compartment other than the one set apart for his race liable to fine or imprisonment, does not violate Const. Amend. 14, by a abridging the privileges or immunities of United States citizens, or depriving persons of liberty or property without due process of law, or by denying them the equal protection of the laws. 11 South. 948. affirmed.

Mr. Justice Harlan dissenting.

In Error to the Supreme Court of the State of Louisiana.

This was a petition for writs of prohibition and certiorari originally filed in the supreme court of the state by Plessy, the plaintiff in error, against the Hon. John H. Ferguson, judge of the criminal district court for the parish of Orleans, and setting forth, in substance, the following facts:

That petitioner was a citizen of the United States and a resident of the state of Louisiana, of mixed descent, in the proportion of seven-eighths Caucasian and one-eighth African blood; that the mixture of colored blood was not discernible in him, and that he was entitled to every recognition, right, privilege, and immunity secured to the citizens of the United States of the white race by its constitution and laws; that on June 7, 1892, he engaged and paid for a first-class passage on the East Louisiana Railway,

FROM
SEGREGATION
TO CIVIL RIGHTS

PLESSY V.
FERGUSON

from New Orleans to Covington, in the same state, and thereupon entered a passenger train, and took possession of a vacant seat in a coach where passengers of the white race were accommodated; that such railroad company was incorporated by the laws of Louisiana as a common carrier, and was not authorized to distinguish between citizens according to their race, but, withstanding this, petitioner was required by the conductor, under penalty of ejection from said train and imprisonment, to vacate said coach, and occupy another seat, in a coach assigned by said company for persons not of the white race, and for no other reason than that petitioner was of the colored race; that, upon petitioner's refusal to comply with such order, he was, with the aid of a police officer, forcibly ejected from said coach, and hurried off to, and imprisoned in, the parish jail of New Orleans, and there held to answer a charge made by such officer to the effect that he was guilty of having criminally violated an act of the general assembly of the state, approved July 10, 1890, in such case made and provided.

The petitioner was subsequently brought before the recorder of the city of preliminary examination, and committed for trial to the criminal district court for the parish of Orleans, where an information was filed against him in the matter above set forth, for a violation of the above act, which act the petitioner affirmed to be null and void, because in conflict with the constitution of the United States; that petitioner interposed a plea to such information, based upon the unconstitutionality of the act of the general assembly, to which the district attorney, on behalf of the state, filed a demurrer; that, upon issue being joined upon such demurrer and plea, the court sustained the demurrer, overruled the plea, and ordered petitioner to plead over to the facts set forth in the information, and that, unless the judge of the said court be enjoined by a writ of prohibition from further proceeding in such case, the court will proceed to fine and sentence petitioner to imprisonment, and thus deprive him of his constitutional rights set forth in his said plea, notwithstanding the unconstitutionality of the act under which was being prosecuted; that no appeal lay from such sentence, and petitioner was without relief or remedy except by writs of prohibition and certiorari. Copies of the information and other proceedings in the criminal district court were annexed to the petition as an exhibit.

Upon the filing of this petition, an order was issued upon the respondent to show cause why a writ of prohibition should not issue, and be made perpetual, and further order that the record of the proceedings had in the criminal cause be certified and transmitted to the supreme court.

To this order the respondent made answer, transmitting a certified copy of the proceedings, asserting the constitutionality of the law, and averring that, instead of pleading or admitting that he belonged to the colored race, the said Plessy declined and refused, either by pleading or otherwise, to admit that he was in any sense or in any proportion a colored man.

The case coming on for hearing before the supreme court, that court was of opinion that the law under which the prosecution was had was constitutional and denied the relief prayed for by the petitioner (*Ex parte Plessy*, 45 La. Ann. 80, 11 South. 948); whereupon petitioner prayed for a writ of error from this court, which was allowed by the chief justice of the Supreme Court of Louisiana.

A.W. Tourgee and S. F. Phillips, for plaintiff in error. Alex. Porter Morse, for defendant in error.

Mr. Justice Brown, after stating the facts in the foregoing language, delivered the opinion of the court.

This case turns upon the constitutionality of an act of the general assembly of the state of Louisiana, passed in 1890, providing for separate railway carriages for the white and colored races. Acts 1890, No. 111, p. 152.

The first section of the statute enacts

"that all railway companies in this state, shall provide equal but separate accommodations for the white, and colored races, by providing two or more passenger coaches for each passenger train, or by dividing the passenger coaches by a partition so as to secure separate accommodations: provided, that this section shall not be construed to apply to street railroads. No person or persons shall be permitted to occupy seats in coaches, other than the ones assigned to them, on account of the race they belong to."

By the second section it was enacted

"that the officers of such passenger trains shall have power and are hereby required to assign each passenger to the coach or compartment used for the race to which such passenger belongs; any passenger insisting on going into a coach or compartment to which by race he does not belong, shall be liable to a fine of twenty-five dollars, or in lieu thereof to imprisonment for a period of not more than twenty days in the parish prison, and any officer of any railroad insisting on assigning a passenger to a coach or compartment other than the one set aside for the race to which said passenger belongs, shall be liable to a fine of twenty-five dollars, or in lieu thereof to imprisonment for a period of not more than twenty days in the parish prison; and should any passenger refuse to occupy the coach or compartment to which he or she is assigned by the officer of such railway, said officer shall have power to refuse to carry such passenger on his train, and for such refusal neither he nor the railway company which he represents shall be liable for damages in any of the courts of this state."

The third section provides penalties for the refusal or neglect of the officers, directors, conductors, and employes of railway companies to comply with the act, with a proviso that "nothing in this act shall be construed as applying to nurses attending children of the other race." The fourth section is immaterial.

The information filed in the criminal district court charged, in substance, that Plessy, being a passenger between two stations within the state of Louisiana, was assigned by officers of the company to the coach used for the race to which he belonged, but he insisted upon going into a coach used by the race to which he did not belong. Neither in the information nor plea was his particular race or color averred.

The petition for the writ of prohibition averred that petitioner was seven-eighths Caucasian and one-eighth African blood; that the mixture of colored blood was not discernible in him; and that he was entitled to every right, privilege, and immunity secured to citizens of the United States of the white race; and that, upon such theory, he took possession of a vacant seat in a coach where passengers of the white race were accommodated, and was ordered by the conductor to vacate said coach, and take a seat in another, assigned to persons of the colored race, and, having refused to comply with such demand he was forcibly ejected with the aid of a police officer and imprisoned in the parish jail to answer a charge of having violated the above act.

The constitutionality of this act is attacked upon the ground that it conflicts both with the Thirteenth Amendment of the Constitution, abolishing slavery and the Fourteenth Amendment, which prohibits certain restrictive legislation on the part of the states.

1. That is does not conflict with the Thirteenth Amendment, which abolished slavery and involuntary servitude, except as a punishment for crime, is too clear for argument. Slavery implies involuntary servitude—a state of bondage; the ownership of mankind as a chattel, or, at least, the control of the labor and services of one man for the benefit of another, and the absence of a legal right to the disposal of his own person, property, and services. This amendment was said in the *Slaughter-House Cases*, 16 Wall. 36, to have been intended primarily to abolish slavery, as it had been previously known in this country, and that it equally forbade Mexican peonage or the Chinese coolie trade, when they amounted to slavery or involuntary servitude, and that the use of the word "servitude" was intended to prohibit the use of all forms of involuntary slavery, of whatever class or name. It was intimated, however, in that case, that this amendment was regarded by the statesmen of that day as insufficient to protect the colored race from certain laws which had been enacted in the Southern states, imposing upon the colored race onerous disabilities and burdens, and curtailing their rights in the pursuit of life, liberty, and property to such an extent that their freedom was of little value; and that the Fourteenth Amendment was devised to meet this exigency

So, too, in the *Civil Rights Cases*, 100 U.S. 3, 3 Sup. Ct. 18, it was said that the act of a mere individual, the owner of an inn, a public conveyance or place of amusement, refusing accommodations to colored people, cannot be justly regarded as imposing any badge of slavery or servitude upon the applicant, but only as involving an ordinary civil injury, properly cognizable by the laws of the state, and presumably subject to redress by those laws until the contrary appears. "It would be running the slavery question into the ground," said Mr. Justice Bradley,

"to make it apply to every act of discrimination which a person may see fit to make as to the guests he will entertain, or as to the people he will take into his coach or cab or car, or admit to his concert or theater, or deal with in other matters of intercourse or business."

A statute which implies merely a legal distinction between the white and colored races—a distinction which is found in the color of the two races, and which must always exist so long

FROM
SEGREGATION
TO CIVIL RIGHTS

PLESSY V.
FERGUSON

FROM
SEGREGATION
TO CIVIL RIGHTS

PLESSY V.
FERGUSON

as white men are distinguished from the other race by color—has no tendency to destroy the legal equality of the two races, or re-establish a state of involuntary servitude. Indeed, we do not understand that the Thirteenth Amendment is strenuously relied upon by the plaintiff in error in this connection.

2. By the Fourteenth Amendment, all persons born or naturalized in the United States, and subject to the jurisdiction thereof, are made citizens of the United States and of the state wherein they reside; and the states are forbidden from making or enforcing any law which shall abridge the privileges or immunities of citizens of the United States, or shall deprive any person of life, liberty or property without due process of law, or deny to any person within their jurisdiction the equal protection of the laws.

The proper construction of this amendment was first called to the attention of this court in the *Slaughter-House Cases*, 16 Wall. 36, which involved, however, not a question of race, but one of exclusive privileges. The case did not call for any expression of opinion as to the exact rights it was intended to secure to the colored race, but it was said generally that its main purpose was to establish the citizenship of the negro, to give definitions of citizenship of the United States and of the states, and to protect from the hostile legislation of the states the privileges and immunities of citizens of the United States, as distinguished from those of citizens of the states.

The object of the amendment was undoubtedly to enforce the absolute equality of the two races before the law, but, in the nature of things, it could not have been intended to abolish distinctions based upon color, or to enforce social, as distinguished from political, equality, or a commingling of the two races upon terms unsatisfactory to either. Laws permitting, and even requiring, their separation, in places where they are liable to be brought into contact, do not necessarily imply the inferiority of either race to the other, and have been generally, if not universally, recognized as within the competency of the state legislatures in the exercise of their police power. The most common instance of this is connected with the establishment of separate schools for white and colored children, which have been held to be a valid exercise of the legislative power even by courts of states where the political rights of the colored race have been longest and most earnestly enforced.

One of the earliest of these cases is that of *Roberts v. City of Boston*, 5 Cush. 198, in which the supreme judicial court of Massachusetts held that the general school committee of Boston had power to make provision for the instruction of colored children in separate schools established exclusively for them, and to prohibit their attendance upon the other schools. "The great principle," said Chief Justice Shaw,

"advanced by the learned and eloquent advocate for the plaintiff [Mr. Charles Sumner], is that, by the constitution and laws of Massachusetts, all persons, without distinction of age or sex, birth or color, origin or condition, are equal before the law. * * * But, when this great principle comes to be applied to the actual and various conditions of persons in society, it will not warrant the assertion that men and women are legally clothed with the same civil and political powers, and that children and adults are legally to have the same functions and be subject to the same treatment; but only that the rights of all, as they are settled and regulated by law, are equally entitled to the paternal consideration and protection of the law for their maintenance and security."

It was held that the powers of the committee extended to the establishment of separate schools for children of different ages, sexes, and colors, and that they might also establish special schools for poor and neglected children, who have become too old to attend the primary school, and yet not acquired the rudiments of learning, to enable them to enter the ordinary schools. Similar laws have been enacted by Congress under its general power of legislation over the District of Columbia (sections 281–283, 310, 319, Rev. St. D. C.), as well as by the legislatures of many of the states, and have been generally, if not uniformly, sustained by the courts. *State v. McCann* 21 Ohio St. 210; *Lehew v. Brummell* (Mo. Sup.) 15 S. W. 705; *Ward v. Flood*, 48 Cal. 36; *Bertonneau v. Directors of City Schools*, 3 Woods, 177 Fed. Cas. No. 1,361; *People v. Gallagher*, 93 N. Y. 438; *Cory v. Carter*, 48 Ind. 337; *Dawson v. Lee*, 83 Ky. 49.

Laws forbidding the intermarriage of the two races may be said in a technical sense to interfere with the freedom of contract, and yet have been universally recognized as within the police power of the state. *State v. Gibson*, 36 Ind. 389.

The distinction between laws interfering with the political equality of the negro and those requiring the separation of two races in schools, theaters, and railway carriages has been frequently drawn by this court. Thus, in *Strauder v. West Virginia*, 100 U.S. 303, it was held that a law of West Virginia limiting to white male persons 21 years of age, and citizens of the state the right to sit upon juries, was a discrimination which implied a legal inferiority in civil society, which lessened the security of the right of the colored race, and was a step towards reducing them to a condition of servility. Indeed, the right of a colored man that in the selection of jurors to pass upon his life, liberty, and property there shall be no exclusion of his race, and no discrimination against them because of color, has been asserted in a number of cases. *Virginia v. Rives,* 100 U. S. 313; *Neal v. Delaware,* 103 U.S. 370; *Bush v. Com.,* 107 U.S. 110, 1 Sup. Ct. 625; *Gibson v. Mississippi,* 162 U.S. 565, 16 Sup. Ct 904. So, where the laws of a particular locality or the charter of a particular railway corporation has provided that no person shall be excluded from the cars on account of color, we have held that this meant that persons of color should travel in the same car as white ones, and that the enactment was not satisfied by the company providing cars assigned exclusively to white persons. *Railroad Co. v. Brown,* 17 Wall. 445.

Upon the other hand, where a statute of Louisiana required those engaged in the transportation of passengers among the states to give to all persons traveling within that state, upon vessels employed in that business, equal rights and privileges in all parts of the vessel, without distinction on account of race or color, and subjected to an action for damages the owner of such a vessel who excluded colored passengers on account of their color from the cabins set aside by him for the use of whites, it was held to be, so far as it applied to interstate commerce, unconstitutional and void. *Hall v. De Cuir,* 95 U. S. 485. The court in this case, however, expressly disclaimed that it had anything whatever to do with the statute as a regulation of internal commerce, or affecting anything else that commerce among the states.

In the *Civil Rights Cases,* 109 U. S. 3, 3 Sup. Ct. 18, it was held that an act of Congress entitling all persons within the jurisdiction of the United States to the full and equal enjoyment of the accommodations, advantages, facilities, and privileges of inns, public conveyances, on land or water, theaters, and other places of public amusement, and made applicable to citizens of every race and color, regardless of any previous condition of servitude, was unconstitutional and void, upon the ground that the Fourteenth Amendment was prohibitory upon the states only, and the legislation authorized to be adopted by Congress for enforcing it was not direct legislation on matters respecting which the states were prohibited from making or enforcing certain laws, or doing certain acts, but was corrective legislation, such as might be necessary or proper for counteracting and redressing the effect of such laws or acts. In delivering the opinion of the court, Mr. Justice Bradley observed that the Fourteenth Amendment

> "does not invest Congress with power to legislate upon subjects that are within the domain of state legislation, but to provide modes of relief against state legislation or state action of the kind referred to. It does not authorize Congress to create a code of municipal law for the regulation of private rights, but to provide modes to redress against the operation of state laws, and the action of state officers, executive or judicial, when these are subversive of the fundamental rights specified in the amendment. Positive rights and privileges are undoubtedly secured by the Fourteenth Amendment; but they are secured by way of prohibition against state laws and state proceedings affecting those rights and privileges, and by power given to Congress to legislate for the purpose of carrying such prohibition into effect; and such legislation must necessarily be predicated upon such supposed state laws or state proceedings, and be directed to the correction of their operation and effect."

Much nearer, and, indeed, almost directly in point, is the case of the *Louisville, N. O. & T. Ry Co. v. State,* 133 U.S. 587, 10 Sup. Ct. 348, wherein the railway company was indicted for a violation of a statute of Mississippi, enacting that all railroads carrying passengers should provide equal, but separate, accommodations for the white and colored races, by providing two or more passenger cars for each passenger train, or by dividing the passenger cars by a petition, so as to secure separate accommodations. The case was presented in a different aspect from the one under consideration, inasmuch as it was an indictment against the railway company for failing to provide the separate accommodations, but the question considered was the constitutionality of the law. In that case, the Supreme Court of Mississippi (66 Miss. 662, 6 South. 203) had held that the statute applied solely to com-

FROM
SEGREGATION
TO CIVIL RIGHTS

PLESSY V.
FERGUSON

merce within the state, and that being the construction of the state statute by its highest court, was accepted as conclusive. "If it be a matter," said the court (page 591, 133 U.S., and page 348, 10 Sup. Ct.),

> "respecting commerce wholly within a state, and not interfering with commerce between the states, then, obviously, there is no violation of the commerce clause of the federal constitution. * * * No question arises under this section as to the power of the state to separate in different compartments interstate passengers, or affect, in any manner, the privileges and rights of such passengers. All that we can consider is whether the state has the power to require that railroad trains within her limits shall have separate accommodations for the two races. That affecting only commerce within the state is no invasion of the power given to Congress by the commerce clause"

A like course of reasoning applies to the case under consideration, since the Supreme Court of Louisiana, in the case of *State v. Judge*, 44 La. Ann. 770, 11 South, 74, held that the statute in question did not apply to interstate passengers, but was confined in its application to passengers traveling exclusively within the borders of the state. The case was decided largely upon the authority of *Louisville, N. O. & T. Ry. Co. v. State*, 66 Miss. 662, 6 South. 203, and affirmed by this court in 133 U.S. 587, 10 Sup. Ct. 348. In the present case no question of interference with interstate commerce can possibly arise, since the East Louisiana Railway appears to have been purely a local line, with both its termini within the state of Louisiana. Similar statutes for the separation of the two races upon public conveyances were held to be constitutional in *Railroad v. Miles*, 55 Pa. St. 209; *Day v. Owen*, 5 Mich. 520; *Railway Co. v. Williams*, 55 Ill. 185; *Railroad Co. v. Wells*, 85 Tenn. 613; 4 S. W. 5; *Railroad Co. v. Benson*, 85 Tenn. 627, 4 S. W. 5; *The Sue*, 22 Fed. 843; *Logwood v. Railroad Co.*, 23 Fed. 318; *McGuinn v. Forbes*, 37 Fed. 639; *People v. King* (N. Y. App.) 18 N. E. 245; *Houck v. Railway Co.*, 38 Fed. 226; *Heard v. Railroad Co.*, 3 Inter St. Commerce Com. R. 111, 1 Inter St. Commerce Com. R. 428.

While we think the enforced separation of the races, as applied to the internal commerce of the state, neither abridges the privileges or immunities of the colored man, deprives him of his property without due process of law, nor denies him the equal protection of the laws,

within the meaning of the Fourteenth Amendment, we are not prepared to say that the conductor, in assigning passengers to the coaches according to their race, does not act at his peril, or that the provision of the second section of the act that denies to the passenger compensation in damages for a refusal to receive him into the coach in which he properly belongs is a valid exercise of the legislative power. Indeed, we understand it to be conceded by the state's attorney that such part of the act as exempts from liability the railway company and its officers is unconstitutional. The power to assign to a particular coach obviously implies the power to determine to which race the passenger belongs, as well as the power to determine who, under the laws of the particular state is to be deemed a white, and who a colored person. This question, though indicated in the brief of the plaintiff in error, does not properly arise upon the record in this case, since the only issue made is as to the unconstitutionality of the act, so far as it requires the railway to provide separate accommodations, and the conductor to assign passengers according to their race.

It is claimed by the plaintiff in error that, in any mixed community, the reputation of belonging to the dominant race, in this instance the white race, is "property," in the same sense that a right of action or of inheritance is property. Conceding this to be so, for the purposes of this case, we are unable to see how this statute deprives him of, or in any way affects his right to, such property. If he be a white man, and assigned to a colored coach, he may have his action for damages against the company for being deprived of his so-called "property." Upon the other hand, if he be a colored man, and be so assigned, he has been deprived of no property, since he is not lawfully entitled to the reputation of being a white man.

In this connection, it is also suggested by the learned counsel for the plaintiff in error that the same argument that will justify the state legislature in requiring railways to provide separate accommodations for the two races will also authorize them to require separate cars to be provided for people whose hair is of a certain color, or who are aliens, or who belong to certain nationalities, or to enact laws requiring colored people to walk upon one side of the street, and white people upon the other, or requiring white men's houses to be painted white, and colored men's black, or their vehicles or business signs to be of different colors, upon the theory that one side of the street is as good as the other, or that a house or vehicle of one color is as good as one of another color. The reply to all this is that every exercise of the police power must be reasonable, and extend only to such laws as are enacted in good faith for the promotion of the public good, and not for the annoyance or oppression of a particular class. Thus, in *Yick Wo v. Hopkins,* 118 U. S. 356, 6 Sup. Ct. 1064, it was held by this court that a municipal ordinance of the city of San Francisco: to regulate the carrying on of public laundries within the limits of the municipality, violated the provisions of the constitution of the United States, if it conferred upon the municipal authorities arbitrary power, at their own will, and without regard to discretion, in the legal sense of the term, to give or withhold consent as to persons or places, without regard to the competency of the persons applying or the propriety of the places selected for the carrying on of the business. It was held to be a covert attempt on the part of the municipality to make an arbitrary and unjust discrimination against the Chinese race. While this was the case of a municipal ordinance, a like principle has been held to apply to acts of a state legislature passed in the exercise of the police power. *Railroad Co. v. Husen,* 95 U. S. 465; *Louisville & N. R. Co. v. Kentucky,* 161 U. S. 677, 16 Sup. Ct. 714, and cases cited on page 700, 161 U. S., and page 714, 16 Sup. Ct.; *Daggett v. Hudson,* 43 Ohio St. 548, 3 N. E. 538; *Capen v. Foster,* 12 Pick. 485; *State v. Baker,* 38 Wis. 71; *Monroe v. Collins,* 17 Ohio St. 665; *Hulseman v. Gems,* 41 Pa. St. 396; *Osman v. Riley,* 15 Cal. 48

So far, then, as a conflict with the Fourteenth Amendment is concerned, the case reduces itself to the question whether the statute of Louisiana is a reasonable regulation, and with respect to this there must necessarily be a large discretion on the part of the legislature. In determining the question of reasonableness, it is at liberty to act with reference to the established usages, customs, and traditions of the people, and with a view to the promotion of their comfort, and the preservation of the public peace and good order. Gauged by this standard, we cannot say that a law which authorizes or even requires the separation of the two races in public conveyances is unreasonable, or more obnoxious to the Fourteenth Amendment than the acts of Congress requiring separate schools for colored children in the District of Columbia, the constitutionality of which does not seem to have been questioned, or the corresponding acts of state legislatures.

We consider the underlying fallacy of the plaintiff's argument to consist in the assumption that the enforced separation of the two races stamps the colored race with a badge of inferiority. If this be so, it is not by reason of anything found in the act, but solely because the colored race chooses to put that construction upon it. The argument necessarily assumes that if, as has been more than once the case, and is not unlikely to be so again, the colored race should become the dominant power in the state legislature, and should enact a law in precisely similar terms, it would thereby relegate the white race to an inferior position. We imagine that the white race, at least, would not acquiesce in this assumption. The argument also assumes that social prejudices may be overcome by legislation, and that equal rights cannot be secured to the negro except by an enforced commingling of the two races. We cannot accept this proposition. If the two races are to meet upon terms of social equality, it must be the result of natural affinities, a mutual appreciation of each other's merits, and a voluntary consent of individuals. As was said by the court of appeals of New York in *People v. Gallagher,* 93 N. Y. 438, 448:

> "This end can neither be accomplished nor promoted by laws which conflict with the general sentiment of the community upon whom they are designed to operate. When the government, therefore, has secured to each of its citizens equal rights before the law, and equal opportunities for improvement and progress, it has accomplished the end for which it was organized, and performed all of the functions respecting social advantages with which it is endowed."

Legislation is powerless to eradicate racial instincts, or to abolish distinctions based upon physical differences, and the attempt to do so can only result in accentuating the difficulties of the present situation. If the civil and political rights of both races be equal, one cannot be inferior to the other socially, the constitution of the United States cannot put them upon the same plane.

It is true that the question of the proportion of colored blood necessary to constitute a colored person, as distinguished from a white person, is one upon which there is a difference of opinion in the different states; some holding that any visible admixture of black blood stamps the person as belonging to the colored race (*State v. Chavers,* 5 Jones [N. C.] 1); others, that it depends upon the preponderance of blood (*Gray v. State,* 4 Ohio, 354; *Monroe v. Collins,* 17 Ohio St. 665); and still others, that the predominance of white blood must only be in the proportion of three-fourths (*People v. Dean,* 14 Mich. 406; *Jones v. Com.,* 80 Va. 544). But these are questions to be determined under the laws of each state, and are not properly put in issue in this case. Under the allegations of his petition, it may undoubtedly become a question of importance whether, under the laws of Louisiana, the petitioner belongs to the white or colored race.

The judgment of the court below is therefore affirmed.

Mr. Justice BREWER did not hear the argument or participate in the decision of this case.

Mr. Justice HARLAN dissenting.

By the Louisiana statute the validity of which is here involved, all railway companies (other than street-railroad companies) carrying passengers in that state are required to have separate but equal accommodations for white and colored persons, "by providing two or more passenger coaches for each passenger train or by dividing the passenger coaches by a partition so as to secure separate accommodations." Under this statute, no colored person is permitted to occupy a seat in a coach assigned to white persons; nor any white person to occupy a seat in a coach assigned to a colored persons. The managers of the railroad are not allowed to exercise any discretion in the premises, buy are required to assign each passenger to some coach or compartment set apart for the exclusive use of his race. If a passenger insists upon going into a coach or compartment not set apart for persons of his race, he is subject to be fined, or to be imprisoned in the parish jail. Penalties are prescribed for the refusal or neglect of the officers, directors, conductors, and employes of railroad companies to comply with the provisions of the act.

Only "nurses attending children of the other race" are excepted from the operation of the statute. No exception is made of colored attendants traveling with adults. A white man is not permitted to have his colored servant with him in the same coach, even if his condition of health requires the constant personal assistance of such servant. If a colored maid insists upon riding in the same coach with a white woman whom she has been employed to serve, and who may need her personal attention while traveling, she is subject to be fined or imprisoned for such an exhibition of zeal in the discharge of duty.

While there may be in Louisiana person of different races who are not citizens of the United States, the words in the act "white and colored races" necessarily include all citizens of the United States of both races residing in the state. So that we have before us a state enactment that compels, under penalties, the separation of the two races in railroad passenger coaches, and makes it a crime for a citizen of either race to enter a coach that has been assigned to citizens of the other race.

Thus, the state regulates the use of a public highway by citizens of the United States solely upon the basis of race.

However apparent the injustice of such legislation may be, we have only to consider whether it is consistent with the Constitution of the United States.

That a railroad is a public highway, and that the corporation which owns or operates it is in the exercise of public functions, is not, at this day, to be disputed. Mr. Justice Nelson, speaking for this court in *New Jersey Steam Nav. Co. v. Merchants' Bank,* 6 How. 344, 382, said that a common carrier was in the exercise "of a sort of public office, and has public duties to perform, from which he should not be permitted to exonerate himself without the assent of the parties concerned." Mr. Justice Strong, delivering the judgment of this court in *Olcott v. Supervisors,* 16 Wall. 678, 694, said

> "That railroads, though constructed by private corporations, and owned by them, are public highways, has been the doctrine of nearly all the courts ever since such conveniences for passage and transportation have had any existence. Very early the question arose whether a state's right of eminent domain could be exercised by a private corporation created for the purpose of constructing a railroad. Clearly, it could not, unless taking land for such a purpose by such an agency is taking land for public use. The right of eminent domain nowhere justifies taking property for a private use. Yet it is a doctrine universally accepted that a state legislature may authorize a private corporation to take land for the construction of such a road, making compensation to the owner. What else does this doctrine mean if not that building a railroad, though it be built by a private corporation, is an act done for a public use?"

So, in *Township of Pine Grove v. Talcott,* 19 Wall. 666, 676:

> "Though the corporation [a railroad company] was private, its work was public, as much so as if it were to be constructed by the state."

So, in *Inhabitants of Worcester v. Western R. Corp.,* 4 Metc. (Mass.) 564:

> "The establishment of that great thoroughfare is regarded as a public work, established by public authority, intended for the public use and benefit the use of which is secured to the whole community, and constitutes, therefore, like a canal, turnpike, or highway, a public easement."

> "It is true that the real and personal property, necessary to the establishment and management of the railroad, is vested in the corporation; but it is in trust for the public."

In respect of civil rights, common to all citizens, the constitution of the United States does not, I think, permit any public authority to know the race of those entitled to be protected in the enjoyment of such rights. Every true man has pride of race, and under appropriate circumstances, when the rights of others, his equals before the law, are not to be affected, it is his privilege to express such pride and take such action based upon it as to him seems proper. But I can deny that any legislative body or judicial tribunal may have regard to the race of citizens when the civil rights of those citizens are involved. Indeed, such legislation as that here in question is inconsistent not only with that equality of rights which pertains to citizenship, national and state, but with the personal liberty enjoyed by every one within the United States.

The Thirteenth Amendment does not permit the withholding or the deprivation of any right necessarily inhering in freedom. It not only struck down the institution of slavery as previously existing in the United States, but it prevents the imposition of any burdens or disabilities that constitute badges of slavery or servitude. It decreed universal civil freedom in this country. This court has so adjudged. But, that amendment having been found inadequate to the protection of the rights of those who had been in slavery, it was followed by the Fourteenth Amendment, which added greatly to the dignity and glory of American citizenship, and to the security of personal liberty, by declaring that

> "all persons born or naturalized in the United States, and subject to the jurisdiction thereof, are citizens of the United States and of the sate wherein they reside,"

and that

> "no state shall make or enforce any law which shall abridge the privileges or immunities of citizens of the United States; not shall any state deprive any person of life, liberty or property without due process of law, nor deny to any person within its jurisdiction the equal protection of the laws."

These two amendments, if enforced according to their true intent and meaning, will protect all the civil rights that pertain to freedom and citizenship. Finally, and to the end that no citizen should be denied, on account of his race, the privilege of participating in the political control of his country, it was declared by the Fifteenth Amendment that

> "the right of citizens of the United States to vote shall not be denied or abridged by the United States or by any state on account of race, color or previous condition of servitude."

These notable additions to the fundamental law were welcomed by the friends of liberty throughout the world. They removed the race line from our governmental systems. They had, as this court has said, a common purpose, namely, to secure "to a race recently emancipated, a race that through many generations have been held in slavery, all the civil rights that the superior race enjoy." They declared, in legal effect, this court has further said

> "that the law in the states shall be the same for the black as for the white; that all persons, whether colored or white, shall stand equal before the laws of the states; and in regard to the colored race, for whose protection the amendment was primarily designed, that no discrimination shall be made against them by law because of their color."

We also said:

> "The words of the amendment, is true, are prohibitory, but they contain a necessary implication of a positive immunity or right, most valuable to the colored—race the right to exemption from unfriendly legislation against them distinctively as colored; exemption from legal discriminations, implying inferiority in civil society, lessening the security of their enjoyment of the rights which others enjoy; and discriminations which are steps towards reducing them to the condition of a subject."

It was, consequently, adjudged that a state law that excluded citizens of the colored race from juries, because of their race, however well qualified in other respects to discharge the duties of jurymen, was repugnant to the Fourteenth Amendment. *Strauder v. West Virginia,* 100 U.S. 303, 306, 307; *Virginia v. Rives,* Id. 313; *Ex parte Virginia,* Id. 339: *Neal v. Delaware,* 103 U.S. 370, 386; *Bush v. Com.,* 107 U.S. 110, 116, 1 Sup. Ct. 625. At the present term referring to the previous adjudications, this court declared that

> "underlying all of those decisions is the principle that the constitution of the United States, in its present form, forbids, so far as civil and political rights are concerned, discrimination by the general government or the states against any citizen because of his race. All citizens are equal before the law. *Gibson v. State,* 162 U.S. 565, 16 Sup. Ct. 904."

The decisions referred to show the scope of the recent amendments of the constitution. They also show that it is not within the power of a state to prohibit colored citizens, because of their race, from participating as jurors in the administration of justice.

It was said in argument that the statute of Louisiana does not discriminate against either race, but prescribes a rule applicable alike to white and colored citizens. But this argument does not meet the difficulty. Every one knows that the statute in question had its origin in the purpose, not so much to exclude white persons from railroad cars occupied by blacks, as to exclude colored people from coaches occupied by or assigned to white persons. Railroad corporations of Louisiana did not make discrimination among whites in the matter of accommodation for travelers. The thing to accomplish was, under the guise of giving equal accommodation for whites and blacks, to compel the latter to keep to themselves while traveling in railroad passenger coaches. No one would be so wanting in candor as to assert the contrary. The fundamental objection, therefore, to the statute, is that it interferes with the personal freedom of citizens. "Personal liberty," it has been well said, "consists in the power of locomotion, of changing situation, or removing one's person to whatsoever places one's own inclination may direct, without imprisonment or restraint, unless by due course of law." 1. Bl. Comm. *134. If a white man and a black man choose to occupy the same public conveyance on a public highway, it is their right to do so; and no government, proceeding alone on grounds of race, can prevent it without infringing the personal liberty of each.

It is one thing for railroad carriers to furnish, or to be required by law to furnish, equal accommodations for all whom they are under a legal duty to carry. It is quite another thing for government to forbid citizens of the white and black races from traveling in the same public conveyance, and to punish officers of railroad companies for permitting persons of the two races to occupy the same passenger coach. If a state can prescribe, as a rule of civil conduct, that whites and blacks shall not travel as passengers in the same railroad coach, why may it not so regulate the use of the streets of its cities and towns as to compel white citizens to keep on one side of a street, and black citizens to keep on the other? Why may it not, upon like grounds, punish whites and blacks who ride together in street cars or in open vehicles on a public road or street? Why may it not require sheriffs to assign whites to one side of a court room, and blacks to the other? And why may it not also prohibit the commingling of the two races in the galleries of legislative halls or in public assemblages convened for the consideration of the political questions of the day? Furthermore, if this statute of Louisiana is consistent with the personal liberty of citizens, why may not the state require the separation in railroad coaches of native and naturalized citizens of the United States, or of Protestants and Roman Catholics?

The answer given at the argument to these question was that regulations of the kind they suggest would be unreasonable, and could not, therefore, stand before the law. Is it meant that the determination of questions of legislative power depends upon the inquiry whether the statute whose validity is questions is, in the judgment of the courts, a reasonable one, taking all the circumstances into consideration? A statute may be unreasonable merely because a sound public policy forbade its enactment. But I do not understand that the courts have anything to do with the policy or expediency of legislation. A statute may be valid, and yet, upon grounds of public policy, may well be characterized as unreasonable. Mr. Sedgwick correctly states the rule when he says that, the legislative intention being clearly ascertained "the courts have no other duty to perform than to execute the legislative will, without any regard to their views as to the wisdom or justice of the particular enactment." Sedg. St. & Const. Law, 324. There is a dangerous tendency in these latter days to enlarge the functions of the courts, by means of judicial interference with the will of the people as expressed by the legislature. Our institutions have the distinguishing characteristic that the three departments of government are co-ordinate and separate. Each must keep within the limits defined by the constitution. And the courts best discharge their duty by executing the will of the lawmaking power, constitutionally expressed, leaving the results of legislation to be dealt with by the people through their representatives. Statutes must always have a reasonable construction. Sometimes they are to be construed strictly, sometimes literally, in order to carry out the legislative will. But, however construed, the intent of the legislature is to be respected if the particular statute in question is valid, although the courts, looking at the public interests, may conceive the statute to be both unreasonable and impolitic. If the power exists to enact a statute, that ends the matter so far as the courts are concerned. The adjudged cases in which statutes have been held to be void, because unreasonable, are those in which the means employed by the legislature were not at all germane to the end to which the legislature was competent.

The white race deems itself to be the dominant race in this country. And so it is, in prestige, in achievements, in education, in wealth, and in power. So, I doubt not, it will continue to be for all time, if it remains true to its great heritage, and holds fast to the principles of constitutional liberty. But in view of the constitution, in the eye of the law, there is in this country no superior, dominant, ruling class of citizens. There is no caste here. Our constitution is color-blind and neither knows nor tolerates classes among citizens. In respect of civil rights, all citizens are equal before the law. The humblest is the peer of the most powerful. The law regards man as man, and takes no account of his surroundings or of his color when his civil rights as guaranteed by the supreme law of the land are involved. It is therefore to be regretted that this high tribunal, the final expositor of the fundamental law of the land, has reached the conclusion that it is competent for a state to regulate the enjoyment by citizens of their civil rights solely upon the basis of race.

In my opinion, the judgment this day rendered will, in time, prove to be quite as pernicious as the decision made by this tribunal in the *Dred Scott Case.*

It was adjudged in that case that the descendants of Africans who were imported into this country, and sold as slaves, were not included nor intended to be included under the word "citizens" in the constitution, and could not claim any of the rights and privileges which that instrument provided for and secured to citizens of the United States; that, at the time of the adoption of the constitution, they were

> "considered as a subordinate and inferior class of beings, who had been subjugated by the dominant race, and, whether emancipated or not, yet remained subject to their authority, and had no rights or privileges but such as those who held the power and the government might choose to grant them." 17 How. 393, 404.

The recent amendments of the constitution, it was supposed, had eradicated these principles from our institutions. But it seems that we have yet, in some of the states, a dominant race—a superior class of citizens—which assumes to regulate the enjoyment of civil rights, common to all citizens, upon the basis of race. The present decision, it may well be apprehended, will not only stimulate aggressions, more or less brutal and irritating, upon the admitted rights of colored citizens, but will encourage the belief that it is possible, by means of state enactments, to defeat the beneficent purposes which the people of the United States had in view when they adopted the recent amendments of the constitution, by one of which the blacks of this country were made citizens of the United States and of the states in which they respectively reside, and whose privileges and immunities, as citizens, the states are forbidden to abridge. Sixty millions of whites are in no danger from the presence here of eight millions of blacks. The destinies of the two races, in this country, are indissolubly linked together, and the interests of both require that the common government of all shall not permit the seeds of race hate to be planted under the sanction of law. What can more certainly arouse race hate, what more certainly create and perpetuate a feeling of distrust between these races, than state enactments which, in fact, proceed on the ground that colored citizens are so inferior and degraded that they cannot be allowed to sit in public coaches occupied by white citizens? That, as all will admit, is the real meaning of such legislation as was enacted in Louisiana.

The sure guaranty of the peace and security of each race is the clear, distinct, unconditional recognition by our governments, national and state, of every right that inheres in civil freedom, and of the equality before the law of all citizens of the United States, without regard to race. State enactments regulating the enjoyment of civil rights upon the basis of race, and cunningly devised to defeat legitimate results of the war, under the pretense of recognizing equality of rights, can have no other result than to render permanent peace impossible, and to keep alive a conflict of races, the continuance of which must do harm to all concerned. This question is not met by the suggestion that social equality cannot exist between the white and black races in this country. That argument, if it can be properly regarded as one, is scarcely worthy of consideration; for social equality no more exists between two races when traveling in a passenger coach or a public highway than when members of the same races sit by each other in a street car or in the jury box, or stand or sit with each other in a political assembly, or when they use in common the streets of a city or town, or when they are in the same room for the purpose of having their names placed on the registry of voters, or when they approach the ballot box in order to exercise the high privilege of voting.

There is a race so different from our own that we do not permit those belonging to it to become citizens of the United States. Persons belonging to it are, with few exceptions, absolutely excluded from our country. I allude to the Chinese race. But, by the statute in question, a Chinaman can ride in the same passenger coach with white citizens of the United States, while citizens of the black race in Louisiana, many of whom, perhaps, risked their lives for the preservation of the Union, who are entitled, by law, to participate in the political control of the state and nation, who are not excluded, by law or by reason of their race, from public stations from public stations of any kind, and who have all the legal rights that belong to white citizens, are yet declared to be criminals, liable to imprisonment, if they ride in a public coach occupied by citizens of the white race. It is scarcely just to say that a colored citizen should not object to occupying a public coach assigned to his own race. He does not object, nor, perhaps, would he object to separate coaches for his race if his rights under the law were recognized. But he does object, and he ought never to cease objecting, that citizens of the white and black races can be adjudged criminals because they sit, or claim the right to sit, in the same public coach on a public highway.

The arbitrary separation of citizens, on the basis of race, while they are on a public highway, is a badge of servitude wholly inconsistent with the civil freedom and the equality before the law established by the constitution. It cannot be justified upon any legal grounds.

If evils will result from the commingling of the two races upon public highways established for the benefit of all, they will be infinitely less than those that will surely come from state legislation regulating the enjoyment of civil rights upon the basis of race. We boast of the freedom enjoyed by our people above all other peoples. But it is difficult to reconcile that boast with a state of the law which, practically, puts the brand of servitude and degradation upon a large class of our fellow citizens—our equals before the law. The thin disguise of "equal" accommodations for passengers in railroad coaches will not mislead any one, nor atone for the wrong this day done.

The result of the whole matter is that while this court has frequently adjudged, and at the present term has recognized the doctrine, that a state cannot, consistently with the constitution of the United States, prevent white and black citizens, having the required qualifications for jury service, from sitting in the same jury box, it is now solemnly held that a state may prohibit white and black citizens from sitting in the same passenger coach on a public highway, or may require that they be separated by a "partition" when in the same passenger coach. May it not now be reasonably expected that astute men of the dominant race, who affect to be disturbed at the possibility that the integrity of the white race may be corrupted, or that its supremacy will be imperiled by contact on public highways with black people, will endeavor to procure statutes requiring white and black jurors to be separated in the jury box by a "partition," and that, upon retiring from the court room to consult as to their verdict, such partition, if it be a movable one, shall be taken to their consultation room, and set up in such was as to prevent black jurors from coming too close to their brother jurors of the white race. If the "partition" used in the court room happens to be stationary, provision could be made for screens with openings through which jurors of the two races could confer as to their verdict without coming into personal contact with each other. I cannot see but that, according to the principles this day announced, such state legislation, although conceived in hostility to, and enacted for the purpose of humiliating, citizens of the United States of a particular race, would be held to be consistent with the constitution.

I do deem it necessary to review the decisions of state courts to which reference was made in argument. Some, and the most important, of them, are wholly inapplicable, because rendered prior to the adoption of the last amendments of the Constitution, when colored people had very few rights which the dominant race felt obliged to respect. Others were made at a time when public opinion, in many localities, was dominated by the institution of slavery; when it would not have been safe to do justice to the black man; and when, so far as the rights of blacks were concerned, race prejudice was, practically, the supreme law of the land. Those decisions cannot be guides in the era introduced by the recent amendments of the supreme law, which established universal civil freedom, gave citizenship to all born or naturalized in the United States, and residing here, obliterated the race line from our systems of governments, national and state, and placed our free institutions upon the broad and sure foundation of the equality of all men before the law.

I am of opinion that the statute of Louisiana is inconsistent with the personal liberty of citizens, white and black, in that state, and hostile to both the spirit and letter of the constitution of the United States. If laws of like character should be enacted in the several states of the Union, the effect would be in the highest degree mischievous. Slavery, as an institution tolerated by law, would, it is true, have disappeared from our country; but there would remain a power in the states, by sinister legislation, to interfere with the full enjoyment of the blessings of freedom, to regulate .civil rights, common to all citizens, upon the basis of race, and to place in a condition of legal inferiority a large body of American citizens, now constituting a part of the political community, called the "People of the United States," for whom, and by whom through representatives, our government is administered. Such a system is inconsistent with the guaranty given by the Constitution to each state of a republican form of government, and may be stricken down by congressional action, or by the courts in the discharge of their solemn duty to maintain the supreme law of the land, anything in the constitution or laws of any state to the contrary notwithstanding.

For the reason stated, I am constrained to withhold my assent from the opinion and judgment of the majority.

**FROM
SEGREGATION
TO CIVIL RIGHTS**

PLESSY V.
FERGUSON

FROM SEGREGATION TO CIVIL RIGHTS

LETTER FROM BIRMINGHAM CITY JAIL

Martin Luther King Jr., April 16, 1963

The civil rights protest marches and demonstrations led by Martin Luther King Jr. met fierce resistance in Mississippi, Alabama, and Georgia. State and local authorities arrested King on various charges in hopes of driving him out of their states and stopping the civil rights movement. In contrast to the NAACP's methods, which centered on using the courts to strike down discriminatory laws, King and his followers used civil disobedience against white racism.

King's methods were criticized by white southerners who contended that the protests were illegal and that King was a lawbreaker. King was stung, however, by attacks on him by white clergy, who claimed that his methods were immoral. They counseled him to take lawful approaches and to avoid inciting public anger and bloodshed.

In 1963 King responded by writing "Letter from Birmingham City Jail." Imprisoned for failing to file an Alabama tax return, King defended the use of civil disobedience and argued that it was proper when citizens are confronted by unjust laws.

Letter from Birmingham City Jail

My Dear Fellow Clergymen:

While confined here in Birmingham city jail, I came across your recent statement calling my present activities "unwise and untimely." Seldom do I pause to answer criticism of my work and ideas. If I sought to answer all the criticisms that cross my desk, my secretaries would have little time for anything other than such correspondence in the course of the day, and I would have no time for constructive work. But since I feel that you are men of genuine good will and that your criticisms are sincerely set forth, I want to try to answer your statement in what I hope will be patient and reasonable terms.

I think I should indicate why I am here in Birmingham, since you have been influenced by the view which argues against "outsiders coming in." I have the honor of serving as president of the Southern Christian Leadership Conference, an organization operating in every southern state, with headquarters in Atlanta, Georgia. We have some eighty-five affiliated organizations across the South, and one of them is the Alabama Christian Movement for Human Rights. Frequently we share staff, educational and financial resources with our affiliates. Several months ago the affiliate here in Birmingham asked us to be on call to engage in a nonviolent direct-action program if such were deemed necessary. We readily consented, and when the hour came we lived up to our promise. So I, along with several members of my staff, am here because I was invited here. I am here because I have organizational ties here.

Reprinted by arrangement with the Heirs to the Estate of Martin Luther King Jr., c/o Writers House, Inc., as agent for the proprietor. Copyright 1963 by Martin Luther King Jr., copyright renewed 1991 by Coretta Scott King.

But more basically, I am in Birmingham because injustice is here. Just as the prophets of the eighth century B.C. left their villages and carried their "thus saith the Lord" far beyond the boundaries of their home towns, and just as the Apostle Paul left his village of Tarsus and carried the gospel of Jesus Christ to the far corners of the Greco-Roman world, so am I compelled to carry the gospel of freedom beyond my own home town. Like Paul, I must constantly respond to the Macedonian call for aid.

Moreover, I am cognizant of the interrelatedness of all communities and states. I cannot sit idly by in Atlanta and not be concerned about what happens to Birmingham. Injustice anywhere is a threat to justice everywhere. We are caught in an inescapable network of mutuality, tied in a single garment of destiny. Whatever affects one directly, affects all indirectly. Never again can we afford to live with the narrow, provincial "outside agitator" idea. Anyone who lives inside the United States can never be considered an outsider anywhere within its bounds.

You deplore the demonstrations taking place in Birmingham. But your statement, I am sorry to say, fails to express a similar concern for the conditions that brought about the demonstrations. I am sure that none of you would want to rest content with the superficial kind of social analysis that deals merely with effects and does not grapple with underlying causes. It is unfortunate that demonstrations are taking place in Birmingham, but it is even more unfortunate that the city's white power structure left the Negro community with no alternative.

In any nonviolent campaign there are four steps: collection of the facts to determine whether injustices exist; negotiation; self-purification; and direct action. We have gone through all these steps in Birmingham. There can be no gain saying the fact that racial injustice engulfs this community. Birmingham is probably the most thoroughly segregated city in the United States. Its ugly record of brutality is widely known. Negroes have experienced grossly unjust treatment in the courts. There have been more unsolved bombings of Negro homes and churches in Birmingham than in any other city in the nation. These are the hard brutal facts of the case. On the basis of these conditions, Negro leaders sought to negotiate with the city fathers. But the latter consistently refused to engage in good-faith negotiation.

Then, last September, came the opportunity to talk with leaders of Birmingham economic community. In the course of negotiations, certain promises were made by the merchants—for example, to remove the stores' humiliating racial signs. On the basis of these promises, the Reverend Fred Shuttlesworth and the leaders of the Alabama Christian Movement for Human Rights agreed to a moratorium on all demonstrations. As the weeks and months went by, we realized that we were the victims of a broken promise. A few signs, briefly removed, returned; the others remained.

As in so many past experiences, our hopes had been blasted, and the shadow of deep disappointment settled upon us. We had no alternative except to prepare for direct action, whereby we would present our very bodies as a means of laying our case before the conscience of the local and the national community. Mindful of the difficulties involved, we decided to undertake a process of self-purification. We began a series of workshops on nonviolence, and we repeatedly asked ourselves: "Are you able to accept blows without retaliating?" "Are you able to endure the ordeal of jail?" We decided to schedule our direct-action program for the Easter season, realizing that except for Christmas, this is the main shopping period of the year. Knowing that a strong economic-withdrawal program would be the by-product of direct action, we felt that this would be the best time to bring pressure to bear on the merchants for the needed change.

Then it occurred to us that Birmingham's mayoralty election was coming up in March, and we speedily decided to postpone action until after election day. When we discovered that the Commissioner of Public Safety, Eugene "Bull" Connor, had piled up enough votes to be in the run-off, we decided again to postpone action until the day after the run-off so that the demonstrations could not be used to cloud the issues. Like many others, we waited to see Mr. Connor defeated, and to this end we endured postponement after postponement. Having aided in this community need, we felt that our direct-action program could be delayed no longer.

You may well ask: "Why direct action? Why sit-ins, marches and so forth? Isn't negotiation a better path?" You are quite right in calling for negotiation. Indeed, this is the very purpose of direct action. Nonviolent direct action seeks to create such a crisis and foster such a tension that

FROM
SEGREGATION
TO CIVIL RIGHTS

LETTER FROM
BIRMINGHAM
CITY JAIL

FROM
SEGREGATION
TO CIVIL RIGHTS

LETTER FROM
BIRMINGHAM
CITY JAIL

a community which has constantly refused to negotiate is forced to confront the issue. It seeks so to dramatize the issue that it can no longer be ignored. My citing the creation of tension as part of the work of the nonviolent-resister may sound rather shocking. But I must confess that I am not afraid of the word "tension." I have earnestly opposed violent tension, but there is a type of constructive nonviolent tension which is necessary for growth. Just as Socrates felt that it was necessary to create a tension in the mind so that individuals could rise from the bondage of myths and half-truths to the unfettered realm of creative analysis and objective appraisal, so must we see the need for nonviolent gadflies to create the kind of tension in society that will help men rise from the dark depths of prejudice and racism to the majestic heights of understanding and brotherhood.

The purpose of our direct-action program is to create a situation so crisis-packed that it will inevitably open the door to negotiation. I therefore concur with you in your call for negotiation. Too long has our beloved Southland been bogged down in a tragic effort to live in monologue rather than dialogue.

One of the basic points in your statement is that the action that I and my associates have taken in Birmingham is untimely. Some have asked: "Why didn't you give the new city administration time to act?" The only answer that I can give to this query is that the new Birmingham administration must be prodded about as much as the outgoing one, before it will act. We are sadly mistaken if we feel that the election of Albert Boutwell as mayor will bring the millennium to Birmingham. While Mr. Boutwell is a much more gentle person than Mr. Connor, they are both segregationists, dedicated to maintenance of the status quo. I have hope that Mr. Boutwell will be reasonable enough to see the futility of massive resistance to desegregation. But he will not see this without pressure from devotees of civil rights. My friends, I must say to you that we have not made a single gain in civil rights without determined legal and nonviolent pressure. Lamentably, it is an historical fact that privileged groups seldom give up their privileges voluntarily. Individuals may see the moral light and voluntarily give up their unjust posture; but, as Reinhold Niebuhr has reminded us, groups tend to be more immoral than individuals.

We know through painful experience that freedom is never voluntarily given by the oppressor; it must be demanded by the oppressed. Frankly, I have yet to engage in a direct-action campaign that was "well timed" in the view of those who have not suffered unduly from the disease of segregation. For years now I have heard the word "Wait!" It rings in the ear of every Negro with piercing familiarity. This "Wait" has almost always meant "Never." We must come to see, with one of our distinguished jurists, that "justice too long delayed is justice denied."

We have waited for more than 340 years for our constitutional and God-given rights. The nations of Asia and Africa are moving with jet-like speed toward gaining political independence, but we still creep at horse-and-buggy pace toward gaining a cup of coffee at a lunch counter. Perhaps it is easy for those who have never felt the stinging darts of segregation to say, "Wait." But when you have seen vicious mobs lynch your mothers and fathers at will and drown your sisters and brothers at whim; when you have seen hate-filled policemen curse, kick and even kill your black brothers and sisters; when you see the vast majority of your 20 million Negro brothers smothering in an airtight cage of poverty in the midst of an affluent society; when you suddenly find your tongue twisted and your speech stammering as you seek to explain to your 6-year-old daughter why she can't go to the public amusement park that has just been advertised on television, and see tears welling up in her eyes when she is told that Funtown is closed to colored children, and see ominous clouds of inferiority beginning to form in her little mental sky, and see her beginning to distort her personality by developing an unconscious bitterness toward white people; when you have to concoct an answer for a 5-year-old son who is asking: "Daddy, why do white people treat colored people so mean?"; when you take a cross-country drive and find it necessary to sleep night after night in the uncomfortable corners of your automobile because no motel will accept you; when you are humiliated day in and day out by nagging signs reading "white" and "colored"; when your first name becomes "nigger," your middle name becomes "boy" (however old you are) and your last name becomes "John," and your wife and mother are never given the respected title "Mrs."; when you are harried by day and haunted by night by the fact that you are a Negro, living constantly at tiptoe stance, never quite knowing what to expect next, and are plagued with inner fears and outer resentments; when you are forever fighting a degenerating sense of "nobodiness"—then you will understand why we find it difficult to wait. There comes a time when the cup of endurance runs over, and men are no longer willing to be plunged into the abyss of despair. I hope, sirs, you can understand our legitimate and unavoidable impatience.

You express a great deal of anxiety over our willingness to break laws. This is certainly a legitimate concern. Since we so diligently urge people to obey the Supreme Court's decision of 1954 outlawing segregation in the public schools, at first glance it may seem rather paradoxical for us consciously to break laws. One may well ask: "How can you advocate breaking some laws and obeying others?" The answer lies in the fact that there are two types of laws: just and unjust. I would be the first to advocate obeying just laws. One has not only a legal but a moral responsibility to obey just laws. Conversely, one has a moral responsibility to disobey unjust laws. I would agree with St. Augustine that "an unjust law is no law at all."

Now, what is the difference between the two? How does one determine whether a law is just or unjust? A just law is a man-made code that squares with the moral law or the law of God. An unjust law is a code that is out of harmony with the moral law. To put it in the terms of St. Thomas Aquinas: An unjust law is a human law that is not rooted in eternal law and natural law. Any law that uplifts human personality is just. Any law that degrades human personality is unjust. All segregation statues are unjust because segregation distorts the soul and damages the personality. It gives the segregator a false sense of superiority and the segregated a false sense of inferiority. Segregation, to use the terminology of the Jewish philosopher Martin Buber, substitutes an "I-it" relationship for an "I-thou" relationship and ends up relegating persons to the status of things. Hence segregation is not only politically, economically and sociologically unsound, it is morally wrong and sinful. Paul Tillich has said that sin is separation. Is not segregation an existential expression of man's tragic separation, his awful estrangement, his terrible sinfulness? Thus it is that I can urge men to obey the 1954 decision of the Supreme Court, for it is morally right; and I can urge them to disobey segregation ordinances, for they are morally wrong.

Let us consider a more concrete example of just and unjust laws. An unjust law is a code that a numerical or power majority group compels a minority group to obey but does not make binding on itself. This is *difference* made legal. By the same token, a just law is a code that a majority compels a minority to follow and that it is willing to follow itself. This is *sameness* made legal.

Let me give another explanation. A law is unjust if it is inflicted on a minority that, as a result of being denied the right to vote, had no part in enacting or devising the law. Who can say that the legislature of Alabama which set up that state's segregation laws was democratically elected? Throughout Alabama all sorts of devious methods are used to prevent Negroes from becoming registered voters, and there are some counties in which even though Negroes constitute a majority of the population, not a single Negro is registered. Can any law enacted under such circumstances be considered democratically structured?

Sometimes a law is just on its face and unjust in its application. For instance, I have been arrested on a charge of parading without a permit. Now, there is nothing wrong in having an ordinance which requires a permit for a parade. But such an ordinance becomes unjust when it is used to maintain segregation and to deny citizens the First-Amendment privilege of peaceful assembly and protest.

I hope you are able to see the distinction I am trying to point out. In no sense do I advocate evading or defying the law, as would the rabid segregationist. That would lead to anarchy. One who breaks an unjust law must do so openly, lovingly, and with a willingness to accept the penalty. I submit that an individual who breaks a law that conscience tells him is unjust, and who willingly accepts the penalty of imprisonment in order to arouse the conscience of the community over its injustice, is in reality expressing the highest respect for law.

Of course, there is nothing new about this kind of civil disobedience. It was evidenced sublimely in the refusal of Shadrach, Meshach and Abednego to obey the laws of Nebuchadnezzar, on the ground that a higher moral law was at stake. It was practiced superbly by the early Christians, who were willing to face hungry

FROM
SEGREGATION
TO CIVIL RIGHTS

LETTER FROM
BIRMINGHAM
CITY JAIL

FROM
SEGREGATION
TO CIVIL RIGHTS

LETTER FROM
BIRMINGHAM
CITY JAIL

lions and the excruciating pain of chopping blocks rather than submit to certain unjust laws of the Roman Empire. To a degree, academic freedom is a reality today because Socrates practiced civil disobedience. In our own nation, the Boston Tea Party represented a massive act of civil disobedience.

We should never forget that everything Adolf Hitler did in Germany was "legal" and everything the Hungarian freedom fighters did in Hungary was "illegal." It was "illegal" to aid and comfort a Jew in Hitler's Germany. Even so, I am sure that, had I lived in Germany at the time, I would have aided and comforted my Jewish brothers. If today I lived in a Communist country where certain principles dear to the Christian faith are suppressed, I would openly advocate disobeying that country's anti-religious laws.

I must make two honest confessions to you, my Christian and Jewish brothers. First, I must confess that over the past few years I have been gravely disappointed with the white moderate. I have almost reached the regrettable conclusion that the Negro's great stumbling block in his stride toward freedom is not the White Citizen's Counciler or the Ku Klux Klanner, but the white moderate, who is more devoted to "order" than to justice; who prefers a negative peace which is the absence of tension to a positive peace which is the presence of justice; who constantly says: "I agree with you in the goal you seek, but I cannot agree with your methods of direct action"; who paternalistically believes he can set the timetable for another man's freedom; who lives by a mythical concept of time and who constantly advises the Negro to wait for a "more convenient season." Shallow understanding from people of good will is more frustrating than absolute misunderstanding from people of ill will. Lukewarm acceptance is much more bewildering than outright rejection.

I had hoped that the white moderate would understand that law and order exist for the purpose of establishing justice and that when they fail in this purpose they become the dangerously structured dams that block the flow of social progress. I had hoped that the white moderate would understand that the present tension in the South is a necessary phase of the transition from an obnoxious negative peace, in which the Negro passively accepted his unjust plight, to a substantive and positive peace, in which all men will respect the dignity and worth of human personality. Actually, we who engage in nonviolent direct action are not the creators of tension. We merely bring to the surface the hidden tension that is already alive. We bring it out in the open, where it can be seen and dealt with. Like a boil that can never be cured so long as it is covered up but must be opened with all its ugliness to the natural medicines of air and light, injustice must be exposed, with all the tension its exposure creates, to the light of human conscience and the air of national opinion before it can be cured.

In your statement you assert that our actions, even though peaceful, must be condemned because they precipitate violence. But is this a logical assertion? Isn't this like condemning a robbed man because his possession of money precipitated the evil act of robbery? Isn't this like condemning Jesus because his unique God-consciousness and never-ceasing devotion to God's will precipitated the evil act of crucifixion? We must come to see that, as the federal courts have consistently affirmed, it is wrong to urge an individual to cease his efforts to gain his basic constitutional rights because the quest may precipitate violence. Society must protect the robbed and punish the robber.

I had also hoped that the white moderate would reject the myth concerning time in relation to the struggle for freedom. I have just received a letter from a white brother in Texas. He writes: "All Christians know that the colored people will receive equal rights eventually, but it is possible that you are in too great a religious hurry. It has taken Christianity almost two thousand years to accomplish what it has. The teachings of Christ take time to come to earth." Such an attitude stems from a tragic misconception of time, from the strangely irrational notion that there is something in the very flow of time that will inevitably cure all ills. Actually, time itself is neutral; it can be used either destructively or constructively. More and more I feel that the people of ill will have used time much more effectively than have the people of good will. We will have to repent in this generation not merely for the hateful words and actions of the bad people but for the appalling silence of the good people. Human progress never rolls in on wheels of inevitability; it comes through the tireless efforts of men willing to be co-workers with God, and without this hard work, time itself becomes an ally of the forces of social stagnation. We must use time creatively, in the knowledge that the time is always ripe to do right. Now is the time to make real the promise of democracy and transform our pending national elegy into a creative psalm of brotherhood. Now is the time to lift our national policy from the quicksand of racial injustice to the solid rock of human dignity.

You speak of our activity in Birmingham as extreme. At first I was rather disappointed that fellow clergymen would see my nonviolent efforts as those of an extremist. I began thinking about the fact that I stand in the middle of two opposing forces in the Negro community. One is a force of complacency, made up in part of Negroes who, as a result of long years of oppression, are so drained of self-respect and a sense of "somebodiness" that they have adjusted to segregation; and in part of a few middle-class Negroes who, because of a degree of academic and economic security and because in some ways they profit by segregation, have become insensitive to the problems of the masses. The other force is one of bitterness and hatred, and it comes perilously close to advocating violence. It is expressed in the various black nationalist groups that are springing up across the nation, the largest and best-known being Elijah Muhammad's Muslim movement. Nourished by the Negro's frustration over the continued existence of racial discrimination, this movement is made up of people who have lost faith in America, who have absolutely repudiated Christianity, and who have concluded that the white man is an incorrigible "devil."

I have tried to stand between these two forces, saying that we need emulate neither the "do-nothingism" of the complacement nor the hatred and despair of the black nationalist. For there is the more excellent way of love and nonviolent protest. I am grateful to God that, through the influence of the Negro church, the way of nonviolence became an integral part of our struggle.

If this philosophy had not emerged, by now many streets of the South would, I am convinced, be flowing with blood. And I am further convinced that if our white brothers dismiss as "rabble-rousers" and "outside agitators" those of us who employ nonviolent direct action, and if they refuse to support our nonviolent efforts, millions of Negroes will, out of frustration and despair, seek solace and security in black-

nationalist ideologies—a development that would inevitably lead to a frightening racial nightmare.

Oppressed people cannot remain oppressed forever. The yearning for freedom eventually manifests itself, and that is what has happened to the American Negro. Something within has reminded him that it can be gained. Consciously or unconsciously, he has been caught up by the *Zeitgeist*, and with his black brothers of Africa and his brown and yellow brothers of Asia, South America and the Caribbean, the United States Negro is moving with a sense of great urgency toward the promised land of racial justice. If one recognizes this vital urge that has engulfed the Negro community, one should readily understand why public demonstrations are taking place. The Negro has many pent-up resentments and latent frustrations, and he must release them. So let him march; let him make prayer pilgrimages to the city hall; let him go on freedom rides—and try to understand why he must do so. If his repressed emotions are not released in nonviolent ways, they will seek expression through violence; this is not a threat but a fact of history. So I have not said to my people: "Get rid of your discontent." Rather, I have tried to say that this normal and healthy discontent can be channeled into the creative outlet of nonviolent direct action. And now this approach is being termed extremist.

But though I was initially disappointed at being categorized as an extremist, as I continued to think about the matter I gradually gained a measure of satisfaction from the label. Was not Jesus an extremist for love: "Love your enemies, bless them that curse you, do good to them that hate you, and pray for them which despitefully use you, and persecute you." Was not Amos an extremist for justice: "Let justice roll down like waters and righteousness like an ever-flowing stream." Was not Paul an extremist for the Christian gospel: "I bear in my body the marks of the Lord Jesus." Was not Martin Luther an extremist: "Here I stand; I cannot do otherwise, so help me God." And John Bunyan: "I will stay in jail to the end of my days before I make a butchery of my conscience." And Abraham Lincoln: "This nation cannot survive half slave and half free." And Thomas Jefferson: "We hold these truths to be self-evident, that all men are created equal. . . ." So the question is not whether we will be extremists, but what kind of extrem-

FROM
SEGREGATION
TO CIVIL RIGHTS

LETTER FROM
BIRMINGHAM
CITY JAIL

FROM
SEGREGATION
TO CIVIL RIGHTS

LETTER FROM
BIRMINGHAM
CITY JAIL

ists we will be. Will we be extremists for hate or for love? Will we be extremists for the preservation of injustice or for the extension of justice? In that dramatic scene on Calvary's hill three men were crucified. We must never forget that all three were crucified for the same crime—the crime of extremism. Two were extremists for immorality, and thus fell below their environment. The other, Jesus Christ, was an extremist for love, truth and goodness, and thereby rose above his environment. Perhaps the South, the nation and the world are in dire need of creative extremists.

I had hoped that the white moderate would see this need. Perhaps I was too optimistic; perhaps I expected too much. I suppose I should have realized that few members of the oppressor race can understand the deep groans and passionate yearnings of the oppressed race, and still fewer have the vision to see that injustice must be rooted out by strong, persistent and determined action. I am thankful, however, that some of our white brothers in the South have grasped the meaning of this social revolution and committed themselves to it. They are still all too few in quantity, but they are big in quality. Some—such as Ralph McGill, Lillian Smith, Harry Golden, James McBride Dabbs, Ann Braden and Sarah Patton Boyle—have written about our struggle in eloquent and prophetic terms. Others have marched with us down nameless streets of the South. They have languished in filthy, roach-infested jails, suffering the abuse and brutality of policemen who view them as "dirty nigger-lovers." Unlike so many of their moderate brothers and sisters, they have recognized the urgency of the moment and sensed the need for powerful "action" antidotes to combat the disease of segregation.

Let me take note of my other major disappointment. I have been so greatly disappointed with the white church and its leadership. Of course, there are some notable exceptions. I am not unmindful of the fact that each of you has taken some significant stands on this issue. I commend you, Reverend Stallings, for your Christian stand on this past Sunday, in welcoming Negroes to your worship service on a nonsegregated basis. I commend the Catholic leaders of this state for integrating Spring Hill College several years ago.

But despite these notable exceptions, I must honestly reiterate that I have been disappointed with the church. I do not say this as one of those negative critics who can always find something wrong with the church. I say this as a minister of the gospel, who loves the church; who was nurtured in its bosom; who has been sustained by its spiritual blessings and who will remain true to it as long as the cord of life shall lengthen.

When I was suddenly catapulted into the leadership of the bus protest in Montgomery, Ala., a few years ago, I felt we would be supported by the white church. I felt that the white ministers, priests and rabbis of the South would be among our strongest allies. Instead, some have been outright opponents, refusing to understand the freedom movement and misrepresenting its leaders; all too many others have been more cautious than courageous and have remained silent behind the anesthetizing security of stained-glass windows.

In spite of my shattered dreams, I came to Birmingham with the hope that the white religious leadership of this community would see the justice of our cause and, with deep moral concern, would serve as the channel through which our just grievances could reach the power structure. I had hoped that each of you would understand. But again I have been disappointed.

I have heard numerous southern religious leaders admonish their worshipers to comply with a desegregation decision because it is the law, but I have longed to hear white ministers declare: "Follow this decree because integration is morally right and because the Negro is your brother." In the midst of blatant injustices inflicted upon the Negro, I have watched white churchmen stand on the sideline and mouth pious irrelevancies and sanctimonious trivialities. In the midst of a mighty struggle to rid our nation of racial and economic injustice, I have heard many ministers say: "Those are social issues, with which the gospel has no real concern." And I have watched many churches commit themselves to a completely other-worldly religion which makes a strange, un-Biblical distinction between body and soul, between the sacred and the secular.

I have traveled the length and breadth of Alabama, Mississippi and all the other southern states. On sweltering summer days and crisp autumn mornings I have looked at the South's beautiful churches with their lofty spires pointing heavenward. I have beheld the impressive outlines of her massive religious-education buildings. Over and over I have found myself asking: "What kind of people worship here? Who is their God? Where were their voices when the lips of Governor Barnett dripped with words of interposition and nullification? Where were they when Governor Wallace gave a clarion call for defiance and hatred? Where were their voices of support when bruised and weary Negro men and women decided to rise from the dark dungeons of complacency to the bright hills of creative protest?"

Yes, these questions are still in my mind. In deep disappointment I have wept over the laxity of the church. But be assured that my tears have been tears of love. There can be no deep disappointment where there is not deep love. Yes, I love the church. How could I do otherwise? I am in the rather unique position of being the son, the grandson and the great-grandson of preachers. Yes, I see the church as the body of Christ. But, oh! How we have blemished and scarred that body through social neglect and through fear of being nonconformists.

There was a time when the church was very powerful—in the time when the early Christians rejoiced at being deemed worthy to suffer for what they believed. In those days the church was not merely a thermometer that recorded the ideas and principles of popular opinion; it was a thermostat that transformed the mores of society. Whenever the early Christians entered a town, the people in power became disturbed and immediately sought to convict the Christians for being "disturbers of the peace" and "outside agitators." But the Christians pressed on, in the conviction that they were "a colony of heaven," called to obey God rather than man. Small in number, they were big in commitment. They were too God-intoxicated to be "astronomically intimidated." By their effort and example they brought an end to such ancient evils as infanticide and gladiatorial contests.

Things are different now. So often the contemporary church is a weak, ineffectual voice with an uncertain sound. So often it is an archdefender of the status quo. Far from being disturbed by the presence of the church, the power structure of the average community is consoled by the church's silent—and often even vocal—sanction of things as they are.

But the judgment of God is upon the church as never before. If today's church does not recapture the sacrificial spirit of the early church, it will lose its authenticity, forfeit the loyalty of millions, and be dismissed as an irrelevant social club with no meaning for the twentieth century. Every day I meet young people whose disappointment with the church has turned into outright disgust.

Perhaps I have once again been too optimistic. Is organized religion too inextricably bound to the status quo to save our nation and the world? Perhaps I must turn my faith to the inner spiritual church, the church within the church, as the true *ekklesia* and the hope of the world. But again I am thankful to God that some noble souls from the ranks of organized religion have broken loose from the paralyzing chains of conformity and joined us as active partners in the struggle for freedom. They have left their secure congregations and walked the streets of Albany, Ga. with us. They have gone down the highways of the South on tortuous rides for freedom. Yes, they have gone to jail with us. Some have been dismissed from their churches, have lost the support of their bishops and fellow ministers. But they have acted in the faith that right defeated is stronger than evil triumphant. Their witness has been the spiritual salt that has preserved the true meaning of the gospel in these troubled times. They have carved a tunnel of hope through the dark mountain of disappointment.

I hope the church as a whole will meet the challenge of this decisive hour. But even if the church does not come to the aid of justice, I have no despair about the future. I have no fear about the outcome of our struggle in Birmingham, even if our motives are at present misunderstood. We will reach the goal of freedom in Birmingham and all over the nation, because the goal of America is freedom. Abused and scorned though we may be, our destiny is tied up with America's destiny. Before the pilgrims landed at Plymouth, we were here. Before the pen of Jefferson etched the majestic words of the Declaration of Independence across the pages of history, we were here. For more than two centuries our forebears labored in this country without wages; they made cotton king; they built the homes of their masters while suffering gross injustice and shameful humiliation—and yet out of a bottomless vitality they continued to thrive and develop. If the inexpressible cruelties of slavery could not stop us, the opposition we now face will surely fail. We will win our free-

FROM
SEGREGATION
TO CIVIL RIGHTS

LETTER FROM
BIRMINGHAM
CITY JAIL

FROM
SEGREGATION
TO CIVIL RIGHTS

LETTER FROM
BIRMINGHAM
CITY JAIL

dom because the sacred heritage of our nation and the eternal will of God are embodied in our echoing demands.

Before closing I feel impelled to mention one other point in your statement that has troubled me profoundly. You warmly commended the Birmingham police force for keeping "order" and "preventing violence." I doubt that you would have so warmly commended the police force if you had seen its dogs sinking their teeth into unarmed, nonviolent Negroes. I doubt that you would so quickly commend the policemen if you were to observe their ugly and inhumane treatment of Negroes here in the city jail; if you were to watch them push and curse old Negro women and young Negro girls; if you were to see them slap and kick old Negro men and young boys; if you were to observe them as they did on two occasions, refuse to give us food because we wanted to sing our grace together. I cannot join you in your praise of the Birmingham police department.

It is true that the police have exercised a degree of discipline in handling the demonstrators. In this sense they have conducted themselves rather "nonviolently" in public. But for what purpose? To preserve the evil system of segregation. Over the past few years I have consistently preached that nonviolence demands that the means we use must be as pure as the ends we seek. I have tried to make clear that it is wrong to use immoral means to attain moral ends. But now I must affirm that it is just as wrong, or perhaps even more so, to use moral means to preserve immoral ends. Perhaps Mr. Connor and his policemen have been rather nonviolent in public, as was Chief Pritchett in Albany, Ga., but they have used the moral means of nonviolence to maintain the immoral end of racial injustice. As T. S. Eliot has said: "The last temptation is the greatest treason: To do the right deed for the wrong reason."

I wish you had commended the Negro sit-inners and demonstrators of Birmingham for their sublime courage, their willingness to suffer and their amazing discipline in the midst of great provocation. One day the South will recognize its real heroes. They will be the James Merediths, with the noble sense of purpose that enables them to face jeering and hostile mobs, and with the agonizing loneliness that characterizes the life of the pioneer. They will be old, oppressed, battered Negro women, symbolized in a 72-year-old woman in Montgomery, Ala., who rose up with a sense of dignity and with her people decided not to ride segregated buses, and who responded with ungrammatical profundity to one who inquired about her weariness: "My feet is tired, but my soul is at rest." They will be the young high school and college students, the young ministers of the gospel and a host of their elders, courageously and nonviolently sitting in at lunch counters and willingly going to jail for conscience sake. One day the South will know that when these disinherited children of God sat down at lunch counters, they were in reality standing up for what is best in the American dream and for the most sacred values in our Judaeo-Christian heritage, thereby bringing our nation back to those great wells of democracy which were dug deep by the founding fathers in their formulation of the Constitution and the Declaration of Independence.

Never before have I written so long a letter. I'm afraid it is much too long to take your precious time. I can assure you that it would have been much shorter if I had been writing from a comfortable desk, but what else can one do when he is alone in a narrow jail cell, other than write long letters, think long thoughts and pray long prayers?

If I have said anything in this letter that overstates the truth and indicates an unreasonable impatience, I beg you to forgive me. If I have said anything that understates the truth and indicates my having a patience that allows me to settle for anything less than brotherhood, I beg God to forgive me.

I hope this letter finds you strong in the faith. I also hope that circumstances will soon make it possible for me to meet each of you, not as an integrationist or a civil-rights leader but as a fellow clergyman and a Christian brother. Let us all hope that the dark clouds of racial prejudice will soon pass away and the deep fog of misunderstanding will be lifted from our fear-drenched communities, and in some not too distant tomorrow the radiant stars of love and brotherhood will shine over our great nation with all their scintillating beauty.

FROM SEGREGATION TO CIVIL RIGHTS

"I HAVE A DREAM" SPEECH

Martin Luther King Jr., August 28, 1963

Late in 1962, long-time labor and civil rights activist ASA PHILIP RANDOLPH began planning what would become known as the March on Washington. CIVIL RIGHTS protests of increasing size and sophistication were taking place throughout the South, but Randolph wanted a rally at the capital to put pressure directly on the federal government. Most of the major civil rights organizations of the day soon became involved in planning and carrying out the rally, including MARTIN LUTHER KING JR. and the SOUTHERN CHRISTIAN LEADERSHIP CONFERENCE (SCLC).

On August 28, 1963, over 200,000 people gathered on the Mall in Washington, D.C., to protest against the unequal treatment of African Americans in U.S. society and agitate for civil rights reform. King's keynote address, the "I Have a Dream" speech, was delivered to an audience of millions via television and radio. Standing in the shadow of the Lincoln Memorial, one hundred years after the EMANCIPATION PROCLAMATION was issued, King explained how the United States had failed to deliver on its promises of equality for African Americans. He forcefully insisted that the time had come for real change but urged his audience not to give in to violence and hatred in their pursuit of reform. He emphasized the CIVIL RIGHTS MOVEMENT's strong links to American and Christian ideals through the use of religious and patriotic themes. King concluded by describing his dream for the future, where all Americans could live together in equality and harmony.

"I Have a Dream" is an eloquent and articulate description of the goals of the civil rights movement. It added to the pressure on Congress, although it would still be almost a year before the CIVIL RIGHTS ACT of 1964 was enacted. Sadly, widespread and violent opposition to civil rights continued, and King himself was assassinated within four years. It is still King's most famous speech and stands as one of the most famous speeches in U.S. history.

—⁓—

"I Have a Dream" Speech

Five score years ago a great American in whose symbolic shadow we stand [today] signed the Emancipation Proclamation. This momentous decree came as a great beacon light of hope to millions of Negro slaves who had been seared in the flames of withering injustice. It came as a joyous daybreak to end the long night of captivity.

But one hundred years later, we must face the tragic fact that the Negro is still not free. One hundred years later, the life of the Negro is still sadly crippled by the manacles of segregation and the chains of discrimination. One hundred years later, the Negro lives on a lonely island of poverty in the midst of a vast ocean of material prosperity. One hundred years later, the Negro is still languishing in the corners of American society and finds himself an exile in his own land. So we have come here today to dramatize an appalling condition.

FROM
SEGREGATION
TO CIVIL RIGHTS

"I HAVE A
DREAM" SPEECH

In a sense we have come to our nation's capital to cash a check. When the architects of our republic wrote the magnificent words of the Constitution and the Declaration of Independence, they were signing a promissory note to which every American was to fall heir. This note was a promise that all men would be guaranteed the inalienable rights of life, liberty, and the pursuit of happiness.

It is obvious today that America has defaulted on this promissory note insofar as her citizens of color are concerned. Instead of honoring this sacred obligation, America has given the Negro people a bad check which has come back marked "insufficient funds." But we refuse to believe that the bank of justice is bankrupt. We refuse to believe that there are insufficient funds in the great vaults of opportunity of this nation. So we have come to cash this check—a check that will give us upon demand the riches of freedom and the security of justice. We have also come to this hallowed spot to remind America of the fierce urgency of now. This is no time to engage in the luxury of cooling off or to take the tranquilizing drug of gradualism. Now is the time to rise from the dark and desolate valley of segregation to the sunlit path of racial justice. Now is the time to open the doors of opportunity to all of God's children. Now is the time to lift our nation from the quicksands of racial injustice to the solid rock of brotherhood.

It would be fatal for the nation to overlook the urgency of the moment and to underestimate the determination of the Negro. This sweltering summer of the Negro's legitimate discontent will not pass until there is an invigorating autumn of freedom and equality. Nineteen sixty-three is not an end, but a beginning. Those who hope that the Negro needed to blow off steam and will now be content will have a rude awakening if the nation returns to business as usual. There will be neither rest nor tranquility in America until the Negro is granted his citizenship rights. The whirlwinds of revolt will continue to shake the foundations of our nation until the bright day of justice emerges.

But there is something that I must say to my people who stand on the warm threshold which leads into the palace of justice. In the process of gaining our rightful place we must not be guilty of wrongful deeds. Let us not seek to satisfy our thirst for freedom by drinking from the cup of bitterness and hatred.

We must forever conduct our struggle on the high plane of dignity and discipline. We must not allow our creative protest to degenerate into physical violence. Again and again we must rise to the majestic heights of meeting physical force with soul force. The marvelous new militancy which has engulfed the Negro community must not lead us to distrust of all white people, for many of our white brothers, as evidenced by their presence here today, have come to realize that their destiny is tied up with our destiny and their freedom is inextricably bound to our freedom. We cannot walk alone.

And as we walk, we must make the pledge that we shall march ahead. We cannot turn back. There are those who are asking the devotees of civil rights, "When will you be satisfied?" We can never be satisfied as long as our bodies, heavy with the fatigue of travel, can not gain lodging in the motels of the highways and the hotels of the cities. We cannot be satisfied as long as the Negro's basic mobility is from a smaller ghetto to a larger one. We can never be satisfied as long as a Negro in Mississippi cannot vote and a Negro in New York believes he has nothing for which to vote. No, no, we are not satisfied, and we will not be satisfied until justice rolls down like waters and righteousness like a mighty stream.

I am not unmindful that some of you have come here out of great trials and tribulations. Some of you have come fresh from narrow cells. Some of you have come from areas where your quest for freedom left you battered by the storms of persecution and staggered by the winds of police brutality. You have been the veterans of creative suffering. Continue to work with the faith that unearned suffering is redemptive.

Go back to Mississippi, go back to Alabama, go back to Georgia, go back to Louisiana, go back to the slums and ghettos of our northern cities, knowing that somehow this situation can and will be changed. Let us not wallow in the valley of despair.

I say to you today, my friends, that in spite of the difficulties and frustrations of the moment, I still have a dream. It is a dream deeply rooted in the American dream.

I have a dream that one day this nation will rise up and live out the true meaning of its creed: "We hold these truths to be self-evident: that all men are created equal."

I have a dream that one day on the red hills of Georgia the sons of former slaves and the sons of former slaveowners will be able to sit down together at a table of brotherhood.

I have a dream that one day even the state of Mississippi, a desert state, sweltering with the heat of injustice and oppression, will be transformed into an oasis of freedom and justice.

I have a dream that my four children will one day live in a nation where they will not be judged by the color of their skin but by the content of their character.

I have a dream today.

I have a dream that one day the state of Alabama, whose governor's lips are presently dripping with the words of interposition and nullification, will be transformed into a situation where little black boys and black girls will be able to join hands with little white boys and white girls and walk together as sisters and brothers.

I have a dream today.

I have a dream that one day every valley shall be exalted, every hill and mountain shall be made low, the rough places will be made plain, and the crooked places will be made straight, and the glory of the Lord shall be revealed, and all flesh shall see it together.

This is our hope. This is the faith with which I return to the South. With this faith we will be able to hew out of the mountain of despair a stone of hope. With this faith we will be able to transform the jangling discords of our nation into a beautiful symphony of brotherhood. With this faith we will be able to work together, to pray together, to struggle together, to go to jail together, to stand up for freedom together, knowing that we will be free one day.

This will be the day when all of God's children will be able to sing with a new meaning, "My country, 'tis of thee, sweet land of liberty, of thee I sing. Land where my fathers died, land of the pilgrim's pride, from every mountainside, let freedom ring."

And if America is to be a great nation this must become true. So let freedom ring from the prodigious hilltops of New Hampshire. Let freedom ring from the mighty mountains of New York. Let freedom ring from the heightening Alleghenies of Pennsylvania!

Let freedom ring from the snowcapped Rockies of Colorado!

Let freedom ring from the curvaceous peaks of California!

But not only that; let freedom ring from Stone Mountain of Georgia!

Let freedom ring from Lookout Mountain of Tennessee!

Let freedom ring from every hill and every molehill of Mississippi. From every mountainside, let freedom ring.

When we let freedom ring, when we let it ring from every village and every hamlet, from every state and every city, we will be able to speed up that day when all of God's children, black men and white men, Jews and Gentiles, Protestants and Catholics, will be able to join hands and sing in the words of the old Negro spiritual, "Free at last! free at last! thank God Almighty, we are free at last!"

Reprinted by arrangement with The Heirs to the Estate of Martin Luther King Jr., c/o Writers House, Inc., as agent for the proprietor. Copyright ©1963 by Martin Luther King Jr.; copyright renewed 1991 by Coretta Scott King.

FROM SEGREGATION TO CIVIL RIGHTS

CIVIL RIGHTS ACT OF 1964

After the assassination of President John F. Kennedy in 1963, President Lyndon B. Johnson announced his determination to pass a strong civil rights act that would end racial discrimination in employment, education, and other spheres of life. Deputy Attorney General Nicholas D. Katzenbach, Johnson's congressional liaison, worked with Senator Hubert H. Humphrey (D.-Minn.) and Senate minority leader Everett M. Dirksen (R.-Ill.) to achieve a compromise that would assure final passage. The result was the landmark Civil Rights Act of 1964.

Title I of the act guarantees equal voting rights by removing registration requirements and procedures biased against minorities and the underprivileged. Title II prohibits segregation or discrimination in places of public accommodation involved in interstate commerce. Title VII bans discrimination by trade unions, schools, and employers involved in interstate commerce or doing business with the federal government. This section also applies to discrimination on the basis of sex and established the Equal Employment Opportunity Commission to enforce these provisions. The act also calls for the desegregation of public schools (title IV), broadens the duties of the Civil Rights Commission (title V), and assures nondiscrimination in the distribution of funds under federally assisted programs (title VI).

Initially, the most controversial provision was title II. Because the 1883 Civil Rights cases held that the Fourteenth Amendment cannot reach private discrimination in public accommodations, Congress based title II on the Constitution's

Commerce Clause, which gives Congress the authority to regulate interstate commerce. In *Heart of Atlanta Motel v. United States,* 379 U.S. 241, 85 S. Ct. 348, 13 L. Ed. 2d 258 (1964), the Supreme Court upheld title II as a constitutional application of the Commerce Clause.

Civil Rights Act of 1964

For Legislative History of Act, see p. 2355

PUBLIC LAW 88–352; 78 STAT. 241

[H. R. 7152]

An Act to enforce the constitutional right to vote, to confer jurisdiction upon the district courts of the United States to provide injunctive relief against discrimination in public accommodations, to authorize the Attorney General to institute suits to protect constitutional rights in public facilities and public education, to extend the Commission on Civil Rights, to prevent discrimination in federally assisted programs, to establish a Commission on Equal Employment Opportunity, and for other purposes.

Be it enacted by the Senate and House of Representatives of the United States of America in Congress assembled, That:

This Act may be cited as the "Civil Rights Act of 1964."

TITLE I—VOTING RIGHTS

Sec. 101. Section 2004 of the Revised Statutes (42 U.S.C. 1971), as amended by section

1313 of the Civil Rights Act of 1957 (71 Stats. 637), and as further amended by section 601 of the Civil Rights Act of 1960 (74 Stats. 90),[1] is further amended as follows:

(a) Insert "1" after "(a)" in subsection (a) and add at the end of subsection (a) the following new paragraphs:

"(2) No person acting under color of law shall—

"(A) in determining whether any individual is qualified under State law or laws to vote in any Federal election, apply any standard, practice, or procedure different from the standards, practices, or procedures applied under such law or laws to other individuals within the same county, parish, or similar political subdivision who have been found by State officials to be qualified to vote;

"(B) deny the right of any individual to vote in any Federal election because of an error or omission on any record or paper relating to any application, registration, or other act requisite to voting, if such error or omission is not material in determining whether such individual is qualified under State law to vote in such election; or

"(C) employ any literacy test as a qualification for voting in any Federal election unless (i) such test is administered to each individual and is conducted wholly in writing, and (ii) a certified copy of the test and of the answers given by the individual is furnished to him within twenty-five days of the submission of his request made within the period of time during which records and papers are required to be retained and preserved pursuant to title III of the Civil Rights Act of 1960 (42 U.S.C. 1974–74e; 74 Stat. 88): *Provided, however,* That the Attorney General may enter into agreements with appropriate State or local authorities that preparation, conduct, and maintenance of such tests in accordance with the provisions of applicable State or local law, including such special provisions as are necessary in the preparation, conduct, and maintenance of such tests for persons who are blind or otherwise physically handicapped, meet the purposes of this subparagraph and constitute compliance therewith.

"(3) For purposes of this subsection—

"(A) the term 'vote' shall have the same meaning as in subsection (e) of this section;

"(B) the phrase 'literacy test' includes any test of the ability to read, write, understand, or interpret any matter."

(b) Insert immediately following the period at the end of the first sentence of subsection (c) the following new sentence: "If in any such proceeding literacy is a relevant fact there shall be a rebuttable presumption that any person who has not been adjudged an incompetent and who has completed the sixth grade in a public school in, or in a private school accredited by, any State or territory, the District of Columbia, or the Commonwealth of Puerto Rico where instruction is carried on predominantly in the English language, possesses sufficient literacy, comprehension, and intelligence to vote in any Federal election."

(c) Add the following subsection "(f)" and designate the present subsection "(f)" as subsection "(g)":

"(f) When used in subsection (a) or (c) of this section, the words 'Federal election' shall mean any general, special, or primary election held solely or in part for the purpose of electing or selecting any candidate for the office of President, Vice President, presidential elector, Member of the Senate, or Member of the House of Representatives."

(d) Add the following subsection "(h)":

"(h) In any proceeding instituted by the United States in any district court of the United States under this section in which the Attorney General requests a finding of a pattern or practice of discrimination pursuant to subsection (e) of this section the Attorney General, at the time he files the complaint, or any defendant in the proceeding, within twenty days after service upon him of the complaint, may file with the clerk of such court a request that a court of three judges be convened to hear and determine the entire case. A copy of the request for a three-judge court shall be immediately furnished by such clerk to the chief judge of the circuit (or in his absence, the presiding circuit judge of the circuit) in which the case is pending. Upon receipt of the copy of such request it shall be the duty of the chief judge of the circuit or the presiding circuit judge, as the case may be, to designate immediately three judges in such circuit, of whom at least one shall be a circuit judge and another of whom shall be a district judge of the court in which the proceeding was instituted, to hear and determine such case, and it shall be the duty of the judges so designated to assign the case for hearing at the earliest practicable date, to participate in the

---

[1] 42 U.S.C.A. § 1971.

hearing and determination thereof, and to cause the case to be in every way expedited. An appeal from the final judgment of such court will lie to the Supreme Court.

"In any proceeding brought under subsection (c) of this section to enforce subsection (b) of this section, or in the event neither the Attorney General nor any defendant files a request for a three-judge court in any proceeding authorized by this subsection, it shall be the duty of the chief judge of the district (or in his absence, the acting chief judge) in which the case is pending immediately to designate a judge in such district to hear and determine the case. In the event that no judge in the district is available to hear and determine the case, the chief judge of the district, or the acting chief judge, as the case may be, shall certify this fact to the chief judge of the circuit (or, in his absence, the acting chief judge) who shall then designate a district or circuit judge of the circuit to hear and determine the case."

"It shall be the duty of the judge designated pursuant to this section to assign the case for hearing at the earliest practicable date and to cause the case to be in every way expedited."

TITLE II—INJUNCTIVE RELIEF AGAINST DISCRIMINATION IN PLACES OF PUBLIC ACCOMMODATION

Sec. 201. (a) All persons shall be entitled to the full and equal enjoyment of the goods, services, facilities, privileges, advantages, and accommodations of any place of public accommodation, as defined in this section, without discrimination or segregation on the ground of race, color, religion, or national origin.

(b) Each of the following establishments which serves the public is a place of public accommodation within the meaning of this title if its operations affect commerce, or if discrimination or segregation by it is supported by State action:

(1) any inn, hotel, motel, or other establishment which provides lodging to transient guests, other than an establishment located within a building which contains not more than five rooms for rent or hire and which is actually occupied by the proprietor of such establishment as his residence;

(2) any restaurant, cafeteria, lunchroom, lunch counter, soda fountain, or other facility principally engaged in selling food for consumption on the premises, including, but not limited to, any such facility located on the prem-

ises of any retail establishment; or any gasoline station;

(3) any motion picture house, theater, concert hall, sports arena, stadium or other place of exhibition or entertainment; and

(4) any establishment (A) (i) which is physically located within the premises of any establishment otherwise covered by this subsection, or (ii) within the premises of which is physically located any such covered establishment, and (B) which holds itself out as serving patrons of such covered establishment.

(c) The operations of an establishment affect commerce within the meaning of this title if (1) it is one of the establishments described in paragraph (1) of subsection (b); (2) in the case of an establishment described in paragraph (2) of subsection (b), it serves or offers to serve interstate travelers or a substantial portion of the food which it serves, or gasoline or other products which it sells, has moved in commerce; (3) in the case of an establishment described in paragraph (3) of subsection (b), it customarily presents films, performances, athletic teams, exhibitions, or other sources of entertainment which move in commerce; and (4) in the case of an establishment described in paragraph (4) of subsection (b), it is physically located within the premises of, or there is physically located within its premises, an establishment the operations of which affect commerce within the meaning of this subsection. For purposes of this section, "commerce" means travel, trade, traffic, commerce, transportation, or communication among the several States, or between the District of Columbia and any State, or between any foreign country or any territory or possession and any State or the District of Columbia, or between points in the same State but through any other State or the District of Columbia or a foreign country.

(d) Discrimination or segregation by an establishment is supported by State action within the meaning of this title if such discrimination or segregation (1) is carried on under color of any law, statute, ordinance, or regulation; or (2) is carried on under color of any custom or usage required or enforced by officials of the State or political subdivision thereof; or (3) is required by action of the State or political subdivision thereof.

(e) The provisions of this title shall not apply to a private club or other establishment not in fact open to the public, except to the extent that the facilities of such establishment are made available to the customers or patrons of an establishment within the scope of subsections (b).

Sec. 202. All persons shall be entitled to be free, at any establishment or place, from discrimination or segregation of any kind on the ground of race, color, religion, or national origin, if such discrimination or segregation is or purports to be required by any law, statute, ordinance, regulation, rule, or order of a State or any agency or political subdivision thereof.

Sec. 203. No person shall (a) withhold, deny, or attempt to withhold or deny, or deprive or attempt to deprive, any person of any right or privilege secured by section 201 or 202, or (b) intimidate, threaten, or coerce, or attempt to intimidate, threaten, or coerce any person with the purpose of interfering with any right or privilege secured by section 201 or 202, or (c) punish or attempt to punish any person for exercising or attempting to exercise any right or privilege secured by section 201 or 202.

Sec. 204. (a) Whenever any person has engaged or there are reasonable grounds to believe that any person is about to engage in any act or practice prohibited by section 203, a civil action for preventive relief, including an application for a permanent or temporary injunction, restraining order, or other order, may be instituted by the person aggrieved and, upon timely application, the court may, in its discretion, permit the Attorney General to intervene in such civil action if he certifies that the case is of general public importance. Upon application by the complaint and in such circumstances as the court may deem just, the court may appoint an attorney for such complainant and may authorize the commencement of the civil action without the payment of fees, costs, or security.

(b) In any action commenced pursuant to this title, the court, in its discretion, may allow the prevailing party, other than the United States, a reasonable attorney's fee as part of the costs, and the United States shall be liable for costs the same as a private person.

(c) In the case of an alleged act or practice prohibited by this title which occurs in a State, or political subdivision of a State, which has a State or local law prohibiting such act or practice and establishing or authorizing a State or local authority to grant or seek relief from such practice or to institute criminal proceedings

with respect thereto upon receiving notice thereof, no civil action may be brought under subsection (a) before the expiration of thirty days after written notice of such alleged act or practice has been given to the appropriate State or local authority by registered mail or in person, provided that the court may stay proceedings in such civil action pending the termination of State or local enforcement proceedings.

(d) In the case of an alleged act or practice prohibited by this title which occurs in a State, or political subdivision of a State, which has no State or local law prohibiting such act or practice, a civil action may be brought under subsection (a): *Provided*, That the court may refer the matter to the Community Relations Service established by title X of this Act for as long as the court believes there is a reasonable possibility of obtaining voluntarily compliance, but for not more than sixty days: *Provided further*, That upon expiration of such sixty-day period, the court may extend such period for an additional period, not to exceed a cumulative total of one hundred and twenty days, if it believes there then exists a reasonable possibility of securing voluntary compliance.

Sec. 205. The Service is authorized to make a full investigation of any complaint referred to it by the court under section 204(d) and may hold such hearings with respect thereto as may be necessary. The Service shall conduct any hearings with respect to any such complaint in executive session, and shall not release any testimony given therein except by agreement of all parties involved in the complaint with the permission of the court, and the Service shall endeavor to bring about a voluntary settlement between the parties.

Sec. 206 (a) Whenever the Attorney General has reasonable cause to believe that any person or group of persons is engaged in a pattern or practice of resistance to the full enjoyment of any of the rights secured by this title, and that the pattern or practice is of such a nature and is intended to deny the full exercise of the rights herein described, the Attorney General may bring a civil action in the appropriate district court of the United States by filing with it a complaint (1) signed by him (or in his absence the Acting Attorney General), (2) setting forth facts pertaining to such pattern or practice, and (3) requesting such preventive relief, including an application for a permanent or temporary injunction, restraining order or other order against the person or persons responsible for such pattern or practice, as he deems necessary to insure the full enjoyment of the rights herein described.

(b) In any such proceeding the Attorney General may file with the clerk of such court a request that a court of three judges be convened to hear and determine the case. Such request by the Attorney General shall be accompanied by a certificate that, in his opinion, the case is of general public importance. A copy of the certificate and request for a three-judge court shall be immediately furnished by such clerk to the chief judge of the circuit (or in his absence, the presiding circuit judge of the circuit) in which the case is pending. Upon receipt of the copy of such request it shall be the duty of the chief judge of the circuit or the presiding circuit judge, as the case may be, to designate immediately three judges in such circuit, of whom at least one shall be a circuit judge and another of whom shall be a district judge of the court in which the proceeding was instituted, to hear and determine such case, and it shall be the duty of the judges so designated to assign the case for hearing at the earliest practicable date, to participate in the hearing and determination thereof, and to cause the case to be in every way expedited. An appeal from the final judgment of such court will lie to the Supreme Court.

In the event the Attorney General fails to file such a request in any such proceeding, it shall be the duty of the chief judge of the district (or in his absence, the acting chief judge) in which the case is pending immediately to designate a judge in such district to hear and determine the case. In the event that no judge in the district is available to hear and determine the case, the chief judge of the district, or the acting chief judge, as the case may be, shall certify this fact to the chief judge of the circuit (or in his absence, the acting chief judge) who shall then designate a district or circuit judge of the circuit to hear and determine the case.

It shall be the duty of the judge designated pursuant to this section to assign the case for hearing at the earliest practicable date and to cause the case to be in every way expedited.

Sec. 207. (a) The district courts of the United States shall have jurisdiction of proceedings instituted pursuant to this title and shall exercise the same without regard to whether the aggrieved party shall have exhausted any administrative or other remedies that may be provided by law.

(b) The remedies provided in this title shall be the exclusive means of enforcing the rights based on this title, but nothing in this title shall prelude any individual or any State or local agency from asserting any right based on any other Federal or State law not inconsistent with this title, including any statute or ordinance requiring nondiscrimination in public establishments or accommodations, or from pursuing any remedy, civil or criminal, which may be available for the vindication or enforcement of such right.

TITLE III—DESEGREGATION OF PUBLIC FACILITIES

Sec. 301. (a) Whenever the Attorney General receives a complaint in writing signed by an individual to the effect that he is being deprived of or threatened with the loss of his right to the equal protection of the laws, on account of his race, color, religion, or national origin, by being denied equal utilization of any public facility which is owned, operated, or managed by or on behalf of any State or subdivision thereof, other than a public school or public college as defined in section 401 of title IV hereof, and the Attorney General believes the complaint is meritorious and certifies that the signer or signers of such complaint are unable, in his judgment, to initiate and maintain appropriate legal proceedings for relief and that the institution of an action will materially further the orderly progress of desegregation in public facilities, the Attorney General is authorized to institute for or in the name of the United States a civil action in any appropriate district court of the United States against such parties and for such relief as may be appropriate, and such court shall have and shall exercise jurisdiction of proceedings instituted pursuant to this section. The Attorney General may implead as defendants such additional parties as are or become necessary to the grant of effective relief hereunder.

(b) The Attorney General may deem a person or persons unable to initiate and maintain appropriate legal proceedings within the meaning of subsection (a) of this section when such person or persons are unable, either directly or through other interested persons or organizations, to bear the expense of the litigation or to obtain effective legal representation; or whenever he is satisfied that the institution of such litigation would jeopardize the personal safety, employment, or economic standing of such person or persons, their families, or their property.

Sec. 302. In any action or proceeding under this title the United States shall be liable for costs, including a reasonable attorney's fee, the same as a private person.

Sec. 303. Nothing in this title shall affect adversely the right of any person to sue for or obtain relief in any court against discrimination in any facility covered by this title.

Sec. 304. A complaint as used in this title is a writing or document within the meaning of section 1001, title 18, United States Code.

TITLE IV—DESEGREGATION OF PUBLIC EDUCATION

DEFINITIONS

Sec. 401. As used in this title—

(a) "Commissioner" means the Commissioner of Education.

(b) "Desegregation" means the assignment of students to public schools and within such schools without regard to their race, color, religion, or national origin, but "desegregation" shall not mean the assignment of students to public schools in order to overcome racial imbalance.

(c) "Public school" means any elementary or secondary educational institution, and "public college" means any institution of higher education or any technical or vocational school above the secondary school level, provided that such public school or public college is operated by a State, subdivision of a State, or governmental agency within a State, or operated wholly or predominantly from or through the use of governmental funds or property, or funds or property derived from a governmental source.

(d) "School board" means any agency or agencies which administer a system of one or more public schools and any other agency which is responsible for the assignment of students to or within such system.

SURVEY AND REPORT OF EDUCATIONAL OPPORTUNITIES

Sec. 402. The Commissioner shall conduct a survey and make a report to the President and the Congress, with two years of the enactment of this title, concerning the lack of availability of equal educational opportunities for individuals by reason of race, color, religion, or national origin in public educational institutions at all levels in the United States, its territories and possessions, and the District of Columbia.

TECHNICAL ASSISTANCE

Sec. 403. The Commissioner is authorized, upon the application of any school board, State, municipality, school district, or other governmental unit legally responsible for operating a public school or schools, to render technical assistance to such applicant in the preparation, adoption, and implementation of plans for the desegregation of public schools. Such technical assistance may, among other activities, include making available to such agencies information regarding effective methods of coping with special educational problems occasioned by desegregation, and making available to such agencies personnel of the Office of Education or other persons specially equipped to advise and assist them in coping with such problems.

TRAINING INSTITUTES

Sec. 404. The Commissioner is authorized to arrange, through grants or contracts, with institutions of higher education for the operation of short-term or regular session institutes for special training designed to improve the ability of teachers, supervisors, counselors, and other elementary or secondary school personnel to deal effectively with special educational problems occasioned by desegregation. Individuals who attend such an institute on a full-time basis may be paid stipends for the period of their attendance at such institute in amounts specified by the Commissioner in regulations, including allowances for travel to attend such institute.

GRANTS

Sec. 405. (a) The Commissioner is authorized, upon the application of a school board, to make grants to such board to pay, in whole in part, the cost of—

(1) giving to teachers and others school personnel inservice training in dealing with problems incident to desegregation, and

(2) employing specialists to advise in problems incident to desegregation.

(b) In determining whether to make a grant, and in fixing the amount thereof and the terms and conditions on which it will be made, the

FROM SEGREGATION TO CIVIL RIGHTS

CIVIL RIGHTS ACT OF 1964

Commissioner shall take into consideration the amount available for grants under this section and the other applications which are pending before him; the financial condition of the applicant and the other resources available to it; the nature, extent, and gravity of its problems incident to desegregation; and such other factors as he finds relevant.

PAYMENTS

Sec. 406. Payments pursuant to a grant or contract under this title may be made (after necessary adjustments on account of previously made overpayments or underpayments) in advance or by way of reimbursement, and in such installments, as the Commissioner may determine.

SUITS BY THE ATTORNEY GENERAL

Sec. 407. (a) Whenever the Attorney General receives a complaint in writing—

(1) signed by a parent or group of parents to the effect that his or their minor children, as members of a class of persons similarly situated, are being deprived by a school board of the equal protection of the laws, or

(2) signed by an individual, or his parent, to the effect that he has been denied admission to or not permitted to continue in attendance at a public college by reason of race, color, religion, or national origin, and the Attorney General believes the complaint is meritorious and certifies that the signer or signers of such complaint are unable, in his judgment, to initiate and maintain appropriate legal proceedings for relief and that the institution of an action will materially further the orderly achievement of desegregation in public education, the Attorney General is authorized, after giving notice of such complaint to the appropriate school board or college authority and after certifying that he is satisfied that such board or authority has had a reasonable time to adjust the conditions alleged in such complaint, to institute for or in the name of the United States a civil action in any appropriate district court of the United States against such parties and for such relief as may be appropriate, and such court shall have and shall exercise jurisdiction of proceedings instituted pursuant to this section, provided that nothing herein shall empower any official or court of the United States to issue any order seeking to achieve a racial balance in any school by requiring the transportation of pupils or students from one

school to another or one school district to another in order to achieve such racial balance, or otherwise enlarge the existing power of the court to insure compliance with constitutional standards. The Attorney General may implead as defendants such additional parties as are or become necessary to the grant of effective relief hereunder.

(b) The Attorney General may deem a person or persons unable to initiate and maintain appropriate legal proceedings within the meaning of subsection (a) of this section when such person or persons are unable, either directly or through other interested persons or organizations, to bear the expense of the litigation or to obtain effective legal representation; or whenever he is satisfied that the institution of such litigation would jeopardize the personal safety, employment, or economic standing of such person or persons, their families, or their property.

(c) The term "parent" as used in this section includes any person standing in loco parentis. A "complaint" as used in this section is a writing or document within the meaning of section 1001, title 18, United States Code.

Sec. 408. In any action or proceeding under this title the United States shall be liable for costs the same as a private person.

Sec. 409. Nothing in this title shall affect adversely the right of any person to sue for or obtain relief in any court against discrimination in public education.

Sec. 410. Nothing in this title shall prohibit classification and assignment for reasons other than race, color, religion, or national origin.

TITLE V—COMMISSION ON CIVIL RIGHTS

Sec. 501. Section 102 of the Civil Rights Act of 1957 (42 U.S.C. 1975a; 71 Stat. 634)[2] is amended to read as follows:

"RULES OF PROCEDURE OF THE COMMISSION
HEARINGS

"Sec. 102. (a) At least thirty days prior to the commencement of any hearing, the Commission shall cause to be published in the Federal Register notice of the date on which such hearing is to commence, the place at which it is to be held and the subject of the hearing. The Chairman, or one designated by him to act

[2] 42 U.S.C.A. § 1975a.

as Chairman at a hearing of the Commission, shall announce in an opening statement the subject of the hearing.

"(b) A copy of the Commission's rules shall be made available to any witness before the Commission, and a witness compelled to appear before the Commission or required to produce written or other matter shall be served with a copy of the Commission's rules at the time of service of the subpoena.

"(c) Any person compelled to appear in person before the Commission shall be accorded the right to be accompanied and advised by counsel, who shall have the right to subject his client to reasonable examination, and to make objections on the record and to argue briefly the basis for such objections. The Commission shall proceed with reasonable dispatch to conclude any hearing in which it is engaged. Due regard be had for the convenience and necessity of witnesses.

"(d) The Chairman or Acting Chairman may punish breaches of order and decorum by censure and exclusion from the hearings.

"(e) If the Commission determines that evidence or testimony at any hearing may tend to defame, degrade, or incriminate any person, it shall receive such evidence or testimony or summary of such evidence or testimony in executive session. The Commission shall afford any person defamed, degraded, or incriminate by such evidence or testimony an opportunity to appear and be heard in executive session, with a reasonable number of additional witnesses requested by him, before deciding to use such evidence or testimony. In the event the Commission determines to release or use such evidence or testimony in such manner as to reveal publicly the identity of the person defamed, degraded, or incriminate, such evidence or testimony, prior to such public release or use, shall be given at a public session, and the Commission shall afford such person an opportunity to appear as a voluntary witness or to file a sworn statement in his behalf and to submit brief and pertinent sworn statements of others. The Commission shall receive and dispose of requests from such person to subpoena additional witnesses.

"(f) Except as provided in sections 102 and 105(f) of this Act, the Chairman shall receive and the Commission shall dispose of requests to subpoena additional witnesses.

"(g) No evidence or testimony or summary of evidence or testimony taken in executive session may be released or used in public sessions without the consent of the Commission. Whoever releases or uses in public without the consent of the Commission such evidence or testimony taken in executive session shall be fined not more than $1,000, or imprisoned for not more than one year.

"(h) In the discretion of the Commission, witnesses may submit brief and pertinent sworn statements in writing for inclusion in the record. The Commission shall determine the pertinency of testimony and evidence adduced at its hearings.

"(i) Every person who submits data or evidence shall be entitled to retain or, on payment of lawfully prescribed costs, procure a copy or transcript thereof, except that a witness in a hearing held in executive session may for good cause be limited to inspection of the official transcript of his testimony. Transcript copies of public sessions may be obtained by the public upon the payment of the cost thereof. An accurate transcript shall be made of the testimony of all witnesses at all hearings, either public or executive sessions, of the Commission or of any subcommittee thereof.

"(j) A witness attending any session of the Commission shall receive $6 for each day's attendance and for the time necessarily occupied in going to and returning from the same, and 10 cents per mile for going from and returning to his place of residence. Witnesses who attend at points so far removed from their respective residences as to prohibit return thereto from day to day shall be entitled to an additional allowance of $10 per day for expenses of subsistence, including the time necessarily occupied in going to an returning from the place of attendance. Mileage payments shall be tendered to the witness upon service of a subpoena issued on behalf of the Commission or any subcommittee thereof.

"(k) The commission shall not issue any subpoena for the attendance and testimony of witnesses or for the production of written or other matter which would require the presence of the party subpoenaed at a hearing to be held outside of the State wherein the witness is found or resides or is domiciled or transacts business, or has appointed an agent for receipt of service of process except that, in any event, the Commission may issue subpoenas for the attendance and testimony of witnesses and the production of written or other matter at a hearing held within fifty miles of the place where the witness is found or resides or is domiciled or transacts business or has appointed an agent for receipt of service of process.

"(l) The Commission shall separately state and currently publish in the Federal Register (1) descriptions of its central and field organization including the established places at which, and methods whereby, the public may secure information or make requests; (2) statements of the general course and method by which its functions are channeled and determined, and (3) rules adopted as authorized by law. No person shall in any manner be subject to or required to resort to rules, organization, or procedure not so published."

Sec. 502. Section 103(a) of the Civil Rights Act of 1957 (42 U.S.C. 1975b(a); 71 Stat. 634)[3] is amended to read as follows:

"Sec. 103. (a) Each member of the Commission who is not otherwise in the service of the Government of the United States shall receive the sum of $75 per day for each day spent in the work of the Commission, shall be paid actual travel expenses, and per diem in lieu of subsistence expenses when away from his usual place of residence, in accordance with section 5 of the Administrative Expenses Act of 1946, as amended (5 U.S.C. 73b-2; 60 Stat. 808)."

Sec. 503. Section 103(b) of the Civil Rights Act of 1957 (42 U.S.C. 1975b(b); 71 Stat. 634)[4] is amended to read as follows:

"(b) Each member of the Commission who is otherwise in the service of the Government of the United States shall serve without compensation in addition to that received for such other service, but while engaged in the work of the Commission shall be paid actual travel expenses, and per diem in lieu of subsistence expenses when away from his usual place of residence, in accordance with the provisions of the Travel Expenses Act of 1949, as amended (5 U.S.C. 835–42; 63 Stat. 166)."

Sec. 504. (a) Section 104(a) of the Civil Rights Act of 1957 (42 U.S.C. 1975c(a); 71 Stat. 635), as amended,[5] is further amended to read as follows:

"DUTIES OF THE COMMISSION

"Sec. 104 (a) The Commission shall—

"(1) investigate allegations in writing under oath or affirmation that certain citizens of the United States are being deprived of their right to vote and have that vote counted by reason of their color, race, religion, or national origin; which writing, under oath or affirmation, shall set forth the facts upon which such belief or beliefs are based;

"(2) study and collect information concerning legal developments constituting a denial of equal protection of the laws under the Constitution because of race, color, religion or national origin or in the administration of justice;

"(3) appraise the laws and policies of the Federal Government with respect to denials of equal protection of the laws under the Constitution because of race, color, religion or national origin or in the administration of justice;

"(4) serve as a national clearinghouse for information in respect to denials of equal protection of the laws because of race, color, religion or national origin, including but not limited to the fields of voting, education, housing, employment, the use of public facilities, and transportation, or in the administration of justice;

"(5) investigate allegations, made in writing and under oath or affirmation, that citizens of the United States are unlawfully being accorded or denied the right to vote, or to have their votes properly counted, in any election of presidential electors, Members of the United States Senate, or of the House of Representatives, as a result of any pattern or practice of fraud or discrimination in the conduct of such election; and

"(6) Nothing in this or any other Act shall be construed as authorizing the Commission, its Advisory Committees, or any person under its supervision or control to inquire into or investigate any membership practices or internal operations of any fraternal organization, any college or university fraternity or sorority, any private club or any religious organization."

(b) Section 104(b) of the Civil Rights Act of 1957 (42 U.S.C. 1975c(b); 71 Stat. 635), as amended,[6] is further amended by striking out the present subsection "(b)" and by substituting therefor:

"(b) The Commission shall submit interim reports to the President and to the Congress at

[3] 42 U.S.C.A. § 1975b(a).
[4] 42 U.S.C.A. § 1975b(b).
[5] 42 U.S.C.A. § 1975c(a).
[6] 42 U.S.C.A. § 1975c(b).

such times as the Commission, the Congress or the President shall deem desirable, and shall submit to the President and to the Congress a final report of its activities, findings, and recommendations not later than January 31, 1968."

Sec. 505. Section 105(a) of the Civil Rights Act of 1957 (42 U.S.C. 1975d(a); 71 Stat. 636)[7] is amended by striking out in the last sentence thereof "$50 per diem" and inserting in lieu thereof "$75 per diem."

Sec. 506. Section 105(f) and section 105(g) of the Civil Rights Act of 1957 (42 U.S.C. 1975d(f) and (g); 71 Stat. 636)[8] are amended to read as follows:

"(f) The Commission, or on the authorization of the Commission any subcommittee of two or more members, at least one of whom shall be of each major political party, may, for the purpose of carrying out the provisions of this Act, hold such hearings and act at such times and places as the Commission or such authorized subcommittee may deem advisable. Subpoenas for the attendance and testimony of witnesses or the production of written or other matter may be issued in accordance with the rules of the Commission as contained in section 102(j) and (k) of this Act, over the signature of the Chairman of the Commission or of such subcommittee, and may be served by any person designated by such Chairman. The holding of hearings by the Commission, or the appointment of a subcommittee to hold hearings pursuant to this subparagraph, must by approved by a majority of the Commission, or by a majority of the members present at a meeting at which at least a quorum of four members is present.

"(g) In case of contumacy or refusal to obey a subpoena, any district court of the United States or the United States court of any territory or possession, or the District Court of the United States for the District of Columbia, within the jurisdiction of which said person guilty of contumacy or refusal to obey is found or resides or is domiciled or transacts business, or has appointed an agent for receipt of service of process, upon application by the Attorney General of the United States shall have jurisdiction to issue to such person an order requiring such person to appear before the Commission or a subcommittee thereof, there to produce pertinent, relevant and nonprivileged evidence if so ordered, or there to give testimony touching the matter under investigation; and any fail-

ure to obey such order of the court may be punished by said court as a contempt thereof."

Sec. 507. Section 105 of the Civil Rights Act of 1957 (42 U.S.C. 1975d; 71 Stat. 636), as amended by section 401 of the Civil Rights Act of 1960 (42 U.S.C. 1975d(h); 74 Stat. 89),[9] is further amended by adding a new subsection at the end to read as follows:

"(i) The Commission shall have the power to make such rules and regulations as are necessary to carry out the purposes of this Act."

TITLE VI—NONDISCRIMINATION IN FEDERALLY ASSISTED PROGRAMS

Sec. 601. No person in the United States shall, on the ground of race, color, or national origin, be excluded from participation in, be denied the benefits of, or be subjected to discrimination under any program or activity receiving Federal financial assistance.

Sec. 602. Each Federal department and agency which is empowered to extend Federal financial assistance to any program or activity, by way of grant, loan, or contract other than a contract of insurance of guaranty, is authorized and directed to effectuate the provisions of section 601 with respect to such program or activity by issuing rules, regulations, or orders of general applicability which shall be consistent with achievement of the objectives of the statute authorizing the financial assistance in connection with which the action is taken. No such rule, regulation, or order shall become effective unless and until approved by the President. Compliance with any requirement adopted of or refusal to grant or to continue assistance under such program or activity to any recipient as to whom there has been an express finding on the record, after opportunity for hearing, of a failure to comply with such requirement, but such termination or refusal shall be limited to the particular political entity, or part thereof, in which such noncompliance has been so found, or (2) by any other means authorized by law: *Provided, however,* That no such action shall be taken until the department or agency concerned has advised the appropriate person or persons of the failure to comply with the requirement and has determined that compliance cannot be secured

FROM
SEGREGATION
TO CIVIL RIGHTS

CIVIL RIGHTS
ACT OF 1964

---

[7] 42 U.S.C.A. § 1975d(a).
[8] 42 U.S.C.A. § 1975d(g).
[9] 42 U.S.C.A. § 1975d(h).

FROM
SEGREGATION
TO CIVIL RIGHTS

CIVIL RIGHTS
ACT OF 1964

by voluntary means. In the case of any action terminating, or refusing to grant or continue, assistance because failure to comply with a requirement imposed pursuant to this section, the head of the Federal department or agency shall file with the committees of the House and Senate having legislative jurisdiction over the program of activity involved a full written report of the circumstances and the grounds for such action. No such action shall become effective until thirty days have elapsed after the filing of such report.

Sec. 603. Any department or agency action taken pursuant to section 602 shall be subject to such judicial review as may otherwise be provided by law for similar action taken by such department or agency on other grounds. In the case of action, not otherwise subject to judicial review, terminating or refusing to grant or to continue financial assistance upon a finding of failure to comply with any requirement imposed pursuant to section 602, any person aggrieved (including any State or political subdivision thereof and any agency of either) may obtain judicial review of such action in accordance with section 10 of the Administrative Procedure Act, and such action shall not be deemed committed to unreviewable agency discretion within the meaning of that section.

Sec. 604. Nothing contained in this title shall be construed to authorize action under this title by any department or agency with respect to any employment practice of any employer, employment agency, or labor organization except where a primary objective of the Federal financial assistance is extended by way of a contract of insurance or guaranty.

Sec. 605. Nothing contained in this title shall add to or detract from any existing authority with respect to any program or activity under which Federal financial assistance is extended by way of a contract of insurance or guaranty.

TITLE VII—EQUAL EMPLOYMENT OPPORTUNITY

DEFINITIONS

Sec. 701. For the purposes of this title—

(a) The term "person" includes one or more individuals, labor unions, partnerships, associations, corporations, legal representatives, mutual companies, joint-stock companies, trusts, unincorporated organizations, trustees, trustees in bankruptcy, or receivers.

(b) The term "employer" means a person engaged in an industry affecting commerce who has twenty-five or more employees for each working day in each of twenty or more calendar weeks in the current or preceding calendar year, and any agent of such a person, but such term does not include (1) the United States, a corporation wholly owned by the Government of the United States, an Indian tribe, or a State or political subdivision thereof, (2) a bona fide private membership club (other than a labor organization) which is exempt from taxation under section 501(c) of the Internal Revenue Code of 1954; *Provided*, That during the first year after the effective date prescribed in subsection (a) of section 716, persons having fewer than one hundred employees (and their agents) shall not be considered employers, and, during the second year after such date, persons having fewer than fifty employees (and their agents) shall not be considered employers: *Provided further*, That it shall be the policy of the United States to insure equal employment opportunities for Federal employees without discrimination because of race, color, religion, sex or national origin and the President shall utilize his existing authority to effectuate this policy.

(c) The term "employment agency" means any person regularly undertaking with or without compensation to procure employees for an employer or to procure for employees opportunities to work for an employer and includes an agent of such a person; but shall not include an agency of the United States, or an agency of a State or political subdivision of a State, except that such term shall include the United States Employment Service and the system of State and local employment services receiving Federal assistance.

(d) The term "labor organization" means a labor organization engaged in an industry affecting commerce, and any agent of such an organization, and includes any organization of any kind, any agency, or employee representation committee, group, association, or plan so engaged in which employees participate and which exists for the purpose, in whole or in part, of dealing with employers concerning grievances, labor disputes, wages, rates of pay, hours, or other terms or conditions of employment, and any conference, general committee, joint or system board, or joint council so engaged which is subordinate to a national or international labor organization.

(e) A labor organization shall be deemed to be engaged in an industry affecting commerce if (1) it maintains or operates a hiring hall or hiring office which procures employees for an employer or procures for employees opportunities to work for an employer, or (2) the number of its members (or, where it is a labor organization composed of other labor organizations or their representatives, if the aggregate number of the members of such other labor organization) is (A) one hundred or more during the first year after the effective date prescribed in subsection (a) of section 716, (B) seventy-five or more during the second year after such date or fifty or more during the third year, or (c) twenty-five or more thereafter, and such labor organization—

(1) is the certified representative of employees under the provisions of the National Labor Relations Act, as amended, or the Railway Labor Act, as amended;

(2) although not certified, is a national or international labor organization or a local labor organization recognized or acting as the representative of employees of an employer or employers engaged in an industry affecting commerce;

(3) has chartered a local labor organization or subsidiary body which representing or actively seeking to represent employees of employers within the meaning of paragraph (1) or (2); or

(4) has been chartered by a labor organization representing or actively seeking to represent employees within the meaning of paragraph (1) or (2) as the local or subordinate body through which such employees may enjoy membership or become affiliated with such labor organization; or

(5) is a conference, general committee, joint or system board, or joint council subordinate to a national or international labor organization, which includes a labor organization engaged in an industry affecting commerce within the meaning of any of the preceding paragraphs of this subsection.

(f) The term "employee" means an individual employed by an employer.

(g) The term "commerce" means trade, traffic, commerce, transportation, transmission, or communication among the several States; or between a State and any place outside thereof; or

within the District of Columbia, or a possession of the United States; or between points in the same State but through a point outside thereof.

(h) The term "industry affecting commerce" means any activity, business, or industry in commerce or in which a labor dispute would hinder or obstruct commerce or the free flow of commerce and includes any activity or industry "affecting commerce" within the meaning of the Labor-Management Reporting and Disclosure Act of 1959.

(i) The term "State" includes a State of the United States, the District of Columbia, Puerto Rico, the Virgin Islands, American Samoa, Guam, Wake Island, the Canal Zone, and Outer Continental Shelf lands defined in the Outer Continental Shelf Lands Act.

EXEMPTION

Sec. 702. This title shall not apply to an employer with respect the employment of aliens outside any State, or to a religious corporation, association, or society with respect to the employment of individuals of a particular religion to perform work connected with the carrying on by such corporation, association, or society of its religious activities or to an educational institution with respect to the employment of individuals to perform work connected with the educational activities of such institution.

DISCRIMINATION BECAUSE OF RACE, COLOR, RELIGION, SEX, OR NATIONAL ORIGIN

Sec. 703. (a) It shall be an unlawful employment practice for an employer—

(1) to fail or refuse to hire or to discharge any individual, or otherwise to discriminate against any individual with respect to his compensation, terms, conditions, or privileges of employment, because of such individual's race, color, religion, sex, or national origin;

(2) to limit, segregate, or classify his employees in any way which would deprive or tend to deprive any individual of employment opportunities or otherwise adversely affect his status as an employee, because of such individual's race, color, religion, sex, or national origin.

(b) It shall be an unlawful employment practice for an employment agency to fail or refuse to refer for employment, or otherwise to discriminate against, any individual because of his race, color, religion, sex, or national origin, or to classify or refer for employment and individual on the basis of his race, color, religion, sex, or national origin.

(c) It shall be an unlawful employment practice for a labor organization—

(1) to exclude or to expel from its membership, or otherwise to discriminate against, any individual because of his race, color, religion, sex, or national origin;

(2) to limit, segregate, or classify its membership, or to classify or fail or refuse to refer for employment any individual, in any way which would deprive or tend to deprive any individual of employment opportunities, or would limit such employment opportunities or otherwise adversely affect his status as an employee or as an applicant for employment, because of such individual's race, color, religion, sex, or national origin; or

(3) to cause or attempt to cause an employer to discriminate against an individual in violation of this section.

(d) It shall be an unlawful employment practice for any employer, labor organization, or joint labor-management committee controlling apprenticeship or other training or retraining, including on-the-job training programs to discriminate against any individual because of his race, color, religion, sex, or national origin in admission to, or employment in, any program established to provide apprenticeship or other training.

(e) Notwithstanding any other provision of this title, (1) it shall not be an unlawful employment practice for an employer to hire and employ employees, for an employment agency to classify, or refer for employment any individual, for a labor organization to classify its membership or to classify or refer for employment any individual, or for an employer, labor organization, or joint labor-management committee controlling apprenticeship or other training or retraining programs to admit or employ any individual in any such program, on the basis of his religion, sex, or national origin in those certain instances where religion, sex, or national origin is a bona fide occupational qualification reasonably necessary to the normal operation of that particular business or enterprise, and (2) it shall not be an unlawful employment practice for a school, college, university, or other educational institution or institution of learning to hire and employ employees of a particular reli-

gion if such school, college, university, or other educational institution or institution of learning is, in whole or in substantial part, owned, supported, controlled, or managed by a particular religion or by a particular religious corporation, association, or society, or if the curriculum, of such school, college, university, or other educational institution or institution of learning is directed toward the propagation of a particular religion.

(f) As used in this title, the phrase "unlawful employment practice" shall not be deemed to include any action or measure taken by an employer, labor organization, joint labor-management committee, employment agency with respect to an individual who is a member of the Communist Party of the United States or of any other organization required to register as a Communist-action or Communist-front organization by final order of the Subversive Activities Control Board pursuant to the Subversive Activities Control Act of 1950.

(g) Notwithstanding any other provision of this title, it shall not be an unlawful employment practice for an employer to fail or refuse to hire and employ any individual for any position, for an employer to discharge any individual from any position, or for an employment agency to fail or refuse to refer any individual for employment in any position, or for a labor organization to fail or refuse to refer any individual for employment in any position, if—

(1) the occupancy of such position, or access to the premises in or upon which any part of the duties of such position is performed or is to be performed, is subject to any requirement imposed in the interest of the national security of the United States under any security program in effect pursuant to or administered under any statute of the United States or any Executive order of the President; and

(2) such individual has not fulfilled or has ceased to fulfill that requirement.

(h) Notwithstanding any other provision of this title, it shall not be an unlawful employment practice for an employer to apply different standards of compensation, or different terms, conditions, or privileges of employment pursuant to a bona fide seniority or merit system, or a system which measures earnings by quantity or quality of productions or to employees who work in different locations, provided that such differences are not the result of an intention to discrimination because of race, color, religion, sex, or national origin, nor shall it be an unlawful employment practice for an employer to give and to act upon the results of any professionally developed ability test provided that such test, its administration or action upon the results is not designed, intended or used to discriminate because of race, color, religion, sex or national origin. It shall not be an unlawful employment practice under this title for any employer to differentiate upon the basis of sex in determining the amount of the wages or compensation paid or to be paid to employees of such employer if such differentiate is authorized by the provisions of section 6(d) of the Fair Labor Standards Act of 1938, as amended (29 U.S.C. 206(d).[10]

(i) Nothing contained in this title shall apply to any business or enterprise on or near an Indian reservation with respect to any publicly announced employment practice of such business or enterprise under which preferential treatment is given to any individual because he is an Indian living on or near a reservation.

(j) Nothing contained in this title shall be interpreted to require any employer, employment agency, labor organization, or joint labor-management committee subject to this title to grant preferential treatment to any individual or to any group because of the race, color, religion, sex, or national origin of such individual or group on account of an imbalance which may exist with respect to the to any group because of race, color, religion, sex, or national origin employed by an employer, referred or classified for employment by any employment agency or labor organization, or admitted to membership or classified by any labor organization, or admitted to, or employed in, any apprenticeship or other training program, in comparison with the total number of percentage of persons of such race, color, religion, sex, or national origin in any community, State, section, or other area, or in the available work force in any community, State, section, or other area.

OTHER UNLAWFUL EMPLOYMENT PRACTICES

Sec. 704. (a) It shall be an unlawful employment practice for an employer to discriminate against any of his employees or applicants for employment, for an employment agency to discriminate against an individual, or for a labor organization to discriminate against any mem-

ber thereof or applicant for membership, because he has opposed any practice made an unlawful employment practice by this title, or because he has made a charge, testified, assisted, or participated in any manner in an investigation, proceeding, or hearing under this title.

(b) It shall be an unlawful employment practice for an employer, labor organization, or employment agency to print or publish or cause to be printed or published any notice or advertisement relating to employment by such an employer or membership in or any classification or referral for employment by such labor organization, or relating to any classification or referral for employment by such an employment agency, indicating any preference, limitation, specification, or discrimination, based on race, color, religion, sex, or national origin, except that such a notice or advertisement may indicate preference, limitation, specification, or discrimination, based on race, color, religion, sex, or national origin is a bona fide occupational qualification for employment.

EQUAL EMPLOYMENT OPPORTUNITY COMMISSION

Sec. 705. (a) There is hereby created a Commission to be known as the Equal Employment Opportunity Commission, which shall be composed of five members, not more than three of whom shall be members of the same political party, who shall be appointed by the President by and with the advice and consent of the Senate. One of the original members shall be appointed for a term of one year, one for a term of two years, one for a term of three year, one for a term of four years, one for a term of five years, beginning from the date of enactment of this title, but their successors shall be appointed for terms of five years, except that any individual chosen to fill a vacancy shall be appointed only for the unexpired term of the member whom he shall succeed. The President shall designate one member to serve as Chairman of the Commission, and one member to serve as Vice Chairman. The Chairman shall be responsible on behalf of the Commission for the administrative operations of the Commissions, and shall appoint, in accordance with the civil service laws, such officers, agents, attorneys, and employees as it deems necessary to assist it in the performance of its functions and to fix their compensation in accordance with the Classification Act of 1949, as amended. The Vice Chairman shall act as Chairman in the absence or disability of the

[10] 29 U.S.C.A. § 206(d).

Chairman or in the event of a vacancy in that office.

(b) A vacancy in the Commission shall not impair the right of the remaining members to exercise all the powers of the Commission and three members thereof shall constitute a quorum.

(c) The Commission shall have an official seal which shall be judicially noticed.

(d) The Commission shall at the close of each fiscal year report to the Congress and to the President concerning the action it has taken; the names, salaries, and duties of all individuals in its employ and the moneys it has disbursed; and shall make such further reports on the cause of and means of eliminating discrimination and such recommendations for further legislation as may appear desirable.

(e) The Federal Executive Pay Act of 1956, as amended (5 U.S.C. 2201–2209),[11] is further amended—

(1) by adding to section 105 thereof (5 U.S.C. 2204) the following clause:

"(32) Chairman, Equal Employment Opportunity Commission"; and

(2) by adding to clause (45) of section 106(a) thereof (5 U.S.C. 2205(a)) the following: "Equal Employment Opportunity Commission (4)."

(f) The principal office of the Commission shall be in or near the District of Columbia, but it may meet or exercise any or all its powers at any other place. The Commission may establish such regional or State offices as it deems necessary to accomplish the purpose of this title.

(g) The Commission shall have power—

(1) to cooperate with and, with their consent, utilize regional State, local, and other agencies, both public and private, and individuals;

(2) to pay to witnesses whose depositions are taken, or who are summoned before the Commission or any of its agents the same witness and mileage fees as are paid to witnesses in the courts of the United States;

(3) to furnish to persons subject to this title such technical assistance as they may request to further their compliance with this title or an order issued thereunder;

(4) upon the request of (i) any employer, whose employees or some of them, or (ii) any

labor organization, whose members or some of them, refuse or threaten to refuse to cooperate in effectuating the provisions of this title, to assist in such effectuation by conciliation or such other remedial action as is provided by this title;

(5) to make such technical studies as are appropriate to effectuate the purposes and policies of this title and to make the results of such studies available to the public.

(6) to refer matters to the Attorney General with recommendations for intervention in a civil action brought by an aggrieved party under section 706, or for the institution of a civil action by the Attorney General under Section 707, and to advise, consult, and assist the Attorney General on such matters.

(h) Attorneys appointed under this section may, at the direction of the Commission, appear for and represent the Commission in any case in court.

(i) The Commission shall, in any of its educational or promotional activities, cooperate with other departments and agencies in the performance of such educational and promotional activities.

(j) All officers, agents, attorneys, and employees of the Commission shall be subject to the provisions of section 9 of the Act of August 2, 1939, as amended (the Hatch Act), notwithstanding any exemption contained in such section.

PREVENTION OF UNLAWFUL EMPLOYMENT
PRACTICES

Sec. 706 (a) Whenever it is charged in writing under oath by a person claiming to be aggrieved, or a written charge has been filed by a member of the Commission where he has reasonable cause to believe a violation of this title has occurred (and such charge sets for the facts upon which it is based) that an employer, employment agency, or labor organization has engaged in an unlawful employment practice, the Commission shall furnish such employer, employment agency, or labor organization (hereinafter referred to as the "respondent") with a copy of such charge and shall make an investigation of such charge, provided that such charge shall not be made public by the Commission. If the Commission shall determine, after such investigation, that there is reasonable cause to believe that the charge is true, the Commission shall endeavor to eliminate any such alleged unlawful employment practice by

---

[11] 5 U.S.C.A. § 2201 et seq.

informal methods of conference, conciliation, and persuasion. Nothing said or done during and as a part of such endeavors may be made public by the Commission, without the written consent of the parties, or used as evidence in a subsequent proceeding. Any officer or employee of the Commission, who shall make public in any manner whatever any information in violation of this subsection shall be deemed guilty of a misdemeanor and upon conviction thereof shall be fined not more than $1,000 or imprisoned not more than one year.

(b) In the case of an alleged unlawful employment practice occurring in a State, or political subdivision of a State, which has a State or local law prohibiting the unlawful employment practice alleged and establishing or authorizing a State or local authority to grant or seek relief from such practice or to institute criminal proceedings with respect thereto upon receiving notice thereof, no charge may be filed under subsection (a) by the person aggrieved before the expiration of sixty days after proceedings have been commenced under the State or local law, unless such proceedings have been earlier terminated, provided that such sixty-day period shall be extended to one hundred and twenty days during the first year after the effective date such State or local law. If any requirement for the commencement of such proceedings is imposed by a State or local authority other than a requirement of the filing of a written and signed statement of the facts upon which the proceeding is based, the proceeding shall be deemed to have been commenced for the purposes of this subsection at the time such statement is sent by registered mail to the appropriate State or local authority.

(c) In the case of any charge filed by a member of the Commission alleging an unlawful employment practice occurring in a State or political subdivision of a State, which has a State or local law prohibiting the practice alleged and establishing or authorizing a State or local authority to grant or seek relief from such practice or to institute criminal proceedings with respect thereto upon receiving notice thereof, the Commission shall, before taking ay action with respect to such charge, notify the appropriate State or local officials and, upon request, afford them a reasonable time, but not less than sixty days (provided that such sixty-day period shall be extended to one hundred and twenty days during the first year after the effective day of such State or local law), unless a shorter period is requested, to act under such State or local law to remedy the practice alleged.

(d) A charge under subsection (a) shall be filed within ninety days after the alleged unlawful employment practice occurred, except that in the case of an unlawful employment practice with respect to which the person aggrieved has followed the procedure set out in subsection (b), such charge shall be filed by the person aggrieved within two hundred and ten days after the alleged unlawful employment practice occurred, or within thirty days after receiving notice that the State or local agency has terminated the proceedings under the State or local law, whichever is earlier, and a copy such charge shall be filed by the Commission with the State or local agency.

(e) If within thirty days after a charge is filed with the Commission or within thirty days after expiration of any period of reference under subsection (c) (except that in either case such period may be extended to not more than sixty days upon a determination by the Commission that further efforts to secure voluntary compliance are warranted), the Commission has been unable to obtain voluntary compliance with this title, the Commission shall so notify the person aggrieved and a civil action may, within thirty days thereafter, be brought against the respondent named in the charge (1) by person claiming to be aggrieved, or (2) if such charge was filed by a member of the Commission, by any person whom the charge alleges was aggrieved by the alleged unlawful employment practice. Upon application by the complainant and in such circumstances as the court may deem just, the court may appoint an attorney for such complainant and may authorize the commencement of the action without the payment of fees, costs, or security. Upon timely application, the court may, in its discretion, permit the Attorney General to intervene in such civil action if he certifies that the case is of general public importance. Upon request, the court may, in its discretion, stay further proceedings for not more than sixty days pending the termination of State or local proceedings described in subsection (b) or the efforts of the Commission to obtain voluntary compliance.

(f) Each United States district court and each United States court of a place subject to the jurisdiction of the United States shall have jurisdiction of actions brought under this title. Such an action may be brought in any judicial district in the State in which the unlawful employment practice is alleged to have been committed, in judicial district in which the employment records relevant to such practice are maintained and administered, or in the judicial district which the plaintiff would have worked but for the alleged unlawful employment practice, but if the respondent is not found within any such district, such an action may be brought within the judicial district in which the respondent has his principal office. For purposes of sections 1404 and 1406 of title 28 of the United States Code, the judicial district in which the respondent has his principal office shall in all cases be considered a district in which the action might have been brought.

(g) If the court finds that the respondent has intentionally engaged in or is intentionally engaging in an unlawful employment practice charged in the complaint, the court may enjoin the respondent from engaging in such unlawful employment practice, and order such affirmative action as may be appropriate, which may include reinstatement or hiring of employees, with or without back pay (payable by the employer, employment agency, or labor organization, as the case may be, responsible for the unlawful employment practice). Interim earnings or amounts earnable with reasonable diligence by the person or persons discriminated against shall operate to reduce the back pay otherwise allowable. No order of the court shall require the admission or reinstatement of an individual as a member as an employee, or the payment to him of any back pay, if such individual was refused admission, suspended, or expelled or was refused employment or advancement or was suspended or discharged for any reason other than discrimination on account of race, color, religion, sex, or national origin or in violation of section 704(a).

(h) The provisions of the Act entitled "An Act to amend the Judicial Code and to define and limit the jurisdiction of courts sitting in equity, and for other purposes," approved March 23, 1932 (29 U.S.C. 101–115), shall not apply with respect to civil actions brought under this section.

(i) In any case in which an employer, employment agency, or labor organization fails to comply with an order of a court issued a civil action brought under subsection (e), the Commission may commence proceedings to compel compliance with such order.

(j) Any civil action brought under subsection (e) and any proceedings brought under subsection (i) shall be subject to appeal as provided in sections 1291 and 1292, title 28, United States Code.

(k) In any action or proceeding under this title the court, in its discretion, may allow the prevailing party, other than the Commission or the United States, a reasonable attorney's fee as part of the costs, and the Commission and the United States shall be liable for costs the same as a private person.

Sec. 707 (a) Whenever the Attorney General has reasonable cause to believe of resistance to the full enjoyment of any of the rights secured by this title, and that the pattern or practice is of such a nature and is intended to deny the full exercise of the rights herein described, the Attorney General may bring a civil action in the appropriate district court of the United States by filing with it a complaint (1) signed by him (or in his absence the Acting Attorney General), (2) setting forth facts pertaining to such pattern or practice, and (3) requesting such relief, including an application for a permanent or temporary injunction, restraining order or other order against the person or persons responsible for such pattern or practice, as he deems necessary to insure the full enjoyment of the rights herein described.

(b) The district courts of the United States shall have and shall exercise jurisdiction of proceedings instituted pursuant to this section, and in any such proceeding the Attorney General may file with the clerk of such court a request that a court of three judges be convened to hear and determine the case. Such request by the Attorney General shall be accompanied by a certificate that, in his opinion, the case is of general public importance. A copy of the certificate and request for a three-judge court shall be immediately furnished by such clerk to the chief judge of the circuit (or in his absence, the presiding circuit judge of the circuit) in which the case is pending. Upon receipt of such request it shall be the duty of the chief judge of the circuit or the presiding circuit judge, as the case may be, to designate immediately three judges in such circuit, of whom at least one shall be a circuit judge and another of whom shall be a district judge of the court in which the proceeding was instituted, to hear and determine such case, and it shall be the duty of the judges so designated to assign the case for hearing at the earliest practicable date, to participate in the hearing and determination thereof, and to cause the case to be in every way expedited. An appeal from the final judgment of such court will lie to the Supreme Court.

In the event the Attorney General fails to file such a request in any such proceeding, it shall be the duty of the chief judge of the district (or in his absence, the acting chief judge) in which the case is pending immediately to designate a judge in such district to hear and determine the case. In the event that no judge in the district is available to hear and determine the case, the chief judge of the district, or the acting chief judge, as the case may be, shall certify this fact to the chief judge of the circuit (or in his absence, the acting chief judge) who shall then designate a district or circuit judge of the circuit to hear and determine the case.

It shall be the duty of the judge designated pursuant to this section to assign the case of hearing at the earliest practicable date and to cause the case to be in every way expedited.

EFFECT ON STATE LAWS

Sec. 708. Nothing in this title shall be deemed to exempt or relieve any person from any liability, duty, penalty, or punishment provided by any present or future law of any State or political subdivision of a State, other than any such law which purports to require or permit the doing of any act which would be an unlawful employment practice under this title.

INVESTIGATIONS, INSPECTIONS, RECORDS, STATE AGENCIES

Sec. 709 (a) In connection with any investigation of a charge filed under section 706, the Commission or its designated representative shall at all reasonable times have access to, for the purposes of examination, and the right to copy any evidence of any person being investigated or proceeded against that relates to unlawful employment practices covered by this title and is relevant to the charge under investigation.

(b) The Commission may cooperate with State and local agencies charged with the administration of State fair employment practices laws and, with the consent of such agencies, may for the purpose of carrying out its functions and duties under this title and within the limitation of funds appropriated specifically for such purpose, utilize the services of such agencies and their employees and, notwithstanding any other provision of law, may reimburse such agencies and their employees for services rendered to assist the Commission in carrying out this title. In furtherance of such cooperative efforts, the Commission may enter into written agreements with such State or local agencies and such agreements may include provisions under which the Commission shall refrain from processing a charge in any cases or class of cases specified in such agreements and under which no person may bring a civil action under section 706 in any cases or class of cases specified, or under which the Commission shall relieve any person or class of persons in such State or locality from requirements imposed under this section. The Commission shall rescind any such agreement whenever it determines that the agreement no longer serves the interest of effective enforcement of this title.

(c) Except as provided in subsection (d), every employer, employment agency, and labor organization subject to this title shall (1) make and keep such records relevant to the determinations of whether unlawful employment practices have been or are being committed, (2) preserve such records for such periods, and (3) make such reports therefrom, as the Commission shall prescribe by regulation or order, after public hearing, as reasonable, necessary, or appropriate for the enforcement of this title or the regulations or orders thereunder. The Commission shall, by regulation, require each employer, labor organization, and joint labor-management committee subject to this title which controls and apprenticeship or other training program to maintain such records as are reasonably necessary to carry out the purpose of this title, including, but not limited to, a list of applicants who wish to participate in such program, including the chronological order in which such applications were received, and shall furnish to the Commission, upon request, a detailed description of the manner in which persons are selected to participate in the apprenticeship or other training program. Any employer, employment agency, labor organization, or joint labor-management committee which believes that the application to it of any regulation or order issued under this section would result in undue hardship may (1) apply to the Commission for an exemption from the application of such regulation or order, or (2) bring a civil action in the United States district court for the district where such records are kept. If the Commission or the court, as the case may be, finds that the application of the regulation or order to the employer, employment agency, and labor organization in question would impose an undue hardship, the Commission or the court, as the case may be, may grant appropriate relief.

(d) The provisions of subsection (c) shall not apply to any employer, employment agency, and labor organization, or joint labor-management committee with respect to matters occurring in any State or political subdivision thereof which has a fair employment practice law during any period in which such employer, employment agency, and labor organization, or joint labor-management committee keeps or is required to keep as are necessary because of differences in coverage or methods of enforcement between the State or local law and the provisions of this title. Where an employer is required by Executive Order 10925, issued March, 6, 1961, or by any other Executive order prescribing fair employment practices for Government contractors and subcontractors, or by rules or regulations issued thereunder, to file reports relating to his employment practices with any Federal agency or committee, and he substantially in compliance with such requirements, the Commission shall not require him to file additional reports pursuant to subsection (c) of this section.

(e) It shall be unlawful for any officer or employee of the Commission to make public in any manner whatever any information obtained by the Commission pursuant to its authority under this section prior to the institution of any proceeding under this title involving such information. Any officer or employee of the Commission who shall make public in any manner whatever any information in violation of this subsection shall be guilty of a misdemeanor and upon conviction thereof, shall be fined not more than $1,000, or imprisoned not more than one year.

INVESTIGATORY POWERS

Sec. 710 (a) For the purposes of any investigation of a charge filed under the authority contained in section 706, the Commission shall have authority to examine witnesses under oath and to require the production of documentary evi-

dence relevant or material to the charge under investigation.

(b) If the respondent named in a charge filed under section 706 fails or refuses to comply with a demand of the Commission for permission to examine or to copy evidence in conformity with the provisions of section 709 (a), or if any person required to comply with the provisions of section 709 (c) or (d) fails or refuse to do so, or if any person fails or refuses to comply with a demand by the Commission to give testimony under oath, the United States district court for the district in which such person is found, resides, or transacts business, shall, upon application of the Commission have jurisdiction to issue to such person an order requiring him to comply with the provisions of section 709 (c) or (d) or to comply with the demand of the Commission, but the attendance of a witness may not be required outside the State where he is found, resides, or transacts business and the production of evidence may not be required outside the State where such evidence is kept.

(c) Within twenty days after the service upon any person charged under section 706 of a demand by the Commission for the production of documentary evidence or for permission to examine or to copy evidence in conformity with the provisions of section 709(a), such person may file in the district court of the United States for the judicial district in which he resides, is found, or transacts business, and serve upon the Commission a petition for an order of such court modifying or setting aside such demand. The time allowed for compliance with the demand in whole or in part as deemed proper and ordered by the court shall not run during the pendency of such petition in the court. Such petition shall specify each ground upon which the petitioner relies in seeking such relief, and may be based upon any failure of such demand to comply with the provisions of this title or with the limitations generally applicable to compulsory process or upon any constitutional or other legal right or privilege of such person. No objection which is not raised by such a petition may be urged in the defense to a proceeding initiated by the Commission under subsection (b) for enforcement of such a demand unless such proceeding is commenced by the Commission prior to the expiration of the twenty-day period, or unless the court determines that the defendant could not reasonably have been aware of the availability of such ground of objection.

(d) In any proceeding brought by the Commission under subsection (b), except as provided in subsection (c) of this section, the defendant may petition the court for an order modifying or setting aside the demand of the Commission.

NOTICES TO BE POSTED

Sec. 711. (a) Every employer, employment agency, labor organization, as the case may be, shall post and keep posted in conspicuous places upon its premises where notices to employees, applicants for employment, and members are customarily posted a notice to be prepared or approved by the Commission setting forth excerpts from or, summaries of, the pertinent provisions of this title and information pertinent to the filing of a complaint.

(b) A willful violation of this section shall be punishable by a fine of not more than $100 for each separate offense.

VETERANS' PREFERENCE

Sec. 712. Nothing contained in this title shall be construed to repeal or modify any Federal, State, territorial, or local law creating special rights or preference for veterans.

RULES AND REGULATIONS

Sec. 713. (a) The Commission shall have authority from time to time to issue, amend, or rescind suitable procedural regulations to carry out the provisions of this title. Regulations issued under this section shall be in conformity with the standards and limitations of the Administrative Procedure Act.

(b) In any action or proceeding based on any alleged unlawful employment practice, no person shall be subject to any liability or punishment for or on account of (1) the commission by such person of unlawful employment practice if he pleads and proves that the act or omission complained of was in good faith, in conformity with, and in reliance on any written interpretation or opinion of the Commission, or (2) the failure of such person to publish and file any information required by any provision of this title if he pleads and proves that he failed to publish and file such information in good faith, in conformity with the instructions of the Commission issued under this title regarding the filing of such information. Such a defense, if

established, shall be a bar to the action or proceeding, notwithstanding that (A) after such act or omission, such interpretation or opinion is modified or rescinded or is determined by judicial authority to be invalid or of no legal effect, or (B) after publishing or filing the description and annual reports, such publication or filing is determined by judicial authority not to be in conformity with the requirements of this title.

FORCIBLY RESISTING THE COMMISSION OR ITS REPRESENTATIVES

Sec. 714. The provisions of section 111, title 18, United States Code, shall apply to officers, agents, and employees of the Commission in the performance of their official duties.

SPECIAL STUDY BY SECRETARY OF LABOR

Sec. 715. The Secretary of Labor shall make a full and complete study of the factors which might tend to result in discrimination in employment because of age and of the consequences of such discrimination on the economy and individuals affected. The Secretary of Labor shall make a report to the Congress not later than June 30, 1965, containing the results of such study and shall include in such report such recommendations for legislation to prevent arbitrary discrimination in employment because of age as he determines advisable.

EFFECTIVE DATE

Sec. 716. (a) This title shall become effective one year after the date of its enactment.

(b) Notwithstanding subsection (a), sections of this title other than sections 703, 704, 706, and 707 shall become effective immediately.

(c) The President shall, as soon as feasible after the enactment of this title, convene one or more conferences for the purposes of enabling the leaders of groups whose members will be affected by this title to become familiar with the rights afforded and obligations imposed by its provisions, and for the purpose of making plans which will result in the fair and effective administration of this title when all of its provisions become effective. The President shall invite the participation in such conference or conferences of (1) the members of the President's Committee on Equal Employment Opportunity, (2) the members of the Commission on Civil Rights, (3) representatives of State and local agencies engaged in furthering equal employment opportunity, (4) representatives of private agencies engaged in furthering equal employment

FROM
SEGREGATION
TO CIVIL RIGHTS

CIVIL RIGHTS
ACT OF 1964

opportunity, and (5) representatives of employers, labor organizations, and employment agencies who will be subject to this title.

TITLE VIII—REGISTRATION AND VOTING STATISTICS

Sec. 801. The Secretary of Commerce shall promptly conduct a survey to compile registration and voting statistics in such geographic areas as may be recommended by the Commission on Civil Rights. Such a survey and compilation shall, to the extent recommended by the Commission on Civil Rights, only include a count of persons of voting age by race, color, and national origin, and determination of the extent to which such persons are registered to vote, and have voted in any statewide primary or general election in which the Members of the United States House of Representatives are nominated or elected, since January 1, 1960. Such information shall also be collected and compiled in connection with the Nineteenth Decennial Census, and at such other times as the Congress may prescribe. The provisions of section 9 and chapter 7 of title 13, United States Code, shall apply to any survey, collection, or compilation of registration and voting statistics carried out under this title: *Provided, however*, That no person shall be compelled to disclose his race, color, and national origin, or questioned about his political party affiliation, how he voted, or the reasons therefore, nor shall any penalty be imposed for his failure or refusal to make such disclosure. Every person interrogated orally, by written survey or questionnaire or by any other means with respect to such information shall be fully advised with respect to his right to fail or refuse to furnish such information.

TITLE IX—INTERVENTION AND PROCEDURE AFTER REMOVAL IN CIVIL RIGHTS CASES

Sec. 901. Title 28 of the United States Code, section 1447(d)[12] is amended to read as follows:

"An order remanding a case to the State court from which it was removed is not reviewable on appeal or otherwise, except that an order remanding a case to the State court from which it was removed pursuant to section 1443 of this title shall be reviewable by appeal or otherwise."

Sec. 902. Whenever an action has been commenced in any court of the United States seeking relief from the denial of equal protection of the laws under the fourteenth amendment to the Constitution on account of race, color, and national origin, the Attorney General for or in the name of the United States may intervene in such action upon timely application if the Attorney General certifies that the case is of general public importance. In such action the United States shall be entitled to the same relief as if it had instituted the action.

TITLE X—ESTABLISHMENT OF COMMUNITY RELATIONS SERVICE

Sec. 1001. (a) There is hereby established in and as a part of the Department of Commerce a Community Relations Service (hereinafter referred to as the "Service"), which shall be headed by a Director who shall be appointed by the President with the advice and consent of the Senate for a term of four years. The Director is authorized to appoint, subject to the civil service laws and regulations, such other personnel as may be necessary to enable the Service to carry out its functions and duties, and to fix their compensation in accordance with the Classification, Act of 1949, as amended. The Director is further authorized to procure services as authorized by section 15 of the Act of August 2, 1946 (60 Stat. 810; 5 U.S.C. 55(a)), but at rates for individuals not in excess of $75 per diem.

(b) Section 106(a) of the Federal Executive Pay Act of 1956, as amended (5 U.S.C. 2205(a))[13] is further amended by adding the following clause thereto:

"(52) Director, Community Relations Service."

Sec. 1002. It shall be the function of the Service to provide assistance to communities and persons therein in resolving disputes, disagreements, or difficulties relating to discriminatory practices based on race, color, and national origin which impair the rights of persons in such communities under the Constitution or laws of the United States or which affect interstate commerce. The Service may offer its services in cases of such disputes, disagreements, or difficulties whenever, in its judgment, peaceful relations among the citizens of the community involved are threatened thereby, and it may offer its services either upon its own motion or upon the request of an appropriate State or local official or other interested person.

---

[12] 28 U.S.C.A. § 1447(d).

[13] 5 U.S.C.A. § 2205(a).

Sec. 1003. (a) The Service shall, whenever possible, in performing its function, seek and utilize the cooperation of appropriate State or local, public, or private agencies.

(b) The activities of all officers and employees of the Service in providing conciliation assistance shall be conducted in confidence and without publicity, and the Service shall hold confidential any information acquired in the regular performance of its duties upon the understanding it would be so held. No officer or employee of the Service shall engage in the performance of investigative or prosecuting functions of any department or agency in any litigation arising out of a dispute in which he acted on behalf of the Service. Any officer or other employee of the Service, who shall make public in any manner whatever any information in violation of this subsection, shall be deemed guilty of a misdemeanor and, upon conviction thereof, shall be fined not more than $1,000 or imprisoned not more than one year.

Sec. 1004. Subject to the provisions of sections 205 and 1003(b) the Director shall, on or before January 31 of each year, submit to the Congress a report of the activities of the Service during the preceding fiscal year.

TITLE XI—MISCELLANEOUS

Sec. 1101. In any proceeding for criminal contempt arising under title II, III, IV, V, VI, VII of this Act, the accused, upon demand therefor, shall be entitled to a trial by jury, which shall conform as near as may be to the practice in criminal cases. Upon conviction, the accused shall not be fined more than $1,000 or imprisoned for more than six months.

This section shall not apply to contempts committed in the presence of the court, or so near thereto as to obstruct the administration of justice, nor to the misbehavior, misconduct, or disobedience of any officer of the court in respect to writs, orders, or process of the court. No person shall be convicted of criminal contempt hereunder unless the act or omission constituting such contempt shall have been intentional, as required in other cases of criminal contempt.

Nor shall anything herein be construed to deprive courts of their power, by civil contempt proceedings, without a jury, to secure compliance with or to prevent obstruction of, as distinguished from punishment for violations of, any lawful writ, process, order, rule, decree, or command of the court in accordance with the prevailing usages of law and equity, including the power of detention.

Sec. 1102. No person should be put twice in jeopardy under the laws of the United States for the same act or omission. For this reason, an acquittal or conviction in a prosecution for a specific crime under the laws of the United States shall bar a proceeding for criminal contempt, which is based upon the same act or omission and which arises under the provisions of this Act; and an acquittal or conviction in a proceeding for criminal contempt, which arises under the provisions of this Act, shall bar a prosecution for a specific crime under the laws of the United States based upon the same act or omission.

Sec. 1103. Nothing in this Act shall be construed to deny, impair, or otherwise affect any right or authority of the Attorney General or of the United States or any agency or officer thereof under existing law to institute or intervene in any action or proceeding.

Sec. 1104. Nothing contained in any title of this Act shall be construed as indicating an intent on the part of Congress to occupy the field in which any such title operates to the exclusion of State laws on the same subject matter, nor shall any provision of this Act be construed as invalidating any provision of State law unless such provision is inconsistent with any of the purposes of this Act, or any provision thereof.

Sec. 1105. There are hereby authorized to be appropriated such sums as are necessary to carry out the provisions of this Act.

Sec. 1106. If any provision of this Act or the application thereof to any person or circumstances is held invalid, the remainder of the Act and the application of the provision to other persons not similarly situated or to other circumstances shall not be affected thereby.

Approved July 2, 1964.

From Segregation to Civil Rights

Voting Rights Act of 1965

The Voting Rights Act of 1965 is a sweeping federal law that seeks to prevent voting discrimination based on race, color, or membership in a language minority group. The act was passed in the aftermath of one of the more violent episodes in the history of the civil rights movement. In 1965 Dr. Martin Luther King Jr., led a group of civil rights supporters on a march to Selma, Alabama, to demand voting rights. They were met by police violence that resulted in the deaths of several marchers. The Selma violence galvanized voting rights supporters in Congress. President Lyndon B. Johnson responded by introducing the Voting Rights Act, the most sweeping piece of civil rights law in one hundred years. Congress enacted the measure five months later.

The passage of the Voting Rights Act was a watershed event in U.S. history. For the first time the federal government undertook voting reforms that had traditionally been left to the states. The act prohibits the states and their political subdivisions from imposing voting qualifications or prerequisites to voting or from imposing standards, practices, or procedures that deny or curtail the right of a U.S. citizen to vote because of race, color, or membership in a language minority group. The act was extended in 1970 and again in 1982, when its provisions were given an additional term of twenty-five years.

Southern states challenged the legislation as a dangerous attack on states' rights, but in *South Carolina v. Katzenbach,* 383 U.S. 301, 86 S. Ct. 803, 15 L. Ed. 2d 769 (1966), the U.S. Supreme Court upheld the constitutionality of the act, even though it was, in the words of Chief Justice Earl Warren, "inventive."

The initial act covered the seven states in the South that had used poll taxes, literacy tests, and other devices to obstruct registration by African Americans. Under the law a federal court can appoint federal examiners, who are authorized to place qualified persons on the list of eligible voters. The act waived accumulated poll taxes and abolished literacy tests and similar devices in the states to which it applied.

In addition, the act requires the seven states to obtain "preclearance" from the Justice Department or the U.S. District Court for the District of Columbia before changing the electoral system. The 1982 extension of the act expanded this provision to include all the states. Thus, a voter in any state may challenge a voting practice or procedure on the grounds that it is racially discriminatory either by intent or by effect.

The act has been used to create congressional districts that have a majority of minority voters so as to ensure minority representation. In *Shaw v. Hunt,* 517 U.S. 899 116 S. Ct. 1894, 135 L. Ed. 2d 207 (1996), however, the Supreme Court ruled that the redrawing of a North Carolina congressional district into a "bizarre-looking" shape so as to include a majority of African Americans violated the Equal Protection Clause of the Fourteenth Amendment and therefore could not be justified by the Voting Rights Act.

Voting Rights Act of 1965

For Legislative History of Act, see p. 2437

Public Law 89–100; 79 Stat. 437

[S. 1564]

An Act to enforce the Fifteenth Amendment to the Constitution of the United States, and for other purposes.

Be it enacted by the Senate and House of Representatives of the United States of America in Congress assembled, That:

This Act shall be known as the "Voting Rights Act of 1965."

Sec. 2. No voting qualifications or prerequisite to voting, or standard, practice, or procedure shall be imposed or applied by any State or political subdivision to deny or abridge the right of any citizen of the United States to vote on account of race or color.

Sec. 3 (a) Whenever the Attorney General institutes a proceeding under any statute to enforce the guarantees of the fifteenth amendment in any State or political subdivision the Court shall authorize the appointment of Federal examiners by the United States Civil Service Commission in accordance withe section 6 to serve for such period of time and for such political subdivisions as the court shall determine is appropriate to enforce the guarantees of the fifteenth amendment (1) as part of any interlocutory order if the court determines that the appointment of such examiners is necessary to enforce such guarantees or (2) as part of any final judgment if the court finds that violations of the Fifteenth Amendment justifying equitable relief have occurred in such State or subdivision: *Provided,* That the court need not authorize the appointment of examiners if any incidents of denial or abridgement of the right to vote on account of race or color (1) have been few in number and have been promptly and effectively corrected by State or local action, (2) the continuing of effect of such incidents has been eliminated, and (3) there is no reasonable probability of their recurrence in the future.

(b) If in a proceeding instituted by the Attorney General under any statute to enforce the guarantees of the Fifteenth Amendment in any State or political subdivision the court finds that a test or device has been used for the purpose or with the effect of denying or abridging the right of any citizen of the United States to vote on account of race or color, it shall suspend the use of tests and devices in such State or political subdivisions as the court shall determine is appropriate and for such period as it deems necessary.

(c) If in any proceeding instituted by the Attorney General under any statute to enforce the guarantees of the Fifteenth Amendment in any State or political subdivision the court finds that violations of the Fifteenth Amendment justifying equitable relief have occurred within the territory of such State or political subdivision, the court, in addition to such relief as it may grant, shall retain jurisdiction for such period as it may deem appropriate and during such period no voting qualification or prerequisite to voting, or standard, practice, or procedure with respect to voting different from that in force or effect at the time the proceeding was commenced shall be enforced unless and until the court finds that such qualification, prerequisite, standard, practice, or procedure does not have the purpose and will not have the effect of denying abridging the right to vote on account of race or color: *Provided,* That such qualification, prerequisite, standard, practice, or procedure may be enforced if the qualification, prerequisite, standard, practice, or procedure has been submitted by the chief legal officer or other appropriate official of such State or subdivision to the Attorney General and the Attorney General has not interposed an objection within sixty days after such submission, except that neither the court's finding nor the Attorney General's failure to object shall bar a subsequent action to enjoin enforcement of such qualification, prerequisite, standard, practice, or procedure.

Sec. 4 (a) To assure that the right of citizens of the United States to vote is not denied or abridged on account of race or color, no citizen shall be denied the right to vote in any Federal, State, or local election because of his failure to comply with any test or device in any State with respect to which the determinations have been made under subsection (b) or in political subdivision with respect to which such determinations have been made as a separate unit, unless the United States District Court for the District of Columbia in an action for a declaratory judgment brought by such State or subdivision against the United States has determined that no such test or device has been used during the five years preceding the filing of the action for the purpose or with the effect of denying or abridging the right to vote on account of race or color: *Provided*, That no such declaratory judgment shall issue with respect to any plaintiff for a period of five years after the entry of a final judgment of any court of the United States, other than the denial of a declaratory judgment under this section, whether entered prior to or after the enactment of this Act, determining that denials or abridgments of the right to vote on account of race or color through the use of such tests or devices have occurred anywhere in the territory of such plaintiff.

An action pursuant to this subsection shall be heard and determined by a court of three judges in accordance with the provisions of section 2284 of title 28 of the United States Code and any appeal shall lie to the Supreme Court. The court shall retain jurisdiction of any action pursuant to this subsection for five years after judgment and shall reopen the action upon motion of the Attorney General alleging that a test or device has been used for the purpose or with the effect of denying or abridging the right to vote on account of race or color.

If the Attorney General determines that he has no reasons to believe that any such test or device has been used during the five years preceding the filing of the action for the purpose or with the effect of denying or abridging the right to vote on account of race or color, he shall consent to the entry of such judgment.

(b) The provisions of subsection (a) shall apply in any State or in any political subdivision of a state which (1) the Attorney General determines maintained on November 1, 1964, any test or device, and with respect to which (2) the Director of the Census determines that less than 50 per centum of the persons of voting age residing therein were registered on November 1, 1964, or that less than 50 per centum of such persons voted in the presidential election of November 1, 1964.

A determination or certification of the Attorney General or of the Director of the Census under this section or under section 6 or section 13 shall not be reviewable in any court and shall be effective upon publication in the Federal Register.

(c) The phrase "test or device" shall mean any requirement that a person as a prerequisite for voting or registration for voting (1) demonstrate the ability to read, write, understand, or interpret any matter, (2) demonstrate any edu-

cational achievement or his knowledge of any particular subject, (3) possess good moral character, or (4) prove his qualifications by the voucher of registered voters or members of any other class.

(d) For purposes of this section no State or political subdivision shall be determined to have engaged in the use of tests or devices for the purpose or with the effect of denying or abridging the right to vote on account of race or color if (1) incidents of such use have been few in number and have been promptly and effectively corrected by State or local action, (2) the continuing effect of such incidents has been eliminated, and (3) there is no reasonable probability of their recurrence in the future.

(e) (1) Congress hereby declares that to secure the rights under the Fourteenth Amendment of persons educated in American-flag schools in which the predominant classroom language was other than English, it is necessary to prohibit the States from conditioning the right to vote of such persons on ability to read, write, understand, or interpret any matter in the English language.

(2) No person who demonstrates that he has successfully completed the sixth primary grade in a public school in, or a private school accredited by, any State or territory, the District of Columbia, or the Commonwealth of Puerto Rico in which the predominant classroom language was other than English, shall be denied the right to vote in any Federal, State, or local election because of his inability to read, write, understand, or interpret any matter in the English language, except that in States in which State law provides that a different level of education is presumptive of literacy, he shall demonstrate that he has successfully completed an equivalent level of education in a public school in, or a private school accredited by, any State or territory, the District of Columbia, or the Commonwealth of Puerto Rico in which the predominant classroom language was other than English.

Sec. 5. Whenever a State or political subdivision with respect to which the prohibitions set forth in section 4(a) are in effect shall enact or seek to administer any voting qualification or prerequisite to voting, or standard, practice, or procedure with respect to voting different from that in force or effect on November 1, 1964, such State or subdivision may institute an action in the United States District Court for the District of Columbia for a declaratory judgment that such qualification, prerequisite, standard, practice, or procedure does not have the purpose and will not have the effect of denying or abridging the right to vote on account of race or color, and unless and until the court enters such judgment no person shall be denied the right to vote for failure to comply with such qualification, prerequisite, standard, practice, or procedure: *Provided*, That such qualification, prerequisite, standard, practice, or procedure may be enforced without such proceeding if the qualification, prerequisite, standard, practice, or procedure has been submitted by the chief legal officer or other appropriate official of such State or subdivision to the Attorney General and the Attorney General has not interposed an objection within sixty days after such submission, except that neither the Attorney General's failure to object nor a declaratory judgment entered under this section shall bar a subsequent action to enjoin enforcement of such qualification, prerequisite, standard, practice, or procedure. Any action under this section shall be heard and determined by a court of three judges in accordance with the provisions of section 2284 of title 28 of the United States Code and any appeal shall lie to the Supreme Court.

Sec. 6. Whenever (a) a court has authorized the appointment of examiners pursuant to the provisions of section 3(a), or (b) unless a declaratory judgment has been rendered under section 4(a), the Attorney General certifies with respect to any political subdivision named in, or included within the scope of, determinations made under section 4(b) that (1) he has received complaints in writing from twenty or more residents of such political subdivision alleging that they have been denied the right to vote under color of law on account of race or color, and that he believes such complaints to be meritorious, or (2) that in his judgment (considering, among other factors, whether the ration of nonwhite persons to white persons registered to vote within such subdivision appears to him to be reasonably attributable to violations of the Fifteenth Amendment or whether substantial evidence exists that bona fide efforts are being made within such subdivision to comply with the fifteenth amendment), the appointment of examiners is otherwise necessary to enforce the guarantees of the Fifteenth Amendment, the Civil Service Commission shall appoint as many examiners for such subdivision as it may deem appropriate to prepare and maintain lists of persons eligible to vote in Federal, State and local elections. Such examiners, hearing officers provided for in section 9(a), and other persons deemed necessary by the Commission to carry out the provisions and purposes of this Act shall be appointed, compensated, and separated without regard to the provisions of any statute administered by the Civil Service Commission, and service under this Act shall not be considered employment for the purposes of any statute administered by the Civil Service Commission, except the provisions of section 9 of the Act of August 2, 1939, as amended (5 U.S.C. 118i), prohibiting partisan political activity: *Provided*, That the Commission is authorized, after consulting the head of the appropriate department or agency, to designate suitable persons in the official service of the United States, with their consent, to serve in these positions. Examiners and hearing officers shall have the power to administer oaths.

Sec. 7. (a) The examiners for each political subdivision shall, at such places as the Civil Service Commission shall by regulation designate, examine applicants concerning their qualifications for voting. An application to an examiner shall be in such form as the Commissioner may require and shall contain allegations that the applicant is not otherwise registered to vote.

(b) Any person whom the examiner finds, in accordance with instructions received under section 9(b), to have the qualifications prescribed by State law not inconsistent with the Constitution and laws of the United States shall promptly be placed on a list of eligible voters. A challenge to such listing may be made in accordance with section 9(a) and shall not be the basis for a prosecution under section 12 of this Act. The examiner shall certify and transmit such list, and any supplements as appropriate, at least once a month, to the offices of the appropriate election officials, with copies to the Attorney General and the attorney general of the State, and any such lists and supplements thereto transmitted during the month shall be available for public inspection on the last business day of the month and in any event not later than the forty-fifth day prior to any election. The appropriate State or local election official shall place such names on the official voting list. Any person whose name appears on the examiner's

FROM
SEGREGATION
TO CIVIL RIGHTS

VOTING RIGHTS
ACT OF 1965

FROM
SEGREGATION
TO CIVIL RIGHTS

VOTING RIGHTS
ACT OF 1965

list shall be entitled and allowed to vote in the election district of his residence unless and until the appropriate election officials shall have been notified that such person has been removed from such list in accordance with subsection (d): *Provided*, That no person shall be entitled to vote in any election by virtue of this Act unless his name shall have been certified and transmitted on such a list to the offices of the appropriate election officials at least forty-five days prior to such election.

(c) The examiner shall issue to each person who name appears on such a list a certificate evidencing his eligibility to vote.

(d) A person whose name appears on such a list shall be removed therefrom by an examiner if (1) such person has been successfully challenged in accordance with the procedure prescribed in section 9, or (2) he has been determined by an examiner to have lost his eligibility to vote under State law not inconsistent with the Constitution and the laws of the United States.

Sec. 8. Whenever an examiner is serving under this Act in any political subdivision, the Civil Service Commission may assign, at the request of the Attorney General, one or more persons, who may be officers of the United States, (1) to enter and attend at any place for holding an election in such subdivision for the purpose of observing whether persons who are entitled to vote are being permitted to vote, and (2) to enter and attend at any place for tabulating the votes cast at any election held in such subdivision for the purpose of observing whether votes cast by persons entitled to vote are being properly tabulated. Such persons so assigned shall report to an examiner appointed for such political subdivision, to the Attorney General, and if the appointment of examiners has been authorized pursuant to section 3(a), to the court.

Sec. 9. (a) Any challenge to a listing on an eligibility list prepared by an examiner shall be heard and determined by a hearing officer appointed by and responsible to the Civil Service Commission and under such rules as the Commission shall by regulation designate, and within ten days after the listing of the challenged person is made available for public inspection, and if supported by (1) the affidavits of at least two persons having personal knowledge of the facts constituting grounds for the challenge, and (2) a certification that a copy of the challenge and affidavits have been served by mail or in person upon the person challenged at his place of residence set out in the application. Such challenge shall be determined within fifteen days after has been filed. A petition for review of the decision of the hearing officer may be filed in the United States court of appeals for the circuit in which the person challenged resides within fifteen days after service of such decision by mail on the person petitioning for review but no decision of a hearing officer shall be reversed unless clearly erroneous. Any person listed shall be entitled and allowed to vote pending final determination by the hearing officer and by the court.

(b) The times, places, procedures, and form for application and listing pursuant to this Act and removal from eligibility lists shall be prescribed by regulations promulgated by the Civil Service Commission and the Commission shall, after consultation with Attorney General, instruct examiners concerning applicable State law not inconsistent with the Constitution and laws of the United States with respect to (1) the qualifications required for listing, and (2) loss of eligibility to vote.

(c) Upon the request of the applicant or challenge or on its own motion the Civil Service Commission shall have the power to require by subpoena the attendance and testimony of witnesses and the production of documentary evidence relating to any matter pending before it under the authority of this section. In case of contumacy or refusal to obey a subpoena, any district court of the United States or the United States court of any territory or possession, or the District Court of the United States for the District of Columbia, within the jurisdiction of which said person guilty of contumacy or refusal to obey is found or resides of is domiciled or transacts business, or has appointed an agent for receipt of service of process, upon application by the Attorney General of the United States shall have jurisdiction to issue to such person an order requiring such person to appear before the Commission or a hearing officer, there to produce pertinent, relevant, and nonprivileged documentary evidence if so ordered, or there to give testimony touching the matter under investigation; and any failure to obey such order of the court may be punished by said court as a contempt thereof.

Sec. 10. (a) The Congress finds that the requirement of the payment of a poll tax as a precondition to voting (i) precludes persons of limited means from voting or imposes unreasonable financial hardship upon such persons as a precondition to their exercise of the franchise, (ii) does not bear a reasonable relationship to any legitimate State interest in the conduct of elections, and (iii) in some areas has the purpose or effect of denying persons the right to vote because of race color. Upon the basis of these findings, Congress declares the constitutional right of citizens to vote is denied or abridged in some areas by the requirement of the payment of a poll tax as a precondition to voting.

(b) In the exercise of the powers of Congress under section 5 of the Fourteenth Amendment and section 2 of the Fifteenth Amendment, the Attorney General is authorized and directed to institute forthwith in the name of the United States such actions, including actions against States or political subdivisions, for declaratory judgment or injunctive relief against the enforcement of any requirement of the payment of a poll tax as a precondition to voting, or substitute therefore enacted after November 1, 1964, as will be necessary to implement the declaration of subsection (a) and the purposes of this section.

(c) The district courts of the United States shall have jurisdiction of such actions which shall be heard and determined by a court of three judges in accordance with the provisions of section 2284 of title 28 of the United States Code and any appeal shall lie to the Supreme Court. It shall be the duty of the judges designates to hear the case to assign the case for hearing at the earliest practicable date, to participate in the hearing and determination thereof, and to cause the case to be in every way expedited.

(d) During the pendency of such actions, and thereafter if the courts, notwithstanding this action by the Congress, should declare the requirement of the payment of a poll tax to be constitutional, no citizen of the United States who is a resident of a State or political subdivision with respect to which determinations have been made under subsection 4(b) and declaratory judgment has not been entered under subsection 4(a), during the first year he becomes otherwise entitled to vote by reason of registration by State or local officials or listing by an examiner, shall be denied the right to vote for failure to pay a poll tax if he tenders payment of such tax for the current year to an examiner or to the appropriate State or local official at least forty-five days prior to election, whether or not such tender would be timely or adequate under State law. An examiner shall have authority to accept such payment from any person authorized by this Act to make an application for listing, and shall issue a receipt for such payment. The examiner shall transmit promptly any such poll tax payment to the office of the State or local official authorized to receive such payment under State law, together with the name and address of the applicant.

Sec. 11. (a) No person acting under color of law shall fail or refuse to permit any person to vote who is entitled to vote under any provision of this Act or is otherwise qualified to vote, or willfully fail or refuse to tabulate, count, and report such person's vote.

(b) No person, whether acting under color of law or otherwise, shall intimidate, threaten, or coerce, or attempt to intimidate, threaten, or coerce any person for urging or aiding any person to vote or attempt to vote, or intimidate, threaten, or coerce any person for exercising any powers or duties under section 3(a), 6, 8, 9, 10, or 12(e).

(c) Whoever knowingly or willfully gives false information as to his name, address, or period of residence in the voting district for the purpose of establishing his eligibility to register or vote, or conspires with another individual for the purpose of encouraging his false registration to vote or illegal voting, or pays or offers to pay or accepts payment either for registration to vote or for voting shall be fined not more than $10,000 or imprisoned not more than five years, or both: *Provided, however,* That this provision shall be applicable only to general, special, or primary elections held solely or in part for the purpose of selecting or electing any candidate for the office of President, Vice President, presidential elector, Member of the United States Senate, Member of the United States House of Representatives, or Delegates or Commissioners from the territories or possessions, or Resident Commissioner of the Commonwealth of Puerto Rico.

(d) Whoever, in any matter within the jurisdiction of an examiner or hearing officer knowingly and willfully falsifies or conceals a material fact, or makes any false, fictitious, or fraudulent statements or representations, or makes or uses any false writing or document knowing the same be fined not more than $10,000 or imprisoned not more than five years, or both.

Sec. 12. (a) Whoever shall deprive or attempt to deprive any person of any right secured by section 2, 3, 4, 5, 7, or 10 or shall violate section 11(a) or (b), shall be fined not more than $5,000, or imprisoned not more than five years, or both.

(b) Whoever, within a year following an election in a political subdivision in which an examiner has been appointed (1) destroys, defaces, mutilates, or otherwise alters the marking of a paper ballot which has been cast in such election, or (2) alters any official record of voting in such election tabulated from a voting machine or otherwise, shall be fined not more than $5,000, or imprisoned not more than five years, or both.

(c) Whoever conspires to violate the provisions of subsection (a) or (b) of this section, or interface with any right secured by section 2, 3, 4, 5, 7, 10, or 11(a) or (b) shall be fined not more than $5,000, or imprisoned not more than five years, or both.

(d) Whenever any person has engaged or there are reasonable grounds to believe that any person is about to engage in any act or practice prohibited by section 2, 3, 4, 5, 7, 10, 11, or subsection (b) of this section, the Attorney General may institute for the United States, or in the name of the United States, an action for preventive relief, including an application for a temporary or permanent injunction, restraining order, or other order, and including an order directed to the State and State or local election officials to require them (1) to permit persons listed under this Act to vote and (2) to count such votes.

(e) Whenever in any political subdivision in which there are examiners appointed pursuant to this Act any persons allege to such an examiner within forty-eight hours after the closing of the polls that notwithstanding (1) their listing under this Act or registration by an appropriate election official and (2) their eligibility to vote, they have not been permitted to vote in such election, the examiner shall forthwith notify then Attorney General may forthwith file with the district court and application for an order providing for the marking, casting, and counting of the ballots of such persons and requiring the inclusion of their votes in the total vote before the results of such election shall be deemed final and any force or effect given there-

to. The district court shall hear and determine such matters immediately after the filing of such application. The remedy provided in this subsection shall not preclude any remedy available under State of Federal law.

(f) The district courts of the United States shall have jurisdiction of proceedings instituted pursuant to this section and shall exercise the same without regard to whether a person asserting rights under the provisions of this Act shall have exhausted any administrative or other remedies that may be provided by law.

Sec. 13. Listing procedures shall be terminated in any political subdivision of any State (a) with respect to examiners appointed pursuant to clause (b) of section 6 whenever the Attorney General notifies the Civil Service Commission, or whether the District Court for the District of Columbia determines in an action for declaratory judgment brought by any political subdivision with respect to which the Director of the Census has determined that more than 50 per centum of the nonwhite persons of voting age residing therein are registered to vote, (1) that all persons listed by an examiner for such subdivision have been placed on the appropriate voting registration roll, and (2) that there is no longer reasonable cause to believe that persons will be deprived of or denied the right to vote on account of race or color in such subdivision, and (b), with respect to examiners appointed pursuant to section 3(a), upon order of the authorizing court. A political subdivision may petition the Attorney General for the termination of listing procedures under clause (a) of this section, and may petition the Attorney General to request the Director of the Census to take such survey or census as may be appropriate for the making of the determination provided for in this section. The District Court for the District of Columbia shall have jurisdiction to require such survey or census to be made by the Director of the Census and it shall require him to do so if it deems the Attorney General's refusal to request such survey or census to be arbitrary or unreasonable.

Sec. 14. (a) All cases of criminal contempt arising under the provisions of this Act shall be governed by section 151 of the Civil Rights Act of 1957 (42 U.S.C. 1995).

(b) No court other than the District Court for the District of Columbia or a court of appeals in any proceeding under section 9 shall have jurisdiction to issue any declaratory judgment pursuant to section 4 or section 5 or any restraining order or temporary or permanent injunction against the execution or enforcement of any provision of this Act or any action of any Federal officer or employee pursuant hereto.

(c) (1) The terms "vote" or "voting" shall include all action necessary to make a vote effective in any primary, special, or general election, including, but not limited to, registration, listing pursuant to this Act, or other action required by law prerequisite to voting, casting a ballot, and having such ballot counted properly and included in the appropriate totals of votes cast with respect to candidates for public or party office and propositions for which votes are received in an election.

(2) The term "political subdivision" shall mean any county or parish, except that where registration for voting is not conducted under the supervision of a county or parish, the term shall include any other subdivision of a State which conducts registration for voting.

(d) In any action for a declaratory judgment brought pursuant to section 4 or section 5 of this Act, subpoenas for witnesses who are required to attend the District Court for the District of Columbia may be served in any judicial district of the United States: *Provided*, That no writ of subpoena shall issue for witnesses without the District of Columbia at a greater distance than one hundred miles from the place of holding court without the permission of the District Court for the District of Columbia being first upon proper application and cause shown.

Sec. 15. Section 2004 of the Revised Statutes (42 U.S.C. 1971),[1] as amended by section 131 of the Civil Rights Act of 1957 (71 Stat. 637), and

---

[1] 42 U.S.C.A. § 1971.

amended by section 601 of the Civil Rights Act of 1960 (74 Stat. 90), and as further amended by section 101 of the Civil Rights Act of 1964 (78 Stat. 241), is further amended as follows:

(a) Delete the word "Federal" wherever it appears in subsections (a) and (c);

(b) Repeal subsection (f) and designate the present subsections (g) and (h) as (f) and (g), respectively.

Sec. 16. The Attorney General and the Secretary of Defense, jointly, shall make a full and complete study to determine whether, under the laws or practices of any State or States, there are preconditions to voting, which might tend to result in discrimination against citizens serving in the Armed Forces of the United States seeking to vote. Such officials shall, jointly, make a report to the Congress not later than June 30, 1966, containing the results of such study, together with a list of any States in which such preconditions exist, and shall include in such report such recommendations for legislation as they deem advisable to prevent discrimination in voting against citizens serving in the Armed Forces of the United States.

Sec. 17. Nothing in this Act shall be construed to deny, impair, or otherwise adversely affect the right to vote of any person registered to vote under the law of any State or political subdivision.

Sec. 18. There are hereby authorized to be appropriate such sums as are necessary to carry out the provisions of this Act.

Sec. 19. If any provision of this Act or the application thereof to any person or circumstances is held invalid, the remainder of the Act and the application of the provision to other persons not similarly situated or to other circumstances shall not be not be affected thereby.

Approved August 6, 1965.

WOMEN'S RIGHTS

The women's rights movement in the United States began in the nineteenth century when some women reformers demanded the right to vote and the same legal rights as men. The participation of women in the abolitionist movement played a crucial role in crystallizing their dissatisfaction with the lack of rights accorded to females. Some, like Lucy Stone, saw parallels between women and slaves: both were expected to be passive, cooperative, and obedient. In addition, the legal status of both slaves and women was unequal to that of white men. Sojourner Truth, an African American evangelist and reformer, also recognized this connection and soon was speaking before women's rights groups, advocating the right to vote.

After the Civil War ended in 1865, many of these women reformers devoted their energies to gaining women's suffrage. Susan B. Anthony, Elizabeth Cady Stanton, and Lucy Stone were the best-known suffrage leaders. Anthony and Stanton fought for a federal constitutional amendment granting women the right to vote, while Stone and her followers sought amendments in state constitutions. The Nineteenth Amendment to the U.S. Constitution, ratified in 1920, finally gave women the right to vote.

During the nineteenth century, women encountered rigid cultural and legal barriers when they sought to enter business and the professions. Women who married had traditionally suffered a loss of legal status, as the identity of the wife merged into that of the husband. He was a legal person but she was not. A married woman could not sign a contract without the signature of her husband. Upon marriage, he received all her personal property and managed all property that she owned. In return, the husband was obliged to support his wife and children. By the 1850s women's rights supporters had convinced many state legislatures to pass married women's separate property acts. These acts gave women the legal right to retain ownership and control of property they brought into the marriage.

Women also had difficulty entering the professions, because the cultural stereotypes of the period dictated that the proper role of an adult woman was to be a wife and mother. According to the prevailing viewpoint, the rough-and-tumble world of business and the professions was no place for women, who had more delicate natures than men. In addition, the male-dominated world believed women to be intellectually inferior and fundamentally incapable of handling the demands of white-collar jobs and the professions. This view was reinforced by the decision in *Bradwell v. Illinois,* 83 U.S. 130, 21 L. Ed. 442 (1872), when the U.S. Supreme Court ruled that it was not unconstitutional for Illinois to deny a woman a license to practice law solely on the basis of her gender.

The quest for women's rights reignited in the 1960s, fueled by the participation of women in the civil rights movement. Just as in the nineteenth century, women compared their legal, economic, and social status with that of persons of color and found similar problems. The National Organization for Women was established in 1966. It quickly became the nation's largest and most influential feminist organization, but in the process it stimulated opponents of modern feminism to organize as well.

Reproductive rights became a key issue for women in the 1960s. At that time the distribution of birth control devices and information was illegal in many states. In *Griswold v. Connecticut,* 381 U.S. 479, 85 S. Ct. 1678, 14 L. Ed. 2d 510 (1965), the Supreme Court struck down a Connecticut law that made the sale and possession of birth control devices a misdemeanor. More importantly, the Court declared that the Constitution contained a right to privacy. In *Eisenstadt v. Baird,* 405 U.S. 438, 92 S. Ct. 1029, 31 L. Ed. 2d 349 (1972), the Court established that the right of privacy is an individual right and is not limited to married couples.

The *Griswold* and *Eisenstadt* decisions paved the way for *Roe v. Wade,* 410 U.S. 113, 93 S. Ct. 705, 35 L. Ed. 2d 147 (1973), which struck down a Texas law that banned abortions. Justice Harry A. Blackmun concluded that the right to privacy "is broad enough to encompass a woman's decision whether or not to terminate her pregnancy." The *Roe* decision provided women with the right to continue or terminate a pregnancy, at least up to the point of viability. By the 1980s, however, a more conservative Supreme Court began upholding state laws that placed restrictions on this right.

WOMEN'S RIGHTS

SENECA FALLS DECLARATION OF SENTIMENTS

The feminist political movement began in the nineteenth century with the call for female suffrage. At a convention in Seneca Falls, New York, in July 1848, a group of 240 people (200 women and 40 men) drafted and approved the Declaration of Sentiments. Among those present was Frederick Douglass, a former slave who was now an abolitionist leader. The convention was organized by Lucretia Mott and Elizabeth Cady Stanton, two Quakers whose concern for women's rights was aroused when Mott was denied a seat at an international anti-slavery meeting in London because she was a woman. The delegates adopted a statement of women's rights, deliberately modeled on the Declaration of Independence, as well as a series of resolutions calling for women's suffrage and the reform of marital and property laws that kept women in an inferior status.

—⚍—

Seneca Falls Declaration of Sentiments

When, in the course of human events, it becomes necessary for one portion of the family of man to assume among the people of the earth a position different from that which they have hitherto occupied, but one to which the laws of nature and of nature's God entitle them, a decent respect to the opinions of mankind requires that they should declare the causes that impel them to such a course.

We hold these truths to be self-evident: that all men and women are created equal; that they are endowed by their Creator with certain inalienable rights; that among these are life, liberty, and the pursuit of happiness; that to secure these rights governments are instituted, deriving their just powers from the consent of the governed. Whenever any form of government becomes destructive of these ends, it is the right of those who suffer from it to refuse allegiance to it, and to insist upon the institution of a new government, laying its foundation on such principles, and organizing its powers in such form, as to them shall seem most likely to effect their safety and happiness. Prudence, indeed, will dictate that governments long established should not be changed for light and transient causes; and accordingly all experience hath shown that mankind are more disposed to suffer, while evils are sufferable, than to right themselves by abolishing the forms to which they were accustomed. But when a long train of abuses and usurpations, pursuing invariably the same object evinces a design to reduce them under absolute despotism, it is their duty to throw off such government, and to provide new guards for their future security. Such has been the patient sufferance of the women under this government, and such is now the necessity which constrains them to demand the equal station to which they are entitled.

The history of mankind is a history of repeated injuries and usurpations on the part of man toward woman, having in direct object the establishment of an absolute tyranny over her. To prove this, let facts be submitted to a candid world.

He has never permitted her to exercise her inalienable right to the elective franchise.

He has compelled her to submit to laws, in the formation of which she had no voice.

He has withheld from her rights which are given to the most ignorant and degraded men—both natives and foreigners.

Having deprived her of this first right of a citizen, the elective franchise, thereby leaving her without representation in the halls of legislation, he has oppressed her on all sides.

He has made her, if married, in the eye of the law, civilly dead.

He has taken from her all right in property, even to the wages she earns.

He has made her, morally, an irresponsible being, as she can commit many crimes with impunity, provided they be done in the presence of her husband. In the covenant of marriage, she is compelled to promise obedience to her husband, he becoming, to all intents and purposes, her master—the law giving him power to deprive her of her liberty, and to administer chastisement.

He has so framed the laws of divorce, as to what shall be the proper causes, and in case of separation, to whom the guardianship of the children shall be given, as to be wholly regardless of the happiness of women—the law, in all cases, going upon a false supposition of the supremacy of man, and giving all power into his hands.

After depriving her of all rights as a married woman, if single, and the owner of property, he has taxed her to support a government which recognizes her only when her property can be made profitable to it.

He has monopolized nearly all the profitable employments, and from those she is permitted to follow, she receives but a scanty remuneration. He closes against her all the avenues to

wealth and distinction which he considers most honorable to himself. As a teacher of theology, medicine, or law, she is not known.

He has denied her the facilities for obtaining a thorough education, all colleges being closed against her.

He allows her in Church, as well as State, but a subordinate position, claiming Apostolic authority for her exclusion from the ministry, and, with some exceptions, from any public participation in the affairs of the Church.

He has created a false public sentiment by giving to the world a different code of morals for men and women, by which moral delinquencies which exclude women from society, are not only tolerated, but deemed of little account in man.

He has usurped the prerogative of Jehovah himself, claiming it as his right to assign for her a sphere of action, when that belongs to her conscience and to her God.

He has endeavored, in every way that he could, to destroy her confidence in her own powers, to lessen her self-respect, and to make her willing to lead a dependent and abject life.

Now, in view of this entire disfranchisement of one-half the people of this country, their social and religious degradation—in view of the unjust laws above mentioned, and because women do feel themselves aggrieved, oppressed, and fraudulently deprived of their most sacred rights, we insist that they have immediate admission to all the rights and privileges which belong to them as citizens of the United States.

In entering upon the great work before us, we anticipate no small amount of misconception, misrepresentation, and ridicule; but we shall use every instrumentality within our power to effect our object. We shall employ agents, circulate tracts, petition the State and National legislatures, and endeavor to enlist the pulpit and the press in our behalf. We hope this Convention will be followed by a series of Conventions embracing every part of the country.

WOMEN'S RIGHTS

SENECA FALLS
DECLARATION
OF SENTIMENTS

WOMEN'S RIGHTS

AIN'T I A WOMAN?

Sojourner Truth, 1851

Sojourner Truth was a nineteenth-century African American evangelist who embraced abolitionism and women's rights. A charismatic speaker, she became one of the best-known abolitionists of her day. Born a slave and given the name Isabella Baumfree, she was freed in 1828 when a New York law abolished slavery within the state.

In 1843 she had a religious experience and came to believe that God had commanded her to travel beyond New York to spread the Christian gospel. She took the name Sojourner Truth and traveled throughout the eastern states as an evangelist. Truth soon became acquainted with the abolitionist movement and its leaders. She adopted their message, speaking out against slavery. Her speaking tours expanded as abolitionists realized her effectiveness as a lecturer. Though illiterate, she dictated her life story, *The Narrative of Sojourner Truth*, and sold the book at her lectures as a means of supporting herself.

In the early 1850s, she met leaders of the emerging women's rights movement, most notably Lucretia Mott. Truth recognized the connection between the inferior legal status of African Americans and women in general. Her most famous speech, "Ain't I a Woman?" first given in 1851, challenged cultural beliefs, including the natural inferiority of women, and biblical justifications for the second-class status of women.

Ain't I a Woman?

Well, children, where there is so much racket there must be something out of kilter. I think that 'twixt the negroes of the South and the women at the North, all talking about rights, the white men will be in a fix pretty soon. But what's all this here talking about?

That man over there says that women need to be helped into carriages, and lifted over ditches, and to have the best place everywhere. Nobody ever helps me into carriages, or over mud-puddles, or gives me any best place! And ain't I a woman? Look at me! Look at my arm! I have ploughed and planted, and gathered into barns, and no man could head me! And ain't I a woman? I could work as much and eat as much as a man—when I could get it—and bear the lash as well! And ain't I a woman? I have borne thirteen children, and seen most all sold off to slavery, and when I cried out with my mother's grief, none but Jesus heard me! And ain't I a woman?

Then they talk about this thing in the head; what's this they call it? [member of audience whispers, "intellect"] That's it, honey. What's that got to do with women's rights or negroes' rights? If my cup won't hold but a pint, and yours holds a quart, wouldn't you be mean not to let me have my little half measure full?

Then that little man in black there, he says women can't have as much rights as men, 'cause Christ wasn't a woman! Where did your Christ come from? Where did your Christ come from?

From God and a woman! Man had nothing to do with Him.

If the first woman God ever made was strong enough to turn the world upside down all alone, these women together ought to be able to turn it back, and get it right side up again! And now they is asking to do it, the men better let them.

Obliged to you for hearing me, and now old Sojourner ain't got nothing more to say.

WOMEN'S RIGHTS

BRADWELL V. ILLINOIS

Myra Bradwell's efforts to gain admission to the Illinois bar resulted in a Supreme Court decision. Bradwell had married a lawyer and read the law with her husband. In 1869 she passed the Illinois bar examination but was refused admission to the bar. She appealed to the Supreme Court, arguing that the Fourteenth Amendment's Equal Protection Clause prevented the state from imposing admission requirements based on gender.

In *Bradwell v. Illinois* in 1872, the Court rejected her constitutional argument. In a concurring opinion that revealed the cultural underpinnings of the period, Justice Joseph P. Bradley supported the Illinois Supreme Court's denial of Bradwell's application to practice law in the state. Bradley articulated the widely held view that the "natural and proper timidity and delicacy which belongs to the female sex evidently unfits it for many of the occupations of civil life." He further concluded that the "paramount destiny and mission of woman is to fulfill the noble and benign offices of wife and mother. This is the law of the Creator."

—⁓—

Myra Bradwell, Plff. in Err., v. State of Illinois

(See S. C. 16 Wall. 130–142.)

* 1. The supreme court of Illinois having refused to grant to plaintiff a license to practice

_____

*Headnotes by Mr. Justice Miller.

law in the courts of that state, on the ground that females are not eligible under the laws of that state, such a decision violates no provision of the Federal Constitution.

2. The 2d section of the 4th article is inapplicable, because plaintiff is a citizen of the state whose action she complains, and that section only other states, in that state.

3. Nor is the right to practice law in the state courts a privileges and immunity of a citizen of the United States within the meaning of the 1st section of the 14th article of Amendment of the Constitution of the United States.

4. The power of a state to prescribe the qualifications for admissions to the bar of its own courts, is unaffected by the 14th Amendment, and this court cannot inquire into the reasonableness or properly of the rules it may be prescribe.

[No. 12.]

Argued Jan. 18, 1873. Decided Apr. 15, 1873.

In Error to the Supreme Court of the State of Illinois.

The petition in this case was filed in the court below, by the plaintiff in error, for license to practice law. The said application having been denied, the petitioner sued out this writ of error.

The case is stated by the court.

Mr. Matt. H. Carpenter, for plaintiff in error:

The plaintiff in error is a married woman, of full age, a citizen of the United States, and of the state of Illinois; was ascertained and certified to be duly qualified in respect to character and attainments; but was denied admission to the bar for the sole reason that she was a married woman. This is the error relied upon to reverse the proceedings below.

By the rules of this court, no person can be admitted to practice at the bar without service for a fixed term in the highest court of the state in which such person resides. Consequently a denial of admission in the highest court of the state is an insurmountable obstacle to admission to the bar of this court.

This record, therefore, presents the broad question whether a married woman, being a citizen of the United States and of a state, and possessing the necessary qualifications, is entitled by the Constitution of the United States to be admitted to practice as an attorney and counselor at law in the courts of the state in which she resides. This is a question, not taste, propriety or politeness, but of civil right.

I have more faith in female suffrage, to reform the abuse of our election system in the large cities, than I have in the penal election laws to be enforced by soldiers and marines. Who believes that if ladies were admitted to seats in Congress, or upon the bench, or were participating in discussions at the bar, such proceedings would thereby be rendered less refined, or that less regard would be paid to the rights of all?

But whether women should be admitted to right of suffrage is one thing and whether this end has already been accomplished is quite another. The 14th Amendment forbids the states to make or enforce any law which shall abridge the privileges or immunities of a citizen. But whether the right to vote is covered by the phrase "the privileges and immunities" was much discussed under the provisions of the old Constitution; and at least one of the earliest decisions drew a distinction between "privileges and immunities" and political rights. On the other hand, Mr. Justice Washington, in a celebrated case, expressed the opinion that the right to vote and hold office was included in this phrase. But in neither of the cases was this point directly involved, and both opinions are *obiter dicta* in relation to it.

But the 14th and 15th Amendments seem to settle this question against the right of female suffrage. These Amendments seem to recognize the distinction at first pointed out between "privileges and immunities" and the right to vote.

The 14th Amendment declares "All persons born and naturalized in the United States, etc., are citizens of the United States, and of the state wherein they reside." Of course women, as well as men, are included in this provision, and recognized as citizens. This Amendment further decisions: "No state shall make or enforce any law which shall abridge the privileges or immunities of citizens of the United States." If the privileges and immunities of a citizen cannot be abridged, then, of course, the privileges and immunities of all citizens must be the same. The 2d section of this Amendment provides, that

> "representatives shall be apportioned among the several states according to their respective numbers, counting the whole number of persons in each state, excluding Indians, not taxed. But when the right to vote at an election, etc., denied to any of the male inhabitants, being twenty-one years of age, etc., the basis of representation therein shall be reduced in the proportion which the number of such male citizens shall bear to the whole number of male citizens twenty-one years of age in such state."

It cannot be denied that the right or power of a state to exclude a portion of its male citizens from the right to vote is recognized by this 2d section; from which it follows that the right to vote is not one of the privileges and immunities which the 1st section declared shall not be abridged by any state.

The 14th Amendment executes itself in every state of the Union. Whatever are the privileges and immunities of a citizen in the state of New York, such citizen emigrating, carries them with him into any other state of the Union. It utters the will of the United States in every state, and silences every state Constitution, usage or law which conflicts with it. If to be admitted to the bar, on attaining the age and learning required by law, be one of the privileges of a white citizen in the state of New York, it is equally the privilege of a colored citizen in that state; and if in that state, then in any state. If no state may make or enforce any law to abridge the privileges of a citizen, it must follows that the privileges of all citizens are the same.

The 14th and 15th Amendments distinguish between privileges and rights, and it must be confessed that it is paradoxical to say, as the 14th Amendment clearly does, that the privileges of a citizen shall not be abridged, while his right to vote may be. But a judicial construction of the

WOMEN'S RIGHTS

BRADWELL V. ILLINOIS

Constitution is wholly different from a mere exercise is philology. The question is not whether certain words are aptly employed, but the context must be searched to ascertain the sense in which such words were used.

It is evident that there are certain privileges and immunities which belong to a citizen of the United States, as such; otherwise it would be nonsense for the 14th Amendment to prohibit a state from abridging them; and it is equally evident from the 14th Amendment that the right to vote is not one of those privileges. And the question recurs, whether or not admission to the bar, the proper qualification being possessed, is one of the privileges which a state may not deny.

In *Cummings v. Mo.* 4 Wall. 321, 18 L. ed. 362, this court says:

"In France, deprivation or suspension of the civil rights or some of them—and among these the right of voting, of eligibility to office, of taking part in family councils, of being guardian or trustee, of bearing arms, and of teaching or being employed in a school or seminary of learning—are punishments prescribed by her Code.

The theory upon which our political institutions rest is, that all men have certain inalienable rights; that among these are life, liberty, and the pursuit of happiness, all avocations, all honors, all positions are alike open to every one, and that in the protection of these rights are all equal before the law. Any deprivation or extension of any of these rights for past conduct is punishment, and can be in no otherwise defined."

No broader or better enumeration of the privileges which pertain to American citizenship could be given. "Life, liberty, and the pursuit of happiness; and in the pursuit of happiness all avocations, all honors, all positions are alike open to every one; and in the protection of these rights all are equal before the law."

In *Ex parte Garland*, 4 Wall. 378, 18 L. ed. 370, this court says:

"The profession of an attorney and counselor is not, like an office, created by Congress. which depends for its continuance, its powers and its emoluments upon the will of its creator, and the possession of which may be burdened with any conditions not prohibited by the Constitution. Attorneys and counselors are not officers of the United States; they are not elected or appointed in the manner prescribed by the Constitution for the election and appointment of such officers. They are officers of the court admitted as such by its

order. upon evidence of their possessing sufficient legal learning and fair private character; . . . they hold their office during good behavior and can only be deprived of it for misconduct ascertained and declared by the judgment of the court, after opportunity to be heard has been offered." *Ex parte Heyfron*, 7 How. (Miss.) 127; *Fletcher v. Daingerfield*, 20 Cal. 430.

"Their admissions or their exclusion is not the exercise of a mere ministerial power. It is exercise of judicial power, and has been so held in numerous cases."

It is now well settled that the courts in admitting attorneys to and in expelling them from the bar, act judicially, and that such proceedings are subject to review on writ of error or appeal. as the case may be. *In re Cooper*, 22 N. Y. 67, *Strother v, Mo.* 1 Mo. 005; *Ex parte Secombe*, 19 How. 9, 15 L. ed. 565; *Ex parte Garland*, supra.

From these cases the conclusion is irresistible that the profession of the law, like the clerical profession and that of medicine, is an avocation open to every citizen of the United States. And while the legislature may prescribe qualifications for entering upon this pursuit, it cannot, under the guise of fixing qualifications, exclude a class of citizens from admission to the bar. The legislature may say at what age candidates shall be admitted; may elevate or depress the standard of learning required. But a qualification to which a whole class of citizens can never attain is not a regulation of admission to the bar, but is, as to such citizens, a prohibition. For instance, a state legislature could not, in enumerating the qualifications, require the candidate to be a white citizen. I presume it will be admitted that such an act would be void. The only provisions in the Constitution of the United States which secures to colored male citizens the privilege of admission to the bar, or the pursuit of the other ordinary avocations of life is the provision that "No state shall make or enforce any law which shall abridge the privileges or immunities of the citizens." If this provision protects the colored citizen, then it protects every citizen, black or white, male or female.

Why may a colored citizen buy, hold and sell land in any state of the Union? Because he is a citizen of the United States, and that is one of the privileges of a citizen. Why may a colored citizen be admitted to the bar? Because he is a citizen, and that is one of the avocations open to every citizen, and no state can abridge his right to pursue it. Certainly no other reason can be given.

Now, let us come to the case of Myra Bradwell. She is a citizen of the United States and of the state of Illinois, residing therein. She has been judicially ascertained to be of full age, and to possess the requisite character and learning. Indeed, the court below in its opinion found in the record says: "Of the ample qualifications of the applicant we have no doubt." Still, admission to the bar was denied the petitioner; not upon the ground that she was not a citizen; not for want of age or qualification; not because the profession of the law is not one of those avocations which are open to every American citizen as a matter of right, upon complying with the reasonable regulations prescribed by the legislature; but upon the sole ground that inconvenience would result from permitting her to enjoy her legal rights in this, to wit: that her clients might have difficulty in enforcing the contracts they might make with her as their attorney, because of her being a married woman.

Now, with entire respect to that court, it is submitted that this argument *ab inconvenienti*, which might have been urged with whatever force belongs to it against adopting the 14th Amendment in the full and proper operation, now that it has been adopted.

I maintain that the 14th Amendment opens to every citizen of the United States, male or female, black or white, married or single, the honorable professions as well as the servile employments of life; and that no citizen can be excluded from any one of them. Intelligence, integrity and honor are the only qualifications that can be prescribed as conditions precedent to an entry upon any honorable pursuit or profitable avocation, and all the privileges and immunities which I vindicate to a colored citizen. I vindicate to our mothers, our sisters and our daughters.

Of a bar composed of men and women of equal integrity and learning, women might be more or less frequently retained as the taste or judgment of clients might dictate; but the broad shield of the Constitution is over all, and protects each in that measure of success which his or her individual merits may secure.

(No counsel appeared for the defendant in error.)

Mr. Justice Miller delivered the opinion of the court:

The plaintiff in error, residing in the state of Illinois, made application to the judges of the supreme court of that state for a license to practice law. She accompanied her petition with the usual certificate from an inferior court, of her good character, and that on due examination she had been found to possess the requisite qualifications. Pending this application, she also filed an affidavit to the effect "that she was born in the state of Vermont; that she was (had been) a citizen of that state; that she is now a citizen of the United States, and has been for many years past a resident of the city of Chicago in the state of Illinois." And with this affidavit she also filed a paper claiming that under the foregoing facts she was entitled to the license paid for, by virtue of the 2d section of the 4th article of the Constitution of the United States, and of the 14th article of Amendment of that instrument.

The statute of Illinois on this subject enacts that no person shall be permitted to practice as an attorney or counselor at law, or the commence, conduct, or defend any action, suit, or plaint, in which he is not a party concerned, in any court of record within this state, either by using or subscribing his own name or the name of any other person, without having previously obtained a license for that purpose from two justices of the supreme court, which license shall constitute the person receiving the same an attorney and counselor at law, and shall authorize him to appear in all the courts of record within this state and there to practice as an attorney and counselor at law according to the laws and customs thereof.

The supreme court denied the application apparently upon the ground that it was a woman who made it.

The record is not very perfect, but it may be fairly taken that the plaintiff asserted her right to a license on the grounds, among others, that she was a citizen of the United States, and that having been a citizen of Vermont at one time, she was, in the state of Illinois, entitled to any right granted to citizens of the latter state.

The court having overruled these claims of right founded on the clauses of the Federal Constitution before referred to, those propositions may be considered as properly before this court.

As regards the provision of the Constitution that citizens of each state shall be entitled to all the privileges and immunities of citizens in the several states, the plaintiff in her affidavit has stated very clearly a case to which it is inapplicable.

The protection designed by that clause, as has been repeatedly held, has no application to a citizen of the state whose laws are complained of. If the plaintiff was a citizen of the state of Illinois, that provision of the Constitution gave her no protection against its courts or it legislation.

The plaintiff seems to have seen this difficulty, and attempts to avoid it by stating that she was born in Vermont.

While she remained in Vermont that circumstance made her a citizen of that state. But she states, at the same time, that she is a citizen of the United States, and that she is now, and has been for many years past, a resident of Chicago, in the state of Illinois.

The 14th Amendment declares that citizens of the United States are citizens of the state within which they reside; therefore the plaintiff was, at the time of making her application, a citizen of the United States and a citizen of the state of Illinois.

We do not here mean to say that there may not be a temporary residence in one state, with intent to return to another, which will not create citizenship in the former. But plaintiff states nothing to take her case out of the definition of citizenship of a state as defined by the 1st section of the 14th Amendment.

In regard to that Amendment counsel for the plaintiff in this court truly says that there are certain privileges and immunities which belong to a citizen in the United States as such; otherwise it would be nonsense for the 14th Amendment to prohibit a state from abridging them, and he proceeds to argue that admission to the bar of a state, of a person who possesses the requisite learning and character, is one of those which a state may not deny.

In this latter proposition we are not able to concur with counsel. We agree with him that there are privileges and immunities belonging to citizens of the United States, in that relation and character, and that it is these and these alone which a state is forbidden to abridge. But the right to admission to practice in the courts of a state is not one of them. This right in no sense depends on citizenship of the United States. It has not, as far as we know, ever been made in any state or in any case to depend on citizenship at all. Certainly many prominent and distinguished lawyers have been admitted to practice, both in the state and Federal courts, who were not citizens of the United States or of any state. But, on whatever basis this right may be placed, so far as it can have any relation to citizenship at all, it would seem that, as to the courts of a state, it would relate to citizenship of that state, and as to Federal courts, it would relate to citizenship of the United States.

The opinion just delivered in the *Slaughter-House Cases*, from Louisiana, *ante*, 394, renders elaborate argument in the present case unnecessary; for, unless we are wholly and radically mistaken in the principles on which those cases are decided, the right to control and regulate the granting of license to practice law in the courts of a state is one of those powers which are not transferred for its protection to the Federal government, and its exercise is in no manner governed or controlled by citizenship of the United States in the partly seeking such license.

It is unnecessary to repeat the argument on which the judgment in those cases is founded. It is sufficient to say, they are conclusive of the present case.

The judgment of the State Court is, therefore, affirmed.

Mr. Justice Bradley:

I concur in the judgment of the court in this case, by which the judgment of the supreme court of Illinois is affirmed, but not for reason specified in the opinion just read.

The claim of the plaintiff, who is a married woman, to be admitted to practice as an attorney and counselor at law, is based upon the supposed right of every person, man or woman, to engage in any lawful employment for a livelihood. The supreme court of Illinois denied the application on the ground that, by the common law, which is the basis of the laws of Illinois, only men were admitted to the bar, and the legislature had not made any change in this respect, but had simply provided that no person should be submitted to practice as attorney or counselor without having previously obtained a license for that purpose from two justices of the supreme court, and that no person should receive a license without first obtaining a certificate from the court of some county of his good moral character. In other respects it was left to the discretion of the court to establish the rules by which admission to the profession should be determined. The court, however, regarded itself as bound by at least two limitations. One was that it should establish such terms of admission as would promote the proper administration of justice, and the other that it should not admit any persons or class of person not intended by the legislature to be admitted, even though not expressly excluded by statute. In view of this latter limitation the court felt compelled to deny the application of females to be admitted as members of the bar. Being contrary to the rules of the common law and the usages of Westminister Hall from time immemorial, it could not be supposed that the legislature had intended to adopt any different rule.

The claim that, under the 14th Amendment of the Constitution, which declares that no state shall make or enforce any law which shall abridge the privileges and immunities of citizens of the United States, and the statute law of Illinois, or the common law prevailing in that state, can no longer be set up as a barrier against the right of females to pursue any lawful employment for a livelihood (the practice of law included), assumes that it is one of the privileges and immunities of women as citizens to engage in any and every profession, occupation or employment in civil life.

It certainly cannot be affirmed, as a historical fact, that this has ever been established as one of the fundamental privileges and immunities of the sex. On the contrary, the civil law, as well as nature herself, has always recognized a wide difference in the respective spheres and destinies of man and woman. Man is, or should be, woman's protector and defender. The natural and proper timidity and delicacy which belongs to the female sex evidently unfits it for many of the occupations of civil life. The constitution of the family organization, which is founded in the divine ordinance, as well as in the nature of things, indicates the domestic sphere as that which properly belongs to the domain and functions of womanhood. The harmony, not to say identity, of interests and views which belong or should belong to the family institution, is repugnant to the idea of a woman adopting a distinct and independent career from that of her husband. So firmly fixed was this sentiment in the founders of the common law that it became a maxim of that system of jurisprudence that a woman had no legal existence separate from her husband, who was regarded as her head and representative in the social state; and, notwithstanding some recent modifications of this civil status, many of the special rules of the law flowing from and dependent upon this cardinal principle still exist in full force in most states. One of these is, that a married woman is incapable, without her husband's consent, of making contracts which shall be binding on her or him. This very incapacity was one circumstance which the supreme court of Illinois deemed important in rendering a married woman incompetent fully to perform the duties and trusts that belong to the office of an attorney and counselor.

It is true that many women are unmarried and not affected by any of the duties, complications, and incapacities arising out of the married state, but these are exceptions to the general rule. The paramount destiny and mission of woman are to fulfill the noble and benign offices of wife and mother. This is the law of the Creator. And the rules of civil society must be adapted to the general constitution of things, and cannot be based upon exceptional cases.

The humane movements of modern society, which have for their object the multiplication of avenues for woman's advancement, and of occupation adapted to her condition and sex, have my heartiest concurrence. But I am prepared to say that is one of her fundamental rights and privileges to be admitted into every office and position. It is not every citizen of every calling and position. It is the prerogative of the legislator to prescribe regulations founded on nature, reason, and experience for the due admission of qualified persons to professions and callings demanding special skill and confidence. This fairly belongs to the police power of the state; and, in my opinion, in view of the peculiar characteristics, destiny, and mission of woman, it is within the province of the legislature to ordain what offices, positions, and callings shall be filled and discharged by men, and shall receive the benefit of those energies and responsibilities, and that decision and firmness which presumed to predominate in the sterner sex.

For these reasons I think that the laws of Illinois now complained of are not obnoxious to the charge of abridging any of the privileges and immunities of citizens of the United States.

Mr. Justice Field and Mr. Justice Swayne; We concur in the opinion of Mr. Justice Bradley.

Dissenting, Mr. Chief Justice Chase.

WOMEN'S RIGHTS

NATIONAL ORGANIZATION FOR WOMEN STATEMENT OF PURPOSE

The establishment of the National Organization for Women (NOW) in 1966 signaled the growing strength of modern feminism. Initially, NOW directed most of its resources toward the needs of working women. It attacked the exclusion of women from the professions, politics, and other areas of society because of outdated male views about women. It also denounced and attacked legal and economic discrimination, such as bank practices that denied married women credit in their own names.

NOW's Statement of Purpose defined the mainstream of the modern feminist movement. Though many women and men refused to be labeled "feminists," they agreed with NOW's basic demand that women in the workforce be treated equally with men, receive equal pay for equal work, and enjoy access to jobs and promotions to which their talents entitled them.

—w—

National Organization for Women Statement of Purpose

We, men and women who hereby constitute ourselves as the National Organization for Women, believe that the time has come for a new movement toward true equality for all women in America, and toward a fully equal partnership of the sexes, as part of the worldwide revolution of human rights now taking place within and beyond our national borders.

The purpose of NOW is to take action to bring women into full participation in the mainstream of American society now, exercising all the privileges and responsibilities thereof in truly equal partnership with men.

We believe the time has come to move beyond the abstract argument, discussion and symposia over the status and special nature of women which has raged in America in recent years; the time has come to confront, with concrete action, the conditions that now prevent women from enjoying the equality of opportunity and freedom of choice which is their right as individual Americans, and as human beings.

NOW is dedicated to the proposition that women first and foremost, are human beings, who, like all other people in our society, must have the chance to develop their fullest human potential. We believe that women can achieve such equality only by accepting to the full the challenges and responsibilities they share with all other people in our society, as part of the decision-making mainstream of American political, economic and social life.

We organize to initiate or support action, nationally or in any part of this nation, by individuals or organizations, to break through the silken curtain of prejudice and discrimination against women in government, industry, the professions, the churches, the political parties, the judiciary, the labor unions, in education, sci-

Reprinted by permission of the National Organization for Women. This is a historical document (1966) and does not reflect the current language or priorities of the organization.

ence, medicine, law, religion and every other field of importance in American society.... .

There is no civil rights movement to speak for women, as there has been for Negroes and other victims of discrimination. The National Organization for Women must therefore begin to speak.

WE BELIEVE that the power of American law, and the protection guaranteed by the U.S. Constitution to the civil rights of all individuals, must be effectively applied and enforced to isolate and remove patterns of sex discrimination, to ensure equality of opportunity in employment and education, and equality of civil and political rights and responsibilities on behalf of women, as well as for Negroes and other deprived groups.

We realize that women's problems are linked to many broader questions of social justice; their solution will require concerted action by many groups. Therefore, convinced that human rights for all are indivisible, we expect to give active support to the common cause of equal rights for all those who suffer discrimination and deprivation, and we call upon other organizations committed to such goals to support our efforts toward equality for women.

WE DO NOT ACCEPT the token appointment of a few women to high-level positions in government and industry as a substitute for a serious continuing effort to recruit and advance women according to their individual abilities. To this end, we urge American government and industry to mobilize the same resources of ingenuity and command with which they have solved problems of far greater difficulty than those now impeding the progress of women.

WE BELIEVE that this nation has a capacity at least as great as other nations, to innovate new social institutions which will enable women to enjoy true equality of opportunity and responsibility in society, without conflict with their responsibilities as mothers and homemakers. In such innovations, America does not lead the Western world, but lags by decades behind many European countries. We do not accept the traditional assumption that a woman has to choose between marriage and motherhood, on the one hand, and serious participation in industry or the professions on the other. We question the present expectation that all normal women will retire from job or profession for ten or fifteen years, to devote their full time to raising chil-

dren, only to reenter the job market at a relatively minor level. This, in itself, is a deterrent to the aspirations of women, to their acceptance into management or professional training courses, and to the very possibility of equality of opportunity or real choice, for all but a few women. Above all, we reject the assumption that these problems are the unique responsibility of each individual woman, rather than a basic social dilemma which society must solve. True equality of opportunity and freedom of choice for women requires such practical and possible innovations as a nationwide network of child-care centers, which will make it unnecessary for women to retire completely from society until their children are grown, and national programs to provide retraining for women who have chosen to care for their own children full time.

WE BELIEVE that it is as essential for every girl to be educated to her full potential of human ability as it is for every boy—with the knowledge that such education is the key to effective participation in today's economy and that, for a girl as for a boy, education can only be serious where there is expectation that it will be used in society. We believe that American educators are capable of devising means of imparting such expectations to girl students. Moreover, we consider the decline in the proportion of women receiving higher and professional education to be evidence of discrimination. This discrimination may take the form of quotas against the admission of women to colleges and professional schools; lack of encouragement by parents, counselors and educators; denial of loans or fellowships; or the traditional or arbitrary procedures in graduate and professional training geared in terms of men, which inadvertently discriminate against women. We believe that the same serious attention must be given to high school dropouts who are girls as to boys.

WE REJECT the current assumptions that a man must carry the sole burden of supporting himself, his wife, and family, and that a woman is automatically entitled to lifelong support by a man upon her marriage, or that marriage, home and family are primarily woman's world and responsibility—hers, to dominate, his to support. We believe that a true partnership between the sexes demands a different concept of marriage, an equitable sharing of the responsibilities of home and children and of the economic burdens of their support. We believe that proper

WOMEN'S RIGHTS

NATIONAL
ORGANIZATION
FOR WOMEN
STATEMENT OF
PURPOSE

WOMEN'S RIGHTS

NATIONAL
ORGANIZATION
FOR WOMEN
STATEMENT OF
PURPOSE

recognition should be given to the economic and social value of homemaking and child care. To these ends, we will seek to open a reexamination of laws and mores governing marriage and divorce, for we believe that the current state of "half-equality" between the sexes discriminates against both men and women, and is the cause of much unnecessary hostility between the sexes.

WE BELIEVE that women must now exercise their political rights and responsibilities as American citizens. They must refuse to be segregated on the basis of sex into separate-and-not-equal ladies' auxiliaries in the political parties, and they must demand representation according to their numbers in the regularly constituted party committees—at local, state, and national levels—and in the informal power structure, participating fully in the selection of candidates and political decision-making, and running for office themselves.

IN THE INTERESTS OF THE HUMAN DIGNITY OF WOMEN, we will protest and endeavor to change the false image of women now prevalent in the mass media, and in the texts, ceremonies, laws, and practices of our major social institutions. Such images perpetuate contempt for women by society and by women for themselves. We are similarly opposed to all policies and practices—in church, state, college, factory, or office—which, in the guise of protectiveness, not only deny opportunities but also foster in women self-denigration, dependence, and evasion of responsibility, undermine their confidence in their own abilities and foster contempt for women.

NOW WILL HOLD ITSELF INDEPENDENT OF ANY POLITICAL PARTY in order to mobilize the political power of all women and men intent on our goals. We will strive to ensure that no party, candidate, president, senator, governor, congressman, or any public official who betrays or ignores the principle of full equality between the sexes is elected or appointed to office. If it is necessary to mobilize the votes of men and women who believe in our cause, in order to win for women the final right to be fully free and equal human beings, we so commit ourselves.

WE BELIEVE THAT women will do most to create a new image of women by acting now, and by speaking out in behalf of their own equality, freedom, and human dignity—not in pleas for special privilege, nor in enmity toward men, who are also victims of the current half-equality between the sexes—but in an active, self-respecting partnership with men. By so doing, women will develop confidence in their own ability to determine actively, in partnership with men, the conditions of their life, their choices, their future and their society.

NATIVE AMERICAN RIGHTS

When Europeans arrived in North America in the 1600s, they discovered that Native American tribes already occupied the land. Between the 1630s and the War of Independence, white settlers gradually pushed the Native Americans, whom they called "Indians," westward. The goals of the settlers, which included colonization, land exploitation, and religious conversion, led to cultural and social conflict that erupted in periodic "Indian wars."

After the formation of the United States, state and federal government leaders agreed that the nation needed to establish a national policy toward Native Americans. By the 1820s the government's policy was to remove Native Americans from their lands and resettle them in the "Great American Desert" to the west. In 1830 Congress passed the Indian Removal Act (4 Stat. 411) and appropriated $500,000 for this purpose. During the presidency of Andrew Jackson (1829–1837), ninety-four removal treaties were negotiated. By 1840 most of the Native Americans in the more settled states and territories had been sent west.

The U.S. Supreme Court confronted the issue of Native American rights in the *Cherokee* cases, the collective name for two cases of the 1830s: *Cherokee Nation v. Georgia*, 30 U.S. 1, 8 L. Ed. 25 (1831), and *Worcester v. Georgia*, 31 U.S. 515, 8 L. Ed. 483 (1832). In *Cherokee Nation*, Chief Justice John Marshall ruled that the Cherokee Indians were not a sovereign nation. The following year Marshall issued an opinion that, while not overruling *Cherokee Nation*, held that the Cherokees were a nation with the right to retain independent political communities. President Jackson refused to abide by this ruling and supported the removal of the Cherokees to Oklahoma, which took place in 1838–1839.

Few tribes willingly moved westward, resulting in more Indian wars. The Black Hawk War of 1832, fought in Illinois, illustrates the situation Native Americans faced. The Sauk and Fox tribes, who had been forced from their lands by white settlers, faced the prospect of famine but were reluctant to move west where they would have to confront the hostile Sioux nation. Accordingly, Chief Black Hawk led the Sauk and Fox in an unsuccessful campaign to reoccupy their former lands.

Throughout the nineteenth century, treaties were made in which tribes ceded areas of land to the federal government in return for compensation in the form of livestock, merchandise, and annuities. These agreements were often accompanied by the establishment of reservations. All treaties that the United States entered into prior to 1871 were written in the formal language of international covenants. The parties would sign the draft treaty, and the document would be submitted to the U.S. Senate for ratification. After 1871 formal treaty arrangements were abandoned in favor of simple agreements between the government and Native American tribes. These agreements required the approval of both houses of Congress and had the same authority as the previous treaty forms, but they effectively abandoned the idea that Native American tribes were independent. For their part, the tribes came to distrust the federal government for not honoring the treaties, confining them to reservations, and ending a way of life that had endured for centuries. Not until the twentieth century, after the continent had been settled and the tribes restricted to reservations, did the federal government attempt to seek a different policy.

NATIVE AMERICAN RIGHTS

WORCESTER V. THE STATE OF GEORGIA

The Cherokee nation, located in the state of Georgia, sought to remain on its territory and be viewed legally as an independent, sovereign nation. In *Cherokee Nation v. Georgia* (1831), the tribe fought the state of Georgia's attempts to assert jurisdiction over Cherokee lands. The Cherokees appealed to the U.S. Supreme Court, arguing that they were protected by treaties negotiated with the U.S. government. Chief Justice John Marshall, writing for the majority, ruled that the Court had no jurisdiction to hear the Cherokees' lawsuit. Marshall defined the Cherokees as a "domestic, dependent nation," rather than a sovereign nation. Therefore, under Article III of the Constitution, the Court had no basis for entertaining the lawsuit.

The following year, however, in *Worcester v. Georgia* (1832), the Court modified its holding. In *Worcester*, Georgia sought to prevent white persons from living in Cherokee country without first obtaining a license from the state. The Cherokees challenged this license requirement. The Supreme Court agreed with the Cherokees, ruling that the Georgia laws were unconstitutional because they violated treaties, the Contract and Commerce Clauses of the Constitution, and the sovereign authority of the Cherokee nation.

In his majority opinion, Chief Justice Marshall placed emphasis on the tribe's standing as a nation. He pointed out that the U.S. government had applied the words *treaty* and *nation* "to Indians as we have applied them to the other nations of the earth." In addition, he ruled that Indian nations were distinct peoples with the right to retain independent political communities.

Worcester's affirmation of the validity of the treaty the Cherokees had signed with the United States did not protect them. President Andrew Jackson refused to enforce the Court's ruling and encouraged the removal of the Cherokees. Nearly a quarter of the 15,000 Cherokees died during the relocation, which began in 1838. The Cherokee called the western trek to Oklahoma and Indian Territory the "Trail of Tears." Nevertheless, *Worcester* remains an important decision, for it endorsed the sovereignty of Native American nations and the need to respect the terms and conditions negotiated by treaty.

—⁓—

Samuel A. Worcester, Plaintiff in Error, v. the State of Georgia

A writ of error was issued to "the judges of the Superior Court of Gwinnett in the State of Georgia," commanding them to send to the Supreme Court of the United States, the record and proceedings in the said Superior Court of the County of Gwinnett, between the State of Georgia, plaintiff, and Samuel A. Worcester, defendant, on an indictment in that court. The record of the court of Gwinnett was returned, certified by the clerk, of the court, and was also authenticated by the seal of the court. It was returned with, and annexed to a writ of error issued in regular form, the citation being signed

NATIVE
AMERICAN
RIGHTS

WORCESTER V.
THE STATE OF
GEORGIA

by one of the associate justices of the Supreme Court, and served on the Governor and Attorney-General of the State more than thirty days before the commencement of the term to which the writ of error was returnable.

By the Court: The judicial Act, so far as it prescribes the mode of proceeding, appears to have been literally pursued. In February, 1797, a rule was made on this subject in the following words:

> "It is ordered by the court that the clerk of the court to which any writ of error shall be directed, may make return of the same by transmitting a true copy of the record, and of all proceedings in the same, under his hand and the seal of the court."

This has been done. But the signature of the judge has not been added to that of the clerk. The law does not require it. The rule does not require it.

The plaintiff in error was indicted in the Superior Court of the County of Gwinnett in the State of Georgia,

> "for residing on the 15th July, 1831, in that part of the Cherokee Nation attached by the laws of the State of Georgia to that county, without a license or permit from the Governor of the State, or from any one authorized to grant it, and without having taken the oath to support and defend the constitution and laws of the State of Georgia, and uprightly to demean himself as a citizen thereof, contrary to the laws of the said State."

To this indictment he pleaded that he was, on the 15th July, 1531, in the Cherokee Nation, out of the jurisdiction of the court of Gwinnett County; that he was a citizen of Vermont, and entered the Cherokee Nation as a missionary under the authority of the President of the United States, and has not been required by him to leave it, and that with the permission and approval of the Cherokee Nation he was engaged in preaching the gospel: that the State of Georgia ought not to maintain the prosecution, as several treaties had been entered into by the United States with the Cherokee Nation, by which that nation was acknowledged to be a sovereign nation, and by which the territory occupied by them was guaranteed to them by the United States, and that the laws of Georgia, under which the plaintiff in error was indicted, are repugnant to the treaties, and unconstitutional and void, and also that they are repugnant to the Act of Congress of March, 1802, entitled "An Act to regulate trade and intercourse with

the Indian tribes." The Superior Court of Gwinnett overruled the plea, and the plaintiff in error was tried and convicted and sentenced "to hard labor in the penitentiary for four years." Held, that this was a case in which the Supreme Court of the United States jurisdiction by writ of error, under the twenty-fifth section of the "Act to establish the judicial court of the United States" passed in 1789.

The indictment and plea in this case draw in question the validity of the treaties made by the United States with the Cherokee Indians: if not so, their construction is certainly drawn in question; and the decision has been, if not against their validity, "against the right, privilege or exemption specially set up and claimed under them." They also draw into question the validity of a statue of the State of Georgia, "on the ground of its being repugnant to the Constitution, treaties and laws of the United States, and the decision is in favor of its validity."

It is too clear for controversy that the act of Congress by which this court is constituted has given it the power, and of course imposed on it the duty of exercising jurisdiction in this case. The record, according to the judiciary act and the rule and practice of the court, is regularly before the court.

The Act of Legislature of Georgia, passed 22 December, 1830, entitled "An Act to prevent the exercise of assumed and arbitrary power by all persons, under pretext of authority from the Cherokee Indians," etc., enacts that

> "all white persons residing within the limits of the Cherokee Nation, on the first day of March next, or at any time thereafter, without a license or permit from his excellency the governor, shall authorize to grant such permit or license, and who shall not have taken the oath hereinafter required, shall be guilty of a high misdemeanor, and upon conviction thereof shall be punished by confinement to the penitentiary at hard labor, for a term not less than four years." The eleventh section authorizes the governor, should he deem it necessary for the protection of the mines or the enforcement of the laws in force within the Cherokee Nation, to raise and organize a guard,"

etc. The thirteenth section enacts,

> "that the said guard or any member of them shall be, and they are hereby authorized and empowered to arrest any person legally charged with or detected in a violation of the laws of this State, and to convey, as soon as practicable, the person so arrested before a

NATIVE
AMERICAN
RIGHTS

WORCESTER V.
THE STATE OF
GEORGIA

justice of the peace, judge of the superior, justice of inferior court of this State, to be dealt with according to law." The extraterritorial power of every legislature being limited in its action to its own citizens or subjects, the very passage of this act is an assertion of jurisdiction over the Cherokee Nation, and of the rights and powers consequent thereto.

The principle, "that the discovery of parts of the continent of America gave title to the government by whose subjects, or by whose authority it was made, against all other European governments, which title might be consummated by possession," acknowledged by all Europeans, because it was the interest of all to acknowledge it; gave to the nation making the discovery, as its inevitable consequence, the sole right of acquiring the soil, and of making settlements on it. It was an exclusive principle, which shut out the right of competition among those who had agreed to it; not one which could annul the previous right of those who had not agreed to it. It regulated the right given by discovery among the European discoverers, but could not affect the rights of those already in possession, either as aboriginal occupants or as occupants by virtue of a discovery made before the memory of man. It gave the exclusive right to purchase, but did not found that right on a denial of the right of the possessor to sell.

The relations between the Europeans and the natives was determined in each case by the particular government which asserted and could maintain this pre-emptive privilege in the particular place. The United States succeeded to all the claims of Great Britain, both territorial and political, but no attempt, so far as is known, has been made to enlarge them. So as they existed merely in theory, or were in their nature only exclusive of the claims of other European nations, they still retain their original character, and remain dormant. So far as they have been practically exerted, they exist in fact, are understood by both parties, are asserted by the one, and admitted by the other.

Soon after Great Britain determined on planting colonies in America, the king granted charters to companies of his subjects, who associated for the purpose of carrying the views of the crown into effect, and of enriching themselves. The first of these charters was made before possession was taken of any part of the country. They purport generally to convey the soil, from the Atlantic to the South Sea. This soil was occu-pied by numerous and warlike nations, equally willing and able to defend their possessions. The extravagant and absurd idea that the feeble settlements made on the sea-coast, or the companies under whom they were made, acquired legitimate power by them to govern the people, or occupy the lands from sea to sea, did not enter the mind of any man. They were well understood to convey the title which, according the common law of European sovereigns respecting America, they might rightfully convey, and no more. This was the exclusive right of purchasing such lands as the natives were willing to sell. The crown could not be understood to grant what the crown did not affect to claim, nor was it so understood.

Certain it is, that our history furnishes no example, from the first settlement of our country, of any attempt, on the part of the crown, to interfere with the internal affairs of the Indians farther than to keep out the agents of foreign powers, who, as traders or otherwise, might seduce them into foreign alliances. The king purchased their lands when they were willing to sell, at a price they were willing to take; but never coerced a surrender of them. He also purchased their alliance and dependence by subsidies, but never intruded with their self-government, so far as respected themselves only.

The third article of the Treaty of Hopewell acknowledges the Cherokees to be under the protection of the United States of America, and of no other power.

This stipulation is found in Indian treaties generally. It was introduced into their treaties with Great Britain; and may probably be found in those with other European powers. Its origin may be traced to the nature of their connection with those powers; and its true meaning is discerned in their relative situation.

The general law of European sovereigns respecting their claims in America, limited the intercourse of Indians, in a great degree, to the particular potentate whose ultimate right of domain was acknowledged by the others. This was the general state of things in time of peace. It was sometimes changed in war. The consequence was that their supplies were derived chiefly from that nation, and their trade confined to it. Goods, indispensable to their comfort, in the shape of presents, were received from the same hand. What was of still more importance, the strong hand of government was interposed to restrain the disorderly and licentious

NATIVE
AMERICAN
RIGHTS

WORCESTER V.
THE STATE OF
GEORGIA

from intrusions into their country, from encroachments on their lands, and from those acts of violence which were often attended by reciprocal murder. The Indians perceived in this protection only what was beneficial to themselves—an engagement to punish aggressions on them. It involved practically no claim to their lands, no dominion over their persons. It merely bound the nation to the British crown, as a dependent ally claiming the protection of a powerful friend and neighbor, and receiving the advantages of that protection, without involving a surrender of their national character.

This is the true meaning of the stipulation, and is undoubtedly the sense in which it was made. Neither the British government nor the Cherokees ever understood it otherwise.

The same stipulation entered into with the United States is undoubtedly to be construed in the same manner. They receive the Cherokee Nation into their favor and protection. The Cherokees acknowledge themselves to be under the protection of the United States, and of no other power. Protection does not imply the destruction of the protected. The manner in which this stipulation was understood by the American government, is explained by the language and acts of our first president.

So with respect to the words "hunting-grounds." Hunting was at that time the principal occupation of the Indians, and their land was more used for that purpose than for any other. It could not, however, be supposed, that any intention existed of restricting the full use of the lands they reserved.

To the United States, it could be a matter of no concern whether their whole territory was devoted to hunting-grounds, or whether an occasional village, and an occasional corn field interrupted, and gave some variety to the scene.

These terms had been used in their treaties with Great Britain, and had never been misunderstood. They had never been supposed to imply a right in the British government to take their lands, or to interfere with their internal government.

The sixth and seventh articles stipulate for the punishment of the citizens of either country who may commit offenses on or against the citizens of the other. The only inference to be drawn from them is, that the United States considered the Cherokees as a nation.

The ninth article is in these words:

"For the benefit and comfort of the Indians, and for the prevention of injuries or oppressions on the part of the citizens or Indians, the United States, in Congress assembled, shall have the sole and exclusive right of regulating the trade with the Indians, and managing all their affairs, as they think proper."

To construe the expression "managing all their affairs," into a surrender of self-government would be a departure from the construction which has been uniformly put on them. The great subject of the article is the Indian trade. The influence it gave made it desirable that Congress should possess it. The commissioners brought forward the claim, with the profession that their motive was "the benefit and comfort of the Indians, and the prevention of injuries or oppressions." This may be true, as respects the regulation of all affairs connected with their trade; but cannot be true, as respects the management of all their affairs. The most important of these is the cession of their lands and security against intruders on them. Is it credible that they could have considered themselves as surrendering to the United States the right to dictate their future cessions, and the terms on which they should be made; or to compel their submission to the violence of disorderly and licentious intruders? It is equally inconceivable that they could have supposed themselves, by a phrase thus slipped into an article, on another and more interesting subject, to have devested themselves of the right of self-government on subjects not connected with trade. Such a measure could not be for their benefit and comfort," or for "the prevention of injuries and oppression." Such a construction would be inconsistent with the spirit of this and of all subsequent treaties; especially of those articles which recognize the right of the Cherokees to declare hostilities and to make war. It would convert a treaty of peace covertly into an act annihilating the political existence of one of the parties. Had such a result been intended, it would have been openly avowed.

This treaty contains a few terms capable of being used in a sense which could not have been intended at the time, and which is inconsistent with the practical construction which has always been put on them; but its essential articles treat the Cherokees as a nation capable of maintaining the relations of peace and war, and ascertain boundaries between them and the United States.

The treaty of Holston, negotiated with the Cherokees in July, 1791, explicitly recognizing the national character of the Cherokees, and their right of self-government, thus guarantying their lands; assuming the duty of protection, and of course pledging the faith of the United States for that protection, has been frequently renewed, and is now in full force.

To the general pledge of protection have been added several specific pledges, deemed valuable by the Indians. Some of these restrain the citizens of the United States from encroachments on the Cherokee country, and provide for the punishment of intruders.

The treaties and laws of the United States contemplate the Indian territory as completely separated from that of the States; and provide that all intercourse with them shall be carried on exclusively by the government of the Union.

The Indian nations had always been considered as distinct, independent political communities, retaining their original natural rights, as the undisputed possessors of the soil, from time immemorial; with the single exception of that imposed by irresistible power, which excluded them from intercourse with any other European potentate than the first discoverer of the coast of the particular region claimed: and this was a restriction which those European potentates imposed on themselves as well as on the Indians. The very term "nation," so generally applied to them, means "a people distinct from others." The Constitution, by declaring treaties already made, as well as those to be made, to be the supreme law of the land, has adopted and sanctioned the previous treaties, with the Indian nations, and consequently, admits their rank among those powers who are capable of making treaties. The words "treaty" and "nation" are words of our own language, selected in our diplomatic and legislative proceedings, by ourselves, having each a definite and well understood meaning. We have applied them to Indians, as we have applied them to other nations of the earth. They are applied to all in the same sense.

Georgia, herself, has furnished conclusive evidence that her former opinions on this subject concurred with those entertained by her sister States, and by the government of the United States. Various acts of her Legislature have been cited in the argument, including the contract of cession made in the year 1802, all tending to prove her acquiescence in the universal conviction that the Indian nations possessed a full right to the lands they occupied, until that right should be extinguished by the United States with their

consent; that their territory was separated from that of any State within whose chartered limits they might reside, by a boundary line, established by treaties; that, within their boundary, they possessed rights with which no State could interfere; and that the whole power of regulating the intercourse with them was vested in the United States.

In opposition to the original right possessed by the undisputed occupants of every country to this recognition of that right, which is evidenced by our history in every change through which we have passed, are placed the charters granted by the monarch of a distant and distinct region, parceling out a territory in possession of others, whom he could not remove, and did not attempt to remove, and the cession made of his claims, by the Treaty of Peace. The actual state of things at the time, and all history since, explain these charters; and the King of Great Britain, at the Treaty of Peace, could cede only what belonged to his crown. These newly asserted titles can derive no aid from the articles so often repeated in Indian treaties, extending to them, first, the protection of Great Britain, and afterwards that of the United States. These articles are associated with others, recognizing their title to self-government. The very fact of repeated treaties with them recognizes it; and the settled doctrine of the law of nations is, that a weaker power does not surrender its independence—its right to self-government, by associating with a stronger, and taking its protection. A weak state, in order to provide for its safety, may place itself under the protection of one more powerful, without stripping itself of the right of government and ceasing to be a state. Examples of this kind are not wanting in Europe. "Tributary and feudatory states," says Vattel, "do not thereby cease to be sovereign and independent states, so long as self-government and sovereign and independent authority are left in the administration of the state." At the present day, more than one state may be considered as holding its right to self-government under the guarantee and protection of one or more allies.

The Cherokee Nation, then, is a distinct community, occupying its own territory, with boundaries accurately described in which the laws of Georgia can have no force, and which the citizens of Georgia have no right to enter but with the assent of the Cherokees themselves, or in conformity with treaties, and with the acts of Congress. The whole intercourse between the United States and this nation is, by

NATIVE
AMERICAN
RIGHTS

WORCESTER V.
THE STATE OF
GEORGIA

our Constitution and laws, vested in the government of the United States.

The act of the State of Georgia under which the plaintiff in error was prosecuted, is consequently void, and the judgment a nullity.

The acts of the Legislature of Georgia interfere forcibly with the relations established between the United States and the Cherokee Nation, the regulation of which, according to the settled principles of our Constitution, is committed exclusively to the government of the Union.

They are in direct hostility with treaties, repeated in a succession of years, which mark out the boundary that separates the Cherokee country from Georgia; guaranty to them all the land within their boundary; solemnly pledge the faith of the United States to restrain their citizens from trespassing on it; and recognize the pre-existing power of the nation to govern itself.

They are in equal hostility with the acts of Congress for regulating the intercourse and giving effect to the treaties.

The forcible seizure and abduction of the plaintiff in error, who was residing in the nation, with its permission, and by authority of the President of the United States, is also a violation of the acts which authorize the chief magistrate to exercise this authority.

Will these powerful considerations avail the plaintiff in error? We think they will. He was seized and forcibly carried away, while under guardianship of treaties guarantying the country in which he resided and taking it under the protection of the United States. He was seized while performing, under the sanction of the chief magistrate of the Union, those duties which the humane policy adopted by Congress had recommended, under color of a law which has been shown to repugnant to the Constitution, laws, and treaties of the United States. Had a judgment, liable to the same objections, been rendered for liable to the same objections, been rendered for property, none would question the jurisdiction of this court. It cannot be less clear when the judgment affects personal liberty, and inflicts disgraceful punishment; if punishment could disgrace when inflicted on innocence. The plaintiff in error is not less interested in the operation of this unconstitutional law than if it affected his property. He is not less entitled to the protection of the Constitution, laws, and treaties of his country.

This was a writ of error to the Superior Court for the County of Gwinnett, in the State of Georgia.

On the 22d December, 1830, the Legislature of the State of Georgia passed the following act:

"An act to prevent the exercise of assumed and arbitrary power of all persons, under pretext of authority from the Cherokee Indians and their laws, and to prevent white persons from residing within that part of the chartered limits of Georgia occupied by the Cherokee Indians, and to provide a guard for the protection of the gold mines, and to enforce the laws of the State within the aforesaid territory.

"Be it enacted by the Senate and House of Representatives of the State of Georgia in General Assembly met, and it is hereby enacted by the authority of the same that, after the 1st day of February, 1831, it shall not be lawful for any person or persons, under color or pretense of authority from said Cherokee tribe, to cause or procure by any means the assembling of any council or other pretended legislative body of the said Indians or others living among them, for the purpose of legislating (or for any other purpose whatever). And persons offending against the provisions of this section shall be guilty of a high misdemeanor, and subject to indictment therefor, and, on conviction, shall be punished by confinement at hard labor in the penitentiary for the space of four years.

"Sec. 2. And be it further enacted by the authority aforesaid that, after the time aforesaid, it shall not be lawful for any person or persons, under pretext of authority from the Cherokee tribe, or as representatives, chiefs, headman or warriors of said tribe, to meet or assemble as a council, assembly, convention, or in any other capacity, for the purpose of making laws, orders or regulations for said tribe. And all persons offending against the provisions of this section shall be guilty of a high misdemeanor, and subject to an indictment, and, on conviction thereof, shall undergo an imprisonment in the penitentiary at hard labor for the space of four years.

"Sec. 3. And be it further enacted by the authority aforesaid that, after the time aforesaid, it shall not be lawful for any person or persons, under color or by authority of the Cherokee tribe, or any of its laws or regulations, to hold any court of tribunal whatever, for the purpose of hearing and determining causes, either civil or criminal, or to give any judgment in such cases, or to issue, or cause to issue, any process against the person or property of any of said tribe. And all persons offending against the provisions of this section shall be guilty of a high misdemeanor, and subject to indictment, and, on conviction thereof, shall be imprisoned in the penitentiary at hard labor for the space of four years.

"Sec. 4. And be it further enacted by the authority aforesaid that, after the time aforesaid, it shall not be lawful for any person or persons, as a ministerial officer, or in any other capacity, to execute any precept, command or process issued by any court or tribunal in the Cherokee tribe, on the persons or property of any of said tribe. And all persons offending against the provisions of this section, shall be guilty of a trespass, and subject to indictment, and, on conviction thereof, shall be punished by fine and imprisonment in the jail or in the penitentiary, not longer than four years, at the discretion of the court.

"Sec. 5. And be it further enacted by the authority aforesaid that, after the time aforesaid, it shall not be lawful for any person or persons to confiscate, or attempt to confiscate, or otherwise to cause a forfeiture of the property or estate of any Indian of said tribe, in consequence of his enrolling himself and family for emigration, or offering to enroll for emigration, or any other act of said Indian, in furtherance of his intention to emigrate. And persons offending against the provisions of this section shall be guilty of high misdemeanor, and, on conviction, shall undergo an imprisonment in the penitentiary at hard labor for the space of four years.

"Sec. 6. And be it further enacted by the authority aforesaid that none of the provisions of this act shall be so construed as to prevent said tribe, its headmen, chiefs or other representatives, from meeting any agent or commissioner, on the part of the State or the United States, for any purpose whatever.

"Sec. 7. And be it further enacted by the authority aforesaid that all white persons residing within the limits of the Cherokee Nation on the 1st day of March next, or at any time thereafter, without a license or permit from his excellency the governor shall authorize to grant such a permit or license, and who shall not have taken the oath hereinafter required, shall be guilty of a high misdemeanor, and, upon conviction thereof, shall be punished by confinement to the penitentiary at hard labor for a term not less than four years; provided, that the provisions of this section shall not be so construed as to extend to any authorized agent or agents of the government of the United States or of this State, or to any person or persons who may rent any of those improvements which have been abandoned by Indians who have emigrated west of the Mississippi; provided, nothing contained in this section shall be so construed as to extend to white females, and all male children under twenty-one years of age.

"Sec. 8. And be it further enacted by the authority aforesaid that all white persons, citizens of the State of Georgia, who have procured a license in writing from his excellency the governor, or from such agent as his excellency the governor shall authorize to grant such permit or license, to reside within the limits of the Cherokee Nation, and who have taken the following oath, viz.: 'I, A. B., do solemnly swear (or affirm, as the case may be) that I will support and defend the constitution and laws of the State of Georgia, and uprightly demean myself as a citizen thereof, so help me God,' shall be, and the same are hereby declared, exempt and free from the operation of the seventh section of this act.

"Sec. 9. And be it further enacted that his excellency the governor be, and he is hereby authorized to grant licenses to reside within the limits of the Cherokee Nation, according to the provisions of the eighth section of this act.

"Sec. 10. And be it further enacted by the authority aforesaid that no person shall collect or claim any toll from any person for passing any turnpike gate or toll bridge, by authority of any act or law of the Cherokee tribe, or any chief or headman or men of the same.

"Sec. 11. And be it further enacted by the authority aforesaid that his excellency the governor be, and he is hereby empowered, should he deem it necessary, either for the protection of the mines, or for the enforcement of the laws of force within the Cherokee Nation, to raise and organize a guard, to be employed on foot or mounted, as occasion may require, which shall not consist of more than sixty persons, which guard shall be under the command of the commissioner or agent appointed by the governor to protect the mines, with power to dismiss from the service any member of said guard (on paying the wages due for services rendered) for disorderly conduct, and make appointments to fill the vacancies occasioned by such dismissal.

"Sec. 12. And be it further enacted by the authority aforesaid that each person who may belong to said guard, shall receive for his compensation at the rate of fifteen dollars per month when on foot, and at the rate of twenty dollars per month when mounted, for every month when mounted, for every month that such person is engaged in actual service; and, in the event that the commis-

NATIVE
AMERICAN
RIGHTS

WORCESTER V.
THE STATE OF
GEORGIA

NATIVE
AMERICAN
RIGHTS

WORCESTER V.
THE STATE OF
GEORGIA

sioner or agent herein referred to should die, resign, or fail to perform the duties herein required of him, his excellency the governor is hereby authorized and required to appoint, in his stead, some other fit and proper person to the command of said guard; and the commissioner or agent, having the command of the guard aforesaid, for the better discipline thereof, shall appoint three sergeants, who shall receive at the rate of twenty dollars per month while serving on foot, and twenty-five dollars per month when mounted, as compensation whilst in actual service.

"Sec. 13. And be it further enacted by the authority aforesaid that the said guard, or any member of them, shall be, and they are hereby authorized and empowered to arrest any person legally charged with, or detected in, a violation of the laws of this State, and to convey as soon as practicable the person so arrested before a justice of the peace, judge of the superior or justice of inferior court of this State, to be dealt with according to law; and the pay and support of said guard be provided out of the fund already appropriated for the protection of the gold mines."

The Legislature of Georgia, on the 19th December, 1829, passed the following Act:

"An Act to add the territory lying within the chartered limits of Georgia, and now in the occupancy of the Cherokee Indians, to the counties of Carroll, DeKalb, Gwinnett, Hall, and Habersham, and to extend the laws of this State over the same, and to annul all laws and ordinances made by the Cherokee Nation of Indians, and to provide for the compensation of officers serving legal process in said territory, and to regulate the testimony of Indians, and to repeal the ninth section of the Act of 1828 upon this subject.

"Sec. 1. Be it enacted by the Senate and House of Representatives of the State of Georgia in General Assembly met, and it is hereby enacted by the authority of the same, that from and after the passing of this act, all that part of the unlocated territory within the limits of this State, and which lies between the Alabama line and the old path leading from the Buzzard Roost on the Chattahoochee, to Sally Hughes's on the Hightower River; thence to Thomas Pelet's on the old federal road; thence with said road to the Alabama line be, and the same is hereby added to, and shall become a part of, the County of Carroll.

"Sec. 2. And be it further enacted that all that part of said territory lying and being north of the last-mentioned line, and south of the road running from Charles Gait's ferry, on the Chattahoochee River, to Dick Roe's, to

where it intersects with the path aforesaid, be, and the same is hereby added to, and shall become a part of, the County of DeKalb.

"Sec. 3. And be it further enacted that all that part of said territory lying north of the last-mentioned line, and south of a line commencing at the mouth of Baldridge's Creek; thence up said creek to its source; from thence to where the federal road crosses the Hightower; thence with said road to the Tennessee line, be, and the same is hereby added to, and shall become part of, the County of Gwinnett.

"Sec. 4. And be it further enacted that all that part of said territory lying north of the last-mentioned line, and south of a line commence on the Chestatee River, at the mouth of Yoholo Creek; thence up said creek to the top of the Blue Ridge; thence to the headwaters of Notley River; thence down said river to the boundary line of Georgia, be, and the same is hereby added to, and shall become a part of, the County of Hall.

"Sec. 5. And be it further enacted that all that part of said territory lying north of the last-mentioned line, within the limits of this State, be, and the same is hereby added to, and shall become a part of, the County of Habersham.

"Sec. 6. And be it further enacted that all the laws, both civil and criminal, of this State, be, and the same are hereby extended over said portions of territory, respectively; and all persons whatever residing within the same, shall, after the 1st day of June next, be subject and liable to the operation of said laws, in the same manner as other citizens of this State, or the citizens of said counties, respectively; and all writs and processes whatever, issued by the courts or officers of said courts, shall extend over, and operate on, the portions of territory hereby added to the same, respectively.

"Sec. 7. And be it further enacted that after the 1st day of June next, all laws, ordinances, orders and regulations, of any kind whatever, made, passed or enacted, by the Cherokee Indians, either in general council or in any other way whatever, or by any authority whatever of said tribe, be, and the same are hereby declared to be, null and void, and of no effect, as if the same had never existed; and in all cases of indictment or civil suits, it shall not be lawful for the defendant to justify under any of said laws, ordinances, orders of regulations; nor shall the courts of this State permit the same to be given in evidence on the trial of any suit whatever.

"Sec. 8. And be it further enacted that it shall not be lawful for any person or body of per-

NATIVE
AMERICAN
RIGHTS

WORCESTER V.
THE STATE OF
GEORGIA

sons, by arbitrary power or by virtue of any pretended rule, ordinance, law or custom of said Cherokee Nation, to prevent by threats, menaces or other means, or endeavor to prevent, any Indian of said nation, residing within the chartered limits of this State, from enrolling as an emigrant, or actually emigrating or removing from said nation; nor shall it be lawful for any person or body of persons, by arbitrary power or by virtue of any pretended rule ordinance, law or custom of said nation, to punish, in any manner, or to molest either the person or property, or to abridge the rights or privileges of any Indian, for enrolling his or her name as an emigrant, or for emigrating or intending to emigrate, from said nation.

"Sec. 9. And be it further enacted that any person or body of persons offending against the provisions of the foregoing section, shall be guilty of a high misdemeanor, subject to indictment, and on conviction shall be punished by confinement in the common jail of any county of this State, or by confinement at hard labor in the penitentiary, for a term not exceeding four years, at the discretion of the court.

"Sec. 10. And be it further enacted that it shall not be lawful for any person or body of persons, by arbitrary power, or under color of any pretended rule, ordinance, law or custom of said nation, to prevent or offer to prevent, or deter any Indian headman, chief or warrior of said nation, residing within the chartered limits of this State, from selling or ceding to the United States, for the use of Georgia, the whole or any part of said territory, or to prevent or offer to prevent, any Indian, headman, chief or warrior of said nation, residing as aforesaid, from meeting in council or treaty any commissioner or commissioners on the part of the United States, for any purpose whatever.

"Sec. 11. And be it further enacted that any person or body of persons offending against the provisions of the foregoing sections, shall be guilty of a high misdemeanor, subject to indictment, and on conviction shall be confined at hard labor in the penitentiary for not less than four nor longer than six years, at the discretion of the court.

"Sec. 12. And be it further enacted that it shall not be lawful for any person or body of persons, by arbitrary force, or under color of any pretended rules, ordinances, law or custom of said nation, to take the life of any Indian residing as aforesaid, for enlisting as an emigrant; attempting to emigrate, ceding, or attempting to cede, as aforesaid, the whole or any part of the said territory; or meeting or attempting

meet, in treaty or in council, as aforesaid, any commissioner or commissioners aforesaid; and any person or body of persons offending against the provisions of this section, shall be guilty of murder, subject to indictment, and on conviction, shall suffer death by hanging.

"Sec. 13. And be it further enacted that, should any of the foregoing offenses be committed under color of any pretended rules, ordinances, custom or law of said nation, all persons acting therein, either as individuals or as pretended executive, ministerial or judicial officers, shall be deemed and considered as principals, and subject to the pains and penalties hereinbefore described.

"Sec. 14. And be it further enacted that for all demands which may come within the jurisdiction of a magistrate's court, suit may be brought for the same in the nearest district of the county to which the territory is hereby annexed; and all officers serving any legal process on any person living on any portion of the territory herein named, shall be entitled to recover the sum of five cents for every mile he may ride to serve the same, after crossing the present limits of the said counties, in addition to the fees already allowed by law; and in case any of the said officers should be resisted in the execution of any legal process, issued by any court or magistrate, justice of the inferior court or judge of the Superior Court of any of said counties, he is hereby authorized to call out a sufficient number of the militia of said counties to aid and protect him in the execution of this duty.

"Sec. 15. And be it further enacted that no Indian or descendant of any Indian, residing within the Creek or Cherokee nations of Indians, shall be deemed a competent witness in any court of this State to which a white person may be a party, except such white person resides within the said nation."

In September, 1831, the grand jurors for the County of Gwinnett in the State of Georgia, presented to the Superior Court of the county the following indictment:

Georgia, Gwinnett County: The Grand Jurors, sworn, chosen and selected for the County of Gwinnett, in the name and behalf of the citizens of Georgia, charge and accuse Elizur Butler, Samuel A. Worcester, James Trott, Samuel Mays, Surry Eaton, Austin Copeland, and Edward D. Losure, white persons of said county, with the offense of residing within the limits of the Cherokee Nation without a license:' For that the said Elizur Butler, Samuel A. Worcester, James Trott, Samuel Mays, Surry Easton, Austin Copeland, and Edward D. Losure, white persons, as aforesaid, on the

NATIVE
AMERICAN
RIGHTS

WORCESTER V.
THE STATE OF
GEORGIA

15th day of July, 1831, did reside in that part of the Cherokee Nation attached by the laws of said State to the said county, and in the county aforesaid, without a license or permit from his excellency the governor of said State, or from any agent authorized by his excellency the governor aforesaid to grant such permit or license, and without having taken the oath to support and defend the constitution and laws of the State of Georgia, and uprightly to demean themselves as citizens thereof, contrary to the laws of said State, the good order, peace and dignity thereof."

To this indictment the plaintiff in error pleaded specially as follows:

"And the said Samuel A. Worcester, in his own proper person, comes and says, that this court ought not to take further cognizance of the action and prosecution aforesaid, because he says, that, on the 15th day of July, in the year 1831, he was and still is, a resident in the Cherokee Nation; and that the said supposed crime or crimes, and each of them, were committed, if committed at all, at the town of New Echota, in the said Cherokee Nation, out of the jurisdiction of this court. And this defendant saith that he is a citizen of the State of Vermont, one of the United States of America, and that he entered the aforesaid Cherokee Nation in the capacity of a duly authorized missionary of the American Board of Commissioners for Foreign Missions, under the authority of the President of the United States, and has not since been required by him to leave it: that he was, at the time of his arrest, engaged in preaching the Gospel to the Cherokee Indians, and in translating the sacred Scriptures into their language, with the permission and approval of the said Cherokee Nation, and in accordance with the humane policy of the government of the United States for the civilization and improvement of the Indians; and that his residence there, for this purpose, is the residence charged in the aforesaid indictment: and this defendant further saith, that this prosecution the State of Georgia ought not to have or maintain, because, he saith, that several treaties have, from time to time, been entered into between the United States and the Cherokee Nation of Indians, to wit: at Hopewell, on the 28th day of November, 1785; at Holston, on the 2d day of July, 1791; at Philadelphia, on the 26th day of June, 1794; at Tellico, on the 2d day of October, 1798; at Tellico, on the 24th day of October, 1804; at Tellico, on the 25th day of October, 1805; at Tellico, on the 27th day of October, 1805; at Washington city on the 22d day of March, 1816; at the Chickasaw Council House, on the 14th day

of September, 1816; at the Cherokee Agency, on the 8th day of July, 1817, and at Washington city, on the 27th day of February, 1819; all which treaties have been duly ratified by the Senate of the United States of America acknowledge the said Cherokee Nation to be a sovereign nation, authorized to govern themselves, and all persons who have settled within their territory, free from any right of legislative interference by the several States composing the United States of America, in reference to acts done within their own territory; and by which treaties the whole of the territory now occupied by the Cherokee Nation, on the east of the Mississippi, has been solemly guaranteed to them; all of which treaties of Hopewell and Holston, the aforesaid territory is acknowledged to lie without the jurisdiction of the several States composing the Union of the United States; and it is thereby especially stipulated that the citizens of the United States shall not enter the aforesaid territory, even on a visit, without a passport from the governor of a State, or from some one duly authorized thereto by the President of the United States; all of which will more fully and at large appear, by reference to the aforesaid treaties. And this defendant saith that the several acts charged in the bill of indictment were done, or omitted to be done, if at all, within the said territory so recognized as belonging to the said nation, and so, as aforesaid, held by them, under the guaranty of the United States: that for those acts the defendant is not amenable to the laws of Georgia, nor to the jurisdiction of the courts of the said State; and that the laws of the State of Georgia, which profess to add the said territory to the several adjacent counties of the said State, and to extend the laws of Georgia over the said territory and persons inhabiting the same; and, in particular, the act on which this indictment against this defendant is grounded, to wit: 'An Act entitled and Act to prevent the exercise of assumed, and arbitrary power by all persons under pretext of authority from the Cherokee Indians and their laws, and to prevent white persons from residing within that part of the chartered limits of Georgia occupied by the Cherokee Indians, and to provide a guard for the protection of the gold mines, and to enforce the laws of the State within the aforesaid territory,' are repugnant to the aforesaid treaties; which according to the Constitution of the United States, compose a part of the supreme law of the land; and that these laws of Georgia are, therefore, unconstitutional, void, and of no effect: that the said laws of Georgia are also unconstitutional and void, because they impair the obligation of the various contracts formed by and between the aforesaid Cherokee Nation and the said United States of America, as above recited: also, that the said laws of Georgia are unconstitutional and void, because they interfere with, and attempt to regulate and control the intercourse with the said Cherokee Nation, which, by the said Constitution, belongs exclusively to the Congress of the United States; and because the said laws are repugnant to the statute of the United States passed on the —— day of March, 1802, entitled 'An Act to regulate trade and intercourse with the Indian tribes, and to preserve peace on the frontiers:' and that, therefore, this court has no jurisdiction to cause this defendant to make further or other answer to the said bill of indictment, or further to try and punish this defendant for the said supposed offense or offenses alleged in the bill of indictment, or any of them; and, therefore, this defendant prays judgment whether he shall be held bound to answer further to said indictment."

This plea was overruled by the court, and the jurisdiction of the Superior Court of the County of Gwinnett was sustained by the judgment of the court.

The defendant was then arraigned, and pleaded "not guilty;" and the case came on for trial on the 15th of September, 1831, when the jury found the defendants in the indictment guilty. On the same day the court pronounced sentence on the parties so convicted, as follows:

> The *State v. B.F. Thompson et al.* Indictment for residing in the Cherokee Nation without license. Verdict, Guilty."

> The *State v. Elizur Butler, Samuel A. Worcester et al.* Indictment for residing in the Cherokee Nation without license. Verdict, Guilty."

> "The defendants in both of the above cases shall be kept in close custody by the sheriff of this county until they can be transported to the penitentiary of this State, and the keeper thereof is hereby directed to receive them, and each of them, at hard labor in said penitentiary for and during the term of four years."

A writ of error was issued on the application of the plaintiff in error, on the 27th of October, 1831, which, with the following proceedings thereon, was returned to this court:

> "United States of America, ss.—The President of the United States to the honorable the judges of the Superior Court for the County of Gwinnett, in the State of Georgia, greeting:

> "Because in the record and proceedings, as also in the rendition of the judgment of a plea

which is in the said Superior Court for the County of Gwinnett, before you, or some of you between the State of Georgia, plaintiff, and Samuel A. Worcester, defendant, on an indictment, being the highest court of law in said State in which a decision could be had in said suit, a manifest error hath happened, to the great damage of said Samuel A. Worcester, as by his complaint appears. We being willing that error, if any hath been, should be duly corrected, and full and speedy justice done to the parties aforesaid in this behalf, do command you, if judgment be therein given, that then under your seal distinctly and openly, you send the record and proceedings aforesaid, with all things concerning the same, to the Supreme Court of the United States, together with this writ, so that you have the same at Washington on the second Monday of January next, in the said Supreme Court, to be then and there held; that the record and proceedings aforesaid being inspected, the said Supreme Court may cause further to be done therein, to correct that error, what of right, and according to the laws and custom of the United States, should be done.

> "Witness, the Honorable John Marshall, Chief Justice of the said Supreme Court, the first Monday of August, in the year of our Lord one thousand eight hundred and thirty one.

Wm. Thos. Carroll.

Clerk of the Supreme Court of the United States.

> "Allowed by Henry Baldwin.

> "United States of America to the State of Georgia, greeting:

> "You are hereby cited and admonished to be and appear at a Supreme Court of the United States to be holden at Washington on the second Monday of January next, pursuant to a writ of error filed in the clerk's office of the Superior Court for the County of Gwinnett, in the State of Georgia, wherein Samuel A. Worcester is plaintiff in error, and the State of Georgia is defendant in error, to show cause, if any there be, why judgment rendered against the said Samuel A. Worcester, as in the said writ of error mentioned, should not be corrected, and why speedy justice should not be corrected, and why speedy justice should not be done to parties in that behalf.

> "Witness, the Honorable Henry Baldwin, one of the justices of the Supreme Court of the United States, this 27th day of October, in the year of our Lord one thousand eight hundred and thirty-one.

Henry Baldwin.

NATIVE
AMERICAN
RIGHTS

WORCESTER V.
THE STATE OF
GEORGIA

"State of Georgia, County of Gwinnett, sct.— On this 26th day of November, in the year of our Lord eighteen hundred and thirty one. William Potter personally appeared before the subscriber, John Mills, a justice of the peace in and fore said country, and being duly sworn on the holy evangelists of Almighty God, deposeth and saith, that on the 24th day of November instant, be delivered a true copy of the within citation to His Excellency Wilson Lumpkin, Governor of the State of Georgia, and another true copy thereof he delivered, on the 22d day of November, instant, to Charles J. Jenkins, Esq., Attorney-General of the State aforesaid, showing to the said governor and attorney-general, respectively, at the times of delivery herein stated, the within situation.

Wm. Potter.

"Sworn to and subscribed before me, the day and year above written.

John Mills, J.P."

This writ of error was returned to the Supreme Court with copies of all the proceedings in the Superior Court of the county of Gwinnett, as stated, and accompanied with certificates of the clerk of that court in the following terms:

"Georgia, Gwinnett County. I, John G. Park, clerk of the Superior Court of the County of Gwinnett and State aforesaid, do certify that the annexed and foregoing is a full and complete exemplification of the proceedings and judgments had in said court against Samuel A. Worcester, one of the defendants in the case therein mentioned, as they remain, of record, in the said Superior Court.

"Given under my hand, and seal of the court, this 28th day of November, 1831.

John G. Park, Clerk.

"I also certify that the original bond, of which copy is annexed (the bond was in the usual form), and also a copy of the annexed writ of error, were duly deposited and filed in the clerk's office of said court on the 10th day of November, in the year of our Lord eighteen hundred and thirty-one.

"Given under my hand and seal aforesaid, the day and date above written.

John G. Park, Clerk.

The case of *Elizur Butler, plaintiff in error, v. State of Georgia,* was brought before the Supreme Court in the same manner.

The case was argued for the plaintiffs in error by Mr. Sergeant and Mr. Writ, with whom also was Mr. Elisha W. Chester.

The following positions were laid down and supported by Mr. Sergeant and Mr. Wirt:

That the court had jurisdiction of the question brought before them by the writ of error; and the jurisdiction extended equally to criminal and to civil cases.

That the writ of error was duly issued, and duly returned, so as to-bring the question regularly before the court, under the Constitution and laws of the United States, and oblige the court to take cognizance of it.

That the statute of Georgia under which the plaintiff's in error were indicted and convicted was unconstitutional and void; because;

By the Constitution of the United States, the establishment and regulation of intercourse with the Indians belonged exclusively to the government of the United States.

The power thus given, exclusively, to the government of the United States had been exercised by treaties and by acts of Congress, now in force, and applying directly to the case of the Cherokees; and that no State could interfere, without a manifest violation of such treaties and laws, which by the Constitution were the supreme law of the land.

The statute of Georgia assumed the power to change these regulations and laws: to prohibit that which they permitted; and to make that criminal which they declared innocent or meritorious; and to subject to condemnation and punishment, free citizens of the United States who had committed no offense. That the indictment, conviction, and sentence being founded upon a statute of Georgia, which was unconstitutional and void; were themselves also void and of no effect, and ought to be reversed.

These several positions were supported, enforced and illustrated by argument and authority.

The following authorities were referred to: 2 Laws U. S. 65, sec. 25; Judiciary Act of 1789; *Miller v. Nicholls,* 4 Wheat. 311; *Craig v. State of Missouri,* 4 Peters, 400, 429; *Fisher v. Cockerell,* 5 Peters, 248; *Ex-parte Kearney,* 7 wheat. 38; *Cohens v. Virginia,* 6 Wheat. 264; *Martin v. Hunter,* 1 Wheat. 304, 315, 361; 1 Laws U. S. 488,

470, 472, 482, 484, 486, 453; Blunt's Historical Sketch, 106, 107; Treaties with the Cherokees, 28th Nov. 1785; 2d July, 1791; 26th July, 1794; 2d Oct. 1798; 3 Laws U. S. 27, 125, 284, 303, 344, 400; 12 Journ. Congress, 82; Blunt's Hist. Sketch, 113, 110, 111, 114; *Federalist*, No. 42; Laws U. S. 454; *Holland v. Pack,* Peck's Rep. 151; *Johnson v. M'Intosh,* 8 Wheat. 543; *Cherokee Nation v. State of Georgia,* 5 Peters, 1, 16, 27, 31, 48; *Ware v. Hylton,* 3 Dall. 199; *Hughes v. Edwards,* 9 Wheat. 489; *Fisher v. Hamden,* 1 Paine, 55; *Hamilton v. Eaton,* North Carolina Cases, 79; *M'Culloch v. State of Maryland,* 4 Wheat. 316; 2 Laws U. S. 121; 3 Laws U.S. 460; 3 Laws U. S. 750; *Gibbons v. Odgen,* 9 Wheat. 1.

Mr. Chief Justice Marshall delivered the opinion of the court:

This cause, in every point of view in which it can be placed, is of the deepest interest.

The defendant is a State, a member of the Union, which has exercised the powers of government over a people who deny its jurisdiction, and are under the protection of the United States.

The plaintiff is a citizen of the State of Vermont, condemned to hard labor for four years in the penitentiary of Georgia, under color of an act which he alleges to be repugnant to the Constitution, laws, and treaties of the United States.

The legislative power of the State, the controlling power of the Constitution and laws of the United States, the rights, if they have any, the political existence of a once numerous and powerful people, the personal liberty of a citizen, are all involved in the subject now to be considered.

It behooves this court in every case, more especially in this, to examine into its jurisdiction with scrutinizing eyes, before it proceeds to the exercise of a power which is controverted.

The first step in the performance of this duty is the inquiry whether the record is properly before the court.

It is certified by the clerk of the court which pronounced the judgment of condemnation under which the plaintiff in error is imprisoned, and is also authenticated by the seal of the court. It is returned with, and annexed to, a writ of error issued in regular form, the citation being signed by one of the associate justices of the Supreme Court, and served on the Governor and Attorney-General of the State more than thirty days before the commencement of the term of which the writ of error was returnable.

The Judicial Act (sec. 22, 25, 2 Laws U. S. 64, 65), so far as it prescribes the mode of proceeding, appears to have been literally pursued.

In February, 1797, a rule (6 Wheat. Rules) was made on this subject in the following words: "It is so ordered by the court that the clerk of the court to which any writ of error shall be directed, may make return of the same by transmitting a true copy of the record, and of all proceedings in the same, under his hand and the seal of the court."

This has been done. But the signature of the judge has not been added to that of the clerk. The law does not require it. The rule does not require it.

In the case of *Martin v. Hunter's Lessee,* 1 Wheat. 304, 361, an exception was taken to the return of the refusal of the State court to enter a prior judgment of reversal by this court, because it was not made by the judge of the State court to which the writ was directed; but the exception was overruled, and the return was held sufficient. In *Buel v. Van Ness,* 8 Wheat, 312, also, a writ of error to a State court, the record was authenticated in the same manner. No exception was taken to it. These were civil cases. But it has been truly said at the bar that, in regard to this process, the law makes no distinction between a criminal and civil cases. The same return is required in both. If the sanction of the court could be necessary for the establishment of this position, it has been silently given.

M'Culloch v. The State of Maryland, 4 Wheat. 316, was a *qui tam* action, brought to recover a penalty, and the record was authenticated by the seal of the court and the signature of the clerk, without that of a judge. *Brown et al. v. State of Maryland* was an indictment for a fine and forfeiture. The record in this case, too, was authenticated by the seal of the court and the certificate of the clerk. The practice is both ways.

The record, then, according to the Judiciary Act, and the rule and the practice of the court, is regularly before us. The more important inquiry is, does it exhibit a case cognizable by this tribunal?

The indictment charges the plaintiff in error and others, being white persons, with the offense of "residing within the limits of the Cherokee Nation without a license," and "without having

NATIVE
AMERICAN
RIGHTS

WORCESTER V.
THE STATE OF
GEORGIA

taken the oath to support and defend the constitution and the laws of the State of Georgia."

The defendant in the State court appeared in proper, person, and filed the following plea:

"And the said Samuel A. Worcester, in his own proper person, comes and says that this court ought not to take further cognizance of the action and prosecution aforesaid, because, he says, that on the 15th day of July, in the year 1831, he was, and still is, a resident in the Cherokee Nation; and that the said supposed crime or crimes, and each of them, were committed, if committed at all, at the Town of New Echota, in the said Cherokee Nation, out of the jurisdiction of this court, and not in the county of Gwinnett, or elsewhere, within the jurisdiction of this court; and this defendant saith that he is a citizen of the State of Vermont, one of the United States of America, and that he entered the aforesaid Cherokee Nation in the capacity of a duly authorized missionary of the American Board of Commissioners for Foreign Missions, under the authority of the President of the United States, and has not since been required by him to leave it; that he was, at the time of his arrest, engaged in preaching the Gospel to the Cherokee Indians, and in translating the sacred Scriptures into their language, with the permission and approval of the said Cherokee Nation, and in accordance with the humane policy of the government of the United States for the civilization and improvement of the Indians; and that his residence there, for this purpose, is the residence charged in the aforesaid indictment; and this defendant further said that this prosecution the State of Georgia ought not to have or maintain, because, he saith, that several treaties have, from time to time, been entered into between the United States and the Cherokee Nation of Indians, to wit, at Hopewell, on the 28th day of November, 1785; at Holston, on the 2d day of July, 1791; at Philadelphia, on the 26th day of June, 1794; at Tellico, on the 2d of October, 1798; at Tellico, on the 24th day of October, 1804; at Tellico, on the 25th day of October, 1805; at Tellico, on the 27th day of October, 1805; at Washington city, on the 22d day of March, 1816; at the Chickasaw Council House, on the 14th day of September, 1816; at the Cherokee Agency, on the 8th day of July, 1817; and at Washington city, on the 27th day of February, 1819; all which treaties have been duly ratified by the Senate of the United States of America, and by which treaties the United States of America acknowledge the said Cherokee Nation to be a sovereign nation, authorized to govern themselves, and all persons who have settled within their territory, free from any right of legislative interference by the several States composing the United States of America, in reference to acts done within their own territory; and by which treaties the whole of the territory now occupied by the Cherokee Nation on the east of the Mississippi has been solemly guaranteed to them; all of which treaties are existing treaties at this day, and in full force.

By these treaties, and particularly by the treaties of Hopewell and Holston, the aforesaid territory is acknowledged to lie without the jurisdiction of the several States composing the Union of the United States; and it is thereby specially stipulated that the citizens of the United States shall not enter the aforesaid territory, even on a visit, without a passport from the governor of a State, or from some one duly authorized thereto by the President of the United States; all of which will more fully and at large appear by references to the aforesaid treaties. And this defendant saith, that the several acts charged in the bill of indictment were done, or omitted to de done, if at all, within the said nation, and so, as aforesaid, held by them, under the guarantee of the United States; that, for those acts, the defendant is not amenable to the laws of Georgia, nor to the jurisdiction of the courts of the said State; and that the laws of the State of Georgia, which profess to add the said territory to the several adjacent counties of the said State, and to extend the laws of Georgia over the said territory and persons inhabiting the same; and, in particular, the act on which this indictment against this defendant is grounded, to wit, 'An Act entitled an Act to prevent the exercise of assumed and arbitrary power by all persons under a pretext of authority from the Cherokee Indians, and their laws, and to prevent white persons from residing within that part of the chartered limits of Georgia occupied by the Cherokee Indians, and to provide a guard for the protection of the gold mines, and to enforce the laws of the State within the aforesaid territory,' are repugnant to the aforesaid treaties; which, according to the Constitution of the United States, compose a part of the supreme law of the land; and that these laws of Georgia are, therefore, unconstitutional, and void, and of no effect; that the said laws of Georgia are also unconstitutional and void, because they impair the obligation of the various contracts formed by and between the aforesaid Cherokee Nation and the said United States of America, as above recited; also, that the said laws of Georgia are unconstitutional and void, because they interfere with, and attempt to regulate and control the intercourse with the said Cherokee Nation, which, by the said Constitution, belongs exclusively to the Congress of the United States; and because the said laws are repugnant to the statue of the United States, passed on the — day of March, 1802, entitled 'An Act to regulate trade and intercourse with the Indian tribes and to preserve peace on the frontier;' and that, therefore, this court has no jurisdiction to cause this defendant to make further or other answer to the said bill of indictment, or further to try and punish this defendant for the said supposed offense or offenses alleged in the bill of indictment, or any of them; and, therefore, this defendant prays judgment whether he shall be held bound to answer further to said indictment."

This plea was overruled by the court, and the prisoner, being arraigned pleaded not guilty. The jury found a verdict against him, and the court sentenced him to hard labor in the penitentiary for the term of four years.

By overruling this plea, the court decided that the matter if contained was not a bar to the action. The plea, therefore, must be examined for the purpose of determining whether it makes a case which brings the party within the provisions of the twenty-fifth section of the "Act to establish the judicial courts of the United States."

The plea avers that the residence charged in the indictment was under the authority of the President of the United States, and with the permission and approval of the Cherokee Nation. That the treaties subsisting between the United States and the Cherokees, acknowledge their right as a sovereign nation to govern themselves and all persons who have settled within their territory, free from any right of legislative interference by the several States composing the United States of America. That the act under which the prosecution was instituted is repugnant to the said treaties, and is, therefore, unconstitutional and void. That the said act is also unconstitutional, because it interferes with, and attempts to regulate and control the intercourse with the Cherokee Nation which belongs exclusively to Congress, and, because, also, it is repugnant to the statute of the United States, entitled "An Act to regulate trade and intercourse with the Indian tribes, and to preserve peace on the frontiers."

Let the averments of this plea be compared with the twenty-fifth section of the Judicial Act.

That section enumerates the cases in which the final judgment or decree of a State court may be revised in the Supreme Court of the United States. These are,

> "where is drawn in question the validity of a treaty, or statute of, or an authority exercised under the United States, and the decision is against their validity of a statute of, or an authority exercised under any State, on the ground of their being repugnant to the Constitution, treaties or laws of the United States, and the decision is in favor of such their validity; or where is drawn in question the construction of any clause of the Constitution, or of a treaty, or statute of, or commission held under the United States, and the decision is against the title, right, privilege or exemption, especially set up or claimed by either party under such clause of the said Constitution, treaty, statute or commission."

The indictment and plea in this case draw in question, we think, the validity of the treaties made by the United States with the Cherokee Indians; if not so, their construction is certainly drawn in question; and the decision has been, if not against their validity, "against the right, privilege or exemption, specially set up and claimed under them." They also draw into question the validity of a statute of the State of Georgia, "on the ground of its being repugnant to the Constitution, treaties and laws of the United States, and the decision is in favor of its validity."

It is, then, we think, too clear for controversy, that the act of Congress by which this court is constituted, has given it the power, and of course imposed on it the duty, of exercising jurisdiction in this case. This duty, however unpleasant, cannot be avoided. Those who fill the judicial department have no discretion in selecting the subjects to be brought before them. We must explain the defense set up in this plea. We must inquire and decide whether the act of the Legislature of Georgia under which the plaintiff in error has been prosecuted and condemned, be consistent with, or repugnant to the Constitution, laws and treaties of the United States.

It has been said at the bar that the acts of the Legislature of Georgia seize on the whole Cherokee country, parcel it out among the neighboring counties of the State, extend her code over the whole country, abolish its institutions and its laws, and annihilate its political existence.

NATIVE
AMERICAN
RIGHTS

WORCESTER V.
THE STATE OF
GEORGIA

If this be the general effect of the system, let us inquire into the effect of the particular statute and section on which the indictment is founded.

It enacts that

"all white persons, residing within the limits of the Cherokee Nation on the 1st day of March next, or at any time thereafter, without a license or permit from his excellency the governor, or from such agent as his excellency the governor shall authorize to grant such permit or license, and who shall not have taken the oath hereinafter required, shall be guilty of a high misdemeanor, and, upon conviction thereof, shall be punished by confinement to the penitentiary, at hard labor for a term not less than four years."

The eleventh section authorizes the governor, should he deem it necessary for the protection of the mines, or the enforcement of the laws in force within the Cherokee Nation, "to raise and organize a guard," etc.

The thirteenth section enacts,

"that the said guard or any member of them, shall be, and they are hereby authorized and empowered to arrest any person legally charged with or detected in a violation of the laws of this State, and to convey, as soon as practicable,, the person so arrested, before a justice of the peace, judge of the superior, or justice of inferior court of this State, to be dealt with according to law."

The extraterritorial power of every Legislation being limited in its action to its own citizens or subjects, the very passage of this act is an assertion of jurisdiction over the Cherokee Nation, and of the rights and powers consequent on jurisdiction.

The first step, then in the inquiry which the Constitution and laws impose on this court, is an examination of the rightfulness of this claim.

America, separated from Europe by a wide ocean, was inhabited by a distinct people, divided into separate nations, independent of each other and of the rest of the world, having institutions of their own, and governing themselves by their own laws. It is difficult to comprehend the proposition that the inhabitants of either quarter of the globe could have rightful original claims of dominion over the inhabitants of the other, or over the lands they occupied; or that the discovery of either by the other should give the discoverer rights in the country discovered which annulled the pre-existing rights of its ancient possessors.

After lying concealed for a series of ages, the enterprise of Europe, guided by nautical science, conducted some of her adventurous sons into this western world. They found it in possession of a people who had made small progress in agriculture or manufacturers, and whose general employment was war, hunting, and fishing.

Did these adventurers, by sailing along the coast and occasionally landing on it, acquire for the several governments to whom they belonged, or by whom they were commissioned, a rightful property in the soil from the Atlantic to the Pacific; or rightful dominion over the numerous people who occupied it? Or has nature, or the great Creator of all things, conferred these rights over hunters and fishermen, on agriculturists and manufacturers?

But power, war, conquest, give rights, which, after possession, are conceded by the world; and which can never be controverted by those on whom they descend. We proceed, then, to the actual state of things, having glanced at their origin, because holding it in our recollection might shed some light on existing pretensions.

The great maritime powers of Europe discovered and visited different parts of this continent at nearly the same time. The object was too immense for any one of them to grasp the whole, and the claimants were too powerful to submit to the exclusive or unreasonable pretensions of any single potentate. To avoid bloody conflicts, which might terminate disastrously to all, it was necessary for the nations of Europe to establish some principle which all would acknowledge, and which should decide their respective rights as between themselves. This principle, suggested by the actual state of things, was, "that discovery gave title to the government by whose subjects or by whose authority it was made, against all other European governments, which title might be consummated by possession." 8 Wheat. 573.

This principle, acknowledged by all Europeans, because it was the interest of all to acknowledge it, gave to the nation making the discovery, as its inevitable consequence, the sole right of acquiring the soil and of making settlements on it. It was an exclusive principle which shut out the right of competition among those who had argued to it; not one which could annul the previous rights of those who had not agreed to it; not one which could annul the previous rights of those who had not agreed to it. It regulated the right given by discovery among the European discoverers, but could not affect the rights of those already in possession, either as aboriginal occupants, or as occupants by virtue of a discovery made before the memory of man. It gave the exclusive right to purchase, but did not found that right on a denial of the right of the possessor to sell.

The relation between the Europeans and the natives was determined in each case by the particular government which asserted and could maintain this pre-emptive privilege in the particular place. The United States succeeded to all the claims of Great Britain, both territorial and political; but no attempt, so far as is known, has been made to enlarge them. So far as they existed merely in theory, or were in their nature only exclusive of the claims of other European nations, they still retain their original character, and remain dormant. So far as they have been practically exerted, they exist in fact, are understood by both parties, are asserted by the one, and admitted by the other.

Soon after Great Britain determined on planting colonies in America, the king granted charters to companies of his subjects, who associated for the purpose of carrying the views of the crown into effect, and of enriching themselves. The first of these charters was made before possession was taken of any part of the country. They purport, generally, to convey the soil, from the Atlantic to the South Sea. This soil was occupied by numerous and warlike nations, equally willing and able to defend their possessions. The extravagant and absurd idea that the feeble settlements made on the sea-coast, or the companies under whom they were made, acquired legitimate power by them to govern the people, or occupy the lands from sea to sea, did not enter the mind of any man. They were well understood to convey the title which, according to the common law of European sovereigns respecting America, they might rightfully convey, and no more. This was the exclusive right of purchasing such lands as the natives were willing to sell. The crown could not be understood to grant what the crown did not affect to claim, nor was it so understood.

The power of making war is conferred by these charters on the colonies, but defensive war alone seems to have been contemplated. In the first charter to the first and second colonies, they are empowered, "for their several defenses, to encounter, expulse, repel, and resist, all persons who shall, without license," attempt to inhabit "within the said precincts and limits of the said several colonies, or that shall enterprise or attempt at any time hereafter the least detriment or annoyance of the said several colonies or plantations."

The charter to Connecticut concludes a general power to make defensive war with these terms: "and upon just cause to invade and destroy the natives or other enemies of the said colony."

The same power, in the same words, is conferred on the government of Rhode Island.

This power to repel invasion, and, upon just cause, to invade and destroy the natives, authorizes offensive as well as defensive war, but only "on just cause." The very terms imply the existence of a country to be invaded, and of an enemy who has given just cause of war.

The charter to William Penn contains the following recital: "and because, in so remote a country, near so many barbarous nations, the incursions, as well as the savages themselves, as of other enemies, pirates, and robbers, may probably be feared, therefore we haven given," etc. The instrument then confers the power of war.

These barbarous nations, whose incursions were feared, and to repel whose incursions the power to make was given, were surely not considered as the subjects of Penn, or occupying his lands during his pleasure.

The same clause is introduced into the charter to Lord Baltimore.

The charter to Georgia professes to be granted for the charitable purpose of enabling poor subjects to gain a comfortable subsistence by cultivating lands in the American provinces, "at present waste and desolate." It recites:

> "and whereas our provinces in North America have been frequently ravaged by Indian enemies, more especially that of South Carolina, which in the late war by the neighboring savages, was laid waste by fire and sword, and great numbers of the English inhabitants miserably massacred; and our loving subjects, who now inhabit there, by reason of the smallness of their numbers, will, in case of any new war, be exposed to the like calamities, inasmuch as their whole southern frontier continueth unsettled, and lieth open to the said savages."

NATIVE
AMERICAN
RIGHTS

WORCESTER V.
THE STATE OF
GEORGIA

These motives for planting the new colony are incompatible with the lofty ideas of granting the soil and all its inhabitants from sea to sea. They demonstrate the truth that these grants asserted a title against Europeans only, and were considered as blank paper so far as the rights of the natives were concerned. The power of war is given only for defense, not for conquest.

The charters contain passages showing one of their objects to be the civilization of the Indians and their conversion to Christianity—objects to be accomplished by conciliatory conduct and good example; not by extermination.

The actual state of things, and the practice of European nations, on so much of the American continent as lies between the Mississippi and the Atlantic, explain their claims, and the charters they granted. Their pretensions unavoidably interfered with each other; though the discovery of one was admitted by all to exclude the claim of any other, the extent of that discovery was the subject of unceasing contest. Bloody conflicts arose between them, which gave importance and security to the neighboring nations. Fierce and warlike in their character, they might be formidable enemies or effective friends. Instead of rousing their resentments by asserting claims to their lands, or to dominion over their persons their alliance was sought by flattering professions, and purchased by rich presents. The English, the French, and the Spaniards, were equally competitors for their friendship and their aid. Not well acquainted with the exact meaning of words, nor supposing it to be material whether they were called the subjects, or the children of their father in Europe; lavish in professions of duty and affection, in return for the rich presents they received; so long as their actual independence was untouched, and their right to self-government acknowledged they were willing to profess dependence on the power which furnished supplies of which they were in absolute need, and restrained dangerous intruders from entering their country; and this was probably the sense in which the term was understood by them.

Certain it is, that our history furnishes no example, from the first settlement of our country, of any attempt on the part of the crown to interfere with the internal affairs of the Indians, farther than to keep out the agents of foreign powers, who, as traders or otherwise, might seduce them into foreign alliances. The king purchased their lands when they were willing to sell, at a price they were willing to take; but never coerced a surrender of them. He also purchased their alliance and dependence by subsides; but never intruded into the interior of their affairs, or interfered with their self-government, so far as respected themselves only.

The general views of Great Britain with regard to the Indians were detailed by Mr. Stuart, Superintendent of Indian Affairs, in a speech delivered at Mobile, in presence of several persons of distinction, soon after the peace of 1763. Towards the conclusion he says,

"lastly, I inform you that it is the king's order to all his governors and subjects to treat Indians with justice and humanity, and to forbear all encroachments on the territories alloted to them; accordingly, all individuals are prohibited from purchasing any of your lands; but, as you know that, as your white brethren cannot feed you when you visit them unless you give them ground to plant, it is expected that you will cede lands to the king for that purpose. But, whenever you shall be pleased to surrender any of your territories to his majesty, it must be done, for the future, at a public meeting of your nation, when the governors of the provinces, or the superintendent shall be present, and obtain the consent of all your people. The boundaries of your hunting-grounds will be accurately fixed, and no settlement permitted to be made upon them. As you may be assured that all treaties with your people will be faithfully kept, so it is expected that you, also, will be careful strictly to observe them."

The proclamation issued by the King of Great Britain in 1763, soon after the ratification of the articles of peace, forbids the governors of any of the colonies to grant warrants of survey, or pass patents upon any lands whatever, which, not having been ceded to, or purchased by, us (the King), as aforesaid, are reserved to the said Indians, or any of them.

The proclamation proceeds:

"And we do further declare it to be our royal will and pleasure, for the present, as aforesaid, to reserve, under our sovereignty, protection, and dominion, for the use of the said Indians, all the lands and territories lying to the westward of the sources of the rivers which fall into the sea, from the west and north-west as aforesaid; and we do hereby strictly forbid, on pain of our displeasure, all our loving subjects from making any purchases or settlements whatever, or taking possession of any of the lands above reserved, without our special leave and license for that purpose first obtained."

"And we do further strictly enjoin and require all persons whatever, who have, either willfully or inadvertently, seated themselves upon any lands within the countries above described, or upon any other lands within the countries above described, or upon any other lands which, not having been ceded to, or purchased by us, are still reserved to the said Indians, as aforesaid, forthwith to remove themselves from such settlements."

A proclamation issued by Governor Gage, in 1772, contains the following passage:

"Whereas many persons, contrary to the positive orders of the king upon this subject, have undertaken to make settlements beyond the boundaries fixed by the treaties made with the Indian nations, which boundaries ought to serve nations, particularly on the Ouabache." The proclamation orders such persons to quit those countries without delay.

Such was the policy of Great Britain towards the Indian nations inhabiting the territory from which she excluded all other Europeans; such her claims, and such her practical exposition of the charters she had granted: she considered them as nations capable of maintaining the relations of peace and war; of governing themselves, under her protection; and she made treaties with them, the obligation of which she acknowledged.

This was the settled state of things when the war of our Revolution commenced. The influence of our enemy was established; her resources enabled her to keep up that influence, and the colonist had much cause for the apprehension that the Indian nations would, as the allies of Great Britain, add their arms to hers. This, as was to be expected, became an object of great solicitude to Congress. Far from advancing a claim to their lands, or asserting any right of dominion over them, Congress resolved "that the securing and preserving the friendship of the Indian nations appears to be a subject of the utmost moment to these colonies."

The early journals of Congress exhibit the most anxious desire to conciliate the Indian nations. Three Indian departments were established, and commissioners appointed in each, "to treat with the Indians in their respective departments, in the name and on the behalf of the United Colonies, in order to preserve peace and friendship with the said Indians, and to prevent their taking any part in the present commotions."

The most strenuous exertions were made to procure those supplies on which Indian friendships were supposed to depend; and everything were supposed to depend; and everything which might excite hostility was avoided.

The first treaty was made with the Delawares, in September, 1778.

The language of equality in which it is drawn evinces the temper with which the negotiation was undertaken, and the opinion which then prevailed in the United States.

"That all offenses or acts of hostilities, by one or either of the contracting parties against the other, be mutually forgiven, and buried in the depth of oblivion, never more to be had in remembrance.

"That a perpetual peace and friendship shall, from henceforth, take place and subsist between the contracting parties aforesaid, through all succeeding generations; and if either of the parties are engaged in a just and necessary war, with any other nation or nations, that then each shall assist the other, in due proportion to their abilities, till their enemies are brought to reasonable terms of accommodation," etc.

The third article stipulates, among other things, a free passage for the American troops through the Delaware Nation; and engages that they shall be furnished with provisions and other necessaries at their value.

"For the better security of the peace and friendship now entered into by the contracting parties against all infractions of the same by the citizens of either party; to the prejudice of the other, neither party shall proceed to the infliction of punishments on the citizens of the other, otherwise than by securing the offender or offenders, by imprisonment or any other competent means, till a fair and impartial trial can be had by judges or juries of both parties, as near as can be to the laws, customs and usages of the contracting parties, and natural justice," etc.

The fifth article regulates the trade between the contracting parties, in a manner entirely equal.

The sixth article is entitled to peculiar attention, as it contains a disclaimer of designs which were, at that time, ascribed to the United States by their enemies, and from the impu-

NATIVE
AMERICAN
RIGHTS

WORCESTER V.
THE STATE OF
GEORGIA

tation of which Congress was then peculiarly anxious to free the government. It is in these words: "Whereas the enemies of the United States have endeavored, by every artifice in their power, to possess the Indians in general with an opinion that it is the design of the States aforesaid to extirpate the Indians and take possession of their country; to obviate such false suggestion the United States do engage to guaranty to the aforesaid nation of Delawares, and their heirs, all their territorial rights, in the fullest and most ample manner, as it hath been bounded by former treaties, as long as the said Delaware Nation shall abide by, and hold fast the chain of friendship now entered into."

The parties further agree that other tribes, friendly to the interest of the United States, may be invited to form a State, whereof the Delaware Nation shall be the heads, and have a representation in Congress.

This treaty, in its language and in its provisions, is formed as near as may be, on the model of treaties between the crowned heads of Europe.

The sixth article shows how Congress then treated the injurious calumny of cherishing designs unfriendly to the political and civil rights of the Indians.

During the war of the Revolution, the Cherokees took part with the British. After its termination, the United States, through desirous of peace, did not feel its necessity so strongly as while the war continued. Their political situation being changed, they might very well think it advisable to assume a higher tone, and to impress on the Cherokees the same respect for Congress which was before felt for the King of Great Britain. This may account for the language of the Treaty of Hopewell. There is the more reason for supposing that the Cherokee chiefs were not very critical judges of the language, from the fact that every one makes his mark; no chief was capable of signing his name. It is probable the treaty was interpreted to them.

The treaty is introduced with the declaration that "the commissioners plenipotentiary of the United States give peace to all the Cherokees, and receive them into the favor and protection of the United States of America, on the following conditions."

When the United States gave peace, did they not also receive it? Were not both parties desirous of it? If we consult the history of the day, does it not inform us that the United States were at least as anxious to obtain it as the Cherokees? We may ask, further, did the Cherokees come to the seat of the American government to solicit peace; or, did the American commissioners go to them to obtain it? The treaty was made at Hopewell, not at New York. The word "give," then, has no real importance attached to it.

The first and second articles stipulate for the mutual restoration of prisoners, and are of course equal.

The third article acknowledges the Cherokees to be under the protection of the United States of America, and of no other power.

This stipulation is found in Indian treaties generally. It was introduced into their treaties with Great Britain; and may probably be found in those with other European powers. Its origin may be traced to the nature of their connection with those powers; and its true meaning is discerned in their relative situation.

The general law of European sovereigns, respecting their claims in America, limited the intercourse of Indians, in a great degree, to the particular potentate whose ultimate right of domain was acknowledged by the others. This was the general state of things in time of peace. It was sometimes changed in war. The consequence was that their supplies were derived chiefly from that nation, and their trade confined to it. Goods, indispensable to their comfort, in the shape of presents, were received from the same hand. What was of still more importance, the strong hand of government was interposed to restrain the disorderly and licentious from intrusions into their country, from encroachments on their lands, and from those acts of violence which were often attended by reciprocal murder. The Indians perceived in this protection only what was beneficial to themselves—an engagement to punish aggressions on them. It involved, practically, no claim to their lands, no dominion over their persons. It merely bound the nation to the British crown as a dependent ally, claiming the protection of a powerful friend and neighbor, and receiving the advantages of that protection, without involving a surrender of their national character.

This is the true meaning of the stipulation, and is undoubtedly the sense in which it was made. Neither the British government nor the Cherokees ever understood it otherwise.

The same stipulation entered into with the United States, is undoubtedly to be construed in the same manner. They receive the Cherokee Nation into their favor and protection. The Cherokees acknowledge themselves to be under the protection of the United States, and of no other power. Protection does not imply the destruction of the protected. The manner in which this stipulation was understood by the American government is explained by the language and acts of our first President.

The fourth article draws the boundary between the Indians and the citizens of the United States. But, in describing this boundary, the term "alloted" and the term "hunting ground" are used.

Is it reasonable to suppose that the Indians, who could not write, and most probably could not read, who certainly were not critical judges of our languages, should distinguish the word "alloted" from the words "marked out." The actual subject of contract was the dividing line 'between the two nations, and their attention may very well be supposed to have been confined to that subject. When, in fact they were ceding lands to the United States, and describing the extent of their cession, it may very well be supposed that they might not understand the term employed as indicating that instead of granting they were receiving lands. If the term would admit of no other signification, which is not conceded, its being misunderstood is so apparent, results so necessarily from the whole transaction, that it must, we think, be taken in the sense in which it was most obviously used.

So with respect to the words "hunting-grounds." Hunting was at that time the principal occupation of the Indians, and their land was more used for that purpose than for any other. It could not, however, be supposed that any intention existed of restricting the full use of the lands they reserved.

To the United States, it could be a matter of no concern whether their whole territory was devoted to hunting-grounds, or whether an occasional village, and an occasional corn field, interrupted and gave some variety to the scene.

These terms had been used in their treaties with Great Britain, and had never been misunderstood. They had never been supposed to imply a right in the British government to take their lands, or to interfere with their internal government.

The fifth article withdraws the protection of the United States from any citizen who has settled, or shall settle, on the lands allotted to the Indians, for their hunting-grounds; and stipulates that if he shall not remove within six months the Indians may punish him.

The sixth and seventh articles stipulate for the punishment of the citizens of either country, who may commit offenses on or against the citizens of the other. The only inference to be drawn from them is, that the United States considered the Cherokees as a nation.

The ninth article is in these words:

"For the benefit and comfort of the Indians, and for the prevention of injuries or oppressions on the part of the citizens or Indians, the United States in Congress assembled, shall have the sole and exclusive right of regulating the trade with the Indians, and managing all their affairs, as they think proper.

To construe the expression "managing all their affairs," into a surrender of self-government, would be, we think a perversion of their necessary meaning, and a departure from the construction which has been uniformly put on them. The great subject of the article is the Indian trade. The influence it gave made it desirable that Congress should possess it. The commissioners brought forward the claim, with the profession that their motive was "the benefit and comfort of the Indians, and the prevention of injuries or oppressions." This may be true, as respects the regulation of their trade, and as respects the regulation of all affairs connected with their trade, but cannot be true as respects the management of all their affairs. The most important of these are the cession of their lands, and security against intruders on them. Is it credible that they should have considered themselves as surrendering to the United States the right to dictate their future cessions, and the terms on which they should be made? or to compel their submission to the violence of disorderly and licentious intruders? It is equally inconceivable that they could have supposed themselves, by a phrase thus slipped into an article on another and most interesting subject, to

NATIVE
AMERICAN
RIGHTS

WORCESTER V.
THE STATE OF
GEORGIA

NATIVE
AMERICAN
RIGHTS

WORCESTER V.
THE STATE OF
GEORGIA

have devested themselves of the right of self-government on subjects not connected with trade. Such a measure could not be "for their benefit and comfort," or for "the prevention of injuries and oppression." Such a construction would be inconsistent with the spirit of this and of all subsequent treaties; especially of those articles which recognize the right of the Cherokees to declare hostilities and to make war. It would convert a treaty of peace covertly into an act annihilating the political existence of one of the parties. Had such a result been intended, it would have been openly avowed.

This treaty contains a few terms capable of being used in a sense which could not have been intended at the time, and which is inconsistent with the practical construction which has always been put on them; but its essential articles treat the Cherokees as a nation capable of maintaining the relations of peace and war, and ascertain the boundaries between them and the United States.

The Treaty of Hopewell seems not to have established a solid peace. To accommodate the differences still existing between the State of Georgia and the Cherokee Nation, the Treaty of Holston was negotiated in July, 1791. The existing Constitution of the United States had been then adopted, and the government, having more intrinsic capacity to enforce its just claims, was perhaps less mindful of high sounding expressions denoting superiority. We hear no more of giving peace to the Cherokees. The mutual desire of establishing permanent peace and friendship, and of removing all causes of war, is honestly avowed, and, in pursuance of their desire, the first article declares that there shall be perpetual peace and friendship between all the citizens of the United States of America and all the individuals composing the Cherokee Nation.

The second article repeats the important acknowledgment that the Cherokee Nation is under the protection of the United States of America, and of no other sovereign whosoever.

The meaning of this has been already explained. The Indian nations were, from their situation, necessarily dependent on some foreign potentate for the supply of their essential wants, and for their protection from lawless and injurious intrusions into their country. That power was naturally termed their protector. They had been arranged under the protection of Great Britain; but the extinguishment of the British power in their neighborhood, and the

establishment of that of the United States in its place, led naturally to the declaration, on the part of the Cherokees, that they were under the protection of the United States, and of no other power. They assumed the relation with the United States which had before subsisted with Great Britain.

This relation was that of nation claiming and receiving the protection of one more powerful, not that of individuals abandoning their national character, and submitting as subjects to the laws of a master.

The third article contains a perfectly equal stipulation for the surrender of prisoners.

The fourth article declares that "the boundary between the United States and the Cherokee Nation shall be as follows: beginning," etc. We hear no more of "allotments" or of "hunting-grounds." A boundary is described, between nation and nation, by mutual consent. The national character of each; ability of each to establish this boundary, is acknowledged by the other. To preclude forever all disputes, it is agreed that it shall be plainly marked by commissioners, to be appointed by each party; and, in order to extinguish forever all claim of the Cherokees to the ceded lands, an additional consideration is to be paid by the United States. For this additional consideration the Cherokees release and right to the ceded land, forever.

By the fifth article, the Cherokees allow the United States a road through their country, and the navigation of the Tennessee River. The acceptance of these cessions is an acknowledgment of the right of the Cherokees to make or withhold them.

By the sixth article, it is agreed, on the part of the Cherokees, that the United States shall have the sole and exclusive right of regulating their trade. No claim is made to the management of all their affairs. This stipulation has already been explained. The observation may be repeated, that the stipulation is itself an admission of their right to make or refuse it.

By the seventh article, the United States solemnly guaranty to the Cherokee Nation all their lands not hereby ceded.

The eighth article relinquishes to the Cherokees any citizens of the United States who may settle on their lands; and the ninth forbids any citizen of the United States to hunt on their lands or to enter their country without a passport.

The remaining articles are equal, and contain stipulations which could be made only with a nation admitted to be capable of governing itself.

This treaty, thus explicitly recognizing the national character of the Cherokees, and their right to self-government, thus guarantying their lands; assuming the duty of protection, and of course, pledging the faith of the United States for that protection, has been frequently renewed and is now in full force.

To the general pledge of protection have been added several specific pledges, deemed valuable by the Indians. Some of these restrain the citizens of the United States from encroachments on the Cherokee country, and provide for the punishment of intruders.

From the commencement of our government Congress has passed acts to regulate trade and intercourse with the Indians; which treat them as nations, respect their rights, and manifest a firm purpose to afford that protection which treaties stipulate. All these acts, and especially that of 1802, which is still in force, manifestly consider the several Indian nations as distinct political communities, having territorial boundaries, within which their authority is exclusive, and having a right to all the lands within those boundaries, which is not only acknowledged, but guaranteed by the United States.

In 1819, Congress passed an Act for promoting those humane designs of civilizing the neighboring Indians, which had long been cherished by the executive. It enacts,

> "that, for the purpose of providing against the further settlements of the United States, and for introducing among them the habits and arts of civilization, the President of the United States shall be, and he is hereby authorized, in every case where he shall judge improvement in the habits and condition of such Indians practicable, and that the means of instruction can be introduced with their own consent, to employ capable persons, of good moral character, to instruct them in the mode of agriculture suited to their situation; and for teaching their children in reading, writing and arithmetic; and for performing such other duties as may be enjoined, according to such instructions and rules as the President may give and prescribe for the regulation of their conduct in the discharge of their duties."

This act avowedly contemplates the preservation of the Indian nations as an object sought by the United States, and purposes to effect this object by civilizing and converting them from hunters into agriculturists. Though the Cherokees had already made considerable progress in this improvement, it cannot be doubted that the general words of the act comprehend them. Their advance in the "habits and arts of civilization," rather encouraged perseverance in the laudable exertions still farther to meliorate their condition. This act furnishes strong additional evidence of a settled purpose to fix the Indians in their country by giving them security at home.

The treaties and laws of the United States contemplate the Indian territory as completely separated from that of the States; and provide that all intercourse with them shall be carried on exclusively by the government of the Union. Is this the rightful exercise of power, or is it usurpation?

While these States were colonies, this power, in its utmost extent, was admitted to reside in the crown. When our revolutionary struggle commenced, Congress was composed of an assemblage of deputies acting under specific powers granted by the legislatures, or conventions of the several colonies. It was a great popular movement, not perfectly organized; nor were intrusted with the management of affairs accurately defined. The necessities of our situation produced a general conviction that those measures which concerned all, must be transacted by a body in which the representatives of all were assembled, and which could command the confidence of all: Congress, therefore, was considered as invested with all the powers of war and peace, and Congress dissolved our connection with the mother country, and declared these United Colonies to be independent States. Without any written definition of powers, they employed diplomatic agents to represent the United States at the several courts of Europe; offered to negotiate treaties with them, and did actually negotiate treaties with France. From the same necessity, and on the same principles, Congress assumed the management of Indian affairs; first in the name of these United Colonies, and afterwards in the name of the United States. Early attempts were made at negotiation, and to regulate trade with them. These not proving successful, war was carried on under direction, and with the forces of the United States, and the efforts to make peace by

NATIVE
AMERICAN
RIGHTS

WORCESTER V.
THE STATE OF
GEORGIA

NATIVE
AMERICAN
RIGHTS

WORCESTER V.
THE STATE OF
GEORGIA

treaty were earnest and incessant. The confederation found Congress in the exercise of the same powers of peace and war, in our relations with Indian nations, as with those of Europe.

Such was the state of things when the confederation was adopted. That instrument surrendered the powers of peace and war to Congress and prohibited them to the States, respectively, unless a State be actually invaded, "or shall have received certain advice of a resolution being formed by some nation of Indians to invade such State, and the danger is so imminent as not to admit of delay till the United States in Congress assembled can be consulted." This instrument also gave the United States in Congress assembled the sole and exclusive right of "regulating the trade and managing all the affairs with the Indians, not members of any of the States: provided that the legislative power of any State within its own limits be not infringed or violated."

The ambiguous phrases which follow the grant of power to the United States were so construed by the States of North Carolina and Georgia as to annul the power itself. The discontent and confusion resulting from these conflicting claims produced representations to Congress, which were referred to a committee, who made their report in 1787. The report does not assent to the construction of the two States, but recommends an accommodation, by liberal cessions of territory, or by an admission on their part of the powers claimed by Congress. The correct exposition of this article is rendered unnecessary by the adoption of our existing Constitution. That instrument confers on Congress the powers of war and peace; of making treaties, and of regulating commerce with foreign nations, and among the several States, and with the Indian tribes. These powers comprehend all that is required for the regulation of our intercourse with the Indians. They are not limited by any restrictions on their free actions. The shackles imposed on this power, in the confederation, are discarded.

The Indian nations had always been considered as distinct, independent political communities, as distinct, retaining their original natural rights, as the undisputed possessors of the soil from time immemorial, with the single exception of that imposed by irresistible power, which excluded them from intercourse with any other European potentate than the first discoverer of the coast of the particular region claimed: and this was a restriction which those European potentates imposed on themselves, as well as on the Indians. The very term "nation," so generally applied to them, means "a people distinct from others." The Constitution, by declaring treaties already made, as well as those to be made, to be the supreme law of the land, has adopted and sanctioned the previous treaties with the Indian nations, and consequently admits their rank among those powers who are capable of making treaties. The words "treaty" and "nation" are words of our own language, selected in our diplomatic and legislative proceedings, by ourselves, having each a definite and well understood meaning. We have applied them to Indians, as we have applied them to the other nations of the earth. They are applied to all in the same scene.

Georgia herself has furnished conclusive evidence that her former opinions on this subject concurred with those entertained by her sister States, and by the government of the United States. Various acts of her Legislature have been cited in the argument, including the contract of cession made in the year 1802, all tending to prove her acquiescence in the universal conviction that the Indian nations possessed a full right to the lands they occupied, until that right should be extinguished by the United States, with their consent; that their territory was separated from that of any State within whose chartered limits they might reside, by a boundary line, established by treaties; that, within their boundary, they possessed rights with which no State could interfere, and that the whole power of regulating the intercourse with them was vested in the United States. A review of these acts, on the part of Georgia, would occupy too much time, and is the less necessary because they have been accurately detailed in the argument at the bar. Her new series of laws, manifesting her abandonment of these opinions, appears to have commenced in December, 1828.

In opposition to this original right, possessed by the undisputed occupants of every country; to this recognition of that right, which is evidenced by our history, in every change through which we have passed, is placed the charters granted by the monarch of a distant and distinct region, parcelling out a territory in possession of others whom he could not remove and did not attempt to remove, and the cession made of his claims by the Treaty of Peace.

The actual state of things at the time, and all history since, explain these charters; and the King of Great Britain, at the Treaty of Peace, could cede only what belonged to his crown. These newly asserted titles can derive no aid from the articles so often repeated in Indian treaties; extending to them, first, the protection of Great Britain, and afterwards that of the United States. These articles are associated with others, recognizing their title to self-government. The very fact of repeated treaties with them recognizes it; and the settled doctrine of the law of nations is that a weaker power does not surrender its independence—its right to self-government, by associating with a stronger and taking its protection. A weak State in order to provide for its safety, may place itself under the protection of one more powerful without stripping itself of the right of government, and ceasing to be a State. Examples of this kind are not wanting in Europe. "Tributary and feudatory states," says Vattel, "do not thereby cease to be sovereign and independent states so long as self-government and sovereign and independent authority are left in the administration of the state." At the present day, more than one State may be considered as holding its right of self-government under the guaranty and protection of one or more allies.

The Cherokee nation, then, is a distinct community, occupying its own territory, with boundaries accurately described, in which the laws of Georgia can have no force, and which the citizens of Georgia have no right to enter but with the assent of the Cherokees themselves or in conformity with treaties and with the acts of Congress. The whole intercourse between the United States and this nation is, by our Constitution and laws, vested in the government of the United States.

The act of the State of Georgia under which the plaintiff in error was prosecuted is consequently void, and the judgment a nullity. Can this court revise and reverse it?

If the objection to the system of legislation lately adopted by the Legislature of Georgia in relation to the Cherokee Nation was confined to its extraterritorial operation, the objection, though complete, so far as respected mere right, would give this court no power over the subject. But it goes much further. If the review which has

been taken be correct, and we think it is, the acts of Georgia are repugnant to the Constitution, laws, and treaties of the United States.

They interfere forcibly with the relations established between the United States and the Cherokee Nation, the regulation of which, according to the settled principles of our Constitution, are committed exclusively to the government of the Union.

They are in direct hostility with treaties, repeated in a succession of years, which mark out the boundary that separates the Cherokee country from Georgia; guaranty to them all the land within their boundary; solemnly pledge the faith of the United States to restrain their citizens from trespassing on it; and recognize the pre-existing power of the nation to govern itself.

They are in equal hostility with the acts of Congress for regulating this intercourse, and giving effect to the treaties.

The forcible seizure and abduction of the plaintiff in error, who was residing in the nation with its permission, and by authority of the President of the United States, is also a violation of the acts which authorize the chief magistrate to exercise this authority.

Will these powerful considerations avail the plaintiff in error? We think they will. He was seized and forcibly carried away while under guardianship of treaties guarantying the country in which he resided, and taking it under the protection of the United States. He was seized while performing, under the sanction of the Chief magistrate of the Union those duties which the humane policy adopted by Congress had recommended. He was apprehended, tried, and condemned, under color of a law which has been shown to be repugnant to the Constitution, laws, and treaties of the United States. Had a judgment, liable to the same objections, been rendered for property, none would question the jurisdiction of this court. It cannot be less clear when the judgment affects personal liberty, and inflicts disgraceful punishment, if punishment could disgrace when inflicted on innocence. The plaintiff in error is not less interested in the operation of this unconstitutional law than if it affected his property. He is not less entitled to the protection of the Constitution, laws, and treaties of his country.

This point has been elaborately argued and, after deliberate consideration, decided, in the

NATIVE
AMERICAN
RIGHTS

WORCESTER V.
THE STATE OF
GEORGIA

NATIVE
AMERICAN
RIGHTS

WORCESTER V.
THE STATE OF
GEORGIA

case of *Cohens v. The Commonwealth of Virginia* 6, Wheat. 264.

It is the opinion of this court that the judgment of the Superior Court for the County of Gwinett, in the State of Georgia, condemning Samuel A. Worcester to hard labor in the penitentiary of the State of Georgia for four years, was pronounced by that court under color of a law which is void, as being repugnant to the Constitution, treaties, and laws of the United States, and ought, therefore, to be reversed and annulled.

Mr. Justice M'Lean.

As this case involves principles of the highest importance, and may lead to consequences which shall have an enduring influence on the institutions of this country; and as there are some points in the case on which I wish to state, distinctly, my opinion, I embrace the privilege of doing so.

With the decision just given, I concur.

The plaintiff in error was indicted under a law of Georgia

"for residing in that part of the Cherokee Nation attached, by the laws of said State, to the County of Gwinnett, without a license or permit from his excellency the governor of the State, or from any agent authorized by his excellency the governor to grant such permit, or license and without having taken the oath to support and defend the constitution and laws of the State of Georgia, and uprightly to demean himself as a citizen thereof."

On this indictment the defendant was arrested, and, on being arraigned before the Superior Court for Gwinnett County, he filed, in substance, the following plea:

He admits that, on the 15th of July, 1831, he was, and still continued to be, a resident in the Cherokee Nation, and that the crime, if any were committed, was committed at the town of New Echota, in said nation, out of the jurisdiction of the court. That he is a citizen of Vermont, and that he entered the Indian country in the capacity of a duly authorized missionary of the American Board of Commissioners for Foreign Missions, under the authority of the President of the United States, and has not since been required by him to leave it. That he was, at the time of his arrest engaged in preaching the Gospel to the Cherokee Indians, and in translating the sacred Scriptures into their language, with the permission and approval of the Cherokee Nation, and in accordance with the humane policy of the government of the United States for the improvement of the Indians.

He then states, as a bar to the prosecution, certain treaties made between the United States and the Cherokee Indians, by which the possession of the territory they now inhabit was solemly guaranteed to them; and also a certain Act of Congress, passed in March, 1802, entitled "An Act to regulate trade and intercourse with the Indian tribes." He also alleges that this subject, by the Constitution of the United States, is exclusively vested in Congress; and that the law of Georgia, being repugnant to the Constitution of the United States, to the treaties referred to, and to the act of Congress specified, is void, and cannot be enforced against him.

This plea was overruled by the court, and the defendant pleaded not guilty.

The jury returned a verdict of guilty, and the defendant was sentenced by the court to be kept in close custody by the sheriff of the county until he could be transported to the penitentiary of the State, and the keeper thereof was directed to receive him into the custody, and keep him at hard labor in the penitentiary, during the term of four years.

Another individual was included in the same indictment, and joined in the plea to the jurisdiction of the court, and was also included in the sentence; but his name is not adverted to, because the principles of the case are fully presented in the above statement.

To reverse this judgment, a writ of error was obtained, which, having been returned with the record of the proceedings, is now before this court.

The first question which it becomes necessary to examine is, whether the record has been duly certified, so as to bring the proceedings regularly before this tribunal.

A writ of error was allowed in this case by one of the justices of this court, and the requisite security taken. A citation was also issued, in the form prescribed, to the State of Georgia, a true copy of which, as appears by the oath of William Patten, was delivered to the governor on the 24th day of November last; and another true copy was delivered on the 22 day of the same month to the Attorney-General of the State.

The record was returned by the clerk, under the seal of the court, who certifies that it is a full and complete exemplification of the proceedings and judgment had in the case; and he further certifies that the original bond, and a copy of the writ of error, were duly deposited and filed in the clerk's office of said court, on the 10th day of November last.

Is it necessary, in such a case, that the record should be certified by the judge who held the court?

In the case of *Martin v. Hunter's Lessee,* which was a writ of error to the Court of Appeals of Virginia, it was objected that the return to the writ of error was defective, because the record was not so certified; but the court in that case said, "the forms of process, and the modes of proceeding in the exercise of jurisdiction, are, with few exceptions, left by the Legislature to be regulated and changed, as this court may, in its discretion, deem expedient." By a rule of this court,

> "the return of a copy of a record, of the proper court, annexed to the writ of error, is declared to be a sufficient compliance with the mandate of the writ. The record in this case is duly certified by the clerk of the Court of Appeals, and annexed to the writ of error. The objection, therefore, which has been urged to the sufficiency of the return cannot prevail." 1 Wheat. 304.

In 9 Wheat. 526, in case of *Stewart v. Ingle et al.,* which was a writ of error to the Circuit Court for the District Columbia, a certiorari was issued upon a suggestion of diminution in the record, which was returned by the clerk with another record; whereupon a motion was made for a new certiorari, on the ground that the return ought to have been made by the judge of the court below, and not by the clerk. The writ of certiorari, it is known, like the writ of error, is directed to the court.

Mr. Justice Washington, after consultation with the judges, stated that according to the rules and practice of the court, a return made by the clerk was a sufficient return.

To ascertain what has been the general course of practice on this subject, an examination has been made into the manner in which records have been certified from State courts to this court; and it appears that, in the year 1817, six causes were certified, in obedience to writs of error, by the clerk, under the seal of this court. In the year 1819, two were so certified, one of them

being the case of *M'Culloch v. The State of Maryland.*

In the year 1821 three cases were so certified; and in the year 1823 there was one. In 1827 there were five, and in the ensuing year, seven.

In the year 1830 there were eight causes so certified, in five of which a State was a party on the record. There were three causes thus certified in the year 1831, and five in the present year.

During the above periods, there were only fifteen causes from State courts where the records were certified by the court or the presiding judge, and one of these was the case of *Cohens v. The State of Virginia.*

This court adopted the following rule on this subject in 1797:

> "It is ordered by the court that the clerk of the court to which any writ of error shall be directed, may make the return of the same by transmitting a true copy of the record, and of all proceedings in the cause, under his hand, and the seal of the court."

The power of the court to adopt this rule cannot be questioned; and it seems to have regulated the practice ever since its adoption. In some cases, the certificate of the court, or the presiding judge has been affixed to the record; but this court has decided, where the question has been raised, that such certificate is unnecessary.

So far as the authentication of the record is concerned, it is impossible to make a distinction between a civil and a criminal case. What may be sufficient to authenticate the proceedings in a civil case, must be equally so in a criminal one. The verity of the record is of as much importance in the one case as in the other.

This is a question of practice; and it would seem that, if any one point in the practice of this court can be considered as settled, this one must be so considered.

In the progress of the investigation, the next inquiry which seems naturally to arise, is, whether this is a case in which a writ of error may be issued.

By the twenty-fifth section of the Judiciary Act of 1789, it is provided

> "that a final judgment or decree in any suit in the highest court of law or equity of a State, in which a decision in the suit could be had, where is drawn in question the validity of a treaty, or statute of, or an authority exercised under, the United States, and the decision is against their validity; or where is drawn in

NATIVE
AMERICAN
RIGHTS

WORCESTER V.
THE STATE OF
GEORGIA

NATIVE
AMERICAN
RIGHTS

WORCESTER V.
THE STATE OF
GEORGIA

question the validity of a statute of, or an authority exercised under, any State, on the ground of their being repugnant to the Constitution, treaties, or laws of the United States, and the decision is in favor of such their validity; or where is drawn in question the construction of any clause of the Constitution, or of a treaty or statute of, or commission held under, the United States, and the decision is against the title, right, privilege, or exemption, specially set up or claimed by either party under such clause of the said constitution, treaty, statute, or commission, may be re-examined, and reversed or affirmed, in the Supreme Court of the United States."

Doubts have been expressed whether a writ of error to a State court is not limited to civil cases. These doubts could not have arisen from reading the above section. Is not a criminal case as much a suit as a civil case? What is a suit but a prosecution; and can anyone suppose that it was the intention of Congress, in using the word "suit," to make a distinction between a civil prosecution and a criminal one?

It is more important that jurisdiction should be given to this court in criminal than in civil cases, under the twenty-fifth section of the Judiciary Act. Would it not be inconsistent both with the spirit and letter of this law, to revise the judgment of a State court, in a matter of controversy respecting damages, where the decision is against a right asserted under the Constitution or a law of the United States; but to deny the jurisdiction, in a case where the property, the character, the liberty and life of a citizen may be destroyed, though protected by the solemn guarantees of the Constitution?

But this is not an open question; it has long since been settled by the solemn adjudications of this court. The above construction, therefore, is sustained both on principle and authority. The provisions of the section apply as well to criminal as to civil cases, where the Constitution, treaties, or laws of the United States come in conflict with the laws of a State, and the latter is sustained by the decision of the court.

It has been said that this court can have no power to arrest the proceedings of a State tribunal in the enforcement of the criminal laws of the State. This is undoubtedly true, so long as a State court, in the execution of its penal laws, shall not infringe upon the Constitution of the United States, or some treaty or law of the Union.

Suppose a State should make it penal for an officer of the United States to discharge his duties within its jurisdiction; as for instance, a land officer, an officer of the customs, or a postmaster, and punish the offender by confinement in the penitentiary; could not the Supreme Court of the United States interpose their power, and arrest or reverse the State proceedings? Cases of this kind are so palpable, that they need only to be stated to gain the assent of every judicious mind. And would not this be an interference with the administration of the criminal laws of a State?

This court have repeatedly decided that they have no appellate jurisdiction in criminal cases from the circuit courts of the United States; writs of error and appeals are given from those courts only in civil cases. But, even in those courts, where the judges are divided on any point in a criminal case, the point may be brought before this court, under a general provision in cases of division of opinion.

Jurisdiction is taken in the case under consideration exclusively by the provisions of the twenty-fifth section of the law which has been quoted. These provisions, as has been remarked, apply indiscriminately to criminal and civil cases, wherever a right is claimed under the Constitution, treaties, or laws of the United States, and the decision, by the State Court, is against such right. In the present case, the decision was against the right expressly set up by the defendant, and it was made by the highest judicial tribunal of Georgia.

To give jurisdiction in such a case, this court need look no further than to ascertain whether the right, thus asserted, was decided against by the State court. The case is clear of difficulty on this point.

The name of the State of Georgia is used in this case because such was the designation given to the cause in the State court. No one ever supposed that the State, in its sovereign capacity, in such a case, is a party to the cause. The form of the prosecution here must be the same as it was in the State court; but so far as the name of the State is used, it is a matter of form. Under a rule of this court, notice was given to the governor and Attorney-General of the State because it is a part of their duty to see that the laws of the State are executed.

In prosecutions for violations of the penal laws of the Union, the name of the United States

NATIVE
AMERICAN
RIGHTS

WORCESTER V.
THE STATE OF
GEORGIA

is used in the same manner. Whether the prosecution be under a federal or State law, the defendant has a right to question the constitutionality of the law.

Can any doubt exist as to the power of Congress to pass the law under which jurisdiction is taken in this case? Since its passage, in 1789, it has been the law of the land; and has been sanctioned by an uninterrupted course of decisions in this court, and acquiesced in by the State tribunals, with perhaps a solitary exception; and whenever the attention of the national Legislature has been called to the subject, their sanction has been given to the law by so large a majority as to approach almost to unanimity.

Of the policy of this act there can be as little doubt as of the right of Congress to pass it.

The Constitution of the United States was formed, not, in my opinion, as some have contended, by the people of the United States, nor, as others, by the States; but by a combined power exercised by the people through their delegates, limited in their sanctions, to the respective States.

Had the Constitution emanated from the people, and the States had been referred to merely as convenient districts by which the public expression could be ascertained, the popular vote throughout the Union would have been the only rule for the adoption of the Constitution. This course was not pursued; and in this fact, it clearly appears that our fundamental law was not formed, exclusively, by the popular suffrage of the people.

The vote of the people was limited to the respective States in which they resided. So that it appears there was an expression of popular suffrage and State sanction, most happily united, in the adoption of the Constitution of the Union.

Whatever differences of opinion may exist as to the means by which the Constitution was adopted, there would seem to be no ground for any difference as to certain powers conferred by it.

Three co-ordinate branches of the government were established—the executive, legislative and judicial. These branches are essential to the existence of any free government, and that they should possess powers, in their respective spheres, co-extensive with each other.

If the executive have not powers which will enable him to execute the functions of his office,

the system is essentially defective; as those duties must, in such a case, be discharged by one of the other branches. This would destroy that balance which is admitted to be essential to the existence of free government, by the wisest and most enlightened statesman of the present day.

It is not less important that the legislative power should be exercised by the appropriate branch of the government, than that the executive duties should devolve upon the proper functionary. And if the judicial power fall short of giving effect to the laws of the Union, the existence of the federal government is at an end.

It is in vain, and worse than in vain, that the national Legislature enact laws, if those laws are to remain upon the statute book as monuments of the imbecility of the national power. It is in vain that the executive is called to superintend the execution of the laws, if he have no power to aid in their enforcement.

Such weakness and folly are in no degree chargeable to the distinguished men through whose instrumentality the Constitution was formed. The powers given, it is true, are limited; and no powers, which are not expressly given, can be exercised by the federal government; but, where given, they are supreme. Within the sphere alloted to them, the co-ordinate branches of the general government revolve, unobstructed by any legitimate exercise of power by the State governments. The powers exclusively given to the federal government are limitations upon the State authorities. But, with the exception of these limitations, the States are supreme; and their sovereignty can be no more invaded by the action of the general government, than the action of the State governments can arrest or obstruct the course of the national power.

It has been asserted that the federal government is foreign to the State governments, and that it must consequently be hostile to them. Such an opinion could not have resulted from a thorough investigation of the great principles which lie at the foundation of our system. The federal government is neither foreign to the State governments, nor is it hostile to them. It proceeds from the same people, and is as much under their control as the State governments.

Where, by the Constitution, the power of legislation is exclusively vested in Congress, they legislate for the people of the Union, and their acts are as binding as are the constitutional enactments of a State Legislature on the people

NATIVE
AMERICAN
RIGHTS

WORCESTER V.
THE STATE OF
GEORGIA

of the State. If this were not so, the federal government would exist only in name. Instead of being the proudest monument of human wisdom and patriotism, it would be the frail memorial of the ignorance and mental imbecility of its framers.

In the discharge of his constitutional duties, the federal executive acts upon the people of the Union the same as a governor of a State, in the performance of his duties, acts upon the people of the State. And the judicial power of the United States acts in the same manner on the people. It rests upon the same basis as the other departments of the government. The powers of each are derived from the same source, and are conferred by the same instrument. They have the same limitations and extent.

The Supreme Court of a State, when required to give effect to a statute of the State, will examine its constitution, which they are sworn to maintain, to see if the legislative act be repugnant to it; and if the repugnancy exist, the statute must yield to the paramount law.

The same principle governs the supreme tribunal of the Union. No one can deny that the Constitution of the United States is the supreme law of the land; and, consequently, no act of any State Legislature or of Congress, which is repugnant to it, can be of any validity.

Now, if an act of a State Legislature be repugnant to the constitution of the State, the State court will declare it void; and if such act be repugnant to the Constitution of the Union, or a law made under that Constitution which is declared to be the supreme law of the land, is it not equally void? And, under such circumstances, if this court should shrink from a discharge of their duty in giving effect to the supreme law of the land, would they not violate their oaths, prove traitors to the Constitution, and forfeit all just claim to the public confidence?

It is sometimes objected, if the federal judiciary may declare an act of a State Legislature void, because it is repugnant to the Constitution of the United States, it places the legislation of a State within the power of this court. And might not the same argument must end in the destruction of all constitutions, and the will of the Legislature, like the acts of the Parliament of Great Britain, must be the supreme, and only law of the land.

It is impossible to guard an investiture of power so that it may not, in some form, be abused: an argument, therefore, against the exercise of power, because it is liable to abuse, would go to the destruction of all governments.

The powers of this court are expressly, not constructively, given by the Constitution; and within this delegation of power, this court are the Supreme Court of the people of the United States, and they are bound to discharge their duties, under the same responsibilities as the Supreme Court of a State; and are equally, within their powers, the Supreme Court of the people of each State.

When this court are required to enforce the laws of any State, they are governed by those laws. So closely do they adhere, to this rule, that during the present term, a judgment of a Circuit Court of the United States, made in pursuance of decisions of this court, has been reversed and annulled because it did not conform to the decisions of the State Court, in giving a construction to a local law. But while this court conforms its decisions to those of the State courts on all questions arising under the statutes and constitutions of the respective States, they are bound to revise and correct those decisions, if they annul either the Constitution of the United States or the laws made under it.

It appears, then, that on all questions arising under the laws of a State, the decisions of the courts of such State form a rule for the decisions of this court, and that on all questions arising under the laws of the United States, the decisions of the State courts. Is there anything unreasonable in this? Have not the federal, as well as the State courts, been constituted by the people? Why, then, should one tribunal more than the other be deemed hostile to the interests of the people?

In the second section of the third article of the Constitution, it is declared that "the judicial power shall extend to all cases in law and equity arising under the Constitution, the laws of the United States, and treaties made, or which shall be made, under their authority."

Having shown that a writ of error will lie in this case, and that the record has been duly certified, the next inquiry that arises is, what are the acts of the United States which relate to the Cherokee Indians and the acts of Georgia; and were these acts of the United States sanctioned by the federal Constitution?

Among the enumerated powers of Congress contained in the eighth section of the first article of the Constitution, it is declared that "Congress shall have power to regulate commerce with foreign nations, and among the Indian tribes." By the Articles of Confederation, which were adopted on the 9th day of July, 1778, it was provided that

"the United States, in Congress assembled, shall also have the sole and exclusive right and power of regulating the alloy and value of coin struck, by their own authority, or by that of the respective States; fixing the standard of weights and measures throughout the United States; regulating the trade and management of all affairs with the Indians, not members of any of the States: Provided, that the legislative right of any State, within its own limits, be not infringed or violated."

As early as June 1775, and before the adoption of the Articles of Confederation, Congress took into their consideration the subject of Indian affairs. The Indian country was divided into three departments, and the superintendence of each was committed to commissioners, who were authorized to hold treaties with the Indians, make disbursements of money for their use, and to discharge various duties designed to preserve peace and cultivate a friendly feeling with them towards the colonies. No person was permitted to trade with them without a license from one or more of the commissioners of the respective departments.

In April, 1776, it was

"resolved, that the commissioners of Indian affairs in the middle department, or any one of them, be desired to employ, for reasonable salaries, a minister of the Gospel, to reside among the Delaware Indians, and instruct them in the Christian religion; a schoolmaster to teach their youth reading, writing, and arithmetic; also a blacksmith. to do the work of the Indians." The general intercourse with the Indians continued to be managed under the superintendence of the continental Congress.

On the 28th of November, 1785, the Treaty of Hopewell was formed which was the first treaty made with the Cherokee Indians. The commissioners of the United States were required to give notice to the executives of Virginia, North Carolina, South Carolina, and Georgia, in order that each might appoint one or more persons to attend the treaty, but they seem to have had no power to act on the occasion.

In this treaty it is stipulated that

"the commissioners plenipotentiary of the United States in Congress assembled, give peace to all the Cherokees, and receive them into the favor and protection of the United States of America, on the following conditions:"

The Cherokees to restore all prisoners and property taken during the war.

The United States to restore to the Cherokees all prisoners.

The Cherokees acknowledge themselves to be under the protection to the United States, and of no other sovereign whatsoever.

The boundary line between the Cherokees and the citizens of the United States was agreed to as designated.

If any person, not being an Indian, intrude upon the land "alloted" to the Indians, or, being settled on it, shall refuse to remove within six months after the ratification of the treaty, he forfeits the protection of the United States, and the Indians were at liberty to punish him as they might think proper.

The Indians are bound to deliver up to the United States any Indian who shall commit robbery, or other capital crime, on a white person, lying within their protection.

If the same offense be committed on an Indian by a citizen of the United States, he is to be punished.

It is understood that the punishment of the innocent, under the idea of retaliation, is unjust, and shall not be practiced on either side, except where there is a manifest violation of this treaty; and then it shall be preceded, first, by a demand of justice; and, if refused, then by a declaration of hostilities.

"That the Indians may have full confidence in the justice of the United States respecting their interests, they shall have a right to send a deputy of their choice whenever they think fit, to Congress.

The Treaty of Holston was entered into with the same people, on the 2d day of July, 1791.

This was a treaty of peace, in which the Cherokees again placed themselves under the protection of the United States, and engaged to hold no treaty with any foreign power, individual State, or with individuals of any State. Prisoners were agreed to be delivered up on both sides; a new Indian boundary was fixed, and a

NATIVE
AMERICAN
RIGHTS

WORCESTER V.
THE STATE OF
GEORGIA

NATIVE
AMERICAN
RIGHTS

WORCESTER V.
THE STATE OF
GEORGIA

cession of land made to the United States on the payment of a stipulated consideration.

A free, unmolested road, was agreed to be given through the Indian lands, and the free navigation of the Tennessee River. It was agreed that the United States should have the exclusive right of regulating their trade, and a solemn guarantee of their land, not ceded; was made. A similar provision was made as to all persons who might enter the Indian territory, as was contained in the Treaty of Hopewell. Also, that reprisal or retaliation shall not be committed until satisfaction shall have been demanded of the aggressor.

On the 7th day of August, 1786, an ordinance for the regulation of Indian affairs adopted, which repealed the former system.

In 1794 another treaty was made with the Cherokees, the object of which was to carry into effect the Treaty of Holston. And on the plains of Tellico, on the 2d of October, 1798, the Cherokees, in another treaty, agreed to give a right of way, in a certain direction, over their lands. Other engagements were also entered into, which need not be referred to.

Various other treaties were made by the United States with the Cherokee Indians, by which, among other arrangements, cessions of territory were procured and boundaries agreed on.

In a treaty made in 1817, a distinct wish is expressed by the Cherokees to assume a more regular form of government, in which they are encouraged by the United States. By a treaty held at Washington on the 27th day of February, 1819, a reservation of land is made by the Cherokees for a school fund, which was to be surveyed and sold by the United States for that purpose. And it was agreed that all white persons, who had intruded on the Indian lands should be removed.

To give effect to various treaties with this people, the power of the executive has frequently been exercised; and at one time General Washington expressed a firm determination to resort to military force to remove intruders from the Indian territories.

On the 30th of March, 1802, Congress passed an Act to regulate trade and intercourse with the Indian tribes, and to preserve peace on the frontiers.

In this act it is provided that any citizen or resident of the United States, who shall enter into the Indian lands to hunt, or for any other purpose, without a license, shall be subject to a fine and imprisonment. And if any person shall attempt to survey, or actually survey, the Indian lands, shall be liable to forfeit a sum not exceeding one thousand dollars, and be imprisoned not exceeding twelve months. No person is permitted to reside as a trader within the Indian boundaries, without a license or permit. All persons are prohibited, under a heavy penalty, from purchasing the Indian lands; and all such purchases are declared to be void. And it is made lawful for the military force of the United States to arrest offenders against the provisions of the act.

By the seventeenth section, it is provided that the act shall not be construed as to

"prevent any trade or intercourse with Indians living on lands surrounded by settlements of the citizens of the United States, and being within the ordinary jurisdiction of any of the individual States; or the unmolested use of a road, from Washington district to Metro district, or to prevent the said road." Nor was the act to be construed as to prevent persons from traveling from Knoxville to Price's settlement, provided they shall travel in the tract or path which is usually traveled, and the Indians do not object; but if they object, then all travel on this road to be prohibited, after proclamation by the President, under the penalties provided in the act.

Several acts, having the same object in view, were passed prior to this one; but as they were repealed either before, or by the Act of 1802, their provisions need not be specially noticed.

The acts of the State of Georgia, which the plaintiff in error complains of as being repugnant to the Constitution, treaties, and laws of the United States are found in two statutes.

The first Act was passed the 12th of December, 1829, and is entitled

"An Act to add the territory lying within the chartered limits of Georgia, and now in the occupancy of the Cherokee Indians, to the counties of Carroll, DeKalb, Gwinnett and Habersham; and to extend the laws of the State over the same, and to annul all laws made by the Cherokee Nation of Indians, and to provide for the compensation of officers serving legal process in said territory, and to regulate the testimony of Indians, and to repeal the ninth section of the Act of 1828 on this subject."

This act annexes the territory to the Indians within the limits of Georgia to the counties named in the title, and extends the jurisdiction of the State over it. It annuls the laws, ordinances, orders and regulations, of any kind, made by the Cherokees, either in council or in any other way, and they are not permitted to be given in evidence in the courts of the State. By this law, no Indian, or the descendant of an Indian, residing within the Creek or Cherokee Nation of Indians, shall be deemed a competent witness in any court of the State to which a white person may be a party, except such white person reside within the nation. Offenses under the act are to be punished by confinement in the penitentiary, in some cases not less than four nor more than six years, and others not exceeding four years.

The second Act was passed on the 22d day of December, 1830, and is entitled

> "An Act to prevent the exercise of assumed and arbitrary power, by all persons, on pretext of authority from the Cherokee Indians and their laws; and to prevent white persons from residing within that part of the chartered limits of Georgia occupied by the Cherokee Indians; and to provide a guard for the protection to the gold mines, and to enforce the laws of the State without the aforesaid territory."

By the first section of this act, it is made a penitentiary offense, after the 1st day of February, 1831, for any person or persons, under color or pretense of authority from the said Cherokee tribe, or as headmen, chiefs or warriors of said tribe, to cause or procure, by any means, the assembling of any council or other pretended legislative body of the said Indians, for the purpose of legislating, etc.

They are prohibited from making laws, holding courts of justice, or executing process. And all white persons, after the 1st of March, 1831, who shall reside within the limits of the Cherokee Nation without a license or permit from his excellency the governor, or from such agent as his excellency the governor shall authorize to grant such permit or license, or who shall not have taken the oath hereinafter required, shall be guilty of a high misdemeanor; and, upon conviction thereof shall be punished by confinement to the penitentiary at hard labor, for a term not less than four years. From this punishment, agents of the United States are

excepted, white females, and male children under twenty-one years of age.

Persons who have obtained license, are required to take the following oath:

> "I. A. B. do solemnly swear that I will support and defend the constitution and laws of the State of Georgia, and uprightly demean myself as a citizen thereof. So help me God."

The governor is authorized to organize a guard, which shall not consist of more than sixty persons, to protect the mines in the Indian territory, and the guard is authorized to arrest all offenders under the act.

It is apparent that these laws are repugnant to the treaties with the Cherokee Indians which have been referred to, and to the law of 1802. This repugnance is made so clear by an exhibition of the respective acts, that no force of demonstration can make it more palpable.

By the treaties and laws of the United States, rights are guaranteed to the Cherokees, both as it respects their territory and internal polity. By the laws of Georgia these rights are abolished; and not only abolished, but an ignominious punishment is inflicted on the Indians and others, for the exercise of them. The important question then arises, which shall stand, the laws of the United States, or the laws of Georgia? No rule of construction, or this question. The response must be, so far as the punishment of the plaintiff in error is concerned, in favor of the one or the other.

Not to feel the full weight of this momentous subject would evidence an ignorance of that high responsibility which is devolved upon this tribunal, and upon its humblest member, in giving a decision in this case.

Are the treaties and law which have been cited, in force? and what, if any obligations, do they impose on the federal government within the limits of Georgia?

A reference had been made to the policy of the United States on the subject of Indian affairs before the adoption of the Constitution, with a view to ascertaining in what light the Indians have been considered by the first official acts, in relation to them, by the United States. For this object, it might not be improper to notice how they were considered by the European inhabitants, who first formed settlements in this part of the continent of America.

NATIVE
AMERICAN
RIGHTS

WORCESTER V.
THE STATE OF
GEORGIA

NATIVE
AMERICAN
RIGHTS

WORCESTER V.
THE STATE OF
GEORGIA

The abstract right of every section of the human race to a reasonable portion of the soil, by which to acquire the means of subsistence, cannot be controverted. And it is equally clear that the range of nations or tribes, who exist in the hunter state, may be restricted within reasonable limits. They shall not be permitted to roam, in the pursuit of game, over an extensive and rich country, whilst in other parts, human beings are crowded so closely together, as to render the means of subsistence precarious. The law of nature, which is paramount to all other laws, gives the right to every nation to the enjoyment of a reasonable extent of country, so as to derive the means of subsistence from the soil.

In this view, perhaps, our ancestors, when they first migrated to this country, might have taken possession of a limited extent of the domain, had they been sufficiently powerful, without negotiation or purchase from the native Indians. But this course is believed to have been nowhere taken. A more conciliatory mode was preferred, and one which was better calculated to impress the Indians, who where then powerful, with a sense of the justice of their white neighbors. The occupancy of their lands was never assumed, except upon the basis of contract, and on the payment of a valuable consideration.

This policy has obtained from the earliest white settlements in this country down to the present time. Some cessions of territory may have been made by the Indians, in compliance with the terms on which peace was offered by the whites, but the soil thus taken was taken by the laws of conquest, and always as an indemnity for the expense of the war commenced by the Indians.

At no time has the sovereignty of the country been recognized as existing in the Indians, but they have been always admitted to possess many of the attributes of sovereignty. All the rights which belong to self-government have been recognized as vested in them. Their right of occupancy has never been questioned, but the fee in the soil has been considered in the government. This may be called the right to the ultimate domain, but the Indians have a present right of possession.

In some of the old States—Massachusetts, Connecticut, Rhode Island and others—where small remnants of tribes remain, surrounded by white population, and who, by their reduced numbers, had lost the power of self-

government—the laws of the State have been extended over them, for the protection of their persons and property.

Before the adoption of the Constitution, the mode of treating with the Indians was various. After the formation of the confederacy, this subject was placed under the special superintendence of the United Colonies, though, subsequent to that time, treaties may have been occasionally entered into between a State and the Indians in its neighborhood. It is not considered to be at all important to go into a minute inquiry on this subject.

By the Constitution, the regulation of commerce among the Indian tribes given to Congress. This power must be considered as exclusively vested in Congress, as the power to regulate commerce with foreign nations, to coin money, to establish post-offices, and to declare war. It is enumerated in the same class of powers.

This investiture of power has been exercised in the regulation of commerce with the Indians, sometimes by treaty, and, at other times, by enactments of Congress. In this respect they have been placed by the federal authority, with but few exceptions, on the same footing as foreign nations.

It is said that these treaties are nothing more than compacts, which cannot be considered as obligatory on the United States, from a want of power in the Indians to enter into them.

What is a treaty? The answer is, it is a compact formed between two nations or communities, having the right of self-government.

Is it essential that each party shall possess the same attributes of sovereignty to give force to the treaty? This will not be pretended; for, on this ground, very few valid treaties could be formed. The only requisite is, that each of the contracting parties shall possess the right of self-government, and the power to perform the stipulations of the treaty.

Under the Constitution, no State can enter into any treaty; and it is believed that, since its adoption, no State, under its own authority, had held a treaty with the Indians.

It must be admitted that the Indians sustain a peculiar relation to the United States. They do not constitute, as was decided at the last term, a foreign state, so as to claim the right to sue in the Supreme Court of the United States; and yet, having the right of self-government, they, in some sense, form a State. In the management of their internal concerns, they are dependent on no power. They punish offenses under their own laws, and, in doing so, they are responsible to no earthly tribunal. They make war and form treaties of peace. The exercise of these and other powers gives to them a distinct character as a people, and constitutes them, in some respects, a state, although they may not be admitted to possess the right of soil.

By various treaties, the Cherokees have placed themselves under the protection of the United States; they have agreed to trade with no other people, nor to invoke the protection of any other sovereignty. But such engagements do not devest them of the right of self-government, nor destroy their capacity to enter into treaties or compacts.

Every State is more or less dependent on those which surround it; but, unless this dependence shall extend so far as to merge the political existence of the protected people into that of their protectors, they may still constitute a state. They may exercise the powers not relinquished, and bind themselves as a distinct and separate community.

The language used in treaties with the Indians should never be construed to their prejudice. If words be made use of which are susceptible of a more extended meaning than their plain import, as connected with the tenor of the treaty, they should be considered as used only in the latter sense. To contend that the word "allotted," in reference to the land guaranteed to the Indians in certain treaties, indicates a favor conferred rather than a right acknowledged, would, it would seem to me, do injustice to the understanding of the parties. How the words of the treaty were understood by this unlettered people, rather than their critical meaning, should form the rule of construction.

The question may be asked, is no distinction to be made between a civilized and savage people? Are our Indians to be placed upon a footing with the nations of Europe, with whom we have made treaties?

The inquiry is not what station shall now be given to the Indian tribes in our country? but, what relation have they sustained to us, since the commencement of our government.

We have made treaties with them; and are those treaties to be disregarded on our part because they were entered into with an uncivilized people? Does this lessen the obligation of such treaties? By entering into them, have we not admitted the power of this people to bind themselves, and to impose obligations on us?

The President of the Senate, except under the treaty-making power, cannot enter into compacts with the Indians, or with foreign nations. This power has been uniformly exercised in forming treaties with the Indians.

Nations differ from each other in condition, and that of the same nation may change by the revolutions of time, but the principles of justice are the same. They rest upon a base which will remain beyond the endurance of time.

After a lapse of more than forty years since treaties with the Indians have been solemnly ratified by the general government, it is too late to deny their binding force. Have the numerous treaties which have been formed with them, and the ratifications by the President and Senate, been nothing more than an idle pageantry?

By numerous treaties with the Indian tribes we have acquired accessions of territory of incalculable value to the Union. Except by compact, we have not even claimed a right of way through the Indian lands. We have recognized in them the right to make war. No one has ever supposed that the Indians could commit treason against the United States. We have punished them for their violation of treaties; be we have inflicted the punishment on them as a nation and not on individual offenders among them as traitors.

In the executive, legislative, and judicial branches of our government, we have admitted, by the most solemn sanctions, the existence of the Indians as a separate and distinct people, and as being vested with rights which constitute them a state, or separate community—not as belonging to the confederacy, but as existing within it, and, of necessity, bearing to it a peculiar relation.

But, can the treaties which have been referred to, and law of 1802, be considered in force within the limits of the State of Georgia?

In the act of cession made by Georgia to the United States in 1802, of all lands claimed by her west of the line designated, one of the conditions was, "that the United States should, at their own expense, extinguish, for the use of Georgia, as early as the same can be peaceably obtained,

NATIVE
AMERICAN
RIGHTS

WORCESTER V.
THE STATE OF
GEORGIA

NATIVE
AMERICAN
RIGHTS

WORCESTER V.
THE STATE OF
GEORGIA

on reasonable terms, the Indian title to lands within the State of Georgia."

One of the counsel, in the argument, endeavored to show that no part of the country now inhabited by the Cherokee Indians is within what is called the chartered limits of Georgia.

It appears that the charter of Georgia was surrendered by the trustees, and that, like the State of South Carolina, she became a regal colony. The effect of this change was to authorize the crown to alter the boundaries, in the exercise of its discretion. Certain alterations, it seems, were subsequently made; but I do not conceive it can be of any importance to enter into a minute consideration of them. Under its charter, it may be observed that Georgia derived a right to the soil, subject to the Indian title, by occupancy. By the act of cession, Georgia designated a certain line as the limit of that cession, and this line, unless subsequently altered, with the assent of the parties interested, must be considered as the boundary of the State of Georgia. This line having been thus recognized, cannot be contested on any question which may incidentally arise for judicial decision.

It is important, on this part of the case to ascertain in what light Georgia has considered the Indian title to lands generally, and particularly within her own boundaries; and also, as to the right, of the Indians to self-government.

In the first place, she was a party to all the treaties entered into between the United States and the Indians since the adoption of the Constitution. And prior to that period she was represented in making them, and was bound by their provisions, although it is alleged that she remonstrated against the Treaty of Hopewell. In the passage of the intercourse law of 1802, as one of the constituent parts of the Union, she was also a party.

The stipulation made in her act of cession, that the United States should extinguish the Indian title to lands within the State, was a distinct recognition of the right in the federal government to make the extinguishment; and also that, until it should be made, the right of occupancy should remain in the Indians.

In a law of the State of Georgia, "for opening the land-office, and for other purposes," passed in 1783, it is declared that surveys made on Indians lands were null and void; a fine was inflicted on the person making the survey, which

if not paid by the offender, he was punished by imprisonment. By a subsequent act, a line was fixed for the Indians, which was a boundary between them and the whites. A similar provision is found in other laws of Georgia, passed before the adoption of the Constitution. By an act of 1787, severe corporeal punishment was inflicted on those who made or attempted to make surveys, "beyond the temporary line designating the Indian hunting-ground."

On the 19th of November, 1814, the following resolutions were adopted by the Georgia Legislature:

> Whereas, many of the citizens of this State, without regard to existing treaties between the friendly Indians and the United States, and contrary to the interest and good policy of this State, have gone, and are frequently going over, and settling and cultivating the lands allotted to the friendly Indians for their hunting-ground, by which means the State is not only deprived of their services in the army, but considerable feuds are engendered between us and our friendly neighboring Indians:

> "Resolved, therefore, by the Senate and House of Representatives of the State of Georgia in General Assembly met, that his excellency the governor, be, and is hereby requested to take the necessary means to have all intruders removed off the Indian lands, and that proper steps be taken to prevent future aggressions."

In 1817 the Legislature refused to take any steps to dispose of lands acquired by treaty with the Indians until the treaty had been ratified by the Senate; and, by a resolution, the governor was directed to have the line run between the State of Georgia and the Indians, according to the late treaty. The same thing was again done in the year 1819, under a recent treaty.

In a memorial to the President of the United States by the Legislature of Georgia in 1819, they say,

> "it has long been the desire of Georgia that her settlements should be extended to her ultimate limits.... ...The the soil within her boundaries should be subjected to her control, and that her police organization and government should be fixed and permanent.... ...That the State of Georgia claims a right to the jurisdiction and soil of the territory within her limits.... ...She admits, however, that the right is inchoate—remaining to be perfected by the United States, in the extinction of the Indian title; the United States *pro hac vice* as their agents."

NATIVE
AMERICAN
RIGHTS

WORCESTER V.
THE STATE OF
GEORGIA

The Indian title was also distinctly acknowledge by the Act of 1796 repealing the Yazoo Act. It is there declared, in reference to certain lands, that "they are the sole property of the State, subject only to the right of the treaty of the United States, to enable the State to purchase, under its pre-emption right, the Indian title to the same;" and, also that the land is vested in the "State, to whom the right of pre-emption to the same belongs, subject only to the controlling power of the United States, to authorize any treaties for, and to superintend the same." This language, it will be observed, was used long before the act of cession.

On the 25th of March, 1825, the Governor of Georgia issued the following proclamation:

"Whereas it is provided in said treaty that the United States shall protect the Indians against the encroachments, hostilities, and impositions of the whites, so that they suffer no imposition, molestation, or injury in their persons, goods, effects, their dwellings, or the lands that they occupy, until their removal shall have been accomplished according to the terms of the treaty" which had been recently made with the Indians.

"I have therefore thought proper to issue this, my proclamation, warning all persons, citizens of Georgia or others, against trespassing or intruding upon lands occupied by the Indians, within the limits of Georgia, either for the purpose of settlement or otherwise, as every such act will be in direct violation of the provisions of the treaty aforesaid, and will expose the aggressors to the most certain and summary punishment by the authorities of the State and the United States.... ...All good citizens, therefore, pursuing the dictates of good faith, will unite in enforcing the obligations of the treaty, as the supreme law," etc.

Many other references might be made to the public acts of the State of Georgia to show that she admitted the obligation of Indian treaties, but the above are believed to be sufficient. These acts did honor to the character of that highly respectable State.

Under the act of cession, the United States were bound, in good faith, to extinguish the Indian title to lands within the limits of Georgia, so soon as it could be done peaceably and on reasonable terms.

The State of Georgia has repeatedly remonstrated to the President on this subject, and called upon the government to take the necessary steps to fulfill its engagement. She complained that, whilst the Indian title to immense tracts of country had been extinguished elsewhere, within the limits of Georgia but little progress had been made; and this was attributed either to a want of effort on the part of the federal government, or to the effect of its policy towards the Indians. In one or more of the treaties, titles in fee-simple were given to the Indians to certain reservations of land; and this was complained of by Georgia as a direct infraction of the condition of the cession. It has also been asserted that the policy of the government, in advancing the cause of civilization among the Cherokees, and inducing them to assume the forms of a regular government and of civilized life, was calculated to increase their attachment to the soil they inhabit, and to render the purchase of their title more difficult, it not impracticable.

A full investigation of this subject may not be considered as strictly within the scope of the judicial inquiry which belongs to the present case. But, to some extent, it has a direct bearing on the question before the court, as it tends to show how the rights and powers of Georgia were construed by her public functionaries.

By the first President of the United States, and by every succeeding one, a strong solicitude has been expressed for the civilization of the Indians. Through the agency of the government, they have been partially induced, in some parts of the Union, to change the hunter state for that of the agriculturist and herdsman.

In a letter addressed by Mr. Jefferson to the Cherokees, dated the 9th of January, 1809, he recommends them to adopt a regular government, that crimes might be punished and property protected. He points out the mode by which a council should be chosen, who should have power to enact laws; and he also recommended the appointment of judicial and executive agents, through whom the law might be enforced. The agent of the government, who resided among them, was recommended to be associated with their council, that he might give the necessary advice on all subjects relating to their government.

In the Treaty of 1817, the Cherokees are encouraged to adopt a regular form of government.

Since that time, a law has been passed making an annual appropriation of the sum of ten thousand dollars, as a school fund for the education of Indian youths, which has been distrib-

NATIVE
AMERICAN
RIGHTS

WORCESTER V.
THE STATE OF
GEORGIA

uted among the different tribes where schools had been established. Missionary labors among the Indians have also been sanctioned by the government, by granting permits to those who were disposed to engage in such a work, to reside in the Indian country.

That the means adopted by the general government to reclaim the savage from his erratic life, and induce him to assume the forms of civilization, have had a tendency to increase the attachment of the Cherokees to the country they now inhabit is extremely probable; and that it increased the difficulty of purchasing their lands, as by act of cession the general government agreed to do, is equally probable.

Neither Georgia nor the United States, when the cession was made, contemplated that force should be used in the extinguishment of the Indian title, nor that it should be procured on terms that are not reasonable. But, may it not be said, with equal truth, that it was not contemplated by either party that any obstructions to the fulfillment of the compact should be allowed, much less sanctioned, by the United States?

The humane policy of the government towards these children of the wilderness must afford pleasure to every benevolent feeling; and if the efforts made have not proved as successful as was anticipated, still much has been done. Whether the advantages of this policy should not have been held out by the government to the Cherokees within the limits of Georgia, as an inducement for them to change their residence and fix it elsewhere, rather than by such means to increase their attachment to their present home, as has been insisted on, is a question which may be considered by another branch of the government. Such a course might, perhaps, have secured to the Cherokee Indians all the advantages they have realized from the paternal superintendence of the government; and have enabled it, on peaceable and reasonable terms, to comply with the act of cession.

Does the intercourse law of 1802 apply to the Indians who live within the limits of Georgia? The nineteenth section of that act provides

> "that it shall not be construed to prevent any trade or intercourse with Indians living on lands surrounded by settlements of the citizens of the United States, and being within the ordinary jurisdiction of any of the individual States? This provision, it has been sup-

posed, excepts from the operation of the law the Indian lands which lie within any State. A moment's reflection will show that this construction is most clearly erroneous.

To constitute an exception to the provisions of this act, the Indian settlement, at the time of its passage, must have been surrounded by settlements of the citizens of the United States, and within the ordinary jurisdiction of a State; not only within the limits of a State, but within the common exercise of its jurisdiction.

No one will pretend that this was the situation of the Cherokees who lived, within the State of Georgia in 1802; or, indeed, that such is their present situation. If then, they are not embraced by the exception, all the provisions of the Act of 1802 apply to them.

In the very section which contains the exception, it is provided that the use of the road from Washington district to Mero district should be enjoyed, and that the citizens of Tennessee, under the orders of the governor, might keep the road in repair. And in the same section, the navigation of the Tennessee River is reserved, and a right to travel from Knoxville to Price's settlement, provided the Indians should not object.

Now, all these provisions relate to the Cherokee country; and can it be supposed, by anyone, that such provisions would have been made in the act if Congress had not considered it as applying to the Cherokee country, whether in the State of Georgia or in the State of Tennessee?

The exception applied exclusively to those fragments of tribes which are found in several of the States, and which came literally within the description used.

Much has been said against the existence of an independent power within a sovereign State; and the conclusion has been drawn that the Indians, as a matter of right, cannot enforce their own laws, within the territorial limits of a State. The refutation of this argument is found in our past history.

The fragments of tribes, having lost the power of self-government, and who lived within the ordinary jurisdiction of a State, have been taken under the protection of the laws, has already been admitted. But there has been no instance where the State laws have been generally extended over a numerous tribe of Indians living within the State and exercising the right of self-government, until recently.

Has Georgia ever, before her late laws, attempted to regulate the Indian communities within her limits? It is true, New York extended her criminal laws over the remains of the tribes within that State, more for their protection than for any other purpose. These tribes were few in number, and were surrounded by a white population. But, even the State of New York has never asserted the power, it is believed, to regulate their concerns beyond the suppression of crime.

Might not the same objection to this interior independent power by Georgia have been urged with as much force as at present, ever since the adoption of the Constitution? Her chartered limits, to the extent claimed, embraced a great number of different nations of Indians, all of whom were governed by their own laws, and were amenable only to them. Has not this been the condition of the Indians with Tennessee, Ohio, and other States?

The exercise of this independent power surely does not become more objectionable, as it assumes the basis of justice and the forms of civilization. Would it not be a singular argument to admit that, so long as the Indians govern by the rifle and the tomahawk, their government may be tolerated, but that it must be suppressed so soon as it shall be administered upon the enlightened principles of reason and justice?

Are not those nations of Indians who have made some advances in civilization better neighbors than those who are still a savage state? And is not the principle, as to their self-government, within the jurisdiction of a State, the same?

When Georgia sanctioned the Constitution, and conferred on the national Legislature the exclusive right to regulate intercourse with the Indians within her limits? This will not be pretended. If such had been the construction of her own powers would they not have been exercised? Did her senators object to the numerous treaties which have been formed with the different tribes who lived within her acknowledged boundaries? Why did she apply to the executive of the Union, repeatedly, to have the Indian title extinguished; to establish a line between the Indians and the State, and to procure a right of way through the Indian lands?

The residence of Indians, governed by their own laws, within the limits of a State, has never been deemed incompatible with State sovereignty until recently. And yet, this has been the condition of many distinct tribes of Indians, since the foundation of the federal government.

How is the question varied by the residence of the Indians in a territory of the United States? Are not the United States sovereign within their territories? And has it ever been conceived by anyone that the Indian governments which exist in the territories are incompatible with the sovereignty of the Union?

A State claims the right of sovereignty commensurate with her territory, as the United States claim it, in their proper sphere, to the extent of the federal limits. This right or power, in some cases, may be exercised, but not in others. Should a hostile force invade the country, at its most remote boundary, it would become the duty of the general government to expel the invaders. But it would violate the solemn compacts with the Indians, without cause, to dispossess them of rights which they possess by nature, and have been uniformly acknowledged by the federal government.

Is it incompatible with State sovereignty to grant exclusive jurisdiction to the federal government over a number of acres of land for military purposes? Our forts and arsenals, though situated in the different States, are not within their jurisdiction.

Does not the constitution give to the United States as exclusive jurisdiction in regulating intercourse with the Indians as has been given to them over any other subjects? Is there any doubt as to this investiture of power? Has it not been exercised by the federal government ever since its formation, not only without objection, but under the express sanction of all the States?

The power to dispose of the pubic domain is an attribute of sovereignty. Can the new States dispose of the lands within their limits which are owned by the federal government? The power to tax is also an attribute of sovereignty; but can the new States tax the lands of the United States? Have they not bound themselves, by compact, not to tax the public lands, nor until five years after they shall have been sold? May they violate this compact at discretion?

Why may not these powers be exercised by the respective States? The answer is, because they have parted with them, expressly for the general good. Why may not a State coin money, issue bills of credit, enter into a treaty of alliance or confederation, or regulate commerce with

NATIVE
AMERICAN
RIGHTS

WORCESTER V.
THE STATE OF
GEORGIA

NATIVE
AMERICAN
RIGHTS

WORCESTER V.
THE STATE OF
GEORGIA

foreign nations? Because these powers have been expressly and exclusively given to the federal government.

Has not the power been as expressly conferred on the federal government to regulate intercourse with the Indians, and is it not as exclusively given as any of the powers above enumerated? There being no exception to the exercise of this power, it must operate on all communities of Indians exercising the right of self-government; and consequently, include those who reside within the limits of a State, as well as others. Such has been the uniform construction of this power by the federal government, and of every State government, until the question was raised by the State of Georgia.

Under this clause of the Constitution, no political jurisdiction over the Indians has been claimed or exercised. The restrictions imposed by the law of 1802 come strictly within the power to regulate trade; not as an incident, but as a part of the principal power. It is the same power, and is conferred in the same words, that has often been exercised in regulating trade with foreign countries. Embargoes have been imposed, laws of non-intercourse have been passed, and numerous acts restrictive of trade, under the power to regulate commerce with foreign nations.

In the regulation of commerce with the Indians, Congress have exercised a more limited power than has been exercised in reference to foreign countries. The law acts upon our own citizens, and not upon the Indian, the same as the laws referred to act upon our own citizens in their foreign commercial intercourse.

It will scarcely be doubted by anyone that, so far as the Indians, as distinct communities, have formed a connection with the federal government by treaties; that such connection is political, and is equally binding on both parties. This cannot be questioned, except upon the ground that in making these treaties, the federal government has transcended the treaty-making power. Such an objection, it is true, has been stated, but it is one of modern invention, which arises out of local circumstances; and is not only opposed to the uniform practice of the government, but also to the letter and spirit of the Constitution.

But the inquiry may be made, is there no end to the exercise of this power over Indians within the limits of a State, by the general government?

The answer is, that, in its nature, it must be limited by circumstances.

If a tribe of Indians shall become so degraded or reduced in numbers as to lose the power of self-government, the protection of the local law, of necessity, must be extended over them. The point at which this exercise of power by a State would be proper, need not now be considered; if, indeed, it be a judicial question. Such a question does not seem to arise in this case. So long as treaties and laws remain in full force, and apply to Indian nations exercising the right of self-government within the limits of a State, the judicial power can exercise no discretion in refusing to give effect to those laws, when questions arise under them, unless they shall be deemed unconstitutional.

The exercise of the power of self-government by the Indians within a State, is undoubtedly contemplated to be temporary. This is shown by the settled policy of the government in the extinguishment of their title, and especially by the compact with the State of Georgia. It is a question, not of abstract right, but of public policy. I do not mean to say that the same moral rule which should regulate the affairs of private life should not be regarded by communities or nations. But, a sound national policy does require that the Indian tribes within our States should exchange their territories, upon equitable principles, or, eventually, consent to become amalgamated in our political communities.

At best they can enjoy a very limited independence within the boundaries of a State, and such a residence must always subject them to encroachments from the settlements around them; and their existence within a State as a separate and independent community, may seriously embarrass or obstruct the operation of the State laws. If, therefore, it would be inconsistent with the political welfare of the States and the social advance of their citizens that an independent and permanent power should exist within their limits, this power must give way to the greater power which surrounds it, or seek its exercise beyond the sphere of State authority.

This state of things can only be produced by a co-operation of the State and federal governments. The latter has the exclusive regulation of intercourse with the Indians; and so long as this power shall be exercised, it cannot be obstructed by the State. It is a power given by the Constitution and sanctioned by the most solemn

NATIVE
AMERICAN
RIGHTS

WORCESTER V.
THE STATE OF
GEORGIA

acts of both the federal and State governments: consequently, it cannot be abrogated at the will of a State. It is one of the powers parted with by the States and vested in the federal government. But, if a contingency shall occur which shall render the Indians who reside in a State incapable of self-government, either by moral degradation or a reduction of their numbers, it would undoubtedly be in the power of a State government to extend to them the aegis of its laws. Under such circumstances, the agency of the general government, of necessity, must cease.

But, if it shall be the policy of the government to withdraw its protection from the Indians who reside within the limits of the respective States, and who not only claim the right of self-government but have uniformly exercised it; the laws and treaties which impose duties and obligations on the general government should be abrogated by the powers competent to do so. So long as those laws and treaties exist, having been formed within the sphere of the federal powers, they must be respected and enforced by the appropriate organs of the federal government.

The plaintiff, who prosecutes this writ of error, entered the Cherokee country, as it appears, with the express permission of the President, and under the protection of the treaties of the United States and the law of 1802. He entered, not to corrupt the morals of this people, nor to profit by their substance; but to teach them, by precept and example, the Christian religion. If he be unworthy of this sacred office; if he had any other object than the one professed; if he sought, by his influence, to counteract the humane policy of the federal government towards the Indians, and to embarrass its efforts to comply with its solemn engagement with Georgia; though his sufferings be illegal, he is not a proper object of public sympathy.

It has been shown that the treaties and laws referred to come within the due exercise of the constitutional powers of the federal government; that they remain in full force, and consequently must be considered as the supreme laws of the land. These laws throw a shield over the Cherokee Indians. They guaranteed to them their rights of occupancy, of self-government, and the full enjoyment of those blessings which might be attained in their humble condition. But, by the enactments of the State of Georgia, this shield is broken in pieces—the infant institutions of the Cherokees are abolished, and their

laws annulled. Infamous punishment is denounced against them for the exercise of those rights which have been most solemnly guaranteed to them by the national faith.

Of these enactments, however, the plaintiff in error has no right to complain, nor can he question their validity, except in so far as they affect his interests. In this view and in this view only, has it become necessary, in the present case, to consider the repugnancy of the laws of Georgia to those of the Union.

Of the justice or policy of these laws it is not my province to speak; such considerations belonging to the Legislature by whom they were passed. They have, no doubt, been enacted under a conviction of right, by a sovereign and independent State, and their policy may have been recommended by a sense of wrong under the compact. Thirty years have elapsed since the federal government engaged to extinguish the Indian title within the limits of Georgia. That she has strong ground of complaint arising from this delay must be admitted; but such considerations are not involved in the present case; they belong to another branch of the government. We can look only to the law, which defines our power, and marks out the path of out duty.

Under the administration of the laws of Georgia, a citizen of the United States has been deprived of his liberty; and, claiming protection under the treaties and laws of the United States, he makes the question, as he has a right to make it, whether the laws of Georgia, under which he is now suffering an ignominious punishment, are not repugnant to the Constitution of the United States, and the treaties and laws made under it. This repugnancy has been shown; and it remains only to say, what has before been often said by this tribunal of the local laws of many of the States in this Union, that being repugnant to the Constitution of the United States, and to the laws made under it, they can have no force to devest the plaintiff in error of his property or liberty.

Mr. Justice Baldwin dissented, stating that in his opinion the record was not properly returned upon the writ of error, and ought to have been returned by the State court, and not by the clerk of that court. As to the merits, he said his opinion remained the same as was expressed by him in the case of *The Cherokee Nation v. The State of Georgia,* at the last term.

NATIVE
AMERICAN
RIGHTS

WORCESTER V.
THE STATE OF
GEORGIA

The opinion of Mr. Justice Baldwin was not delivered to the reporter.

This cause came on to be heard on the transcript of the record from the Superior Court for the County of Gwinnett, in the State of Georgia, and was argued by counsel; on consideration whereof, it is the opinion of this court that the act of the Legislature of the State of Georgia upon which the indictment in this case is founded, is contrary to the Constitution, treaties, and laws of the United States; and that the special plea in bar pleaded by the said Samuel A. Worcester, in manner aforesaid, and relying upon the Constitution, treaties, and laws of the United States aforesaid, is a good bar and defense to the said indictment, by the Samuel A. Worcester; and as such ought to have been allowed and admitted by the said Superior Court for the County of Gwinnett, in the State of Georgia, before which the said indictment was pending and tried; and that there was error in the said Superior Court of the State of Georgia in overruling the plea so pleaded as aforesaid. It is therefore ordered and adjudged that the judgment rendered in the premises by the said Superior Court of Georgia, upon the verdict upon the plea of "not guilty" afterwards pleaded by the said Samuel A. Worcester, whereby the said Samuel A. Worcester is sentenced to hard labor in the penitentiary of the State of Georgia, ought to be reversed and annulled. And this court proceeding to render such judgment as the said Superior Court of the State of Georgia should have rendered, it is further ordered and adjudged that the said judgment of the said Superior Court be, and hereby is reversed and annulled; and that judgment be, and hereby is, awarded, that the special plea, in bar, so as aforesaid pleaded, is a good sufficient plea in bar in law to the indictment aforesaid; and that all proceedings on the said indictment do forever surcease; and that the said Samuel A. Worcester be, and hereby is henceforth dismissed therefrom, and that he go thereof quit without day. And that a special mandate do go from this court to the said Superior Court, to carry this judgment into execution.

In the case of *Butler, Plaintiff in Error, v. The State of Georgia,* the same judgment was given by the court, and a special mandate was ordered from the court to the Superior Court of Gwinnett County, to carry the judgment into execution.

NATIVE AMERICAN RIGHTS

SURRENDER SPEECH

Black Hawk, 1832

From April to August 1832, an armed band of Sauk and Fox Indians under Chief Black Hawk sought to reoccupy the lands they had held in the Illinois and Wisconsin Territory. The tribes, who faced famine and hostile Sioux to the west, wanted a place with decent land in which to plant their corn. The Illinois militia chased them into Wisconsin, killing women and children as the tribe attempted to escape across the Mississippi River.

Faced with annihilation, Black Hawk had no choice but to surrender. In his speech he recounted the history of lies and betrayal the white men had perpetuated on Native Americans. President Jackson then sent Black Hawk and his son Whirling Thunder on tour to be displayed as "trophies" of war. But the two prisoners showed such dignity in their ordeal that the public quickly began to sympathize with them.

Surrender Speech

Black-hawk is an Indian. He has done nothing for which an Indian ought to be ashamed. He has fought for his countrymen, the squaws and papooses, against white men, who came, year after year, to cheat them and take away their lands. You know the cause of our making war. It is known to all white men. They ought to be ashamed of it. The white men despise the Indians, and drive them from their homes. But the Indians are not deceitful. The white men speak bad of the Indian, and look at him spitefully. But the Indian does not tell lies; Indians do not steal.

An Indian, who is as bad as the white men, could not live in our nation; he would be put to death, and eat up by the wolves. The white men are bad schoolmasters; they carry false looks, and deal in false actions; they smile in the face of the poor Indian to cheat him; they shake them by the hand to gain their confidence, to make them drunk, to deceive them, and ruin our wives. We told them to let us alone, and keep away from us; but they followed on, and beset our paths, and they coiled themselves among us, like the snake. They poisoned us by their touch. We were not safe. We lived in danger. We were becoming like them, hypocrites and liars, adulterers, lazy drones, all talkers, and no workers.

We looked up to the Great Spirit. We went to our great father. We were encouraged. His great council gave us fair words and big promises; but we got no satisfaction. Things were growing worse. There were no deer in the forest. The opossum and beaver were fled; the springs were drying up, and our squaws and papooses without victuals to keep them from starving; we called a great council, and built a large fire. The spirit of our fathers arose and spoke to us to avenge our wrongs or die. We all spoke before the council fire. It was warm and pleasant. We set up the war-whoop, and dug up the tomahawk; our knives were ready, and the heart of Black-hawk swelled high in his bosom, when he led his warriors to battle. He is satisfied. He will go to the world of spirits contented. He has done his duty. His father will meet him there, and commend him.

NATIVE AMERICAN RIGHTS

TREATY WITH SIOUX NATION

The Sioux were an important confederacy of the North American Indian tribes that inhabited the Great Plains. In the seventeenth century the Sioux had comprised small bands of Woodland Indians in the Mille Lacs region of present-day Minnesota. Conflict with the Ojibwa (also called Chippewa or Anishinabe) forced the Sioux to move to the buffalo ranges of the Great Plains. As they became adept buffalo hunters, the tribes grew and prospered. By 1750 the Sioux comprised some 30,000 persons firmly established in the heartland of the northern plains.

An 1825 treaty confirmed Sioux possession of an immense territory including much of present-day Minnesota, the Dakotas, Wisconsin, Iowa, Missouri, and Wyoming. As white settlers moved onto Sioux lands, violence erupted. Red Cloud's War (1866–1867) resulted in a treaty granting the Black Hills in perpetuity to the Sioux. The United States failed to honor the treaty, however, and allowed gold prospectors and miners to invade the territory in the 1870s. These events were the backdrop for the Battle of Little Bighorn on June 25, 1876, in which General George Armstrong Custer and three hundred troops were killed by Chief Sitting Bull and his Sioux warriors.

In 1877 Congress approved a treaty with certain bands of the Sioux (19 Stat. 254), which changed the terms of the treaty ratified in 1869. Because of pressure by white miners and settlers, the Great Sioux Reservation was reduced, three roads were to be constructed and maintained through the reservation, and the free navigation of the Missouri River was mandated.

In return, the Sioux nation continued to receive annuities negotiated in the 1869 treaty. More importantly, the Sioux were required to select land for a reservation "located in a country where they may eventually become self-supporting and acquire the arts of civilized life." The U.S. government promised the Sioux schools, instruction in "mechanical and agricultural arts," a ration of food, and a "comfortable house." The removal to the reservation meant the end of the Sioux people's traditional way of life. Sporadic resistance continued until the massacre at Wounded Knee, South Dakota, in December 1890, when U.S. troops slaughtered more than two hundred Sioux men, women, and children.

—◊◊◊—

Treaty with Sioux Nation

FORTIETH CONGRESS SECOND SESSION

CHAPTER 72, AN ACT TO RATIFY AN AGREEMENT WITH CERTAIN BANDS OF THE SIOUX NATION OF INDIANS AND ALSO WITH THE NORTHERN ARAPAHO AND CHEYENNE INDIANS.

BE IT ENACTED BY THE SENATE AND THE HOUSE OF REPRESENTATIVES OF THE UNITED STATES OF AMERICA IN CONGRESS ASSEMBLED,

that a certain agreement made by George W. Manypenny, Henry B. Whipple, Jared W. Daniels, Albert G. Boone, Henry C. Bulis, Newton Edumunds, and Augustine S. Gaylord, commissioners on the part of the United States, with the different bands of the Sioux Nation of Indians, and also the Northern Arapaho and Cheyenne Indians, be, and the same is hereby, ratified and confirmed:

PROVIDED, that nothing in this act shall be construed to authorize the removal of Sioux Indians to the Indian Territory and the President of the United States is hereby directed to prohibit the removal of any portion of the Sioux Indians to the Indian Territory until the same shall be authorized by an act of Congress hereafter enacted, except article four, except also the following portion of article six: "And if said Indians shall remove to said Indian Territory as hereinbefore provided, the Government shall erect for each of the principal chiefs a good and comfortable dwelling house" and said article not having been agreed to by the Sioux Nation: said agreement is in words and figures following: namely: "Articles of agreement made pursuant to the provisions of an act of Congress entitled "An act making appropriations for the current and contingent expenses of the Indian Department, and for fulfilling treaty stipulations with various Indian tribes, for the year ending June thirtieth, eighteen hundred and seventy-seven, and for other purposes," approved August 15, 1876, by and between George W. Manypenny, Henry B. Whipple, Jared W. Daniels, Albert G. Boone, Henry C. Bulis, Newton Edumunds, and Augustine S. Gaylord, commissioners on the part of the United States, with the different bands of the Sioux Nation of Indians, and also the Northern Arapaho and Cheyenne Indians, by their chiefs and headmen, whose names are hereto subscribed, they being duly authorized to act in the premises.

ARTICLE 1

[Reduction of the Great Sioux Reservation]

The said parties hereby agree that the northern and western boundaries of the reservation defined by article 2 of the treaty between the United States and different tribes of Sioux Indians, concluded April 29, 1868, and proclaimed February 24, 1869, shall be as follows: The western boundaries shall commence at the intersection of the one hundred and third meridian of longitude with the northern border of the State of Nebraska; thence north along said meridian to its intersection with the South Fork of the Cheyenne River; thence down said stream

to its junction with the North Fork; thence up the North Fork of said Cheyenne River to the said one hundred and third meridian; thence north along said meridian to the South Branch of Cannon Ball River or Cedar Creek; and the northern boundary of the said reservation shall follow the said South Branch to its intersection with the main Cannon Ball River, and thence down the said main Cannon Ball River to the Missouri River; and the said Indians do hereby relinquish and cede to the United States all territory lying outside the said reservation, as herein, modified and described, including all privileges of hunting; and article 16 of said treaty is hereby abrogated.

ARTICLE 2

[Roads Through Reservation]

The said Indians also agree and consent that wagon and other roads, not exceeding three in number, may be constructed and maintained, from convenient and accessible points on the Missouri River, through said reservation, to the country lying immediately west thereof, upon such routes as shall be designated by the President of the United States; and they also consent and agree to the free navigation of the Missouri River.

ARTICLE 3

[Distribution Points for Annuities to Be Designated]

The said Indians also agree that they will hereafter receive all annuities provided by the said treaty of 1868, and all subsistence and supplies which may be provided for them under the present or any future act of Congress, at such points and places on the said reservation, and in the vicinity of the Missouri River.

ARTICLE 4

[Delegation to Select Home in Indian Territory]

The Government of the United States and the said Indians, being mutually desirous that the latter shall be located in a country where they may eventually become self-supporting and acquire the arts of civilized life, it is therefore agreed that the said Indians shall select a delegation of five or more chiefs and principal men from each band, who shall, without delay, visit the Indian Territory under the guidance and protection of suitable persons, to be appointed for that purpose by the Department of the Interior, with a view to selecting therein a permanent home for said Indians. If such delegation shall make a selection which shall be satisfactory to themselves, the people whom they represent, and to the United States, then the said Indians agree that they will remove to the country so selected within one year from this date. And the said Indians do further agree in all things to submit themselves to such beneficent plans as the Government may provide for them in the selection of a country suitable for a permanent home, where they may live like white men.

ARTICLE 5

[Assistance, Schools, Rations, Purchase of Surplus, Employment]

In consideration of the foregoing cession of territory and rights, and upon full compliance with each and every obligation assumed by the said Indians, the United States does agree to provide all necessary aid to assist the said Indians in the work of civilization; to furnish to them schools and instruction in mechanical and agricultural arts, as provided for by the treaty of 1868. Also to provide the said Indians with subsistence consisting of a ration for each individual of a pound and a half of beef, (or in lieu thereof, one half pound of bacon,) one-half pound of flour, and one-half pound of corn; and for every one hundred rations, four pounds of coffee, eight pounds of sugar, and three pounds of beans, or in lieu of said articles the equivalent thereof, in the discretion of the Commissioner of Indian Affairs. Such rations, or so much thereof as may be necessary, shall be continued until the Indians are able to support themselves. Rations shall, in all cases, be issued to the head of each separate family; and whenever schools shall have been provided by the Government for said Indians, no rations shall be issued for children between the ages of six and fourteen years (the sick and infirm excepted) unless such children shall regularly attend school. Whenever the said Indians shall be located upon lands which are suitable for cultivation, rations shall be issued only to the persons and families of those persons who labor, (the aged, sick, and infirm excepted;) and may provide that such persons be furnished in payment for their labor such other necessary

articles as are requisite for civilized life. The Government will aid said Indians as far as possible in finding a market for their surplus productions, and in finding employment, and will purchase such surplus, as far as may be required, for supplying food to those Indians, parties to this agreement, who are unable to sustain themselves; and will also employ Indians, so far as practicable, in the performance of Government work upon their reservation.

ARTICLE 6

[Erection of Homes]

Whenever the head of a family shall, in good faith, select an allotment of land upon such reservation and engage in the cultivation thereof, the Government shall, with his aid, erect a comfortable house on such allotment; and if said Indians shall remove to said Indian Territory as hereinbefore provided, the Government shall erect for each of the principal chiefs a good and comfortable dwelling house.

ARTICLE 7

[Agency Employees to Be Married]

To improve the morals and industrious habits of said Indians, it is agreed that the agent, trader, farmer, carpenter, blacksmith, and other artisans employed or permitted to reside within the reservation belonging to the Indians, parties to this agreement, shall be lawfully married and living with their respective families on the reservation; and no person other than an Indian of full blood, whose fitness, morally or otherwise, is not, in the opinion of the Commissioner of Indian Affairs, conducive to the welfare of said Indians, shall receive any benefit from this agreement or former treaties, and may be expelled from the reservation.

ARTICLE 8

[Indians Subject to the Laws of the United States]

The provisions of the said treaty of 1868, except as herein modified, shall continue in full force, and, with the provisions of this agreement, shall apply to any country which may hereafter be occupied by the said Indians as a home; and Congress shall, by appropriate legislation, secure to them an orderly government; they shall be subject to the laws of the United

States, and each individual shall be protected in his rights, property, person and life.

ARTICLE 9

[Indians Pledged to this Agreement]

The Indians, parties to this agreement, do hereby solemnly pledge themselves, individually and collectively, to observe each and all of the stipulations herein contained, to select allotments of land as soon as possible after their removal to their permanent home, and to use their best efforts to learn to cultivate the same. And they do solemnly pledge themselves that they will at all times maintain peace with the citizens and Government of the United States; that they will observe the laws thereof and loyally endeavor to fulfill all the obligations assumed by them under the treaty of 1868 and the present agreement, and to this end will, whenever called requested by the President of the United States, select so many suitable men from each band to co-operate with him in maintaining order and peace on the reservation as the President may deem necessary, who shall receive such compensation for their services as Congress may provide.

ARTICLE 10

[Annual Census]

In order that the Government may faithfully fulfill the stipulations contained in this agreement, it is mutually agreed that a census of all Indians affected hereby shall be taken in the month of December of each year, and the names of each head of family and adult person registered; said census to be taken in such manner as the Commissioner of Indian Affairs may provide.

ARTICLE 11

[Term "Reservation" Defined]

It is understood that the term reservation herein contained shall be held to apply to any country which shall be selected under the authority of the United States as the future home of said Indians.

This agreement shall not be binding upon either party until it shall have received the approval of the President and Congress of the United States.

Dated and signed at Red Cloud agency, Nebraska, September 26, 1876.

NATIVE
AMERICAN
RIGHTS

TREATY WITH
SIOUX NATION

NATIVE AMERICAN RIGHTS

MY SON, STOP YOUR EARS

Chief Joseph, Nez Percé leader, 1879 Address to Congress

On January 14, 1879, Chief Joseph, leader of the Nez Percé nation of the Northwest, addressed Congress to explain why his people had declared war on U.S. troops in 1877. Chief Joseph explained that he and his band had refused to leave their Oregon homes despite the yearly demands of U.S. Indian agents. In 1877, after local cowboys stole Nez Percé horses, the Native Americans struck back. For four months and over thirteen hundred miles, they conducted guerrilla warfare against U.S. troops as they sought to escape into Canada. Chief Joseph surrendered just before reaching the border. In this excerpt of his remarks, Chief Joseph discusses the treaties that the tribe had signed with the U.S. government and the subsequent efforts of the government to send his people to a reservation.

—⁂—

My Son, Stop Your Ears

It has always been the pride of the Nez Percés that they were the friends of the white men. When my father was a young man there came to our country a white man [the Reverend Mr. Spaulding] who talked spirit law. He won the affections of our people because he spoke good things to them. At first he did not say anything about white men wanting to settle on our lands. Nothing was said about that until about twenty winters ago, when a number of white people came into our country and built houses and made farms. At first our people made no complaint. They thought there was room enough for all to live in peace, and they were learning many things from the white men that seemed to be good. But we soon found that the white men were growing rich very fast, and were greedy to possess everything the Indian had. My father was the first to see through the schemes of the white men, and he warned his tribe to be careful about trading with them. He had suspicion of men who seemed so anxious to make money. I was a boy then, but I remember well my father's caution. He had sharper eyes than the rest of our people.

Next there came a white officer [Governor Stevens], who invited all the Nez Percés to a treaty council. After the council was opened he made known his heart. He said there were a great many white people in the country, and many more would come; that he wanted the land marked out so that the Indians and white men could be separated. If they were to live in peace it was necessary, he said, that the Indians should have a country set apart for them, and in that country they must stay. My father, who represented his band, refused to have anything to do with the council, because he wished to be a free man. He claimed that no man owned any part of the earth, and a man could not sell what he did not own.

Mr. Spaulding took hold of my father's arm and said, "Come and sign the treaty." My father pushed him away, and said: "Why do you ask me to sign away my country? It is your business to talk to us about spirit matters, and not to talk to us about parting with our land." Governor Stevens urged my father to sign his treaty, but he refused. "I will not sign your paper," he said; "you go where you please, so do I; you are not a child. I am no child; I can think for myself. No man can think for me. I have no other home than this. I will not give it up to any man. My people would have no home. Take away your paper. I will not touch it with my hand."

My father left the council. Some of the chiefs of the other bands of the Nez Percés signed the treaty, and then Governor Stevens gave them presents of blankets. My father cautioned his people to take no presents, for "after a while," he said, "they will claim that you have accepted pay for your country." Since that time four bands of the Nez Percés have received annuities from the United States. My father was invited to many councils, and they tried hard to make him sign the treaty, but he was firm as the rock, and would not sign away his home. His refusal caused a difference among the Nez Percés.

Eight years later (1863) was the next treaty council. A chief called Lawyer, because he was a great talker, took the lead in this council, and sold nearly all the Nez Percés' country. My father was not there. He said to me: "When you go into council with the white man, always remember your country. Do not give it away. The white man will cheat you out of your home. I have taken no pay from the United States. I have never sold our land." In this treaty Lawyer acted without authority from our band. He had no right to sell the Wallowa [*winding water*] country. That had always belonged to my father's own people, and the other bands had never disputed our right to it. No other Indians ever claimed Wallowa.

In order to have all people understand how much land we owned, my father planted poles around it and said: "Inside is the home of my people—the white man may take the land outside. Inside this boundary all our people were born. It circles around the graves of our fathers, and we will never give up these graves to any man."

The United States claimed they had bought all the Nez Percés' country outside of Lapwai Reservation, from Lawyer and other chiefs, but we continued to live in this land in peace until eight years ago, when white men began to come inside the bounds my father had set. We warned them against this great wrong, but they would not leave our land, and some bad blood was raised. The white men represented that we were going upon the warpath. They reported many things that were false.

The United States Government again asked for a treaty council. My father had become blind and feeble. He could no longer speak for his people. It was then that I took my father's place as chief.

In this council I made my first speech to white men. I said to the agent who held the council: "I did not want to come to this council, but I came hoping that we could save blood. The white man has no right to come here and take our country. We have never accepted any presents from the Government. Neither Lawyer nor any other chief had authority to sell this land. It has always belonged to my people. It came unclouded to them from our fathers, and we will defend this land as long as a drop of Indian blood warms the hearts of our men."

The agent said he had orders, from the Great White Chief at Washington, for us to go upon the Lapwai Reservation, and that if we obeyed he would help us in many ways. "You *must* move to the agency," he said. I answered him: "I will not. I do not need your help; we have plenty and we are contented and happy if the white man will let us alone. The reservation is too small for so many people with all their stock. You can keep your presents; we can go to your towns and pay for all we need; we have plenty of horses and cattle to sell, and we won't have any help from you; we are free now; we can go where we please. Our fathers were born here. Here they lived, here they died, here are their graves. We will never leave them." The agent went away, and we had peace for a little while.

Soon after this my father sent for me. I saw he was dying. I took his hand in mine. He said: "My son, my body is returning to my mother earth, and my spirit is going very soon to see the Great Spirit Chief. When I am gone, think of your country. You are the chief of these people. They look to you to guide them. Always remember that your father never sold his country. You must stop your ears whenever you are asked to sign a treaty selling your home. A few years more, and white men will be all around you. They have their eyes on this land. My son, never forget my dying words. This country holds your father's body. Never sell the bones of your father and your mother." I pressed my father's hand and told him I would protect his grave with my life. My father smiled and passed away to the spirit-land.

NATIVE
AMERICAN
RIGHTS

MY SON, STOP
YOUR EARS

NATIVE
AMERICAN
RIGHTS

MY SON, STOP
YOUR EARS

I buried him in that beautiful valley of winding waters. I love that land more than all the rest of the world. A man who would not love his father's grave is worse than a wild animal.

For a short time we lived quietly. But this could not last. White men had found gold in the mountains around the land of winding water. They stole a great many horses from us, and we could not get them back because we were Indians. The white men told lies for each other. They drove off a great many of our cattle. Some white men branded our young cattle so they could claim them. We had no friend who would plead our cause before the law councils. It seemed to me that some of the white men in Wallowa were doing these things on purpose to get up a war. They knew that we were not strong enough to fight them. I labored hard to avoid trouble and bloodshed. We gave up some of our country to the white men, thinking that then we could have peace. We were mistaken. The white man would not let us alone. We could have avenged our wrongs many times, but we did not.

Whenever the Government has asked us to help them against other Indians, we have never refused. When the white men were few and we were strong, we could have killed them all off, but the Nez Percés wished to live at peace.

If we have not done so, we have not been to blame. I believe that the old treaty has never been correctly reported. If we ever owned the land we own it still, for we never sold it. In the treaty councils the commissioners have claimed that our country had been sold to the Government. Suppose a white man should come to me and say, "Joseph, I like your horses, and I want to buy them." I say to him, "No, my horses suit me, I will not sell them." Then he goes to my neighbor, and says to him: "Joseph has some good horses. I want to buy them, but he refuses to sell." My neighbor answers, "Pay me the money, and I will sell you Joseph's horses." The white man returns to me, and says, "Joseph, I have bought your horses, and you must let me have them." If we sold our lands to the Government, this is the way they were bought.

REFLECTIONS ON
LAW AND SOCIETY

PRESIDENTIAL SPEECHES

LEGAL SCHOLARSHIP

PRESIDENTIAL SPEECHES

- GEORGE WASHINGTON: FAREWELL ADDRESS

- ABRAHAM LINCOLN: GETTYSBURG ADDRESS

- ABRAHAM LINCOLN: SECOND INAUGURAL ADDRESS

- WOODROW WILSON: FOURTEEN POINTS

- FRANKLIN D. ROOSEVELT: FIRST INAUGURAL ADDRESS

- JOHN F. KENNEDY: INAUGURAL ADDRESS

- LYNDON B. JOHNSON: VOTING RIGHTS ACT ADDRESS

- RONALD W. REAGAN: FIRST INAUGURAL ADDRESS

- GEORGE W. BUSH: ADDRESS TO CONGRESS, SEPTEMBER 20, 2001

Beginning with George Washington, U.S. presidents have addressed the nation concerning various issues of domestic and international policy. A small number of these speeches have become important documents in their own right. They contain ideas, symbols, and memorable statements that have captured the public's imagination and led to significant changes in U.S. law and government.

PRESIDENTIAL SPEECHES

GEORGE WASHINGTON: FAREWELL ADDRESS

On September 17, 1796, leading newspapers published President George Washington's Farewell Address to the nation. Washington, who was nearing the end of his second four-year term, had rejected pleas by members of the Federalist party to seek a third term. The address, which was never delivered orally, is now remembered for its comments on foreign policy, but in 1796 Washington was also concerned with domestic politics.

Alexander Hamilton, who helped draft the Constitution and who wrote many of the essays contained in the *Federalist Papers*, prepared an initial version of the speech. Washington then revised and reshaped it into its final form. The president used the address both to end speculation that he would seek a third term and to help the chances of the Federalists in the forthcoming election.

Washington discussed the state of U.S. politics and lamented the bitter rivalry that had developed between the Federalists and the Republicans, who were led by Thomas Jefferson. A proponent of a strong national government, he warned against the dangers of sectionalism, political revenge, and "the insidious wiles of foreign influence." The latter statement referred to the pro-French sentiments of Jefferson and the Republicans. Washington's policy during the wars between Great Britain and France in the early 1790s had been one of strict neutrality.

The most important section of the address dealt with U.S. foreign relations. Washington stated that the "true policy [of the United States] is to steer clear of permanent alliances with any parts of the foreign world." His views provided support and inspiration for U.S. isolationists who sought to prevent the United States from becoming involved with European governments. U.S. isolationism did not disappear as a viable political viewpoint until the nation's entry into World War II in 1941.

—ɯ—

George Washington: Farewell Address

Friends and fellow citizens:

The period for a new election of a citizen to administer the executive government of the United States being not far distant, and the time actually arrived when your thoughts must be employed in designating the person who is to be clothed with that important trust, it appears to me proper, especially as it may conduce to a more distinct expression of the public voice, that I should now apprise you of the resolution I have formed to decline being considered among the number of those out of whom a choice is to be made.

I beg you at the same time to do me the justice to be assured that this resolution has not been taken without a strict regard to all the considerations appertaining to the relation which binds a dutiful citizen to his country; and that in

Source: James D. Richardson, ed., *A Compilation of the Messages and Papers of the Presidents*, vol. 1 (1896), pp. 213–24.

PRESIDENTIAL
SPEECHES

GEORGE
WASHINGTON:
FAREWELL
ADDRESS

withdrawing the tender of service, which silence in my situation might imply, I am influenced by no diminution of zeal for your future interest, no deficiency of grateful respect for your past kindness, but am supported by a full conviction that the step is compatible with both.

The acceptance of and continuance hitherto in the office to which your suffrages have twice called me have been a uniform sacrifice of inclination to the opinion of duty and to a deference for what appeared to be your desire. I constantly hoped that it would have been much earlier in my power, consistently with motives which I was not at liberty to disregard, to return to that retirement from which I had been reluctantly drawn. The strength of my inclination to do this previous to the last election had even led to the preparation of an address to declare it to you; but mature reflection on the then perplexed and critical posture of our affairs with foreign nations and the unanimous advice of persons entitled to my confidence impelled me to abandon the idea. I rejoice that the state of your concerns, external as well as internal, no longer tenders the pursuit of inclination incompatible with the sentiment of duty or propriety, and am persuaded, whatever partiality may be retained for my services, that in the present circumstances of our country you will not disapprove my determination to retire.

The impressions with which I first undertook the arduous trust were explained on the proper occasion. In the discharge of this trust I will only say that I have, with good intentions, contributed toward the organization and administration of the government the best exertions of which a very fallible judgment was capable. Not unconscious in the outset of the inferiority of my qualifications, experience in my own eyes, perhaps still more in the eyes of others, has strengthened the motives to diffidence of myself; and everyday the increasing weight of years admonishes me more and more that the shade of retirement is as necessary to me as it will be welcome. Satisfied that if any circumstances have given peculiar value to my services they were temporary, I have the consolation to believe that, while choice and prudence invite me to quit the political scene, patriotism does not forbid it.

In looking forward to the moment which is intended to terminate the career of my political life, my feelings do not permit me to suspend the deep acknowledgment of that debt of gratitude which I owe to my beloved country for the many honors it has conferred upon me; still more for the steadfast confidence with which it has supported me, and for the opportunities I have thence enjoyed of manifesting my inviolable attachment by services faithful and persevering, though in usefulness unequal to my zeal. If benefits have resulted to our country from these services, let it always be remembered to your praise and as an instructive example in our annals that under circumstances in which the passions, agitated in every direction, were liable to mislead; amidst appearances sometimes dubious; vicissitudes of fortune often discouraging; in situations in which not unfrequently want of success has countenanced the spirit of criticism, the constancy of your support was the essential prop of the efforts and a guaranty of the plans by which they were effected. Profoundly penetrated with this idea, I shall carry it with me to my grave as a strong incitement to unceasing vows that Heaven may continue to you the choicest tokens of its beneficence; that your union and brotherly affection may be perpetual; that the free Constitution which is the work of your hands may be sacredly maintained; that its administration in every department may be stamped with wisdom and virtue; that, in time the happiness of the people of these states, under the auspices of liberty may be made complete by so careful a preservation and so prudent a use of this blessing as will acquire to them the glory of recommending it to the applause, the affection, and adoption of every nation which is yet a stranger to it.

Here, perhaps, I ought to stop. But a solicitude for your welfare which can not end but with my life, and the apprehension of danger natural to that solicitude, urge me on an occasion like the present to offer to your solemn contemplation and to recommend to your frequent review some sentiments which are the result of much reflection, of no inconsiderable observation, and which appear to me all important to the permanency of your felicity as a people. These will be offered to you with the more freedom as you can only see in them the disinterested warnings of a parting friend, who can possibly have no personal motive to bias his counsel. Nor can I forget as an encouragement to it your indulgent reception of my sentiments on a former and not dissimilar occasion.

Interwoven as is the love of liberty with every ligament of your hearts, no recommendation of mine is necessary to fortify or confirm the attachment.

The unity of government which constitutes you one people is also now dear to you. It is justly so, for it is a main pillar in the edifice of your real independence, the support of your tranquillity at home, your peace abroad, of your safety, of your prosperity, of that very liberty which you so highly prize. But as it is easy to foresee that from different causes and from different quarters much pains will be taken, many artifices employed, to weaken in your minds the conviction of this truth, as this is the point in your political fortress against which the batteries of internal and external enemies will be most constantly and actively (though often covertly and insidiously) directed, it is of infinite moment that you should properly estimate the immense value of your national union to your collective and individual happiness; that you should cherish a cordial, habitual, and immovable attachment to it; accustoming yourselves to think and speak of it as of the palladium of your political safety and prosperity; watching for its preservation with jealous anxiety; discountenancing whatever may suggest even a suspicion that it can in any event be abandoned, and indignantly frowning upon the first dawning of every attempt to alienate any portion of our country from the rest or to enfeeble the sacred ties which now link together the various parts.

For this you have every inducement of sympathy and interest. Citizens by birth or choice of a common country, that country has a right to concentrate your affections. The name of American, which belongs to you in your national capacity, must always exalt the just pride of patriotism more than any appellation derived from local discriminations. With slight shades of difference, you have the same religion, manners, habits, and political principles. You have in a common cause fought and triumphed together. The independence and liberty you possess are the work of joint councils and joint efforts, of common dangers, sufferings, and successes.

But these considerations, however powerfully they address themselves to your sensibility, are greatly outweighed by those which apply more immediately to your interest. Here every portion of our country finds the most commanding motives for carefully guarding and preserving the union of the whole.

The North, in an unrestrained intercourse with the South, protected by the equal laws of a common government, finds in the productions of the latter great additional resources of maritime and commercial enterprise and precious materials of manufacturing industry. The South, in the same intercourse, benefiting by the same agency of the North, sees its agriculture grow and its commerce expand. Turning partly into its own channels the seamen of the North, it finds its particular navigation invigorated; and while it contributes in different ways to nourish and increase the general mass of the national navigation, it looks forward to the protection of a maritime strength to which itself is unequally adapted. The East, in a like intercourse with the West, already finds, and in the progressive improvement of interior communications by land and water will more and more find, a valuable vent for the commodities which it brings from abroad or manufactures at home. The West derives from the East supplies requisite to its growth and comfort, and what is perhaps of still greater consequence, it must of necessity owe the secure enjoyment of indispensable outlets for its own productions to the weight, influence, and the future maritime strength of the Atlantic side of the Union, directed by an indissoluble community of interest as one nation. Any other tenure by which the West can hold this essential advantage, whether derived from its own separate strength or from an apostate and unnatural connection with any foreign power, must be intrinsically precarious.

While, then, every part of our country thus feels an immediate and particular interest in union, all the parts combined cannot fail to find in the united mass of means and efforts greater strength, greater resource, proportionably greater security from external danger, a less frequent interruption of their peace by foreign nations, and what is of inestimable value, they must derive from union an exemption from those broils and wars between themselves which so frequently afflict neighboring countries not tied together by the same governments, which their own rivalships alone would be sufficient to produce, but which opposite foreign alliances, attachments, and intrigues would stimulate and embitter. Hence, likewise, they will avoid the necessity of those overgrown military establish-

PRESIDENTIAL
SPEECHES

GEORGE
WASHINGTON:
FAREWELL
ADDRESS

PRESIDENTIAL
SPEECHES

GEORGE
WASHINGTON:
FAREWELL
ADDRESS

ments which, under any form of government, are inauspicious to liberty, and which are to be regarded as particularly hostile to republican liberty. In this sense, it is that your union ought to be considered as a main prop of your liberty, and that the love of the one ought to endear to you the preservation of the other.

These considerations speak a persuasive language to every reflecting and virtuous mind, and exhibit the continuance of the union as a primary object of patriotic desire. Is there a doubt whether a common government can embrace so large a sphere? Let experience solve it. To listen to mere speculation in such a case were criminal. We are authorized to hope that a proper organization of the whole, with the auxiliary agency of governments for the respective subdivisions, will afford a happy issue to the experiment. It is well worth a fair and full experiment. With such powerful and obvious motives to union affecting all parts of our country, while experience shall not have demonstrated its impracticability, there will always be reason to distrust the patriotism of those who in any quarter may endeavor to weaken its bands.

In contemplating the causes which may disturb our union it occurs as matter of serious concern that any ground should have been furnished for characterizing parties by geographical discriminations—northern and southern, Atlantic and western—whence designing men may endeavor to excite a belief that there is a real difference of local interests and views. One of the expedients of party to acquire influence within particular districts is to misrepresent the opinions and aims of other districts. You cannot shield yourselves too much against the jealousies and heartburnings which spring from these misrepresentations; they tend to render alien to each other those who ought to be bound together by fraternal affection. The inhabitants of our western country have lately had a useful lesson on this head. They have seen in the negotiation by the executive and in the unanimous ratification by the Senate of the treaty with Spain, and in the universal satisfaction at that event throughout the United States, a decisive proof how unfounded were the suspicions propagated among them of a policy in the general government and in the Atlantic states unfriendly to their interests in regard to the Mississippi. They have been witnesses to the formation of two treaties—that with Great Britain and that with

Spain—which secure to them everything they could desire in respect to our foreign relations toward confirming their prosperity. Will it not be their wisdom to rely for the preservation of these advantages on the union by which they were procured? Will they not henceforth be deaf to those advisers, if such there are, who would sever them from their brethren and connect them with aliens?

To the efficacy and permanency of your union a government for the whole is indispensable. No alliances, however strict, between the parts can be an adequate substitute. They must inevitably experience the infractions and interruptions which all alliances in all times have experienced. Sensible of this momentous truth, you have improved upon your first essay by the adoption of a Constitution of government better calculated than your former for an intimate union and for the efficacious management of your common concerns. This government, the offspring of our own choice, uninfluenced and unawed, adopted upon full investigation and mature deliberation, completely free in its principles, in the distribution of its powers, uniting security with energy, and containing within itself a provision for its own amendment, has a just claim to your confidence and your support. Respect for its authority, compliance with its laws, acquiescence in its measures, are duties enjoined by the fundamental maxims of true liberty. The basis of our political systems is the right of the people to make and to alter their constitutions of government. But the constitution which at any time exists till changed by an explicit and authentic act of the whole people is sacredly obligatory upon all. The very idea of the power and the right of the people to establish government presupposes the duty of every individual to obey the established government.

All obstructions to the execution of the laws, all combinations and associations, under whatever plausible character, with the real design to direct, control, counteract, or awe the regular deliberation and action of the constituted authorities, are destructive of this fundamental principle and of fatal tendency. They serve to organize faction; to give it an artificial and extraordinary force; to put in the place of the delegated will of the nation the will of a party, often a small but artful and enterprising minority of the community, and, according to the alternate triumphs of different parties, to make the public administration the mirror of the ill-concerted and incongruous projects of faction rather than the organ of consistent and wholesome plans, digested by common counsels and modified by mutual interests.

However combinations or associations of the above description may now and then answer popular ends, they are likely in the course of time and things to become potent engines by which cunning, ambitious, and unprincipled men will be enabled to subvert the power of the people, and to usurp for themselves the reins of government, destroying afterwards the very engines which have lifted them to unjust dominion.

Toward the preservation of your government and the permanency of your present happy state, it is requisite not only that you steadily discountenance irregular oppositions to its acknowledged authority, but also that you resist with care the spirit of innovation upon its principles, however specious the pretexts. One method of assault may be to effect in the forms of the Constitution alterations which will impair the energy of the system, and thus to undermine what can not be directly overthrown. In all the changes to which you may be invited remember that time and habit are at least as necessary to fix the true character of governments as of other human institutions; that experience is the surest standard by which to test the real tendency of the existing constitution of a country; that facility in changes upon the credit of mere hypothesis and opinion exposes to perpetual change, from the endless variety of hypothesis and opinion; and remember especially that for the efficient management of your common interests in a country so extensive as ours a government of as much vigor as is consistent with the perfect security of liberty is indispensable. Liberty itself will find in such a government, with powers properly distributed and adjusted, its surest guardian. It is, indeed, little else than a name where the government is too feeble to withstand the enterprises of faction, to confine each member of the society within the limits prescribed by the laws, and to maintain all in the secure and tranquil enjoyment of the rights of person and property.

I have already intimated to you the danger of parties in the state, with particular reference to the founding of them on geographical discriminations. Let me now take a more comprehensive view, and warn you in the most solemn manner against the baneful effects of the spirit of party generally.

This spirit, unfortunately, is inseparable from our nature, having its root in the strongest passions of the human mind. It exists under different shapes in all governments, more or less stifled, controlled, or repressed; but in those of the popular form it is seen in its greatest rankness and is truly their worst enemy.

The alternate domination of one faction over another, sharpened by the spirit of revenge natural to party dissension, which in different ages and countries has perpetrated the most horrid enormities, is itself a frightful despotism. But this leads at length to a more formal and permanent despotism. The disorders and miseries which result gradually incline the minds of men to seek security and repose in the absolute power of an individual, and sooner or later the chief of some prevailing faction, more able or more fortunate than his competitors, turns this disposition to the purposes of his own elevation on the ruins of public liberty.

Without looking forward to an extremity of this kind (which nevertheless ought not to be entirely out of sight), the common and continual mischiefs of the spirit of party are sufficient to make it the interest and duty of a wise people to discourage and restrain it.

It serves always to distract the public councils and enfeeble the public administration. It agitates the community with ill-founded jealousies and false alarms; kindles the animosity of one part against another; foments occasionally riot and insurrection. It opens the door to foreign influence and corruption, which find a facilitated access to the government itself through the channels of party passion. Thus the policy and the will of one country are subjected to the policy and will of another.

There is an opinion that parties in free countries are useful checks upon the administration of the government, and serve to keep alive the spirit of liberty. This within certain limits is probably true; and in governments of a monarchical cast patriotism may look with indulgence, if not with favor, upon the spirit of party. But in those of the popular character, in governments purely elective, it is a spirit not to be encouraged. From their natural tendency it is certain there will always be enough of that spirit for every salutary purpose; and there being constant danger of excess, the effort ought to be by force of

PRESIDENTIAL
SPEECHES

GEORGE
WASHINGTON:
FAREWELL
ADDRESS

PRESIDENTIAL
SPEECHES

GEORGE
WASHINGTON:
FAREWELL
ADDRESS

public opinion to mitigate and assuage it. A fire not to be quenched, it demands a uniform vigilance to prevent its bursting into a flame, lest, instead of warming, it should consume.

It is important, likewise, that the habits of thinking in a free country should inspire caution in those entrusted with its administration to confine themselves within their respective constitutional spheres, avoiding in the exercise of the powers of one department to encroach upon another. The spirit of encroachment tends to consolidate the powers of all the departments in one, and thus to create, whatever the form of government, a real despotism. A just estimate of that love of power and proneness to abuse it which predominates in the human heart is sufficient to satisfy us of the truth of this position. The necessity of reciprocal checks in the exercise of political power, by dividing and distributing it into different depositories, and constituting each the guardian of the public weal against invasions by the others, has been evinced by experiments ancient and modern, some of them in our country and under our own eyes. To preserve them must be as necessary as to institute them. If in the opinion of the people the distribution or modification of the constitutional powers be in any particular wrong, let it be corrected by an amendment in the way which the Constitution designates. But let there be no change by usurpation; for though this in one instance may be the instrument of good, it is the customary weapon by which free governments are destroyed. The precedent must always greatly overbalance in permanent evil any partial or transient benefit which the use can at any time yield.

Of all the dispositions and habits which lead to political prosperity, religion and morality are indispensable supports. In vain would that man claim the tribute of patriotism who should labor to subvert these great pillars of human happiness—these firmest props of the duties of men and citizens. The mere politician, equally with the pious man, ought to respect and to cherish them. A volume could not trace all their connections with private and public felicity. Let it simply be asked, Where is the security for property, for reputation, for life, if the sense of religious obligations desert the oaths which are the instruments of investigation in courts of justice? And let us with caution indulge the supposition that morality can be maintained without religion. Whatever may be conceded to the influence of refined education on minds of peculiar structure, reason and experience both forbid us to expect that national morality can prevail in exclusion of religious principle.

It is substantially true that virtue or morality is a necessary spring of popular government. The rule indeed extends with more or less force to every species of free government. Who that is a sincere friend to it can look with indifference upon attempts to shake the foundation of the fabric? Promote, then, as an object of primary importance, institutions for the general diffusion of knowledge. In proportion as the structure of a government gives force to public opinion, it is essential that public opinion should be enlightened.

As a very important source of strength and security, cherish public credit. One method of preserving it is to use it as sparingly as possible, avoiding occasions of expense by cultivating peace, but remembering also that timely disbursements to prepare for danger frequently prevent much greater disbursements to repeal it; avoiding likewise the accumulation of debt, not only by shunning occasions of expense, but by vigorous exertions in time of peace to discharge the debts which unavoidable wars have occasioned, not ungenerously throwing upon posterity the burthen which we ourselves ought to bear. The execution of these maxims belongs to your representatives; but it is necessary that public opinion should cooperate. To facilitate to them the performance of their duty, it is essential that you should practically bear in mind that toward the payment of debts there must be revenue; that to have revenue there must be taxes; that no taxes can be devised which are not more or less inconvenient and unpleasant; that the intrinsic embarrassment inseparable from the selection of the proper objects (which is always a choice of difficulties), ought to be a decisive motive for a candid construction of the conduct of the government in making it, and for a spirit of acquiescence in the measures for obtaining revenue which the public exigencies may at any time dictate.

Observe good faith and justice toward all nations. Cultivate peace and harmony with all. Religion and morality enjoin this conduct. And can it be that good policy does not equally enjoin it? It will be worthy of a free, enlightened, and at no distant period a great nation to give to mankind the magnanimous and too novel exam-

PRESIDENTIAL
SPEECHES

GEORGE
WASHINGTON:
FAREWELL
ADDRESS

ple of a people always guided by an exalted justice and benevolence. Who can doubt that in the course of time and things the fruits of such a plan would richly repay any temporary advantages which might be lost by a steady adherence to it? Can it be that Providence has not connected the permanent felicity of a nation with its virtue? The experiment, at least, is recommended by every sentiment which ennobles human nature. Alas! is it rendered impossible by its vices?

In the execution of such a plan nothing is more essential than that permanent, inveterate antipathies against particular nations and passionate attachments for others should be excluded, and that in place of them just and amicable feelings toward all should be cultivated. The nation which indulges toward another in habitual hatred or an habitual fondness is in some degree a slave. It is a slave to its animosity or to its affection, either of which is sufficient to lead it astray from its duty and its interest. Antipathy in one nation against another disposes each more readily to offer insult and injury, to lay hold of slight causes of umbrage, and to be haughty and intractable when accidental or trifling occasions of dispute occur.

Hence frequent collisions, obstinate, envenomed, and bloody contests. The nation prompted by ill will and resentment sometimes impels to war the government contrary to the best calculations of policy. The government sometimes participates in the national propensity, and adopts through passion what reason would reject. At other times it makes the animosity of the nation subservient to projects of hostility, instigated by pride, ambition, and other sinister and pernicious motives. The peace often, sometimes perhaps the liberty, of nations has been the victim.

So, likewise, a passionate attachment of one nation for another produces a variety of evils. Sympathy for the favorite nation, facilitating the illusion of an imaginary common interest in cases where no real common interest exists, and infusing into one the enmities of the other, betrays the former into a participation in the quarrels and wars of the latter without adequate inducement or justification. It leads also to concessions to the favorite nation of privileges denied to others, which is apt doubly to injure the nation making the concessions by unnecessarily parting with what ought to have been retained, and by exciting jealousy, ill will, and a

disposition to retaliate in the parties from whom equal privileges are withheld; and it gives to ambitious, corrupted, or deluded citizens (who devote themselves to the favorite nation) facility to betray or sacrifice the interests of their own country without odium, sometimes even with popularity, gilding with the appearances of a virtuous sense of obligation, a commendable deference for public opinion, or a laudable zeal for public good the base or foolish compliances of ambition, corruption, or infatuation.

As avenues to foreign influence in innumerable ways, such attachments are particularly alarming to the truly enlightened and independent patriot. How many opportunities do they afford to tamper with domestic factions, to practice the arts of seduction, to mislead public opinion, to influence or awe the public councils! Such an attachment of a small or weak toward a great and powerful nation dooms the former to be the satellite of the latter. Against the insidious wiles of foreign influence (I conjure you to believe me, fellow citizens), the jealousy of a free people ought to be constantly awake, since history and experience prove that foreign influence is one of the most baneful foes of republican government. But that jealousy, to be useful, must be impartial, else it becomes the instrument of the very influence to be avoided, instead of a defense against it. Excessive partiality for one foreign nation and excessive dislike of another cause those whom they actuate to see danger only on one side, and serve to veil and even second the arts of influence on the other. Real patriots who may resist the intrigues of the favorite are liable to become suspected and odious, while its tools and dupes usurp the applause and confidence of the people to surrender their interests.

The great rule of conduct for us in regard to foreign nations is, in extending our commercial relations to have with them as little political connection as possible. So far as we have already formed engagements let them be fulfilled with perfect good faith. Here let us stop.

Europe has a set of primary interests which to us have none or a very remote relation. Hence she must be engaged in frequent controversies, the causes of which are essentially foreign to our concerns. Hence, therefore, it must be unwise in us to implicate ourselves by artificial ties in the ordinary vicissitudes of her politics or the ordi-

PRESIDENTIAL
SPEECHES

GEORGE
WASHINGTON:
FAREWELL
ADDRESS

nary combinations and collisions of her friendships or enmities.

Our detached and distant situation invites and enables us to pursue a different course. If we remain one people, under an efficient government, the period is not far off when we may defy material injury from external annoyance; when we may take such an attitude as will cause the neutrality we may at any time resolve upon to be scrupulously respected; when belligerent nations, under the impossibility of making acquisitions upon us, will not lightly hazard the giving us provocation; when we may choose peace or war, as our interest, guided by justice, shall counsel.

Why forgo the advantages of so peculiar a situation? Why quit our own to stand upon foreign ground? Why, by interweaving our destiny with that of any part of Europe, entangle our peace and prosperity in the toils of European ambition, rivalship, interest, humor, or caprice?

It is our true policy to steer clear of permanent alliances with any portion of the foreign world, so far, I mean, as we are now at liberty to do it; for let me not be understood as capable of patronizing infidelity to existing engagements. I hold the maxim no less applicable to public than to private affairs that honesty is always the best policy. I repeat, therefore, let those engagements be observed in their genuine sense. But in my opinion it is unnecessary and would be unwise to extend them.

Taking care always to keep ourselves by suitable establishments on a respectable defensive posture, we may safely trust to temporary alliances for extraordinary emergencies.

Harmony, liberal intercourse with all nations are recommended by policy, humanity, and interest. But even our commercial policy should hold an equal and impartial hand, neither seeking nor granting exclusive favors or preferences; consulting the natural course of things; diffusing and diversifying by gentle means the streams of commerce, but forcing nothing; establishing with powers so disposed, in order to give trade a stable course, to define the rights of our merchants, and to enable the government to support them, conventional rules of intercourse, the best that present circumstances and mutual opinion will permit, but temporary and liable to be from time to time abandoned or varied as experience and circumstances shall dictate; constantly keeping in view that it is folly in one nation to look

for disinterested favors from another; that it must pay with a portion of its independence for whatever it may accept under that character; that by such acceptance it may place itself in the condition of having given equivalents for nominal favors, and yet of being reproached with ingratitude for not giving more. There can be no greater error than to expect or calculate upon real favors from nation to nation. It is an illusion which experience must cure, which a just pride ought to discard.

In offering to you, my countrymen, these counsels of an old and affectionate friend I dare not hope they will make the strong and lasting impression I could wish—that they will control the usual current of the passions or prevent our nation from running the course which has hitherto marked the destiny of nations. But if I may even flatter myself that they may be productive of some partial benefit, some occasional good— that they may now and then recur to moderate the fury of party spirit, to warn against the mischiefs of foreign intrigue, to guard against the impostures of pretended patriotism—this hope will be a full recompense for the solicitude for your welfare by which they have been dictated.

How far in the discharge of my official duties I have been guided by the principles which have been delineated the public records and other evidences of my conduct must witness to you and to the world. To myself, the assurance of my own conscience is that I have at least believed myself to be guided by them.

In relation to the still subsisting war in Europe, my proclamation of the 22d of April 1793 is the index to my plan. Sanctioned by your approving voice and by that of your representatives in both houses of Congress, the spirit of that measure has continually governed me, uninfluenced by any attempts to deter or divert me from it.

After deliberate examination, with the aid of the best lights I could obtain, I was well satisfied that our country, under all the circumstances of the case, had a right to take, and was bound in duty and interest to take, a neutral position. Having taken it, I determined as far as should depend upon me to maintain it with moderation, perseverance, and firmness.

The considerations which respect the right to hold this conduct it is not necessary on this occasion to detail. I will only observe that, according to my understanding of the matter, that right, so far from being denied by any of the belligerent powers, has been virtually admitted by all.

The duty of holding a neutral conduct may be inferred, without anything more, from the obligation which justice and humanity impose on every nation, in cases in which it is free to act, to maintain inviolate the relations of peace and amity toward other nations.

The inducements of interest for observing that conduct will best be referred to your own reflections and experience. With me a predominant motive has been to endeavor to gain time to our country to settle and mature its yet recent institutions, and to progress without interruption to that degree of strength and consistency which is necessary to give it, humanly speaking, the command of its own fortunes.

Though in reviewing the incidents of my administration I am unconscious of intentional error, I am nevertheless too sensible of my defects not to think it probable that I may have committed many errors. Whatever they may be, I fervently beseech the Almighty to avert or mitigate the evils to which they may tend. I shall also carry with me the hope that my country will never cease to view them with indulgence, and that, after forty-five years of my life dedicated to its service with an upright zeal, the faults of incompetent abilities will be consigned to oblivion, as myself must soon be to the mansions of rest.

Relying on its kindness in this as in other things, and actuated by that fervent love toward it which is so natural to a man who views in it the native soil of himself and his progenitors for several generations, I anticipate with pleasing expectation that retreat in which I promise myself to realize without alloy the sweet enjoyment of partaking in the midst of my fellow citizens the benign influence of good laws under a free government—the ever-favorite object of my heart, and the happy reward, as I trust, of our mutual cares, labors, and dangers.

PRESIDENTIAL
SPEECHES

GEORGE
WASHINGTON:
FAREWELL
ADDRESS

PRESIDENTIAL SPEECHES

ABRAHAM LINCOLN: GETTYSBURG ADDRESS

On November 19, 1863, President Abraham Lincoln delivered an address at the dedication of the national cemetery in Gettysburg, Pennsylvania, that has become one of the most famous speeches of U.S. history. Lincoln's speech came less than six months after the conclusion of the Gettysburg campaign (June 27–July 4, 1863), one of the bloodiest battles of the U.S. Civil War. Confederate General Robert E. Lee and his forces were defeated by Union forces led by General George Meade. The losses for both sides were immense with more than 7,000 killed and 44,000 wounded or missing.

The principal orator at the dedication was Edward Everett, a senator, preacher, and scholar who spoke for more than two hours in the florid style of the time. Lincoln, who presided at the dedication, followed with a few brief remarks in a speech he had written in Washington and then revised slightly before the ceremony. Lincoln honored those who had died at Gettysburg and proclaimed that the cause for which they had died had given the nation a "new birth of freedom."

Lucid, terse, and precise, Lincoln's speech stood in stark contrast to Everett's. Though the crowd that day applauded Lincoln's address without enthusiasm, generations of schoolchildren have memorized and recited it, while Everett's speech was quickly forgotten.

—⁓—

Source: *The Writings of Abraham Lincoln,* Constitutional ed., vol. 7 (G. P. Putnam's Sons, 1906), p. 20.

Abraham Lincoln: Gettysburg Address

Fourscore and seven years ago our fathers brought forth on this continent a new nation, conceived in liberty, and dedicated to the proposition that all men are created equal.

Now we are engaged in a great civil war, testing whether that nation, or any nation so conceived and so dedicated, can long endure. We are met on a great battlefield of that war. We have come to dedicate a portion of that field as a final resting-place for those who here gave their lives that that nation might live. It is altogether fitting and proper that we should do this.

But, in a larger sense, we cannot dedicate—we cannot consecrate—we cannot hallow—this ground. The brave men, living and dead, who struggled here, have consecrated it far above our poor power to add or detract. The world will little note nor long remember what we say here, but it can never forget what they did here. It is for us, the living, rather, to be dedicated here to the unfinished work which they who fought here have thus far so nobly advanced. It is rather for us to be here dedicated to the great task remaining before us—that from these honored dead we take increased devotion to that cause for which they gave the last full measure of devotion; that we here highly resolve that these dead shall not have died in vain; that this nation, under God, shall have a new birth of freedom; and that government of the people, by the people, for the people, shall not perish from the earth.

PRESIDENTIAL SPEECHES

ABRAHAM LINCOLN: SECOND INAUGURAL ADDRESS

Abraham Lincoln gave many memorable addresses during his political career, but his second inaugural address is ranked as perhaps his greatest speech. On March 4, 1865, as he began his second term as president, Lincoln delivered the address at the Capitol in Washington, D.C. With the Union forces close to victory—the Civil War would end the following month—Lincoln's address looked forward to the peace that would follow. Throughout the war Lincoln had expressed his desire to preserve the Union. In his address he reminded his listeners that the issue of slavery had been central to the Civil War and suggested that slavery had offended God and brought forth divine retribution in the form of the conflict. Now, with peace at hand, he urged a national reconciliation "with malice toward none, with charity for all." Lincoln did not have the opportunity to shape Reconstruction. He was shot on April 14, 1865, by John Wilkes Booth during the performance of a play at Ford's Theater in Washington, D.C. He died the next day.

—⚬⚬⚬—

Abraham Lincoln: Second Inaugural Address

Fellow countrymen:

At this second appearing to take the oath of the presidential office, there is less occasion for an extended address than there was at the first. Then a statement somewhat in detail of a course to be pursued seemed fitting and proper. Now, at the expiration of four years, during which public declarations have been constantly called forth on every point and phase of the great contest which still absorbs the attention and engrosses the energies of the nation, little that is new could be presented. The progress of our arms, upon which all else chiefly depends, is as well known to the public as to myself, and it is, I trust, reasonably satisfactory and encouraging to all. With high hope for the future, no prediction in regard to it is ventured.

On the occasion corresponding to this four years ago, all thoughts were anxiously directed to an impending civil war. All dreaded it, all sought to avert it. While the inaugural address was being delivered from this place, devoted altogether to saving the Union without war, insurgent agents were in the city seeking to destroy it without war—seeking to dissolve the Union and divide effects by negotiation. Both parties deprecated war, but one of them would make war rather than let the nation survive, and the other would accept war rather than let it perish, and the war came.

One-eighth of the whole population were colored slaves, not distributed generally over the Union, but localized in the southern part of it. These slaves constituted a peculiar and powerful interest. All knew that this interest was somehow the cause of the war. To strengthen, perpetuate, and extend this interest was the object for which the insurgents would rend the Union even by

Source: James D. Richardson, ed. *Messages and Papers of the Presidents: 1789–1897*, vol. 6 (1900), pp. 276–277.

PRESIDENTIAL
SPEECHES

ABRAHAM
LINCOLN:
SECOND
INAUGURAL
ADDRESS

war, while the government claimed no right to do more than to restrict the territorial enlargement of it. Neither party expected for the war the magnitude or the duration which it has already attained. Neither anticipated that the cause of the conflict might cease with or even before the conflict itself should cease. Each looked for an easier triumph, and a result less fundamental and astounding. Both read the same Bible and pray to the same God, and each invokes His aid against the other. It may seem strange that any men should dare to ask a just God's assistance in wringing their bread from the sweat of other men's faces, but let us judge not, that we be not judged. The prayers of both could not be answered. That of neither has been answered fully. The Almighty has His own purposes. "Woe unto the world because of offenses; for it must needs be that offenses come, but woe to that man by whom the offense cometh." If we shall suppose that American slavery is one of those offenses which, in the providence of God, must needs come, but which, having continued through His appointed time, He now wills to remove, and that He gives to both North and South this terrible war as the woe due to those by whom the offense came, shall we discern therein any departure from those divine attributes which the believers in a living God always ascribe to Him? Fondly do we hope, fervently do we pray, that this mighty scourge of war may speedily pass away. Yet, if God wills that it continue until all the wealth piled by the bondsman's two hundred and fifty years of unrequited toil shall be sunk, and until every drop of blood drawn with the lash shall be paid by another drawn with the sword, as was said three thousand years ago, so still it must be said, "the judgments of the Lord are true and righteous altogether."

With malice toward none, with charity for all, with firmness in the right as God gives us to see the right, let us strive on to finish the work we are in, to bind up the nation's wounds, to care for him who shall have borne the battle and for his widow and his orphan, to do all which may achieve and cherish a just and lasting peace among ourselves and with all nations.

PRESIDENTIAL SPEECHES

WOODROW WILSON: FOURTEEN POINTS

By the end of the nineteenth century, U.S. presidents had begun to relax the traditional isolationism of U.S. foreign policy. Nevertheless, when World War I began in 1914, the United States remained aloof from the conflict. President Woodrow Wilson was reelected to a second term in 1916 on the slogan "He kept us out of war." Wilson and U.S. public opinion shifted, however, when Germany announced that it would engage in unrestricted submarine warfare beginning on February 1, 1917. On April 6, 1917, Wilson signed the congressional declaration of war against Germany.

Wilson, who had attempted to negotiate a peace among the belligerents in 1916, renewed his efforts by proposing a new framework for negotiations. On January 8, 1918, he delivered an address to Congress that named fourteen points to be used as the guide for a peace settlement. The speech became known as the Fourteen Points and served as a distillation of Wilson's vision of a postwar world. In the address Wilson said that the secret alliances that triggered the war must be replaced with "open covenants of peace, openly arrived at." He proclaimed the need to demilitarize the ocean and reduce military armaments. He also articulated the desire to end European colonialism and allow the various nationalities of the Austro-Hungarian and Ottoman Empires to create their own states. The most important point was the last, which called for a general association of nations that would guarantee political independence and territorial integrity for all countries.

Following the armistice that ended the war on November 9, 1918, President Wilson led the U.S. delegation to the Paris Peace Conference. Wilson was the only representative of the great powers (which also included Great Britain, France, and Italy) who truly wanted an international organization. His influence was instrumental in persuading the delegates to establish the League of Nations. At home, however, he was unable to secure Senate ratification of the peace treaty that included the league. He was opposed both by Republicans who did not want to commit the United States to supporting the league with financial resources and by isolationists from both major political parties who argued that the United States should not interfere in European affairs.

—∽∿∾—

Woodrow Wilson: Fourteen Points

It will be our wish and purpose that the processes of peace, when they are begun, shall be absolutely open and that they shall involve and permit henceforth no secret understandings of any kind. The day of conquest and aggrandizement is gone by; so is also the day of secret covenants entered into in the interest of particular governments and likely at some unlooked-for moment to upset the peace of the world. It is this happy fact, now clear to the view of every public man whose thoughts do not still linger in an age that is dead and gone, which makes it possible for every nation whose purposes are

PRESIDENTIAL
SPEECHES

WOODROW
WILSON:
FOURTEEN
POINTS

consistent with justice and the peace of the world to avow now or at any other time the objects it has in view.

We entered this war because violations of right had occurred which touched us to the quick and made the life of our own people impossible unless they were corrected and the world secure once for all against their recurrence. What we demand in this war, therefore, is nothing peculiar to ourselves. It is that the world be made fit and safe to live in; and particularly that it be made safe for every peace-loving nation which, like our own, wishes to live its own life, determine its own institutions, be assured of justice and fair dealing by the other peoples of the world as against force and selfish aggression. All the peoples of the world are in effect partners in this interest, and for our own part we see very clearly that unless justice be done to others it will not be done to us. The programme of the world's peace, therefore, is our programme; and that programme, the only possible programme, as we see it, is this:

I. Open covenants of peace, openly arrived at, after which there shall be no private international understandings of any kind but diplomacy shall proceed always frankly and in the public view.

II. Absolute freedom of navigation upon the seas, outside territorial waters, alike in peace and in war, except as the seas may be closed in whole or in part by international action for the enforcement of international covenants.

III. The removal, so far as possible, of all economic barriers and the establishment of an equality of trade conditions among all the nations consenting to the peace and associating themselves for its maintenance.

IV. Adequate guarantees given and taken that national armaments will be reduced to the lowest point consistent with domestic safety.

V. A free, open-minded, and absolutely impartial adjustment of all colonial claims, based upon a strict observance of the principle that in determining all such questions of sovereignty the interests of the populations concerned must have equal weight with the equitable claims of the government whose title is to be determined.

VI. The evacuation of all Russian territory and such a settlement of all questions affecting Russia as will secure the best and freest cooperation of the other nations of the world in obtaining for her an unhampered and unembarrassed opportunity for the independent determination of her own political development and national policy and assure her of a sincere welcome into the society of free nations under institutions of her own choosing; and, more than a welcome, assistance also of every kind that she may need and may herself desire. The treatment accorded Russia by her sister nations in the months to come will be the acid test of their good will, of their comprehension of her needs as distinguished from their own interests, and of their intelligent and unselfish sympathy.

VII. Belgium, the whole world will agree, must be evacuated and restored, without any attempt to limit the sovereignty which she enjoys in common with all other free nations. No other single act will serve as this will serve to restore confidence among the nations in the laws which they have themselves set and determined for the government of their relations with one another. Without this healing act the whole structure and validity of international law is forever impaired.

VIII. All French territory should be freed and the invaded portions restored, and the wrong done to France by Prussia in 1871 in the matter of Alsace-Lorraine, which has unsettled the peace of the world for nearly fifty years, should be righted, in order that peace may once more be made secure in the interest of all.

IX. A readjustment of the frontiers of Italy should be effected along clearly recognizable lines of nationality.

X. The peoples of Austria-Hungary, whose place among the nations we wish to see safeguarded and assured, should be accorded the freest opportunity to autonomous development.

XI. Rumania, Serbia, and Montenegro should be evacuated; occupied territories restored; Serbia accorded free and secure access to the sea; and the relations of the several Balkan states to one another determined by friendly counsel along historically established lines of allegiance and nationality; and international guarantees of the political and economic independence and territorial integrity of the several Balkan states should be entered into.

XII. The Turkish portion of the present Ottoman Empire should be assured a secure sovereignty, but the other nationalities which are now under Turkish rule should be assured an undoubted security of life and an absolutely unmolested opportunity of autonomous development, and the Dardanelles should be permanently opened as a free passage to the ships and commerce of all nations under international guarantees.

XIII. An independent Polish state should be erected which should include the territories inhabited by indisputably Polish populations, which should be assured a free and secure access to the sea, and whose political and economic independence and territorial integrity should be guaranteed by international covenant.

XIV. A general association of nations must be formed under specific covenants for the purpose of affording mutual guarantees of political independence and territorial integrity to great and small states alike.

In regard to these essential rectifications of wrong and assertions of right we feel ourselves to be intimate partners of all the governments and peoples associated together against the Imperialists. We cannot be separated in interest or divided in purpose. We stand together until the end.

For such arrangements and covenants we are willing to fight and to continue to fight until they are achieved; but only because we wish the right to prevail and desire a just and stable peace such as can be secured only by removing the chief provocations to war, which this programme does remove. We have no jealousy of German greatness, and there is nothing in this programme that impairs it. We grudge her no achievement or distinction of learning or of pacific enterprise such as have made her record very bright and very enviable. We do not wish to injure her or to block in any way her legitimate influence or power. We do not wish to fight her either with arms or with hostile arrangements of trade if she is willing to associate herself with us and the other peace-loving nations of the world in covenants of justice and law and fair dealing. We wish her only to accept a place of equality among the peoples of the world,—the new world in which we now live,—instead of a place of mastery.

PRESIDENTIAL SPEECHES

FRANKLIN D. ROOSEVELT: FIRST INAUGURAL ADDRESS

During the presidential campaign of 1932, with the United States mired in the Great Depression, Franklin D. Roosevelt called for action by the federal government to revive the economy and end the suffering of the thirteen million people who were unemployed. When he took office on March 4, 1933, the national mood was bleak. In his first inaugural address, Roosevelt reassured the nation that "the only thing we have to fear is fear itself." He proposed a New Deal for the people of the United States and promised he would use the power of the executive branch to address the economic crisis.

In his speech Roosevelt criticized the financial community for breeding a culture of greed during the 1920s that led to the economic depression. Declaring that "our greatest task is to put people to work," he proposed to use the government to reinvigorate the economy. He acknowledged that the need for "undelayed action" might require disturbing the "normal balance of executive and legislative authority."

Roosevelt's address helped rally the nation. His call for sweeping actions by the federal government produced a torrent of legislation from Congress in his first hundred days in office. Though the Supreme Court initially struck down many of these acts as unconstitutional, within a few years the Court changed its view. As a result, the federal government greatly expanded its power to regulate the economy. Through Roosevelt's bold initiatives, many U.S. citizens came to view the federal government in a new way—as the catalyst of progressive social change.

Franklin D. Roosevelt: First Inaugural Address

I am certain that my fellow Americans expect that on my induction into the Presidency I will address them with a candor and a decision which the present situation of our Nation impels. This is preeminently the time to speak the truth, the whole truth, frankly and boldly. Nor need we shrink from honestly facing conditions in our country today. This great Nation will endure as it has endured, will revive and will prosper.

So, first of all, let me assert my firm belief that the only thing we have to fear is fear itself—nameless, unreasoning, unjustified terror which paralyzes needed efforts to convert retreat into advance. In every dark hour of our national life a leadership of frankness and vigor has met with that understanding and support of the people themselves which is essential to victory. I am convinced that you will again give that support to leadership in these critical days.

In such a spirit on my part and on yours we face our common difficulties. They concern, thank God, only material things. Values have shrunken to fantastic levels; taxes have risen; our ability to pay has fallen; government of all kinds is faced by serious curtailment of income; the means of exchange are frozen in the currents of trade; the withered leaves of industrial enterprise lie on every side; farmers find no markets for their produce; the savings of many years in thousands of families are gone.

PRESIDENTIAL
SPEECHES

FRANKLIN D.
ROOSEVELT:
FIRST
INAUGURAL
ADDRESS

More important, a host of unemployed citizens face the grim problem of existence, and an equally great number toil with little return. Only a foolish optimist can deny the dark realities of the moment.

Yet our distress comes from no failure of substance. We are stricken by no plague of locusts. Compared with the perils which our forefathers conquered because they believed and were not afraid, we have still much to be thankful for. Nature still offers her bounty and human efforts have multiplied it. Plenty is at our doorstep, but a generous use of it languishes in the very sight of the supply. Primarily this is because the rulers of the exchange of mankind's goods have failed, through their own stubbornness and their own incompetence, have admitted their failure, and abdicated. Practices of the unscrupulous money changers stand indicted in the court of public opinion, rejected by the hearts and minds of men.

True they have tried, but their efforts have been cast in the pattern of an outworn tradition. Faced by failure of credit they have proposed only the lending of more money. Stripped of the lure of profit by which to induce our people to follow their false leadership, they have resorted to exhortations, pleading tearfully for restored confidence. They know only the rules of a generation of self-seekers. They have no vision, and when there is no vision the people perish.

The money changers have fled from their high seats in the temple of our civilization. We may now restore that temple to the ancient truths. The measure of the restoration lies in the extent to which we apply social values more noble than mere monetary profit.

Happiness lies not in the mere possession of money; it lies in the joy of achievement, in the thrill of creative effort. The joy and moral stimulation of work no longer must be forgotten in the mad chase of evanescent profits. These dark days will be worth all they cost us if they teach us that our true destiny is not to be ministered unto but to minister to ourselves and to our fellow men.

Recognition of the falsity of material wealth as the standard of success goes hand in hand with the abandonment of the false belief that public office and high political position are to be valued only by the standards of pride of place and personal profit; and there must be an end to a conduct in banking and in business which too often has given to a sacred trust the likeness of callous and selfish wrongdoing. Small wonder that confidence languishes, for it thrives only on honesty, on honor, on the sacredness of obligations, on faithful protection, on unselfish performance; without them it cannot live.

Restoration calls, however, not for changes in ethics alone. This Nation asks for action, and action now.

Our greatest primary task is to put people to work. This is no unsolvable problem if we face it wisely and courageously. It can be accomplished in part by direct recruiting by the Government itself, treating the task as we would treat the emergency of a war, but at the same time, through this employment, accomplishing greatly needed projects to stimulate and reorganize the use of our natural resources.

Hand in hand with this we must frankly recognize the overbalance of population in our industrial centers and, by engaging on a national scale in a redistribution, endeavor to provide a better use of the land for those best fitted for the land. The task can be helped by definite efforts to raise the values of agricultural products and with this the power to purchase the output of our cities. It can be helped by preventing realistically the tragedy of the growing loss through foreclosure of our small homes and our farms. It can be helped by insistence that the Federal, State, and local governments act forthwith on the demand that their cost be drastically reduced. It can be helped by the unifying of relief activities which today are often scattered, uneconomical, and unequal. It can be helped by national planning for and supervision of all forms of transportation and of communications and other utilities which have a definitely public character. There are many ways in which it can be helped, but it can never be helped merely by talking about it. We must act and act quickly.

Finally, in our progress toward a resumption of work we require two safeguards against a return of the evils of the old order; there must be a strict supervision of all banking and credits and investments; there must be an end to speculation with other people's money, and there must be provision for an adequate but sound currency.

There are the lines of attack. I shall presently urge upon a new Congress in special session detailed measures for their fulfillment, and I shall seek the immediate assistance of the several States.

PRESIDENTIAL
SPEECHES

FRANKLIN D.
ROOSEVELT:
FIRST
INAUGURAL
ADDRESS

Through this program of action we address ourselves to putting our own national house in order and making income balance outgo. Our international trade relations, though vastly important, are in point of time and necessity secondary to the establishment of a sound national economy. I favor as a practical policy the putting of first things first. I shall spare no effort to restore world trade by international economic readjustment, but the emergency at home cannot wait on that accomplishment.

The basic thought that guides these specific means of national recovery is not narrowly nationalistic. It is the insistence, as a first consideration, upon the interdependence of the various elements in all parts of the United States—a recognition of the old and permanently important manifestation of the American spirit of the pioneer. It is the way to recovery. It is the immediate way. It is the strongest assurance that the recovery will endure.

In the field of world policy I would dedicate this Nation to the policy of the good neighbor— the neighbor who resolutely respects himself and, because he does so, respects the rights of others—the neighbor who respects his obligations and respects the sanctity of his agreements in and with a world of neighbors.

If I read the temper of our people correctly, we now realize as we have never realized before our interdependence on each other; that we can not merely take but we must give as well; that if we are to go forward, we must move as a trained and loyal army willing to sacrifice for the good of a common discipline, because without such discipline no progress is made, no leadership becomes effective. We are, I know, ready and willing to submit our lives and property to such discipline, because it makes possible a leadership which aims at a larger good. This I propose to offer, pledging that the larger purposes will bind upon us all as a sacred obligation with a unity of duty hitherto evoked only in time of armed strife.

With this pledge taken, I assume unhesitatingly the leadership of this great army of our people dedicated to a disciplined attack upon our common problems.

Action in this image and to this end is feasible under the form of government which we have inherited from our ancestors. Our Constitution is so simple and practical that it is possible always to meet extraordinary needs by changes in emphasis and arrangement without loss of essential form. That is why our constitutional system has proved itself the most superbly enduring political mechanism the modern world has produced. It has met every stress of vast expansion of territory, of foreign wars, of bitter internal strife, of world relations.

It is to be hoped that the normal balance of executive and legislative authority may be wholly adequate to meet the unprecedented task before us. But it may be that an unprecedented demand and need for undelayed action may call for temporary departure from that normal balance of public procedure.

I am prepared under my constitutional duty to recommend the measures that a stricken nation in the midst of a stricken world may require. These measures, or such other measures as the Congress may build out of its experience and wisdom, I shall seek, within my constitutional authority, to bring to speedy adoption.

But in the event that the Congress shall fail to take one of these two courses, and in the event that the national emergency is still critical, I shall not evade the clear course of duty that will then confront me. I shall ask the Congress for the one remaining instrument to meet the crisis—broad Executive power to wage a war against the emergency, as great as the power that would be given to me if we were in fact invaded by a foreign foe. For the trust reposed in me I will return the courage and the devotion that befit the time. I can do no less.

We face the arduous days that lie before us in the warm courage of the national unity; with the clear consciousness of seeking old and precious moral values; with the clean satisfaction that comes from the stem performance of duty by old and young alike. We aim at the assurance of a rounded and permanent national life.

We do not distrust the future of essential democracy. The people of the United States have not failed. In their need they have registered a mandate that they want direct, vigorous action. They have asked for discipline and direction under leadership. They have made me the present instrument of their wishes. In the spirit of the gift I take it.

In this dedication of a Nation we humbly ask the blessing of God. May He protect each and every one of us. May He guide me in the days to come.

PRESIDENTIAL SPEECHES

JOHN F. KENNEDY: INAUGURAL ADDRESS

John F. Kennedy was elected president in 1960 by a slim margin over Vice President Richard M. Nixon. During the campaign Kennedy had charged that the United States had fallen militarily behind the Soviet Union during the administration of President Dwight D. Eisenhower. Therefore, when Kennedy gave his inaugural address on January 20, 1961, he focused on U.S. foreign policy.

Kennedy's address revealed how far the United States had moved in international affairs. The isolationism of the 1930s had given way to a foreign policy based on fighting Communism anywhere in the world. He declared that "the torch has been passed to a new generation of Americans" committed to defending liberty.

The most quoted lines of the address—"ask not what your country can do for you, ask what you can do for your country"—became the patriotic rallying cry for Kennedy's New Frontier initiatives, which emphasized the space program, the Peace Corps, and increased defense spending.

—⁓—

John F. Kennedy: Inaugural Address

We observe today not a victory of party but a celebration of freedom—symbolizing an end as well as a beginning—signifying renewal as well as change. For I have sworn before you and Almighty God the same solemn oath our forebears prescribed nearly a century and three-quarters ago.

The world is very different now. For man holds in his mortal hands the power to abolish all forms of human poverty and all forms of human life. And yet the same revolutionary beliefs for which our forebears fought are still at issue around the globe—the belief that the rights of man come not from the generosity of the state but from the hand of God.

We dare not forget today that we are the heirs of that first revolution. Let the word go forth from this time and place, to friend and foe alike, that the torch has been passed to a new generation of Americans—born in this century, tempered by war, disciplined by a hard and bitter peace, proud of our ancient heritage—and unwilling to witness to or permit the slow undoing of those human rights to which this nation has always been committed, and to which we are committed today at home and around the world.

Let every nation know, whether it wishes us well or ill, that we shall pay any price, bear any burden, meet any hardship, support any friend, oppose any foe to assure the survival and the success of liberty.

This much we pledge—and more.

To those old allies whose cultural and spiritual origins we share, we pledge the loyalty of faithful friends. United, there is little we cannot do in a host of new cooperative ventures. Divided, there is little we can do—for we dare not meet a powerful challenge at odds and split asunder.

To those new states whom we welcome to the ranks of the free, we pledge our word that one form of colonial control shall not have

PRESIDENTIAL
SPEECHES

JOHN F.
KENNEDY:
INAUGURAL
ADDRESS

passed away merely to be replaced by a far more iron tyranny. We shall not always expect to find them supporting our view. But we shall always hope to find them strongly supporting their own freedom—and to remember that, in the past, those who foolishly sought power by riding the back of the tiger ended up inside.

To those people in the huts and villages of half the globe struggling to break the bonds of mass misery, we pledge our best efforts to help them help themselves, for whatever period is required—not because the Communists may be doing it, not because we seek their votes, but because it is right. If a free society cannot help the many who are poor, it cannot save the few who are rich.

To our sister republics south of our border, we offer a special pledge—to convert our good words into good deeds—in a new alliance for progress—to assist free men and free governments in casting off the chains of poverty. But this peaceful revolution of hope cannot become the prey of hostile powers. Let all our neighbors know that we shall join with them to oppose aggression or subversion anywhere in the Americas. And let every other power know that this hemisphere intends to remain the master of its own house.

To that world assembly of sovereign states, the United Nations, our last best hope in an age where the instruments of war have far outpaced the instruments of peace, we renew our pledge of support—to prevent it from becoming merely a forum for invective—to strengthen its shield of the new and the weak—and to enlarge the area in which its writ may run.

Finally, to those nations who would make themselves our adversary, we offer not a pledge but a request: that both sides begin anew the quest for peace, before the dark powers of destruction unleashed by science engulf all humanity in planned or accidental self-destruction.

We dare not tempt them with weakness. For only when our arms are sufficient beyond doubt can we be certain beyond doubt that they will never be employed.

But neither can two great and powerful groups of nations take comfort from our present course—both sides overburdened by the cost of modern weapons, both rightly alarmed by the steady spread of the deadly atom, yet both racing to alter that uncertain balance of terror that stays the hand of mankind's final war.

So let us begin anew—remembering on both sides that civility is not a sign of weakness, and sincerity is always subject to proof. Let us never negotiate out of fear. But let us never fear to negotiate.

Let both sides explore what problems unite us instead of belaboring those problems which divide us.

Let both sides, for the first time, formulate serious and precise proposals for the inspection and control of arms—and bring the absolute power to destroy other nations under the absolute control of all nations.

Let both sides seek to invoke the wonders of science instead of its terrors. Together let us explore the stars, conquer the deserts, eradicate disease, tap the ocean depths and encourage the arts and commerce.

Let both sides unite to heed in all corners of the earth the command of Isaiah—to "undo the heavy burdens … [and] let the oppressed go free."

And if a beachhead of cooperation may push back the jungles of suspicion, let both sides join in creating a new endeavor—not a new balance of power, but a new world of law, where the strong are just and the weak secure and the peace preserved.

All this will not be finished in the first 100 days. Nor will it be finished in the first 1,000 days, nor in the life of this Administration, nor even perhaps in our lifetime on this planet. But let us begin.

In your hands, my fellow citizens, more than mine, will rest the final success or failure of our course. Since this country was founded, each generation of Americans has been summoned to give testimony to its national loyalty. The graves of young Americans who answered the call to service surround the globe.

Now the trumpet summons us again—not as a call to bear arms, though arms we need—not as a call to battle, though embattled we are—but a call to bear the burden of a long twilight struggle year in and year out, "rejoicing in hope, patient in tribulation"—a struggle against the common enemies of man: tyranny, poverty, disease and war itself.

Can we forge against these enemies a grand and global alliance, north and south, east and west, that can assure a more fruitful life for all mankind? Will you join in that historic effort?

In the long history of the world, only a few generations have been granted the role of defending freedom in its hour of maximum danger. I do not shrink from this responsibility—I welcome it. I do not believe that any of us would exchange places with any other people or any other generation. The energy, the faith, the devotion which we bring to this endeavor will light our country and all who serve it—and the glow from that fire can truly light the world.

And so, my fellow Americans: ask not what your country can do for you—ask what you can do for your country.

My fellow citizens of the world: ask not what America will do for you, but what together we can do for the freedom of man.

Finally, whether you are citizens of America or citizens of the world, ask of us here the same high standards of strength and sacrifice which we ask of you. With a good conscience our only sure reward, with history the final judge of our deeds, let us go forth to lead the land we love, asking His blessing and His help, but knowing that here on earth God's work must truly be our own.

PRESIDENTIAL
SPEECHES

JOHN F.
KENNEDY:
INAUGURAL
ADDRESS

PRESIDENTIAL SPEECHES

LYNDON B. JOHNSON: VOTING RIGHTS ACT ADDRESS

On March 15, 1965, President Lyndon B. Johnson addressed a joint session of Congress to urge the passage of new voting rights legislation. Although Johnson had successfully engineered the passage of the landmark Civil Rights Act of 1964 (42 U.S.C.A. § 2000a et seq.) the year before, problems remained. Dr. Martin Luther King Jr., and other civil rights leaders demanded an end to racially discriminatory voting practices in the South. They organized public protests and voter registration drives that were met with intense resistance from local authorities.

When King and civil rights supporters marched to Selma, Alabama, in 1965 to demand voting rights, police met them with violence, and several marchers were murdered. The Selma violence, which was broadcast on television news programs, galvanized voting rights supporters in Congress. One week later, President Johnson responded by introducing the Voting Rights Act (42 U.S.C.A. § 1973 et seq.), which included the harshest penalties ever imposed for denials of civil rights. Congress enacted the measure five months later.

In his address Johnson confronted the problem of racism and racial discrimination. He declared that "every American citizen must have an equal right to vote. There is no reason which can excuse the denial of that right." Johnson reminded the nation that the Fifteenth Amendment, which was passed after the Civil War, gives all citizens the right to vote regardless of race or color, yet states had defied the Constitution and erected barriers based on

those forbidden grounds. In Johnson's view no constitutional or moral issue was at stake. Congress simply needed to enforce the amendment with strict penalties.

Johnson, a native of Texas, surprised the nation near the close of his speech when he invoked the famous civil rights anthem and declared "we shall overcome." He was greeted by stunned silence, followed by thunderous applause and tears. It was reported that Dr. King, watching the speech on television from Selma, wept. Many historians view the speech as the watershed moment of the civil rights revolution of the 1960s.

———✺———

Lyndon B. Johnson: Voting Rights Act Address

I speak tonight for the dignity of man and the destiny of democracy.

I urge every member of both parties—Americans of all religions and of all colors—from every section of this country—to join me in that cause.

At times history and fate meet at a single time in a single place to shape a turning point in man's unending search for freedom. So it was at Lexington and Concord. So it was a century ago at Appomattox. So it was last week in Selma, Alabama.

There is no Negro problem. There is no southern problem. There is no northern problem. There is only an American problem.

And we are met here tonight as Americans—not as Democrats or Republicans—we are met here as Americans to solve that problem.

This was the first nation in the history of the world to be founded with a purpose. The great phrases of that purpose still sound in every American heart, north and south: "All men are created equal"—"Government by consent of the governed"—"Give me liberty or give me death.". . .

Those words are a promise to every citizen that he shall share in the dignity of man. This dignity cannot be found in man's possessions. It cannot be found in his power or in his position. It really rests on his right to be treated as a man equal in opportunity to all others. It says that he shall share in freedom, he shall choose his leaders, educate his children, provide for his family according to his ability and his merits as a human being. . . .

Many of the issues of civil rights are very complex and most difficult. But about this there can and should be no argument. Every American citizen must have an equal right to vote. There is no reason which can excuse the denial of that right. There is no duty which weighs more heavily on us than the duty we have to ensure that right.

Yet the harsh fact is that in many places in this country men and women are kept from voting simply because they are Negroes. . . .

Experience has clearly shown that the existing process of law cannot overcome systematic and ingenious discrimination. No law that we now have on the books—and I have helped to put three of them there—can ensure the right to vote when local officials are determined to deny it.

In such a case our duty must be clear to all of us. The Constitution says that no person shall be kept from voting because of his race or his color.

We have all sworn an oath before God to support and to defend that Constitution.

We must now act in obedience to that oath.

Wednesday I will send to Congress a law designed to eliminate illegal barriers to the right to vote. . . .

To those who seek to avoid action by their National Government in their home communities—who want to and who seek to maintain purely local control over elections—the answer is simple. Open your polling places to all your people. Allow men and women to register and vote whatever the color of their skin. Extend the rights of citizenship to every citizen of this land. There is no constitutional issue here. The command of the Constitution is plain. There is no moral issue. It is wrong—deadly wrong—to deny any of your fellow Americans the right to vote in this country. There is no issue of States rights or National rights. There is only the struggle for human rights.

I have not the slightest doubt what will be your answer. . . .

But even if we pass this bill, the battle will not be over. What happened in Selma is part of a far larger movement which reaches into every section and State of America. It is the effort of American Negroes to secure for themselves the full blessings of American life.

Their cause must be our cause too, because it is not just Negroes but really it is all of us, who must overcome the crippling legacy of bigotry and injustice. And we shall overcome. . . .

This great, rich, restless country can offer opportunity and education and hope to all—all black and white, all North and South, sharecropper and city dweller. These are the enemies—poverty, ignorance, disease—they are our enemies, not our fellow man, not our neighbor. And these enemies too—poverty, disease, and ignorance—we shall overcome.

PRESIDENTIAL
SPEECHES

LYNDON B.
JOHNSON:
VOTING RIGHTS
ACT ADDRESS

PRESIDENTIAL SPEECHES

RONALD REAGAN: FIRST INAUGURAL ADDRESS

RONALD REAGAN was elected president in 1980, defeating the incumbent JIMMY CARTER. Reagan, a Republican from California, had campaigned as much against the federal government as against his opponent. He charged that the federal government had become a bloated bureaucracy since its dramatic growth under FRANKLIN D. ROOSEVELT in the 1930s and 1940s. He proposed to cut the size of the federal government and its budget and return power to the states.

In his first inaugural address, delivered on January 20, 1981, Reagan reaffirmed his campaign pledges. With the nation in an economic recession, he declared that "government is not the solution to our problem." Instead, he proposed to remove "the roadblocks that have slowed our economy and reduced productivity," reawaken "this industrial giant," get "government back within its means," and reduce "punitive tax burdens."

In addition, Reagan announced that he would restore the balance between the various levels of government. The federal government's growth would be reversed, and power would be returned to the states and the people. Though he denied any intention of doing away with government, Reagan made clear that "we are a nation that has a government—not the other way around."

Reagan's address signaled a turning point in modern U.S. history, as conservative political views became more popular with the electorate. Almost every facet of modern U.S. government became the subject of a conservative reevaluation that resulted in significant changes in the regulation of the economy and social welfare programs.

—✺—

Ronald Reagan: First Inaugural Address

To a few of us here today, this is a solemn and most momentous occasion; and yet, in the history of our Nation, it is a commonplace occurrence. The orderly transfer of authority as called for in the Constitution routinely takes place as it has for almost two centuries and few of us stop to think how unique we really are. In the eyes of many in the world, this every-4-year ceremony we accept as normal is nothing less than a miracle.

Mr. President, I want our fellow citizens to know how much you did to carry on this tradition. By your gracious cooperation in the transition process, you have shown a watching world that we are a united people pledged to maintaining a political system which guarantees individual liberty to a greater degree than any other, and I thank you and your people for all your help in maintaining the continuity which is the bulwark of our Republic.

The business of our nation goes forward. These United States are confronted with an economic affliction of great proportions. We suffer from the longest and one of the worst sustained inflations in our national history. It distorts our economic decisions, penalizes thrift, and crushes the struggling young and the fixed-income elderly alike. It threatens to shatter the lives of millions of our people. Idle industries have cast workers into unemployment, causing human misery and personal indignity.

Those who do work are denied a fair return for their labor by a tax system which penalizes successful achievement and keeps us from maintaining full productivity. But great as our tax burden is, it has not kept pace with public spending. For decades, we have piled deficit upon deficit, mortgaging our future and our children's future for the temporary convenience of the present. To continue this long trend is to guarantee tremendous social, cultural, political, and economic upheavals. You and I, as individuals, can, by borrowing, live beyond our means, but for only a limited period of time.

Why, then, should we think that collectively, as a nation, we are not bound by that same limitation? We must act today in order to preserve tomorrow. And let there be no misunderstanding—we are going to begin to act, beginning today. The economic ills we suffer have come upon us over several decades. They will not go away in days, weeks, or months, but they will go away. They will go away because we, as Americans, have the capacity now, as we have had in the past, to do whatever needs to be done to preserve this last and greatest bastion of freedom.

In this present crisis, government is not the solution to our problem. From time to time, we have been tempted to believe that society has become too complex to be managed by self-rule, that government by an elite group is superior to government for, by, and of the people. But if no one among us is capable of governing himself, then who among us has the capacity to govern someone else? All of us together, in and out of government, must bear the burden. The solutions we seek must be equitable, with no one group singled out to pay a higher price.

We hear much of special interest groups. Our concern must be for a special interest group that has been too long neglected. It knows no sectional boundaries or ethnic and racial divisions, and it crosses political party lines. It is made up of men and women who raise our food, patrol our streets, man our mines and our factories, teach our children, keep our homes, and heal us when we are sick—professionals, industrialists, shopkeepers, clerks, cabbies, and truckdrivers. They are, in short, "We the people," this breed called Americans.

Well, this administration's objective will be a healthy, vigorous, growing economy that provides equal opportunity for all Americans, with no barriers born of bigotry or discrimination. Putting America back to work means putting all Americans back to work. Ending inflation means freeing all Americans from the terror of runaway living costs. All must share in the productive work of this "new beginning" and all must share in the bounty of a revived economy. With the idealism and fair play which are the core of our system and our strength, we can have a strong and prosperous America at peace with itself and the world. So, as we begin, let us take inventory.

We are a nation that has a government—not the other way around. And this makes us special among the nations of the Earth. Our Government has no power except that granted it by the people. It is time to check and reverse the growth of government which shows signs of having grown beyond the consent of the governed.

It is my intention to curb the size and influence of the Federal establishment and to demand recognition of the distinction between the powers granted to the Federal Government and those reserved to the States or to the people. All of us need to be reminded that the Federal Government did not create the States; the States created the Federal Government. Now, so there will be no misunderstanding, it is not my intention to do away with government. It is, rather, to make it work—work with us, not over us; to stand by our side, not ride on our back. Government can and must provide opportunity, not smother it; foster productivity, not stifle it.

If we look to the answer as to why, for so many years, we achieved so much, prospered as no other people on Earth, it was because here, in this land, we unleashed the energy and individual genius of man to a greater extent than has ever been done before. Freedom and the dignity of the individual have been more available and assured here than in any other place on Earth. The price for this freedom at times has been high, but we have never been unwilling to pay that price. It is no coincidence that our present troubles parallel and are proportionate to the intervention and intrusion in our lives that result from unnecessary and excessive growth of government.

It is time for us to realize that we are too great a nation to limit ourselves to small dreams.

PRESIDENTIAL
SPEECHES

RONALD
REAGAN: FIRST
INAUGURAL
ADDRESS

PRESIDENTIAL
SPEECHES

RONALD
REAGAN: FIRST
INAUGURAL
ADDRESS

We are not, as some would have us believe, loomed to an inevitable decline. I do not believe in a fate that will fall on us no matter what we do. I do believe in a fate that will fall on us if we do nothing.

So, with all the creative energy at our command, let us begin an era of national renewal. Let us renew our determination, our courage, and our strength. And let us renew; our faith and our hope. We have every right to dream heroic dreams. Those who say that we are in a time when there are no heroes just don't know where to look. You can see heroes every day going in and out of factory gates. Others, a handful in number, produce enough food to feed all of us and then the world beyond. You meet heroes across a counter—and they are on both sides of that counter. There are entrepreneurs with faith in themselves and faith in an idea who create new jobs, new wealth and opportunity. They are individuals and families whose taxes support the Government and whose voluntary gifts support church, charity, culture, art, and education. Their patriotism is quiet but deep. Their values sustain our national life.

I have used the words "they" and "their" in speaking of these heroes. I could say "you" and "your" because I am addressing the heroes of whom I speak—you, the citizens of this blessed land. Your dreams, your hopes, your goals are going to be the dreams, the hopes, and the goals of this administration, so help me God. We shall reflect the compassion that is so much a part of your makeup. How can we love our country and not love our countrymen, and loving them, reach out a hand when they fall, heal them when they are sick, and provide opportunities to make them self-sufficient so they will be equal in fact and not just in theory? Can we solve the problems confronting us? Well, the answer is an unequivocal and emphatic "yes." To paraphrase Winston Churchill, I did not take the oath I have just taken with the intention of presiding over the dissolution of the world's strongest economy. In the days ahead I will propose removing the roadblocks that have slowed our economy and reduced productivity. Steps will be taken aimed at restoring the balance between the various levels of government. Progress may be slow—measured in inches and feet, not miles—but we will progress.

It is time to reawaken this industrial giant, to get government back within its means, and to lighten our punitive tax burden. And these will be our first priorities, and on these principles, there will be no compromise. On the eve of our struggle for independence a man who might have been one of the greatest among the Founding Fathers, Dr. Joseph Warren, President of the Massachusetts Congress, said to his fellow Americans, "Our country is in danger, but not to be despaired of.... On you depend the fortunes of America. You are to decide the important questions upon which rests the happiness and the liberty of millions yet unborn. Act worthy of yourselves."

Well, I believe we, the Americans of today, are ready to act worthy of ourselves, ready to do what must be done to ensure happiness and liberty for ourselves, our children and our children's children. And as we renew ourselves here in our own land, we will be seen as having greater strength throughout the world. We will again be the exemplar of freedom and a beacon of hope for those who do not now have freedom.

To those neighbors and allies who share our freedom, we will strengthen our historic ties and assure them of our support and firm commitment. We will match loyalty with loyalty. We will strive for mutually beneficial relations. We will not use our friendship to impose on their sovereignty, for our own sovereignty is not for sale.

As for the enemies of freedom, those who are potential adversaries, they will be reminded that peace is the highest aspiration of the American people. We will negotiate for it, sacrifice for it; we will not surrender for it—now or ever. Our forbearance should never be misunderstood. Our reluctance for conflict should not be misjudged as a failure of will. When action is required to preserve our national security, we will act. We will maintain sufficient strength to prevail if need be, knowing that if we do so we have the best chance of never having to use that strength.

Above all, we must realize that no arsenal, or no weapon in the arsenals of the world, is so formidable as the will and moral courage of free men and women. It is a weapon our adversaries in today's world do not have. It is a weapon that we as Americans do have. Let that be understood by those who practice terrorism and prey upon their neighbors. I am told that tens of thousands of prayer meetings are being held on this day, and for that I am deeply grateful. We are a nation under God, and I believe God intended for us to be free. It would be fitting and good, I think, if on each Inauguration Day in future years it should be declared a day of prayer.

This is the first time in history that this ceremony has been held, as you have been told, on this West Front of the Capitol. Standing here, one faces a magnificent vista, opening up on this city's special beauty and history. At the end of this open mall are those shrines to the giants on whose shoulders we stand. Directly in front of me, the monument to a monumental man: George Washington, Father of our country. A man of humility who came to greatness reluctantly. He led America out of revolutionary victory into infant nationhood. Off to one side, the stately memorial to Thomas Jefferson. The Declaration of Independence flames with his eloquence. And then beyond the Reflecting Pool the dignified columns of the Lincoln Memorial. Whoever would understand in his heart the meaning of America will find it in the life of Abraham Lincoln. Beyond those monuments to heroism is the Potomac River, and on the far shore the sloping hills of Arlington National Cemetery with its row on row of simple white markers bearing crosses or Stars of David. They add up to only a tiny fraction of the price that has been paid for our freedom. Each one of those markers is a monument to the kinds of heroes I spoke of earlier. Their lives ended in places called Belleau Wood. The Argonne, Omaha Beach, Salerno and halfway around the world on Guadalcanal, Tarawa, Pork Chop Hill, the Chosin Reservoir, and in a hundred rice paddies and jungles of a place called Vietnam.

Under one such marker lies a young man—Martin Treptow—who left his job in a small town barber shop in 1917 to go to France with the famed Rainbow Division. There, on the western front, he was killed trying to carry a message between battalions under heavy artillery fire. We are told that on his body was found a diary. On the flyleaf under the heading, "My Pledge," he had written these words: "America must win this war. Therefore, I will work, I will save, I will sacrifice, I will endure, I will fight cheerfully and do my utmost, as if the issue of the whole struggle depended on me alone."

The crisis we are facing today does not require of us the kind of sacrifice that Martin Treptow and so many thousands of others were called upon to make. It does require, however, our best effort, and our willingness to believe in ourselves and to believe in our capacity to perform great deeds; to believe that together, with God's help, we can and will resolve the problems which now confront us. And, after all, why shouldn't we believe that? We are Americans. God bless you, and thank you.

PRESIDENTIAL
SPEECHES

RONALD
REAGAN: FIRST
INAUGURAL
ADDRESS

PRESIDENTIAL SPEECHES

GEORGE W. BUSH: ADDRESS TO CONGRESS, SEPTEMBER 20, 2001

On September 11, 2001, two hijacked aircraft crashed into the World Trade Center in New York City, destroying the complex. Another plane hit the Pentagon, headquarters for the U.S. military, outside Washington, D.C. A fourth plane, also believed to be heading for Washington, D.C., crashed in rural Pennsylvania when passengers attempted to retake control from the hijackers. Almost 3,000 people were killed in the attacks.

Within hours of the attacks, the U.S. government had blamed them on terrorists. Speculation centered around the al Qaeda organization and its leader Osama bin Laden. Bin Laden was believed to be operating out of Afghanistan, a nation controlled by the Taliban, a radical Islamic group sympathetic with bin Laden's ideals. President GEORGE W. BUSH and other administration figures were soon on television and radio telling the nation not to fear and warning the world that the United States would respond to the attacks with determination and vigor.

On September 20th, President Bush spoke before a joint session of Congress in the U.S. Capitol. His speech served many purposes. It honored those who had died in the attacks, and those who were struggling to deal with the aftermath. Bush also sought to reassure Americans that they were safe and that steps were being taken to prevent future attacks. The central message of the speech, however, was that the United States remained strong and unafraid, and that it intended to eliminate terrorist threats through a WAR ON TERROR. President Bush identified al Qaeda as being behind the September 11th attacks and warned the Taliban in Afghanistan that if they failed to cooperate in stopping al Qaeda they would be viewed as collaborators. President Bush went on to make it clear to the American people and the world that a protracted struggle against not just al Qaeda, but world terrorism as a whole, was underway.

President Bush's speech helped honor the fallen and reassure the living, but it did not convince the Taliban to give in to his demands. On October 7, 2001, the United States and its allies began a military campaign against the Taliban and terrorists in Afghanistan. It was eventually successful in driving the Taliban out of power and destroying much of the terrorist's infrastructure in that country.

—␣␣␣—

Mr. Speaker, Mr. President Pro Tempore, members of Congress, and fellow Americans:

In the normal course of events, Presidents come to this chamber to report on the state of the Union. Tonight, no such report is needed. It has already been delivered by the American people.

We have seen it in the courage of passengers, who rushed terrorists to save others on the ground—passengers like an exceptional man named Todd Beamer. And would you please help me to welcome his wife, Lisa Beamer, here tonight.

We have seen the state of our Union in the endurance of rescuers, working past exhaustion.

PRESIDENTIAL
SPEECHES

GEORGE W.
BUSH: ADDRESS
TO CONGRESS,
SEPTEMBER 20,
2001

We have seen the unfurling of flags, the lighting of candles, the giving of blood, the saying of prayers—in English, Hebrew, and Arabic. We have seen the decency of a loving and giving people who have made the grief of strangers their own.

My fellow citizens, for the last nine days, the entire world has seen for itself the state of our Union—and it is strong.

Tonight we are a country awakened to danger and called to defend freedom. Our grief has turned to anger, and anger to resolution. Whether we bring our enemies to justice, or bring justice to our enemies, justice will be done.

I thank the Congress for its leadership at such an important time. All of America was touched on the evening of the tragedy to see Republicans and Democrats joined together on the steps of this Capitol, singing "God Bless America." And you did more than sing; you acted, by delivering $40 billion to rebuild our communities and meet the needs of our military.

Speaker Hastert, Minority Leader Gephardt, Majority Leader Daschle and Senator Lott, I thank you for your friendship, for your leadership and for your service to our country.

And on behalf of the American people, I thank the world for its outpouring of support. America will never forget the sounds of our National Anthem playing at Buckingham Palace, on the streets of Paris, and at Berlin's Brandenburg Gate.

We will not forget South Korean children gathering to pray outside our embassy in Seoul, or the prayers of sympathy offered at a mosque in Cairo. We will not forget moments of silence and days of mourning in Australia and Africa and Latin America.

Nor will we forget the citizens of 80 other nations who died with our own: dozens of Pakistanis; more than 130 Israelis; more than 250 citizens of India; men and women from El Salvador, Iran, Mexico and Japan; and hundreds of British citizens. America has no truer friend than Great Britain. Once again, we are joined together in a great cause—so honored the British Prime Minister has crossed an ocean to show his unity of purpose with America. Thank you for coming, friend.

On September the 11th, enemies of freedom committed an act of war against our country. Americans have known wars—but for the past 136 years, they have been wars on foreign soil, except for one Sunday in 1941. Americans have known the casualties of war—but not at the center of a great city on a peaceful morning. Americans have known surprise attacks—but never before on thousands of civilians. All of this was brought upon us in a single day—and night fell on a different world, a world where freedom itself is under attack.

Americans have many questions tonight. Americans are asking: Who attacked our country? The evidence we have gathered all points to a collection of loosely affiliated terrorist organizations known as al Qaeda. They are the same murderers indicted for bombing American embassies in Tanzania and Kenya, and responsible for bombing the USS *Cole*.

Al Qaeda is to terror what the mafia is to crime. But its goal is not making money; its goal is remaking the world—and imposing its radical beliefs on people everywhere.

The terrorists practice a fringe form of Islamic extremism that has been rejected by Muslim scholars and the vast majority of Muslim clerics—a fringe movement that perverts the peaceful teachings of Islam. The terrorists' directive commands them to kill Christians and Jews, to kill all Americans, and make no distinction among military and civilians, including women and children.

This group and its leader—a person named Osama bin Laden—are linked to many other organizations in different countries, including the Egyptian Islamic Jihad and the Islamic Movement of Uzbekistan. There are thousands of these terrorists in more than 60 countries. They are recruited from their own nations and neighborhoods and brought to camps in places like Afghanistan, where they are trained in the tactics of terror. They are sent back to their homes or sent to hide in countries around the world to plot evil and destruction.

The leadership of al Qaeda has great influence in Afghanistan and supports the Taliban regime in controlling most of that country. In Afghanistan, we see al Qaeda's vision for the world.

Afghanistan's people have been brutalized—many are starving and many have fled. Women are not allowed to attend school. You can be jailed for owning a television. Religion can be practiced only as their leaders dictate. A man can

PRESIDENTIAL
SPEECHES

GEORGE W.
BUSH: ADDRESS
TO CONGRESS,
SEPTEMBER 20,
2001

be jailed in Afghanistan if his beard is not long enough.

The United States respects the people of Afghanistan—after all, we are currently its largest source of humanitarian aid—but we condemn the Taliban regime. It is not only repressing its own people, it is threatening people everywhere by sponsoring and sheltering and supplying terrorists. By aiding and abetting murder, the Taliban regime is committing murder.

And tonight, the United States of America makes the following demands on the Taliban: Deliver to United States authorities all the leaders of al Qaeda who hide in your land. Release all foreign nationals, including American citizens, you have unjustly imprisoned. Protect foreign journalists, diplomats and aid workers in your country. Close immediately and permanently every terrorist training camp in Afghanistan, and hand over every terrorist, and every person in their support structure, to appropriate authorities. Give the United States full access to terrorist training camps, so we can make sure they are no longer operating.

These demands are not open to negotiation or discussion. The Taliban must act, and act immediately. They will hand over the terrorists, or they will share in their fate.

I also want to speak tonight directly to Muslims throughout the world. We respect your faith. It's practiced freely by many millions of Americans, and by millions more in countries that America counts as friends. Its teachings are good and peaceful, and those who commit evil in the name of Allah blaspheme the name of Allah. The terrorists are traitors to their own faith, trying, in effect, to hijack Islam itself. The enemy of America is not our many Muslim friends; it is not our many Arab friends. Our enemy is a radical network of terrorists, and every government that supports them.

Our war on terror begins with al Qaeda, but it does not end there. It will not end until every terrorist group of global reach has been found, stopped and defeated.

Americans are asking, why do they hate us? They hate what we see right here in this chamber—a democratically elected government. Their leaders are self-appointed. They hate our freedoms—our freedom of religion, our freedom of speech, our freedom to vote and assemble and disagree with each other.

They want to overthrow existing governments in many Muslim countries, such as Egypt, Saudi Arabia, and Jordan. They want to drive Israel out of the Middle East. They want to drive Christians and Jews out of vast regions of Asia and Africa.

These terrorists kill not merely to end lives, but to disrupt and end a way of life. With every atrocity, they hope that America grows fearful, retreating from the world and forsaking our friends. They stand against us, because we stand in their way.

We are not deceived by their pretenses to piety. We have seen their kind before. They are the heirs of all the murderous ideologies of the 20th century. By sacrificing human life to serve their radical visions—by abandoning every value except the will to power—they follow in the path of fascism, and Nazism, and totalitarianism. And they will follow that path all the way, to where it ends: in history's unmarked grave of discarded lies.

Americans are asking: How will we fight and win this war? We will direct every resource at our command—every means of diplomacy, every tool of intelligence, every instrument of law enforcement, every financial influence, and every necessary weapon of war—to the disruption and to the defeat of the global terror network.

This war will not be like the war against Iraq a decade ago, with a decisive liberation of territory and a swift conclusion. It will not look like the air war above Kosovo two years ago, where no ground troops were used and not a single American was lost in combat.

Our response involves far more than instant retaliation and isolated strikes. Americans should not expect one battle, but a lengthy campaign, unlike any other we have ever seen. It may include dramatic strikes, visible on TV, and covert operations, secret even in success. We will starve terrorists of funding, turn them one against another, drive them from place to place, until there is no refuge or no rest. And we will pursue nations that provide aid or safe haven to terrorism. Every nation, in every region, now has a decision to make. Either you are with us, or you are with the terrorists. From this day forward, any nation that continues to harbor or support terrorism will be regarded by the United States as a hostile regime.

Our nation has been put on notice: We are not immune from attack. We will take defensive measures against terrorism to protect Americans. Today, dozens of federal departments and agencies, as well as state and local governments, have responsibilities affecting homeland security. These efforts must be coordinated at the highest level. So tonight I announce the creation of a Cabinet-level position reporting directly to me—the Office of Homeland Security.

And tonight I also announce a distinguished American to lead this effort, to strengthen American security: a military veteran, an effective governor, a true patriot, a trusted friend—Pennsylvania's Tom Ridge. He will lead, oversee and coordinate a comprehensive national strategy to safeguard our country against terrorism, and respond to any attacks that may come.

These measures are essential. But the only way to defeat terrorism as a threat to our way of life is to stop it, eliminate it, and destroy it where it grows.

Many will be involved in this effort, from FBI agents to intelligence operatives to the reservists we have called to active duty. All deserve our thanks, and all have our prayers. And tonight, a few miles from the damaged Pentagon, I have a message for our military: Be ready. I've called the Armed Forces to alert, and there is a reason. The hour is coming when America will act, and you will make us proud.

This is not, however, just America's fight. And what is at stake is not just America's freedom. This is the world's fight. This is civilization's fight. This is the fight of all who believe in progress and pluralism, tolerance and freedom.

We ask every nation to join us. We will ask, and we will need, the help of police forces, intelligence services, and banking systems around the world. The United States is grateful that many nations and many international organizations have already responded—with sympathy and with support. Nations from Latin America, to Asia, to Africa, to Europe, to the Islamic world. Perhaps the NATO Charter reflects best the attitude of the world: An attack on one is an attack on all.

The civilized world is rallying to America's side. They understand that if this terror goes unpunished, their own cities, their own citizens may be next. Terror, unanswered, can not only bring down buildings, it can threaten the stability of legitimate governments. And you know what—we're not going to allow it.

Americans are asking: What is expected of us? I ask you to live your lives, and hug your children. I know many citizens have fears tonight, and I ask you to be calm and resolute, even in the face of a continuing threat.

I ask you to uphold the values of America, and remember why so many have come here. We are in a fight for our principles, and our first responsibility is to live by them. No one should be singled out for unfair treatment or unkind words because of their ethnic background or religious faith.

I ask you to continue to support the victims of this tragedy with your contributions. Those who want to give can go to a central source of information, <libertyunites.org>, to find the names of groups providing direct help in New York, Pennsylvania, and Virginia.

The thousands of FBI agents who are now at work in this investigation may need your cooperation, and I ask you to give it.

I ask for your patience, with the delays and inconveniences that may accompany tighter security; and for your patience in what will be a long struggle.

I ask your continued participation and confidence in the American economy. Terrorists attacked a symbol of American prosperity. They did not touch its source. America is successful because of the hard work, and creativity, and enterprise of our people. These were the true strengths of our economy before September 11th, and they are our strengths today.

And, finally, please continue praying for the victims of terror and their families, for those in uniform, and for our great country. Prayer has comforted us in sorrow, and will help strengthen us for the journey ahead.

Tonight I thank my fellow Americans for what you have already done and for what you will do. And ladies and gentlemen of the Congress, I thank you, their representatives, for what you have already done and for what we will do together.

Tonight, we face new and sudden national challenges. We will come together to improve air safety, to dramatically expand the number of air marshals on domestic flights, and take new measures to prevent hijacking. We will come

PRESIDENTIAL
SPEECHES

GEORGE W.
BUSH: ADDRESS
TO CONGRESS,
SEPTEMBER 20,
2001

PRESIDENTIAL
SPEECHES

GEORGE W.
BUSH: ADDRESS
TO CONGRESS,
SEPTEMBER 20,
2001

together to promote stability and keep our airlines flying, with direct assistance during this emergency.

We will come together to give law enforcement the additional tools it needs to track down terror here at home. We will come together to strengthen our intelligence capabilities to know the plans of terrorists before they act, and find them before they strike.

We will come together to take active steps that strengthen America's economy, and put our people back to work.

Tonight we welcome two leaders who embody the extraordinary spirit of all New Yorkers: Governor George Pataki, and Mayor Rudolph Giuliani. As a symbol of America's resolve, my administration will work with Congress, and these two leaders, to show the world that we will rebuild New York City.

After all that has just passed—all the lives taken, and all the possibilities and hopes that died with them—it is natural to wonder if America's future is one of fear. Some speak of an age of terror. I know there are struggles ahead, and dangers to face. But this country will define our times, not be defined by them. As long as the United States of America is determined and strong, this will not be an age of terror; this will be an age of liberty, here and across the world.

Great harm has been done to us. We have suffered great loss. And in our grief and anger we have found our mission and our moment. Freedom and fear are at war. The advance of human freedom—the great achievement of our time, and the great hope of every time—now depends on us. Our nation—this generation—

will lift a dark threat of violence from our people and our future. We will rally the world to this cause by our efforts, by our courage. We will not tire, we will not falter, and we will not fail.

It is my hope that in the months and years ahead, life will return almost to normal. We'll go back to our lives and routines, and that is good. Even grief recedes with time and grace. But our resolve must not pass. Each of us will remember what happened that day, and to whom it happened. We'll remember the moment the news came—where we were and what we were doing. Some will remember an image of a fire, or a story of rescue. Some will carry memories of a face and a voice gone forever.

And I will carry this: It is the police shield of a man named George Howard, who died at the World Trade Center trying to save others. It was given to me by his mom, Arlene, as a proud memorial to her son. This is my reminder of lives that ended, and a task that does not end.

I will not forget this wound to our country or those who inflicted it. I will not yield; I will not rest; I will not relent in waging this struggle for freedom and security for the American people.

The course of this conflict is not known, yet its outcome is certain. Freedom and fear, justice and cruelty, have always been at war, and we know that God is not neutral between them.

Fellow citizens, we'll meet violence with patient justice—assured of the rightness of our cause, and confident of the victories to come. In all that lies before us, may God grant us wisdom, and may He watch over the United States of America.

Thank you.

LEGAL SCHOLARSHIP

Since the nineteenth century, the role of lawyers and the nature of law in U.S. society have been the subject of ongoing debate and scrutiny. Legal scholars and practitioners have discussed whether the law is a self-contained body of rules, displaying logic and reason. Some have embraced this view and have aspired to make law a science. Since the early twentieth century, however, other important legal figures have expressed skepticism about the inner logic of the law, preferring to see legal rulings as responses to immediate social, political, and economic pressures. These skeptics eventually became known as legal realists, a school of thought that can be traced to the scholar and jurist Oliver Wendell Holmes Jr.

The French writer Alexis de Tocqueville visited the United States in the 1830s and wrote about his travels in *Democracy in America* (1835), one of the classic works of social analysis. Tocqueville, a nobleman, was struck by the democratic character of U.S. society and devoted a section of his work to the role of lawyers and judges. He concluded that lawyers were vital to the preservation of civil order and democracy.

Lawyers have also been the target of popular criticism. In the late eighteenth and early nineteenth century, U.S. critics contended that lawyers and judges conspired to make the law a mysterious body of arcane language and procedures that needlessly complicated problems. Robert Rantoul Jr., a Massachusetts attorney and member of Congress, was a prominent spokesman for the codification movement, which attacked the common law as unsuitable for a democratic republic. In a famous 1836 oration, Rantoul charged that "judge-made law is *ex post facto* law, and therefore unjust." People could not know the law because "no one knows what the law is before [the judge] lays it down." Moreover, a judge was able to rule differently from case to case.

For Rantoul and others, the only solution was to abandon the common-law system and codify all laws into one book that everyone could read and understand. The codification movement had limited success during the nineteenth century. Rantoul advocated a code but never tried to write one. David Dudley Field, a New York attorney, wrote what became known as the Field Code of civil procedure. His code was enacted in twenty-four states, most of them in the West.

The education and training of lawyers began to change in the nineteenth century. Traditionally, the most popular method of becoming a lawyer had been "reading the law" in a law office, learning legal rules and procedures under the tutelage of a practicing attorney. As the century progressed, however, more law schools were opened. The law school curriculum consisted of attending lectures, reading legal treatises, and memorizing legal rules and concepts. Christopher Columbus Langdell changed the course of U.S. legal education when he published his contracts casebook in 1871. Langdell, a professor and dean of Harvard Law School, introduced the case method, which required students to read judicial opinions and analyze the key points of each case. The Socratic method of logical inquiry was an integral part of the program: professors called on students in class, asked them to present their analysis, and challenged their presentation.

Langdell also embraced the nineteenth century's belief in progress and in the superiority of scientific inquiry. Langdell's conclusion that the law could be a science became a tenet of legal scholarship, but he was eventually challenged by Oliver Wendell Holmes Jr. Holmes, a professor and scholar before serving on the Supreme Judicial Court of Massachusetts and the U.S. Supreme Court, rejected the assumption that law was a science or a logical system.

Holmes wrote a set of legal essays that was published in 1881 as *The Common Law*. In this volume, which is the most renowned work of legal philosophy in U.S. history, Holmes systematically analyzed, classified, and explained various aspects of U.S. common law, ranging from torts to contracts to crime and punishment. He concluded that:

> The life of the law has not been logic: it has been experience. The felt necessities of the time, the prevalent moral and political theories, intuitions of public policy, avowed or unconscious, even the prejudices which judges share with their fellow-men, have had a good deal more to do than the syllogism in determining the rules by which men should be governed.

By the beginning of the twentieth century, the United States had become an industrialized, urban nation. Some lawyers and legal scholars attempted to inject new ideas and information into the law in hopes of overturning stubbornly held doctrines and restoring public confidence in a legal system that appeared to be unprepared to face the realities of the new century. Famed

lawyer and later Supreme Court justice Louis D. Brandeis revolutionized the law by submitting what has come to be known as the "Brandeis brief" in *Muller v. Oregon*, 208 U.S. 412, 28 S. Ct. 324, 52 L. Ed. 551 (1908). The brief contained sociological information on the health and well-being of women that Brandeis believed was relevant to deciding whether an Oregon law limiting work hours for women was constitutional. The U.S. Supreme Court upheld the law, lending credibility to Brandeis's use of nonlegal information.

Roscoe Pound, a scholar, teacher, reformer, and dean of Harvard Law School, worked to link law and society through his sociological jurisprudence and to improve the administration of the judicial system. His 1906 speech, "The Causes of Popular Dissatisfaction with the Administration of Justice," was a call to improve court administration and a preview of his theory of law. In 1908 he published "Mechanical Jurisprudence," attacking the notion that an unchanging and inflexible natural law formed the basis for the common law.

The twentieth century also saw the growth of law through legislation. As state legislatures and the U.S. Congress enacted more statutes containing complex and often unclear provisions, the courts were called upon to interpret these laws by using various rules of statutory construction to determine legislative purpose. In 1947, Harvard law professor and later Supreme Court justice Felix Frankfurter delivered a lecture entitled "Some Reflections on the Reading of Statutes," which expounds on the effect that legislative law has on the courts. Fifty years later, the torrent of legislation remains unabated.

LEGAL SCHOLARSHIP

LAWYERS AND JUDGES

Alexis de Tocqueville, 1835

Alexis de Tocqueville, a French political scientist, historian, and politician, is best known for *Democracy in America* (1835). A believer in democracy, he was concerned about the concentration of power in the hands of a centralized government. During his visit to the United States in 1831 and 1832, Tocqueville observed the deep social and political divisions produced by slavery. He was impressed, however, by the power of a free press and the importance that citizens placed upon the legal system.

In his observations on lawyers and judges, Tocqueville noted that U.S. courts of law possessed enormous political power. Judges had the power of judicial review, which allowed them to strike down laws as unconstitutional. He also observed that lawyers were active in politics, bringing to government and the political arena the knowledge, skills, and temperament peculiar to their profession. Tocqueville pointed out that lawyers are wedded to the public order and are often conservative. He concluded that "lawyers belong to the people by birth and interest, and to the aristocracy by habit and taste; they may be looked upon as the connecting link between the two great classes of society."

Lawyers and Judges

Whenever a law that the judge holds to be unconstitutional is invoked in a tribunal of the United States, he may refuse to admit it as a rule; this power is the only one peculiar to the American magistrate, but it gives rise to immense political influence. In truth, few laws can escape the searching analysis of the judicial power for any length of time, for there are few that are not prejudicial to some private interest or other, and none that may not be brought before a court of justice by the choice of parties or by the necessity of the case. But as soon as a judge has refused to apply any given law in a case, that law immediately loses a portion of its moral force.

* * *

Within these limits the power vested in the American courts of justice of pronouncing a statute to be unconstitutional forms one of the most powerful barriers that have ever been devised against the tyranny of political assemblies.

* * *

When we have examined in detail the organization of the [United States] Supreme Court and the entire prerogatives which it exercises, we shall readily admit that a more imposing judicial power was never constituted by any people. The Supreme Court is placed higher than any other known tribunal, both by the nature of its rights and the class of justiciable parties which it controls.

* * *

The peace, the prosperity, and the very existence of the Union are vested in the hands of the seven Federal judges [of the United States Supreme Court]. Without them the Constitu-

---

From *Democracy in America.*

tion would be a dead letter: the executive appeals to them for assistance against the encroachments of the legislative power; the legislature demands their protection against the assaults of the executive; they defend the Union from the disobedience of the states, the states from the exaggerated claims of the Union, the public interest against private interests, and the conservative spirit of stability against the fickleness of the democracy. Their power is enormous, but it is the power of public opinion. They are all-powerful as long as the people respect the law; but they would be impotent against popular neglect or contempt of the law. The force of public opinion is the most intractable of agents, because its exact limits cannot be defined; and it is not less dangerous to exceed than to remain below the boundary prescribed.

* * *

Democratic laws generally tend to promote the welfare of the greatest possible number; for they emanate from the majority of the citizens, who are subject to error, but who cannot have an interest opposed to their own advantage. The laws of an aristocracy tend, on the contrary, to concentrate wealth and power in the hands of the minority; because an aristocracy, by its very nature, constitutes a minority. It may therefore be asserted, as a general proposition, that the purpose of a democracy in its legislation is more useful to humanity than that of an aristocracy. This, however, is the sum total of its advantages.

* * *

No political form has hitherto been discovered that is equally favorable to the prosperity and the development of all the classes into which society is divided. These classes continue to form, as it were, so many distinct communities in the same nation; and experience has shown that it is no less dangerous to place the fate of these classes exclusively in the hands of any one of them than it is to make one people the arbiter of the destiny of another. When the rich alone govern, the interest of the poor is always endangered; and when the poor make the laws, that of the rich incurs very serious risks. The advantage of democracy does not consist, therefore, as has sometimes been asserted, in favoring the prosperity of all, but simply in contributing to the well-being of the greatest number.

The men who are entrusted with the direction of public affairs in the United States are fre-

quently inferior, in both capacity and morality, to those whom an aristocracy would raise to power. But their interest is identified and mingled with that of the majority of their fellow citizens. They may frequently be faithless and frequently mistaken, but they will never systematically adopt a line of conduct hostile to the majority; and they cannot give a dangerous or exclusive tendency to the government.

* * *

It is not always feasible to consult the whole people, either directly or indirectly, in the formation of law; but it cannot be denied that, when this is possible, the authority of law is much augmented. This popular origin which impairs the excellence and the wisdom of legislation, contributes much to increase its power. There is an amazing strength in the expression of the will of a whole people; and when it declares itself, even the imagination of those who would wish to contest it is overawed. The truth of this fact is well known by parties, and they consequently strive to make out a majority whenever they can. If they have not the greater number of voters on their side, they assert that the true majority abstained from voting; and if they are foiled even there, they have recourse to those persons who had no right to vote.

In the United States, except slaves, servants, and paupers supported by the townships, there is no class of persons who do not exercise the elective franchise and who do not indirectly contribute to make the laws. Those who wish to attack the laws must consequently either change the opinion of the nation or trample upon its decision.

A second reason, which is still more direct and weighty, may be adduced: in the United States everyone is personally interested in enforcing the obedience of the whole community to the law; for as the minority may shortly rally the majority to its principles, it is interested in professing that respect for the decrees of the legislator which it may soon have occasion to claim for its own. However irksome an enactment may be, the citizen of the United States complies with it, not only because it is the work of the majority, but because it is his own, and he regards it as a contract to which he is himself a party.

In the United States, then, that numerous and turbulent multitude does not exist who, regarding the law as their natural enemy, look upon it with fear and distrust. It is impossible, on the contrary, not to perceive that all classes display the utmost reliance upon the legislation of their country and are attached to it by a kind of parental affection.

* * *

In visiting the Americans and studying their laws, we perceive that the authority they have entrusted to members of the legal profession, and the influence that these individuals exercise in the government, are the most powerful existing security against the excesses of democracy. This effect seems to me to result from a general cause, which it is useful to investigate, as it may be reproduced elsewhere. . . .

Men who have made a special study of the laws derive from [that] occupation certain habits of order, a taste for formalities, and a kind of instinctive regard for the regular connection of ideas, which naturally render them very hostile to the revolutionary spirit and the unreflecting passions of the multitude.

The special information that lawyers derive from their studies ensures them a separate rank in society, and they constitute a sort of privileged body in the scale of intellect. This notion of their superiority perpetually recurs to them in the practice of their profession: they are the masters of a science which is necessary, but not very generally known; they serve as arbiters between the citizens; and the habit of directing to their purpose the blind passions of parties in litigation inspires them with a certain contempt for the judgment of the multitude. Add to this that they naturally constitute a body; not by any previous understanding, or by an agreement that directs them to a common end; but the analogy of their studies and the uniformity of their methods connect their minds as a common interest might unite their endeavors.

Some of the tastes and the habits of the aristocracy may consequently be discovered in the characters of lawyers. They participate in the same instinctive love of order and formalities; and they entertain the same repugnance to the actions of the multitude, and the same secret contempt of the government of the people. I do not mean to say that the natural propensities of lawyers are sufficiently strong to sway them irresistibly; for they, like most other men, are governed by their private interests, and especially by the interests of the moment.

* * *

I do not, then, assert that all the members of the legal profession are at all times the friends of order and the opponents of innovation, but merely that most of them are usually so. In a community to which lawyers are allowed to occupy without opposition that high station which naturally belongs to them, their general spirit will be eminently conservative and antidemocratic. When an aristocracy excludes the leaders of that profession from its ranks, it excites enemies who are the more formidable as they are independent of the nobility by their labors and feel themselves to be their equals in intelligence though inferior in opulence and power.

* * *

Lawyers are attached to public order beyond every other consideration, and the best security of public order is authority. It must not be forgotten, also, that if they prize freedom much, they generally value legality still more; they are less afraid of tyranny than of arbitrary power; and, provided the legislature undertakes of itself to deprive men of their independence, they are not dissatisfied.

* * *

The government of democracy is favorable to the political power of lawyers; for when the wealthy, the noble, and the prince are excluded from the government, the lawyers take possession of it, in their own right, as it were, since they are the only men of information and sagacity, beyond the sphere of the people, who can be the object of the popular choice. If, then, they are led by their tastes towards the aristocracy and the prince, they are brought in contact with the people by their interests. They like the government of democracy without participating in its propensities and without imitating its weaknesses; whence they derive a two-fold authority from it and over it. The people in democratic states do not mistrust the members of the legal profession, because it is known that they are interested to serve the popular cause; and the people listen to them without irritation, because they do not attribute to them any sinister designs. The lawyers do not, indeed, wish to overthrow the institutions of democracy, but they constantly endeavor to turn it away from its real direction by means that are foreign to its nature. Lawyers belong to the people by birth and interest, and to the aristocracy by habit and taste; they may be looked upon as the connecting link between the two great classes of society.

LEGAL
SCHOLARSHIP

LAWYERS AND
JUDGES

LEGAL
SCHOLARSHIP

LAWYERS AND
JUDGES

The profession of the law is the only aristocratic element that can be amalgamated without violence with the natural elements of democracy and be advantageously and permanently combined with them. I am not ignorant of the defects inherent in the character of this body of men; but without this admixture of lawyer-like sobriety with the democratic principle, I question whether democratic institutions could long be maintained; and I cannot believe that a republic could hope to exist at the present time if the influence of lawyers in public business did not increase in proportion to the power of the people.

* * *

In America there are no nobles or literary men, and the people are apt to mistrust the wealthy; lawyers consequently form the highest political class and the most cultivated portion of society. They have therefore nothing to gain by innovation, which adds a conservative interest to their natural taste for public order. If I were asked where I place the American aristocracy, I should reply without hesitation that it is not among the rich, who are united by no common tie, but that it occupies the judicial bench and the bar.

The more we reflect upon all that occurs in the United States, the more we shall be persuaded that the lawyers, as a body, form the most powerful, if not the only, counterpoise to the democratic element. In that country we easily perceive how the legal profession is qualified by its attributes, and even by its faults, to neutralize the vices inherent in popular government. When the American people are intoxicated by passion or carried away by the impetuosity of their ideas, they are checked and stopped by the almost invisible influence of their legal counselors. These secretly oppose their aristocratic propensities to the nation's democratic instincts, their superstitious attachment to what is old to its love of novelty, their narrow views to its immense designs, and their habitual procrastination to its ardent impatience.

The courts of justice are the visible organs by which the legal profession is enabled to control the democracy. The judge is a lawyer who, independently of the taste for regularity and order that he has contracted in the study of law, derives an additional love of stability from the inalienability of his own functions. His legal attainments have already raised him to a distinguished rank among his fellows; his political power completes the distinction of his station and gives him the instincts of the privileged classes.

* * *

It must not be supposed, moreover, that the legal spirit is confined in the United States to the courts of justice; it extends far beyond them. As the lawyers form the only enlightened class whom the people do not mistrust, they are naturally called upon to occupy most of the public stations. They fill the legislative assemblies and are at the head of the administration; they consequently exercise a powerful influence upon the formation of the law and upon its execution. The lawyers are obliged, however, to yield to the current public opinion, which is too strong for them to resist; but it is easy to find indications of what they would do if they were free to act. The Americans, who have made so many innovations in their political laws, have introduced very sparing alterations in their civil laws, and that with great difficulty, although many of these laws are repugnant to their social condition. The reason for this is that in matters of civil law the majority are obliged to defer to the authority of the legal profession, and the American lawyers are disinclined to innovate when they are left to their own choice.

* * *

The influence of legal habits extends beyond the precise limits I have pointed out. Scarcely any political question arises in the United States that is not resolved, sooner or later, into a judicial question. Hence all parties are obliged to borrow, in their daily controversies, the ideas, and even the language, peculiar to judicial proceedings. As most public men are or have been legal practitioners, they introduce the customs and technicalities of their profession into the management of public affairs. The jury extends this habit to all classes. The language of the law thus becomes, in some measure, a vulgar tongue; the spirit of the law, which is produced in the schools and courts of justice, gradually penetrates beyond their walls into the bosom of society, where it descends to the lowest classes, so that at last the whole people contract the habits and the tastes of the judicial magistrate. The lawyers of the United States form a party which is but little feared and scarcely perceived, which has no badge peculiar to itself, which adapts itself with great flexibility to the exigencies of the time and accommodates itself without resistance to all the movements of the social body. But this party extends over the whole community and penetrates into all the classes which compose it; it acts upon the country imperceptibly, but finally fashions it to suit its own purposes.

LEGAL SCHOLARSHIP

WHAT SHALL BE DONE WITH THE PRACTICE OF THE COURTS?

David Dudley Field, 1847

David Dudley Field was an attorney from a prominent New York family. His brother was Stephen J. Field, a U.S. Supreme Court justice. Field was a leading crusader for the codification movement. He attacked the rules of civil procedure of his time, which were based on English common-law pleading practices. Common-law pleading was an arcane practice filled with traps for the uninitiated that could result in the dismissal of the case on procedural grounds. Field's essay of 1847, "What Shall Be Done with the Practice of the Courts," presented his case for what is now known as code pleading.

As a member of the New York pleading and practice commission, Field prepared a civil procedure code that the legislature adopted in 1848. The code simplified the filing and prosecution of lawsuits. It was a significant improvement over common-law systems of procedure, in that it required that the complaint contain "a plain and concise statement of the facts constituting plaintiff's cause of action." The code used the pleading as a way of narrowing and defining the dispute rather than as a general means of initiating a civil action.

The Field Code was later adopted by Missouri, California, and many other states. In time, however, code pleading became very technical, requiring the pleader to set forth the facts underlying and demonstrating the existence of the cause of action. Matters were simplified in 1938, when the Federal Rules of Civil Procedure were adopted. Rule 8(a) provides that the complaint shall contain "a short and plain statement of the claim showing that the pleader is entitled

to relief." Likewise, the defendant "shall state in short and plain terms" the defenses to the plaintiff's complaint. There is no requirement that facts be alleged.

In the twentieth century, the desire for codification led to the drafting of various sets of uniform laws, including the Uniform Commercial Code and the Uniform Probate Code.

—⁓—

What Shall Be Done with the Practice of the Courts?

The Constitution of this State [New York, 1846], which goes into effect to-day, will render great changes necessary in our system of legal procedure. It remodels our Courts; unites the administration of law and equity in the same tribunal; directs testimony to be taken in like manner in both classes of cases; abolishes the offices of Master and Examiner in Chancery, hitherto important parts of our equity system; and, finally, directs that the next Legislature shall provide for the appointment of three commissioners, "whose duty it shall be to revise, reform, simplify, and abridge the rules of practice, pleadings, forms, and proceedings of the courts of record," and report thereon to the Legislature for its action.

Important modifications of the equity practice are thus made indispensable, in order to adapt it to the new mode of taking testimony. But I think that the Convention intended, and that the people expect, much greater changes than these. We know that radical reform in legal proceedings has long been demanded by no inconsiderable number of the people; that a more determined agitation of the subject has been postponed by its friends, till such time as there should be a reorganization of the judicial establishment, upon the idea that a new system of procedure and a new system of Courts ought to come in together; that it was a prominent topic in the Convention itself, where its friends were in an undoubted majority; and that the manifestations of public sentiment out of doors were no less clear than were the sentiments of that body. Indeed, if now, after all that has been done within the last five years, there should be made only such changes as the Constitution absolutely commands, there will be great and general disappointment.

* * *

Every consideration, as it seems to me, makes it expedient for us all now to enter heartily upon the work of amendment. Those of us who have long been laboring for a radical reformation of the law, and those who have felt less inclination for it, should find this an occasion to act together in the common pursuit of thorough and wise reforms. We feel the inconvenience of the present state of things. We know that the technicality and the drudgery of legal proceedings are discreditable to our profession. Justice is entangled in the net of forms.

* * *

Believing, therefore, that great changes are inevitable in any event, and that this is a period favorable to the adoption of all the reforms which are really required, I wish it were possible to engage every member of the legal profession in the promotion of a wise, safe, and radical reform. Radical reform will come sooner or later, with us or without us. Shall we cooperate to make it at the same time wise and safe?

Such a reform, I am persuaded, should have in view nothing less than a uniform course of proceeding, in all cases, legal and equitable.

* * *

What I propose, then, in respect to cases of legal cognizance, is this: that the present forms of action be abolished, and in their stead a complaint and answer required, each setting forth the real claim and defense of the parties. Such pleadings would be precisely similar to those proposed for equity cases, and we should thus have a uniform course of pleading for all cases, legal and equitable. The distinction between the two classes of cases is now merely a distinction in the forms of proceeding. The Court of Chancery has existed only in consequence of the narrow and fixed forms of the common law. If those forms had been abolished, and a natural procedure adopted, the course of the two Courts would long ago have been assimilated.

Let the plaintiff set forth his cause of action in his complaint briefly, in ordinary language, and without repetition; and let the defendant make his answer in the same way. Let each party verify his allegation by making oath that he believes it to be true. The complaint will then acquaint the defendant with the real charge, while the answer will inform the plaintiff of the real defense. The disputed facts will be sifted from the undisputed, and the parties will go to trial knowing what they have to answer. The plaintiff will state his case as he believes it, and as he expects to prove it. The defendant, on his part, will set forth what he believes and expects to establish, and he need set forth no more. He will not be likely to aver what he does not believe. His answer will disclose the whole of his defense, because he will not be allowed to prove anything which the answer does not contain. He will not be perplexed with questions of double pleading, nor shackled by ancient technical rules.

* * *

The legitimate end of every administration of law is to do justice, with the least possible delay and expense. Every system of pleading is useful only as it tends to this end. This it can do but one of two ways: either by enabling the parties the better to prepare for trial, or by assisting the jury and the Court in judging the causes.

* * *

If we adopt the plan of pleading which I propose, we shall save both time and expense. We shall avoid the risk of losing causes from mistaking the rules of pleading; and we take one step, and that a great one, toward introducing simplicity and directness into the machinery of the law.

* * *

And is, indeed, the learning of the profession bound up with the system of common-law pleading? Is the noble science of jurisprudence—the fruit of the experience of ages, at once the monument and the record of civiliza-

LEGAL
SCHOLARSHIP

WHAT SHALL BE
DONE WITH THE
PRACTICE OF
THE COURTS?

tion—inseparable from such paltry learning as that, "after the declaration, the parties must at each stage demur, or plead by way of traverse, or by way of confession and avoidance," or that "upon a traverse issue must be tendered," or anything of that sort? Lawyers have enough to learn if their studies are confined to useful knowledge. To assert that the great body of the law, civil and criminal—the law which defines rights and punishes crimes; the law which regulates the proprietorship, the enjoyment, and the transmission of property in all its forms; which explains the nature and the obligations of contracts through all their changes; the law that prevails equally on the sea and the land; the law that is enforced in courts of chancery and courts of admiralty, as well as in the courts of common law—to assert that this vast body of law requires the aid of that small portion which regulates the written statement of the parties in the courts of common law, is to assert a monstrous paradox, fitter for ridicule than for argument.

LEGAL SCHOLARSHIP

CONTRACTS

Christopher C. Langdell, 1871

The 1871 publication of *A Selection of Cases on the Law of Contracts* by Christopher Columbus Langdell revolutionized legal education. The book, which consisted of a collection of mostly English judicial opinions, was meant to assist the professor in developing within the student a scientific approach to the law. Langdell chose the cases for the fundamental principles they contained. Students were expected to dispense with the idea that they were attending a vocational school. Instead, they were to apply the principles they learned in the scientific search for truth. In his preface Langdell said that he sought to "select, classify, and arrange all cases which had contributed in any important degree to the growth, development, or establishment of any of its essential doctrines."

—⚶—

Contracts

PREFACE

I entered upon the duties of my present position, a year and a half ago, with a settled conviction that law could only be taught or learned effectively by means of cases in some form. I had entertained such an opinion ever since I knew anything of the nature of law or legal study; but it was chiefly through my experience as a learner that it was formed, as well as subsequently strengthened and confirmed. Of teaching indeed, as a business, I was entirely without experience; nor had I given much consideration to that subject, except so far as proper methods of teaching are involved in proper methods of study.

Now, however, I was called upon to consider directly the subject of teaching, not theoretically but practically, in connection with a large school with its more or less complicated organization, its daily routine, and daily duties. I was expected to take a large class of pupils, meet them regularly from day to day, and give them systematic instruction in such branches of law as had been assigned to me. To accomplish this successfully, it was necessary, first, that the efforts of the pupils should go hand in hand with mine, that is, that they should study with direct reference to my instruction; secondly, that the study thus required of them should be of the kind from which they might reap the greatest and most lasting benefit; thirdly, that the instruction should be of such a character that the pupils might at least derive a greater advantage from attending it than from devoting the same time to private study. How could this threefold object be accomplished? Only one mode occurred to me which seemed to hold out any reasonable prospect of success; and that was, to make a series of cases, carefully selected from the books of reports, the subject alike of study and instruction. But here I was met by what seemed at first to be an insuperable practical difficulty, namely, the want of books; for though it might be practicable, in case of private pupils having free access to a complete library, to refer them directly to the books of reports, such a course was quite out of the question with a large class, all of whom would want the same books at the same time. Nor would such a course be without great drawbacks and inconveniences, even in the case of a single pupil. As he would always have to go

503

LEGAL
SCHOLARSHIP

CONTRACTS

where the books were, and could only have access to them there during certain prescribed hours, it would be impossible for him to economize his time or work to the best advantage; and he would be liable to be constantly haunted by the apprehension that he was spending time, labor, and money in studying cases which would be inaccessible to him in after life.

It was with a view to removing these obstacles, that I was first led to inquire into the feasibility of preparing and publishing such a selection of cases as would be adapted to my purpose as a teacher. The most important element in that inquiry was the great and rapidly increasing number of reported cases in every department of law. In view of this fact, was there any satisfactory principle upon which such a selection could be made? It seemed to me that there was. Law, considered as a science, consists of certain principles or doctrines. To have such a mastery of these as to be able to apply them with constant facility and certainly to the ever-tangled skein of human affairs, is what constitutes a true lawyer; and hence to acquire that mastery should be the business of every earnest student of law. Each of these doctrines has arrived at its present state by slow degrees; in other words, it is a growth, extending in many cases through centuries. This growth is to be traced in the

main through a series of cases; and much the shortest and best, if not the only way of mastering the doctrine effectually is by studying the cases in which it is embodied. But the cases which are useful and necessary for this purpose at the present day bear an exceedingly small proportion to all that have been reported. The vast majority are useless and worse than useless for any purpose of systematic study. Moreover, the number of fundamental legal doctrines is much less than is commonly supposed; the many different guises in which the same doctrine is constantly making its appearance, and the great extent to which legal treatises are a repetition of each other, being the cause of much misapprehension. If these doctrines could be so classified and arranged that each should be found in its proper place, and nowhere else, they would cease to be formidable from their number. It seemed to me, therefore, to be possible to take such a branch of the law as Contracts, for example, and, without exceeding comparatively moderate limits, to select, classify, and arrange all the cases which had contributed in any important degree to the growth, development, or establishment of any of its essential doctrines; and that such a work could not fail to be of material service to all who desire to study that branch of law systematically and in its original sources.

LEGAL SCHOLARSHIP

THE PATH OF THE LAW

Oliver Wendell Holmes Jr., 1897

Oliver Wendell Holmes Jr. is one of the most celebrated legal figures in U.S. history. His writings on jurisprudence have shaped discussions on the nature of law, and his court opinions have been studied as much for their style as their intellectual content.

Holmes rejected the idea that law could be studied as a science. He also emphatically dismissed Langdell's belief that legal systems obey rules of logic. While his book, *The Common Law* (1881), is a scholarly tour de force, his 1897 essay, "The Path of the Law," has proved to be one of the most influential works in legal theory. In the essay Holmes builds on the themes of *The Common Law*, which included his disassociation of law from morality and his emphasis on policy over logic. He went on to define the law as a prediction of what the courts would do in a particular situation. He proposed a "bad man" theory of justice: a bad man will want to know only what the material consequences of his conduct will be; he will not be motivated by morality or conscience.

Holmes's jurisprudence led to the conclusion that judges make decisions first and then come up with reasons to explain them. His approach, which has been characterized as cynical, touched a nerve with succeeding generations of legal scholars.

⁓⁓⁓

The Path of the Law

When we study law we are not studying a mystery but a well known profession. We are study-ing what we shall want in order to appear before judges, or to advise people in such a way as to keep them out of court. The reason why it is a profession, why people will pay lawyers to argue for them or to advise them, is that in societies like ours the command of the public force is intrusted to the judges in certain cases, and the whole power of the state will be put forth, if necessary, to carry out their judgments and decrees. People want to know under what circumstances and how far they will run the risk of coming against what is so much stronger than themselves, and hence it becomes a business to find out when this danger is to be feared. The object of our study, then, is prediction, the prediction of the incidence of the public force through the instrumentality of the courts.

The means of the study are a body of reports, of treatises, and of statutes, in this country and in England, extending back for six hundred years, and now increasing annually by hundreds. In these sibylline leaves are gathered the scattered prophesies of the past upon the cases in which the ax will fall. These are what properly have been called the oracles of the law. Far the most important and pretty nearly the whole meaning of every new effort of legal thought is to make these prophecies more precise, and to generalize them into a thoroughly connected system. The process is one, from a lawyer's statement of a case, eliminating as it

Source: Reprinted in its entirety from O. W. Holmes, Jr., *The Path of the Law*, 10 HARVARD LAW REVIEW 457 (1897). The footnotes have been renumbered.

does all the dramatic elements with which his client's story has clothed it, and retaining only the facts of legal import, up to the final analyses and abstract universals of theoretic jurisprudence. The reason why a lawyer does not mention that his client wore a white hat when he made a contract, while Mrs. Quickly would be sure to dwell upon it along with the parcel gilt goblet and the sea-coal fire, is that he foresees that the public force will act in the same way whatever his client had upon his head. It is to make the prophecies easier to be remembered and to be understood that the teachings of the decisions of the past are put into general propositions and gathered into textbooks, or that statutes are passed in a general form. The primary rights and duties with which jurisprudence busies itself again are nothing but prophecies. One of the many evil effects of the confusion between legal and moral ideas, about which I shall have something to say in a moment, is that theory is apt to get the cart before the horse, and to consider the right or the duty as something existing apart from and independent of the consequences of its breach, to which certain sanctions are added afterward. But, as I shall try to show, a legal duty so called is nothing but a prediction that if a man does or omits certain things he will be made to suffer in this or that way by judgment of the court;—and so of a legal right.

The number of our predictions when generalized and reduced to a system is not unmanageably large. They present themselves as a finite body of dogma which may be mastered within a reasonable time. It is a great mistake to be frightened by the ever increasing number of reports. The reports of a given jurisdiction in the course of a generation take up pretty much the whole body of the law, and restate it from the present point of view. We could reconstruct the corpus from them if all that went before were burned. The use of the earlier reports is mainly historical, a use about which I shall have something to say before I have finished.

I wish, if I can, to lay down some first principles for the study of this body of dogma or systematized prediction which we call the law, for men who want to use it as the instrument of their business to enable them to prophesy in their turn, and, as bearing upon the study, I wish to point out an ideal which as yet our law has not attained.

The first thing for a business-like understanding of the matter is to understand its limits, and therefore I think it desirable at once to point out and dispel a confusion between morality and law, which sometimes rises to the height of conscious theory, and more often and indeed constantly is making trouble in detail without reaching the point of consciousness. You can see very plainly that a bad man has as much reason as a good one for wishing to avoid an encounter with the public force, and therefore you can see the practical importance of the distinction between morality and law. A man who cares nothing for an ethical rule which is believed and practised by his neighbors is likely nevertheless to care a good deal to avoid being made to pay money, and will want to keep out of jail if he can.

I take it for granted that no hearer of mine will misinterpret what I have to say as the language of cynicism. The law is the witness and external deposit of our moral life. Its history is the history of the moral development of the race. The practice of it, in spite of popular jests, tends to make good citizens and good men. When I emphasize the difference between law and morals I do so with reference to a single end, that of learning and understanding the law. For that purpose you must definitely master its specific marks, and it is for that that I ask you for the moment to imagine yourselves indifferent to other and greater things.

I do not say that there is not a wider point of view from which the distinction between law and morals becomes of secondary or no importance, as all mathematical distinctions vanish in presence of the infinite. But I do say that that distinction is of the first importance for the object which we are here to consider,—a right study and mastery of the law as a business with well understood limits, a body of dogma enclosed within definite lines. I have just shown the practical reason for saying so. If you want to know the law and nothing else, you must look at it as a bad man, who cares only for the material consequences which such knowledge enables him to predict, not as a good one, who finds his reasons for conduct, whether inside the law or outside of it, in the vaguer sanctions of conscience. The theoretical importance of the distinction is no less, if you would reason on your subject aright. The law is full of phraseology drawn from morals, and by the mere force of language continually invites us to pass from one domain to the other without perceiving it, as we are sure to do unless we have the boundary constantly before our minds. The law talks about rights, and duties, and malice, and intent, and negligence, and so forth, and nothing is easier, or, I may say, more common in legal reasoning, than to take these words in their moral sense, at some stage of the argument, and so to drop into fallacy. For instance, when we speak of the rights of man in a moral sense, we mean to mark the limits of interference with individual freedom which we think are prescribed by conscience, or by our ideal, however reached. Yet it is certain that many laws have been enforced in the past, and it is likely that some are enforced now, which are condemned by the most enlightened opinion of the time, or which at all events pass the limit of interference as many consciences would draw it. Manifestly, therefore, nothing but confusion of thought can result from assuming that the rights of man in a moral sense are equally rights in the sense of the Constitution and the law. No doubt simple and extreme cases can be put of imaginable laws which the statute-making power would not dare to enact, even in the absence of written constitutional prohibitions, because the community would rise in rebellion and fight; and this gives some plausibility to the proposition that the law, if not a part of morality, is limited by it. But this limit of power is not coextensive with any system of morals. For the most part it falls far within the lines of any such system, and in some cases may extend beyond them, for reasons drawn from the habits of a particular people at a particular time. I once heard the late Professor Agassiz[29] say that a German population would rise if you added two cents to the price of a glass of beer. A statute in such a case would be empty words, not because it was wrong, but because it could not be enforced. No one will deny that wrong statutes can be and are enforced, and we should not all agree as to which were the wrong ones.

The confusion with which I am dealing besets confessedly legal conceptions. Take the fundamental question, What constitutes the law? You will find some text writers telling you

that it is something different from what is decided by the courts of Massachusetts or England, that it is a system of reason, that it is a deduction from principles of ethics or admitted axioms or what not, which may or may not coincide with the decisions. But if we take the view of our friend the bad man we shall find that he does not care two straws for the axioms or deductions, but that he does want to know what the Massachusetts or English courts are likely to do in fact. I am much of his mind. The prophecies of what the courts will do in fact, and nothing more pretentious, are what I mean by the law.

Take again a notion which as popularly understood is the widest conception which the law contains;—the notion of legal duty, to which already I have referred. We fill the word with all the content which we draw from morals. But what does it mean to a bad man? Mainly, and in the first place, a prophecy that if he does certain things he will be subjected to disagreeable consequences by way of imprisonment or compulsory payment of money. But from his point of view, what is the difference between being fined and being taxed a certain sum for doing a certain thing? That his point of view is the test of legal principles is shown by the many discussions which have arisen in the courts on the very question whether a given statutory liability is a penalty or a tax. On the answer to this question depends the decision whether conduct is legally wrong or right, and also whether a man is under compulsion or free. Leaving the criminal law on one side, what is the difference between the liability under the mill acts or statutes authorizing a taking by eminent domain and the liability for what we call a wrongful conversion of property where restoration is out of the question? In both cases the party taking another man's property has to pay its fair value as assessed by a jury, and no more. What significance is there in calling one taking right and another wrong from the point of view of the law? It does not matter, so far as the given consequence, the compulsory payment, is concerned, whether the act to which it is attached is described in terms of praise or in terms of blame, or whether the law purports to prohibit it or to allow it. If it matters at all, still speaking from the bad man's point of view, it must be because in one case and not in the other some further disadvantages, or at least further consequences, are attached to the act by the law. The only other disadvantages thus attached to it which I ever have been able to think of are

---

[29] [Ed. note] Jean Louis Rodolphe Agassiz (1807–73), a Swiss born naturalist and, *inter alia*, Professor of Natural History at Harvard. His second wife, Elizabeth Cabot (née Cary) (1822–1907) was one of the founders of Radcliffe College and its president from 1894 until 1902.

to be found in two somewhat insignificant legal doctrines, both of which might be abolished without much disturbance. One is, that a contract to do a prohibited act is unlawful, and the other, that, if one of two or more joint wrongdoers has to pay all the damages, he cannot recover contribution from his fellows. And that I believe is all. You see how the vague circumference of the notion of duty shrinks and at the same time grows more precise when we wash it with cynical acid and expel everything except the object of our study, the operations of the law.

Nowhere is the confusion between legal and moral ideas more manifest than in the law of contract. Among other things, here again the so called primary rights and duties are invested with a mystic significance beyond what can be assigned and explained. The duty to keep a contract at common law means a prediction that you must pay damages if you do not keep it,—and nothing else. If you commit a tort, you are liable to pay a compensatory sum. If you commit a contract, you are liable to pay a compensatory sum unless the promised event comes to pass, and that is all the difference. But such a mode of looking at the matter stinks in the nostrils of those who think it advantageous to get as much ethics into the law as they can. It was good enough for Lord Coke, however, and here, as in many other cases, I am content to abide with him. In Bromage v. Genning,[30] a prohibition was sought in the King's Bench against a suit in the marches of Wales for the specific performance of a covenant to grant a lease, and Coke said that it would subvert the intention of the covenantor, since he intends it to be at his election either to lose the damages or to make the lease. Sergeant Harris for the plaintiff confessed that he moved the matter against his conscience, and a prohibition was granted. This goes further than we should go now, but it shows what I venture to say has been the common law point of view from the beginning, although Mr. Harriman, in his very able little book upon Contracts has been misled, as I humbly think, to a different conclusion.

I have spoken only of the common law, because there are some cases in which a logical justification can be found for speaking of civil liabilities as imposing duties in an intelligible sense. These are the relatively few in which equity will grant an injunction, and will enforce it by putting the defendant in prison or otherwise punishing him unless he complies with the

order of the court. But I hardly think it advisable to shape general theory from the exception, and I think it would be better to cease troubling ourselves about primary rights and sanctions altogether, than to describe our prophecies concerning the liabilities commonly imposed by the law in those inappropriate terms.

I mentioned, as other examples of the use by the law of words drawn from morals, malice, intent, and negligence. It is enough to take malice as it is used in the law of civil liability for wrongs,—what we lawyers call the law of torts,—to show you that it means something different in law from what it means in morals, and also to show how the difference has been obscured by giving to principles which have little or nothing to do with each other the same name. Three hundred years ago a parson preached a sermon and told a story out of Fox's Book of Martyrs of a man who had assisted at the torture of one of the saints, and afterward died, suffering compensatory inward torment. It happened that Fox was wrong. The man was alive and chanced to hear the sermon, and thereupon he sued the parson. Chief Justice Wray instructed the jury that the defendant was not liable, because the story was told innocently, without malice. He took malice in the moral sense, as importing a malevolent motive. But nowadays no one doubts that a man may be liable, without any malevolent motive at all, for false statements manifestly calculated to inflict temporal damage. In stating the case in pleading, we still should call the defendant's conduct malicious; but, in my opinion at least, the word means nothing about motives, or even about the defendant's attitude toward the future, but only signifies that the tendency of his conduct under the known circumstances was very plainly to cause the plaintiff temporal harm.[31]

In the law of contract the use of moral phraseology has led to equal confusion, as I have shown in part already, but only in part. Morals deal with the actual internal state of the individual's mind, what he actually intends. From the time of the Romans down to now, this mode of dealing has affected the language of the law as to contract, and the language used has reacted upon the thought. We talk about a contract as a

---

[30] 1 Roll[e] Rep. 368 [81 Eng.Rep. 540 (1616)].
[31] See Hanson v. Globe Newspaper Co., 159 Mass. 293, 302 [34 N.E. 462, 465 (1893)].

meeting of the minds of the parties, and thence it is inferred in various cases that there is no contract because their minds have not met; that is, because they have intended different things or because one party has not known of the assent of the other. Yet nothing is more certain than that parties may be bound by a contract to things which neither of them intended, and when one does not know of the other's assent. Suppose a contract is executed in due form and in writing to deliver a lecture, mentioning no time. One of the parties thinks that the promise will be construed to mean at once, within a week. The other thinks that it means when he is ready. The court says that it means within a reasonable time. The parties are bound by the contract as it is interpreted by the court, yet neither of them meant what the court declares that they have said. In my opinion no one will understand the true theory of contract or be able even to discuss some fundamental questions intelligently until he has understood that all contracts are formal, that the making of a contract depends not on the agreement of two minds in one intention, but on the agreement of two sets of external signs,—not on the parties' having *meant* the same thing but on their having *said* the same thing. Furthermore, as the signs may be addressed to one sense or another,—to sight or to hearing,—on the nature of the sign will depend the moment when the contract is made. If the sign is tangible, for instance, a letter, the contract is made when the letter of acceptance is delivered. If it is necessary that the minds of the parties meet, there will be no contract until the acceptance can be read,—none, for example, if the acceptance be snatched from the hand of the offerer by a third person.

This is not the time to work out a theory in detail, or to answer many obvious doubts and questions which are suggested by these general views. I know of none which are not easy to answer, but what I am trying to do now is only by a series of hints to throw some light on the narrow path of legal doctrine, and upon two pitfalls which, as it seems to me, lie perilously near to it. Of the first of these I have said enough. I hope that my illustrations have shown the danger, both to speculation and to practice, of confounding morality with law, and the trap which legal language lays for us on that side of our way. For my own part, I often doubt whether it would not be a gain if every word of moral significance could be banished from the law altogether, and

other words adopted which should convey legal ideas uncolored by anything outside the law. We should lose the fossil records of a good deal of history and the majesty got from ethical associations, but by ridding ourselves of an unnecessary confusion we should gain very much in the clearness of our thought.

So much for the limits of the law. The next thing which I wish to consider is what are the forces which determine its content and its growth. You may assume, with Hobbes and Bentham and Austin, that all law emanates from the sovereign, even when the first human beings to enunciate it are the judges, or you may think that law is the voice of the Zeitgeist, or what you like. It is all one to my present purpose. Even if every decision required the sanction of an emperor with despotic power and a whimsical turn of mind, we should be interested none the less, still with a view to prediction, in discovering some order, some rational explanation, and some principle of growth for the rules which he laid down. In every system there are such explanations and principles to be found. It is with regard to them that a second fallacy comes in, which I think it important to expose.

The fallacy to which I refer is the notion that the only force at work in the development of the law is logic. In the broadest sense, indeed, that notion would be true. The postulate on which we think about the universe is that there is a fixed quantitative relation between every phenomenon and its antecedents and consequents. If there is such a thing as a phenomenon without these fixed quantitative relations, it is a miracle. It is outside the law of cause and effect, and as such transcends our power of thought, or at least is something to or from which we cannot reason. The condition of our thinking about the universe is that it is capable of being thought about rationally, or, in other words, that every part of it is effect and cause in the same sense in which those parts are with which we are most familiar. So in the broadest sense it is true that the law is a logical development, like everything else. The danger of which I speak is not the admission that the principles governing other phenomena also govern the law, but the notion that a given system, ours, for instance, can be worked out like mathematics from some general axioms of conduct. This is the natural error of the schools, but it is not confined to them. I once heard a very eminent judge say that he never let a decision go until he was absolutely sure that it was right. So judicial dissent often is blamed, as if it meant simply that one side or the other were not doing their sums right, and, if they would take more trouble, agreement inevitably would come.

This mode of thinking is entirely natural. The training of lawyers is a training in logic. The processes of analogy, discrimination, and deduction are those in which they are most at home. The language of judicial decision is mainly the language of logic. And the logical method and form flatter that longing for certainty and for repose which is in every human mind. But certainty generally is illusion, and repose is not the destiny of man. Behind the logical form lies a judgment as to the relative worth and importance of competing legislative grounds, often an inarticulate and unconscious judgment, it is true, and yet the very root and nerve of the whole proceeding.[32]

You can give any conclusion a logical form. You always can imply a condition in a contract. But why do you imply it? It is because of some belief as to the practice of the community or of a class, or because of some opinion as to policy, or, in short, because of some attitude of yours upon a matter not capable of exact quantitative measurement, and therefore not capable of founding exact logical conclusions. Such matters really are battle grounds where the means do not exist for determinations that shall be good for all time, and where the decision can do no more than embody the preference of a given body in a given time and place. We do not realize how large a part of our law is open to reconsideration upon a slight change in the habit of the public mind. No concrete proposition is self-evident, no matter how ready we may be to accept it, not even Mr. Herbert Spencer's Every man has a right to do what he wills, provided he interferes not with a like right on the part of his neighbors.

Why is a false and injurious statement privileged, if it is made honestly in giving information about a servant? It is because it has been thought more important that information should be given freely, than that a man should be protected from what under other circumstances would be an actionable wrong. Why is a man at liberty to set up a business which he knows will ruin his neighbor? It is because the public good is supposed to be best subserved by free competition. Obviously such judgments of relative importance may vary in different times and places. Why does a judge instruct a jury that an employer is not liable to an employee for an injury received in the course of his employment unless he is negligent, and why do the jury generally find for the plaintiff if the case is allowed to go to them? It is because the traditional policy of our law is to confine liability to cases where a prudent man might have foreseen the injury, or at least the danger, while the inclination of a very large part of the community is to make certain classes of persons insure the safety of those with whom they deal. Since the last words were written, I have seen the requirement of such insurance put forth as part of the programme of one of the best known labor organizations. There is a concealed, half conscious battle on the question of legislative policy, and if any one thinks that it can be settled deductively, or once for all, I only can say that I think he is theoretically wrong, and that I am certain that his conclusion will not be accepted in practice *semper ubique et ab omnibus.*[33]

Indeed, I think that even now our theory upon this matter is open to reconsideration, although I am not prepared to say how I should decide if a reconsideration were proposed. Our law of torts comes from the old days of isolated, ungeneralized wrongs, assaults, slanders, and the like, where the damages might be taken to lie where they fell by legal judgment. But the torts with which our courts are kept busy to-day are mainly the incidents of certain well known businesses. They are injuries to person or property by railroads, factories, and the like. The liability

---

[32] [Ed. note] Cf. the famous opening lines from *The Common Law:*

The object of this book is to present a general view of the Common Law. To accomplish the task, other tools are needed besides logic. It is something to show that the consistency of a system requires a particular result, but it is not all. The life of the law has not been logic: it has been experience. The felt necessities of the time, the prevalent moral and political theories, intuitions of public policy, avowed or unconscious, even the prejudices which judges share with their fellow-men, have had a good deal more to do than the syllogism in determining the rules by which men should be governed. The law embodies the story of a nation's development through many centuries, and it cannot be dealt with as if it contained only the axioms and corollaries of a book of mathematics. In order to know what it is, we must know what it has been, and what it tends to become. We must alternately consult history and existing theories of legislation. But the most difficult labor will be to understand the combination of the two into new products at every stage... .

O. W. Holmes, Jr., THE COMMON LAW 1 (1881).

[33] [Ed. note] Literally "forever, everywhere and by everyone."

for them is estimated, and sooner or later goes into the price paid by the public. The public really pays the damages, and the question of liability, if pressed far enough, is really the question how far it is desirable that the public should insure the safety of those whose work it uses. It might be said that in such cases the chance of a jury finding for the defendant is merely a chance, once in a while rather arbitrarily interrupting the regular course of recovery, most likely in the case of an unusually conscientious plaintiff, and therefore better done away with. On the other hand, the economic value even of a life to the community can be estimated, and no recovery, it may be said, ought to go beyond that amount. It is conceivable that some day in certain cases we may find ourselves imitating, on a higher plane, the tariff for life and limb which we see in the Leges Barbarorum.

I think that the judges themselves have failed adequately to recognize their duty of weighing considerations of social advantage. The duty is inevitable, and the result of the often proclaimed judicial aversion to deal with such considerations is simply to leave the very ground and foundation of judgments inarticulate, and often unconscious, as I have said. When socialism first began to be talked about, the comfortable classes of the community were a good deal frightened. I suspect that this fear has influenced judicial action both here and in England, yet it is certain that it is not a conscious factor in the decisions to which I refer. I think that something similar has led people who no longer hope to control the legislatures to look to the courts as expounders of the Constitutions, and that in some courts new principles have been discovered outside the bodies of those instruments, which may be generalized into acceptance of the economic doctrines which prevailed about fifty years ago, and a wholesale prohibition of what a tribunal of lawyers does not think about right. I cannot but believe that if the training of lawyers led them habitually to consider more definitely and explicitly the social advantage on which the rule they lay down must be justified, they sometimes would hesitate where now they are confident, and see that really they were taking sides upon debatable and often burning questions.

So much for the fallacy of logical form. Now let us consider the present condition of the law as a subject for study, and the ideal toward which it tends. We still are far from the point of view which I desire to see reached. No one has reached it or can reach it as yet. We are only at the beginning of a philosophical reaction, and of a reconsideration of the worth of doctrines which for the most part still are taken for granted without any deliberate, conscious, and systematic questioning of their grounds. The development of our law has gone on for nearly a thousand years, like the development of a plant, each generation taking the inevitable next step, mind, like matter, simply obeying a law of spontaneous growth. It is perfectly natural and right that it should have been so. Imitation is a necessity of human nature, as has been illustrated by a remarkable French writer, M. Tarde,[34] in an admirable book, "Les Lois de l'Imitation." Most of the things we do, we do for no better reason than that our fathers have done them or that our neighbors do them, and the same is true of a larger part than we suspect of what we think. The reason is a good one, because our short life gives us no time for a better, but it is not the best. It does not follow, because we all are compelled to take on faith at second hand most of the rules on which we base our action and our thought, that each of us may not try to set some corner of his world in the order of reason, or that all of us collectively should not aspire to carry reason as far as it will go throughout the whole domain. In regard to the law, it is true, no doubt, that an evolutionist will hesitate to affirm universal validity for his social ideals, or for the principles which he thinks should be embodied in legislation. He is content if he can prove them best for here and now. He may be ready to admit that he knows nothing about an absolute best in the cosmos, and even that he knows next to nothing about a permanent best for men. Still it is true that a body of law is more rational and more civilized when every rule it contains is referred articulately and definitely to an end which it subserves, and when the grounds for desiring that end are stated or are ready to be stated in words.

At present, in very many cases, if we want to know why a rule of law has taken its particular shape, and more or less if we want to know why it exists at all, we go to tradition. We follow it

---

[34] [Ed. note] Gabriel Tarde (1843–1904). French sociologist and criminologist and from 1899 until his death Professor of Modern Philosophy, College de France. Tarde regarded man as an agent striving to realize ends suggested by the social environment and either sanctioned or rejected by that enactment. *Les Lois de l'Imitation* was published in 1890.

into the Year Books, and perhaps beyond them to the customs of the Salian Franks, and somewhere in the past, in the German forests, in the needs of Norman kings, in the assumptions of a dominant class, in the absence of generalized ideas, we find out the practical motive for what now best is justified by the mere fact of its acceptance and that men are accustomed to it. The rational study of law is still to a large extent the study of history. History must be a part of the study, because without it we cannot know the precise scope of rules which it is our business to know. It is a part of the rational study, because it is the first step toward an enlightened scepticism, that is, toward a deliberate reconsideration of the worth of those rules. When you get the dragon out of his cave on to the plain and in the daylight, you can count his teeth and claws, and see just what is his strength. But to get him out is only the first step. The next is either to kill him, or to tame him and make him a useful animal. For the rational study of the law the black-letter man may be the man of the present, but the man of the future is the man of statistics and the master of economics. It is revolting to have no better reason for a rule of law than that so it was laid down in the time of Henry IV. It is still more revolting if the grounds upon which it was laid down have vanished long since, and the rule simply persists from blind imitation of the past. I am thinking of the technical rule as to trespass *ab initio*, as it is called, which I attempted to explain in a recent Massachusetts case.[35]

Let me take an illustration, which can be stated in a few words, to show how the social end which is aimed at by a rule of law is obscured and only partially attained in consequence of the fact that the rule owes its form to a gradual historical development, instead of being reshaped as a whole, with conscious articulate reference to the end in view. We think it desirable to prevent one man's property being misappropriated by another, and so we make larceny a crime. The evil is the same whether the misappropriation is made by a man into whose hands the owner has put the property, or by one who wrongfully takes it away. But primitive law in its weakness did not get much beyond an effort to prevent violence, and very naturally made a wrongful taking, a trespass, part of its definition of the crime. In modern times the judges enlarged the definition a little by holding that, if the wrong-doer gets possession by a trick or device, the crime is committed. This really was giving up

the requirement of a trespass, and it would have been more logical, as well as truer to the present object of the law, to abandon the requirement altogether. That, however, would have seemed too bold, and was left to statute. Statutes were passed making embezzlement a crime. But the force of tradition caused the crime of embezzlement to be regarded as so far distinct from larceny that to this day, in some jurisdictions at least, a slip corner is kept open for thieves to contend, if indicted for larceny, that they should have been indicted for embezzlement, and if indicted for embezzlement, that they should have been indicted for larceny, and to escape on that ground.

Far more fundamental questions still await a better answer than that we do as our fathers have done. What have we better than a blind guess to show that the criminal law in its present form does more good than harm? I do not stop to refer to the effect which it has had in degrading prisoners and in plunging them further into crime, or to the question whether fine and imprisonment do not fall more heavily on a criminal's wife and children than on himself. I have in mind more far-reaching questions. Does punishment deter? Do we deal with criminals on proper principles? A modern school of Continental criminalists plumes itself on the formula, first suggested, it is said, by Gall,[36] that we must consider the criminal rather than the crime. The formula does not carry us very far, but the inquiries which have been started look toward an answer of my questions based on science for the first time. If the typical criminal is a degenerate, bound to swindle or to murder by as deep seated an organic necessity as that which makes the rattlesnake bite, it is idle to talk of deterring him by the classical method of imprisonment. He must be got rid of; he cannot be improved, or frightened out of his structural reaction. If, on the other hand, crime, like normal human conduct, is mainly a matter of imitation, punishment fairly may be expected to help to keep it out of fashion. The study of criminals has been thought by some well known men of science to sustain the former hypothesis. The statistics of the relative increase of crime in

---

[35] Commonwealth v. Rubin, 165 Mass. 453, [43 N.E. 200 (1896)].

[36] [Ed. note] Probably Franz Joseph Gall (1758–1828), a German physician who eventually settled first in Vienna and later in Paris and was the founder of phrenology.

crowded places like large cities, where example has the greatest chance to work, and in less populated parts, where the contagion spreads more slowly, have been used with great force in favor of the latter view. But there is weighty authority for the belief that, however this may be, "not the nature of the crime, but the dangerousness of the criminal, constitutes the only reasonable legal criterion to guide the inevitable social reaction against the criminal."[37]

The impediments to rational generalization, which I illustrated from the law of larceny, are shown in the other branches of the law, as well as in that of crime. Take the law of tort or civil liability for damages apart from contract and the like. Is there any general theory of such liability, or are the cases in which it exists simply to be enumerated, and to be explained each on its special ground, as is easy to believe from the fact that the right of action for certain well known classes of wrongs like trespass or slander has its special history for each class? I think that there is a general theory to be discovered, although resting in tendency rather than established and accepted. I think that the law regards the infliction of temporal damage by a responsible person as actionable, if under the circumstances known to him the danger of his act is manifest according to common experience, or according to his own experience if it is more than common, except in cases where upon special grounds of policy the law refuses to protect the plaintiff or grants a privilege to the defendant.[38] I think that commonly malice, intent, and negligence mean only that the danger was manifest to a greater or less degree, under the circumstances known to the actor, although in some cases of privilege malice may mean an actual malevolent motive, and such a motive may take away a permission knowingly to inflict harm, which otherwise would be granted on this or that ground of dominant public good. But when I stated my view to a very eminent English judge the other day, he said: "You are discussing what the law ought to be; as the law is, you must show a right. A man is not liable for negligence unless he is subject to a duty." If our difference was more than a difference in words, or with regard to the proportion between the exceptions and the rule, then, in his opinion, liability for an act cannot be referred to the manifest tendency of the act to cause temporal damage in general as a sufficient explanation, but must be referred to the special nature of the damage, or must be derived from some special circumstances outside of the tendency of the act, for which no generalized explanation exists. I think that such a view is wrong, but it is familiar, and I dare say generally is accepted in England.

Everywhere the basis of principle is tradition, to such an extent that we even are in danger of making the rôole of history more important than it is. The other day Professor Ames wrote a learned article[39] to show, among other things, that the common law did not recognize the defence of fraud in actions upon specialties, and the moral might seem to be that the personal character of that defence is due to its equitable origin. But if, as I have said, all contracts are formal, the difference is not merely historical, but theoretic, between defects of form which prevent a contract from being made, and mistaken motives which manifestly could not be considered in any system that we should call rational except against one who was privy to those motives. It is not confined to specialties, but is of universal application. I ought to add that I do not suppose that Mr. Ames would disagree with what I suggest.

However, if we consider the law of contract, we find it full of history. The distinctions between debt, covenant, and assumpsit are merely historical. The classification of certain obligations to pay money, imposed by the law irrespective of any bargain as quasi contracts, is merely historical. The doctrine of consideration is merely historical. The effect given to a seal is to be explained by history alone.—Consideration is a mere form. Is it a useful form? If so, why should it not be required in all contracts? A seal is a mere form, and is vanishing in the scroll and in enactments that a consideration must be given, seal or no seal.—Why should any merely historical distinction be allowed to affect the rights and obligations of business men?

Since I wrote this discourse I have come on a very good example of the way in which tradition

---

[37] Havelock Ellis, "The Criminal," 41, citing Garofalo [Baron Raffaele, 1851–1934, Italian statesman, jurist, and criminologist].

[38] An example of the law's refusing to protect the plaintiff is when he is interrupted by a stranger in the use of a valuable way, which he has traveled adversely for a week less than the period of prescription. A week later he will have gained a right, but now he is only a trespasser. Examples of privilege I have given already. One of the best is competition in business.

[39] [Ed. note] Unquestionably, *Specialty Contracts and Equitable Defences*, 9 HARV. L.REV. 49 (1895).

not only overrides rational policy, but overrides it after first having been misunderstood and having been given a new and broader scope than it had when it had a meaning. It is the settled law of England that a material alteration of a written contract by a party avoids it as against him. The doctrine is contrary to the general tendency of the law. We do not tell a jury that if a man ever has lied in one particular he is to be presumed to lie in all. Even if a man has tried to defraud, it seems no sufficient reason for preventing him from proving the truth. Objections of like nature in general go to the weight, not to the admissibility, of evidence. Moreover, this rule is irrespective of fraud, and is not confined to evidence. It is not merely that you cannot use the writing, but that the contract is at an end. What does this mean? The existence of a written contract depends on the fact that the offeror and offeree have interchanged their written expressions, not on the continued existence of those expressions. But in the case of a bond the primitive notion was different. The contract was inseparable from the parchment. If a stranger destroyed it, or tore off the seal, or altered it, the obligee could not recover, however free from fault, because the defendant's contract, that is, the actual tangible bond which he had sealed, could not be produced in the form in which it bound him. About a hundred years ago Lord Kenyon undertook to use his reason on this tradition, as he sometimes did to the detriment of the law, and, not understanding it, said he could see no reason why what was true of a bond should not be true of other contracts. His decision happened to be right, as it concerned a promissory note, where again the common law regarded the contract as inseparable from the paper on which it was written, but the reasoning was general, and soon was extended to other written contracts, and various absurd and unreal grounds of policy were invented to account for the enlarged rule.

I trust that no one will understand me to be speaking with disrespect of the law, because I criticise it so freely. I venerate the law, and especially our system of law, as one of the vastest products of the human mind. No one knows better than I do the countless number of great intellects that have spent themselves in making some addition or improvement, the greatest of which is trifling when compared with the mighty whole. It has the final title to respect that it exists, that it is not a Hegelian dream, but a

part of the lives of men. But one may criticise even what one reveres. Law is the business to which my life is devoted, and I should show less than devotion if I did not do what in me lies to improve it, and, when I perceive what seems to me the ideal of its future, if I hesitated to point it out and to press toward it with all my heart.

Perhaps I have said enough to show the part which the study of history necessarily plays in the intelligent study of the law as it is to-day. In the teaching of this school and at Cambridge it is in no danger of being undervalued. Mr. Bigelow here and Mr. Ames and Mr. Thayer there have made important contributions which will not be forgotten, and in England the recent history of early English law by Sir Frederick Pollock and Mr. Maitland has lent the subject an almost deceptive charm. We must beware of the pitfall of antiquarianism, and must remember that for our purposes our only interest in the past is for the light it throws upon the present. I look forward to a time when the part played by history in the explanation of dogma shall be very small, and instead of ingenious research we shall spend our energy on a study of the ends sought to be attained and the reasons for desiring them. As a step toward that ideal it seems to me that every lawyer ought to seek an understanding of economics. The present divorce between the schools of political economy and law seems to me an evidence of how much progress in philosophical study still remains to be made. In the present state of political economy, indeed, we come again upon history on a larger scale, but there we are called on to consider and weigh the ends of legislation, the means of attaining them, and the cost. We learn that for everything we have to give up something else, and we are taught to set the advantage we gain against the other advantage we lose, and to know what we are doing when we elect.

There is another study which sometimes is undervalued by the practical minded, for which I wish to say a good word, although I think a good deal of pretty poor stuff goes under that name. I mean the study of what is called jurisprudence. Jurisprudence, as I look at it, is simply law in its most generalized part. Every effort to reduce a case to a rule is an effort of jurisprudence, although the name as used in English is confined to the broadest rules and most fundamental conceptions. One mark of a great lawyer is that he sees the application of the broadest rules. There is a story of a Vermont justice of the peace before whom a suit was brought by one farmer against another for breaking a churn. The justice took time to consider, and then said that he had looked through the statutes and could find nothing about churns, and gave judgment for the defendant. The same state of mind is shown in all our common digests and text-books. Applications of rudimentary rules of contract or tort are tucked away under the head of Railroads or Telegraphs or go to swell treatises on historical subdivisions, such as Shipping or Equity, or are gathered under an arbitrary title which is thought likely to appeal to the practical mind, such as Mercantile Law. If a man goes into law it pays to be a master of it, and to be a master of it means to look straight through all the dramatic incidents and to discern the true basis for prophecy. Therefore, it is well to have an accurate notion of what you mean by law, by a right, by a duty, by malice, intent, and negligence, by ownership, by possession, and so forth. I have in my mind cases in which the highest courts seem to me to have floundered because they had no clear ideas on some of these themes. I have illustrated their importance already. If a further illustration is wished, it may be found by reading the Appendix to Sir James Stephen's Criminal Law on the subject of possession, and then turning to Pollock and Wright's enlightened book.[40] Sir James Stephen is not the only writer whose attempts to analyze legal ideas have been confused by striving for a useless quintessence of all systems, instead of an accurate anatomy of one. The trouble with Austin was that he did not know enough English law. But still it is a practical advantage to master Austin, and his predecessors, Hobbes and Bentham, and his worthy successors, Holland and Pollock. Sir Frederick Pollock's recent little book is touched with the felicity which marks all his works, and is wholly free from the perverting influence of Roman models.

The advice of the elders to young men is very apt to be as unreal as a list of the hundred best books. At least in my day I had my share of such counsels, and high among the unrealities I place the recommendation to study the Roman law. I assume that such advice means more than collecting a few Latin maxims with which to ornament the discourse,—the purpose for which Lord Coke recommended Bracton. If that is all that is wanted, the title "De Regulis Juris Antiqui" can be read in an hour. I assume that, if it is well to study the Roman law, it is well to study it as a working system. That means mas-

tering a set of technicalities more difficult and less understood than our own, and studying another course of history by which even more than our own the Roman law must be explained. If any one doubts me, let him read Keller's[41] "Der Römische Civil Process und die Actionen," a treatise on the pr;aetor's edict, Muirhead's most interesting "Historical Introduction to the Private Law of Rome," and, to give him the best chance possible, Sohm's[42] admirable Institutes. No. The way to gain a liberal view of your subject is not to read something else, but to get to the bottom of the subject itself. The means of doing that are, in the first place, to follow the existing body of dogma into its highest generalizations by the help of jurisprudence; next, to discover from history how it has come to be what it is; and, finally, so far as you can, to consider the ends which the several rules seek to accomplish, the reasons why those ends are desired, what is given up to gain them, and whether they are worth the price.

We have too little theory in the law rather than too much, especially on this final branch of study. When I was speaking of history, I mentioned larceny as an example to show how the law suffered from not having embodied in a clear form a rule which will accomplish its manifest purpose. In that case the trouble was due to the survival of forms coming from a time when a more limited purpose was entertained. Let me now give an example to show the practical importance, for the decision of actual cases, of understanding the reasons of the law, by taking an example from rules which, so far as I know, never have been explained or theorized about in any adequate way. I refer to statutes of limitation and the law of prescription. The end of such rules is obvious, but what is the justification for depriving a man of his rights, a pure evil as far as it goes, in consequence of the lapse of time? Sometimes the loss of evidence is referred to, but that is a secondary matter. Sometimes the desirability of peace, but why is peace more desirable after twenty years than before? It is increasingly likely to come without the aid of legislation. Sometimes it is said that, if a man neglects to enforce his rights, he cannot complain if, after a while, the law follows his example. Now if this is

---

[40] [Ed. note] AN ESSAY ON POSSESSION IN THE COMMON LAW (1888).

[41] [Ed. note] Friedrich Ludwig von Keller (1799–1860).

[42] [Ed. note] Rudolph Sohm (1841–1917).

LEGAL
SCHOLARSHIP

THE PATH OF
THE LAW

all that can be said about it, you probably will decide a case I am going to put, for the plaintiff; if you take the view which I shall suggest, you possibly will decide it for the defendant. A man is sued for trespass upon land, and justifies under a right of way. He proves that he has used the way openly and adversely for twenty years, but it turns out that the plaintiff had granted a license to a person whom he reasonably supposed to be the defendant's agent, although not so in fact, and therefore had assumed that the use of the way was permissive, in which case no right would be gained. Has the defendant gained a right or not? If his gaining it stands on the fault and neglect of the landowner in the ordinary sense, as seems commonly to be supposed, there has been no such neglect, and the right of way has not been acquired. But if I were the defendant's counsel, I should suggest that the foundation of the acquisition of rights by lapse of time is to be looked for in the position of the person who gains them, not in that of the loser. Sir Henry Maine has made it fashionable to connect the archaic notion of property with prescription. But the connection is further back than the first recorded history. It is in the nature of man's mind. A thing which you have enjoyed and used as your own for a long time, whether property or an opinion, takes root in your being and cannot be torn away without your resenting the act and trying to defend yourself, however you came by it. The law can ask no better justification than the deepest instincts of man. It is only by way of reply to the suggestion that you are disappointing the former owner, that you refer to his neglect having allowed the gradual dissociation between himself and what he claims, and the gradual association of it with another. If he knows that another is doing acts which on their face show that he is on the way toward establishing such an association, I should argue that in justice to that other he was bound at his peril to find out whether the other was acting under his permission, to see that he was warned, and, if necessary, stopped.

I have been speaking about the study of the law, and I have said next to nothing of what commonly is talked about in that connection,—text-books and the case system, and all the machinery with which a student comes most immediately in contact. Nor shall I say anything about them. Theory is my subject, not practical details. The modes of teaching have been improved since my time, no doubt, but

ability and industry will master the raw material with any mode. Theory is the most important part of the dogma of the law, as the architect is the most important man who takes part in the building of a house. The most important improvements of the last twenty-five years are improvements in theory. It is not to be feared as unpractical, for, to the competent, it simply means going to the bottom of the subject. For the incompetent, it sometimes is true, as has been said, that an interest in general ideas means an absence of particular knowledge. I remember in army days reading of a youth who, being examined for the lowest grade and being asked a question about squadron drill, answered that he never had considered the evolutions of less than ten thousand men. But the weak and foolish must be left to their folly. The danger is that the able and practical minded should look with indifference or distrust upon ideas the connection of which with their business is remote. I heard a story, the other day, of a man who had a valet to whom he paid high wages, subject to deduction for faults. One of his deductions was, "For lack of imagination, five dollars." The lack is not confined to valets. The object of ambition, power, generally presents itself nowadays in the form of money alone. Money is the most immediate form, and is a proper object of desire. "The fortune," said Rachel, "is the measure of the intelligence." That is a good text to waken people out of a fool's paradise. But, as Hegel says,[43] "It is in the end not the appetite, but the opinion, which has to be satisfied." To an imagination of any scope the most far-reaching form of power is not money, it is the command of ideas. If you want great examples read Mr. Leslie Stephen's "History of English Thought in the Eighteenth Century," and see how a hundred years after his death the abstract speculations of Descartes had become a practical force controlling the conduct of men. Read the works of the great German jurists, and see how much more the world is governed to-day by Kant than by Bonaparte. We cannot all be Descartes or Kant, but we all want happiness. And happiness, I am sure from having known many successful men, cannot be won simply by being counsel for great corporations and having an income of fifty thousand dollars. An intellect great enough to win the

---

[43] Phil. des Rechts, § 190.

prize needs other food beside success. The remoter and more general aspects of the law are those which give it universal interest. It is through them that you not only become a great master in your calling, but connect your subject with the universe and catch an echo of the infinite, a glimpse of its unfathomable process, a hint of the universal law.

LEGAL SCHOLARSHIP

BRIEF FOR THE DEFENDANT IN ERROR, MULLER V. OREGON

Louis D. Brandeis, October Term, 1907

The World's Experience Upon Which the Legislation Limiting the Hours of Labor for Women is Based

In MULLER V. OREGON in 1908, the U.S. Supreme Court upheld an Oregon law that prohibited the employment of women for more than ten hours a day. The decision was based in large part on a brief submitted by LOUIS D. BRANDEIS in support of the law. The brief emphasized the differences between women and men and presented information showing that long work hours could have injurious effects on the health and welfare of women and their children, including their unborn children. The Court unanimously agreed, noting that "woman's physical structure and the performance of maternal functions place her at a disadvantage in the struggle for subsistence."

The Brandeis brief signaled a change in the type of evidence a court would consider in determining a case. With the growth of the social sciences, quantitative and qualitative studies conducted by researchers would increasingly find their way into U.S. courtrooms.

Brief for the Defendant in Error, *Muller v. Oregon*

I. THE DANGERS OF LONG HOURS

A. Causes

(1) Physical Differences Between Men and Women. The dangers of long hours for women arise from their special physical organization taken in connection with the strain incident to factory and similar work.

Long hours of labor are dangerous for women primarily because of their special physical organization. In structure and function women are differentiated from men. Besides these anatomical and physiological differences, physicians are agreed that women are fundamentally weaker than men in all that makes for endurance: in muscular strength, in nervous energy, in the powers of persistent attention and application. Overwork, therefore, which strains endurance to the utmost, is more disastrous to the health of women than of men, and entails upon them more lasting injury.

Report of Select Committee on Shops Early Closing Bill, British House of Commons, 1895.

Dr. Percy Kidd, physician in Brompton and London Hospitals:

The most common effect I have noticed of the long hours is general deterioration of health; very general symptoms which we medically attribute to over-action, and debility of the nervous system; that includes a great deal more than what is called nervous disease, such as indigestion, constipation, a general slackness, and a great many other indefinite symptoms.

Are those symptoms more marked in women than in men?

I think they are much more marked in women. I should say one sees a great many more women of this class than men; but I have seen precisely the same symptoms in men, I should not say in the same proportion, because one has not been able to make anything like a statistical inquiry. There are other symptoms, but I mention those as being the most common. Another symptom especially among women is anemia, blood-lessness or pallor, that I have no doubt is con-nected with long hours indoors.

Report of the Maine Bureau of Industrial and Labor Statistics, 1888.

Let me quote from Dr. Ely Van der Warker (1875):

Woman is badly constructed for the purposes of standing eight or ten hours upon her feet. I do not intend to bring into evidence the pecu-liar position and nature of the organs contained in the pelvis, but to call attention to the peculiar construction of the knee and the shallowness of the pelvis, and the delicate nature of the foot as part of a sustaining column. The knee joint of woman is a sexual characteristic. Viewed in front and extended, the joint in but a slight degree interrupts the gradual taper of the thigh into the leg. Viewed in a semi-flexed position, the joint forms a smooth ovate spheroid. The reason of this lies in the smallness of the patella in front, and the narrowness of the articular surfaces of the tibia and femur, and which in man form the lateral prominences, and thus is much more perfect as a sustaining column than that of a woman. The muscles which keep the body fixed upon the thighs in the erect posi-tion labor under the disadvantage of short-ness of purchase, owing to the short distance, compared to that of man, between the crest of the ilium and the great trochanter of the femur, thus giving to man a much larger pur-chase in the leverage existing between the trunk and the extremities. Comparatively the foot is less able to sustain weight than that of man, owing to its shortness and the more delicate formation of the tarsus and metatarsus.

Report of the Massachusetts Bureau of Labor Statistics, 1875.

A "lady operator," many years in the business, informed us: "I have had hundreds of lady compositors in my employ, and they all exhibited, in a marked manner, both in the way they performed their work and in its results, the difference in physical ability between themselves and men. They cannot endure the prolonged close attention and confinement which is a great part of type-setting. I have few girls with me more than two or three years at a time; they must have vacations, and they break down in health rapidly. I know no reason why a girl could not set as much type as a man, if she were as strong to endure the demand on mind and body."

Report of the Nebraska Bureau of Labor and Industrial Statistics, 1901–1902.

They (women) are unable, by reason of their physical limitations, to endure the same hours of exhaustive labor as may be endured by men without injury to their health would wreck the constitution and destroy the health of women, and render them incapable of bearing their share of the burdens of the fam-ily and the home. The State must be accord-ed the right to guard and protect women as a class against such a condition, and the law in question to that extent conserves the public health and welfare.

In strength as well as in rapidity and preci-sion of movement women are inferior to men. This is not a conclusion that has ever been contested. It is in harmony with all the practical experience of life. It is perhaps also in harmony with the results of those investi-gators . . . who have found that, as in the blood of women, so also in their muscles, there is more water than in those of men. To a very great extent it is a certainty, a matter of difference in exercise and environment. It is probably, also, partly a matter of organic con-stitution.

The motor superiority of men, and to some extent of males generally, is, it can scarcely be doubted, a deep-lying fact. It is related to what is most fundamental in men and in women, and to their whole psychic organization.

There appears to be a general agreement that women are more docile and amenable to dis-cipline; that they can do light work equally well; that they are steadier in some respects; but that, on the other hand, they are often absent on account of slight indisposition, and they break down sooner under strain.

* * *

It has been estimated that out of every one hundred days women are in a semipathological state of health for from fourteen to sixteen days. The natural congestion of the pelvic organs dur-ing menstruation is augmented and favored by work on sewing machines and other industrial occupations necessitating the constant use of the lower part of the body. Work during these periods tends to induce chronic congestion of the uterus and appendages, and dysmenorrhea and flexion of the uterus are well known affec-tions of working girls.

VII. Laundries

The specific prohibition in the Oregon Act of more than ten hours' work in laundries is not an arbitrary discrimination against that trade. Laundries would probably not be included under the general terms of "manufacturing" or

LEGAL
SCHOLARSHIP

BRIEF FOR THE
DEFENDANT IN
ERROR, MULLER
V. OREGON

LEGAL
SCHOLARSHIP

BRIEF FOR THE
DEFENDANT IN
ERROR. MULLER
V. OREGON

"mechanical establishments"; and yet the special dangers of long hours in laundries, as the business is now conducted, present strong reasons for providing a legal limitation of the hours of work in that business.

DANGEROUS TRADES. THOMAS OLIVER, MEDICAL EXPERT ON DANGEROUS TRADES COMMITTEES OF THE HOME OFFICE. 1902.

Chapter XLVII. Laundry Workers.

It is perhaps difficult to realize that the radical change which has everywhere transformed industrial conditions has already affected this occupation (laundry work) also, and that for good or for evil the washerwoman is passing under the influences which have so profoundly modified the circumstances of her sister of the spinning-wheel and the sewing needle. When the first washing machine and ironing roller were applied to this occupation, alteration in the conditions became as much a foregone conclusion as it did in the case of the textile or the clothing manufactures, when the spinning frame, the power loom, or the sewing machine appeared.

Meanwhile, few industries afford at the present time a more interesting study. From a simple home occupation it is steadily being transformed by the application of power-driven machinery and by the division of labor into a highly organized factory industry, in which complicated labor-saving contrivances of all kinds play a prominent part. The tremendous impetus in the adoption of machinery, and the consequent modification of the system of employment so striking in the large laundries, is not greater than the less obvious but even more important development in the same direction among small laundries. Indeed the difference is rapidly becoming one of degree only. In the large laundries may be found perhaps more machinery and a greater number of the newest devices, but the fundamental change has affected all alike.

* * *

D. BAD EFFECT UPON MORALS

Report of British Chief Inspector of Factories and Workshops, 1900.

One of the most unsatisfactory results of the present system of lack of working hours in laundries is the unfortunate moral effect on the women and girls. . . . Women who are employed at arduous work till far into the night are not likely to be early risers nor given to punctual attendance in the mornings, and workers who on one or two days in the week are dismissed to idleness or to other occupations, while on the remaining days they are expected to work for abnormally long hours, are not rendered methodical, industrious, or dependable workers by such an unsatisfactory training. The self-control and good habits engendered by a regular and definite period of moderate daily employment, which affords an excellent training for the young worker in all organized industries, is sadly lacking, and, instead, one finds periods of violent overwork alternating with hours of exhaustion. The result is the establishment of a kind of "vicious circle"; bad habits among workers make compliance by their employers with any regulation as to hours very difficult while a lack of loyal adherence to reasonable hours of employment by many laundry occupiers increases the difficulty for those who make the attempt in real earnestness.

LEGAL SCHOLARSHIP

MECHANICAL JURISPRUDENCE

Roscoe Pound, 1908

ROSCOE POUND followed in Oliver Wendell Holmes's footsteps. In "Mechanical Jurisprudence" (1908), Pound coined the term *mechanical jurisprudence* to refer to the common but odious practice whereby judges woodenly applied previous precedents to the facts of cases without regard to the consequences. For Pound, the logic of previous precedents alone would not solve jurisprudential problems. The essay decries the ossification of legal concepts into self-evident truths.

In opposition to mechanical jurisprudence, Pound offered his theory of sociological jurisprudence. He acknowledged that the common law contains some constant principles, particularly in regard to methods. He gave these principles the name "taught legal tradition." Pound believed that the implementation of this taught legal tradition by wise common-law judges resulted in substantive change, which reflected changes in society. As the interpreters of the common law, judges had a special duty to consider the practical effects of their decisions and to strive to ensure that they facilitated rather than hindered societal growth.

—⟶—

Mechanical Jurisprudence

"There is no way," says Sir Frederick Pollock, "by which modern law can escape from the scientific and artificial character imposed on it by the demand of modern societies for full, equal, and exact justice:" An Australian judge has stated the same proposition in these words: "The public is more interested than it knows in maintaining the highest scientific standard in the administration of justice." Every lawyer feels this, and every thoughtful student of institutions must admit it. But what do we mean by the word "scientific" in this connection? What is scientific law? What constitutes science in the administration of justice? Sir Frederick Pollock gives us the clue when he defines the reasons that compel law to take on this scientific character as three: the demand for full justice, that is for solutions that go to the root of controversies; the demand for equal justice, that is a like adjustment of like relations under like conditions; and the demand for exact justice, that is for a justice whose operations, within reasonable limits, may be predicted in advance of action. In other words, the marks of a scientific law are, conformity to reason, uniformity, and certainty. Scientific law is a reasoned body of principles for the administration of justice, and its antithesis is a system of enforcing magisterial caprice, however honest, and however much disguised under the name of justice or equity or natural law. But this scientific character of law is a means—a means toward the end of law, which is the administration of justice. Law is forced to take on this character in order to accomplish its end fully, equally, and exactly; and in so far as it fails to perform its function fully, equally, and exactly, it fails in the end for which it exists. Law is scientific in order to eliminate so far as may be the personal equation in judicial administration, to preclude cor-

---

Source: Reprinted from 8 *Columbia Law Review* 605.

LEGAL
SCHOLARSHIP

MECHANICAL
JURISPRUDENCE

ruption and to limit the dangerous possibilities of magisterial ignorance. Law is not scientific for the sake of science. Being scientific as a means toward an end, it must be judged by the results it achieves, not by the niceties of its internal structure; it must be valued by the extent to which it meets its end, not by the beauty of its logical processes or the strictness with which its rules proceed from the dogmas it takes for its foundation.

Two dangers have to be guarded against in a scientific legal system, one of them in the direction of the effect of its scientific and artificial character upon the public, the other in the direction of its effect upon the courts and the legal profession. With respect to the first danger, it is well to remember that law must not become too scientific for the people to appreciate its workings. Law has the practical function of adjusting everyday relations so as to meet current ideas of fair play. It must not become so completely artificial that the public is led to regard it as wholly arbitrary. No institution can stand upon such a basis today. Reverence for institutions of the past will not preserve, of itself, an institution that touches everyday life as profoundly as does the law. Legal theory can no more stand as a sacred tradition in the modern world than can political theory. It has been one of the great merits of English law that its votaries have always borne this in mind. When Lord Esher said, "the law of England is not a science," he meant to protest against a pseudo-science of technical rules existing for their own sake and subserving supposed ends of science, while defeating justice. And it is the importance of the role of jurors in tempering the administration of justice with common-sense and preserving a due connection of the rules governing everyday relations with everyday needs of ordinary men that has atoned for the manifold and conspicuous defects of trial by jury and is keeping it alive. In Germany today one of the problems of law reform is how to achieve a similar tempering of the justice administered by highly trained specialists.

In the other direction, the effect of a scientific legal system upon the courts and upon the legal profession is more subtle and far-reaching. The effect of all systems is apt to be petrifaction of the subject systematized. Perfection of scientific system and exposition tends to cut off individual initiative in the future, to stifle independent consideration of new problems

and of new phases of old problems, and to impose the ideas of one generation upon another. This is so in all departments of learning. One of the obstacles to advance in every science is the domination of the ghosts of departed masters. Their sound methods are forgotten, while their unsound conclusions are held for gospel. Legal science is not exempt from this tendency. Legal systems have their periods in which science degenerates, in which system decays into technicality, in which a scientific jurisprudence becomes a mechanical jurisprudence.

Roman law in its decadence furnishes a striking example. The Valentinian "law of citations" made a selection of jurisconsults of the past and allowed their writings only to be cited. It declared them, with the exception of Papinian, equal in authority. It confined the judge, when questions of law were in issue, to the purely mechanical task of counting and of determining the numerical preponderance of authority. Principles were no longer resorted to in order to make rules to fit cases. The rules were at hand in a fixed and final form, and cases were to be fitted to the rules. The classical jurisprudence of principles had developed, by the very weight of its authority, a jurisprudence of rules; and it is in the nature of rules to operate mechanically.

Undoubtedly one cause of the tendency of scientific law to become mechanical is to be found in the average man's admiration for the ingenious in any direction, his love of technicality as a manifestation of cleverness, his feeling that law, as a developed institution, ought to have a certain ballast of mysterious technicality. "Philosophy's queerest arguments," says James, "tickle agreeably our sense of subtlety and ingenuity." Every practitioner has encountered the lay obsession as to invalidity of a signing with a lead pencil. Every law teacher has had to combat the student obsession that notice, however cogent, may be disregarded unless it is "official." Lay hair-splitting over rules and regulations goes far beyond anything of which lawyers are capable. Experienced advocates have insisted that in argument to a jury, along with a just, common-sense theory of the merits, one ought to have a specious technicality for good measure. But apart from this general human tendency, there is the special tendency of the lawyer to regard artificiality in law as an end, to hold science something to be pursued for its own sake, to forget in this pursuit the purpose of law and hence of scientific law, and to judge rules and doctrines by their conformity to a supposed science and not by the results to which they lead. In periods of growth and expansion, this tendency is repressed. In periods of maturity and stability, when the opportunity for constructive work is largely eliminated, it becomes very marked.

> I have known judges, [said Chief Justice Erle] bred in the world of legal studies, who delighted in nothing so much as in a strong decision. Now a strong decision is a decision opposed to common-sense and to common convenience. . . . A great part of the law made by judges consists of strong decisions, and as one strong decision is a precedent for another a little stronger, the law at last, on some matters, becomes such a nuisance that equity intervenes, or an Act of Parliament must be passed to sweep the whole away.

The instance suggested in the conversation from which the foregoing extract is taken illustrates very well the development of a mechanical legal doctrine. Successive decisions upon the construction of wills had passed upon the meaning of particular words and phrases in particular wills. These decisions were used as guides in the construction of other wills. Presently rules grew up whereby it was settled that particular words and phrases had prescribed hard and fast meanings, and the construction of wills became so artificial, so scientific, that it defeated the very end of construction and compelled a series of sections in the Wills Act of 1836.

I have referred to mechanical jurisprudence as scientific because those who administer it believe it such. But in truth it is not science at all. We no longer hold anything scientific merely because it exhibits a rigid scheme of deductions from *a priori* conceptions. In the philosophy of today, theories are "instruments, not answers to enigmas, in which we can rest." The idea of science as a system of deductions has become obsolete, and the revolution which has taken place in other sciences in this regard must take place and is taking place in jurisprudence also. This revolution in science at large was achieved in the middle of the nineteenth century. In the first half of that century, scientific method in every department of learning was dominated by the classical German philosophy. Men conceived that by dialectics and deduction from controlling conceptions they could construe the whole content of knowledge. Even in the natural sciences this belief prevailed and had long dictated theories of nature and of natural phenomena.

Linnaeus, for instance, lays down a proposition, *omne vivum ex ovo,* and from this fundamental conception deduces a theory of homologies between animal and vegetable organs. He deemed no study of the organisms and the organs themselves necessary to reach or to sustain these conclusions. Yet, today, study of the organisms themselves has overthrown his fundamental proposition. The substitution of efficient for final causes as explanations of natural phenomena has been paralleled by a revolution in political thought. We do not base institutions upon deduction from assumed principles of human nature; we require them to exhibit practical utility, and we rest them upon a foundation of policy and established adaptation to human needs. It has been asserted that to no small extent the old mode of procedure was borrowed from the law. We are told that it involved a "fundamentally juristic conception of the world in which all kinds of action and every sort of judgment was expressed in legal phraseology." We are told that "in the Middle Ages human welfare and even religion was conceived under the form of legality, and in the modern world this has given place to utility." We have, then, the same task in jurisprudence that has been achieved in philosophy, in the natural sciences and in politics. We have to rid ourselves of this sort of legality and to attain a pragmatic, a sociological legal science.

> What is needed nowadays, [it has been said] is that as against an abstract and unreal theory of State omnipotence on the one hand, and an atomistic and artificial view of individual independence on the other, the facts of the world with its innumerable bonds of association and the naturalness of social authority should be generally recognized, and become the basis of our laws, as it is of our life.

Herein is the task of the sociological jurist. Professor Small defines the sociological movement as "a frank endeavor to secure for the human factor in experience the central place which belongs to it in our whole scheme of thought and action." The sociological movement in jurisprudence is a movement for pragmatism as a philosophy of law; for the adjustment of principles and doctrines to the human conditions they are to govern rather than to assumed first principles; for putting the human factor in the central place and relegating logic to its true position as an instrument.

Jurisprudence is last in the march of the sciences away from the method of deduction from

LEGAL
SCHOLARSHIP

MECHANICAL
JURISPRUDENCE

predetermined conceptions. On the continent of Europe, both the historical school of jurists and the philosophical school, which were dominant until at least the last quarter of the nineteenth century, proceeded in this way. The difference between them lay in the manner in which they arrived at their fundamental conceptions. The former derived them from the history of juristic speculation and the historical development of the Roman sources. The latter, through metaphysical inquiries, arrived at certain propositions as to human nature, and deduced a system from them. This was the philosophical theory behind the eighteenth-century movement for codification. Ihering was the pioneer in the work of superseding this jurisprudence of conceptions (*Begriffsjurisrudenz*) by a jurisprudence of results (*Wirklichkeitsjurisprudenz*). He insisted that we should begin at the other end; that the first question should be, how will a rule or a decision operate in practice? For instance, if a rule of commercial law were in question, the search should be for the rule that best accords with and gives effect to sound business practice. In the Civil Law, the doctrine as to mistake in the formation of a contract affords an example of the working of the two methods. Savigny treated the subject according to the jurisprudence of conceptions. He worked out historically and analytically the conception of a contract and deduced therefrom the rules to govern cases of mistake. It followed, from his conception, that if *A* telegraphed *B* to *buy* shares and the telegram as delivered to *B* read *sell*, there was no contract between *A* and *B*, and hence no liability of *A* to *B*; and for a time it was so held. But this and some of the other resulting rules were so far from just in their practical operation that, following the lead of Ihering, they have been abandoned and the ordinary understanding of businessmen has been given effect. And, in this same connection, the new German code has introduced, as a criterion of error in the content of an expression of the will, the question, what would be regarded as essential in the ordinary understanding of business. Even better examples of the workings of a jurisprudence of conceptions, for our purposes, may be found in the manner in which common-law courts have dealt with points of mercantile law. For instance, the law of partnership is made difficult and often unjust by the insistence of the courts upon deducing its rules from a conception of joint ownership and joint obligation, instead of ascer-

taining and giving effect to the actual situation as understood and practiced by merchants. The legal theory does not affect the actual course of business an iota. But it leads to unfortunate results when that course of business, for some reason, comes before the courts. Again, the refusal of Lord Holt to recognize the negotiability of promissory notes proceeded upon a deduction from the conception of a chose in action. A jurisprudence of ends would have avoided each of these errors.

In periods of legal development through juristic speculation and judicial decision, we have a jurisprudence of ends in fact, even if in form it is a jurisprudence of conceptions. The Roman *jus gentium* was worked out for concrete causes and the conceptions were later generalizations from its results. The *jus naturale* was a system of reaching reasonable ends by bringing philosophical theory into the scale against the hard and fast rules of antiquity. The development of equity in England was attained by a method of seeking results in concrete causes. The liberalizing of English law through the law merchant was brought about by substituting business practice for juridical conceptions. The development of the common law in America was a period of growth because the doctrine that the common law was received only so far as applicable led the courts, in adapting English case-law to American conditions, to study the conditions of application as well as the conceptions and their logical consequences. Whenever such a period has come to an end, when its work has been done and its legal theories have come to maturity, the jurisprudence of conceptions tends to decay. Conceptions are fixed. The premises are no longer to be examined. Everything is reduced to simple deduction from them. Principles cease to have importance. The law becomes a body of rules. This is the condition against which sociologists now protest, and protest rightly.

A period of legislative activity supervenes to supply, first new rules, then new premises, and finally a systematic body of principles as a fresh start for juristic development. But such periods hitherto have not been periods of growth. Usually legislative activity has not gone beyond the introduction of new rules or of new premises, and the chief result has been a summing up of the juristic accomplishment of the past in improved form. The further step, which is beginning to be taken in our present era of legal development through legislation, is in reality an awakening of juristic activity, as jurists perceive that they may effect results through the legislator as well as through the judge or the doctrinal writer. This step has yet to be taken outside of Germany. And in the first and second stages of a period of legislation the mechanical character of legal science is aggravated by the imperative theory, which is a concomitant of legislative activity. Austin's proposition that law is command so complete that even the unwritten law must be given this character, since whatever the sovereign permits he commands, was simply rediscovered during the legislative ferment of the reform movement in English law. In the flowering-time of Papal legislation the canon law had already asserted it. Moreover, a period of legislation and codification has brought German jurists to a like conclusion. At such times, when law is felt to be positive, to be the command of the law-maker, a tendency to enact rules as such becomes manifest. Roman law, in its period of legislation, can furnish more than one example of the sort of law-making of which we complain to-day.

Before the analytical school, which revived the imperative theory to meet the facts of an age of legislation, had become established, historical jurists led a revolt. But their jurisprudence is a jurisprudence of conceptions. Moreover, they have had little effect upon the actual course of Anglo-American law. The philosophical jurists have protested also and have appealed from purely legal considerations to considerations of reason and of natural law. But theirs, too, is a jurisprudence of conceptions, and their method, of itself, offers no relief. Their service has been in connection with the general sociological movement, in giving natural law a new and a modern aspect, and in promoting a general agreement among jurists on a sociological basis. In Europe, it is obvious that the different schools are coming together in a new sociological school that is to dominate juristic thought. Instead of seeking for an ideal universal law by metaphysical methods, the idea of all schools is to turn "the community of fact of mankind into a community of law in accord with the reasonable ordering of active life." Hence they hold that "the less arbitrary the character of a rule and the more clearly it conforms to the nature of things, the more nearly does it approach to the norm of a perfect law." The utilitarian theory of Bentham was a theory of legislation. The sociological theory of

the present is a theory of legal science. Probably the chief merit of the new German code lies in its conformity in so large a degree to this theory. It lays down principles from which to deduce, not rules, but decisions; and decisions will indicate a rule only so long as the conditions to which they are applied cause them to express the principle. This, and not lax methods of equitable application, into which American courts are falling so generally, is the true way to make rules fit cases instead of making cases fit rules.

An efficient cause of the failure of much American legislation is that it is founded on an assumption that it is enough for the State to command. Legislation has not been the product of preliminary study of the conditions to which it was to apply. It has not expressed social standards accurately. It has not responded accurately to social needs. Hence a large proportion has been nugatory in practice. But the difficulty is not, as some have assumed, that matters of private law are not within the legitimate scope of legislation. It is rather that legislation has approached them upon a false theory. Judicial law-making also has acted upon an erroneous theory; and its results are often quite as much disregarded in practice as are statutes. Judicial law-making, however, cannot escape, except within very narrow limits, until it is given a new starting point from without. Legislative law-making, on the contrary, may do so and is beginning to do so.

That our case law at its maturity has acquired the sterility of a fully developed system, may be shown by abundant examples of its failure to respond to vital needs of present-day life. Its inadequacy to deal with employers' liability; the failure of the theory of "general jurisprudence" of the Supreme Court of the United States to give us a uniform commercial law; the failure of American courts, with centuries of discussion before them, to work out a reasonable or certain law of future interests in land; the breakdown of the common law in the matter of discrimination by public service companies because of inability to make procedure enforce its doctrines and rules; its breakdown in the attempt to adjust water rights in our newer states, where there was opportunity for free development; its inability to hold promoters to their duty and to protect the interests of those who invest in corporate enterprises against mismanagement and breach of trust; its failure to

LEGAL SCHOLARSHIP

MECHANICAL JURISPRUDENCE

work out a scheme of responsibility that will hold legal entities, or those who hide behind their skirts, to their duty to the public—all these failures, and many more might be adduced, speak for themselves. But compare these failures with the great achievements of the youth of our case-law, with Lord Mansfield's development of a law of quasi-contracts from the fictions of the common counts, with Lord Mansfield's development of mercantile law by judicial decision, with Kent's working out of equity for America from a handful of English decisions, with Marshall's work in giving us a living constitution by judicial interpretation. Now and then, at present, we see vigorous life in remote corners of our case law, as, for instance, in the newer decisions as to surface and underground waters. But judicial revolt from mechanical methods to-day is more likely to take the form of "officious kindness" and flabby equitable application of law. Our judge-made law is losing its vitality, and it is a normal phenomenon that it should do so.

I have suggested some examples of the failure of our case law to rise to social and legal emergencies. Let me point to some phases of its active operation which lead to the same conclusion.

The manner in which the Fourteenth Amendment is applied affords a striking instance of the workings today of a jurisprudence of conceptions. Starting with the conception that it was intended to incorporate Spencer's Social Statics in the fundamental law of the United States, rules have been deduced that obstruct the way of social progress. The conception of liberty of contract, in particular, has given rise to rules and decisions which, tested by their practical operation, defeat liberty. As Mr. Olney says of the *Adair* Case, "it is archaic, it is a long step into the past, to conceive of and deal with the relations between the employer in such industries and the employee, as if the parties were individuals." The conception of freedom of contract is made the basis of a logical deduction. The court does not inquire what the effect of such a deduction will be, when applied to the actual situation. It does not observe that the result will be to produce a condition precisely the reverse of that which the conception originally contemplated. Again, the Commerce Clause of the Federal Constitution has been taken by one judge, at least, to be a constitutional enactment of a conception of free trade among the states. Deductions from this and like

conceptions, assumed to express the meaning and the sole meaning of the clause, have given us rules which, when applied to the existing commercial and industrial situation, are wholly inadequate.

Procedure, with respect to which every thoughtful lawyer must feel that we are inexcusably behind the rest of the English-speaking world, suffers especially from mechanical jurisprudence. The conception of a theory of the case, developed by the common-law forms of action, has, in nearly half of our code jurisdictions, nullified the legislative intent and made the practice more rigid than at common law. But this conception is regarded by many as fundamental. In deductions from this conception they lose sight of the end of procedure, they make scientific procedure an end of itself, and thus, in the result, make adjective law an agency for defeating or delaying substantive law and justice instead of one for enforcing and speeding them. Aristotle discusses a project of a Greek reformer for enabling tribunals to render what he called a divided judgment. At that time, the judgment had to be absolute one way or the other. If a plaintiff claimed twenty *minæ:* when but eighteen were proved to be due him, there was no course but to find for the defendant. The proposal to correct this and to allow a finding for the eighteen *minæ:* due did not meet with Aristotle's approval. He said:

> A juror who votes acquittal decides, not that the defendant owes nothing, but that he does not owe the twenty *minæ:* claimed.

We smile now at Aristotle's hard and fast deduction, in the face of a manifestly absurd result, from his conception of the trial of an issue. But at least half our jurisdictions do the same thing essentially in this matter of the theory of a plaintiff's case. That his pleadings and proofs disclose a case and a good case is not enough. The courts say they are not foreclosing that case; they are merely deciding upon the theory he has chosen to advance.

Again, in the practice as to parties, the common-law conception that there must be a joint interest or a joint liability, because there must be one controversy and joint parties are as one party, has seriously interfered with the liberal plan of the framers of the original Code of Civil Procedure. I can only cite some of the cases. But let me compare with our American cases a recent English decision. In that case two plaintiffs sued for an injunction against infringement of copyright and for an accounting of profits. Only one was owner of the copyright; the other was a mere licensee. But which one was owner was not clear. The court did not deem it necessary to take up this question and determine whether one only was owner and if so which, although a money recovery was to be had. So long as the plaintiffs were agreed among themselves and the defendant had wronged and owed money to one or the other of them, it affirmed a decree for an injunction and accounting. Although in strictness it might be that only *one* was entitled to judgment and so it would be necessary to determine *which* one, the court wasted no time on that question so long as nothing turned on it. Here the court was conscious that procedure was a mere means. It strove to vindicate the substantive law. It was not set upon adhering with scrupulous exactness to logical deductions from a conception of adjective law at the expense of the merits the latter exists to give effect to.

Trial procedure is full of mechanical jurisprudence born of deduction from conceptions. The decisions as to the effect of a view of the *locus* by a jury, in which judgments are reversed unless jurors are told, in the face of common-sense, not to use what they see as evidence, in order to vindicate a conception of the duty of a court of review; the wilderness of decisions as to the province of court and jury, in which, carrying a conception of distinction between law and fact to extreme logical results, the courts at one moment assume that jurors are perfect and will absolutely follow an abstract instruction to its logical consequences, in the face of common-sense and the evidence, and at the next assume that they are fools and will be misled by anything not relevant that drops from the court; and the practice of instructions, one way or the other, when doubtful points of law arise, a general verdict, and a new trial, if the court of review takes another view of the point, when the verdict could have been taken quite as well subject to the point of law reserved, and a new trial obviated, illustrate forcibly the extent to which procedural conceptions, pursued for their own sake, may defeat the end of procedure and defeat the substance of the law. For delay of justice is denial of justice. Every time a party goes out of court on a mere point of practice, substantive law suffers an injury. The life of the law is in its enforcement.

Evidence also has been a prolific field for the unchecked jurisprudence of conceptions. But one example must suffice. The decisions by which in a majority of jurisdictions jurors are not permitted to learn directly the views of standard texts upon scientific and technical subjects, but must pass upon the conflicting opinions of experts without the aid of the impartial sources of information to which any common-sense man would resort in practice, carry out a conception of the competency of evidence at the expense of the end of evidence. In one case, the question was whether death had taken place from strangulation. The trial was held in a rural community, and the medical experts accessible had had no actual experience of cases of strangulation of the sort involved. But standard medical works did relate cases precisely in point, and, after proof that they were standard authorities, a physician was allowed to testify with respect to the symptoms disclosed in the light of the recorded experience of mankind. For this, the judgment was reversed. To vindicate a juridical conception, the court shut out the best possible means of information, in the circumstances of the case in hand, and allowed an accused person to escape because of the inevitable limits of experience of a rural physician.

How far the mechanical jurisprudence, of which the example just given is an extreme case, forgets the end in the means, is made manifest by the stock objection to attempts at introducing a common-sense and business-like procedure. We are told that formal and technical procedure "makes better lawyers." One might ask whether the making of good lawyers is the end of law. But what is a good lawyer? Let Ulpian answer:

> *Ius est ars boni et æqui. Cuius merito quis nos sacerdotes appellet; iustitiam namque colimus et boni et æqui, notitiam profitemur, æquum ab iniquo separantes, licitum ab illicto discernentes, bonos non solum metu pœnarum, verum etiam præmiorum quoque exhortatione efficere cupientes veram, nisi fallor, philosophiam, non simulatam affectantes.*

The nadir of mechanical jurisprudence is reached when conceptions are used, not as premises from which to reason, but as ultimate solutions. So used, they cease to be conceptions and become empty words. James has called attention to a like vice in philosophical thought:

> Metaphysics has usually followed a very primitive kind of quest. You know how men have always hankered after unlawful magic,

LEGAL
SCHOLARSHIP

MECHANICAL
JURISPRUDENCE

and you know what a great part in magic *words* have always played. If you have his name, or the formula of incantation that binds him, you can control the spirit, genie, afrite, or whatever the power may be. . . . So the universe has always appeared to the natural mind as a kind of enigma of which the key must be sought in the shape of some illuminating or power-bringing word or name. That word names the universe's *principle*, and to possess it is after a fashion to possess the universe itself. "God," "Matter," "Reason," "the Absolute," "Energy," are so many solving names. You can rest when you have them. You are at the end of your metaphysical quest.

Current decisions and discussions are full of such solving words: estoppel, malice, privity, implied, intention of the testator, vested and contingent—when we arrive at these we are assumed to be at the end of our juristic search. Like Habib in the Arabian Nights, we wave aloft our scimitar and pronounce the talismanic word.

With legislative law-making in the grip of the imperative theory and its arbitrary results, and judicial decision in the grip of a jurisprudence of conceptions and its equally arbitrary results, whither are we to turn? Judicial law-making cannot serve us. As things are, the cure would be worse than the disease. No court could hold such hearings as those had by legislative committees upon measures for the protection of operatives, described by Mrs. Kelley, or that recently had before the Interstate Commerce Commission as to uniform bills of lading. We must soon have a new starting-point that only legislation can afford. That we may put the sociological, the pragmatic theory behind legislation, is demonstrated every day. Legislative reference bureaus, the Comparative Law Bureau, the Conferences of Commissioners on Uniform State Laws, such hearings as the one before the Interstate Commerce Commission already referred to, hearings before legislative committees, such conferences as the one held recently with respect to the Sherman Anti-trust Law, bar-association discussions of reforms in procedure—all these are furnishing abundant material for legislation of the best type. No such resources are open to the courts. Hence common-law lawyers will some day abandon their traditional attitude toward legislation; will welcome legislation and will make it what it should be. The part played by jurists in the best days of Roman legislation, and the part they have taken in modern Continental legislation, should convince us, if need be, that juristic principles may be recognized and juristic speculation may be put into effect quite as well by legislation as by judicial decision.

Herein is a noble task for the legal scholars of America. To test the conceptions worked out in the common law by the requirements of the new juristic theory, to lay sure foundations for the ultimate legislative restatement of the law, from which judicial decision shall start afresh—this is as great an opportunity as has fallen to the jurists of any age. The end of a period of development by judicial decision is marked by the prevalence of two types of judges; those who think it a great display of learning and of judicial independence to render what Chief Justice Erle called "strong decisions," and those who fix their gaze upon the raw equities of a cause and forage in the books for cases to sustain the desired result. But the task of a judge is to make a principle living, not by deducing from it rules, to be, like the Freshman's hero, "immortal for a great many years," but by achieving thoroughly the less ambitious but more useful labor of giving a fresh illustration of the intelligent application of the principle to a concrete cause, producing a workable and a just result. The real genius of our common law is in this, not in an eternal case-law. Let the principles be formulated by whom or derived from whence you will. The Common Law will look to courts to develop and expound them, the Civil Law to doctrinal treatises. It is only a lip service to our common law that would condemn it to a perpetuity of mechanical jurisprudence through distrust of legislation.

LEGAL SCHOLARSHIP

THE CAUSES OF POPULAR DISSATISFACTION WITH THE ADMINISTRATION OF JUSTICE

Roscoe Pound, 1906

ROSCOE POUND presented "The Causes of Popular Dissatisfaction with the Administration of Justice" at the annual convention of the American Bar Association in 1906. The lecture was a call to improve court administration and a preview of his theory of law. It has remained a classic statement on the need for efficient and equitable judicial administration.

Pound acknowledged that some people have always been dissatisfied with the law, but he contended that the courts did indeed need to be administered more effectively. He also noted that the adversary system often turned litigation into a game, irritating parties, jurors, and witnesses and giving the public the "false notion of the purpose and end of law." In addition, he attacked the overlapping jurisdiction of courts and argued that each state had too many courts.

In 1909 Pound organized the First National Conference on Criminal Law and Criminology, which gathered participants from many professions to discuss ways to reform the criminal law. The conference was one of the first of Pound's efforts to give practical application to sociological jurisprudence. Later, in 1929 President HERBERT HOOVER appointed Pound to the Wickersham Commission, the popular name for the National Commission on Law Observance and Enforcement. This commission conducted the first comprehensive national study of crime and law enforcement in U.S. history. The findings of the commission, which were published in fourteen volumes in 1931 and 1932, covered every aspect of the criminal justice system, including the causes of crime, police and prose-

cutorial procedures, and the importance of probation and parole.

Pound's lecture is a treasure trove of ideas concerning the management of courts. The area of court administration has grown since the 1960s, and court administrators now play an active role in monitoring and managing caseloads. Many states have also heeded Pound's advice and unified their trial courts, thereby eliminating several layers of courts.

—⚭—

The Causes of Popular Dissatisfaction with the Administration of Justice

Dissatisfaction with the administration of justice is as old as law. Not to go outside of our own legal system, discontent has an ancient and unbroken pedigree. The Anglo-Saxon laws continually direct that justice is to be done equally to rich and to poor and the king exhorts that the peace be kept better than has been wont, and that "men of every order readily submit ... each to that law which is appropriate to him." The author of the apocryphal *Mirror of Justices* gives a list of one hundred and fifty-five abuses in legal administration, and names it as one of the chief abuses of the degenerate times in which he lived that executions of judges for corrupt or illegal decisions had ceased. Wyclif complains

Source: Reprinted from 29 *A.B.A. Rep.*, pt. I, 395–417, 1906.

LEGAL
SCHOLARSHIP

THE CAUSES OF
POPULAR
DISSATISFACTION
WITH THE
ADMINISTRATION
OF JUSTICE

that "lawyers make process by subtlety and cavilations of law civil, that is much heathen men's law, and do not accept the form of the gospel, as if the gospel were not so good as pagan's law." Starkey, in the reign of Henry VIII, says: "Everyone that can color reason maketh a stop to the best law that is beforetime devised." James I reminded his judges that "the law was founded upon reason, and that he and others had reason as well as the judges." In the eighteenth century, it was complained that the bench was occupied by "legal monks, utterly ignorant of human nature and of the affairs of men." In the nineteenth century the vehement criticism of the period of the reform movement needs only to be mentioned. In other words, as long as there have been laws and lawyers, conscientious and well-meaning men have believed that laws were mere arbitrary technicalities, and that the attempt to regulate the relations of mankind in accordance with them resulted largely in injustice. But we must not be deceived by this innocuous and inevitable discontent with all law into overlooking or underrating the real and serious dissatisfaction with courts and lack of respect for law which exists in the United States today.

In spite of the violent opposition which the doctrine of judicial power over unconstitutional legislation at first encountered, the tendency to give the fullest scope to the common law doctrine of supremacy of law and to tie down administration by common law liabilities and judicial review, was, until recently, very marked. Today, the contrary tendency is no less marked. Courts are distrusted, and executive boards and commissions with summary and plenary powers, freed, so far as constitutions will permit, from judicial review, have become the fashion. It will be assumed, then, that there is more than the normal amount of dissatisfaction with the present-day administration of justice in America. Assuming this, the first step must be diagnosis, and diagnosis will be the sole purpose of this paper. It will attempt only to discover and to point out the causes of current popular dissatisfaction. The inquiry will be limited, moreover, to civil justice. For while the criminal law attracts more notice, and punishment seems to have greater interest for the lay mind than the civil remedies of prevention and compensation, the true interest of the modern community is in the civil administration of justice. Revenge and its modern outgrowth, punishment, belong to the past of legal history. The rules which define

these invisible boundaries, within which each may act without conflict with the activities of his fellows in a busy and crowded world, upon which investor, promoter, buyer, seller, employer, and employee must rely consciously or subconsciously in their every-day transactions, are conditions precedent of modern social and industrial organization.

With the scope of inquiry so limited, the causes of dissatisfaction with the administration of justice may be grouped under four main heads: (1) Causes for dissatisfaction with *any* legal system, (2) causes lying in the peculiarities of our Anglo-American legal system, (3) causes lying in our American judicial organization and procedure, and (4) causes lying in the environment of our judicial administration.

It needs but a superficial acquaintance with literature to show that all legal systems among all peoples have given rise to the same complaints. Even the wonderful mechanism of modern German judicial administration is said to be distrusted by the people on the time-worn ground that there is one law for the rich and another for the poor. It is obvious, therefore, that there must be some cause or causes inherent in all law and in all legal systems in order to produce this universal and invariable effect. These causes of dissatisfaction with any system of law I believe to be the following: (1) The necessarily mechanical operation of rules, and hence of laws; (2) the inevitable difference in rate of progress between law and public opinion; (3) the general popular assumption that the administration of justice is an easy task, to which anyone is competent; and (4) popular impatience of restraint.

The most important and most constant cause of dissatisfaction with all law at all times is to be found in the necessarily mechanical operation of legal rules. This is one of the penalties of uniformity. Legal history shows an oscillation between wide judicial discretion on the one hand and strict confinement of the magistrate by minute and detailed rules upon the other hand. From time to time more or less reversion to justice without law becomes necessary in order to bring the public administration of justice into touch with changed moral, social, or political conditions. But such periods of reversion result only in new rules or changed rules. In time the modes of exercising discretion become fixed, the course of judicial action becomes stable and uniform, and the new element, whether custom or equity or natural law, becomes as rigid and mechanical as the old. This mechanical action of the law may be minimized, but it cannot be obviated. Laws are general rules; and the process of making them general involves elimination of the immaterial elements of particular controversies. If all controversies were alike or if the degree in which actual controversies approximate to the recognized types could be calculated with precision, this would not matter. The difficulty is that in practice they approximate to these types in infinite gradations. When we eliminate immaterial factors to reach a general rule, we can never entirely avoid eliminating factors which will be more or less material in some particular controversy. If to meet this inherent difficulty in administering justice according to law we introduce a judicial dispensing power, the result is uncertainty and an intolerable scope for the personal equation of the magistrate. If we turn to the other extreme and pile up exceptions and qualifications and provisos, the legal system becomes cumbrous and unworkable. Hence the law has always ended in a compromise, in a middle course between wide discretion and over-minute legislation. In reaching this middle ground, some sacrifice of flexibility of application to particular cases is inevitable. In consequence, the adjustment of the relations of man and man according to these rules will of necessity appear more or less arbitrary and more or less in conflict with the ethical notions of individuals.

In periods of absolute or generally received moral systems, the contrast between legal results and strict ethical requirements will appeal only to individuals. In periods of free individual thought in morals and ethics, and especially in an age of social and industrial transition, this contrast is greatly intensified and appeals to large classes of society. Justice, which is the end of law, is the ideal compromise between the activities of all in a crowded world. The law seeks to harmonize these activities and to adjust the relations of every man with his fellows so as to accord with the moral sense of the community. When the community is at one in its ideas of justice, this is possible. When the community is divided and diversified, and groups and classes and interests, understanding each other none too well, have conflicting ideas of justice, the task is extremely difficult. It is impossible that legal and ethical ideas should be in entire accord

in such a society. The individual looks at cases one by one and measures them by his individual sense of right and wrong. The lawyer must look at cases in gross and must measure them largely by an artificial standard. He must apply the ethics of the community, not his own. If discretion is given him, his view will be that of the class from which he comes. If his hands are tied by law, he must apply the ethics of the past as formulated in common law and legislation. In either event, judicial and individual ethical standards will diverge. And this divergence between the ethical and the legal, as each individual sees it, makes him say with Luther, "Good jurist, bad Christian."

A closely related cause of dissatisfaction with the administration of justice according to law is to be found in the inevitable difference in rate of progress between law and public opinion. In order to preclude corruption, to exclude the personal prejudices of magistrates, and to minimize individual incompetency, law formulates the moral sentiments of the community in rules to which the judgments of tribunals must conform. These rules, being formulations of public opinion, cannot exist until public opinion has become fixed and settled, and cannot change until a change of public opinion has become complete. It follows that this difficulty in the judicial administration of justice, like the preceding, may be minimized, but not obviated. In a rude age the Teutonic moots in which every free man took a hand might be possible. But these tribunals broke under pressure of business and became ordinary courts with permanent judges. The Athenians conceived that the people themselves should decide each case. But the Athenian dikastery, in which controversies were submitted to blocks of several hundred citizens by way of reaching the will of the democracy, proved to register its caprice for the moment rather than its permanent will. Modern experience with juries, especially in commercial causes, does not warrant us in hoping much from any form of judicial referendum. Public opinion must affect the administration of justice through the rules by which justice is administered rather than through the direct administration. All interference with the uniform and automatic application of these rules, when actual controversies arise, introduces an anti-legal element which becomes intolerable. But, as public opinion affects tribunals through the rules by which they decide and these rules once made, stand till abro-

LEGAL
SCHOLARSHIP

THE CAUSES OF
POPULAR
DISSATISFACTION
WITH THE
ADMINISTRATION
OF JUSTICE

LEGAL
SCHOLARSHIP

THE CAUSES OF
POPULAR
DISSATISFACTION
WITH THE
ADMINISTRATION
OF JUSTICE

gated or altered, any system of law will be made up of successive strata of rules and doctrines representing successive and often widely divergent periods of public opinion. In this sense, law is often in very truth a government of the living by the dead. The unconscious changes of judicial law making and the direct alterations of legislation and codification operate to make this government by the dead reasonably tolerable. But here again we must pay a price for certainty and uniformity. The law does not respond quickly to new conditions. It does not change until ill effects are felt; often not until they are felt acutely. The moral or intellectual or economic change must come first. While it is coming, and until it is so complete as to affect the law and formulate itself therein, friction must ensue. In an age of rapid moral, intellectual, and economic changes, often crossing one another and producing numerous minor resultants, this friction cannot fail to be in excess.

A third perennial source of popular dissatisfaction with the administration of justice according to law may be found in the popular assumption that the administration of justice is an easy task to which anyone is competent. Laws may be compared to the formulas of engineers. They sum up the experience of many courts with many cases and enable the magistrate to apply that experience subconsciously. So, the formula enables the engineer to make use of the accumulated experience of past builders, even though he could not work out a step in its evolution by himself. A layman is no more competent to construct or to apply the one formula than the other. Each requires special knowledge and special preparation. Nonetheless, the notion that anyone is competent to adjudicate the intricate controversies of a modern community contributes to the unsatisfactory administration of justice in many parts of the United States. The older states have generally outgrown it. But it is felt in extravagant powers of juries, lay judges of probate and legislative or judicial law making against *stare decisis,* in most of the commonwealths of the South and West. The public seldom realizes how much it is interested in maintaining the highest scientific standard in the administration of justice. There is no more certain protection against corruption, prejudice, class feeling, or incompetence. Publicity will avail something. But the daily criticism of trained minds, the knowledge that nothing which does not conform to the principles and

received doctrines of scientific jurisprudence will escape notice, does more than any other agency for the every-day purity and efficiency of courts of justice.

Another necessary source of dissatisfaction with judicial administration of justice is to be found in popular impatience of restraint. Law involves restraint and regulation, with the sheriff and his posse in the background to enforce it. But, however necessary and salutary this restraint, men have never been reconciled to it entirely. The very fact that it is a compromise between the individual and his fellows makes the individual, who must abate some part of his activities in the interest of his fellows, more or less restive. In an age of absolute theories, monarchical or democratic, this restiveness is acute. A conspicuous example is to be seen in the contest between the king and the common law courts in the seventeenth century. An equally conspicuous example is to be seen in the attitude of the frontiersman toward state-imposed justice. "The unthinking sons of the sage brush," says Owen Wister, "ill tolerate anything which stands for discipline, good order and obedience; and the man who lets another command him they despise. I can think of no threat more evil for our democracy, for it is a fine thing diseased and perverted, namely, the spirit of independence gone drunk." This is an extreme case. But in a lesser degree the feeling that each individual, as an organ of the sovereign democracy, is above the law he helps to make, fosters everywhere a disrespect for legal methods and institutions and a spirit of resistance to them. It is "the reason of this our artificial man the commonwealth," says Hobbes, "and his command that maketh law." This man, however, is abstract. The concrete man in the street or the concrete mob is much more obvious; and it is no wonder that individuals and even classes of individuals fail to draw the distinction.

A considerable portion of current dissatisfaction with the administration of justice must be attributed to the universal causes just considered. Conceding this, we have next to recognize that there are potent causes in operation of a character entirely different.

Under the second main head, causes lying in our peculiar legal system, I should enumerate five: (1) The individualist spirit of our common law, which agrees ill with a collectivist age; (2) the common law doctrine of contentious proce-

LEGAL
SCHOLARSHIP

THE CAUSES OF
POPULAR
DISSATISFACTION
WITH THE
ADMINISTRATION
OF JUSTICE

dure, which turns litigation into a game; (3) political jealousy, due to the strain put upon our legal system by the doctrine of supremacy of law; (4) the lack of general ideas or legal philosophy, so characteristic of Anglo-American law, which gives us petty tinkering where comprehensive reform is needed; and (5) defects of form due to the circumstance that the bulk of our legal system is still case law.

The first of these, conflict between the individualist spirit of the common law and the collectivist spirit of the present age, has been treated of on another occasion. What was said then need not be repeated. Suffice it to point out two examples. From the beginning, the main reliance of our common law system has been individual initiative. The main security for the peace at common law is private prosecution of offenders. The chief security for the efficiency and honesty of public officers is mandamus or injunction by a taxpayer to prevent waste of the proceeds of taxation. The reliance for keeping public service companies to their duty in treating all alike at reasonable price is an action to recover damages. Moreover, the individual is supposed at common law to be able to look out for himself and to need no administrative protection. If he is injured through contributory negligence, no theory of comparative negligence comes to his relief; if he hires as an employee, he assumes the risk of the employment; if he buys goods, the rule is *caveat emptor*. In our modern industrial society, this whole scheme of individual initiative is breaking down. Private prosecution has become obsolete. Mandamus and injunction have failed to prevent rings and bosses from plundering public funds. Private suits against carriers for damages have proved no preventive of discrimination and extortionate rates. The doctrine of assumption of risk becomes brutal under modern conditions of employment. An action for damages is no comfort to us when we are sold diseased beef or poisonous canned goods. At all these points, and they are points of every-day contact with the most vital public interests, common law methods of relief have failed. The courts have not been able to do the work which the common law doctrine of supremacy of law imposed on them. A widespread feeling that the courts are inefficient has been a necessary result. But, along with this, another phase of the individualism of the common law has served to increase public irritation. At the very time the courts have appeared powerless themselves to give relief, they have seemed to obstruct public efforts to get relief by legislation. The chief concern of the common law is to secure and protect individual rights. "The public good," says Blackstone, "is in nothing more essentially interested than in the protection of every individual's private rights." Such, it goes without saying, is not the popular view today. Today we look to society for protection against individuals, natural or artificial, and we resent doctrines that protect these individuals against society for fear society will oppress us. But the common law guaranties of individual rights are established in our constitutions, state and federal. So that, while in England these common law dogmas have had to give way to modern legislation, in America they stand continually between the people, or large classes of the people, and legislation they desire. In consequence, the courts have been put in a false position of doing nothing and obstructing everything, which it is impossible for the layman to interpret aright.

A no less potent source of irritation lies in our American exaggerations of the common law contentious procedure. The sporting theory of justice, the "instinct of giving the game fair play," as Professor Wigmore has put it, is so rooted in the profession in America that most of us take it for a fundamental legal tenet. But it is probably only a survival of the days when a lawsuit was a fight between two clans in which change of venue had been taken to the forum. So far from being a fundamental fact of jurisprudence, it is peculiar to Anglo-American law; and it has been strongly curbed in modern English practice. With us, it is not merely in full acceptance, it has been developed and its collateral possibilities have been cultivated to the furthest extent. Hence in America we take it as a matter of course that a judge should be a mere umpire, to pass upon objections and hold counsel to the rules of the game, and that the parties should fight out their own game in their own way without judicial interference. We resent such interference as unfair, even when in the interests of justice. The idea that procedure must of necessity be wholly contentious disfigures our judicial administration at every point. It leads the most conscientious judge to feel that he is merely to decide the contest, as counsel present it, according to the rules of the game, not to search independently for truth and justice. It leads counsel to forget that they are officers of the court and to deal with the rules of law and procedure exactly

LEGAL
SCHOLARSHIP

THE CAUSES OF
POPULAR
DISSATISFACTION
WITH THE
ADMINISTRATION
OF JUSTICE

as the professional football coach with the rules of the sport. It leads to exertion to "get error into the record" rather than to dispose of the controversy finally and upon its merits. It turns witnesses, and especially expert witnesses, into partisans pure and simple. It leads to sensational cross-examinations "to affect credit," which have made the witness stand "the slaughter house of reputations." It prevents the trial court from restraining the bullying of witnesses and creates a general dislike, if not fear, of the witness function which impairs the administration of justice. It keeps alive the unfortunate exchequer rule, dead in the country of its origin, according to which errors in the admission or rejection of evidence are presumed to be prejudicial and hence demand a new trial. It grants new trials because by inability to procure a bill of exceptions a party has lost the chance to play another inning in the game of justice. It creates vested rights in errors of procedure, of the benefit whereof parties are not to be deprived. The inquiry is not, What do substantive law and justice require? Instead, the inquiry is: Have the rules of the game been carried out strictly? If any material infraction is discovered, just as the football rules put back the offending team five or ten or fifteen yards, as the case may be, our sporting theory of justice awards new trials, or reverses judgments, or sustains demurrers in the interest of regular play.

The effect of our exaggerated contentious procedure is not only to irritate parties, witnesses and jurors in particular cases, but to give to the whole community a false notion of the purpose and end of law. Hence comes, in large measure, the modern American race to beat the law. If the law is a mere game, neither the players who take part in it nor the public who witness it can be expected to yield to its spirit when their interests are served by evading it. And this is doubly true in a time which requires all institutions to be economically efficient and socially useful. We need not wonder that one part of the community strain their oaths in the jury box and find verdicts against unpopular litigants in the teeth of law and evidence, while another part retain lawyers by the year to advise how to evade what to them are unintelligent and unreasonable restrictions upon necessary modes of doing business. Thus the courts, instituted to administer justice according to law, are made agents or abettors of lawlessness.

Another source of irritation at our American courts is political jealousy due to the strain put upon our legal system by the doctrine of the supremacy of law. By virtue of this doctrine, which has become fundamental in our polity, the law restrains, not individuals alone, but a whole people. The people so restrained would be likely in any event to be jealous of the visible agents of restraint. Even more is this true in that the subjects which our constitutional polity commits to the courts are largely matters of economics, politics, and sociology upon which a democracy is peculiarly sensitive. Not only are these matters made into legal questions, but they are tried as incidents of private litigation. This phase of the common law doctrine was felt as a grievance in the seventeenth century. "I tell you plainly," said Bacon, as attorney general, in arguing a question of prerogative to the judges, "I tell you plainly it is little better than a by-let or crooked creek to try whether the king hath power to erect this office in an assize between Brownlow and Michell." King Demos must feel much the same at seeing the constitutionality of the Missouri Compromise tried in an action of trespass, at seeing the validity of the legal tender laws tried on pleas of payment in private litigation, at seeing the power of the federal government to carry on the Civil War tried judicially in admiralty, at seeing the income tax overthrown in a stockholder's bill to enjoin waste of corporate assets and at seeing the important political questions in the Insular Cases disposed of in forfeiture proceedings against a few trifling imports. Nor is this the only phase of the common law doctrine of supremacy of law which produces political jealousy of the courts. Even more must the layman be struck with the spectacle of law paralyzing administration which our polity so frequently presents. The difficulties with writs of *habeas corpus* which the federal government encountered during the Civil War and the recent case of the income tax will occur to you at once. In my own state, in a few years we have seen a freight-rate law suspended by decree of a court and have seen the collection of taxes from railroad companies, needed for the everyday conduct of public business, tied up by an injunction. The strain put upon judicial institutions by such litigation is obviously very great.

Lack of general ideas and absence of any philosophy of law, which has been characteristic of our law from the beginning and has been a point of pride at least since the time of Coke,

LEGAL
SCHOLARSHIP

THE CAUSES OF
POPULAR
DISSATISFACTION
WITH THE
ADMINISTRATION
OF JUSTICE

contributes its mite also toward the causes of dissatisfaction with courts. For one thing, it keeps us in the thrall of a fiction. There is a strong aversion to straightforward change of any important legal doctrine. The cry is *interpret it.* But such interpretation is spurious. It is legislation. And to interpret an obnoxious rule out of existence rather than to meet it fairly and squarely by legislation is a fruitful source of confusion. Yet the Bar are trained to it as an ancient common law doctrine, and it has a great hold upon the public. Hence if the law does not work well, says Bentham, with fine sarcasm, "it is never the law itself that is in the wrong; it is always some wicked interpreter of the law that has corrupted and abused it." Thus another unnecessary strain is imposed upon our judicial system and courts are held for what should be the work of the legislature.

The defects of form inherent in our system of case law have been the subject of discussion and controversy too often to require extended consideration. Suffice it to say that the want of certainty, confusion and incompleteness inherent in all case law, and the waste of labor entailed by the prodigious bulk to which ours has attained, appeal strongly to the layman. The compensating advantages of this system, as seen by the lawyer and by the scientific investigator, are not apparent to him. What he sees is another phase of the great game; a citation match between counsel, with a certainty that diligence can rake up a decision *somewhere* in support of any conceivable proposition.

Passing to the third head, causes lying in our judicial organization and procedure, we come upon the most efficient causes of dissatisfaction with the present administration of justice in America. For I venture to say that our system of courts is archaic and our procedure behind the times. Uncertainty, delay and expense, and above all the injustice of deciding cases upon points of practice, which are the mere etiquette of justice, direct results of the organization of our courts and the backwardness of our procedure, have created a deep-seated desire to keep out of court, right or wrong, on the part of every sensible business man in the community.

Our system of courts is archaic in three respects: (1) In its multiplicity of courts, (2) in preserving concurrent jurisdictions, (3) in the waste of judicial power which it involves. The judicial organizations of the several states exhib-

it many differences of detail. But they agree in these three respects. Multiplicity of courts is characteristic of archaic law. In Anglo-Saxon law, one might apply to the Hundred, the Shire, the Witan, or the king in person. Until Edward I broke up private jurisdictions, there were the king's superior courts of law, the itinerant justices, the county courts, the local or communal courts, and the private courts of lordships; besides which one might always apply to the king or to the Great Council for extraordinary relief. When later the royal courts had superseded all others, there were the concurrent jurisdictions of King's Bench, Common Pleas, and Exchequer, all doing the same work, while appellate jurisdiction was divided by King's Bench, Exchequer Chamber, and Parliament. In the Fourth Institute, Coke enumerates seventy-four courts. Of these, seventeen did the work that is now done by three, the County Courts, the Supreme Court of Judicature, and the House of Lords. At the time of the reorganization by the Judicature Act of 1873, five appellate courts and eight courts of first instance were consolidated into the one Supreme Court of Judicature. It was the intention of those who devised the plan of the Judicature Act to extend the principle of unity of jurisdiction by cutting off the appellate jurisdiction of the House of Lords and by incorporating the County Courts in the newly formed Supreme Court as branches thereof. The recommendation as to the County Courts was not adopted, and the appellate jurisdiction of the House of Lords was restored in 1875. In this way the unity and simplicity of the original design were impaired. But the plan, although adopted in part only, deserves the careful study of American lawyers as a model modern judicial organization. Its chief features were (1) to set up a single court, complete in itself, embracing all superior courts and jurisdictions; (2) to include in this one court, as a branch thereof, a single court of final appeal. In the one branch, the court of first instance, all original jurisdiction at law, in equity, in admiralty, in bankruptcy, in probate, and in divorce was to be consolidated; in the other branch, the court of appeal, the whole reviewing jurisdiction was to be established. This idea of unification, although not carried out completely, has proved most effective. Indeed, its advantages are self-evident. Where the appellate tribunal and the court of first instance are branches of one court, all expense of transfer of record, of transcripts, bills of exceptions, writs of error, and citations is

LEGAL
SCHOLARSHIP

THE CAUSES OF
POPULAR
DISSATISFACTION
WITH THE
ADMINISTRATION
OF JUSTICE

wiped out. The records are the records of the court, of which each tribunal is but a branch. The court and each branch thereof knows its own records, and no duplication and certification is required. Again, all appellate practice, with its attendant pitfalls, and all waste of judicial time in ascertaining how or whether a case has been brought into the court of review is done away with. One may search the recent English reports in vain for a case where an appeal has miscarried on a point of practice. Cases on appellate procedure are wanting. In effect there is no such thing. The whole attention of the court and of counsel is concentrated upon the cause. On the other hand, our American reports bristle with fine points of appellate procedure. More than four per cent of the digest paragraphs of the last ten volumes of the *American Digest* have to do with Appeal and Error. In ten volumes of the *Federal Reporter*, namely volumes 129 to 139, covering decisions of the Circuit Courts of Appeals from 1903 till the present, there is an average of ten decisions upon points of appellate practice to the volume. Two cases to the volume, on the average, turn wholly upon appellate procedure. In the ten volumes there are six civil cases turning upon the question whether error or appeal was the proper mode of review, and in two civil cases the question was whether the Circuit Court of Appeals was the proper tribunal. I have referred to these reports because they represent courts in which only causes of importance may be brought. The state reports exhibit the same condition. In ten volumes of the Southwestern Reporter, the decisions of the Supreme Court and Courts of Appeals of Missouri show that nearly twenty per cent involve points of appellate procedure. In volume 87, of fifty-three decisions of the Supreme Court and ninety-seven of the Courts of Appeals, twenty-eight are taken up in whole or in part with the mere technics of obtaining a review. All of this is sheer waste, which a modern judicial organization would obviate.

Even more archaic is our system of concurrent jurisdiction of state and federal courts in causes involving diversity of citizenship; a system by virtue of which causes continually hang in the air between two courts, or, if they do stick in one court or the other, are liable to an ultimate overturning because they stuck in the wrong court. A few statistics on this point may be worth while. In the ten volumes of the Federal Reporter referred to, the decisions of the Circuit Courts of Appeals in civil cases average

seventy-six to the volume. Of these, on the average, between four and five in a volume are decided on points of federal jurisdiction. In a little more than one to each volume, judgments of Circuit Courts are reversed on points of jurisdiction. The same volumes contain on the average seventy-three decisions of Circuit Courts in civil cases to each volume. Of these, six, on the average, are upon motions to remand to the state courts, and between eight and nine are upon other points of federal jurisdiction. Moreover, twelve cases in the ten volumes were remanded on the *form* of the petition for removal. In other words, in nineteen and three-tenths per cent of the reported decisions of the Circuit Courts the question was whether those courts had jurisdiction at all; and in seven per cent of these that question depended on the form of the pleadings. A system that permits this and reverses four judgments a year because the cause was brought in or removed to the wrong tribunal is out of place in a modern business community. All original jurisdiction should be concentrated. It ought to be impossible for a cause to fail because brought in the wrong place. A simple order of transfer from one docket to another in the same court ought to be enough. There should be no need of new papers, no transcripts, no bandying of cases from one court to another on orders of removal and of remand, no beginnings again with new process.

Judicial power may be wasted in three ways: (1) By rigid districts or courts or jurisdictions, so that business may be congested in one court while judges in another are idle; (2) by consuming the time of courts with points of pure practice, when they ought to be investigating substantial controversies; and (3) by nullifying the results of judicial action by unnecessary retrials. American judicial systems are defective in all three respects. The Federal Circuit Courts and Circuit Courts of Appeals are conspicuous exceptions in the first respect, affording a model of flexible judicial organization. But in nearly all of the states, rigid districts and hard and fast lines between courts operate to delay business in one court while judges in another have ample leisure. In the second respect, waste of judicial time upon points of practice, the intricacies of federal jurisdiction, and the survival of the obsolete Chinese Wall between law and equity in procedure make our federal courts no less conspicuous sinners. In the ten volumes of the *Federal Reporter* examined, of an average of sev-

LEGAL
SCHOLARSHIP

THE CAUSES OF
POPULAR
DISSATISFACTION
WITH THE
ADMINISTRATION
OF JUSTICE

enty-six decisions of the Circuit Courts of Appeals in each volume, two turn upon the distinction between law and equity in procedure and not quite one judgment to each volume is reversed on this distinction. In an average of seventy-three decisions a volume by the Circuit Courts, more than three in each volume involve this same distinction, and not quite two in each volume turn upon it. But many states that are supposed to have reformed procedure scarcely make a better showing.

Each state has to a great extent its own procedure. But it is not too much to say that all of them are behind the times. We struck one great stroke in 1848 and have rested complacently or contented ourselves with patchwork amendment ever since. The leading ideas of the New York Code of Civil Procedure marked a long step forward. But the work was done too hurriedly and the plan of a rigid code, going into minute detail, was clearly wrong. A modern practice act lays down the general principles of practice and leaves details to rules of court. The New York Code Commission was appointed in 1847 and reported in 1848. If we except the Connecticut Practice Act of 1878, which shows English influence, American reform in procedure has stopped substantially where that commission left it. In England, beginning with 1826 and ending with 1874, *five* commissions have put forth *nine* reports upon this subject. As a consequence we have nothing in America to compare with the radical treatment of pleading in the English Judicature Act and the orders based thereon. We still try the *record*, not the *case*. We are still reversing judgments for nonjoinder and misjoinder. The English practice of joinder of parties against whom relief is claimed in the alternative, rendering judgment against any that the proof shows to be liable and dismissing the rest, makes an American lawyer rub his eyes. We are still reversing judgments for variances. We still reverse them because the recovery is in excess of the prayer, though sustained by the evidence.

But the worst feature of American procedure is the lavish granting of new trials. In the ten volumes of the *Federal Reporter* referred to, there are, on the average, twenty-five writs of error in civil cases to the volume. New trials are awarded on the average in eight cases a volume, or nearly twenty-nine per cent. In the state courts the proportion of new trials to causes reviewed, as

ascertained from investigation of the last five volumes of each series of the National Reporter system, runs over forty per cent. In the last three volumes of the *New York Reports* (180–182), covering the period from December 6, 1904, to October 24, 1905, forty-five new trials are awarded. Nor is this all. In one case in my own state an action for personal injuries was tried six times, and one for breach of contract was tried three times and was four times in the Supreme Court. When with this we compare the statistics of the English Court of Appeal, which does not grant to exceed twelve new trials a year, or new trials in about three per cent of the cases reviewed, it is evident that our methods of trial and review are out of date.

A comparison of the volume of business disposed of by English and by American courts will illustrate the waste and delay caused by archaic judicial organization and obsolete procedure. In England there are twenty-three judges of the High Court who dispose on the average of fifty-six hundred *contested* cases, and have before them, in one form or another, some eighty thousand cases each year. In Nebraska there are twenty-eight district judges who have no original probate jurisdiction and no jurisdiction in bankruptcy or admiralty, and they had upon their dockets last year forty-three hundred and twenty cases, of which they disposed of about seventy per cent. England and Wales, with a population in 1900 of 32,000,000, employ for their whole civil litigation ninety-five judges, that is, thirty-seven in the Supreme Court and House of Lords and fifty-eight county judges. Nebraska, with a population in 1900 of 1,066,000, employs for the same purpose one hundred and twenty-nine. But these one hundred and twenty-nine are organized on an antiquated system and their time is frittered away on mere points of legal etiquette.

Finally, under the fourth and last head, causes lying in the environment of our judicial administration, we may distinguish six: (1) Popular lack of interest in justice, which makes jury service a bore and the vindication of right and law secondary to the trouble and expense involved; (2) the strain put upon law in that it has today to do the work of morals also; (3) the effect of transition to a period of legislation; (4) the putting of our courts into politics; (5) the making the legal profession into a trade, which has superseded the relation of attorney and

LEGAL
SCHOLARSHIP

THE CAUSES OF
POPULAR
DISSATISFACTION
WITH THE
ADMINISTRATION
OF JUSTICE

client by that of employer and employee; and (6) public ignorance of the real workings of courts due to ignorant and sensational reports in the press. Each of these deserves consideration, but a few points only may be noticed. Law is the skeleton of social order. It must be "clothed upon by the flesh and blood of morality." The present is a time of transition in the very foundations of belief and of conduct. Absolute theories of morals and supernatural sanctions have lost their hold. Conscience and individual responsibility are relaxed. In other words, the law is strained to do double duty, and more is expected of it than in a time when morals as a regulating agency are more efficacious. Another strain upon our judicial system results from the crude and unorganized character of American legislation in a period when the growing point of law has shifted to legislation. When, in consequence, laws fail to produce the anticipated effects, judicial administration shares the blame. Worse than this is the effect of laws not intended to be enforced. These parodies, like the common law branding of felons, in which a piece of bacon used to be interposed between the branding iron and the criminal's skin, breed disrespect for law. Putting courts into politics and compelling judges to become politicians, in many jurisdictions has almost destroyed the traditional respect for the Bench. Finally, the ignorant and sensational reports of judicial proceedings, from which alone a great part of the public may judge of the daily work of the courts, completes the impression that the administration of justice is but a game. There are honorable exceptions, but the average press reports distract attention from the real proceeding to petty tilts of counsel, encounters with witnesses and sensational by-incidents. In Nebraska, not many years since, the federal court enjoined the execution of an act to regulate insurance companies. In press accounts of the proceeding, the conspiracy clause of the bill was copied *in extenso* under the headline "Conspiracy Charged," and it was made to appear that the ground of the injunction was a conspiracy between the state officers and some

persons unknown. It cannot be expected that the public shall form any just estimate of our courts of justice from such data.

Reviewing the several causes for dissatisfaction with the administration of justice which have been touched upon, it will have been observed that some inhere in all law and are the penalty we pay for uniformity; that some inhere in our political institutions and are the penalty we pay for local self-government and independence from bureaucratic control; that some inhere in the circumstances of an age of transition and are the penalty we pay for individual freedom of thought and universal education. These will take care of themselves. But too much of the current dissatisfaction has a just origin in our judicial organization and procedure. The causes that lie here must be heeded. Our administration of justice is not decadent. It is simply behind the times. Political judges were known in England down to the last century. Lord Kenyon, as Master of the Rolls, sat in Parliament and took as active a part in political squabbles in the House of Commons as our state judges today in party conventions. Dodson and Fogg and Sergeant Buzzfuzz wrought in an atmosphere of contentious procedure. Bentham tells us that in 1797, out of five hundred and fifty pending writs of error, five hundred and forty-three were shams or vexatious contrivances for delay. Jarndyce and Jarndyce dragged out its weary course in chancery only half a century ago. We are simply stationary in that period of legal history. With law schools that are rivaling the achievements of Bologna and of Bourges to promote scientific study of the law; with active Bar Associations in every state to revive professional feeling and throw off the yoke of commercialism; with the passing of the doctrine that politics, too, is a mere game to be played for its own sake, we may look forward confidently to deliverance from the sporting theory of justice; we may look forward to a near future when our courts will be swift and certain agents of justice, whose decisions will be acquiesced in and respected by all.

LEGAL SCHOLARSHIP

SOME REFLECTIONS ON THE READING OF STATUTES

Felix Frankfurter, 1947

By 1947, when FELIX FRANKFURTER delivered "Some Reflections on the Reading of Statutes" to New York City's bar association, he had been on the U.S. Supreme Court eight years. From 1914 until his appointment to the Court in 1939, Frankfurter had been a professor at Harvard Law School.

In his reflections Frankfurter noted that the work of the Supreme Court had changed over the years. In the nineteenth and early twentieth centuries, it heard a declining number of common-law cases. By the 1940s, not one case involved common law. This meant that the Supreme Court had become primarily an interpreter of statutes.

Frankfurter's essay discusses issues that have remained contentious. How does a judge divine legislative intent? What rules of construction should a judge apply to a statute? In the act of interpreting a statute, is the judge identifying legislative intent or acting as a surrogate legislator?

—∽∾—

Some Reflections on the Reading of Statutes

A single volume of 320 octavo pages contains all the laws passed by Congress during its first five years, when measures were devised for getting the new government under way; 26 acts were passed in the 1789 session, 66 in 1790, 94 in 1791, 38 in 1792, 63 in 1793. For the single session of the 70th Congress, to take a predepression period, there are 993 enactments in a monstrous vol-

ume of 1014 pages—quarto not octavo—with a comparable range of subject matter. Do you wonder that one for whom the Statutes at Large constitute his staple reading should have sympathy, at least in his moments of baying at the moon, with the touching Congressman who not so long ago proposed a "Commission on Centralization" to report whether "the Government has departed from the concept of the founding fathers" and what steps should be taken "to restore the Government to its original purposes and sphere of activity"? Inevitably the work of the Supreme Court reflects the great shift in the center of gravity of lawmaking. Broadly speaking, the number of cases disposed of by opinions has not changed from term to term. But even as late as 1875 more than 40 per cent of the controversies before the Court were common-law litigation, fifty years later only five per cent, while today cases not resting on statutes are reduced almost to zero. It is therefore accurate to say that courts have ceased to be the primary makers of law in the sense in which they "legislated" the common law. It is certainly true of the Supreme Court, that almost every case has a statute at its heart or close to it.

This does not mean that every case before the Court involves questions of statutory construction. If only literary perversity or jaundiced partisanship can sponsor a particular rendering of a statute there is no problem. When we talk of

Source: Reprinted with permission from *The Record* of the Association of the Bar of the City of New York, © 1947. 2 *The Record* 213.

LEGAL
SCHOLARSHIP

SOME
REFLECTIONS
ON THE READING
OF STATUTES

statutory construction we have in mind cases in which there is a fair contest between two readings, neither of which comes without respectable title deeds. A problem in statutory construction can seriously bother courts only when there is a contest between probabilities of meaning.

DIFFICULTIES OF CONSTRUCTION

Though it has its own preoccupations and its own mysteries, and above all its own jargon, judicial construction ought not to be torn from its wider, nonlegal context. Anything that is written may present a problem of meaning, and that is the essence of the business of judges in construing legislation. The problem derives from the very nature of words. They are symbols of meaning. But unlike mathematical symbols, the phrasing of a document, especially a complicated enactment, seldom attains more than approximate precision. If individual words are inexact symbols, with shifting variables, their configuration can hardly achieve invariant meaning or assured definiteness. Apart from the ambiguity inherent in its symbols, a statute suffers from dubieties. It is not an equation or a formula representing a clearly marked process, nor is it an expression of individual thought to which is imparted the definiteness a single authorship can give. A statute is an instrument of government partaking of its practical purposes but also of its infirmities and limitations, of its awkward and groping efforts. With one of his flashes of insight, Mr. Justice Johnson called the science of government "the science of experiment." Anderson v. Dunn, 6 Wheat. 204, 226. The phrase, uttered a hundred and twenty-five years ago, has a very modern ring, for time has only served to emphasize its accuracy. To be sure, laws can measurably be improved with improvement in the mechanics of legislation, and the need for interpretation is usually in inverse ratio to the care and imagination of draftsmen. The area for judicial construction may be contracted. A large area is bound to remain.

The difficulties are inherent not only in the nature of words, of composition, and of legislation generally. They are often intensified by the subject matter of an enactment. The imagination which can draw an income tax statute to cover the myriad transactions of a society like ours, capable of producing the necessary revenue without producing a flood of litigation, has not yet revealed itself. (See 1 Report of Income Tax Codification Committee, Cmd. 5131, [1936]

pp. 16 to 19.) Moreover, government sometimes solves problems by shelving them temporarily. The legislative process reflects that attitude. Statutes as well as constitutional provisions at times embody purposeful ambiguity or are expressed with a generality for future unfolding. "The prohibition contained in the Fifth Amendment refers to infamous crimes—a term obviously inviting interpretation in harmony with conditions and opinions prevailing from time to time." Mr. Justice Brandeis in United States v. Moreland, 258 U.S. 433, 451. And Mr. Justice Cardozo once remarked, "a great principle of constitutional law is not susceptible of comprehensive statement in an adjective." Carter v. Carter Coal Co., 298 U.S. 238, 327.

The intrinsic difficulties of language and the emergence after enactment of situations not anticipated by the most gifted legislative imagination, reveal doubts and ambiguities in statutes that compel judicial construction. The process of construction, therefore, is not an exercise in logic or dialectic. The aids of formal reasoning are not irrelevant; they may simply be inadequate. The purpose of construction being the ascertainment of meaning, every consideration brought to bear for the solution of that problem must be devoted to that end alone. To speak of it as a practical problem is not to indulge a fashion in words. It must be that, not something else. Not, for instance, an opportunity for a judge to use words as "empty vessels into which he can pour anything he will"—his caprices, fixed notions, even statesmanlike beliefs in a particular policy. Nor, on the other hand, is the process a ritual to be observed by unimaginative adherence to well-worn professional phrases. To be sure, it is inescapably a problem in the keeping of the legal profession and subject to all the limitations of our adversary system of adjudication. When the judge, selected by society to give meaning to what the legislature has done, examines the statute, he does so not in a laboratory or in a classroom. Damage has been done or exactions made, interests are divided, passions have been aroused, sides have been taken. But the judge, if he is worth his salt, must be above the battle. We must assume in him not only personal impartiality but intellectual disinterestedness. In matters of statutory construction also it makes a great deal of difference whether you start with an answer or with a problem.

THE JUDGE'S TASK

Everyone has his own way of phrasing the task confronting judges when the meaning of a statute is in controversy. Judge Learned Hand speaks of the art of interpretation as "the proliferation of purpose." Who am I not to be satisfied with Learned Hand's felicities? And yet that phrase might mislead judges intellectually less disciplined than Judge Hand. It might justify interpretations by judicial libertines, not merely judicial libertarians. My own rephrasing of what we are driving at is probably no more helpful, and is much longer than Judge Hand's epigram. I should say that the troublesome phase of construction is the determination of the extent to which extraneous documentation and external circumstances may be allowed to infiltrate the text on the theory that they were part of it, written in ink discernible to the judicial eye.

Chief Justice White was happily endowed with the gift of finding the answer to problems by merely stating them. Often have I envied him this faculty but never more than in recent years. No matter how one states the problem of statutory construction, for me, at least, it does not carry its own answer. Though my business throughout most of my professional life has been with statutes, I come to you empty-handed. I bring no answers. I suspect the answers to the problems of an art are in its exercise. Not that one does not inherit, if one is capable of receiving it, the wisdom of the wise. But I confess unashamedly that I do not get much nourishment from books on statutory construction, and I say this after freshly reexamining them all, scores of them.

When one wants to understand or at least get the feeling of great painting, one does not go to books on the art of painting. One goes to the great masters. And so I have gone to great masters to get a sense of their practise of the art of interpretation. However, the art of painting and the art of interpretation are very different arts. Law, Holmes told us, becomes civilized to the extent that it is self-conscious of what it is doing. And so the avowals of great judges regarding their process of interpretation and the considerations that enter into it are of vital importance, though that ultimate something called the judgment upon the avowed factors escapes formulation and often, I suspect, even awareness. Nevertheless, an examination of some 2,000 cases, the bulk of which directly or

indirectly involves matters of construction, ought to shed light on the encounter between the judicial and the legislative processes, whether that light be conveyed by hints, by explicit elucidation, or, to mix the metaphor, through the ancient test, by their fruits.

And so I have examined the opinions of Holmes, Brandeis, and Cardozo and sought to derive from their treatment of legislation what conclusions I could fairly draw, freed as much as I could be from impressions I had formed in the course of the years.

Holmes came to the Supreme Court before the great flood of recent legislation, while the other two, especially Cardozo, appeared at its full tide. The shift in the nature of the Court's business led to changes in its jurisdiction, resulting in a concentration of cases involving the legislative process. Proportionately to their length of service and the number of opinions, Brandeis and Cardozo had many more statutes to construe. And the statutes presented for their interpretation became increasingly complex, bringing in their train a quantitatively new role for administrative regulations. Nevertheless, the earliest opinions of Holmes on statutory construction, insofar as he reveals himself, cannot be distinguished from Cardozo's last opinion, though the latter's process is more explicit.

A judge of marked individuality stamps his individuality on what he writes, no matter what the subject. What is however striking about the opinions of the three Justices in this field is the essential similarity of their attitude and of their appraisal of the relevant. Their opinions do not disclose a private attitude for or against extension of governmental authority by legislation, or towards the policy of particular legislation, which consciously or imperceptibly affected their judicial function in construing laws. It would thus be a shallow judgment that found in Mr. Justice Holmes' dissent in the Northern Securities case (193 U.S. 197, 400) an expression of his disapproval of the policy behind the Sherman Law. His habit of mind—to be as accurate as one can—had a natural tendency to confine what seemed to him familiar language in a statute to its familiar scope. But the proof of the pudding is that his private feelings did not lead him to invoke the rule of indefiniteness to invalidate legislation of which he strongly disapproved (Compare Nash *v.* United States, 229 U.S. 373, and International Harvester Co. *v.*

LEGAL
SCHOLARSHIP

SOME
REFLECTIONS
ON THE READING
OF STATUTES

LEGAL
SCHOLARSHIP

SOME
REFLECTIONS
ON THE READING
OF STATUTES

Kentucky, 234 U.S. 216), or to confine language in a constitution within the restrictions which he gave to the same language in a statute. (Compare Towne *v.* Eisner, 245 U.S. 418, and Eisner *v.* Macomber, 252 U.S. 189.)

The reservations I have just made indicate that such differences as emerge in the opinions of the three Justices on statutory construction, are differences that characterize all of their opinions, whether they are concerned with interpretation or constitutionality, with admiralty or patent law. They are differences of style. In the case of each, the style is the man.

If it be suggested that Mr. Justice Holmes is often swift, if not cavalier, in his treatment of statutes, there are those who level the same criticism against his opinions generally. It is merited in the sense that he wrote, as he said, for those learned in the art. I need hardly add that for him "learned" was not a formal term comprehending the whole legal fraternity. When dealing with problems of statutory construction also he illumined whole areas of doubt and darkness with insights enduringly expressed, however briefly. To say "We agree to all the generalities about not supplying criminal laws with what they omit, but there is no canon against using common-sense in construing laws as saying what they obviously mean," Rochen *v.* Ward, 279 U.S. 337, 339, is worth more than most of the dreary writing on how to construe penal legislation. Again when he said that "the meaning of a sentence is to be felt rather than to be proved," United States *v.* Johnson, 221, U.S. 448, 496, he expressed the wholesome truth that the final rendering of the meaning of a statute is an act of judgment. He would shudder at the thought that by such a statement he was giving comfort to the school of visceral jurisprudence. Judgment is not drawn out of the void but is based on the correlation of imponderables all of which need not, because they cannot, be made explicit. He was expressing the humility of the intellectual that he was, whose standards of exactitude distrusted pretensions of certainty, believing that legal controversies that are not frivolous almost always involve matters of degree, and often degree of the nicest sort. Statutory construction implied the exercise of choice, but precluded the notion of capricious choice as much as choice based on private notions of policy. One gets the impression that in interpreting statutes, Mr. Justice Holmes reached meaning easily, as was true of most of

his results, with emphasis on the language in the totality of the enactment and the felt reasonableness of the chosen construction. He had a lively awareness that a statute was expressive of purpose and policy, but in his reading of it he tended to hug the shores of the statute itself, without much re-enforcement from without.

Mr. Justice Brandeis, on the other hand, in dealing with these problems as with others, would elucidate the judgment he was exercising by proof or detailed argument. In such instances, especially when in dissent, his opinions would draw on the whole arsenal of aids to construction. More often than either Holmes or Cardozo, Brandeis would invoke the additional weight of some "rule" of construction. But he never lost sight of the limited scope and function of such "rules." Occasionally, however, perhaps because of the nature of a particular statute, the minor importance of its incidence, the pressure of judicial business or even the temperament of his law clerk, whom he always treated as a co-worker, Brandeis disposed of a statute even more dogmatically, with less explicit elucidation, than did Holmes.

For Cardozo, statutory construction was an acquired taste. He preferred common law subtleties, having great skill in bending them to modern uses. But he came to realize that problems of statutory construction had their own exciting subtleties and gave ample employment to philosophic and literary talents. Cardozo's elucidation of how meaning is drawn out of a statute gives proof of the wisdom and balance which, combined with his learning, made him a great judge. While the austere style of Brandeis seldom mitigated the dry aspect of so many problems of statutory construction, Cardozo managed to endow even these with the glow and softness of his writing. The differences in the tone and color of their style as well as in the moral intensity of Brandeis and Cardozo made itself felt when they wrote full-dress opinions on problems of statutory construction. Brandeis almost compels by demonstration; Cardozo woos by persuasion.

SCOPE OF THE JUDICIAL FUNCTION

From the hundreds of cases in which our three Justices construed statutes one thing clearly emerges. The area of free judicial movement is considerable. These three remembered that laws are not abstract propositions. They are expressions of policy arising out of specific situations and addressed to the attainment of particular ends. The difficulty is that the legislative ideas which laws embody are both explicit and immanent. And so the bottom problem is: What is below the surface of the words and yet fairly a part of them? Words in statutes are not unlike words in a foreign language in that they too have "associations, echoes, and overtones." (See Sir Ernest Barker's Introduction to his translation of Aristotle's Politics, p. 1xiii.) Judges must retain the associations, hear the echoes, and capture the overtones. In one of his last opinions, dealing with legislation taxing the husband on the basis of the combined income of husband and wife, Holmes wrote: "The statutes are the outcome of a thousand years of history. . . . They form a system with echoes of different moments, none of which is entitled to prevail over the other." Hoeper *v.* Tax Commission, 284 U.S. 206, 219.

What exactions such a duty of construction places upon judges, and with what freedom it entrusts them! John Chipman Gray was fond of quoting from a sermon by Bishop Hoadley that "Whoever hath an *absolute authority* to *interpret* any written or spoken laws, it is he who is truly the law-giver to all intents and purposes, and not the person who first wrote or spoke them." Gray, *Nature and Sources of the Law* (2nd ed. 1921) 102, 125, 172. By admitting that there is some substance to the good Bishop's statement, one does not subscribe to the notion that they are lawgivers in any but a very qualified sense.

Even within their area of choice the courts are not at large. They are confined by the nature and scope of the judicial function in its particular exercise in the field of interpretation. They are under the constraints imposed by the judicial function in our democratic society. As a matter of verbal recognition certainly, no one will gainsay that the function in construing a statute is to ascertain the meaning of words used by the legislature. To go beyond it is to usurp a power which our democracy has lodged in its elected legislature. The great judges have constantly admonished their brethren of the need for discipline in observing the limitations. A judge must not rewrite a statute, neither to enlarge nor to contract it. Whatever temptations the statesmanship of policymaking might wisely suggest, construction must eschew interpolation and evisceration. He must not read in by way of creation. He must not read out except to avoid

patent nonsense or internal contradiction. "If there is no meaning in it," said Alice's King, "that saves a world of trouble, you know, as we needn't try to find any." Legislative words presumably have meaning and so we must try to find it.

This duty of restraint, this humility of function as merely the translator of another's command, is a constant theme of our Justices. It is on the lips of all judges, but seldom, I venture to believe, has the restraint which it expresses, or the duty which it enjoins, been observed with so consistent a realization that its observance depends on self-conscious discipline. Cardozo put it this way: "We do not pause to consider whether a statute differently conceived and framed would yield results more consonant with fairness and reason. We take this statute as we find it." Anderson *v.* Wilson, 289 U.S. 20, 27. It was expressed more fully by Mr. Justice Brandeis when the temptation to give what might be called a more liberal interpretation could not have been wanting.

> The particularization and detail with which the scope of each provision, the amount of the tax thereby imposed, and the incidence of the tax, were specified, preclude an extension of any provision by implication to any other subject. . . . What the Government asks is not a construction of a statute, but, in effect, an enlargement of it by the court, so that what was omitted, presumably by inadvertence, may be included within its scope. (Iselin *v.* United States, 270 U.S. 245, 250-51.)

An omission, at the time of enactment, whether careless or calculated, cannot be judicially supplied however much later wisdom may recommend the inclusion.

The vital difference between initiating policy, often involving a decided break with the past, and merely carrying out a formulated policy, indicates the relatively narrow limits within which choice is fairly open to courts and the extent to which interpreting law is inescapably making law. To say that, because of this restricted field of interpretive declaration, courts make law just as do legislatures is to deny essential features in the history of our democracy. It denies that legislation and adjudication have had different lines of growth, serve vitally different purposes, function under different conditions, and bear different responsibilities. The judicial process of dealing with words is not at all Alice in Wonderland's way of dealing with them. Even in matters legal some words and phrases, though

LEGAL
SCHOLARSHIP

SOME
REFLECTIONS
ON THE READING
OF STATUTES

LEGAL
SCHOLARSHIP

SOME
REFLECTIONS
ON THE READING
OF STATUTES

very few, approach mathematical symbols and mean substantially the same to all who have occasion to use them. Other law terms like "police power" are not symbols at all but labels for the results of the whole process of adjudication. In between lies a gamut of words with different denotations as well as connotations. There are varying shades of compulsion for judges behind different words, differences that are due to the words themselves, their setting in a text, their setting in history. In short, judges are not unfettered glossators. They are under a special duty not to overemphasize the episodic aspects of life and not to undervalue its organic processes—its continuities and relationships. For judges at least it is important to remember that continuity with the past is not only a necessity but even a duty.

There are not wanting those who deem naïve the notion that judges are expected to refrain from legislating in construing statutes. They may point to cases where even our three Justices apparently supplied an omission or engrafted a limitation. Such an accusation cannot be rebutted or judged in the abstract. In some ways, as Holmes once remarked, every statute is unique. Whether a judge does violence to language in its total context is not always free from doubt. Statutes come out of the past and aim at the future. They may carry implicit residues or mere hints of purpose. Perhaps the most delicate aspect of statutory construction is not to find more residues than are implicit nor purposes beyond the bound of hints. Even for a judge most sensitive to the traditional limitation of his function, this is a matter for judgment not always easy of answer. But a line does exist between omission and what Holmes called "misprision or abbreviation that does not conceal the purpose." St. Louis–San Francisco Ry. *v.* Middlekamp, 256 U.S. 226, 232. Judges may differ as to the point at which the line should be drawn, but the only sure safeguard against crossing the line between adjudication and legislation is an alert recognition of the necessity not to cross it and instinctive, as well as trained, reluctance to do so.

In those realms where judges directly formulate law because the chosen lawmakers have not acted, judges have the duty of adaptation and adjustment of old principles to new conditions. But where policy is expressed by the primary lawmaking agency in a democracy, that is by the

legislature, judges must respect such expressions by adding to or subtracting from the explicit terms which the lawmakers used no more than is called for by the shorthand nature of language. Admonitions, like that of Justice Brandeis in the Iselin case, that courts should leave even desirable enlargement to Congress will not by itself furnish the meaning appropriate for the next statute under scrutiny. But as is true of other important principles, the intensity with which it is believed may be decisive of the outcome.

THE PROCESS OF CONSTRUCTION

Let me descend to some particulars.

The Text. Though we may not end with the words in construing a disputed statute, one certainly begins there. You have a right to think that a hoary platitude, but it is a platitude too often not observed at the bar. In any event, it may not take you to the end of the road. The Court no doubt must listen to the voice of Congress. But often Congress cannot be heard clearly because its speech is muffled. Even when it has spoken, it is as true of Congress as of others that what is said is what the listener hears. Like others, judges too listen with what psychologists used to call the apperception mass, which I take it means in plain English that one listens with what is already in one's head. One more caution is relevant when one is admonished to listen attentively to what a statute says. One must also listen attentively to what it does not say.

We must, no doubt, accord the words the sense in which Congress used them. That is only another way of stating the central problem of decoding the symbols. It will help to determine for whom they were meant. Statutes are not archaeological documents to be studied in a library. They are written to guide the actions of men. As Mr. Justice Holmes remarked upon some Indian legislation "The word was addressed to the Indian mind," Fleming *v.* McCurtain, 215 U.S. 56, 60. If a statute is written for ordinary folk, it would be arbitrary not to assume that Congress intended its words to be read with the minds of ordinary men. If they are addressed to specialists, they must be read by judges with the minds of the specialists.

And so we assume that Congress uses common words in their popular meaning, as used in the common speech of men. The cases speak of the "meaning of common understanding," "the normal and spontaneous meaning of language," "the common and appropriate use," "the natural straight-forward and literal sense," and similar variants. In McBoyle *v.* United States, 283 U.S. 25, 26, Mr. Justice Holmes had to decide whether an aeroplane is a "motor vehicle" within the meaning of the Motor Vehicle Theft Act. He thus disposed of it: "No doubt etymologically it is possible to use the word to signify a conveyance working on land, water or air, and sometimes legislation extends the use in that direction. . . . But in everyday speech 'vehicles' calls up a picture of a thing moving on land."

Sometimes Congress supplies its own dictionary. It did so in 1871 in a statute defining a limited number of words for use as to all future enactments. It may do so, as in recent legislation, by a section within the statute containing detailed definitions. Or there may be indications from the statute that words in it are the considered language of legislation. "If Congress has been accustomed to use a certain phrase with a more limited meaning than might be attributed to it by common practice, it would be arbitrary to refuse to consider that fact when we come to interpret a statute. But, as we have said, the usage of Congress simply shows that it has spoken with careful precision, that its words mark the exact spot at which it stops." Boston Sand Co. *v.* United States, 278 U.S. 41, 48. Or words may acquire scope and function from the history of events which they summarize or from the purpose which they serve.

> However colloquial and uncertain the words had been in the beginning, they had won for themselves finally an acceptance and a definiteness that made them fit to play a part in the legislative process. They came into the statute . . . freighted with the meaning imparted to them by the mischief to be remedied and by contemporaneous discussion. . . . In such conditions history is a teacher that is not to be ignored. (*Cardozo,* Duparquet Co. *v.* Evans, 297 U.S. 216, 220-21.)

Words of art bring their art with them. They bear the meaning of their habitat whether it be a phrase or technical significance in the scientific or business world, or whether it be loaded with the recondite connotations of feudalism. Holmes made short shrift of a contention by remarking that statutes used "familiar legal expressions in their familiar legal sense." Henry *v.* United States, 251 U.S. 393, 395. The peculiar idiom of business or of administrative practice often modifies the meaning that ordinary

speech assigns to language. And if a word is obviously transplanted from another legal source, whether the common law or other legislation, it brings the old soil with it.

The Context. Legislation is a form of literary composition. But construction is not an abstract process equally valid for every composition, not even for every composition whose meaning must be judicially ascertained. The nature of the composition demands awareness of certain presuppositions. For instance, the words in a constitution may carry different meanings from the same words in a statute precisely because "it is a constitution we are expounding." The reach of this consideration was indicated by Mr. Justice Holmes in language that remains fresh no matter how often repeated:

> "When we are dealing with words that also are a constituent act, like the Constitution of the United States, we must realize that they have called into life being the development of which could not have been foreseen completely by the most gifted of its begetters. It was enough for them to realize or to hope that they had created an organism; it has taken a century and has cost their successors much sweat and blood to prove that they created a nation. The case before us must be considered in the light of our whole experience and not merely in that of what was said a hundred years ago. (Missouri *v.* Holland, 252 U.S. 416, 433.)

And so, the significance of an enactment, its antecedents as well as its later history, its relation to other enactments, all may be relevant to the construction of words for one purpose and in one setting but not for another. Some words are confined to their history; some are starting points for history. Words are intellectual and moral currency. They come from the legislative mint with some intrinsic meaning. Sometimes it remains unchanged. Like currency, words sometimes appreciate or depreciate in value.

Frequently the sense of a word cannot be got except by fashioning a mosaic of significance out of the innuendoes of disjointed bits of statute. Cardozo phrased this familiar phenomenon by stating that "the meaning of a statute is to be looked for, not in any single section, but in all the parts together and in their relation to the end in view." Panama Refining Co. *v.* Ryan, 293 U.S. 388, 433, 439. And to quote Cardozo once more on this phase of our problem: "There is need to keep in view also the structure of the statute, and the relation, physical and logical,

LEGAL
SCHOLARSHIP

SOME
REFLECTIONS
ON THE READING
OF STATUTES

LEGAL
SCHOLARSHIP

SOME
REFLECTIONS
ON THE READING
OF STATUTES

between its several parts." Duparquet Co. *v.* Evans, 297 U.S. 216, 218.

The generating consideration is that legislation is more than composition. It is an active instrument of government which, for purposes of interpretation, means that laws have ends to be achieved. It is in this connection that Holmes said "words are flexible." International Stevedoring Co. *v.* Haverty, 272 U.S. 50, 58. Again it was Holmes, the last judge to give quarter to loose thinking or vague yearning, who said that "the general purpose is a more important aid to the meaning than any rule which grammar or formal logic may lay down." United States *v.* Whitridge, 197 U.S. 135, 143. And it was Holmes who chided courts for being "apt to err by sticking too closely to the words of a law where those words import a policy that goes beyond them." Olmstead *v.* United States, 277 U.S. 438, 469. Note, however, that he found the policy in "those words"!

PROLIFERATION OF PURPOSE

You may have observed that I have not yet used the word "intention." All these years I have avoided speaking of the "legislative intent" and I shall continue to be on my guard against using it. The objection to "intention" was indicated in a letter by Mr. Justice Holmes which the recipient kindly put at my disposal:

> Only a day or two ago—when counsel talked of the intention of a legislature, I was indiscreet enough to say I don't care what their intention was. I only want to know what the words mean. Of course the phrase often is used to express a conviction not exactly thought out—that you construe a particular clause or expression by considering the whole instrument and any dominant purposes that it may express. In fact intention is a residuary clause intended to gather up whatever other aids there may be to interpretation beside the particular words and the dictionary.

If that is what the term means, it is better to use a less beclouding characterization. Legislation has an aim; it seeks to obviate some mischief, to supply an inadequacy, to effect a change or policy, to formulate a plan of government. That aim, that policy is not drawn, like nitrogen, out of the air; it is evinced in the language of the statute, as read in the light of other external manifestations of purpose. That is what the judge must seek and effectuate, and he ought not be led off the trail by tests that have overtones of subjective design. We are not concerned with anything subjective. We do not delve into

the mind of legislators or their draftsmen, or committee members. Against what he believed to be such an attempt Cardozo once protested:

> The judgment of the court, if I interpret the reasoning aright, does not rest upon a ruling that Congress would have gone beyond its power if the purpose that it professed was the purpose truly cherished. The judgment of the court rests upon the ruling that another purpose, not professed, may be read beneath the surface, and by the purpose so imputed the statute is destroyed. Thus the process of psychoanalysis has spread to unaccustomed fields. There is a wise and ancient doctrine that a court will not inquire into the motives of a legislative body. . . . (United States *v.* Constantine, 269 U.S. 287 at 298-99.)

The difficulty in many instances where a problem of meaning arises is that the enactment was not directed towards the troubling question. The problem might then be stated, as once it was by Mr. Justice Cardozo, "which choice is it the more likely that Congress would have made?" Burnet *v.* Guggenheim, 288 U.S. 280, 285. While in its context the significance and limitations of this question are clear, thus to frame the question too often tempts inquiry into the subjective and might seem to warrant the court in giving answers based on an unmanifested legislative state of mind. But the purpose which a court must effectuate is not that which Congress should have enacted, or would have. It is that which it did enact, however inaptly, because it may fairly be said to be imbedded in the statute, even if a specific manifestation was not thought of, as is often the very reason for casting a statute in very general terms.

Often the purpose or policy that controls is not directly displayed in the particular enactment. Statutes cannot be read intelligently if the eye is closed to considerations evidenced in affiliated statutes, or in the known temper of legislative opinion. Thus, for example, it is not lightly to be presumed that Congress sought to infringe on "very sacred rights." Milwaukee Publishing Co. *v.* Burleson, 255 U.S. 407, 438. This improbability will be a factor in determining whether language, though it should be so read if standing alone, was used to effect such a drastic change.

More frequently still, in the interpretation of recent regulatory statutes, it becomes important to remember that the judicial task in marking out the extent to which Congress has exercised its constitutional power over commerce, is not that of devising an abstract formula. The task is one of accommodation as between assertions of new federal authority and historic functions of the individual States. Federal legislation of this character cannot therefore be construed without regard to the implications of our dual system of government. In such cases, for example, it is not to be assumed as a matter of course that when Congress adopts a new scheme for federal industrial regulation, it deals with all situations falling within the general mischief which gave rise to the legislation. The underlying assumptions of our dual form of government, and the consequent presuppositions of legislative draftsmanship which are expressive of our history and habits, cut across what might otherwise be the implied range of legislation. The history of congressional legislation regulating not only interstate commerce as such but also activities intertwined with it, justify the generalization that, when the federal government takes over such local radiations in the vast network of our national economic enterprise and thereby radically readjusts the balance of State and national authority, those charged with the duty of legislating are reasonably explicit and do not entrust its attainment to that retrospective expansion of meaning which properly deserves the stigma of judicial legislation.

SEARCH FOR PURPOSE

How then does the purpose which a statute expresses reveal itself, particularly when the path of purpose is not straight and narrow? The English courts say: look at the statute and look at nothing else. Lord Reading so advised the House of Lords when a bill was before it as to which the Attorney General had given an interpretative explanation during its passage in the House of Commons:

> Neither the words of the Attorney General nor the words of an ex-Lord Chancellor, spoken in this House, as to the meaning intended to be given to language used in a Bill, have the slightest effect or relevance when the matter comes to be considered by a Court of Law. The one thing which stands out beyond all question is that in a Court of Law you are not allowed to introduce observations made either by the Government or by anybody else, but the Court will only give consideration to the Statute itself. That is elementary, but I think it is necessary to bring it home to your Lordships because I think too much importance can be attached to language which fell from the Attorney-General. (94 Parl. Deb. 5th Series, Lords, col. 232, Nov. 8, 1934.)

How narrowly the English courts confine their search for understanding an English enactment is vividly illustrated by the pronouncements of Lord Haldane, surely one of the most broadminded of all modern judges.

> My Lords, (*Viscountess Rhondda's Claim*, [1922] 2 A. C. 339 at 383) the only other point made on the construction of the Act was that this Committee might be entitled to look at what passed while the Bill was still a Bill and in the Committee stage in the House. It was said that there amendments were moved and discussions took place which indicated that the general words of s. 1 were not regarded by your Lordships' House as covering the title to a seat in it. But even assuming that to be certain, I do not think, sitting as we do with the obligation to administer the principles of the law, that we have the least right to look at what happened while the Bill was being discussed in Committee and before the Act was passed. Decisions of the highest authority show that the interpretation of an Act of Parliament must be collected from the words in which the Sovereign has made into law the words agreed upon by both Houses. The history of previous changes made or discussed cannot be taken to have been known or to have been in view when the Royal assent was given. The contrary was suggested at the Bar, though I do not think the point was pressed, and I hope that it will not be thought that in its decision this Committee has given any countenance to it. To have done so would, I venture to say, have been to introduce confusion into well-settled law. In Millar *v.* Taylor the principle of construction was laid down in words, which have never, so far as I know, been seriously challenged, by Willes J. as long ago as in 1769: "The sense and meaning of an Act of Parliament must be collected from what it says when passed into a law; and not from the history of changes it underwent in the house where it took its rise. That history is not known to the other house or to the sovereign."

These current English rules of construction are simple. They are too simple. If the purpose of construction is the ascertainment of meaning, nothing that is logically relevant should be excluded. The rigidity of English courts in interpreting language merely by reading it disregards the fact that enactments are, as it were, organisms which exist in their environment. One wonders whether English judges are confined psychologically as they purport to be legally. The judges deem themselves limited to reading the words of a statute. But can they really escape placing the words in the context of their minds,

LEGAL
SCHOLARSHIP

SOME
REFLECTIONS
ON THE READING
OF STATUTES

which after all are not automata applying legal logic but repositories of all sorts of assumptions and impressions? Such a modest if not mechanical view of the task of construction disregards legal history. In earlier centuries the judges recognized that the exercise of their judicial function to understand and apply legislative policy is not to be hindered by artificial canons and limitations. The well-known resolutions in Heydon's Case, 3 Co. Rep. 7a, have the flavor of Elizabethan English but they express the substance of a current volume of U.S. Reports as to the considerations relevant to statutory interpretation. To be sure, early English legislation helped ascertainment of purpose by explicit recitals; at least to the extent of defining the mischief against which the enactment was directed. To take a random instance, an act in the reign of Edward VI reads: "'Forasmuch as intolerable Hurts and Troubles to the Commonwealth of this Realm doth daily grow and increase through such Abuses and Disorders as are had and used in common Alehouses and other Houses called Tipling houses': (2) it is therefore enacted by the King our Sovereign Lord, etc." 6 Edward VI c. 25 (1552); 2 Stats. at Large 458. Judicial construction certainly became more artificial after the practice of elucidating recitals ceased. It is to be noted that Macaulay, a great legislative draftsman, did not think much of preambles. He believed that too often they are jejune because legislators may agree on what ought to be done, while disagreeing about the reasons for doing it. At the same time he deemed it most important that in some manner governments should give reasons for their legislative course. (See Lord Macaulay's Legislative Minutes (ed. by C. D. Dharker) pp. 145 et seq.) When not so long ago the Parliamentary mechanism was under scrutiny of the Lord Chancellor's Committee, dissatisfaction was expressed with the prevailing practice of English courts not to go outside the statutes. It was urged that the old practice of preambles be restored or that a memorandum of explanation go with proposed legislation. (See Professor Laski's Note to the Report of the Committee on Ministers' Powers, Cmd. 4060, Annex V, p. 135, 1932.)

At the beginning, the Supreme Court reflected the early English attitude. With characteristic hardheadedness Chief Justice Marshall struck at the core of the matter with the observation "Where the mind labours to discover the design of the legislature, it seizes everything from

which aid can be derived." United States *v.* Fisher, 2 Cranch 358, 386. This commonsensical way of dealing with statutes fell into disuse, and more or less catchpenny canons of construction did service instead. To no small degree a more wooden treatment of legislation was due, I suspect, to the fact that the need for keeping vividly in mind the occasions for drawing on all aids in the process of distilling meaning from legislation was comparatively limited. As the area of regulation steadily widened, the impact of the legislative process upon the judicial brought into being, and compelled consideration of, all that convincingly illumines an enactment, instead of merely that which is called, with delusive simplicity, "the end result." Legislatures themselves provided illumination by general definitions, special definitions, explicit recitals of policy, and even directions of attitudes appropriate for judicial construction. Legislative reports were increasingly drawn upon, statements by those in charge of legislation, reports of investigating committees, recommendations of agencies entrusted with the enforcement of laws, etc., etc. When Mr. Justice Holmes came to the Court, the U.S. Reports were practically barren of references to legislative materials. These swarm in current volumes. And let me say in passing that the importance that such materials play in Supreme Court litigation carry far-reaching implications for bench and bar.

The change I have summarized was gradual. Undue limitations were applied even after Courts broke out of the mere language of a law. We find Mr. Justice Holmes saying, "It is a delicate business to base speculations about the purposes or construction of a statute upon the vicissitudes of its passage." Pine Hill Co. *v.* United States 259 U.S. 191, 196. And as late as 1925 he referred to earlier bills relating to a statute under review, with the reservation "If it be legitimate to look at them." Davis *v.* Pringle, 268 U.S. 315, 318.

Such hesitations and restraints are in limbo. Courts examine the forms rejected in favor of the words chosen. They look at later statutes "considered to throw a cross light" upon an earlier enactment. See United States *v.* Aluminum Co. Of America, 148 F. 2d. 416, 429. The consistent construction by an administrative agency charged with effectuating the policy of an enactment carries very considerable weight. While assertion of authority does not demonstrate its existence, long-continued, uncontested assertion is at least evidence that the legislature conveyed the authority. Similarly, while authority conferred does not atrophy by disuse, failure over an extended period to exercise it is some proof that it was not given. And since "a page of history is worth a volume of logic," N.Y. Trust Co. *v.* Eisner, 256 U.S. 345, 349, courts have looked into the background of statutes, the mischief to be checked and the good that was designed, looking sometimes far afield and taking notice also as judges of what is generally known by men.

Unhappily, there is no table of logarithms for statutory construction. No item of evidence has a fixed or even average weight. One or another may be decisive in one set of circumstances, while of little value elsewhere. A painstaking, detailed report by a Senate Committee bearing directly on the immediate question may settle the matter. A loose statement even by a chairman of a committee, made impromptu in the heat of debate, less informing in cold type than when heard on the floor, will hardly be accorded the weight of an encyclical.

Spurious use of legislative history must not swallow the legislation so as to give point to the quip that only when legislative history is doubtful do you go to the statute. While courts are no longer confined to the language, they are still confined by it. Violence must not be done to the words chosen by the legislature. Unless indeed no doubt can be left that the legislature has in fact used a private code, so that what appears to be violence to language is merely respect to special usage. In the end, language and external aids, each accorded the authority deserved in the circumstances, must be weighed in the balance of judicial judgment. Only if its premises are emptied of their human variables, can the process of statutory construction have the precision of a syllogism. We cannot avoid what Mr. Justice Cardozo deemed inherent in the problem of construction, making "a choice between uncertainties. We must be content to choose the lesser." Burnet *v.* Guggenheim, 288 U.S. 280, 288. But to the careful and disinterested eye, the scales will hardly escape appearing to tip slightly on the side of a more probable meaning.

CANONS OF CONSTRUCTION

Nor can canons of construction save us from the anguish of judgment. Such canons give an air of abstract intellectual compulsion to what is in fact a delicate judgment, concluding a complicated process of balancing subtle and elusive elements. All our three Justices have at one time or another leaned on the crutch of a canon. But they have done so only rarely, and with a recognition that these rules of construction are not in any true sense rules of law. So far as valid, they are what Mr. Justice Holmes called them, axioms of experience. See Boston Sand Co. *v.* United States, 278 U.S. 41, 48. In many instances, these canons originated as observations in specific cases from which they were abstracted, taken out of the context of actuality, and, as it were, codified in treatises. We owe the first known systematic discussion of statutory interpretation in England to the scholarship of Professor Samuel T. Thorne, Yale's Law Librarian. According to Professor Thorne, it was written probably prior to 1567. The latest American treatise on the subject was published in 1943. It is not unfair to say that in the four intervening centuries not much new wisdom has been garnered. But there has been an enormous quantitative difference in expounding the wisdom. "A Discourse upon the Exposicion & Understandinge of Statutes" is a charming essay of not more than thirty pages. Not even the freest use of words would describe as charming the latest edition of Sutherland's Statutory Construction, with its three volumes of more than 1500 pages.

Insofar as canons of construction are generalizations of experience, they all have worth. In the abstract, they rarely arouse controversy. Difficulties emerge when canons compete in soliciting judgment, because they conflict rather than converge. For the demands of judgment underlying the art of interpretation, there is no vade-mecum.

But even generalized restatements from time to time may not be wholly wasteful. Out of them may come a sharper rephrasing of the conscious factors of interpretation; new instances may make them more vivid but also disclose more clearly their limitations. Thereby we may avoid rigidities which, while they afford more precise formulas, do so at the price of cramping the life of law. To strip the task of judicial reading of statutes of rules that partake of the mysteries of a craft serves to reveal the true elements of our problem. It defines more accurately the nature of the intellectual responsibility of a judge and thereby subjects him to more relevant criteria of criticism. Rigorous analysis also sharpens the

LEGAL
SCHOLARSHIP

SOME
REFLECTIONS
ON THE READING
OF STATUTES

LEGAL
SCHOLARSHIP

SOME
REFLECTIONS
ON THE READING
OF STATUTES

respective duties of legislature and courts in relation to the making of laws and to their enforcement.

FAIR CONSTRUCTION AND FIT LEGISLATION

The quality of legislative organization and procedure is inevitably reflected in the quality of legislative draftsmanship. Representative Monroney told the House last July that "95 percent of all the legislation that becomes law passes the Congress in the shape that it came from our committees. Therefore if our committee work is sloppy, if it is bad, if it is inadequate, our legislation in 95 percent of the cases will be bad and inadequate as well." And Representative Lane added that "In the second session of the 78th Congress 953 bills and resolutions were passed, of which only 86 were subject to any real discussion." See 92 Cong. Rec. pp. 10040 and 10054, July 25, 1946. But what courts do with legislation may in turn deeply affect what Congress will do in the future. Emerson says somewhere that mankind is as lazy as it dares to be. Loose judicial reading makes for loose legislative writing. It encourages the practise illustrated in a recent cartoon in which a senator tells his colleagues "I admit this new bill is too complicated to understand. We'll just have to pass it to find out what it means." A modern Pascal might be tempted at times to say of legislation what Pascal said of students of theology when he charged them with "a looseness of thought and language that would pass nowhere else in making what are professedly very fine distinctions." And it is conceivable that he might go on and speak, as did Pascal, of the "insincerity with which terms are carefully chosen to cover oppo-

site meanings." See Pater, *Miscellaneous Studies*, "Essay on Pascal," pp. 48, 51.

But there are more fundamental objections to loose judicial reading. In a democracy the legislative impulse and its expression should come from those popularly chosen to legislate, and equipped to devise policy, as courts are not. The pressure on legislatures to discharge their responsibility with care, understanding and imagination should be stiffened, not relaxed. Above all, they must not be encouraged in irresponsible or undisciplined use of language. In the keeping of legislatures perhaps more than of any other group is the well-being of their fellow-men. Their responsibility is discharged ultimately by words. They are under a special duty therefore to observe that "Exactness in the use of words is the basis of all serious thinking. You will get nowhere without it. Words are clumsy tools, and it is very easy to cut one's fingers with them, and they need the closest attention in handling; but they are the only tools we have, and imagination itself cannot work without them. You must master the use of them, or you will wander forever guessing at the mercy of mere impulse and unrecognized assumptions and arbitrary associations, carried away with every wind of doctrine." (See J. W. Allen's "Essay on Jeremy Bentham," in *The Social and Political Ideals of the Revolutionary Era* (ed. by Hearnshaw), pp. 181, 199.)

Perfection of draftsmanship is as unattainable as demonstrable correctness of judicial reading of legislation. Fit legislation and fair adjudication are attainable. The ultimate reliance of society for the proper fulfilment of both these august functions is to entrust them only to those who are equal to their demands.

LEGAL MISCELLANY

PRESIDENTS AND VICE
PRESIDENTS OF THE UNITED
STATES

PRESIDENTIAL NOMINATIONS TO
THE SUPREME COURT

TIME CHART OF THE SUPREME
COURT

SUCCESSION OF SUPREME
COURT JUSTICES

U.S. ATTORNEYS GENERAL

CONGRESSIONAL TIMELINE:
NINETEENTH CENTURY

CONGRESSIONAL TIMELINE:
TWENTIETH AND TWENTY-FIRST
CENTURIES

BRITISH REGNAL YEARS

LEGAL MISCELLANY

This section contains a diverse collection of legal, political, and historical information, most of which is organized in tabular form and in chronological order.

The tables provide readers with precise dates of the reigns of British monarchs and the terms of service of U.S. Supreme Court justices, presidents, vice presidents, and attorneys general. Readers may, for example, consult the succession of Supreme Court justices to determine which justices were on the Court when a major case was decided.

Using a chronological sequence, the congressional timeline links pertinent information about the House of Representatives and the Senate (size, political parties, procedural matters) with major court cases, laws, and investigations. Wars, presidential eras, and developments in science, technology, and communications are included as well.

The following tables are included:

- Presidents and Vice Presidents of the United States
- Presidential Nominations to the Supreme Court
- Time Chart of the Supreme Court
- Succession of Supreme Court Justices
- U.S. Attorneys General
- Congressional Timeline: Nineteenth Century
- Congressional Timeline: Twentieth Century
- British Regnal Years

Presidents and Vice Presidents of the United States

President	Service			Vice President		Congress
1 George Washington, F	April 30, 1789	to	March 3, 1797	1 John Adams		1, 2, 3, 4
2 John Adams, F	March 4, 1797		March 3, 1801	2 Thomas Jefferson		5, 6
3 Thomas Jefferson, D-R	March 4, 1801		March 3, 1805	3 Aaron Burr		7, 8
Thomas Jefferson, D-R	March 4, 1805		March 3, 1809	4 George Clinton		9, 10
4 James Madison, D-R	March 4, 1809		March 3, 1813	George Clinton		11, 12
James Madison, D-R	March 4, 1813		March 3, 1817	5 Elbridge Gerry		13, 14
5 James Monroe, D-R	March 4, 1817		March 3, 1825	6 Daniel D. Tompkins		15, 16, 17, 18
6 John Quincy Adams, D-R	March 4, 1825		March 3, 1829	7 John C. Calhoun		19, 20
7 Andrew Jackson, D	March 4, 1829		March 3, 1833	John C. Calhoun		21, 22
Andrew Jackson, D	March 4, 1833		March 3, 1837	8 Martin Van Buren		23, 24
8 Martin Van Buren, D	March 4, 1837		March 3, 1841	9 Richard M. Johnson		25, 26
9 William Henry Harrison[a], W	March 4, 1841		April 4, 1841	10 John Tyler		27
10 John Tyler, W	April 6, 1841		March 3, 1845			27, 28
11 James K. Polk, D	March 4, 1845		March 3, 1849	11 George M. Dallas		29, 30
12 Zachary Taylor[a], W	March 5, 1849		July 9, 1850	12 Millard Fillmore		31
13 Millard Fillmore, W	July 10, 1850		March 3, 1853			31, 32
14 Franklin Pierce, D	March 4, 1853		March 3, 1857	13 William R. King		33, 34
15 James Buchanan, D	March 4, 1857		March 3, 1861	14 John C. Breckinridge		35, 36
16 Abraham Lincoln, R	March 4, 1861		March 3, 1865	15 Hannibal Hamlin		37, 38
Abraham Lincoln[a], R	March 4, 1865		April 15, 1865	16 Andrew Johnson		39
17 Andrew Johnson, R	April 15, 1865		March 3, 1869			39, 40
18 Ulysses S. Grant, R	March 4, 1869		March 3, 1873	17 Schuyler Colfax		41, 42
Ulysses S. Grant, R	March 4, 1873		March 3, 1877	18 Henry Wilson		43, 44
19 Rutherford B. Hayes, R	March 4, 1877		March 3, 1881	19 William A. Wheeler		45, 46
20 James A. Garfield[a], R	March 4, 1881		September 19, 1881	20 Chester A. Arthur		47
21 Chester A. Arthur, R	September 20, 1881		March 3, 1885			47, 48
22 Grover Cleveland, D	March 4, 1885		March 3, 1889	21 Thomas A. Hendricks		49, 50
23 Benjamin Harrison, R	March 4, 1889		March 3, 1893	22 Levi P. Morton		51, 52
24 Grover Cleveland, D	March 4, 1893		March 3, 1897	23 Adlai E. Stevenson		53, 54
25 William McKinley, R	March 4, 1897		March 3, 1901	24 Garret A. Hobart		55, 56
William McKinley[a], R	March 4, 1901		September 14, 1901	25 Theodore Roosevelt		57
26 Theodore Roosevelt, R	September 14, 1901		March 3, 1905			57, 58
Theodore Roosevelt, R	March 4, 1905		March 3, 1909	26 Charles W. Fairbanks		59, 60
27 William H. Taft, R	March 4, 1909		March 3, 1913	27 James S. Sherman		61, 62
28 Woodrow Wilson, D	March 4, 1913		March 3, 1921	28 Thomas R. Marshall		63, 64, 65, 66
29 Warren G. Harding[a], R	March 4, 1921		August 2, 1923	29 Calvin Coolidge		67
30 Calvin Coolidge, R	August 3, 1923		March 3, 1925			68
Calvin Coolidge, R	March 4, 1925		March 3, 1929	30 Charles G. Dawes		69, 70
31 Herbert C. Hoover, R	March 4, 1929		March 3, 1933	31 Charles Curtis		71, 72
32 Franklin D. Roosevelt[b], D	March 4, 1933		January 20, 1941	32 John N. Garner		73, 74, 75, 76
Franklin D. Roosevelt, D	January 20, 1941		January 20, 1945	33 Henry A. Wallace		77, 78
Franklin D. Roosevelt[a], D	January 20, 1945		April 12, 1945	34 Harry S. Truman		79
33 Harry S. Truman, D	April 12, 1945		January 20, 1949			79, 80
Harry S. Truman, D	January 20, 1949		January 20, 1953	35 Alben W. Barkley		81, 82
34 Dwight D. Eisenhower, R	January 20, 1953		January 20, 1961	36 Richard M. Nixon		83, 84, 85, 86
35 John F. Kennedy[a], D	January 20, 1961		November 22, 1963	37 Lyndon B. Johnson		87, 88
36 Lyndon B. Johnson, D	November 22, 1963		January 20, 1965			88
Lyndon B. Johnson, D	January 20, 1965		January 20, 1969	38 Hubert H. Humphrey		89, 90
37 Richard M. Nixon, R	January 20, 1969		January 20, 1973	39 Spiro T. Agnew		91, 92, 93
Richard M. Nixon[c], R	January 20, 1973		August 9, 1974	40 Gerald R. Ford[d]		93
38 Gerald R. Ford[e], R	August 9, 1974		January 20, 1977	41 Nelson A. Rockefeller		93, 94
39 Jimmy Carter, D	January 20, 1977		January 20, 1981	42 Walter F. Mondale		95, 96
40 Ronald Reagan, R	January 20, 1981		January 20, 1989	43 George H. W. Bush		97, 98, 99, 100
41 George H. W. Bush, R	January 20, 1989		January 20, 1993	44 Dan Quayle		101, 102
42 Bill Clinton, D	January 20, 1993		January 20, 2001	45 Al Gore		103, 104, 105, 106
43 George W. Bush, R	January 20, 2001			46 Dick Cheney		107, 108

[a]Died in office.
[b]First president to be inaugurated under 20th Amendment, Jan. 20, 1937.
[c]Resigned Aug. 9, 1974.
[d]First nonelected vice president, chosen under 25th Amendment procedure.
[e]First nonelected president.
Party affiliation follows each president's name. F = Federalist, D-R = Democratic-Republican, D = Democrat, W = Whig, R = Republican.

SOURCE: *The World Almanac 1997*, White House web page, and U.S. House of Representatives web page.

Presidential Nominations to the Supreme Court

The following table shows the presidents who nominated the various Supreme Court justices and the states from which the justices were appointed. The names of chief justices are followed by an asterisk.

President	Nominee	Year Nominated
George Washington	John Jay (N.Y.)*	1789
	John Rutledge (S.C.)	1789
	William Cushing (Mass.)	1789
	James Wilson (Pa.)	1789
	Robert H. Harrison (Md.)[a]	1789
	John Blair (Va.)	1789
	James Iredell (N.C.)	1790
	Thomas Johnson (Md.)	1791
	William Paterson (N.J.)	1793
	John Rutledge (S.C)*[b]	1795
	Samuel Chase (Md.)	1796
	Oliver Ellsworth (Conn.)*	1796
John Adams	Bushrod Washington (Va.)	1798
	Alfred Moore (N.C.)	1799
	John Marshall (Va.)*	1801
Thomas Jefferson	William Johnson (S.C.)	1804
	Henry Brockholst Livingston (N.Y.)	1806
	Thomas Todd (Ky.)	1807
James Madison	Joseph Story (Mass.)	1811
	Gabriel Duvall (Md.)	1811
James Monroe	Smith Thomson (N.Y.)	1823
John Quincy Adams	Robert Trimble (Ky.)	1826
Andrew Jackson	John McLean (Ohio)	1829
	Henry Baldwin (Pa.)	1830
	James M. Wayne (Ga.)	1835
	Roger B. Taney (Md.)*	1836
	Philip B. Barbour (Va.)	1836
	John Catron (Tenn.)	1837
Martin Van Buren	John McKinley (Ala.)	1837
	Peter V. Daniel (Va.)	1841
John Tyler	Samuel Nelson (N.Y.)	1845
James Polk	Levi Woodbury (N.H.)	1845
	Robert C. Grier (Pa.)	1846
Millard Fillmore	Benjamin R. Curtis (Mass.)	1851
Franklin Pierce	John A. Campbell (Ala.)	1853
James Buchanan	Nathan Clifford (Me.)	1858
Abraham Lincoln	Noah H. Swayne (Ohio)	1862
	Samuel F. Miller (Iowa)	1862
	David Davis (Ill.)	1862
	Stephen J. Field (Calif.)	1863
	Salmon P. Chase (Ohio)*	1864
Ulysses S. Grant	William Strong (Pa.)	1870
	Joseph P. Bradley (N.J.)	1870
	Ward Hunt (N.Y.)	1873
	Morrison R. Waite (Ohio)*	1874
Rutherford Hayes	John M. Harlan (Ky.)	1877
	William B. Woods (Ga.)	1881
James Garfield	Stanley Matthews (Ohio)	1881
Chester Arthur	Horace Gray (Mass.)	1882
	Samuel Blatchford (N.Y.)	1882
Grover Cleveland	Lucius Q. C. Lamar (Miss.)	1888
	Melville W. Fuller (Ill.)*	1888
Benjamin Harrison	David J. Brewer (Kan.)	1889
	Henry B. Brown (Mich.)	1891
	George Shiras Jr. (Pa.)	1892
	Howell E. Jackson (Tenn.)	1893
Grover Cleveland	Edward D. White (La.)	1894
	Rufus W. Peckham (N.Y.)	1895
William McKinley	Joseph McKenna (Calif.)	1898

[continued]

[a]Declined appointment.
[b]Accepted appointment but delayed taking his seat and later resigned.

Presidential Nominations to the Supreme Court

The following table shows the presidents who nominated the various Supreme Court justices and the states from which the justices were appointed. The names of chief justices are followed by an asterisk.

President	Nominee	Year Nominated
Theodore Roosevelt	Oliver Wendell Holmes Jr. (Mass.)	1902
	William R. Day (Ohio)	1903
	William H. Moody (Mass.)	1906
William Taft	Horace H. Lurton (Tenn.)	1910
	Edward D. White (La.)*	1910
	Charles E. Hughes (N.Y.)	1910
	Willis Van Devanter (Wyo.)	1911
	Joseph R. Lamar (Ga.)	1911
	Mahlon Pitney (N.J.)	1912
Woodrow Wilson	James C. McReynolds (Tenn.)	1914
	Louis D. Brandeis (Mass.)	1916
	John H. Clarke (Ohio)	1916
Warren Harding	William H. Taft (Conn.)*	1921
	George Sutherland (Utah)	1922
	Pierce Butler (Minn.)	1922
	Edward T. Sanford (Tenn.)	1923
Calvin Coolidge	Harlan F. Stone (N.Y.)	1925
Herbert Hoover	Charles E. Hughes (N.Y.)*	1930
	Owen J. Roberts (Pa.)	1930
	Benjamin N. Cardozo (N.Y.)	1932
Franklin D. Roosevelt	Hugo L. Black (Ala.)	1937
	Stanley F. Reed (Ky.)	1938
	Felix Frankfurter (Mass.)	1939
	William O. Douglas (Conn.)	1939
	Frank Murphy (Mich.)	1940
	Harlan F. Stone (N.Y.)*	1941
	James F. Byrnes (S.C.)	1941
	Robert H. Jackson (N.Y.)	1941
	Wiley B. Rutledge (Iowa)	1943
Harry S. Truman	Harold H. Burton (Ohio)	1945
	Fred M. Vinson (Ky.)*	1946
	Tom C. Clark (Tex.)	1946
	Sherman Minton (Ind.)	1949
Dwight D. Eisenhower	Earl Warren (Calif.)*	1953
	John M. Harlan (N.Y.)	1955
	William J. Brennan Jr. (Ind.)	1956
	Charles E. Whittaker (Mo.)	1957
	Potter Stewart (Ohio)	1958
John F. Kennedy	Byron R. White (Colo.)	1962
	Arthur J. Goldberg (Ill.)	1962
Lyndon B. Johnson	Abe Fortas (Tenn.)	1965
	Thurgood Marshall (N.Y.)	1967
Richard M. Nixon	Warren Earl Burger (Minn.)*	1969
	Harry A. Blackmun (Minn.)	1970
	Lewis F. Powell (Va.)	1971
	William H. Rehnquist (Ariz.)	1971
Gerald Ford	John Paul Stevens (Ill.)	1976
Ronald Reagan	Sandra Day O'Conner (Ariz.)	1981
	William H. Rehnquist (Ariz.)*	1986
	Antonin Scalia (Va.)	1986
	Anthony M. Kennedy (Calif.)	1988
George H. W. Bush	David H. Souter (N.H.)	1990
	Clarence Thomas (Va.)	1991
Bill Clinton	Ruth Bader Ginsburg (D.C.)	1993
	Stephen Breyer (Mass.)	1994

Time Chart of the Supreme Court

This table is designed to aid the user in identifying the composition of the Supreme Court at any given time in U.S. history. Each listing is headed by the chief justice, whose name is italicized. Associate justices are listed following the chief justice in order of seniority. The name of each justice is followed by a symbol representing his or her party affiliation at the time of appointment.

F = Federalist
DR = Democratic-Republican (Jeffersonian)
D = Democrat

W = Whig
R = Republican
I = Independent

1789	1790–91	1792	1793–94	1795	1796–97	1798–99
Jay (F)	*Jay* (F)	*Jay* (F)	*Jay* (F)	*J. Rutledge* (F)[a]	*Ellsworth* (F)	*Ellsworth* (F)
J. Rutledge (F)	J. Rutledge (F)	Cushing (F)	Cushing (F)	Cushing (F)	Cushing (F)	Cushing (F)
Cushing (F)	Cushing (F)	Wilson (F)	Wilson (F)	Wilson (F)	Wilson (F)	Iredell (F)
Wilson (F)	Wilson (F)	Blair (F)	Blair (F)	Blair (F)	Iredell (F)	Paterson (F)
Blair (F)	Blair (F)	Iredell (F)	Iredell (F)	Iredell (F)	Paterson (F)	S. Chase (F)
	Iredell (F)	T. Johnson (F)	Paterson (F)	Paterson (F)	S. Chase (F)	Washington (F)

1823–25	1811–22	1807–10	1806	1804–05	1801–03	1800
J. Marshall (F)	*J. Marshall* (F)	*J. Marshall* (F)	*J. Marshall* (F)	*J. Marshall* (F)	*J. Marshall* (F)	*Ellsworth* (F)
Washington (F)	Washington (F)	Cushing (F)	Cushing (F)	Cushing (F)	Cushing (F)	Cushing (F)
W. Johnson (DR)	W. Johnson (DR)	S. Chase (F)	S. Chase (F)	Paterson (F)	Paterson (F)	Paterson (F)
Todd (DR)	Livingston (DR)	Washington (F)	Washington (F)	S. Chase (F)	S. Chase (F)	S. Chase (F)
Duval (DR)	Todd (DR)	W. Johnson (DR)	W. Johnson (DR)	Washington (F)	Washington (F)	Washington (F)
Story (DR)	Duval (DR)	Livingston (DR)	Livingston (DR)	W. Johnson (DR)	Moore (F)	Moore (F)
Thompson (DR)	Story (DR)	Todd (DR)				

1826–28	1829	1830–34	1835	1836	1837–40	1841–43
J. Marshall (F)	*J. Marshall* (F)	*J. Marshall* (F)	*J. Marshall* (F)	*Taney* (D)	*Taney* (D)	*Taney* (D)
Washington (F)	Washington (F)	W. Johnson (DR)	Duval (DR)	Story (DR)	Story (DR)	Story (DR)
W. Johnson (DR)	W. Johnson (DR)	Duval (DR)	Story (DR)	Thompson (DR)	Thompson (DR)	Thompson (DR)
Duval (DR)	Duval (DR)	Story (DR)	Thompson (DR)	McLean (D)	McLean (D)	McLean (D)
Story (DR)	Story (DR)	Thompson (DR)	McLean (D)	Baldwin (D)	Baldwin (D)	Baldwin (D)
Thompson (DR)	Thompson (DR)	McLean (D)	Baldwin (D)	Wayne (D)	Wayne (D)	Wayne (D)
Trimble (DR)	McLean (D)	Baldwin (D)	Wayne (D)	Barbour (D)	Barbour (D)	Catron (D)
					Catron (D)	McKinley (D)
					McKinley (D)	Daniel (D)

1861	1858–60	1853–57	1851–52	1846–50	1845	1844
Taney (D)	*Taney* (D)	*Taney* (D)	*Taney* (D)	*Taney* (D)	*Taney* (D)	*Taney* (D)
McLean (D)	McLean (D)	McLean (D)	McLean (D)	McLean (D)	McLean (D)	Story (DR)
Wayne (D)	Wayne (D)	Wayne (D)	Wayne (D)	Wayne (D)	Wayne (D)	McLean (D)
Catron (D)	Catron (D)	Catron (D)	Catron (D)	Catron (D)	Catron (D)	Baldwin (D)
Nelson (D)	Daniel (D)	Daniel (D)	McKinley (D)	McKinley (D)	McKinley (D)	Wayne (D)
Grier (D)	Nelson (D)	Nelson (D)	Daniel (D)	Daniel (D)	Daniel (D)	Catron (D)
Campbell (D)	Grier (D)	Grier (D)	Nelson (D)	Nelson (D)	Nelson (D)	McKinley (D)
Clifford (D)	Campbell (D)	Curtis (W)	Grier (D)	Woodbury (D)	Woodbury (D)	Daniel (D)
	Clifford (D)	Campbell (D)	Curtis (W)	Grier (D)		

1862	1863	1864–65	1866	1867–69	1870–71	1872–73
Taney (D)	*Taney* (D)	*S. P. Chase* (R)	*S. P. Chase* (R)	*S. P. Chase* (R)	*S. P. Chase* (R)	*S. P. Chase* (R)
Wayne (D)	Wayne (D)	Wayne (D)	Wayne (D)[b]	Nelson (D)	Nelson (D)	Clifford (D)
Catron (D)	Catron (D)	Catron (D)[b]	Nelson (D)	Grier (D)	Clifford (D)	Swayne (R)
Nelson (D)	Nelson (D)	Nelson (D)	Grier (D)	Clifford (D)	Swayne (R)	Miller (R)
Grier (D)	Grier (D)	Grier (D)	Clifford (D)	Swayne (R)	Miller (R)	Davis (R)
Clifford (D)	Clifford (D)	Clifford (D)	Swayne (R)	Miller (R)	Davis (R)	Field (D)
Swayne (R)	Swayne (R)	Swayne (R)	Miller (R)	Davis (R)	Field (D)	Strong (R)
Miller (R)	Miller (R)	Miller (R)	Davis (R)	Field (D)	Strong (R)	Bradley (R)
Davis (R)	Davis (R)	Davis (R)	Field (D)		Bradley (R)	Hunt (R)
	Field (D)	Field (D)				

[continued]

[a]Rutledge was a recess appointment whose confirmation was rejected by the Senate after the 1795 term.
[b]Upon the death of Catron in 1865 and Wayne in 1867, their positions were abolished according to a congressional act of 1866. The Court's membership was reduced to eight until a new position was created by Congress in 1869. The new seat has generally been regarded as a re-creation of Wayne's set.

Time Chart of the Supreme Court

This table is designed to aid the user in identifying the composition of the Supreme Court at any given time in U.S. history. Each listing is headed by the chief justice, whose name is italicized. Associate justices are listed following the chief justice in order of seniority. The name of each justice is followed by a symbol representing his or her party affiliation at the time of appointment.

F = Federalist
DR = Democratic-Republican (Jeffersonian)
D = Democrat

W = Whig
R = Republican
I = Independent

1889	1888	1882–87	1881	1880	1877–79	1874–76
Fuller (D)	*Fuller* (D)	*Waite* (R)	*Waite* (R)	*Waite* (R)	*Waite* (R)	*Waite* (R)
Miller (R)	Miller (R)	Miller (R)	Miller (R)	Clifford (D)	Clifford (D)	Clifford (D)
Field (D)	Field (D)	Field (D)	Field (D)	Swayne (R)	Swayne (R)	Swayne (R)
Bradley (R)	Bradley (R)	Bradley (R)	Bradley (R)	Miller (R)	Miller (R)	Miller (R)
Harlan (Ky.) (R)	Harlan (Ky.) (R)	Harlan (Ky.) (R)	Hunt (R)	Field (D)	Field (D)	Davis (R)
Gray (R)	Matthews (R)	Woods (R)	Harlan (Ky.) (R)	Bradley (R)	Strong (R)	Field (D)
Blatchford (R)	Gray (R)	Matthews (R)	Woods (R)	Hunt (R)	Bradley (R)	Strong (R)
L. Lamar (D)	Blatchford (R)	Gray (R)	Matthews (R)	Harlan (Ky.) (R)	Hunt (R)	Bradley (R)
Brewer (R)	L. Lamar (D)	Blatchford (R)	Gray (R)	Woods (R)	Harlan (Ky.) (R)	Hunt (R)

1890–91	1892	1893	1894	1895–97	1898–1901	1902
Fuller (D)	*Fuller* (D)	*Fuller* (D)	*Fuller* (D)	*Fuller* (D)	*Fuller* (D)	*Fuller* (D)
Field (D)	Field (D)	Field (D)	Field (D)	Field (D)	Harlan (Ky.) (R)	Harlan (Ky.) (R)
Bradley (R)	Harlan (Ky.) (R)	Harlan (Ky.) (R)	Harlan (Ky.) (R)	Harlan (Ky.) (R)	Gray (R)	Brewer (R)
Harlan (Ky.) (R)	Gray (R)	Gray (R)	Gray (R)	Gray (R)	Brewer (R)	Brown (R)
Gray (R)	Blatchford (R)	Blatchford (R)	Brewer (R)	Brewer (R)	Brown (R)	Shiras (R)
Blatchford (R)	L. Lamar (D)	Brewer (R)	Brown (R)	Brown (R)	Shiras (R)	E. White (D)
L. Lamar (D)	Brewer (R)	Brown (R)	Shiras (R)	Shiras (R)	E. White (D)	Peckham (D)
Brewer (R)	Brown (R)	Shiras (R)	H. Jackson (D)	E. White (D)	Peckham (D)	McKenna (R)
Brown (R)	Shiras (R)	H. Jackson (D)	E. White (D)	Peckham (D)	McKenna (R)	Holmes (R)

1916–20	1914–15	1912–13	1910–11	1909	1906–08	1903–05
E. White (D)	*E. White* (D)	*E. White* (D)	*E. White* (D)	*Fuller* (D)	*Fuller* (D)	*Fuller* (D)
McKenna (R)	McKenna (R)	McKenna (R)	Harlan (Ky.) (R)	Harlan (Ky.) (R)	Harlan (Ky.) (R)	Harlan (Ky.) (R)
Holmes (R)	Holmes (R)	Holmes (R)	McKenna (R)	Brewer (R)	Brewer (R)	Brewer (R)
Day (R)	Day (R)	Day (R)	Holmes (R)	E. White (D)	E. White (D)	Brown (R)
Van Devanter (R)	Hughes (R)	Lurton (D)	Day (R)	McKenna (R)	Peckham (D)	E. White (D)
Pitney (R)	Van Devanter (R)	Hughes (R)	Lurton (D)	Holmes (R)	McKenna (R)	Peckham (D)
McReynolds (D)	J. Lamar (D)	Van Devanter (R)	Hughes (R)	Day (R)	Holmes (R)	McKenna (R)
Brandeis (R)c	Pitney (R)	J. Lamar (D)	Van Devanter (R)	Moody (R)	Day (R)	Holmes (R)
Clarke (D)	McReynolds (D)	Pitney (R)	J. Lamar (D)	Lurton (D)	Moody (R)	Day (R)

1921	1922	1923–24	1925–29	1930–31	1932–36	1937
Taft (R)	*Taft* (R)	*Taft* (R)	*Taft* (R)	*Hughes* (R)	*Hughes* (R)	*Hughes* (R)
McKenna (R)	McKenna (R)	McKenna (R)	Holmes (R)	Holmes (R)	Van Devanter (R)	McReynolds (D)
Holmes (R)	Holmes (R)	Holmes (R)	Van Devanter (R)	Van Devanter (R)	McReynolds (D)	Brandeis (R)
Day (R)	Van Devanter (R)	Van Devanter (R)	McReynolds (D)	McReynolds (D)	Brandeis (R)	Sutherland (R)
Van Devanter (R)	Pitney (R)	McReynolds (D)	Brandeis (R)	Brandeis (R)	Sutherland (R)	Butler (D)
Pitney (R)	McReynolds (D)	Brandeis (R)	Sutherland (R)	Sutherland (R)	Butler (D)	Stone (R)
McReynolds (D)	Brandeis (R)	Sutherland (R)	Butler (D)	Butler (D)	Stone (R)	Roberts (R)
Brandeis (R)	Sutherland (R)	Butler (D)	Sanford (R)	Stone (R)	Roberts (R)	Cardozo (D)
Clarke (D)	Butler (D)	Sanford (R)	Stone (R)	Roberts (R)	Cardozo (D)	Black (D)

1946–48	1945	1943–44	1941–42	1940	1939	1938
Vinson (D)	*Stone* (R)	*Stone* (R)	*Stone* (R)	*Hughes* (R)	*Hughes* (R)	*Hughes* (R)
Black (D)	Black (D)	Roberts (R)	Roberts (R)	McReynolds (D)	McReynolds (D)	McReynolds (D)
Reed (D)	Reed (D)	Black (D)	Black (D)	Stone (R)	Butler (D)	Brandeis (R)
Frankfurter (I)	Frankfurter (I)	Reed (D)	Reed (D)	Roberts (R)	Stone (R)	Butler (D)
Douglas (D)	Douglas (D)	Frankfurter (I)	Frankfurter (I)	Black (D)	Roberts (R)	Stone (R)
Murphy (D)	Murphy (D)	Douglas (D)	Douglas (D)	Reed (D)	Black (D)	Roberts (R)
R. Jackson (D)	R. Jackson (D)	Murphy (D)	Murphy (D)	Frankfurter (I)	Reed (D)	Cardozo (D)
W. Rutledge (D)	W. Rutledge (D)	R. Jackson (D)	Byrnes (D)	Douglas (D)	Frankfurter (I)	Black (D)
Burton (R)	Burton (R)	W. Rutledge (D)	R. Jackson (D)	Murphy (D)	Douglas (D)	Reed (D)

[continued]

cAccording to Professor Henry Abraham, "Many—and with some justice—consider Brandeis a Democrat, however, he was in fact a registered Republican when nominated" (Henry Abraham, *Freedom and the Court*, 3d ed. 455 [1977]).

Time Chart of the Supreme Court

This table is designed to aid the user in identifying the composition of the Supreme Court at any given time in U.S. history. Each listing is headed by the chief justice, whose name is italicized. Associate justices are listed following the chief justice in order of seniority. The name of each justice is followed by a symbol representing his or her party affiliation at the time of appointment.

F = Federalist
DR = Democratic-Republican (Jeffersonian)
D = Democrat

W = Whig
R = Republican
I = Independent

1949–52	1953–54	1955	1956	1957	1958–61	1962–65
Vinson (D)	*Warren* (R)	*Warren* (R)	*Warren* (R)	*Warren* (R)	*Warren* (R)	*Warren* (R)
Black (D)	Black (D)	Black (D)	Black (D)	Black (D)	Black (D)	Black (D)
Reed (D)	Reed (D)	Reed (D)	Reed (D)	Frankfurter (I)	Frankfurter (I)	Douglas (D)
Frankfurter (I)	Frankfurter (I)	Frankfurter (I)	Frankfurter (I)	Douglas (D)	Douglas (D)	Clark (D)
Douglas (D)	Douglas (D)	Douglas (D)	Douglas (D)	Burton (R)	Clark (D)	Harlan (N.Y.) (R)
R. Jackson (D)	R. Jackson (D)	Burton (R)	Burton (R)	Clark (D)	Harlan (N.Y.) (R)	Brennan (D)
Burton (R)	Burton (R)	Clark (D)	Clark (D)	Harlan (N.Y.) (R)	Brennan (D)	Stewart (R)
Clark (D)	Clark (D)	Minton (D)	Harlan (N.Y.) (R)	Brennan (D)	Whittaker (R)	B. White (D)
Minton (D)	Minton (D)	Harlan (N.Y.) (R)	Brennan (D)	Whittaker (R)	Stewart (R)	Goldberg (D)

1972–75	1971	1970	1969–70	1969	1967–69	1965–67
Burger (R)	*Burger* (R)	*Burger* (R)	*Burger* (R)	*Burger* (R)	*Warren* (R)	*Warren* (R)
Douglas (D)	Douglas (D)	Black (D)	Black (D)	Black (D)	Black (D)	Black (D)
Brennan (D)	Brennan (D)	Douglas (D)	Douglas (D)	Douglas (D)	Douglas (D)	Douglas (D)
Stewart (R)	Stewart (R)	Harlan (N.Y.) (R)	Harlan (N.Y.) (R)	Harlan (N.Y.) (R)	Harlan (N.Y.) (R)	Clark (D)
B. White (D)	B. White (D)	Brennan (D)	Brennan (D)	Brennan (D)	Brennan (D)	Harlan (N.Y.) (R)
T. Marshall (D)	T. Marshall (D)	Stewart (R)	Stewart (R)	Stewart (R)	Stewart (R)	Brennan (D)
Blackmun (R)	Blackmun (R)	B. White (D)	B. White (D)	B. White (D)	B. White (D)	Stewart (R)
Powell (D)		T. Marshall (D)	T. Marshall (D)	Fortas (D)	Fortas (D)	B. White (D)
Rehnquist (R)		Blackmun (R)		T. Marshall (D)	T. Marshall (D)	Fortas (D)

1975–81	1981–85	1986–87	1988–89	1990	1991–92	1993
Burger (R)	*Burger* (R)	*Rehnquist* (R)	*Rehnquist* (R)	*Rehnquist* (R)	*Rehnquist* (R)	*Rehnquist* (R)
Brennan (D)	Brennan (D)	Brennan (D)	Brennan (D)	B. White (D)	B. White (D)	Blackmun (R)
Stewart (R)	B. White (D)	B. White (D)	B. White (D)	T. Marshall (D)	Blackmun (R)	Stevens (R)
B. White (D)	T. Marshall (D)	T. Marshall (D)	T. Marshall (D)	Blackmun (R)	Stevens (R)	O'Connor (R)
T. Marshall (D)	Blackmun (R)	Blackmun (R)	Blackmun (R)	Stevens (R)	O'Connor (R)	Scalia (R)
Blackmun (R)	Powell (D)	Powell (D)	Stevens (R)	O'Connor (R)	Scalia (R)	Kennedy (R)
Powell (D)	Rehnquist (R)	Stevens (R)	O'Connor (R)	Scalia (R)	Kennedy (R)	Souter (R)
Rehnquist (R)	Stevens (R)	O'Connor (R)	Scalia (R)	Kennedy (R)	Souter (R)	Thomas (R)
Stevens (R)	O'Connor (R)	Scalia (R)	Kennedy (R)	Souter (R)	Thomas (R)	Ginsburg (D)

1994–2003
Rehnquist (R)
Stevens (R)
O'Connor (R)
Scalia (R)
Kennedy (R)
Souter (R)
Thomas (R)
Ginsburg (D)
Breyer (D)

Succession of Supreme Court Justices

This table is designed to aid the user in identifying the succession of justices on the Supreme Court. Read vertically, the table lists the succession of justices in each position of the Court and the years served by each.

The number of justices constituting the Supreme Court has varied. Initially, the Court comprised six justices, but Congress increased the number to seven in 1807, to nine in 1837, and then to ten in 1863. In 1866, Congress reduced the number of justices to eight in an effort to prevent President Andrew Johnson from making any appointments to the Court. As a result, the positions of John Catron, who died in 1865, and James M. Wayne, who died in 1867, were abolished. In 1869, Congress raised the number of justices to nine, where it has remained. William Strong, the first justice appointed under the new statute, has generally been considered to have succeeded Wayne. Thus, Catron is the only person who has held the tenth seat on the Court.

Chief Justices	Associate Justices								
Jay 1789–1795	J. Rutledge 1789–1791	Cushing 1789–1810	Wilson 1789–1798	Harrison[f] 1789	Iredell 1790–1798	Todd 1807–1826	Field 1863–1897	McKinley 1837–1852	Catron 1837–1865
J. Rutledge[a] 1795	T. Johnson 1791–1793	Story 1811–1845	Washington 1798–1829	Blair 1789–1796	Moore 1799–1804	Trimble 1826–1828	McKenna 1898–1925	Campbell 1853–1861	
Ellsworth 1796–1799	Paterson 1793–1806	Woodbury 1845–1851	Baldwin 1830–1844	S. Chase 1796–1811	W. Johnson 1804–1834	McLean 1829–1861	Stone[h] 1925–1941	Davis 1862–1877	
J. Marshall 1801–1835	Livingston 1806–1823	Curtis 1851–1857	Grier 1846–1870	Duvall 1812–1835	Wayne 1835–1867	Swayne 1862–1881	R. Jackson 1941–1954	Harlan 1877–1911	
Taney 1836–1864	Thomson 1823–1843	Clifford 1858–1881	Bradley 1870–1892	Barbour 1836–1841	Strong 1870–1880	Matthews 1881–1889	Harlan 1955–1971	Pitney 1912–1922	
S. P. Chase 1864–1873	Nelson 1845–1872	Gray 1882–1902	Woods 1881–1887	Daniel 1841–1860	Shiras 1892–1903	Brewer 1889–1910	Rehnquist[i] 1971–1986	Sanford 1923–1930	
Waite 1874–1888	Hunt 1873–1882	Holmes 1902–1932	L. Lamar 1888–1893	Miller 1862–1890	Day 1903–1922	Hughes 1910–1916	Scalia 1986–	Roberts 1930–1945	
Fuller 1888–1910	Blatchford 1882–1893	Cardozo 1932–1938	H. Jackson 1893–1895	Brown 1891–1906	Butler 1922–1939	Clarke 1916–1922		Burton 1945–1958	
E. White[b] 1910–1921	E. White[d] 1894–1910	Frankfurter 1939–1962	Peckham 1895–1909	Moody 1906–1910	Murphy 1940–1949	Sutherland 1922–1938		Stewart 1958–1981	
Taft 1921–1930	Van Devanter 1911–1937	Goldberg 1962–1965	Lurton 1910–1914	J. Lamar 1911–1916	Clark 1949–1967	Reed 1938–1957		O'Connor 1981–	
Hughes 1930–1941	Black 1937–1971	Fortas[e] 1965–1969	McReynolds 1914–1941	Brandeis 1916–1939	T. Marshall 1967–1991	Whittaker 1957–1962			
Stone[c] 1941–1946	Powell 1971–1988	Blackmun 1970–1994	Byrnes 1941–1942	Douglas 1939–1975	Thomas 1991–	B. White 1962–1993			
Vinson 1946–1953	Kennedy 1988–	Breyer 1994–	W. Rutledge 1943–1949	Stevens 1976–		Ginsburg 1993–			
Warren 1953–1969			Minton 1949–1956						
Burger 1969–1986			Brennan 1956–1990						
Rehnquist[g] 1986–			Souter 1990–						

[a]Appointment not confirmed.
[b]Associate justice, 1894–1910.
[c]Associate justice, 1925–1941.
[d]Later chief justice, 1910–1921.
[e]Appointment as chief justice but not confirmed; resigned.
[f]Declined appointment.
[g]Associate justice, 1971–1986.
[h]Later chief justice, 1941–1946.
[i]Later chief justice, 1986–.

U.S. Attorneys General

Name	Term	President
Edmund Randolph	1789-1794	Washington
William Bradford	1794-1795	Washington
Charles Lee	1795-1801	Washington & John Adams
Levi Lincoln	1801-1805	Jefferson
John Breckenridge	1805-1806	Jefferson
Caesar A. Rodney	1807-1811	Jefferson & Madison
William Pinkney	1811-1814	Madison
Richard Rush	1814-1817	Madison
William Wirt	1817-1829	Monroe & John Q. Adams
John M. Berrien	1829-1831	Jackson
Roger B. Taney	1831-1833	Jackson
Benjamin F. Butler	1833-1838	Jackson & Van Buren
Felix Grundy	1838-1839	Van Buren
Henry D. Gilpin	1840-1841	Van Buren
John J. Crittenden	1841	Harrison & Tyler
Hugh S. Legare	1841-1843	Tyler
John Nelson	1843-1845	Tyler
John Y. Mason	1845-1846	Polk
Nathan Clifford	1846-1848	Polk
Issac Toucey	1848-1849	Polk
Reverdy Johnson	1849-1850	Taylor
John J. Crittenden	1850-1853	Fillmore
Caleb Cushing	1853-1857	Pierce
Jeremiah S. Black	1857-1860	Buchanan
Edwin M. Stanton	1860-1861	Buchanan
Edward Bates	1861-1864	Lincoln
James Speed	1864-1866	Lincoln & Johnson
Henry Stanberry	1866-1868	Johnson
William M. Evarts	1868-1869	Johnson
Ebenezer R. Hoar	1869-1870	Grant
Amos T. Akerman	1870-1872	Grant
George H. Williams	1871-1875	Grant
Edwards Pierrepont	1875-1876	Grant
Alphonso Taft	1876-1877	Grant
Charles Devens	1877-1881	Hayes
Wayne MacVeagh	1881	Garfield
Benjamin H. Brewster	1881-1885	Arthur
Augustus H. Garland	1885-1889	Cleveland
William H.H. Miller	1889-1893	Harrison
Richard Olney	1893-1895	Cleveland
Judson Harmon	1895-1897	Cleveland
Joseph McKenna	1897-1898	McKinley
John W. Griggs	1898-1901	McKinley
Philander C. Knox	1901-1904	McKinley
William H. Moody	1904-1906	Roosevelt
Charles J. Bonaparte	1906-1909	Roosevelt
George W. Wickersham	1909-1913	Taft
James C. McReynolds	1913-1914	Wilson
Thomas Watt Gregory	1914-1919	Wilson
A. Mitchell Palmer	1919-1921	Wilson
Harry M. Daugherty	1921-1924	Harding
Harlan Fiske Stone	1924-1925	Coolidge
John G. Sargent	1925-1929	Coolidge
William D. Mitchell	1929-1933	Hoover
Homer S. Cummings	1933-1939	Roosevelt
Frank Murphy	1939-1940	Roosevelt
Robert H. Jackson	1940-1941	Roosevelt
Francis Biddle	1941-1945	Roosevelt
Tom C. Clark	1945-1949	Truman
J. Howard McGrath	1949-1952	Truman
James P. McGranery	1952-1953	Truman
Herbert Brownell Jr.	1953-1957	Eisenhower
William P. Rogers	1957-1961	Eisenhower

[CONTINUED]

U.S. Attorneys General

Name	Term	President
Robert F. Kennedy	1961-1964	Kennedy
Nicholas deB. Katzenbach	1965-1966	Johnson
Ramsey Clark	1967-1969	Johnson
John N. Mitchell	1969-1972	Nixon
Richard G. Kleindienst	1972-1973	Nixon
Elliot L. Richardson	1973	Nixon
William B. Saxbe	1974-1975	Nixon
Edward H. Levi	1975-1977	Ford
Griffin B. Bell	1977-1979	Carter
Benjamin R. Civiletti	1979-1981	Carter
William French Smith	1981-1985	Reagan
Edwin Meese III	1985-1988	Reagan
Richard Thornburgh	1988-1991	Reagan & George Bush
William Barr	1991-1993	George Bush
Janet Reno	1993-2001	Clinton
John Ashcroft	2001-	George W. Bush

SOURCE: U.S. Department of Justice.

Congressional Timeline: Nineteenth Century

SOURCE: *Congress and Its Members*, reprinted with the permission of the Congressional Quarterly, Inc.

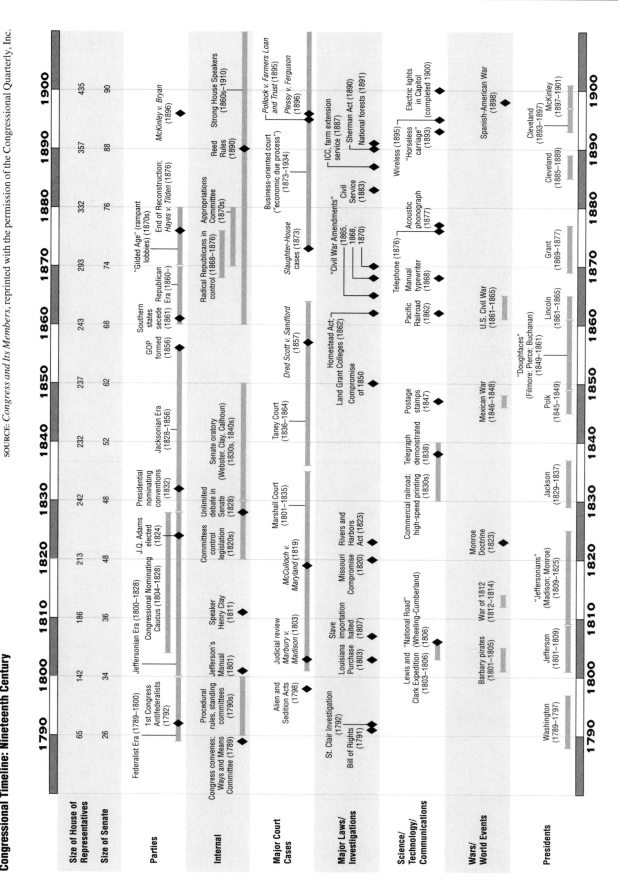

Congressional Timeline: Twentieth and Twenty-first Centuries

SOURCE: *Congress and Its Members*, reprinted with the permission of the Congressional Quarterly, Inc.

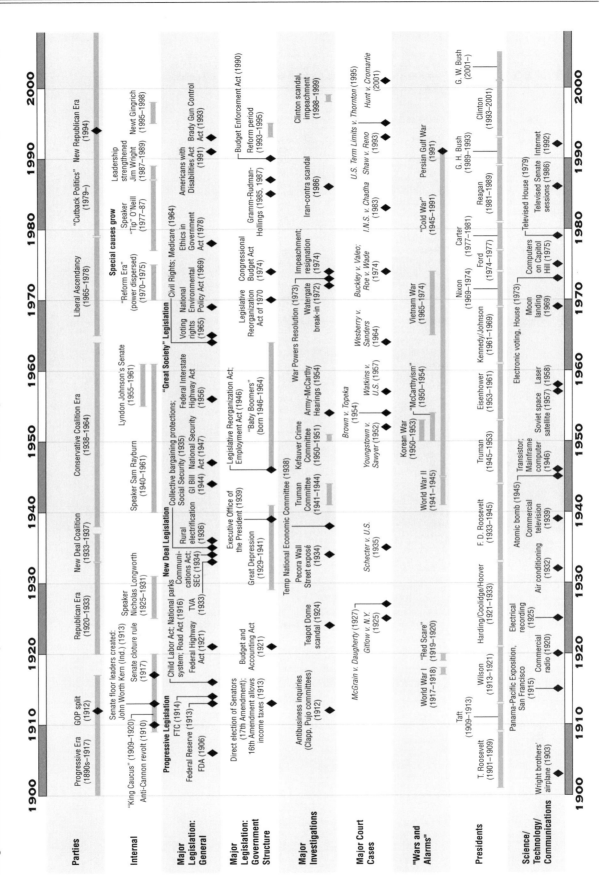

British Regnal Years

Regnal years run from the date of the monarch's accession to the throne until the same date in the next calendar year. Thus an event occurring on March 24, 1626, would be the first regnal year of King Charles I who acceded to the throne on March 27, 1625. British statutes are usually cited by regnal years.

Sovereign	Accession	Length of reign
William I	Oct. 14, 1066	21
William II	Sept. 26, 1087	13
Henry I	Aug. 5, 1100	36
Stephen	Dec. 26, 1135	19
Henry II	Dec. 19, 1154	35
Richard I	Sept. 23, 1189	10
John	May 27, 1199	18
Henry III	Oct. 28, 1216	57
Edward I	Nov. 20, 1272	35
Edward II	July 8, 1307	20
Edward III	Jan. 25, 1326	51
Richard II	June 22, 1377	23
Henry IV	Sept. 30, 1399	14
Henry V	March 21, 1413	10
Henry VI	Sept. 1, 1422	39
Edward IV	March 4, 1461	23
Edward V	April 9, 1483	—
Richard III	June 26, 1483	3
Henry VII	Aug. 22, 1485	24
Henry VIII	April 22, 1509	38
Edward VI	Jan. 28, 1547	7
Mary	July 6, 1553	6
Elizabeth	Nov. 17, 1558	45
James I	March 24, 1603	23
Charles I	March 27, 1625	24
The Commonwealth[a]	Jan. 30, 1649	11
Charles II	May 29, 1660	37
James II	Feb. 6, 1685	4
William III and Mary II	Feb. 13, 1689	14
Anne	March 8, 1702	13
George I	Aug. 1, 1714	13
George II	June 11, 1727	34
George III	Oct. 25, 1760	60
George IV	Jan. 29, 1820	11
William IV	June 26, 1830	7
Victoria	June 20, 1837	64
Edward VII	Jan. 22, 1901	9
George V	May 6, 1910	25
Edward VIII	Jan. 20, 1936	1
George VI	Dec. 11, 1936	15
Elizabeth II	Feb. 6, 1952	—

[a]The government established by Parliament after the abolition of the monarchy. The government of Oliver Cromwell and his son (1653–1658) is also known as the Protectorate.

ISBN 0-7876-6379-4

9 780787 663797

90000